METHODS FOR COMPUTER DESIGN OF DIFFRACTIVE OPTICAL ELEMENTS

WILEY SERIES IN LASERS AND APPLICATIONS

D.R.VIJ, Editor
Kurukshetra University

OPTICS OF NANOSTRUCTURED MATERIALS ● Vadim Markel

LASER REMOTE SENSING OF THE OCEAN: METHODS AND APPLICATIONS ● Alexey B. Bunkin

COHERENCE AND STATISTICS OF PHOTONICS AND ATOMS ● Jan Perina

METHODS FOR COMPUTER DESIGN OF DIFFRACTIVE OPTICAL ELEMENTS ● Victor A. Soifer

METHODS FOR COMPUTER DESIGN OF DIFFRACTIVE OPTICAL ELEMENTS

Edited by

Victor A. Soifer

A WILEY-INTERSCIENCE PUBLICATION

JOHN WILEY & SONS, INC.

For ordering and customer service, call 1-800-CALL-WILEY.

Library of Congress Cataloging-in-Publication Data:

Methods for computer design of diffractive optical elements / edited by Victor A. Soifer.
    p. cm. — (Wiley series in lasers and applications)
   "A Wiley-Interscience publication."
   Includes bibliographical references and index.
   ISBN 978-0-471-09533-0
    1. Optical data processing. 2. Diffraction. I. Soifer, V. A. (Victor Aleksandrovich) II. Series.

TA1630 .M45 2002
621.36'7–dc21

2001045400

CONTENTS

Chapter 4. Technology of DOE fabrication   267

Golovashkin D.L., Kazanskiy N.L., Pavelyev V. S., Soifer V.A., Solovyev V.S., Usplenyev G.V., and Volkov A.V.

Chapter 7. Light beams with periodic properties   **535**

Khonina S.N., Kotlyar V.V., and Soifer V.A.

Chapter 8. Wave front correction   **607**

Kazanskiy N.L., Kotlyar V.V., and Soifer V.A.

Chapter   9. DOE-based lighting devices   **651**

Kazanskiy N.L.

This book covers a fast growing area of Optics with a variety of names still used by different authors to identify the subject, such as "Binary Optics," "Computer-generated Optics," "Planar Optics," "Computer Optics," and "Diffractive Optics," of which, the latter tends to be most firmly established worldwide. In any case, these names define various features of the optical elements in question. Optical elements of this kind are represented by the refraction or reflection plate coated with a thin phase microrelief that is computed using diffraction theory. The diffraction grating invented more than 200 years ago was the first-ever optical element of this class. Next came a zone plate. These types of diffractive optical elements (DOEs) featured the binary-amplitude or binary-phase transmittance. Although diffraction gratings have found wide use in optical instrumentation, the major niche for the zone plates was in optical laboratories for educational purposes.

The use of computers has revolutionized the DOE fabrication techniques. In the 1970s, computers were used to synthesize holograms of mathematically defined objects. As a result, the key problem of coding — writing the complex function in a physical medium and fabricating the corresponding amplitude-phase transparencies — was resolved. This provided an impetus to computer-aided synthesis of binary-amplitude phase and phase spatial filters, with photo-plotters used for writing the DOE in a physical medium. In the late 1980s, progress in microelectronics and laser machinery resulted in the advent of precision photo-plotters and e-beam lithographers, thus making the fabrication of DOEs with complex zone profile practically feasible. These advances have provided a wide range of activities for physicists, opticists, applied mathematicians, electronics and process engineers, and automatization specialists. DOEs with unique characteristics that are unattainable using the conventional optics were developed; for example, DOEs to focus the laser light and DOEs to select laser light modes called *modans*.

The book is constructed in such a manner that the basics of the subject may be derived from Chapter 1, while the following chapters may be read out of order according to the reader's personal professional preferences.

The book was written by the employees of Samara Image Processing Systems Institute of the Russian Academy of Sciences: Chapter 1 by V.A. Soifer; Chapter 2 by L.L. Doskolovich, V.V. Kotlyar, and V.A. Soifer; Chapter 3, Sections 3.1 to 3.4 by L.L. Doskolovich, Sections 3.5 to 3.7 by S.I. Kharitonov, Section 3.8 by D.L. Golovashkin, and Section 3.9 by D.L. Golovashkin and V.S. Pavelyev; Chapter 4 by A.V. Volkov, N.L. Kazanskiy, V.A. Soifer, and G.V. Usplenyev, with the exception of Section 4.4 by V.S. Solovyev and Section 4.6 by D.L. Golovashkin and V.S. Pavelyev; Chapter 5 by L.L. Doskolovich, N.L. Kazanskiy, and V.A. Soifer, Chapter 6 by V.S. Pavelyev and V.A. Soifer; Chapter 7 by V.V. Kotlyar, V.A. Soifer, and S.N. Khonina; Chapter 8 by N.L. Kazanskiy, V.V. Kotlyar, and V.A. Soifer;

Chapter 9 by N.L. Kazanskiy; and Chapter 10 by V.V. Kotlyar, V.A. Soifer, R.V. Skidanov, and S.N. Khonina.

The authors wish to thank

- the Board of Directors of the Russian Federal Program "Integration" and Director-general, Academician, Professor V.P. Shorin in person for the financial support at the stage of preparing the book manuscript in Russian;
- the employees of the Laboratory of Diffractive Optics and the Laboratory of Laser Measurements and, personally, S.G. Volotovsky and P.G. Seraphimovich for conducting a great bulk of computer-aided and physical experiments;
- the employees of the Institute of General Physics of the Russian Academy of Sciences, Professors V.I. Konov and V.V. Kononenko for kindly providing the materials for Section 4.6 of the book;
- the international partners from the FIAT Research Center, Italy (the research group of Dr. P. Perlo), Applied Optics Institute of Friedrich Schiller University, Jena, Germany (Professor Kowarschik's group and Dr. M. Duparre's), Joensuu University, Finland (Professor Turunen's group) for their assistance in fabricating various types of DOEs and joint experimental studies;
- S.V. Smagin and Ya.Ye. Takhtarov for preparing the computer version of the book and M.I. Kotlyar for translating the book into English.

The book is based on the original research papers published during the last 20 years by the contributors to the book, a number of papers used in writing this book being in co-authorship with Academician A.M. Prokhorov, Professors I.N. Sisakian and M.A. Golub, and Doctors V.A. Danilov and S.V. Karpeyev.

LIST OF CONTRIBUTORS

Victor A. Soifer, Image Processing Systems Institute, 151 Molodogvardejskaya str., Samara 443001, Russia; Phone (07) (8462) 325620; E-mail: soifer@ssau.ru

Victor V. Kotlyar, Image Processing Systems Institute, 151 Molodogvardejskaya str., Samara 443001, Russia; Phone (07) (8462) 325787; E-mail: kotlyar@smr.ru

Nikolai L. Kazanskiy, Image Processing Systems Institute, 151 Molodogvardejskaya str., Samara 443001, Russia; Phone (07) (8462) 325783; E-mail: kazansky@smr.ru

Leonid L. Doskolovich, Image Processing Systems Institute, 151 Molodogvardejskaya str., Samara 443001, Russia; Phone (07) (8462) 325783; E-mail: ipsi@smr.ru

Sergei I. Kharitonov, Image Processing Systems Institute, 151 Molodogvardejskaya str., Samara 443001, Russia; Phone (07) (8462) 325783; E-mail: ipsi@smr.ru

Svetlana N. Khonina, Image Processing Systems Institute, 151 Molodogvardejskaya str., Samara 443001, Russia; Phone (07) (8462) 325622; E-mail: khonina@smr.ru

Vladimir S. Pavelyev, Image Processing Systems Institute, 151 Molodogvardejskaya str., Samara 443001, Russia; Phone (07) (8462) 325783; E-mail: pavelyev@smr.ru

Roman V. Skidanov, Image Processing Systems Institute, 151 Molodogvardejskaya str., Samara 443001, Russia; Phone (07) (8462) 325622; E-mail: ipsi@smr.ru

Aleksey V. Volkov, Image Processing Systems Institute, 151 Molodogvardejskaya str., Samara 443001, Russia; Phone (07) (8462) 358659; E-mail: ipsi@smr.ru

Dimitriy L. Golovashkin, Image Processing Systems Institute, 151 Molodogvardejskaya str., Samara 443001, Russia; Phone (07) (8462) 325783; E-mail: ipsi@smr.ru

Vladimir S. Solovyev, Image Processing Systems Institute, 151 Molodogvardejskaya str., Samara 443001, Russia; Phone (07) (8462) 358659; E-mail: ipsi@smr.ru

Gleb V. Usplenyev, Image Processing Systems Institute, 151 Molodogvardejskaya str., Samara 443001, Russia; Phone (07) (8462) 325783; E-mail: ipsi@smr.ru

CHAPTER 1

Introduction to Diffractive Optics

1.1 FUNCTIONAL CAPABILITIES OF ZONED DIFFRACTIVE OPTICAL ELEMENTS

The first diffractive optical elements (DOEs), called *diffraction gratings*, were invented more than 200 years ago. The one-dimensional (1D) amplitude diffraction grating is a planar transparency with alternating dark and light parallel strips (grooves and slits). The strips are of the same width. Figure 1.1 depicts a fragment of a binary amplitude diffraction grating and Figure 1.2 illustrates the light-transmission function over the grating. If such a grating is illuminated by a monochromatic light beam of wavelength λ that strikes the grating's plane perpendicularly, the light diffracted by a periodic structure will generate a set of light beams emerging at different angles α and corresponding to different diffraction orders. The angle α depends on the grating period and, with the supposition of small angles, is defined by

$$\alpha^p = p\frac{\lambda}{T}, \quad p = 0, \pm1, \pm2, \ldots, \tag{1.1}$$

where T is period. The light intensity decreases as the absolute value of p increases. From the theory of diffraction gratings it follows that when the groove's width is equal to the slit width, the decrease is defined by

$$I(\alpha^p) \sim \left(\frac{\sin(a\alpha^p)}{a\alpha^p}\right)^2 \approx \frac{1}{(2p+1)^2} \tag{1.2}$$

Because a significant portion of light is absorbed by the amplitude transparency, the diffraction efficiency in the first order does not exceed 10 percent. Note that for a

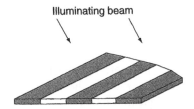

Illuminating beam

Figure 1.1. Fragment of a binary-amplitude diffraction grating.

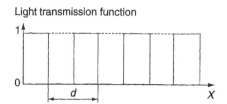

Figure 1.2. Transmission function of the amplitude diffraction grating.

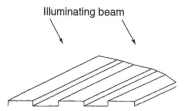

Figure 1.3. Fragment of a binary-phase diffraction grating.

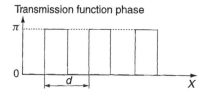

Figure 1.4. Transmission function phase of the phase diffraction grating.

1D phase grating this parameter is approximately four times greater. A fragment of a binary phase diffraction grating is schematically shown in Figure 1.3. In this case, the transmission function is purely phase, periodic (period T), and skipping by π (Fig. 1.4). Functionally, the phase and the amplitude diffraction gratings are equivalent. Corresponding two-dimensional (2D) radially symmetric gratings (zone plates) have come as a natural outgrowth of 1D binary-amplitude and binary-phase diffraction gratings.

Figure 1.5 depicts the central fragment of the Rayleigh-Soreau zone plate, and Figure 1.6 depicts the transmission function versus radius. Let us clarify the notion termed as *zone*. The zone is a limited domain on the DOE on which the transmission function undergoes a simple change of its value from maximum to minimum. For the amplitude diffraction grating, the zone is a combination of dark and light strips within one grating period (Fig. 1.1), with the zone fringe represented by a straight line. For a Rayleigh-Soreau [1] zone plate, the zone is a combination of dark and light rings of varied thickness (Fig. 1.5), and the zone fringe is represented by a circumference of varying diameter.

Further, we consider DOEs with more complicated zones and, respectively, with more complicated zone fringes. The radii of the circumferences are changed proportionally to the square roots of sequential integers p

$$\rho_p = \sqrt{p\lambda f}, \tag{1.3}$$

Figure 1.5. Central fragment of the Rayleigh-Soreau zone plate.

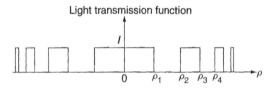

Figure 1.6. Transmission function of the amplitude zone plate.

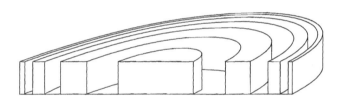

Figure 1.7. Fragment of a binary-phase zone plate.

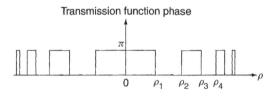

Figure 1.8. Transmission function phase of a binary-phase zone plate.

where f is the focal length. A fragment of a 2D phase zone plate and the corresponding transmission function are shown in Figures 1.7 and 1.8.

The zone plate serves to focus light and behaves as a lens with a set of foci f_{-2}, f_{-1}, f_0, f_1, f_2 corresponding to different diffraction orders and found along the axis of light propagation:

$$f_n = \frac{f}{2n + 1}, \quad n = 0, \pm 1, \pm 2, \ldots \tag{1.4}$$

The light intensity decreases with decreasing order number by the rule

$$I_{2n+1} = \frac{4}{\pi^2} \frac{1}{(2n+1)^2}.$$

(1.5)

Improvement of "base" DOEs represented by 1D diffraction gratings is possible through changing of the zone profile. By this means, we obtain the so-called *blazed gratings*. For example, we may consider an amplitude 1D diffraction grating with the transmission function given by the rule $\cos^2[2\pi(\lambda/T)]$. Theoretical investigations suggest that after the light is diffracted by such a grating, besides zero order, we will only obtain $\pm$1st diffraction orders. However, in practice, when we take into account DOE fabrication errors, the result will be much more complicated.

For 2D diffraction gratings, it seems reasonable to try and construct zones that would be different from periodic slitlike and ringlike ones, with a view of achieving novel functional capabilities of DOEs. Despite the fact that such a challenge is seemingly obvious, it had not been undertaken for years since the invention of the zone plate because it was impossible by then to practically implement zone plates with varying character of zones. The emergence of computers and technical means for machine graphics (writing machines and photoplotters) made this possible.

In 1967, Lohmann and Paris [2] proposed 2D diffraction gratings with varying Fresnel zones fabricated by superposition of a pair of synthesized masks producing Moiré effects. The synthesized masks contain binary images periodic in one coordinate (e.g., in x-coordinate) and described by a specially selected algebraic function $\varphi(x, y)$. By varying the form and parameters of the $\varphi(x, y)$ function as well as parameters with respect to the shift Δx and the rotation of the masks, one can obtain a number of 2D amplitude diffraction gratings with an individual diffraction pattern corresponding to each of them. Unfortunately, the described procedure involves a regular method of synthesis only for cylindrical and spherical Fresnel zones. An example of a cylindrical amplitude zone plate is shown in Figure 1.9. The result of focusing is a straight focal line. It is also feasible to construct conical zone plates by means of an optical registration of the result of physical superposition of a cylindrical and plane wave, the result of focusing being an inclined straight line in a plane parallel to the zone plate.

The examples considered here show a possibility of obtaining zone plates of different zone shapes. At the same time, it is of interest to construct 2D zone patterns of Fresnel zones for more complicated cases, for example, for a zone plate focusing into a longitudinal and transverse line-segment of desired length, into a ring, or into another geometric configuration.

By way of example, let us consider a DOE focusing into a ring. The relevant pattern of Fresnel zones of the grating can be obtained by combination of a 1D diffraction

Figure 1.9. Binary cylindrical zone plate.

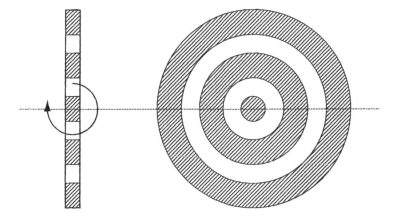

Figure 1.10. A narrow fragment of a 1D diffraction grating.

Figure 1.11. Axicon.

grating and a zone plate. Let us take a fairly narrow segment of a 1D diffraction grating (Fig. 1.10) whose action is identical to that of the entire diffraction grating, implying that it deflects an input monochromatic beam at a definite angle in the plane (we consider the first diffraction order). Rotating the segment about the center in the manner shown in Figure 1.10 yields a DOE whose Fresnel zones are represented by a set of concentric black-white rings of the same width (Fig. 1.11). This DOE will be denoted as a *diffraction axicon*. It can easily be seen that such a DOE will deflect the input beam at a definite solid angle in space. A zone plate is used to collect the diffracted beam in the focal plane. Note that the diffraction axicon and the zone plate can be superposed in a single plane and then written in a single substrate. In this case, a set of concentric, unequally spaced rings of varying width will be generated in the DOE plane (Fig. 1.12). Thus, we have synthesized an amplitude DOE focusing into a ring.

On the basis of the described technique, we can construct different focusing DOEs. For example, if we record two crossed cylindrical lenses of different focal length onto the same substrate, we shall obtain a DOE focusing into a segment lying in a plane perpendicular to the propagation axis (Fig. 1.13). There is no special need

Figure 1.12. DOE focusing into a ring.

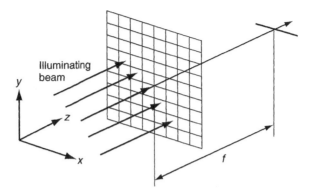

Figure 1.13. The result of focusing by two crossed cylindrical lenses.

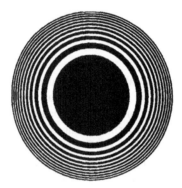

Figure 1.14. DOE focusing into a coaxial line-segment.

to point to the fact that both a DOE focusing into a ring and a DOE focusing into a transverse segment can be realized as phase DOEs. The simplest way to do so is to use a photographic bleaching of corresponding amplitude masks (photomasks). Generally speaking, in the two aforementioned examples, we are dealing with phase modulation, which implies that one binary function describing the diffraction grating is multiplied by another one. However, it should be noted that the process of modulating parameters of the diffraction grating may also be implemented for a wider class of modulating functions. In particular, by modulating the radii of zone plate rings, we can design a DOE focusing into a coaxial segment of definite length in the form of a zone plate with extended longitudinal aberration. While synthesizing the relevant radially symmetric DOE, the main idea is to make its peripheral part correspond to a zone plate of focal length F_1 and its central part correspond to a zone plate of focal length $F_2 > F_1$. Between the central and peripheral part, one should record rings corresponding to zone plates with focal lengths decreasing from F_2 to F_1. The result will be a focuser into a coaxial line-segment of length $\ell = F_2 - F_1$. The photomask of such a DOE is shown in Figure 1.14, and the process of focusing is shown in Figure 1.15.

General methods for designing modulated diffraction gratings with pregiven functional properties require solving inverse problems of the diffraction theory and are dealt with in the subsequent chapters. Here, we only mention that the inverse problem of

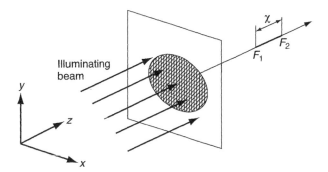

Figure 1.15. The result of focusing into a coaxial line-segment.

diffraction is solved with reference to the phase of a DOE that performs the required transformation of light beam. This phase function has to be recorded into an optical medium as a regular zoned structure with phase microrelief to yield a DOE.

1.2   ZONE FRINGES AND PHASE FUNCTIONS OF OPTICAL ELEMENTS

1.2.1   Reduction of Phase Functions to the Interval

The phase function $\varphi(u, v)$ of an optical element represents a function that describes how the value of the phase detour generated by the optical element at point (u, v) depends on spatial coordinates. In a number of cases, the zone fringes of DOE can be derived from the phase functions of the corresponding conventional (refractive) optical elements. A conventional optical element is characterized by the smooth phase function $\varphi(\vec{u})$, where $\vec{u} = (u, v)$ are transverse coordinates of the point lying in the plane of the optical element. If we illuminate an optical element by a beam of complex amplitude $W_0(\vec{u})$, we will obtain, immediately behind the optical element, the field

$$W(\vec{u}) = \exp[i\varphi(\vec{u})]W_0(\vec{u}). \tag{1.6}$$

By way of illustration, the phase function of a spherical lens is shown in Figure 1.16.

The thickness H of a conventional lens may amount to thousands of wavelengths, with phase values φ ranging from zero to thousands of 2π. At the same time, phase variations range from 0 to 2π for the previously considered DOEs. Because the complex component in Eq. (1.6) is a periodic function of period 2π, the phase can be reduced to the interval $(0, 2\pi)$. Reduction to the interval can be implemented by the formula

$$\Phi = \text{mod}_{2\pi}\varphi, \tag{1.7}$$

where
$$\text{mod}_{2\pi}\varphi = \varphi - 2\pi j$$

for
$$j2\pi \leq \varphi \leq (j+1)2\pi, \quad j = 0, \pm1, \pm2, \dots \tag{1.8}$$

From practical considerations, the reduction of phase to the interval $(0, 2\pi m)$ using the relation

$$\Phi = \text{mod}_{2\pi m}\varphi, \tag{1.9}$$

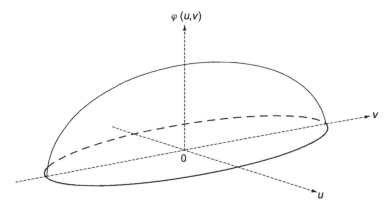

Figure 1.16. Phase function of a spherical lens.

where usually $m \sim 1$–100, may appear to be inconvenient. Equivalency of the initial smooth phase φ and a piecewise phase Φ reduced to the interval is given by the equation

$$\partial \equiv \exp(i\Phi) = \exp(i\varphi). \tag{1.10}$$

1.2.2 Planar Spherical Lens

In a paraxial approximation, the phase function of a spherical lens is given by

$$\varphi(u, v) = \varphi(r) = -k\frac{u^2 + v^2}{2f}, \quad r \leq \frac{D}{2}, \tag{1.11}$$

where $k = 2\pi/\lambda$ is the wavelength, f is the focal length, D is the lens diameter, and $r = (u^2 + v^2)^{1/2}$.

Reduction of the phase function of Eq. (1.11) to the interval $(0, 2\pi)$ is shown in Figure 1.17. If the refractive index of the lens material is n, the maximum relief height equals

$$h_{\max} = \frac{\lambda}{n - 1},$$

$$h(r) = \frac{\lambda}{n - 1}\frac{1}{2\pi}\mathrm{mod}_{2\pi}\,\varphi(r). \tag{1.12}$$

The radii of Fresnel zones can be found from the relation

$$\varphi(r_j) = -2\pi j, \tag{1.13}$$

whence it follows

$$r_j = \sqrt{2\lambda f j}. \tag{1.14}$$

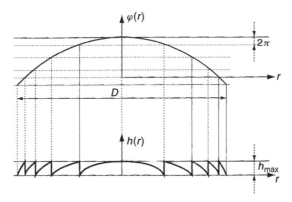

Figure 1.17. Reduction of the phase function of lens to the interval $(0, 2\pi)$.

The number j_0 of complete zones on the lens is found from the condition $r_{j_0} \leq D/2$ and satisfies the relation

$$j_0 = \,]\frac{D^2}{8\lambda f}[\,, \tag{1.15}$$

where $]D^2/8\lambda f[$ denotes the integer part of the number rounded off to the lesser number.

The zone width of a planar spherical lens

$$\Delta_j = r_j - r_{j-1}, \quad j = \overline{1, j} \tag{1.16}$$

is variable and decreases toward the lens's periphery. The characteristic parameter Δ is the width of the narrowest (in the present case, the last) peripheral zone, because it is this that imposes requirements on the technological equipment. In a more general case of a DOE with phase function $\varphi(u, v)$, one can determine the width of the narrowest microrelief zone with the maximum phase height of $2\pi m$. Employing the linear approximation of the phase function within this zone, we shall obtain the relation

$$\Delta = \frac{2\pi m}{\max |\nabla_\perp \varphi|}, \tag{1.17}$$

where max is taken along the DOE's surface and $\nabla_\perp = (\partial/\partial u, \partial/\partial v)$ is the gradient of the function $\varphi(u, v)$.

Let us compare the equations for the ring radii of a Rayleigh-Soreau zone plate of Eq. (1.3) and a spherical planar lens of Eq. (1.14). Zones' radii on the lens are seen to be $\sqrt{2}$ times as large as rings' radii on the zone plate. Accordingly, at a pregiven diameter, the number of rings on the zone plate is twice as large, that is, to each ring of the spherical planar lens there correspond two rings of the zone plate, a dark one and a light one. Within zones, the relief of the planar lens is continuous, whereas the zone plate has a binary-phase relief approximating the continuous one (Fig. 1.18).

If in designing a DOE we proceed from the general considerations of discrete approximation of the continuous phase function, the procedure of a stepwise approximation of the original continuous phase function within Fresnel zone limits can be extended. An example of a planar Fresnel lens with its phase uniformly quantized into

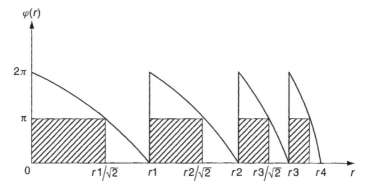

Figure 1.18. Phase function of the Fresnel lens and a binary zone plate.

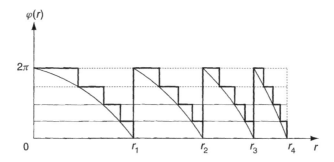

Figure 1.19. Stepwise approximation of radial section of the phase function of a spherical lens.

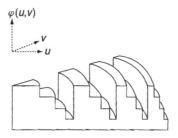

Figure 1.20. Stepwise approximation of the phase function of the spherical lens.

four levels is shown in Figure 1.19. Figure 1.20 illustrates the corresponding phase function.

An amplitude mask with N levels of intensity can be practically implemented using $(N - 1)$ binary-amplitude masks in a sequential photoprocess. It is also possible to reduce the number of binary masks to $n = \log_2 N$. It presents no problem to calculate the ring radii corresponding to phase gradations in different zones. Although their knowledge is necessary while designing binary-amplitude masks, they have no such clear physical meaning as is the case with the zone plate. Also, note that the equation of rings of the Rayleigh-Soreau zone plate is impossible to obtain using an equidistant sampling of the phase function of a planar spherical lens.

1.2.3 Planar Cylindrical Lens

Consider a cylindrical lens (Fig. 1.21) described by the phase function

$$\varphi(u) = -k\frac{u^2}{2f}, \quad |u| \le \frac{D}{2}. \tag{1.18}$$

Reduction of the phase function to the interval $[0, 2\pi]$ is analogous to the earlier-described procedure with reference to the spherical lens. In this case, zone fringes are straight lines, with the distance between them determined by Eq. (1.14) and r_j replaced by u_j. The photomask of a planar cylindrical lens is shown in Figure 1.22.

1.2.4 Reflection Zone Plate

Let us consider a reflection zone plate designed to operate the incident light at some angle of α (Figs. 1.23 and 1.24) and focusing the light into point F.

With normal incidence, the maximum relief height of the reflection zone plate has to be $\lambda/2$ in order that the phase shift under the direct and reverse passage be equal to 2π. In the meantime, with inclined incidence we have

$$h_{\max} = \frac{\lambda}{2\cos\alpha}.$$

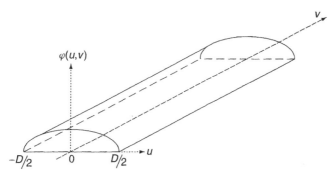

Figure 1.21. Cylindrical lens.

Figure 1.22. Photomask of a planar cylindrical lens.

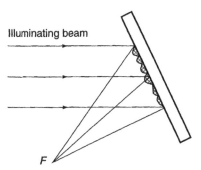

Figure 1.23. Reflection zone plate.

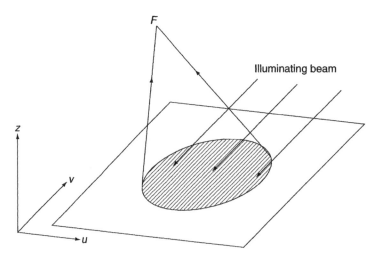

Figure 1.24. Focusing into a point at an angle.

With normal incidence, the equations for zone fringes of a reflection zone plate exactly correspond to those of a refraction plate, the zone height being different by a factor of $2/(n-1)$. With inclined incidence, the equation for zone fringes may be deduced by straightforward reasoning. The inclined incidence is equivalent to the introduction of a turning mirror. If we project rings of a Rayleigh-Soreau plate onto this mirror, we shall obtain the equation of zone fringes of a reflection zone plate for the inclined light incidence at angle α. Obviously, these will be ellipses with the extention factor along the u-axis of $\cos \alpha$ (Fig. 1.25).

The relief height of a reflection DOE focusing into a point at an angle α is defined by the equation

$$h(u, v) = \frac{\lambda}{2 \cos \alpha} \frac{1}{2\pi} \mathrm{mod}_{2\pi} \, \varphi(u \cos \alpha, v), \qquad (1.19)$$

where $\varphi(u, v)$ is determined by Eq. (1.11).

In deriving Eq. (1.19), we made use of the plane wave approximation for the incident and reflected beams.

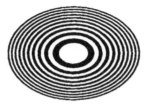

Figure 1.25. Photomask of a reflection zone plate with inclination angle $\alpha = 45°$.

1.2.5 Planar Prism

Let us consider a prism of angle α (Fig. 1.26).

The prism provides a phase shift linearly dependent on the coordinate and characterized by a phase function

$$\varphi(u) = \frac{2\pi}{\lambda} u\theta, \qquad (1.20)$$

where $\theta = (n-1)\mathrm{tg}\,\alpha$.

Reducing the phase function $\varphi(u)$ to the interval $(0, 2\pi)$ (Fig. 1.27), we obtain a 1D blazed diffraction grating (Fig. 1.28). The maximum relief height is $h_{\max} = \lambda/(n-1)$

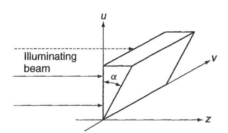

Figure 1.26. Prism.

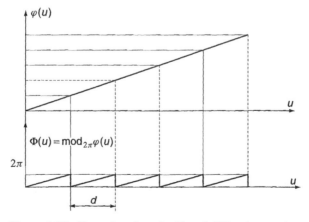

Figure 1.27. Phase function of a blazed diffraction grating.

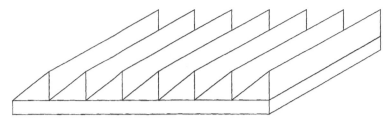

Figure 1.28. Blazed diffraction grating.

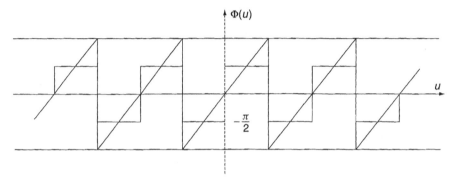

Figure 1.29. Comparison of a binary diffraction grating and a blazed diffraction grating.

and the equation of the relief height is given by

$$h(u) = \frac{\lambda}{n-1}\frac{1}{2\pi}\mathrm{mod}_{2\pi}\varphi(u). \tag{1.21}$$

For different deviation angles β, there are corresponding different periods of grating

$$d = \frac{\lambda}{\sin\beta}, \tag{1.22}$$

where $\sin\beta = (n-1)\mathrm{tg}\,\alpha$.

We shall derive a 1D amplitude diffraction grating if we replace a linearly varying phase function within a single period by a binary function taking the values $\pm\pi/2$ (Fig. 1.29).

1.2.6 Combined and Segmentized DOEs

We have already mentioned the possibility of obtaining combined zone plates being a superposition of two original zone plates. If two coaxial zone plates have respective phase functions of φ_1 and φ_2, they may be replaced by a combined optical element with phase function $\varphi = \varphi_1 + \varphi_2$. By way of illustration, consider two crossed cylindrical

lenses of different focal length

$$\left.\begin{array}{l} \varphi_1(u, v) = -k\dfrac{u^2}{2f_1} \\[12pt] \varphi_2(u, v) = -k\dfrac{v^2}{2f_2} \end{array}\right\}.$$

(1.23)

The photomask of a combined DOE corresponding to the phase function

$$\varphi(u, v) = -k\left(\frac{u^2}{2f_1} + \frac{v^2}{2f_2}\right)$$

(1.24)

is shown in Figure 1.30. The zone fringes are seen to be elliptical, the DOE performing focusing into a line-segment. Within aperture, the plane of a segmentized DOE is broken into two or more segments (Fig. 1.31), with a zone plate recorded in each

Figure 1.30. Two crossed cylindrical lenses.

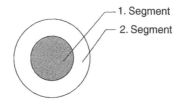

Figure 1.31. Segmentation of a DOE.

Figure 1.32. Photomask of a DOE focusing into the letter "R".

segment and corresponding to a definite phase function. For example, in such a manner one can obtain a DOE focusing into the letter "R," whose photomask is given in Figure 1.32.

1.3 IMPLEMENTATION OF DOEs USING DIGITAL HOLOGRAPHY METHODS

1.3.1 Fourier and Fresnel Holograms

The development of digital holography methods began in the late 1960s because of the extensive use of computers and computer graphics in optics. The advent of computers provided a real opportunity to derive amplitude-phase characteristics of light field in the element's plane from the characteristics of the object under reconstruction. The development of computer graphics tools presented wide possibilities for recording encoded values of the calculated transmission function of a holographic element into a physical medium. The emergence of digital holography methods for the first time made it possible to synthesize the holograms of mathematically defined objects. Fundamental papers on digital holography have been written by Lohmann, Lee, Lesem, Gallagher, and a number of other authors [3–9]. At present, publications on digital holography number in thousands. There are detailed reviews and monographs devoted to this subject.

It has been known that the propagation of a light wave in space is described in the paraxial approximation by the Fresnel transform. Note that if the far-field condition is fulfilled, the Fresnel transform may be reduced to the Fourier transform. The knowledge of the operator describing the light wave propagation in space and characteristics of the object under reconstruction make it possible to calculate the complex amplitude of a light wave in the holographic element's plane.

$$T(\vec{u}) = a_T(\vec{u}) \exp[i\varphi_T(\vec{u})], \tag{1.25}$$

where $|T(\vec{u})| \equiv a_T(\vec{u}) \leq 1$. Sampling of the transmission function $T(\vec{u})$ leads to the emergence of a corresponding matrix of field pixels:

$$T_{mn} \equiv T(m, n) = a_T(m, n) \exp[i\varphi_T(m, n)]$$

$$= a_T(u, v) \exp[i\varphi_T(u, v)]|_{\substack{u=m\delta u \\ v=n\delta v}} \tag{1.26}$$

$$T = \{T_{mn}\} \quad m = \overline{1, N_u}, n = \overline{1, N_v} \tag{1.27}$$

If we then apply the calculated and properly encoded pixels onto a physical medium, the reconstructing wave will produce the image of the holographic object at the output plane. Shown in Figures 1.33 and 1.34 are schemes of imaging by the Fourier and Fresnel holograms, respectively.

By digital holography methods is meant a set of approaches to encoding the pixels T_{mn} and their recording on a physical carrier, aimed at synthesizing digital holograms with the transmission function of Eq. (1.25). The amplitude-phase character of Eq. (1.25) has resulted in the emergence of three major available types of digital holograms: (*1*) *Amplitude holograms*—Encoded pixels T_{mn} are recorded on an amplitude carrier, (2) *Phase holograms*—Encoded pixels are recorded on a phase carrier,

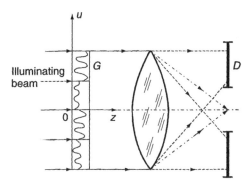

Figure 1.33. Encoding for Fourier holograms.

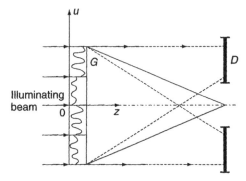

Figure 1.34. Encoding for Fresnel holograms.

(*3*) *Combined holograms* — The amplitude information $a_T(m, n)$ is applied onto a carrier with amplitude transmittance, while the phase information $\varphi_T(m, n)$ is recorded onto a carrier with phase transmittance. After recording, the carriers are overlapped.

At present, there are a great number of methods for encoding amplitude-phase characteristics into both the amplitude and the phase. Phase holograms have become the most popular because the transparency of phase medium allows a desired image to be generated at comparatively small energy losses.

When reducing the field in the hologram plane to the amplitude-only or the phase-only, the main approach is the introduction of auxiliary image elements or parity elements in the plane of object reconstruction. These elements are spatially separated from the principal image and therefore do not affect its quality. They just redistribute the beam energy, thus decreasing the brightness of the image to be reconstructed. The process of synthesizing and reconstructing the phase hologram using the auxiliary elements is shown in Figures 1.35 and 1.36.

The transmission function may be encoded with introduction of parity elements either analytically (e.g., by introducing a carrier frequency into the phase or into the amplitude, thus producing auxiliary diffraction orders) or in the course of iteration process. If the initial object is specified only by its amplitude (phase) distribution, one may reduce the hologram transmission function to the amplitude-only or the phase-only by means of the phase (amplitude) distribution on the object. A brief review

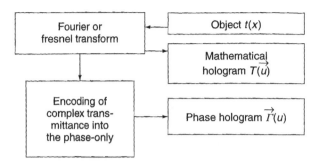

Figure 1.35. Synthesis of phase holograms.

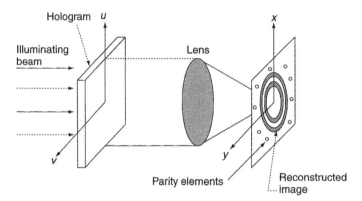

Figure 1.36. Reconstruction of a phase hologram.

of available methods for encoding the complex transmission function is given in the following text.

1.3.2 Amplitude Holograms

Historically, the first method for designing the amplitude hologram was proposed by Lohmann [2], and it employed properties of irregular amplitude diffraction gratings. Lohmann held that, in principle, any hologram may be looked upon as a distorted diffraction grating. Thus, according to Lohmann, the essence of digital holography is the calculation of these distortions based on the characteristics of the object under holography. The Lohmann hologram represents an array of cells in the form shown in Figure 1.37, with each of them corresponding to one pixel of matrix **T**. If we consider the digital hologram as a distorted grating, it becomes clear that shifting the cell pinhole with respect to a central position would proportionally change the phase of the incident light wave. Therefore, the shift is chosen as follows:

$$C_{u,v} = \frac{\varphi_T(u, v)}{2\pi} \cdot (\Delta b - 2d) + d, \tag{1.28}$$

where $2d$ is the window size of Lohmann's hologram cell. At the same time, changing the size of each pinhole would result in the changed amplitude of the incident wave.

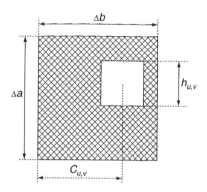

Figure 1.37. Lohmann's hologram cell.

The pinhole's size is given by

$$h_{u,v} = \frac{a_T(u, v)}{a_{T \max}} \Delta a.$$ (1.29)

The approaches proposed by Lee [6] and Burckhardt [10] are conceptually similar to the Lohmann method. Lee's approach is as follows: to each pixel T_{mn} of the complex-valued matrix **T** are assigned two pairs of real pixels $T_{m,n}^1$, $T_{m,n}^2$, $T_{m,n}^3$, and $T_{m,n}^4$ with their values fixed within the cells of two neighboring rows of an amplitude hologram

$$T_{m,n}^1 = \begin{cases} T_{m,n}^r, & T_{m,n}^r \geq 0 \\ 0, & T_{m,n}^r < 0 \end{cases},$$ (1.30)

$$T_{m,n}^2 = \begin{cases} -T_{m,n}^r, & T_{m,n}^r < 0 \\ 0, & T_{m,n}^r \geq 0 \end{cases},$$ (1.31)

$$T_{m,n}^3 = \begin{cases} T_{m,n}^i, & T_{m,n}^i \geq 0 \\ 0, & T_{m,n}^i < 0 \end{cases},$$ (1.32)

$$T_{m,n}^4 = \begin{cases} -T_{m,n}^i, & T_{m,n}^i \geq 0 \\ 0, & T_{m,n}^i < 0 \end{cases},$$ (1.33)

where $T_{m,n}^r = \mathrm{Re}(T_{m,n}), T_{m,n}^i = \mathrm{Im}(T_{m,n}).$ (1.34)

According to Burckhardt, to each complex-valued pixel T_m are assigned three real pixels fixed in neighboring cells of the hologram

$$T_{m,n}^1 = a_T(m, n) \sin[\phi_T(m, n)],$$ (1.35)

$$T_{m,n}^2 = a_T(m, n) \cos\left[\frac{\pi}{6} - \phi_T(m, n)\right],$$ (1.36)

$$T_{m,n}^3 = a_T(m, n) \cos\left[\frac{\pi}{6} + \phi_T(m, n)\right].$$ (1.37)

The common disadvantage of Lohmann's, Lee's, and Burckhardt's methods is their low energy efficiency, which is the result of the amplitude character of the hologram and the emergence of higher diffraction orders because of the implicit introduction of the carrier frequency.

1.3.3 Phase Holograms

The invention of kinoform (Lesem, Hirsh, Jordan, 1969 [3]) was a real breakthrough in the synthesis of phase holograms. The kinoform is a thin phase plate of uniform amplitude transmittance and a phase transmittance determined by the phase $\phi_T(u, v)$ of the complex transmission function. Figure 1.38 depicts the photomask of a kinoform generating a cross-shaped image.

Theoretical studies have shown that if we neglect the amplitude information, 80 percent of the field energy in the plane of the reconstructed image will correspond to the useful information on the object, with the remaining 20 percent responsible for the noise deteriorating the reconstructed object quality. In 1971, Kirk and Jones [4] proposed that holograms of higher reconstruction quality may be synthesized by reducing the complex transmission function to the phase-only transmission function with introduction of a sinusoidal carrier into the plane of the element under design. The useful image is reconstructed in the "working" diffraction order, while the remaining diffraction orders, as in the case of the Lohmann method, are used as auxiliary elements. Shown in Figure 1.39 is an object image reconstructed from the Kirk-Jones hologram. One can clearly see the working diffraction order (at the center) as well as the auxiliary diffraction orders.

The Kirk-Jones method was later generalized onto the case of a periodic carrier of arbitrary form

$$\Gamma(\vec{u}) = \exp[i\varphi(\vec{u})], \tag{1.38}$$

$$\varphi(\vec{u}) = \varphi_T(\vec{u}) + \varphi_{\max}\beta a(\vec{u})q[\vec{v}\vec{u} + \alpha(\vec{u})], \tag{1.39}$$

where q is an arbitrary periodic function of period 1 that takes values from the interval $q(t) \in [-1, 1]$, $\varphi_{\max}$ is the maximum phase shift on the microrelief height, $\vec{v}$ is the carrier frequency, $a(\vec{u})$ is the modulation function of microrelief height nonlinearly related to $a_T(\vec{u})$ at each point $\vec{u}$, and $\beta \in [0, 1]$ is the coefficient of modulation depth.

Figure 1.38. Kinoform.

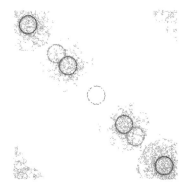

Figure 1.39. Object image reconstructed from the Kirk-Jones hologram.

The optical element of Eq. (1.38) is represented by an irregular diffraction grating changing to a regular one at $\varphi_T \equiv 0$, $\alpha \equiv 0$, $a \equiv 1$. Variations in any of these parameters will result in the redistribution of light field between different diffraction orders, which is equivalent to directing a portion of light beam energy to "auxiliary" elements. In that case, different energy portions go to the useful "working" diffraction order from different cells. This phenomenon is equivalent to the implicit introduction of amplitude transmittance alongside the phase one, but on the basis of a purely phase structure. Equation (1.39) for phase transmittance makes it possible to construct various encoding methods. For any periodic function q, one may determine a specific form of the nonlinear dependence of the normalized amplitude distribution on the modulation function of microrelief height:

$$a_T(\vec{u}) = B(\beta a(\vec{u})). \tag{1.40}$$

Figure 1.40 shows diffraction gratings corresponding to the most popular carriers. Table 1.1 gives calculational formulae for various types of base diffraction gratings. Note that in the particular case of the sinusoidal carrier, $n = 0$, $\vec{v}_1 = (v_1, 0)$, we get

TABLE 1.1. Calculational Formulae for Various Types of Grating

Type of Base Grating $q0(t)$	φ max	B (βa) for n-th Diffraction Order
Sinusoidal;		$i^n J_n\left(\frac{1}{2}\varphi_{\max}\beta a\right)$
$\frac{1}{2}\cos(2\pi t)$	$\sim \pi$	
Rectangular;		$\cos\left(\frac{\pi}{2}\beta a\right)$ at $n = 0$
0.5 at $1 \leq t < 0.5 + 1$		
-0.5 at $0.5 + 1 \leq t < 1 + 1$	π	$\frac{2}{\pi n}\sin\left(\frac{\pi}{2}\beta a\right)$ at $n = \pm 1, \pm 3, \ldots$
$1 = 0, \pm 1, \pm 2, \ldots$		0 at $n = \pm 2, \pm 4, \ldots$
Sawtooth;		
$(t - 0.5 - 1)$ at $1 \leq t < 1 + 1$	2π	$(-1)^n \sin c(\beta a - n)$
$1 = 0, \pm 1, \pm 2, \ldots$		

$$a_T(\vec{u}) = B(\beta a(\vec{u}))$$

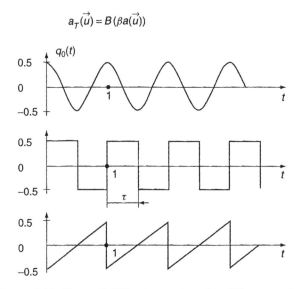

Figure 1.40. Types of diffraction gratings for different carriers.

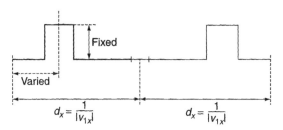

Figure 1.41. Modulation of shift of diffraction microrelief groove center.

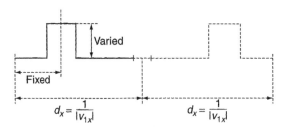

Figure 1.42. Modulation of groove height of diffraction microrelief.

the same equations as in the Kirk-Jones method [4]. In another particular case of the rectangular grating, we come to the method of synthetic coefficients [7].

Encoding the amplitude distribution into the phase one may be implemented not only by modulating the microrelief height but also by modulating other parameters of the carrier (Figs. 1.41–1.43)[11]. Just as with Lohmann's, Lee's, and Burkhardt's holograms, the disadvantage of phase holograms built up by introducing the carrier

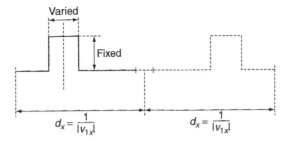

Figure 1.43. Modulation of relative pulse duration of diffraction microrelief grooves.

is a decrease in the energy efficiency caused by the emergence of higher diffraction orders.

1.3.4 Combined Holograms

The advantages of combined holograms are as follows. They generate a unique working order and produce no noise related to the loss of amplitude information. However, because of the technological complexity of fabrication and alignment of a pair of substrates and energy losses related to the transmission of amplitude distribution, such holograms have not found wide practical use.

1.3.5 Iterative Approach to the Design of Holograms

Iterative approach to the design of holograms has found wide use [12–15]. This became possible because of the steady enhancement of computer performance and the high quality of holograms that are calculated using this approach. Nowadays there are plenty of techniques for designing both amplitude and phase holograms developed within the previously mentioned approach. Problems related to the convergence and applicability of iterative procedures have been given thoughtful study. Figure 1.44 depicts the most general scheme of an iterative process of calculating the transmission function of a DOE.

The iterative process of designing DOEs usually proceeds through either the consecutive construction of projections onto closed sets corresponding to the limitations imposed on the complex amplitude in the focal and the DOE planes (Stark, Levi,

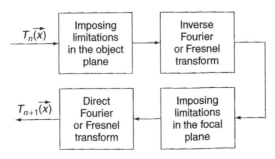

Figure 1.44. Scheme of iterative process.

1984 [14]) or a widely known gradient procedure of searching for the functional minimum [13].

In the simplest and most popular case, when the object is specified by its amplitude distribution, one may design a holographic element using an iterative procedure known as the *error-reduction procedure* (Fienup, 1980 [12]). The desired phase amplitude is complemented with a stochastic or a specially calculated determinate phase and is recalculated into the hologram plane. The resulting amplitude distribution in the hologram plane is replaced by the amplitude distribution of an illuminating beam and then the reverse calculation is performed. The phase of a reconstructed object serves as complement to the original amplitude distribution in the next iteration. Fienup has shown that such a procedure has a property of nonincreasing error.

Note that we may interpret the design of a kinoform as the result of the zero iteration in the iterative design of the phase hologram of an object specified by its amplitude distribution. Holographic elements designed via iterative procedures feature high energy efficiency and relatively small error in formation of the desired distribution. Among the disadvantages of the iterative approach are high computational efforts and development of the stagnation effect after 10 to 30 iterations when a further increase in the number of iterations does not result in a significant decrease in the error of the desired distribution formation. Technological problems resulting from an extremely irregular structure of the elements are common to iteratively designed phase holographic elements and kinoforms.

In Ref. [14], it has been demonstrated that the use of the Fienup procedure is equivalent to searching for the DOE phase function by constructing sequential mathematical projections onto sets that meet the limitations imposed on the DOE and the image under synthesis. As a possible reason for stagnation, the authors call either the absence of solution (the set of admissible solutions is empty) or a special character of these sets' topology — so-called "traps" and "tunnels " [14]. In Refs. [14,15], the authors try to rule out the stagnation caused by the "traps" and "tunnels" using a number of approaches that involve alternative search for the solutions. Such an approach may involve individual fitting of parameters and is not always effective. Another possibility is the releasing of the limitations imposed in the focal plane and in the DOE aperture, the inevitable consequence being the emergence of additional noise of reconstruction caused by a change in a priori limitations. Besides, the question of what limitation and to what extent needs to be released is answered through numerical simulations that have been repeated many times. When the straightforward problem of diffraction requires no great computational efforts (e.g., the desired distribution should be radially symmetric or factorable in coordinates) or high-performance hardware is available (working station or supercomputer), the use of stochastic or heuristic, "unidirectional," algorithms is expedient [16–21]. Among the most familiar heuristic "unidirectional" methods are the simulated annealing algorithm [16,17] and genetics algorithm [17–21]. References [17–21] discuss the use of so-called "genetics" algorithms in the DOE design. The term *genetics algorithms* refers to the application of heuristic approaches based on the principles of nature evolution. The evolution algorithms came out as an attempt to describe some processes found in nature development. The genetics algorithm (GA) is an iterative stochastic process that works with a set of individuals (populations). Every individual represents the potential solution to a problem (e.g., the phase problem of diffraction optics). The solution is found as a result of coding-decoding procedure. At the beginning, the population is generated at random (possibly by heuristic construction). Some evaluating function J is used to assign each individual the measure of individual value with respect to the problem under study (for the phase problem, this may be the energy efficiency or signal-to-noise ratio). This value serves as a quantitative information that the algorithm uses for directing the search. The frame of the GA is as follows:

```
Creation of the first generation [P(0)]
t=0
WHILE NOT the stop criterion [P(t)] DO
Estimate [P(t)]
P'(t)=Selection of [P(...)] from the evaluating function J
P''(t)=Application of the reproduction operator [P'(t)]
P(t+1)=Replacement [P(t),P''(t)]
t=t+1
END
RETURN Best solution
```

Note that the GA establishes the relation between the "development" of the good solution (selection phase) and the investigation of new zones of a pregiven space (reproduction phase), on the understanding that the replacement policy allows new solutions to be assumed, which are not necessarily better than the existing ones. The GA are heuristic and hence (in the general case) do not guarantee the optimal solution. The algorithms demonstrate irregular behavior, thus producing different outcomes at various passages of the same algorithm. However, in Ref. [21] the conditions under which the implementation of the GA results in the global maximum are discussed. There is a possibility of constructing an iterative procedure with the choice of an initial guess. In this case, the algorithm for constructing an iterative procedure is as follows: in one way or another, the phase of an element that generates a nearly desired distribution is computed. This phase is then used as one of the "parents" of the initial population, with the remaining members of the population obtained, for example, by adding noise to the estimated result. By way of example (Figs. 1.45 and 1.46), consider the construction of a GA for designing a binary DOE capable of generating a desired

Figure 1.45. Phase of a binary element designed by use of the genetics algorithm.

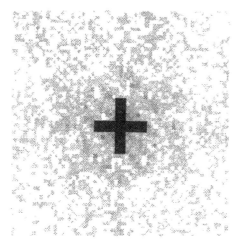

Figure 1.46. The result of operation of the optical element with the phase depicted in Fig. 1.45.

uniform intensity distribution in some domain D of the output plane (x, y). The DOE is supposed to have a binary structure, thus implying the use of the conventional binary coding, that is, the pixel with a phase equal to π is denoted as one, whereas the zero phase is denoted as 0. Such a coding technique can be easily generalized to the number of levels equal to 2^n, (i.e., for 2, 4, 8, etc. levels), but in this case, every pixel of the optical element will account for 2, 4, and so forth "chromosomes," respectively. It seems natural to choose the following functional as maximizing:

$$J = 1/\delta \rightarrow \max, \quad \delta = \iint\limits_{D} (I(x, y) - I_{cp})^2 \, dx, \tag{1.41}$$

where D is the object domain, and

$$I_{cp} = \frac{C_{max}}{\|D\|} \iint\limits_{M} I_0(u, v) \, du \, dv, \tag{1.42}$$

where M is the aperture domain, $I_0(u, v)$ is the intensity distribution on the aperture, and $C_{max} \approx 0, 8$ is the theoretical maximum of energy efficiency with binary quantization. This criterion allows both the intensity leveling and the energy efficiency variation to be taken into account jointly in a single functional. It is also necessary to work out a certain heuristic mechanism of "chromosome exchange," $P''(t) = [P'(t)]$.

It should, however, be noted that heuristic character of the algorithms [17–21] and generally great computational efforts hamper their use for synthesis of phase DOEs. The error-diffusion procedure [22–24] realizes another approach to eliminating (or rather neutralizing) noise on the reconstructed object that appears as the result of the absence of the exact solution to the problem of synthesis of phase DOEs. Using this algorithm in the DOE phase function, a predistortion is introduced and aimed at spatially separating the object under reconstruction and the noise in the DOE output plane.

1.4   RAY-TRACING APPROACH TO THE DOE DESIGN

1.4.1   Designing a DOE Using Ray-Tracing Optics

In geometric optics, the energy is assumed to propagate along certain curves called *light beams*. In the homogeneous medium, the light beams are straight lines. The distance between two points on the ray multiplied by the refractive index is called an *optical path length*. The optical path length as a function of point coordinates on the ray is designated the *eikonal*. The eikonal function multiplied by the wave number is spoken of as the phase. The argument of a complex function describing any projection of the electric or magnetic vector of the electromagnetic wave is also termed *the phase*. The locus of points of equal phase or equal eikonal is called the *wave front*. The rays are always perpendicular to the wave front. A beam coming out of a small domain of one and the same wave front and coming into the corresponding domain of another wave front is called the *ray pipe*. The intensity flux (the product of intensity by the light pipe area) is conserved along the ray pipe. Within the ray-tracing approach, the problem of focusing the laser light is equivalent to searching for a function of mapping (or transformation) of coordinates (u, v) into coordinates (x, y) separated by the distance f. This mapping is constructed with the use of straight light beams connecting the points on both planes. The ray is perpendicular to the wave front surface, and, therefore, knowing the ray path between two planes, we can uniquely find the wave front equation $W(x, y, z) = 0$.

An optical element is a surface on which the eikonal function suffers a discontinuity. The magnitude of this discontinuity is called the *eikonal of an optical element*. In the general case, this magnitude depends not only on the height of an optical element's microrelief, but also on the eikonal of an incident light wave.

By way of illustration, we shall find the eikonal function of an optical element represented as a domain filled with a material of refractive index n and limited by the surfaces $z = 0$ and $z = h(x, y)$ (Fig. 1.47). Without loss of generality, we shall consider a plane wave illuminating the optical element on the plane $z = 0$ side.

Let us consider two reference planes: the input plane $z = 0$ and the output plane $z = L$, $L = \max h(x, y)$. We shall find the eikonal in the plane $z = L$. Assume that

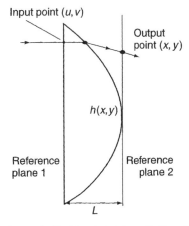

Figure 1.47. The definition of eikonal.

u, v are the coordinates of the input ray point and that x, y are the coordinates of the output ray point. The eikonal in the output plane is given by

$$W(u + N_x\ell, v + N_y\ell) = nh(u, v) + \ell$$
$$L = h(u, v) + N_z\ell, \tag{1.43}$$

where (N_x, N_y, N_z) are coordinates of the unit vector $\vec{N}$ directed from a point where the ray intersects the output surface limiting the optical element to a point of the ray exit and l is the length of the vector directed from a point where the ray intersects the optical element's surface to the point (x, y). Decomposing the expression for W into a Taylor series up to linear terms yields

$$W(u, v) + \frac{\partial W}{\partial u}N_x\ell + \frac{\partial W}{\partial v}N_y\ell = nh(u, v) + \ell. \tag{1.44}$$

Taking into account that $\ell = \dfrac{L - h(u, v)}{N_z}$, we obtain the final expression for the eikonal of an optical element

$$W(u, v) = nh(u, v) + \frac{L - h(u, v)}{N_z} - \left(\frac{\partial W}{\partial u}N_x + \frac{\partial W}{\partial v}N_y\right)\frac{L - h(u, v)}{N_z}. \tag{1.45}$$

In the paraxial approximation,

$$N_z \approx 1$$
$$N_x = \frac{\partial W}{\partial u} \ll 1 \tag{1.46}$$
$$N_y = \frac{\partial W}{\partial v} \ll 1$$

In view of the preceding relations, the expression for the eikonal of the optical element takes the following simple form:

$$W(u, v) = L + (n - 1)h(u, v). \tag{1.47}$$

When passing through the optical element, the magnitude of jump of this element's eikonal is

$$\psi(u, v) = (n - 1)h(u, v). \tag{1.48}$$

By way of example, let us consider a spherical plane convex lens (Fig. 1.48).

$$h(x, y) = R - d + \sqrt{R^2 - x^2 - y^2}$$
$$\psi(u, v) = C + (n - 1)\sqrt{R^2 - u^2 - v^2} \tag{1.49}$$

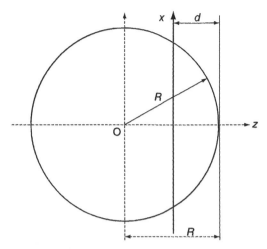

Figure 1.48. Spherical plane convex lens.

where R is the lens curvature radius and d is the lens thickness. For the thin lens

$$\sqrt{R^2 - u^2 - v^2} \approx R - \frac{u^2 + v^2}{2R}(d \approx 0), \qquad (1.50)$$

the expression for the eikonal takes the form

$$\psi(u, v) = C - \frac{u^2 + v^2}{2f}, \qquad (1.51)$$

where $f = R/(n - 1)$ is the focal length of the thin spherical lens. Equation (1.51) is different from the phase in Eq. (1.11) by an arbitrary constant C and a constant multiplier k.

It can easily be seen that the mapping of a circle into the point is carried out with a spherical wave front that is formed by a conventional spherical lens. The mapping of a rectangle into a straight-line segment is conducted with a cylindrical wave front that is formed by a spherical lens. In the general case, a domain with coordinates (u, v) is mapped into a domain with coordinates (x, y) with a DOE that may be considered as an aspheric lens with aberrations.

1.4.2 Deducing an Inclinations Equation for the Design of DOEs

Figure 1.49 shows the angles α and β for defining a unit vector $\vec{N}$ directed from an arbitrary point (u, v) in the DOE plane to the corresponding point (x, y) in the plane of focusing. Coordinates of the aforementioned unit vector are

$$N_u = \sin \alpha \sin \beta, \quad N_v = \sin \alpha \cos \beta, \quad N_z = \cos \alpha. \qquad (1.52)$$

Expressing the coordinates of vector $\vec{N}$ through the length L of a segment connecting points (u, v) and (x, y) and through the coordinates of the projection of point (x, y)

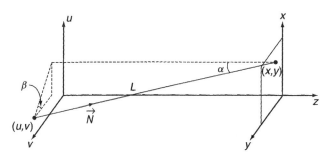

Figure 1.49. Schematic layout of the ray path from the plane (u, v) onto the plane (x, y).

onto the plane (u, v) produces

$$N_u = \frac{x - u}{L}, \quad N_v = \frac{y - v}{L}, \quad N_z = \frac{z}{L},$$

$$L = \sqrt{(x - u)^2 + (y - v)^2 + z^2}. \tag{1.53}$$

Next, we shall make use of a reference formula connecting the coordinates of the unit normal vector to a surface with the function of that surface. In this case, this surface is represented by a wave front. Let the wave front surface be specified in an implicit form

$$W(u, v, z) = 0. \tag{1.54}$$

In this case, vector $\vec{N}$ has coordinates

$$N_u = \frac{\partial W/\partial x}{P}, \quad N_v = -\frac{\partial W/\partial y}{P}, \quad N_z = \frac{\partial W/\partial z}{P}, \tag{1.55}$$

where $\quad P = \sqrt{\left(\frac{\partial W}{\partial x}\right)^2 + \left(\frac{\partial W}{\partial y}\right)^2 + \left(\frac{\partial W}{\partial z}\right)^2}. \tag{1.56}$

Using Eq. (1.55) it should be noted that the $W(x, y, z)$ function is an eikonal and should satisfy the eikonal equation

$$\left(\frac{\partial W}{\partial x}\right)^2 + \left(\frac{\partial W}{\partial y}\right)^2 + \left(\frac{\partial W}{\partial z}\right)^2 = 1. \tag{1.57}$$

The last equation immediately follows from the definition of the eikonal function. Actually, the product of refractive index $n(x, y, z)$ by a small distance ds along the ray is equal to the increment of an optical path length or the eikonal increment $dW(x, y, z)$ (Fig. 1.50):

$$dW(x, y, z) = n(x, y, z) \, dS. \tag{1.58}$$

Expressing the directional derivative in Eq. (1.58) by the gradient of eikonal function, we get

$$n = \frac{dW}{dS} = \vec{\nabla} W \cdot \vec{N}. \tag{1.59}$$

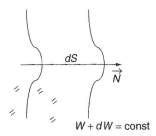

Figure 1.50. Derivation of eikonal equation.

We can also write the expression for dW/dS in the form $dW/dS = \vec{\nabla}W \cdot \vec{N}$, where $\vec{N} = (N_x, N_y, N_z)$ is a unit vector directed along the ray and $\vec{\nabla} = (\partial/\partial x, \partial/\partial y, \partial/\partial z)$ is the gradient.

By comparing modules on both sides of the last equality and assuming a homogeneous character of optical medium, $n(u, v, z) = 1$, we get the eikonal equation in the vector form:

$$|\vec{\nabla}W|^2 = 1. \tag{1.60}$$

The foregoing considerations taken into account, we shall infer the equation of inclinations that allows the DOE phase function to be derived:

$$\varphi(u, v) = kW(x, y, z)|_{x=u, y=v, z=0},$$

$$\frac{\partial \varphi}{\partial u} = \frac{k(x - u)}{L}, \quad \frac{\partial \varphi}{\partial u} = \frac{k(y - v)}{L}, \tag{1.61}$$

$$\frac{\partial \varphi}{\partial z} = \sqrt{k^2 - \left(\frac{\partial \varphi}{\partial u}\right)^2 + \left(\frac{\partial \varphi}{\partial v}\right)^2} = \frac{kz}{L}.$$

1.4.3 Designing a Focusing DOE Using Geometric Optics

We need to focus an incident beam of intensity $I_0(\vec{u})$ and phase $\psi_0(\vec{u})$ into a focal curve $z = f$ specified by the parametric equation

$$\vec{x} = \vec{X}(\xi), \quad \xi \in [0, \ell], \tag{1.62}$$

and a linear energy density of $I(\xi)$ along the curve (Fig. 1.51) [25–27].

The linear density function $I(\xi)$ characterizes the energy distribution along the focal curve. Examples of the linear density function when focusing into a straight-line segment are shown in Figure 1.52. Since the DOE is 2D and the focal line is 1D, there is a 1D set of points, $\Gamma(\xi)$, on the DOE that directs the light at the same point $\vec{X}(\xi)$ on the curve. We shall call this set of points *a layer*. The ray pipe is here sheetlike and passes between the points $\vec{X}(\xi)$ and $\vec{X}(\xi + d\xi)$ of the focal curve and between $\Gamma(\xi)$ and $\Gamma(\xi + d\xi)$ in the domain $D(\xi, \xi + d\xi)$ (Fig. 1.51a).

It has been theoretically shown that the layers are represented by a family of hyperbolas. In the paraxial approximation, the hyperbola degenerates into a straight line

$$\vec{u}\vec{X}'(\xi) = P(\xi), \tag{1.63}$$

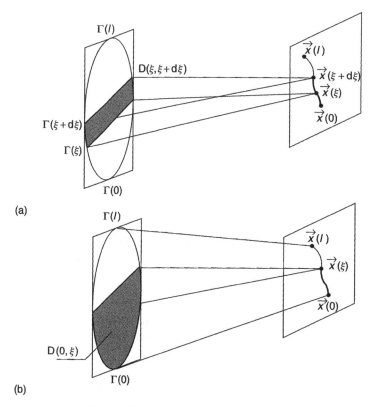

Figure 1.51. Focusing into a focal curve.

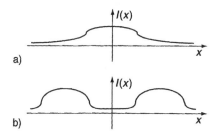

Figure 1.52. Examples of the linear density function when focusing into a line-segment.

The $P(\xi)$ function determines the energy distribution along the focal curve. A specific form of the linear density may be found from the energy conservation law.

Let us consider points $\vec{X}(0)$ and $\vec{X}(\xi)$ on the focal curve and the corresponding layers $\Gamma(0)$ and $\Gamma(\xi)$ on the DOE. In this case, the light flux conservation law may be written in the integral form (see Fig. 1.51b):

$$\int_0^t I(\xi)\,d\xi = E[t, c(t)] = \int_{D(0,t)} I_0(\vec{u})\,d^2\vec{u}. \tag{1.64}$$

The inverse problem of focusing has a solution if the energy conservation law holds for the total light flux. Substituting the derived form of $P(\xi)$ into the layer equation and solving the resulting algebraic equation for ξ produces a relationship $\xi = \xi(\vec{u})$ between points on the focal curve and points on the optical element. Substituting this relationship into the inclinations equation we can find

$$\nabla_{\perp}\varphi = \frac{\vec{X}[\xi(\vec{u})] - \vec{u}}{(f^2 + \{\vec{X}[\xi(\vec{u})] - \vec{u}\}^2)^{\frac{1}{2}}} \cong \frac{1}{f}\{\vec{X}[\xi(\vec{u})] - \vec{u}\} \tag{1.65}$$

and reconstruct $\varphi(\vec{u})$ using potential theory methods:

$$\varphi(\vec{u}) = \varphi(\vec{u}_0) + \int_{\vec{u}_0}^{\vec{u}} \nabla_{\perp}\varphi \, d\vec{u}, \tag{1.66}$$

where integration is over an arbitrary curve connecting point u with some initial point $\vec{u}_0$, $\nabla_{\perp} = (\partial/\partial u, \partial/\partial v)$.

Examples 1.1   Let us consider some examples [28–33]. Of particular interest is focusing into a straight-line segment $|x| \leq (\ell/2)$ parallel to the x-axis:

$$\vec{X}(\xi) = (-l/2 + \xi, 0); \xi \in (0, l). \tag{1.67}$$

In this case, $\Gamma(\xi)$ is a straight line $u = P(\xi)$ parallel to the Ov.

Consider a simplest DOE focusing from a beam of rectangular cross section $D = [-A, A] \times [-B, B]$, plane wave front and uniform intensity $I_0(\vec{u}) = 1/4AB$ over D into the aforementioned straight-line segment of uniform intensity distribution. Equations (1.64) to (1.66) yield

$$\varphi(\vec{u}) = k\left\{ -\frac{u^2}{2f}\left(1 - \frac{\ell}{2A}\right) - \frac{v^2}{2f} \right\}. \tag{1.68}$$

and describe, as one might expect, an astigmatic beam with the foci $f/[1 - (\ell/2A)]^{-1}$ and f. The photomask corresponding to Eq. (1.68) is shown in Figure 1.53.

Example 1.2   As a more complicated example, we shall take a geometric DOE focusing the rectangular Gaussian beam into the same straight-line segment for which

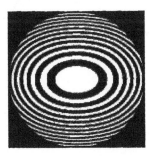

Figure 1.53. Photomask of a geometric DOE focusing into a line-segment.

Eqs. (1.64) to (1.66) produce the phase function in the form

$$\varphi(\vec{u}) = -\frac{k\vec{u}^2}{2f} + \frac{k\ell\sigma}{\sqrt{2}f\,\mathrm{erf}\left(\dfrac{A}{\sigma\sqrt{2}}\right)}$$

$$\times \left\{ \frac{u}{\sigma\sqrt{2}}\mathrm{erf}\left(\frac{u}{\sigma\sqrt{2}}\right) - \frac{1}{\pi}\left[1 - \exp\left(-\frac{u^2}{2\sigma^2}\right)\right]\right\}, \qquad (1.69)$$

where $\quad \mathrm{erf}(x) = \dfrac{1}{\sqrt{2\pi}}\displaystyle\int_{-\infty}^{x}\exp\left(-\frac{t^2}{2}\right)dt. \qquad (1.70)$

Here, a more complicated character of the phase function is due to the combination of astigmatism with the diffractive redistribution of energy from the center to the periphery of the beam.

1.4.4 Geometric-Optical Design of Wave Front Compensators

Compensators [34–37] are intended to transform the shape of the illuminating-beam wave front. For example, they serve to transform a spherical wave front into an aspheric one. Figure 1.54 depicts how a compensator forms the wave front.

Let us specify a wave front σ by the equation $z = f(\vec{x})$. We shall introduce a three-dimensional (3D) normalized gradient of a surface defined by the function $f(x)$ as follows:

$$\vec{N} = \frac{(-\nabla_{\perp}f, 1)}{\sqrt{1 + |\nabla_{\perp}f|^2}}. \qquad (1.71)$$

We shall use the solution of the task to select the compensator's phase function in the form

$$\psi_0(\vec{u}) + \frac{\varphi(\vec{u})}{k} + L = \varphi_0 = \mathrm{const}, \qquad (1.72)$$

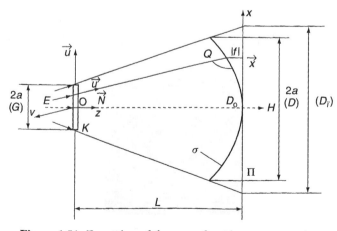

Figure 1.54. Formation of the wave front by a compensator.

where L is the distance between a point on the compensator and a point on the wave front measured along the ray and $k\psi_0$ is the illuminating-beam phase.

According to Eq. (1.71), we can express the quantity L from the ray optics as follows:

$$L = [\ell - f(\vec{x})]\sqrt{1 + |\nabla_\perp f(\vec{x})|^2} \qquad (1.73)$$

From Eqs. (1.72) and (1.73) follows an equation of the compensator's phase function

$$\varphi(\vec{u}) = \varphi_0 - k\left[\psi_0(\vec{u}) + [\ell - f(\vec{x})]\sqrt{1 + |\nabla_\perp f(\vec{x})|^2}\right] \qquad (1.74)$$

and an equation relating the coordinates of point $\vec{u}$ on the compensator and point $\vec{x}$ on the surface σ:

$$\vec{u} = \vec{x} + [\ell + f(\vec{x})]\nabla_\perp f(\vec{x}). \qquad (1.75)$$

For actually symmetric compensators generating rotating wave fronts, the relationships (1.74) and (1.75) change to

$$\varphi(r) = \varphi_0 - k\left[\psi_0(r) + [\ell + f(\rho)]\sqrt{1 + (f'(\rho))^2}\right], \qquad (1.76)$$

$$r = \rho + [\ell + f(\rho)]f'(\rho), \qquad (1.77)$$

where

$$\rho = (x^2 + y^2)^{1/2}, \quad r = (u^2 + v^2)^{1/2}, \quad z = f(\rho), \quad 0 \le \rho \le \frac{D}{2},$$

$$\ell = -f(D/2) - (D - d)[2f'(D/2)], \qquad (1.78)$$

and d is the diameter of the compensator. Shown in Fig. 1.55 is the photomask of a compensator transforming a spherical wave front into a parabolic one.

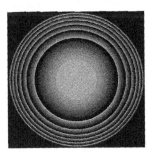

Figure 1.55. Photomask of the compensator "sphere-paraboloid".

1.5 SAMPLING AND QUANTIZATION OF PHASE IN DIFFRACTIVE OPTICS

1.5.1 Model of Sampling and Quantizing the Phase in the Process of DOE Fabrication

Great potentialities of diffractive optics are restricted by the resolution of devices for designing and generating the diffraction microrelief of an optical element. Sampling and quantization of the phase transmission function eventually leads to the deviation of real characteristics of a DOE from the designed ones [38–43].

In this chapter, we deal with the techniques for the computer-aided synthesis of optical elements using computer-controlled raster pattern generators. At the first stage, a mathematical model of sampling and quantization is set up. Next, we analyze the properties of sampling and quantization perturbations and estimate the phase error directly in the input plane of the optical element under synthesis. Finally, the field structure in the output plane, which is parallel to the synthesized element, is estimated.

All major stages of computer-aided synthesis of phase diffractive optical elements are related in one way or another to phase sampling and quantization. The smooth phase $\varphi(u, v) = \varphi(\vec{u})$ is calculated as an array of pixels and brought to the interval $(0, 2\pi m)$, thereby resulting in the reduced phase $\Phi(u, v) \equiv \Phi(\vec{u})$, Eq. (1.9), whose values are then quantized in M levels and passed to a photomask generator. This represents the phase in the form of varying blackening densities: halftone or binary.

Next is a technological process of microrelief formation: halftone photomasks may be used for generating a continuous diffraction phase microrelief, whereas a set of binary photomasks allows a stepwise phase microrelief to be lithographically obtained.

Sampling and quantization perturbations are principally unavoidable in computer-generated optical elements and should be estimated. We shall consider a sampling model for optical elements fabricated with a raster pattern generator or a raster lithographer. Photomasks synthesized with a scanning raster generator are made up of a set of J nonintersecting resolution cells, $G_{\vec{j}}$. When combined, they form a working area of the photomask (Figs. 1.56 and 1.57); here $\vec{j} = (j_1, j_2)$ is a 2D index number of the resolution cell with the center $\vec{u}_{\vec{j}}$. Dimension of the cells $G_{\vec{j}}$ determines the resolution of both the photomask and the resulting optical element.

The critical characteristic of a raster generator is the function of acting energy distribution over the scanning spot $E_j(\vec{u})$. The extension of this function must be exactly equal to the resolution cell dimension, otherwise, phases in neighboring cells will overlap.

We shall consider most interesting particular cases of the raster generator. Rectangular raster photomask generators with a $\delta_1 \times \delta_2$ uniform rectangular spot and a $2a \times 2b$ field (Fig. 1.56) allow the following sampling model to be used:

$$G_{\vec{j}} = \left\{ (u, v) : u_{j_1} - \frac{\delta_1}{2} \leq u \leq u_{j_1} + \frac{\delta_1}{2}, v_{j_2} - \frac{\delta_2}{2} \leq v \leq v_{j_2} + \frac{\delta_2}{2} \right\}$$

$$\vec{u}_{\vec{j}} = (u_{j_1}, v_{j_2}); \quad j_1 = \overline{1, N_1}, \quad j_2 = \overline{1, N_2}, \tag{1.79}$$

where the numbers u_{j_1}, v_{j_2} form arithmetic progressions with the step δ_1, δ_2, respectively, $N_1 \delta_1 = 2a$, $N_2 \delta_2 = 2b$. In that case,

$$E_{\vec{j}}(u, v) = \text{rect}\left(\frac{u - u_{j_1}}{\delta_1}\right) \text{rect}\left(\frac{v - v_{j_2}}{\delta_2}\right), \tag{1.80}$$

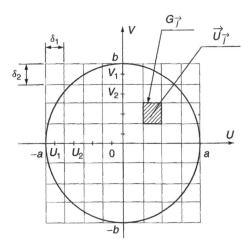

Figure 1.56. Rectangular raster photomask structure.

where

$$\text{rect}(t) = \begin{cases} 1, & |t| < \frac{1}{2} \\ 0, & |t| \geq \frac{1}{2} \end{cases}. \tag{1.81}$$

Note that within the limits of the rectangular field $2a \times 2b$ there are $N_1 \times N_2$ possible positions of the spot, of which only a portion $|J|$ corresponds to the domain G (a circle). Using rectangular raster generators, one can fabricate photomasks of arbitrary DOEs, the phase function being expressed through the interpolation formula

$$\Phi(\vec{u}) = \sum_{\vec{j} \in J} \Phi_{\vec{j}} E_{\vec{j}}(\vec{u}), \tag{1.82}$$

where $\Phi_{\vec{j}} \equiv \Phi(\vec{u})|_{\vec{u}=\vec{u}_{\vec{j}}}$. Accordingly, the DOE transmission function will take the form

$$\partial(\vec{u}) = \exp[i\,\Phi(\vec{u})]. \tag{1.83}$$

With a circular raster photomask generator (Fig. 1.57), the domain G is represented by a circle of radius a, the cells G_j numbered with the same index $j = 1, N$ and shaped as rings

$$G_j = \left\{ \vec{u} : r_j - \frac{\delta}{2} \leq |\vec{u}| \leq r_j + \frac{\delta}{2} \right\}, \tag{1.84}$$

$$E_j(\vec{u}) \equiv E_j(r) = \text{rect}\left(\frac{r - r_j}{\delta}\right). \tag{1.85}$$

The numbers r_j form an arithmetic progression with the step δ, $r = |\vec{u}|$. The circular generators are oriented to the fabrication of photomasks for radially symmetric optical elements with the transmission function given by

$$\partial(\vec{u}) = \partial(r), \tag{1.86}$$

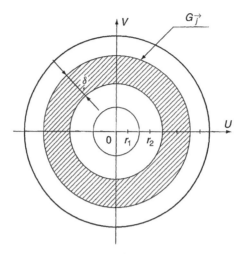

Figure 1.57. Circular raster photomask structure.

where $r = (u^2 + v^2)^{1/2}$, and the phase function

$$\Phi(\vec{u}) = \Phi(r) = \sum_{j=1}^{N} \Phi_j E_j(r). \tag{1.87}$$

Let us now consider a model of phase quantization. When generating photomasks, phase pixels Φ_j are quantized in M equidistant levels with a constant step

$$h_m = \frac{2\pi m}{M} \tag{1.88}$$

and transformed into pixels $\hat{\Phi}_j$, $j \in J$, of the quantized phase (Fig. 1.59)

$$\hat{\Phi}_j = \hat{\Phi}(\Phi_j). \tag{1.89}$$

The quantized values $\hat{\Phi}_j$ serve as control signals of a raster photomask generator. In view of the phase quantization in levels, the phase and transmission functions are given by

$$\hat{\Phi}(\vec{u}) = \sum_{j \in J} \hat{\Phi}_j E_j(\vec{u}), \tag{1.90}$$

$$\hat{\Gamma}(\vec{u}) = \exp[i\hat{\Phi}(\vec{u})]. \tag{1.91}$$

1.5.2 Estimating the Error in Sampling and Quantizing the Phase in a DOE Plane

Figure 1.58 illustrates the procedure of sampling and quantizing the DOE phase. Let us introduce an error in sampling and quantizing

$$\Delta\Phi(\vec{u}) = \Phi(\vec{u}) - \hat{\Phi}(\vec{u}). \tag{1.92}$$

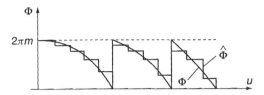

Figure 1.58. Sampling (quantization) of phase.

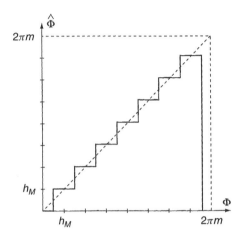

Figure 1.59. Equidistant phase quantization.

From Figure 1.58 and previous comments, its value is seen to depend on the sampling step with respect to the arguments δ_1, δ_2, and on the number of quantization levels M. Therefore, one should distinguish between the sampling error and the quantization error.

In a number of cases, the sampling error is practically not found. In particular, if a radially symmetric optical element is fabricated using a raster circular generator with a proper choice of ring's radii, we can bring the sampling error to a negligibly small value.

In any case, one is striving to bring the sampling error to a minimum, but limitations are dictated here by the resolution of a photomask generator. If the resolution of the available photomask generator does not allow obtaining a sufficiently small quantization error, the generator must be ruled out.

Let us give some considerations concerning the choice of the sampling step. We shall consider a continuous phase function $f(u)$, $-a \leq u \leq a$, that should be sampled with the step Δ

$$f(n) = f(u)|_{u=n\Delta}, \quad n = 0, 1, \ldots, N, \tag{1.93}$$

$$N = \left\lfloor \frac{2a}{\Delta} \right\rfloor. \tag{1.94}$$

From the theory of signals it has been known that if one wants the sampling to be reversible, that is, it should be possible to reconstruct the function $f(n)$ from the function $f(u)$, the following condition should be fulfilled:

$$\Delta < \frac{1}{2F},\tag{1.95}$$

where F is the width of the $f(u)$ function spectrum.

Inequality (1.95) is the starting point in the procedure of choosing the sampling step, but it gives no quantitative value of the step.

We shall additionally provide some quantitative estimates. Consider the phase function $\varphi(u, v)$ and impose a fairly obvious condition of sampling admissibility in the form

$$\left|\delta_1 \frac{\partial \varphi(u, v)}{\partial u} + \delta_2 \frac{\partial \varphi(u, v)}{\partial v}\right| \ll 2\pi \tag{1.96}$$

or in shorthand form

$$|\nabla_\delta \varphi| \ll 2\pi.$$

Let us estimate the error of a piecewise-constant approximation of the function $\varphi(\vec{u})$ (Fig. 1.56). In each cell $G_{\vec{j}}$, the function φ can be expanded into the Macloren series and approximated by the relation

$$\varphi(u, v) = \varphi(u_{j_1}, v_{j_2}) + (u - u_{j_1})\varphi_u + (v - v_{j_2})\varphi_v \tag{1.97}$$

where

$$\varphi_u = \left.\frac{\partial \varphi(\vec{u})}{\partial u}\right|_{\vec{u}=\vec{u}_j}; \quad \varphi_v = \left.\frac{\partial \varphi(\vec{u})}{\partial v}\right|_{\vec{u}=\vec{u}_j}. \tag{1.98}$$

These relations allow the sampling error to be expressed in the form

$$\Delta \varphi_{\vec{j}}(\vec{u}) = -(\vec{u} - \vec{u}_{\vec{j}})\nabla_\perp \varphi(\vec{u}_{\vec{j}}); \quad \nabla_\perp = \left(\frac{\partial}{\partial u}, \frac{\partial}{\partial v}\right). \tag{1.99}$$

Note that owing to the condition (1.96) the following inequality takes place:

$$|\Delta \varphi_{\vec{j}}(\vec{u})| \ll 2\pi. \tag{1.100}$$

The sampling effect may be characterized by the maximum or root-mean-square (rms) deviation (fluctuation) of phase given by

$$\Delta \varphi_{\max} = \max_{\vec{u} \in G} |\Delta \varphi(\vec{u})|, \tag{1.101}$$

$$\Delta \varphi_s = \left[\frac{1}{|G|} \int_G |\Delta \varphi(\vec{u})|^2 d^2 u\right]^{\frac{1}{2}}, \tag{1.102}$$

where $|G|$ is the area of the domain G.

Let us estimate the quantities in Eqs. (1.101) and (1.102) for the case of rectangular scanning spot, Eq. (1.80), and smooth function $\varphi(u, v)$. Substituting Eqs. (1.97) and (1.99) into (1.101) yields

$$\Delta\varphi_{max} = \max_{\vec{j}\in J} \max_{\vec{u}\in G_{\vec{j}}} |\Delta\varphi_{\vec{j}}(\vec{u})|$$

$$= \max_{\vec{j}\in J} \max_{\vec{u}\in G_{\vec{j}}} |\Delta\varphi_{\vec{j}}(\vec{u})| \leq \max_{\vec{j}\in J} \max_{\vec{u}\in G_{\vec{j}}} |(\vec{u} - \vec{u}_{\vec{j}})\nabla_{\perp}\varphi(\vec{u}_{\vec{j}})|. \qquad (1.103)$$

Since the minimum of the linear function

$$(u - u_{j_1})\varphi_u + (v - v_{j_2})\varphi_v \qquad (1.104)$$

on the rectangle G_j, Eq. (1.79), is achieved at

$$u - u_{j_1} = \frac{\delta_1}{2}\text{sign}(\varphi_u); \quad v - v_{j_2} = \frac{\delta_2}{2}\text{sign}(\varphi_v); \quad \text{sign}(t) = \begin{cases} 1, & t \geq 0 \\ 0, & t < 0 \end{cases} \qquad (1.105)$$

and accounts for

$$\frac{1}{2}(\delta_1|\varphi_u| + \delta_2|\varphi_v|), \qquad (1.106)$$

Eq. (1.103) may be used to derive a convenient estimate of the maximum error in phase sampling:

$$\Delta\varphi_{max} \leq \frac{1}{2} \max_{\vec{u}\in G} |\nabla_{\perp}\varphi(\vec{u})|_{+} \qquad (1.107)$$

where the symbol $|\cdot|_{+}$ denotes the sum of vector component's modules.

Similarly, for $\Delta\varphi_s$ we have

$$|G| \cdot (\Delta\varphi_s)^2 = \sum_{j\in 1} \int_{G_{\vec{j}}} < [\Delta\varphi_{\vec{j}}(\vec{u})]^2 > d^2\vec{u}. \qquad (1.108)$$

Integrating with respect to Eq. (1.85) and relations

$$\int_{G_{\vec{j}}} (\vec{u} - \vec{u}_{\vec{j}})\, d^2\vec{u} = 0, \qquad (1.109)$$

$$\int_{G_{\vec{j}}} (u - u_{j_1})^2\, d^2\vec{u} = \frac{\delta_1^3\delta_2}{12}; \quad \int_{G_{\vec{j}}} (v - v_{j_2})^2\, d^2\vec{u} = \frac{\delta_1\delta_2^3}{12}, \qquad (1.110)$$

we get

$$|G| \cdot (\Delta\varphi_s)^2 = \frac{1}{12} \sum_{\vec{j}\in J} [\nabla_{\delta}\varphi(\vec{u}_{\vec{j}})]^2\delta_1\delta_2. \qquad (1.111)$$

Replacing the sum by the corresponding integral gives a convenient estimate of the rms error in the sampling of phase

$$\Delta\varphi_s = \left\{ \frac{1}{12|G|} \int_G [\nabla_{\delta}\varphi(\vec{u})]^2 d^2\vec{u} \right\}^{\frac{1}{2}}. \qquad (1.112)$$

The estimates (1.107) and (1.112) allow the sampling errors $\Delta\varphi_s$ to be calculated directly from the sampling parameters δ_1, δ_2 and from the first-phase derivatives. An interesting particular case corresponds to "cylindrical optics," when $\varphi(\vec{u}) \equiv \varphi(u)$, $|u| \leq a$. In this case, the aforementioned formulae take the form

$$\Delta\varphi_{\max} \leq \frac{\delta}{2|} \max_{|u| \leq a} |\varphi'(\vec{u})|, \quad \varphi' = \frac{d\varphi}{du}, \tag{1.113}$$

$$\Delta\varphi_s = \left\{ \frac{\delta^2}{24a} \int_{-a}^{a} [\varphi'(\vec{u})]^2 \, du \right\}^{\frac{1}{2}}. \tag{1.114}$$

Another important particular case corresponds to the radially symmetric phase function

$$\varphi(\vec{u}) \equiv \varphi(r), \quad r = |\vec{u}| \leq a. \tag{1.115}$$

In that case,

$$\Delta\varphi_{\max} \leq \frac{\delta}{2} \max_{0 \leq r \leq a} |\varphi'(r)|, \quad \varphi' = \frac{d\varphi}{dr}, \tag{1.116}$$

$$\Delta\varphi_s = \left\{ \frac{\delta^2}{6a^2} \int_{0}^{a} [\varphi'(r)]^2 r \, dr \right\}^{\frac{1}{2}}. \tag{1.117}$$

The estimates in Eqs. (1.107) and (1.113) to (1.117) provide the direct correlation between the sampling perturbations and the derivatives of the smooth phase function. By way of example, Figure 1.58 shows the plots of the rms deviation $\Delta\varphi_s$ upon phase sampling

$$\varphi(r) = -k \frac{1 + (n-1)^{-2}}{8 f_0^3} r^4 \tag{1.118}$$

with the parameters $\lambda = 0.63$ μm, $m = 1$, $n = 1.5$, the resolution δ being a variable parameter.

From the plots in Figure 1.58, it is seen, for example, that if the resolution of a photomask generator is $\delta = 6$ μm, it is possible to implement the optical element of Eq. (1.118) with the error in phase sampling less than 5 percent in the range of variations of the "relative pinhole" parameter of $0 < 2a/f < 0.8$, whereas for $\delta = 24$ μm the corresponding range is half as wide.

Let us consider quantization effects. One should distinguish between the binary quantization ($M = 2$), the adjacent "rough" quantization characterized by a small number of levels ($M = 3, 4$), and quantization with a large number of levels ($M \gg 2$). For the binary quantization, the DOE phase assumes two values: 0 and π (hence the term *binary optics*).

The DOE operates as a phase diffraction grating (or a zone plate), that is, it gives a great number of the diffraction orders. The first order usually serves as a working order into which up to 40 percent of energy falls, thus determining the ultimate diffraction efficiency of the DOE in the present case.

If the number of quantization levels is large, one may introduce quantization noise $\Delta\varphi$. From Figure 1.60 it is seen that if the quantization step is defined by Eq. (1.88),

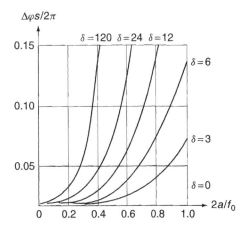

Figure 1.60. Root-mean-square deviation upon phase sampling.

the maximum value of phase quantization error is given by

$$\Delta\varphi_{\max}^{k} = \frac{\pi m}{M}. \tag{1.119}$$

Assuming that $\Delta\varphi_k$ can, with equal probability, take values from the range $[-\pi m/M, \pi m/M]$, we can easily find the rms error of phase quantization

$$\Delta\varphi_{s}^{k} = \frac{1}{2\pi m/M} \int_{-\pi m/M}^{\pi m/M} (\Delta\varphi^{k})^{2} d(\Delta\varphi^{k}) = \frac{1}{3}\left(\frac{\pi m}{M}\right)^{2}. \tag{1.120}$$

For large M, the rms error of phase quantization amounts to fractions of a percent. In this case, the quantization effect may be reduced to the emergence in the DOE plane of an additional phase transparency with the phase random over the aperture field and varying in the narrow range $[-\pi m/M, \pi m/M]$. Note that the quantization effect is described here by the model of a stochastic phase diffuser.

1.5.3 Influence of Phase Sampling and Quantization on DOE Characteristics

To find out how the sampling and quantization of the phase function affect DOE parameters, one should consider the diffraction of light by the synthesized optical element.

Consider a plane monochromatic wave

$$W(u, v, z, t) = f(u, v)e^{-i\omega(t-z/c)}, \tag{1.121}$$

propagating along the z-axis with the velocity c. Assume that a DOE of transmittance $\partial(u, v)$ and aperture G is placed in the plane $z = 0$ (Fig. 1.61). We seek to find the diffraction field

$$S(x, y, z, t) = g(x, y, z)e^{-i\omega t} \tag{1.122}$$

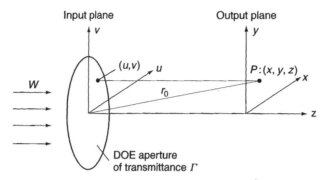

Figure 1.61. Diffraction of light by a DOE.

at large distances from the DOE plane. Let r_0 be the distance from the origin of coordinates to point P: (x, y, z) and $\alpha = x/r_0$, $\beta = y/r_0$ are the directing cosines of the line OP. Then, if r_0 is great as compared with the area of domain G, the field $g(x, y, z)$ will be expressed at point P by the relation

$$g(x, y, z) = Ae^{ikr_0} \iint\limits_G \partial(u, v) \exp[-ik(\alpha u + \beta v)] du\, dv. \tag{1.123}$$

The result arrived at may be expressed by a 2D Fourier transform of the function $\partial(u, v)$:

$$F(\omega_x, \omega_y) = \int_{-\infty}^{\infty} \int_{-\infty}^{\infty} \partial(u, v) \exp[-i(\omega_x u + \omega_y v)] du\, dv, \tag{1.124}$$

or

$$g(x, y, z) = Ae^{ikr_0} F(k\alpha, k\beta). \tag{1.125}$$

Thus, on the surface of a sphere centered at the origin of coordinates, the complex amplitude of the diffraction field is proportional to the Fourier transform $F(\omega_x, \omega_y)$ of the DOE transmission function $\Gamma(u, v)$. Bearing this in mind, we shall find out how the sampling and quantization affect DOE parameters.

For a diffractive optical element whose complex transmission function is sampled with the rectangular raster of Eq. (1.80), the output field is given by

$$g(x, y, z) = g(\omega_x, \omega_y)$$

$$= A \frac{e^{ikR_0}}{R_0} \sum_{j_1=0}^{N_1-1} \sum_{j_2=0}^{N_2-1} \partial(u_{j'}, v_j) \int_{u_{j_1}}^{u_{j_1+1}} \int_{v_{j_2}}^{v_{j_2+1}} e^{-i\omega_x u} e^{-i\omega_y v} du\, dv, \tag{1.126}$$

where $u_{j_1} = -A_1 + j_1(2A_1/N_1)$, $v_{j_2} = -A_2 + j(2A_2/N_2)$; $\omega_x = k\alpha$, $\omega_y = k\beta$; A_1, A_2 are the dimensions of the optical element, and N_1, N_2 are the number of pixels along the coordinate axes. After a simple manipulation, the previous expression takes the form

$$
g(\omega_x, \omega_y) = A \frac{e^{ikR_0}}{R_0} \exp\left[-i\omega_x \left(-A_1 + \frac{A_1}{N_1}\right)\right.
$$
$$
\left. -i\omega_y \left(-A_2 + \frac{A_2}{N_2}\right)\right] P(\omega_x, \omega_y) Q(\omega_x, \omega_y), \qquad (1.127)
$$

where

$$
Q(\omega_x, \omega_y) = \sum_{j_1=0}^{N_1-1} \sum_{j_2=0}^{N_2-1} \partial(u_{j_1}, v_{j_2}) e^{-ij_1 \omega_x 2A_1/N_1} e^{-ij_2 \omega_y 2A_2/N_2}, \qquad (1.128)
$$

$$
P(\omega_x, \omega_y) = 4 \frac{A_1 A_2}{N_1 N_2} \operatorname{sinc}\left[\frac{\omega_x A_1}{N_1}\right] \operatorname{sinc}\left[\frac{\omega_x A_2}{N_2}\right]. \qquad (1.129)
$$

The function $Q(\omega_x, \omega_y)$, Eq. (1.128), is a 2D periodic function with periods of $\pi N_1/A_1$ and $\pi N_2/A_2$ along the axes. This function describes a well-known effect of spectrum multiplication that occurs upon sampling the initial spectrum. As the number of sampling points N_1 and N_2 of the initial optical element increases, the distance between different orders also increases. In practice, the number of samplings should be chosen in such a manner that different orders in spectrum be spatially separated and not overlapped [Eq. (1.95)]. The $P(\omega_x, \omega_y)$ function describes the light diffraction by a rectangular raster when sampling a DOE. This function causes the energy portion spent on additional spectra to decrease. As the number of sampling points on the DOE increases, this energy portion decreases. The relation between the quantity P and N_1, N_2 is given by $[P \sim (1/N_1 N_2)]$.

Consider physical effects taking place in quantizing the phase function of a DOE. By $\varphi(u, v)$ we shall denote the phase function of a DOE focusing a beam of complex amplitude $W(u, v)$ into a domain S in the focal plane. We shall consider the DOE as a complement to a lens of focal length f. The criterion of the DOE functional quality is the diffractive efficiency

$$
\varepsilon = \frac{\iint\limits_{S} I(x, y)\,dx\,dy}{\iint\limits_{D} |W(x, y)|^2\,du\,dv}, \qquad (1.130)
$$

where $I(x, y)$ is the intensity in the focal plane, D is the DOE aperture, and S is the domain of focusing.

The quantity ε indicates what portion of the illuminating beam is focused into a desired domain on the focal plane. The quantization of the DOE phase function may be described as the result of application of a nonlinear transform $\hat{\Phi}(\varphi)$ to the phase function $\varphi(u, v)$ of the optical element. When quantizing the phase function $\varphi(u, v)$ reduced to the interval 2π with respect to M levels, the nonlinear predistortion takes the form

$$
\hat{\Phi}(\varphi) = \operatorname{int}\left[\frac{\varphi}{\Delta}\right]\Delta; \quad \Delta = 2\pi/M, \qquad (1.131)
$$

where int[x] denotes the whole part of the number x, M is the number of phase quantization levels (Fig. 1.57). For quantization, the function of complex transmission is given by

$$\partial(u, v) = \exp\{i\hat{\Phi}[\varphi(u, v)]\}. \tag{1.132}$$

To describe the operation of a DOE, we shall expand the complex transmission function into a Fourier series in terms of $\varphi(u, v)$:

$$\partial(u, v) = \sum_{n=-\infty}^{n=\infty} c_n \exp\left[i\frac{n}{m}\varphi(u, v)\right], \tag{1.133}$$

where $2\pi m$ is the maximum phase on the optical element,

$$c_n = \frac{1}{2\pi m} \int_0^{2\pi m} \exp\left(i\hat{\Phi}(\xi) - i\frac{n}{m}\xi\right) d\xi. \tag{1.134}$$

In view of Eq. (1.133), the field complex amplitude in the element's focal plane is represented by

$$W(x, y) = \sum_{n=-\infty}^{n=\infty} c_n W_n(x, y). \tag{1.135}$$

In the Fresnel-Kirchhoff approximation, the W_n takes the form

$$W_n(\vec{x}) = \frac{1}{i\lambda f} \exp\left(i\frac{k}{2f}x^2\right) \iint_D E_0(\vec{u}) \exp\left(i\frac{n}{m}\varphi(\vec{u}) - i\frac{kxu}{f}\right) d^2u, \tag{1.136}$$

where (u, v) is the adjacent plane of the optical element and (x, y) is the plane of focusing.

According to the aforementioned formulae, the DOE generates the diffraction orders $W_n(x, y)$, $n = -\infty, \infty$. The desired process of focusing in the m-th working (useful) order is described by the quantity $W_m(x, y)$. From the general form of the phase function, it follows that the terms with different n correspond to defocused images whose size is n/m times greater.

In the general case, the defocused images $W_n(x, y)$ affect the $W_m(x, y)$, whereas in view of Eq. (1.135) the intensity estimate will be given by

$$I(x, y) \geq |c_m|^2 I_m(x, y), \tag{1.137}$$

where

$$I(x, y) = |W(x, y)|^2, \quad I_m(x, y) = |W_m(x, y)|^2. \tag{1.138}$$

The estimate of the DOE energy efficiency will be given by

$$\varepsilon \leq |C_{nm}|^2 \varepsilon_0, \tag{1.139}$$

where ε_0 is the energy efficiency of a DOE with the continuous (nonquantized) phase function $\varphi(u, v)$.

Let us next consider quantizing the phase function of an optical element of maximum phase 2π (i.e., $m = 1$). Assume that the number of levels is M. Then, the relation for c_n takes the form

$$c_n = \frac{1}{2\pi} \sum_{k=0}^{M-1} \int_{2\pi k/M}^{2\pi(k+1)/M} \exp\left(i\frac{2\pi k}{M} - in\xi\right) d\xi. \qquad (1.140)$$

It is interesting to note that the relation for the diffraction order intensity does not contain the phase function of the original DOE. After integration, the aforementioned relation takes the form

$$c_n = i\frac{\left[\exp\left(-\dfrac{2\pi ni}{M}\right) - 1\right]}{2\pi n} \sum_{k=0}^{M-1}\left[\exp\left(-\frac{2\pi i(n-1)}{M}\right)\right]^k. \qquad (1.141)$$

Using the geometric-progression formula, we may simplify this expression

$$c_n = i\frac{\left[\exp\left(-\dfrac{2\pi ni}{M}\right) - 1\right]}{2\pi n} \frac{1 - \exp(-2\pi i(n-1))}{1 - \exp\left(-\dfrac{2\pi i(n-1)}{M}\right)}. \qquad (1.142)$$

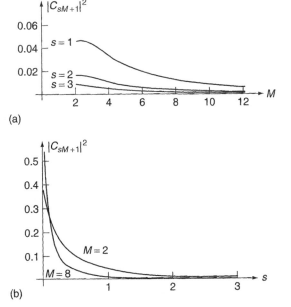

Figure 1.62. (a) Coefficient c_{sM+1} versus the number of quantization levels, (b) Coefficient c_{sM+1} versus the parameter s.

On evaluating an underterminate form, we shall obtain the final relation for the c_n:

$$c_n = \begin{cases} \dfrac{iM}{2\pi n}\left[\exp\left(-\dfrac{2\pi in}{M}\right) - 1\right], & \text{if } (n-1)/M \text{ is integer} \\ 0, & \text{if } (n-1)/M \text{ is noninteger.} \end{cases} \tag{1.143}$$

Let $n = sM + 1$ (according to (1.143), for the other n we have $c_n = 0$), where s is an arbitrary integer determining nonzero diffraction orders:

$$c_{sM+1} = \frac{i}{2\pi(s + 1/M)}\left[\exp\left(-\frac{2\pi i}{M}\right) - 1\right]. \tag{1.144}$$

From Figure 1.62 it is seen that when the number of quantization levels is small ($M = 2$–6), it is the first two to three orders that have an essential weight, the absolute value of the corresponding coefficients being comparable with $|c_1|^2$. As the number M of phase quantization levels of the DOE increases, all coefficients (except the first one) tend to zero, meaning that the contribution of auxiliary orders becomes very small (Fig. 1.62).

1.6 COMPUTER-AIDED DESIGN OF DOEs

Computer-aided design of DOEs is a complicated process. It involves solving the inverse problem of the diffraction theory, using optical-electronic facilities for recording images, and utilizing a variety of techniques for generating the phase microrelief. Each of these aforementioned stages affect the quality of the optical element to be manufactured considerably, making it difficult to predict its future performances exactly (e.g., the thickness of focusing line or the diffraction efficiency of the optical element). In this connection, the process of computer-aided synthesis of optical elements becomes iterative; studying the parameters of the element under synthesis at different fabrication stages, one produces recommendations for their improvement (Fig. 1.63). Such a situation is typical of the design process generally and of the automated design specifically. It can be seen that the investigation of characteristics of the DOEs obtained by experimenting is of great significance here. In computer optics, one needs to conduct two

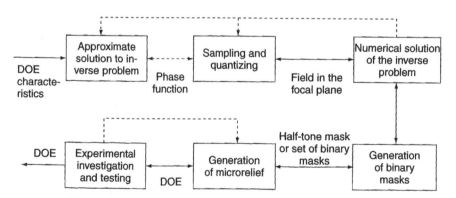

Figure 1.63. Main stages of computer-aided synthesis of DOEs.

types of experiments: computational and real experiments. Note that both types call for the use of computer, the former by definition and the latter because of high informativeness of the object under study and sophisticated processing of optical images.

Let us first dwell on the numerical simulation (computational experiment) in diffractive optics. By way of example, we shall consider a focusing DOE. Assume that as a result of solving the inverse task of focusing we have obtained the phase function of the DOE and recorded it as a number array in the computer memory. To make sure that the inverse task is solved correctly and to predict parameters of the DOE under synthesis, one need not directly proceed to the fabrication of a "hard copy" and conduct real experiments in an optical system. However, the real experiment will allow one to study characteristics of the DOE obtained as a joint result of implementing all fabrication stages, including technology. We will see whether the DOE is operative or inoperative, but we will be unable to conduct a fine investigation into how the light intensity distribution in the focal plane depends on the inverse task solution. One should bear in mind that the results are better to represent not as huge number arrays that make one dazzled but in a form habitual for the optician-experimenter, namely, as halftone intensity distributions on the screen of a monitor, plots, or compact tables of the experimental data processed. It is also desirable that 3D distributions be represented in isomery and color. Hence, it follows that the computer on which one conducts numerical simulation should be equipped with computer graphics and image-visualization facilities. It is the combination of mathematical methods and programs for solving a variety of problems on diffraction and tools for image visualization that make it possible to incorporate numerical simulation in the DOE fabrication technology. Shown in Figure 1.64 is the result of numerical simulation of a DOE focusing into a half-ring. The DOE designed using the ray-tracing approach as an addition to a lens redistributes a converging spherical light beam into a semiring. The numerical simulation is based on the mathematical methods for sampling and quantizing the phase function dealt with in Chapter 5. The field in the DOE's focal plane is calculated in the diffraction approximation using the Kirchhoff integral as a sum of the analytically derived fields produced by separate DOE modules (sampling elements) shaped as a line, a ring, or a rectangle.

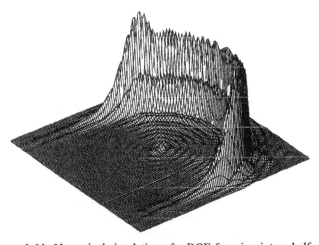

Figure 1.64. Numerical simulation of a DOE focusing into a half-ring.

The result of the numerical simulation allows the solution to the inverse problem of focusing to be optimized and characteristics of the synthesized optical elements to be predicted. At the next stage, the numerical simulation looks into how an optical system that involves the DOEs operates. In the course of simulation, the optical system is represented as light sources, a set of optical media, reflecting and refracting surfaces, and DOEs. The simulation uses the equation of ray propagation and the derivation of ray paths through the optical system from the source to the registration plane. The more rays have been drawn through the system, the more accurate is the result of simulation.

1.6.1 Different Approaches to the Microrelief Generation

The DOE is a zone plate in which the phase function $\varphi(u, v)$ is represented by a phase microrelief. There are a variety of automated technologies for translating the phase function onto an optical medium. For example, dividing machines allow the diffraction gratings (including the blazed ones) to be generated directly. Because in this case the zone fringes are represented by straight lines, the divider may be controlled without the use of sophisticated algorithms. Techniques are also available for directly translating radially symmetric and even more complex phase functions onto a physical medium using precision mechanical computer-controlled lathes. These techniques are employed for the fabrication of submillimeter and far-infrared (IR) DOEs.

The interest of specialists working in diffractive optics has recently been focused on the techniques for microrelief generation based on the achievements and facilities of microelectronics, because these can essentially add to new functionality of diffractive optics due to the following benefits:

- Similar geometric size of the DOE and microcircuits;
- Similar requirements on spatial resolution;
- High-level automatization and feasibility of topological realization of complex-shaped zones;
- Feasibility of obtaining a variety of phase microrelief levels;
- Availability of technological facilities and possibility of leasing the equipment;
- High-level reliability of technological automatic units and repeatability of results;
- Possibility of utilizing microelectronic expendable materials (substrates, resists, etc.).

However, it is important to bear in mind that microelectronic technologies are not the unique method for generating DOEs. There are also other techniques for translating a multilevel amplitude mask corresponding to the $\varphi(u, v)$ function into a phase microrelief.

1.6.2 Conducting Real Experiments in Diffractive Optics

For conducting real experiments in diffractive optics, a computer should be matched to devices for entering an optical image into the digital memory. For this purpose, one may use various converters of the optical signal to the electrical one: vidifon-based transmitting TV tubes, photodiode arrays, and charge transfer devices. The electrical signal

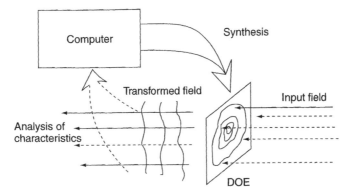

Figure 1.65. Computer in the synthesis of the DOE.

is then digitally coded and recorded in the computer memory. The technical aspect of this procedure presents no problems. The main difficulty is in the development of digital methods for analyzing the optical signal. In this situation, as in the synthesis of optical elements, we face the necessity of computer processing of 2D number arrays and solving ill-posed inverse problems. The process of solving is complicated by the fact that alongside the useful information, a 2D signal stored in the computer memory contains various interfering factors: perturbation and distortion errors. There are many causes that may lead to the emergence of the interfering factors: a nonuniform illumination of the object under registration, vibrations, instrumentational voltage jumps, continuous signal quantization, and so on.

Generation of DOEs imposes fairly hard requirements on the computer both in terms of calculating and storing the phase functions and in terms of controlling the pattern generator. The dedicated software for synthesis of DOEs should cover the following aspects:

- Determination of the DOE phase function, solutions based on the inverse problem of diffraction to be included;
- Solution of the direct problem of diffraction aimed at evaluating the DOE operational performances (numerical simulation);
- Formation of files for the pattern generator;
- Software for controlling the pattern generator;
- Programs for entering and processing the experimental data obtained in the course of testing a DOE.

The role the computer plays in synthesizing the DOE is illustrated in Figure 1.65.

REFERENCES

1. M. Born and E. Wolf, *Principles of Optics*, Pergamon Press, Oxford, 1968.
2. A.W. Lohmann and D.P. Paris, Binary Fraunhofer holograms generated by computer, *Appl. Opt.* **6**(10), 1739–1748 (1967).
3. L.B. Lesem, P.M. Hirsh, and J.A. Jordan, The kinoform; a new wave front reconstruction device IBM, *J. Res. Develop.* **13**(3), 150–155 (1969).

4. J.P. Kirk and A.L. Jones, Phase-only complex valued spatial filter, *J. Opt. Soc. Am.* **61**(8), 1023–1028 (1971).

5. W.H. Lee, Binary computer-generated holograms, *Appl. Opt.* **18**(21), 3661–3669 (1979).

6. W.H. Lee, Sampled Fourier-transform hologram generated by computer, *Appl. Opt.* **9**(3), 639–643 (1970).

7. D.C. Chu and J.R. Fienup, Recent approaches to computer-generated holograms, *Opt. Eng.* **13**(3), 189–195 (1974).

8. N.C. Gallagher and B. Liu, Method for computing kinoform that reduces image reconstruction errors, *Appl. Opt.* **12**(10), 2328–2355 (1973).

9. R.W. Gerchberg and W.O. Saxton, A practical algorithm for the determination of phase from image and diffraction plane pictures, *Optik* **35**, 237–242 (1972).

10. C.B. Burckhardt, A simplification of Lee's method of generating holograms by computer, *Appl. Opt.* **9**(8), 1949–1953 1949 (1970).

11. M.A. Golub, Generalized complex-to-phase coding for computer-generated holograms, *Proceedings of the 3rd International Seminar on Digital Image Processing in Medicine, Remote Sensing and Visualization of Information*, Riga, Latvia, 1992, p. 77.

12. J.R. Fienup, Iterative method applied to image reconstruction and to computer-generated holograms, *Opt. Eng.* **19**, 297–303 (1980).

13. J.R. Fienup, Phase retrieval algorithms: a comparison, *Appl. opt.* **21**(15), 2758–2769 (1982).

14. G. Stark, ed., *Image Reconstruction*, Mir Publishers, Moscow, Russia, 1992.

15. V.V. Kotlyar, I.V. Nikolski, and V.A. Soifer, Adaptive iterative algorithm for focusators synthesis, *Optik* **88**(1), 17–19 (1991).

16. S. Kirkpatrick, C.D. Gelatt Jr., and M.P. Vecchi, Optimization by simulated annealing, *Science* **220**, 671–680 (1983).

17. L. Davis, *Genetic Algorithms and Simulated Annealing*, Chapter 1, Pitman, London, 1987, pp. 1–11.

18. J.E. Baker, Adaptive selection methods for genetics algorithm, in *Proceedings of the First International Conference on Genetic Algorithms*, J.J. Grefenstette, ed., Lawrence Erlbaum Associates, London, 1985, pp.101–111.

19. D.E. Goldberg, *Genetic Algorithms in Search, Optimization, and Machine Learning*, Chapter 4, Addison-Wesley, Reading, Mass. 1989, p. 125–129.

20. D. Brown and A. Kathman, Multi-element diffractive optical designs using evolutionary programming, *Proc. SPIE* **2404**, 17–27 (1995).

21. C.Y. Lu, H.Z. Liao, C.K. Lee, and J.S. Wang, Energy control by linking individual patterns to self-repeating diffractive optical elements, *Appl. Opt.* **36**(20), 713–718 (1997).

22. S. Weissbach and F. Wyrowski, Error-diffusion procedure: theory and applications in optical signal processing, *Appl. Opt.* **31**(14), 2518–2534 (1992).

23. S. Weissbach, F. Wyrowski, and O. Bryngdahl, Digital phase holograms: coding and quantization with an error-diffusion concept, *Opt. commun.* **72**(1–3), 37–41 (1989).

24. F. Wyrowski and O. Bryngdahl, Digital holography as part of diffractive optics, *Rep. Prog. Phys.* **54**(12), 1481–1571 (1991).

25. A.V. Goncharsky, Mathematical models in the synthesis of planar optical elements, *J. Comput. Opt.* (Moscow) **1**, 19–31 (1987).

26. V.A. Danilov et al., Synthesis of optical elements to focus onto arbitrary-shape line, *Lett. J. Tech. Phys.* **54**(12), 1481–1571 (1982) (in Russian).

27. V.A. Danilov, K.A. Kulkin, and I.N. Sisakian, Optical elements to focus onto geometric figures composed of spatial curves, *J. Comput. Opt.* (Moscow) **13**, 3–11 (1993).

28. L.L. Doskolovich et al., Focusators into a ring, *Opt. Quant. Elect.* **25**, 801–814 (1993).

29. M. Duparre et al., Investigation of computer-generated diffractive beam shapers for flattening of single-modal CO2-laser beams, *Appl. Opt.* **34**(1), 2489–2497 (1995).

30. M.A. Golub, I.N. Sisakyan, and V.A. Soifer, Infrared radiation focusators, *Opt. Lasers Eng.* **15**, 297–309 (1991).

31. A.M. Prokhorov et al., Optical Phase Element for Focusing Monochromatic Radiation. Patent GB 2185126, Printing 08.07.87, Patent publ. 24.05.89.

32. V.A. Danilov et al., Optical elements to focus coherent light onto an arbitrary focal line, Lebedev Physical Institute, Moscow, Preprint No. 69 (in Russian).

33. M.A. Golub et al., Focusing the light onto a desired space domain using computer-synthesized holograms, *Lett. J. Tech. Phys.* **7**(10), 619–623 (1981).

34. M.A. Golub et al., Generation of aspheric wave fronts using computer-synthesized holograms, *Dokl. U.S.S.R. Acad. Sci.* **253**(5), 1104–1108 (1980) (in Russian).

35. N.P. Larionov, A.V. Lukin, and K.S. Mustafin, Artificial hologram as an optical compensator, *J. Opt. Spectrosc.* **32**(2), 396–399 (1972) (in Russian).

36. I.N. Sisakian and V.A. Soifer, Computer Optics: achievements and problems, *J. Comput. Opt.* (Moscow) **1**, 5–19 (1987).

37. V.A. Soifer, *Introduction into Diffractive Optics*, Samara State Aerospace University Publishers, Samara, 1996, 95 pages (in Russian).

38. L.P. Yaroslavsky, N.S. Merzlyakov, *Methods of Digital Holography*, Nauka Publishers, Moscow, Russia, 1977, 192 pages (in Russian).

39. I.J. Kabo, Evaluating quantizing errors resulting from digital synthesis of amplitude holograms, *J. Hologr. Probl.* **2**, 25–27 (1973).

40. V.I. Mandrosov, Influence of quantizing the transmission function on the reconstructed image quality, *J. Opt. Spectrosc.* **32**(1), 174–177 (1972) (in Russian).

41. M.A. Golub, Studies of characteristics and fabrication of coherent computer-synthesized optical spatial filters, Ph.D. thesis, Kuibyshev, U.S.S.R., 1981 (in Russian).

42. M.A. Golub, I.N. Sisakyan, and V.A. Soifer, Phase quantization and discretization in diffractive optics, *Proc. SPIE*, San-Diego-90, **1334**, 188–199 (1990).

43. D.D. Klovsky and V.A. Soifer, *Space-time signal processing*, Svyaz Publishers, Moscow, Russia, 208 pages (1976) (in Russian).

CHAPTER 2

Iterative Methods for Designing DOEs

2.1 INTRODUCTION

In image processing and reconstruction, iterative methods have found wide use. For their review see Ref. [1]. Iterative methods may be divided into several classes: (*1*) methods using compressing or nonexpanding operators — the Burger-van Zittert algorithm and the superresolution Gerchberg-Papoulis algorithm; (*2*) methods using projections onto convex sets — Stark and Jula algorithms; (*3*) iterative methods comprising pseudodifferential limitation operators — the Gerchberg-Saxton (GS) algorithm and the Fienup algorithm; (*4*) methods of nonlinear programming or optimization — the fastest descent algorithm, the conjugate gradients method, and the method of modified Lagrange functions. Application of these iterative methods to solving the problems of diffractive optical element's (DOEs) design requires special studies. The reason is that, as a rule, when reconstructing distorted images, one has to solve a linear convolution-type integral equation with additive noise. Whereas, when synthesizing a DOE, one has to solve a nonlinear integral equation whose nonlinearity is due to taking the modulus of the complex amplitude of coherent light.

In this chapter, we discuss iterative methods for solving inverse problems of the scalar diffraction theory applied to the synthesis of optical elements. Solutions arrived at through iterative methods are quasi-optimal, since they lead to the attainment of the local minimum of a criterion-functional or a goal function. At the same time, the iterative methods themselves appear as the result of solving a variation task on minimum or maximum of the goal function. As the goal function, one usually takes the root-mean-square (rms) deviation of desired light field amplitude at some point of space from the calculated one. Sometimes, instead of amplitudes one compares intensities and instead of the rms criterion one chooses higher-order criteria. The iterative methods discussed in this chapter may be divided into two groups: the parametric and gradient ones. In the parametric algorithms, one or two parameters affecting the convergence rate of the algorithm remain unchanged within several iterations. In the gradient algorithms (of conjugate gradient or fastest descent), the optimal value is found in every iteration. In addition to the familiar uniparametric iterative methods for designing DOEs, we also discuss two-parameter algorithms obtained by minimizing the criterion-functional by a regularizing parameter. Chapter 2 is constructed as follows. In Sections 2.2–2.7, we describe general aspects relating to various types of iterative algorithms that are applied to designing DOEs in scalar approximation. These include the nonparametric algorithm of error-reduction (Section 2.2), one-parameter iterative algorithms (Sections 2.3–2.5), the regularization two-parameter method (Section 2.6), and gradient algorithms for DOEs' design (Section 2.7). In Section 2.8 are given numerous examples of designing various DOE types. The design of a DOE with radially symmetric phase (subsection 2.8.1) is peculiar for the use of the Hankel transform. The design of a DOE generating axial-light line-segments (subsection 2.8.2) is reduced to a problem of focusing into a transverse light segment. A special algorithm is required to design radially symmetric DOEs with aperture divided into several circular subapertures (Section 2.8.3). Application of gradient and parametric iterative algorithms to designing binary and multigradation diffraction gratings with pregiven number of orders and desired intensity is dealt with in Sections 2.8.4 and 2.8.5. The design of special-purpose DOEs is expanded upon in the final sections of this chapter. Iterative algorithms for designing DOEs focusing the laser light into three-dimensional (3D) spatial domains or onto two-dimensional (2D) surfaces of rotational bodies (cone, cylinder) is treated in subsection 2.8.6. Subsection 2.8.7 deals with comparison of different iterative methods intended for the DOE-aided leveling of the Gaussian intensity of laser beam. The ray-tracing approach is shown to give the best initial approximation for the iterative design of a DOE focusing the Gaussian intensity distribution into a uniform light square. Iterative algorithms for DOEs focusing the coherent light into a ring or a contour image (e.g., a letter) are discussed in subsections 2.8.8 and 2.8.9. Subsections 2.8.10 and 2.8.11 are devoted to the gradient methods for DOEs with quantized phase.

2.2   ERROR-REDUCTION ALGORITHM

In what follows, we discuss algorithms for solving a nonlinear integral Fresnel equation intended for designing phase optical elements, generating a desired arbitrary intensity distribution of coherent monochromatic light in a plane perpendicular to the optical axis.

Assume that the light is monochromatic and coherent and is described by a complex function and an integral Fresnel transform. Polarization effects are considered in Chapter 3.

The algorithms under study are adaptive because a new estimate of the desired function at every iteration is chosen not only in correspondence with the required intensity function but also in relation with the previous estimate.

These algorithms are also termed as *parametric ones* because their convergence rate depends on the choice of particular values of some weight or regularization parameters. In the scalar diffraction theory, the light complex amplitude in the optical element plane

$$W(u, v) = A(u, v)e^{i\varphi(u,v)}$$

is related to the light complex amplitude

$$F(\xi, \eta) = B(\xi, \eta)e^{i\psi(\xi, \eta)}$$

in the observation plane, in which a desired intensity distribution $I_0(\xi, \eta)$ is formed, through the Fresnel transform [2]

$$F(\xi, \eta) = -\frac{ik}{2\pi z} e^{ikz} \iint\limits_{-\infty}^{\infty} W(u, v)H(u - \xi, v - \eta, z)\, du\, dv, \qquad (2.1)$$

where

$$H(u - \xi, v - \eta, z) = \exp\left\{\frac{ik}{2z}\left[(u - \xi)^2 + (v - \eta)^2\right]\right\} \qquad (2.2)$$

is the impulse response function of free space in the Fresnel approximation, z is the distance between the DOE and the observation plane, and $k = 2\pi/\lambda$ is the wave number of the light of wavelength λ.

In Eq. (2.1), the complex amplitude $W(u, v)$ in the thin optical element approximation (transparency approximation), which disregards the ray refraction, is equal to the product of the complex amplitude $W_0(u, v)$ of the illuminating beam by the eigenfunction of the DOE transmission $\tau(u, v)$:

$$W(u, v) = W_0(u, v)\,\tau(u, v). \qquad (2.3)$$

Because we propose to consider only phase optical elements hereafter (if not specified otherwise), the DOE transmission function is chosen in the form:

$$\tau(u, v) = e^{ig(u,v)}, \qquad (2.4)$$

where $g(u, v)$ is the sought-for DOE phase. For illustration of the preceding notation, see Figure 2.1. The calculation of the DOE phase function $g(u, v)$ may be reduced to solving a nonlinear integral equation

$$I_0(\xi, \eta) = |F(\xi, \eta)|^2 = \left|\iint\limits_{-\infty}^{\infty} A_0(u, v)\,e^{i\varphi(u,v)}H(u - \xi, v - \eta, z)\,du\,dv\right|^2, \qquad (2.5)$$

where $I_0(\xi, \eta)$ is the desired intensity in the image domain, $A_0(u, v)$ is the illuminating beam amplitude, and $\varphi(u, v) = g(u, v) + g_0(u, v)$, where $g_0(u, v)$ is the illuminating beam phase. An iterative calculation of the phase $\varphi(u, v)$, and simultaneously the phase $g(u, v)$, consists in solving Eq. (2.5) by a successive approximation's method. The GS algorithm, or the error-reduction algorithm [3], involves the following steps (for the diagram see Fig. 2.2):

1. The initial phase estimate $\varphi_0(u, v)$ is chosen;
2. The $A_0(u, v)\exp[i\varphi_0(u, v)]$ function is integrally transformed using Eq. (2.1);

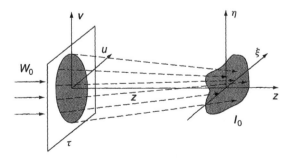

Figure 2.1. Schematic picture of the DOE-aided image formation.

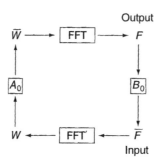

Figure 2.2. Diagram of the Gerchberg–Saxton error-reduction algorithm.

3. The resulting complex amplitude $F(\xi, \eta)$ in the image-formation plane is replaced by $\overline{F}(\xi, \eta)$ by the rule

$$\overline{F}(\xi, \eta) = B_0(\xi, \eta)F(\xi, \eta)|F(\xi, \eta)|^{-1}, \tag{2.6}$$

where $B_0(\xi, \eta) = \sqrt{I_0(\xi, \eta)}$;

4. A transform inverse to (2.1) relative to the $\overline{F}(\xi, \eta)$ function is taken:

$$W(u, v) = \frac{ik}{2\pi z} e^{-ikz} \iint\limits_{-\infty}^{\infty} \overline{F}(\xi, \eta)H^*(\xi - u, \eta - v, z)\,d\xi\,d\eta; \tag{2.7}$$

5. The derived complex amplitude $W(u, v)$ in the DOE plane is replaced by $\overline{W}(u, v)$ by the rule

$$\overline{W}(u, v) = \begin{cases} A_0(u, v)W(u, v)|W(u, v)|^{-1}, & (u, v) \in Q \\ 0, & (u, v) \notin Q \end{cases} \tag{2.8}$$

where Q is the DOE aperture shape;

6. Passage to step 2.

The procedure is repeated until the errors δ_F and δ_W cease to vary significantly:

$$\delta_F^2 = \frac{\displaystyle\iint\limits_{-\infty}^{\infty} [|F(\xi, \eta)| - B_0(\xi, \eta)]^2\,d\xi\,d\eta}{\displaystyle\iint\limits_{-\infty}^{\infty} B_0^2(\xi, \eta)\,d\xi\,d\eta}, \tag{2.9}$$

$$\delta_W^2 = \frac{\displaystyle\iint\limits_{-\infty}^{\infty} [|W(u, v)| - A_0(u, v)]^2\,du\,dv}{\displaystyle\iint\limits_{-\infty}^{\infty} A_0^2(u, v)\,du\,dv}. \tag{2.10}$$

The GS algorithm has been given the name error-reduction algorithm because the errors in Eqs. (2.9) and (2.10) have been shown not to increase with increasing number of iterations [4]. Besides, it has been shown that the GS algorithm is a variant of the gradient method [5] or the gradient method of fastest descent [6], using which one can minimize the functional of the rms deviation of the reconstructed image amplitude from the desired value

$$\varepsilon_0 = \iint\limits_{-\infty}^{\infty} [|F(\xi, \eta)| - B_0(\xi, \eta)]^2 \, d\xi \, d\eta. \tag{2.11}$$

Note, however, that the convergence process of the GS algorithm is characterized by the stagnation effect, which means that after a rapid decrease of the error δ_F (or δ_W) in the course of several initial iterations, further iterations do not result in its significant decrease. The stagnation effect implies that the algorithm reaches a local minimum of the functional (2.11), and it is in this sense that we may call it quasi-optimal. To increase the convergence rate and partially avoid the stagnation effect, one usually uses a diversity of adaptive algorithms with certain parameters controlling the convergence rate; hence these algorithms are sometimes called *parametric*.

2.3 INPUT-OUTPUT ALGORITHM

In Refs. [5,7,8], Fienup proposed an input-output method in which the phase is reconstructed from a single measurement of intensity in the domain of spatial spectrum. We shall consider this algorithm. The functions of complex amplitude in the DOE plane $W(u, v)$ and in the Fourier plane $F(\xi, \eta)$ (in the rear focal plane of a spherical lens), in which the desired image is formed are related through a 2D Fourier transform

$$F(\xi, \eta) = \iint\limits_{-\infty}^{\infty} W(u, v) \exp\left[-i\frac{k}{f}(u\xi + v\eta)\right] du \, dv, \tag{2.12}$$

where f is the focal length of a thin lens generating the Fourier spectrum. The conversion from the Fresnel transform of Eqs. (2.1) and (2.2) to the Fourier transform of Eq. (2.12) means that in the latter case one should employ a DOE and lens combination.

An iterative reconstruction of the light field phase (i.e., the argument of the $F(\xi, \eta)$ function) from the known amplitude (i.e., the modulus $|F(\xi, \eta)|$) using a modernized variant of the input-output algorithm takes the form

$$\overline{F}_{n+1}(\xi, \eta) = \overline{F}_n(\xi, \eta) + \beta \delta F_n(\xi, \eta), \tag{2.13}$$

where

$$\delta F_n(\xi, \eta) = \begin{cases} 0, & (\xi, \eta) \notin \gamma \\ -F_n(\xi, \eta), & (\xi, \eta) \in \gamma \end{cases}, \tag{2.14}$$

$$F_n(\xi, \eta) = \Im D_A \Im^{-1}\left\{\overline{F}_n(\xi, \eta)\right\} \tag{2.15}$$

is the output function, $\Im$ and $\Im^{-1}$ are the direct Fourier transform and its inverse, D_A is a limiting operator in the DOE domain allowing the representation

$$D_A W_n = A_0 \frac{W_n}{|W_n|}, \tag{2.16}$$

where $0.5 \le \beta \le 1$ is some parameter, and γ is the domain of violation of the limitations imposed on the pregiven field function.

Especially, for solving the problem of the DOE synthesis, it is proposed that the function increment δF_n in the input-output algorithm should be chosen as follows [8]:

$$\delta F = \left[B_0 F |F|^{-1} - F \right] + \left[B_0 F |F|^{-1} - B_0 \overline{F} |\overline{F}|^{-1} \right], \tag{2.17}$$

where $B_0^2(\xi, \eta)$ is the desired intensity distribution in the Fourier plane, $\overline{F}$ and F are the input and output functions, or the complex amplitude functions in the Fourier image plane before and after imposing the limitations.

In Ref. [9] a new variant is reported of the iterative input-output algorithm for synthesizing the DOE in which the phase is supposed to be independent of the modulus of light complex amplitude, $F(\xi, \eta)$. The optimal choice of the modulus and the phase at the $(n + 1)$th iteration step is shown to take the form $(\overline{F}(\xi, \eta) = \overline{F})$

$$\begin{cases} |\overline{F}_{n+1}| = B_0 + \beta[|F_n| - B_0] \\ \arg \overline{F}_{n+1} = \arg F_n + \alpha[\arg F_n - \arg \overline{F}_n] \end{cases}. \tag{2.18}$$

Also, numerical examples were used in Ref. [9] to demonstrate that the best values of α and β are equal to 2. Note that the iterative algorithm that employs the first equation in (2.18) is similar to the earlier algorithm described in Refs. [10,11].

The authors of Ref. [9] named this algorithm a pendulum algorithm. In our opinion, this is different from the original input-output algorithm of Eq. (2.14) since it takes explicit account of the limitation imposed on the amplitude in the Fourier plane B_0.

2.4 ADAPTIVE-ADDITIVE ALGORITHM

The initial application of the input-output algorithm [5,7] was to reconstruct the light field phase from one measurement of intensity distribution in the spatial frequencies plane. Such a problem is typical of stellar interferometry. The same algorithm was successfully applied to computing the DOE phase [8]. Note, however, that the algorithm is lacking an adequate theoretical substantiation.

In the following paragraphs, it has been shown that the algorithm in Eq. (2.18) (only the first equation), further referred to as an adaptive-additive algorithm (AA algorithm), can be arrived at by minimizing a certain criterion-functional. One can also demonstrate that for the AA algorithm some characteristic rms deviation does not increase with increasing number of iterations.

Let us consider in more detail the replacement in Eq. (2.6) for the GS algorithm. This replacement implies that the light amplitude $|F_n(\xi, \eta)|$ in the observation plane derived in the nth iteration step is replaced by a pregiven value of amplitude, $B_0(\xi, \eta)$. It should be noted that despite the fact that the Fourier (or Fresnel) transform of a function with limited definition domain is an analytical integer and exponential function, the $B_0(\xi, \eta)$ function may not be an analytical function and may be specified arbitrarily.

Hence, it would be better to try a replacement in which both functions (the desired one and the analytical one) are found as a linear combination with different weights instead of the replacement (2.6) [12]:

$$|\overline{F}_n(\xi, \eta)| = |\lambda B_0(\xi, \eta) + (1 - \lambda)|F_n(\xi, \eta)||. \tag{2.19}$$

In this case, the replacement (2.6) in the iterative GS algorithm takes the form:

$$\overline{F}_n(\xi, \eta) = |\overline{F}_n(\xi, \eta)|F_n(\xi, \eta)|F_n(\xi, \eta)|^{-1}. \tag{2.20}$$

The range of values of the parameter λ is found from the condition that the average deviation ε_0 in Eq. (2.11) is not increased when using the replacement (2.19), which means that the following condition is fulfilled:

$$
\begin{aligned}
\overline{\varepsilon}_0 &= \iint\limits_{-\infty}^{\infty} \left[|\overline{F}_n| - B_0 \right]^2 d\xi \, d\eta \\
&= \iint\limits_{-\infty}^{\infty} \left[\lambda B_0 + (1 - \lambda)|F_n| - B_0 \right]^2 d\xi \, d\eta \\
&= (1 - \lambda)^2 \iint\limits_{-\infty}^{\infty} \left[|F_n| - B_0 \right]^2 d\xi \, d\eta \leq \varepsilon_0 \\
&= \iint\limits_{-\infty}^{\infty} \left[|F_n| - B_0 \right]^2 d\xi \, d\eta.
\end{aligned} \tag{2.21}
$$

From Eq. (2.21) it follows that the weight coefficient is to be chosen from the condition $0 \leq \lambda \leq 2$. Note that at $\lambda = 1$ the replacement (2.19) changes to Eq. (2.6) of the GS algorithm, whereas at $\lambda = 2$, we come to the "mirror image" replacement

$$|\overline{F}_n(\xi, \eta)| = |2B_0(\xi, \eta) - |F_n(\xi, \eta)||. \tag{2.22}$$

In the latter case ($\lambda = 2$), the amplitude $|F_n(\xi, \eta)|$ calculated in the nth iteration in the observation plane is replaced by a "mirror image" relative to a desired amplitude distribution $B_0(\xi, \eta)$.

It is noteworthy that the initial "mirror image" replacement in Eq. (2.22) was as follows [10,11]

$$\overline{I}_n(\xi, \eta) = \begin{cases} |2I_0(\xi, \eta) - I_n(\xi, \eta)|, & (\xi, \eta) \in \Omega \\ I_n(\xi, \eta), & (\xi, \eta) \notin \Omega, \end{cases} \tag{2.23}$$

where I_n is the intensity distribution obtained in the nth step, $I_n = |F_n(\xi, \eta)|^2$, I_0 is a desired intensity distribution, $I_0 = B_0^2$, Ω is the domain of image definition. If $I_n \geq 2I_0$, then $\overline{I}_n = 0$.

Let us demonstrate that the replacement (2.19) in the AA algorithm minimizes the residual functional ε_1, which is the rms deviation of the calculated amplitude from the desired one in the DOE plane:

$$\varepsilon_1 = \iint\limits_{-\infty}^{\infty} [A_0(u, v) - |W(u, v)|]^2 \, du \, dv, \tag{2.24}$$

where $A_0(u, v)$ is the amplitude of light illuminating the DOE. The variation of the functional ε_1 relative to the W function is given by

$$\delta\varepsilon_1 = 2\mathrm{Re}\left\{ \iint\limits_{-\infty}^{\infty} \left[W_n - A_0 W_n |W_n|^{-1} \right] \delta W_n^* \, du \, dv \right\}, \tag{2.25}$$

where $\mathrm{Re}\{\}$ denotes the real part of number and * denotes complex conjugation.

When deriving Eq. (2.25), the following relations were employed:

$$\delta\left\{ \iint\limits_{-\infty}^{\infty} A_0^2(u, v) \, du \, dv \right\} = 0, \tag{2.26}$$

$$\delta\left\{ \iint\limits_{-\infty}^{\infty} |W(u, v)|^2 \, du \, dv \right\} \neq 0, \tag{2.27}$$

$$\delta(WW^*) = W\delta W^* + W^*\delta W = 2\mathrm{Re}\left\{ W\delta W^* \right\}. \tag{2.28}$$

Using the Parseval equations,

$$\iint\limits_{-\infty}^{\infty} |W(u, v)|^2 \, du \, dv = \iint\limits_{-\infty}^{\infty} |\overline{F}(\xi, \eta)|^2 \, d\xi \, d\eta, \tag{2.29}$$

$$\iint\limits_{-\infty}^{\infty} |\overline{W}(u, v)|^2 \, du \, dv = \iint\limits_{-\infty}^{\infty} |F(\xi, \eta)|^2 \, d\xi \, d\eta, \tag{2.30}$$

where $\overline{W} = D_A W = AW|W|^{-1}$ is the light amplitude in the DOE plane after performing the replacement (2.8), we can show that the following relationship will hold:

$$\mathrm{Re}\left\{ \iint\limits_{-\infty}^{\infty} \left[W_n - A_0 W_n |W_n|^{-1} \right] \delta W_n^* \, du \, dv \right\} = \mathrm{Re}\left\{ \iint\limits_{-\infty}^{\infty} [\overline{F}_n - F_n] \delta \overline{F}_n^* \, d\xi \, d\eta \right\}, \tag{2.31}$$

where $\overline{F}_n = \Im\{W_n\}$, $F_n = \Im D_A \Im^{-1}\{\overline{F}_n\} = \Im\{A_0 W_n |W_n|^{-1}\}$, and $\Im$ denotes the Fourier transform.

The increment $\delta\varepsilon_1$ of the error functional ε_1 takes its maximum negative value in the nth iteration under the following parametrically termed condition:

$$\delta\overline{F}_n = \overline{F}_{n+1} - \overline{F}_n = \lambda(F_n - \overline{F}_n), \quad \lambda > 0. \tag{2.32}$$

In view of Eq. (2.32), instead of Eq. (2.25), we get

$$\delta\varepsilon_1 = -2\lambda \iint\limits_{-\infty}^{\infty} |\overline{F}_n - F_n|^2 \, d\xi \, d\eta < 0. \tag{2.33}$$

From Eq. (2.32) follows the parametrical equation for the integral calculation of the function $F(\xi, \eta)$:

$$\overline{F}_{n+1} = (1 - \lambda)\overline{F}_n + \lambda F_n = (1 - \lambda)\overline{F}_n + \lambda \Im D_A \Im^{-1}\left\{\overline{F}_n\right\}. \tag{2.34}$$

Equation (2.34) implies that in the $(n + 1)$th iteration the input amplitude is a linear combination of the nth input and output amplitudes. The algorithm (2.34) is similar to the input-output algorithm [5] and the preceding reasoning should be considered as a theoretical substantiation of its optimality.

For the algorithm (2.34) the rms error of amplitude does not increase with increasing number of iterations on the condition that the λ parameter satisfies the inequality

$$0 < \lambda \leq 2. \tag{2.35}$$

Actually, introducing the designations

$$F_n = B_n \, e^{i\varphi_n}, \quad \overline{F}_n = \overline{B}_n \, e^{i\overline{\varphi}_n}, \quad W_n = A_n \, e^{i\psi_n}, \quad \overline{W}_n = A_0 \, e^{i\psi_n} \tag{2.36}$$

yields a sequence in which the equalities 1, 3, and 5 are evident, the equalities 2 and 4 are the Parseval equality, and the inequality is that of triangle ($|a| - |b| \leq |a - b|$):

$$\iint\limits_{-\infty}^{\infty} |A_0 - A_{n+1}|^2 \, du \, dv = \iint\limits_{-\infty}^{\infty} |A_0 \, e^{i\psi_{n+1}} - A_{n+1} \, e^{i\psi_{n+1}}|^2 \, du \, dv$$

$$\leq \iint\limits_{-\infty}^{\infty} |A_0 \, e^{i\psi_n} - A_{n+1} \, e^{i\psi_{n+1}}|^2 \, du \, dv$$

$$= \iint\limits_{-\infty}^{\infty} |B_n \, e^{i\varphi_n} - [(1 - \lambda)\overline{B}_n \, e^{i\overline{\varphi}_n} + \lambda B_n \, e^{i\varphi_n}]|^2 \, d\xi \, d\eta$$

$$= (1 - \lambda)^2 \iint\limits_{-\infty}^{\infty} |B_n \, e^{i\varphi_n} - \overline{B}_n \, e^{i\overline{\varphi}_n}|^2 \, d\xi \, d\eta$$

$$= (1 - \lambda)^2 \iint\limits_{-\infty}^{\infty} |A_0 \, e^{i\psi_n} - A_n \, e^{i\psi_n}|^2 \, du \, dv$$

$$= (1 - \lambda)^2 \iint\limits_{-\infty}^{\infty} |A_0 - A_n|^2 \, du \, dv. \tag{2.37}$$

From Eq. (2.37) it follows that given the condition (2.35), there takes place a relaxation of the rms error

$$\iint\limits_{-\infty}^{\infty} |A_0 - A_{n+1}|^2 \, du \, dv \le \iint\limits_{-\infty}^{\infty} |A_0 - A_n|^2 \, du \, dv. \tag{2.38}$$

The algorithm (2.34) takes into account that the complex amplitude satisfies the limitation in the DOE plane but disregards that the modules of input and output functions of the complex amplitude in the Fourier plane, that is, $\overline{F}(\xi, \eta)$ and $F(\xi, \eta)$, must tend to a desired function $B_0(\xi, \eta)$. In order that this condition can be used in the algorithm (2.34), we assume that the input function in the nth iteration obeys the following limitation:

$$\overline{F}_n(\xi, \eta) = D_B F(\xi, \eta) = B_0(\xi, \eta) F(\xi, \eta) |F(\xi, \eta)|^{-1}, \tag{2.39}$$

and that in the $(n + 1)$th step it obeys Eq. (2.34). Because of this, the combination of Eqs. (2.34) and (2.39) leads to the AA algorithm:

$$\overline{F}_{n+1}(\xi, \eta) = (1 - \lambda) B_0(\xi, \eta) \frac{F_n(\xi, \eta)}{|F_n(\xi, \eta)|} + \lambda F_n(\xi, \eta), \tag{2.40}$$

Note that Eq. (2.40) differs from Eq. (2.19) by the permutation of weight coefficients $\lambda \to 1 - \lambda$.

It is also noteworthy that a similar technique was employed in the Ref. [9] with the aim to get the algorithm (2.40) from the algorithm (2.34). In the Ref. [13] the algorithm (2.19) was derived as a weight algorithm. Let us consider the residual functional ε_0, but with the weight function given by

$$\overline{\varepsilon}_0 = \iint\limits_{-\infty}^{\infty} S(\xi, \eta) [|F(\xi, \eta)| - B_0(\xi, \eta)]^2 \, d\xi \, d\eta, \tag{2.41}$$

where $S(\xi, \eta)$ is a real, positively defined weight function, which specifies, for example, the domain of definition of the synthesized image:

$$S(\xi, \eta) = \begin{cases} \lambda, & (\xi, \eta) \in \Omega \\ 0, & (\xi, \eta) \notin \Omega, \end{cases} \tag{2.42}$$

where λ is constant.

The variation of the functional (2.41) takes the form

$$\delta \overline{\varepsilon}_0 = 2 \mathrm{Re} \iint\limits_{-\infty}^{\infty} S(\xi, \eta) \left[F - B_0 \frac{F}{|F|} \right] \delta F^* \, d\xi \, d\eta. \tag{2.43}$$

An iterative equation which makes it possible to get the function $F(\xi, \eta)$ minimizing the functional (2.41) follows from the requirement that the integrand in Eq. (2.43) be equal to zero and takes the form

$$\overline{F}_{n+1} = F_n + S\left[B_0\frac{F_n}{|F_n|} - F_n\right] = (1 - S)F_n + SB_0\frac{F_n}{|F_n|}, \tag{2.44}$$

where F_n and $\overline{F}_{n+1}$ are the functions of input in the nth step and of output in the $(n + 1)$th step, respectively. In getting Eq. (2.44), we made use of a nontraditional concept of function variation. In the traditional notion the variation is a change of amplitude at the input or output from iteration to iteration: $\delta F_n = F_{n+1} - F_n$. We think of the function variation as a passage from the input to the output: $\delta F_n = \overline{F}_{n+1} - F_n$. Benefits of the AA algorithm may be illustrated by the following examples.

Example 2.1   Let us design a DOE illuminated by a laser-light beam with Gaussian intensity [14]

$$A_0(u, v) = \exp\left[-\frac{u^2 + v^2}{r^2}\right] \tag{2.45}$$

and capable of forming an image of a "soft square" for the far-field diffraction zone; this means that the pregiven intensity distribution in the observation plane is chosen as a super-Gaussian function:

$$B_0(\xi, \eta) = \exp\left[-\frac{\xi^{2n} + \eta^{2n}}{a^{2n}}\right], \quad n = 1, 2, \ldots, \tag{2.46}$$

where $2a$ is the effective side of the square and r is the Gaussian beam radius.

Such a task of leveling the Gaussian beam intensity is topical in many applications: laser printing, laser heat treatment of surface, and the like. This task is treated in more detail in subsection 2.8.7.

The Fresnel transform (2.1) and its inverse (2.7) were taken using the FFT. The array was 256×256 pixels. The illuminating Gaussian beam intensity along boundaries of the DOE square aperture was 10 percent of the maximum value in the center. The side of the square image was about 10 airy-disk diameters (a minimal diffraction spot), the number of iterations being 10.

Shown in Figure 2.3 are (a) the 2π-modulo DOE phase (halftone, 16 gradations) calculated using the GS algorithm, (b) the image for far-field diffraction, and (c) the horizontal section of the image intensity distribution.

Figure 2.4 depicts similar results obtained by the AA algorithm ($\lambda = 2$): (a) the DOE phase, (b) the resulting image, and (c) the horizontal section of the image intensity. The rms deviations calculated by Eq. (2.9) for the examples discussed were as follows: 27.2 percent (Fig. 2.3) and 5.1 percent (Fig. 2.4).

Let us introduce the notion of the energy efficiency of generating the desired image. This is a fraction of light energy coming to a desired domain of image definition:

$$E = \frac{\displaystyle\iint_\Omega |F(x, y)|^2 \, dx \, dy}{\displaystyle\iint_{-\infty}^{\infty} |F(x, y)|^2 \, dx \, dy}, \tag{2.47}$$

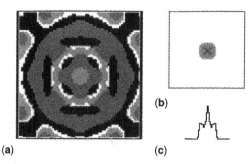

Figure 2.3. DOE design using the GS algorithm: (**a**) the DOE phase from 0 to 2π, (**b**) the resulting image, and (**c**) the central horizontal section of the image intensity.

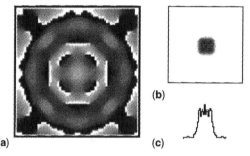

Figure 2.4. DOE design using the AA algorithm: (**a**) the DOE phase from 0 to 2π, (**b**) the resulting image, and (**c**) the central horizontal section of the image intensity.

where Ω is the shape of the domain of image definition. For the preceding examples, the energy efficiency was 96.4 percent (Fig. 2.3) and 91.5 percent (Fig. 2.4). From Figures 2.3 and 2.4, the phases obtained using the aforementioned two methods are seen to differ insignificantly. But this insignificant difference leads to the essential difference in the images formed. Simulation has shown that the convergence rate of the iterative algorithm increases as the relaxation parameter increases from 0 to 2.

Example 2.2 In this example we shall design an optical element capable of effectively locating the light source in space [15]. This element is part of a device for determining the coordinates of center of the cross section of a point source image. The schematic view of the device is shown in Figure 2.5.

A point source of light, S, illuminates a spherical lens behind which a DOE is found (Fig. 2.5). The DOE is designed in such a manner that the point source image has the cross-shape intensity distribution. Each side of the cross image intersects a linear photosensor, as is shown in Figure 2.6. As a linear photosensor, with characteristic side of the input window of 10 mm, one may use a silicon semiconducting structure whose output analogous signal in terms of voltage drop is proportional to the distance between the point of maximum light intensity and the initial point of the photosensor. Technical parameters of such a photosensor are as follows: voltage variation by 0.1 mV is equivalent to the axial shift of maximum light intensity by 0.2 μm.

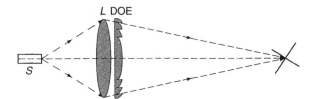

Figure 2.5. Optical setup for the formation of a cross-like image.

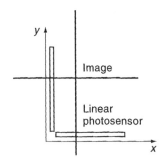

Figure 2.6. The device imaging plane.

To design a DOE for the aforementioned parameters, we used a paraxial relationship connecting the intensity distribution in the source plane to that in the cross plane [16]:

$$F(\xi, \eta) = \frac{k^2}{ab} \exp\left[i\frac{k}{2b}(\xi^2 + \eta^2)\right] \iint\limits_{-\infty}^{\infty} W_o(u, v) \exp\left[i\frac{k}{2a}(u^2 + v^2)\right]$$

$$\times H\left(u + \frac{b}{a}\xi, v + \frac{b}{a}\eta\right) du\, dv \tag{2.48}$$

where a and b are the source-to-lens and the lens-to-image distances (Fig. 2.5) related to each other by the thin lens relation

$$\frac{1}{a} + \frac{1}{b} = \frac{1}{f}, \tag{2.49}$$

where f is the lens's focal length and $H(u, v)$ is the impulse response function specified in the form

$$H(u, v) = \iint\limits_{Q} P(\xi, \eta)\tau(\xi, \eta) \exp\left[-i\frac{k}{b}(u\xi + v\eta)\right] d\xi\, d\eta. \tag{2.50}$$

The function $P(\xi, \eta)$ in (2.50) is termed the *lens pupil function*, Q determines the shape of the diaphragm aperture limiting the lens. The function $\tau(\xi, \eta)$ is the complex transmission function(CTF), which is purely the phase:

$$\tau(\xi, \eta) = e^{i\varphi(\xi,\eta)}. \tag{2.51}$$

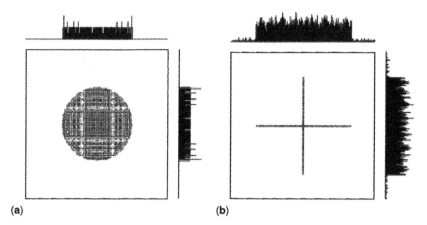

Figure 2.7. (a) The DOE phase, five gradations, and (b) the cross in the image plane.

The phase $\varphi(\xi, \eta)$ of the optical element is found as a solution of the integral equation

$$I(u, v) = |H(u, v)|^2, \tag{2.52}$$

where $I(u, v)$ is the desired intensity distribution for the impulse response function or a pregiven function of point dissipation. For the cross, this intensity function takes the form

$$I(u, v) = \begin{cases} I_0; & -l \leq u \leq l, v = 0 \text{ and } u = 0, -l \leq v \leq l \\ 0; & \text{else} \end{cases} \tag{2.53}$$

where I_0 is constant and $2l$ is the length of vertical and horizontal fragment of the cross. Equation (2.52) was solved using the AA algorithm (2.19) at $\lambda = 2$.

The design parameters are as follows: the DOE was limited by a circular diaphragm, 64 pixels in radius; for taking the Fourier transform, an array of 256×256 pixels was chosen; each side of the cross was 170 pixels; and the width was 1 pixel. Figure 2.7a shows the optical element phase calculated during 25 iterations with five gradations. The squared modulus of the impulse response for the "Lens + DOE" combination is depicted in Figure 2.7b. Horizontal and vertical profiles for the resulting diffraction patterns are also shown in Figure 2.7.

2.5 ADAPTIVE-MULTIPLICATIVE ALGORITHM

In this section we consider another iterative algorithm for DOE design that also features a convergence rate larger than that of the GS algorithm. This algorithm can be arrived at by using an identity that is to be true in the image-formation plane

$$I_0(\xi, \eta) = F(\xi, \eta) F^*(\xi, \eta). \tag{2.54}$$

In other words, the desired intensity $I_0(\xi, \eta)$ must be generated by a light field with complex amplitude $F(\xi, \eta)$. Making use of an inverse operator, we obtain in the DOE plane

$$W(u, v) = \hat{L}^{-1} \left[\frac{I_0(\xi, \eta)}{F^*(\xi, \eta)} \right] = \hat{L}^{-1} \left[\frac{I_0 F}{|F^2|} \right], \tag{2.55}$$

where $\hat{L}^{-1}$ is the inverse Fresnel transform.

Equation (2.55) suggests an iterative procedure for searching for a DOE phase (argument of the $W(u, v)$ function), very similar to that used in the GS algorithm, but with the following replacement used instead of Eq. (2.6):

$$\overline{F}(\xi, \eta) = I_0(\xi, \eta) F(\xi, \eta) |F(\xi, \eta)|^{-2}. \tag{2.56}$$

Equation (2.56) is ill-posed since the modulus $F(\xi,\eta)$ in the denominator can take zero value. The well-posed statement of the task of finding the DOE phase should rest upon the consideration of some residual functional with regularization [17]. Having this in view, we shall consider the functional

$$\varepsilon_2 = \iint\limits_{-\infty}^{\infty} \left[|F|^2 - I_0 \right]^2 d\xi \, d\eta + \alpha \iint\limits_{-\infty}^{\infty} Q|F|^2 \, d\xi \, d\eta. \tag{2.57}$$

The first term in Eq. (2.57) is the rms deviation of the generated intensity in the observation plane from the desired one $I_0(\xi, \eta)$. As distinct from the functional (2.11), this term represents a functional of the fourth order with respect to the light field amplitude. The second term in Eq. (2.57) is stabilizing. Note that the real, positively defined function Q in Eq. (2.57) in the Tikhonov regularization method [18] is specified as follows:

$$Q(\xi, \eta) = \sum_{n=0}^{N} |C_n|(\xi^{2n} + \eta^{2n}), \tag{2.58}$$

where C_n are arbitrary coefficients. The stabilizing constant $\alpha \geq 0$ determines the lower boundary of variation of the functional ε_2. Minimization of ε_2 denotes that from a set of functions F most close to the modulus of the function $\sqrt{I_0(\xi, \eta)}$, the smoothest function is chosen. The iterative procedure of minimizing of the functional (2.57) is constructed using interim functionals, quadratic with respect to the desired function $G_n(\xi, \eta)$

$$\varepsilon_{2n} = \iint\limits_{-\infty}^{\infty} |F_n G_n^* - I_0|^2 \, d\xi \, d\eta + \alpha \iint\limits_{-\infty}^{\infty} Q|G_n|^2 \, d\xi \, d\eta, \tag{2.59}$$

where $F_n(\xi, \eta)$ is the complex amplitude found in the nth iteration in the observation plane and $G_n(\xi, \eta)$ is a function minimizing the functional ε_{2n}. The variation of the functional (2.59) with respect to the G_n function is

$$\delta\varepsilon_{2n} = 2\text{Re} \left\{ \iint\limits_{-\infty}^{\infty} [|F_n|^2 G_n - I_0 F_n + \alpha Q G_n] \delta G_n^* \, d\xi \, d\eta \right\}. \tag{2.60}$$

The functional (2.59) attains its minimum on the condition that the variation (2.60) becomes equal to zero. From (2.60) it is seen that this becomes possible if

$$G_n = \frac{I_0 F_n}{|F_n|^2 + \alpha Q}.$$

(2.61)

By comparing Eqs. (2.61) and (2.56) it can be seen that the $G_n(\xi, \eta)$ function is a regular analog of the $\overline{F}(\xi, h)$ function. The replacement (2.61) minimizes interim functionals ε_{2n} at each iteration. However, because of the convergence of the iterative procedure, the difference $|F_n - G_n|$ decreases as n increases, whereas the functionals ε_{2n} tend to the functional ε_2. Hence, one can conclude that, in the limit the replacement (2.61) minimizes the initial functional (2.57). The foregoing reasoning confirms that the DOE phase can be derived iteratively using a method similar to the GS algorithm but with the replacement (2.61) taken instead of the replacement (2.6).

This algorithm has been given the name *adaptive-multiplicative* (AM) *algorithm*, as distinguished from the AA algorithm. Its benefits over the GS algorithm are seen from the following example.

Example 2.3 Let us design a DOE intended to generate a "soft circle" image for the far-field diffraction. The element is illuminated by a laser beam with the Gaussian intensity distribution (2.45). The desired intensity in the observation plane is given by

$$I_0(\xi, \eta) = \exp\left[-2\left\{\frac{\xi^2 + \eta^2}{a^2}\right\}^n\right],$$

(2.62)

where a is the effective radius of the "soft circle," $n = 1, 2, 3, \ldots$. The radius was chosen to be approximately equal to two airy-disk radii, the pixel array being 256×256.

Figure 2.8 depicts (a) the modulo-2π DOE phase (16 gradations) calculated during 20 iterations using the GS algorithm, (b) the resulting diffraction pattern, and (c) the light intensity distribution in the pattern's central cross section.

Shown in Figure 2.9 are the analogous results obtained by the AM algorithm: (a) the phase calculated during 20 iterations, (b) the diffraction pattern, and (c) the pattern's central cross section in per unit.

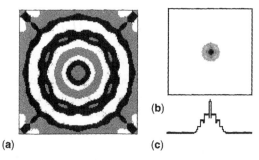

(a) (b) (c)

Figure 2.8. Design using the GS algorithm: (a) the DOE phase ranging from 0 to 2π, (b) the diffraction pattern, and (c) the intensity distribution in the central cross section.

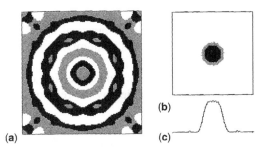

Figure 2.9. Design using the AM-algorithm: (**a**) the DOE phase ranging from 0 to 2π, (**b**) the diffraction pattern, and (**c**) the intensity distribution in the central section.

For the foregoing example, the energy efficiencies calculated by formula (2.47) were 97.1 percent (Fig. 2.8) and 91.8 percent (Fig. 2.9). The rms errors calculated by Eq. (2.9) were 22.9 percent (Fig. 2.8) and 3.6 percent (Fig. 2.9).

From comparison of Figures 2.8 and 2.9, the phases are seen to differ insignificantly. Nevertheless, this insignificant difference results in the formation of fairly different diffraction patterns.

Figure 2.10 shows the functional ε_2 in Eq. (2.57) as a function of the number of iterations: curve 1 for the GS algorithm ($\alpha = 0$) and curve 2 for the AM algorithm ($\alpha = 10^{-8}$). From Figure 2.10, it is seen that the adaptive algorithm features a better convergence: curve 2 attains the value of 1 after 4 iterations, whereas curve 1 attains the value 1.2 after 20 iterations.

Note, however, that Figure 2.10 reveals a disadvantage of the AM algorithm: its nonmonotone convergence. It is noteworthy that, if taking the values of the functional (2.57) in every other iteration (Fig. 2.10, curve 2), they will decrease monotonically. For all examples considered, the initial phase estimate was chosen to be random, with results practically independent of its specific value.

Note that the lack of circular symmetry in the phase patterns in Figures 2.8a. and 2.9a may be because of the violation of circular symmetry of the function $I_0(\xi, \eta)$ in Eq. (2.62), for discrete values of the variables ξ and η, which causes the circles to change into polygonals. Also, note that it appears to be difficult to give a theoretical substantiation of the optimal choice of the stabilizing constant α and the degree

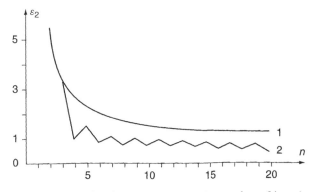

Figure 2.10. Functional as a function of the number of iterations.

of the polynomial N for the function $Q(\xi, \eta)$, which affect the minimization of the functional (2.57). However, for a number of practical applications it turns out to be possible to choose the function $Q(\xi, \eta)$ as a monomial $(\xi^2 + \eta^2)^n$ at $n = 1, 2$ and find the constant α by fitting.

Putting $\alpha = 0$ in Eq. (2.57), we obtain another version of the multiplicative algorithm. Consider the error functional specified by the relation

$$\varepsilon_{2p} = \iint\limits_{-\infty}^{\infty} [B_0^2(\xi, \eta) - |F(\xi, \eta)|^2]^p \, d\xi \, d\eta. \tag{2.63}$$

Variation of this functional by $F(\xi, \eta)$ is given by

$$\delta\varepsilon_{2p} = 2\mathrm{Re} \iint p \left[B_0^2(\xi, \eta) - |F(\xi, \eta)|^2 \right]^{p-1} F(\xi, \eta) \delta F^*(\xi, \eta) \, d\xi \, d\eta, \tag{2.64}$$

where $\delta F = \overline{F} - F$ is the difference between the input $\overline{F}$ and output F complex amplitudes in the Fourier image plane. From the condition that the integrand in (2.64) should be zero, there follows an iterative equation for finding an input function $\overline{F}$ minimizing the functional (2.63):

$$\overline{F}_{n+1} - F_n = \lambda p \left[B_0^2 - |F_n|^2 \right]^{p-1} F_n,$$

$$\text{or } \overline{F}_{n+1} = \left\{ 1 + \lambda p \left[B_0^2 - |F_n|^2 \right]^{p-1} \right\} F_n, \tag{2.65}$$

where λ is the relaxation constant.

Equation (2.65) nonlinearly relates the output amplitude function F_n in the nth iteration step with the input function $\overline{F}_{n+1}$. Note that the F_n function is found from the relation

$$F_n = \Im D_A \Im^{-1} \left\{ \overline{F}_n \right\}, \tag{2.66}$$

where the limiting operator D_A in the DOE plane is specified by Eq. (2.16).

In conclusion, it may be mentioned that the cooperative application of the AA algorithm, Eq. (2.40), and the AM-algorithm, Eq. (2.61), originates a new two-parameter iterative algorithm, which may be put down as follows:

$$\overline{F}_{n+1}(\xi, \eta) = \frac{(1 - \lambda) I_0 F_n(\xi, \eta)}{|F_n(\xi, \eta)|^2 + \alpha Q(\xi, \eta)} + \lambda F_n(\xi, \eta). \tag{2.67}$$

2.6 ADAPTIVE-REGULARIZATION ALGORITHM

Because, as a rule, DOEs generate spatially limited images, there is some freedom in choosing the light field behavior beyond the domain of image definition. This additional degree of freedom is employed both in early algorithms of Gerchberg [19] and Papoulis [20] as well as in later works by Wyrowski [21] and Fienup [13], thus allowing partially to eliminate the stagnation effect typical of the GS algorithm.

In this section, we deal with an algorithm representing a generalization of the afore-mentioned methods, as it includes the relaxation constant, accounts for the fact that the image-under-synthesis domain is spatially limited, and uses an additional parameter called the *regularization parameter.*

Becuase the DOE under synthesis should generate a required image at some distance and in a certain pregiven space domain, the light field beyond this domain may be considered as some noise. The energy contribution beyond the separated domain may be controlled by the Tikhonov regularization method [18] through a stabilizing term. We shall state the problem of designing a DOE focusing the incident laser light into a small area of the Fourier plane as a variation task of minimization of the criterion-functional (for the sake of designation simplicity, we shall consider a 1D case)

$$\varepsilon(\alpha) = \int_{-\infty}^{\infty} [|F_0(u)| - D_A|F(u)|]^2 \, du + \alpha \int_{-\infty}^{\infty} Q(u)|F(u)|^2 du, \qquad (2.68)$$

where $Q(u) = \sum_{n=0}^{N} |c_n| u^{2n}$ is a stabilizing function analogous to the function of Eq. (2.58), $D_A f = \begin{cases} f, & u \in \Omega_A \\ 0, & u \notin \Omega_A \end{cases}$ is the space limitation operator, $|F_0(u)|$ is the desired amplitude distribution in the domain Ω_A, $|\alpha|$ is the regularization parameter, and $F(u)$ is the light complex amplitude in the Fourier spectrum plane, in which the desired image $|F_0(u)|$ is to be formed. As distinct from the functional (2.57), the functional (2.68) is quadratic with respect to the light field amplitude.

The variation of the functional is written by

$$\delta\varepsilon = 2\text{Re}\left[\int_{\infty}^{\infty}\left(-|F_0(u)|\frac{F(u)}{|F(u)|} + D_A F(u) + \alpha Q(u)F(u)\right)\delta F^*(u)du\right]. \quad (2.69)$$

where $\text{Re}[\ldots]$ is the real part of the complex number.

If we choose the variation δF as a difference of complex amplitudes before and after satisfying the spatial limitations

$$\delta F = \overline{F} - F, \qquad (2.70)$$

the maximum negative variation (2.69) of the functional (2.68) is attained under the condition

$$\overline{F} - F = \lambda G(u) = \lambda\left(|F_0(u)|\frac{F(u)}{|F(u)|} - D_A F(u) - \alpha Q(u)F(u)\right), \qquad (2.71)$$

where $\lambda > 0$ is the parameter of the algorithm adaptation or the relaxation parameter. Actually, given the condition (2.71), the variation (2.69) takes the form

$$\delta\varepsilon = -2\lambda\int_{-\infty}^{\infty} |G(u)|^2 \, du \le 0. \qquad (2.72)$$

From the condition (2.71) follows a two-parameter iterative equation for designing a DOE [22]:

$$\overline{F}_{n+1} = [1 - \lambda(D_A + \alpha Q(u))]F_n + \lambda|F_0(u)|\frac{F_n(u)}{|F_n(u)|}. \qquad (2.73)$$

Note that in Eq. (2.73), the complex amplitude $F_n(u)$ in the nth iteration step results from satisfying the limitations imposed in the DOE plane and may be represented by

$$F_n(u) = \Im D_B W_B \Im^{-1} \overline{F}_n(u), \tag{2.74}$$

where $\overline{F}_n(u)$ is the complex amplitude in the nth step after the replacement of Eq. (2.73), $D_B f = \begin{cases} f, & x \in \Omega_B \\ 0, & x \notin \Omega_B \end{cases}$ is the spatial limitation operator, Ω_B is the DOE aperture shape, and $W_B f = |f_0|(f/|f|)$ is the operator that assigns the desired illuminating beam amplitude, $|f_0|$, to the complex function $f(x)$ describing the light field in the DOE plane.

Thus, Eqs. (2.73) and (2.74) describe an iterative two-parameter algorithm for designing a DOE that forms a desired intensity distribution (image) in a limited domain Ω_A of spatial spectrum. We shall term this algorithm as an *adaptive-regularization* (AR) *algorithm*.

In the following section, we shall demonstrate that the familiar algorithms for designing DOEs are a particular case of the AR algorithm.

Putting $\lambda = 1$ and $\alpha = 0$ instead of Eq. (2.73), we shall get the following relationship:

$$\overline{F}_{n+1} = [1 - D_A]F_n + |F_0(n)|\frac{F_n(n)}{|F_n(n)|} = \begin{cases} |F_0(n)|\dfrac{F_n(n)}{|F_n(n)|}, & u \in \Omega_A \\ F_n(n), & u \notin \Omega_A \end{cases} \tag{2.75}$$

Algorithm (2.75) combines the properties of the GS algorithm [3] and Gerchberg-Papoulis algorithm [19,20]. Actually, in accordance with Eq. (2.75) in the Fourier plane of a pregiven domain Ω_A, the calculated modulus of complex amplitude, $|F_n(u)|$, is replaced by the desired one, $|F_0(u)|$, whereas beyond the domain Ω_A, the calculated function $F_n(u)$ remains unchanged. Therefore, Eq. (2.75) may be interpreted as a GS algorithm possessing the superresolution property of the Gerchberg-Papoulis algorithm. Eq. (2.75) was treated in Ref. [21] as a realization of the idea of an additional degree of freedom aimed at eliminating the iterative algorithm stagnation [3].

Putting $\lambda \neq 1$ and $\alpha = 0$ instead of Eq. (2.73), we get the relation

$$\overline{F}_{n+1} = \begin{cases} \lambda|F_0(u)|\dfrac{F_n(u)}{|F_n(u)|} + (1 - \lambda)F_n, & u \in \Omega_A \\ F_n(u), & u \notin \Omega_A \end{cases}. \tag{2.76}$$

Equation (2.76) is an analog of the input-output algorithm [7], the method of orthogonal projections [23], the adaptive [10,11] and pendulum [9] algorithms and reflects the idea of the "soft" coding of complex amplitude, advanced in [24]. The relaxation parameter λ in Eq. (2.76) allows the algorithm convergence rate to be controlled and putting $\lambda = 2$, this rate is usually maximum [9,10].

When choosing $\lambda = 1$ and $\alpha \neq 0$ instead of Eq. (2.73), we shall get the expression

$$\overline{F}_{n+1} = [(1 - \alpha) - D_A]F_n + |F_0(u)|\frac{F_n(u)}{|F_n(u)|}$$

$$= \begin{cases} |F_0(u)|\dfrac{F_n(u)}{|F_n(u)|} - \alpha F_n, & u \in \Omega_A \\ (1 - \alpha)F_n(u), & u \notin \Omega_A \end{cases} \tag{2.77}$$

The algorithm (2.77) is analogous to the regularized Gerchberg–Papoulis algorithm, proposed in Ref. [25], and intended to reconstruct a real object from the noised image. The regularization parameter in Eq. (2.77) controls the contribution of the calculated light amplitude $F_n(u)$ into and beyond a pregiven domain Ω_A.

In the general case, the AR algorithm of Eq. (2.73) can be recast as follows:

$$\overline{F}_{n+1} = \begin{cases} \lambda |F_0(u)| \dfrac{F_n(u)}{|F_n(u)|} + (1 - \lambda - \lambda\alpha)F_n, & u \in \Omega_A \\ (1 - \lambda\alpha)F_n(u), & u \notin \Omega_A \end{cases} \qquad (2.78)$$

It would be of interest to note that under no values of the parameters α and λ one can change from the AR algorithm of Eq. (2.78) to the error-reduction algorithm [3], which in the present terms is given by

$$\overline{F}_{n+1} = \begin{cases} |F_0(u)| \dfrac{F_n(u)}{|F_n(u)|}, & u \in \Omega_A \\ 0 & u \notin \Omega_A \end{cases} \qquad (2.79)$$

The change from Eq. (2.78) to Eq. (2.79) is only possible if one considers the relaxation constant as a dual constant taking different values within and out of the pregiven domain

$$\lambda = \begin{cases} (1 + \alpha)^{-1}, & u \in \Omega_A \\ \alpha^{-1}, & u \notin \Omega_A \end{cases} \qquad (2.80)$$

Example 2.4   Advantages of the algorithm (2.73) or (2.78) over the base GS algorithm of Eq. (2.79) are shown for the case of formation in the lens's focal plane of the intensity distribution in the form $I(x) = I_0\mathrm{rect}(x/a)$. The Fourier transform relating to the light field complex amplitudes in the DOE plane and in the lens's focal plane was derived using the Fast Fourier Transform algorithm on an array of 256 pixels. The initial phase for the iterative process was chosen as a realization of some stochastic value.

Figure 2.11 depicts (a) the DOE phase derived after 30 iterations by the algorithm (2.79) and (b) the normalized intensity distribution in the lens's focal plane generated by the DOE with the aforementioned phase. The optical element occupied 64 of 256 pixels. The dotted line in Figure 2.11b shows the desired intensity distribution specified on a segment of 16 to 48 pixels. This segment accounts for 97.5 percent

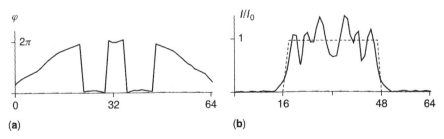

Figure 2.11. (a) The DOE phase derived via the algorithm (2.79) and (b) the intensity distribution in the Fourier plane.

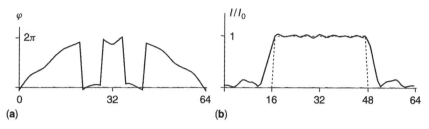

Figure 2.12. (**a**) The DOE phase derived using the algorithm (2.78) and (**b**) the intensity in the focal plane.

of the light energy illuminating the DOE, and the rms deviation of the resulting intensity distribution (Fig. 2.11b) from constant value is 27.2 percent. If the phase shown in Figure 2.11a is used as an initial phase guess for the algorithm (2.78), then after the following 100 iterations one gets the result shown in Figure 2.12. Figure 2.12 depicts (a) the DOE phase and (b) the normalized intensity distribution generated in the focal plane, the parameters being $\lambda = 1$ and $\alpha = 0.1$. About 92.7 percent of the entire light energy comes to a segment of 16 to 48 pixels, the rms deviation of the intensity from a constant value being 2 percent.

Thus, the two-parameter algorithm of Eq. (2.78) makes possible an essential reduction of the deviation of the generated diffraction pattern from a desired one (more than 10 times for our example) at the expense of an unessential reduction in the energy efficiency (by 5 percent in our example).

2.7   A GRADIENT ALGORITHM FOR COMPUTING A DOE PHASE

A review of nonlinear programming algorithms intended for image reconstruction may be found in Ref. [1]. The problem is how to minimize the purpose functional in view of limitations imposed on the entering functions. If the limitations imposed allow the resulting functional to be represented as a sum of the linear and quadratic functional, the solution to the problem may be found analytically. Otherwise, one will have to construct calculational algorithms. Among them are the direct optimization method, the gradient descent method, the fastest descent method, and the conjugate gradient method. Of the methods listed, the last one has the best convergence. Still faster convergence is found with the Lagrange method of modified functions, which implies the addition into the functional of terms with the limitation functions being squared. However, one iteration of the gradient method requires taking from three to five integral transforms of convolution type or Fourier type. Therefore, the more complex is the algorithm, the longer it takes for the computer to implement. The use of gradient methods for designing DOEs has some peculiarities, that are dealt with in the following section.

Following Ref. [5], we shall consider how the gradient method of fastest descent applies to the DOE design.

Assume that the variables x and $u = 0, 1, 2, \ldots, N - 1$ are arrays of discrete coordinates. To do the computer-aided design, it is necessary to sample the variables.

This being the case, the functional (2.11) takes the form

$$\varepsilon = \sum_u (|G(u)| - |F(u)|)^2, \tag{2.81}$$

where $|F|$ and $|G|$ are the desired and the calculated light amplitudes in the spatial spectrum plane and the Fourier transform (2.12) is brought to the discrete Fourier transform (DFT):

$$G(u) = \Im\{g(x)\} = \sum_{u=0}^{N-1} g(x) \exp[-i2\pi xu/N]. \tag{2.82}$$

The inverse to the DFT is given by

$$g(x) = \Im^{-1}\{G(u)\} = \frac{1}{N}\sum_{u=0}^{N-1} G(u) \exp[i2\pi xu/N]. \tag{2.83}$$

The gradient of the functional (2.81) is equal to the sum of partial derivatives of this functional with respect to unknown parameter p (for p one may take the DOE phase, the illuminating beam amplitude, and the like):

$$\frac{\partial\varepsilon}{\partial p} = 2\sum_u [|G(u)| - |F(u)|]\frac{\partial|G(u)|}{\partial p}$$

$$= \sum_u \left[G^*(u) - \frac{|F(u)|}{|G(u)|}G^*(u)\right]\frac{\partial G(u)}{\partial p} + \text{c.c}$$

$$= -\sum_u G^{w*}(u)\frac{\partial G(u)}{\partial p} + \text{c.c.}, \tag{2.84}$$

where $*$ denotes the complex conjugation, c.c. is the complex conjugated previous term, and the function $G^w(u)$ takes the form

$$G^w(u) = |F(u)|\frac{G(u)}{|G(u)|} - G(u). \tag{2.85}$$

Making use of the linearity of the Fourier transform we find the relation between the derivatives of complex amplitudes in the DOE plane and in the Fourier spectrum plane:

$$\frac{\partial G(u)}{\partial p} = \frac{\partial}{\partial p}\{\Im[g(x)]\} = \Im\left\{\frac{\partial g(x)}{\partial p}\right\}. \tag{2.86}$$

Substituting the above relation into Eq. (2.84) and doing some rearrangements yields

$$\frac{\partial\varepsilon}{\partial p} = -\sum_u G^{w*}(u)\Im\left(\frac{\partial g(x)}{\partial p}\right) + \text{c.c.}$$

$$= -\sum_x \left[\frac{\partial g(x)}{\partial p}\right]^* \Im^{-1}[G^w(u)] + \text{c.c.}$$

$$= -2\mathrm{Re}\left\{\sum_x \left[\frac{\partial g(x)}{\partial p}\right]^* \Im^{-1}[G^w(u)]\right\}$$

$$= -2\mathrm{Re}\left(\sum_x \frac{\partial g(x)}{\partial p}\Im^{-1}[G^{w*}(u)]\right) \tag{2.87}$$

The calculation of (2.87) involves taking the Fourier transform of $g(x)$ in order to get $G(u)$; obtaining $G^w(u)$ from (2.85); conjugating the derived result; taking the inverse Fourier transform, and the scalar multiplication of the result by the function $(\partial g(x)/\partial p)$.

Consider now a particular instance when the p parameter represents samples of the phase function $\theta(x)$. Then we have $g(x) = |g(x)| \exp[i\theta(x)]$

$$\frac{\partial g(x')}{\partial \theta(x)} = ig(x)\delta(x', x), \tag{2.88}$$

where

$$\delta(x', x) = \begin{cases} 1, & x = x' \\ 0, & x \neq x' \end{cases} \tag{2.89}$$

is the Cronecker function. Substituting (2.88) into (2.84) yields

$$\frac{\partial \varepsilon}{\partial \theta(x)} = -2\mathrm{Re}\left\{\sum_x ig(x')\delta(x', x)g^{w*}(x)\right\}$$

$$= 2\mathrm{Im}\left\{g(x)g^{w*}(x)\right\}, \tag{2.90}$$

where

$$g^w(x) = \Im^{-1}\left\{G^w(u)\right\}. \tag{2.91}$$

The gradient found may be employed in any gradient method for calculating the phase function $\theta(x)$, for example, in the fastest descent method. With this method, starting from some initial phase guess $\theta_0(x)$, each subsequent approximation is found from the iterative equation

$$\theta_{n+1}(x) = \theta_n(x) + s\frac{\partial \varepsilon}{\partial \theta_n(x)} \tag{2.92}$$

(n is the iteration number) by way of a 1D minimization with respect to s of the purpose function ε as a function of $\theta_{n+1}(x)$.

With a view of avoiding the 1D minimization with respect to s of the purpose function ε, we shall follow the Ref. [5] and get the estimate of an optimal step s based on the first-order Taylor expansion of ε about the point $\theta(x)$, as a function of $\theta_n(x)$:

$$\varepsilon \approx \varepsilon_n + \sum_x \frac{\partial \varepsilon}{\partial \theta_n(x)}[\theta(x) - \theta_n(x)]. \tag{2.93}$$

This expression is equal to zero if

$$\theta(x) - \theta_n(x) = -\varepsilon_n \frac{\partial \varepsilon}{\partial \theta_n(x)} \left\| \frac{\partial \varepsilon}{\partial \theta_n(x)} \right\|^{-2}. \tag{2.94}$$

Thus, on the assumption (2.93), the optimal value of the gradient method step is given by

$$s_n = -\varepsilon_n \left\| \frac{\partial \varepsilon}{\partial \theta_n(x)} \right\|^{-2}. \tag{2.95}$$

The convergence rate of the algorithm may also be enhanced using other gradient methods.

Consider, for example, the conjugate gradient method. For its Flatcher-Reevse variant [26], every subsequent approximation is given by

$$\theta_{n+1}(x) = \theta_n(x) + s d_n, \tag{2.96}$$

$$d_{n+1} = -\frac{\partial \varepsilon}{\partial \theta_{n+1}(x)} + \beta_n d_n, \tag{2.97}$$

$$\beta_n = \frac{\left\| \dfrac{\partial \varepsilon}{\partial \theta_{n+1}(x)} \right\|^2}{\left\| \dfrac{\partial \varepsilon}{\partial \theta_n(x)} \right\|^2}, \tag{2.98}$$

where $\left\| \dfrac{\partial \varepsilon}{\partial \theta_n(x)} \right\|^2 = \sum_{x=0}^{N-1} \left(\dfrac{\partial \varepsilon}{\partial \theta_n(x)} \right)^2$ is the Euclidean norm.

2.8   APPLICATION OF ITERATIVE ALGORITHMS FOR DESIGNING DOEs

In this section, we deal with particular realizations of the aforementioned algorithms for designing various DOE types.

In subsection 2.8.2, the problems of designing radially symmetric DOEs generating axial light segments, and multifocus lenses are brought to one-dimensional (1D) problems of focusing the light into a transverse segment and designing a multiorder diffraction grating. In subsection 2.8.3, the algorithm for DOE design is adapted in such a manner as to calculate the phase of a radial element as a piecewise-constant function, with the DOE surface divided into rings of constant phase. Binary and multi-level diffraction gratings are designed in subsections 2.8.4 and 2.8.5 using gradient methods.

In subsection 2.8.6, we discuss peculiarities of iterative algorithms for designing DOEs focusing the light into a 3D domain and onto a pregiven 2D surface. Two practically important problems are highlighted in separate subsections: the leveling of the Gaussian beam profile (subsection 2.8.7) and the focusing of light into narrowing and widening rings (subsection 2.8.8).

Composite DOEs intended for focusing the light into contour images (e.g., a set of letters for laser branding) are dealt with in subsection 2.8.9. Gradient iterative method modernizations for designing DOEs with a small number of phase levels are discussed in subsections 2.8.10 and 2.8.11. Such DOEs are termed *quantized*.

2.8.1 Design of DOEs Focusing into Radially Symmetric Domains of Fourier Spectrum

When designing a DOE forming in a certain spatial domain an intensity distribution with circular symmetry, it seems useful to employ polar coordinates (r, φ) and (ρ, θ) in the DOE plane and in the observation plane, respectively:

$$\begin{cases} u = r \cos \varphi \\ v = r \sin \varphi \end{cases} \quad \begin{cases} \xi = \rho \cos \theta \\ \eta = \rho \sin \theta \end{cases} . \tag{2.99}$$

In this case, the integral Fresnel transform (2.1) in polar coordinates takes the form

$$F(\rho, \theta) = \frac{ik}{2\pi z} e^{ikz} \int_0^\infty \int_0^{2\pi} W(r, \varphi)$$

$$\times \exp\left\{ \frac{ik}{2z} \left[r^2 + \rho^2 - 2r\rho \cos(\varphi - \theta) \right] \right\} r \, dr \, d\varphi. \tag{2.100}$$

To enable the modulus of the complex function $F(\rho, \theta)$ in the observation plane not to depend on the azimuth angle θ, we shall restrict ourselves to the consideration of a set of functions given as

$$W(r, \varphi) = g(r) e^{im\varphi}, \quad m = 1, 2, 3, \ldots. \tag{2.101}$$

Then, instead of Eq. (2.100), we get

$$F(\rho, \theta) = (-i)^{m-1} k z^{-1} e^{ikz} e^{im\theta} \int_0^\infty g(r) e^{\frac{ik}{2z}(r^2 + \rho^2)} J_m\left(\frac{kr\rho}{z} \right) r \, dr, \tag{2.102}$$

where

$$J_m(x) = \frac{(-i)^m}{2\pi} \int_0^{2\pi} e^{i(mt + x \cos t)} \, dt \tag{2.103}$$

are the Bessel functions of first kind and of mth order.

Equation (2.102) suggests that the DOE phase may be found using the scalar theory of Fresnel diffraction if we solve the following integral equation:

$$I_0(\rho) = |F(\rho, \theta)|^2 = \left| kz^{-1} \int_0^R A_0(r) e^{i\psi(r)} e^{\frac{ikr^2}{2z}} J_m\left(\frac{kr\rho}{z} \right) r \, dr \right|^2, \tag{2.104}$$

where $I_0(\rho)$ is the image's radial intensity distribution to be generated at the distance z from the DOE plane, $A_0(r)$ is the radial amplitude distribution of the illuminating beam, and $\psi(r)$ is the sought-for DOE phase function. In the following section, we discuss iterative techniques for solving Eq. (2.104) aimed at the generation of a desired image in the spatial spectrum plane. From Eq. (2.104) it follows that the DOE phase function can be iteratively found if we take the direct Hankel transform and its inverse:

$$H(\rho) = \int_0^\infty h(r) J_m(r\rho) r \, dr, \tag{2.105}$$

$$h(r) = \int_0^\infty H(\rho) J_m(r\rho) \rho \, d\rho. \tag{2.106}$$

The Hankel transforms of Eqs. (2.105) and (2.106) can be quickly calculated using the method of exponential replacement of variables [27]. With this method, by the exponential replacement of variables, we change from the Hankel transform (HT) to a correlation, which may be calculated through the Fourier transform. Actually, after the replacement,

$$r = r_0 \, e^x, \quad \rho = \rho_0 \, e^y, \tag{2.107}$$

where r_0 and ρ_0 are constant, and instead of (2.105), we obtain

$$\overline{H}(y) = r_0^2 \int_{-\infty}^{\infty} \overline{h}(x) S(x+y) \, e^{2x} \, dx, \tag{2.108}$$

where

$$\overline{h}(x) = h(r_0 \, e^x), \quad S(x+y) = J_m(r_0 \rho_0 \, e^{x+y}), \quad \overline{H}(y) = H(\rho_0 \, e^y). \tag{2.109}$$

For $m = 0$, the Bessel function tends to one as $x \to -\infty$. Therefore, in order for the function $S(x)$ to tend to zero as $x \to \pm\infty$, it should be multiplied by $\exp(x/4)$, and in order for the integrand in Eq. (2.108) not to change, the function $h(x)$ also should be multiplied by $\exp(-x/4)$. Since the DOE transmission function $h(r)$ is limited by an aperture $r \in [0, R]$, where R is the aperture radius, there is no divergence for the function $\overline{h}(x)$ as $x \to \pm\infty$.

After redesignation, we get the following relations:

$$h_1(x) = \overline{h}(x) r_0^2 \, e^{7x/4}, \quad S_1(x+y) = S(x+y) \exp\left(\frac{x+y}{4}\right),$$

$$H_1(y) = \overline{H}(y) \, e^{y/4}, \tag{2.110}$$

and instead of (2.105) we get the correlation integral

$$H_1(y) = \int_{-\infty}^{a} h_1(x) S_1(x+y) \, dx, \quad a = \ln \frac{R}{r_0}. \tag{2.111}$$

The integral (2.111) may be expressed by the Fourier transform in the form

$$H(\rho) = \left[\frac{\rho}{\rho_0}\right]^{-\frac{1}{4}} \int_{-\infty}^{\infty} P(-w) U(w) \, e^{iw \ln \frac{\rho}{\rho_0}} \, dw, \tag{2.112}$$

where $P(w)$ is the Fourier image of the $h_1(x)$ function and $U(w)$ is the Fourier image of $S_1(y)$. In a similar way, we may represent the inverse HT of Eq. (2.106). Note that there are also other methods for fast calculation of the HT [28].

We revert to the solution of Eq. (2.104) and combine both functions in the exponent into a single function that is to be derived:

$$\overline{\psi}(r) = \psi(r) + \frac{k}{2z} r^2. \tag{2.113}$$

The procedure of iteratively solving Eq. (2.104) is realized similarly to the GS algorithm, Eq. (2.6), and successively uses a pair of direct and inverse HTs. In the process, in the nth iteration step, one performs a limiting replacement of variables both in the optical element plane and in the observation plane. The $g_n(r)$ function calculated in the DOE plane is replaced by $\overline{g}_n(r)$ by the rule

$$\overline{g}_n(r) = \begin{cases} A_0(r)g_n(r)|g_n(r)|^{-1}, & r \in [0, R] \\ 0, & r \notin [0, R] \end{cases}, \qquad (2.114)$$

whereas the calculated amplitude $F_n(\rho)$ in the observation plane is replaced by $\overline{F}_n(\rho)$ using the relation

$$\overline{F}_n(\rho) = \sqrt{I_0(\rho)}F_n(\rho)|F_n(\rho)|^{-1}. \qquad (2.115)$$

There is no essential difference between the preceding replacements, Eqs. (2.114) and (2.115), and the corresponding replacements for the 2D error-reduction algorithm, Eqs. (2.6) and (2.8). The convergence rate of the algorithm may be increased, if, instead of Eq. (2.115), one uses the AA algorithm of Eq. (2.19) when changing from the 2D case to the radial one.

The algorithm considered allows one to design DOEs intended for the formation of the images such as a circle, a ring, or a set of rings [29,30].

Example 2.5   Shown in Figure 2.13 is the phase (after 22 iterations) of a DOE capable of transforming the laser light with Gaussian intensity distribution into a circle of uniform intensity in a lens's focal plane. The Gaussian beam intensity on the DOE aperture boundaries is 0.1 of its maximum value at the center. The DOE radius is $R = 0.4$ mm; the number of pixels along the radius is 256, $k/f = 100$ mm^{-2}, f is the lens's focal length; the circle radius in the image plane is 0.3 mm and approximately equal to three radii of the minimal diffraction spot (airy disk). Figure 2.13b depicts the radial section of the DOE phase.

Figure 2.14 illustrates (a) the diffraction pattern generated in the focal plane by the DOE with such a phase and (b) its radial section. The rms deviation of intensity in the circle produced, from a constant value is 6 percent, whereas the energy efficiency of focusing into a circle is 91 percent. In our case, the design was performed using the HT (for $m = 0$, the Fourier–Bessel transform). If one needs to design a DOE with radial

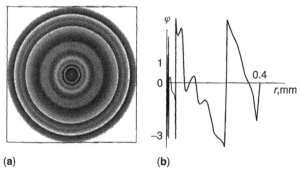

(a)   (b)

Figure 2.13. Phase of a DOE focusing into a circle: (a) the DOE phase and (b) its radial section.

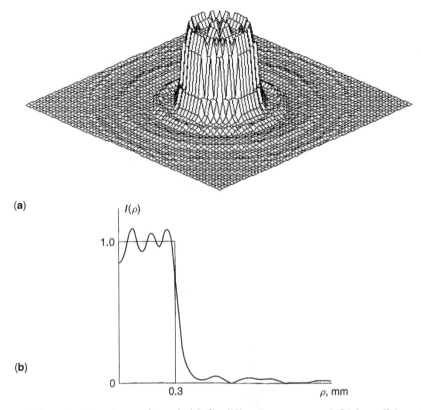

Figure 2.14. The circle image formed: (**a**) the diffraction pattern and (**b**) its radial section.

phase generating a ringlike intensity distribution, then the use of the HT will result in the formation of an intensity peak at the center of the ring. This may be eliminated by the use of a higher order HT.

Example 2.6 Figure 2.15 depicts the result of designing a DOE focusing into a wide ring of uniform intensity. The design was performed using a HT of the 8th order (in Eq. (2.101), $m = 8$), the DOE radius being $R = 5$ mm, and the radii of the ring being $r_1 = 0.1$ mm and $r_2 = 0.2$ mm, and the number of pixels being 256.

The energy efficiency of focusing into a ring was 83 percent and the rms deviation was eight percent.

Note that the azimuth term in Eq. (2.101) in the form $e^{im\varphi}$ is of interest by itself as the transmission function of a phase optical element that may be utilized for the implementation of a variety of optical transforms: the HT of mth order [31], the generation of Bessel beams of higher orders [32,33], and a radial analog of the Hilbert transform [34].

2.8.2 Design of Diffractive Axicons Generating Axial Light Segments

A novel optical element in the form of a transparent cone is proposed in the Ref. [35]. Such an element is used for producing a narrow axial light beam with the cross section diameter proportional to the angle at the cone apex and with the length

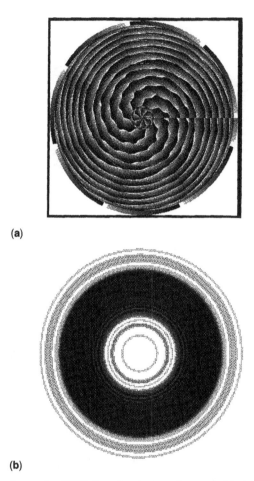

(a)

(b)

Figure 2.15. (a) The phase of a DOE focusing into a ring and (b) the diffraction pattern at $m = 8$.

proportional to the illuminating beam diameter and inversely proportional to the angle at the cone apex (the light beam must fall perpendicularly to the cone base). In parallel with a spherical lens, the axicon is used for the formation of a narrow light ring [36].

In following section, we consider DOEs similar in properties to axicons. Phase optical elements capable, in combination with a spherical lens, of producing the light field with enhanced focal depth have been given the name *DOE-to-focus* into an axial line-segment [37] and may be treated as generalized axicons [36]. They have found wide practical use in studying the charge in gases [38], in reading data out of or into optical disks [39], and in surface testing [40].

In the subsequent text, we consider iterative techniques for designing DOEs (generalized axicons) capable of forming axial light beams of desired intensity distribution.

Assume that it is necessary to find the radial phase function of an optical element that forms an axial light segment lying between the points z_1 and z_2 and with a desired intensity distribution along the axis $I_0(z)$, $z \in [z_1, z_2]$. Then, Eq. (2.102) will take the form

$$F(\rho, z) = \frac{ik}{z} e^{ikz} e^{ik\rho^2/2z} \int_0^R \exp\left[i\varphi(r) + i\frac{kr^2}{2z}\right] J_0\left(\frac{kr\rho}{z}\right) r \, dr, \qquad (2.116)$$

where R is the DOE radius, $\varphi(r)$ is the unknown phase, and $J_0(x)$ is the Bessel function of zero order. In Eq. (2.116), the optical element is supposed to be illuminated by a plane light wave. Because the intensity is known only along the z-axis, one may put in Eq. (2.116) $\rho = 0$ and get [omitting a trivial term $i \exp(ikz)$] the equation

$$F(0, z) = \frac{k}{z} \int_0^R \exp\left[i\varphi(r) + i\frac{kr^2}{2z}\right] r \, dr. \qquad (2.117)$$

Introduce redesignations

$$\xi = \frac{k}{z}, \qquad x = \frac{r^2}{2}, \qquad (2.118)$$

and recast Eq. (2.117) as follows

$$\frac{1}{\xi} F(\xi) = \int_0^a e^{i\varphi(x) + ix\xi} dx, \qquad a = \frac{R^2}{2}. \qquad (2.119)$$

From Eq. (2.119) the desired function of the axicon-DOE transmission, $e^{i\varphi(r)}$ is seen to be related to the axial complex light amplitude, $F(\xi)$, through a one-dimensional Fourier transform. Hence, the challenge now is to solve a 1D integral equation

$$\frac{1}{\xi^2} I_0(\xi) = \left|\int_0^a e^{i\varphi(x) + ix\xi} dx\right|^2. \qquad (2.120)$$

We shall make use of the error-reduction algorithm and all its modifications. If it is required to design an axicon as an addition to a spherical lens, the phase in Eq. (2.117) must be given by

$$\varphi(r) = \varphi_0(r) - \frac{kr^2}{2f}, \qquad (2.121)$$

where f is the focal length of the spherical lens, from which, instead of (2.117), we may write

$$F(0, z) = \frac{k}{z} \int_0^R \exp\left[i\varphi_0(r) + i\frac{kr^2}{2}\left(\frac{1}{z} - \frac{1}{f}\right)\right] r \, dr. \qquad (2.122)$$

Equation (2.122) with respect to $\varphi_0(r)$ will be equivalent to Eq. (2.119) with the following replacement of variables

$$\xi = k\left(\frac{1}{z} - \frac{1}{f}\right), \qquad x = \frac{r^2}{2}. \qquad (2.123)$$

In order to form short line-segment (given that $2d = z_2 - z_1 \ll f$, where $2d$ is the length focal depth or the length of the desired light line) instead of Eq. (2.122), one may use a simpler relation

$$F(\Delta z) = \frac{k}{f} \int_0^R \exp\left[i\varphi_0(r) + i\frac{k\Delta z}{2f^2}r^2\right] r\, dr, \tag{2.124}$$

where $\Delta z \in [-d, d]$, $f = (z_1 + z_2)/2$.
After the replacement of variables

$$\xi = \frac{k\Delta z}{f^2}, \qquad x = \frac{r^2}{2},$$

we get the equation for the derivation of the DOE phase

$$I_0(\xi) = \left|\frac{k}{f}\int_0^a e^{i\varphi_0(x)+ix\xi}\, dx\right|^2. \tag{2.125}$$

The solution to Eq. (2.125) may be found by an iterative procedure [41,42,43], the degree of closeness of the evaluating function $I_n(\xi) = |F_n(\xi)|^2$ to the desired function $I_0(\xi)$ is determined from the rms deviation

$$\delta = \left[\int_{\xi_1}^{\xi_2} |I_n(\xi) - I_0(\xi)|^2 d\xi\right]^{\frac{1}{2}} \left[\int_{\xi_1}^{\xi_2} I_0^2(\xi) d\xi\right]^{-\frac{1}{2}}. \tag{2.126}$$

The efficiency of production of the axial light segment can be specified by

$$E_k = \int_0^{\rho_0} I(\rho, z_k)\rho\, d\rho \bigg/ \int_0^{\infty} I(\rho, z_k)\rho\, d\rho, \tag{2.127}$$

where $I_0(\rho, z_k)$ is the intensity calculated in a plane located at the distance z_k from the DOE, and ρ_0 is the radius of the first local intensity minimum $I(\rho, z_k)$. The function E_k specifies the portion of light energy that contributes to the formation of the minimal diffraction spot in a pregiven observation plane. Note that if the desired intensity $I_0(z)$ is given by

$$I_0(z) = I_0 \sum_{n=1}^{N} \delta(z - z_n), \tag{2.128}$$

where $\delta(x)$ is the Dirac function, the solution to Eq. (2.125), $\varphi_0(r)$, will be the phase of an N-focus lens with N longitudinal foci of equal intensity I_0.

Example 2.7   Figure 2.16a depicts the DOE phase calculated during 100 iterations, with the GS algorithm employed for solving Eq. (2.125). This DOE produces a light beam with the axial intensity distribution shaped as a rectangular impulse (Fig. 2.16b). The calculational parameters are as follows: 256 is the total number of pixels; $R = 6$ mm is the DOE radius and $f = 400$ mm is the focal length of a lens which in the vicinity of its focal plane contains the produced line-segment of length $2a = 40$ mm,

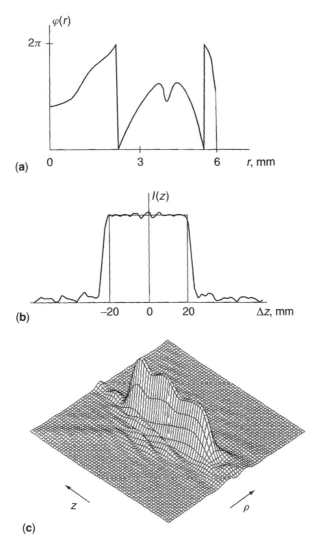

Figure 2.16. A DOE focusing into an axial line-segment: (**a**) the phase radial section, (**b**) the axial intensity, and (**c**) the intensity distribution in the plane (z, ρ).

and 0.63 µm is the wavelength. The illuminating light beam is assumed to be plane. The error of Eq. (2.126) is two percent, whereas the efficiency of focusing of Eq. (2.127) varies along the line in a complicated manner and lies within the range from 15 percent to 85 percent. The line length is about eight Fresnel lengths. Shown in Figure 2.16c is a 3D intensity distribution.

Figure 2.17a shows the DOE phase in the form of an amplitude mask that forms 10 axial foci of equal intensity (Fig. 2.17b).

The phase of a multifocus lens is approximated by the sum of phases of two different axicons or two different DOEs, producing axial lines of different length. As a result, two conical waves with different tilt to the optical axis are propagated in space. It is because of interference of these waves that the axial foci appear.

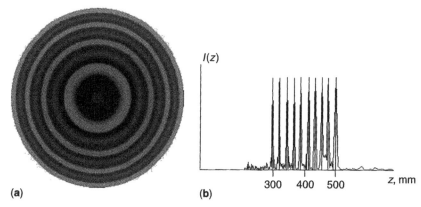

(a)   **(b)**

Figure 2.17. Design of a multifocus lens: (**a**) the DOE phase and (**b**) the axial intensity distribution.

2.8.3 Designing Radially Symmetric DOEs with Quantized Phase

In this section, we deal with an iterative algorithm allowing one to design radially symmetric DOEs with a small number of phase levels, thus providing an essential advantage in fabricating DOEs by photolithography and e-beam-lithography methods. Widening the diffraction spot may serve as an example of practical application of such DOEs. This problem is of interest for laser printing. It stands to reason that a twofold expansion of diffraction spot (Airy disk) can be implemented without the use of a DOE by way of a twofold increase in the lens's focal length or by a twofold reduction of the lens aperture radius. However, the former approach may cause undesirable modifications to the equipment, whereas the latter reduces the focusing efficiency by four times.

We propose a "DOE + lens" combination to be employed for the effective solution of this problem [44]: suppose that we must calculate a DOE phase, $\varphi(r)$, which depends only on the radial variable, and that the DOE produces a desired intensity distribution $I_0(\rho)$ in the lens's focal plane, then, instead of Eq. (2.104) one may write down the following equation for determining the phase $\varphi(r)$:

$$I_0(\rho) = \left| \frac{k}{2\pi f} \int A_0(r)\, e^{i\varphi(r)} J_0\left(\frac{kr\rho}{f}\right) r\, dr \right|^2, \tag{2.129}$$

where $A_0(r)$ is the illuminating beam amplitude and f is the lens's focal length. Also, suppose the fulfillment of the condition $A_0(r) = 1$. The function $\varphi(r)$ will be sought in a piecewise form (Fig. 2.18). Then, we can represent the light complex amplitude, $F(\rho)$, in the lens's focal plane as a sum of the amplitudes resulting from the diffraction of the plane wave by a circular aperture:

$$F(\rho) = 2\pi \sum_{n=0}^{N-1} e^{i\varphi_{n+1}} \left[r_{n+1} \frac{J_1(k\rho r_{n+1}/f)}{\rho} - r_n \frac{J_1(k\rho r_n/f)}{\rho} \right], \tag{2.130}$$

where φ_{n+1} is the value of $\varphi(r)$ at $r \in [r_n, r_{n+1}]$, $n = 0, 1, \ldots, N-1$; $r_0 = 0$, $r_N = R$, R is the DOE radius, and N is the number of partition points on the DOE radius.

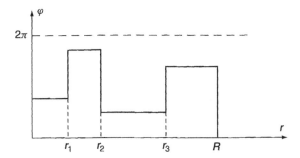

Figure 2.18. Piecewise-constant phase.

After the corresponding transformation of Eq. (2.130), we get

$$F(\rho) = \frac{2\pi}{\rho} \sum_{n=1}^{N} C_n J_1\left(\frac{\gamma_n \rho}{a}\right), \qquad (2.131)$$

where

$$\begin{cases} C_n = r_n[e^{i\varphi_n} - e^{i\varphi_{n+1}}] \\ C_N = Re^{i\varphi_N} \end{cases}, \qquad (2.132)$$

γ_n are zeros of the Bessel function of first order $J_1(\gamma_n) = 0$. Comparison of Eqs. (2.130) and (2.131) suggests that the partition points r_n should satisfy the following condition

$$r_n = \frac{\gamma_n f}{ka}, \qquad a \geq R, \qquad (2.133)$$

where a is a constant that controls the scale of dividing the DOE into rings.

By introducing the designations $\overline{F}(\rho) = (2\pi)^{-1}\rho F(\rho)$, instead of (2.131), we get

$$\overline{F}(\rho) = \sum_{n=1}^{N} C_n J_1\left(\frac{\gamma_n \rho}{a}\right). \qquad (2.134)$$

Using the property of orthogonality of the Bessel function

$$\int_0^1 J_m(\gamma_p x) J_m(\gamma_q x) x\, dx = \begin{cases} [J'_m(\gamma_p)]^2 /2, & p = q \\ 0, & p \neq q \end{cases}, \qquad (2.135)$$

where $J'_m(\gamma_p)$ is the derivative of the Bessel function at point γ_p, one can represent the sum (2.134) in the form

$$C_n = 2\left[aJ'_1(\gamma_n)\right]^{-2} \int_0^a \overline{F}(\rho) J_1\left(\frac{\gamma_n \rho}{a}\right) \rho\, d\rho. \qquad (2.136)$$

The relationships (2.134) and (2.136) may form a basis for constructing an iterative procedure for solving Eq. (2.129):

(1) The initial estimate $\overline{F}(\rho)$ of complex amplitude is taken in the form

$$\overline{F}(\rho) = \sqrt{I_1(\rho)}\, e^{i\psi_0(\rho)}, \qquad (2.137)$$

where $I_1(\rho) = (2\pi)^{-2}\rho^2 I_0(\rho)$, $I_0(\rho)$ is a desired light intensity in the lens's focal plane, and $\varphi_0(\rho)$ is a stochastic phase guess.

(2) In the kth iteration step the $\overline{F}_k(\rho)$ function is represented as the sum in Eq. (2.134) with the coefficients $C_n^{(k)}$ derived from Eq. (2.136) and then replaced by the rule

$$\overline{C}_n^{(k)} = B_n\, e^{i\nu_{nk}}, \quad n = \overline{1, N}, \tag{2.138}$$

where

$$B_n = 2r_n \sin\left[\frac{\varphi_n - \varphi_{n+1}}{2}\right], \tag{2.139}$$

$$\begin{cases} \varphi_n = -\pi - \varphi_{n+1} + 2\nu_{nk}, & n = N-1, N-2, \dots, 1 \\ \varphi_N = \nu_{Nk}, \end{cases} \tag{2.140}$$

where $\nu_{nk} = \arg C_n^{(k)}$. The phases φ_n are derived by the recurrent relationships (2.140) following from Eq. (2.132).

(3) The $(k+1)$th estimate of the function $\overline{F}_{k+1}(\rho)$ is constructed:

$$\overline{F}_{k+1} = \sum_{n=1}^{N} \overline{C}_n^{(k)} J_1\left(\frac{\gamma_n \rho}{a}\right). \tag{2.141}$$

(4) The calculated function $\overline{F}_{k+1}(\rho)$ is replaced by the function $\hat{F}_{k+1}(\rho)$ by the rule

$$\hat{F}_{k+1}(\rho) = \sqrt{I_1(\rho)}\,\overline{F}_{k+1}(\rho)|\overline{F}_{k+1}(\rho)|^{-1}. \tag{2.142}$$

(5) Passage to step 2, and so on.

The algorithm considered is not converging: as the number of iterations increases the error changes quasi-periodically. However, after a limited number of iterations, one manages to obtain practically significant results.

Figure 2.19 depicts the rms error as a function of the number of iterations in Example 2.8. From Figure 2.19, the plot of the error is seen to have several local minima.

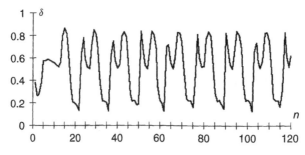

Figure 2.19. Error as a function of the number of iterations.

Example 2.8. Let us design a DOE with quantized phase, focusing the light into a ring [45]. The calculation parameters are as follows: $k/f = 100\,\text{mm}^{-2}$, $R = 0.5$ mm is the DOE radius, the discreteness along ρ is 2 μm, and the total number of pixels is 256, the ring's radii being $R_1 = 0.3$ mm and $R_2 = 0.5$ mm. Figure 2.20 illustrates the result of designing when parting the radius into several rings $N = 15$. Shown in Figure 2.20 are (a) a 2D phase distribution found after 12 iterations, (b) its radial section (both having five levels of gradation), (c) the diffraction pattern in the lens's focal plane, and (d) its radial profile (curve 2 corresponds to the calculated intensity and curve 1 corresponds to the desired one).

The energy efficiency of focusing into a ring is 89 percent (Fig. 2.20). It is noteworthy that, as distinct from a common practice, the phase quantization is not equidistant here. Actually, it is a common practice that the calculated continuous-phase function $\varphi(x)$ is subjected to the equidistant quantization in N levels.

$$\varphi_n = \left\{ \frac{2\pi}{N} n; \quad \frac{2\pi}{N} n < \varphi(x) < \frac{2\pi}{N}(n+1), \quad n = 0, 1, \ldots (N-1) \right\}$$

In the algorithm (2.140), there are already N phase pixels, φ_n, connected with the number of rings of a radial DOE, and they are nonequidistant as a rule.

2.8.4 Multiorder Binary-Phase Diffraction Gratings

Multiorder phase diffraction gratings are represented by the diffraction structure with a periodic phase relief and intended for the production of a 1D or a 2D array of plane

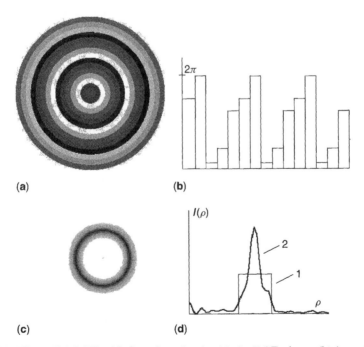

Figure 2.20. The radial DOE with five phase levels: (**a**) the DOE phase, (**b**) its radial profile, (**c**) the diffraction pattern, and (**d**) its radial profile.

beams with pregiven energy ratio between the beams. Multiorder diffraction gratings have found use in optical devices for image multiplication, optical connectors for optical fibers and free space, in optical communications and data processing devices, and in coherent optical processors [46–51].

Binary diffraction gratings are of interest because of the simplicity of their fabrication by photolithography methods: the binary microrelief is generated within one cycle of the chemical etching of substrate. The binary gratings are usually designed using stochastic optimization methods such as the direct binary search [52,53], the annealing simulation algorithm [54–58], and iterative algorithms [59–62]. In the Refs. [63,64], the design of the binary gratings is built upon the solution of a set of nonlinear equations relating the intensities in orders to the coordinates of the phase profile. Designing a binary grating with a number of orders of $2N + 1$ is brought to solving a nonlinear set of N equations.

The application of binary diffraction gratings as laser-beam transformers and beam formers (shapers) in optical fiber networks makes it necessary that the number of orders of the binary grating be increased up to several hundreds. As the number of orders increases, the algorithms for stochastic search of diffraction grating profile will take greater time and lead to unstable convergence. At the same time, the calculational methods based on the solution of a set of nonlinear equations become numerically unstable. In this subsection, we base the procedure of designing multiorder binary gratings on a gradient method, with the initial guess of grating profile chosen in a special manner. The choice of the initial guess is based on the properties of a 1D binary element focusing into a line-segment.

The phase profile of a binary grating is composed of K rectangular grooves of equal height φ, but different width (Fig. 2.21). The coordinates $x_1 \ldots x_{2K}$ of the groove boundaries are optimization parameters and determine the intensity values in diffraction orders.

To make a proper initial guess of the binary grating profile, let us consider, before hand, the design of a 1D phase DOE with aperture d focusing at $z = f$ into a line-segment with intensity distribution $I(\xi)$ (Fig. 2.22). The segment of focusing $\xi \in [n_1\Delta, n_2\Delta]$, where $\Delta = \lambda f/d$ is the size of diffraction spot, may be interpreted as a set of $(n_2 - n_1 + 1)$ diffraction spots. The phase function $\varphi(x)$ $(0 \le x \le d)$ of a 1D DOE may be derived analytically using the ray-tracing approach [65–67].

For a converging cylindrical illuminating beam of focus f

$$W_0(x) = \exp\left(-\frac{ikx^2}{2f}\right), \quad k = \frac{2\pi}{\lambda},$$

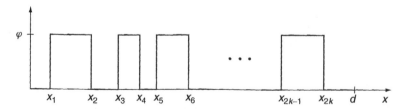

Figure 2.21. The phase function of a single period of binary grating.

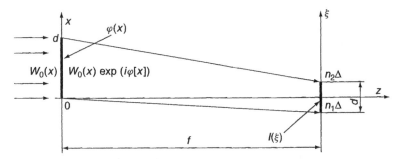

Figure 2.22. Geometry of focusing into a transverse line.

the geometro-optical function $\varphi(x)$ takes the form

$$\varphi(x) = \frac{2\pi}{d}(n_2 - n_1)\int_0^x \kappa(\alpha)\,d\alpha + \frac{2\pi}{d}n_1 x. \tag{2.143}$$

The $\kappa(\alpha)$ function in Eq. (2.143) is sought from the solution of the following differential equation:

$$\frac{d\kappa(\alpha)}{d\alpha} = \left[I\left(\frac{\kappa(\alpha) - n_1\Delta}{(n_2 - n_1)\Delta} \right) \right]^{-1} \tag{2.144}$$

with boundary conditions $\kappa(0) = 0$, $\kappa(1) = 1$. The $\varphi(x)$ function corresponds to the phase function of a nonbinary diffraction grating forming $(n_2 - n_1 + 1)$ diffraction orders. Actually, in the Fresnel-Kirchhoff approximation, the values of intensity at points $\xi = \xi_j = j\Delta$ in the plane $z = f$,

$$I(\xi_j) = \frac{1}{\lambda f} \left| \int_0^d \exp\left(i\varphi(x) - i\frac{2\pi j}{d}x \right) dx \right|^2 \tag{2.145}$$

are in direct proportion to squared modules of the Fourier coefficients in the decomposition of the function $\exp[i\varphi(x)]$. Hence, the continuous function $\varphi(x)$ may be treated as the phase function of a diffraction grating of period d and diffraction order intensities

$$I_j = \begin{cases} I(j\Delta), & n_1 \le j \le n_2 \\ 0, & \text{else.} \end{cases} \tag{2.146}$$

With a view to designing a binary grating forming $2N + 1$ diffraction orders in the range $[-N\Delta, +N\Delta]$, we shall define the binary-phase function in the form [68,69]

$$\varphi_b(x) = \Phi[\overline{\varphi}(x)], \tag{2.147}$$

where $\overline{\varphi}(x)$ is the continuous function of Eqs. (2.143) and (2.144) calculated on the assumption of generation of $(N + 1)$ orders in the range $[0, N\Delta]$ and reduced to the interval $[0, 2\pi)$, whereas

$$\Phi[\eta] = \begin{cases} 0, & \eta \in (0, \pi) \\ \pi, & \eta \in (\pi, 2\pi) \end{cases} \tag{2.148}$$

is a binary function describing quantization of the phase $\overline{\varphi}(x)$ in two levels. To describe operation of the binary grating (2.147), we shall expand the function $\exp[i\Phi(\eta)]$ on the interval $[0, 2\pi)$ into a Fourier series

$$\exp(i\Phi[\eta]) = \sum_{n=-\infty}^{\infty} c_n \exp(in\eta), \tag{2.149}$$

where

$$c_n = \begin{cases} \dfrac{1-(-1)^n}{i\pi n}, & n \neq 0, \ n = \pm 1, \ \pm 2, \ \dots \\ 0, & n = 0 \end{cases} \tag{2.150}$$

are the Fourier coefficients. Assuming $\eta = \overline{\varphi}(x)$ in (2.149) and considering a 2π-periodicity, we shall represent the complex transmittance of the binary grating, $\varphi_b(x)$, in the form

$$\exp\{i\Phi[\overline{\varphi}(x)]\} = \sum_{n=-\infty}^{\infty} c_n \exp[in\varphi(x)]. \tag{2.151}$$

Equation (2.151) corresponds to a superposition of the beams with the phase functions

$$\varphi_n(x) = n\varphi(x). \tag{2.152}$$

The beams of Eq. (2.151) are the result of a nonlinear operation of binarization, Eq. (2.148), and are also called *diffraction orders*. The squared modules of the Fourier coefficients in (2.150) depict the energy distribution between the beams in Eq. (2.152). Since $|c_1|^2 = |c_{-1}|^2 = 0.405$, 81 percent of the incident beam energy goes into the $+1$st and -1st diffraction orders. The images produced in the main $+1$st and -1st orders are determined by the functions $-\varphi(x)$ and $+\varphi(x)$. The functions $-\varphi(x)$ and $+\varphi(x)$ are continuous-phase functions of the diffraction gratings, each generating N orders in the intervals $[-N\Delta, 0]$ and $[0, N\Delta]$, respectively. The summation of the intervals $[-N\Delta, 0]$ and $[0, N\Delta]$ yields $2n + 1$ orders in the interval $[-N\Delta, N\Delta]$. The binary grating of Eq. (2.147) may be considered only as an approximate solution. Actually, the function $\varphi(x)$ was found using the ray-tracing approach, whereas in the analysis of operation of the grating (2.147), only the two main diffraction orders were taken into account, without regard for their interference. Therefore, even if the approximate solution enables a 80 percent efficiency ($|c_1|^2 + |c_{-1}|^2 = 0.81$), the rms error remains within the limits of 40–50 percent. In what follows, the approximate solution (2.147) is used as an initial guess of profile for the gradient algorithm.

According to Eqs. (2.141)–(2.148), the coordinates of the initial profile of the grating for the production of $2N + 1$ orders of equal intensity are given by

$$x_i = \sqrt{\frac{i}{N}}, \quad i = \overline{1, N}. \tag{2.153}$$

Similarly, for a grating with symmetric linear intensity distribution in the orders

$$I_i = I_0 + c|i|, \quad i = \overline{-N, N},$$

the coordinates of the initial profile of the grating are found from the following equation:

$$\frac{2N}{(b-1)(b^2-1)}\left\{-3x_i(b^2-1)-2+2\left[1+(b^2-1)x_i\right]^{\frac{3}{2}}\right\} = i, \quad i = 1, 2, \ldots,$$

(2.154)

where $b = 1 + cN/I_0$.

For optimization of the grating structure, we shall introduce an error function specifying the difference between the desired values of intensity in orders, and the calculated values, I_j, in the form

$$\varepsilon(x) = \sum_{j=-N}^{N}\left[I_j(x) - \hat{I}_j\right]^2,$$

(2.155)

where $\mathbf{x} = (x_1, \ldots, x_{2K})$ is the vector of coordinates of the groove boundaries. Without loss of generality, the grating period d will be taken to be equal to one. For $d = 1$, the order intensities corresponding to the squared modules of Fourier coefficients in the decomposition of the grating transmittance are given by [54,64]

$$\begin{cases} I_j(x) = \sin^2(\varphi/2)\dfrac{(C_j^2 + S_j^2)}{(\pi j)^2}, & j \neq 0, \quad j = \pm 1 \pm 2, \ldots \\ I_0(x) = 1 - 4Q(1-Q)\sin^2(\varphi/2), \end{cases}$$

(2.156)

where

$$C_j = \sum_{i=1}^{2K}(-1)^i\cos(2\pi j x_i),$$

$$S_j = \sum_{i=1}^{2K}(-1)^i\sin(2\pi j x_i),$$

(2.157)

$$Q = \sum_{i=1}^{2K}(-1)^i x_i.$$

From Eqs. (2.156) and (2.157) it follows that $I_j = I_{-j}$. Owing to symmetry, the design of a binary grating with $2N + 1$ orders requires, as a minimum, $N + 1$ free parameters; accordingly, the number of grooves, K, on a period should be no less than $N/2$ [54,64]. To design the grating profile, we shall employ a gradient method for minimizing the error function $\varepsilon(\mathbf{x})$. With the gradient procedures, the main problem is how to choose an initial profile resulting in the stable convergence. As a rule, the stochastic choice of the initial profile leads to the stagnation of the gradient algorithms at the rms error on the order of 75–85 percent. The use of the analytical initial approximation of Eqs. (2.147), (2.153), and (2.154) yields quick and stable convergence of the gradient procedure alongside high efficiency and low rms error. Let us consider a conjugate gradient method for minimizing the error function $\varepsilon(\mathbf{x})$. The method involves the correction of coordinates of the grating profile by the rule [70]

$$\mathbf{x}_{n+1} = \mathbf{x}_n + \mathbf{h}(\mathbf{x}_n)t,$$

(2.158)

where $\mathbf{h}(\mathbf{x}_n) = -\mathbf{g}(\mathbf{x}_n) + \gamma_n \mathbf{h}(\mathbf{x}_{n-1})$, $\mathbf{g}(\mathbf{x}) = [\partial\varepsilon(\mathbf{x})/\partial x_1, \ldots, \partial\varepsilon(\mathbf{x})/\partial x_{2K}] = [g_1(\mathbf{x}),$ $\ldots, g_{2K}(\mathbf{x})]$ is the gradient of the function $\varepsilon(\mathbf{x})$, t is the gradient method step, and

$$\gamma_n = -\frac{[\mathbf{g}(\mathbf{x}_n), \mathbf{g}(\mathbf{x}_n) - \mathbf{g}(\mathbf{x}_{n-1})]}{|\mathbf{g}(\mathbf{x}_{n-1})|^2},$$

where (f, g) is the scalar product of vectors.

According to Eqs. (2.155)–(2.157) and the symmetry relation, at $\varphi = \pi$, the components of the gradient vector may be represented as

$$g_i(x) = 16\frac{(-1)^i}{\pi}\sum_{p=1}^{N}\frac{1}{p}\left[S_p\cos(2\pi px_i) - C_p\sin(2\pi px_i)\right]$$

$$\times [I_p(x) - \hat{I}_p] + 4(-1)^i(2Q - 1)[I_0(x) - \hat{I}_0], \tag{2.159}$$

where S_p, C_p, and Q are specified in Eq. (2.157).

To find the step t of the gradient method, we shall consider the error function along the conjugate direction as a function of t:

$$\varepsilon[x_n + h(x_n)t] = \varepsilon_1(t).$$

An optimal size of the step t may be found by approximating the function $\varepsilon_1(t)$ by a Fourier series truncated up to second-order terms relative to point $t = 0$:

$$\varepsilon_1(t) = \varepsilon_1(0) + \varepsilon_1'(0)\,t + \frac{\varepsilon''_1(0)\,t^2}{2}.$$

Then, the step value may be easily obtained from the condition of minimum of the second-order decomposition in the form

$$t = -\frac{\varepsilon_1'(0)}{\varepsilon_1''(0)}. \tag{2.160}$$

Analytical formulae for the derivatives $\varepsilon_1'(0)$ and $\varepsilon_1''(0)$ may be easily obtained from Eqs. (2.155)–(2.157).

The groove phase may be treated as an additional parameter in the optimization algorithm. According to Eqs. (2.156) and (2.157), the value $\varphi = \pi$ is optimal when designing a grating without the zero order. When designing a grating with the zero order, the required value of zero order may be arrived at by a proper choice of φ. In particular, when designing a grating with equal order-intensities, we shall determine the value of φ in Eq. (2.156) in the form [52,68]

$$\varphi = 2\arcsin\left(\sqrt{\frac{2N}{E_0 + 8Q(1 - Q)N}}\right), \tag{2.161}$$

where

$$E_0 = \sum_{\substack{j=-N \\ j\neq 0}}^{N} I_j$$

The quantity E_0 is called *energy efficiency* and corresponds to the energy portion coming to the desired orders. Substituting the value of φ determined according to Eq. (2.161) into Eq. (1.156), we find that the zero-order value becomes equal to an average intensity value in the orders. In view of the zero order, the grating energy efficiency increases by the magnitude of

$$\Delta E = E_0 \frac{2N + 1 - E_0 - \gamma N}{E_0 - \gamma N}, \tag{2.162}$$

where $\gamma = 8Q(1 - Q)$.

Table 2.1 gives the results of designing binary gratings for various numbers of orders $M = 2N + 1$ of equal intensity. The rms error in column 4 takes the form

$$\delta = \frac{1}{\overline{I}} \left[\frac{1}{M} \sum_{j=-N}^{N} (I_j - \overline{I})^2 \right]^{\frac{1}{2}},$$

where $\overline{I} = (1/M) \sum_{j=-N}^{N} I_j$ is an average value. High energy efficiency E and low rms error δ that have been obtained for any gratings with the number of orders of

TABLE 2.1. Results of Designing Binary Diffraction Gratings

Number of Orders M	Number of Grooves K	Energy Efficiency E(%)	Rms Error (%)
1	**2**	**3**	**4**
5	2	77.5	0.7
7	2	81.2	1.4
9	3	78.2	2.6
11	4	84.6	0.5
15	4	84.6	0.5
19	5	82.4	1.1
25	7	80.3	3.8
31	8	83.4	3.1
41	11	82.0	4.7
51	14	82.3	3.7
61	16	80.7	2.1
71	19	80.4	1.3
81	22	82.8	3.7
91	25	81.0	2.5
101	27	81.4	2.4
151	40	82.8	4.9
181	44	82.7	3.9
201	54	81.4	4.6
251	69	82.2	4.7
281	74	82.4	4.0 ·
301	81	83.3	3.7
451	118	85.1	3.2

up to 451 confirm the high efficiency of the gradient procedure with the analytically obtained initial profile of Eq. (2.153).

Note that the method proposed may, without limitations, apply to designing the gratings with up to 1001 orders, or more, which still will take several minutes of computer-aided computation. The gratings with the number of orders of $M > 15$ were calculated at $\varphi = \pi$. In the process of computation, it was found that at $M \leq 15$ it appears more convenient to generate the zero order, choosing the value of φ from Eq. (2.161). Such a choice of φ makes possible a 2 to 4 percent increase in the energy efficiency for the gratings with the number of orders of 5–11. The step t for the gradient method (2.158) was derived from the condition of minimum of the squared approximation of the error function along the conjugate direction, thus considerably increasing the convergence rate.

An important technological characteristic of grating is the size of the minimal groove, specified as a minimal distance between the neighboring coordinates. In the process of calculation, it was found that the minimal width of groove, $\Delta_{min} \approx 1/M$, of the initial binary profile (2.153) remains almost the same after the iterative correction (2.158). For example, for a 101-order grating the Δ_{min}/period ratio is 0.01.

Figure 2.23 depicts the calculated profiles for 101-order gratings forming a uniform and a linear intensity distribution in diffraction orders. The intensity distributions in orders for the gratings in Figure 2.23 are shown in Figure 2.24. Symmetry of the pattern made it possible to present in Figure 2.24 only half of the diffraction orders.

Note, in conclusion, that the proposed method for choosing the initial profile of the diffraction grating admits the generalization onto a 2D case. In the 2D case, the initial profile may be derived through binarization of the phase function of a 2D DOE focusing into a rectangular domain [71].

2.8.5 Multilevel Phase Diffraction Gratings

According to Eqs. (2.156) and (2.157), what the binary diffraction gratings allow one to form is only symmetric intensity distributions of diffraction orders. The diffraction

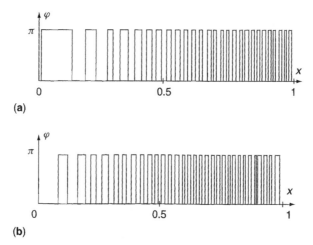

Figure 2.23. The calculated profile of a 101-order grating forming: (**a**) a uniform intensity distribution and (**b**) a linear intensity distribution.

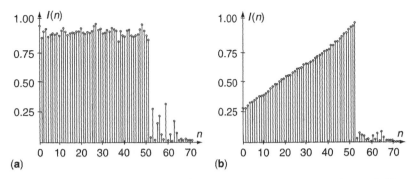

Figure 2.24. (a) A uniform intensity distribution for the 101-order grating and (b) a linear intensity distribution for the 101-order grating.

gratings with continuous-phase function allow the formation of asymmetric, or arbitrarily complex, intensity distributions in diffraction orders. In designing the diffraction gratings with continuous-phase function φ, the GS algorithm is in most common use. For the 1D diffraction gratings designed using the GS algorithm, the energy efficiency is more than 90 percent, the rms error of formation of the desired intensity $\hat{I}_j$ of diffraction orders being 10–12 percent.

In Ref. [20], it has been shown that the GS algorithm may be looked upon as a gradient method for optimizing the functional $\varepsilon(\varphi)$ describing the squared error

$$\varepsilon(\varphi) = \sum_{j=-\infty}^{\infty} \left(\sqrt{I_j} - \sqrt{\hat{I}_j} \right)^2 . \tag{2.163}$$

The diffraction order intensities in Eq. (2.163) are in direct proportion to the squared modules of the Fourier coefficients in the decomposition of the grating complex transmittance $\exp[i\varphi(x)]$:

$$I_j = \left| \frac{1}{d} \int_0^d \exp\left(i\varphi(x) - i\frac{2\pi}{d} jx \right) dx \right|^2 , \tag{2.164}$$

where d is the grating period. For future purposes we shall assume that $d = 1$. The GS algorithm is characterized by the stagnation effect: after several initial iterations, the error in Eq. (2.163) decreases very slowly. The structure of the iterative algorithm and its convergence rate considerably depend on the choice of the error functional. The convergence rate of the iterative process may be considerably augmented by changing the form of the functional (2.163).

In this connection, we shall consider the gradient method for calculating the grating phase function $\varphi(x)$ for a general form error functional. Assume that $\varepsilon(\varphi)$ is some functional characterizing the difference of the calculated intensity distribution in diffraction orders from the desired one:

$$\varepsilon(\varphi) = \hat{\varepsilon}(\mathbf{I}, \mathbf{I}_d), \tag{2.165}$$

where $\mathbf{I}$ and $\mathbf{I}_d$ are the vectors whose components correspond to the calculated and desired intensities of diffraction orders. According to Eq. (2.164), the components of the **I** vector are the functionals of the grating phase function $\varphi(x)$. In the gradient method for minimizing the functional $\varepsilon(\varphi)$, the desired function $\hat{\varphi}(x)$ is sought as a limit of a sequence of functions $\varphi_n(x)$ derived by the rule

$$\varphi_{n+1}(x) = \varphi_n(x) - t_n \varepsilon'(\varphi_n), \tag{2.166}$$

where $\varepsilon'(\varphi_n)$ is the functional gradient in the nth step of optimization process and t_n is the step of the gradient method. For the calculation of the functional gradient $\varepsilon'(\rho)$ in (2.166), let us consider the functional $\varepsilon(\varphi)$ increment caused by a small phase change $\Delta\varphi$. According to Eq. (2.164), the functional increment takes the form

$$\Delta\varepsilon(\varphi) = \varepsilon(\varphi + \Delta\varphi) - \varepsilon(\varphi) = \sum_j \frac{\partial \hat{\varepsilon}(\mathbf{I}, \mathbf{I}_d)}{\partial I_j} \Delta I_j(\varphi). \tag{2.167}$$

The intensity increment $\Delta I_j(\varphi)$ in Eq. (2.167), up to the second-order terms, may be represented in the form

$$\Delta I_j(\varphi) = 2\text{Re}[F_j^*(\varphi)\Delta F_j(\varphi)], \tag{2.168}$$

where $F_j(\varphi)$ is the field complex amplitude in the jth diffraction order:

$$F_j(\varphi) = \int_0^1 \exp[i\varphi(x) - i2\pi jx]\,dx. \tag{2.169}$$

According to (2.169), the increment $\Delta F_j(\varphi)$ takes the form

$$\Delta F_j(\varphi) = \int_0^1 \{\exp[i\varphi(x) + i\Delta\varphi(x)] - \exp[i\varphi(x)]\}\exp(-i2\pi jx)\,dx$$

$$\approx \int_0^1 i\Delta\varphi(x)\exp[i\varphi(x) - i2\pi jx]\,dx. \tag{2.170}$$

Substituting Eqs. (2.168)–(2.170) into (2.167), we get the functional increment in the form

$$\Delta\varepsilon(\varphi) = 2\text{Re}\left(\sum_j \frac{\partial \hat{\varepsilon}(\mathbf{I}, \mathbf{I}_d)}{\partial I_j} F_j^*(\varphi) \int_0^1 i\Delta\varphi(x)\exp[i\varphi(x) - i2\pi jx]\,dx\right). \tag{2.171}$$

According to Eq. (2.171), the functional gradient $\varepsilon'(\varphi)$ is given by

$$\varepsilon'(\varphi) = 2\text{Re}\left(i\sum_j \frac{\partial \hat{\varepsilon}(\mathbf{I}, \mathbf{I}_d)}{\partial I_j} F_j^*(\varphi)\exp[i\varphi(x) - i2\pi jx]\right). \tag{2.172}$$

For the sake of convenience of the subsequent analysis, let us represent Eq. (2.172) in the form

$$\varepsilon'(\varphi) = 2\text{Re}\left\{i\exp[i\varphi(x)]\Psi^*(x)\right\}$$

$$= -2|\Psi(x)|\sin\left\{\varphi(x) - \arg[\Psi(x)]\right\}, \tag{2.173}$$

where

$$\Psi(x) = \int_{-\infty}^{\infty} f(\xi) \exp(i2\pi x\xi) \, d\xi$$

is the inverse Fourier transform of the function

$$f(\xi) = \sum_{j} \frac{\partial \hat{\varepsilon}(\mathbf{I}, \mathbf{I}_d)}{\partial I_j} F_j(\varphi) \, \delta(\xi + j), \tag{2.174}$$

where $\delta(\varepsilon)$ is the delta function.

The calculation of the $\Psi(x)$ function in Eq. (2.173) is analogous to the first three steps of the GS algorithm. Actually, the derivation of $\Psi(x)$ in (2.173) is reduced to the following steps:

1. Taking the direct Fourier transform for the computation of the field values F_j in diffraction orders;
2. The replacement of the field pixels F_j by the function $f(\xi)$; and
3. Taking the inverse Fourier transform of the function $f(\xi)$.

The difference of the GS algorithm from the gradient procedure is in the form of the replacement (2.174). In the GS algorithm, the field values F_j are replaced not by the function $f(\xi)$ in Eq. (2.174) but by the following values:

$$\hat{F}_j = \sqrt{\hat{I}_j} \cdot F_j / |F_j|.$$

To calculate the gradient method step t, let us consider a functional $\varepsilon(\varphi)$ along the antigradient direction as a function of t:

$$\varepsilon(\varphi) = \varepsilon(\varphi - t\varepsilon'(\varphi)) = \varepsilon_1(t).$$

The value of the step t may be found from the decomposition of the function $\varepsilon_1(t)$ into a Taylor series up to linear terms in the vicinity of point $t = 0$

$$\varepsilon_1(t) = \varepsilon_1(0) + \varepsilon_1'(0) \, t. \tag{2.175}$$

Assuming the extreme value of the functional $\varepsilon(\varphi)$ to be equal to zero, we can find the step t from the assumption that the Eq. (2.175) is equal to zero:

$$t_f = -\frac{\varepsilon_1(0)}{\varepsilon_1'(0)}. \tag{2.176}$$

The derivative $\varepsilon_1'(0)$ in (2.176) may be found from Eqs. (2.171) and (2.172) in the form

$$\varepsilon_1'(0) = -4 \int_0^1 |\Psi(x)|^2 \sin^2 \{\varphi(x) - \arg[\Psi(x)]\} \, dx. \tag{2.177}$$

Assuming the $\varepsilon_1(t)$ function to be quadratic along the antigradient direction, we can easily get an estimate for the optimal step value t_s in the form

$$t_s = -\frac{[\varepsilon_1(0)]^2}{2\varepsilon_1(t_f)\varepsilon_1'(0)}. \tag{2.178}$$

To determine the step t_s, one needs to recalculate the order intensities to find $\varepsilon_1(t_f)$. Once the convergence process is stabilized, the functional $\varepsilon(\varphi)$ varies insignificantly from iteration to iteration. Assuming $\varepsilon_1(t_f) \approx \varepsilon_1(0)$, the estimate for the step t_s upon the stabilization of the convergence process is as follows:

$$t_s = \frac{t_f}{2} = \varepsilon_1(0) \left(8 \int_0^1 |\Psi(x)|^2 \sin^2\{\varphi(x) - \arg[\Psi(x)]\}dx \right)^{-1}. \tag{2.179}$$

Note that the previously derived equations for the functional gradient and the value of the gradient method step are general and independent of the functional $\varepsilon(\varphi)$ form.

Let us consider the relation between the GS algorithm and the gradient procedure of minimization of the functional (2.163). The minimization of the functional (2.163) is equivalent to the maximization of the following functional:

$$\hat{\varepsilon}(\varphi) = 2 \sum_j \sqrt{I_j \hat{I}_j}. \tag{2.180}$$

The gradient of the functional (2.180) takes the form of Eq. (2.173), if the function $f(\xi)$ is given by

$$f(\xi) = \sum_j \sqrt{\hat{I}_j} \frac{F_j(\varphi)}{|F_j(\varphi)|} \delta(\xi + j). \tag{2.181}$$

The function (2.181) corresponds to the replacement implemented in the Fourier plane for the GS algorithm.

Accordingly, the derivation of the $\Psi(x)$ function in Eq. (2.173) coincides with the first three steps of the GS algorithm. The difference of the gradient procedure (2.166), (2.173), and (2.181) from the GS algorithm is in the calculation of a new phase guess $\varphi_{n+1}(x)$ in the nth iteration step. For the GS algorithm, the new phase guess is calculated by the rule $\varphi_{n+1}(x) = \arg[(\Psi_n(x)]$, whereas for the gradient procedure it is found from Eq. (2.166). Suppose that after performing the initial iterations, the gradient process has been stabilized and the error functional (2.180) came to vary slowly. In this case, for the majority of values x in (2.173) we have

$$\sin\{\varphi_n(x) - \arg[\Psi_n(x)]\} \approx \varphi_n(x) - \arg[\Psi_n(x)]. \tag{2.182}$$

From Eqs. (2.166) and (2.173) it follows that for the gradient method the difference $\varphi_{n+1}(x) - \varphi_n(x)$ is approximately proportional to the value of $\varphi_n(x) - \arg[\Psi_n(x)]$. Because the arg $[\Psi_n(x)]$ function is a new phase estimate for the GS algorithm, one may conclude that the gradient procedure (2.166), (2.171), and (2.181) at $t = 1$ and $|\Psi_n(x)| \approx 1$ calculates the new phase $\varphi_{n+1}(x)$ following much the same procedure as the GS algorithm.

As distinct from the GS algorithm, the gradient procedure of Eqs. (2.166), and (2.173) allows the choice of various functionals $\varepsilon(\varphi)$. The form of the functional $\varepsilon(\varphi)$ considerably affects the iterative process convergence. It seems appropriate to study the gradient procedure convergence for the error functional in the form:

$$\varepsilon(\varphi, p) = \sum_j (I_j - \hat{I}_j)^p. \tag{2.183}$$

As distinct from the functional (2.163), the functional $\varepsilon(\varphi, p)$ in Eq. (2.183) at $p > 1$ shows a greater sensitivity to the deviation of the intensity distribution in diffraction orders from a desired distribution. The gradient of the functional (2.183) is described by Eq. (2.173), given that the $f(\xi)$ function is specified in the form:

$$f(\xi) = p \sum_j (I_j - \hat{I}_j)^{p-1} F_j \delta(\xi + j). \tag{2.184}$$

With a view of choosing an optimal method for designing multiorder diffraction gratings, let us compare efficiencies of the following iterative procedures: the GS algorithm, the AA algorithm dealt with in Section 2.4, and the gradient method of Eqs. (2.166) and (2.176) with the error functional given by Eq. (2.183).

Let us recall that the only distinction between the GS algorithm and the AA algorithm is in the form of replacement of the calculated values F_j of the field complex amplitude in the Fourier plane. In the GS algorithm, the values F_j are replaced by the values $\hat{F}_j$ by the rule

$$\hat{F}_j = \begin{cases} \sqrt{\hat{I}_j} \dfrac{F_j}{|F_j|}, & j \in Q \\ 0, & j \notin Q \end{cases}, \tag{2.185}$$

where $Q = \{n_1, n_2, \ldots, n_M\}$ are the indices of pregiven diffraction orders.

In the AA algorithm of Eq. (2.40), the replacement (2.185) takes the form [10]:

$$\hat{F}_j = \begin{cases} |\alpha\sqrt{\hat{I}_j} + (1 - \alpha)\sqrt{I_j}| \dfrac{F_j}{|F_j|}, & j \in Q \\ F_j, & j \notin Q \end{cases}, \tag{2.186}$$

where α is the coefficient to be chosen.

To characterize the efficiency of diffraction gratings, we shall use the energy efficiency

$$E = \sum_{j \in Q} I_j$$

and the rms error

$$\delta = \frac{1}{\bar{I}} \left[\frac{1}{M} \sum_{j \in Q} (I_j - \hat{I}_j)^2 \right]^{\frac{1}{2}},$$

where $\bar{I} = \dfrac{1}{M} \sum_{j \in Q} I_j$ is an average value and M is the total number of orders.

TABLE 2.2. Results of Iterative Design of Multiorder Diffraction Gratings

Number of Orders	GS Algorithm		AA Algorithm		Gradient Method for the Functional (2.182) at $p = 2$	
	$E(\%)$	$\delta(\%)$	$E(\%)$	$\delta\ (\%)$	$E(\%)$	$\delta\ (\%)$
5	90.1	14.7	88.5	0.1	91.5	0.5
9	95.6	17.5	93.5	0.2	93.8	0.2
15	97.9	15.5	93.6	0.1	94.0	0.8
19	97.2	14.9	94.1	0.1	94.5	0.7
23	95.1	16.9	93.9	0.1	94.8	0.6
27	98.3	18.7	93.3	0.1	94.4	1.2
33	97.9	14.8	94.5	0.1	96.2	1.8
39	99.2	11.5	94.2	0.2	96.3	1.5
45	99.6	10.8	96.1	0.4	97.5	1.2
51	99.7	9.8	95.9	0.7	98.3	1.8

Table 2.2 gives the values of E and δ for the designed diffraction gratings with various numbers of symmetrically spaced orders of equal intensity. In designing, the FFT algorithm was used, the number of samplings of the grating phase function being $n = 64$. For the diffraction by the raster to be taken into account, the desired order intensities $\hat{I}_j$ were assumed to be not uniform but inversely proportional to the values of $f(j) = \sin c^2(\pi j/n)$, $j = -n/2$, $n/2$ [59]. As an initial phase for the iterative procedures, we used a stochastic phase uniformly distributed in the interval $[0,2\pi)$. In the course of computations, we found that 80–100 iterations will suffice to stabilize the error in the iterative procedures.

In the left of Table 2.2 are the values for E and δ for the gratings designed by the GS algorithm [replacement (2.185)]. In the middle of Table 2.2 are the values of E and δ for the gratings designed by the AA algorithm. When calculating a grating using the AA algorithm, the first 15 to 20 iterations, during which the deviation of calculated intensities in orders from desired ones decreased quickly, were produced using the GS algorithm. After the error in the GS algorithm has been stabilized, we changed to the AA algorithm of Eq. (2.186) at $\alpha = 2$. In the right of Table 2.2 are the values of E and δ for the gratings designed using the gradient method of Eqs. (2.166), (2.173), and (2.174) for the functional (2.183) at $p = 2$. The optimal size of the step (2.166) was determined using the formulae (2.178) and (2.179). While designing it was found that during the first 10 to 20 iterations the step t_n should be derived from a more accurate relation in Eq. (2.178). The use of the simplified formula (2.179) for the value of the step t_n results in oscillations of the criterion (2.183).

Because determining t_n using Eq. (2.178) calls for the calculation of an extra Fourier transform, the procedure may be simplified by using the GS algorithm for the first 10 to 20 iterations. The subsequent employment of the gradient procedure leads to smooth variations in the functional $\varepsilon(\varphi, 2)$, and the use of the simplified formula (2.179) for the determination of the step t_n ensures stable convergence.

Data given in Table 2.2 show that the gratings designed using the GS algorithm have the rms error δ of 10–15 percent and the energy efficiency E of 90–99 percent.

The AA algorithm allows a decrease in the error of up to 0.1 to 0.2%, whereas the energy efficiency is insignificantly decreased by 1 to 3%. For the gratings designed using the gradient method for the functional $\varepsilon(\varphi, 2)$, the error δ is almost by the order less than that for the gratings designed by the GS algorithm. While designing, it was found that the convergence of the gradient method for the functional $\varepsilon(\varphi, 2)$ was best at $p = 2$; in the meantime as p increases the convergence rate decreases.

Also, gratings with asymmetrically located orders were designed. Figure 2.25 depicts the phase functions of diffraction gratings generating 11 asymmetrical orders of equal intensity. The intensity distributions in the Fourier plane for the gratings in Figure 2.25 are shown in Figure 2.26. The values of δ and E for the gratings in

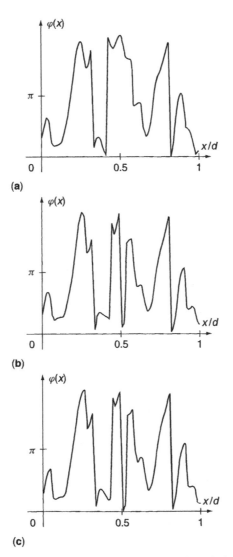

Figure 2.25. Phase functions of 11-order gratings designed by (**a**) the GS algorithm, (**b**) the AA algorithm, and (**c**) the gradient method.

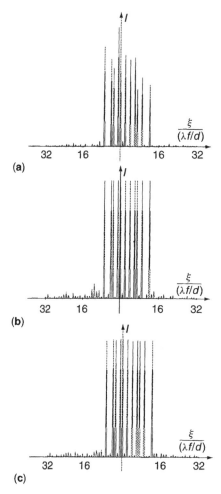

Figure 2.26. Intensity distribution in the Fourier plane for the 11-order gratings composed of four periods: (**a**) the GS algorithm, (**b**) the AA algorithm, and (**c**) the gradient method.

Figure 2.25 amounted to 20.4% and 94.3% for the GS algorithm (Fig. 2.26a), 0.1% and 90.2% for the AA algorithm (Fig. 2.26b), and 0.6% and 92.2% for the gradient method with the functional $\varepsilon(\varphi, 2)$ (Fig. 2.26c).

The computational results (Table 2.2 and Fig. 2.26) suggest that for the design of multiorder diffraction gratings, the AA algorithm and the gradient algorithm for the functional $\varepsilon(\varphi, 2)$ are a great improvement over the GS algorithm. The AA algorithm is also simpler than the gradient method in terms of the program implementation, for it requires no explicit computation of the gradient and the step value in each iteration.

2.8.6 Phase DOEs Focusing into a Spatial Domain and onto the Surface of a Body of Revolution

To design a DOE focusing the light into spatial domains, one breaks down the domain in question into N planes and reduces the problem to the design of a DOE generating plane images. In the Refs. [72,73], different approaches to the solution of this task are proposed. In Ref. [72] the amplitude-phase functions $f_n(x, y)$ whose Fresnel transform is related to the desired intensity distribution $I_n(\xi, \eta)$ on the planes $z = z_n$ (see Fig. 2.27) by the equation

$$I_n(\xi, \eta) = |\Im_n\{f_n(x, y)\}|^2, \tag{2.187}$$

where $\Im_n\{\cdot\}$ is the Fresnel transform onto the plane $z = z_n$, are found separately. The only distinction between this designation of the Fresnel transform and the Fourier transform is the subscript n, which indicates the number of the plane (ξ, η) on which the light complex amplitude is found.

The resulting DOE amplitude-phase transmission function is equal to the arithmetic average

$$f(x, y) = \frac{1}{N} \sum_{n=0}^{N} f_n(x, y). \tag{2.188}$$

Then, the amplitude-phase function $f(x, y)$ is replaced by the phase-only function using common coding procedures of digital holography [74].

In the Ref. [73], the functions $f_n(x, y)$ are calculated not separately, but on the basis of their correlation, thus allowing the derivation of the phase-only function in the course of the iterative process, avoiding additional (low-efficiency) coding procedures.

In Ref. [75], a DOE focusing onto a surface of rotation with the axis z was designed using the ray-tracing approach.

In this section, the authors take another approach to the iterative design of phase DOEs focusing the laser light into a 3D domain and onto the surface of rotation [76] Figure 2.27 shows that a DOE, which is treated in the following text as a thin phase transparency, is illuminated by the plane light wave of wavelength $\lambda = 2\pi/k$, where k is the wave number, and generates at distances z_n, $n = \overline{1, N}$ from the optical axis the desired intensity distributions $I_n(\xi, \eta)$.

The discussion will be held within the Kirchhoff scalar wave theory of diffraction in the Fresnel approximation. In Ref. [73] we find an algorithm for calculating the DOE transmission function using an iterative procedure minimizing the functional

$$M = \sum_{n=1}^{N} \iint_{-\infty}^{\infty} [|F(\xi, \eta, z_n)| - A_n(\xi, \eta)]^2 \, d\xi \, d\eta, \tag{2.189}$$

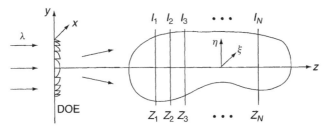

Figure 2.27. Optical scheme for the DOE-aided focusing into a 3D domain.

where

$$A_n(\xi, \eta) = \sqrt{I_n(\xi, \eta)}, \quad n = \overline{1, N},$$

$$F(\xi, \eta, z_n) = \Im_n\{e^{iT(x,y)}\} = \frac{k}{z_n} e^{ikz_n} \iint\limits_{\Omega} \exp\left[iT(x, y)\right.$$

$$\left. + \frac{ik}{2z_n}[(x - \xi)^2 + (y - \eta)^2]\right] dx\,dy, \tag{2.190}$$

where $T(x, y)$ is the desired phase of a DOE that produces the light field with the complex amplitude $F(\xi, \eta, z)$ whose modulus coincides at required distances z_n with the desired amplitude $A_n(\xi, \eta, z_n)$ and Ω is the aperture shape.

The iterative algorithm minimizing the mean-square deviation (2.88) is given by

$$T_p(x, y) = \arg\left[\sum_{n=1}^{N} U_n^{(p)}(x, y)\right], \tag{2.191}$$

$$U_n^{(p)}(x, y) = \Im_n^{-1}\left\{A_n(\xi, \eta) \exp\left[iQ_{n,p}(\xi, \eta)\right]\right\}, \tag{2.192}$$

$$Q_{n,p}(\xi, \eta) = \arg\left[\Im_n\left\{\exp\left[iT_{p-1}(x, y)\right]\right\}\right], \tag{2.193}$$

where p is the number of the iteration, $Q_{n,p}(\xi, \eta)$ is the light field phase on the plane offset by the distance z_n from the DOE and calculated in the pth iteration.

In the following text, we discuss various variants of the iterative algorithm minimizing the functional of the rms deviation in the form

$$\varepsilon_1 = \iint\limits_{\Omega} \left|e^{iT(x,y)} - \sum_{n=1}^{N} C_n U_n(x, y)\right|^2 dx\,dy, \tag{2.194}$$

where C_n are complex-valued weight coefficients.

In further discussions, it is the form of the U_n function that depends on the domain of focusing and will constitute the difference between the problems under consideration. The functional (2.189) written for the planes offset by the distances z_n from the DOE may be put down using the Parseval equality in the form

$$\varepsilon = \sum_{n=1}^{N} \iint\limits_{\Omega} |e^{iT(x,y)} - U_n(x, y)|^2 dx\,dy. \tag{2.195}$$

The functions $U_n(x, y)$ in Eqs. (2.194) and (2.195) are the result of taking the inverse Fresnel transform

$$U_n(x, y) = \Im_n^{-1}\{F_n(\xi, \eta)\}, \tag{2.196}$$

$$F_n(\xi, \eta) = A_n(\xi, \eta) \exp[iQ_n(\xi, \eta)]. \tag{2.197}$$

Recasting the functional (2.195) in the generalized form with weight coefficients

$$\hat{\varepsilon} = \sum_{n=1}^{N} \iint_{\Omega} |e^{iT(x,y)} - C_n U_n(x, y)|^2 dx \, dy \qquad (2.198)$$

easily gives an equation relating the values of both functionals

$$\varepsilon_1 = \hat{\varepsilon} + \sum_{m \neq n}^{N} \sum^{N} C_m C_n^* \iint_{\Omega} U_n^*(x, y) U_m(x, y) \, dx \, dy - (N - 1) \cdot W_0, \qquad (2.199)$$

where

$$W_0 = \iint_{\Omega} |e^{iT(x,y)}|^2 dx \, dy \qquad (2.200)$$

is the total light energy in the DOE plane and Ω is the DOE aperture area.

From Eq. (2.199) it can be seen that if the functions $U_n(x, y)$ are orthogonal, that is,

$$\iint_{\Omega} U_n(x, y) U_m^*(x, y) dx \, dy = \int\!\!\!\int_{-\infty}^{\infty} F_n(\xi, \eta) F_m^*(\xi, \eta) d\xi \, d\eta = W_0 \delta_{mn}, \qquad (2.201)$$

where δ_{mn} denotes the Kronecker delta, the functionals ε_1 and $\hat{\varepsilon}$ are equal up to a insignificant constant $(N - 1) \cdot W_0$. In the general form of the functional, Eq. (2.194), the functions $Q_n(\xi, \eta)$ are specified by an arbitrary rule. The orthogonality condition of Eq. (2.201) can certainly be satisfied by specifying the amplitude functions, $A_n(\xi, \eta)$, on the planes of focusing in the Fresnel diffraction zones with spatially separated carriers, which means that the domains G_n where the amplitudes $A_n(\xi, \eta)$ are not zero do not intersect:

$$G_n \cap G_m = \varnothing, \quad m, n = \overline{1, N}. \qquad (2.202)$$

Such a condition is realized when designing phase DOEs generating Gauss-Hermite and Gauss-Laguerre modes in different diffraction orders [77,78].

The condition (2.201) may also be satisfied if the DOE aperture Ω is divided into N nonintersecting subapertures Ω_n, with the function $U_n(x, y)$ specified in each subaperture

$$\Omega_n \cap \Omega_m = \varnothing, \quad m, n = \overline{1, N}. \qquad (2.203)$$

For example, the DOE aperture is subdivided into ringlike subapertures when designing axicons and Bessel mode formers [79] and also in the finite element method for designing DOEs.

The minimization of the functional (2.194) is equivalent to searching for the coefficients C_n that provide the fulfillment of the following equality:

$$e^{iT(x,y)} = \sum_{n=1}^{N} C_n U_n(x, y), \qquad (2.204)$$

where the functions $U_n(x, y)$ are determined by Eqs. (2.196) and (2.197) and are generally not orthogonal. We may treat Eq. (2.204) as a 2D projection of the 3D task:

$$e^{iT(x,y,z)} = \sum_{n=1}^{N} C_n U_n(x, y)\psi_n(z), \qquad (2.205)$$

where the functions $\psi_n(z)$ are orthogonal:

$$\int_0^1 \psi_n(z)\psi_m^*(z)dz = \delta_{mn}. \qquad (2.206)$$

If, for example, the functions (2.206) are chosen as Fourier harmonics

$$\psi_n(z) = \exp[i2\pi nz], \qquad (2.207)$$

the coefficients of the sum (2.205) are determined from the relations

$$C_n = W_0^{-1} \iint_\Omega L_n(x, y)U_n(x, y)\, dx\, dy, \qquad (2.208)$$

$$L_n(x, y) = \int_0^1 \exp[iT(x, y, z) - i2\pi nz]\, dz. \qquad (2.209)$$

In view of Eqs. (2.204)–(2.209), we get an iterative algorithm for minimizing the functional (2.194) [76]

$$T_p(x, y, z) = \arg\left[\sum_{n=1}^{N} B_n\, e^{iD_{n,p}} U_n(x, y)\, e^{i2\pi nz}\right], \qquad (2.210)$$

$$D_{n,p} = \arg\left[\iint_\Omega L_{n,p}(x, y)U_n(x, y)\, dx\, dy\right], \qquad (2.211)$$

$$L_{n,p}(x, y) = \int_0^1 \exp\left[iT_{p-1}(x, y, z) - i2\pi nz\right]dz, \qquad (2.112)$$

where $B_n \geqslant 0$ are arbitrary positive numbers and p is the number of the iteration. The required DOE's phase function is found as a projection onto the axis $z = 0$:

$$T_p(x, y) = T_p(x, y, z = 0). \qquad (2.213)$$

Note that the set of functions $U_n(x, y)\psi(z)$ will be incomplete, and therefore, not every function $e^{iT(x,y,z)}$ can be decomposed into a series in terms of this set of functions. However, since the algorithm (2.210)–(2.212) is used for numerical simulation and the number N is always finite, the completeness property of basis functions is not utilized.

In what follows, we constrain our discussion to bodies radially symmetric with respect to the z-axis. Figure 2.28 depicts an optical setup for designing a DOE focusing the light into an array of planes, being the circular sections of a body of revolution. The

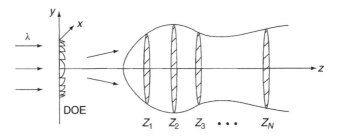

Figure 2.28. DOE-aided focusing onto a body of revolution.

amplitude $A_n(\xi, \eta)$ on every plane depends in the polar coordinates $\xi = \rho \cdot \cos\theta$, $\eta = \rho \cdot \sin\theta$, only on the radial variable $\rho : A_n(\rho)$.

In this case, instead of Eqs. (2.205) and (2.206) we can write down

$$e^{iT(r,\varphi)} = \sum_{n=1}^{N} C_n U_n(r) e^{in\varphi}, \tag{2.214}$$

$$C_n = (2\pi W_0)^{-1} \int_0^R \int_0^{2\pi} e^{iT(r,\varphi)} U_n^*(r) e^{-in\varphi} r \, dr \, d\varphi, \tag{2.215}$$

$$U_n(r) = \mathfrak{S}_n^{-1}\{A_n(\rho) e^{iQ_n(\rho)}\} = \frac{k}{z_n} \exp\left[-i\frac{kr^2}{2z_n}\right], e^{-ikz_n}$$

$$\times \int_0^{\infty} A_n(\rho) \exp\left[iQ_n(\rho) - i\frac{k\rho^2}{2z_n}\right] J_0\left(\frac{kr\rho}{z_n}\right) \cdot \rho d\rho, \tag{2.216}$$

where (r, φ) are polar coordinates in the DOE plane and $J_0(x)$ is the Bessel function of zero order. Eq. (2.216) is an inverse Fresnel transform in polar coordinates.

If intensity across the sections of the axial symmetric body is uniform, we may choose the amplitude $A_n(\rho)$ as follows

$$A_n(\rho) = \sqrt{I_n} \text{circ}\left(\frac{\rho}{\rho_n}\right), \tag{2.217}$$

where

$$\text{circ}\left(\frac{\rho}{\rho_n}\right) = \begin{cases} 1, & \rho \le \rho_n \\ 0, & \rho > \rho_n \end{cases} \tag{2.218}$$

and I_n are constant intensity values within the circle of each plane.

In Eq. (2.215), the arbitrary phases $Q_n(\rho)$ may be chosen to be quadratic because the parabolic wave is an eigenfunction of the Fresnel transform:

$$Q_n(\rho) = \frac{k\rho^2}{2z_n}, \tag{2.219}$$

and the uniform intensities I_n are chosen from the condition of energy conservation

$$\pi\rho_n^2 I_n = W_0, \quad n = \overline{1, N}. \tag{2.220}$$

Substituting the expressions (2.217)–(2.219) into Eq. (2.216) gives a particular form of the decomposition functions

$$U_n(r) = 2\pi\rho_n\sqrt{I_n}\, r^{-1} J_1\left(\frac{kr\rho_n}{z_n}\right) \exp\left[-i\frac{kr^2}{2z_n}\right], \tag{2.221}$$

where $J_1(x)$ is the Bessel function of the first order.

The desired phase function $T(r, \varphi)$ of a DOE focusing into a set of circles of uniform intensities and pregiven radii, and located along the optical axis at desired distances z_n, may be sought as a sum with incompletely defined coefficients

$$e^{iT(r,\varphi)} = r^{-1} \sum_{n=1}^{N} C_n J_1(\alpha_n r) \exp[-i\beta_n r^2 + in\varphi], \tag{2.222}$$

where C_n are constants whose modules are specified in view of the choice of the intensities I_n and the phase is a free parameter,

$$\alpha_n = \frac{k\rho_n}{z_n}, \quad \beta_n = \frac{k}{2z_n}.$$

From Eq. (2.222), the expression for the coefficient's computation is

$$C_n = W^{-1} \int_0^R \int_0^{2\pi} e^{iT(r,\varphi)} J_1(\alpha_n r) \exp[i\beta_n r^2 - in\varphi] \cdot r^2\, dr\, d\varphi, \tag{2.223}$$

$$W = 2\pi \int_0^R J_1^2(\alpha_n r) \cdot r\, dr. \tag{2.224}$$

Equations (2.222)–(2.224) allow us to construct an iterative algorithm for computing the DOE's phase function, analogous to the algorithms (2.210)–(2.212). These two algorithms are similar in structure and differ only in the basis functions (2.221).

Consider a special case of this algorithm aimed at designing a DOE focusing the light into an array of axial points. Similar to (2.222) we can easily obtain an equation to design multifocus diffractive lenses that form along the optical axis z a desired number of foci at desired distances and of desired intensity. Different approaches to the design of multifocus-lens-type DOEs are discussed in Refs. [80,81]. The DOEs designed using the method of Eq. (2.222) possess the properties of holograms. By way of illustration, a small fragment of such a DOE is capable of reconstructing the required image with minimal distortions, all factors being equal.

In this case, instead of Eq. (2.217) for focusing into a set of circles, one should use the equation for focusing into a set of delta impulses:

$$A_n(\rho) = \sqrt{I_n}\delta(\rho). \tag{2.225}$$

Then, instead of Eqs. (2.221) and (2.222) we get, respectively,

$$U_n(r) = \frac{k}{z_n}\sqrt{I_n} \exp\left[-i\frac{kr^2}{2z_n}\right], \tag{2.226}$$

and $$e^{iT(r,\varphi)} = \sum_{n=1}^{N} C_n \exp[-i\beta_n r^2 + in\varphi], \quad \beta_n = \frac{k}{2z_n}. \tag{2.227}$$

Instead of Eq. (2.223), the coefficients in the sum (2.227) are derived from the formulae

$$C_n = (\pi R^2)^{-1} \int_0^R \int_0^{2\pi} e^{iT(r,\varphi)} \exp\left[i\frac{kr^2}{2z_n} - in\varphi\right] \cdot r \, dr \, d\varphi. \tag{2.228}$$

From Eq. (2.228), it can be seen that the coefficients C_n are deduced using a 2D Fourier transform. Note that instead of the sum (2.227) for the iterative design of multifocus lenses, one may use a simpler radial-only equation

$$e^{iT(r)} = \sum_{n=1}^N C_n \exp[-i\beta_n r^2]. \tag{2.229}$$

Note, however, that the Gaussian exponents in Eq. (2.229) will be orthogonal only under the condition

$$\int_0^R \exp[-i(\beta_m - \beta_n)r^2] \cdot r \, dr = \delta_{mn}, \tag{2.230}$$

which is valid if

$$z_n = n^{-1} z_0, \quad z_0 = \frac{R^2}{2\lambda}. \tag{2.231}$$

From (2.231) it follows that Eq. (2.229) is convenient to employ for the computation of the DOE phase if the desired foci are located only at definite distances z_n.

Following is an algorithm for designing a DOE focusing the laser light onto the surface of a body of rotation. A DOE focusing the laser light onto the surface of a body of rotation, with the axis coincident with an optical axis, was designed by the ray-tracing method in Ref. [75]. Let us construct a diffractive iterative algorithm. If a rotational body with the axis z is represented as an array of its cross sections, its surface can be approximated by a set of rings. Therefore, in order to design a DOE forming a set of light rings, with preset radii ρ_n and located at required distances z_n, one may derive an equation similar to Eq. (2.222). For this, instead of Eq. (2.217) for the desired amplitude on the nth plane, let us write down the following:

$$A_n(\rho, \psi) = \sqrt{I_n} \cdot \delta(\rho - \rho_n) \cdot e^{in\psi}. \tag{2.232}$$

Substituting Eq. (2.232) into (2.216), instead of Eq. (2.221), we get the following expression for the complex amplitude in the DOE plane:

$$U_n(r, \varphi) = \frac{(-i)^n k}{z_n} \sqrt{I_n} J_n\left(\frac{kr\rho_n}{z_n}\right) \exp\left[-i\frac{k}{2z_n}(r^2 + \rho_n^2) + in\varphi\right]. \tag{2.233}$$

Combining under the sign of the constant C_n the terms in Eq. (2.233), independent of the variables r and φ, we get the following relation instead of Eq. (2.222):

$$e^{iT(r,\varphi)} = \sum_{n=1}^N C_n J_n(\alpha_n r) \exp[-i\beta_n r^2 + in\varphi], \tag{2.234}$$

with the coefficients derived from the relations similar to (2.224) and (2.225)

$$C_n = W_n^{-1} \int_0^R \int_0^{2\pi} e^{iT(r,\varphi)} J_n(\alpha_n r) \exp[i\beta_n r^2 - in\varphi] \cdot r \, dr \, d\varphi, \qquad (2.235)$$

$$W_n = 2\pi \int_0^R J_n^2(\alpha_n r) \cdot r \, dr,$$

where $J_n(x)$ is the Bessel function of the nth order.

With a view to speeding up the computation, instead of the decomposition (2.234), one may employ, in practice the following equation:

$$e^{iT(r)} = \sum_{n=1}^{N} C_n J_0(\alpha_n r) \exp[-i\beta_n r^2]. \qquad (2.236)$$

Note, however, that in that case the terms in Eq. (2.236) are not mutually orthogonal in the general case. The condition to be imposed on the parameters α_n and β_n for the achievement of orthogonality of the terms in Eq. (2.236) may be found from the following reference integral [82]:

$$\int_0^{\infty} e^{iax^2} J_v(bx) J_v(cx) x \, dx = \frac{i}{2a} J_v\left(\frac{bc}{2a}\right) e^{ih}, \quad h = \frac{b^2 + c^2}{4a} - \frac{v\pi}{2}. \qquad (2.237)$$

For the functions entering into Eq. (2.236), instead of (2.237), we get

$$\int_0^{\infty} J_0(\alpha_n r) J_0(\alpha_m r) \exp[-i(\beta_n - \beta_m)r^2] r \, dr$$

$$= \frac{i}{2}(\beta_n - \beta_m)^{-1} J_0\left(\frac{\alpha_n \alpha_m}{2(\beta_n - \beta_m)}\right) \exp\left[-i\frac{\alpha_n^2 + \alpha_m^2}{4(\beta_n - \beta_m)}\right], \quad \beta_n > \beta_m. \ (2.238)$$

From Eq. (2.238) it follows that if the parameters α_n and β_n satisfy the condition

$$\frac{\alpha_n \alpha_m}{2(\beta_n - \beta_m)} = \gamma_p; \quad n, m = \overline{1, N}, \quad p = \overline{1, N^2}, \qquad (2.239)$$

where γ_p are the roots of the Bessel function $J_0(\gamma_p) = 0$, the terms in the sum (2.236) will be orthogonal and the coefficients may be deduced from the relations

$$C_n = W_n^{-1} \int_0^R e^{iT(r)} J_0(\alpha_n r) \exp[i\beta_n r^2] \cdot r \, dr, \qquad (2.240)$$

$$W_n = 2\pi \int_0^R J_0^2(\alpha_n r) \cdot r \, dr. \qquad (2.241)$$

The condition in Eq. (2.239) limits the choice of values of the distance z_n and the ring radii ρ_n. However, from numerical simulation, it follows that one may achieve good results assuming the terms in Eq. (2.236) to be orthogonal and deriving the coefficients from Eq. (2.240).

Example 2.9 The numerical results given subsequently pertain to focusing onto a surface of rotation, with the DOE phase found using an iterative method of Eqs. (2.236) and (2.240). The calculation parameters are as follows: $R = 1$ mm is the DOE radius, $k = 10^4$ mm^{-1}, and $n = 256$ is the number of pixels along the radial variable. A conical surface was described by the equation

$$\rho_n = \alpha(z_n - z_0) + \rho_0, \qquad (2.242)$$

where $\alpha = \pm 5 \times 10^{-3}$, $z_0 = 100$ mm, $\Delta z = 5$ mm is the distance between the cone cross section planes, and $n = 1, \ldots, 10$. Figure 2.29 shows (a) a halftone DOE phase with respect to level 2π and (b) its radial section computed after 10 iterations by the algorithm of Eqs. (2.236) and (2.240).

Figure 2.30 depicts the energy distributions (the upper row) and their sections (the bottom row) generated by a DOE with the phase shown in Figure 2.29 and computed for different distances along the z-axis in the range [100 mm, 150 mm] with a 10-mm step, the variable z increasing from left to right.

Figure 2.31 depicts how the normalized intensity on the conic surface (Fig. 2.30, $\alpha > 0$) varies along the z-axis: curve 1, the desired intensity distribution, curve 2, the computed one.

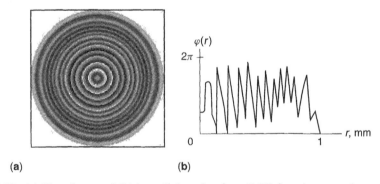

(a)   (b)

Figure 2.29. (a) The phase and (b) its radial section for a DOE focusing onto the surface of a diverging cone.

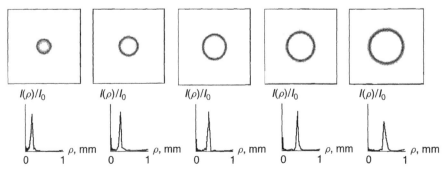

Figure 2.30. Intensity distributions (the upper row) and their radial sections (the bottom row) generated by a DOE with the phase in Figure 2.29.

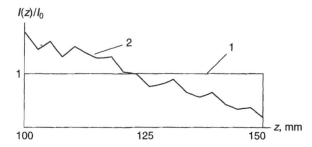

Figure 2.31. Relative intensity distribution on the surface of a diverging cone.

Example 2.10   Figures 2.32–2.34 illustrate the results of a numerically simulated focusing onto a cylinder of radius $\rho_0 = 0.5$ mm. Shown in Figure 2.32 are (a) the DOE phase and (b) its section computed during 10 iterations using Eqs. (2.236) and (2.240) at $\alpha = 0$.

In Figure 2.33 are depicted the intensity distributions and their sections found on the same planes as is the case in Figure 2.30. The computation was conducted using the Fresnel integral transform that in turn was taken using the FFT.

Figure 2.34 shows the relative light intensity on the cylinder surface as a function of the distance z to the optical element. The results presented demonstrate that the proposed algorithms can be used for design of phase optical elements intended to focus the laser light onto the surface of a body of revolution.

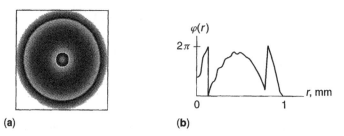

(a)   (b)

Figure 2.32. (a) The phase and (b) its radial section for a DOE focusing onto a cylinder surface.

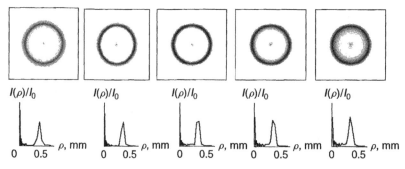

Figure 2.33. The intensity distributions (the upper row) and radial sections (the bottom row) produced by a DOE with the phase in Figure 2.32.

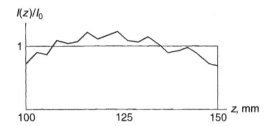

Figure 2.34. Relative intensity distribution on the cylinder surface.

2.8.7 Focusing the Gaussian Beam into a Square

Leveling the energy density over the coherent light beam cross section is of great importance for technological and information laser applications. To accomplish this, DOEs that transform the wave front into a desired intensity distribution in the pregiven plane are used.

The background to this problem is as follows. In Ref. [83], a binary diffraction grating was employed to redistribute the energy in the beam with the aim of its leveling. In Ref. [84], a DOE capable of leveling the transverse intensity distribution of a collimated Gaussian beam was designed using the geometric optics approach. In Ref. [85], a kinoform lens was used for the experimental leveling of the Gaussian beam intensity for the far-field diffraction. An iterative approach to designing a phase DOE transforming the Gaussian intensity distribution into a super Gaussian intensity distribution in a lens focus has been proposed in Ref. [86]. In this case, it was numerically demonstrated that the algorithm developed can effectively operate if the size of a domain of focusing is greater than several (4–5) minimal diffraction spots.

Reference [87] is devoted to the geometric optical-based computation of a holographic filter for leveling the profile of the light beam intensity. A disadvantage of the holographic filter is its low energy intensity. In Ref. [88], the holographic filter for leveling the beam transverse intensity was designed iteratively using the scalar diffraction approximation, thus providing a more accurate formation of the required intensity distribution. In particular, it has been shown that the geometric optics method is applicable if the size of a focusing domain is greater than seven diffraction spots.

In [90] two holographic filters were used in an experiment with transformation of an elliptical Gaussian beam into a square of uniform intensity and constant phase for far-field diffraction. In the papers [90] and [91] analytical formulae for the phase of a DOE focusing the Gaussian beam into a small square of uniform intensity have been obtained independently. In [92] a numerical simulation of the DOE design was conducted to compare two techniques, a geometric optical technique and an iterative technique in the Fresnel approximation. It has been shown that the leveling of the Gaussian beam is best accomplished by taking the geometric optical solution [90,91] as an initial guess for the iterative procedure.

Leveling the intensity profile of a semiconductor laser beam using binary-phase diffraction optics has been demonstrated in Ref. [93]. In Ref. [94] a binary reflecting DOE with grazing incidence was used in the experimental leveling of a He-Ne laser beam in the plane of defocusing. Experimental studies on focusing the Gaussian CO_2-laser beam into a rectangle of uniform intensity with the aid of a binary and a multilevel DOE were conducted, respectively, in Refs. [95] and [96].

In all the references cited, except Ref. [85], the DOE-focused rectangular or circular domain of uniform intensity distribution measured several minimal diffraction spots; this means that a complete focusing of the Gaussian beam did not take place. In Ref. [97] it was mentioned that the Gaussian beam in the focal plane of the domain of minimal diffraction spot may be leveled using a binary-phase plate with cylindrical step.

In Refs. [89,90] it has been demonstrated that if a DOE generates a uniform rectangular intensity distribution given by

$$I(x, y) = \begin{cases} 1, & |x| \le d_1, \quad |y| \le d_2 \\ 0, & |x| > d_1, \quad |y| > d_2 \end{cases},$$

it is capable of transforming (when combined with a lens) a Gaussian intensity distribution

$$I_0(u, v) = I_0 \exp\left[-\frac{u^2 + v^2}{\sigma^2} \right]$$

in such a way that its phase function can be represented as a sum of phases along the corresponding coordinates:

$$\Phi(u, v) = \Phi_1(u) + \Phi_2(v),$$

with the sum terms satisfying the following set of two equations

$$\begin{cases} \dfrac{dx}{du} = \dfrac{I_0(u)}{I(x)} \\ x = u + fk^{-1}\dfrac{d\Phi(u)}{du} \end{cases} \tag{2.243}$$

where f is the focal length of the lens in whose focal plane the light rectangle is produced; k is the light wave number; (u, v), and (x, y) are the coordinates in the DOE plane and in the Fourier plane, respectively; $2d_1$, and $2d_2$ are the rectangle measures; and σ is the Gaussian beam parameter.

The first equation in (2.243) sets the equality between the light energy density of a 1D DOE and that of the corresponding parts of the line-segment. The second equation in (2.243) describes stationary points in the paraxial approximation. For more detailed discussion of the set (2.243) and its continuous solution [Eq. (1.58)], refer to Chapter 1.

The discrete variant of the solution of the set (2.243) may be written as follows:

$$\Phi_{mn} = \ln 10 \left[M_x \left[\frac{6n}{N} \text{erf}\left(\frac{6n}{N} \right) + \frac{1}{\sqrt{\pi}} e^{-36n^2/N^2} \right] \right.$$
$$\left. + M_y \left[\frac{6m}{N} \text{erf}\left(\frac{6m}{N} \right) + \frac{1}{\sqrt{\pi}} e^{-36m^2/N^2} \right] \right], \tag{2.244}$$

where

$$\text{erf}(x) = \frac{2}{\sqrt{\pi}} \int_0^x e^{-t^2} dt, \quad m = 0, \pm 1, \pm 2, \ldots, \pm \frac{N}{2}, \quad n = 0, \pm 1, \pm 2, \ldots, \pm \frac{N}{2},$$

$$M_x = \frac{\pi N_x}{6\sqrt{\ln 10}}, \quad M_y = \frac{\pi N_y}{6\sqrt{\ln 10}},$$

M_x and M_y are the number of minimal diffraction spots caught by the rectangle $N_x \times N_y$. Then, a DOE of size $N \times N$ has the square aperture of size 6σ: $N\Delta = 6\sigma$, where Δ is the distance between the neighboring pixels in the DOE plane, when the illuminating collimated Gaussian beam produces an intensity distribution given by

$$I_{0mn} = \exp[-36N^{-2}(n^2 + m^2)]. \tag{2.245}$$

In further discussion, a geometric optics DOE is numerically simulated using the phase (2.244). Following the procedures described in Refs. [10,11], let us briefly outline iterative techniques for DOE design. Assume that we are given the complex amplitude of an illuminating beam, $A(u)$, and a desired intensity distribution, $I(x)$, in the lens's focal plane. The complex amplitude $F(x)$ in the focal plane is related to the complex amplitude

$$f(u) = a(u) \exp[i\,\Phi(u)]$$

directly behind the DOE through the Fourier transform

$$F(x) = \int_{-b}^{b} f(u)\,e^{-ikxu/f} dx,$$

where $2b$ is the DOE aperture size. The DOE equation takes the form

$$|F(x)|^2 = I(x). \tag{2.246}$$

Equation (2.246) can be solved iteratively with respect to the phase $\Phi(u)$ if we find a preliminary phase guess $\Phi_0(u)$ and then determine the light complex amplitude in the focal plane. In this case, the complex amplitude $F_n(x)$ found in the nth iteration is replaced by the function $F_n^0(x)$ by the rule

$$F_n^0(x) = \begin{cases} \sqrt{I_n(x)}\, \dfrac{F_n(x)}{|F_n(x)|}, & |x| \le d \\ \sqrt{a}\, F_n(x), & |x| > d \end{cases} \tag{2.247}$$

where $I_n(x) = (1 + \alpha)I(x) - \alpha|F_n(x)|^2$, $I(x)$ is the desired intensity distribution in the focal plane interval $[-d, d]$, and α is a parameter that controls the convergence rate of the calculated intensity to the desired one. For $\alpha = 0$, the replacement (2.247) changes to the standard replacement in the GS algorithm [3]. The light amplitude $f_n(u)$ in the DOE plane derived using the inverse Fourier transform is replaced by the function $f_n^0(x)$ by the rule

$$f_n^0(x) = \begin{cases} A(u)\, \dfrac{f_n(u)}{|f_n(u)|}, & |u| \le b \\ 0, & |u| > b \end{cases} \tag{2.248}$$

As distinct from conditional-gradient algorithms [98], the α-parameter in this case is introduced directly into the intensity function. The convergence rate of intensity

$|F_n(x)|^2$ to the desired intensity is checked using the rms deviation

$$\delta = \left[\frac{\int_{-d}^{d} [I(x) - |F_n(x)|^2]^2 \, dx}{\int_{-d}^{d} I^2(x) \, dx} \right]^{12}. \tag{2.249}$$

Equation (2.249) determines the error of intensity, as opposed to Eqs. (2.9) and (2.10) that determine the error of amplitude. Besides, an additional parameter E is introduced, and it characterizes the energy efficiency of focusing:

$$E = \frac{\int_{-d}^{d} |F_n(x)|^2 \, dx}{\int_{-\infty}^{\infty} |F_n(x)|^2 \, dx}. \tag{2.250}$$

Equation (2.250) is a 1D analog of Eq. (2.47). In following text, by way of illustration, we employ the phase derived from Eqs. (2.246)–(2.248) to numerically simulate the operation of DOEs [92].

Example 2.11   Consider a DOE of 32×32 pixels focusing into a square of 10 minimal diffraction spots. For a DOE that transforms the collimated Gaussian beam into a square, the modulo 2π phase derived from Eq. (2.244) on the 256×256 array is presented by a set of rings (lines of equal phase) changing to the lines of square perimeter (Fig. 2.35). Figure 2.36 illustrates the light intensity distribution in the lens's

Figure 2.35. Geometric optical phase of a DOE focusing into a square.

Figure 2.36. Intensity distribution produced by the geometric optical DOE in the lens's focal plane.

focal plane, derived as the Fourier transform for the amplitude

$$f_{mn} = \sqrt{I_{0mn}}\, e^{i\Phi_{mn}},$$

where I_{0mn} is taken from (2.245) and Φ_{mn} from (2.244). The rms deviation of the resulting distribution from the uniform one is 5 percent, whereas the efficiency is 91 percent.

When designing a DOE focusing the Gaussian beam into a square of uniform intensity, the aforementioned geometric optical phase (Fig. 2.35) is taken as an initial guess. The subsequent iterative procedure employed the following three techniques. The first approach to the computation of the phase relied on the standard variant of the GS algorithm with the replacement (2.247) for $\alpha = 0$. After the first iterations, the error δ increased but then it slowly decreased with iterations (Fig. 2.37a, curve 1). With this method, after 10 iterations the error did not decrease below 13 percent, although the efficiency increased up to 98.9 percent (Fig. 2.37b, curve 1).

The second approach was combined: the first three iterations were performed using the replacement (2.247) for $\alpha = 0$, whereas for the remaining seven iterations, was taken $\alpha = 1$ (Fig. 2.37a, curve 2). The latter approach is seen to be more effective as compared to the former because it yields the error reduction from 13 percent to 2 percent (6 times) without an essential decrease in the energy efficiency.

The third technique was adaptive, which means that the replacement in Eq. (2.247), for $\alpha = 1$ was performed in every iteration step (Fig. 2.37a, curve 3). With this approach, the error decreases monotonically, becoming equal to 0.1 percent after 10 iterations, but the efficiency drops to 92.2 percent (Fig. 2.37b, curve 3). Figure 2.38 depicts the modulo 2π DOE phase derived from the geometric optical phase of Eq. (2.244) during 10 iterations using the third approach. First, one can see that the use of the adaptive algorithm does not result in an essential change in the initial phase.

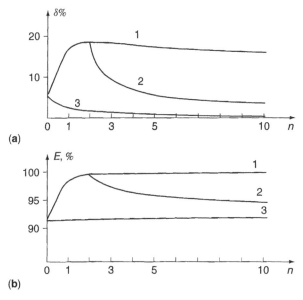

(a)

(b)

Figure 2.37. (a) Root-mean-square error and (b) the energy efficiency as a function of the number of iterations for various variants of the iterative algorithm: (1) the GS algorithm, (2) the combined algorithm, and (3) the adaptive algorithm..

Figure 2.38. Phase of a DOE focusing into a square, derived from the geometric optical initial phase guess after 10 iterations.

Pronounced changes of the phase (Fig. 2.35) take place only on the peripheral parts of the DOE (Fig. 2.38). Second, we may conclude that the adaptive algorithm based on the replacement (2.247), at $\alpha = 1$, makes it possible to enhance the geometric optical phase in such a manner that the error in the light square formation decreases by more than an order; in the meantime the efficiency changes insignificantly.

Figure 2.39. An initial phase guess with random radius.

Figure 2.40. Phase of a DOE focusing into a square, derived from the random initial phase guess after 10 iterations.

For the sake of comparison, in another numerical experiment, a phase function with random radius was used as the initial phase guess (Fig. 2.39). The intensity distribution produced by a DOE with the aforementioned phase is shown in Figure 2.41, the error being $\delta = 6.4$ percent and the efficiency being $E = 80.8$ percent. Further iterations did not produce an essential change in these values. From what has been said, it might be assumed that an iterative algorithm based on the random initial phase guess results in an irregular structure of the DOE zones and produces somewhat smaller accuracies and efficiencies than the geometric optical DOE.

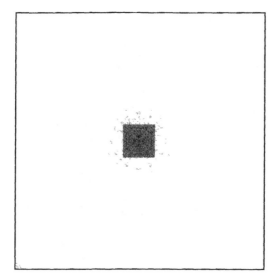

Figure 2.41. Intensity distribution in the lens's focal plane derived from a DOE with the phase shown in Figure 2.40.

TABLE 2.4. Comparison of DOEs

Type of the DOE and the Phase	Energy Efficiency $E(\%)$	Relative Root-Mean-Square Error $\delta(\%)$
Geometric optical phase	91.6	5.0
10 iterations of the GS algorithm with the geometric optical phase	98.9	13.0
10 iterations of the adaptive-iterative algorithm with the geometric optical phase	92.2	0.1
10 combined iterations with the geometric optical phase	96.4	2.4
10 iterations with the random-radius phase	80.8	6.4

Table 2.4 gives a summary of all the DOEs described in this section. From this table one can see the advantage in terms of uniformity, efficiency, and zone structure regularity of a physically justified initial estimate in the form of the geometric optical phase (compare rows 1–4 with row 5). Comparison between rows 1 and 2 of Table 2.4 suggests that the GS method provides a 7 percent increase in the energy efficiency with the geometric optical approximation (row 1), but results in a significantly nonuniform intensity across the square (13 percent instead of 5 percent).

By contrast, the adaptive method provides high degree of uniform intensity (0.1%), though it does not enhance the efficiency as compared with the geometric optical approach (row 3). The combined method unites a fairly high efficiency and an acceptable intensity uniformity (row 4). Row 5 suggests that not knowing the geometric optical solution, but instead relying on a stochastic initial phase guess of a DOE and using an iterative technique one manages to get results plausible in terms of both the accuracy and efficiency of generating a desired intensity distribution.

Thus, it has numerically been demonstrated that when designing DOEs focusing the light into small areas of spatial spectrum, the best result is attained by the use of the adaptive-iterative algorithm, with the initial DOE phase guess being the result of solving an inverse problem via geometric optical ray tracing. In the course of iterations, the regular structure of phase zones undergoes main changes in peripheral parts of the DOE aperture.

2.8.8 Focusing into a Ring

In common practice, the coherent light is focused into a narrow ring using conic axicons in combination with spherical lenses [36] and binary axicons [99]. If to the phase function specifying the axicon transmittance a term that is linearly dependent on the azimuth angle is added, the resulting optical element will feature new properties [100].

For focusing into a wide ring of desired intensity distribution along the radius, we design a DOE focusing into a circular off-axis domain. The method combines the reduction of focusing into a radial off-axis domain to a 1D focusing into a line-segment and the use of iterative techniques for the 1D focusing into a line-segment. This method requires taking only two Fourier transforms in each iteration, thus reducing the computation time by a factor of 3 as compared to the HT based iterative procedure, described in subsection 2.8.1.

By a narrow light ring in the focal plane [30] is meant the ring whose width is smaller than the Fraunhofer diffraction limit for a conic wave of limited aperture diffracted by the DOE.

Focusing into a narrow ring may be implemented by an optical element in the form of a conic axicon with the CTF given by

$$\tau(r) = \exp(-i\alpha r), \tag{2.251}$$

where α is the characteristic of the axicon resolution and r is the radial coordinate. If the element of Eq. (2.251) is illuminated by a plane monochromatic light beam of wave number $k = 2\pi/\lambda$ (where λ is the wavelength) and if there is a spherical lens of focus f placed behind this element, then a light ring of radius $R = \alpha f/k$ and width $b = 2\lambda f/a$, (where a is the aperture radius) will be formed in the lens's rear focal plane. The light complex amplitude in the lens focal plane is specified by the Fraunhofer diffraction integral expressed in polar coordinates:

$$F_0(\rho) = \frac{k}{f} \int_0^a e^{-i\alpha r} J_0\left(\frac{k}{f}r\rho\right) r \, dr, \tag{2.252}$$

where $J_0(x)$ is the Bessel function of zero order. The light amplitude over the ring is derived from the relation

$$
\begin{aligned}
F_0(R) &= \frac{k}{f} \int_0^a e^{-i\alpha r} J_0(\alpha r) r \, dr \\
&= \frac{k}{f\alpha^2} e^{i\xi} \left\{ \left[\xi J_1(\xi) - \frac{\xi^2}{3} J_2(\xi) \right] + i\frac{\xi^2}{3} J_1(\xi) \right\},
\end{aligned} \tag{2.253}
$$

where $\xi = \alpha a$ and $J_1(x)$ and $J_2(x)$ are the Bessel functions of the first and second order. The light intensity at the ring center is computed as

$$I_0(0) = \left| \frac{k}{f} \int_0^a e^{-i\alpha r} r \, dr \right|^2 = \left(\frac{ka^2}{2f} \right)^2 \left[\left(\frac{\sin \nu}{\nu} \right)^2 + \left(\frac{\cos \nu}{\nu} - \frac{\sin \nu}{\nu^2} \right)^2 \right], \quad (2.254)$$

where $\nu = \alpha a/2$.

From the last term in Eq. (2.254), the central intensity is seen to take its maximum value at $\alpha = 0$:

$$I_0(0)|_{\max} = \left(\frac{ka^2}{2f} \right)^2. \quad (2.255)$$

The intensity at the ring center asymptotically tends to zero as α tends to infinity. One may derive values that will yield local maxima and minima of intensity as a solution to the following equation:

$$\frac{dI_0}{d\nu} = \left(\frac{ka^2}{2f} \right)^2 \left[\frac{-4}{\nu} \left(\frac{\cos \nu}{\nu} - \frac{\sin \nu}{\nu^2} \right)^2 \right] = 0. \quad (2.256)$$

The solution to Eq. (2.256) takes the form

$$\nu = \tan \nu. \quad (2.257)$$

The energy efficiency of an axicon-aided focusing into a narrow ring is found from the relation

$$\varepsilon_0 = 2\pi Rb I_0(R) [2\pi Rb I_0(R) + \pi b^2 I_0(0)]^{-1}, \quad (2.258)$$

where $b = 2\lambda f/a$ is the ring width that practically coincides with the central light spot's radius, when $I_0(R)$ is taken from Eq. (2.253) and is equal to

$$I_0(R) = \left(\frac{k}{f} \right)^2 \frac{a^4}{9} [J_1^2(\xi) + J_2^2(\xi)] + \left(\frac{k}{f} \right)^2 a^4 \frac{J_1(\xi)}{\xi} \left[\frac{J_1(\xi)}{\xi} - \frac{2}{3} J_2(\xi) \right]. \quad (2.259)$$

For focusing into a narrow ring, one may also use a helical axicon with the transmission function given by [30,32]

$$\tau(r, \varphi) = \exp[-i\alpha r + im\varphi], \quad (2.260)$$

where $m = 0, 1, 2, \ldots$, and φ is the azimuth angle. Note that α may assume both positive and negative values. Then, the light complex amplitude in the lens's focal plane is described instead of Eq. (2. 252) by

$$F_m(\rho, \psi) = \frac{k}{f} i^m e^{im\psi} \int_0^a e^{-i\alpha r} J_m \left(\frac{k}{f} r\rho \right) r \, dr, \quad (2.261)$$

where $J_m(x)$ is the Bessel function of the mth order and (ρ, ψ) are the polar coordinates in the Fourier plane. From Eq. (2.261), the central intensity is seen to be equal to zero irrespective of the values of α and a: $J_m(0) = 0$, $m > 0$. For $m = 1$, the intensity across the ring is derived from the relation

$$I_1(R) = |F_1(R, \psi)|^2 = \left(\frac{k}{f}\right)^2 \frac{a^4}{9}[J_1^2(\xi) + J_2^2(\xi)]. \tag{2.262}$$

Comparison of Eqs. (2.259) and (2.262) suggests that when using the helical axicon of Eq(2. 260) the light intensity across the ring may be both greater and smaller than that produced by the axicon of Eq. (2.251), which depends on the sign of the second term in the expression

$$I_0(R) = I_1(R) + \left(\frac{k}{f}\right)^2 a^4 \frac{J_1(\xi)}{\xi}\left[\frac{J_1(\xi)}{\xi} - \frac{2}{3}J_2(\xi)\right].$$

The helical axicon does not result in an essential gain in the energy efficiency as compared to the conventional axicon.

We discuss an approximate method for design of DOEs focusing into radially symmetric domains in the following section. Assume that a laser beam of complex amplitude

$$W_0(r) = \sqrt{I_0(r)}\exp(i\varphi_0(r)),$$

where $I_0(r)$ is the illuminating beam intensity and $\varphi_0(r)$ is the phase, falls onto a DOE of CTF $\exp[i\tilde{\varphi}(r)]$, $r \leqslant a$. It is required to find a DOE phase function, $\tilde{\varphi}(r)$, that provides the generation of a desired circular intensity distribution $I(\rho)$, $\rho_1 \leqslant \rho \leqslant \rho_2$, in the focal plane $z = f$ (Fig. 2.42).

In what follows, we assume the phase function to take the form

$$\tilde{\varphi}(r) = \varphi(r) - \varphi_0(r). \tag{2.263}$$

The representation in Eq. (2.263) allows a DOE to be designed without regard for the illuminating beam phase. The field complex amplitude in the DOE's focal plane is specified by the Fresnel-Kirchhoff integral of Eq. (2.1) in polar coordinates

$$F(\rho) = \frac{k}{f}\exp\left(i\frac{k\rho^2}{2f}\right)\int_0^a \sqrt{I_0(r)}\exp[i\varphi(r)]\exp\left(i\frac{kr^2}{2f}\right)J_0\left(\frac{k}{f}r\rho\right)r\,dr. \tag{2.264}$$

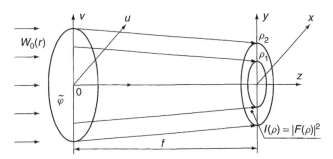

Figure 2.42. Geometry of focusing into a ringlike domain.

Using an asymptotic representation of the Bessel function $J_0(\xi)$ at $\xi \gg 0$

$$J_0(\xi) = \sqrt{\frac{2}{\pi\xi}} \cos\left(\xi - \frac{\pi}{4}\right), \quad \xi \to \infty, \tag{2.265}$$

yields the following approximation for $F(\rho)$ at $\rho \gg 0$:

$$F(\rho) = \exp(-i\pi/4)(F_1(\rho)/\sqrt{\rho} + iF_2(\rho)/\sqrt{\rho}), \tag{2.266}$$

where

$$F_1(\rho) = \sqrt{\frac{k}{2\pi if}} \int_0^a \sqrt{I_0(r)r} \exp[i\varphi(r)] \exp\left(\frac{ik(\rho-r)^2}{2f}\right) dr, \tag{2.267}$$

$$F_2(\rho) = F_1(-\rho). \tag{2.268}$$

The function $F_1(\rho)$ corresponds to the field complex amplitude produced by a 1D DOE illuminated by the beam of intensity

$$\tilde{I}(r) = I_0(r)r. \tag{2.269}$$

Focusing into a radial domain with the intensity distribution $I(\rho)$, $\rho \gg 0$, may be reduced to a 1D focusing into a line-segment. Actually, assume that $\varphi(r)$ is the phase function of a 1D DOE focusing the beam (2.269) into a line-segment of intensity distribution

$$I_1(\rho) = I(\rho)\rho, \quad \rho_1 \leqslant \rho \leqslant \rho_2. \tag{2.270}$$

According to Eq. (2.268), the term $F_2(\rho)$ corresponds to the field complex amplitude when focusing into a line-segment at $-\rho_2 < \rho < -\rho_1$ and does not affect the field $F_1(\rho)$ at $\rho_1 \leqslant \rho \leqslant \rho_2$ (see Fig. 2.43).

Therefore, the approximation of $F(\rho)$ takes the form

$$F(\rho) \approx \exp(-i\pi/4)F_1(\rho)/\sqrt{\rho}. \tag{2.271}$$

Accordingly, the $|F_1(\rho)|^2/\rho$ function, being the intensity distribution in the focal plane of a radial DOE, changes to a desired intensity distribution $I(\rho)$, for $I_1(\rho) = |F_1(\rho)|^2$,

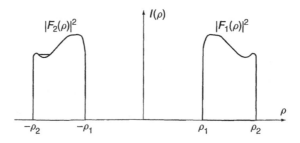

Figure 2.43. The field structure described by the terms $F_1(\rho)$ and $F_2(\rho)$ of Eq. (2.268).

specified by Eq. (2.270). It is noteworthy that when computing the integral (2.264) by the stationary phase method, the approximation (2.271) leads to the familiar formulae for the phase function [30,66,67]:

$$\varphi(r) = -\frac{kr^2}{2f} + \frac{k}{f}\int_0^r \tilde{\rho}(\xi)\,d\xi, \quad r \in [0, a], \tag{2.272}$$

where the $(\tilde{\rho})$ function in Eq. (2.272) is derived from the following relationship:

$$\int_0^r I_0(\zeta)\zeta\,d\zeta = \int_{\rho_1}^{\tilde{\rho}(r)} I(\xi)\xi\,d\xi. \tag{2.273}$$

In Refs. [30,66], Eq. (2.272) has been derived from the eikonal equation, whereas Eq. (2.273) is derived from the transfer equation and corresponds to the integral form of the law of light flux conservation.

For example, the phase function of a DOE focusing the plane beam into a wide ring with uniform intensity distribution may be found from Eqs. (2.272) and (2.273) in the form

$$\varphi(r) = -\frac{kr^2}{2f} + \frac{k\rho_1}{2fc}[cr(c^2r^2 + 1)^{1/2} + \ln(cr + (c^2r^2 + 1)^{1/2})], \tag{2.274}$$

where $c = (\rho_2^2 - \rho_1^2)^{1/2}/(a\rho_1)$, and ρ_1, and ρ_2 are the inner and outer radii of the ring, respectively.

Numerical estimates make it possible to define the off-axis domain of focusing, as a domain with inner radius four to five times greater than the diffraction size $\Delta = \lambda f/a$.

The geometric optical method for calculating the $\varphi(r)$ leads to the familiar Eqs. (2.272) and (2.273) for the focuser's phase function. The computation of $\varphi(r)$ through the 1D iterative algorithm corresponds to a new iterative technique of designing a DOE focusing into an off-axis domain.

Subsection 2.8.1 is concerned with an iterative design of DOEs focusing into a radial domain that involves the computation of the field between the DOE and the focal plane by the HT. The HT is realized through three Fourier transforms with the exponential replacement of variables. Hence, the iterative approach described in subsection 2.8.1 requires the computation of six Fourier transforms in each iteration step, whereas the iterative approach dealt with in this subsection requires taking only two Fourier transforms per iteration. In the subsequent text, the HT–based iterative approach will be referred to as a radial iterative approach. The design of a radial DOE relied on the iterative computation of a DOE focusing into a line-segment will be called the linear iterative approach. In the following text, we make a comparison between the DOEs focusing into a wide ring whose phase $\varphi(r)$ [Eq. (2.272)] was derived using a geometric optical approach, a linear iterative approach, and a radial iterative approach.

In estimating the DOE characteristics, we shall make use of the values of energy efficiency E and rms deviation δ. The quantity

$$E = \int_{\rho_1}^{\rho_2} I(\rho)\rho\,d\rho \Big/ \int_0^a I_0(r)r\,dr$$

characterizes the illuminating beam energy portion coming to a desired focal domain. The quantity

$$\delta = \frac{1}{\overline{I}}\sqrt{\frac{2}{(\rho_2^2 - \rho_1^2)}\int_{\rho_1}^{\rho_2} [I(\rho) - \overline{I}]^2 \rho\, d\rho}$$

characterizes the rms deviation of the intensity distribution from an average value

$$\overline{I} = \frac{2}{(\rho_2^2 - \rho_1^2)}\int_{\rho_1}^{\rho_2} I(\rho)\rho\, d\rho.$$

Example 2.12 The linear-approach- and radial-approach-based computation of $\varphi(r)$ was implemented using the AA algorithm (2.40), treated in Section 2.4. The geometric optical function of Eq. (2.272) was chosen as an initial phase guess in the iterative procedure. The field between the planes was determined using the FFT for the following parameters: the number of pixels is $N = 256$, $\lambda = 1.06$ µm, $a = 2.5$ mm, and $f = 250$ mm. In Table 2.5 the values of E and δ are given versus the parameter $S = (\rho_2 - \rho_1)/\Delta$, $\Delta = \lambda f/a$, for $\rho_1 = 28\Delta$. The quantity S characterizes the width of the focal ring in comparison with the diffraction size Δ.

The data given in Table 2.5 suggest that the rms error for DOEs designed using the linear iterative algorithm is three to five times less than that for a DOE designed by use of the geometric optical approach; at the same time the energy efficiency E is seen to change insignificantly. The radial iterative algorithm fails to essentially increase the values of E and δ as compared to the DOEs designed using the linear algorithm.

Shown in Figure 2.44 are the phase functions of the DOEs designed using the linear and the radial algorithm, respectively, for $S=10$. The calculated values for the energy efficiency in Figure 2.45 bring out almost total absence of intensity fluctuations on the focal ring for the "linear" and the "radial" DOE. The geometric optical DOE and the linear DOE produce intensity peaks at $\rho = 0$. The presence of the peaks is due to the fact that both the geometric optical and the linear iterative algorithm do not control the intensity distribution near the optical axis. For the radial DOE the central peak did not occur.

TABLE 2.5. The Parameters E and δ for the DOEs Designed Using the Geometric Optical, Linear, and Radial Algorithms

S	Geometric Optical Method		Linear Iterative Method		Radial Iterative Method	
	$E(\%)$	$\delta(\%)$	$E(\%)$	$\delta(\%)$	$E(\%)$	$\delta(\%)$
8	90.4	48.0	89.1	13.1	89.2	13.3
10	89.9	39.4	92.5	11.1	92.6	11.0
12	90.7	37.4	89.4	9.7	89.5	9.6
14	90.9	40.0	91.3	9.1	91.5	9.2
16	90.2	37.7	90.4	7.8	90.7	7.7
18	89.7	34.5	90.8	7.4	90.7	7.2
20	89.7	32.4	90.1	6.9	90.2	6.6

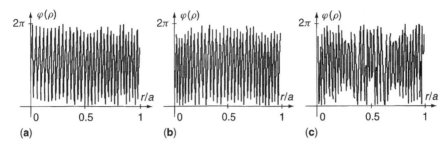

Figure 2.44. Phase functions of the (**a**) geometric optical DOE, (**b**) linear DOE, and (**c**) radial DOE.

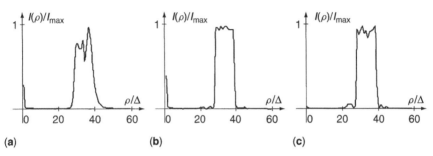

Figure 2.45. The intensity distribution in the focal plane of the (**a**) geometric optics DOE, (**b**) linear DOE, and (**c**) radial DOE.

2.8.9   Composite DOEs Generating Contour Images

In Ref. [101], the laser light has been focused into letters and figures using "combined" DOE. The aperture of such DOEs is composed of N nonintersecting subapertures, each focusing the light either into a straight-line segment or into a narrow semiring, as fragments of letters. A demerit of such "combined" DOEs is that the width of the lines of focusing is determined not by the size of the DOE aperture but by the size of the subaperture. As a result, the letters' elements are broadened and the light energy density is decreased. Besides, the DOE phase jumps present on the common lines of the adjacent subapertures make the light scatter, the result being a decrease in the energy efficiency.

In Ref. [76], an iterative algorithm for design of a DOE focusing the laser light into a spatial domain with desired intensity distribution in N cross sections perpendicular to the axis of light propagation is discussed. In this algorithm, the DOE transmission function is represented as a linear combination of the complex amplitudes appearing as the result of taking an inverse Fresnel transform of the functions describing the light field in pregiven cross sections of the object of focusing.

In this section, we discuss a method to design composite DOEs, proposed in Ref. [102]. The transmission function of such a DOE is a linear combination of the complex amplitudes being the Fourier images of N mutually disjoint images. The modules of the linear combination coefficients characterize the light beam energy distribution between N images, whereas the arguments of the coefficients are free parameters of the task. The phase of a composite DOE may be searched for using a successive approximation method based on an iterative algorithm analogous to that described in Refs. [3,77,79] or the fastest descent gradient algorithm [5].

In Ref. [91], the phase function of a DOE that transforms the plane light wave at a desired distance into a transverse straight-line segment of uniform intensity is derived using the geometric optical ray tracing. Limiting our consideration to the DOE-aided generation of contour images made up only of straight-line segments (e.g., letters), the ray-tracing solution of Ref. [91] may be chosen as basic. In this case, any segment in the Fourier plane may be derived through expanding (compressing), shifting, and turning a basic line-segment. At the same time, the phase of a DOE focusing into an arbitrary line-segment is derived through expanding (compressing), shifting, and turning a basic solution for the phase [91].

Assume that a DOE with transmission function $\exp[i\varphi(x, y)]$ transforms a plane-laser light beam at a distance f_0 in the plane (ξ, η) into a contour image made up of an array of line-segments of length d_n centered at points (ξ_n, η_n) and set at the angles φ_n to the ξ- axis.

Assume then that the complex amplitude $f_n(\xi, \eta)$, $(\xi, \eta) \in \Omega_n$, specifies the light field in the plane (ξ, η). Let the squared modulus of this function define the intensity distribution across the nth image contained in the domain Ω_n. Let the set of those domains be mutually disjoint: $\Omega_n \cap \Omega_m = 0$. In this case, the functions $f_n(\xi, \eta)$ and their Fresnel images $F_n(x, y)$ will be orthogonal:

$$\int\!\!\!\int_{-\infty}^{\infty} f_n(\xi, \eta) f_m^*(\xi, \eta) \, d\xi \, d\eta = \int\!\!\!\int_{-\infty}^{\infty} F_n(x, y) F_m^*(x, y) \, dx \, dy = Q_n \delta_{nm}, \quad (2.275)$$

$$Q_n = \int\!\!\!\int_{\Omega_n} |f_n(\xi, \eta)|^2 \, d\xi \, d\eta = \int\!\!\!\int_{-\infty}^{\infty} |F_n(x, y)|^2 \, dx \, dy, \quad (2.276)$$

$$F_n(x, y) = \frac{ike^{ikf_0}}{2\pi f_0} \int\!\!\!\int_{\Omega_n} f_n(\xi, \eta) \, e^{i\frac{k}{2f_0}[(x-\xi)^2+(y-\eta)^2]} \, d\xi \, d\eta, \quad k = \frac{2\pi}{\lambda}. \quad (2.277)$$

The relationship (2.277) is the Fresnel transform of Eq. (2.1) written in different notation. Based on Eqs. (2.275)–(2.277) we may formulate the problem of computing the phase function $\varphi(x,y)$ of a diffractive element transforming a light field of known amplitude $A_0(x, y)$ into an array of mutually disjoint images, $f_n(\xi,\eta)$, in the plane (ξ,η) at distance f_0 from the DOE:

$$A_0(x, y) \, e^{i\varphi(x,y)} = \sum_{n=1}^{N} C_n F_n(x, y), \quad (2.278)$$

$$C_n = Q_n^{-1} \int\!\!\!\int_{W} A_0(x, y) \, e^{i\varphi(x,y)} F_n^*(x, y) \, dx \, dy, \quad (2.279)$$

where W is the DOE aperture function. In Eq. (2.278), the squared modules of coefficients $|C_n|^2$ are assumed to be pregiven numbers proportional to the energy portion going to the formation of the nth image $f_n(\xi,\eta)$. The arguments of the coefficients, $\nu_n = \arg C_n$, and the function $\varphi(x,y)$ are the unknown parameters of the task.

When designing the composite DOEs, instead of Eq. (2.278), one may rely upon the functional of the rms residual ε:

$$\varepsilon = \iint\limits_{W} \left[A_0(x, y) - \left| \sum_{n=0}^{N} C_n F_n(x, y) \right| \right]^2 dx\, dy. \tag{2.280}$$

Solving Eq. (2.278) is equivalent to minimizing the functional (2.280). The criterion minimum may be found using the gradient method of fastest descent. In particular, following Ref. [5], the gradient method may be represented in the form

$$v_n^{(p+1)} = v_n^{(p)} + t_p \frac{\partial \varepsilon}{\partial v_n^{(p)}}, \tag{2.281}$$

$$\frac{\partial \varepsilon}{\partial v_n^{(p)}} = 2 |C_n \overline{C}_n^{(p)}| \sin(v_n^{(p)} - \overline{v}_n^{(p)}), \tag{2.282}$$

$$\overline{C}_n^{(p)} = Q_n^{-1} \iint\limits_{W} R^{(p)}(x, y) F_n^*(x, y)\, dx\, dy, \tag{2.283}$$

$$R^{(p)}(x, y) = A_0(x, y) \frac{U^{(p)}(x, y)}{|U^{(p)}(x, y)|} - U^{(p)}(x, y), \tag{2.284}$$

$$U^{(p)}(x, y) = \sum_{n=1}^{N} |C_n| e^{i v_n^{(p)}} F_n(x, y), \tag{2.285}$$

where $|C_n|$ are arbitrary numbers. The step t_p of the algorithm (2.281) in the pth iteration may be chosen as [5]:

$$t_p = \varepsilon_p \overline{\varepsilon}_p^{-1}, \tag{2.286}$$

$$\overline{\varepsilon}_p = -\sum_{n=1}^{N} \left| \frac{\partial \varepsilon}{\partial v_n^{(p)}} \right|^2 . \tag{2.287}$$

Because in this algorithm the phases of the images $f_n(x, y)$ are given arbitrarily, Eq. (2.278) may have a variety of solutions of which we may choose that with maximum efficiency

$$E = \left[\sum_{n=1}^{N} |C_n|^2 \iint\limits_{\Omega_n} |f_n(\xi, \eta)|^2 d\xi d\eta \right] \left[\iint\limits_{W} A_0^2(x, y)\, dx\, dy \right]^{-1} \tag{2.288}$$

or minimal error

$$\delta = \left[\sum_{n=1}^{N} \iint\limits_{\Omega_n} [|f_n(\xi, \eta)| - |f_n^{(p)}(\xi, \eta)|]^2 d\xi\, d\eta \right] \left[\sum_{n=1}^{N} \iint\limits_{\Omega_n} |f_n(\xi, \eta)|^2 d\xi d\eta \right]^{-1}, \tag{2.289}$$

where $|f_n(\xi, \eta)|$ and $|f_n^{(p)}(\xi, \eta)|$ are the desired and calculated values in the pth iteration image modules.

If the image $f(x, y)$ is made up of N similar elementary images $f_n(x, y)$, all the images can be obtained through a single similarity transformation. For instance, if a contour image is made up of N line-segments, all functions $f_n(x, y), n = \overline{1, N}$, of these line-segments can be derived from a certain basic function $f_0(x, y)$ through shifting T, turning R, and scaling D (compression and expansion):

$$f_n(\xi, \eta) = DTRf_0(\xi, \eta), \tag{2.290}$$

$$Rf_0(\xi, \eta) = f_0(\xi', \eta'), \tag{2.291}$$

$$\begin{cases} \xi' = \xi \cos \varphi_n + \eta \sin \varphi_n \\ \eta' = -\xi \sin \varphi_n + \eta \cos \varphi_n \end{cases}, \tag{2.292}$$

$$Tf_0(\xi, \eta) = f_0(\xi - \xi_n, \eta - \eta_n), \tag{2.293}$$

$$Df_0(\xi, \eta) = Df_0(\alpha_n \xi, \alpha_n \eta), \tag{2.294}$$

where φ_n is the angle of turning, (ξ_n, η_n) are the coordinates of center, and α_n is the scaling coefficient for the nth image.

With a contour image composed of a set of line-segments, we can make use of the results reported in Ref. [91] where the phase of a DOE focusing a plane wave into a straight-line segment of uniform intensity is given by

$$\varphi_0(x, y) = -\frac{k}{2f_0} \left[x^2 \left(1 - \frac{a}{2A} \right) + y^2 \right], \tag{2.295}$$

where a is the length of the segment stretched along the ξ-axis and having the minimal diffraction width along the η-axis, and $2A$ is the size of the square DOE aperture.

Putting the phase function of Eq. (2.295) as a basic solution, it is not difficult to find the phase of a DOE generating an arbitrary thin line-segment in the plane (ξ, η)

$$\varphi_n(x, y) = -\frac{k}{2} [A_n (x - x_n)^2 + B_n (y - y_n)^2 + C_n (x - x_n)(y - y_n)], \tag{2.296}$$

$$A_n = b_n^{-1} \cos^2 \varphi_n + a^{-1} \sin^2 \varphi_n, \quad B_n = b_n^{-1} \sin^2 \varphi_n + a^{-1} \cos^2 \varphi_n,$$

$$C_n = (ab_n)^{-1} \sin(2\varphi_n)(a - b_n), \quad a = f_0, \quad b_n = f_0 \left(1 - \frac{a_n}{2R} \right)^{-1};$$

where R is the radius of the DOE circular aperture. Then, Eq. (2.278) for the phase function of a DOE $\overline{\varphi}(x, y)$ focusing into a segmented contour takes the form

$$A_0(x, y)e^{i\overline{\varphi}(x, y)} = \sum_{n=1}^{N} C_n e^{i\varphi_n(x, y)}, \tag{2.297}$$

where the $\varphi_n(x, y)$ function is defined by Eq. (2.296). Analytical definition of the phase $\varphi_n(x, y)$ of elementary images is practically convenient. Actually, Eq. (2.297) can be numerically solved by the iterative gradient algorithm (2.281)–(2.285) with small-dimension number arrays (e.g., 256×256) used with a view of reducing the time needed for the determination of arguments of the coefficients C_n. At the same time, when computing the function $\overline{\varphi}(x, y)$ in Eq. (2.297) for generating a photomask, the sum in the right-hand side of Eq. (2.297) is computed using a large-dimension number array ($10^4 \times 10^4$ pixels, or greater).

The solutions in Eqs. (2.295) and (2.296) have been found by the geometric optical ray-tracing and provide high energy efficiency of focusing into a desired line-segment, but fail to provide a highly uniform intensity along the segment. Highly uniform focusing along the segment may be provided with the use of the scalar diffraction approach. In this case, instead of the function in Eq. (2.295), the basic solution is given by the following complex amplitude:

$$
f_0(\xi, \eta) = \text{rect}\left(\frac{\xi}{a}\right) \text{rect}\left(\frac{\eta}{b}\right),
\tag{2.298}
$$

whence it is not difficult to find the functions describing an arbitrary line-segment in the plane (ξ, η):

$$
f_n(\xi, \eta) = \text{rect}\left(\frac{\xi \cos \varphi_n + \eta \sin \varphi_n - \xi_n}{b_n}\right) \text{rect}\left(\frac{-\xi \sin \varphi_n + \eta \cos \varphi_n - \eta_n}{a}\right).
\tag{2.299}
$$

Then, the equation for the phase of a DOE focusing the light into a contour composed of N segments will take the form [instead of Eq. (2.297)]:

$$
A_0(x, y) e^{i\overline{\varphi}(x,y)} = \sum_{n=1}^{N} C_n \text{sinc}\left[\frac{b_n k}{2f_0}(x \cos \varphi_n + y \sin \varphi_n)\right]
$$

$$
\times \text{sinc}\left[\frac{ak}{2f_0}(-x \sin \varphi_n + y \cos \varphi_n)\right] \cdot e^{-i\frac{k}{f_0}(x\xi_n + y\eta_n)}
\tag{2.300}
$$

where $\text{sin } c(x) = \sin(x)/x$, b_n is the length of the nth segment, and a is the diffraction width of all the segments.

Example 2.13 In numerical simulation, the following parameters were used in Eq. (2.296): $f_0 = 100$ mm, $R = 10$ mm, x_n, y_n, $a_n \in [0, 0.5 \text{ mm}]$, $\varphi_n \in [0, \pi]$, and the discrete matrix was 256×256 pixels. Figures 2.46–2.48 depict the results of designing DOEs (Figs. 2.46a–2.48a) focusing into various contour figures: the letter A (Fig. 2.46), Y (Fig. 2.47), O (Fig. 2.48), and the results of simulation of the DOE operation through the Fresnel transform–based determination of the light field intensity distribution at the distance f_0 (Fig. 2.46b–2.48b).

Note that each illustration shows in the upper row the DOE designed using Eq. (2.297) and in the bottom row the DOE being a simple combination of the angular segments derived from Eq. (2.295). Figures suggest that the greater number of line elements in a contour image implies the greater number of the segments building the DOE. As a consequence, a smaller fragment of the DOE's useful area will contribute to each image line, the result being broadened lines and the decreased light energy density. This effect may even be observed in the presented pictures with a limited number of lines. Another disadvantage of the combined DOE is the necessity of fitting the best combination of the elements, while Eq. (2.297) provides the complete automatism.

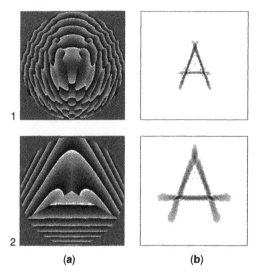

(a)   (b)

Figure 2.46. Design of DOEs focusing into the letter "A": the phase of (**1a**) the composite DOE, (**2a**) the combined DOE, and the corresponding diffraction patterns: (**1b**) and (**2b**).

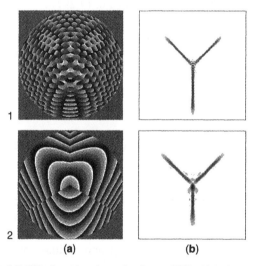

(a)   (b)

Figure 2.47. Design of DOEs focusing into the letter "Y": (**1a**) the composite DOE phase, (**2a**) the combined DOE phase, and the corresponding diffraction patterns: (**1b**) and (**2b**).

2.8.10 Quantized DOEs Focusing onto a Desired 2D Domain

Among other things, the phase DOEs intended to focus onto a pregiven 2D domain with desired intensity distribution hold significance in transforming and leveling the laser light intensity.

The photolithographic technology traditionally used in the DOE fabrication provides the quantization of the DOE phase function in M levels. Quantized DOEs with a small number of quantization levels ($M = 3, 4$), and especially binary DOEs ($M = 2$) are of

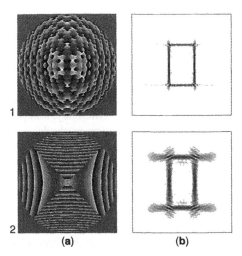

(a)   (b)

Figure 2.48. Design of DOEs producing a rectangular contour; the phase of (**1a**) the composite DOE and (**2a**) the combined DOE, and the corresponding diffraction patterns: (**1b**) and (**2b**).

interest because of simple photolithographic fabrication techniques. In particular, the binary relief is produced in a single process of substrate etching.

The well-known iterative algorithms, such as the error-reduction algorithm, the GS algorithm, and gradient algorithms [2,5,7,98,103] intended to design DOEs with continuous-phase functions break down when applied to the design of DOEs with a small number of quantization levels ($M = 2, 3, 4$). In the papers by Wirowsky [21,104–106], a modification of the iterative GS algorithm for designing quantized DOEs with $M > 2$ is proposed. The above modification employs a partial quantization operation in the iterative process and shows a fairly good convergence when applied to focusing onto off-axis focal domains even if the number of quantization levels is equal to $M = 3, 4$. However, when applied to designing quantized DOEs focusing onto near-axis domains, the convergence of the aforementioned algorithm becomes significantly worse. In particular, for $M = 3, 4$, the rms error of generation of a desired intensity distribution in the domain of focusing is, as a rule, 25–30 percent.

The computation of binary DOEs ($M = 2$) is based on the methods essentially different from fast iterative algorithms, such as the GS algorithm. For example, multi-order binary diffraction gratings are usually designed using stochastic optimization methods, such as the direct binary search and the simulated annealing algorithm [52–58]. The gradient method for designing binary gratings dealt with in subsection 2.8.4 turns out to be efficient only for the 1D gratings. The stochastic optimization methods, in the general 2D case, require great computational efforts and are of little use when focusing onto the domains of size by an order of magnitude greater than the diffraction spot size.

In this section, an iterative method for designing quantized DOEs is discussed. In terms of complexity and computational efforts, the method is equivalent to the GS algorithm and involves the following steps: *(1)* Approximation of the complex transmission function (CTF) of the quantized DOE by a continuous CTF; *(2)* The gradient method for the optimization of the continuous CTF; *(3)* Return to the quantized CTF.

In comparison with the algorithm discussed in the papers by Wirowsky, the method under consideration is of greater generality and suitable for designing both quantized and binary DOEs. As compared with the familiar methods [52–58] oriented to the design of binary-phase diffraction gratings (PDG) the advantages of the proposed method are as follows: they allow for the illuminating beam intensity distribution, are essentially two-dimensional, which proves to be critical for unfactorable domains of focusing and for the attainment of high energy efficiency, and possess high convergence rate as compared with the stochastic optimization methods.

Let it be required to design a DOE with the phase function $\varphi_M(\mathbf{u})$ quantized in M levels. The illuminating beam with intensity distribution $I_o(\mathbf{u})$ and a converging spherical wave front (focus f) passes through this DOE and generates in the plane $z = f$ a domain D with desired intensity distribution $I_D(\mathbf{x}), \mathbf{x} \in D$ (Fig. 2.49). From this point on, we shall use bold type to denote vectors.

In the scalar approximation, the intensity distribution $I(\mathbf{x})$ in the plane $z = f$ is related to the DOE phase function $\varphi_M(\mathbf{u})$ through the Fresnel-Kirchhoff integral:

$$I(\mathbf{x}) = \left| \frac{1}{\lambda f} \int_G \sqrt{I_0(\mathbf{u})} \exp\left(i\varphi_M(\mathbf{u}) - i\frac{k}{f}\mathbf{xu} \right) d^2\mathbf{u} \right|^2, \qquad (2.301)$$

where G is the DOE aperture. Equation (2.301) differs from Eq. (2.5) only in designations.

The CTF of a DOE with the phase function $\varphi_M(\mathbf{u})$ quantized in M levels and taking the values $\varphi_j = j(2\pi/M)$, $j = \overline{0, M-1}$, may be written in the form

$$A_M(\mathbf{u}) = \exp(i\Phi_M[\varphi(\mathbf{u})]), \qquad (2.302)$$

where $\varphi(\mathbf{u})$ is a continuous function defined in the interval $[0,2\pi)$, and the function

$$\Phi_M[\xi] = \frac{2\pi}{M} \text{int}\left(\frac{\xi M}{2\pi} \right), \qquad (2.303)$$

describes the quantization in M levels. The function int(x) in Eq. (2.303) is the function of separation of the integral part x.

Thus, Eq. (2.302) represents the CTF of the quantized DOE as a quantized function $\Phi_M[\xi]$ of the continuous argument $\varphi(\mathbf{u})$.

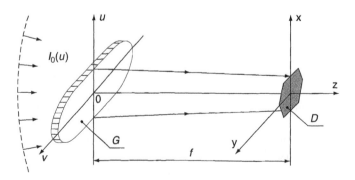

Figure 2.49. Geometry of the task on focusing.

The main idea of the method for designing quantized DOEs is in the introduction of a continuous function $\tilde{A}_M(\mathbf{u})$, approximating the discontinuous CTF $A_M(\mathbf{u})$ of the quantized DOE [107–110]. The subsequent use of fast gradient algorithms for the optimization of the continuous function $\tilde{A}_M(\mathbf{u})$ makes it possible to suggest an effective method for the computation of the quantized CTF in Eq. (2.302).

To construct the continuous approximation $\tilde{A}_M(\mathbf{u})$, we shall decompose the function $\exp(i\Phi_M[\xi])$ into the Fourier series:

$$\exp(i\Phi_M[\xi]) = \sum_{n=-\infty}^{\infty} c_n \exp(in\,\xi), \tag{2.304}$$

where
$$c_n = \begin{cases} (-1)^{(n-1)/M} \sin c\left(\frac{\pi n}{M}\right) \exp\left(i\frac{-\pi n}{M}\right), \\ \qquad n = 1 + pM, \quad p = \pm 1, \pm 2, \ldots \\ 0, \quad \text{else} \end{cases} \tag{2.305}$$

are the Fourier coefficients. Assuming $\xi = \mathrm{mod}_{2\pi}[\varphi(\mathbf{u})]$ in Eq. (2.304) and taking account of 2π-periodicity, the CTF of the quantized DOE is given by

$$\exp(i\Phi_M[\varphi(\mathbf{u})]) = \sum_{n=-\infty}^{\infty} c_n \exp[in\,\varphi(\mathbf{u})]. \tag{2.306}$$

The decomposition Eq. (2.306) corresponds to the superposition of beams with the phase functions

$$\varphi_n(\mathbf{x}) = n\varphi(\mathbf{x}). \tag{2.307}$$

The squared modules of the Fourier coefficients in Eq. (2.305) define the energy distribution between the beams, whereas the functions in Eq. (2.307) specify the structure of images generated in the diffraction orders of the quantized DOE [111,112]. Introduce an auxiliary function

$$\tilde{A}_M(\mathbf{u}; L_1, L_2) = \sum_{p=-L_1}^{L_2} c_{1+pM} \exp[i(1 + pM)\varphi(\mathbf{u})] \tag{2.308}$$

Formally speaking, the function $\tilde{A}_M(\mathbf{u}; L_1, L_2)$ is a truncated series of Eq. (2.308) approximating the CTF of the quantized DOE. With the $\tilde{A}_M(\mathbf{u}; L_1, L_2)$ function of Eq. (2.308), the intensity distribution in the plane $z = f$

$$I(\mathbf{x}; M) = \left| \frac{1}{\lambda f} \int_G \sqrt{I_0(\mathbf{u})}\, \tilde{A}_M(\mathbf{u}; L_1, L_2) \exp\left(-i\frac{k}{f}\mathbf{x}\mathbf{u}\right) d^2\mathbf{u} \right|^2 \tag{2.309}$$

takes into account the contribution of $K = L_2 - L_1 + 1$, nonzero orders of the quantized DOE of Eq. (2.302), and their mutual interference. The introduction of the function $\tilde{A}_M(\mathbf{u}; L_1, L_2)$ of Eq. (2.308) makes it possible to change from the quantized CTF, Eq. (2.302), to the continuous function. With a reasonable choice of the parameters L_1, L_2, it will pay to use highly elaborated iterative algorithms [3,5,7,8,98,103] intended for the optimization of continuous functions.

We propose that the process of designing the quantized DOE of Eq. (2.302) be replaced by that of designing a DOE with the continuous CTF of Eq. (2.308) that generates a required intensity distribution $I_D(\mathbf{x})$ at $\mathbf{x} \in D$ [107–110]. Then, the design of the quantized DOE will involve the following steps:

1. The replacement of the CTF of the quantized DOE by the function $\tilde{A}_M(\mathbf{u}; L_1, L_2)$;
2. The derivation of the function $\varphi(\mathbf{u})$ on the condition that the DOE with the CTF of Eq. (2.308) will generate a required intensity distribution $I_D(\mathbf{x})$, $\mathbf{x} \in D$;
3. Backward jump from the function $\tilde{A}_M(\mathbf{u}; L_1, L_2)$, Eq. (2.308), to the quantized function of Eq. (2.302).

The phase function $\varphi(\mathbf{u})$ in step 2 may be derived using a variety of iterative algorithms [3,5,7,8]. Let us analyze how the $\varphi(\mathbf{u})$ function can be derived using gradient algorithms [98].

Introduce some integral functional $\varepsilon(\varphi)$ that characterizes the difference between the intensity distribution of Eq. (2.309) generated by the DOE with the continuous CTF of Eq. (2.308) and a desired intensity distribution $I_D(\mathbf{x})$

$$\varepsilon(\varphi) = \bar{\varepsilon}[\tilde{I}_M(\mathbf{x}), I_D(\mathbf{x})]. \tag{2.310}$$

The gradient minimization of the functional in Eq. (2.310) consists in the iterative correction of the function $\varphi(\mathbf{x})$ by the rule

$$\varphi_{n+1}(\mathbf{u}) = \varphi_n(\mathbf{u}) - \varepsilon'(\varphi_n) \cdot t, \tag{2.311}$$

where n denotes the number of the iteration, $\varepsilon'(\varphi_n)$ is the functional gradient, and t is the gradient method's step. Calculations similar to those discussed in sections 2.7 and 2.8.5 easily give the increment of the functional $\varepsilon(\varphi)$ caused by a small variation $\Delta\varphi$ of the phase $\varphi(\mathbf{u})$

$$\Delta\varepsilon(\varphi) = \varepsilon(\varphi + \Delta\varphi) - \varepsilon(\varphi) = 2\mathrm{Re}\left(\int_{-\infty}^{\infty} \sqrt{I_0(\mathbf{u})} \Psi^*(\mathbf{u})(\Delta\phi) \, d^2\mathbf{u}\right), \tag{2.312}$$

where $\Delta\phi = \Delta\tilde{A}_M(\mathbf{u}; L_1, L_2)$ is the increment of the CTF of DOE caused by a small phase variation $\Delta\varphi$.

The calculation of the function $\Psi(\mathbf{u})$ in Eq. (2.312) is performed in three stages:

1. Calculation of the field complex amplitude $W(\mathbf{x})$ in the plane $z = f$;
2. Replacement of the function $W(\mathbf{x})$ by the function

$$W_1(\mathbf{x}) = \frac{d\bar{\varepsilon}(\tilde{I}_M, I_D)}{d\tilde{I}_M} W(\mathbf{x}); \tag{2.313}$$

3. Backward recalculation of the field into the plane $z = 0$.

The recalculation of the field between the planes $z = 0$ and $z = f$ is done by taking the direct and inverse Fourier transform of the functions $W_0(\mathbf{u}) = \tilde{A}_M(\mathbf{u}; L_1, L_2)\sqrt{I_0(\mathbf{u})}$

and $W_1(\mathbf{x})$, respectively. Designating the direct and inverse Fourier transforms as $\Im\{\}$ and $\Im^{-1}\{\}$, the $\Psi(\mathbf{u})$ function may be written as

$$\Psi(\mathbf{x}) = \Im^{-1}\left\{\frac{d\bar{\varepsilon}(\tilde{I}_M, I_D)}{d\tilde{I}_M}\Im[\sqrt{I_0(\mathbf{u})}\tilde{A}_M(\mathbf{u}; L_1, L_2)]\right\}. \qquad (2.314)$$

Interestingly, the computation procedure of the function $\Psi(\mathbf{u})$ coincides with the first three steps of the GS algorithm up to the replacement in the plane $z = f$.

According to Eq. (2.308), the increment $\Delta\tilde{A}_M(\mathbf{u}; L_1, L_2)$ caused by the small phase variation $\Delta\varphi$ takes the form

$$\Delta\tilde{A}_M(\mathbf{u}; L_1, L_2) = \sum_{p=-L_1}^{L_2} c_{1+pM} \cdot i(1+pM)\exp[i(1+pM)\varphi(\mathbf{u})]\Delta\varphi(\mathbf{u}). \qquad (2.315)$$

Substituting Eq. (2.315) in (2.312), we get the functional gradient in the form

$$\varepsilon'(\varphi) = 2\,\mathrm{Re}\left(\sqrt{I_0(\mathbf{u})}\Psi^*(\mathbf{u})\sum_{p=-L_1}^{L_2} c_{1+pM} \cdot i(1+pM)\exp[i(1+pM)]\varphi(\mathbf{u})\right). \qquad (2.316)$$

Equations (2.314) and (2.316) specify the gradient for the continuous functional in Eqs. (2.310) and (2.309). Note that when defining the function $\Psi(\mathbf{u})$ in the form

$$\Psi(\mathbf{x}) = \Im^{-1}\left\{\frac{d\bar{\varepsilon}(I, I_D)}{dI}\Im\left[\sqrt{I_0(\mathbf{u})}A_M(\mathbf{u})\right]\right\}, \qquad (2.317)$$

Equation (2.316) may be treated as the gradient of a discontinuous functional

$$\varepsilon(\varphi) = \bar{\varepsilon}[I(\mathbf{x}), I_D(\mathbf{x})], \qquad (2.318)$$

that determines the difference between the intensity distribution $I(\mathbf{x})$ in Eq. (2.301) for the quantized DOE of Eq. (2.302) and the desired intensity distribution $I_D(\mathbf{x})$.

Actually, the functional of Eq. (2.318) is a limiting case of the functional of Eq. (2.310) as $L_1 \to \infty$ and $L_2 \to \infty$. For this limiting case, the functional increment $\Delta\varepsilon(\varphi)$ may also be represented as Eq. (2.312). The function $\Psi(\mathbf{u})$ in Eq. (2.312) takes the form of Eq. (2.313), whereas the increment $\Delta\Phi$ corresponds to the increment of the quantized CTF $A_M(\mathbf{u})$ caused by a small variation of the phase $\Delta\varphi$

$$\Delta A_M(\mathbf{u}) = \exp\{i\Phi_M[\varphi(\mathbf{u}) + \Delta\varphi(\mathbf{u})]\} - \exp\{i\Phi_M[\varphi(\mathbf{u})]\}. \qquad (2.319)$$

Using in Eq. (2.302) the continuous approximation $\Delta A_M(\mathbf{u}) \approx \Delta\tilde{A}_M(\mathbf{u}, L_1, L_2)$ of Eq. (2.315) for the increment of the discontinuous function $A_M(\mathbf{u})$, the gradient functional will be given by Eq. (2.316).

Note that the computational procedure for the increment $\Delta \tilde{A}_M(\mathbf{u}; L_1, L_2)$ involves the differentiation of a truncated Fourier series

$$S(\xi; L_1, L_2) = \sum_{p=-L_1}^{L_2} c_{1+pM} \exp[i(1 + pM)\xi] \qquad (2.320)$$

for the function $\exp(i\Phi_M[\xi])$. A formal differentiation of the Fourier series may result in a significantly reduced accuracy in the calculation of derivative [113]. To enhance the gradient method stability, it is expedient to differentiate the series in Eq. (2. 319) with the use of regularization methods. One simple regularization technique to enhance the convergence of the differentiated Fourier series is to multiply the coefficients of a formally differentiated series by weight factors monotonically decreasing as d_n increases. Those readers interested in the methods for choosing the weight factors are referred to Refs. [113–115]. For the series in Eq. (2.320), we may choose the following fairly universal weight factors [113]:

$$d_n = \text{Sinc}\left(\frac{\pi n}{m}\right), \quad m = \max(L_1, L_2) + 1, \qquad (2.321)$$

where $\text{Sinc}(x) = \sin(x)/x$. When using the regularization factors of Eq. (2.321), the increments in Eq. (2.315) take the form

$$\Delta \tilde{A}_M(\mathbf{u}; L_1, L_2) = \sum_{p=-L_1}^{L_2} c_{1+pM} d_{1+pM} \cdot i(1 + pM) \exp[i(1 + pM)\varphi(\mathbf{u})]\Delta\varphi(\mathbf{u}),$$

$$(2.322)$$

and the gradient of the functional in Eqs. (2.310) and (2.318) is given by

$$\varepsilon'(\varphi) = 2 \operatorname{Re}\left\{ \sqrt{I_0(\mathbf{u})}\Psi^*(\mathbf{u}) \sum_{p=-L_1}^{L_2} c_{1+pM} \cdot d_{1+pM} \cdot i(1 + pM) \exp[i(1 + pM)\varphi(\mathbf{u})] \right\}.$$

$$(2.323)$$

To illustrate how the regularization factors of Eq. (2.321) affect the accuracy of differentiation, let us differentiate a truncated Fourier series for the function

$$\exp[i\Phi_2(\xi)] = -\text{Sgn}(\xi - \pi). \qquad (2.324)$$

The function

$$\Phi_2[\xi] = \begin{cases} 0, & \xi \in [0, \pi) \\ \pi, & \xi \in [\pi, 2\pi) \end{cases}$$

in Eq. (2.324) describes the binarization operation. According to Eq. (2.324), the derivative $d \exp[i\Phi_2(\xi)]/d\xi$ is equal to zero at every point of the interval $[0, 2\pi)$, except for the point $\xi = \pi$, where the classical derivative is nonexistent. Note that the generalized derivative of the periodically extended function of Eq. (2.324) corresponds to an alternating series composed of δ-functions. Assuming $M = 2$ in Eqs. (2.304) and

(2.305), the truncated Fourier series for the function of Eq. (2.324) at $L_1 = L_2$ is given by

$$S(\xi; L_1, L_1) = \frac{2}{\pi} \sum_{p=1}^{L_1} \frac{1}{(2p-1)} \sin[(2p-1)\xi]. \tag{2.325}$$

The formal differentiation of the truncated Fourier series of Eq. (2.325) yields the series

$$\frac{dS(\xi; L_1, L_1)}{d\xi} = \frac{2}{\pi} \sum_{p=1}^{L_1} \cos[(2p-1)\xi], \tag{2.326}$$

which is converging at all points of the interval $(0, 2\pi)$ as $L_1 \to \infty$ [113]. Multiplying the series in Eq. (2.326) by the factors in Eq. (2.321), we obtain the regularized derivative in the form

$$\frac{dS(\xi; L_1, L_2)}{d\xi} = \frac{2}{\pi} \sum_{p=1}^{L_1} \frac{\sin[\pi(2p-1)/2L_1]}{\pi(2p-1)/2L_1} \sin[(2p-1)\xi]. \tag{2.327}$$

As opposed to the series in Eq. (2.326), the series (2.327) tends to zero at every fixed point $\xi \neq \pi$ as $L_1 \to \infty$ [113]. The series in Eq. (2.236) is trigonometric for the δ-functions. The accuracy of computing the derivative for the function of Eq. (2.324) using the series of Eq. (2.235) and the regularized series of Eq. (2.327) is illustrated by the plots in Figure 2.50. Because of symmetry with respect to the point $\xi = \pi$, the functions in Eqs. (2.326) and (2.327) in Figure 2.50 have been found in the interval $[0, \pi]$. From Figure 2.50 it can clearly be seen that the series of Eq. (2.326) shows much greater oscillations in the vicinity of the required zero value.

To choose the step t for the gradient procedure of Eq. (2.311) consider the functional $\varepsilon(\varphi)$ along the antigradient direction as a function of t:

$$\varepsilon_1(t) = \varepsilon[\varphi - t\varepsilon'(\varphi)]. \tag{2.328}$$

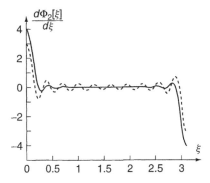

Figure 2.50. The binary function derivatives, Eq. (2.236): the dotted line is the series of Eq. (2.326) at $L_1 = 10$ and the solid line is the regularized series of Eq. (2.327) at $L_1 = 10$.

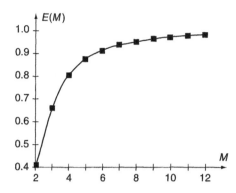

Figure 2.51. The portion of illuminating beam energy focused in the 1st order when quantizing the DOE phase in M levels.

The value of the step t in each iteration may be derived from the condition of minimum of the linear approximation

$$\varepsilon_l(t) = \varepsilon_1(0) - t\varepsilon_1'(0) \tag{2.329}$$

of the function $\varepsilon_1(t)$ [5]. Taking the extreme value of the functional $\varepsilon(t)$ equal to zero, equate the right-hand side of Eq. (2.329) to zero and obtain the optimal step value in the form

$$t = \varepsilon_1(0)/\varepsilon_1'(0). \tag{2.330}$$

To derive the derivative $\varepsilon_1'(0)$, it will suffice to substitute in Eqs. (2.302) and (2.305) the value $\Delta\varphi = -(\Delta t) \cdot \varepsilon'(\varphi)$. Then, the derivative $\varepsilon_1'(0)$ in Eq. (2.330) takes the form

$$\varepsilon_1'(0) = -4\operatorname{Re}\left(I_0(\mathbf{u})\left\{ \Psi^*(\mathbf{u}) \sum_{p=-L_1}^{L_2} \gamma_{1+pM} \cdot i(1+pM)\exp[i(1+pM)\varphi(\mathbf{u})]\right\}^2\right), \tag{2.331}$$

where $\gamma_{1+pM} = c_{1+pM}$, when computing the increment $\Delta\tilde{A}_M(\mathbf{u}; L_1, L_2)$ without regard for the regularizing factors of Eq. (2.321), and $\gamma_{1+pM} = c_{1+pM}d_{1+pM}$ when computing with regard to the regularization.

In conclusion, we shall consider how to choose the initial estimate for the gradient procedure of Eq. (2.311). In designing quantized DOEs with the number of quantization levels of $M > 2$, a continuous function $\varphi_0(\mathbf{u}) \in [0, 2\pi)$ derived from the condition of generation of the desired intensity distribution $I_D(\mathbf{x})$, $x \in D$ may serve as the initial guess for the gradient procedure of Eq. (2.311). The computation of the continuous (nonquantized) function $\varphi_0(\mathbf{u})$ presents no problem and may be based on the use of the fast iterative algorithms discussed in sections 2.2–2.8. The function $\varphi_0(\mathbf{u})$ may also be computed analytically using geometric optical approaches [37,66,116]. The quantization operation of Eqs. (2.302) and (2.303) leads to a decrease in the efficiency of focusing and the advent of new diffraction orders — the beams with the phase functions of Eq. (2.307). The desired domain of focusing is generated in the first order at $n = 1$. The spurious orders of Eq. (2.307), for $n \neq 1$, are overlapped onto the major image and distort it.

The portion of the illuminating beam energy focused in the 1st order corresponds to the squared modulus of the Fourier coefficient c_1 in Eq. (2.305):

$$E(M) = |c_1|^2 = \mathrm{Sinc}^2(\pi/M). \tag{2.332}$$

The function $E(M)$ is plotted in Figure 2.51 and shows that the quantization effects are of most significance for small $M = 2, 3, 4$, whereas for $M > 4$ the quantized DOE directs over 85 percent of energy into the desired domain.

When designing binary DOEs ($M = 2$), the computation of the initial phase $\varphi_0(\mathbf{u}) \in [0, 2\pi)$ should be modified along the lines similar to those adopted in subsection 2.8.4 for the computation of 1D binary diffraction gratings. The intensity distribution produced by a binary DOE is centrally symmetric, $I(\mathbf{x}) = I(-\mathbf{x})$. Therefore, the domain D and the desired intensity distribution $I_D(\mathbf{x})$ are supposed to be centrally symmetric. Represent the domain of focusing D as a union of two centrally symmetric domains, D_1 and D_2. For $M = 2$, the initial phase $\varphi_0(\mathbf{u})$ should be computed on the implication that the focusing is into half the domain D, that is, into the domain D_1 or the domain D_2. Actually, assume that $\varphi_0(\mathbf{u})$ is the initial phase function of a DOE generating the intensity distribution

$$I_{D_1}(\mathbf{x}) = \begin{cases} I_D(\mathbf{x}), & x \in D_1 \\ 0, & x \notin D_1 \end{cases}. \tag{2.333}$$

In this case, the intensities of the fields generated by the binary DOE with the CTF $\exp\{i\,\Phi_2[\varphi_0(\mathbf{u})]\}$ in the 1st and $-$1st orders ($|c_1|^2 = |c_{-1}|^2 = 0.405$) are given by

$$I_1(\mathbf{x}) = \left| \frac{c_1}{\lambda f} \int_G \sqrt{I_0(\mathbf{u})} \exp\left(i\varphi_0(\mathbf{u}) - i\frac{k}{f}\mathbf{x}\mathbf{u} \right) d^2\mathbf{u} \right|^2, \tag{2.334}$$

$$I_{-1}(\mathbf{x}) = \left| \frac{c_{-1}}{\lambda f} \left\{ \int_G \sqrt{I_0(\mathbf{u})} \exp\left[i\varphi_0(\mathbf{u}) - i\frac{k}{f}(-\mathbf{x})\mathbf{u} \right] d^2\mathbf{u} \right\}^* \right|^2. \tag{2.335}$$

According to Eqs. (2.334) and (2.335), the intensity distributions are centrally symmetric:

$$I_1(\mathbf{x}) = I_{-1}(-\mathbf{x}). \tag{2.336}$$

From Eq. (2.336) it follows that if $I_1(\mathbf{x})$ is the desired intensity distribution $I_D(\mathbf{x})$ for $x \in D_1$, then the intensity distribution $I_{-1}(\mathbf{x}) \equiv I_D(\mathbf{x})$, for $\mathbf{x} \in D_2$, will be generated in the $-$1st order. The summation of the field intensities generated in the 1st and $-$1st orders produces the desired intensity distribution $I_D(\mathbf{x})$, for $\mathbf{x} \in D$. Because $|c_1|^2 + |c_{-1}|^2 = 0.81$, we find that with allowance made only for the main $\pm$1st orders, 81 percent of the illuminating beam energy is focused in the desired domain D. The foregoing choice of the phase function $\varphi_0(\mathbf{u})$ gives an approximate solution $\Phi_2[\varphi_0(\mathbf{u})]$ of the problem of focusing at $M = 2$. We considered only two main orders without regard for the error in the computation of the $\varphi_0(\mathbf{u})$ function. Iterative algorithms for computing $\varphi_0(\mathbf{u})$, as a rule, allow 85–90 percent of the illuminating beam energy to be focused onto the desired domain, the rms error being 10–20 percent. In this case, even with allowance made only for the 1st and $-$1st orders, the intensity distribution on the domain D will differ from $I_D(\mathbf{x})$ not only because of the error in the phase $\varphi_0(\mathbf{u})$ calculation, but also because of interference between the fields generated in the 1st and −1st orders. The order interference may be disregarded only when focusing into specific domains composed of two separated symmetric subdomains. For the domains of practical interest, such as a rectangle, a circle, a line-segment, the binary DOE as a rule offers a 70–75 percent energy efficiency with a fairly great rms error in formation of the desired intensity distribution — 45–55 percent.

Example 2.14   To illustrate the operation of the proposed method, we designed a binary DOE for focusing the Gaussian beam of intensity distribution

$$I_0(\mathbf{u}) = \exp(-\mathbf{u}^2/\sigma^2), \quad |\mathbf{u}| \le \sigma \tag{2.337}$$

into a square $2d \times 2d$ of uniform intensity distribution at $2d = 13\Delta$, where $\Delta = \lambda f/\sigma$ is the diffraction size. The energy efficiency E and the error δ were determined using Eqs. (2.47) and (2.249).

As indicated earlier, the approximate solution for the phase function of a binary DOE may be derived by direct binarization of the phase function $\varphi_0(\mathbf{u})$ computed on the provision of focusing the beam (2.337) into a "semisquare." Figure 2.52(a) shows the binary phase $\varphi_2(\mathbf{u}) = \Phi_2[\varphi_0(\mathbf{u})]$ derived on the assumption that $\varphi_0(\mathbf{u})$ is found from the GS algorithm for focusing into a "semisquare."

The calculated intensity distribution in the plane $z = f$ for a binary DOE shown in Figure 2.52(a) is depicted in Figure 2.52(b). From Figure 2.52(b), it can be seen that although the energy is focused within the limits of the square ($E = 74.8\%$), the intensity distribution is essentially nonuniform ($\delta = 54.5\%$). To get a better solution, the CTF of the binary DOE was approximated by the function $A_2(\mathbf{u}; L1, L2)$, at $L_1 = L_2 = 5$. The function $\varphi(\mathbf{u})$ in Eq. (2.308) was sought for, iteratively, with the use of Eqs. (2.311), (2.323), and the regularization of Eq. (2.322). As the error functional in Eq. (2.310), the following functional of squared error was used:

$$\varepsilon(\varphi) = \int_{-\infty}^{\infty} \left(\sqrt{\tilde{I}_M(\mathbf{x})} - \sqrt{I_D(\mathbf{x})} \right)^2 d^2\mathbf{x}. \tag{2.338}$$

The phase $\varphi(\mathbf{u})$ was used as the initial guess for the function $\varphi_0(\mathbf{u})$ in Eq. (2.308). The foregoing choice of the initial guess allows the number of iterations to be reduced by a factor of 2–3. Shown in Figure 2.53a is the binary phase $\varphi_2(\mathbf{u})$ derived through the binarization of the function $\varphi(\mathbf{u})$ in Eq. (2.308), calculated during 50 iterations. The calculated intensity distribution produced by the binary DOE in Figure 2.53a is

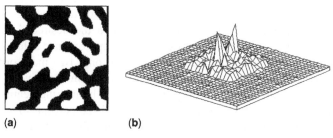

(a)   (b)

Figure 2.52. (a) The binary phase of a DOE focusing onto a square (approximate solution); (b) intensity distribution when focusing onto a square.

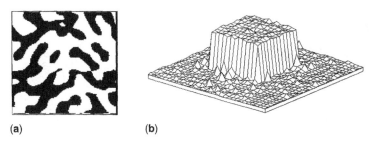

Figure 2.53. (**a**) The binary phase of a DOE focusing onto a square, computed via iterations for $L_1 = L_2 = 5$; (**b**) the intensity distribution when focusing onto a square.

shown in Figure 2.53b. For the DOE with the CTF $A_2(\mathbf{u}; 5, 5)$ and the corresponding binary DOE, the values of E and δ were found to differ insignificantly and amounted to 73.5%, 1.5% and 72.6%, 2.9%, respectively.

Example 2.15   Two other examples illustrate designing DOEs that focus the beam of Eq. (2.337) onto a ring with radii $R_1 = 9\Delta$ and $R_2 = 18\Delta$, and onto the letter "H" made up of three segments of lengths 12Δ, 12Δ, and 7Δ. The calculated binary phases and the intensity distributions produced by the binary DOEs are shown in Figures 2.54 and 2.55. When focusing onto the ring (Fig. 2.54), the efficiency and error were, respectively, 73.2 percent and 3.2 percent, whereas for the letter "H" (Fig. 2.55) these values were 70.2 percent and 2.1 percent.

In the course of computation, it was found that the approximation of the CTF of a binary DOE by the function $A_2(\mathbf{u}; L_1, L_2)$ is fairly good as early as for $L_1 = L_2 > 4, 5$. For the aforementioned examples including the regularized computation of the increment $\Delta \tilde{A}_2(\mathbf{u}; L_1, L_2)$, the return from the function $A_2(\mathbf{u}; L_1, L_2)$ to the binary function at $L_1 = L_2 = 4, 5$ caused an insignificant decrease in the energy efficiency E of just 1 to 2 percent and a small increase in the error δ of 1 to 2 percent. Note that finding the increment $\Delta \tilde{A}_2(\mathbf{u}; L_1, L_2)$ without regularization factors makes the procedure less stable and results in a smaller efficiency E and greater errors δ (by a factor of 2 to 3) when returning to the binary function.

The binary-phase DOEs make it possible to generate only the centrally symmetric intensity distribution $I_D(\mathbf{x})$. To focus onto asymmetric domains D the number of quantization levels M should be greater than 2. To illustrate the focusing onto an asymmetric

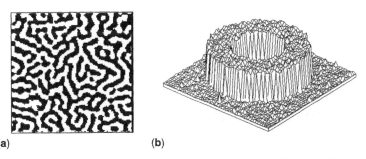

Figure 2.54. (**a**) Binary phase of a DOE focusing onto a ring, (**b**) intensity distribution when focusing onto a ring.

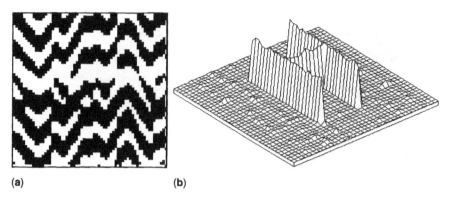

(a)   (b)

Figure 2.55. (a) Binary phase of a DOE focusing onto the letter "H," (b) intensity distribution when focusing onto the letter "H".

domain, a DOE with four quantization levels was computed and focused into the letter "F" composed of three line-segments of lengths 13Δ, 7Δ, and 4Δ.

The calculated phase function and the intensity distribution generated by the 4-level DOE are shown in Figure 2.56. When focusing into the letter "F" the energy efficiency E and the error δ were, respectively, 70.2 percent and 2.1 percent. It is noteworthy that the value of the energy efficiency E for $M = 4$ is approximately the same as for the binary DOEs in Figures 2.52–2.55. This is due to the fact that in computing the binary DOEs two main orders, 1st and -1st, are employed and the portion of energy $E = |c_1|^2 + |c_{-1}|^2 = 0.81$ focused in the main orders, 1st and -1st, of a binary DOE is equal to the portion of energy E, Eq. (2.332), (Fig. 2.51) focused in the main 1st order for $M = 4$.

Note that designing a quantized DOE of square aperture G ($b \times b$) intended to focus the uniform beam onto a rectangle $N\Delta \times K\Delta$, where $\Delta = \lambda f/b$ is the diffraction spot size, is equivalent to designing a PDG that forms $N \times K$ orders. Actually, for $\mathbf{x} = \mathbf{x}_{j,p} = (j\Delta, p\Delta)$, the intensity values in the plane $z = f$

$$I_{j,p} = \left| \frac{1}{\lambda f} \int_G \exp[i\varphi_M(\mathbf{u})] \exp\left(-i\frac{2\pi}{b}(ju + pv)\right) d^2\mathbf{u} \right|^2 \tag{2.339}$$

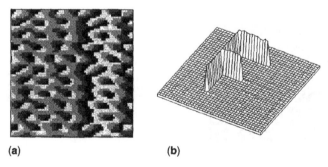

(a)   (b)

Figure 2.56. (a) The 4-level phase of a DOE focusing onto the letter "F"; (b) intensity distribution when focusing onto the letter "F".

are proportional to the squared modules of Fourier coefficients in the decomposition of the function $\exp[i\varphi_M(\mathbf{u})]$. Therefore, the $\varphi_M(\mathbf{u})$ function corresponds to the M-level phase function of a diffraction grating of period $b \times b$ and the intensity in the orders given by

$$I_{j,p} = \begin{cases} I_D(j\Delta, p\Delta), |j| \leq N/2, |p| \leq K/2 \\ 0, \text{ else} \end{cases}. \tag{2.340}$$

Example 2.16 Table 2.6 gives the results of designing binary PDGs for the different number of equal-intensity orders. The energy efficiency E of 73–75 percent and the rms error δ of 3–5 percent confirm high robustness of the method proposed.

In the course of iterative computation of the gratings from Table 2.6, the initial approximation was given by the following phase function $\varphi_0(\mathbf{u})$:

$$\varphi_0(\mathbf{u}) = \text{mod}_{2\pi} \left\{ \frac{\pi N}{4} \left[\left(\frac{u}{b}\right)^2 + 2\left(\frac{v}{b}\right)^2 + 4\left(\frac{u}{b}\right) \right] \right\}, \quad (u, v) \in [-b/2, b/2]. \tag{2.341}$$

The function of Eq. (2.341) is the phase function of a DOE [71,89] designed using the geometric optical ray tracing to focus onto a rectangle $\mathbf{x} \in [0, (N/2)\Delta] \times [-(N/2)\Delta, (N/2)\Delta]$. The phase function of Eq. (2.341) corresponds to the phase of a period of the diffraction grating of $(N/2) \times N$ orders and provides the focusing onto half the initial domain of $N \times N$ orders. The use of the analytical initial approximation, Eq. (2.341) simplifies the design procedure and provides a better convergence of the iterative process of Eq. (2.311).

Figure 2.57 depicts the computed one period's binary phase of a diffraction grating that generates 33×33 orders of equal intensity. A quasi-regular form of the derived binary phase in Figure 2.57(a) is due to the use of the smooth function of Eq. (2.341) as an initial approximation. The intensity distribution in the plane $z = f$ for the PDG in Figure 2.57a is shown in Figure 2.57b, with the number of the grating periods being 2×2.

2.8.11 Quantized DOEs for Generating Amplitude-Phase Distributions

The use of the method dealt with in subsection 2.8.10 is not restricted to designing quantized DOEs focusing onto a desired domain. The method also applies well to the

TABLE 2.6. Results of Computation of Binary PDGs

Number of Orders	Energy Efficiency, E (%)	Root-Mean-Square Error, (%)
5×5	74.4	3.1
7×7	73.7	3.1
9×9	72.6	2.9
11×11	73.8	3.6
15×15	74.7	3.4
21×21	73.8	3.7
33×33	75.1	4.8
51×51	74.2	4.9

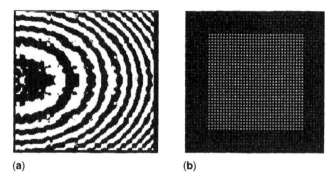

(a)   **(b)**

Figure 2.57. (a) One period's binary phase of a PDG with 33×33 orders; (b) intensity distribution in the Fourier plane for the grating in Figure 2.57a.

design of binary and quantized DOEs that generate required amplitude-phase distributions.

Assume that we need to design a DOE with the phase function $\varphi_M(\mathbf{u})$, quantized in M levels, that generates at $z = f$ a desired complex intensity distribution $W_D(\mathbf{x})$ in the domain D. Considering a special character of the task, the DOE is supposed to be found in the front plane of a Fourier lens (at $z = -f$). In this case, the complex amplitude in the output plane (at $z = f$) corresponds to the Fourier transform of the output field

$$W(\mathbf{x}) = \frac{1}{\lambda f} \int_G \sqrt{I_0(\mathbf{u})} \exp\left(i\varphi_M(\mathbf{u}) - i\frac{k}{f}\mathbf{x}\mathbf{u}\right) d^2\mathbf{u}. \tag{2.342}$$

The design of DOEs that generate fields with a required complex amplitude distribution is also relied on the optimization of the continuous function $\tilde{A}_M(\mathbf{u}; L_1, L_2)$ of Eq. (2.308). The computation of the function $\varphi(\mathbf{u})$ in Eq. (2.308) is conducted using a gradient method and consists in the iterative correction of the $\varphi(\mathbf{u})$ function by the rule (2.311). Then, the functional $\varepsilon(\varphi)$ corresponds to a certain integral functional

$$\varepsilon(\varphi) = \overline{\varepsilon}[\tilde{W}_M(\mathbf{x}), W_D(\mathbf{x})],$$

that characterizes the difference between the complex amplitude distribution generated by the DOE with the continuous CTF of Eq. (2.308)

$$\tilde{W}_M(\mathbf{x}) = \frac{1}{\lambda f} \int_G \sqrt{I_0(\mathbf{u})} \tilde{A}_M(\mathbf{u}; L_1, L_2) \exp\left(-i\frac{k}{f}\mathbf{x}\mathbf{u}\right) d^2\mathbf{u}, \tag{2.343}$$

and the required amplitude-phase distribution $W_D(\mathbf{x})$, $\mathbf{x} \in D$.

The gradient $\varepsilon'(\varphi)$ of the functional is also represented by Eqs. (2.316) and (2.323) given the function $\Psi(\mathbf{u})$ defined in the form

$$\Psi(\mathbf{x}) = \Im^{-1}\left\{\frac{d\overline{\varepsilon}(\tilde{W}_M, W_D)}{d\tilde{W}_M}\right\}. \tag{2.344}$$

The return from the continuous function $\tilde{A}_M(\mathbf{u}; L_1, L_2)$ to the quantized function of Eq. (2.302) yields an M-level phase function.

Note in conclusion that the method may also be extended onto the case of designing a DOE with the following general CTF:

$$A(\mathbf{u}) = \Phi[\varphi(\mathbf{u})], \tag{2.345}$$

where $\varphi(\mathbf{u})$ is the continuous function defined in the interval $[0, 2\pi)$ and $\Phi[\xi], \xi \in [0, 2\pi]$ is a certain discontinuous complex-valued function that defines the point-by-point transformation of the $\varphi(\mathbf{u})$ function. The CTF of the quantized DOE of Eqs. (2.302) and (2.303) is a special case of Eq. (2.345) given that the $\Phi[\xi]$ function is defined by

$$\Phi[\xi] = \exp(i\,\Phi_M[\xi]) = \exp\left[i\frac{2\pi}{M} \cdot int\left(\frac{\xi M}{2\pi}\right)\right]. \tag{2.346}$$

The CTF of Eq. (2.345) may also be represented as a series in terms of the diffraction orders of Eq. (2.306), with the coefficients c_n being the coefficients of the Fourier function $\Phi[\xi]$. The use of the truncated series expanded in diffraction orders for the CTF of Eq. (2.345) also makes it possible to replace the optimization of the discontinuous CTF in Eq. (2.345) by the optimization of the continuous truncated series in Eq. (2.306). The specific form of the $\Phi[\xi]$ function in Eq. (2.345) depends on the problem to be solved. By way of illustration, when designing quantized amplitude filters, the function $\Phi[\xi] = (1/2\pi)\Phi_M[\xi]$ may be used.

Example 2.17   To demonstrate the robustness of the method for designing quantized DOEs capable of generating the field with desired complex amplitude distribution we shall consider the design of DOEs that generate fields with the complex amplitude corresponding to the mode functions of the operator of light propagation [10,117]. The method was applied to the design of binary DOE that transform the Gaussian beam of Eq. (2.337) into a unimode Gauss-Hermite distribution

$$M_{(p'l)}(\mathbf{x}) = H_p(\sqrt{2}x/\sigma)H_l(\sqrt{2}y/\sigma)\exp(-\mathbf{x}^2/\sigma^2), \tag{2.347}$$

where (p, l) is the mode index and $H_p(x)$ is the Hermite polynomial of power p. The computation was conducted for the mode distributions (1, 0) and (1, 1) and employed the gradient procedure of Eqs. (2.311), (2.316), (2.322), (2.323), and (2.344) at $L_1 = L_2 = 5$ and the following error functional:

$$\varepsilon(\varphi) = \int_{-\infty}^{\infty} |\tilde{W}_M(\mathbf{x}) - W_D(\mathbf{x})|^2 d^2\mathbf{x}. \tag{2.348}$$

The physical parameters were as follows: the wavelength is $\lambda = 0.63$ μm, the Gaussian beam parameter is $\sigma = 1.41$ mm, the fundamental mode radii are (1, 0) and (1, 1), $\sigma_{0,1} = \sigma_{1,1} = 0.123$ mm, the focal length of the Fourier lens is $f = 500$ mm, and the size of the domain D in which the mode distributions are generated is 0.2 mm × 0.2 mm.

The computed binary-phase DOEs that generate the Gauss-Hermite modes (0, 1) and (1, 1) are shown in Figures 2.58a and 2.58b, respectively.

The amplitude and phase distributions for the fields generated by the DOE in Figure 2.58 in the output plane of the Fourier lens are shown in Figure 2.59.

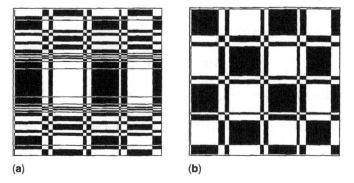

(a)   (b)

Figure 2.58. Binary phases of DOE that transform the Gaussian beam into the (**a**) Gauss-Hermite (0, 1) and (**b**) Gauss-Hermite (1, 1) mode beams.

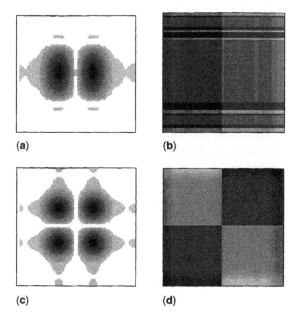

(a)   (b)

(c)   (d)

Figure 2.59. Amplitude and phase distributions in the Fourier plane: (**a, b**) for the binary DOE in Figure 2.58a, and (**c, d**) for the binary DOE in Figure 2.58b.

Figure 2.59 clearly demonstrates the field structure typical of the mode distributions (0, 1) (Fig. 2.59a) and (1, 1) (Fig. 2.59c, d).

The DOE robustness was evaluated using the values of the energy efficiency

$$E_m = \int_D |W_D(\mathbf{x})|^2 \, d^2\mathbf{x} / \int_G I_0(\mathbf{u}) \, d^2\mathbf{u} \qquad (2.349)$$

and the mode coefficient

$$\gamma = \left| \int_D W(\mathbf{x}) W_D^*(\mathbf{x}) \, d^2\mathbf{x} \right| / \int\int_D |W(\mathbf{x})|^2 \, d^2\mathbf{x}, \qquad (2.350)$$

characterizing the content of the mode in the useful domain D [117]. The calculated values of E_m and γ were 47.7 percent and 0.958 for the (0, 1) mode, and 43.9 percent and 0.947 for the (1, 1) mode.

It is noteworthy that the generalized Kirk-Jones method of coding, which is commonly used for the design of DOEs fails when applied to designing binary DOEs. For comparison, the generalized Kirk-Jones method was applied to designing continuous-phase DOEs for the aforementioned physical parameters [117]. The energy efficiency of the DOEs computed by the Kirk-Jones method was 1.5 times less than it was for the binary DOEs in Figure 2.59, thus testifying to high robustness of the method proposed.

REFERENCES

1. G.I. Vasilenko and A.M. Taratorin, *Image Retrieval*, Radio i Svyaz, (Radio & Communications Publishers), Moscow, 1980 (in Russian).

2. J. Goodman, *Introduction into Fourier Optics*, Mir (World Publishers), Moscow, 1970.

3. R.W. Gerchberg and W.O. Saxton, A practical algorithm for the determination of the phase from image and diffraction plane pictures, *Optik* **35**(2), 237–246 (1972).

4. B. Lin and N.C. Gallagher, Convergence of a spectrum shaping algorithm, *Appl. Opt.* **13**(11), 2470–2471 (1974).

5. J.R. Fienup, Phase retrieval algorithm: a comparison, *Appl. Opt.* **21**(15), 2758–2769 (1982).

6. V.P. Sivokon, Generation of light beams with desired structure in laser technology, Candidate thesis, Moscow State University, Moscow, 1986 (in Russian).

7. J.R. Fienup, Reconstruction of an object from the modulus of its fourier transform, *Opt. Lett.* **3**(1), 27–29 (1978).

8. J.R. Fienup, Iterative method applied to image reconstruction and to computer-generated holograms, *Opt. Eng.* **19**(3), 297–305 (1980).

9. G. Lu et al., Pendulum iterative algorithm for phase retrieval from modulus data, *Opt. Eng.* **33**(2), 548–555 (1994).

10. V.V. Kotlyar, I.V. Nikolski, and V.A. Soifer, Adaptive iterative algorithm for focusators synthesis, *Optik* **88**(1), 17–19 (1991).

11. V.V. Kotlyar and I.V. Nikolski, Iterative computing of transmittance of optical elements focusing at a predetermined area, *Opt. Laser Eng.* **15**(5), 323–330 (1991).

12. V.V. Kotlyar, P.G. Seraphimovich, and V.A. Soifer, An iterative weight-based method for calculating kinoforms, *Proc. SPIE Image Proc. Comput. Opt.* **2363**, 175–183 (1994).

13. J.R. Fienup, Phase-retrieval algorithm for a complicated optical system, *Appl. Opt.* **32**(10), 1737–1746 (1993).

14. V.V. Kotlyar, P.G. Seraphymovich, and V.A. Soifer, An iterative weight method for kinoforms computation, *Opt. Spectrosc.* **78**(1), 149–151 (1995) (in Russian).

15. E.D. Vasilyev et al., Computer-generated optical element for detecting the position, *Proc. SPIE* **1983**, 1012–1013 (1993).

16. M. Born and E. Wolf, *Principles of optics*, Nauka (Science Publishers), Moscow, 1973 (in Russian).

17. V.V. Kotlyar and P.G. Seraphimovich, An adaptive iterative method for design of kinoforms, *J. Opt. Spectrosc.* **77**(4), 678–681 (1994) (in Russian).

18. A.N. Tikhonov and V.J. Arsenin, *Methods for solving Ill-posed problems*, Nauka (Science Publishers), Moscow, 1979 (in Russian).

19. R.W. Gerchberg, Superresolution through error energy reduction, *Opt. Acta.* **21**, 709–720 (1974).

20. A. Papoulis, A new algorithm in spectral analysis and band-limited extrapolation, *IEEE Trans. Circ. Syst.* **CAS 22**, 735–742 (1975).

21. F. Wyrowski, Diffractive optical elements: iterative calculation of quantized, blazed phase structures, *J. Opt. Soc. Am.* **7**(6), 961–963 (1990).

22. V.V. Kotlyar, P.G. Seraphimovich, and V.A. Soifer, An iterative algorithm for designing diffractive optical elements with regularization, *Opt. Laser Eng.* **29**(4,5), 261–268 (1998).

23. D.C. Youla, Generalized image restoration by the method of alternating orthogonal projections, *IEEE Trans Circ. Syst.* **CAS-25**, 694–702 (1979).

24. H. Aagedal et al., Theory of speckles in diffractive optics and its application to beam shaping, *J. Mod. Opt.* **43**(7), 1409–1421 (1996).

25. J.B. Abbis et al., Regularized iterative and noniterative procedures for object restoration in the presence of noise: an error analysis, *J. Opt. Soc. Am.* **73**, 1470–1475 (1983).

26. M. Minu, *Mathematical Programming*, Nauka (Science Publishers) Moscow, 1990 (in Russian)

27. A.E. Siegman, Quasifast Hankel transform, *Opt. Lett.* **1**(1), 13–15 (1977).

28. V. Magni, G. Gerullo, and S. Desilvestry, High-accuracy fast Hankel transform for optical beam propagation, *J. Opt. Soc. Am.* **9**(11) 2031–2033 (1992).

29. S.N. Khonina, V.V. Kotlyar, and V.A. Soifer, Fast Hankel transform for focusators synthesis, *Optik* **88**(4), 182–184 (1991).

30. L.L. Doskolovich, et al. Focusators into a ring, *Opt. Quant. Electron.* **25**, 801–814 (1993).

31. A.E. Bereznyi et al., Bessel optics, *Sov. Phys. Dokl.* **29**(2), 115–117 (1984).

32. S.N. Khonina et al., Trochoson. *Opt. Commun.* **91**(3,4), 158–162 (1992).

33. V.V. Kotlyar and V.A. Soifer, A spatial filter for differentiating radially symmetric light fields, *Lett. J. Tech. Phys.* **16**(12), 30–33 (1990) (in Russian).

34. S.N. Khonina et al., The phase rotor filter, *J. Mod. Opt.* **39**(5), 1147–1154 (1992).

35. J.H. McLeod, The axicon: a new type optical element, *J. Opt. Soc. Am.* **44**(8), 592–597 (1954).

36. P. Belanger and M. Rioux, Ring pattern of a lens-axicon doublet illuminated by a Gaussian beam, *Appl. Opt.* **17**(7), 1080–1086 (1978).

37. M.A. Golub et al., Focusing the radiation onto a pregiven spatial domain using computer-synthesized holograms, *Lett. J. Techl. Phys.* **7**(10), 618–623 (in Russian).

38. R. Tremblay et al., Laser plasmas-optically pumped by focusing with axicon a CO2-TEA laser beam in a high-pressure gas, *Opt. Commun.* **28**(2), 193 (1979).

39. B.B. Brenden and J.T. Russel, Optical playback apparatus focusing system for producing a prescribed energy distribution along an axial focal zone, *Appl. Opt.* **23**(19), 3250 (1984).

40. I.A. Michaltsova, V.I. Nalivaiko, and I.S. Soldatenkov, Kinoform axicon, *Optik*, **67**(3), 267 (1984).

41. S.N. Khonina, V.V. Kotlyar, and V.A. Soifer, Calculation of the focusator into a longitudinal line-segment and study of a focal area, *J. Mod. Opt.* **40**(5), 761–769 (1993).

42. S.N. Khonina, V.V. Kotlyar, and V.A. Soifer, Diffraction computation of a focusator into a longitudinal segment and multifocal lens, *Proc. SPIE*, **1780**, 263–272 (1993).

43. S.N. Khonina, V.V. Kotlyar, and V.A. Soifer, Focusator into longitudinal segment and multifocal lenses, *Comput. Opt. Moscow*, **13**, 12–15 (1993) (in Russian).

44. V.V. Kotlyar, S.N. Khonina, and V.A. Soifer, Phase optical elements aimed for widening a minimum diffraction spot, *Opt. Lasers Technol.* **27**(4), 235–240 (1995).

45. S.N. Khonina et al., Iterative methods for the kinoforms synthesis, *OSA Proc. Int. Opt. Des. Conf.* **22**, 251–256 (1994).

46. H. Damman and E. Klotz, Coherent optical generation and inspection of two-dimensional periodic structures, *Opt. Acta.* **24**, 505–575 (1977).

47. J.N. Mait and K.H. Brenner, Optical symbolic substitution: system design using phase-only holograms, *Appl. Opt.* **27**, 1692–1700 (1988).

48. W.B. Veldkamp, J.R. Leger, and G.J. Swanson, Coherent summation of laser beams using binary-phase gratings. *Opt. Lett.* **11**, 303–305 (1986).

49. M.J. Simpson, Diffraction pattern sampling using a holographic optical element in an imaging configuration, *Appl. Opt.* **26**(9), 1786–1791 (1987).

50. U. Killat, G. Rabe, and W. Rave, Binary-phase gratings for star couplers with high splitting ratio, *Fiber Integ. Opt.* **4**, 159–167 (1982).

51. H.H. Arsenault, T. Szoplik, and B. Macukow, *Optical Processing and Computing*, San Diego, Academic Press 1989.

52. L.L. Doskolovich, V.A. Soifer, and M.S. Shinkaryev, A method for stochastic synthesis of binary diffraction gratings, *J. Autometr.*, **3**, 104–108 (1992) (in Russian).

53. M.A. Seldowitz, J.P. Allebach, and D.W. Sweeney, Synthesis of digital holograms by direct binary search, *Appl. Opt.* **26**, 2788–2798 (1987).

54. M.R. Feldman and C.C. Gest, Iterative encoding of high-efficiency holograms for generation of spot arrays, *Opt. Lett.* **14**(8) 479–481 (1989).

55. J. Turunen, A. Vasara, and J. Westerholm, Kinoform phase relief synthesis, *Opt. Eng.* **28**(11), 1162–1167 (1989).

56. R.L. Morrison, S.L. Walker, and T.J. Cloonan, Beam array generation and holographic interconnections in a free-space optical network, *Appl. Opt.* **32**, 2512–2518 (1993).

57. J. Turunen, A. Vasara, and J. Westerholm, Stripe-geometry two-dimensional Dammann gratings, *Opt. Commun.* **74**, 245–252 (1990).

58. J.N. Mait, Design of binary-phase and multiphase fourier gratings for array generation, *J. Opt. Soc. Am.* **7**(8), 1514–1528 (1990).

59. A.Ye. Bereyezny et al., Phase diffraction gratings with desired parameters on one inverse problem in optics, *Rep. USSR Acad. Sci.* **287**(3), 623–627 (1986) (in Russian).

60. L.L. Doskolovich, V.V. Kotlyar, and V.A. Soifer, Phase diffraction gratings with desired intensity distribution in orders, *Lett. J. Tech. Phys.* **17**(21), 54–57 (1991) (in Russian).

61. H. Dammann and K. Gortler, High-efficiency in-line multiple imaging by means of multiple phase holograms. *Opt. Commun.* **3**(5), 312–315 (1971).

62. J. Jahns et al., Dammann gratings for laser beam shaping, *Opt. Eng.* **28**, 1267–1275 (1988).

63. S.T. Bobrov and Yu.G. Turkevich, Multiorder diffraction gratings with asymmetric period profile, *J. Comput. Opt. M., ICSTI*, **4**, 38–45 (1989) (in Russian).

64. S. Bobrov, B. Kotletsov, and Y. Turkevich, New diffractive optical elements. *Proc. SPIE*, **1751**, 154–165 (1992).

65. A.D. Pommet, M.G. Moharam, and E.B. Grann, Limits of scalar diffraction theory for diffractive phase elements, *J. Opt. Soc. Am.* **11**(6), 1827–1834 (1994).

66. M.A. Golub, I.N. Sisakyan, and V.A. Soifer. Infrared radiation focusators. *Opt. Las. Eng.* **15**(5), 297–309 (1991).

67. V. Soifer and M. Golub, Diffractive micro-optical elements with non-point response. *Proc. SPIE*, **1751**, 140–154 (1992).

68. L.L. Doskolovich et al., Analytical initial approximation for multiorder binary gratings design, *Pure Appl. Opt.* **3**, 921–930 (1994).

69. L.L. Doskolovich et al., Microfabricated multiorder diffraction gratings for fiber networks and broad to broad interconnects, Proc. ISHM "The many aspects of microelectronics," Pavia, Italy (1994).

70. V.G. Karmanov, *Mathematical Programming*, Nauka (Science Publishers), Moscow, 1986 (in Russian).

71. M.A. Golub et al., A method of coordinated rectangles for designing focusers onto a plane domain, *J. Comput. Opt. M., ICSTI*, **10–11**, 100–110 (1992) (in Russian).

72. D. Leseberg, Computer-generated three-dimensional image holograms, *Appl. Opt.* **31**(2), 223–229 (1992).

73. M.A. Vorontzov, A.V. Koryabin, and V.I. Shmalgausen, *Controlled Optical Systems*, Nauka, Moscow, 1988 (in Russian).

74. O. Bryngdahl and F. Wyrowski, Digital holography-computer-generated holograms, *Prog. Opt.* Ed. by E. Wolf, **28**, 3–86 1990.

75. L.L. Doskolovich et al., Focusing the laser light onto a 3D surface of rotation, *J. Comput. Opt. ICSTI*, **12**, 8–14 (1992) (in Russian).

76. V.V. Kotlyar, S.N. Khonina, and V.A. Soifer, Iterative calculation of diffractive optical elements focusing into a three-dimensional domain and into the surface of the body of rotation. *J. Mod. Opt.* **43**(7), 1509–1524 (1996).

77. V.V. Kotlyar, I.V. Nikolsky, and V.A. Soifer, An algorithm for calculating multichannel formers of Gaussian modes, *Optik* **98**(1), 26–30 (1994).

78. N.L. Kazanskiy, V.V. Kotlyar, and V.A. Soifer. Computer-aided design of diffractive optical elements, *Opt. Eng.* **33**(10), 3156–3166 (1994).

79. S.N. Khonina, V.V. Kotlyar, and V.A. Soifer, Algorithm for the generation of nondiffracting Bessel modes. *J. Mod. Opt.* **42**(6), 1231–1239 (1995).

80. M.A. Golub et al., Computer-generated diffractive multifocal lens, *J. Mod. Opt.* **39**(6), 1245–1251(1992).

81. S.N. Khonina, V.V. Kotlyar, and V.A. Soifer, Diffraction computation of focusator into a longitudinal segment and multifocal lens, *Proc. SPIE*, **1780**, 263–272 (1993).

82. A.P. Prudnikov, Yu.A. Brychkov, and O.I. Marychev, *Integrals and Series*, *Special Functions*, Nauka, Moscow, 1983 (in Russian).

83. W.P. Veldcamp, Laser beam profile shaping with interplaced binary diffraction gratings, *Appl. Opt.* **21**(17), 3209 (1982).

84. C.-Y. Han, Y. Ishii, and K. Murata, Reshaping collimated laser beams with Gaussian profile to uniform profiles, *Appl. Opt.* **22**(22), 3644–3647 (1983).

85. V.P. Koronkevich et al., Kinoform optical elements: methods of design, fabrication technology, and optical applications, *Autometry*, **1**, 4–25 (1985) (in Russian).

86. M.A. Vorontzov, A.I. Matveyev, and V.P. Sivokon, On the design of laser light focusers using the diffraction approximation, *J. Comput. Opt. ICSTI*, **1**, 74–78 (1987) (in Russian).

87. N.C. Roberts, Beam shaping by holographic filters, *Appl. Opt.* **28**(1), 31–32 (1989).

88. M.T. Eismann, A.M. Tai, and J.N. Cederquist, Iterative design of holographic beam former, *Appl. Opt.* **28**(15), 2641–2650 (1989).

89. M.A. Golub et al., Computer simulation of a focuser of Gaussian beam onto a uniform-intensity rectangle, *J. Comput. Opt. ICSTI* **7**, 42–49 (1990) (in Russian).

90. C.C. Aleksoff, K.K. Ellis, and S.D. Neagle, Holographic conversion of a Gaussian beam to a near-field uniform beam. *Opt. Eng.* **30**(5), 537–543 (1991).

91. M.A. Golub, I.N. Sisakyan, and V.A. Soifer, Infrared radiation focusators, *Opt. Lasers Eng.* **15**(5), 297–309 (1991).

92. M.A. Golub et al., Iterative-phase method for diffractively levelling the Gaussian beam intensity, *J. Comput. Opt. ICSTI*, **13**, 30–33 (1993) (in Russian).

93. J. Cordingley, Application of a binary diffractive optics for beam shaping a semiconductor processing by lasers. *Appl. Opt.* **32**(14), 2538–2542 (1994).

94. A.G. Seduhkin and Y.G. Churin, Shape transformation of a grazing incidence laser Gaussian beam, *Autometry*, **6**, 75–81 (1995) (in Russian).

95. M. Duparre et al., Investigation of computer-generated diffractive beam shapers for flattening of single-modal CO2 laser beam, *Appl. Opt.* **34**(14), 2488–2497 (1995).

96. M.A. Golub et al., New diffractive beam shaper generated with the aid of e-beam lithography, *Opt. Eng.* **35**(5), 1400–1406 (1996).

97. M.W. Farn, Modeling of diffractive optics, *OSA Proc. Int. Opt. Design Conf.* **22**, 246–250 (1994).

98. M.A. Vorontzov and V.I. Shmalgausen, *Adaptive optics principles*, Nauka, Moscow, 1985 (in Russian).

99. A. Fedotovsky and H. Lehovec, Optimal filter design for annular imaging, *Appl. Opt.* **13**(12), 2919–2923 (1974).

100. I.G. Palchikova, Kinoform optical elements with enhanced focal depth, *J. Comput. Opt. ICSTI*, **6**, 9–19 (1989)(in Russian).

101. L.L. Doskolovich et al., Focusators for laser branding, *Opt. Lasers Eng.* **15**(5), 311–322 (1991).

102. S.N. Khonina et al., A method for design of composite DOEs for the generation of letter images, *Opt. Memory Neural Networks*, **6**(3), 213–220 (1997).

103. V.A. Soifer, V.V. Kotlyar, and L.L. Doskolovich, *Iterative Methods for Diffractive Optical Elements Computation*, Taylor & Francis, London, 1997.

104. F. Wyrowski, Iterative quantization of digital amplitude holograms, *Appl.Opt.* **28**, 3864–3871 (1989).

105. S. Weissbach, F. Wirowski, and O. Bringdahl, Digital phase holograms: Coding and quantization with an error-diffusion concept, *Opt. Comm.* **72**(1,2), 37–41 (1989).

106. F. Wyrowski and O. Bryngdahl, Digital holography as part of diffractive optics, *Int. Rep. Prog. Phys.* (UK), **28**, 1481–1571 (1991).

107. L.L. Doskolovich et al., Direct 2D calculation of quantized DOEs on the basis of a continuous series approach, *J. Mod. Opt.* **44**(4), 685–695 (1997).

108. L.L. Doskolovich et al., Direct two-dimensional calculation of binary DOEs using a nonbinary series expression approach, *Int. J. Opto electron.* **10**, N4, 243–249 (1995).

109. L.L. Doskolovich, N.L. Kazanskiy, and V.A. Soifer, Design of binary diffractive optica elements for focusing onto a desired 2D domain, Autometry, **5**, 42–50 (1995) (in Russian).

110. P. Repetto et al., Metodi iterativi nel calcolo ottico. Un esempio: l'ottimizzazione diretta di reticoli di diffrazione 2D, Workshop on Diffractive Optics and Microoptics, Firenze, Italy, March 1998, **7**.

111. J.M. Dallas, Phase quantization — a compact derivation, *Appl. Opt.* **14**, 674–676 (1971).

112. J.M. Goodman and A.M. Silvestri, Some effects of fourier-domain phase quantization IBM, *J. Res. Develop.* **14**, 478–484 (1969).

113. K. Lantzosh, *Practical Methods of Applied Analysis*, State Publishers of Physical & Mathematical Literature Moscow, 1961 (in Russian).

114. A.V. Oppenheim and R.V. Shaffer, *Digital Image Processing* Svyaz (Communications Publishers) Moscow, 1979 (in Russian).

115. G. Stark, Theory and measurements of optical fourier-spectra, application of fourier-optics methods, Radio i Svyaz (Radio & Communications Publishers), Moscow, 1988 (in Russian).

116. I.N. Sisakyan and V.A. Soifer, Infrared focusators, new optical elements, *Infrared Phys.* **32**, 435–438 (1991).

117. V.A. Soifer and M.A. Golub, *Laser beam mode selection by computer-generated holograms.* CRC Press, Boca Raton, FA, 1994.

CHAPTER 3

Design of DOE Using Electromagnetic Theory

If the medium the light is diffracted by has subwavelength parameters (average depth and modulation period of microrelief), the scalar approximation dealt with in Chapter 2 becomes invalid. In this situation, the light diffraction can be adequately described using the general electromagnetic theory of light on the basis of Maxwell equations. A concise discussion of the electromagnetic theory of light diffraction is found in Refs. [1–3].

This chapter uses the rigorous theory to give solutions to specific, direct, and inverse problems of light diffraction. The diffraction of the plane wave by a one-dimensional (1D) reflection diffraction grating with the period in the form of a special multistep microrelief is discussed in Section 3.1. This problem serves as a generalization of the problem on light diffraction by a perfectly reflecting binary grating [4,5]. Section 3.2 considers the plane wave diffraction by a continuous-profile reflection grating in the Rayleigh approximation. The Rayleigh approximation is a combination of the rigorous theory and an approximate boundary condition. Section 3.3 covers the plane wave diffraction by a continuous-profile dielectric transmission grating, with the continuous-profile grating replaced by a step-relief grating. As distinct from the familiar method for solving the problem [6], a more convenient matrix formalism is used. The numerical examples illustrate the operation of a transmission binary grating and allow the comparison with the results discussed in Ref. [6]. Section 3.4 deals with methods for solving the inverse problem of designing 1D diffraction gratings, such as reflection (subsection 3.4.1) and transmission multistep gratings (subsection 3.4.2) and reflection continuous-profile gratings. Within the electromagnetic theory, the diffraction grating relief is synthesized through the minimizing of functionals-criteria by the use of a gradient procedure. The methods discussed in Section 3.4 are a generalization of the iterative algorithms treated in Chapter 2. The generalization consists in the passage from a scalar approximation to the rigorous solution of an electromagnetic problem. In Section 3.5, we discuss the plane wave diffraction by two-dimensional (2D) diffractive structures, both perfectly reflecting (subsection 3.5.1) and transmission dielectric ones (subsection 3.5.2). Section 3.6 deals with a gradient method for synthesis of the electromagnetic field in the vicinity of a 2D DOE. The method makes it possible to calculate what electromagnetic field should be produced near the DOE surface to generate a desired intensity distribution in the focal plane. Section 3.7 discusses an asymptotic method for analysis of the light diffraction by reflection zoned structures. The method uses the replacement of the diffraction structure under analysis by the equivalent set of binary diffraction gratings. In Section 3.8, a method of finite differences is used to model the electromagnetic impulse diffraction by a 1D continuous-relief and

159

binary-relief microlens placed in a waveguide with perfectly conducting walls. Two implicit difference schemes featured by a different degree of approximation accuracy are compared. In Section 3.9, antireflection subwavelength structures are modeled using a difference solution of Maxwell equations. The problem shows potential for enhancement of the efficiency of antireflection periodic microstructures coated on a diamond film using a selective laser etching.

3.1   DIFFRACTION BY REFLECTION GRATINGS WITH STEPWISE PROFILE

The general set of Maxwell equations for the electromagnetic field in Gaussian units is given by

$$\text{rot } \mathbf{H} = \frac{4\pi \mathbf{j}}{c} + \frac{1}{c}\frac{\partial \mathbf{D}}{\partial t}; \tag{3.1}$$

$$\text{rot } \mathbf{E} = -\frac{1}{c}\frac{\partial \mathbf{B}}{\partial t}; \tag{3.2}$$

$$\text{div } \mathbf{D} = 4\pi\rho; \tag{3.3}$$

$$\text{div } \mathbf{B} = 0, \tag{3.4}$$

where $\mathbf{E}$, $\mathbf{H}$ are the strengths of the electric and magnetic field, respectively, $\mathbf{D}$, $\mathbf{B}$ are the inductions of the electric and magnetic field, $\mathbf{j}$ is the density of the electric conduction current, and ρ is the density of electric charges.

The equations relating the field inductions to the field strengths and the density of the conduction current to the electric field strength are called *the material equations*. In this section, the relation between these quantities is assumed to be linear: $\mathbf{j} = \sigma\mathbf{E}$, $\mathbf{D} = \varepsilon\mathbf{E}$, and $\mathbf{B} = \mu\mathbf{H}$, where the coefficients of proportionality, ε and μ, describe the permittivity and magnetic permeability of medium.

The space components of the monochromatic electromagnetic field (ω is the cyclic frequency in a space with constant permittivity), in the absence of currents and charge sources, instead of Eqs. (3.1) and (3.2) are given by

$$\text{rot } \mathbf{H} = \frac{4\pi j}{c} - \frac{i\omega}{c}\varepsilon\mathbf{E}, \tag{3.5}$$

$$\text{rot } \mathbf{E} = \frac{i\omega}{c}\mathbf{H}. \tag{3.6}$$

Consider a perfectly conducting diffraction grating with K rectangular grooves per period d (Fig. 3.1). The position of the lth groove is defined by the initial coordinate x_l of the groove, the groove width c_l, and the groove depth h_l. Suppose that the diffraction grating is illuminated by a plane monochromatic wave of unit amplitude and the wave vector $\mathbf{k} = k[\sin(\theta)\cos(\gamma_0), -\cos(\theta)\cos(\gamma_0), \sin(\gamma_0)]$, where $k = 2\pi/\lambda$, λ is the wavelength, and the angles θ and γ_0 define the direction of the incident wave (Fig. 3.1).

The z-dependence of the electric and magnetic fields generated upon the reflection of the plane wave from the grating is described by the function $\exp(ik\gamma z)$ [4,5]:

$$\mathbf{E}(x, y, z) = \mathbf{E}(x, y)\exp(ik\gamma z),$$

$$\mathbf{H}(x, y, z) = \mathbf{H}(x, y)\exp(ik\gamma z), \tag{3.7}$$

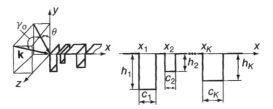

Figure 3.1. Diffraction grating with a stepwise relief.

where $\gamma = \sin(\gamma_0)$. Substituting Eq. (3.7) into Eqs. (3.5) and (3.6) gives Maxwell equations for projections of the electric and magnetic vectors of the monochromatic wave:

$$\partial_y E_z - ik\gamma E_y = ikH_x; \quad \partial_y H_z - ik\gamma H_y = -ik\varepsilon E_x; \quad ik\gamma E_x - \partial_x E_z = ikH_x;$$

$$ik\gamma H_x - \partial_x H_z = -ik\varepsilon E_y; \quad \partial_x E_y - \partial_y E_x = ikH_z; \quad \partial_x H_y - \partial_y H_x = -ik\varepsilon E_z;$$

(3.8)

where $\partial_x H_z = \partial H_z/\partial x_x$, and so on. From analysis of Eq. (3.8), the vector components of $\mathbf{E}(x, y)$ and $\mathbf{H}(x, y)$ are seen to be expressed through the components $E_z(x, y)$, $H_z(x, y)$ in the form

$$E_x = \frac{-1}{ik - ik\gamma^2}(\partial_y H_z + \gamma \partial_x E_z), \quad H_x = \frac{1}{ik - ik\gamma^2}(\partial_y E_z - \gamma \partial_x H_z),$$

$$E_y = \frac{1}{ik - ik\gamma^2}(\partial_x H_z - \gamma \partial_y E_z), \quad H_y = \frac{-1}{ik - ik\gamma^2}(\partial_x E_z + \gamma \partial_y H_z), \quad (3.9)$$

where the components $E_z(x, y)$, $H_z(x, y)$ satisfy the 2D Helmholtz equation

$$\frac{\partial^2 E_z}{\partial x^2} + \frac{\partial^2 E_z}{\partial y^2} + k^2(1 - \gamma^2)E_z = 0,$$

$$\frac{\partial^2 H_z}{\partial x^2} + \frac{\partial^2 H_z}{\partial y^2} + k^2(1 - \gamma^2)H_z = 0. \quad (3.10)$$

According to Eqs. (3.9) and (3.10), the problem of diffraction of the plane wave by a 1D diffraction grating can be brought to two independent problems: diffraction of the plane wave with TE-polarization ($E_z \neq 0$, $H_z = 0$) and diffraction of the plane wave with TM-polarization ($H_z \neq 0$, $E_z = 0$) [4,5]. Note that any plane wave can be represented as a linear combination of the two earlier wave types. The Helmholtz equations, Eq. (3.10), should be completed by the boundary conditions. The boundary condition on a perfectly conducting surface takes the form

$$E_t = 0, \quad (3.11)$$

where E_t is the tangential component of the electric field. In view of Eq. (3.9), Eq. (3.11) takes the form

$$\begin{cases} E_x \sim \partial_y H_z + \gamma \partial_x E_z = 0 \\ E_z = 0 \end{cases} \quad (3.12)$$

for horizontal parts of the grating profile and

$$\begin{cases} E_z = 0 \\ E_y \sim \partial_x H_z - \gamma \partial_y E_z = 0 \end{cases} \tag{3.13}$$

for vertical parts of the grating profile. Besides, the electric field should be continuous at $y = 0$. The boundary conditions in Eqs. (3.12) and (3.13) should also be completed by the condition of continuity of the tangential components H_x, H_z of the magnetic field at $y = 0$ within the grooves, that is, for $x_i \leq x \leq x_i + c_i$, $i = \overline{1, K}$ [4–7]. As distinct from the electric field, the magnetic field at $y = 0$ suffers a discontinuity that amounts to the surface current density.

In further discussion, we constrain our consideration to the case of $\gamma = 0$, corresponding to a "plane incidence." For $\gamma = 0$, TE-polarization gives $E_z \neq 0$, $E_x = E_y = H_z = 0$ and TM-polarization gives $H_z \neq 0$, $H_x = H_y = E_z = 0$. Consider how the diffraction problem is solved using a method of modal decomposition [4–7]. With this method, two fields are sewed together at $y = 0$, with the first field being the solution of the Helmholtz equation within the diffraction grating grooves at $x_i \leq x \leq x_i + c_i$, $-h_i \leq y < 0$, $i = \overline{1, K}$ and the second field being the solution of the Helmholtz equation outside the grooves at $y > 0$.

The out-of-groove field is represented as a Rayleigh expansion

$$u(x, y) = \exp[ik(\alpha_0 x - \beta_0 y)] + \sum_{n=-\infty}^{\infty} R_n \exp[ik(\alpha_n x + \beta_n y)], \tag{3.14}$$

where

$$\alpha_n = \sin(\theta) + n\frac{\lambda}{d}, \tag{3.15}$$

$$\beta_n = \sqrt{1 - \alpha_n^2}. \tag{3.16}$$

The scalar function $u(x, y)$ corresponds to the $E_z(x, y)$ component for TE-polarization and the $H_z(x, y)$ component for TM-polarization. The Rayleigh expansion in Eq. (3.14) provides the solution to the Helmholtz equation and contains homogeneous plane waves ($\alpha_n^2 < 1$) and inhomogeneous plane waves ($\alpha_n^2 > 1$), which are exponentially damped out as the distance from the grating surface increases. The term $n\lambda/d$ in Eq. (3.15) follows from the Floceaut theorem and characterizes the presence of a constant phase shift between the neighboring periods of the grating.

The field within the diffraction grating grooves is described differently for TE-polarization and TM-polarization.

3.1.1 TE-Polarization

For TE-polarization, the electric field $E_z^l(x, y)$ within the lth groove satisfies the Helmholtz equation

$$\Delta E_z^l + k^2 E_z^l = 0 \tag{3.17}$$

with the boundary condition

$$E_z^l(x, y)\big|_{(x,y)\in C_l} = 0, \qquad (3.18)$$

where C_l is the groove contour made up of three segments: $x = x_l$, $y \in [-h_l, 0]$, $x = x_l + c_l$, $y \in [-h_l, 0]$, and $y = -h_l$, $x \in [x_l, x_l + c_l]$. Condition in Eq. (3.18) is a specific form of conditions in Eqs. (3.12) and (3.13). Using the method of separation of variables to solve the Helmholtz equation in (3.17), the field within the lth groove is given by the following expansion in terms of orthogonal functions:

$$E_z^l(x, y) = \sum_{n=1}^{\infty} B_n^l \sin\left(\frac{\pi n}{c_l}(x - x_l)\right) \sin[\mu_{ln}(y + h_l)], \qquad (3.19)$$

where

$$\mu_{ln}^2 = k^2 - \left(\frac{\pi n}{c_l}\right)^2. \qquad (3.20)$$

Proceeding with the solution of the diffraction problem, we seek to find the coefficients R_n and B_n^l from the boundary conditions at $y = 0$. The condition for the field continuity at $y = 0$ are

$$\exp(ik\alpha_0 x) + \sum_{n=-\infty}^{\infty} R_n \exp(ik\alpha_n x) = \sum_{l=1}^{K} \text{rect}\left(\frac{1}{c_l}(x - x_l - c_l/2)\right)$$

$$\times \sum_{n=1}^{\infty} B_n^l \sin\left(\frac{\pi n}{c_l}(x - x_l)\right) \sin(\mu_{ln} h_l), \qquad (3.21)$$

where $\qquad \text{rect}(x) = \begin{cases} 1, & |x| \leq 0,5 \\ 0, & |x| > 0,5 \end{cases}$

Multiplying Eq. (3.21) by $\exp(-ik\alpha_p x)$, $(p = -\infty, \infty)$ and integrating over the period, Eq. (3.21) can be replaced by the condition of equality of the Fourier coefficients in the expansion of the left and right sides of the equation. As a result, we get the following set of linear equations:

$$R_p + \delta(p) = \sum_{l=1}^{K} \sum_{n=1}^{\infty} AA_{pn}^l B_n^l, \quad (p = -\infty, \infty), \qquad (3.22)$$

where $\qquad \delta(p) = \begin{cases} 1, & p = 0, \\ 0, & p \neq 0, \end{cases}$

$$AA_{pm}^l = \frac{\sin(\mu_{lm} h_l)}{kd} \exp(-ik\alpha_p x_l) \int_0^{kc_l} \sin\left(\frac{\pi m}{kc_l}\xi\right) \exp(-i\alpha_p \xi)\, d\xi. \qquad (3.23)$$

The system in Eq. (3.21) contains two sequences of coefficients: $\mathbf{R} = (R_n)$ and $\mathbf{B} = (B_n^l)$. To find the second equation relating the coefficients $\mathbf{R}$ and $\mathbf{B}$, make use of the condition of continuity for the tangent components of the magnetic field. The magnetic field tangent component, $H_x \sim \partial E_z / \partial y$, should be continuous at $y = 0$ within the grooves, that is, at $x_l \leq x \leq x_l + c_l, l = \overline{1, K}$. Applying the condition of continuity for the derivative $\partial E_z / \partial y$ at $y = 0$, we find that

$$
-ik\beta_0 \exp(ik\alpha_0 x) + \sum_{n=-\infty}^{\infty} R_n ik\beta_n \exp(ik\alpha_n x)
$$

$$
= \sum_{m=1}^{\infty} B_m^l \mu_{lm} \sin\left(\frac{\pi m}{c_l}(x - x_l)\right) \cos(\mu_{lm} h_l) \tag{3.24}
$$

at $x_l \leq x \leq x_l + c_l, l = \overline{1, K}$. Multiplying Eq. (3.24) by $\sin[\pi m(x - x_l)/c_l], m = -\infty, \infty$ and integrating over x on the segment $[x_l, x_l + c_l]$, we get the following expression for the coefficients of the field expansion within the lth groove:

$$
B_m^l = \frac{2ik}{\mu_{lm} \cos(\mu_{lm} h_l)} \sum_{n=-\infty}^{\infty} \beta_n [R_n - \delta(n)] DD_{mn}^l, \tag{3.25}
$$

where

$$
DD_{mn}^l = \frac{1}{kc_l} \exp(ik\alpha_n x_l) \int_0^{kc_l} \sin\left(\frac{\pi m}{kc_l}\xi\right) \exp(i\alpha_n \xi)\, d\xi. \tag{3.26}
$$

Substituting Eqs. (3.25) and (3.26) into Eq. (3.22) produces the following set of linear equations for the derivation of the Rayleigh coefficients:

$$
\sum_{s=-\infty}^{\infty} AA_{ps} \cdot R_s = D_p, \quad p = -\infty, \infty, \tag{3.27}
$$

where

$$
AA_{ps} = \beta_s M_{ps} - \delta(p - s), \tag{3.28}
$$

$$
M_{ps} = \frac{2ik}{d} \sum_{l=1}^{K} \sum_{n=1}^{\infty} c_l \frac{\text{tg}(\mu_{ln} h_l)}{\mu_{ln}} DD_{ns}^l (DD_{np}^l)^*, \tag{3.29}
$$

$$
D_p = \beta_0 M_{p0} + \delta(p). \tag{3.30}
$$

For practical purposes, the infinite set of linear equations Eq. (3.27) is replaced by a finite set of $2N + 1$ equations

$$
\mathbf{AA} \cdot \mathbf{R} = \mathbf{D}, \tag{3.31}
$$

where

$$
\mathbf{AA} = (AA_{ps})_{-N}^{N}, \quad \mathbf{R} = (R_p)_{-N}^{N}, \quad \mathbf{D} = (D_p)_{-N}^{N} \tag{3.32}
$$

with the series in Eq. (3.29) replaced by sums composed of $n_l, l = \overline{1, K}$ terms. It should be noted that the replacement of the lth series in Eq. (3.29) by a sum of n_l terms implies that the field within the lth groove is properly described by the sum of n terms.

3.1.2 TM-Polarization

The case of TM-polarization is, in many respects, analogous to TE-polarization. The magnetic field $H_z^l(x, y)$ within the lth groove of the diffraction grating satisfies the Helmholtz equation

$$\Delta H_z^l + k^2 H_z^l = 0 \tag{3.33}$$

with the boundary conditions

$$\frac{\partial H_z^l(x, y)}{\partial \mathbf{n}}\bigg|_{(x,y)\in C_l} = 0, \tag{3.34}$$

where $\mathbf{n}$ is the normal vector to the groove contour C_l. The conditions in Eq. (3.34) follow from the general boundary conditions in Eqs. (3.12) and (3.13).

Using the method of separation of variables to solve the Helmholtz equation, Eq. (3.33), the field within the lth groove is given by the following expansion:

$$H_z^l(x, y) = \sum_{n=1}^{\infty} B_n^l \cos\left(\frac{\pi n}{c_l}(x - x_l)\right) \cos[\mu_{ln}(y + h_l)], \tag{3.35}$$

with the coefficients μ_{ln} defined in Eq. (3.20).

To derive the Rayleigh coefficients R_n and the coefficients B_n^l of the field expansion within the grooves, make use of the "sewing" conditions at $y = 0$. The condition of continuous magnetic field at $y = 0$ within the grooves results in the following functional equation:

$$\exp(ik\alpha_0 x) + \sum_{n=-\infty}^{\infty} R_n \exp(ik\alpha_n x) = \sum_{n=1}^{\infty} B_n^l \cos\left(\frac{\pi n}{c_l}(x - x_l)\right) \cos(\mu_{ln} h_l), \tag{3.36}$$

where $x_l \leq x \leq x_l + c_l$ and $l = \overline{1, K}$. The boundary condition for the tangential component of the electric field (in this case, for $E_x \sim \partial H_z/\partial y$) requires that at $y = 0$ the derivative $\partial H_z/\partial y$ be equal to zero on horizontal parts of the profile and the derivative $\partial H_z/\partial y$ be continuous within the grooves ($x_l \leq x \leq x_l + c_l$, $l = \overline{1, K}$). These stipulations provide the other functional equation for the coefficients R_n and B_n^l in the form

$$-ik\beta_0 \exp(ik\alpha_0 x) + \sum_{n=-\infty}^{\infty} R_n ik\beta_n \exp(ik\alpha_n x) = -\sum_{l=1}^{K} \mathrm{rect}\left(\frac{1}{c_l}(x - x_l - c_l/2)\right)$$

$$\times \sum_{m=1}^{\infty} B_m^l \mu_{lm} \cos\left(\frac{\pi m}{c_l}(x - x_l)\right) \sin(\mu_{lm} h_l). \tag{3.37}$$

Multiplying Eq. (3.36) by $\cos[\pi m(x - x_l)/c_l]$, $m = -\infty, \infty$ and integrating over x on the segment $[x_l, x_l + c_l]$ yields the following equation for the coefficients of the field expansion within the lth groove:

$$B_m^l = \frac{2}{\cos(\mu_{lm} h_l)} \sum_{n=-\infty}^{\infty} [R_n + \delta(n)] D D_{mn}^l, \tag{3.38}$$

where

$$D D_{mn}^l = \frac{1}{kc_l} \exp(ik\alpha_n x_l) \int_0^{kc_l} \cos\left(\frac{\pi m}{kc_l}\xi\right) \exp(i\alpha_n \xi) \, d\xi. \tag{3.39}$$

Then, replacing Eq. (3.37) by the condition of equality of the Fourier coefficients for the right and left sides of this equation, we get the following set of linear equations:

$$-\beta_0 \delta(p) + \beta_p R_p = i \sum_{l=1}^{K} \sum_{m=1}^{\infty} B_m^l A A_{pm}^l, \quad p = -\infty, \infty \tag{3.40}$$

$$A A_{pm}^l = \frac{\sin(\mu_{lm} h_l)}{kd} \left(\frac{\mu_{lm}}{k}\right) \exp(-ik\alpha_p x_l)$$

$$\times \int_0^{kc_l} \cos\left(\frac{\pi m}{kc_l}\xi\right) \exp(-i\alpha_p \xi) \, d\xi. \tag{3.41}$$

Substituting Eqs. (3.38) and (3.39) into Eq. (3.40), the set of linear equations relative to the Rayleigh coefficients will take the form of Eqs. (3.27) and (3.31), where

$$A A_{ps} = M_{ps} - \beta_p \delta(p - s), \tag{3.42}$$

$$M_{ps} = \frac{2ki}{d} \sum_{l=1}^{K} \sum_{n=1}^{\infty} \frac{c_l}{\mu_{ln}} \mathrm{tg}(\mu_{ln} h_l) D D_{ns}^l (D D_{np}^l)^*, \tag{3.43}$$

$$D_p = -M_{p0} - \beta_0 \delta(p). \tag{3.44}$$

In the Kirchhoff approximation, by the diffraction order intensities are meant squared modules of the Fourier coefficients, $|c_n|^2$, in the decomposition of the function $\exp[i\varphi(x)]$, with the function $\varphi(x)$ describing the phase lead acquired by the plane wave upon reflection from the grating. Let us define the notion "order intensity" within the electromagnetic theory approach. Consider a domain D limited from bottom by the grating profile, from top by the straight-line segment $x = p$, $p > 0$, from the right and left by the straight-line segments $x = 0$ and $x = d$, respectively. Using the law of energy conservation, make the flux of the Umov-Poynting vector $\mathbf{S} = (c/8\pi)\mathrm{re}[\mathbf{E}, \mathbf{H}^*]$ over the domain D equal to zero [8]. Then, the normalization condition will be given by

$$\beta_0 = \sum_{n \in U} |R_n|^2 \beta_n, \tag{3.45}$$

where $U = \{n | \alpha_n^2 < 1\}$ is a set of indices corresponding to the propagated reflected waves (orders) in Eq. (3.14), whereas β_n are defined in Eq. (3.16) and are equal to the cosines of angles between the Oy-axis and the reflected waves (orders) directions. Equation (3.45) has an explicit physical meaning: the energy of an incident wave is equal to the sum of the energies of reflected orders. According to Eq. (3.45), by the order intensities, one should mean the following normalized Rayleigh coefficients:

$$I_n = |R_n|^2 \frac{\beta_n}{\beta_0}, \quad \left(\sum_{n \in U} I_n = 1 \right). \tag{3.46}$$

Example 3.1   Consider the operation of a simplest binary grating with a single groove of length $d/2$ per period d. Figure 3.2 depicts the plots for the intensities of the 0th and -1st orders as a function of the groove depth h. The order intensities were estimated using Eqs. (3.31), (3.42)–(3.44) for the period $d = \lambda$, the inclination angle $\theta = 30°$, and TM-polarization. Note that for the earlier parameters the Bragg condition [6] is satisfied:

$$m \cdot \lambda = -2d \cdot \sin(\theta) \tag{3.47}$$

at $m = -1$. In that case, there are only 0th and -1st propagated orders, with the -1st diffraction order being opposite to the incident wave direction. The remaining orders correspond to inhomogeneous waves ($\alpha_n^2 > 1$) exponentially damped out as the distance from the grating surface increases. The plot in Figure 3.2 reveals the following interesting peculiarities of the grating operation. First, for the groove depths of $h \approx 0.1\lambda$, 0.42λ, 0.57λ, and 0.93λ, the energy is divided equally between the 0th and -1st orders, thus implying that the grating operates as a beam splitter. Second, for the groove depths of 0.22λ and 0.72λ, the energy is concentrated in the -1st order, which means that the grating serves as a beam deflector. From the general form of the plots in Figure 3.2, the intensities of the 0th and -1st orders are seen to be periodically changing. The order intensity of the binary grating as a function of the groove depth for TM-polarization is shown in Figure 3.3. For TE-polarization, the binary grating is not able to concentrate light in the -1st order. At the groove depth of $h \approx 0.55\lambda$, the grating operates as a beam splitter.

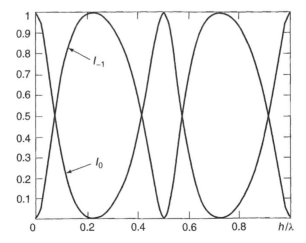

Figure 3.2. The intensity in the -1st (I_{-1}) and 0th (I_0) orders for the binary grating, as a function of groove height for TM-polarization at $d = \lambda$, $\theta = 30°$.

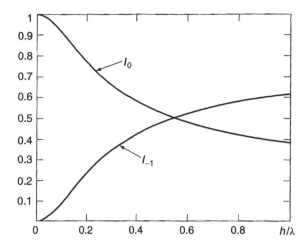

Figure 3.3. The intensities in the −1st (I_{-1}) and 0th (I_0) orders for the binary grating, as a function of groove height for TE-polarization at $d = \lambda$, $\theta = 30°$.

3.2 DIFFRACTION BY CONTINUOUS-PROFILE REFLECTION GRATINGS

Before solving the problem of the plane wave diffraction by a 1D perfectly conducting diffraction grating, consider the derivation of the integral equation relating the light field and the current density on a perfectly conducting surface.

The integral equations are derived using the vector form of the second Green formula:

$$\int_V (\mathbf{Q} \operatorname{rot} \operatorname{rot} \mathbf{P} - \mathbf{P} \operatorname{rot} \operatorname{rot} \mathbf{Q}) dV = \oint_S \{[\mathbf{P}, \operatorname{rot} \mathbf{Q}] - [\mathbf{Q}, \operatorname{rot} \mathbf{P}]\}\mathbf{n}\, dS. \tag{3.48}$$

Transform the integrand in Eq. (3.48) to the form

$$\mathbf{Q} \operatorname{rot} \operatorname{rot} \mathbf{P} - \mathbf{P} \operatorname{rot} \operatorname{rot} \mathbf{Q} = \mathbf{P}\Delta\mathbf{Q} - \mathbf{Q}\Delta\mathbf{P} + \mathbf{Q} \operatorname{grad} \operatorname{div} \mathbf{P} - \mathbf{P} \operatorname{grad} \operatorname{div} \mathbf{Q}$$

$$= \mathbf{P}\Delta\mathbf{Q} - \mathbf{Q}\Delta\mathbf{P} + \operatorname{div}(\mathbf{Q} \operatorname{div} \mathbf{P} - \mathbf{P} \operatorname{div} \mathbf{Q}). \tag{3.49}$$

Then, utilizing the Ostrogradsky-Gauss formula we get

$$\int_V (\mathbf{P}\Delta\mathbf{Q} - \mathbf{Q}\Delta\mathbf{P})\, dV = \oint_S \{\mathbf{n}[\mathbf{P}, \operatorname{rot} \mathbf{Q}] - \mathbf{n}[\mathbf{Q}, \operatorname{rot} \mathbf{P}] + \mathbf{n}\mathbf{P} \operatorname{div} \mathbf{Q} - \mathbf{n}\mathbf{Q} \operatorname{div} \mathbf{P}\}\, dS. \tag{3.50}$$

Equations (3.48) and (3.50) can be easily transformed to the integral relations for the electromagnetic field in space. Assume that $\mathbf{P} = \mathbf{E}$, $\mathbf{Q} = \mathbf{a}G$, $G(\mathbf{x} - \mathbf{x}_0) = \exp(ikR)/R$, $\mathbf{a}$ is a unit vector of arbitrary direction, $R = |\mathbf{x} - \mathbf{x_0}|$, $\mathbf{x}$ is the radius vector of the observation point, $\mathbf{x}_0$ is a point on the surface S. In that case, the $\mathbf{Q}$ function satisfies the equation

$$\Delta\mathbf{Q} + k^2\mathbf{Q} = -4\pi \mathbf{a}\delta(\mathbf{x} - \mathbf{x}_0), \tag{3.51}$$

where $\operatorname{rot} \mathbf{Q} = [\operatorname{grad} G, \mathbf{a}]$, $\operatorname{div} \mathbf{Q} = (\mathbf{a}, \operatorname{grad} G)$, and $k^2 = \omega^2\bar{\varepsilon}\mu/c^2$.

Equation for the vector of the electric field strength follows from the Maxwell equations, Eqs. (3.5) and (3.6), but with due allowance for the presence of the permittivity μ and complex permeability $\bar{\varepsilon} = \varepsilon + (4\pi i\sigma/w)$, where σ is the medium specific conductivity:

$$\text{rot } \mathbf{H} = +\frac{4\pi}{c}j - \frac{i\omega}{c}\bar{\varepsilon}\,\mathbf{E}, \tag{3.52}$$

$$\text{rot } \mathbf{E} = \frac{i\omega}{c}\mu\mathbf{H}. \tag{3.53}$$

We will assume the medium of electromagnetic field propagation to be homogeneous and isotropic. Applying the operation rot to the left and right side of Eq. (3.53) and using the relation $\text{rot rot } \mathbf{A} = \text{grad div } \mathbf{A} - \Delta\mathbf{A}$ and Eq. (3.52) yields

$$\Delta\mathbf{E} + \frac{\omega^2\bar{\varepsilon}\mu}{c^2}\mathbf{E} = -4\pi\mathbf{J}_2,$$

$$\mathbf{J}_2 = \frac{i\omega\mu}{c^2}j - \frac{\text{grad div } j}{i\omega\bar{\varepsilon}}, \tag{3.54}$$

where j is the electric current density.

Multiply Eq. (3.51) by E(x) and Eq. (3.54) for the electric field by $\mathbf{Q}(\mathbf{x} - \mathbf{x}_0)$. Utilizing Eq. (3.50) and the relation $\{\mathbf{n}, [\mathbf{E}, (\text{grad } G, \mathbf{a})]\} = \{\mathbf{a}, [\text{grad } G, (\mathbf{E}, \mathbf{n})]\}$ produces the expression

$$\mathbf{E}(x)\mathbf{a} = \mathbf{a}\left\{\int_V \mathbf{J}_2(\mathbf{x}_0)G(\mathbf{x} - \mathbf{x}_0)\,dV + \frac{1}{4\pi}\oint_S [\mathbf{n}G(\mathbf{x} - \mathbf{x}_0)\,\text{div}_0\,\mathbf{E}(\mathbf{x}_0)]\,dS\right.$$

$$+ \frac{1}{4\pi}\oint_S ((\text{grad}_0\,G(\mathbf{x} - \mathbf{x}_0), [\mathbf{n}, \mathbf{E}(\mathbf{x}_0)]) + [\text{rot}_0\,\mathbf{E}(\mathbf{x}_0), \mathbf{n}]$$

$$\left.\times\, G(\mathbf{x} - \mathbf{x}_0) - \text{grad}_0\,G(\mathbf{x} - \mathbf{x}_0)(\mathbf{n}, \mathbf{E}(\mathbf{x}_0)))\,dS\right\}. \tag{3.55}$$

Taking into account that div E = 0 and the vector **a** is arbitrary, we get the following integral representation:

$$\mathbf{E}(\mathbf{x}) = \mathbf{E}_0(\mathbf{x}) + \frac{1}{4\pi}\oint_S \{[\text{grad}_0\,G(\mathbf{x} - \mathbf{x}_0), [\mathbf{n}, \mathbf{E}]] + [\text{rot}_0\,\mathbf{E}, \mathbf{n}]G(\mathbf{x} - \mathbf{x}_0)$$

$$- \text{grad}_0\,G(\mathbf{x} - \mathbf{x}_0)(\mathbf{n}, \mathbf{E})\}\,dS, \tag{3.56}$$

where

$$\mathbf{E}_0(\mathbf{x}) = \int_V \mathbf{J}_2(\mathbf{x}_0)G(\mathbf{x} - \mathbf{x}_0)\,dV. \tag{3.57}$$

By analogy with Eq. (3.57), the integral form for the magnetic field can be given by

$$\mathbf{H}(\mathbf{x}) = \mathbf{H}_0(\mathbf{x}) + \frac{1}{4\pi}\oint_S ([\text{grad}_0\,G(\mathbf{x} - \mathbf{x}_0)[\mathbf{n}, \mathbf{H}(x_0)]]$$

$$+ [\text{rot}_0\,\mathbf{H}(\mathbf{x}_0), \mathbf{n}]G(\mathbf{x} - \mathbf{x}_0) - \text{grad}_0\,G(\mathbf{x} - \mathbf{x}_0)[\mathbf{n}, \mathbf{H}(\mathbf{x}_0)])\,dS, \tag{3.58}$$

where $\mathbf{H}_0(\mathbf{x})$ is the magnetic field strength of the incident light. Equations (3.57) and (3.58) are referred to as *Stretton-Chu formulae*.

Introduce the designations for the surface densities of the electric and magnetic currents $(4\pi/c)\mathbf{j}_e(\mathbf{x}_0) = [\mathbf{n}, \mathbf{H}(\mathbf{x}_0)]$, $(4\pi/c)\mathbf{j}_m(\mathbf{x}_0) = [\mathbf{n}, \mathbf{E}(\mathbf{x}_0)]$. Take into account that $\operatorname{grad} G(\mathbf{x} - \mathbf{x}_0) = -\operatorname{grad}_0 G(\mathbf{x} - \mathbf{x}_0)$, $\operatorname{rot}(\Phi\mathbf{F}) = \Phi\operatorname{rot}\mathbf{F} + [\operatorname{grad}\Phi, \mathbf{F}]$, $\operatorname{rot} j_m(\mathbf{x}_0) = 0$, $\operatorname{rot}\mathbf{E} = ik\mathbf{H}$,

$$[\operatorname{grad}_0 G(\mathbf{x} - \mathbf{x}_0), j_m(\mathbf{x}_0)] = -[\operatorname{grad} G(\mathbf{x} - \mathbf{x}_0), j_m(\mathbf{x}_0)]$$

$$= -\operatorname{rot}(G(\mathbf{x} - \mathbf{x}_0) j_m(\mathbf{x}_0)) + G(\mathbf{x} - \mathbf{x}_0)\operatorname{rot} j_m(\mathbf{x}_0). \quad (3.59)$$

As a result, instead of Eq. (3.57), the electric field can be given by

$$\mathbf{E}(\mathbf{x}) = \mathbf{E}_0(\mathbf{x}) - \frac{1}{4\pi}\operatorname{rot}\oint_S j_m(\mathbf{x}_0)G(\mathbf{x} - \mathbf{x}_0)\,dS - \frac{ik}{4\pi}\oint_S j_e(\mathbf{x}_0)$$

$$\times G(\mathbf{x} - \mathbf{x}_0)\,dS + \frac{1}{4\pi}\operatorname{grad}\oint_S G(\mathbf{x} - \mathbf{x}_0)(\mathbf{n}, \mathbf{E}(\mathbf{x}_0))\,dS. \quad (3.60)$$

Applying the operation rot to both the sides of Eq. (3.60) and utilizing the relation $\operatorname{rot}(\operatorname{grad}\Phi) = 0$ yields the following expression comprising only tangential field components:

$$\mathbf{H}(\mathbf{x}) = \mathbf{H}_0(\mathbf{x}) - \frac{1}{4\pi ik}\operatorname{rot}\operatorname{rot}\oint_S \mathbf{j}_m(\mathbf{x}_0)G(\mathbf{x} - \mathbf{x}_0)\,dS - \frac{1}{4\pi}\operatorname{rot}\oint_S \mathbf{j}_e(\mathbf{x}_0)G(\mathbf{x} - \mathbf{x}_0)\,dS. \quad (3.61)$$

By analogy with Eq. (3.58), the integral form of the electric field is given by

$$\mathbf{E}(\mathbf{x}) = \mathbf{E}_0(\mathbf{x}) + \frac{1}{4\pi ik}\operatorname{rot}\operatorname{rot}\oint_S \mathbf{j}_e(\mathbf{x}_0)G(\mathbf{x} - \mathbf{x}_0)\,dS - \frac{1}{4\pi}\operatorname{rot}\oint_S \mathbf{j}_m(\mathbf{x}_0)G(\mathbf{x} - \mathbf{x}_0)\,dS. \quad (3.62)$$

Taking account of the boundary conditions on a perfectly conducting surface, $[\mathbf{n}, \mathbf{E}] = 0$, $(\mathbf{n}, \mathbf{H}) = 0$, Eqs. (3.61) and (3.62) can be rewritten as follows:

$$\mathbf{H}(\mathbf{x}) = \mathbf{H}_0(\mathbf{x}) - \frac{1}{4\pi}\operatorname{rot}\oint_S \mathbf{j}_e(\mathbf{x}_0)G(\mathbf{x} - \mathbf{x}_0)\,dS, \quad (3.63)$$

$$\mathbf{E}(\mathbf{x}) = \mathbf{E}_0(\mathbf{x}) + \frac{1}{4\pi ik}\operatorname{rot}\operatorname{rot}\oint_S \mathbf{j}_e(\mathbf{x}_0)G(\mathbf{x} - \mathbf{x}_0)\,dS. \quad (3.64)$$

For deriving the integral equation of first kind for the electric current density on a perfectly conducting surface, the vector $\mathbf{x}$ is considered to belong to the surface. Multiplying Eq. (3.64) by the normal vector at point $\mathbf{x}$ and taking account of the boundary condition for the perfect conductor, we get

$$[\mathbf{E}_0(\mathbf{x})\mathbf{n}(\mathbf{x})] = -\frac{1}{4\pi ik}\operatorname{rot}\operatorname{rot}\oint_S [\mathbf{j}_e(\mathbf{x}_0)\mathbf{n}(\mathbf{x})]G(\mathbf{x} - \mathbf{x}_0)\,dS. \quad (3.65)$$

Thus, the problem of determination of the electromagnetic field is broken down into two stages:

(1) Solution of the integral Eq. (3.65) relative to $\mathbf{j}_e(\mathbf{x}_0)$,
(2) Derivation of the field using Eqs. (3.64) and (3.63).

Next, utilize Eq. (3.65) for solving the problem of the plane wave diffraction by a cylindrical surface whose element is parallel to the z-axis. Let the electric field vector be parallel to the cylinder element (TE-polarization). Make use of the familiar formulae of vector analysis:

$$\operatorname{rot} \operatorname{rot}[\mathbf{j}_e(\mathbf{x}_0)G(\mathbf{x} - \mathbf{x}_0)] = \operatorname{grad} \operatorname{div}[\mathbf{j}_e(\mathbf{x}_0)G(\mathbf{x} - \mathbf{x}_0)] - \Delta[\mathbf{j}_e(\mathbf{x}_0)G(\mathbf{x} - \mathbf{x}_0)],$$

$$\operatorname{div}[\mathbf{j}_e(\mathbf{x}_0)G(\mathbf{x} - \mathbf{x}_0)] = [\operatorname{grad} G(\mathbf{x} - \mathbf{x}_0)j_e(\mathbf{x}_0)];$$

$$\operatorname{grad}(\operatorname{grad} G(\mathbf{x} - \mathbf{x}_0), \mathbf{j}_e(\mathbf{x}_0)) = (j_e(\mathbf{x}_0), \nabla) \operatorname{grad} G(\mathbf{x} - \mathbf{x}_0)$$

$$+ [j_e(\mathbf{x}_0), \operatorname{rot} \operatorname{grad} G(\mathbf{x} - \mathbf{x}_0)];$$

$$\Delta G(\mathbf{x} - \mathbf{x}_0) = -k^2 G(\mathbf{x} - \mathbf{x}_0). \tag{3.66}$$

Next, substituting these formulae into Eq. (3.65) and integrating along the cylindrical element z produces

$$E_z(\mathbf{x}) = E_{0z}(\mathbf{x}) - ik \oint_l j_{ze}(\mathbf{x}_0)G_2(\mathbf{x} - \mathbf{x}_0)\, dl, \tag{3.67}$$

where $G_2(\mathbf{x} - \mathbf{x}_0) = (i/4)H_0^1(k\sqrt{(\mathbf{x} - \mathbf{x}_0)^2})$ is a 2D Green formula, $H_0^1(x)$ is the Hankel formula of the first kind and of zero order, and $\mathbf{x} = (x_1, x_2)$ is a transverse vector.

The integral equation for the current density on the cylindrical surface takes the form

$$E_{0z}(\mathbf{x}) = ik \oint_l j_{ez}(\mathbf{x}_0)G_2(\mathbf{x} - \mathbf{x}_0)\, dl, \tag{3.68}$$

where $\mathbf{x}$ is a transverse vector that defines the point on the surface. The integral in Eq. (3.68) is taken along the generating surface.

Further, to solve the problem of diffraction by a diffraction grating (of period d) of continuous profile $y = f(x)$, make use of Eq. (3.68) with due account of the relation

$$dl = \sqrt{1 + \left(\frac{df(x_0)}{dx}\right)^2}\, dx_0. \tag{3.69}$$

According to the method of integral equations, the diffraction problem for TE-polarization is solved in the following two stages:

(1) Solving the integral equation relative to the z-component of the vector of surface current density, Eq. (3.63)

$$E_{0z}[x, f(x)] = \frac{ik}{c} \int_{-\infty}^{\infty} j_z(x_0)G_2[x - x_0, f(x_0) - f(x)]\sqrt{1 + \left(\frac{df(x_0)}{dx}\right)^2}\, dx_0, \tag{3.70}$$

where $E_{0z}(x, y) = \exp(ik\alpha_0 x - ik\beta_0 y)$ is the z-component of the electric field vector of the incident wave;

(2) Deriving the scattered field

$$E_z(x, y) = -\frac{ik}{c} \int_{-\infty}^{\infty} j_z(x_0) G_2[x - x_0, y - f(x_0)] \sqrt{1 + \left(\frac{df(x_0)}{dx}\right)^2} \, dx_0.$$

$$(3.71)$$

In Eqs. (3.70) and (3.71), the integration is in infinite limits. Let us derive integral relations in which the integration is performed only over the period d. When diffraction is caused by a diffraction grating, the surface current density is a quasi-periodic function

$$j_z(x + nd) = \exp(ik\alpha_0 nd) j_z(x).$$

$$(3.72)$$

In view of the current periodicity, Eq. (3.71) takes the form

$$E_z(x, y) = -\frac{ik}{c} \sum_{n=-\infty}^{\infty} \exp(ik\alpha_0 nd)$$

$$\times \int_0^d j_z(x_0) G_2[x - x_0 - nd, y - f(x_o)] \sqrt{1 + \left(\frac{df(x_0)}{dx_0}\right)^2} \, dx_0$$

$$(3.73)$$

In Eq. (3.73), the integration is performed only over the period d of the diffraction grating. Next, using the familiar Hankel integral

$$H_0^1\left(k\sqrt{x^2 + y^2}\right) = \frac{1}{\pi} \int_{-\infty}^{\infty} \frac{\exp[i(|y|\sqrt{k^2 - u^2} + ux)]}{\sqrt{k^2 - u^2}} \, du$$

$$(3.74)$$

and the formula for the "comb" function from the theory of generalized functions

$$\sum_{l=-\infty}^{\infty} \exp[i(x - y)la] = \frac{2\pi}{a} \sum_{m=-\infty}^{\infty} \delta\left[y - \left(x + \frac{2\pi m}{a}\right)\right],$$

$$(3.75)$$

the final expression for the scattered field is given by

$$E_z(x, y) = -\frac{ik}{c} \int_0^d j_z(x_0) G[x - x_0, y - f(x_0)] \sqrt{1 + \left(\frac{df(x_0)}{dx_0}\right)} dx_0, \quad (3.76)$$

where the Green function takes the form

$$G(x - x_0, y - y_0) = \frac{i}{2kd} \sum_{n=-\infty}^{\infty} \frac{\exp[ik\alpha_n(x - x_0)]}{\sqrt{1 - \alpha_n^2}} \exp\left[ik\sqrt{1 - \alpha_n^2}|y - f(x_0)|\right],$$

$$(3.77)$$

where α_n is defined in Eq. (3.15).

Replacing the observation point (x, y) in Eq. (3.76) by the point $[x, f(x)]$ of the diffraction grating profile and utilizing the boundary condition stipulating that the full electric field $E_z(x, y) + E_{0z}(x, y)$ on the grating surface [at $y = f(x)$] is equal to zero, we get the integral equation for the surface current density

$$E_{0z}[x, f(x)] = \frac{ik}{c} \int_0^d j_z(x) G[x - x_0, f(x) - f(x_0)] \sqrt{1 + \left(\frac{df(x_0)}{dx_0}\right)^2} \, dx_0. \quad (3.78)$$

According to Eqs. (3.76) and (3.77), the scattered field over the diffraction grating profile (at $y > \max[f(x_0)], x_0 \in [0, d]$) is the Rayleigh expansion

$$E_z(x, y) = \sum_{n=-\infty}^{\infty} R_n \exp[ik(\alpha_n x + \beta_n y)], \quad (3.79)$$

with the coefficients

$$R_n = \frac{1}{2cd\sqrt{1 - \alpha_n^2}} \int_0^d j_z(x_0) \exp[-ik\alpha_n x_0 - ik\beta_n f(x_0)] \sqrt{1 + \left(\frac{df(x_0)}{dx_0}\right)^2} \, dx_0 \quad (3.80)$$

expressed through the current densities on the grating surface.

Thus, solving the diffraction problem is implemented through solving the integral Eq. (3.78), followed by the derivation of the Rayleigh coefficients from Eq. (3.80).

We shall seek the solution of the integral equation (3.78) using the Fourier method [5] in which the sought-for function of the current density is represented as a quasi-periodic expansion

$$j_z(x) = \sum_{-\infty}^{\infty} c_n \exp(ik\alpha_n x). \quad (3.81)$$

Substituting Eq. (3.81) into Eq. (3.78) gives the following functional equation:

$$\frac{c}{ik} \exp[ik\alpha_0 x - ik\beta_0 f(x)] = \sum_{-\infty}^{\infty} c_n \int_0^d G[x - x_0, f(x) - f(x_0)]$$

$$\times \exp(ik\alpha_n x_0) \sqrt{1 + \left(\frac{df(x_0)}{dx_0}\right)^2} \, dx_0. \quad (3.82)$$

Multiplying both the sides of Eq. (3.82) by $\exp(-ik\alpha_p x)$, $p = -\infty, \infty$ and integrating over period, we get a set of linear equations for the derivation of the desired current expansion coefficients in the form

$$\sum_{n=-\infty}^{\infty} AA_{pn} \cdot c_n = d_p, \quad p = -\infty, \infty \quad (3.83)$$

where

$$d_p = \frac{c}{ik} \int_0^d \exp[-ik\beta_0 f(x)] \exp(-2\pi i p/d) \, dx, \quad (3.84)$$

$$AA_{pn} = \int_0^d \int_0^d \exp(-ik\alpha_p x_0) G[x_0 - x, f(x_0) - f(x)]$$

$$\times \exp(ik\alpha_n x)\sqrt{1 + \left(\frac{df(x)}{dx}\right)^2}\, dx\, dx_0. \tag{3.85}$$

According to Eqs. (3.71) and (3.85), the derivation of the matrix elements AA_{pn} in Eq. (3.83) is reduced to the computation of a series composed of double integrals. Therefore, in the general case, the derivation of the matrix elements AA_{pn} is a complicated computational task. If the grating profile is represented by a piecewise linear function

$$f(x) = \xi_m + \eta_m x, \quad x \in [x_m, x_{m+1}], \quad m = \overline{1, K}, \tag{3.86}$$

the matrix elements in Eq. (3.85) can be rearranged to give

$$AA_{pn} = \frac{1}{2ikd} \sum_{j=-\infty}^{\infty} \sum_{m=1}^{K-1} \sum_{k=1}^{K-1} \frac{\sqrt{1+\eta_k^2}}{\beta_j} I_{pn}^{jmk}, \tag{3.87}$$

where the integrals

$$I_{pn}^{jmk} = \int_{x_k}^{x_{k+1}} \int_{x_m}^{x_{m+1}} \exp\left\{-ik(\alpha_p - \alpha_j)x_0 + ik(\alpha_n - \alpha_j)x\right.$$

$$\left. +ik\beta_j \,|\xi_m - \xi_k + \eta_m x_0 - \eta_k x|\right\} dx dx_0 \tag{3.88}$$

are derived analytically. Equations (3.87) and (3.88) can be applied for designing common continuous-profile diffraction gratings. All one has to do is to approximate the continuous function by a piecewise-constant function.

3.2.1   Rayleigh Approximation

Although solving the integral Eq. (3.78) is rather a complicated mathematical problem, in a number of cases the field generated by the diffraction grating is calculated using the Rayleigh approximation [5]. According to Eq. (3.79), the field over the diffraction grating profile (at $y > a = \max[f(x_0)]$, $x_0 \in [0, d]$) is represented by a Rayleigh expansion. From this it cannot be inferred that the field at $y < a$ is also described by the Rayleigh expansion. Note, however, that with a shallow and smooth profile, the use of the Rayleigh approximation may be justified and implies that the expansion in Eqs. (3.79) and (3.14) describes the field not only over the grating at $y > a$ but also within the grating at $y < a$. Recall that the scalar function $u(x, y)$ in Eq. (3.14) corresponds to the E_z-component of the electric field for TE-polarization or the H_z-component of the magnetic field for TM-polarization.

To calculate the Rayleigh coefficients R_n in Eq. (3.14), it will suffice to use the boundary condition in Eq. (3.11) at $y = f(x)$. According to Eq. (3.11), the field in Eq. (3.14) should satisfy the boundary condition

$$u(x, y)|_{y=f(x)} = 0 \tag{3.89}$$

for TE-polarization and the boundary condition

$$\frac{du(x, y)}{d\mathbf{n}}\bigg|_{y=f(x)} = 0 \tag{3.90}$$

for TM-polarization, where $\mathbf{n}$ is the unit normal vector to the grating profile.

Substituting Eq. (3.14) into Eq. (3.89), the coefficients R_n for TE-polarization are derived from

$$\sum_{n=-\infty}^{\infty} R_n \exp\{ik[(\alpha_n - \alpha_0)x + (\beta_n - \beta_0)f(x)]\} = -\exp[-2ik\beta_0 f(x)]. \tag{3.91}$$

Replacing Eq. (3.91) by the condition of equality of the Fourier coefficients in the expansion of the left and right sides of this equation, the coefficients R_n are derived from the following set of linear equations:

$$\sum_{n=-\infty}^{\infty} AA_{pn} \cdot R_n = B_p, \quad p = -\infty, \infty, \tag{3.92}$$

where

$$AA_{pn} = \int_0^{2\pi} \exp[i\xi(n - p) + i(\beta_n - \beta_0)H(\xi)] \, d\xi, \tag{3.93}$$

$$B_p = -\int_0^{2\pi} \exp[-2i\beta_0 H(\xi) - ip\xi] \, d\xi, \tag{3.94}$$

$$H(\xi) = kf\left(\frac{\xi d}{2\pi}\right) \tag{3.95}$$

is the normalized height.

For TM-polarization, similar rearrangements produce for the coefficients R_n a set of linear equations analogous to Eq. (3.91), but with the following equations in place of Eqs. (3.93) and (3.94):

$$AA_{pn} = \int_0^{2\pi} \left(\beta_n - \alpha_n \frac{\lambda}{d} H'(\xi)\right) \exp[i\xi(n - p) + i(\beta_n - \beta_0)H(\xi)] \, d\xi, \tag{3.96}$$

$$B_p = \int_0^{2\pi} \left(\beta_0 + \alpha_0 \frac{\lambda}{d} H'(\xi)\right) \exp[-2i\beta_0 H(\xi) - ip\xi] \, d\xi. \tag{3.97}$$

For practical purposes, the coefficients R_n are derived using a finite set of $2N + 1$ equations

$$\mathbf{AA} \cdot \mathbf{R} = \mathbf{B}, \tag{3.98}$$

where $\mathbf{AA} = (AA_{pn})_{-N}^{N}$, $\mathbf{R} = (R_n)_{-N}^{N}$, $\mathbf{B} = (B_n)_{-N}^{N}$.

At $d \gg \lambda$, the Rayleigh approximation changes to the Fraunhofer approximation. Actually, at $d \gg \lambda$, we obtain that $(\beta_n - \beta_0) \approx 0$ and $(\lambda/d)H'(\xi) \approx 0$. In that case, the matrices in Eqs. (3.92) and (3.98) become diagonal ($\mathbf{AA} = 2\pi \mathbf{E}$) with the Rayleigh coefficients being proportional to the Fourier coefficients in the expansion of the function $\exp[i\varphi(\xi)]$, where the function

$$\varphi(x) = -2\beta_0 k f \left(\frac{xd}{2\pi}\right) \tag{3.99}$$

describes the phase lead acquired upon the reflection of the plane wave from the grating of height $f(xd/2\pi)$.

It would be interesting to note that the Fraunhofer approximation corresponds to the choice of the first term in the asymptotic expansion for the Rayleigh coefficients. Actually, using the matrix expansion $(\mathbf{E} + \mathbf{C})^{-1} = \sum_{j=0}^{\infty}(-\mathbf{C})^j$, the Rayleigh coefficients are represented as follows:

$$\mathbf{R} = \mathbf{A}\mathbf{A}^{-1} \cdot \mathbf{B} = \frac{1}{2\pi}(\mathbf{E} + \mathbf{A}\mathbf{A}_1)^{-1}\mathbf{B} = \frac{1}{2\pi}\sum_{j=0}^{\infty}(-\mathbf{A}\mathbf{A}_1)^j \cdot \mathbf{B} = \pm\mathbf{F} - \sum_{j=1}^{\infty}(-AA_1)^k \cdot \mathbf{F},$$

$$\tag{3.100}$$

where $\mathbf{F}$ is the vector of the Fourier coefficients and $\mathbf{AA}_1$ is the matrix with the elements

$$AA_{1pn} = \begin{cases} AA_{pn}/2\pi, & p \neq n, \\ AA_{pn}/2\pi - 1, & p = n. \end{cases} \tag{3.101}$$

Example 3.2 To estimate the accuracy of the Rayleigh approximation, examine the operation of a cosine grating with profile

$$f(x) = \frac{h}{2} \cdot \cos\left(\frac{2\pi x}{d}\right). \tag{3.102}$$

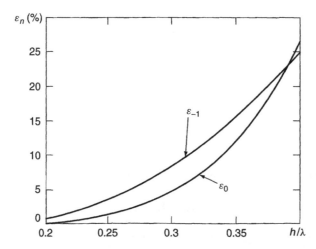

Figure 3.4. Error of the Rayleigh approximation for the intensities of the -1st $[\varepsilon_{-1}(h)]$ and 0th $[\varepsilon_0(h)]$ orders of the cosine grating as a function of depth for TE-polarization at $d = \lambda$, $\theta = 30°$.

The Rayleigh approximation accuracy is characterized by the relative error

$$\varepsilon_n(h) = \frac{|I_n^{\text{Int}}(h) - I_n^{\text{Rel}}(h)|}{I_n^{\text{Int}}(h)} \tag{3.103}$$

where h is the profile amplitude, $I_n^{\text{Int}}(h)$, $I_n^{\text{Rel}}(h)$ are the intensities of the nth order derived, respectively, using the accurate integral method of Eqs. (3.83)–(3.85) and the Rayleigh approximation of Eqs. (3.92)–(3.94). Figure 3.4 depicts the plots of the relative error $\varepsilon_n(h/\lambda)$ for the intensities of the 0th and the -1st orders as a function of profile depth h at a period of $d = \lambda$ and an incidence angle of $\theta = 30°$ for TE-polarization. From the plots in Figure 3.4, the Rayleigh approximation is seen to give the error of less than 10 percent at $h < 0.325\lambda$. The earlier example demonstrates that the Rayleigh approximation is suitable for smooth shallow profiles ($h < d/3$) even for subwavelength periods.

3.3 DIFFRACTION BY TRANSMISSION DIELECTRIC GRATINGS

Consider the diffraction of a plane wave with wave vector $\mathbf{k} = k[\sin(\theta), -\cos(\theta), 0]$ by a dielectric grating of profile $y = f(x)$ and period d. The geometry of the diffraction task is shown in Figure 3.5, where R_n and T_n are the coefficients of reflection and transmission of diffraction orders. In this case, there are three zones differing in the permittivity ε. The permittivity is constant in zones 1 and 3, that is, for $y > a$ (a is the grating profile maximum height) and for $y < 0$. Without loss of generality, we shall assume that $\varepsilon = 1$ in zone 1 and $\varepsilon > 1$ in zone 3. In zone 2, or modulation zone, where $y \in (0, a)$, the permittivity is represented by a function $\varepsilon = \varepsilon(x, y)$.

Consider the diffraction of two independent plane waves with TE-polarization and TM-polarization. In zone 1 ($y > a$) and zone 3 ($y < 0$), the field is represented by the Rayleigh expansion of Eq. (3.14). For $y > a$, the field takes the form

$$u(x, y) = \exp[i(\alpha_0 x - \beta_0 y)] + \sum_{n=-\infty}^{\infty} R_n \exp[i(\alpha_n x + \beta_n y)], \tag{3.104}$$

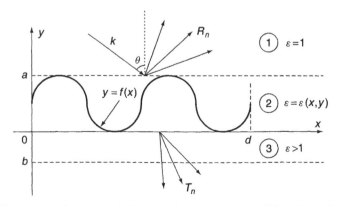

Figure 3.5. Geometry of the task of diffraction by a dielectric grating.

where

$$\begin{cases} \alpha_n = k_0 \sin(\theta) + n\dfrac{2\pi}{d}, & k_0^2 = \omega^2/c^2 = (2\pi/\lambda_0)^2, \\ \beta_n = \sqrt{k_0^2 - \alpha_n^2}, \end{cases} \tag{3.105}$$

whereas the scalar function $u(x, y)$ corresponds to the $E_z(x, y)$-component of the electric field for TE-polarization and the $H_z(x, y)$-component of the magnetic field for TM-polarization. Note that as distinct from Eqs. (3.14)–(3.16), k_0 is introduced into make the notation shorter, which means that α_n and β_n do not correspond to sines and cosines of diffraction angles any more. For $y < 0$, the field takes the form [5]

$$u(x, y) = \sum_{n=-\infty}^{\infty} T_n \exp\left[i\left(\alpha_n x - \tilde{\beta}_n y\right)\right], \tag{3.106}$$

where

$$\tilde{\beta}_n = \sqrt{k_0^2 \varepsilon - \alpha_n^2}. \tag{3.107}$$

The Rayleigh expansions in Eqs. (3.104) and (3.106) are the solutions to the Helmholtz equation

$$\Delta u + k^2 u = 0 \tag{3.108}$$

at $k^2 = k_0^2$ and $k^2 = k_0^2 \varepsilon$, respectively. In the modulation zone [at $y \in (0, a)$], the field is defined by a set of differential equations that are different for TE-polarization and TM-polarization.

3.3.1 TM-Polarization

Rearrange the Maxwell equations for a monochromatic electromagnetic wave traveling in a homogeneous dielectric medium, Eqs. (3.5) and (3.6), as follows:

$$\left.\begin{aligned} \mathrm{rot}\, H &= -ik_0 \varepsilon E \\ \mathrm{rot}\, E &= ik_0 H \end{aligned}\right\} \tag{3.109}$$

For TM-polarization (at $\mathbf{H}(x, y) = [0, 0, H_z(x, y)]$), we get

$$\begin{aligned} \frac{\partial H_z(x, y)}{\partial y} &= -ik_0 \varepsilon E_x(x, y), & \frac{\partial E_y(x, y)}{\partial z} &= 0, \\ -\frac{\partial H_z(x, y)}{\partial x} &= -ik_0 \varepsilon E_y(x, y), & \frac{\partial E_x(x, y)}{\partial z} &= 0, \\ E_z(x, y) &= 0, & \frac{\partial E_y(x, y)}{\partial x} - \frac{\partial E_x(x, y)}{\partial y} &= -ik_0 H_z(x, y). \end{aligned}$$

$$\tag{3.110}$$

At the interface of two media with permittivities ε_1 and ε_2 the tangential components of the vectors $\mathbf{E}$ and $\mathbf{H}$ are continuous. Without loss of generality, the Ox-axis can be considered as the interface, with the tangential components of the vectors $\mathbf{E}$ and $\mathbf{H}$ corresponding to the components $H_z(x, y)$ and $E_x(x, y)$. The condition for continuity of the $E_x(x, y)$-component is given by

$$\frac{1}{ik_0\varepsilon_1}\frac{\partial H_z(x, +0)}{\partial y} = E_x(x, +0) = E_x(x, -0) = \frac{1}{ik_0\varepsilon_2}\frac{\partial H_z(x, -0)}{\partial y}. \tag{3.111}$$

According to Eq. (3.111), while passing through the interface (the Ox-axis), the function $\partial H_z(x, y)/\partial y$ suffers a discontinuity, a break, thus preventing the common Helmholtz equation from being used for TM-polarization. It is the functions $(1/ik_0\varepsilon) \cdot [\partial H_z(x, y)/\partial y]$ and

$$\tilde{E}_x(x, y) = \frac{1}{k_0^2\varepsilon}\frac{\partial H_z(x, y)}{\partial y} = \frac{1}{k^2}\frac{\partial H_z(x, y)}{\partial y} \tag{3.112}$$

that are continuous in passing through the interface.

From Eq. (3.109) and (3.110) we derive an analog of the Helmholtz equation for the continuous function $H_z(x, y)$:

$$\frac{\partial}{\partial x}\left(\frac{1}{k^2}\frac{\partial H_z(x, y)}{\partial x}\right) + \frac{\partial}{\partial y}\left(\frac{1}{k^2}\frac{\partial H_z(x, y)}{\partial y}\right) + H_z(x, y) = 0. \tag{3.113}$$

While taking account of Eq. (3.112), we shall represent Eq. (3.113) as a set of two equations:

$$\begin{cases} \dfrac{\partial H_z(x, y)}{\partial y} = k^2\tilde{E}(x, y), \\[2mm] \dfrac{\partial \tilde{E}(x, y)}{\partial y} = -\dfrac{\partial}{\partial x}\left(\dfrac{1}{k^2}\dfrac{\partial H_z(x, y)}{\partial x}\right) - H_z(x, y). \end{cases} \tag{3.114}$$

The $H_z(x, y)$ function is quasi-periodic [5]:

$$H_z(x, y) = v(x, y)\exp(i\alpha_0 x), \quad \alpha_0 = k_0\sin(\theta), \tag{3.115}$$

where $v(x, y)$ is a function periodic in x, of period d. Expanding the $v(x, y)$ function into a Fourier series with respect to the variable x, the $H_z(x, y)$ function is given by

$$H_z(x, y) = \sum_{m=-\infty}^{\infty} H_m(y)\exp(i\alpha_m x), \quad \alpha_m = \alpha_0 + 2\pi m/d. \tag{3.116}$$

The $\tilde{E}_x(x, y)$ function is also quasi-periodic:

$$\tilde{E}_x(x, y) = \sum_{m=-\infty}^{\infty} \tilde{E}_m(y)\exp(i\alpha_m x). \tag{3.117}$$

For further purposes, assume that the functions $\tilde{E}_x(x, y)$ and $H_z(x, y)$ in the modulation zone can be approximated by their truncated series in Eqs. (3.116) and (3.117) with $2N + 1$ terms retained.

The functions $k^2(x, y) = k_0^2 \cdot \varepsilon(x, y)$ and $1/k^2(x, y)$ are periodic in x, of period d:

$$
\left.
\begin{aligned}
k^2(x, y) &= \sum_{n=-\infty}^{\infty} c_n^{(1)}(y) \exp\left(i\frac{2\pi}{d}nx\right), \\
\frac{1}{k^2(x, y)} &= \sum_{n=-\infty}^{\infty} c_n^{(2)}(y) \exp\left(i\frac{2\pi}{d}nx\right).
\end{aligned}
\right\}
\tag{3.118}
$$

Substituting Eqs. (3.116)–(3.118) into the set in Eq. (3.114) yields (with $2N + 1$ terms retained in the expansions (3.116) and (3.117)) the following set of $4N + 2$ differential equations:

$$
\left.
\begin{aligned}
\sum_{m=-N}^{N} \frac{dH_m(y)}{dy} \exp(i\alpha_m x) &= \sum_{l=-N}^{N} \tilde{E}_l(y) \exp(i\alpha_l x) \cdot \sum_{n=-\infty}^{\infty} c_n^{(1)}(y) \exp\left(i\frac{2\pi}{d}nx\right), \\
\sum_{m=-N}^{N} \frac{d\tilde{E}_m(y)}{dy} \exp(i\alpha_m x) &= -\frac{\partial}{\partial x}\left(\sum_{n=-\infty}^{\infty} c_n^{(2)}(y) \exp\left(i\frac{2\pi}{d}nx\right)\right. \\
&\quad \left. \times \sum_{l=-N}^{N} i\alpha_l H_l(y) \exp(i\alpha_l x)\right) - \sum_{m=-N}^{N} H_m(y) \exp(i\alpha_m x).
\end{aligned}
\right\}
\tag{3.119}
$$

Multiplying every equation in the set (3.119) by $\exp(-i\alpha_p x)$, $p = -N, N$, and integrating with respect to x over the period, the set (3.119) can be brought to a set of equations irrespective of the variable x

$$
\left.
\begin{aligned}
\frac{dH_p(y)}{dy} &= \sum_{l=-N}^{N} \tilde{E}_l(y) c_{p-l}^{(1)}(y), \quad p = -N, N, \\
\frac{d\tilde{E}_p(y)}{dy} &= \alpha_p \sum_{l=-N}^{N} \alpha_l c_{p-l}^{(2)}(y) H_l(y) - H_p(y), \quad p = -\overline{N, N}.
\end{aligned}
\right\}
\tag{3.120}
$$

For a binary grating, the Fourier coefficients in Eq. (3.120) are not dependent on the variable y

$$
c_n^{(1)} =
\begin{cases}
\dfrac{ik_0^2(\varepsilon - 1)}{2\pi n} \displaystyle\sum_{j=1}^{2K}(-1)^j \exp\left(-i\frac{2\pi}{d}nx_j\right), & n \neq 0 \\[3mm]
k_0^2 + \dfrac{k_0^2(\varepsilon - 1)}{d} \displaystyle\sum_{j=1}^{2K}(-1)^j x_j, & n = 0
\end{cases}
\tag{3.121}
$$

$$
c_n^{(2)} =
\begin{cases}
\dfrac{i(1/\varepsilon - 1)}{2\pi n k_0^2} \displaystyle\sum_{j=1}^{2K}(-1)^j \exp\left(-i\frac{2\pi}{d}nx_j\right), & n \neq 0 \\[3mm]
1/k_0^2 + \dfrac{(1/\varepsilon - 1)}{k_0^2 d} \displaystyle\sum_{j=1}^{2K}(-1)^j x_j, & n = 0
\end{cases}
\tag{3.122}
$$

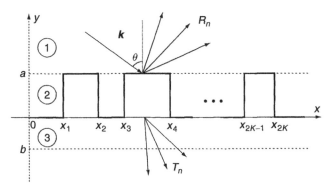

Figure 3.6. Geometry of the task of diffraction by a dielectric binary grating.

where K is the number of grooves in the grating and $x_1, \ldots, x_{2K}$ are the coordinates of the groove boundaries (Fig. 3.6).

Thus, in zones 1 and 3 the solutions are given by Eqs. (3.104) and (3.106), whereas in the modulation zone the solution is found from the set (3.120).

To find the general solution of the set (3.120), one needs to find $4N + 2$ linearly independent partial solutions. With no modulation $[\varepsilon(x, y) = \varepsilon]$, the basis solutions to the set (3.120) take the form

$$\left.\begin{aligned}
H_p^{\pm}(y) &= \exp(\pm i\tilde{\beta}_p y), \quad p = -\overline{N, N}, \\
\tilde{E}_p^{\pm}(y) &= \pm \frac{i\tilde{\beta}_p}{k_0^2 \varepsilon} \exp(\pm i\tilde{\beta}_p y), \quad p = -\overline{N, N}.
\end{aligned}\right\} \tag{3.123}$$

To match the solutions in the modulation zone 2 with the solution in Eq. (3.123) in zone 2, the boundary conditions for the set (3.120) should be given by

$$\left.\begin{aligned}
H^{\mp}{}_{mj}(0) &= \delta_{m-j}, \quad m, j = -\overline{N, N}, \\
\tilde{E}^{\mp}{}_{mj}(0) &= \mp i\tilde{\beta}_m \delta_{m-j}/(k_0^2 \varepsilon), \quad m, j = -\overline{N, N},
\end{aligned}\right\} \tag{3.124}$$

where $\delta_m = \begin{cases} 1, & m = 0, \\ 0, & m \neq 0. \end{cases}$

For convenience of mathematical treatment, we shall introduce $4N+2$ combined vectors of initial conditions in the form

$$\left[\begin{pmatrix} \mathbf{H}_{-N}^+(0) \\ \tilde{\mathbf{E}}_{-N}^+(0) \end{pmatrix}, \ldots, \begin{pmatrix} \mathbf{H}_N^+(0) \\ \tilde{\mathbf{E}}_N^+(0) \end{pmatrix}, \begin{pmatrix} \mathbf{H}_{-N}^-(0) \\ \tilde{\mathbf{E}}_{-N}^-(0) \end{pmatrix}, \ldots, \begin{pmatrix} \mathbf{H}_N^-(0) \\ \tilde{\mathbf{E}}_N^-(0) \end{pmatrix} \right]. \tag{3.125}$$

Let $\Psi_i(y), i = \overline{1, 4N + 2}$ stand for the basis functions vectors

$$\left[\begin{pmatrix} \Psi_{-N}^+(y) \\ \tilde{\Psi}_{-N}^+(y) \end{pmatrix}, \ldots, \begin{pmatrix} \Psi_N^+(y) \\ \tilde{\Psi}_N^+(y) \end{pmatrix}, \begin{pmatrix} \Psi_{-N}^-(y) \\ \tilde{\Psi}_{-N}^-(y) \end{pmatrix}, \ldots, \begin{pmatrix} \Psi_N^-(y) \\ \tilde{\Psi}_N^-(y) \end{pmatrix} \right] \tag{3.126}$$

deduced from solving the set (3.120) with the initial conditions in Eq. (3.125). Then, the general solution to the set takes the form

$$H_m(y) = \sum_{j=-N}^{N} C_j^- \Psi_{mj}^-(y) + \sum_{j=-N}^{N} C_j^+ \Psi_{mj}^+(y), \quad m = -\overline{N, N}, \quad (3.127)$$

$$\tilde{E}_m(y) = \sum_{j=-N}^{N} C_j^- \tilde{\Psi}_{mj}^-(y) + \sum_{j=-N}^{N} C_j^+ \tilde{\Psi}_{mj}^+(y), \quad m = -\overline{N, N}. \quad (3.128)$$

In the search for the Rayleigh coefficients of transmission, T_n, and reflection, R_n, in Eqs. (3.104) and (3.106), utilize the condition that the field $H_z(x, y)$ and the function $\tilde{E}_x(x, y)$ are continuous on the boundaries of the modulation zone at $y = 0$ and at $y = a$.

The continuity conditions at $y = 0$ produce the following functional equations:

$$\sum_{n=-N}^{N} T_n \exp(i\alpha_n x) = \sum_{n=-N}^{N} H_n(0) \exp(i\alpha_n x)$$

$$= \sum_{n=-N}^{N} \left(\sum_{j=-N}^{N} C_j^- \Psi_{nj}^-(0) + \sum_{j=-N}^{N} C_j^+ \Psi_{nj}^+(0) \right) \exp(i\alpha_n x)$$

$$= \sum_{n=-N}^{N} (C_n^- + C_n^+) \exp(i\alpha_n x), \quad (3.129)$$

$$-\frac{i}{k_0^2 \varepsilon} \sum_{n=-N}^{N} \tilde{\beta}_n T_n \exp(i\alpha_n x) = \sum_{n=-N}^{N} \tilde{E}_n(0) \exp(i\alpha_n x)$$

$$= \sum_{n=-N}^{N} \left(\sum_{j=-N}^{N} C_j^- \tilde{\Psi}_{nj}^-(0) + \sum_{j=-N}^{N} C_j^+ \tilde{\Psi}_{nj}^+(0) \right) \exp(i\alpha_n x)$$

$$= \sum_{n=-N}^{N} \frac{i\tilde{\beta}_n}{k_0^2 \varepsilon} (C_n^+ - C_n^-) \exp(i\alpha_n x). \quad (3.130)$$

Multiplying both sides of Eqs. (3.129) and (3.130) by $\exp(-i\alpha_p x)$, $p = -\overline{N, N}$ and integrating over period produces

$$\left. \begin{aligned} T_p &= C_p^- + C_p^+, \\ -T_p &= -C_p^- + C_p^+. \end{aligned} \right\} \quad (3.131)$$

The solution to the set (3.131) takes the form

$$\left. \begin{aligned} T_p &= C_p^-, \\ C_p^+ &= 0. \end{aligned} \right\} \quad (3.132)$$

According to Eq. (3.132), we find that in the modulation zone the field is given by

$$
\begin{pmatrix} H_m(y) \\ \tilde{E}_m(y) \end{pmatrix} = \sum_{j=-N}^{N} C_j^- \begin{pmatrix} \Psi_{mj}^-(y) \\ \tilde{\Psi}_{mj}^-(y) \end{pmatrix} = \sum_{j=-N}^{N} T_j \begin{pmatrix} \Psi_{mj}^-(y) \\ \tilde{\Psi}_{mj}^-(y) \end{pmatrix}, \quad m = -\overline{N, N}. \quad (3.133)
$$

The conditions that the functions $H_z(x, y)$ and $\tilde{E}_x(x, y)$ should be continuous on the upper boundary of the modulation zone (at $y = a$) produce the following equations:

$$
\sum_{n=-N}^{N} R_n \exp(i\alpha_n x + i\beta_n a) + \exp(i\alpha_0 x - i\beta_0 a) = \sum_{n=-N}^{N} H_n(a) \exp(i\alpha_n x)
$$

$$
= \sum_{n=-N}^{N} \left(\sum_{j=-N}^{N} T_j \Psi_{nj}^-(a) \right) \exp(i\alpha_n x), \quad (3.134)
$$

$$
\frac{i\beta_n}{k_0^2} \sum_{n=-N}^{N} R_n \exp(i\alpha_n x + i\beta_n a) - \frac{i\beta_0}{k_0^2} \exp(i\alpha_0 x - i\beta_0 a)
$$

$$
= \sum_{n=-N}^{N} \tilde{E}_n(a) \exp(i\alpha_n x) = \sum_{n=-N}^{N} \left(\sum_{j=-N}^{N} T_j \tilde{\Psi}_{nj}^-(a) \right) \exp(i\alpha_n x). \quad (3.135)
$$

Multiplying both sides of Eqs. (3.134) and (3.135) by $\exp(-i\alpha_p x)$ and integrating over the period produces two sets of linear equations:

$$
\sum_{j=-N}^{N} T_j \Psi_{pj}^-(a) = R_p \exp(i\beta_p a) + \delta_p \exp(-i\beta_0 a), \quad p = -\overline{N, N}, \quad (3.136)
$$

$$
\sum_{j=-N}^{N} T_j \tilde{\Psi}_{pj}^-(a) = R_p \exp(i\beta_p a) \frac{i\beta_p}{k_0^2} - \delta_p \exp(-i\beta_0 a) \frac{i\beta_0}{k_0^2}, \quad p = -\overline{N, N}. \quad (3.137)
$$

The sets of linear equations (3.136) and (3.137) can be put in a matrix form:

$$
\mathbf{H}_{01} \cdot \mathbf{T} = \mathbf{H}_{02} \mathbf{R} + \exp(-i\beta_0 a) \cdot \boldsymbol{\delta},
$$

$$
H_{01pj} = \Psi_{pj}^-(a), \quad H_{02pj} = \delta_{p-j} \cdot \exp(i\beta_p a), \quad p, j = -\overline{N, N}, \quad (3.138)
$$

$$
\mathbf{H}_{11} \cdot \mathbf{T} = \mathbf{H}_{12} \mathbf{R} - \frac{i\beta_0}{k_0^2} \exp(-i\beta_0 a) \cdot \boldsymbol{\delta},
$$

$$
H_{11pj} = \tilde{\Psi}_{pj}^-(a), \quad H_{12pj} = \delta_{p-j} \cdot \frac{i\beta_p}{k_0^2} \exp(i\beta_p a), \quad p, j = -\overline{N, N}. \quad (3.139)
$$

Here $\boldsymbol{\delta}$ is a column vector whose central element is unit and the remaining elements are equal to zero. From Eqs. (3.138) and (3.139), the Rayleigh coefficient vectors are given by

$$
\mathbf{T} = 2 \exp(-i\beta_0 a)(\mathbf{H}_{01} - \mathbf{D}_\beta \cdot \mathbf{H}_{11})^{-1} \cdot \boldsymbol{\delta}, \quad (3.140)
$$

$$
\mathbf{R} = \mathbf{H}_{12}^{-1} \mathbf{H}_{11} \cdot \mathbf{T} + \exp(-2i\beta_0 a) \cdot \boldsymbol{\delta}, \quad (3.141)
$$

where $\mathbf{D}_\beta$ is a diagonal matrix with elements $k_0^2/i\beta_p$, $p = -\overline{N, N}$.

For the earlier discussed diffraction problem, the effect of the substrate on the grating operation can be easily estimated. The substrate is designated by a dashed line in Figure 3.5. We shall assume that $\varepsilon = 1$ below the substrate. Then, the field behind the substrate (at $y < b$) takes the form

$$H_z(x, y) = \sum_{n=-\infty}^{\infty} T_n \exp[i(\alpha_n x - \beta_n y)]. \tag{3.142}$$

The field of Eq. (3.142) differs from the field of Eq. (3.106) in zone 3 by the form of the coefficient β_n. According to Eq. (3.123), the general solution to the set (3.120) at $b < y < 0$ is given by

$$\begin{cases} H_p(y) = C_p^+ \exp(i\tilde{\beta}_p y) + C_p^- \exp(-i\tilde{\beta}_p y), & p = \overline{-N, N}, \\ \tilde{E}_p(y) = C_p^+ \dfrac{i\tilde{\beta}_p}{k_0^2 \varepsilon} \exp(i\tilde{\beta}_p y) - C_p^- \dfrac{i\tilde{\beta}_p}{k_0^2 \varepsilon} \exp(-i\tilde{\beta}_p y), & p = \overline{-N, N}. \end{cases} \tag{3.143}$$

Utilize the condition that the functions $H_z(x, y)$ and $\tilde{E}_x(x, y)$ are continuous on the substrate–air interface to express the coefficients $C_p^\pm$ in Eq. (3.143) through the coefficients T_n

$$\sum_{n=-N}^{N} T_n \exp(i\alpha_n x - i\beta_n b) = \sum_{n=-N}^{N} H_n(b) \exp(i\alpha_n x)$$

$$= \sum_{n=-N}^{N} [C_n^+ \exp(i\tilde{\beta}_n b) + C_n^- \exp(-i\tilde{\beta}_n b)] \exp(i\alpha_n x),$$

$$\frac{-i}{k_0^2} \sum_{n=-N}^{N} \beta_n T_n \exp(i\alpha_n x - i\beta_n b) = \sum_{n=-N}^{N} \tilde{E}_n(b) \exp(i\alpha_n x)$$

$$= \frac{i}{k_0^2 \varepsilon} \sum_{n=-N}^{N} \tilde{\beta}_n [C_n^+ \exp(i\tilde{\beta}_n b)$$

$$- C_n^- \exp(-i\tilde{\beta}_n b)] \exp(i\alpha_n x). \tag{3.144}$$

Multiplying the preceding functional equation by $\exp(-i\alpha_p x)$ and integrating over period produces the relation between the coefficients $C_p^\pm$ and T_n in the form

$$\begin{cases} T_p \exp(-i\beta_p b) = C_p^+ \exp(i\tilde{\beta}_p b) + C_p^- \exp(-i\tilde{\beta}_p b), \\ -T_p \exp(-i\beta_p b) = \dfrac{\tilde{\beta}_p}{\beta_p \varepsilon} (C_p^+ \exp(i\tilde{\beta}_p b) - C_p^- \exp(-i\tilde{\beta}_p b)), & p = \overline{-N, N}. \end{cases} \tag{3.145}$$

From Eq. (3.145) it follows that

$$\begin{cases} C_p^- = T_p \cdot \gamma_p, \\ C_p^+ = T_p \cdot \mu_p, & p = \overline{-N, N}, \end{cases} \tag{3.146}$$

where

$$\begin{cases} \gamma_p = \dfrac{\tilde{\beta}_p + \varepsilon\beta_p}{2\tilde{\beta}_p} \cdot \exp[-ib(\beta_p - \tilde{\beta}_p)], \\[4mm] \mu_p = \exp(-2i\tilde{\beta}_p b)\dfrac{\tilde{\beta}_p - \varepsilon\beta_p}{2\tilde{\beta}_p} \cdot \exp[-ib(\beta_p + \tilde{\beta}_p)]. \end{cases} \tag{3.147}$$

Substituting Eq. (3.146) into Eq. (3.143) yields the functions $H_p(y)$, $\tilde{E}_p(y)$ in the explicit form:

$$\begin{cases} H_p(y) = T_p[\mu_p \exp(i\tilde{\beta}_p y) + \gamma_p \exp(-i\tilde{\beta}_p y)], & p = -\overline{N, N}, \\[4mm] \tilde{E}_p(y) = T_p \dfrac{i\tilde{\beta}_p}{k_0^2 \varepsilon}[\mu_p \exp(i\tilde{\beta}_p y) - \gamma_p \exp(-i\tilde{\beta}_p y)], & p = -\overline{N, N}. \end{cases} \tag{3.148}$$

Thus, with the substrate taken into account, in zone 3 there are both transmitted waves propagated in opposition to the Oy-axis and those reflected from the substrate–air interface propagated along the Oy-axis. To match the solution for the modulation zone with the solution for zone 3, Eq. (3.148), we shall define the boundary conditions for the set (3.120) as follows:

$$\begin{cases} H_{mj}^+(0) = \mu_m \delta_{m-j}, & H_{mj}^-(0) = \gamma_m \delta_{m-j}, \\[2mm] \tilde{E}_{mj}^+(0) = i\chi_m \mu_m \delta_{mj}, & \tilde{E}_{mj}^-(0) = -i\chi_m \gamma_m \delta_{m-j}, & m, j = -\overline{N, N}, \\[2mm] \chi_m = \tilde{\beta}_m/(k_0^2 \varepsilon). \end{cases} \tag{3.149}$$

From the condition that the functions $H_z(x, y)$ and $\tilde{E}_x(x, y)$ are continuous on the low boundary of the modulation zone, it follows that

$$\left.\begin{array}{l} T_p(\mu_p + \gamma_p) = \mu_p C_p^+ + \gamma_p C_p^-, \\[2mm] T_p(\mu_p - \gamma_p) = \mu_p C_p^+ - \gamma_p C_p^-. \end{array}\right\} \tag{3.150}$$

The solution to Eq. (3.150) takes the form

$$T_p = C_p^+ = C_p^-. \tag{3.151}$$

The general solution to the set (3.120) is given by

$$H_m(y) = \sum_{j=-N}^{N} T_j[\Psi_{mj}^-(y) + \Psi_{mj}^+(y)], \quad m = -\overline{N, N}, \tag{3.152}$$

$$\tilde{E}_m(y) = \sum_{j=-N}^{N} T_j[\tilde{\Psi}_{mj}^-(y) + \tilde{\Psi}_{mj}^+(y)], \quad m = -\overline{N, N}. \tag{3.153}$$

Next, we shall determine the Rayleigh coefficients of transmission, T_n, and reflection, R_n, in Eqs. (3.104) and (3.140) from the condition of the continuous field $H_z(x, y)$ and function $\tilde{E}_x(x, y)$ on the upper boundary of the modulation zone (at $y = a$). From the continuity condition, the coefficients T_n and R_n are easily derived in the form of Eqs. (3.140) and (3.141) with the matrices $\mathbf{H}_{01}$ and $\mathbf{H}_{11}$ given by

$$\mathbf{H}_{01pj} = \Psi_{pj}^+(a) + \Psi_{pj}^-(a), \quad p, j = -\overline{N, N},$$

$$\mathbf{H}_{11pj} = \tilde{\Psi}_{pj}^+(a) + \tilde{\Psi}_{pj}^-(a), \quad p, j = -\overline{N, N}. \tag{3.154}$$

For a continuous-profile grating, the set (3.120) is treated using numerical methods similar to the Ruhnge-Kutt method. For a binary grating, the Fourier coefficients in Eqs. (3.121) and (3.122) are not dependent on the variable y. In this case, the field within the modulation zone is defined by a set of differential equations of the first order with constant coefficients. The solution to the set (3.120) with constant coefficients and with the boundary condition $\mathbf{X}_0$ defined in Eq. (3.125) or Eq. (3.149) can be represented in a compact matrix form

$$\begin{pmatrix} \Psi_p^-(y) \\ \tilde{\Psi}_p^-(y) \end{pmatrix} = \exp(\mathbf{A}^{TM} \cdot y)\mathbf{X}_0, \tag{3.155}$$

where $\mathbf{A}^{TM}$ is the matrix of the set (3.120) with the constant Fourier coefficients $c_n^{(1)}$, $c_n^{(2)}$ defined in Eqs. (3.121) and (3.122). According to Eq. (3.120), the $\mathbf{A}^{TM}$ matrix takes the form

$$\mathbf{A}^{TM} = \begin{pmatrix} \mathbf{NU} & \mathbf{F}_1 \\ \mathbf{F}_2 & \mathbf{NU} \end{pmatrix}, \tag{3.156}$$

where $\mathbf{NU}$ are zero matrices of size $(2N + 1) \times (2N + 1)$ and $\mathbf{F}_1$ and $\mathbf{F}_2$ are matrices composed of the Fourier coefficients

$$F_{1_{i,j}} = c_{i-j}^{(1)}, \quad F_{2_{i,j}} = \alpha_{-(N+1)+i}\alpha_{-(N+1)+j}c_{i-j}^{(2)} - \delta_{i-j}, \quad i, j = \overline{1, 2N + 1}. \tag{3.157}$$

The matrix representation in Eq. (3.155) allows the matrices $\mathbf{H}_{01}$ and $\mathbf{H}_{11}$ in Eqs. (3.140) and (3.141) to be compactly expressed through the system matrix and boundary conditions in Eq. (3.125) or (3.149) as follows:

$$\begin{pmatrix} \mathbf{H}_{01} \\ \mathbf{H}_{11} \end{pmatrix} = \exp(\mathbf{A}^{TM} \cdot a) \cdot \mathbf{BC}, \tag{3.158}$$

where the $\mathbf{BC}$ matrix is made up of the second half of the initial conditions vectors in Eq. (3.125):

$$\mathbf{BC} = \left[\begin{pmatrix} \mathbf{H}_{-N}^-(0) \\ \tilde{\mathbf{E}}_{-N}^-(0) \end{pmatrix}, \ldots, \begin{pmatrix} \mathbf{H}_N^-(0) \\ \tilde{\mathbf{E}}_N^-(0) \end{pmatrix} \right] = \begin{pmatrix} \mathbf{E} \\ \mathbf{DE} \end{pmatrix} \tag{3.159}$$

provided that the computation is carried out without regard to the substrate effect, with $\mathbf{E}$ being a unit matrix of size $(2N + 1) \times (2N + 1)$ and $\mathbf{DE}$ being a diagonal matrix with elements

$$DE_{jj} = -i\tilde{\beta}_j/k_0^2\varepsilon, \quad j = -\overline{N, N}. \tag{3.160}$$

With due regard for the substrate effect, the **BC** matrix is made up of the initial conditions vectors in Eq. (3.149)

$$\mathbf{BC} = \left[\begin{pmatrix} \mathbf{H}_{-N}^{-}(0) + \mathbf{H}_{-N}^{+}(0) \\ \tilde{\mathbf{E}}_{-N}^{-}(0) + \tilde{\mathbf{E}}_{-N}^{+}(0) \end{pmatrix}, \ldots, \begin{pmatrix} \mathbf{H}_{N}^{-}(0) + \mathbf{H}_{N}^{+}(0) \\ \tilde{\mathbf{E}}_{N}^{-}(0) + \tilde{\mathbf{E}}_{N}^{+}(0) \end{pmatrix} \right]. \tag{3.161}$$

The matrix form in Eq. (3.158) for a binary grating may be used to solve the problem of diffraction by a continuous-profile grating. Actually, introduce the breakdown y_i, $i = \overline{0, N}$, $y_0 = 0$, $y_N = a$, of the modulation zone onto N layers. In every layer $y_{i-1} \leq y \leq y_i$, the continuous profile can be approximated by a binary profile. Putting in Eq. (3.120) at $y_{i-1} \leq y \leq y_i$

$$c_n^{(1)}(y) \approx c_n^{(1)}(\tilde{y}_i), \quad c_n^{(2)}(y) \approx c_n^{(2)}(\tilde{y}_i) \tag{3.162}$$

where $\tilde{y}_i = (y_{i-1} + y_i)/2$, we shall approximate at $y_{i-1} \leq y \leq y_i$ the set of differential equations in Eq. (3.120) with variable coefficients with a set of equations with constant coefficients. Putting the solutions to the set of differential equations as analytical matrices, the $\mathbf{H}_{01}$ and $\mathbf{H}_{11}$ matrices are given by

$$\begin{pmatrix} \mathbf{H}_{01} \\ \mathbf{H}_{11} \end{pmatrix} = \{ \exp[\mathbf{A}^{TM}(\tilde{y}_N) \cdot (a - y_{N-1})] \times \cdots$$

$$\times \exp[A^{TM}(\tilde{y}_2) \cdot (y_2 - y_1)] \exp[A^{TM}(\tilde{y}_1) \cdot y_1] \} \cdot$$

$$\cdot \mathbf{BC} = \left(\prod_{i=N}^{1} \exp[A^{TM}(\tilde{y}_i) \cdot (y_i - y_{i-1})] \right) \cdot \mathbf{BC}, \tag{3.163}$$

where **BC** is the matrix of initial conditions in Eq. (3.159) or (3.161) and $\mathbf{A}^{TM}(\tilde{y}_i)$ is the matrix of the set (3.120) at $c_n^{(1)}(y) = c_n^{(1)}(\tilde{y}_i)$ and $c_n^{(2)}(y) = c_n^{(2)}(\tilde{y}_i)$. The Rayleigh coefficients, R_n and T_n, are also determined from Eqs. (3.140) and (3.141). Note that the limit of the matrix product

$$\Omega_N(\mathbf{A}^{TM}) = \prod_{i=N}^{1} \exp[\mathbf{A}^{TM}(\tilde{y}_i) \cdot (y_i - y_{i-1})] \tag{3.164}$$

in the right side of Eq. (3.163) at $\Delta y_i = (y_i - y_{i-1}) \to 0$ and $N \to \infty$ corresponds to a multiplicative integral $\Omega_0^a(\mathbf{A}^{TM})$ [9], which is the solution to the set of differential equations with variable coefficients. The product in Eq. (3.164) corresponds to a standard approximation of the multiplicative integral when the set of differential equations with variable coefficients is solved by solving N sets of differential equations with constant coefficients [9].

3.3.2 TE-Polarization

Consider TE-polarization. Assuming in the basis equations (3.109) that $\mathbf{E}(x, y) = [0, 0, E_z(x, y)]$, we obtain

$$\frac{\partial E_z(x, y)}{\partial y} = ik_0 H_x(x, y), \quad \frac{\partial H_y(x, y)}{\partial z} = 0,$$

$$\frac{\partial E_z(x, y)}{\partial x} = -ik_0 H_y(x, y), \quad \frac{\partial H_x(x, y)}{\partial z} = 0,$$

$$H_z(x, y) = 0 \qquad \frac{\partial H_y(x, y)}{\partial x} - \frac{\partial H_x(x, y)}{\partial y} = -ik_0 \varepsilon E_z(x, y). \qquad (3.165)$$

On the interface of two dielectrics, the tangential components $E_z(x, y)$ and $H_x(x, y)$ of the vectors $\mathbf{E}$ and $\mathbf{H}$ are continuous. As distinct from TM-polarization, the derivative $(\partial E_z(x, y)/\partial y) = ik_0 H_x(x, y)$ on the interface (at $x = 0$) is continuous:

$$\frac{1}{ik_0} \frac{\partial E_z(x, +0)}{\partial y} = H_x(x, +0) = H_x(x, -0) = \frac{1}{ik_0} \frac{\partial E_z(x, -0)}{\partial y}. \qquad (3.166)$$

Hence, the $E_z(x, y)$ component in the modulation zone satisfies the Helmholtz equation

$$\Delta E_z(x, y) + k^2(x, y) E_z(x, y) = 0. \qquad (3.167)$$

The $E_z(x, y)$ function is quasi-periodic [5]:

$$E_z(x, y) = \sum_{m=-\infty}^{\infty} E_m(y) \exp(i\alpha_m x). \qquad (3.168)$$

Substituting Eqs. (3.168) and (3.118) into Eq. (3. 167) yields a set of $2N + 1$ differential equations of second order

$$\frac{d^2 E_n(y)}{dy^2} - \alpha_n^2 E_n(y) + \sum_{m=-N}^{N} c_{n-m}^{(1)}(y) E_m(y) = 0, \quad n = -\overline{N, N}. \qquad (3.169)$$

To find the general solution to the set (3.169), one needs to find $2(2N + 1)$ linearly independent partial solutions. Without modulation [$\varepsilon(x, y) = \varepsilon$], the basis solutions to the set (3.169) take the form

$$E_p^{\pm}(y) = \exp(\pm i\tilde{\beta}_p y), \quad p = -\overline{N, N}. \qquad (3.170)$$

To match the solution in the modulation zone with the solution in Eq. (3.170) in zone 3, define $2(2N + 1)$ vectors of the boundary conditions for the set in Eq. (3.169) as follows:

$$\left. \begin{array}{l} E_{mj}^{\mp}(0) = \delta_{m-j}, \\[2mm] \dfrac{\partial E_{mj}^{\mp}(0)}{\partial y} = \mp i\beta_m \delta_{m-j}, \quad m, j = -\overline{N, N}. \end{array} \right\} \qquad (3.171)$$

The general solution to the set (3.169) takes the form

$$E_m(y) = \sum_{j=-N}^{N} C_j^- E_{mj}^-(y) + \sum_{j=-N}^{N} C_j^+ E_{mj}^+(y), \quad m = -\overline{N, N}. \qquad (3.172)$$

Substituting Eq. (3.172) into Eq. (3.168) produces the field in the modulation zone

$$E_z(x, y) = \sum_{m=-N}^{N} \left(\sum_{j=-N}^{N} C_j^- E_{mj}^-(y) + \sum_{j=-N}^{N} C_j^+ E_{mj}^+(y) \right) \exp(ik\alpha_m x). \qquad (3.173)$$

To derive the Rayleigh coefficients of transmission, T_n, and reflection, R_n, in Eqs. (3.104) and (3.106) put down the condition of continuity for the field $E_z(x, y)$ and the derivative $\partial E_z(x, y)/\partial y$ along the modulation zone boundary at $y = 0$ and $y = a$. As in the case with TM-polarization, the condition of continuity of the field and the derivative easily gives $T_p = C_p^-$ and $C_p^+ = 0$ at $y = 0$, with the field in the modulation zone taking the form

$$E(x, y) = \sum_{m=-N}^{N} \sum_{j=-N}^{N} T_j E_{mj}^-(y) \exp(ik\alpha_m x). \qquad (3.174)$$

On the upper boundary of the modulation zone, the conditions of continuity of the field and derivative are given by

$$\sum_{m=-N}^{N} \left(\sum_{j=-N}^{N} T_j E_{mj}^-(a) \right) \exp(ik\alpha_m x) = \sum_{m=-N}^{N} R_m \exp(i\beta_m a) \exp(i\alpha_m x)$$
$$+ \exp(-i\beta_0 a) \exp(i\alpha_0 x), \qquad (3.175)$$

$$\sum_{m=-N}^{N} \left(\sum_{j=-N}^{N} T_j \frac{\partial E_{mj}^-(a)}{\partial y} \right) \exp(i\alpha_m x) = \sum_{m=-N}^{N} i\beta_m R_m \exp(i\beta_m a) \exp(i\alpha_m x)$$
$$- i\beta_0 \exp(-i\beta_0 a) \exp(i\alpha_0 x). \qquad (3.176)$$

Multiplying both sides in Eqs. (3.175) and (3.176) by $\exp(-i\alpha_p x)$ and integrating with respect to period yields two sets of linear equations in the form

$$\sum_{j=-N}^{N} T_j E_{pj}^-(a) = R_p \exp(i\beta_p a) + \delta_p \exp(-i\beta_0 a), \quad p = -\overline{N, N}, \qquad (3.177)$$

$$\sum_{j=-N}^{N} T_j \frac{\partial E_{pj}^-(a)}{\partial y} = i\beta_p R_p \exp(i\beta_p a) - \delta_p i\beta_0 \exp(-i\beta_0 a), \quad p = -\overline{N, N}, \qquad (3.178)$$

which in the matrix form are given by

$$\mathbf{E}_{01} \cdot \mathbf{T} = \mathbf{E}_{02}\mathbf{R} + \exp(-i\beta_0 a)\boldsymbol{\delta},$$
$$E_{01pj} = E_{pj}^-(a), \quad E_{02pj} = \delta_{p-j} \cdot \exp(i\beta_p a), \quad p, j = -N, N, \qquad (3.179)$$
$$\mathbf{E}_{11} \cdot \mathbf{T} = \mathbf{E}_{12}\mathbf{R} - i\beta_0 \exp(-i\beta_0 a)\boldsymbol{\delta},$$
$$E_{11pj} = \frac{\partial E_{pj}^-(a)}{\partial y}, \quad E_{12pj} = \delta_{p-j} \cdot i\beta_p \exp(i\beta_p a), \quad p, j = -N, N. \qquad (3.180)$$

From Eqs. (3.179) and (3.180), the Rayleigh coefficients are given by

$$\mathbf{T} = -2i\beta_0 \exp(-i\beta_0 a)(\mathbf{E}_{11} - \mathbf{D}_\beta \cdot \mathbf{E}_{01})^{-1}\boldsymbol{\delta}, \qquad (3.181)$$

$$\mathbf{R} = \mathbf{E}_{02}^{-1}\mathbf{E}_{01} \cdot \mathbf{T} + \exp(-2i\beta_0 a)\boldsymbol{\delta}, \qquad (3.182)$$

where $\mathbf{D}_\beta$ is a diagonal matrix with the elements $i\beta_p$, $p = \overline{-N, N}$ and $\boldsymbol{\delta}$ is a column vector composed of zeros, excepting the "one" at the center.

Consider the diffraction by the grating with due account for the substrate. The field in the zone behind the substrate is given by

$$E_z(x, y) = \sum_{n=-\infty}^{\infty} T_n \exp[i(\alpha_n x - \beta_n y)]. \qquad (3.183)$$

where the coefficients β_n defined in Eq. (3.105).

The general solution to the set in Eq. (3.169) in zone 3 takes the form

$$E_p^{\pm}(y) = C_p^{+} \exp(i\tilde{\beta}_p y) + C_p^{-} \exp(-i\tilde{\beta}_p y), \quad p = \overline{-N, N}. \qquad (3.184)$$

Using the condition of continuity for the function $E_z(x, y)$ and its derivative on the substrate–air interface, the $E_p(y)$ functions are given in an explicit form

$$E_p(y) = T_p[\mu_p \exp(i\tilde{\beta}_p y) + \gamma_p \exp(-i\tilde{\beta}_p y)], \quad p = \overline{-N, N}, \qquad (3.185)$$

where

$$\left.\begin{aligned}
\gamma_p &= \frac{\tilde{\beta}_p + \beta_p}{2\tilde{\beta}_p} \cdot \exp[-ib(\beta_p - \tilde{\beta}_p)], \\
\mu_p &= \exp(-2i\tilde{\beta}_p b)\frac{\tilde{\beta}_p - \beta_p}{2\tilde{\beta}_p} \cdot \exp[-ib(\beta_p + \tilde{\beta}_p)].
\end{aligned}\right\} \qquad (3.186)$$

To match the solution in the modulation zone with the solution (3.185) in zone 3, let us define the boundary conditions for the set in Eq. (3.169) as follows:

$$\left.\begin{aligned}
E_{mj}^{+}(0) &= \mu_m\delta_{m-j}, \quad E_{mj}^{-}(0) = \gamma_m\delta_{m-j}, \\
\frac{\partial E_{mj}^{+}(0)}{\partial y} &= i\tilde{\beta}_m\mu_m\delta_{m-j}, \quad \frac{\partial E_{mj}^{-}(0)}{\partial y} = -i\tilde{\beta}_m\gamma_m\delta_{m-j}, \quad m, j = \overline{-N, N}.
\end{aligned}\right\} \qquad (3.187)$$

Using the continuity condition for the field and derivative on the low boundary of the modulation zone, we find, as for TM-polarization, that

$$T_p = C_p^{+} = C_p^{-}, \qquad (3.188)$$

with the general solution to the set (3.169) taking the form

$$E_m(y) = \sum_{j=-N}^{N} T_j[E_{mj}^{-}(y) + E_{mj}^{+}(y)], \quad m = -N, N. \qquad (3.189)$$

Next, the Rayleigh coefficients of transmission, T_n, and reflection, R_n, in Eqs. (3.104) and (3.183) are derived from the continuity condition for the field and derivative on the upper boundary of the modulation zone. From the continuity conditions, the relations for the vectors of the Rayleigh coefficients are easily derived in the form of Eqs. (3.181) and (3.182), where the matrices $\mathbf{E}_{01}$ and $\mathbf{E}_{11}$ take the form

$$\mathbf{E}_{01pj} = E_{pj}^{-}(a) + E_{pj}^{+}(a), \quad p, j = -\overline{N, N},$$

$$\mathbf{E}_{11pj} = \frac{\partial E_{pj}^{-}(a)}{\partial y} + \frac{\partial E_{pj}^{+}(a)}{\partial y}, \quad p, j = -\overline{N, N}. \tag{3.190}$$

For a binary grating, the Fourier coefficients of Eq. (3.121) are z-independent. In this case, the field in the modulation zone is described by a set of differential equations of second order with constant coefficients. Write down the solution to the set of equations with constant coefficients for a boundary condition number m in Eq. (3.171) or (3.187) in a matrix form

$$\mathbf{E}_{m}^{-}(y) = \cos\left(\sqrt{\mathbf{A}^{TE}} \cdot y\right) \mathbf{E}_{m}^{-}(0) + \frac{\sin\left(\sqrt{\mathbf{A}^{TE}} \cdot y\right)}{\sqrt{\mathbf{A}^{TE}}} \frac{\partial \mathbf{E}_{m}^{-}(0)}{\partial y}, \tag{3.191}$$

where

$$\mathbf{A}_{i,j}^{TE} = -\alpha_{-(N+1)+i}^{2}\delta_{i,j} + c_{i-j}^{(1)}, \quad i, j = \overline{1, 2N+1} \tag{3.192}$$

is the matrix of the set (3.169) with constant Fourier coefficients $c_n^{(1)}$ defined in Eq. (3.121). The preceding matrix representation allows the $\mathbf{E}_{01}$ and $\mathbf{E}_{11}$ matrices in Eqs. (3.181) and (3.182) to be expressed through the matrix of Eq. (3.192) and the boundary conditions in Eqs. (3.171) and (3.187) are as follows:

$$\left.\begin{array}{l} \mathbf{E}_{01} = \cos\left(\sqrt{\mathbf{A}^{TE}} \cdot a\right) \mathbf{E} + \dfrac{\sin\left(\sqrt{\mathbf{A}^{TE}} \cdot a\right)}{\sqrt{\mathbf{A}}^{TE}} \cdot \mathbf{DE}, \\[4mm] \mathbf{E}_{11} = -\sqrt{\mathbf{A}^{TE}} \sin\left(\sqrt{\mathbf{A}^{TE}} \cdot a\right) \mathbf{E} + \cos\left(\sqrt{\mathbf{A}^{TE}} \cdot a\right) \cdot \mathbf{DE}. \end{array}\right\} \tag{3.193}$$

When calculating with no substrate, the matrices $\mathbf{E}$ and $\mathbf{DE}$ in Eq. (3.193) are the unit and diagonal matrices with the elements $DE_{jj} = -i\beta_j$, $j = -\overline{N, N}$, respectively. When taking the substrate into account, the $\mathbf{E}$ and $\mathbf{DE}$ matrices are diagonal, with their elements given by $E_{jj} = \mu_j + \gamma_j$, $j = -\overline{N, N}$ and $DE_{jj} = i\tilde{\beta}_j(\mu_j - \gamma_j)$, $j = -\overline{N, N}$, respectively.

The $\mathbf{E}_{01}$ and $\mathbf{E}_{11}$ matrices can also be expressed through the matrix exponent in a form similar to Eq. (3.158) for TM-polarization. Actually, replacing the set of $2N + 1$ differential equations of second order, Eq. (3.169), by the equivalent set of $4N + 2$ differential equations of first order gives

$$\begin{pmatrix} \mathbf{E}_{01} \\ \mathbf{E}_{11} \end{pmatrix} = \exp(\mathbf{A}_{1}^{TE} \cdot a) \begin{pmatrix} \mathbf{E} \\ \mathbf{DE} \end{pmatrix}, \tag{3.194}$$

where $\mathbf{A}_1^{TE} = \begin{pmatrix} \mathbf{NU} & \mathbf{E} \\ -\mathbf{A}^{TE} & \mathbf{NU} \end{pmatrix}$, $\mathbf{NU}$ are zero matrices of size $(2N+1) \times (2N+1)$ and $\mathbf{E}$ is a unit matrix.

The matrix relations in Eqs. (3.193) and (3.194) for a binary grating can be used for solving the problem of diffraction by a continuous-profile grating. Actually, similar to TM-polarization, approximating the continuous profile by a set of N binary layers and deriving the relations for the diffraction by layer from Eqs. (3.193) and (3.194) produces the Rayleigh coefficients R_n and T_n in the form of Eqs. (3.181) and (3.182). When calculating the diffraction by a binary layer using Eq. (3.194), the matrices $\mathbf{E}_{01} = \mathbf{E}_{01}(a)$ and $\mathbf{E}_{11} = \mathbf{E}_{11}(a)$ in Eq. (3.181) and (3.182) are derived from the multiplicative integral, as is the case with TM-polarization. When calculating the diffraction by a layer using Eq. (3.193), the matrices $\mathbf{E}_{01}(a)$ and $\mathbf{E}_{11}(a)$ are found using the following recurrent relations:

$$\mathbf{E}_{01}(y_i) = \cos\left(\sqrt{\mathbf{A}^{TE}(\tilde{y}_i)} \cdot \Delta y_i\right) \mathbf{E}_{01}(y_{i-1}) + \frac{\sin\left(\sqrt{\mathbf{A}^{TE}(\tilde{y}_i)} \cdot \Delta y_i\right)}{\sqrt{\mathbf{A}^{TE}(\tilde{y}_i)}} \cdot \mathbf{E}_{11}(y_{i-1}),$$

$$\mathbf{E}_{11}(y_i) = -\sqrt{\mathbf{A}^{TE}(\tilde{y}_i)} \sin\left(\sqrt{\mathbf{A}^{TE}(\tilde{y}_i)} \cdot \Delta y_i\right) \mathbf{E}_{01}(y_{i-1})$$

$$+ \cos\left(\sqrt{\mathbf{A}^{TE}(\tilde{y}_i)} \cdot \Delta y_i\right) \cdot \mathbf{E}_{11}(y_{i-1}),$$

$$i = \overline{1, N}, \quad \mathbf{E}_{01}(y_0) = \mathbf{E}_{01}(0) = \mathbf{E}, \quad \mathbf{E}_{11}(y_0) = \mathbf{E}_{11}(0) = \mathbf{DE}, \qquad (3.195)$$

where y_i, $i = \overline{0, N}$, $y_0 = 0$, $y_N = a$ is the breakdown of the modulation zone into N layers, $\Delta y_i = y_{i+1} - y_i$, $\tilde{y}_i = (y_{i+1} + y_i)/2$, and $\mathbf{A}^{TE}(\tilde{y}_i)$ is the matrix of the set (3.169) at $c_n^{(1)}(y) = c_n^{(1)}(\tilde{y}_i)$ and $\mathbf{E}$ and $\mathbf{DE}$ are the initial conditions matrices.

Let us use the energy conservation law to determine intensities of the orders corresponding to the transmitted and reflected waves in Eqs. (3.104) and (3.106). Let U_1 and U_2 denote sets of indices corresponding to the transmitted and reflected propagated waves

$$U_1 = \left\{ n \left| \left(\frac{\alpha_n}{k_0}\right)^2 < 1 \right. \right\}, \quad U_2 = \left\{ n \left| \left(\frac{\alpha_n}{k_0\sqrt{\varepsilon}}\right)^2 < 1 \right. \right\}. \qquad (3.196)$$

Consider a rectangle D limited by the straight-line segments $y = 0$, $y = a$ and $x = 0$, $x = d$. On the basis of the energy conservation law, make the Umov-Poynting vector flux, $\mathbf{S} = (c/8\pi)\mathrm{Re}[\mathbf{E}, \mathbf{H}^*]$, over the domain D equal to zero [8] and, thus, get the following normalization conditions for TE-polarization and TM-polarization, respectively:

$$\cos(\theta) = \sum_{n \in U_1} |R_n|^2 \cos(\theta_n) + \sqrt{\varepsilon} \sum_{n \in U_2} |T_n|^2 \cos(\tilde{\theta}_n), \qquad (3.197)$$

$$\cos(\theta) = \sum_{n \in U_1} |R_n|^2 \cos(\theta_n) + \frac{1}{\sqrt{\varepsilon}} \sum_{n \in U_2} |T_n|^2 \cos(\tilde{\theta}_n). \qquad (3.198)$$

The angles θ_n, $\tilde{\theta}_n$ in Eqs. (3.197) and (3.198) correspond to the directions of reflected and transmitted waves in Eqs. (3.104) and (3.106).

According to Eqs. (3.197) and (3.198), the intensities of the reflected and transmitted orders will be denoted by the following normalized values of the Rayleigh coefficients for TE-polarization and TM-polarization, respectively:

$$I_n^R = |R_n|^2 \frac{\cos(\theta_n)}{\cos(\theta)}, \quad I_n^T = \sqrt{\varepsilon} |T_n|^2 \frac{\cos(\tilde{\theta}_n)}{\cos(\theta)}, \quad \left(\sum_{n \in U_1} I_n^R + \sum_{n \in U_2} I_n^T = 1 \right), \quad (3.199)$$

$$I_n^R = |R_n|^2 \frac{\cos(\theta_n)}{\cos(\theta)}, \quad I_n^T = |T_n|^2 \frac{\cos(\tilde{\theta}_n)}{\sqrt{\varepsilon}\cos(\theta)}, \quad \left(\sum_{n \in U_1} I_n^R + \sum_{n \in U_2} I_n^T = 1 \right). \quad (3.200)$$

These relations are analogous to Eq. (3.46) for the case of diffraction by a perfectly reflecting surface.

When calculating the gratings with due regard for the substrate in Eqs. (3.197) and (3.198), we have $\varepsilon = 1$ and $\theta_n = \tilde{\theta}_n$, with order intensities defined by

$$I_n^R = |R_n|^2 \frac{\cos(\theta_n)}{\cos(\theta)}, \quad I_n^T = |T_n|^2 \frac{\cos(\theta_n)}{\cos(\theta)}, \quad \left(\sum_{n \in U_1} I_n^R + \sum_{n \in U_2} I_n^T = 1 \right) \quad (3.201)$$

both for TE-polarization and TM-polarization.

Example 3.3   Consider the operation of a simplest binary grating with a single groove of width $d/2$ over the period d. Figure 3.7 depicts the plots of intensities for the 0th reflected and 0th and -1st transmitted orders as a function of the groove height a for TE-polarization. The order intensities were found using Eqs. (3.181), (3.182), and (3.194) with no regard to the substrate effect, with the parameters $d = \lambda_0$ and $\theta = 30°$ satisfying the Bragg condition $2d \cdot \sin(\theta) = m \cdot \lambda_0$ at $m = 1$. The plot in Figure 3.7

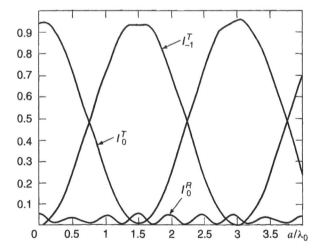

Figure 3.7. Intensities in the -1st and 0th transmitted (I_{-1}^T, I_0^T) and 0th reflected (I_0^R) orders of the binary grating as functions of the groove height for TM-polarization at $d = \lambda_0$, $\theta = 30°$, $\varepsilon = 2.25$.

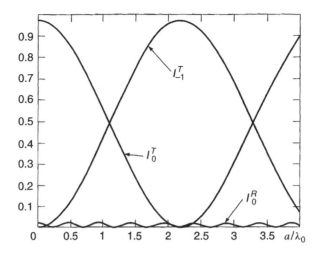

Figure 3.8. Intensities in the −1st and 0th transmitted (I_{-1}^T, I_0^T) and 0th reflected (I_0^R) orders of the binary grating as functions of the groove height for TM-polarization at $d = \lambda_0$, $\theta = 30°$, $\varepsilon = 2.25$.

reveals a number of interesting peculiarities in the binary grating operation. First, for the height of $a \approx 0.75\lambda_0$, the energy is uniformly distributed between the 0th and −1st transmitted orders, that is, at this height the grating may be utilized as a beam splitter. Second, for the groove height of $a \approx 1.6\lambda_0$, about 93 percent of the incident wave energy is redistributed from the 0th to the −1st transmitted order; thus meaning that at the given height the grating may find use as a beam deflector. From the general appearance of the plots in Figure 3.7, one can also suppose that the intensities in the 0th and −1st transmitted orders experience periodic changes.

Figure 3.8 depicts intensities in the binary grating orders as a function of the groove height for TM-polarization. For TM-polarization, the binary grating operates as a beam splitter at a groove height of $a \approx 1.1\lambda_0$. Whereas at $a \approx 2.15\lambda_0$, more than 95 percent of the incident wave energy goes to the −1st transmitted order, thus meaning that the grating operates as a beam deflector.

Figure 3.9 shows intensities of the binary grating orders as a function of the incidence angle θ for TE-polarization. From Figure 3.8, it can be seen that at $\theta \in [25°, 35°]$ more than 80 percent of energy goes to the −1st transmitted order, whereas 0th order has less than 10 percent of energy. This effect allows the binary grating to be utilized as a light shutter, if the incidence angle is varied.

Example 3.4 Consider the operation of a triangle-profile grating

$$f(x) = \begin{cases} ax/d_1, & x \in [0, d_1], \\ -a(x - d)/(d - d_1) + a, & x \in [d, d_1], \end{cases} \tag{3.202}$$

where d_1 is the abscissa of the grating apex.

Figures 3.10–3.12 for TM-polarization show order intensities for a symmetric triangle grating $(d_1 = d/2)$, for a right saw-tooth grating $(d_1 = d)$, and for a left saw-tooth grating $(d_1 = 0)$. The order intensities were estimated using Eqs. (3.140),

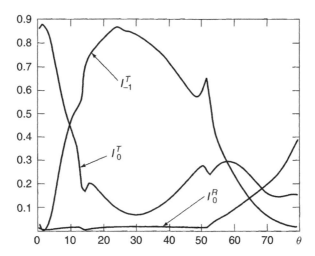

Figure 3.9. Intensities in the -1st and 0th transmitted (I^T_{-1}, I^T_0) and 0th reflected (I^R_0) orders of the binary grating as functions of the incidence angle θ for TE-polarization at $d = \lambda_0$, $a = 1.2\lambda_0$, $\varepsilon = 2.5$.

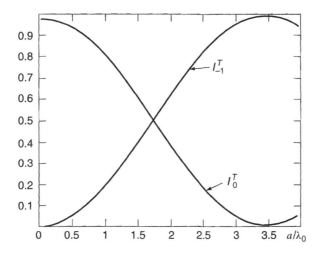

Figure 3.10. Intensities in the -1st and 0th transmitted (I^T_{-1}, I^T_0) of a symmetric triangular grating as functions of the profile height for TM-polarization at $d = \lambda_0$, $\theta = 30°$, $\varepsilon = 2.25$.

(3.141), (3.163) with no regard for the substrate for a period of $d = \lambda_0$ and an incidence angle of $\theta = 30°$. In the course of calculation, in Eq. (3.163) the triangular profile was approximated by 16 binary layers, which corresponds to quantizing the triangular grating profile in 17 levels.

It can be seen from Figure 3.10 that at the profile height of $a \approx 1.7\lambda$ the energy is uniformly distributed between the 0th and -1st transmitted orders, that is the grating operates as a beam splitter. At $a \approx 3.35\lambda$, more than 95 percent of energy goes to the -1st transmitted order, and the grating serves as a beam deflector. Thus, the symmetric triangular and binary gratings in Figures 3.7 and 3.8 are able to split the beam and collect the energy in the -1st order. For a symmetric grating, these effects take place at about 1.6 times greater profile's height. The intensity plots for the right and left saw-tooth gratings in Figures 3.11 and 3.12 show that while varying the profile height it appears impossible to concentrate the energy in the -1st transmitted order. Thus, as distinct from the symmetric binary and triangular gratings, the asymmetric gratings fail to operate as beam deflectors. Note that opposite to the right saw-tooth grating (Fig. 3.11), the left saw-tooth grating (Fig. 3.12) does not allow the energy to be uniformly distributed between the 0th and -1st transmitted orders.

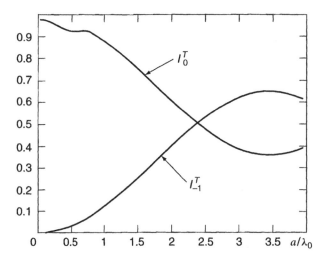

Figure 3.11. Intensities of the -1st and 0th transmitted orders (I^T_{-1}, I^T_0) of the right saw-tooth grating as functions of the groove height for TM-polarization at $d = \lambda_0 = 30°, \varepsilon = 2.25$.

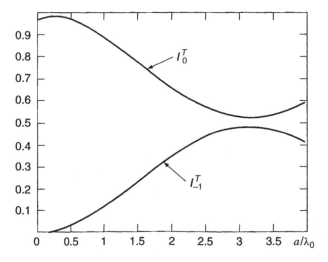

Figure 3.12. Intensities in the -1st and 0th transmitted orders (I^T_{-1}, I^T_0) of the left saw-tooth grating as functions of the groove height for TM-polarization at $d = \lambda_0, \theta = 30°, \varepsilon = 2.25$.

3.4 GRADIENT TECHNIQUES FOR SOLVING THE INVERSE PROBLEM OF DESIGNING DIFFRACTION GRATINGS

3.4.1 Designing Reflection Gratings with a Stepwise Profile

The solution to the direct problem of diffraction by a stepwise-profile grating made of a perfectly conducting material has been discussed in Section 3.1. In this section, we consider a gradient method for solving the inverse problem involving the calculation of the parameters $(x_1, \ldots, x_K, c_1, \ldots, c_K, h_1, \ldots, h_K)$ of the grating profile (Fig. 3.1) on the condition of generation of desired intensities in diffraction orders [10]. The order intensities are defined in Eq. (3.46) and are proportional to the squared modules of the Rayleigh coefficients.

To construct the gradient procedure of designing a diffraction grating profile, we shall introduce an error function, $\varepsilon(\mathbf{p})$, that characterizes the difference of the estimated intensity values, I_n, in the diffraction orders from the desired ones, $\tilde{I}_n$

$$\varepsilon(\mathbf{p}) = \varepsilon[\mathbf{I}(\mathbf{p}), \tilde{\mathbf{I}}], \tag{3.203}$$

where $\mathbf{p} = (x_1, \ldots, x_K, c_1, \ldots, c_K, h_1, \ldots, h_K)$ is the vector of the diffraction grating parameters, K is the number of grooves on a grating period, and $\mathbf{I} = (I_n)_{-M}^{M}$, $\tilde{\mathbf{I}} = (\tilde{I}_n)_{-M}^{M}$ are the vectors of the estimated and desired intensities in the orders.

The gradient procedure of minimizing the error function $\varepsilon(\mathbf{p})$ involves iterative correction of the grating profile parameters by the rule

$$\mathbf{p}_{n+1} = \mathbf{p}_n - t \cdot \nabla \varepsilon(\mathbf{p}), \tag{3.204}$$

where n is the number of the iteration, t is the gradient algorithm step, and

$$\nabla \varepsilon(\mathbf{p}) = \left(\frac{\partial \varepsilon(\mathbf{p})}{\partial x_1}, \ldots, \frac{\partial \varepsilon(\mathbf{p})}{\partial x_K}, \frac{\partial \varepsilon(\mathbf{p})}{\partial c_1}, \ldots, \frac{\partial \varepsilon(\mathbf{p})}{\partial c_K}, \frac{\partial \varepsilon(\mathbf{p})}{\partial h_1}, \ldots, \frac{\partial \varepsilon(\mathbf{p})}{\partial h_K} \right)$$

is the error function gradient. Consider the calculation of the error function gradient, $\nabla \varepsilon(\mathbf{p})$. According to Eqs. (3.203) and (3.46), the gradient vector elements, $\partial \varepsilon(\mathbf{p})/\partial p_i$, where p_i is the $(x_i, c_i$ or $h_i)$ component of the vector $\mathbf{p}$, take the form

$$\frac{\partial \varepsilon(\mathbf{p})}{\partial p_i} = \sum_{j=-M}^{M} \frac{\partial \varepsilon(\mathbf{I}, \tilde{\mathbf{I}})}{\partial I_j} \frac{\partial I_j(\mathbf{p})}{\partial p_i} = \sum_{j=-M}^{M} \frac{\partial \varepsilon(\mathbf{I}, \tilde{\mathbf{I}})}{\partial I_j} \frac{\partial}{\partial p_i} \left(\frac{\beta_j}{\beta_0} R_j \cdot R_j^* \right)$$

$$= 2 \operatorname{Re} \left(\sum_{j=-M}^{M} \frac{\partial \varepsilon(\mathbf{I}, \tilde{\mathbf{I}})}{\partial I_j} \frac{\beta_j}{\beta_0} R_j^* \frac{\partial R_j(\mathbf{p})}{\partial p_i} \right). \tag{3.205}$$

Equation (3.205) is conveniently represented as a real part of scalar product

$$\frac{\partial \varepsilon(\mathbf{p})}{\partial p_i} = 2 \operatorname{Re} \left(\frac{\partial \mathbf{R}(\mathbf{p})}{\partial p_i}, \mathbf{L} \right), \tag{3.206}$$

of the vectors

$$\frac{\partial \mathbf{R}(\mathbf{p})}{\partial p_j} = \left(\frac{\partial R_j(\mathbf{p})}{\partial p_i} \right)_{-M}^{M}, \quad \mathbf{L} = (L_j)_{-M}^{M}, \quad L_j = \sum_{j=-M}^{M} \frac{\partial \varepsilon(\mathbf{I}, \tilde{\mathbf{I}})}{\partial I_j} \frac{\beta_j}{\beta_0} R_j. \quad (3.207)$$

The Rayleigh coefficients R_j and the cosines of the angles β_j defining the propagation directions for the orders are derived from Eqs. (3.31) and (3.16), respectively. To derive the vector of derivatives of the Rayleigh coefficients in Eq. (3.206), we shall differentiate Eq. (3.31) with respect to the variable p

$$\frac{\partial (\mathbf{AA} \cdot \mathbf{R})}{\partial p_i} = \frac{\partial \mathbf{AA}}{\partial p_i} \cdot \mathbf{R} + \mathbf{AA} \cdot \frac{\partial \mathbf{R}}{\partial p_i} = \frac{\partial \mathbf{D}}{\partial p_i}. \quad (3.208)$$

According to Eq. (3.208), the derivative vector $\partial \mathbf{R}(\mathbf{p})/\partial p_i$ takes the form

$$\frac{\partial \mathbf{R}}{\partial p_i} = \mathbf{AA}^{-1} \left(\frac{\partial \mathbf{D}}{\partial p_i} - \frac{\partial \mathbf{AA}}{\partial p_i} \cdot \mathbf{R} \right). \quad (3.209)$$

Next, substituting Eq. (3.209) into (3.206) gives the components of the error function gradient

$$\frac{\partial \varepsilon(\mathbf{p})}{\partial p_i} = 2 \operatorname{Re} \left[\mathbf{AA}^{-1} \left(\frac{\partial \mathbf{D}}{\partial p_i} - \frac{\partial \mathbf{AA}}{\partial p_i} \cdot \mathbf{R} \right), \mathbf{L} \right]. \quad (3.210)$$

The matrices and vectors in Eq. (3.210) are derived from Eqs. (3.27)–(3.30) for TE-polarization, and from Eqs. (3.27), (3.42)–(3.44) for TM-polarization. In particular, for TE-polarization the derivatives $\partial AA/\partial p_i$ and $\partial D/\partial p_i$ can easily be derived from Eqs. (3.27)–(3.30) in the form

$$\frac{\partial D_p}{\partial p_l} = \frac{\partial AA_{p0}}{\partial p_l}, \quad (3.211)$$

$$\frac{\partial AA_{ps}}{\partial x_l} = -\beta_s \frac{2k^2}{d} (\alpha_s - \alpha_p) c_l \sum_{n=1}^{\infty} \frac{tg(\mu_{ln} h_l)}{\mu_{ln}} DD_{ns}^l (DD_{np}^l)^*, \quad (3.212)$$

$$\frac{\partial AA_{ps}}{\partial h_l} = \beta_s \frac{2ik}{d} c_l \sum_{n=1}^{\infty} \frac{1}{\cos^2(\mu_{ln} h_l)} DD_{ns}^l (DD_{np}^l)^*, \quad (3.213)$$

$$\frac{\partial AA_{ps}}{\partial c_l} = \beta_s \frac{2ik}{d} \sum_{n=1}^{\infty} \left[\left(\frac{tg(\mu_{ln} h_l)}{\mu_{ln}} + \frac{\pi n(-\sin(2\mu_{ln} h_l) + 2\mu_{ln} h_l)}{2c_l^2 \mu_{ln}^3 \cos^2(\mu_{ln} h_l)} \right) DD_{ns}^l (DD_{np}^l)^* \right.$$
$$\left. + ic_l \frac{tg(\mu_{ln} h_l)}{\mu_{ln}} (\alpha_s - \alpha_p) \cdot MD_{ns}^l \cdot (DD_{np}^l)^* \right], \quad (3.214)$$

where

$$MD_{mn}^l = \frac{1}{k} \exp(ik\alpha_n x_l) \int_0^k \sin\left(\frac{\pi m}{k} \xi \right) \exp(i\alpha_n c_l \xi) \, d\xi. \quad (3.215)$$

Note that α_n and β_n in the earlier equations take the form of Eqs. (3.15) and (3.16). For TM-polarization, the derivatives $\partial \mathbf{AA}/\partial p_i$, $\partial \mathbf{D}/\partial p_i$ are derived in a similar manner, by differentiating Eqs. (3.42)–(3.44).

To find out whether it is worthwhile using electromagnetic theory when designing conducting gratings, we shall estimate the efficiency of the gratings designed by use of the Kirchhoff approximation and aimed at generating $M = 2N + 1$ identical orders. We shall characterize the grating operation through the energy efficiency

$$E(M) = \sum_{j=-N}^{N} I_j \tag{3.216}$$

and the root-mean-square error of generating the desired equal intensity in the orders

$$\delta(M) = \frac{1}{\overline{I}} \left[\frac{1}{M} \sum_{j=-N}^{N} (I_j - \overline{I})^2 \right]^{1/2}, \tag{3.217}$$

where $\overline{I} = E(M)/M$ is the average intensity.

Example 3.5   The studies examined an 11-order binary diffraction grating with the groove depth $h = \lambda/4$ and the groove coordinates $(x_1, c_1) = (0, 0.06857)$, $(x_2, c_2) = (0.20885, 0.23582)$, $(x_3, c_3) = (0.5293, 0.19171)$, $(x_4, c_4) = (0.72854, 0.13583)$. These groove coordinates are normalized to the grating period. According to Ref. [11], in the Kirchhoff approximation, the efficiency of this grating is $E = 7.6.6$ percent, the root-mean-square (rms) error in generating equal-order intensity being less than 1 percent. For estimating the applicability of the Kirchhoff approximation, the order intensities of the grating were derived for the following values of period d: 7.2λ, 15.2λ, 25.2λ, 35.2λ. The calculation was carried out for TE-polarization using Eqs. (3.27)–(3.32) at normal incidence of the plane wave. The estimated values of the rms error δ and the energy efficiency E were 30.2% and 83.8% at $d = 7.2\lambda$, 17% and 78.9% at $d = 15.2\lambda$, 12% and 78.5% at $d = 25.2\lambda$, and 10.6% and 83.8% at $d = 35.2\lambda$. From the earlier results, the 11-order grating is seen to operate with an error of about $\delta \sim 15$ percent at the period $d > 15\lambda$, thus testifying to an appropriate accuracy of the scalar approximation. At the same time, at $d = 7.2\lambda$, the scalar approximation gives a considerable error of $\delta > 30$ percent. The example presented clearly demonstrates topicality of the electromagnetic theory in developing exact procedures for synthesizing diffraction gratings with subwavelength grooves.

Example 3.6   The exact gradient method of Eqs. (3.204) and (3.210) was applied to designing binary, equal-order gratings. The error function was found as a square error function

$$\varepsilon(\mathbf{p}) = \sum_{j=-N}^{N} (I_j(\mathbf{p}) - \tilde{I}_j)^2. \tag{3.218}$$

Table 3.1 gives the results of designing the gratings at normal incidence of the plane wave for TE-polarization and testifies to the robustness of the gradient method. In particular, the 11-order grating designed for $d = 7.2\lambda$ provides a four-times less error δ

TABLE 3.1. The Parameters of Reflection Binary Gratings Designed in Electromagnetic Approximation Using the Gradient Method

Number of Orders	Number of Grooves	Period (d/λ)	Groove Depth (h/λ)	Normalized Groove Coordinates $(x_i, c_i)/d$	Energy Efficiency $E(\%)$	Root-Mean-Square Error $\delta(\%)$
3	1	3.2		(0, 0.5)	92	0
5	2	3.2	0.25	(0, 0.089204), (0.397067, 0.29625)	87.2	3.5
7	2	3.2	0.2241	(0.098974, 0.453849), (0.751026, 0.146244)	99.4	1.9
9	3	5.2	0.2450	(0.117498, 0.095706), (0.401101, 0.066281), (0.643485, 0.289262)	91.2	4.1
11	5	7.2	0.2363	(0.043523, 0.030163), (0.196521, 0.094899), (0.331266, 0.013970), (0.381802, 0.161684), (0.651364, 0.282746)	86.5	7.5

relative to the 11-order grating developed using the scalar approximation. The gradient method of Eqs. (3.204) and (3.210) allows not only binary gratings but also varying groove depth gratings to be designed. As illustration, we designed a 5-order grating having a period of $d = 3.2\lambda$ two grooves of depth 0.1λ and 0.2584λ with respective coordinates of $(x_1, c_1) = (0.034224, 0.173889)$ and $(x_2, c_2) = (0.465776, 0.308846)$. The energy efficiency E and the rms error δ were 89.6% and 2.9%. When optimizing with regard to the groove depth h_i, it becomes feasible to achieve high-energy efficiency and small error δ, whereas the minimal groove width, $\Delta = \min_i [c_i, x_{i+1} - (x_i + c_i)]$, is essentially greater. In particular, a 5-order grating with varying groove depth has almost the same values of E and δ as the binary 5-order grating in Table 3.1, but with almost two times increased width of the minimal groove.

3.4.2 Designing Dielectric Binary Gratings

The solution to the direct problem of diffraction by a dielectric grating was discussed in Section 3.3. The gradient method for solving the inverse problem of designing a binary dielectric grating [12] we discuss in this section involves the derivation of the groove coordinates for the grating profile (Fig. 3.6) capable of generating desired diffraction order intensities $\tilde{I}_n$, $n = -\overline{M, M}$, corresponding to the transmitted waves in Eq. (3.106). The diffraction order intensities are proportional to the squared modules of the transmission coefficients T_n in Eq. (3.106):

$$I_n = t_n \cdot |T_n|^2, \tag{3.219}$$

where the t_n coefficients are defined in Eqs. (3.199) and (3.200).

The computation of the grating profile involves a gradient minimization of the error function in Eq. (3.203) that specifies the difference of the estimated order intensity values (vector I) from the desired values (vector $\tilde{I}$). The gradient minimization of the error function in Eq. (3.203) involves an iterative correction of the groove coordinates (of vector $\mathbf{p} = (x_1, \ldots, x_{2K})$) by the rule in Eq. (3.204). Derive the gradient of the error function, $\nabla \varepsilon(\mathbf{p})$, for TM-polarization.

According to Eq. (3.203), the partial derivatives $\partial \varepsilon(\mathbf{p})/\partial x_m$ take the form

$$
\frac{\partial \varepsilon(\mathbf{p})}{\partial x_m} = \sum_{j=-M}^{M} \frac{\partial \varepsilon(\mathbf{I}, \tilde{\mathbf{I}})}{\partial I_j} \frac{\partial I_j(\mathbf{p})}{\partial x_m} = 2 \operatorname{Re} \left(\sum_{j=-M}^{M} \frac{\partial \varepsilon(\mathbf{I}, \tilde{\mathbf{I}})}{\partial I_j} t_j T_j^* \frac{\partial T_j(\mathbf{p})}{\partial x_m} \right)
$$

$$
= 2 \operatorname{Re} \left(\frac{\partial \mathbf{T}(\mathbf{p})}{\partial x_m}, \mathbf{L} \right), \tag{3.220}
$$

where

$$
\frac{\partial \mathbf{T}(\mathbf{p})}{\partial x_m} = \left(\frac{\partial T_j(\mathbf{p})}{\partial x_m} \right)_{-M}^{M}, \tag{3.221}
$$

$$
\mathbf{L} = (L_j)_{-M}^{M}, \qquad L_j = \sum_{j=-M}^{M} \frac{\partial \varepsilon(\mathbf{I}, \tilde{\mathbf{I}})}{\partial I_j} t_j T_j. \tag{3.222}
$$

According to Eqs. (3.199)–(3.201), the coefficients t_j in Eqs. (3.220) and (3.222) are given by

$$
t_j = \frac{\cos(\tilde{\theta}_n)}{\sqrt{\varepsilon} \cos(\theta)} \tag{3.223}
$$

when designing the grating with no regard to the substrate and

$$
t_j = \frac{\cos(\theta_n)}{\cos(\theta)} \tag{3.224}
$$

when designing the grating with regard for the substrate.

To derive the derivative vector $\partial \mathbf{T}(\mathbf{p})/\partial x_m$ in Eq. (3.220), we shall differentiate Eq. (3.140)

$$
\frac{\partial \mathbf{T}}{\partial x_m} = \frac{\partial}{\partial x_m} [2 \cdot \exp(-i\beta_0 a) \cdot (\mathbf{H}_{01} - \mathbf{D}_\beta \cdot \mathbf{H}_{11})^{-1} \cdot \delta]
$$

$$
= -(\mathbf{H}_{01} - \mathbf{D}_\beta \cdot \mathbf{H}_{11})^{-1} \left(\frac{\partial \mathbf{H}_{01}}{\partial x_m} - \mathbf{D}_\beta \cdot \frac{\partial \mathbf{H}_{11}}{\partial x_m} \right) \mathbf{T}. \tag{3.225}
$$

To derive the derivatives $\partial \mathbf{H}_{01}/\partial x_m$, $\partial \mathbf{H}_{11}/\partial x_m$ use the analytical representation of the matrices $\mathbf{H}_{01}$ and $\mathbf{H}_{11}$ in Eq. (3.158). Differentiating Eq. (3.158) gives

$$
\begin{pmatrix} \dfrac{\partial \mathbf{H}_{01}}{\partial x_m} \\[2mm] \dfrac{\partial \mathbf{H}_{11}}{\partial x_m} \end{pmatrix} = \frac{\partial}{\partial x_m} [\exp(\mathbf{A}^{\mathrm{TM}} \cdot a) \cdot \mathbf{BC}] = \frac{\partial}{\partial x_m} \left(\sum_{n=1}^{\infty} \frac{a^n}{n!} (\mathbf{A}^{\mathrm{TM}})^n \right) \cdot \mathbf{BC}
$$

$$
= \left(\sum_{n=1}^{\infty} \frac{a^n}{n!} \frac{\partial}{\partial x_m} (\mathbf{A}^{\mathrm{TM}})^n \right) \cdot \mathbf{BC}
$$

$$
= \left[\sum_{n=1}^{\infty} \frac{a^n}{n!} \left(\sum_{j=0}^{n-1} (\mathbf{A}^{\mathrm{TM}})^{n-j-1} \frac{\partial \mathbf{A}^{\mathrm{TM}}}{\partial x_m} (\mathbf{A}^{\mathrm{TM}})^j \right) \right] \cdot \mathbf{BC}. \tag{3.226}
$$

When summing up the series in Eq. (3.226), the derivatives $\partial(\mathbf{A}^{\mathrm{TM}})^n / \partial x_m$ should be derived using the recurrent relation

$$
\frac{\partial}{\partial x_m} (\mathbf{A})^n = \mathbf{A} \cdot \frac{\partial}{\partial x_m} (\mathbf{A})^{n-1} + \frac{\partial \mathbf{A}}{\partial x_m} \cdot (\mathbf{A})^{n-1}. \tag{3.227}
$$

In terms of complexity, the derivation of derivatives of the matrices $\mathbf{H}_{01}$ and $\mathbf{H}_{11}$ is equivalent to the derivation the matrix exponent through the series. To derive the derivative $\partial \mathbf{A}^{\mathrm{TM}} / \partial x_m$, make use of the $\mathbf{A}^{\mathrm{TM}}$ matrix representation in Eq. (3.156). Differentiating Eq. (3.156) gives

$$
\frac{\partial \mathbf{A}^{\mathrm{TM}}}{\partial x_m} = \begin{pmatrix} \mathbf{NU} & \dfrac{\partial \mathbf{F}_1}{\partial x_m} \\[3mm] \dfrac{\partial \mathbf{F}_2}{\partial x_m} & \mathbf{NU} \end{pmatrix}, \tag{3.228}
$$

where $\mathbf{NU}$ are zero matrices of size $(2N+1) \times (2N+1)$, whereas the matrices $\partial \mathbf{F}_1 / \partial x_m$, $\partial \mathbf{F}_2 / \partial x_m$ can be derived from Eq. (3.157) in the form

$$
\frac{\partial \mathbf{F}_1}{\partial x_m} = \frac{\partial c_{l-j}^{(1)}}{\partial x_m} = (-1)^m \frac{k_0^2 (\varepsilon - 1)}{d} \exp\left(-i \frac{2\pi}{d} (l-j) x_m \right), \quad l, j = \overline{1, 2N+1}, \tag{3.229}
$$

$$
\frac{\partial \mathbf{F}_2}{\partial x_m} = \alpha_{-(N+1)+l} \alpha_{-(N+1)+j} \frac{\partial c_{l-j}^{(2)}}{\partial x_m} = \alpha_{-(N+1)+l} \alpha_{-(N+1)+j} (-1)^m \frac{(1/\varepsilon - 1)}{k_0^2 d}
$$

$$
\times \exp\left(-i \frac{2\pi}{d} (l-j) x_m \right), \quad l, j = \overline{1, 2N+1}. \tag{3.230}
$$

Thus, the vector components of the error function gradient take the form of the real part of a scalar product

$$
\frac{\partial \varepsilon(\mathbf{p})}{\partial x_m} = 2 \operatorname{Re} \left[(\mathbf{H}_{01} - \mathbf{D}_\beta \cdot \mathbf{H}_{11})^{-1} \left(\mathbf{D}_\beta \frac{\partial \mathbf{H}_{11}}{\partial x_m} - \frac{\partial \mathbf{H}_{01}}{\partial x_m} \right) \mathbf{T}, \mathbf{L} \right], \tag{3.231}
$$

where the vector $\mathbf{T}$ is defined in Eq. (3.140), the vector $\mathbf{L}$ is defined in Eq. (3.222), the matrices $\mathbf{H}_{01}$ and $\mathbf{H}_{11}$ are analytically defined through the matrix in Eq. (3.156), and the boundary conditions in Eqs. (3.159) and (3.161) through Eq. (3.158), whereas the matrices of the derivatives $\partial \mathbf{H}_{01} / \partial x_m$, $\partial \mathbf{H}_{11} / \partial x_m$ are specified in Eqs. (3.226)–(3.230).

Note that the grating profile height, a, can also be treated as an optimization parameter. The derivative of the resudial function with regard for the profile height also takes the form of Eq. (3.231), where the matrices $\partial \mathbf{H}_{01}/\partial a$, $\partial \mathbf{H}_{11}/\partial a$ can be derived from Eq. (3.158) in the form

$$
\begin{pmatrix} \dfrac{\partial \mathbf{H}_{01}}{\partial a} \\[2mm] \dfrac{\partial \mathbf{H}_{11}}{\partial a} \end{pmatrix} = \frac{\partial}{\partial a}(\exp(\mathbf{A}^{\mathrm{TM}} \cdot a) \cdot \mathbf{BC}) = \mathbf{A}^{\mathrm{TM}} \cdot \exp(\mathbf{A}^{\mathrm{TM}} \cdot a) \cdot \mathbf{BC}
$$

For TE-polarization, the components of the gradient vector of the error function also take the form of Eqs. (3.220) and (3.222), with the vector $\mathbf{T}$ defined in Eq. (3.181) and the t_j coefficients given by

$$
t_j = \sqrt{\varepsilon}\,\frac{\cos(\tilde{\theta}_n)}{\cos(\theta)} \tag{3.232}
$$

when designing the grating with no regard for the substrate and

$$
t_j = \frac{\cos(\theta_n)}{\cos(\theta)} \tag{3.233}
$$

when designing the grating with regard to the substrate.
To derive the derivatives $\partial T(\mathbf{p})/\partial x_m$ in Eq. (3.220), we shall differentiate Eq. (3.181)

$$
\frac{\partial \mathbf{T}}{\partial x_m} = -(\mathbf{E}_{11} - \mathbf{D}_\beta \cdot \mathbf{E}_{01})^{-1}\left(\frac{\partial \mathbf{E}_{11}}{\partial x_m} - \mathbf{D}_\beta \cdot \frac{\partial \mathbf{E}_{01}}{\partial x_m}\right)\mathbf{T}. \tag{3.234}
$$

To derive the derivatives $\partial \mathbf{E}_{01}/\partial x_m$, $\partial \mathbf{E}_{11}/\partial x_m$ of the matrices $\mathbf{E}_{01}$ and $\mathbf{E}_{11}$, use their analytical representations in Eq. (3.193). According to Eq. (3.193), the matrices $\mathbf{E}_{01}$ and $\mathbf{E}_{11}$ take the form

$$
\begin{aligned}
\frac{\partial \mathbf{E}_{01}}{\partial x_m} &= \frac{\partial}{\partial x_m}\left(\cos\left(\sqrt{\mathbf{A}^{\mathrm{TE}}} \cdot a\right)\mathbf{E} + \frac{\sin\left(\sqrt{\mathbf{A}^{\mathrm{TE}}} \cdot a\right)}{\sqrt{\mathbf{A}^{\mathrm{TE}}}} \cdot \mathbf{DE}\right) \\
&= \frac{\partial}{\partial x_m}\left[\left(\sum_{n=0}^{\infty}(-1)^n\frac{a^{2n}}{(2n)!}\left(\mathbf{A}^{\mathrm{TE}}\right)^n\right)\mathbf{E} + \left(\sum_{n=0}^{\infty}(-1)^n\frac{a^{2n+1}}{(2n+1)!}\left(\mathbf{A}^{\mathrm{TE}}\right)^n\right)\mathbf{DE}\right] \\
&= \left(\sum_{n=0}^{\infty}(-1)^n\frac{a^{2n}}{(2n)!}\frac{\partial\left(\mathbf{A}^{\mathrm{TE}}\right)^n}{\partial x_m}\right)\mathbf{E} + \left(\sum_{n=0}^{\infty}(-1)^n\frac{a^{2n+1}}{(2n+1)!}\frac{\partial\left(\mathbf{A}^{\mathrm{TE}}\right)^n}{\partial x_m}\right)\mathbf{DE},
\end{aligned} \tag{3.235}
$$

$$
\begin{aligned}
\frac{\partial \mathbf{E}_{11}}{\partial x_m} &= \frac{\partial}{\partial x_m}\left[-\sqrt{\mathbf{A}^{\mathrm{TE}}}\sin\left(\sqrt{\mathbf{A}^{\mathrm{TE}}} \cdot a\right)\mathbf{E} + \cos\left(\sqrt{\mathbf{A}^{\mathrm{TE}}} \cdot a\right) \cdot \mathbf{DE}\right] \\
&= \frac{\partial}{\partial x_m}\left[\left(\sum_{n=1}^{\infty}(-1)^n\frac{a^{2n-1}}{(2n-1)!}\left(\mathbf{A}^{\mathrm{TE}}\right)^n\right)\mathbf{E} + \left(\sum_{n=0}^{\infty}(-1)^n\frac{a^{2n}}{(2n)!}\left(\mathbf{A}^{\mathrm{TE}}\right)^n\right) \cdot \mathbf{DE}\right] \\
&= \left(\sum_{n=1}^{\infty}(-1)^n\frac{a^{2n-1}}{(2n-1)!}\frac{\partial\left(\mathbf{A}^{\mathrm{TE}}\right)^n}{\partial x_m}\right)\mathbf{E} + \left(\sum_{n=0}^{\infty}(-1)^n\frac{a^{2n}}{(2n)!}\frac{\partial\left(\mathbf{A}^{\mathrm{TE}}\right)^n}{\partial x_m}\right) \cdot \mathbf{DE},
\end{aligned} \tag{3.236}
$$

where

$$\frac{\partial \left(\mathbf{A}^{\text{TE}}\right)^n}{\partial x_m} = \sum_{j=0}^{n-1} \left(\mathbf{A}^{\text{TE}}\right)^{n-j-1} \frac{\partial \mathbf{A}^{\text{TE}}}{\partial x_m} \left(\mathbf{A}^{\text{TE}}\right)^j. \tag{3.237}$$

When summing up the series in Eqs. (3.235) and (3.236), the derivatives $\partial (\mathbf{A}^{\text{TE}})^n / \partial x_m$ should be sought for using the recurrent relation in Eq. (3.227). Note that in terms of complexity, the derivation of the derivatives of the matrices $\mathbf{E}_{01}$ and $\mathbf{E}_{11}$ is equivalent to the derivation of the matrix through the cosine and sine series. The matrix $\partial \mathbf{A}^{\text{TE}} / \partial x_m$ in Eqs. (3.235) and (3.236) may be derived from Eq. (3.192) in the form

$$\frac{\partial \mathbf{A}^{\text{TE}}}{\partial x_m} = \frac{\partial c_{l-j}^{(1)}}{\partial x_m} = (-1)^m \frac{k_0^2(\varepsilon - 1)}{d} \exp\left(-i\frac{2\pi}{d}(l-j)x_m\right), \quad l, j = \overline{1, 2N+1}. \tag{3.238}$$

Thus, for TE-polarization, the components of the gradient vector are given by

$$\frac{\partial \varepsilon(\mathbf{p})}{\partial x_m} = 2 \operatorname{Re}\left[(\mathbf{E}_{11} - \mathbf{D}_\beta \cdot \mathbf{E}_{01})^{-1} \left(\mathbf{D}_\beta \frac{\partial \mathbf{E}_{01}}{\partial x_m} - \frac{\partial \mathbf{E}_{11}}{\partial x_m}\right) \mathbf{T}, \mathbf{L}\right], \tag{3.239}$$

where the $\mathbf{T}$ vector is defined in Eq. (3.181), the $\mathbf{L}$ vector is defined in Eqs. (3.222) and (3.232), (3.233), the matrices $\mathbf{E}_{01}$ and $\mathbf{E}_{11}$ are analytically defined through the matrix in Eq. (3.192), the boundary conditions of Eqs. (3.171) and (3.187) through Eq. (3.193), and the matrices of the derivatives $\partial \mathbf{E}_{01} / \partial x_m$, $\partial \mathbf{E}_{11} / \partial x_m$ are defined in Eqs. (3.235) and (3.236).

When minimizing the residual function with regard for the profile height, the derivative $\partial \varepsilon(\mathbf{p}) / \partial a$ also takes the form of Eq. (3.239), where the matrices $\partial \mathbf{E}_{01} / \partial a$, $\partial \mathbf{E}_{11} / \partial a$ can be derived from Eq. (3.193) in the form

$$\frac{\partial \mathbf{E}_{01}}{\partial a} = \frac{\partial}{\partial a}\left(\cos\left(\sqrt{\mathbf{A}^{\text{TE}}} \cdot a\right)\mathbf{E} + \frac{\sin\left(\sqrt{\mathbf{A}^{\text{TE}}} \cdot a\right)}{\sqrt{\mathbf{A}^{\text{TE}}}} \cdot \mathbf{DE}\right)$$

$$= -\sqrt{\mathbf{A}^{\text{TE}}} \cdot \sin\left(\sqrt{\mathbf{A}^{\text{TE}}} \cdot a\right)\mathbf{E} + \cos\left(\sqrt{\mathbf{A}^{\text{TE}}} \cdot a\right) \cdot \mathbf{DE}, \tag{3.240}$$

$$\frac{\partial \mathbf{E}_{11}}{\partial a} = \frac{\partial}{\partial a}\left[-\sqrt{\mathbf{A}^{\text{TE}}} \sin\left(\sqrt{\mathbf{A}^{\text{TE}}} \cdot a\right)\mathbf{E} + \cos\left(\sqrt{\mathbf{A}^{\text{TE}}} \cdot a\right) \cdot \mathbf{DE}\right]$$

$$= -\mathbf{A}^{\text{TE}} \cdot \cos\left(\sqrt{\mathbf{A}^{\text{TE}}} \cdot a\right)\mathbf{E} - \sqrt{\mathbf{A}^{\text{TE}}} \cdot \sin\left(\sqrt{\mathbf{A}^{\text{TE}}} \cdot a\right) \cdot \mathbf{DE}. \tag{3.241}$$

To look into whether it is worthwhile designing the dielectric gratings in the electromagnetic approximation, the operation of the gratings designed in the Kirchhoff approximation and intended for generating $M = 2N + 1$ equal orders was analyzed. The grating operation was estimated through the energy efficiency E [Eq. (3.216)] and the rms error δ in the generation of a desired equal intensity in orders [Eq. (3.217)].

Example 3.7 The studies examined an 11-order and a 7-order grating with the groove depth corresponding to the phase π and the respective groove coordinates $(x_1, x_2) = (0, 0.06857)$; $(x_3, x_4) = (0.20885, 0.44467)$; $(x_5, x_6) = (0.5293, 0.72101)$; $(x_7, x_8) = (0.72854, 0.86437)$ and $(x_1, x_2) = (0, 0.23191)$; $(x_3, x_4) = (0.42520, 0.52571)$. The

TABLE 3.2. Functional Characteristics of the Gratings Designed Using the Kirchhoff Approximation ($\varepsilon = 2.25$, $\theta = 0$)

Period of the Grating (d/λ_0)	11-Order Grating		7-Order Grating	
	$E(\%)$ (TM/TE)	$\delta(\%)$ (TM/TE)	$E(\%)$ (TM/TE)	$\delta(\%)$ (TM/TE)
5.5	90.3/82.9	95.9/144.0	81.3/79.0	35.8/38.2
10	78.9/77.6	42.7/52.3	76.2/75.9	19.6/22.2
15	75.9/75.9	28.6/34.2	75.9/75.5	13.4/14.1
20	75.4/75.4	22.4/25.1	75.6/75.5	11.4/11.7
25	74.9/74.8	18.0/20.4	75.5/75.4	9.1/8.4
30	74.6/74.6	16.3/16.9	75.5/75.4	7.8/7.1
50	74.0/74.0	9.9/8.6	75.4/75.4	4.8/4.1

groove coordinates were normalized with respect to the grating period. According to Ref. [11], in the scalar approximation these gratings generate 11- and 7-orders with the energy efficiencies $E(11) = 76.6$ percent and $E(7) = 78.6$ percent, with the nonuniformity of order intensity being less than 1 percent. Table 3.2 gives the values of E and δ the electromagnetic theory predicts for these gratings at different period lengths. The values of E and δ in Table 3.2 are arranged in pairs corresponding to TM-polarization and TE-polarization. The intensities of the transmitted orders were estimated using Eqs. (3.140), (3.158), and (3.181), Eq. (3.193) at $\varepsilon = 2.25$ and $\theta = 0$. According to Table 3.2, the 11-order grating is practically inoperable for the period $d < 20\lambda_0$, whereas the rms error δ becomes less than 10 percent no sooner than for $d \geq 50\lambda_0$. At the same time, for the 7-order grating the error becomes less than 10 percent as early as for $d > 20\lambda_0$. Better operation of the 7-order grating for small values of d/λ_0 is because of the large size of the grooves. In particular, for the 11-order grating the minimal groove width is $\Delta = 0.008d$, whereas for the 7-order grating it is $\Delta = 0.1d$. The simulation conducted clearly testifies in favor of the exact procedures of grating synthesis.

The gradient technique developed was applied to designing dielectric binary gratings ($\varepsilon = 2.25$) with equal orders with no regard to the substrate. The quadratic function of error in Eq. (3.218) was used as a residual function. Table 3.3 gives the estimated characteristics of the gratings of period $d = 5.5\lambda_0$ at normal incidence for TE-polarization and TM-polarization. From the data of Table 3.3, it can be seen that the exact electromagnetic calculation produces the gratings essentially different from the 11-order and 7-order gratings produced using the scalar approach. Similar to the scalar approximation, the use of the gradient procedures within the electromagnetic approach reduces the rms error up to $1-5$ percent, whereas the energy efficiency is greater by $5-10$ percent [11,13–15]. In particular, 11-order and 3-groove gratings have the energy efficiency over 90 percent.

Example 3.8   In scalar approximation, the intensity distribution in the diffraction orders of a binary grating can only be symmetric. The examples of the exact electromagnetic calculation of the field propagated from simplest gratings dealt with in Sections 3.1–3.3 show that for the parameters $d = \lambda_0$, $\theta = 30°$ satisfying the Bragg condition, the symmetric gratings allow the radiation to be concentrated in the -1st order. Such asymmetry is possible not only for small periods. Table 3.4 gives the

TABLE 3.3. The Results of Designing Dielectric Binary Gratings in the Electromagnetic Approximation Using the Gradient Procedure ($d = 5.5\lambda_0$, $\varepsilon = 2.25$, $\theta = 0$)

Number of Orders M	Number of Grooves K	Height of Grooves (a/λ_0)	Coordinates of Profile	$E(\%)$	$\delta(\%)$
TM-Polarization					
5	2	0.9	(0.1820, 0.4822), (0.5544, 0.8546)	80.1	3.1
7	2	0.9	(0.2454, 0.4367), (0.5999, 0.7912)	85.1	1.0
9	3	1.56	(0.0925, 0.1963), (0.3728, 0.4786), (0.6155, 0.7185)	96.1	0.6
11	3	1.6	(0.1515, 0.3435), (0.4845, 0.5753), (0.7162, 0.9046)	94.0	5.1
TE-Polarization					
5	2	0.8	(0.1798, 0.4816), (0.5550, 0.8567)	80.7	2.5
7	2	0.875	(0.2579, 0.4297), (0.6070, 0.7787)	83.8	1.1
9	3	1.0	(0.0091, 0.1924), (0.3145, 0.4811), (0.7769, 0.9547)	89.7	3.6
11	3	1.57	(0.0444, 0.3390), (0.5033, 0.5567), (0.8259, 0.8792)	91.5	4.3

results of the gradient calculation of binary deflectors that provides the maximum at −1st order at normal incidence for TE-polarization. The following square error function

$$\varepsilon(\mathbf{p}) = [1 - I_{-1}(\mathbf{p})]^2 \rightarrow \min. \tag{3.242}$$

was used as a resudiae function.

It can be seen from Table 3.4 that over 80 percent of energy is possible to concentrate in the −1st order even for "large" periods. The number of grooves of order p on the period $d = p\lambda_0$ is necessary to attain the high efficiency of over 80 percent.

The gratings that allow the radiation to be concentrated in the −1st order are of great practical importance. Examine whether it is feasible to use such gratings when designing various focusing DOEs, for example, lenses. In scalar approximation, the DOE is commonly designed using a thin optical element approximation that describes the DOE through the phase function. Let $\varphi(x)$, $x \in [0, d]$ be the DOE phase function derived in the geometric optical approximation provided the focusing into a desired domain. The geometric optical approximation is based on the inclination equation that

TABLE 3.4. The Results of Designing Binary Deflectors Concentrating the Radiation in the -1st Order Using the Gradient Procedure ($\varepsilon = 2.25$, $\theta = 0$, TE-Polarization)

Period (d/λ_0)	Number of Grooves K	Height of Grooves (a/λ_0)	Profile Coordinates	$E(\%)$
3.5	2	1.68	(0.2596, 0.4378, 0.6082, 0.6754, 0.8469, 0.8780)	83.5
4.5	4	1.69	(0.2617, 0.4009, 0.5426, 0.6043, 0.7001, 0.7361, 0.8521, 0.8734)	87.7
5.5	5	1.78	(0.2714, 0.3982, 0.4997, 0.5565, 0.6100, 0.6473, 0.7243, 0.7560, 0.8793, 0.8984)	87.6
6.5	5	1.5	(0.1809, 0.4334, 0.4717, 0.5302, 0.6113, 0.6530, 0.7566, 0.7845, 0.8997, 0.9142)	80.0

defines the refracted ray direction through the DOE phase function as follows:

$$\sin(\theta_r) = \frac{1}{k_0\sqrt{\varepsilon}} \left(\frac{d\varphi(x)}{dx} + \frac{d\varphi_0(x)}{dx} \right) = \frac{\lambda}{2\pi} \left(\frac{d\varphi(x)}{dx} + \frac{d\varphi_0(x)}{dx} \right), \qquad (3.243)$$

where $\lambda = \lambda_0/\sqrt{\varepsilon}$ is the wavelength in the medium, $\varphi_0(x) = k_0 \sin(\theta) \cdot x$ is the illuminating beam phase function. Equation (3.243) coincides with the equation for the diffraction grating

$$\sqrt{\varepsilon} \cdot \sin(\theta_m) = \sin(\theta) + m\lambda_0/d \qquad (3.244)$$

for a period of $d = 2\pi/|d\varphi(x)/dx|$ and for m equal to 1 or -1. The sign of m is determined by the sign of the phase derivative: $m = \text{sign} [d\varphi(x)/dx]$. This value of period coincides with the size of the DOE zone Δx specified from the condition

$$\Delta\varphi(x) = 2\pi \approx \left| \frac{d\varphi(x)}{dx} \right| \Delta x \Rightarrow \Delta x = 2\pi / \left| \frac{d\varphi(x)}{dx} \right|. \qquad (3.245)$$

Thus, the geometric optical approximation supposes that each DOE zone operates as a "single-order" grating that concentrates the radiation in the -1st and $+1$st orders. In the scalar Kirchhoff approximation, to the single-order grating there corresponds a left or right saw-tooth grating. For small-size zones, the geometric and scalar approximations fail to operate, as the saw-tooth grating becomes inoperative. In particular, for the right

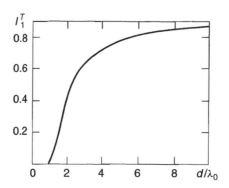

Figure 3.13. First-order intensity for the right saw-tooth grating as a function of the period length for TE-polarization at $\varepsilon = 2.25$, $\theta = 0$, and a profile height of $a = \lambda_0/(\sqrt{\varepsilon} - 1)$.

saw-tooth grating of height $a = \lambda_0/(\sqrt{\varepsilon} - 1)$, the first-order intensity tends to zero as $d \to \lambda_0$ (Fig. 3.13).

It is believed that with the continuous-DOE zones replaced by binary gratings designed in electromagnetic approximation with the proviso that the -1st or $+1$st order intensity is maximum, the resulting binary DOE turns out to be highly efficient. Although Eqs. (3.243) and (3.244) offer just a heuristic verification of the method of replacing DOE zones by a "single-order" grating, the method proves successful in practice. In particular, Ref. [16] reports designing an off-axis segment of the reflection binary lens that shows a nearly 90 percent efficiency for TM-polarization. In Ref. [16], the lens was designed through replacing continuous diffraction lens zones by a simplest reflection binary grating with a single groove. For TM-polarization, at $d \sim \lambda_0$, $\theta \sim 30°$, and a groove height of $a \sim 0.25\lambda_0$, such a grating concentrates the radiation in the -1st order (Fig. 3.2).

Example 3.9   To illustrate the suitability of the method, we shall design a refraction lens. The diffraction lens phase function is

$$\varphi(x) = \mathrm{mod}_{2\pi}\left[\frac{2\pi}{\lambda_0}\left(-x\sin(\theta) - \sqrt{\varepsilon}\sqrt{(x-x_0)^2 + f^2} + \mathrm{const}\right)\right], \quad x \in [0, d],$$

(3.246)

where (x_0, f) are the coordinates of focus. At $d = 20\lambda_0$, $\theta = 30°$, and $(x_0, f) = (-20\lambda_0, -85\lambda_0)$ the lens phase function has 20 zones of size $0.89\lambda_0 \leq \Delta x \leq 1.17\lambda_0$. Replacing the lens zones in Eq. (3.246) by a binary grating

$$h_2(x) = \begin{cases} 0, & x \in [0, \Delta x/2) \\ a \cdot \lambda_0, & x \in [\Delta x/2, \Delta x) \end{cases}$$

(3.247)

produces a binary relief. For TM-polarization, at $a \sim 2\lambda_0$, $\theta = 30°$, and $0.89\,\lambda_0 \leq \Delta x \leq 1, 17\lambda_0$, the grating of Eq. (3.247) concentrates the light in the -1st order (Fig. 3.8). Figures 3.14 and 3.15a depict the resulting binary relief of the lens and the intensity distribution

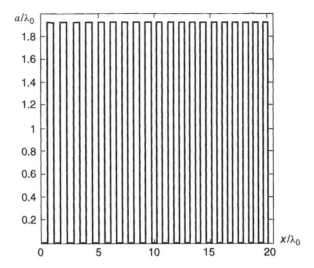

Figure 3.14. Binary lens of aperture $d = 20\lambda_0$ to focus into a point $(x_0, f) = (-20\lambda_0, -85\lambda_0)$ at $\theta = 30°$, $\varepsilon = 2.25$.

$$I(x, f) = \left| \mathrm{Re}\left(E_x(x, f) \cdot H_z^*(x, f) \right) \right|$$

$$= \frac{1}{k_0 \varepsilon} \left| Im\left[\left(\sum_{n=-N}^{N} T_n \tilde{\beta}_n \cdot \exp[i\,(\alpha_n x - \tilde{\beta}_n f)] \right) \right.\right.$$

$$\left.\left. \cdot \left(\sum_{n=-N}^{N} T_n \exp[i\,(\alpha_n x - \tilde{\beta}_n f)] \right)^* \right] \right| \qquad (3.248)$$

in the focal plane $y = -85\lambda_0$ at $N = 57$. The earlier relation for the intensity is proportional to the y-component of the Umov-Poynting vector. For comparison, Figure 3.15b shows the intensity distribution for a continuous-relief lens

$$h(x) = \frac{\sqrt{\varepsilon - \sin(\theta)}}{\varepsilon - \cos(\theta)\sqrt{\varepsilon - \sin(\theta)}} \mathrm{mod}_{\lambda_0}\left(const - x\sin(\theta) \right.$$

$$\left. - \sqrt{\varepsilon}\sqrt{(x - x_0)^2 + f^2} \right), \quad x \in [0, d] \qquad (3.249)$$

derived in the thin optical element approximation. The intensity distribution in Figure 3.15b lacks the pronounced intensity peak of width $5\lambda_0$, produced by the binary lens, as is seen in Figure 3.15a.

The earlier example demonstrates the feasibility and practical importance of the problem of designing gratings that are capable of providing the energy maximum in the -1st and $+1$st orders. Compared to the wavelength, large-size zones require more complex gratings with several grooves. Designing single-order gratings for a certain interval of periods of $[d_{min}, d_{max}]$ that determines the variation of the DOE zone size still remains a topical problem. The binary grating that provides the maximum

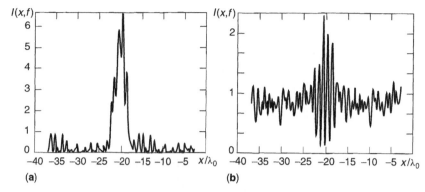

Figure 3.15. Intensity distribution in the focal plane (at $y = -85\lambda_0$) (**a**) for the binary lens in Figure 3.14 and (**b**) for the continuous lens of Eq. (3.333) for TM-polarization.

intensity $I_{-1}(\mathbf{p}, d)$ in the $-$1st order at $d \in [d_{\min}, d_{\max}]$ can be designed using the earlier considered gradient method, with the error function defined, for example, in the form

$$\varepsilon(\mathbf{p}) = \int_{d_{\min}}^{d_{\max}} (1 - I_{-1}(\mathbf{p}, \xi))^2 \, d\xi \to \min, \qquad (3.250)$$

where $\mathbf{p}$ is the vector of the grating groove coordinates.

Example 3.10 The simplest grating in Eq. (3.247) with a single step can only be used for subwavelength zone-sizes. Below, we shall design a more complicated binary lens with large zones and widely ranging zone sizes. Given the parameters: the lens aperture is $d = 30\lambda_0$, the focusing point coordinates are $(x_0, f) = (0, -130\lambda_0)$, $\theta = 10°$, $\varepsilon = 2.25$, the continuous-relief lens of Eq. (3.249) has 10 complete zones of size varying from $5\lambda_0$ at the aperture beginning to $2\lambda_0$ at the aperture edge. To design the binary lens one needs to design a grating capable of providing the intensity maximum in the $-$1st order for a period interval of $[2\lambda_0, 5\lambda_0]$. For TM-polarization, the gradient method produced a three-groove grating capable of providing the maximum

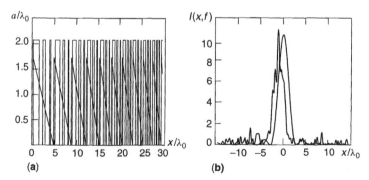

Figure 3.16. (**a**) Binary lens of aperture $d = 30\lambda_0$ to focus into a point $(x_0, f) = (0, -130\lambda_0)$ at $\theta = 10°$, $\varepsilon = 2.25$ and continuous-relief lens of Eq. (3.249), (**b**) Intensity distribution generated by the binary lens for TM-polarization and intensity distribution generated in the focal plane of an ideal spherical front.

in the -1st order for the aforementioned period interval and the error function of Eq. (3.250). The coordinates of the grating grooves normalized with respect to period are equal to $\mathbf{p} = (0.0429, 0.2981, 0.4556, 0.5771, 0.7745, 0.8276)$, with the groove height being $a = 2.07\lambda_0$. At $d \in [2\lambda_0, 5\lambda_0]$, this grating is able to concentrate in the -1st order no less than 80% of energy. Figure 3.16a depicts the binary lens profile obtained as a result of replacing the zones of the lens (3.249) by the calculated binary grating, whereas Figure 3.16b shows the intensity distribution produced by the binary lens at $Y = -130\lambda_0$. For comparison, Figures. 3.16a and 3.16b also depict the profile of the continuous diffraction lens in Eq. (3.249) and the Kirchhoff approximation of the intensity distribution

$$I(x, f) = \frac{\sqrt{\varepsilon}}{\lambda_0 f} \left| \int_0^d \exp\left(-2\pi i \frac{\sqrt{\varepsilon}}{\lambda_0 f} xu\right) du \right|^2 = \frac{d^2 \sqrt{\varepsilon}}{\lambda_0 f} \sin c^2 \left(\frac{\pi \sqrt{\varepsilon} \cdot d \cdot x}{\lambda_0 f}\right),$$
(3.251)

where $\sin c(x) = \sin(x)/x$ generated in the focal plane of an ideal spherical front. From Figure 3.16, the designed binary lens is seen to show high operating capabilities and demonstrates that it is possible to replace the problem of designing a DOE by a much more simple problem of designing a single-order grating even for widely ranging zone sizes.

3.4.3 Designing Continuous-Profile Reflection Gratings Using the Rayleigh Approximation

The problem of diffraction by a perfectly conducting, continuous-profile grating is solved in the Rayleigh approximation in subsection 3.2.3.2. We shall apply the gradient method to designing the grating profile $f(x)$ intended for generating a desired intensity in the diffraction orders [17]. The order intensities, Eq. (3.46), are proportional to the squared modules of the Rayleigh coefficients: $I_n = |R_n|^2 \beta_n/\beta_0$. For the sake of convenience, we shall use the normalized profile function

$$H(x) = k \cdot f\left(\frac{x \cdot d}{2\pi}\right)$$
(3.252)

While constructing the gradient procedure for computing the grating profile $H(x)$, we shall introduce the error functional $\varepsilon(H)$ equal to the difference between the estimated intensities in the orders, I_n and the desired intensities, $\tilde{I}_n$:

$$\varepsilon(H) = \varepsilon[\mathbf{I}(H), \tilde{\mathbf{I}}],$$
(3.253)

where $\mathbf{I}$ and $\tilde{\mathbf{I}}$ are the vectors of the estimated and desired intensities of diffraction orders. Note that the vector $\mathbf{I}$ components are functionals of the grating profile $H(x)$.

The gradient minimization of the functional in Eq. (3.253) involves the iterative correction of the function $H(x)$ by the rule

$$H_{n+1}(x) = H_n(x) - t \cdot \varepsilon'(x),$$
(3.254)

where n is the number of the iteration, t is the gradient method step, and $\varepsilon'(x)$ is the functional gradient. To derive the gradient $\varepsilon'(x)$, consider an increment of the functional $\varepsilon(H)$ caused by a small increment of the profile height, $\Delta H(x)$:

$$\Delta\varepsilon(H) = \varepsilon(H + \Delta H) - \varepsilon(H) = \sum_{j=-M}^{M} \frac{\partial \varepsilon(\mathbf{I}, \tilde{\mathbf{I}})}{\partial I_j} \Delta I_j(H)$$

$$= \sum_{j=-M}^{M} \frac{\partial \varepsilon(\mathbf{I}, \tilde{\mathbf{I}})}{\partial I_j} \Delta \left(\frac{\beta_j}{\beta_0} R_j(H) \cdot R_j^*(H)\right) = 2 \, \text{Re} \, [\Delta\mathbf{R}(H), \mathbf{L}(H)], \quad (3.255)$$

where

$$\Delta\mathbf{R}(H) = [\Delta R_j(H)]_{-M}^{M}, \; \mathbf{L}(H) = [L_j(H)]_{-M}^{M}, \; L_j = \sum_{j=-M}^{M} \frac{\partial \varepsilon(\mathbf{I}, \tilde{\mathbf{I}})}{\partial I_j} \frac{\beta_j}{\beta_0} R_j(H).$$
$$(3.256)$$

According to Eq. (3.98), the increment vector $\Delta\mathbf{R}(H)$ takes the form

$$\Delta\mathbf{R}(H) = \mathbf{AA}^{-1}(\Delta\mathbf{B} - \Delta\mathbf{AA} \cdot \mathbf{R}), \quad (3.257)$$

where the matrix $\mathbf{AA}$ and the vector $\mathbf{B}$ are defined in Eqs. (3.93) and (3.94), for TE-polarization, and in Eqs. (3.96) and (3.97), for TM-polarization. For TE-polarization, we derive the increment vector from Eqs. (3.93) and (3.94) in the form

$$\Delta\mathbf{R}(H) = \mathbf{AA}^{-1} \cdot \int_0^{2\pi} i \, \Delta H(\xi)[\tilde{\mathbf{B}}(\xi) - \tilde{\mathbf{A}}(\xi) \cdot \mathbf{R}] \, d\xi, \quad (3.258)$$

where

$$\tilde{\mathbf{A}}(\xi) = [\tilde{A}_{pn}(\xi)]_{-N}^{N}, \; \tilde{A}_{pn}(\xi) = (\beta_n - \beta_0) \cdot \exp[i\xi(n - p)$$
$$+ i(\beta_n - \beta_0)H(\xi)], \quad (3.259)$$

$$\tilde{\mathbf{B}}(\xi) = [\tilde{B}_p(\xi)]_{-N}^{N}, \; \tilde{B}_p(\xi) = -2\beta_0 \exp[-2i\beta_0 H(\xi) - ip\xi]. \quad (3.260)$$

Substituting Eq. (3.258) into (3.255), we obtain the increment of the error functional $\varepsilon(H)$ in the form

$$\Delta\varepsilon(H) = -2 \int_0^{2\pi} \Delta H \cdot \text{Im} \, (\mathbf{AA}^{-1}[\tilde{B}(\xi) - \tilde{\mathbf{A}}(\xi) \cdot \mathbf{R}], \mathbf{L}) \, d\xi. \quad (3.261)$$

According to Eq. (3.261), the functional gradient takes the form of the imaginary part of the scalar product

$$\varepsilon'(x) = -2 \cdot \text{Im} \, (\mathbf{AA}^{-1}[\tilde{\mathbf{B}}(x) - \tilde{\mathbf{A}}(x) \cdot \mathbf{R}], \mathbf{L}). \quad (3.262)$$

For TM-polarization, similar mathematical treatment easily yields the gradient of the error functional in the form of Eq. (3.262), where $\mathbf{R}$ is sought from Eqs. (3.96)–(3.98), whereas the matrix $\tilde{\mathbf{A}}(\xi)$ and the vector $\tilde{\mathbf{B}}(\xi)$ take the form

$$\tilde{\mathbf{A}}(\xi) = [\tilde{A}_{pn}(\xi)]_{-N}^{N}, \; \tilde{A}_{pn}(\xi) = \left(\beta_n(\beta_n - \beta_0) + \frac{\alpha_n\lambda}{d}(n - p)\right)$$
$$\times \exp[i\xi(n - p) + i(\beta_n - \beta_0)H(\xi)], \quad (3.263)$$

$$\tilde{B}(\xi) = [\tilde{B}_p(\xi)]_{-N}^{N}, \quad \tilde{B}_p(\xi) = \left(-2\beta_0^2 + \frac{\alpha_0\lambda}{d}p\right)$$

$$\times \exp[-2i\beta_0 H(\xi) - ip\xi]. \tag{3.264}$$

Let us determine the step t for the gradient procedure of Eq. (3.254). In doing so, the functional $\varepsilon(H)$ along the antigradient direction is treated as a function of t:

$$\varepsilon_1(t) = \varepsilon[H - t \cdot \varepsilon'(H)]. \tag{3.265}$$

Expand the function $\varepsilon_1(t)$ into the Taylor series in the vicinity of point $t = 0$:

$$\varepsilon_1(t) = \varepsilon_1(0) + \varepsilon_1'(0) \cdot t. \tag{3.266}$$

Assuming the minimal value of the functional $\varepsilon(H)$ to be equal to zero, make the right-hand side in Eq. (3.266) be equal to zero and obtain the value of step t in the form

$$t = -\varepsilon_1(0)/\varepsilon_1'(0). \tag{3.267}$$

According to Eq. (3.261), the derivative $\varepsilon_1'(0)$ is given by

$$\varepsilon_1'(0) = -4 \int_0^{2\pi} [\mathrm{Im}\,(\mathbf{A}\mathbf{A}^{-1} \cdot [\tilde{\mathbf{B}}(\xi) - \tilde{A}(\xi) \cdot \mathbf{R}], \mathbf{L})]^2 \, d\xi, \tag{3.268}$$

and the step value is determined from

$$t = \varepsilon_1(0) \cdot \left[\int_0^{2\pi} (2 \cdot \mathrm{Im}\,(\mathbf{A}\mathbf{A}^{-1}[\tilde{\mathbf{B}}(\xi) - \tilde{\mathbf{A}}(\xi) \cdot \mathbf{R}], \mathbf{L}))^2 \, d\xi \right]^{-1}. \tag{3.269}$$

The matrix $\tilde{\mathbf{A}}(x)$ and the vector $\tilde{\mathbf{B}}(x)$ in Eq. (3.269) are defined in Eqs. (3.259) and (3.260), for TE-polarization, and in Eqs. (3.263) and (3.264), for TM-polarization.

In Section 3.2, the Rayleigh approximation is shown to change to the Fraunhofer approximation at $d \gg \lambda$, for which the Rayleigh coefficients correspond to the Fourier coefficients in the decomposition of the function $\exp[i\varphi(x)]$, where $\varphi(x)$ is the phase lead function of Eq. (3.99). This allows the widely used gradient methods for grating synthesis in the Fraunhofer approximation to be treated as a particular case of the general gradient algorithm of Eqs. (3.254) and (3.262) that uses the Rayleigh approximation.

The earlier-considered gradient method was used to design gratings with $2M + 1$ equal orders, with a quadratic functional

$$\varepsilon(H) = \sum_{j=-M}^{M} (I_j(H) - \tilde{I}_j)^2. \tag{3.270}$$

serving as the error functional.

The gradient method step t was determined from the condition of minimum of a function being a linear approximation of the functional $\varepsilon(H)$ along the antigradient direction.

Example 3.11   The simulated experiment was conducted for TE-polarization and normal incidence of the plane wave. Figures 3.17–3.20 show the estimated profiles $H(x)$ and intensities in diffraction orders for a 5-order, 7-order, 9-order, and 11-order grating of period 3.6λ, 5.2λ, 6.2λ, and 7.2λ, respectively. As the initial guess for the gradient procedure in the Rayleigh approximation, we used profiles calculated by the gradient method in scalar approximation. The initial profiles are shown in Figures. 3.17a–3.20a by dashed lines. The energy efficiency E (Eq. (3.216)) and the rms error δ (Eq. (3.217)) for the initial profiles in scalar approximation were found to be 95.2% and 1.1%, for the 5-order grating, 98.1% and 1.4%, for the 7-order grating, 99.6% and 1.9%, for the 9-order grating, and 98.6% and 0.8%, for the 11-order grating.

Order intensities for the initial profiles, calculated in the Rayleigh approximation are shown by the dashed line in Figures 3.17b–3.20b. The Rayleigh approximation for the initial profiles results in the error increase by 25–30 percent, whereas the energy efficiency E decreases by 1.5–2.5 percent.

The use of the gradient method in the Rayleigh approximation allows the scalar solution to be corrected. The grating profiles and order intensities calculated in the Rayleigh approximation are shown by solid lines in Figures 3.17–3.20.

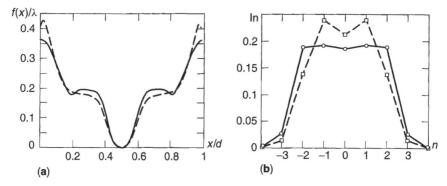

Figure 3.17. Five-order grating (**a**) profiles and (**b**) order intensities calculated in scalar approximation (dashed line) and in the Rayleigh approximation (solid line).

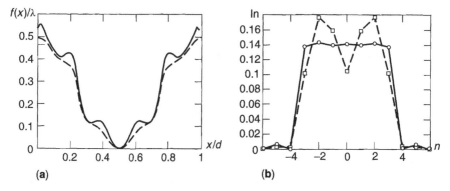

Figure 3.18. Seven-order grating (**a**) profiles and (**b**) order intensities calculated in scalar approximation (dashed line) and in the Rayleigh approximation (solid line).

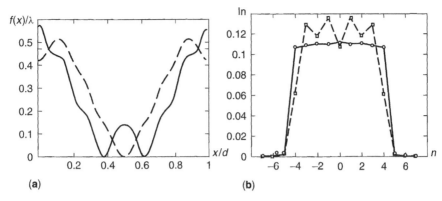

(a)   **(b)**

Figure 3.19. Nine-order grating (**a**) profiles and (**b**) order intensities calculated in scalar approximation (dashed line) and in the Rayleigh approximation (solid line).

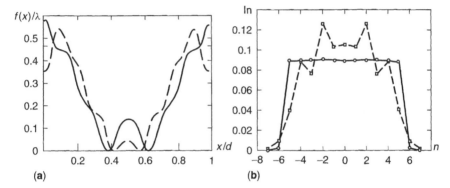

(a)   **(b)**

Figure 3.20. Eleven-order grating (**a**) profiles and (**b**) order intensities calculated in scalar approximation (dashed line) and in the Rayleigh approximation (solid line).

The values of E and δ for the gratings designed in the Rayleigh approximation run at 92.5% and 1.7%, for 5-order grating, 94.2% and 0.8%, for 7-order grating, 99.3% and 0.5%, for 9-order grating, and 96.3% and 0.7%, for 11-order grating. To estimate the accuracy of the derived solutions, the order intensities were calculated using the exact integral method treated in Section 3.2. The results of the calculation have shown that for the Rayleigh-approximation-based profile the error δ increase is only about 2 to 3 percent as compared to the exact solution. The examples considered demonstrate both a fairly good convergence and accuracy of the gradient procedure in the Rayleigh approximation and the need for correcting the profiles calculated in scalar approximation.

3.5 DIFFRACTION BY 2D REFLECTION STRUCTURES

3.5.1 Light Diffraction by a Curvilinear Zone

Consider the diffraction of a monochromatic electromagnetic wave by a groove curved within a perfectly conducting material in plane $z = 0$, where (x, y, z) are the Cartesian coordinates. The groove walls are parallel to the z-axis, whereas the groove bottom is parallel to plane (x, y). This problem bears importance for a variety of applications, for example, for computing the field produced by the binary Fresnel lens. In further discussion, the curvilinear groove is referred to as *zone*. The problem is tackled using the method of mode expansions [5]. A particular case of the mode expansions method has been dealt with in Section 3.1 devoted to solving the problem of diffraction by perfectly conducting diffraction gratings with stepwise profile.

The electric and magnetic fields satisfy a set of Maxwell equations analogous to Eqs. (3.5) and (3.6) at

$$\text{rot } \mathbf{H} = -ik\mathbf{E}, \tag{3.271}$$

$$\text{rot } \mathbf{E} = ik\mathbf{H}, \tag{3.272}$$

where k is the wave number. The boundary conditions on the perfectly conducting surface take the form of Eq. (3.11). Besides, the tangential components of the electric field should be continuous while passing through the plane $z = 0$ corresponding to the upper rim of the groove:

$$[\mathbf{n}, \mathbf{E}_1(z = 0)] = [\mathbf{n}, \mathbf{E}_2(z = 0)], \tag{3.273}$$

where $\mathbf{n}$ is the normal to the plane $z = 0$, $\mathbf{E}_1$, $\mathbf{E}_2$ are the fields in domains above (at $z > 0$) and within the groove. The tangential components of the magnetic field are not continuous while passing through the plane $z = 0$:

$$[\mathbf{n}, \mathbf{H}] = 4\pi\mathbf{j}/c, \tag{3.274}$$

where $\mathbf{j}$ is the surface current density. However, at $z = 0$, the magnetic field tangential component within the groove is also continuous:

$$[\mathbf{n}, \mathbf{H}_1(z = 0)] = [\mathbf{n}, \mathbf{H}_2(z = 0)]. \tag{3.275}$$

To solve the Maxwell equations in Eqs. (3.271) and (3.272), we shall make use of the method of separation of variables as it has been set forth in Section 3.1. The solution to the Maxwell equation is presented as a wave propagating along the z-axis:

$$\mathbf{E}(\mathbf{x}; \chi) = \tilde{\mathbf{E}}(x, y, \chi)e^{ik\Gamma z},$$

$$\mathbf{H}(\mathbf{x}; \chi) = \tilde{\mathbf{H}}(x, y, \chi)e^{ik\Gamma z}, \tag{3.276}$$

where $x = (x, y, z)$, $\Gamma = \pm\sqrt{1 - \chi^2}$ is the constant of propagation along the z-axis. Note that contrary to Eq. (3.7) of Section 3.1 where the Oz-axis was parallel to the grating grooves, in Eq. (3.261) the Oz-axis is directed perpendicularly to the groove bottom plane.

Substituting Eq. (3.276) in the set (3.271) and (3.272), we obtain the relation for $\tilde{\mathbf{E}}(x, y, \chi)$ and $\tilde{\mathbf{H}}(x, y, \chi)$ expressed through $\tilde{E}_z(x, y, \chi)$ and $\tilde{H}_z(x, y, \chi)$:

$$\tilde{\mathbf{E}}(x, y, \chi) = -\frac{\Gamma}{ik(1 - \Gamma^2)}\nabla_\perp \tilde{E}_z(x, y, \chi) - \frac{1}{ik(1 - \Gamma^2)}\text{rot}_\perp \tilde{H}_z(x, y, \chi)$$

$$+ \tilde{E}_z(x, y, \chi)\mathbf{e}_z,$$

$$\tilde{\mathbf{H}}(x, y, \chi) = -\frac{\Gamma}{ik(1 - \Gamma^2)} \nabla_\perp \tilde{H}_z(x, y, \chi) + \frac{1}{ik(1 - \Gamma^2)} \operatorname{rot}_\perp \tilde{E}_z(x, y, \chi)$$

$$+ \tilde{H}_z(x, y, \chi)\mathbf{e}_z, \tag{3.277}$$

where $\mathbf{e}_x$, $\mathbf{e}_y$, $\mathbf{e}_z$ are the basis vectors of the coordinate system,

$$\nabla_\perp F = \frac{\partial F}{\partial x}\mathbf{e}_x + \frac{\partial F}{\partial y}\mathbf{e}_y, \tag{3.278}$$

$$\operatorname{rot}_\perp F = \frac{\partial F}{\partial y}\mathbf{e}_x - \frac{\partial F}{\partial x}\mathbf{e}_y. \tag{3.279}$$

Note that the operations $\operatorname{rot}_\perp F$ and $\operatorname{rot} \mathbf{A}$ should not be confused, the former being applied to the scalar function and the latter being applied to the vector function. The $\tilde{E}_z$ and $\tilde{H}_z$ component sin Eq. (3.277) satisfy 2D Helmholtz equations

$$\Delta_\perp \tilde{E}_z(x, y) + k^2\chi^2 \tilde{E}_z(x, y) = 0,$$

$$\Delta_\perp \tilde{H}_z(x, y) + k^2\chi^2 \tilde{H}_z(x, y) = 0. \tag{3.280}$$

The Helmholtz equation is an equation in eigenvalues. For free space, the eigenvalues have a continuous spectrum. At the same time, for guiding structures, such as waveguides, the eigenvalues spectrum is discrete. Substituting Eq. (3.277) into Eq. (3.276), we put down the expressions for the traveling waves

$$\mathbf{E}^s(\mathbf{x}, \chi) = \left[-\frac{s\sqrt{1 - \chi^2}}{ik\chi^2} \nabla_\perp \tilde{E}_z(x, y, z) - \frac{1}{ik\chi^2} \operatorname{rot}_\perp \tilde{H}_z(x, y, \chi) + \tilde{E}_z(x, y, \chi)\mathbf{e}_z \right]$$

$$\times e^{sik\sqrt{1-\chi^2}z},$$

$$\mathbf{H}^s(\mathbf{x}, \chi) = \left[-\frac{s\sqrt{1 - \chi^2}}{ik\chi^2} \nabla_\perp \tilde{H}_z(x, y, z) - \frac{1}{ik\chi^2} \operatorname{rot}_\perp \tilde{E}_z(x, y, \chi) + \tilde{H}_z(x, y, \chi)\mathbf{e}_z \right]$$

$$\times e^{sik\sqrt{1-\chi^2}z}. \tag{3.281}$$

Here, $s = \pm 1$, with $s = 1$ describing the waves propagated along the z-axis and $s = -1$ describing the waves propagated contrary to the z-axis. In free space, the solutions to the Helmholtz equation, Eq. (3.280), take the form

$$\tilde{E}_z(x, y, \chi) = E^s(\alpha, \beta)F_0(\alpha, \beta, x, y),$$

$$\tilde{H}_z(x, y, \chi) = H^s(\alpha, \beta)F_0(\alpha, \beta, x, y). \tag{3.282}$$

Substituting Eq. (3.282) into Eq. (3.281), we obtain the partial solutions of the Maxwell equations (3.271) and (3.272) as functions of the parameters (α, β) in the form

$$\mathbf{E}^s(x, \chi) = \mathbf{E}^s(x, \alpha, \beta)$$

$$= \left[-\frac{s\sqrt{1 - \chi^2}}{\chi^2} E^s(\alpha, \beta)\mathbf{F}_1(\alpha, \beta, x, y) - \frac{1}{\chi^2} H^s(\alpha, \beta)\mathbf{F}_2(\alpha, \beta, x, y) \right]$$

$$\times e^{sik\sqrt{1-\chi^2}z} + \mathbf{e}_z E^s(\alpha, \beta)F_0(\alpha, \beta, x, y)e^{sik\sqrt{1-\chi^2}z},$$

$$\mathbf{H}^s(\mathbf{x}, \chi) = \mathbf{H}^s(\mathbf{x}, \alpha, \beta)$$

$$= \left[-\frac{s\sqrt{1-\chi^2}}{\chi^2} H^s(\alpha, \beta)\mathbf{F}_1(\alpha, \beta, x, y) + \frac{1}{\chi^2} E^s(\alpha, \beta)\mathbf{F}_2(\alpha, \beta, x, y) \right]$$

$$\times e^{sik\sqrt{1-\chi^2}z} + \mathbf{e}_z H^s(\alpha, \beta)F_0(\alpha, \beta, x, y)e^{sik\sqrt{1-\chi^2}z}, \tag{3.283}$$

where

$$\mathbf{F}_1(\alpha, \beta, x, y) = (1/ik)\nabla_\perp e^{ik(\alpha x + \beta y)},$$

$$\mathbf{F}_2(\alpha, \beta, x, y) = (1/ik)\nabla_\perp \times e^{ik(\alpha x + \beta y)}.$$

The solutions in Eq. (3.283) correspond to linearly polarized plane waves with the propagation direction $(\alpha, \beta, s\sqrt{1-\alpha^2-\beta^2})$. According to the superposition principle, the general solution to Eqs. (3.271) and (3.272) in free space is represented as a superposition of plane waves of Eq. (3.283) at $s = \pm 1$ and various (α, β). Although (α, β) take values from a continuous range, such a superposition takes the form of the integral

$$\mathbf{E}(\mathbf{x}) = \sum_s \int_{-\infty}^{\infty} \left[-\frac{s\sqrt{1-\chi^2}}{\chi^2} E^s(\alpha, \beta)\mathbf{F}_1(\alpha, \beta, x, y) - \frac{1}{\chi^2} H^s(\alpha, \beta)\mathbf{F}_2(\alpha, \beta, x, y) \right]$$

$$\times e^{sik\sqrt{1-\chi^2}z}\, d\alpha\, d\beta + \sum_s \int_{-\infty}^{\infty} \mathbf{e}_z E^s(\alpha, \beta)F_0(\alpha, \beta, x, y)e^{sik\sqrt{1-\chi^2}z}\, d\alpha\, d\beta, \tag{3.284}$$

$$\mathbf{H}(\mathbf{x}) = \sum_s \int_{-\infty}^{\infty} \left[-\frac{s\sqrt{1-\chi^2}}{\chi^2} H^s(\alpha, \beta)\mathbf{F}_1(\alpha, \beta, x, y) + \frac{1}{\chi^2} E^s(\alpha, \beta)\mathbf{F}_2(\alpha, \beta, x, y) \right]$$

$$\times e^{sik\sqrt{1-\chi^2}z}\, d\alpha\, d\beta + \sum_s \int_{-\infty}^{\infty} \mathbf{e}_z H^s(\alpha, \beta)F_0(\alpha, \beta, x, y)e^{sik\sqrt{1-\chi^2}z}\, d\alpha\, d\beta.$$

For the purposes of further discussion, of special interest is a quasi-periodic field whose spectrum is given by

$$E^s(\alpha, \beta) = \sum_{mn} R_{mn}^{se}\delta(\alpha - \alpha_n)\delta(\alpha - \beta_n), \tag{3.285}$$

where $\quad H^s(\alpha, \beta) = \sum_{mn} R_{mn}^{sh}\delta(\alpha - \alpha_n)\delta(\alpha - \beta_n), \quad -\infty < m, \ n < \infty,$

$\alpha_n = \alpha_0 - \lambda n/d_x$, $\beta_m = \alpha_0 - \lambda m/d_y$, $\chi_{mn}^2 = \alpha_{mn}^2 + \beta_{mn}^2$, d_x, d_y is the period of quasi-periodicity.
Substituting Eq. (3.285) into Eq. (3.284), we obtain the following decomposition of quasi-periodic fields:

$$\mathbf{E}(\mathbf{x}) = \sum_s \sum_{mn} \left[-\frac{s\sqrt{1-\chi_{mn}^2}}{\chi_{mn}^2} R_{nm}^{se}\mathbf{F}_1(\alpha_n, \beta_m, x, y) - \frac{1}{\chi_{mn}^2} R_{nm}^{sh}\mathbf{F}_2(\alpha_n, \beta_n, x, y) \right]$$

$$\times e^{sik\sqrt{1-\chi_{mn}^2}z} + \sum_s \sum_{mn} \mathbf{e}_z R_{nm}^{sh}F_0(\alpha_n, \beta_m, x, y)e^{sik\sqrt{1-\chi_{mn}^2}z}, \tag{3.286}$$

$$\mathbf{H}(\mathbf{x}) = \sum_{s} \sum_{mn} \left[-\frac{s\sqrt{1-\chi_{mn}^2}}{\chi_{mn}^2} R_{nm}^{sh} \mathbf{F}_1(\alpha_n, \beta_m, x, y) + \frac{1}{\chi_{mn}^2} R_{nm}^{se} \mathbf{F}_2(\alpha_n, \beta_m, x, y) \right]$$

$$\times e^{sik\sqrt{1-\chi_{mn}^2}z} + \sum_{s} \sum_{mn} \mathbf{e}_z R_{nm}^{sh} F_0(\alpha, \beta, x, y) e^{sik\sqrt{1-\chi_{mn}^2}z}.$$

Quasi-periodic decompositions are found when the electromagnetic wave is diffracted by a 2D diffraction grating of periods d_x, d_y. In the earlier-described case, $s = 1$ describes waves reflected from the diffraction grating, whereas $s = 1$ describes waves incident on the diffraction grating.

Consider now how the Maxwell equations in Eqs. (3.271) and (3.272) are solved within the zone groove. In doing so, let us first treat the problem of the electromagnetic wave propagation within a waveguide. Assume that the waveguide cross section is a domain located between two pairs of curves, which are the coordinate lines of a curvilinear system: elliptical, parabolic, cylindrical, or Cartesian. The name of the coordinate system coincides with the name of a second-order curve that defines the guiding structure cross section. The waveguide walls are assumed to be perfectly conducting. Introduce the curvilinear coordinates by the formulae

$$x = x(u, v), \quad y = y(u, v). \tag{3.287}$$

The waveguide cross section is a domain limited by the coordinate curves, with their Cartesian parametric equations given by

$$x = x(t) = x(u_1, t), \ y = y(t) = y(u_1, t),$$
$$x = x(t) = x(u_2, t), \ y = y(t) = y(u_2, t),$$
$$x = x(t) = x(t, v_1), \ y = y(t) = y(t, v_1),$$
$$x = x(t) = x(t, v_2), \ y = y(t) = y(t, v_2). \tag{3.288}$$

The expressions for vector operations in the orthogonal curvilinear coordinate system take the form

$$\nabla_{\perp} F = \frac{1}{\sqrt{g_{11}}} \frac{\partial F}{\partial u} \mathbf{e}_u + \frac{1}{\sqrt{g_{22}}} \frac{\partial F}{\partial v} \mathbf{e}_v,$$

$$\nabla_{\perp} \times F = \frac{1}{\sqrt{g_{22}}} \frac{\partial F}{\partial v} \mathbf{e}_u - \frac{1}{\sqrt{g_{11}}} \frac{\partial F}{\partial u} \mathbf{e}_v, \tag{3.289}$$

where g_{ij} are the components of a metric tensor in the curvilinear coordinate system. In this situation, the full field is also expressed through $\tilde{E}_z$ and $\tilde{H}_z$ using formulae (3.277). The $\tilde{E}_z$ and $\tilde{H}_z$ functions themselves satisfy *(1)* the Helmholtz equations written in the curvilinear coordinates

$$\frac{1}{\sqrt{g}} \left[\frac{\partial}{\partial u} \left(\frac{\sqrt{g}}{g_{11}} \right) \frac{\partial \tilde{E}_z}{\partial u} + \frac{\partial}{\partial v} \left(\frac{\sqrt{g}}{g_{22}} \right) \frac{\partial \tilde{E}_z}{\partial v} \right] + k^2 \chi^2 \tilde{E}_z = 0,$$

$$\frac{1}{\sqrt{g}} \left[\frac{\partial}{\partial u} \left(\frac{\sqrt{g}}{g_{11}} \right) \frac{\partial \tilde{H}_z}{\partial u} + \frac{\partial}{\partial v} \left(\frac{\sqrt{g}}{g_{22}} \right) \frac{\partial \tilde{H}_z}{\partial v} \right] + k^2 \eta^2 \tilde{H}_z = 0, \tag{3.290}$$

where χ and η define the phase velocities of propagation of the electric and magnetic field within the groove and *(2)* the boundary conditions on the waveguide structure surface

$$(\nabla_\perp \tilde{E}_z, \ \mathbf{e}_v) = 0, \ \text{if } u = u_1, \ u = u_2,$$

$$(\nabla_\perp \tilde{E}_z, \ \mathbf{e}_u) = 0, \ \text{if } v = v_1, \ v = v_2, \tag{3.291}$$

for the electric field and

$$(\nabla_\perp \times \tilde{H}_z, \ \mathbf{e}_v) = 0, \quad \text{if } u = u_1, \ u = u_2,$$

$$(\nabla_\perp \times \tilde{H}_z, \ \mathbf{e}_u) = 0, \quad \text{if } v = v_1, \ v = v_2, \tag{3.292}$$

for the magnetic field.

The boundary-value problem for Eq. (3.290) with the boundary conditions in Eqs. (3.291) and (3.292) is a problem on eigenvalues (χ, η are the eigen-numbers of the boundary-value problem). In this case, the range of eigenvalues is discrete. Denote the solution to Eq. (3.290) for $\tilde{E}_z$ corresponding to the eigenvalue χ_{nm} as $E_{nm}(u, v, \chi_{nm})$ and the solution to Eq. (3.290) for $\tilde{H}_z$ corresponding to the eigenvalue η_{nm} as $H_{nm}(u, v, \eta_{nm})$. The general solution to the Maxwell equations in Eqs. (3.271) and (3.272) can be expressed through the superposition of solutions of the problem on eigenvalues

$$\mathbf{E}^\pm(u, v, z) = \sum_m C_{nm}^{\pm e}\left[-\frac{\pm\sqrt{1-\chi_{nm}^2}}{k\chi_m^2}\nabla_\perp E_{nm}(u, v, \chi_{nm})\exp(\pm ik\sqrt{1-\chi_{nm}^2}z) \right.$$

$$\left. + \mathbf{e}_z E_{nm}(u, v, \chi_{nm})\exp(\pm ik\sqrt{1-\chi_{nm}^2}z) \right]$$

$$- \sum_m \frac{C_{nm}^{\pm h}}{k\eta_{nm}^2}\nabla_\perp \times H_{nm}(u, v, \eta_{nm})\exp(\pm ik\sqrt{1-\eta_{nm}^2}z),$$

$$\mathbf{H}^\pm(u, v, z) = \sum_m C_{nm}^{\pm h}\left[-\frac{\pm\sqrt{1-\eta_m^2}}{ik\eta_{\sim m}^2}\nabla_\perp H_{nm}(u, v, \eta_{nm})\exp(\pm ik\sqrt{1-\eta_{nm}^2}z) \right.$$

$$\left. + \mathbf{e}_z H_{nm}(u, v, \eta_{nm})\exp\left(\pm ik\sqrt{1-\eta_{nm}^2}z\right) \right]$$

$$+ \sum_m \frac{C_{nm}^{\pm e}}{k\chi_{nm}^2}\nabla_\perp \times E_{nm}(u, v, \chi_{nm})\exp\left(\pm ik\sqrt{1-\chi_{nm}^2}z\right), \tag{3.293}$$

where C_{nm} are arbitrary coefficients, with the upper sign describing the waves propagating along the z-axis and the lower sign describing the waves propagating contrary to the z-axis direction. Within the zone, there are waves propagating in both directions (the waves propagating contrary to the z-axis are caused by the reflection from the curvilinear groove bottom). The boundary condition on the groove bottom takes the form $[E(z = -h), \mathbf{e}] = 0$, where h is the groove depth.

In view of Eq. (3.293) and the boundary condition on the groove bottom, we obtain the expression for the vectors of the electric and magnetic field in the following form:

$$
\mathbf{E}(u, v, z) = \sum_m C_{nm}^e \left\{ -\frac{\sqrt{1 - \chi_{nm}^2}}{k\chi_m^2} \nabla_\perp E_{nm}(u, v, \chi_{nm}) \sin\left[k\sqrt{1 - \chi_{nm}^2}(z + h)\right] \right.
$$

$$
\left. + e_z E_{nm}(u, v, \chi_{nm}) \cos\left[k\sqrt{1 - \chi_{nm}^2}(z + h)\right] \right\}
$$

$$
- \sum_m \frac{C_{nm}^h}{k\eta_{nm}^2} \nabla_\perp \times H_{nm}(u, v, \eta_{nm}) \sin\left[k\sqrt{1 - \eta_{nm}^2}(z + h)\right],
$$

$$
\mathbf{H}(u, v, z) = \sum_m C_{nm}^h \left\{ -\frac{\sqrt{1 - \eta_m^2}}{ik\eta_{\sim m}^2} \nabla_\perp H_{nm}(u, v, \eta_{nm}) \cos\left[k\sqrt{1 - \eta_{nm}^2}(z + h)\right] \right.
$$

$$
\left. + e_z i H_{nm}(u, v, \eta_{nm}) \sin\left[k\sqrt{1 - \eta_{nm}^2}(z + h)\right] \right\}
$$

$$
+ \sum_m \frac{C_{nm}^e}{k\chi_{nm}^2} \nabla_\perp \times E_{nm}(u, v, \chi_{nm}) \cos\left[k\sqrt{1 - \chi_{nm}^2}(z + h)\right]. \quad (3.294)
$$

The mode functions satisfy the orthogonality relations:

$$
\int E_{ms}(u, v) E_{nk}^*(u, v) \, du \, dv = 0,
$$

$$
\int [\nabla_\perp E_{ms}(u, v), \nabla_\perp E_{nk}^*(u, v)] \, du \, dv = 0,
$$

$$
\int [\nabla_\perp \times E_{ms}(u, v), \nabla_\perp \times E_{nk}^*(u, v)] \, du \, dv = 0,
$$

$$
\int [\nabla_\perp H_{ms}(u, v), \nabla_\perp H_{nk}^*(u, v) \, du \, dv] = 0,
$$

$$
\int [\nabla_\perp \times H_{ms}(u, v), \nabla_\perp \times H_{nk}^*(u, v)] \, du \, dv = 0,
$$

$$
\int [\nabla_\perp \times E_{ms}(u, v), \nabla_\perp H_{nk}^*(u, v)] \, du \, dv = 0. \quad (3.295)
$$

In further discussion, we will need to use expressions for the tangential components of the electric and magnetic field at $z = 0$. The tangential components of the electric field should be continuous when going across the medium interface $z = 0$ [Eq. (3.273)]. In view of Eq. (3.284), we can write down

$$
\sum_s \int_{-\infty}^\infty \left[-\frac{s\sqrt{1 - \chi^2}}{\chi^2} E^s(\alpha, \beta)\mathbf{F}_1(\alpha, \beta, x, y) - \frac{1}{\chi^2} H^s(\alpha, \beta)\mathbf{F}_2(\alpha, \beta, x, y) \right] d\alpha \, d\beta
$$

$$
= \sum_m C_{nm}^e \left[-\frac{\sqrt{1 - \chi_{nm}^2}}{k\chi_m^2} \nabla_\perp E_{nm}(u, v, \chi_{nm}) \sin(k\sqrt{1 - \chi_{nm}^2}h) \right.
$$

$$
\left. - \sum_m \frac{C_{nm}^h}{k\eta_{nm}^2} \nabla_\perp \times H_{nm}(u, v, \eta_{nm}) \sin(k\sqrt{1 - \eta_{nm}^2}h) \right]. \quad (3.296)
$$

The tangential component of the magnetic field is not continuous, preserving continuity only at points of the plane $z = 0$, where the conductor is absent Eqs. (3.274) and (3.275). In these points, the continuity condition takes the form

$$
\sum_s \int_{-\infty}^{\infty} \left[-\frac{s\sqrt{1-\chi^2}}{\chi^2} H^s(\alpha, \beta) \mathbf{F}_1(\alpha, \beta, x, y) + \frac{1}{\chi^2} E^s(\alpha, \beta) F_2(\alpha, \beta, x, y) \right] d\alpha \, d\beta
$$

$$
= \sum_m C_{nm}^h \left[-\frac{\sqrt{1-\eta_m^2}}{ik\eta_{nm}^2} \nabla_{\perp} H_{nm}(u, v, \eta_{nm}) \cos(k\sqrt{1-\eta_{nm}^2}\,h) \right.
$$

$$
\left. + \sum_m \frac{C_{nm}^e}{k\chi_{nm}^2} \nabla_{\perp} \times E_{nm}(u, v, \chi_{nm}) \cos(k\sqrt{1-\chi_{nm}^2}\,h) \right]. \tag{3.297}
$$

The functions $E^s(\alpha, \beta)$ and $H^s(\alpha, \beta)$ define a plane wave at $s = \pm 1$.

The relations in Eqs. (3.296) and (3.297) may be treated as a set of integral equations with respect to the functions $E^s(\alpha, \beta)$ and $H^s(\alpha, \beta)$ and the coefficients C_{nm}. Taking into account the orthogonality relations in Eq. (3.295), C_{nm}^e and C_{nm}^e can be derived from Eq. (3.297) and substituted into Eq. (3.296). Then, taking into account the orthogonality relations, we obtain for the functions $F_{1,2}(\alpha, \beta, x)$ of Eq. (3.283) a set of integral equations that comprise only the functions $H^s(\alpha, \beta)$, $E^s(\alpha, \beta)$ at $s = 1$. Solving the constructed set of equations by one of the available methods and substituting the derived functions into Eq. (3.294), we get expressions for the vectors of the electric and magnetic field in a half-space $z > 0$.

3.5.2   Diffraction by a 2D Reflection Binary Grating

The algorithm of the earlier section may be used to compute a field diffracted by a 2D diffraction grating. Let the diffraction grating be represented by a periodic structure of periods d_x, d_y along the corresponding coordinate axes. The grating period is composed of a set of curvilinear grooves with vertical walls and a flat bottom, as those treated in the earlier section. A typical example of such a structure is represented by an array of reflection binary lenses. Let such a 2D diffraction grating be illuminated by a quasi-periodic electromagnetic wave, with the electric and magnetic field vectors defined by

$$
\mathbf{E}(\mathbf{x}) = \sum_{mn} \left[\frac{\sqrt{1-\chi^2}}{\chi^2} R_{nm}^{se} \mathbf{F}_1(\alpha_n, \beta_m, x, y) - \frac{1}{\chi^2} R_{nm}^{sh} \mathbf{F}_2(\alpha_n, \beta_n, x, y) \right] e^{-ik\sqrt{1-\chi^2}z}
$$

$$
+ \sum_{mn} \mathbf{e}_z R_{nm}^{sh} F_0(\alpha_n, \beta_m, x, y) e^{-ik\sqrt{1-\chi^2}z},
$$

$$
\mathbf{H}(\mathbf{x}) = \sum_{mn} \left[\frac{\sqrt{1-\chi^2}}{\chi^2} R_{nm}^{sh} \mathbf{F}_1(\alpha_n, \beta_m, x, y) + \frac{1}{\chi^2} R_{nm}^{se} \mathbf{F}_2(\alpha_n, \beta_m, x, y) \right] e^{-ik\sqrt{1-\chi^2}z}
$$

$$
+ \sum_{mn} \mathbf{e}_z R_{nm}^{sh} F_0(\alpha, \beta, x, y) e^{-ik\sqrt{1-\chi^2}z}, \tag{3.298}
$$

where $\alpha_n = \alpha_0 + \lambda n/d_x$, $\beta_m = \alpha_0 + \lambda m/d_y$, and the coefficients R_{nm}^{se} and R_{nm}^{sh} are taken to be known at $s = -1$.

The full field is specified by Eq. (3.286). We seek to find the coefficients R_{nm}^{se} and R_{nm}^{sh} at $s = 1$ in the decomposition of the electric and magnetic field for the reflected wave. The within-groove field takes the form analogous to Eq. (3.294)

$$
\mathbf{E}(u, v, z) = \sum_L \sum_m C_{nm}^{eL} \left(-\frac{\sqrt{1 - \chi^{L_{nm}2}}}{k\chi^L nm2} \nabla_\perp E_{nm}^L(u, v, \chi_{nm}^L) \sin\left[k\sqrt{1 - (\chi_{lm})^2}(z + h)\right] \right.
$$

$$
\left. + \mathbf{e}_z i E_{nm}^L(u, v, \chi_{nm}^L) \cos\left[k\sqrt{1 - (\chi_{nm}^L)^2}(z + h)\right] \right)
$$

$$
+ \sum_m \frac{C_{nm}^{hL}}{k\eta_{nm2}^L} \nabla_\perp \times H_{nm}^L(u, v, \eta_{nm}^L) \sin\left[k\sqrt{1 - (\eta_{nm}^L)^2}(z + h)\right],
$$

$$
\mathbf{H}(u, v, z) = \sum_m C_{nm}^{hL} \left(-\frac{\sqrt{1 - \eta^{L_m2}}}{ik\eta_{\sim m}^2} \nabla_\perp H_{nm}^L(u, v, \eta_{nm}^L) \cos\left[k\sqrt{1 - (\eta_{nm}^L)^2}(z + h)\right] \right.
$$

$$
\left. + \mathbf{e}_z i H_{nm}^L(u, v, \eta_{nm}^L) \sin\left[k\sqrt{1 - (\eta_{nm})^2}(z + h)\right] \right)
$$

$$
+ \sum_m \frac{C_{nm}^{eL}}{k\chi_{nm2}^L} \nabla_\perp \times E_{nm}^L(u, v, \chi_{nm}^L) \cos\left[k\sqrt{1 - (\chi_{nm}^L)^2}(z + h)\right], \quad (3.299)
$$

where L is the groove number.

In this case, the equality of the tangential components takes the form:

$$
\sum_s \sum_{mn} \left[-\frac{s\sqrt{1 - \chi^2}}{\chi_{mn}^2} R_{nm}^{se} F_1(\alpha_n, \beta_m, x, y) - \frac{1}{\chi_{mn}^2} R_{nm}^{sh} F_2(\alpha_n, \beta_n, x, y) \right]
$$

$$
= \sum_L \sum_m C_{nm}^{eL} \left[-\frac{\sqrt{1 - \chi_{nm2}^L}}{k\chi_{nm2}^L} \nabla_\perp E_{nm}^L(u, v, \chi_{nm}) \sin(k\sqrt{1 - (\chi_{nm}^L)^2}h) \right]
$$

$$
- \sum_m \frac{C_{nm}^{hL}}{k\eta_{nm2}^{L2}} \nabla_\perp \times H_{nm}^L(u, v, \eta_{nm}^L) \sin\left(k\sqrt{1 - \eta_{nm2}^L {}^2}h\right) \quad (3.300)
$$

for the electric field and

$$
\sum_s \sum_{mn} \left[-\frac{s\sqrt{1 - \chi^2}}{\chi_{mn}^2} R_{nm}^{sh} \mathbf{F}_1(\alpha_n, \beta_m, x, y) + \frac{1}{\chi_{mn}^2} R_{nm}^{se} \mathbf{F}_2(\alpha_n, \beta_m, x, y) \right]
$$

$$
= \sum_m -C_{nm}^{hL} \frac{\sqrt{1 - \eta_{m2}^L}}{ik(\eta_{nm})^2} \nabla_\perp H_{nm}^L(u, v, \eta_{nm}^L) \cos\left(k\sqrt{1 - (\eta_{nm}^L)^2}h\right)
$$

$$
+ \sum_m \frac{C_{nm}^{eL}}{k\chi_{nm}^2} \nabla_\perp \times E_{nm}^L(u, v, \chi_{nm}^L) \cos\left(k\sqrt{1 - (\chi_{nm}^L)^2}h\right), \quad (3.301)
$$

for the magnetic field.

The set of functional equations in Eqs. (3.300) and (3.301) can be easily reduced to a set of linear algebraic equations. Making use of the orthogonality relations for modal functions, Eq. (3.295), the coefficients C_{nm}^{eL} and C_{nm}^{hL} can be derived from Eq. (3.300) and substituted in Eq. (3.300). Then, making use of the orthogonality relations for the functions F_1 and F_2, we obtain a set of linear equations for the derivation of the coefficients R_{nm}^{se} and R_{nm}^{sh}.

3.5.3 Diffraction by 2D Transmission Dielectric Structures

A method for analyzing the diffraction of the light wave by a 2D transmission dielectric structure dealt with in this section uses the numerical solution of the Maxwell equations written in terms of impulse (in the spatial-frequency coordinates). The set of Maxwell equations in Eqs. (3.5) and (3.6) may be rewritten in the following form, expanding the vector operator:

$$\partial_z E_x = \frac{i}{k}\partial_x\left(\frac{1}{\varepsilon}(\partial_x H_y - \partial_y H_x)\right) + ikH_y,$$

$$\partial_z E_y = \frac{i}{k}\partial_y\left(\frac{1}{\varepsilon}(\partial_x H_y - \partial_y H_x)\right) - ikH_x,$$

$$\partial_z H_x = \frac{1}{ik}\partial_x(\partial_x E_y - \partial_y E_x) - ik\varepsilon E_y,$$

$$\partial_z H_y = \frac{1}{ik}\partial_y(\partial_x E_y - \partial_y E_x) + ik\varepsilon E_x. \tag{3.302}$$

We shall represent the vectors of the electric and magnetic field and the permittivity function as a Fourier expansion with respect to the transverse coordinates:

$$\mathbf{E}(x, y, z) = \int_{-\infty}^{\infty} \mathbf{E}(\alpha, \beta, z)\exp[ik(\alpha x + \beta y)]\, d\alpha\, d\beta,$$

$$\mathbf{H}(x, y, z) = \int_{-\infty}^{\infty} \mathbf{H}(\alpha, \beta, z)\exp[ik(\alpha x + \beta y)]\, d\alpha\, d\beta,$$

$$\varepsilon(x, y, z) = \int_{-\infty}^{\infty} \varepsilon(\alpha, \beta, z)\exp[ik(\alpha x + \beta y)]\, d\alpha\, d\beta,$$

$$\varepsilon^{-1}(x, y, z) = \int_{-\infty}^{\infty} \varepsilon^{-1}(\alpha, \beta, z)\exp[ik(\alpha x + \beta y)]\, d\alpha\, d\beta, \tag{3.303}$$

where $\varepsilon^{-1}(x, y, z) = 1/\varepsilon(x, y, z)$, but $\varepsilon^{-1}(\alpha, \beta, z) \neq 1/\varepsilon(\alpha, \beta, z)$, and $\varepsilon^{-1}(\alpha, \beta, z)$ is simply a convenient designation. In further discussion, the functions $\mathbf{E}(\alpha, \beta, z)$ and $\mathbf{H}(\alpha, \beta, z)$ will be referred to as transverse spatial-frequency components.

Substituting the expansions in Eq. (3.303) into the Maxwell equations in Eq. (3.302) yields the Maxwell equation in terms of impulse (in the spatial-frequency coordinates)

$$\partial_z E_x(\alpha, \beta, z) = -ik\alpha \int_{-\infty}^{\infty}[\omega_x H_y(\omega_x, \omega_y, z) - \omega_y H_x(\omega_x, \omega_y, z)]\varepsilon(\alpha - \omega_x, \beta - \omega_y)$$

$$\times\, d\omega_x\, d\omega_y + ikH_y(\alpha, \beta, z),$$

$$\partial_z E_y(\alpha, \beta, z) = -ik\beta \int_{-\infty}^{\infty} [\omega_x H_y(\omega_x, \omega_y, z) - \omega_y H_x(\omega_x, \omega_y, z)] \varepsilon(\alpha - \omega_x, \beta - \omega_y)$$
$$\times \, d\omega_x \, d\omega_y + ik H_x(\alpha, \beta, z),$$

$$\partial_z H_x(\alpha, \beta, z) = ik\alpha[\alpha E_y(\alpha, \beta, z) - \beta E_x(\alpha, \beta, z)] - ik \int_{-\infty}^{\infty} \varepsilon(\alpha - \omega_x, \beta - \omega_y)$$
$$\times \, E_y(\omega_x, \omega_y, z) \, d\omega_x \, d\omega_y,$$

$$\partial_z H_y(\alpha, \beta, z) = ik\beta[\alpha E_y(\alpha, \beta, z) - \beta E_x(\alpha, \beta, z)] + ik \int_{-\infty}^{\infty} \varepsilon(\alpha - \omega_x, \beta - \omega_y)$$
$$\times \, E_x(\omega_x, \omega_y, z) \, d\omega_x \, d\omega_y. \tag{3.304}$$

Consider now the diffraction by a 2D transmission diffractive optical element. The procedure of solving this problem is, in many respects, analogous to that of solving the problem of diffraction by a 1D transmission diffraction grating having been treated in Section 3.3. The difference is in a manner the coordinate axes in Figures 3.5 and 3.6 are located: the z-axis is perpendicular to the optical element plane or the diffractive structure plane. Assume then that the first and the third zones in Figure 3.5 correspond, respectively, to the domains at $z > a$, where a is a maximum structure relief height, and $z < 0$ of uniform permittivity. In the second zone, the modulation zone, where $z \in (0, a)$ the permittivity is a function of coordinates: $\varepsilon = \varepsilon(x, y, z)$.

The zone-1 field is a combination of the incident field, with its frequency components given by (designations in Eq. (3.284))

$$\mathbf{E}(\alpha, \beta, z) = \left\{ \frac{-\sqrt{1 - \alpha^2 - \beta^2}}{\alpha^2 + \beta^2}(\alpha\mathbf{e}_x + \beta\mathbf{e}_y)I^e(\alpha, \beta) - \frac{\beta\mathbf{e}_x - \alpha\mathbf{e}_y}{\alpha^2 + \beta^2}I^h(\alpha, \beta) \right.$$
$$\left. + I^e(\alpha, \beta)\mathbf{e}_z \right\} \exp\left[ik\left(-\sqrt{1 - \alpha^2 - \beta^2}z \right) \right],$$

$$\mathbf{H}(\alpha, \beta, z) = \left\{ \frac{-\sqrt{1 - \alpha^2 - \beta^2}}{\alpha^2 + \beta^2}(\alpha\mathbf{e}_x + \beta\mathbf{e}_y)I^h(\alpha, \beta) + \frac{\beta\mathbf{e}_x - \alpha\mathbf{e}_y}{\alpha^2 + \beta^2}I^e(\alpha, \beta) \right.$$
$$\left. + I^h(\alpha, \beta)\mathbf{e}_z \right\} \exp\left[ik\left(-\sqrt{1 - \alpha^2 - \beta^2}z \right) \right], \tag{3.305}$$

and the reflected field, with its frequency components given by

$$\mathbf{E}(\alpha, \beta, z) = \left\{ \frac{-\sqrt{1 - \alpha^2 - \beta^2}}{\alpha^2 + \beta^2}(\alpha\mathbf{e}_x + \beta\mathbf{e}_y)R^e(\alpha, \beta) \right.$$
$$\left. - \frac{\beta\mathbf{e}_x - \alpha\mathbf{e}_y}{\alpha^2 + \beta^2}R^h(\alpha, \beta) + R^e(\alpha, \beta)\mathbf{e}_z \right\} \exp\left[ik\left(\sqrt{1 - \alpha^2 - \beta^2}z \right) \right],$$

$$\mathbf{H}(\alpha, \beta, z) = \left\{ \frac{-\sqrt{1 - \alpha^2 - \beta^2}}{\alpha^2 + \beta^2}(\alpha\mathbf{e}_x + \beta\mathbf{e}_y)R^h(\alpha, \beta) + \frac{\beta\mathbf{e}_x - \alpha\mathbf{e}_y}{\alpha^2 + \beta^2}R^e(\alpha, \beta) \right.$$
$$\left. + R^h(\alpha, \beta)\mathbf{e}_z \right\} \exp\left[ik\left(-\sqrt{1 - \alpha^2 - \beta^2}z \right) \right]. \tag{3.306}$$

The zone-3 field comprises the transmitted field, with its frequency components given by

$$
\mathbf{E}(\alpha, \beta, z) = \left\{ \frac{-\sqrt{1 - \alpha^2 - \beta^2}}{\alpha^2 + \beta^2} (\alpha \mathbf{e}_x + \beta \mathbf{e}_y) T^e(\alpha, \beta) - \frac{\beta \mathbf{e}_x - \alpha \mathbf{e}_y}{\alpha^2 + \beta^2} \right.
$$

$$
\left. \times T^h(\alpha, \beta) + T^e(\alpha, \beta) \mathbf{e}_z \right\} \exp \left[ik \left(-\sqrt{1 - \alpha^2 - \beta^2} z \right) \right],
$$

$$
\mathbf{H}(\alpha, \beta, z) = \left\{ \frac{-\sqrt{1 - \alpha^2 - \beta^2}}{\alpha^2 + \beta^2} (\alpha \mathbf{e}_x + \beta \mathbf{e}_y) T^h(\alpha, \beta) + \frac{\beta \mathbf{e}_x - \alpha \mathbf{e}_y}{\alpha^2 + \beta^2} T^e(\alpha, \beta) \right.
$$

$$
\left. \times T^h(\alpha, \beta) \mathbf{e}_z \right\} \exp \left[ik \left(-\sqrt{1 - \alpha^2 - \beta^2} z \right) \right]. \tag{3.307}
$$

The spatial-frequency components in the modulation zone satisfy a set of integral-differential equations of Eq. (3.305).

For the sake of further analysis, it is convenient to represent the equations in terms of operator and matrix. In terms of operator, the set of Maxwell equations in (3.302) takes the form

$$
\partial_z \mathbf{W} = \mathbf{H} \mathbf{W}, \tag{3.308}
$$

where $\mathbf{W}$ is a 4-component column-matrix: $W = \begin{pmatrix} E_x \\ E_y \\ H_x \\ H_y \end{pmatrix}$, $\mathbf{H}$ is a block-matrix differential operator:

$$
\mathbf{H} = \begin{pmatrix} \mathbf{A} & 0 \\ 0 & \mathbf{B} \end{pmatrix} \begin{pmatrix} 0 & 1 \\ 1 & 0 \end{pmatrix},
$$

$$
\mathbf{A} = \frac{i}{k} \begin{pmatrix} \partial_x & 0 \\ 0 & \partial_y \end{pmatrix} \begin{pmatrix} \varepsilon^{-1} & 0 \\ 0 & \varepsilon^{-1} \end{pmatrix} \begin{pmatrix} -\partial_y & \partial_x \\ -\partial_y & \partial_x \end{pmatrix} + ik \begin{pmatrix} 0 & 1 \\ -1 & 0 \end{pmatrix},
$$

$$
\mathbf{B} = \frac{1}{ik} \begin{pmatrix} \partial_x & 0 \\ 0 & \partial_y \end{pmatrix} \begin{pmatrix} -\partial_y & \partial_x \\ -\partial_y & \partial_x \end{pmatrix} + ik \begin{pmatrix} \varepsilon & 0 \\ 0 & \varepsilon \end{pmatrix} \begin{pmatrix} 0 & -1 \\ 1 & 0 \end{pmatrix}. \tag{3.309}
$$

In terms of matrix, Eq. (3.303) takes the form

$$
\mathbf{W}(x, y, z) = \int_{-\infty}^{\infty} \mathbf{W}(\alpha, \beta, z) \exp[ik(\alpha x + \beta y)] \, d\alpha \, d\beta. \tag{3.310}
$$

In spatial-frequency designations, the set of equations in Eq. (3.304) takes the form

$$
\partial_z \mathbf{W}(\alpha, \beta, z) = \mathbf{H}(\alpha, \beta, z) \mathbf{W}(\alpha, \beta, z),
$$

$$
\mathbf{H}(\alpha, \beta, z) = \begin{pmatrix} \mathbf{A}(\alpha, \beta, z) & 0 \\ 0 & \mathbf{B}(\alpha, \beta, z) \end{pmatrix} \begin{pmatrix} 0 & 1 \\ 1 & 0 \end{pmatrix}, \tag{3.311}
$$

where the 2D matrix operators operate on the 2D column-matrices by the formulae

$$
\mathbf{A}(\alpha, \beta) \begin{pmatrix} \varphi \\ \psi \end{pmatrix} = \frac{i}{k} \begin{pmatrix} ik\alpha & 0 \\ 0 & ik\beta \end{pmatrix} \int_{-\infty}^{\infty} \varepsilon^{-1}(\alpha - \omega_x, \beta - \omega_y, z) \begin{pmatrix} -ik\omega_y & ik\omega_x \\ -ik\omega_y & ik\omega_x \end{pmatrix}
$$

$$
\times \begin{pmatrix} \varphi(\omega_x, \omega_y, z) \\ \psi(\omega_x, \omega_y, z) \end{pmatrix} d\omega_x \, d\omega_y + ik \begin{pmatrix} 0 & 1 \\ -1 & 0 \end{pmatrix} \begin{pmatrix} \varphi \\ \psi \end{pmatrix},
$$

$$
\mathbf{B}(\alpha, \beta) \begin{pmatrix} \varphi \\ \psi \end{pmatrix} = \frac{1}{ik} \begin{pmatrix} ik\alpha & 0 \\ 0 & ik\beta \end{pmatrix} \begin{pmatrix} -ik\beta & ik\alpha \\ -ik\beta & ik\alpha \end{pmatrix} \begin{pmatrix} \varphi \\ \psi \end{pmatrix} + ik \int_{-\infty}^{\infty} \varepsilon(\alpha - \omega_x, \beta - \omega_y)
$$

$$
\times \begin{pmatrix} 0 & -1 \\ 1 & 0 \end{pmatrix} \begin{pmatrix} \varphi(\omega_x, \omega_y) \\ \psi(\omega_x, \omega_y) \end{pmatrix} d\omega_x \, d\omega_y. \tag{3.312}
$$

Consider in more details how the electromagnetic field propagates in vacuum. In this case, the set of integral-differential equations reduces to a set of common differential equations:

$$
\partial_z E_x(\alpha, \beta, z) = -ik\alpha[\alpha H_y(\alpha, \beta, z) - \beta H_x(\alpha, \beta, z)] + ik H_y(\alpha, \beta, z),
$$

$$
\partial_z E_y(\alpha, \beta, z) = -ik\beta[\alpha H_y(\alpha, \beta, z) - \beta H_x(\alpha, \beta, z)] - ik H_x(\alpha, \beta, z),
$$

$$
\partial_z H_x(\alpha, \beta, z) = ik\alpha[\alpha E_y(\alpha, \beta, z) - \beta E_x(\alpha, \beta, z)] - ik E_y(\alpha, \beta, z),
$$

$$
\partial_z H_y(\alpha, \beta, z) = ik\beta[\alpha E_y(\alpha, \beta, z) - \beta E_x(\alpha, \beta, z)] + ik E_x(\alpha, \beta, z). \tag{3.313}
$$

The general solution to the set in Eq. (3.313) is given by

$$
\mathbf{W}(\alpha, \beta, z) = [E^+(\alpha, \beta)\mathbf{W}^{+e}(\alpha, \beta) + H^+(\alpha, \beta)\mathbf{W}^{+h}(\alpha, \beta)] \exp\left(ik\sqrt{1 - \alpha^2 - \beta^2}z\right)
$$

$$
+ [E^-(\alpha, \beta)\mathbf{W}^{-e}(\alpha, \beta) + H^-(\alpha, \beta)\mathbf{W}^{-h}(\alpha, \beta)]
$$

$$
\times \exp\left(-ik\sqrt{1 - \alpha^2 - \beta^2}z\right),
$$

$$
\mathbf{W}^{\pm e}(\alpha, \beta) = \begin{pmatrix} \mp\sqrt{1 - \alpha^2 - \beta^2}\alpha \\ \mp\sqrt{1 - \alpha^2 - \beta^2}\beta \\ \beta \\ -\alpha \end{pmatrix} \bullet \|W\|^{-1},
$$

$$
\mathbf{W}^{\pm h}(\alpha, \beta) = \begin{pmatrix} -\beta \\ \alpha \\ \mp\sqrt{1 - \alpha^2 - \beta^2}\alpha \\ \mp\sqrt{1 - \alpha^2 - \beta^2}\beta \end{pmatrix} \bullet \|W\|^{-1},
$$

$$
\mathbf{W} = \sqrt{(\alpha^2 + \beta^2)\left(1 + \sqrt{|1 - \alpha^2 - \beta^2|}\right)}, \tag{3.314}
$$

where E^+, E^-, H^+, H^- define the contribution of the electric and magnetic waves into a desired direction. The upper sign corresponds to waves propagating in positive direction of the z-axis, whereas the lower sign corresponds to the negative direction. For the sake of completeness sake, note that the changeover to the uniform dielectric medium of permittivity E is implemented by use of the following transform:

$$\alpha \to \frac{\alpha}{\sqrt{\varepsilon}}, \ \beta \to \frac{\beta}{\sqrt{\varepsilon}}, \ z \to \sqrt{\varepsilon}z, \ H_x \to \sqrt{\varepsilon}H_x, \ H_y \to \sqrt{\varepsilon}H_y. \tag{3.315}$$

Recast Eq. (3.314) in a block-matrix form:

$$W(\alpha, \beta, z) = \mathbf{W}_1\mathbf{SP},$$

$$\mathbf{P} = \begin{pmatrix} E^+(\alpha, \beta) \\ H^+(\alpha, \beta) \\ E^-(\alpha, \beta) \\ H^-(\alpha, \beta) \end{pmatrix},$$

$$\mathbf{S} = \begin{pmatrix} \exp\left(ik\sqrt{1 - \alpha^2 - \beta^2}z\right)E_2 & 0 \\ 0 & \exp\left(-ik\sqrt{1 - \alpha^2 - \beta^2}z\right)E_2 \end{pmatrix},$$

$$\tag{3.316}$$

where $\mathbf{W}_1 = [W^{+e}(\alpha, \beta) \ W^{+h}(\alpha, \beta) \ W^{-e}(\alpha, \beta)W^{-h}(\alpha, \beta)]$ is a quadratic matrix composed of columns:

$$E_2 = \begin{pmatrix} 1 & 0 \\ 0 & 1 \end{pmatrix}. \tag{3.317}$$

The relation between the spatial-frequency components in different planes along the propagation direction Z takes the form

$$W(\alpha, \beta, z) = \mathbf{W}_1\mathbf{SM}^{-1}\overline{\mathbf{W}}_1 W(\alpha, \beta, 0), \tag{3.318}$$

where $\overline{\mathbf{W}}_1$ is a matrix conjugate to $\mathbf{W}_1$ in the Hermitean sense:

$$\mathbf{M} = \begin{pmatrix} E_2 & W^{\pm}E_2 \\ W^{\pm}E_2 & E_2 \end{pmatrix}, \ W^{\pm} = \overline{W}^{+e}W^{-e} = \frac{(\alpha^2 + \beta^2)^2}{\|W\|^2}. \tag{3.319}$$

Substituting Eq. (3.316) into (3.303) yields the expression for the operator of propagation of the electromagnetic field in free space:

$$\mathbf{W}(x, y, z) = T\mathbf{W}(x, y, 0) = \frac{k^2}{4\pi^2} \int_{-\infty}^{\infty} \mathbf{W}_1\mathbf{SM}^{-1}\overline{\mathbf{W}}_1 \left(\int_{-\infty}^{\infty} \mathbf{W}(x', y', 0) \right.$$

$$\left. \times \exp\{ik[\alpha(x - x') + \beta(y - y')]\} dx' dy' \right) d\alpha \, d\beta. \tag{3.320}$$

The advantage of the integral method of Eq. (3.320) is as follows: the direct and inverse Fourier transforms that form its basis allow the fast Fourier transform algorithm to be employed, resulting in a significantly reduced computational time relative to solving the Maxwell equations through the difference methods.

Introduce the notion of a scalar product in the space of 4-component vectors of the W functions. Assume the scalar product not to depend on the z-coordinate and, at the same time, the product of vector by itself to be proportional to the Umov-Poynting vector flux. To do this, we shall use the common form of the Maxwell equations in Eqs. (3.271) and (3.272) for the field $\mathbf{E}_1$, $\mathbf{H}_2$ and for the complex conjugate field:

$$\operatorname{rot} \mathbf{E}_1 = ik\mathbf{H}_1, \quad \operatorname{rot} \mathbf{E}_2^* = -ik\mathbf{H}_2^*,$$

$$\operatorname{rot} \mathbf{H}_1 = -ikE_1, \quad \operatorname{rot} \mathbf{H}_2^* = ik\mathbf{E}_2^*. \tag{3.321}$$

Using the well-known formula of vector analysis, $\operatorname{div}[\mathbf{a}, \mathbf{b}] = \mathbf{b}\operatorname{rot}\mathbf{a} - \mathbf{a}\operatorname{rot}\mathbf{b}$, we obtain

$$\operatorname{div}[(\mathbf{E}_1, \mathbf{H}_2^*) + (\mathbf{E}_2^*, \mathbf{H}_1)] = 0. \tag{3.322}$$

Then, using the Ostrogradsky-Gauss theorem and taking account of the radiation condition (so as to make the integral over the side surface zero), we obtain

$$\iint \{[\mathbf{E_1}(x, y, z_1), \mathbf{H_2^*}(x, y, z_1)] + [\mathbf{E_2^*}(x, y, z_1), \mathbf{H_1}(x, y, z_1)]\}\, dx\, dy$$

$$= \iint \{[\mathbf{E_1}(x, y, z_2), \mathbf{H_2^*}(x, y, z_2)] + [\mathbf{E_2^*}(x, y, z_2), \mathbf{H_1}(x, y, z_2)]\}\, dx\, dy. \tag{3.323}$$

Recast Eq. (3.323) as follows:

$$\iint A^T(x, y, z_1)\Omega B^*(x, y, z_1)\, dx\, dy = \iint A^T(x, y, z_2)\Omega B^*(x, y, z_2)\, dx\, dy,$$

$$\tag{3.324}$$

where

$$\Omega = \begin{pmatrix} 0 & 0 & 0 & 1 \\ 0 & 0 & -1 & 0 \\ 0 & -1 & 0 & 0 \\ 1 & 0 & 0 & 0 \end{pmatrix}, \tag{3.325}$$

or

$$\iint \langle A(x, y, z_2), B(x, y, z_2)\rangle\, dx\, dy = \iint \langle A(x, y, z_1), B(x, y, z_1)\rangle\, dx\, dy, \tag{3.326}$$

where $\langle A, B\rangle = (A^T)^*\Omega B$, $(A^T)^*$ is a pseudo-scalar product in the space of 4-component column-matrices. Equation (3.326) denotes that the propagation operator in Eq. (3.320) preserves the scalar product

$$\langle A \circ B\rangle = \iint \langle A, B\rangle\, dx\, dy, \tag{3.327}$$

that is, it is a unitary operator in the space with the scalar product. This property of preserving the scalar operator can be applied to solving the inverse diffraction problem, thus essentially simplifying the derivation of the residual functional gradient, similarly to the procedure adopted in the scalar approximation [13,14]. In addition, the availability of a preserving magnitude may be used to control whether the direct diffraction problem is solved correctly.

Example 3.12   Consider the field (Fig. 3.21) produced by a geometric optical DOE (Chapter 5) focusing the Gaussian beam into a thin ring and into a square. The field in the plane behind the optical element takes the form

$$\mathbf{W}(x, y, 0) = \frac{1}{2}\sqrt{I_0(x, y)}\, \exp[i\varphi(x, y)] \begin{pmatrix} 1 \\ 0 \\ 0 \\ 1 \end{pmatrix}, \tag{3.328}$$

where $I_0(x, y)$ is the incident beam intensity and $\varphi(x, y)$ is the phase function of the geometric optical focusing element. The light propagation within the optical element is estimated in the geometric optical approximation. In this case, the relation between the phase function and relief is given by $\varphi(x, y) = 2\pi(n - 1)h(x, y)$, where n is the refractive index of the material the element is made of and $h(x, y)$ is the relief height at a given point. The field was calculated for the following parameters: the DOE size is $D_x = 256\lambda$, $D_y = 256\lambda$, the Gaussian beam parameter (waist radius) is $\sigma = 64\lambda$, and the focal length is $f = 512\lambda$.

Figure 3.21 depicts the results of the numerical simulation: (*1*) the sampling step is $\Delta = \lambda$, the ring radius is $r_0 = 32\lambda$; (*2*) the sampling step is $\Delta = 4\lambda$, the ring radius

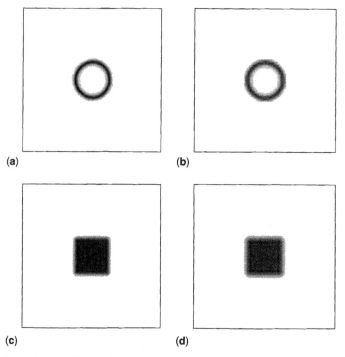

(a)   (b)

(c)   (d)

Figure 3.21. Intensity distribution from a geometric optical element focusing into a ring and into a square.

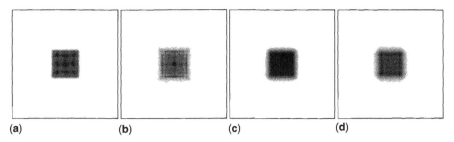

(a)   (b)   (c)   (d)

Figure 3.22. Intensity distribution from an element focusing into a square for various parameters and various calculation techniques.

is $r_0 = 32\lambda$; (*3*) the sampling step is $\Delta = \lambda$, the square size is $a \times b = 32\lambda \times 32\lambda$, (**4**) the sampling step is $\Delta = 4\lambda$, the square size is $a \times b = 32\lambda \times 32\lambda$.

Example 3.13 Compare the results of numerical simulation of the field (Fig. 3.22) produced by a geometric optical element focusing the Gaussian light into a square using the Fresnel approximation and the electromagnetic theory for the following parameters: the sampling step on the element is $\Delta = \lambda$, the element aperture is $D_x = 64\lambda$, $D_y = 64\lambda$, the focal length is $f = 64\lambda$, and the square size in the plane of focusing is $a \times b = 16\lambda \times 16\lambda$. Figure 3.22 depicts the results of numerical simulation: (a) the Gaussian beam parameter is $\sigma = 16\lambda$, the diffraction efficiency is 93 percent, the rms deviation is 20 percent (electromagnetic theory); (b) the Gaussian beam parameter is $\sigma = 16\lambda$, the diffraction efficiency is 94 percent, the rms deviation is 17 percent (scalar theory); (c) the Gaussian beam parameter is $\sigma = 32\lambda$, the diffraction efficiency is 96 percent, the rms deviation is 49 percent (electromagnetic theory); (d) the Gaussian beam parameter is $\sigma = 32\lambda$, the diffraction efficiency is 91 percent, and the rms deviation is 26 percent (scalar theory).

The results obtained suggest that given the earlier parameters, taking account of the electromagnetic nature of light does not result in essentially improved parameters of focusing relative to those provided by a geometric optical DOE (Chapter 5). Although, strictly speaking, it is only in free space where the electromagnetic properties of light are regarded in full measure in this example, whereas the light propagated in the DOE medium is treated using the geometric optical approximation. From the earlier examples it follows that the distinction is greatest when the illuminating beam size is greater than the DOE aperture.

Let us return to the problem of the electromagnetic wave diffraction by a transmission dielectric optical element. Rewrite Eqs. (3.305)–(3.307) in the matrix form. The zone-1 field is a superposition of the incident field, with its frequency components given by

$$\mathbf{W}(\alpha, \beta, z) = [I^e(\alpha, \beta)\mathbf{W}^{-\mathbf{e}}(\alpha, \beta) + I^h(\alpha, \beta)\mathbf{W}^{-\mathbf{h}}(\alpha, \beta)]\exp(-ik\sqrt{1 - \alpha^2 - \beta^2}z)$$

(3.329)

and the field reflected from the optical element surface

$$\mathbf{W}(\alpha, \beta, z) = [R^e(\alpha, \beta)\mathbf{W}^{+\mathbf{e}}(\alpha, \beta) + R^h(\alpha, \beta)\mathbf{W}^{+\mathbf{h}}(\alpha, \beta)]\exp\left(ik\sqrt{1 - \alpha^2 - \beta^2}z\right).$$

(3.330)

The zone-3 field (Fig. 3.6) behind the optical element is given by

$$\mathbf{W}(\alpha, \beta, z) = [T^e(\alpha, \beta)\mathbf{W}^{-\mathbf{e}}(\alpha, \beta) + T^h(\alpha, \beta)\mathbf{W}^{-\mathbf{h}}(\alpha, \beta)]$$

$$\times \exp\left(-ik\sqrt{1 - \alpha^2 - \beta^2}z\right). \tag{3.331}$$

The field in the modulation zone satisfies a set of integral-differential equations, Eq. (3.311). Consider a technique for solving the set (3.311). Instead of continuous functions, we shall introduce their values at points:

$$\alpha_n = \alpha_0 + \frac{\lambda n}{d_x}, \quad \beta_m = \beta_0 + \frac{\lambda m}{d_y},$$

$$\mathbf{W}_{nm}^{\pm e} = \mathbf{W}^{\pm e}(\alpha_n, \beta_m), \quad \mathbf{W}_{nm}^{\pm h} = \mathbf{W}^{\pm h}(\alpha_n, \beta_m),$$

$$I_{nm}^e = I^e(\alpha_n, \beta_m)\lambda^2/(d_x\, d_y), \quad I_{nm}^h = I^h(\alpha_n, \beta_m)\lambda^2/(d_x\, d_y),$$

$$R_{nm}^e = R^e(\alpha_n, \beta_m)\lambda^2/(d_x\, d_y), \quad R_{nm}^h = R^h(\alpha_n, \beta_m)\lambda^2/(d_x\, d_y),$$

$$T_{nm}^e = T^e(\alpha_n, \beta_m)\lambda^2/(d_x\, d_y), \quad T_{nm}^h = T^h(\alpha_n, \beta_m)\lambda^2/(d_x\, d_y). \tag{3.332}$$

The set of integral-differential equations in (3.308) reduces to a set of first-order differential equations with respect to the function $\mathbf{W}_{nm}(z)$:

$$\partial_z \mathbf{W}_{nm}(z) = \sum_{sk} \mathbf{H}_{nm,sk}(z)\mathbf{W}_{sk}(z),$$

$$\mathbf{H}_{nm,sk}(z) = \begin{pmatrix} \mathbf{A}_{nm,sk}(z) & 0 \\ 0 & \mathbf{B}_{nm,sk}(z) \end{pmatrix} \begin{pmatrix} 0 & 1 \\ 1 & 0 \end{pmatrix}, \tag{3.333}$$

where the 2D matrix operators operate on 2D column-matrices by the formulae following from Eqs. (3.312):

$$\mathbf{A}_{nm,sk}\begin{pmatrix} \varphi_{sk}(z) \\ \psi_{sk}(z) \end{pmatrix} = \frac{i}{k}\begin{pmatrix} ik\alpha_n & 0 \\ 0 & ik\beta_m \end{pmatrix} \varepsilon_{n-s,m-k}^{-1} \begin{pmatrix} -ik\beta_k & ik\alpha_s \\ -ik\beta_k & ik\alpha_s \end{pmatrix} \begin{pmatrix} \varphi_{sk}(z) \\ \psi_{sk}(z) \end{pmatrix}$$

$$+ ik\delta_{ns,mk}\begin{pmatrix} 0 & 1 \\ -1 & 0 \end{pmatrix} \begin{pmatrix} \varphi_{sk}(z) \\ \psi_{sk}(z) \end{pmatrix},$$

$$\mathbf{B}_{nm,sk}\begin{pmatrix} \varphi_{sk}(z) \\ \psi_{sk}(z) \end{pmatrix} = \frac{1}{ik}\begin{pmatrix} ik\alpha_n & 0 \\ 0 & ik\beta_m \end{pmatrix} \delta_{nm,sk} \begin{pmatrix} -ik\beta_k & ik\alpha_s \\ -ik\beta_k & ik\alpha_s \end{pmatrix} \begin{pmatrix} \varphi_{sk} \\ \psi_{sk} \end{pmatrix}$$

$$+ ik\varepsilon_{n-s,m-k}\begin{pmatrix} 0 & -1 \\ 1 & 0 \end{pmatrix} \begin{pmatrix} \varphi_{sk}(z \\ \psi_{sk}(z) \end{pmatrix}. \tag{3.334}$$

The set of solutions to the system of equations in (3.333) with different indices is convenient to combine in a block quadratic matrix $\overline{\mathbf{W}}$, with its elements being 4-component column-matrices. Let $\overline{\mathbf{W}}_{nm}^e(z)$, $\overline{\mathbf{W}}_{nm}^h(z)$ be the solution of the set of equations in (3.333) with the initial conditions given by $\mathbf{W}_{nm}^{-e}(0)$ and $\mathbf{W}_{nm}^{-h}(0)$, where $\mathbf{W}_{nm}^{-e}(0)$ or $\mathbf{W}_{nm}^{-h}(0)$ is a block quadratic matrix whose single nonzero element is found on the intersection of the mth row and nth column. This element is equal to the 4-component column

$\mathbf{W}_{nm}^{-e}$ or $\mathbf{W}_{nm}^{-h}$ (not to be confused with $\mathbf{W}_{nm}^{-e}(0)$, $\mathbf{W}_{nm}^{-h}(0)$, $\mathbf{W}_{nm}^{-e}$, $\mathbf{W}_{nm}^{-h}$). The continuity condition of the spatial-frequency components at $z = a$ is given by

$$\sum_{mn}[T_{nm}^e \mathbf{W}_{nm}^{-e}(a) + T_{nm}^h \mathbf{W}_{nm}^{-h}(a)] = \sum_{mn}[I_{nm}^e \mathbf{W}_{nm}^{-e}(0) + I_{nm}^h \mathbf{W}_{nm}^{-h}(0)]$$

$$\times \exp\left(-ik\sqrt{1 - \alpha_n^2 - \beta_m^2}a\right) + \sum_{mn}[R_{nm}^e \mathbf{W}_{nm}^{+e} + R_{nm}^h \mathbf{W}^{+h}(0)_{nm}]$$

$$\times \exp\left(ik\sqrt{1 - \alpha_n^2 - \beta_m^2}a\right). \tag{3.335}$$

The last relation is a set of linear equations for deriving the transmission and reflection coefficients. The field transmitted through the optical element takes the form

$$\mathbf{W}(x, y, z) = \sum_{nm}(T_{nm}^e \mathbf{W}_{nm}^{-e} + T_{nm}^h \mathbf{W}_{nm}^{-h}) \exp\left(-ik\sqrt{1 - \alpha_n^2 - \beta_m^2}z + ik(\alpha_n x + \beta_m y)\right). \tag{3.336}$$

3.6 GRADIENT TECHNIQUE FOR SYNTHESIZING DOEs

We shall consider a technique that allows wave fields to be reconstructed from the result of measuring the electromagnetic field intensity in two different planes. This technique makes it possible to compute the electromagnetic field, which should occur immediately behind a DOE and generates as it propagates in space, a desired intensity distribution at a desired distance from the DOE. In the subsequent process of DOE synthesis, the estimated field can serve as a boundary condition when solving the Maxwell equations in the transmission dielectric medium of the optical element.

In this case, the projection of the Umov-Poynting vector onto the Cartesian z-coordinate serves as the intensity. Assuming $I_0(x, y)$ to be the intensity distribution in the plane $z = 0$ and $I(x, y)$ to be the intensity distribution in the plane $z = f$, we seek a wave field $W(x, y, z)$ that satisfies the following conditions:

$$\begin{cases} \mathbf{W}(x, y, f) = T\mathbf{W}(x, y, 0) \\ I_0(x, y) = \langle \mathbf{W}(x, y, 0), \mathbf{W}(x, y, 0) \rangle \\ I(x, y) = \langle \mathbf{W}(x, y, f), \mathbf{W}(x, y, f) \rangle \end{cases} \tag{3.337}$$

where T is the propagation operator in Eq. (3.320).

As the general exact solution to the problem does not exist, we shall replace it by an approximation:

$$\begin{cases} \varepsilon[\mathbf{W}(x, y, f)] \to \min, \\ \varepsilon = \int \left[\sqrt{I(x, y)} - \sqrt{\langle \mathbf{W}(x, y, f), \mathbf{W}(x, y, f) \rangle}\right]^2 dx\, dy, \\ \mathbf{W}(x, y, f) = T\mathbf{W}(x, y, 0), \\ I_0(x, y) = \langle \mathbf{W}(x, y, 0), \mathbf{W}(x, y, 0) \rangle. \end{cases} \tag{3.338}$$

For simplicity, the minimum will be sought for in the class of functions given by

$$\mathbf{W}(x, y, 0) = \frac{1}{2}\sqrt{I_0(x, y)} \exp[i\varphi(x, y)] \begin{pmatrix} \cos\alpha(x, y) \\ -\sin\alpha(x, y)\exp[i\delta(x, y)] \\ \sin\alpha(x, y)\exp[i\delta(x, y)] \\ \cos\alpha(x, y) \end{pmatrix}. \tag{3.339}$$

The field has been chosen in the form of Eq. (3.339) because in the geometric optical approximation each parameter has a simple physical meaning. The function $\varphi(x, y)$ defines the wave phase (or eikonal) in the plane $z = 0$ and $\alpha(x, y)$, $\delta(x, y)$ defines the wave polarization.

Find the gradient of the functional of Eq. (3.338):

$$\delta\varepsilon = \text{Re}[\langle \psi(\mathbf{x}, 0), \delta W(\mathbf{x}, 0)\rangle], \tag{3.340}$$

where

$$\psi(x, 0) = T^{-1}\left(\sqrt{\frac{I(\mathbf{x})}{\langle \mathbf{W}(\mathbf{x}, f), \mathbf{W}(x, \mathbf{f})\rangle}}\,\mathbf{W}(x, \mathbf{f})\right),$$

$$\delta W(\mathbf{x}, f) = T[\delta W(x, 0)]. \tag{3.341}$$

In deriving Eq. (3.340), we used the property of conservation of the pseudo-scalar product. Changing to a discrete representation and using Eqs. (3.337)–(3.340), we obtain the relation for the functional gradient at each point (u, v):

$$\nabla\varepsilon(\mathbf{x}, 0) = \langle L(\mathbf{x}, 0), \psi(\mathbf{x}, 0)\rangle + \langle \psi(\mathbf{x}, 0), L(\mathbf{x}, 0)\rangle = 2\psi\langle L(\mathbf{x}, 0), \psi(\mathbf{x}, 0)\rangle, \tag{3.342}$$

where $L(\mathbf{x}, 0) = \dfrac{i}{2}\sqrt{I_0(\mathbf{x}, 0)}\exp[i\varphi(\mathbf{x}, 0)]\mathbf{E}(\mathbf{x}, 0)$, $\mathbf{E}(\mathbf{x}, 0) = \begin{pmatrix} 1 \\ 0 \\ 0 \\ 1 \end{pmatrix}$.

Next, applying the gradient relation in Eq. (3.342), we may use a conventional iterative procedure for minimizing the functional $\varphi_{n+1}(\mathbf{x}, 0) = \varphi_n(\mathbf{x}, 0) - t\nabla\varepsilon$, where t is the gradient algorithm step, with the iterative solution depending on the initial guess. The reason is that the functional commonly have no global minimum, but do have several local ones. When using this technique for designing DOEs, the existence of a set of solutions presents no problem because any solution capable of minimizing the initial functional is suitable.

Example 3.14   Let us compute the output field of a diffractive optical element that focuses the light into a square found at distance f from the DOE plane (Fig. 3.23). Figure 3.23a depicts the intensity distribution produced by a DOE that focuses the Gaussian beam into a square and has been synthesized in the Fresnel approximation. The field is also computed in the Fresnel approximation. Figure 3.23b also depicts the intensity distribution produced by a DOE focusing the Gaussian beam into a square, but with the field computed in the electromagnetic approximation. Figure 3.23c depicts the intensity distribution produced by a DOE that focuses the Gaussian beam and has been synthesized using the electromagnetic theory. The sampling step on the element is $\Delta = \lambda$, the aperture sizes are $D_x = 64\lambda$, $D_y = 64\lambda$, the focal length is $f = 64\lambda$, the square size in the plane of focusing is $a \times b = 16\lambda \times 16\lambda$, the Gaussian beam parameter is $\sigma = 32\lambda$, the diffraction efficiency E and the rms error are δ: $E = 94\%$, $\delta = 16\%$ (Fig. 3.23a), $E = 96\%$, $\delta = 64\%$ (Fig. 3.23b), $E = 97\%$, $\delta = 22\%$ (Fig. 3.23c).

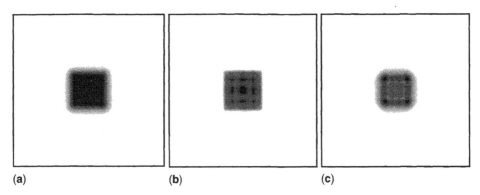

(a)   (b)   (c)

Figure 3.23. Intensity distributions produced by a DOE focusing the Gaussian beam into a square and iteratively designed using various approximations.

The results obtained confirm that describing the light propagation in space in terms of the rigorous electromagnetic theory does not lead to qualitative changes in the result of the inverse problem solution. Quantitative changes depend on the problem parameters to a greater degree. The results obtained in scalar approximation and using the electromagnetic theory turn out to be essentially different when the illuminating beam size is greater than the DOE's aperture size. In the other situations, they coincide up to several percent. Note that for the light diffraction to be adequately described one needs to take account of the electromagnetic wave propagation through the DOE.

3.7 ASYMPTOTIC ANALYSIS OF DIFFRACTION BY ZONED STRUCTURES

3.7.1 Solving the Problem of Diffraction by 1D DOEs Using the Scalar Approximation

Up to date, the problem of light diffraction by simplest structures, such as diffraction gratings [4–7], a ball [8], and others has been solved in the electromagnetic approximation. The main reason is as follows: the computation of the field produced by more complicated structures requires great computational efforts. In this connection, the great part in the theory of diffraction belongs to asymptotic methods. In this section, we discuss an asymptotic technique for evaluating the field when the light is diffracted by a binary quasi-periodic structure composed of an array of diffraction gratings of varying period. This approach successfully applies to the computation of the field produced by DOE.

3.7.1.1 Asymptotic Evaluation of the Field upon Diffraction by a 1D Reflection Quasi-Periodic Binary Structure   Consider a 1D reflection structure composed of an array of diffraction gratings. Introduce the following designations: X_M are local grating's boundaries and N_M is the number of periods of the diffraction

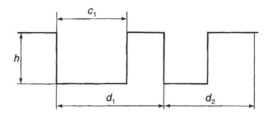

Figure 3.24. Two DOE zones, each having a single period of different diffraction gratings.

grating. As $N_M \to \infty$, the quasi-periodic structure turns into a strictly periodic diffraction grating; if $N_M = 1$, all segments of the quasi-periodic structure are of different period. Let x_m be the boundaries of the period of a local grating (for the period boundaries, a consecutive numeration is used irrespective of the grating to which the period belongs), $d_m = x_{m+1} - x_m$. Without loss of generality, is considered a grating with a single groove per period here [4,5] (Fig. 3.24), and where c_m is the groove width, h is its depth. Assume a plane wave $\exp[ik(\alpha_0 x - \beta_0 z)]$ striking the earlier-described quasi-periodic structure.

Consider two domains: 1 = the domain of $z > 0$ and 2 = the domain of $z < 0$ (Fig. 3.1). In the first domain, the field is a combination of plane waves

$$W(x, z) = \exp[ik(\alpha_0 x - \beta_0 z)] + \overline{W}(x, z),$$

$$\overline{W}(x, z) = \int_{-\infty}^{\infty} A(\alpha) \exp(ik(\alpha x + \beta z)] \, d\alpha, \qquad (3.343)$$

where $\beta = \sqrt{1 - \alpha^2}$. The normal field derivative is

$$\frac{\partial W(x, z)}{\partial z} = -ik\beta_0 \exp[ik(\alpha_0 x - \beta_0 z)] + \int_{-\infty}^{\infty} ik\beta(\alpha) A(\alpha) \exp[ik(\alpha x + \beta z)] \, d\alpha, \qquad (3.344)$$

where $A(\alpha)$ is the spectrum of spatial frequency of the waves reflected from the structure, $|\alpha| < 1$ corresponds to homogeneous plane waves, $|\alpha| < 1$ corresponds to inhomogeneous plane waves, with their amplitude decreasing as the distance from the quasi-periodic structure increases. The spectral function is expressed through the reflected field on the surface as follows:

$$A(\alpha) = \frac{k}{2\pi} \int_{-\infty}^{\infty} \overline{W}(x, 0) \exp(-ik\alpha x) \, dx. \qquad (3.345)$$

Let the reflected field on the structure surface be given by

$$\overline{W}(x) = \exp(ik\alpha_0 x) \sum_m \sum R_n^m \exp\left[ik\frac{\lambda n}{d_m}(x - x_m)\right] \mathrm{rect}(x, x_m, x_{m+1}), \qquad (3.346)$$

$$\mathrm{rect}(x, a, b) = \begin{cases} 1, x \in [a, b], \\ 0, x \notin [a, b]. \end{cases} \qquad (3.347)$$

This form of representation is convenient in that it is identical to the representation of the reflected field resulting from the diffraction by a reflection that is strictly periodic structure. To find the surface field, we should just determine the diffraction coefficients R_n^m. In the following discussion, we shall demonstrate that in the limit the expressions for the diffraction coefficients in the quasi-periodic case coincide with the coefficients derived for a strictly periodic grating with parameters d_m, c_m. This is the major result in asymptotically evaluating the field diffracted by a quasi-periodic structure.

The total field and its normal derivative at $z < 0$ are given by

$$W = \sum_k \sum_q a_q^{\ k} \sin\left(\frac{\pi q(x - x_k)}{c_k}\right) \sin[\Gamma_q^{\ k}(z + h)]S^k(x), \qquad (3.348)$$

$$\frac{\partial W}{\partial z} = \sum_k \sum_q a_q^{\ k}\Gamma_q^{\ k} \sin\left(\frac{\pi q(x - x_k)}{c_k}\right) \cos[\Gamma_q^{\ k}(z + h))S^k(x), \qquad (3.349)$$

$$\Gamma_q^{\ k} = \sqrt{k^2 - \left(\frac{\pi q}{c_k}\right)^2}, \quad q = 1, 2 \ldots, \qquad (3.350)$$

$$S^k(x) = \begin{cases} 1, & x \in [x_k, x_k + c_k], \\ 0, & x \notin [x_k, x_k + c_k]. \end{cases} \qquad (3.351)$$

By analogy with Refs. [4,5], the conditions of continuity of the field $W(x, z)$ and its normal derivative on the interface between the diffraction grating surface and free semispace ($z = 0$) are given by

$$\exp(ik\alpha_0 x)\left(1 + \sum_n \sum_m R_n^m \Phi_n^m(x)\right) = \sum_k \sum_q a_q^k \sin\left(\frac{\pi q(x - x_k)}{bd_k}\right)$$

$$\sin(\Gamma_q^{\ k}h)S^k(x), \qquad (3.352)$$

$$\sum_s ik \exp(ik\alpha_0 x)\left(-\beta(\alpha_0) + \sum_n \sum_m R_n^m F_n^m(x)\right) S^s(x)$$

$$= \sum_k \left(\sum_q a_q^k \sin\left(\frac{\pi q(x - x_k)}{bd_k}\right)\Gamma_q^{\ k} \cos(\Gamma_q^{\ k}h)\right) S^k(x), \qquad (3.353)$$

$$\Phi_n^m = \exp\left(\frac{ik\lambda n}{d_m}(x - x_m)\right) \text{rect}(x, x_m, x_{m+1}), \qquad (3.354)$$

$$F_n^m(x) = \hat{F}_n^m(x) + \tilde{F}_n^m(x),$$

$$\tilde{F}_n^m(x) = \beta\alpha_n^m)\Phi_n^m(x), \qquad (3.355)$$

$$\tilde{F}_n^m(x) = \frac{i}{2\pi} \times \int_{-\infty}^{\infty} (\beta(\alpha) - \beta[\alpha_n^m)]$$

$$\times \frac{\exp[ik(\alpha - \alpha_0)(x - x_{m+1})] - \exp[ik(\alpha - \alpha_0)(x - x_m)]}{(\alpha - \alpha_0) - \dfrac{\lambda n}{d_m}} d\alpha' \qquad (3.356)$$

$$\alpha_n^m = \alpha_0 + \frac{\lambda n}{d_m}, c_k = bd_k. \qquad (3.357)$$

The set of functional equations in Eq. (3.353) reduces to a set of linear algebraic equations

$$\sum_{mn} m_{pn}^k R_n^k = D_p^k, \tag{3.358}$$

where $m_{pn}^k = i A_{pn}^k + k d_k \delta_{pn}$, $D_p^k = i A_{p0}^k + k d_k \delta_{p0} - B_p^k$,

$$A_{pn}^k = \sum_{qn} \frac{tg(\Gamma_q^k h)}{N_q^k \Gamma_q^k} \beta(\alpha_n^k) D_{nq}^k \overline{D}_{pq}^k,$$

$$D_{nq}^k = \int_{x_k}^{x_k+c_k} \{\exp(ik[\alpha_0 x + \lambda n/d_k (x - x_k)])\} \sin\left(\frac{\pi q(x - x_k)}{c_k}\right) dkx, \tag{3.359}$$

$$B_p^k = \sum \frac{tg(\Gamma_q^k h)}{N_q^k \Gamma_q^k} \beta(\alpha_n^k) \Delta_q^k \overline{D}_{pq}^k,$$

$$\Delta_\mu^k = ik \int_{x_k}^{x_k+c_k} \sum_n \exp(ik\alpha_0 x) \tilde{F}_n(x) \sin\left(\frac{\pi q(x - x_k)}{c_k}\right) dx,$$

$$\tilde{F}_n(x) = \sum_m R_n^m \tilde{F}_n^m(x)$$

The resulting set contains an infinite number of linear equations. To derive the diffraction coefficients, a finite number of linear equations should be retained. Let $N = \max(k)$ be the maximum number of periods and $P = \max(n)$ be the maximum number of orders. In this case, the dimensionality of the set is $N \times P$.

Let us find shortwave asymptotics. The last equation in (3.359) describes the impact of different periods of the quasi-periodic structure. Analyzing the set of equations in (3.358) we can see that if $\tilde{F}_n(x) = \sum R_n^m \tilde{F}_n^m(x) \to 0$, the set in (3.358) is disintegrated into **N** independent sets of equations, each having the dimensionality **P**. Each of these subsets coincides with the set of equations found when solving the problem of diffraction by a perfectly reflecting binary grating with parameters $d_m = x_{m+1} - x_m$, c_m, h_m (Section 3.1). This technique allows the computational error in solving the set of equations to be reduced and convenient relations for the field asymptotic estimation to be derived.

For the purpose of further discussion, we shall introduce several auxiliary continuous functions: $v(x)$, $R_n(x)$, $\alpha_n(x)$. The $v(x)$ function defines the zone boundaries of the qausi-periodic grating $v(x_m) = m\Lambda$, where Λ is the quasi-periodic structure parameter (as $\Lambda \to 0$, the zone boundaries tend to each other), $R_n(x_m) = R_n^m$, and $\alpha_n(x_m) = \alpha_n^m$. Rewrite $\tilde{F}_n(x)$ as follows:

$$\tilde{F}_n(x) = \frac{1}{2\pi i} \int_{-\infty}^{\infty} \sum_m \left[\frac{\beta(\alpha) - \beta(\alpha_n^{m+1})}{\alpha - \alpha_n^{m+1}} R_n^{m+1} - \frac{\beta(\alpha) - \beta(\alpha_n^m)}{\alpha - \alpha_n^m} R_n^m \right]$$
$$\times \exp[ik(\alpha - \alpha_0)(x - x_{m+1})] da. \tag{3.360}$$

Consider the limiting cases when the influence of neighboring periods may be neglected, that is, $\tilde{F}_n(x) \to 0$.

1. A periodic structure $\alpha_n^m = \alpha_n^{m+1}$, $R_n^m = R_n^{m+1}$.

   In this case, from Eq. (3.359), it follows that $\tilde{F}_n(x)$ is identically equal to zero.

2. The illuminating beam wavelength tends to zero: $\lambda \to 0$ $(k \to \infty)$, whereas Λ remains finite.

   In this case, Eq. (3.360) presents a Fourier transform (with respect to the variable α) taken over a low-frequency function. As $k(x - x_{m+1}) \to \infty$, the Fourier transform tends to zero.

3. $\Lambda \to 0$, $k \to \infty$, but $k\Lambda$ remains finite.

It can be demonstrated that

$$\sum_m \left[\frac{\beta(\alpha) - \beta(\alpha_n^{m+1})}{\alpha - \alpha_n^{m+1}} R_n^{m+1} - \frac{\beta(\alpha) - \beta(\alpha_n^m)}{\alpha - \alpha_n^m} R_n^m \right] \exp[ik(\alpha - \alpha_0)(x - x_{m+1})] \to 0$$

(3.361)

The proof of the statement in Eq. (3.361) reduces to the proof of the limiting relation

$$\sum_m \left[R\left(\frac{x_{m+2} - x_{m+1}}{\Lambda}\right) - R\left(\frac{x_{m+1} - x_m}{\Lambda}\right) \right] \exp\left(\frac{2\pi i p x_{m+1}}{\Lambda}\right) \to 0 \; \pi p \; \Lambda \to 0,$$

(3.362)

where $v(x_m) = \Lambda m$, $R(x)$ is an arbitrary function. Though the strict proof is possible only for equally-spaced zones (in this case, the expression in square brackets in Eq. (3.361) is identically equal to zero), the numerical simulation shows it to be true for a wide class of sequences x_m and functions $R(x)$.

Supposing Λ to be small, we obtain a convenient expression for amplitude in the vicinity of the quasi-periodic structure. If the $\varphi(x)$ function is monotone and differentiable, within the limits of the segment $[x_m x_{m+1}]$, the following linear approximation will be valid: $v(x) = m\Lambda + [\Lambda(x - x_m)/d_m]$, where $d_m = x_{m+1} - x_m$. Then, substituting this approximation into Eq. (3.347), we get the following:

$$\overline{W}(x) = \exp(ik\alpha_0 x) \sum_m \sum R_n^M \exp\left(ik\frac{\lambda n}{\Lambda}v(x)\right) \text{rect}\,(x, x_m, x_{m+1}). \qquad (3.363)$$

It can be easily noted that the sign of sum can be removed and the field on the quasi-periodic structure surface is given by

$$\overline{W}_0(x) = \exp(ik\alpha_0 x) \sum_n R_n(x) \exp\left(ik\frac{\lambda n}{\Lambda}v(x)\right). \qquad (3.364)$$

The field $W(x,z)$ in semispace over the surface takes the form

$$W(x, z) = \int_{-\infty}^{\infty} G(x - \overline{x}, z) W_0(\overline{x}) \, d\overline{x}, \qquad (3.365)$$

$$G(x, z) = \frac{1}{2i} \frac{\partial H_0^1(k\sqrt{x^2 + z^2})}{\partial z}. \tag{3.366}$$

Substituting Eq. (3.364) into (3.365) yields the final expression for the field anywhere for $z > 0$:

$$\overline{W}(x, z) = \sum_n \int_{-\infty}^{\infty} R_n(\overline{x}) G(x - \overline{x}, z) \exp\left(ik\alpha_0\overline{x} + ik\frac{\lambda n}{\Lambda} v(\overline{x})\right) d\overline{x}. \tag{3.367}$$

Conceptually speaking, this approach is analogous to the method of linear predistortion [15]. The difference is that in Ref. [15] the diffraction coefficients for the grating were derived from the geometric optical approximation of the field within the diffraction grating grooves, which is valid for the grating periods of several tens of wavelengths. With the electromagnetic approach, the coefficient values in Eq. (3.367) depend on the type of polarization and the relative orientation of polarization vectors and grating grooves' direction. The essential difference of Eq. (3.367) from the formulae arrived at using the linear predistortion method is that the former show the dependence of the diffraction coefficients from coordinates.

Example 3.15   Compute the field from a binary quasi-periodic structure, with its zone boundaries defined by $v(x_m) = m\Lambda$, where $v(x)$ takes the form of the phase function of a lens with focal length f:

$$v(x) = x \sin \omega + \sqrt{(x - f \sin q)^2 + f^2 \cos^2 q}, \tag{3.368}$$

where ω is the angle of incidence of the plane wave onto the lens and q is the angle at which the lens focuses.

To utilize Eq. (3.367) for determining the over-lens field we need to define the function $R_n(x)$. It is defined using the values of the diffraction coefficients $R_n^m = Q_n(\lambda/d_m)$, derived from the set (3.353)

$$R_n(x) = Q_n[\lambda/d_m(x)], \tag{3.369}$$

where

$$\frac{\Lambda}{d_m(x)} = \frac{(x - f \sin q)}{\sqrt{(x - f \sin q)^2 + f^2 \cos^2 q}} + \sin \omega. \tag{3.370}$$

The plot of the function

$$Q\left(\frac{\lambda}{d_m}\right) = \frac{\sqrt{1 - (\alpha_0 - \lambda_o/d_m)^2}}{\sqrt{1 - \alpha_o^2}} Q_{-1}(\lambda/d_m), \quad 0.8 < \lambda/d_m < 1.8,$$

$$\alpha_0 = \sin \omega, \omega = 45°.$$

for TM-polarization may be found in Ref. [16]. The results reported in Ref. [16] also suggest that $Q_n = 0$, if $n \neq -1, 0$. The Q_0 function can be derived from the law of energy conservation: $Q_{-1}^2 + Q_0^2 = 1$.

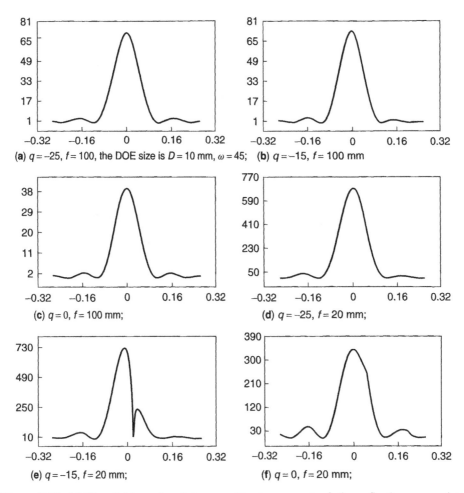

Figure 3.25. (a) The field produced by an off-axis segment of the reflection zone plate, $q = -25$, $f = 100$, the DOE size is $D = 10$ mm, $\omega = 45$; (b) The field from an off-axis segment of the reflection zone plate, $q = -15$, $f = 100$ mm; (c) The field from an off-axis segment of the reflection zone plate, $q = 0$, $f = 100$ mm; (d) The field from an off-axis segment of the reflection zone plate, $q = -25$, $f = 20$ mm; (e) The field from an off-axis segment of the reflection zone plate, $q = -15$, $f = 20$ mm; (f) The field from an off-axis segment of the reflection zone plate, $q = 0$, $f = 20$ mm.

The results of the field computation are shown in Figure. 3.25. Analysis of the derived results suggests that for short focal lengths (that is, comparable with the optical element size) there exists the asymmetry of the focal spot shape and a displacement relative to the point of the expected geometric focus. The displacement is due to changing the phase of the diffraction coefficients on the aperture, small as this change can be.

Example 3.16 A DOE focusing into a transverse line-segment is a more complicated example of the reflection zone structure. Figure 3.26 depicts the examples of focusing into a line-segment for various parameters.

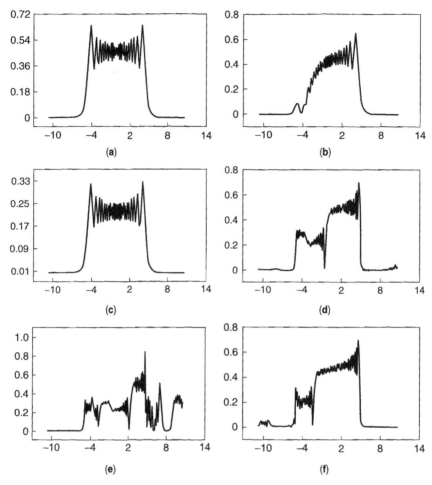

Figure 3.26. (a) The field from a DOE focusing into a line-segment $q = -25$, $f = 100$ mm, the line-segment length is $L = 10$ mm; (b) The field from a DOE focusing into a line-segment $q = -15$, $f = 100$ mm, the line-segment length is $L = 10$ mm; (c) The field from a DOE focusing into a line-segment $q = 0$, $f = 100$ mm, the line-segment length is $L = 10$ mm; (d) The field from a DOE focusing into a line-segment $q = -25$, $f = 10$ mm, the line-segment length is $L = 10$ mm; (e) The field from a DOE focusing into a line-segment $q = -15$, $f = 10$ mm, the line-segment length is $L = 10$ mm; (f) The field from a DOE focusing into a line-segment $q = 0$, $f = 10$ mm, the line-segment length is $L = 10$ mm.

3.7.2 Solving the Problem of Diffraction by 1D DOEs Using the Electromagnetic Approach

Let a plane electromagnetic wave be reflected from a perfectly conducting quasi-periodic structure. Assume that the plane wave $\exp[ik(\alpha_0 x_\nu - \beta_0 x_N + \gamma x_\tau)]$ strikes a 1D optical element, with its zone x_m boundaries defined by $\nu(x_m) = m\lambda$ $m = 1, 2 \ldots$. The 1D case is considered for reasoning simplicity. Introduce the coordinate set x, x_N, x_τ and the following vectors (Fig. 3.27): $\mathbf{s}$ defines the propagation direction, $\mathbf{N}$ is the normal vector to the grating (to the diffractive structure plane), ν is the normal vector to the grating lines, τ is the tangent vector to the grating lines,

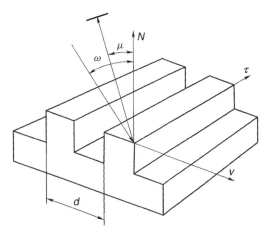

Figure 3.27. The light strikes at an angle to a binary reflection quasi-periodic structure.

$\tau = [\boldsymbol{\nu} \times \mathbf{N}]$, and $\boldsymbol{\nu} = \nabla \varphi(\mathbf{u})/|\nabla \varphi(\mathbf{u})|$ is the vector perpendicular to the grating lines and found in the optical element plane.

Also, introduce the **l** vector found in the plane of the wave incidence (that is, in the plane that goes through the normal vector to the surface and the incident wave vector) and the **t** vector perpendicular to the plane of incidence:

$$\mathbf{t} = \frac{[\mathbf{s}, \mathbf{N}]}{|(\mathbf{s}, \mathbf{N})|}, \quad \mathbf{l} = \frac{[\mathbf{s}, \mathbf{t}]}{|(\mathbf{s}, \mathbf{t})|}. \tag{3.371}$$

The electric vector in the incident wave can be represented as a sum of two vectors that are collinear to the vectors **l** and **t**:

$$\mathbf{E} = \mathbf{E}_t + \mathbf{E}_l. \tag{3.372}$$

Assume that the electric vector lies in the optical element plane:

$$\mathbf{E} = \exp[ik(\mathbf{s}, \mathbf{x})]\mathbf{t}, \tag{3.373}$$

$$\mathbf{H} = \frac{1}{ik} \left[\text{grad} \left\{ \exp[ik(\mathbf{s}, \mathbf{x})] \right\}, \mathbf{t} \right], \tag{3.374}$$

$$\mathbf{H} = \exp[ik(\mathbf{s}, \mathbf{x})][\mathbf{s}, \mathbf{t}] = \exp[ik(\mathbf{s}, \mathbf{x})]\mathbf{l}. \tag{3.375}$$

The electric field component along the grooves is

$$E_\tau^0 = (\mathbf{t}, \boldsymbol{\tau}), \tag{3.376}$$

whereas the magnetic field component along the grooves is

$$H_\tau^0 = (\mathbf{l}, \boldsymbol{\tau}). \tag{3.377}$$

If the vector **H** of the magnetic field is parallel to the optical element plane, Eqs. (3.376) and (3.377) take the form

$$E_\tau^0 = -(\mathbf{l}, \boldsymbol{\tau}), \quad H_\tau^0 = (\mathbf{t}, \boldsymbol{\tau}). \tag{3.378}$$

The electromagnetic field components can be found from the following relations:

$$\mathbf{E} = E_\nu \boldsymbol{\nu} + E_N \mathbf{N} + E_\tau \boldsymbol{\tau}, \quad \mathbf{H} = H_\nu \boldsymbol{\nu} + H_N \mathbf{N} + H_\tau \boldsymbol{\tau}. \tag{3.379}$$

$$\left.\begin{array}{ll} E_\nu = \dfrac{i}{k(1-\gamma^2)}(\partial_N H_\tau - \gamma \partial_\nu E_\tau), & H_\nu = -\dfrac{i}{k(1-\gamma^2)}(\partial_N E_\tau - \gamma \partial_\nu H_\tau), \\[3mm] E_N = -\dfrac{i}{k(1-\gamma^2)}(\partial_\nu H_\tau + \gamma \partial_N E_\tau), & H_N = \dfrac{i}{k(1-\gamma^2)}(\partial_\nu E_\tau + \gamma \partial_N H_\tau) \end{array}\right\} \tag{3.380}$$

$$E_\tau(\mathbf{x}) = |E_\tau^0| \exp(ik\alpha_0 x + ik\gamma x_\tau)$$
$$\times \sum_m \sum_n E_n^m \exp\left(ik\frac{\lambda n}{d_m}(x - x_m) + ik\beta_n x_N\right) \text{rect}(x, x_m, x_{m+1}). \tag{3.381}$$

Consider a zone numbered m that belongs to the interval $[x_m, x_{m+1}]$. The field within this zone for $z = 0$ is thought to coincide with the field of a diffraction grating whose microrelief on period coincides with the microrelief in the present zone, with the microrelief structure in all zones being similar up to a scale. In that case, all the characteristics of the output field (the diffraction coefficients) depend only on the ratio λ/d. Using Eq. (3.381) yields expressions for the field reflected from the grating

$$H_\tau(\mathbf{x}) = |H_\tau^0| \exp(ik\alpha_0 x + ik\gamma x_\tau)$$
$$\times \sum_m \sum_n H_n^m \exp\left(ik\frac{\lambda n}{d_m}(x - x_m) + ik\beta_n x_N\right) \text{rect}(x, x_m, x_{m+1}), \tag{3.382}$$

$$E_\nu(\mathbf{x}) = -\frac{1}{1-\gamma^2}\left\{H_\tau^0 \exp(ik\alpha_0 x + ik\gamma x_\tau) \sum_m \sum_n \beta_n H_n^m \exp\left[ik\frac{\lambda n}{d_m}(x - x_m)\right.\right.$$
$$\left.+ ik\beta_n x_N\right] \text{rect}(x, x_m, x_{m+1}) + \gamma E_\tau^0 \exp(ik\alpha_0 x + ik\gamma x_\tau)$$
$$\left.\times \sum_m \sum_n \alpha_n E_n^m \exp\left[ik\frac{\lambda n}{d_m}(x - x_m) + ik\beta_n x_N\right] \text{rect}(x, x_m, x_{m+1})\right\}, \tag{3.383}$$

$$H_\nu(\mathbf{x}) = \frac{1}{1-\gamma^2}\left\{E_\tau^0 \exp(ik\alpha_0 x + ik\gamma x_\tau) \sum_m \sum_n \beta_n E_n^m \exp\left[ik\frac{\lambda n}{d_m}(x - x_m)\right.\right.$$
$$\left.+ ik\beta_n x_N\right] \text{rect}(x, x_m, x_{m+1}) - \gamma H_\tau^0 \exp(ik\alpha_0 x + ik\gamma x_\tau)$$
$$\left.\times \sum_m \sum_n \alpha_n H_n^m \exp\left[ik\frac{\lambda n}{d_m}(x - x_m) + ik\beta_n x_N\right] \text{rect}(x, x_m, x_{m+1})\right\}, \tag{3.384}$$

$$E_N(\mathbf{x}) = \frac{1}{1 - \gamma^2} \left\{ H_\tau^0 \exp(ik\alpha_0 x + ik\gamma x_\tau) \sum_m \sum_n \alpha_n H_n^m \exp\left[ik\frac{\lambda n}{d_m}(x - x_m) \right.\right.$$

$$\left. + ik\beta_n x_N \right] \text{rect}(x, x_m, x_{m+1}) - \gamma E_\tau^0 \exp(ik\alpha_0 x + ik\gamma x_\tau)$$

$$\left. \times \sum_m \sum_n \beta_n E_n^m \exp\left[ik\frac{\lambda n}{d_m}(x - x_m) + ik\beta_n x_N \right] \text{rect}(x, x_m, x_{m+1}) \right\},$$

(3.385)

$$H_N(\mathbf{x}) = -\frac{1}{1 - \gamma^2} \left\{ E_\tau^0 \exp(ik\alpha_0 x + ik\gamma x_\tau) \sum_m \sum_n \alpha_n E_n^m \exp\left[ik\frac{\lambda n}{d_m}(x - x_m) \right.\right.$$

$$\left. + ik\beta_n x_N \right] \text{rect}(x, x_m, x_{m+1}) + \gamma H_\tau^0 \exp(ik\alpha_0 x + ik\gamma x_\tau)$$

$$\left. \times \sum_m \sum_n \beta_n H_n^m \exp\left[ik\frac{\lambda n}{d_m}(x - x_m) + ik\beta_n x_N \right] \text{rect}(x_m, x_{m+1}) \right\},$$

(3.386)

$$\gamma(\mathbf{u}) = (\mathbf{s}, \tau(\mathbf{u})), \quad \alpha_0(\mathbf{u}) = (\mathbf{s}, \cdot\nu(\mathbf{u})), \quad \alpha_n(\mathbf{u}) = \alpha_0(\mathbf{u}) + \frac{\lambda n}{d}, \quad (3.387)$$

where $\beta_n(\mathbf{u}) = \sqrt{1 - \gamma^2(\mathbf{u}) - \alpha_n^2(\mathbf{u})}$, $\lambda/d = |\nabla\varphi(\mathbf{u})|$.
Taking account of

$$\nabla\nu = \lambda/d_m, \quad \nu(x) = m\lambda + \nabla\nu(x - x_m) \quad (3.388)$$

produces the relation for the field that the optical element generates in the plane $x_N = 0$:

$$E_\nu(\mathbf{x}) = -\frac{1}{(1 - \gamma^2)} \sum_n \left[H_\tau^0(\mathbf{x}) H_n(\mathbf{x})\beta_n(\mathbf{x}) + \gamma(\mathbf{x}) E_\tau^0(\mathbf{x}) E_n(\mathbf{x})\alpha_n(\mathbf{x}) \right]$$

$$\times \exp[ikn\nu(\mathbf{x})] \exp[ik(\mathbf{s}, \mathbf{x})], \quad (3.389)$$

$$H_\nu(\mathbf{x}) = \frac{1}{(1 - \gamma^2)} \sum_n \left[E_\tau^0(\mathbf{x}) E_n(\mathbf{x})\beta_n(\mathbf{x}) - \gamma(\mathbf{x}) H_\tau^0(\mathbf{x}) H_n(\mathbf{x})\alpha_n(\mathbf{x}) \right]$$

$$\times \exp[ikn\nu(\mathbf{x})] \exp[ik(\mathbf{s}, \mathbf{x})], \quad (3.390)$$

$$E_N(\mathbf{x}) = \frac{1}{(1 - \gamma^2)} \sum_n \left[H_\tau^0(\mathbf{x}) H_n(\mathbf{x})\alpha_n(\mathbf{x}) - \gamma(\mathbf{x}) E_\tau^0(\mathbf{x}) E_n(\mathbf{x})\beta_n(\mathbf{x}) \right]$$

$$\times \exp[ikn\nu(\mathbf{x})] \exp(ik(\mathbf{s}, \mathbf{x})), \quad (3.391)$$

$$H_N(\mathbf{x}) = -\frac{1}{(1 - \gamma^2)} \sum_n \left[E_\tau^0(\mathbf{x}) E_n(\mathbf{x})\alpha_n(\mathbf{x}) - \gamma(\mathbf{x}) H_\tau^0(\mathbf{x}) H_n(\mathbf{x})\beta_n(\mathbf{x}) \right]$$

$$\times \exp[ikn\nu(\mathbf{x})] \exp(ik(\mathbf{s}, \mathbf{x})), \quad (3.392)$$

$$E_\tau(\mathbf{x}) = \sum_n E_\tau^0(\mathbf{x}) E_n(\mathbf{x}) \exp[ikn\nu(\mathbf{x})] \exp(ik(\mathbf{s}, \mathbf{x})), \quad (3.393)$$

$$H_\tau(\mathbf{x}) = \sum_n H_\tau^0(\mathbf{x}) H_n(\mathbf{x}) \exp[ikn\nu(\mathbf{x})] \exp(ik(\mathbf{s}, \mathbf{x})). \tag{3.394}$$

The relations in Eqs. (3.389)–(3.394) have been derived for diffraction by a 1D DOE, but they hold for a 2D DOE, too.

To find the electromagnetic field in the entire space we need to represent the field in the Kirchhoff-Kotler form [8]. Taking the Kirchhoff-Kotler integral is computationally complex, as in the general case one cannot use algorithms for the fast Fourier transform. The authors used the Hopkins method to compute the earlier integral. This method is recommended for use when the $\varphi(x, y)$ function is differentiable. Besides, a modified method was employed so that the computation time be reduced and involved the truncation of the integral sum in the Hopkins method when the argument in the function $\sin c(x)$ was greater than 10. This rules out the necessity of time-consuming computing of the diffraction coefficients and the vector products in those points.

Example 3.17   Compute the field from an off-axis segment of the reflection zone plate. Assume that the optical element's zone boundaries are defined by the function $\nu(\mathbf{x}) = m\lambda$:

$$\nu(\mathbf{x}) = x \sin\omega + \sqrt{(x - f\sin q)^2 + y^2 + f^2\cos^2 q}, \tag{3.395}$$

where ω is the angle of incidence of the plane wave onto the lens. The function in Eq. (3.395) is a 2D generalization of Eq. (3.368). Within the zone, the microrelief presents a binary diffraction grating with a single groove. This element is seen to focus the radiation onto a spot with coordinates

$$(x, y, z) = (\mathbf{f}\sin q, 0, \mathbf{f}\cos q). \tag{3.396}$$

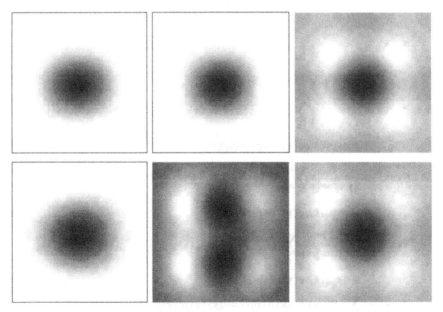

Figure 3.28. The field from an off-axis segment of the reflection zone plate.

The results of computing the field in the lens focal plane are given in Figure 3.28 and pertain to the magnetic field vector found in the optical element plane. Analysis of the results arrived at suggests that the focal spot is asymmetric in shape for short focal lengths.

Figure 3.28 carries the following designations: ω is the light incidence angle, q is the angle between the normal to the plate and the direction to the focus, D is the zone plate size, and f is the focal length.

3.8   MODELING THE ELECTROMAGNETIC RADIATION PROPAGATION USING A METHOD OF FINITE DIFFERENCES

The development of numerical techniques and great strides made in the field of computers made possible the numerical solution of Maxwell's equations. Thus, assuming that the proper boundary conditions have been imposed and the medium parameters have been substituted in the equations allows the process of light propagation in various media to be numerically simulated.

In Ref. [18], they discuss a difference technique for solving the Maxwell equations and report the results for optical integrated circuits. In the present section, gradient-index media and DOE are numerically simulated. This is done through the use of a difference "push-pull" scheme and a scheme of enhanced time-accuracy order because these allow one to study the propagation in a fiber of short impulses and subwave-length diffractive elements. The difference method has been realized for solving the Maxwell equations in the left-hand Cartesian coordinate system for the H-wave (TE-polarization).

The Maxwell equations in the left-hand Cartesian coordinate system for TE-polarization are as follows [18]:

$$\left.\begin{array}{l} \dfrac{\partial E_x}{\partial \tau} = \dfrac{1}{\varepsilon}\left(\dfrac{\partial H_y}{\partial z} - \dfrac{\partial H_z}{\partial y}\right); \\[3mm] \dfrac{\partial H_y}{\partial \tau} = \dfrac{\partial E_x}{\partial z}; \\[3mm] \dfrac{\partial H_z}{\partial \tau} = -\dfrac{\partial E_x}{\partial y}. \end{array}\right\} \qquad (3.397)$$

where H_y, H_z, E_x are the corresponding projections of the vectors of the magnetic and electric field strength, $\tau = ct$, c is the speed of light in free space, t is time, and ε is permittivity. The medium presents a thin layer found in the plane (y, z), whereas the radiation is directed along the z-axis.

Suppose that on the boundary we have $E_x = 0$ (the electric wall) [19]. By way of example, this is true for a coplanar waveguide contained in a metal envelope. Such a waveguide will correspond to an envelopless waveguide if:

- the bend exceeds no critical angle α, which corresponds to a change from the higher-order excited mode to the first air radiation mode;
- nonhomogeneous character of the refractive index responsible for the occurrence of the air modes can be neglected.

We shall tackle the set in Eq. (3.397) using the finite difference "push-pull" method. Consider a set of functions $E_x(z, y, \tau)$, $H_y(z, y, \tau)$, $H_z(z, y, \tau)$ in the domain $D = [0 \le z \le L, -a/2 \le y \le a/2, 0 \le \tau \le T]$, where L is the waveguide length, a is the waveguide width, $T = ct_1$, and t_1 is the duration of the experiment. Let us define in the domain D a grid: $\Omega_{\Delta z \Delta y \Delta \tau} = [(z_i, y_j, \tau_n) \in D]$, where (z_i, y_j, τ_n) are the grid nodes and $0 \le i \le N_1 - 1$; $0 \le j \le N_2 - 1$; $0 \le n \le N_3 - 1$.

The grid steps are defined according to the formulae: $\Delta z = L/(N_1 - 1)$; $\Delta y = a/(N_2 - 1)$; $\Delta \tau = T/(N_3 - 1)$.

Make the splitting in Eq. (3.397):

$$\left.\begin{aligned}
\frac{\partial \tilde{E}_x}{\partial \tau} &= \frac{1}{n^2(y)} \frac{\partial H_y}{\partial z}; \\
\frac{\partial E_x}{\partial \tau} &= \frac{1}{n^2(y)} \frac{\partial H_z}{\partial y} \\
\frac{\partial H_y}{\partial \tau} &= \frac{\partial \tilde{E}_x}{\partial z}; \\
\frac{\partial H_z}{\partial \tau} &= -\frac{\partial E_x}{\partial y},
\end{aligned}\right\} \tag{3.398}$$

where $n^2(y) = \varepsilon$ and $\tilde{E}_x$ is the splitted component E_x.

On the basis of the general principles put forward in Ref. [20], we shall construct an implicit difference scheme of splitting. Put down a set of difference equations:

$$\left.\begin{aligned}
\frac{\tilde{E}_{x_{i,j}}^{n+1} - E_{x_{i,j}}^{n}}{\Delta \tau} &= \frac{1}{n^2(y)} \frac{H_{y_{i,j}}^{n+1} - H_{y_{i-1,j}}^{n+1}}{\Delta z}; \\
\frac{E_{x_{i,j}}^{n+1} - \tilde{E}_{x_{i,j}}^{n+1}}{\Delta \tau} &= -\frac{1}{n^2(y)} \frac{H_{z_{i,j}}^{n+1} - H_{z_{i,j-1}}^{n+1}}{\Delta y}; \\
\frac{H_{y_{i,j}}^{n+1} - H_{y_{i,j}}^{n}}{\Delta \tau} &= \frac{\tilde{E}_{x_{i+1,j}}^{n+1} - \tilde{E}_{x_{i,j}}^{n+1}}{\Delta z}; \\
\frac{H_{z_{i,j}}^{n+1} - H_{z_{i,j}}^{n}}{\Delta \tau} &= -\frac{E_{x_{i,j+1}}^{n+1} - E_{x_{i,j}}^{n+1}}{\Delta y}.
\end{aligned}\right\} \tag{3.399}$$

The set in Eq. (3.399) approximates Eq. (3.398) in the nodes (z_i, y_j, τ_n) for the following index values: $0 \le i \le N_1 - 1$; $1 \le j \le N_2 - 1$; $0 \le n \le N_3 - 1$.

Substituting the third equation of (3.399) into the first and the fourth into the second, we obtain the difference equations

$$\frac{\Delta \tau}{n^2(y) \Delta z^2} \tilde{E}_{x_{i-1,j}}^{n+1} + \left(-\frac{1}{\Delta \tau} - 2\frac{\Delta \tau}{n^2(y) \Delta z^2}\right) \tilde{E}_{x_{i,j}}^{n+1} + \frac{\Delta \tau}{n^2(y) \Delta z^2} \tilde{E}_{x_{i+1,j}}^{n+1}$$

$$= -\frac{1}{\Delta \tau} E_{x_{i,j}}^{n} - \frac{1}{n^2(y) \Delta z} H_{y_{i,j}}^{n} + \frac{1}{n^2(y) \Delta z} H_{y_{i-1,j}}^{n};$$

$$\frac{\Delta \tau}{n^2(y) \Delta y^2} E_{x_{i,j-1}}^{n+1} + \left(-\frac{1}{\Delta \tau} - 2\frac{\Delta \tau}{n^2(y) \Delta y^2}\right) E_{x_{i,j}}^{n+1} + \frac{\Delta \tau}{n^2(y) \Delta y^2} E_{x_{i1,j+1}}^{n+1}$$

$$= -\frac{1}{\Delta \tau} \tilde{E}_{x_{i,j}}^{n+1} - \frac{1}{n^2(y) \Delta y} H_{z_{i,j}}^{n} + \frac{1}{n^2(y) \Delta y} H_{z_{i,j-1}}^{n}, \tag{3.400}$$

that are resolved using the sweep method.

In the nodes (x_i, y_j, τ_k) for the index values $0 \leq i \leq N_1 - 1$; $j = 0$; $0 \leq n \leq N_3 - 1$, we shall construct an alternative set of approximating equations:

$$
\left.
\begin{array}{l}
\dfrac{\tilde{E}^{n+1}_{x_{i,j}} - E^n_{x_{i,j}}}{\Delta \tau} = \dfrac{1}{n^2(y)} \dfrac{H^{n+1}_{y_{i+1,j}} - H^{n+1}_{y_{i,j}}}{\Delta z}; \\[3mm]
\dfrac{E^{n+1}_{x_{i,j}} - \tilde{E}^{n+1}_{x_{i,j}}}{\Delta \tau} = -\dfrac{1}{n^2(y)} \dfrac{H^{n+1}_{z_{i,j+1}} - H^{n+1}_{z_{i,j}}}{\Delta y}; \\[3mm]
\dfrac{H^{n+1}_{y_{i,j}} - H^n_{y_{i,j}}}{\Delta \tau} = \dfrac{\tilde{E}^{n+1}_{x_{i,j}} - \tilde{E}^{n+1}_{x_{i-1,j}}}{\Delta z}; \\[3mm]
\dfrac{H^{n+1}_{z_{i,j}} - H^n_{z_{i,j}}}{\Delta \tau} = -\dfrac{E^{n+1}_{x_{i,j}} - E^{n+1}_{x_{i,j-1}}}{\Delta y}.
\end{array}
\right\}
\tag{3.401}
$$

Substituting the third equation of the set (3.401) into the first and the fourth into the second, we obtain the following difference equations:

$$
\frac{\Delta \tau}{n^2(y)\Delta z^2} \tilde{E}^{n+1}_{x_{i-1,j}} + \left(-\frac{1}{\Delta \tau} - 2\frac{\Delta \tau}{n^2(y)\Delta z^2} \right) \tilde{E}^{n+1}_{x_{i,j}} + \frac{\Delta \tau}{n^2(y)\Delta z^2} \tilde{E}^{n+1}_{x_{i+1,j}}
$$

$$
= -\frac{1}{\Delta \tau} E^n_{x_{i,j}} - \frac{1}{n^2(y)\Delta z} H^n_{y_{i+1,j}} + \frac{1}{n^2(y)\Delta z} H^n_{y_{i,j}};
$$

$$
\frac{\Delta \tau}{n^2(y)\Delta y^2} E^{n+1}_{x_{i,j-1}} + \left(-\frac{1}{\Delta \tau} - 2\frac{\Delta \tau}{n^2(y)\Delta y^2} \right) E^{n+1}_{x_{i,j}} + \frac{\Delta \tau}{n^2(y)\Delta y^2} E^{n+1}_{x_{i,j+1}}
$$

$$
= -\frac{1}{\Delta \tau} \tilde{E}^{n+1}_{x_{i,j}} - \frac{1}{n^2(y)\Delta y} H^n_{z_{i,j+1}} + \frac{1}{n^2(y)\Delta y} H^n_{z_{i,j}},
\tag{3.402}
$$

which can be solved using the sweep method, too. Now, knowing the electric field pixels, $E^{n+1}_{x_{i,j}}$, the magnetic field is defined as

$$
\left.
\begin{array}{l}
\dfrac{H^{n+1}_{y_{i,j}} - H^n_{y_{i,j}}}{\Delta \tau} = \dfrac{E^{n+1}_{x_{i+1,j}} - E^{n+1}_{x_{i,j}}}{\Delta z}; \\[3mm]
\dfrac{H^{n+1}_{z_{i,j}} - H^n_{z_{i,j}}}{\Delta \tau} = -\dfrac{E^{n+1}_{x_{i,j+1}} - E^{n+1}_{x_{i,j}}}{\Delta y}
\end{array}
\right\}
\tag{3.403}
$$

for index values of $0 \leq i \leq N_1 - 1$; $1 \leq j \leq N_2 - 1$; $0 \leq n \leq N_3 - 1$ and

$$
\left.
\begin{array}{l}
\dfrac{H^{n+1}_{y_{i,j}} - H^n_{y_{i,j}}}{\Delta \tau} = \dfrac{E^{n+1}_{x_{i,j}} - E^{n+1}_{x_{i-1,j}}}{\Delta z}; \\[3mm]
\dfrac{H^{n+1}_{z_{i,j}} - H^n_{z_{i,j}}}{\Delta \tau} = -\dfrac{E^{n+1}_{x_{i,j}} - E^{n+1}_{x_{i,j-1}}}{\Delta y}
\end{array}
\right\}
\tag{3.404}
$$

for index values of $0 \leq i \leq N_1 - 1$; $j = 0$; $0 \leq n \leq N_3 - 1$.

Let the boundary condition be given by $E_x \| \Gamma = 0$ (the Γ domain is the boundary) and the end condition (at $z = 0$) be given by $E_x = A(y) \cos(\omega t + \pi/2)$, where A is the real wave amplitude in scalar approximation.

In the set in (3.399), the spatial derivative approximations in equation 1, 2 are left, whereas in equations 3, 4 they are right. In the set in (3.401) the case is vice versa.

Therefore, Eqs. (3.399) and (3.401) can conventionally be referred to as the *push-pull scheme*. While allowing the use of boundary-value conditions to be abandoned for the magnetic field, it essentially simplifies the problem. Scheme of Eqs. (3.399) and (3.401) approximates the boundary-value problem of Eq. (3.398) with an approximation error of $O(\Delta\tau, \Delta z, \Delta y)$.

Below, we give examples that serve to test the developed difference scheme and discuss some practical applications.

Example 3.18 For a planar vacuum waveguide with metallic walls, the mode is represented by the following H-wave [21]:

$$\left.\begin{aligned}
E_x &= \cos(\gamma y) \cdot \cos\left(\sqrt{k^2 - \gamma^2}z - \omega t\right), \\
H_y &= -\frac{1}{k}\sqrt{k^2 - \gamma^2} \cdot \cos(\gamma y) \cdot \cos\left(\sqrt{k^2 - \gamma^2}z - \omega t\right), \\
H_z &= -\frac{1}{k}\gamma \cdot \sin(\gamma y) \cdot \sin\left(\sqrt{k^2 - \gamma^2}z - \omega t\right),
\end{aligned}\right\} \tag{3.405}$$

where k is the wave number and $\gamma = 2\pi/a$. Set the initial condition assuming in Eq. (3.405) that $t = 0$. Figure 3.29 shows the result of numerical simulation for the following parameters: $t_1 = 1 \cdot 10^{-11}$ s, $\Delta t = 4, 2 \cdot 10^{-15}$ s, $a = 60$ μm, $L = 3$ μm, $\Delta x = 2.36 \cdot 10^{-2}$ μm, $\Delta y = 1.935$ μm, and $\lambda = 0.637$ μm.

Visually, the result complies with the expected electric component representation in the form of cosine. Numerical analysis shows the error to depend on the value of the sampling steps $\Delta\tau$, Δz, and Δy.

Example 3.19 Assume that the earlier wave [22] with the identical sampling parameters is propagating in a glass waveguide with refractive index $n = 1.458$. The wave coming from vacuum strikes an infinite glass waveguide.

From Figure 3.30, the impulse shape is seen to be changed because of the n-fold difference in the light speed in vacuum and in the glass. The change appears as n-times compressed impulses.

Example 3.20 Let us look how the Gauss-Laguerre mode [23]

$$\Psi_{10} = \frac{2}{\sigma\sqrt{2\pi}}L_1^0\left(\frac{2y^2}{\sigma^2}\right)e^{-\frac{y^2}{\sigma^2}} \tag{3.406}$$

Figure 3.29. Numerically simulated mode of Eq. (3.405) propagating in a vacuum waveguide: the module of the E_x projection is depicted.

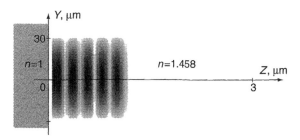

Figure 3.30. Numerically simulated mode of Eq. (3.405) propagating in a glass waveguide with refractive index $n = 1.458$: the module of the $n = 1.458$ projection is depicted.

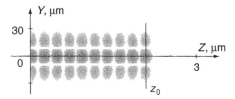

Figure 3.31. Propagation of the Gauss-Laguerre mode in a graded-index waveguide with the module of the E_x projection is shown.

propagates in a graded-index waveguide with refractive index $n^2(y) = n_1^2 \left(1 - 2\Delta (y/d)^2\right)$, where $L_1^0 (\mathbf{x})$ is the generalized Laguerre polynomial, $\sigma = 5, 6$ μm is the mode effective radius, $n_1 = 1.458$, $\Delta = 60$ μm.

The sampling steps were as follows: $\Delta t = 4.2 \cdot 10^{-15}$ s, $d = 60$ μm, $L = 3$ μm, $\Delta x = 1.003 \cdot 10^{-2}$ μm, $\Delta y = 4.72 \cdot 10^{-1}$ μm, $\lambda = 0.63$ μm, and $t = 1 \cdot 10^{-11}$. The results of simulation are shown in Figure 3.31.

To make it more visually clear, consider the amplitude distribution at the waveguide input end ($z = 0$), as shown in Figure 3.32 and within the waveguide ($z = z_0$), as shown in Figure 3.33.

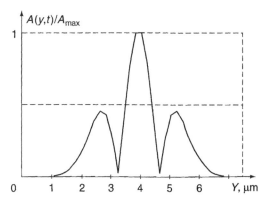

Figure 3.32. Amplitude distribution of the Gauss-Laguerre mode at the input end of the graded-index waveguide.

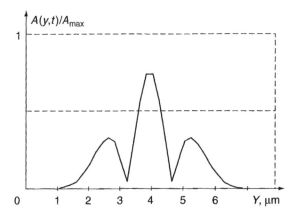

Figure 3.33. Amplitude distribution of the Gauss-Laguerre mode within the graded-index waveguide ($z = z_0$).

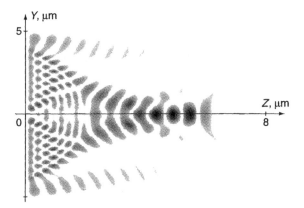

Figure 3.34. Intensity distribution for the electric field in the meridian section of the cylindrical lens.

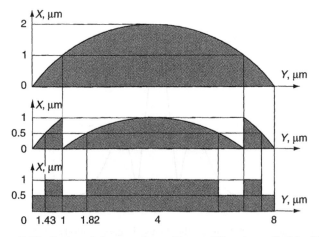

Figure 3.35. Stades of degenerating a binary diffractive cylindrical lens.

From the plots, the mode is seen to preserve the characteristic maxima, though the maximum amplitude value is somewhat reduced. This is due to the sampling errors. Note that as the sampling step is decreased, the accuracy of the simulation is increased.

Example 3.21   This experiment studies the propagation of the H-wave ($\lambda = 1 \ \mu m$) over a planar waveguide through a cylindrical focusing lens. Figure 3.34 depicts the result of numerical simulation of the intensity distribution in the focal plane of lens of radius 5 μm, aperture 8 μm, focal length 5 μm, refractive index 2, with the wave composed of eight tandems. The wave front after the lens is spherical. The intensity distribution in the lens focal plane is shown in Figure 3.34.

Example 3.22   We shall replace the lens by a two-level (binary) DOE corresponding to Figure 3.35. The results of numerical simulation are shown in Figure 3.36.

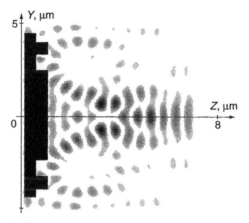

Figure 3.36. Intensity distribution for the electric field in the meridian section of the diffractive lens.

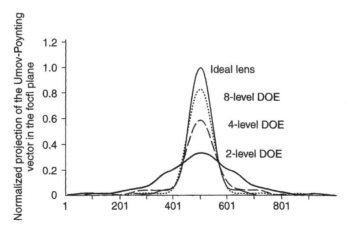

Figure 3.37. Distribution of the Umov-Poynting projection vector along the z-axis in the focal plane.

Figure 3.37 shows the plots of distribution of the Umov-Poynting vectors' projections on the z-axis for four lenses. These may be compared with analogous plots in Ref. [24] in which the lenses with the corresponding quantization levels display a greater efficiency. The differences are because of the fact that in Ref. [24], they study a thin lens in the diffraction approximation unacceptable in the present case when the radiation is studied directly after the optical element.

On the basis of the general principles of constructing the Peaceman-Rackford schemes reported in Ref. [20], we shall build an implicit difference scheme of enhanced time-accuracy rate. Put down the set of difference equations in the form

$$
\left.
\begin{aligned}
\frac{E_{x_{i,j}}^{n+0,5} - E_{x_{i,j}}^{n}}{0.5\Delta\tau} &= \frac{1}{n^2(z,y)}\left(\frac{H_{y_{i+1,j}}^{n+0,5} - H_{y_{i,j}}^{n+0,5}}{\Delta z} - \frac{H_{z_{i,j}}^{n} - H_{z_{i,j-1}}^{n}}{\Delta y}\right); \\[2mm]
\frac{E_{x_{i,j}}^{n+1} - E_{x_{i,j}}^{n+0,5}}{0.5\Delta\tau} &= \frac{1}{n^2(z,y)}\left(\frac{H_{y_{i+1,j}}^{n+0,5} - H_{y_{i,j}}^{n+0,5}}{\Delta z} - \frac{H_{z_{i,j}}^{n+1} - H_{z_{i,j-1}}^{n+1}}{\Delta y}\right); \\[2mm]
\frac{H_{y_{i,j}}^{n+0,5} - H_{y_{i,j}}^{n-0,5}}{\Delta\tau} &= \frac{E_{x_{i,j}}^{n+0,5} - E_{x_{i-1,j}}^{n+0,5}}{\Delta z}; \\[2mm]
\frac{H_{z_{i,j}}^{n+1} - H_{z_{i,j}}^{n}}{\Delta\tau} &= -\frac{E_{x_{i,j+1}}^{n+1} - E_{x_{i,j}}^{n+1}}{\Delta y}.
\end{aligned}
\right\}
\tag{3.407}
$$

The set (3.407) approximates the set in Eq. (3.398) in the nodes z_i, y_j, π_n for the following values of indices: $0 \le i \le N_1 - 1$, $z \le i \le N_2 - 2$, $0 \le n \le N_3 - 3$. Substituting equation 3 of the set (3.407) into equation 1, and equation 2 into equation 4 produces the following difference equations

$$
\frac{\Delta\tau}{n^2(z,y)\Delta z^2}E_{x_{i-1,j}}^{n+0,5} + \left(-\frac{2}{\Delta\tau} - 2\frac{\Delta\tau}{n^2(z,y)\Delta z^2}\right)E_{x_{i,j}}^{n+0,5} + \frac{\Delta\tau}{n^2(z,y)\Delta z^2}E_{x_{i+1,j}}^{n+0,5}
$$

$$
= -\frac{2}{\Delta\tau}E_{x_{i,j}}^{n} - \frac{1}{n^2(z,y)\Delta z}H_{y+1i,j}^{n-0,5} + \frac{1}{n^2(z,y)\Delta z}H_{y_{i,j}}^{n-0,5}
$$

$$
+ \frac{1}{n^2(z,y)\Delta y}H_{z_{i,j}}^{n} - \frac{1}{n^2(z,y)\Delta y}H_{z_{i,j-1}}^{n};
$$

$$
\frac{\Delta\tau}{n^2(z,y)\Delta y^2}E_{x_{i,j-1}}^{n+1} + \left(-\frac{2}{\Delta\tau} - 2\frac{\Delta\tau}{n^2(z,y)\Delta y^2}\right)E_{x_{i,j}}^{n+1} + \frac{\Delta\tau}{n^2(z,y)\Delta y^2}E_{x_{i,j+1}}^{n+1}
$$

$$
= -\frac{2}{\Delta\tau}E_{x_{i,j}}^{n+\frac{1}{2}} + \frac{1}{n^2(z,y)\Delta y}H_{z_{i,j}}^{n} - \frac{1}{n^2(z,y)\Delta y}H_{z_{i,j-1}}^{n}
$$

$$
- \frac{1}{n^2(z,y)\Delta z}H_{y_{i+1,j}}^{n+\frac{1}{2}} + \frac{1}{n^2(z,y)\Delta z}H_{y_{i,j}}^{n+0,5},
\tag{3.408}
$$

which can be solved using the sweep method. In the nodes (x_i, y_j, τ_k), for the index values of $0 \le i \le N_1 - 1$; $j = 1$; $0 \le n \le N_3 - 1$, an alternative set of approximating equations is given by

$$
\left.
\begin{aligned}
\frac{E_{x_{i,j}}^{n+0,5} - E_{x_{i,j}}^{n}}{0.5\Delta\tau} &= \frac{1}{n^2(z,y)}\left(\frac{H_{y_{i+1,j}}^{n+0,5} - H_{y_{i,j}}^{n+0,5}}{\Delta z} - \frac{H_{z_{i,j+1}}^{n} - H_{z_{i,j}}^{n}}{\Delta y}\right); \\
\frac{E_{x_{i,j}}^{n+1} - E_{x_{i,j}}^{n+0,5}}{0.5\Delta\tau} &= \frac{1}{n^2(z,y)}\left(\frac{H_{y_{i+1,j}}^{n+0,5} - H_{y_{i,j}}^{n+0,5}}{\Delta z} - \frac{H_{z_{i,j+1}}^{n+1} - H_{z_{i,j}}^{n+1}}{\Delta y}\right); \\
\frac{H_{y_{i,j}}^{n+0,5} - H_{y_{i,j}}^{n-0,5}}{\Delta\tau} &= \frac{E_{x_{i,j}}^{n+0,5} - E_{x_{i-1,j}}^{n+0,5}}{\Delta z}; \\
\frac{H_{z_{i,j}}^{n+1} - H_{z_{i,j}}^{n}}{\Delta\tau} &= -\frac{E_{x_{i,j}}^{n+1} - E_{x_{i,j-1}}^{n+1}}{\Delta y}.
\end{aligned}
\right\}
\tag{3.409}
$$

Substituting equation 3 of the set (3.409) into equation 1 and equation 4 into equation 2, we get the following difference equations

$$
\frac{\Delta\tau}{n^2(z,y)\Delta z^2}E_{x_{i-1,j}}^{n+0,5} + \left(-\frac{2}{\Delta\tau} - 2\frac{\Delta\tau}{n^2(z,y)\Delta z^2}\right)E_{x_{i,j}}^{n+0,5} + \frac{\Delta\tau}{n^2(z,y)\Delta z^2}E_{x_{i+1,j}}^{n+0,5}
$$

$$
= -\frac{2}{\Delta\tau}E_{x_{i,j}}^{n} - \frac{1}{n^2(z,y)\Delta z}H_{y_{i,j}}^{n-0,5} + \frac{1}{n^2(z,y)\Delta z}H_{y_{i,j}}^{n-0,5}
$$

$$
+ \frac{1}{n^2(z,y)\Delta y}H_{z_{i,j+1}}^{n} - \frac{1}{n^2(z,y)\Delta y}H_{z_{i,j}}^{n};
$$

$$
\frac{\Delta\tau}{n^2(z,y)\Delta y^2}E_{x_{i,j-1}}^{n+1} + \left(-\frac{2}{\Delta\tau} - 2\frac{\Delta\tau}{n^2(z,y)\Delta y^2}\right)E_{x_{i,j}}^{n+1} + \frac{\Delta\tau}{n^2(z,y)\Delta y^2}E_{x_{i,j+1}}^{n+1}
$$

$$
= -\frac{2}{\Delta\tau}E_{x_{i,j}}^{n+0,5} + \frac{1}{n^2(z,y)\Delta y}H_{z_{i,j+1}}^{n} - \frac{1}{n^2(z,y)\Delta y}H_{z_{i,j}}^{n}
$$

$$
- \frac{1}{n^2(z,y)\Delta z}H_{y_{i+1,j}}^{n+0,5} + \frac{1}{n^2(z,y)\Delta z}H_{y_{i,j}}^{n+0,5},
\tag{3.410}
$$

which can be solved using the sweep method, too. Now, knowing the electric field pixels $E_{x_{i,j}}^{n+1}$, the magnetic field is defined as

$$
\left.
\begin{aligned}
\frac{H_{y_{i,j}}^{n+0,5} - H_{y_{i,j}}^{n}}{\Delta\tau} &= \frac{E_{x_{i+1,j}}^{n+0,5} - E_{x_{i,j}}^{n+0,5}}{\Delta z}; \\
\frac{H_{z_{i,j}}^{n+1} - H_{z_{i,j}}^{n}}{\Delta\tau} &= -\frac{E_{x_{i,j+1}}^{n+1} - E_{x_{i,j}}^{n+1}}{\Delta y}
\end{aligned}
\right\},
\tag{3.411}
$$

for the index values of $0 \le i \le N_1 - 1$; $2 \le j \le N_2 - 2$; $0 \le n \le N_3 - 1$ and as

$$
\left.
\begin{aligned}
\frac{H_{y_{i,j}}^{n+0,5} - H_{y_{i,j}}^{n}}{\Delta\tau} &= \frac{E_{x_{i+1,j}}^{n+0,5} - E_{x_{i,j}}^{n+0,5}}{\Delta z}; \\
\frac{H_{z_{i,j}}^{n+1} - H_{z_{i,j}}^{n}}{\Delta\tau} &= -\frac{E_{x_{i,j+1}}^{n+1} - E_{x_{i,j}}^{n+1}}{\Delta y}
\end{aligned}
\right\},
\tag{3.412}
$$

for the index values of $0 \leq i \leq N_1 - 1$; $j = 1$; $0 \leq n \leq N_3 - 1$. The scheme in Eqs. (3.407) and (3.409) approximates the boundary-value problem of Eq. (3.398) with an approximation error of $O(\Delta \tau^2, \Delta z, \Delta y)$. This result has appeared following the use of both projections of H-field while deriving $E^{n+0.5}$ and E^{n+1}, which was not the case with the "push-pull" scheme.

To compare the efficiency of the proposed scheme with the "push-pull' scheme, we shall evaluate the relative error of solving the problem of mode propagation along a vacuum waveguide with metallic walls. Let the error be given by

$$\delta = \max_{z,y} \left| \frac{E_x^{\text{experiment}}(z, y) - E_x^{\text{theoretical}}(z, y)}{E_x^{\text{theoretical}}(z, y)} \right|. \tag{3.413}$$

Figure 3.38 depicts the error as a function of sampling for the "push-pull" scheme and the scheme of enhanced time-accuracy rate $[\Delta t = \lambda/(\text{fc})]$.

The numerical studies were conducted for the following parameters: $t = 10^{-11}$ s, $a = 3$ μm, $L = 3$ μm, $\Delta z = 0.0058$ μm, $\Delta y = 0.023$ μm, $\lambda = 1$ μm, $\Delta t_1 = 0.333 \cdot 10^{-12}$, $0.166 \cdot 10^{-12}$, $0.111 \cdot 10^{-12}$, $0.0833 \cdot 10^{-12}$, $0.0666 \cdot 10^{-12}$, $0.0556 \cdot 10^{-12}$, $0.0476 \cdot 10^{-12}$, $0.0416 \cdot 10^{-12}$, $0.037 \cdot 10^{-12}$, $0.033 \cdot 10^{-12}$ s.

Obviously, with more than 20 time pixels on a given interval, the scheme of enhanced accuracy rate is preferable. Note that in Figure 3.38, the error that occurs when using the enhanced time-accuracy rate depends quadratically on the sampling.

The scheme for the Maxwell equations in a 3D right Cartesian system in SI notation can be written as follows:

$$\left. \begin{aligned}
E_x^{n+1} &= \frac{h_t}{\varepsilon} \left(\frac{H_{z_{j+1}}^{n+1} - H_z^{n+1}}{h_y} - \frac{H_{y_{m+1}}^{n+1} - H_y^{n+1}}{h_z} \right) + E_x; \\[2mm]
H_z^{n+1} &= -\frac{h_t}{\mu} \left(\frac{E_{y_{i+1}}^{n+1} - E_y^{n+1}}{h_x} - \frac{E_x^{n+1} - E_{x_{j-1}}^{n+1}}{h_y} \right) + H_z; \\[2mm]
E_y^{n+1} &= \frac{h_t}{\varepsilon} \left(\frac{H_x^{n+1} - H_{x_{m-1}}^{n+1}}{h_z} - \frac{H_z - H_{z_{i-1}}}{h_x} \right) + E_y; \\[2mm]
H_x^{n+1} &= -\frac{h_t}{\mu} \left(\frac{E_{z_{j+1}}^{n+1} - E_z^{n+1}}{h_y} - \frac{E_{y_{m+1}}^{n+1} - E_y^{n+1}}{h_z} \right) + H_x; \\[2mm]
E_z^{n+1} &= \frac{h_t}{\varepsilon} \left(\frac{H_{y_{i+1}}^{n+1} - H_y^{n+1}}{h_x} - \frac{H_x - H_{x_{j-1}}}{h_y} \right) + E_z; \\[2mm]
H_y^{n+1} &= -\frac{h_t}{\mu} \left(\frac{E_x - E_{x_{m-1}}}{h_z} - \frac{E_z^{n+1} - E_{z_{i-1}}^{n+1}}{h_x} \right) + H_y,
\end{aligned} \right\} \tag{3.414}$$

where H_x, H_y, H_z, E_x, E_y, E_z are the corresponding projections of vectors of the magnetic and electric field strength, h_t, h_x, h_y, h_z are sampling steps on the grid $\Omega_{h_t, h_x, h_y, h_z} = [(x_i, y_j, z_m, t_n) \in D]$ in the domain $D[0 < x < L_x, \ 0 < y < L_y, \ 0 < z < L_z, \ 0 < t < L_t]$, where i, j, m, n are the grid nodes and $0 < i < N_x - 2$; $0 <$

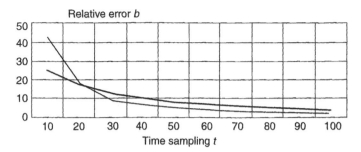

Figure 3.38. Error as a function of time. Thin line corresponds to the error resulting from using the enhanced time-accuracy rate scheme. Thick line is for the error the "push-pull" scheme yields.

$j < N_y - 2; 0 < m < N_z - 2; 0 < n < N_t - 2$. To make the notation simpler, the field values are indexed by letters other than i, j, m, n.

The boundary-value conditions are chosen for each projection from the following considerations: if the examined domain is placed within a perfectly conducting envelope (electric wall), tangential projections of the electric field and normal projections of the magnetic field onto the wall surface are equal to zero (boundary-value condition of first kind), whereas for the normal projections of the electric field, and the tangential projections of the magnetic field, the normal derivatives to the wall are equal to zero (boundary-value condition of second kind).

The scheme developed approximates the boundary-value problem with an approximation error of $O(h_t, h_x, h_y, h_z)$.

A variety of electromagnetic modes propagated in a hollow waveguide with perfectly conducting walls were used as test. The modes are harmonic functions that satisfy boundary conditions. Figure 3.39 depicts the analytical and difference-based solutions for the E_{11}-wave.

Among the disadvantages of the proposed schemes are a rather small order of approximation the difference schemes provide for the initial tasks and considerable computational efforts, which, in particular, does not allow one to use the methods for computing the field in lengthy waveguides.

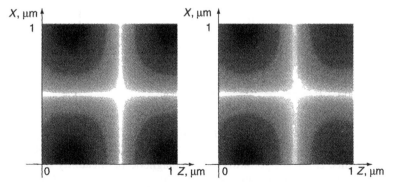

Figure 3.39. Ideal and estimated modal distributions for the wave E_{11} in the XZ-section at $y = Ly/2$.

3.9   ANALYSIS OF ELECTROMAGNETIC IMPULSE TRAVELING THROUGH AN ANTIREFLECTING STRUCTURE

When synthesizing DOE, one is concerned over energy losses related to the Fresnel reflection that is of primary importance for focusing high-power laser light. In Chapter 4 we deal with a technique for synthesizing focusing diffractive components for high-power IR lasers by means of selective ablation of diamond plates. While causing reflection losses, a relatively high diamond refractive index results in transmissions of no higher than 71 percent for the 10.6-μm wavelength. Because of this, the application of an antireflecting coating aimed at fighting the Fresnel reflection losses appears to be a topical task. In Refs. [25,26] they conducted a real experiment to demonstrate the efficiency of antireflecting subwavelength periodic microstructures on a diamond film surface produced by selective laser etching. The operation of antireflecting structures was numerically analyzed [25,26] using the theory of effective media [27]. This theory looks upon the subwavelength diffractive structure as a gradient medium with smoothly varying transverse gradient distribution of refractive index (Fig. 3.40). However, the effective medium theory approximation disregards real electromagnetic effects. In this section, we discuss a technique, which makes it possible to simulate the mechanism of laser light traveling through an antireflecting structure using the rigorous electromagnetic theory of light.

In Ref. [21], they present a difference scheme for the 3D Maxwell equation written in SI notation in the Cartesian coordinate system. Because the diffractive microrelief is applied as a set of fringes, choosing the Cartesian coordinate system's x-axis being parallel to the fringes would allow the following 2D schemes for TE-polarization to be built [19]:

$$
\left.
\begin{aligned}
H_z^{n+1} &= \frac{h_t}{\mu_0 \mu} \frac{E_x^{n+1} - E_{x_{j-1}}^{n+1}}{h_y} + H_z; \\
E_x^{n+1} &= \frac{h_t}{\varepsilon_0 \varepsilon} \left(\frac{H_{z_{j+1}} - H_z}{h_y} - \frac{H_{y_{m+1}}^{n+1} - H_y^{n+1}}{h_z} \right) + E_x; \\
H_y^{n+1} &= -\frac{h_t}{\mu_0 \mu} \frac{E_x^{n+1} - E_{x_{m-1}}^{n+1}}{h_z} + H_y,
\end{aligned}
\right\}
\tag{3.415}
$$

$$
\left.
\begin{aligned}
H_y^{n+1} &= -\frac{h_t}{\mu_0 \mu} \frac{E_x^{n+1} - E_{x_{m-1}}^{n+1}}{h_z} + H_y; \\
E_x^{n+1} &= \frac{h_t}{\varepsilon_0 \varepsilon} \left(\frac{H_{z_{j+1}}^{n+1} - H_z^{n+1}}{h_y} - \frac{H_{y_{m+1}} - H_y}{h_z} \right) + E_x; \\
H_z^{n+1} &= \frac{h_t}{\mu_0 \mu} \frac{E_x^{n+1} - E_{x_{j-1}}^{n+1}}{h_y} + H_z,
\end{aligned}
\right\}
\tag{3.416}
$$

where H_y, H_z, E_x are the corresponding projections of the vectors of the electric and magnetic field strength in the Cartesian coordinate system, ε_0, μ_0 are electric and magnetic constants, ε_0, μ are permittivity and magnetic permeability of vacuum, and the medium, h_t, h_y, h_z are sampling steps on the grid $\Omega_{ht,hy,hz} = [(y_j, z_m, t_n) \in D]$ in the domain $D = [0 < y < L_y, \ 0 < z < L_z, \ 0 < t < L_t]$, where j, m, n are the grid nodes, given $0 < j < N_y - 2$; $0 < k < N_z - 2$; $0 < n < N_t - 2$. For simplicity

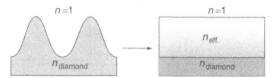

Figure 3.40. An equivalent medium for structured subwavelength gratings on the diamond film surface.

of notation, the indices of field values are other than j, k, m. For E_x and H_y, the boundary-value conditions are of first kind, and for H_z, the boundary-value conditions are of the second kind. The light is considered to propagate along the z-axis. The constructed scheme approximates the boundary-value problem with an approximation error of $O(h_t, h_y, h_z)$.

The set of difference equations is solved as follows: equation 3 is substituted in equation 2, with the resulting equation to be reduced to a three-diagonal form:

$$
E_{x_{m-1}}^{n+1}\left(-\frac{h_t^2}{\mu_0\mu\varepsilon_0\varepsilon h_z^2}\right) + E_x^{n+1}\left(1+2\frac{h_t^2}{\mu_0\mu\varepsilon_0\varepsilon h_z^2}\right) + E_{x_{m+1}}^{n+1}\left(-\frac{h_t^2}{\mu_0\mu\varepsilon_0\varepsilon h_z^2}\right)
$$
$$
= \frac{h_t}{\varepsilon_0\varepsilon h_y}\left(H_{z_{j+1}} - H_z\right) + \frac{h_t}{\varepsilon_0\varepsilon h_z}\left(H_y - H_{y_{m+1}}\right) + E_x \tag{3.417}
$$

and solved by a standard three-diagonal sweep. Having derived the E_x projection, we shall substitute it into equations 1 and 3 of the set (3.415), thus deriving H_y and H_z.

The set (3.416) is solved similarly, with the three-diagonal equation given by

$$
E_{x_{j-1}}^{n+1}\left(-\frac{h_t^2}{\mu_0\mu\varepsilon_0\varepsilon h_y^2}\right) + E_x^{n+1}\left(1+2\frac{h_t^2}{\mu_0\mu\varepsilon_0\varepsilon h_y^2}\right) + E_{x_{j+1}}^{n+1}\left(-\frac{h_t^2}{\mu_0\mu\varepsilon_0\varepsilon h_y^2}\right)
$$
$$
= \frac{h_t}{\varepsilon_0\varepsilon h_y}\left(H_{z_{j+1}} - H_z\right) + \frac{h_t}{\varepsilon_0\varepsilon h_z}\left(H_y - H_{y_{m+1}}\right) + E_x. \tag{3.418}
$$

From Eqs. (3.417) and (3.418), it can be seen that when the number of pixels along the domain of the numerical simulation is considerably greater than that across the domain, the scheme in Eq. (3.416) is preferable, because in that case one can do with a lesser bulk of random access memory. Otherwise, the scheme in Eq. (3.415) is preferable.

Note implicit peculiarities of the schemes (3.415) and (3.416) that make them different from the schemes (3.399), (3.401) and (3.407), (3.407) dealt with in the earlier section. In the Scheme (3.415), the longitudinal component of the magnetic field is computed explicitly, whereas in the Scheme (3.416) it is the transverse component of the magnetic field that is computed explicitly. At the same time, the difference Schemes (3.415) and (3.416) are not explicit because the other components of the electric field are derived implicitly. Though resulting in a 50 percent reduction of computation efforts, this approach is vulnerable to instability.

Example 3.23   Table 3.5 gives the results of a numerical simulation in which H_{01}-waves ($\lambda = 10.6$ μm, one-wavelength tandem) were generated and directed onto the air–plate interface, with one portion to be further propagated and the other portion

TABLE 3.5. Antireflection Effect Manifestation for Various Types of Antireflecting Coating

Number of the Numerical Simulation	Antireflecting Coating Type	Reflected Energy Fraction, %
1	No antireflecting coating	19.24
2	Triangle of base 4 μm and height 2.5 μm	19.24
3	Triangle of base 3 μm and height 2.4 μm	9.8
4	Triangle of base 3 μm and height 3 μm	9.8
5	Triangle of base 3 μm and height 2 μm	11.44
6	Triangle of base 3 μm and height 1.8 μm	12.39
7	Triangle of base 2 μm and height 2.5 μm	9.37
8	Triangle of base 1.5 μm and height 2.5 μm	5.41

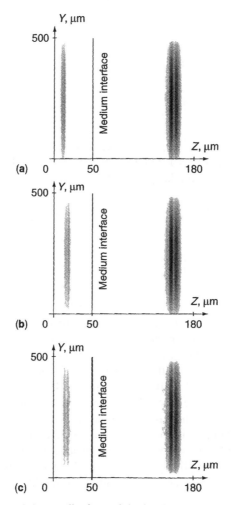

Figure 3.41. Distribution of the amplitude module for E component between the transmitted and reflected wave in experiments 1 (**a**), 3 (**b**), and 8 (**c**).

reflected from the interface. Permittivity of the plate was $\varepsilon = 5.76$. The scheme parameters were as follows: $L_y = 500$ μm, $L_z = 180$ μm, $L_t = 8.1 \cdot 10^{-14}$ s, $h_y = 1/3$ μm, $h_z = 0,2$ μm, $h_t = 3.5 \cdot 10^{-18}$ s. The electromagnetic field energy was defined as [19]

$$W = 1/2 \int_D (\varepsilon_0 \varepsilon |E|^2 + \mu_0 \mu |H|^2) \, dD, \qquad (3.419)$$

where $D = (0 \leq y \leq L_y, \; 0 \leq z \leq L_z)$.

The results of the computer simulations No. 3–6 suggest that there is an optimal height of the isosceles triangle corresponding to the antireflecting structure period. A triangle-shaped structure of less than optimal height displays a lesser antireflecting effect (cp. computer experiment 3 with computer experiments 5, 6), whereas for greater than optimal heights, the antireflecting effect does not increase (cp. experiment 3 with experiment 4).

Figures 3.41, 3.42, and 3.43 depict how the incident wave (experiments 1, 3, and 8) is separated into a wave having passed the diamond–air interface and that reflected from the interface.

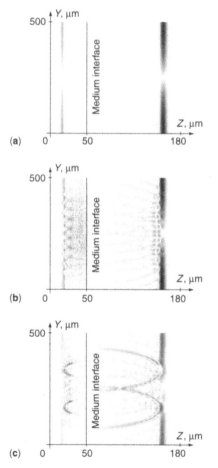

Figure 3.42. Distribution of the amplitude module for Hz component between the transmitted and reflected wave in experiment 1 (**a**), 3 (**b**), and 8 (**c**).

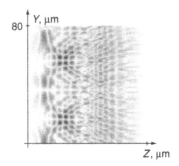

Figure 3.43. Distribution of the amplitude module for Hz component between the transmitted and reflected wave in experiment 8.

Figure 3.44. Distribution of the amplitude module for the H_z-projection of the electromagnetic field in the transmitted and reflected wave in experiment 1.

The size of the triangle base also affects the antireflecting effect. As it decreases, the fraction of energy having passed through the triangle is increased (cp. experiments 2, 3, 7, and 8 and Figs. 3.41, 3.42, and 3.43). Relating to Figure 3.41, the fraction of reflected energy is seen to decrease in Figures 3.42 and 3.43.

Figures 3.42a, d, and c show the mode composition of the electromagnetic wave on both sides of the interface. The mode composition can be clearly traced on the longitudinal projection of the magnetic field component. This is because low-order modes transfer the overwhelming fraction of the wave energy, whereas the longitudinal projection of the magnetic field component contributes insignificantly to the total energy, with low-order modes being predominant over the other modes.

The higher-order modes found in Figures 3.42, (as distinct from lower-order modes in Fig. 3.41) are because of continuous electromagnetic field on the antireflecting structure. Every relief fragment composed of one or more periods generates a set of modes of order $L_z \cdot a/d$, where d is the period of the antireflecting grating and a is the number of periods on the fragment. In more detail, the modal structure is shown in Figures 3.43 and 3.44.

Thus, in this section, we have demonstrated the potentialities of the difference solution of the Maxwell equations for the analysis of antireflecting subwavelength structure operation. The results of computer simulation are in good agreement with the results of real experiments reported in Refs. [25,26] and numerical simulation based on the theory of effective second-order media [27]. Thus, the difference solution of the Maxwell equations for the first time made it possible to computer simulate the antireflecting subwavelength structures, evaluate their efficiency, and analyze the fine structure of the reflected electromagnetic wave within the framework of the electromagnetic field theory.

CONCLUSION

This chapter contains the major relations of electrodynamics used in optics. The general equations have been applied to solving a number of basic problems of diffraction by a variety of optical elements.

Methods for solving the direct problem of diffraction by perfectly reflecting and transmitting dielectric diffraction gratings have been proposed. The electromagnetic analysis of operation of simple diffraction gratings with rectangular and triangular groove profile brings out a number of essential effects that the scalar theory fails to describe. This fact demonstrates that the use of accurate calculational procedures for analysis of DOEs with subwavelength zones is both topical and necessary.

The solution to the direct problem was used to develop, for the first time, electromagnetic gradient techniques for solving the inverse problem that involves designing a diffraction grating profile that is capable of generating desired order intensities. The reported studies of performances of the diffraction gratings designed using the scalar approximation demonstrate the topicality of accurate synthesis procedures. At the same time, the results of calculating the grating profiles confirm the robustness and efficiency of the gradient procedures developed.

It has been shown that the gradient procedure is fairly suitable for designing 1-order binary dielectric gratings aimed at concentrating the light in the 1st and −1st orders. The 1-order gratings have a number of interesting applications. In particular, the DOE relief corresponding to a binary 1-order grating provides an energy efficiency of more than 90 percent.

A number of diffraction problems have been solved in the general 3D case. The derived integral relations for the operator of electromagnetic field propagation allow the solution of the direct problem of field calculation to be reduced to four Fourier transforms. The unitary property of propagation operator that has been demonstrated allows "scalar" iterative algorithms for synthesis of phase wave fields to be extended onto the case of exact electromagnetic calculation. The derived integral relations have formed the basis for a gradient method for solving the inverse problem of wave field reconstruction.

An asymptotic technique for derivation of the field from optical elements on the basis of the local approximation of the element profile by a 2D diffraction grating has been proposed. This technique was used to calculate the field produced by a reflecting lens and an optical element focusing onto a line-segment. The asymptotics obtained have made it possible to evaluate a number of electromagnetic effects omitted in the "scalar case." This appears to be important in the analysis of the operation of a periodic large-aperture DOEs, when great computational complexity makes the exact calculation impossible. A joint use of the asymptotics developed and the gradient methods for designing 1-order gratings shows promise and allows the inverse problem of synthesizing optical elements for focusing light to be solved with due regard for electromagnetic effects.

Difference schemes for the numerical solution of the set of Maxwell equations for all types of electromagnetic waves in a domain limited by the electric or magnetic wall have been developed. In particular, such an approach has made it possible to simulate the propagation of short light impulses through optical elements and waveguides with an arbitrary profile of refractive index. The difference schemes were used to model the propagation of the H-wave (TE-polarization) through cylindrical lenses, including those with antireflecting coating.

REFERENCES

1. M.B. Winogradova et al., *Wave Theory*, Nauka Publishers, Moscow, 1979.
2. A.S. Ilyinsky, V.V. Kravtzov, and A.G. Sveshnikov. *Mathematical models in electrodynamics*, Vysshaya Shkola Publishers, Moscow, 1991.
3. V.A. Zverev. *Radiooptics*, Sovetskoye Radio Publishers, Moscow, 1975.
4. Y.L. Kok, N.C. Gallagher, *J. Opt. Soc. Am. A.* **5**(1), 65–73 (1988).
5. R. Petit, ed., *Electromagnetic Theory of Gratings: Topics in Current Physics*, 22nd Ed., Springer-Verlag, New York, 1980.
6. M.G. Moharam and T.K. Gaylord *J. Opt. Soc. Am, A*, **3**(11), 1780–1787 (1986).
7. Y.L. Kok, *Opt. Eng.* **33**(11), 3604–3609 (1994).
8. M. Born and E. Wolf. *Principles of Optics*, Pergamon Press, London, 1968.
9. F.P. Gantmakher. *Matrix Theory*, Nauka Publishers, Moscow, 1988.
10. L.L. Doskolovich et al., *Opt. Lasers in Eng.* **29**, 249–259 (1998).
11. C. Zhou and L. Liu, *Appl. Opt.* **34**, 5961–5969 (1995).
12. L.L. Doskolovich, *J. Comput. Opt.* **18**, 82–91 (1998).
13. L.L. Doskolovich et al., *Pure Appl. Opt.* **3**, 921–930 (1994).
14. L.L. Doskolovich et al., *Int. J. Optoelectronics* **10**, 243–249 (1995).
15. V. Soifer, V. Kotlyar, L. Doskolovich *Iterative Methods for Diffractive Optical Elements Computation*, Taylor & Francis, London, 1997.
16. W.B. Veldkamp, G.C. Swanson, and D.C. Shaver, *Optics Commun.* **5**(6), 353–358 (1984).
17. L.L. Doskolovich et al., *Proc. SPIE, Opt. Inf. Sci. Tech.* **3348**, 13–19 (1997).
18. S.T. Chu, W.P. Huang, and S.K. Chaudhuri, *Comput. Phys. Commun.* 68. 451–484 (1991).
19. V.V. Nikolsky and N.I. Nikolskaya, *Radiowaves: Electrodynamics and Propagation*, Nauka Publishers, Moscow, 1989, p. 544.
20. A.A. Samarsky. *Theory of Difference Schemes*, Nauka Publishers, Moscow, 1989.
21. D.L. Golovashkin, A difference scheme for the maxwell equations, *Transactions of the 9th Inter-college Students' Conference*, Samara, Russia, 1999.
22. S. Solimeno, B. Kroziniani, and P. Di Porto, *Diffraction and Waveguide Propagation of Optical Radiation*, Mir Publishers, Moscow, 1984.

23. V.A. Soifer and M.A. Golub, *Laser Beam Mode Selection by Computer Generated Holograms*, CRC Press, Boca Raton, Florida, 1994.

24. J.J. Stamnes, T. Gravelsaeter, and O. Bentsen, *Acoustical Imaging* **10**, 587–606 (1982).

25. T.V. Kononenko et al., *Appl. Phys. A* **68**(1), 99–102 (1999).

26. V.V. Kononenko et al., Quantum Electronics, *J. Quant. Electron.* **26** (2), 158–162 (1999).

27. H. Daniel and G. Raguin, *Appl. Opt.* **32**(7), 1154–1167 (1993).

CHAPTER 4

Technology of DOE Fabrication

4.1 TYPES OF PHASE MICRORELIEFS AND TECHNIQUES FOR THEIR FABRICATION

The diffractive optical element (DOE) is a zone plate with the diffractive microrelief corresponding to the phase function. At the design stage, the DOE phase function $\varphi(x, y)$ is derived using one of the methods discussed in the previous Chapters. Assume that a zone plate is found in the plane (x, y). The microrelief $h(x, y)$ is related to the phase function DOE $\varphi(x, y)$ by

$$h(x, y) = \frac{\lambda}{2\pi(\sqrt{n^2 - \sin^2 \alpha} - \cos \alpha)} \, \mathrm{mod}_{2\pi m}[\varphi(x \cos \alpha, y)] \qquad (4.1)$$

for the transmission DOE [1], and by

$$h(x, y) = \frac{\lambda}{4\pi \cos \alpha} \, \mathrm{mod}_{2\pi m} \left[\varphi(x \cos \alpha, y) \right], \qquad (4.2)$$

for the reflection DOE, where $\mathrm{mod}_{2\pi m}(t)$ is a function equal to the least positive remainder of the division of t by $2\pi m$, $m = 1, 2, 3, \ldots$ is the integer, λ is the wavelength, n is the refractive index of the substrate, and α is the angle between the incident beam's optical axis and the normal to the DOE plane (x, y) (Fig. 4.1).

The microrelief derived from Eqs. (4.1) or (4.2) using a continuous-phase function $\varphi(x, y)$, is referred to as a continuous or blazed microrelief [2]. According to Eqs. (4.1) and (4.2), the microrelief height takes maximal values when the phase function $\varphi(x, y)$ values are multiples of $2\pi m$. For the transmission DOE, the maximal microrelief height

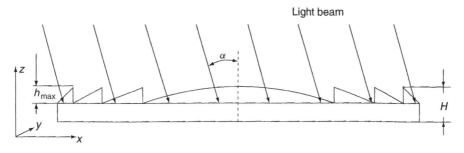

Figure 4.1. Schematic view of DOE operation.

is given by

$$h_{max} = \frac{m\lambda}{\sqrt{n^2 - \sin^2\alpha} - \cos\alpha}, \tag{4.3}$$

whereas for the reflection DOE, the maximal height is

$$h_{max} = \frac{m\lambda}{2\cos\alpha} \tag{4.4}$$

Note that because of the thickness of the substrate, the usual overall thickness H of the optical element is essentially greater than h_{max} (Fig. 4.1).

In terms of practical implementation of the DOE, two types of phase microrelief (Fig. 4.2) have come to be most popular: a stepwise (binary and multilevel) microrelief and continuous microrelief.

The stepwise multilevel microrelief profile (Figs. 1.19 and 1.20) is a realization of the phase function $\hat{\varphi}(x, y)$ quantized in M levels with the step $\Delta\varphi$, specified from the considerations of the DOE manufacturability and efficiency. In terms of technology, the major characteristic of the DOE stepwise microrelief is to what degree it corresponds to the phase function $\hat{\varphi}(x, y)$ profile. Technological errors result in a reduced diffraction efficiency of the DOE.

The binary microrelief height takes two values within a single zone and is defined by

$$h(x, y) = \begin{cases} 0, & \varphi(x, y) < \pi, \\ h_{max}, & \varphi(x, y) \geq \pi. \end{cases} \tag{4.5}$$

where the $\varphi(x, y)$ function is reduced to the interval $[0, 2\pi)$.

For the derivation of values of the binary function in Eq. (4.5) from the initial phase function $\varphi(x, y)$ see, for example, Section 1.2 (Fig. 1.18). The choice of the microrelief type is determined not only by a set of available technologies for the diffractive microrelief fabrication but also by the DOE operation quality and efficiency dictated by the specific optical configuration and the purpose for which the DOE is due to serve. The DOE-dedicated software complexes are certain to include means that allow a decrease in the DOE quality and energy efficiency to be estimated when changing from a continuous to a multilevel or binary microrelief [3]. Dedicated physical and mathematical tools that allow the efficiency of binary and multilevel DOEs to be enhanced are being developed [4].

Whatever technique for the DOE phase function calculation and optimization may be, the eventual quality of the optical element operation is determined by the fabrication accuracy of the diffractive microrelief. There are a variety of technologies to implement the phase function in an optical medium. For example, dividing machines allow the direct fabrication of diffraction gratings (including blazed ones) with straight-line zone boundaries making the control of the dividing machine rather easy, doing without sophisticated algorithms. There are also techniques for directly translating onto a physical medium radially symmetric, and even more complex, phase functions using precision machine tools with numerical control [5,6]. It is by using these techniques that submillimeter and far-infrared (IR) DOEs are fabricated [7,8]. Photolithographic technology also shows promise and involves a multistep etching of glass substrate [9]. Optical elements operating the visible range are fabricated using chalcogenide glassy semiconductors (HGS) [10] and graded-index materials [11]. Methods based on the use of liquid (and dry) photopolymerizable compositions (LPPC) also show considerable promise for fabricating continuous microreliefs [12,13].

Relief-making technologies employing advances and instrumentation of microelectronics have attracted particular attention of diffractive optics researchers [14]. The main factors in favor of this choice are as follows:

- DOEs and microcircuits are similar in size
- The desired spatial resolutions are similar
- High-level automation of microelectronics equipment allows complex-topology zones to be implemented
- There is a feasibility of fabricating multilevel phase reliefs
- Easily available microelectronics technological equipment makes the use of leased equipment feasible
- Microelectronics features high-level reliability of technological automata and repeatability of results
- Microelectronics materials (substrates, resists, and others) are suitable for fabricating DOEs
- The results can be automatically checked

Highly automated technological procedures of microelectronics allow us to speak about the automated design of the diffractive microrelief of optical elements. Such design techniques involve not only the choice of special methods taking account of technological limitations but also the feasibility iteratively to optimize the major DOE parameters according to the results of checking the resulting microrelief quality and the operational efficiency of the DOE in an optical scheme. Note that the choice of the size, shape, and the material used, and the spatial resolution of the microrelief under design (and, hence, the choice of a particular technology) is determined by both the DOE purpose and the working optical range. By way of illustration, feasible range of resolution of a diffraction grating may vary from 0.25 mm^{-1} for IR and submillimeter light to 1200 mm^{-1} for UV light.

Most technologies for generating DOE microreliefs can be generally depicted by a scheme shown in Figure 4.3. Variations of the phase function reduced to the working interval $[0, 2\pi m)$ are represented as variations in transmission of a photomask generated by an automated precision tool. When the energy is delivered through the photomask (exposure) in a special manner, the active medium changes its properties in

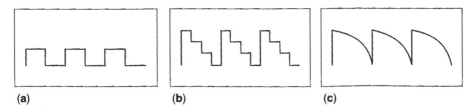

(a)   (b)   (c)

Figure 4.2. Microrelief profiles of the DOE: (a) binary, (b) multilevel, (c) continuous.

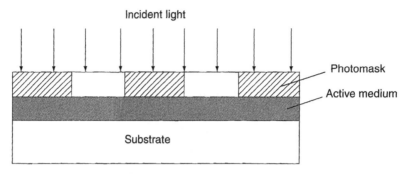

Figure 4.3. Process of the microrelief generation.

exposed places and produces a structure that is either the diffraction grating itself (as is the case with the LPPC layers) or that facilitates its creation by etching the substrate.

At present, a wide variety of technological processes aimed at generating the diffractive microrelief have been evaluated and elaborated. These processes use diverse active media (physical, chemical, and mechanical): focused e-beams and ion-beams, gases, acids, resists, polymeric compositions, and diamond chisels. Different technologies require different photomasks: sets of binary photomasks for photolithography, halftone photomasks for LPPCs and for bleaching the gelatin, a thin-membrane film for X-ray lithography or stencil-photomask to be used in ion-electron lithography. When employing halftone photomasks and appropriate technologies, a continuous microrelief is generated in a single step (for the techniques of generating a continuous relief, see Section 4.4). When using a set of binary photomasks and relevant "binary-active" media for generating a multilevel relief, the process shown in Figure 4.3 has to be reiterated sequentially for all photomasks from the set. A variety of up-to-date technologies (e-beam lithography, numerically controlled tools) do not allow for the physical implementation of the photomask (or photomask set), because in this case the microrelief is generated using a calculated virtual photomask. The most important characteristics of photomasks (both real and virtual) are the parameters of lines found on a photomask, especially the minimal value of the line width and the maximal value of the line curvature. These parameters are better to describe for the lines found on binary photomasks. When fabricating a binary DOE, the photomask is an amplitude zone plate (for various types of the zone plates and for the concept of the zone of an optical element, see Section 1.1). The photomask lines reproduce the zone shape, occupying about half the zone area for a binary DOE. In particular, the phase diffraction grating is fabricated using a photomask in the form of an amplitude diffraction grating, with its dark lines forming the photomask lines (Fig. 1.1). When fabricating more complex DOEs, the photomask lines may vary in thickness and may be significantly curved (e.g., Figs. 1.9 and 1.5).

The mathematical model of the line (Fig. 4.4) is defined by the following functions:

$$x = x(t), \quad y = y(t), \quad Z = Z(t), \quad 0 < t < L, \tag{4.6}$$

where $x(t)$, $y(t)$ are differentiable functions that parametrically describe a curve of the line centers, which is later referred to as a *route*; $Z(t)$ is the function of the line width (the aggregate distance from the route to the line boundaries reckoned along the

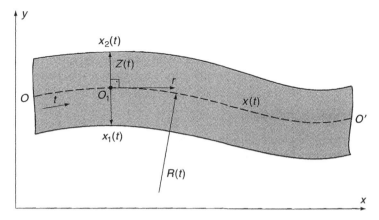

Figure 4.4. Mathematical definition of the line characteristics.

perpendicular to the route); t is the distance from the initial line point measured along the route; and L is the route length.

From Eq. (4.6), we can uniquely derive the line boundaries, the curvature, and the curvature radius of the line at each route point. The line curvature at point t is

$$K(t) = \frac{|y'' \cdot x' - x'' \cdot y'|}{|(x')^2 + (y')^2|} \tag{4.7}$$

where, $\qquad x' = dx(t)/dt, \quad x'' = d^2x(t)/dt^2$

$R(t)$ is the radius of curvature of the t line at point, (a quantity inverse to the curvature — Fig. 4.4). The curvature parameters and the minimal width of photomask lines determine the choice of the technology type and the necessary items of process equipment. Obviously, the lesser the working wavelength and higher the DOE resolution, the lesser is the width of photomask lines and higher are the requirements imposed on the resolution, accuracy of the techniques, and process equipment used.

The choice of the technology and machines for writing photomasks implies an adequate organization of data for the optical element under design. The data organization for machines with circular or line-by-line scanning will differ from that used in the machines with a vector type of writing (a photomask or microrelief). Whether the machine uses a halftone or binary automaton also affects the way in which data will be transmitted: either as a serial set of binary arrays (binary machines) or as a single array with an appropriate number of bytes per pixel (usually, one byte is sufficient) to provide a desired number of phase gradations of the optical element (halftone machines). We consider the most popular technologies for DOE fabrication in the following section.

4.2   FABRICATING DOEs USING PHOTOLITHOGRAPHY

Lithography is a process in which a configuration or a mutual location of elements on the substrate is reproduced by generating a protective relief coating followed by the translation of the microrelief into the substrate. Depending on the type of the radiation used, the lithography is classified as photolithography, e-beamlithography, x-ray lithography, and ion lithography [14–16].

Among the available technologies for fabricating multilevel DOE microrelief, photolithography has become most popular. With photolithography, fabrication of a set of precision photomasks is a key method for generating a DOE microrelief.

4.2.1 Photomask Fabrication

At early stages, the DOEs were fabricated using computer graphics techniques: cathode-ray tubes, plotters, and binary and multilevel photo-plotters [17]. In particular, in the 1970s, electromechanical, computer-controlled photo-plotters were widely used for generating holograms and DOEs (Fig. 4.5).

A pixel coming from the computer is transformed into an analogous electric signal that modulates the intensity of a diode laser beam illuminating a corresponding place on the photofilm. The device provides the generation of a raster image with the following parameters: the raster's step is 12.5, 25, 50, and 100 μm; the optical densities range from 0 to 2D; the number of quantization levels is up to 256; the rate of pixeling is 28 KHz; the maximal image size is 5 in. × 10 in. The pixel field is $N_u \times N_v \sim 10^6$.

The 1980s saw the advent of laser photo-plotters. The He-Ne laser can focus the light into a minimal size of about 10 μm. Depending on the type of the film used, the parameters of recording chosen, and the mode of film development, the line width may vary from 9 to 13 μm.

Because the image is generated through a photochemical process, the development modes heavily affecting the image quality and contrast should be stabilized and fixed. Fitting the parameters to control the recording process occupies a considerable portion of the entire time required to generate a DOE photomask. Because the laser light produces the Gaussian intensity distribution over the spot, the laser light intensity and the spot defocusing parameter are fitted. The line is composed of spots, and for it to be continuous, the spots must overlap. Output test images are often

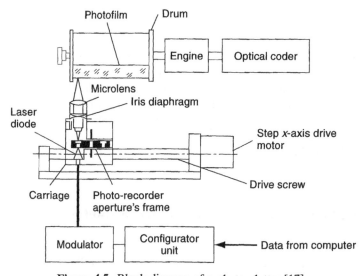

Figure 4.5. Block-diagram of a photo-plotter [17].

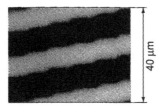

Figure 4.6. A fragment of the DOE photomask fabricated on a grained film.

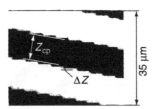

Figure 4.7. The line edge of the metallized DOE photomask is rough.

found to disintegrate into separate spots or be unacceptably thickened. After a series of tests involving a complete cycle of film processing, these problems are overcome to yield stable recording parameters; we may consider these to be finalized for a given type of film and developer. Once any of them is changed, the entire procedure should be reiterated. With film-recorded photomasks, the main disadvantage is a grained film structure that heavily affects the edge irregularity and image contrast (Fig. 4.6).

Later in the process, the DOE photomasks are translated from the film onto glass metallized plates, for example, coated with a chromium layer, thus increasing the image contrast (Fig. 4.7) and making the metallized photomasks suitable for photolithographic processes involving multiple exposure and alignment.

The earlier-described electromechanical systems are called *drum-type devices* because the film is retained against a drum by vacuum and the positioning along a coordinate is implemented by rotating a microscrew with a specified pitch. Laser image generators capable of scanning over the X-Y coordinate grid were specially developed to generate photomasks directly on a glass substrate. Here, step motors control the displacement of a plane table, whereas laser interferometers or a glass coordinate grid are used to control the desired coordinates and the displacement accuracy (Table 4.1). A linear laser image generator was used to synthesize multiorder diffraction gratings with a spatial frequency of 500 lines/mm [18]. The pixel field was $N_u \times N_v \approx 10^8$ in size.

Because most DOEs have complex topology, much attention is paid to the accurate line representation. Figure 4.8 depicts photomask fragments generated by various writing machines.

In Figures 4.8a and 4.8b, DOEs are composed of lines being approximated by sets of elementary images in the form of spots or rectangles oriented along fixed orthogonal axes. When illuminated, such a structure causes the light to be scattered by the corners of the rectangles, resulting in the decreased DOE efficiency and extra noise in the image generated. There is an entire class of optical elements in which such

TABLE 4.1. Comparative Characteristics of Some Types of Laser Image Generators

System	Pixel Size, (μm)	Pixel Generation Rate, (MHz)	Maximal Area, Inch	Positioning
Argis 1	5	25	18 × 32	Glass coordinate grid
Argis 3	5	100	24 × 32	Glass coordinate grid
Argis 4	10	100	24 × 32	Glass coordinate grid
Laserad I	0.5	25	5 × 5	Interferometer
Laserad II	2.5/1.25/0.5	25	8 × 10	Interferometer

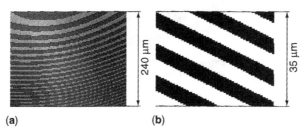

(a)   (b)

Figure 4.8. Photomask fragments generated by various writing machines: (**a**) laser photo-plotter FEAG, (**b**) e-beam lithographer ZBA-20.

errors are intolerable. The greater the edge irregularity, the smaller is the resolution. Besides, in array image generators, heavily curved lines are represented by a set of spots whose coordinates are found within geometric limits of the line. In this case, if the line width becomes comparable with the spot size, computational errors may cause the lines to become discontinuous. Because it is fairly difficult to estimate the probability of discontinuity, they use the software intended to make critical places on the DOE photomask visible on the computer display as early as possible at the design stage [19]. Thus, the DOE parameters can be corrected in advance, doing without fairly costly writing machinery (Fig. 4.9). The line disintegration shown in Figure 4.9 can be remedied by decreasing the aperture or by increasing the focal length.

For radially symmetric (and similar) DOEs, this error can be essentially diminished by using writing machines with a circular laser writing system [20]. Figure 4.10 shows the configuration of such a unit.

Axially symmetric DOE photomasks are written by circular scanning of the outer and inner line boundary, with the internal area filled by spiral scanning. When written

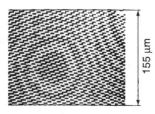

Figure 4.9. Line disintegration on the DOE photomask caused by the limited resolution of the writing machine.

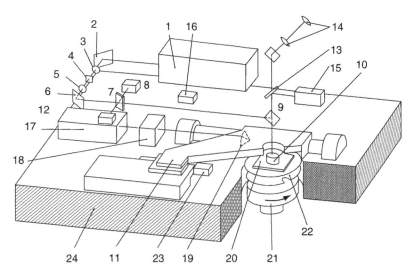

Figure 4.10. Configuration of a circular laser writing system [20]. (1:Ar laser; 2, 6:mirrors; 3, 5:lenses; 7, 9, 13:beam splitters; 8, 12:photo-receivers; 10:focusing lens; 11:platform; 14:microscope; 15:focusing sensor; 16:illuminator; 17:He-Ne laser; 18:interferometer; 19:reflector; 20:substrate; 21:spindle; 22:zero sensor; 23:linear motor; 24:granite plate).

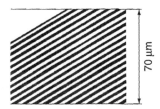

Figure 4.11. A photomask fragment written by a circular laser-writing machine.

by a circular laser writing system, axial photomasks feature smooth line edging and an excellent accuracy in terms of width and position (Fig. 4.11).

When writing an arbitrary DOE, one uses the dedicated software to transform the rectangular coordinate system into the polar one thus ensuring that the writing laser beam is modulated according to the angular position. Both with circular and arbitrary microimages, their spatial resolution is above $1,000$ mm^{-1}. A photoresist or thin amorphous chromium or silicon films are used as a photosensitive material [21]. By way of illustration, binary photomasks of a microlens raster were written on a glass substrate using the circular laser writing machine. A fragment of such a microrelief in which four lenses of microlens raster are combined is shown in Figure. 4.12.

Note, however, that for fabricating visible and even near-IR DOEs, the parameters of the available laser image generators make necessary the use of photoreduction devices or writing systems of higher resolution.

In the 1990s, cathode ray tubes (CRT) have become the most popular type of image generators. The plates are exposed with the aid of the e-beam of a certain width using methods of vector and polar scanning. The dynamic deflection system takes account of the table movement in the course of exposure and determines the

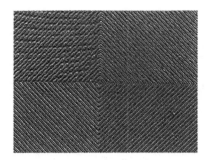

Figure 4.12. A microrelief fragment for the microlens raster.

coordinates of the subsequent stamp. The ray is blanked between two subsequent actions on the photosensitive layer (exposures). While being capable of operating under great current densities of the beam and changing the stamp size in a wide range, the CRTs have high performances of 10 cm^2/min or 10 plates/hour. The CRT has a spatial resolution of 0.1 μm, thus allowing one to do without photoreduction in the visible range (Table 4.2).

Though mainly used to fabricate binary photomasks, the CRTs are also suitable for generating multilevel images. The field size is $N_u \times N_v \sim 10^{10}$ pixels. As distinct from the photo-plotter, the CRTs produce an amplitude DOE photomask on a special photoresist.

When fabricating a DOE by microlithography, the precision microelectronics standards, according to which the ratio between the line edge roughness and its width (Fig. 4.7) should be no less than 1:100, are not observed. With concentric photomasks, this means that the line width should be at least 100 times the resolution of the writing machine. Considering the number of phase levels M, practically manufacturable width of the minimal zone becomes extremely great, thus limiting the DOE applications. Because of this, having in mind the fabrication of short-focus and wide-aperture optical elements, the principles mentioned earlier are deliberately violated. In practice, the ratio $\Delta Z / Z = 1:10$, or even 1:3 for peripheral zones can be considered acceptable. In the

TABLE 4.2. Parameters of Cathode Ray (e-beam) Writing Systems

Parameters	Linear Scanning	Circular Scanning
E-beam:		
Voltage, (kW)	15; 30	15; 30
Current, (nA)	0.1–1.0	0.1–1.0
Beam diameter, (μm)	0.1–1.0	0.1–1.0
Area under scanning, (mm × mm)	3 × 3	3 × 3
Control by	X: analog scanning by rectangular signal Y: digital scanning	XY: analog scanning sinusoidal signal
Resolution (on the area under scanning)	2^{16} pixels	2^{14} pixels (radius)
Scanning time	100 μs—10 s/line	10 ms/circle

limiting case, the curved line of the DOE peripheral zone can be accurately reproduced by a line (lines) of the following width:

$$Z_{\min} = (\Delta_{\text{spot}} + \Delta_{\text{step}}) \leq \frac{f\lambda}{d}\frac{1}{M}, \qquad (4.8)$$

where M is the number of phase quantization levels, Δ_{spot} is the diameter of the focused writing spot; Δ_{step} is the displacement minimal step of the writing machine, f is the focal length of DOE, d is the diameter of DOE, and λ is the DOE operating wavelength. This relation can be used to estimate the minimal line width of arbitrary focusing DOEs.

For instance, if $\Delta_{\text{spot}} = 10\ \mu\text{m}$, $\Delta_{\text{step}} = 10\ \mu\text{m}$, $\lambda = 0.5\ \mu\text{m}$ and an 8-level step microrelief, the minimal realizable ratio of the focal length f to the diameter d equals 320, that is, for a lens of aperture 10 mm, the focal length can be no less than 3200 mm. It stands to reason that in this situation it is impossible to generate a practically suitable visible DOE without taking additional measures, for example, photoreduction. However, for the average IR DOE ($\lambda = 10.6\ \mu\text{m}$) with the aperture of 40 mm in diameter, the focal length may be equal to, or greater than 600 mm, as is the case in a number of practical applications.

When employed in a technological process, the following critical parameters of the photomasks must be checked:

1) The size of the characteristic photomask elements (i.e., thinnest and most peripheral, or curved lines, and thinnest lines of reference marks intended to control the quality of photomask alignment).
2) Density of defects.
3) Accuracy of photomask position.

The minimal size of the characteristic elements (hereafter called *minimal elements*) is the most important characteristic of the photomask. For XY-coordinate image generators [18], the size of minimal elements in the photomasks of linear and concentric pattern may differ essentially. For a line grating or a cylindrical lens, the minimal line width may be equal to the diameter of the writing spot. Curved lines are generated in this case as sets of segments or even points. Identity of the minimal elements is also an important parameter in characterizing the set of DOE photomasks. Both the parameters are of equal importance for the technological process. An adequate determination of the minimal element is critical in providing an appropriate exposure time within which all structural lines of the DOE are written down. Besides, considerably varied minimal elements in the photomask set of a single DOE cause the range of exposures to be changed while changing from one photomask to another.

The relative level of the density of defects on the photomask surface mainly depends on how thoroughly the substrate has been cleaned and prepared before applying the photoresist. Despite the fact that as distinct from the integrated circuit production, minute defects, such as punches and line breaks, are not so critical in the DOE fabrication, they are essentially able to reduce the general efficiency of the optical element.

With photolithography, the process of exposure and alignment makes it necessary for the DOE photomasks to have a fairly rigid surface of the working masking layer.

At the same time, in order to avoid shades on the boundary between the light and dark lines, the masking layer must have minimal thickness. The plane surface of the photomask should provide the best contact over the entire surface of the photomask and the substrate.

The accuracy of photomask positioning describing the quality of alignment of two or more levels from the set of photomasks is usually characterized by the alignment error. This depends on the accuracy and stability of the image generator that provides the maximal linearity in the straight-line image and the perpendicularity of the coordinate grid.

With visual alignment, the accuracy is determined by the quality and the principle of operation of micromanipulators, by the size and contrast of reference marks, their shape, and the stability that the aforementioned parameters show during the technological process. When fabricating optical elements, the critical parameter is the brightness contrast that occurs as a result of the light scatter from the "etching wedge" (i.e., deviation of the microrelief steps from vertical direction). Because of this, the reference marks look dark against the light background. Note that deeper the etching, greater is the blurring. The shape of the reference marks on the photomask and substrate is related to the condition of their alignment, which may imply a contact between the mark elements, an equality of interelement gaps and areas, and, at last, coaxiality of the points of mark intersection (Fig. 4.13).

The marks are considered to be optimal if they are formed upon the alignment of lines inscribed between two other lines. For medium IR DOEs, the line width can be equal to 3 μm, the length is 10 times greater than the width, and the contrast is 0.3–0.4. In DOE fabrication, the reference marks should be chosen with due account for the image structure. By way of illustration, for radially symmetric structures, the angle error is not critical, whereas a small displacement along the X-axis or Y-axis can lead to the complete failure of the DOE. Because of this the Nonius scale is used,

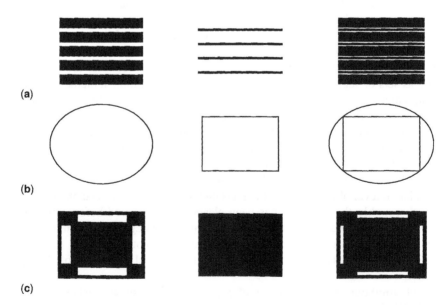

(a)

(b)

(c)

Figure 4.13. Reference marks: (**a**) equal gaps; (**b**) contacts; (**c**) equal areas.

along with the conventional reference marks, thus allowing the error to be evaluated in the process of alignment and eliminated in time (Fig. 4.14).

Such reference marks provide alignment accuracy of not less than 1.0 μm at the line width of about 10 μm.

4.2.2 Exposure and Development of Photoresist Films

Exposing the photoresist through a photomask is the most critical operation of the photolithographic process. During this operation, the photoresist undergoes a physicochemical conversion and grows soluble (or insoluble) in the developing solution, thus implementing the DOE structure.

The image is generated on the substrate surface according to certain optical laws. For example, in projection lithography, characteristics of the objective play the main role, whereas in contact lithography it is the illuminating beam characteristics and the presence and size of the gap between the photomask and the substrate that is of importance. The exposure time and the illuminating beam intensity are determined by the following factors: characteristic of the photosensitive layer — type of the resist and modes of its preliminary processing; parameters of the DOE photomask — properties of the photomask substrate material and acceptable limiting size of the DOE structure; development modes — concentration of reagents in the developing solution, solution temperature, and development time. The exposure and development should result in a DOE pattern generated in the photoresist that determines the topology and size of structural elements. A high-quality pattern is achieved through the use of a variety of exposure techniques and photoresist types.

The maximal spectral photosensitivity of photoresists is in the range $\lambda = 0.3$–0.45 μm. There are photoresists whose maximal photosensitivity is adapted to far UV ($\lambda = 0.193$ μm or $\lambda = 0.248$ μm for KrF- and ArF-lasers, respectively). However, in this case it may be difficult to choose adequate photomask substrates, which would be sufficiently transparent to such wavelengths. It is common to expose the photoresist by the actinic light because its spectral characteristics meet the technological process requirements and have the maximal resolution. By way of illustration, the mercury discharge lamps with the spectral peak at $\lambda = 0.436$ μm (g-line) and at $\lambda = 0.365$ μm (i-line) corresponding to the photoresist maximal photosensitivity (Fig. 4.15) are widely used in exposure units.

When fabricating photomasks and DOE microreliefs, three major techniques for photoresist exposure are as follows: *(1)* scanning by a focused beam; *(2)* contact or noncontact printing; *(3)* projection printing (Fig. 4.16).

With the first method (Fig. 4.16a), an elementary ray beam (e-beam or Gaussian light beam) is focused as a spot on the substrate, with the desired pattern produced by the scanning apparatus. One may use raster scanning in which the entire DOE aperture is scanned with a regular step, or a vector scanning in which the beam scans

Figure 4.14. Reference marks in combination with the Nonius scale.

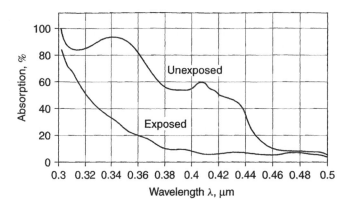

Figure 4.15. Photoresist absorption as a function of the light wavelength (from the technical manual on the Microposite S1218 photoresist by Shipley firm).

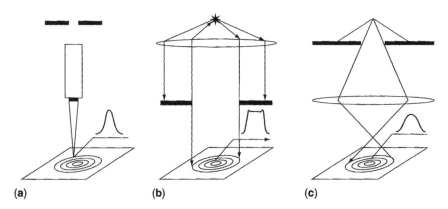

Figure 4.16. Techniques for photoresist exposure: (**a**) scanning; (**b**) noncontact printing; (**c**) projection printing.

only exposed zones, through a continuous trajectory. The second and third exposure methods (Fig. 4.16b and 4.16c) are grouped into so-called parallel-exposure systems (where large areas with a variety of photomasks can be exposed simultaneously) and are classified as follows:

1) Shadow-casting systems (contact and noncontact printing)
2) Imaging systems (projection printing)

With contact printing, the photomask and the sample are in close contact, whereas with noncontact printing, a small gap is introduced specially to avoid damaging the photomask. With projection printing, the illuminating light transmitted by the amplitude photomask is focused by the objective and produces the image on the substrate.

The resolution of modern exposure units amounts to 0.5 μm at a 100×100 mm^2 area. The alignment accuracy is not less than 0.25 μm. A special device allows the gap between the photomask and the sample to be chosen and fixed in the range from 0 to 50 μm, while keeping the planes parallel. Automatic operation of some units is advisable in mass production of integrated microcircuits. However, while fabricating DOEs, one has to use the manual exposure mode, owing to nonstandard substrate size and some techniques for improving image quality. The substrate and photomask are usually fixed by vacuum, although they may be pressed to each other either by vacuum or mechanically, the latter having benefits of allowing a gap between the photomask and the sample. The exposure time is determined by a photosensor according to desired values. The alignment is checked by a binocular microscope, with the reference marks observed in its different fields (Figs. 4.13 and 4.14). In alignment, it is the sample that is shifted and rotated, whereas the photomask remains fixed.

The intensity of the illuminating beam having passed through a photomask is known to be in inverse proportion to the line frequency per unit photomask area. Therefore, the peripheral intensity of the DOE photomask is often several times less than that at the center. In this situation, the overexposure is employed. The difference between the central and peripheral transmitted light intensity caused by diffraction effects becomes still more pronounced in the presence of a gap. Because of air dust, irregular photoresist thickness, and temperature-related surface deformations, full contact over the entire photomask-substrate area is difficult to attain. Even with full contact, the photoresist layer will play the part of a gap, the result being the observation of Fresnel's diffraction conditions [22] for particularly small structures. As a result, narrow zones are etched with distorted shape and size of the microrelief profile or even fully destroyed. One may combat this effect by enhancing the resolution, for example, by decreasing the wavelength of the actinic light used. If for one or another reason one fails to provide full photomask-substrate contact, an immersion layer of liquid introduced into the gap will be able to change the diffraction angle, which is lesser in denser-than-air media (the immersion method of determining the refractive index). The intermediate liquid layer practically exerts no chemical action on the photoresist layer because the dried photoresist surface is hydrophobic. This technique should also be employed for exposing large areas when there are signs of irregular photoresist thickness.

Another reason for narrow zones being irreproducible is the reflection of light wave from the back surface of the glass substrate, especially if the substrate thickness is fairly great and the DOE shows focusing properties, as is the case with a microlens array. The light wave reflected from the back substrate surface interferes with the incident wave, thus forming in the photoresist layer ringlike interference maxima and minima and so increasing or suppressing the light intensity. As a result, even the non-narrowest zones may become irreproducible. Eliminating the back-surface reflection may combat this phenomenon. By way of illustration, one may directly attach to it a thick glass plate with black or frosted back surface, operating like a reflection-free black body (Fig. 4.17). Another way is to coat the substrate with a chromium layer by vacuum deposition. The latter technique is advantageous because it makes the photoresist more adhesives, while the chrome acts as an additional protective layer upon etching the substrate.

4.2.3 Technology of DOE Microrelief Fabrication

For detailed review of factors that affect the inclination angle θ of the photoresist sidewall and the groove width W in the photoresist developed (Fig. 4.18), see Refs. [22–27]. They study how the quality of the resulting patterns is influenced by

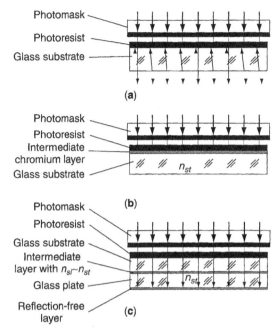

Figure 4.17. (**a**) Repeated reflection and techniques to eliminate the reflection from the substrate back-surface; (**b**) by an intermediate chromium layer; (**c**) attachment of reflection-free glass plate (n_{st} is the refractive index of the glass plate; n_{sl} is the refractive index of the intermediate layer).

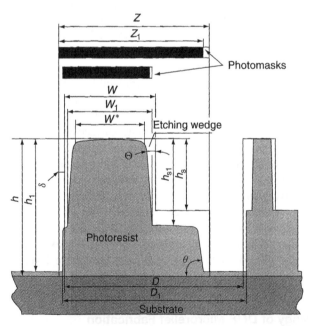

Figure 4.18. Technological profile of the DOE microrelief. Z is the estimated groove width on the photomask; Z_1 is the really generated groove width; D is the zone width for a perfect profile; D_1 is the really generated zone width; h_1 is the derived profile height; h_{s1} is the derived step height; W is the step width; W_1 is the derived step width; W^* is the width of photoresist step plateau; Θ is the etching wedge; θ is the edge deviation.

various factors of the lithographic process (exposure time, time and temperature of thermo-processing, time and temperature of the development process, and the photoresist sensitivity).

In terms of diffractive optics, the realization accuracy of the following parameters is of importance (Fig. 4.18):

- Relief height h and step height h_s;
- Possibly steep slope of the microrelief step (i.e., the angle Θ, characterizing the etching wedge should tend to zero, whereas the angle θ, characterizing the "edge deviation" should tend to $\pi/2$);
- Minimal error of the step width, $\Delta W = W - W_1$.

From analysis of Refs. [22–27], one can infer that to generate a high-quality microrelief with the aforementioned parameters one needs to use a high-contrast photoresist.

The DOE pattern is transferred into a substrate surface layer using photolithography techniques in four stages (Fig. 4.19): the photoresist layer is exposed through a photomask to generate a hidden image; the pattern is developed and hardened (i.e., a protective mask is formed); unprotected segments of the substrate surface are etched; and the substrate is cleaned off from the remains of photoresist [28,29].

At each process stage, there exist factors that cause the distortion of the initial pattern. With exposure, the factors such as light diffraction, refraction, and reflection result in a changed size of image elements and blurred boundaries. At the development and hardening stage, the distortions are due to photoresist swell and photomask shrinkage occurring in the course of thermal processing. In the course of etching, the photomask lateral subetching is an adverse factor. Processing conditions at various stages change both from plate to plate and for a single plate. Because of this, the DOE geometric parameters and performances are varied and should therefore be considered when choosing the DOE fabrication technology.

The photolithographic process is aimed at generating a photoresist mask, which either serves for local processing of the underlying substrate layer or is itself the desired DOE microrelief. Figure 4.18 schematically shows the microrelief profile of a single DOE period or zone.

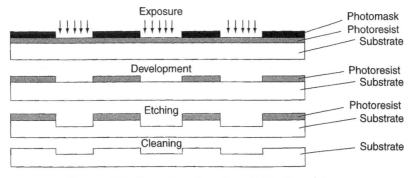

Figure 4.19. Formation of a microrelief in the substrate.

Major types of microrelief distortions that may be caused either by photomask design errors or by inadequate technological process are shown in Figure 4.18. The technological process will be called inadequate if it fails to meet certain parameters (e.g. resolution) or microrelief fabrication conditions. Technological errors may appear for a variety of reasons and include photomask output errors, exposure and alignment errors, as well as photoresist development and etching errors.

Let us define major microrelief errors:

$\Delta Z = Z - Z_1$ is the error of the photomask line width resulting from the discrete data output and/or insufficient resolution of the image generator;

$\Delta D = D - D_1$ is the zone width error (defined as the difference between the estimated and produced width) caused by incorrect photomask size, rough line edging, insufficient steepness of the photoresist mask step, and DOE photomask alignment errors;

$\Delta W = W - W_1$ is the step width error caused by the similar factors (excluding the alignment error);

$\Delta h = h - h_1$ is the relief height error (the difference between the estimated and produced height) caused by errors in substrate etching;

$\Delta h_s = h_s - h_{s1}$ is the step height error caused by errors in step etching;

Θ is the etching wedge resulting from the subetching under the photomask, isotropic character of etching, and insufficient removal of etching products form narrow slits;

θ is the "step edge deviation" characteristic of photoresist DOE profiles;

δ is the displacement of the relief step caused by photomask and exposure system errors.

The quantity

$$\Delta x = \tfrac{1}{2}(W_1 - W^*), \qquad (4.9)$$

where W^* is the width of the photoresist step plateau, is the width of photoresist mask edge whose value is essentially affected by properties of the illuminating system that transmits the DOE photomask image onto the substrate. Besides, the value of W_1 depends on the parameters of processing of the photoresist layer. Uncontrolled variations in the parameters of the photoresist film and its processing modes will result in a scattered size of W_1 even with constant illuminating light intensity. The quantity Δx is considered to define the minimal width of a photoresist mask strip: $W_{\min} = 2\Delta x$. In its turn, the quantity $W_{\min}$ defines the minimal period $d_{\min}$ of a grating generated in the photoresist layer: $d_{\min} = 2W_{\min}$. The quantity that is in inverse proportion to the minimal period is called the *resolution R* of the photolithographic process:

$$R = \frac{1}{d_{\min}} \qquad (4.10)$$

In most cases, it is advisable to use a photoresist mask with near-vertical walls. The relative error of line width in the photoresist mask is generally taken to be not more than 10 percent.

With photolithography, the stepped multilevel DOE microrelief is fabricated using photomask sets generated by one of the two techniques: the linear technique for uniform etching [15] and the dichotomic technique for irregular (gradual) etching [30]. With the linear etching, all microrelief levels are fabricated by etching the substrate to the same depth, $h_s = h_{\max}/M$. The number of photomasks in the set is determined by the

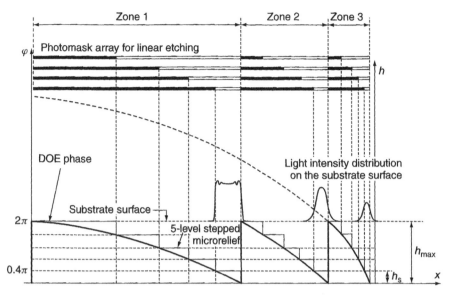

Figure 4.20. Method of linear etching.

number of phase quantization levels M. However, because the first level corresponds to the unprocessed substrate surface (Fig. 4.20), the total number of masks is less by one than the number of phase levels, that is, $M - 1$.

As noted earlier, while synthesizing a DOE photomask, it is essential to check the characteristics of the photomask lines. For a binary DOE, the photomask is an amplitude zone plate (for its various types, see Section 1.1). The photomask lines reproduce the zones in shape, occupying about half the zone area for the binary DOE. When the stepped DOE relief is fabricated by the linear etching, just a solitary line is found on each photomask within the zone. In Figure. 4.20, which depicts photomask profiles, one of the line edges is clearly seen to coincide with the zone edge (this condition may be violated only for central DOE zones), whereas the line width depends on the photomask number and determines the microrelief profile after etching.

By way of illustration, an 8-level optical element requires seven photomasks with different line width. While fabricating such an element, the photolithographic process is reiterated no less than seven times, including seven stages of photomask alignment and exposure. In the meantime, the element becomes operative only after all technological operations have been performed. This method has a variety of advantages. First of all, although it is possible to make peripheral zones fairly thin (of order D_{min}/M, where D_{min} is the minimal zone width), these lines are so separated (Fig. 4.20) that they do not affect each other on exposure through the photomask, thus somewhat enhancing the method resolution. In addition, insignificant errors of aligning the photomask with the previously generated microrelief or the deviation of the photomask zone size from the calculational DOE parameters result in insignificant distortions and in a smoothed zone boundary edge (Fig. 4.21). The interferogram of a DOE microrelief in Figure 4.21 features the boundary of zone-to-zone passage, with the simultaneous emergence of several levels caused by the inclination of the sidewall.

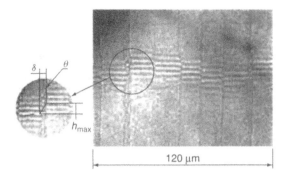

Figure 4.21. Interferogram of a 5-level microrelief of the Fresnel lens. h_{max} corresponds to a phase jump of 4/5 π; θ is the "step edge deviation" on the DOE zone boundary; δ is a 5–8 μm step edge displacement.

When fabricating the DOE microrelief with irregular etching, the depth of substrate etching is halved at every subsequent photolithographic step. At the first stage, the depth of etching of the binary microrelief is $h_{max}/2$, where h_{max} is defined by Eqs. (4.3) and (4.4). The dichotomic method defines not only the depth of microrelief etching at each stage but also the principle of photomask synthesis, with which the line density within a single zone is doubled (Fig. 4.22) while passing from the previous to every subsequent photomask. For M quantization levels, the minimal line width on the final photomask of the dichotomic method is equal to the minimal line width (of order D_{min}/M) on the final photomask of the linear method. In the former case, the number of the photomasks required is significantly $(M - 1)/\log_2 M$ times less, whereas the number of lines within the final photomask zone is $M/2$ times greater as compared with the uniform (linear) etching.

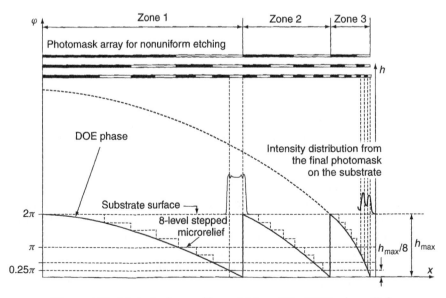

Figure 4.22. Method of nonuniform etching of the DOE microrelief.

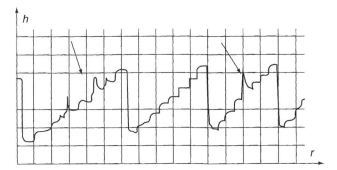

Figure 4.23. A profilogram fragment of an 8-level Fresnel lens shows technological "peaks" in the microrelief.

With irregular etching, the number of phase quantization levels and the number of photomasks in the set are related by the power law

$$M = 2^N \qquad (4.11)$$

where N is the number of photomasks.

An 8-level DOE microrelief can be generated using three photomasks, with each stage resulting in an operative element, while all subsequent etching stages only add to its efficiency. An essential disadvantage of the method is high sensitivity to the alignment error and line-width distortions caused, for example, by exposure or development errors or inaccurate photomask generation by the writing machine. As a result, "peaks" are found on the microrelief profile at the joints of the lines aligned (Fig. 4.23).

Alternating dark and light lines on the photomask far zones act together as a quasi-periodic diffraction grating, and the higher the photomask spatial resolution, the larger is the difference between the amplitude and the intensity profile on the substrate for central and peripheral parts of the DOE.

Speaking about the suitability of photolithography for the DOE fabrication, there are several parameters to characterize both the DOE and the synthesis process. A most critical DOE parameter is the least zone width (usually most peripheral) that can be estimated for the diffraction lens in the paraxial approximation as follows [11]:

$$D_{\min} = \frac{\lambda f}{a} \qquad (4.12)$$

where f is the focal length and a is the DOE aperture radius. This formula is also suitable for other DOEs possessing resolving power, for example, focusing DOEs.

Also, one needs to take into account that for every mask with the number $i = 1, 2, 3, \ldots$ the minimal line width at the DOE extremal zone will be essentially less, amounting, for example, for nonuniform etching to $M = 2^i$, and, thus attaining technologically irreproducible values. In that case, DOE parameters should be chosen in accordance with technology potentialities.

The DOE parameters are chosen on the basis of the DOE manufacturability and maximal efficiency. The photolithographic DOE fabrication technology can be described as the following sequence of operations.

Basic Sequence of Technological Operations:

1. Computer-aided design of DOE photomasks and output of control codes to an image generator.

2. Photomask fabrication (when using optical image generators, intermediate photomasks are fabricated by photoreduction of the original ones).

3. Preparation of substrate plates (chromium-coated glass).

4. Application of photoresist, projection, or contact exposure using a photomask (from a photomask set).

5. Development, drying, and other operations on the photoresist aimed at generating a protective mask on glass plates.

6. Etching of chrome, removal of chrome remains, and generation of a metallized photomask or a photomask array (by reiteration of steps 1–6).

7. Checking of parameters of the metallized photomasks.

8. Preparation of a substrate (glass, quartz, silicon, and so on).

9. Reiteration of steps 4–5 on one and the same substrate involving the alignment of metallized photomasks aimed to generate a stepped microrelief on the substrate surface, and examination of the relief height.

10. Deposition of protective layers, reflecting coatings (for reflection element), replication, electroplating, and mass production.

11. Framing.

12. Assessment in a laser system and certification.

Example 4.1 Generation of a diffraction microrelief by layerwise growth of photoresist. With this method, the stepped microrelief of the DOE is generated by a multiple application of photoresist layers (layer over layer), with each of them exposed to light through the photomask and passing all processing steps [31]. The photoresist is coated by centrifuging onto a glass substrate with planeness of 1–4 Newton rings on the entire surface. The critical factor in this process is the photoresist layer thickness. For a standard photoresist, there are finalized technological processes for generating layers of a desired thickness, with viscosity and centrifuge rotation rate taken in correlation [32].

The stable thickness of the grown layer is ensured by fixed photoresist viscosity and stable rates of centrifuge rotation. Deep thermal hardening of the previous layer prevents destruction while processing the subsequent layer.

Let us consider the fabrication of a DOE focusing into a line-segment. The DOE parameters are as follows:

Aperture's diameter	= 40 mm
Focal length	= 400 mm
Operating angle	= 45 deg.
Wavelength	= 10.6 μm
Segment dimension	= 5 mm × 0.3 mm

The multilevel microrelief was fabricated on an updated industrial exposure and development unit EM-5006A that can fabricate a minimal zone size of about 3 μm over the working field 100 mm in diameter. With this unit, it is possible to apply photoresist films with the following parameters: the photoresist layer thickness is

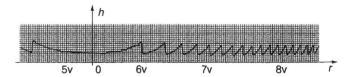

Figure 4.24. Profilogram of a focusing DOE microrelief.

$0.5-1.0$ μm; thickness irregularity is no more than 10 percent; the error of alignment of the photomask and substrate elements on X-Y coordinates is no more than $\pm$ 0.25 μm.

The profilogram of the fabricated 8-level microrelief shown in Figure 4.24 testifies in favor of a high-quality microrelief, whereas the fabrication technology is quite simple.

Example 4.2   DOE fabricated by use of halftone photomasks on direct laser write (DLW) glass photoplates (FIAT Research Center, Orbassano, Italy). It has previously been noted that technologies allowing the element's phase function to be realized as a continuous microrelief show potential in DOE fabrication. At FIAT Research Center, the use of DLW glass photoplates has made it possible to fabricate DOEs through a single-step generation of a halftone photomask [33–35].

DLW glass photoplates are monolithic, coating-free, chemically processed silicate glass plates, with colored Ag microparticles found in a layer of thickness 1 μm. A focused laser beam of arbitrary wavelength in a spectral range of sub-UV, visible ($\lambda = 0.524$; $\lambda = 0.632$; $\lambda = 0.647$ μm), near-IR ($\lambda = 0.82$ and $\lambda = 1.06$ μm) and IR light $\lambda = 10.6$ μm can be used to decolorize those colored Ag microparticles by heating, thus making part (or all) of Ag particles turn into colorless Ag ions. The light transmission of DLW glass photoplates increases with increasing energy density of the writing laser beam.

Exposing this photomask on a laser writing machine allows the available software to be dedicated for binary photomasks to be employed, thus making direct writing over the photoresist possible. Thus, the halftone photomasks generated may find its use in optical lithography (projection or contact printing) for the mass production of photoresist profiles, while doing without alignment errors. While writing the photomask, the gray levels are generated by varying energy densities of the laser beam.

A circular laser writing machine (Fig. 4.10) was used to write halftone DOE photomasks, such as a bifocal lens and a microlens array. In both cases, the elements' phase functions were precalculated and represented as a two-dimensional (2D) data array. The data format used allows the final result of synthesis of the DOE photomask to be visually represented (Fig. 4.25).

For writing the bifocal lens, a one-dimensional (1D) array cut along a line passing through the element's center was used. The calculational parameters of the bifocal lens are as follows: the lens diameter is 10 mm, the first and second focal lengths are 50 mm and 100 mm, respectively, and the number of phase levels is 40. The photomask was written using a symmetric DOE method, with a 0.75 μm minimal radial displacement and a 0.9 μm effective spot size. Figure 4.26a depicts a fragment of the rectangular microlens raster.

The microlens phase function was calculated for the following parameters: the size is 1.4 mm $\times$ 2 mm, the focal length is 25 mm, and the number of levels is eight.

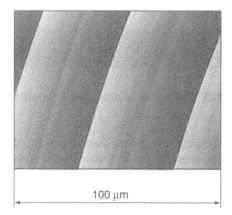

Figure 4.25. A fragment of the bifocal microlens photomask.

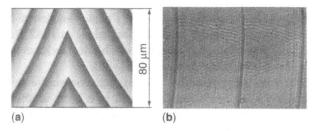

(a)   (b)

Figure 4.26. (**a**) A fragment of a microlens array photomask and (**b**) a microinterferogram of several zones.

The array of nine microlenses was placed on the substrate symmetrically with respect to the center of rotation. The writing was conducted by multipassage exposure with the effective spot radius of 0.9 μm. A computer-aided microinterferogram of several microlens zones as shown in Figure 4.26b was produced using a TV camera attached to the interferometer. Symmetrically located interferogram fringes are produced by the reflection of light from the substrate surface. A micron resolution on the DLW glass photoplates was attained with the use of Ar laser light of visible range and a focusing lens of numerical aperture 0.25.

4.3   DOE FABRICATION USING E-BEAM LITHOGRAPHY

A basic distinction of e-beam lithography from the conventional optical lithography (photolithography) is the use of high-energy electrons for initiating physicochemical processes in the photoresist [36]. Considering diffraction limitations of photolithography in combination with quantum mechanical concept of free movement of microparticles, we can safely say that in generating topological patterns, e-beam lithography has a number of essential advantages in terms of resolution.

In the de Broglie approximation, the movement of a free electron can be described in terms of the wave concept, quantitatively defined in Table 4.3 (with no regard to relativistic effects).

TABLE 4.3. Electronic Movement in Terms of the Wave Concept

Electron energy, (eV)	1	10^2	10^4
Wavelength, (m)	10^{-9}	10^{-10}	10^{-11}

Table 4.3 suggests that the ultimate resolution of e-beam lithography for typical accelerating voltages ($\sim 10^4$ V) is 0.1 Å and that it cannot impose any resolutional limitations even in principle, considering that the electron size is about $\sim 2.8 \cdot 10^{-5}$Å).

The fact that, in the year 2000, a number of manufacturers shifted to the mass production of microcircuits on the basis of multilevel technology with a 0.13 μm resolution testifies in favor of the resolutional and quality capabilities of the e-beam lithography methods. However, essential resolutional benefits that e-beam lithography offers at the stage of photoresist light exposure are diminished at the subsequent technological stages as a result of the special features of diffractive optics technology.

Fundamental and Technological Limitations of e-beam Lithography.

Considering the potentialities of e-beam lithography in the DOE fabrication, it is important to dwell on the most critical limitations:

1. Limitations caused by the electron scattering in the substrate. This type of limitations results from elastic collisions of original electrons with the nuclei of the substrate. Being repulsed from the substrate, the electrons returning to the photoresist possess the energy sufficient to initiate an elementary act of light exposure. In the first approximation, the repulsion efficiency is a linear function of the atomic number of the substrate material.

2. Limitations caused by the statistical character of the electronic flux. The wave nature of the electron beam manifests itself strongly when the pattern size is extremely small. This fact should be taken into account when designing visible and UV DOEs.

3. Limitations caused by aberrations of the focusing system. The aberration of focusing electonic-optical systems is inherent into all e-beam methods and results in a "minimal spot size." The diameter of the "minimal spot" of up-to-date e-beam lithography units is about 0.005–0.01 μm. If a DOE is fabricated by putting together the neighboring patterns, the accuracy is determined by the use of mechanical microdrives whose error is not less than 0.1 μm. Thus, the final error of the pattern is a function of the number of steps of mechanical displacements of the e-beam lithographer's objective table. The number of steps can be diminished by increasing the elementary fragment of the initial pattern to a geometric size within which one can achieve the desired accuracy.

4. Limitations caused by a system that controls the e-beam deflection. The process of controlling the amplifiers of the deflecting system involves the necessity to convert the digital control signal into an analogous form. Thus, the system resolution is determined by the digit capacity of the digital-analog converter (DAC). Besides, the accuracy of the control system is affected by nonlinear and noise effects in the amplifiers of e-beam deflection. From the experience, the influence of nonlinear and noise effects on the operational accuracy of the

TABLE 4.4. Parameters of Up-to-Date e-beam Lithography Systems

Model	EBES4, Lepton Inc.	JBX-6000FS, JEOL Inc.	EBL Nanowriter, Leica Lithography Systems Ltd.	EL-4, IBM Corp.
Type of e-beam control system	Raster scanning	Vector scanning	SEM system	Varied beam shape
Minimal spot size	0.125 μm	0.005 μm	0.1 μm	0.15 μm
Alignment	Automatic	Automatic	Automatic	Automatic
Working field	Fringes 256 × 32 μm in size	Max. 800 μm at 50 kV	Up to 2 mm at 50 kV	Max. 10 mm
Accelerating voltage	20 kV	25, 50, and 100 kV	10–100 kV	75 kV
Current density	1600 A/cm^2	–	–	–
Frequency	500 mHz	12 mHz	1 mHz	2, 3 substrates per hour
Substrate size	150 mm	150 mm	50 mm	200 mm
Platform positioning electrostatic	Laser positioning, a 146 mm max displacement at a minimal step of 0.005 μm	Laser positioning, 150 mm max displacement at a minimal step of 0.0006 μm	Laser positioning,	Laser positioning, using bearings

e-beam lithography is comparable with the minimal information unit of a 16-digit converter. These factors affect the value of the minimal step of beam displacement over the DOE pattern fragment.

Table 4.4 gives parameters of up-to-date e-beam lithography systems [23] varied in the way the e-beam is controlled.

The aforementioned data on the ultimate resolution of e-beam lithography are peculiar to a single exposure without subsequent alignment. When several masks are aligned the requirements on photomask fabrication tolerances are essentially higher. Owing to errors in aligning the lines found in different levels and possible size deviations arising in thermo-processing, there is an uncertainty in the position of each line edge. Thus, for two lines, the number of possible errors is equal to the general number of degrees of freedom. Taking into account that the absolute values of possible errors are equal to each other, the alignment error should not be greater than 0.062 μm at a 0.5-μm line width. Otherwise, both the lines may appear to be completely misaligned. This fact becomes critical for spatially extended structures such as DOEs. In this connection, the DOE structural features may become critical in the DOE efficient implementation.

4.3.1 Generation of Pattern Topology

The e-beam lithography is based on the use of a scanning, sharply focused e-beam, with the computer that is used to control its movement and to modulate the intensity (Fig. 4.27).

While experiencing the e-beam bombardment, the photoresist becomes exposed (the electrons saw together or break down the atomic-molecular bonds) and this changes the local properties of the photoresist [37].

The e-beam dose is controlled by varying the exposure time on a definite domain and is determined using a calibrated curve (the relation between the e-beam dose and the etching depth). This relation is determined by photographing the grating stepped relief with the aid of a scanning e-beam microscope. After exposure, the exposed, or unexposed, areas are washed out during the development (etching) process, depending on the photoresist type used. Having been generated in such a manner, the microrelief presents a topological pattern used for subsequent technological operations. The earlier-described procedure of generating a topological pattern is a key process in e-beam lithography. Depending on the application field, the topological pattern is used in the fabrication and replication (as a rule, with worsened resolution) of photomasks or directly on the substrate under processing.

Implementing e-beam lithography directly on the substrate is especially important when one strives for the flexible technological process and high resolution [38]. The available units for e-beam lithography [23] can be successfully used in small-series and medium-series production of DOEs. The experience gained and the experts' opinion suggests that the performance of units for e-beam lithography can be increased, thus making them profitable for industrial production of DOEs.

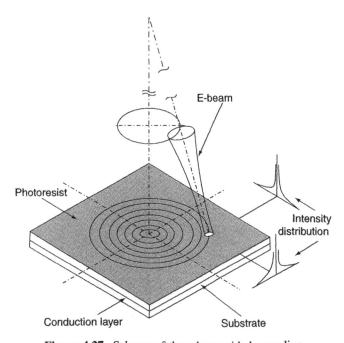

Figure 4.27. Scheme of the e-beam-aided recording.

Note that given the modern requirements on the DOE resolution, the use of standard photomasks produced by e-beam lithography is not ruled out. While making use of optical lithography achievements, so-made photomasks ensure a shorter small-series production cycle and an appropriate DOE quality. By way of illustration, we shall consider particular technological solutions to implement DOEs through e-beam lithography.

4.3.2   DOE Fabrication at the Institute of Applied Physics of Friedrich Schiller University (Jena, Germany)

At the Institute of Applied Physics of Friedrich Schiller University, they have elaborated a variety of technologies for automated design and fabrication of DOEs [39–43]. DOEs designed to operate in visible range with low-energy laser light sources are fabricated using stepwise lithographic etching [40–42]. Such elements are technologically implemented by uniformly etching a polymethylmethacrylate (PMMA) photoresist applied onto a quartz glass according to the desired number of phase quantization levels (2–16 levels, usually). To perform a uniform etching of the photoresist through a calculated halftone photomask, an array of technological binary files (virtual binary photomasks) is calculated, and these determine the process of stepwise lithographic etching of the photoresist. The phase function values ranging from 0 to 2π are being transformed into corresponding values of the microrelief thickness of the transmission element with due regard for the photoresist refractive index.

The virtual binary photomasks have one binary file less, compared to the number of quantization levels. The process of DOE fabrication is schematically shown in Figure 4.28.

It has already been mentioned that the DOE is fabricated on a quartz substrate coated with a PMMA layer 2–3 μm in thickness. The M-level DOE microrelief is fabricated using an $(M - 1)$-step uniform etching on an e-beam microlithographer ZBA-23 by Jenoptik GmbH through relevant virtual binary photomasks. The photoresist heat-up resulting from pixel-by-pixel etching leads to definite deviations from the desired relief [40,41]. Because of this, in order to implement the desired profile, it is recommended that an 80 percent depth etching should first be performed, the really

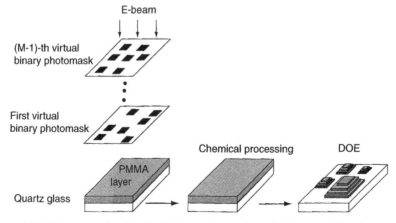

Figure 4.28. Sequence of technological operations of generating a multilevel structure.

achieved maximal etching depth should be measured by an optical microprofilometer, and then the etching procedure should be finished by a single or several extra "etching-profilometry" cycles [41,42]. To increase the efficiency of such a procedure, the etching depth is measured using a regular stepped test structure rather than an irregular complex diffraction profile, which is calculated, for example, through an iterative procedure.

As a rule, such a test structure is located on the substrate beyond the DOE aperture, in order not to distort the DOE complex transmission function, or on the test DOE aperture.

The microrelief generated is examined using an interferometric microprofilometer MICROMAP-512 with a 3 μm resolution. For the examples of DOEs fabricated by the described technology, see Chapter 6.

Example 4.3 Fabrication of the DOE microrelief using a stepped etching technique [43]. Friedrich Schiller University has developed technologies for the fabrication of DOEs operating IR range using the method of stepped etching of a quartz glass and Zn-Se substrates with Au-coatings applied onto the reflecting surface. The fabricated focusing DOEs are replicated through electroplating. As a rule, an 8-level or 16-level DOE microrelief is generated through the plasmo-etching of the substrate, for which purpose a respective set of 3 or 4 binary photomasks is written on the lithographer.

Fabricated visible and IR DOEs have been experimentally studied at the Institute of Applied Physics and Institute of Applied Optics of Friedrich Schiller University. The University is equipped with all relevant facilities — visible and IR range lasers, including those produced by Carl Zeiss Jena, vibration-proof platforms, visible-range CCD cameras (manufactured by SPIRICON Ltd.) and IR-range systems MAC2 (manufactured by ACCS GmbH) with dedicated software.

Figure 4.29 depicts the result of the profilometric studies of the microrelief of a DOE focusing into a rectangle, manufactured through the 16-level etching of a quartz

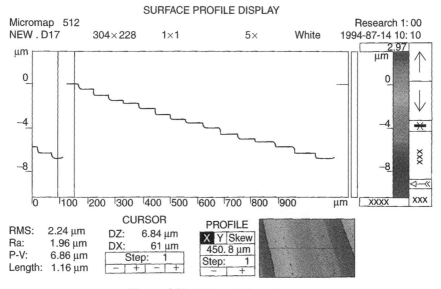

Figure 4.29. Microrelief profilogram.

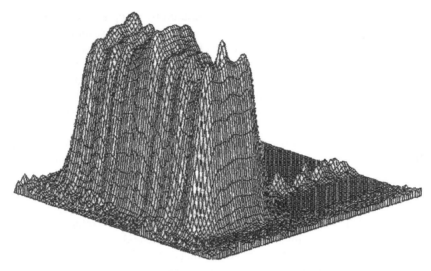

Figure 4.30. Intensity distribution in the focal plane of the DOE focusing into a rectangle.

glass [43]. The profilogram suggests the high quality of the generated DOE microrelief pattern. Figure 4.30 shows the intensity distribution produced by the focusing IR DOE that was measured by the MAC2-camera (of wavelength 10.6 μm).

Example 4.4   Technology of fabrication of binary-phase DOE at the University of Joensuu (Finland). Joensuu University's low-voltage e-beam image generator Leica LION LV1 with an ultimate resolution of about 0.04 μm allows the microrelief to be fabricated using a single photomask [44].

The e-beam produces the image of a binary-phase element in a PMMA layer 0.18 μm in thickness coated on the substrate of fused silica (Fig. 4.31).

Once the image has been developed, the binary structure is coated with a 0.5-μm thick chromium layer through vacuum deposition. Then, the remaining PMMA photoresist and the chromium layer are washed out from the unexposed, areas. Finally, the desired binary profile is generated by the reactive ion etching, with the chromium layer acting as a protective photomask. Fabrication stages of the binary profile are shown in Figure 4.32.

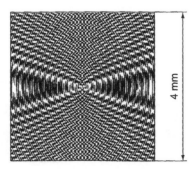

Figure 4.31. A photomask fragment of the binary-phase DOE.

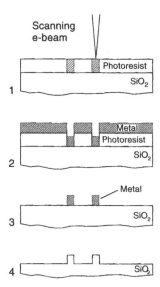

Figure 4.32. Fabrication stages of a binary-phase DOE: 1) the resist is exposed to the e-beam; 2) deposition of chromium and washing-out of the photoresist; 3) reactive ion etching.

The described technology was employed to produce a 4 mm × 4 mm DOE (1,000 pixels × 1,000 pixels) of binary-relief depth $\lambda/[2(n-1)] = 0.675$ μm (the refractive index of quartz is $n = 1.46$) for a He-Ne laser of wavelength 0.633 μm.

4.4   GENERATION OF A CONTINUOUS MICRORELIEF

4.4.1   Techniques for Generating a Continuous Microrelief

When fabricating DOEs, it seems most reasonable to generate a continuous-profile microrelief to get the phase function most close to the desired value. Presently, there are a great variety of methods and technologies that allow the generation of a continuous-profile microrelief of various heights and resolution:

- e-beam etching of PMMA
- Numerically controlled tools with diamond chisel
- Laser-induced etching
- Hard-UV etching of polymeric materials
- Use of mass-transfer in polymeric materials
- Bleaching of photomaterials
- Development of gray-level photoresists
- Washing-out of the hardened gelatin or the "cellophote" material

All these techniques have their advantages and problems. Presently, there is no universal technique that would allow one to create a continuous-profile microrelief with a complicated surface pattern and a height varying from fractions to tens of microns for various optical spectrum regions.

Techniques for generating continuous microrelief on gelatin layers [45–52] are most familiar and available. When using the gelatin as a relief-generating material, this should be strongly hardened in places where one strives to generate large-height relief, with a lesser hardened layer being washed out by hot water. There exist three well-known techniques for selectively hardening the gelatin:

1. Hardening development.
2. Hardening bleaching of photographic layers containing silver halide.
3. Hardening of bichromated gelatin through exposure to light.

High-level spatial frequencies (above 1,000 mm^{-1}) for microrelief heights in the range 0.1–0.3 μm are attained using complex development techniques, including thermo-hardening and processing in a sulfuric acid solution. However, for microrelief heights of several microns, the spatial resolution is sharply decreased, and because of various degree of hardening the maximal microrelief height may vary 2–3 times.

Until recently, the DOE fabrication based on bichromated gelatin (BCG) used to be a popular technology. Figure 4.33a shows the gray-level photomask of a DOE to focus into the letter "π" and the result of focusing the CO_2 laser light [53]. The quality of focusing (Fig. 4.33b) suggests wide potentialities of BCG-aided focusing DOEs.

However, a relatively simple BCG-based technology of microrelief generation has not become widely used in DOE fabrication because it results in a rough microrelief, reducing the DOE efficiency and, in a limited resolution, making it impossible to fabricate elements with the numerical aperture over 0.1.

The first focusing IR DOEs were fabricated using a film photoresist [54,55]. The relief height of a continuous profile is limited by high photoresist contrast. By fitting the contrast range of photomasks, exposure and development modes, they managed to fabricate optical elements with a microrelief height of up to 10 μm and continuously varying profile for the zone size ranging from 5 mm to 150 μm. Unfortunately, the thickness of the film photoresist varies greatly over the DOE aperture ranging from 50 to 100 mm.

Light scattering occurs with all technologies based on washing out of polymeric materials characterized by various degree of polymerization or hardening, which is due to extensive dissolution of the material in the liquid developing solution. Because of this, fabrication of high-quality elements by this technology presents a definite problem.

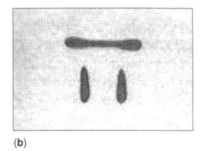

(a)   (b)

Figure 4.33. (**a**) A photomask of the DOE to focus into the letter "π" and (**b**) the result of focusing.

Let us consider in greater detail a method, based on the use of liquid photopolymerizable compositions (LPPC), which is employed at IPSI RAS as a major technological process for DOE fabrication [56 –58].

The LPPC are compositions based on oligomers and monomers of organic origin, with a photoinitiating agent included into them and allowing the solidification to be conducted as a result of a radical polymerization reaction caused by the actinic light radiation. In holography, oligomeric compositions of urethane nature have become widely used [59]. These are inexpensive and easily available materials admitting to the chemical synthesis of high pure composition and the reproducibility of parameters. When solidified, they form netlike polymers in a glasslike or elastic state, characterized by high ray strength of 500 Mw/cm^2 for nanosecond radiation impulses and a transparency window of 0.35–2 µm [60].

4.4.2 Mechanism of LPPC-Based Relief Generation

The liquid light-sensitive layer is composed of oligo-ester-acrylates acting as a polymerizing compound and the isobutyl ester acting as a photoinitiator. The periodic structure is recorded using a projection unit (Fig. 4.34) schematically shown in Figure 4.35. Photomask 1 is projected in UV light onto LPPC layer 5.

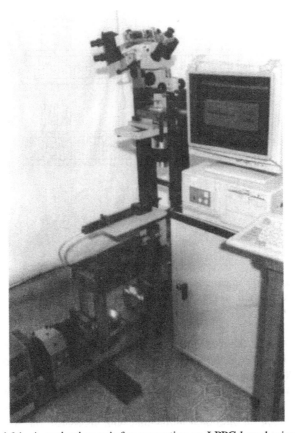

Figure 4.34. A projection unit for generating an LPPC-based microrelief.

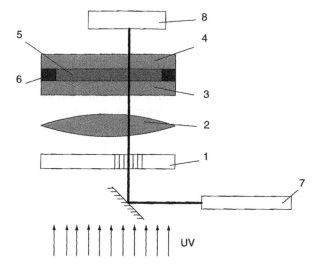

Figure 4.35. An optical scheme of the projection of halftone amplitude photomasks into the LPPC layer. 1: a halftone mask of an optical element with diffraction grating; 2: a lens; 3: a hydrophilic glass plate; 4: a hydrophobic glass plate; 5: an LPPC layer; 6: a gasket; 7: a laser; and 8: a power meter.

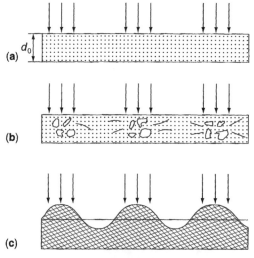

Figure 4.36. A model of microrelief generation: (**a**) the initial stage; (**b**) beginning of mass-transfer; (**c**) completion of mass-transfer.

To explain physics of the recording process, we shall use the thermodynamic concept of three-dimensional (3D) polymerization [61]. We shall limit our consideration to an elementary cell appearing as a domain in which the light field node and antinode are in contact (Fig. 4.36). There is a diffusive particle exchange between the domains.

Being initiated in the domains of maximum exposure to light, the polymerization decreases the number of oligomer molecules and increases the number of polymer molecules, thus leading to the appearance of a polymeric gel.

Once the gel islets have been generated in the places exposed to light, the mobility of polymer molecules becomes limited, with the generated polymer becoming fixed on the surfaces limiting the layer. Then, the process of diffusion of the oligomer into the polymer, and vice versa, starts. The direction of diffusion is determined by the sign of variation of the oligomer chemical potential within the gel. If the sign is negative, the oligomer diffuses into the polymer, and if it is positive, the oligomer is displaced from the gel. If all variations of free energy are mutually compensated, there is no process of mass-transfer. Therefore, the critical factor is the character of interaction between the oligomer and its own polymer, so that the relief formation process is enhanced when oligomers with good thermodynamic affinity [61] to their polymers are used.

Thus, the initially liquid oligomer is exposed to light until it converts into a soft rubber like layer. Then, the upper glass is removed. A relief pattern of the photomask under exposure can be immediately observed on the surface of the layer. The microrelief height measured after the removal of the upper glass amounts to 1/20 of the maximum achievable height and is apt to dark growth because of mass-transfer [62]. The maximal achievable height is equal to 1/3 of the initial liquid layer. So, the sample is placed in darkness for a period ranging from several hours to three days, according to the desired microrelief height. During the dark growth (i.e., spontaneous increase of the relief height in darkness), the relief is periodically measured on the interferometer. Since the LPPC's sensitivity to visible light is insignificant, the sample cannot be spoiled during the period of examination. Once the desired height has been achieved, the microrelief is fixed through the general exposure to UV light in vacuum, resulting in the complete polymerization. Thus, the sample acquires the properties of a rigid plastic suitable for making copies, coating with metal, and so on.

The process of relief formation is checked using a structure (Fig. 4.37) made up of two parallel plates P_1 and P_2 with a gap between them filled with the LPPC.

A plane laser wave is employed. The transmitted light flux generates the zero diffraction order B_0 and the first diffraction orders B_{-1}, B_1. The amplitude sinusoidal modulation in a thin subsurface LPPC layer near the internal surface of the plate P_2

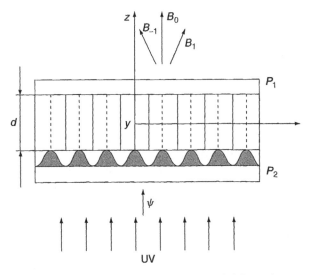

Figure 4.37. Process of checking the relief-formation.

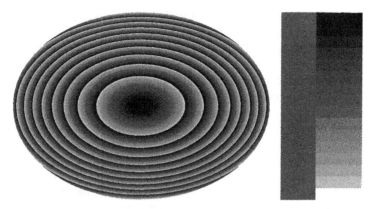

Figure 4.38. Photomask of the 'DOE + diffraction grating' combination.

is rendered by a diffraction grating recorded by the DOE halftone image (Fig. 4.38). The maximal and minimal optical densities, D_{max} and D_{min} of the DOE photomask and the diffraction grating photomask are respectively equal to each other. Thus, the degree of LPPC conversion in the domain of the grating will determine the degree of conversion in the domain of the DOE.

In an effort to get the minimum of zero diffraction order under UV illumination, it is important to attain an optimal degree of LPPC conversion, thus providing optimal conditions for the microrelief dark growth. In the dark-growth mode, the microrelief height is measured on a reflecting microinterferometer.

4.4.3 Determination of an Optimal Optical Density of Photomask in the Course of LPPC-Based Relief Generation

In order to fabricate optical elements with minimal scattering and possibly high transfer of edge contrast, one has to fit an optimal optical density of the photomask. The problem was solved using the photomask of an array of diffraction gratings, with their optical densities covering the range $D = (0.1 - 2)$, while frequencies varied from 1 to 20 mm^{-1}. A thin oligomer sublayer was generated on the photomask (emulsion-coated side of the photoplate). Applying a thin layer of fluoroplast dissolved in a special solvent reduced the adhesion to the photo-emulsion. A diffraction grating of spatial frequency 13 mm^{-1} was chosen experimentally. In further experiments, the optical density drop, C for each grating was measured by a laser scanning densitometer. The plot of the maximum achievable relief height h_{max} versus the optical density drop of the grating is shown in Figure 4.39.

Three sections can be clearly seen on the plot. The first section from point "a" to point "b" is characterized by a fast growth of the maximum achievable relief height h_{max}. The reasons are as follows. Before point "a," when the degree of contrasts of the gratings is very small, a low gradient of the "light-shade" passage results in a negligibly small mass-transfer. Then, as the "light-shade" boundary begins to be seen, the mass-transfer mechanism is initiated (from point "a" to point "b"); hence the sharp growth of height h_{max}. Further, from point "b" to point "c," the height is increasing almost linearly according to the increase of the "light-shade" gradient. From point "d," noise is increased and the relief height h_{max} ceases to grow because of the sharp decrease of

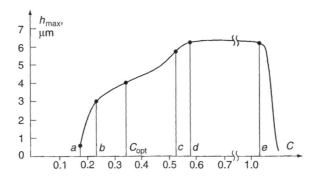

Figure 4.39. A maximum achievable microrelief height h_{max} as a function of the drop C of image optical density.

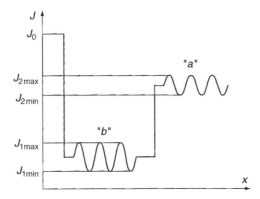

Figure 4.40. Densitogram of two test diffraction gratings "a" and "b" with different contrast, corresponding to points "a" and "C_{opt}" in Figure 4.39.

polymerization in dark areas. Finally, once a definite boundary value of contrast has been achieved, the degree of conversion in dark areas becomes so small that after the system has been disassembled the LPPC layer remains in liquid state. Therefore, after the critical point "e", there is a sharp decrease on the plot.

The drop C is derived as a difference between the optical densities in light and dark places: $C_x = D_{max} - D_{min}$, which were determined from diagrams plotted by a scanning densitometer (Fig. 4.40).

A photo-receiver of the scanning densitometer, recorded a signal proportional to the incident light power. Therefore, the optical density in light and dark areas was derived as a decimal logarithm of the attenuation coefficient K of the light flux J, recorded in the absence of the plate:

$$D_{max} = \lg K_{max}, \quad \text{where} \quad K_{max} = J_o/J_{min}; \ D_{min} = \lg K_{min},$$

where $K_{min} = J_o/J_{max}$; J_{min} is light intensity in dark areas of the grating, J_{max} is the light intensity in light areas of the grating.

While seeking to optimize the following two criteria–the maximal relief height at a minimal layer thickness, on the one hand, and the maximal signal-to-noise ratio, on the other hand, we have chosen point $C_{opt} = D_{max} - D_{min} = 0.79 - 0.45 = 0.34$ on the plot. On the left of this point, the noise is decreased, but the height h_{max} is dropped, whereas on the right the height h_{max} is increased but the noise is also increased. The relief formation mainly takes place during the dark growth. The relief height in the dark mode can increase as much as $1-15$ times, as compared to the initial height recorded immediately after exposure. In order to study how the relief is changed in dark mode, a grating of drop $C_{opt} = 0.34$ was chosen.

4.4.4 Fabrication of Test Samples of Visible-Range Optical Elements

The problem of generating a polymeric layer of uniform thickness and that of projecting the photomask image onto the photopolymeric layer in order to fabricate a DOE of aperture ranging from 40 mm to 100 mm was resolved using a contact method. The structure of a multilayer sandwich designed to generate the DOE microrelief is shown in Figure 4.41.

To keep the structure rigid and deformation-immune (because at the final stage the sandwich is disassembled and the structure is subjected to mechanical stress), the photo-emulsion plate was glued onto a thick glass using a photo-sensitive composition about 10 μm in thickness. The photosensitive composition was solidified using a medium-pressure mercury-vapor lamp. The distance to the illuminating lamp was chosen to prevent excessive heating of the glasses to be glued. It took not less than two hours to glue the surfaces under UV light. Before gluing, the reverse side of the photo-plate and the glass side to be glued were thoroughly degreased and adhesive-processed.

The next critical operation is the formation of so-called rigid polymeric sublayer on the surface of the plate's photosensitive layer. To ensure the desired optical quality of the DOE, the planeness of the sublayer must be maximally high. To these ends, we have chosen an oligomer with minimal shrinkage ability. In terms of the layer's planeness, there is some optimal thickness. On the one hand, all the irregularities caused by the photo-plate optical unplaneness and irregular applying of the photosensitive layer should be eliminated. On the other hand, the sublayer should not be extremely thick to minimize shrinkage effects and irregular conversion degree across the layer

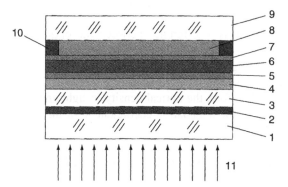

Figure 4.41. Sandwich designed to grow the DOE microrelief using a contact method. 1 is a thick glass, 2 is a layer of glue-base photosensitive composition, 3 is a photoplate substrate, 4 is a photo-emulsion layer, 5 is an adhesive layer, 6 is a polymeric sublayer, 7 is an antiadhesion layer, 8 is a LPPC, 9 is an optical glass, 10 are calibrated gaskets, and 11 is the UV light.

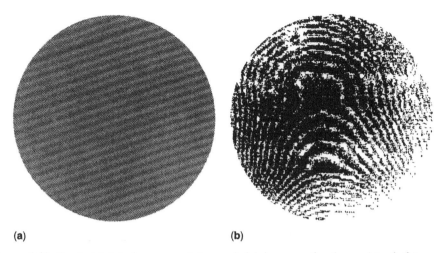

Figure 4.42. Sandwich interferograms: (a) a sandwich incorporating layers 1 to 6; (b) a sandwich with layers 3 to 6, as shown in Figure 4.41.

caused by a layerwise polymerization effect. These factors being considered, it has been experimentally demonstrated that at a thickness of about 10 μm, the planeness is optimal. However, if the sublayer is excessively thin, while the sandwich is dismantled along the 7−8 surface interface (Fig. 4.41), the sublayer is separated from the photoemulsion because of lack of adhesion.

To enhance the adhesion to the photosensitive gelatin layer, an additional adhesive layer (0.1 μm thick) composed of oligomeric solution showing high adhesion to oligoesters (of which the LPPC is composed) was generated. This layer was polymerized in vacuum by a five-minute exposure to a mercury-vapor lamp. In practice, the polymeric sublayer thickness amounts to 20–50 μm, depending on the DOE aperture and the resolution requirements determined by the peripheral zone size. The generated sublayer is checked by an interferometer. Interferograms of two sandwich samples are shown in Figure 4.42.

On comparison of the interferograms, the surface planeness is seen to be considerably improved. From the fringe curvature in Figure 4.42b, we can calculate that the deviation from planeness exceeds 10 fringes at the wavelength of $\lambda = 0.628$ μm, that is, the deviation from planeness amounts to about 3 μm, whereas in Figure 4.42a the planeness is seen to be practically perfect.

After the sublayer is checked for planeness and found to meet the requirements, an antiadhesive layer is applied on it by extracting from solution. After the antiadhesion layer is dried and calibrated, 10 gaskets of about 30 μm thick are inserted, and an LPPC-layer is applied and covered with an adhesive-coated plate. Then, the assembly is exposed to UV light while providing the on-line monitoring using the HE-Ne laser.

Example 4.5 Implementation of LPPC-based technology in DOE fabrication. The aforementioned technology was employed in the fabrication of visible-range DOEs. Shown in Figures 4.43 and 4.44 are lens, photomasks, and profiles.

With a 50-μm thick sublayer, the DOE zone image is being blurred by 2 to 3 μm. Having been passed through the LPPC layer, the edge image becomes degraded still more. At the bottom of the LPPC, the image is defocused by some 4 μm. Thus, we

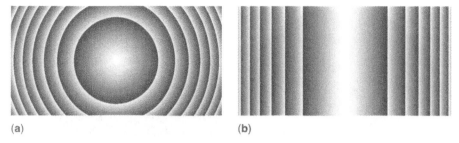

(a)   (b)

Figure 4.43. Microlens photomasks: (a) spherical and (b) cylindrical.

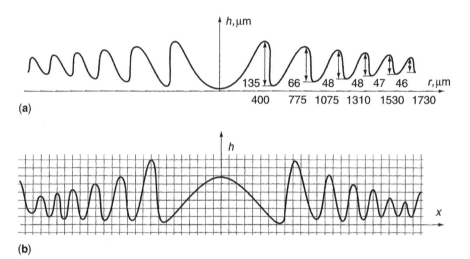

Figure 4.44. Profilograms of the microlenses shown in Figures 4.43 (a) and 4.43 (b), respectively. Vertical scale is 20 μm per cell and horizontal scale is 50 μm per cell (b).

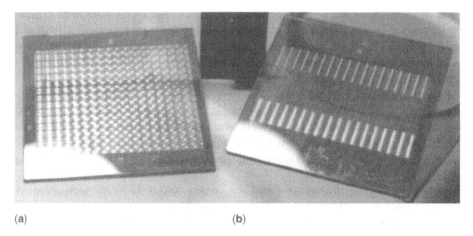

(a)   (b)

Figure 4.45. Light diffusers.

can infer that in our case the contact technique for projecting the image into the LPPC has the resolution of about 200 mm^{-1}.

We fabricated lens arrays designed to generate the radiation with desired angles of the directivity diagram in the vertical and horizontal direction (so-called "light-scatterers," or diffusers; see Fig. 4.45 for their photos). Shown in Figures 4.45a and 4.45b are the diffusers composed of the lens arrays shown in Figures 4.43a and 4.43b, respectively. The maximal angle of light deflection we were able to obtain through this technology amounted to 20 degrees with respect to the normal. For the 135 µm height, first zone at the wavelength of $\lambda = 0.6$ µm and the refractive index of $n = 1.5$, the phase lead amounts to about $112 \times (2\pi)$.

4.5 ETCHING TECHNOLOGY

Etching is a critical stage of the lithographic process. The stage of image transfer through etching dictates the following requirements on the technology, equipment, and materials used:

1. Reproducible and homogeneous etching of a single plate or a batch of plates.
2. Removal of material from sidewalls of the structure to be generated should be insignificant.
3. Removal of material upon etching large-area plates (>200 mm^2) needs to be conducted at an acceptable rate.

Irrespective of the etching environment — gaseous or liquid phase — its efficiency is determined by the type of ions used and the electric field direction found around the etching agent [63,64].

A typical etching process involves the following sequence of reactions:

1. Transfer of the reagent (of a gas in which the etching is to be conducted).
2. Reagent absorption.
3. Reaction on the surface.
4. Desorption of intermediate and final products of reaction.
5. Product transfer.

At the etching stage, the photoresist adhesion, impermeability, planeness, and chemical inertness are toughly tested. For the photoresist, the resistance to etching and the adhesion are, probably, the most critical parameters of the process that contribute to the success to a great degree. Using highly etching-proof photoresists guarantees the minimal image distortion during its transfer onto the substrate. Practical applicability of the method of liquid chemical etching (LCE) is defined by its resolution (1.5–2.0 µm) and size departure upon etching ±(0.2–0.5) µm.

To control the etching process properly, one needs to know its static and dynamic parameters. With the LCE, the critical parameters are the film thickness, as well as time and temperature of processing. To obtain reproducible results, one needs to fix rigidly the moment of etching completion and the change in the reagent chemical composition.

Because of its simplicity, the LCE method stood the test of time, being able to gradually decrease the line width and the distance between them. With LCE, the cooperative influence of interior neighborhood effects that occur upon under-etching and over-etching limits the line spacing on metallic films up to 6 μm. Hence, the use of the LCE for fabricating multilevel DOEs for technological lasers of wavelength less than 10 μm may prove to be impractical.

The minimal DOE zone size and the simplicity of the LCE method have made it suitable for the fabrication of IR DOEs. With shorter wavelengths, when the linear size of the binary microrelief is smaller than 1 μm, one needs to use a plasma-etching (dry) method.

In terms of the physicochemical mechanism of interaction of the material under processing with the surface, there are three major types of plasma etching [65]:

1. Ion etching.
2. Plasmo-chemical etching.
3. Reactive ion-plasma etching.

The dry etching is conducted in a nonisothermal, low-temperature, gas-discharge, low-pressure plasma, with the average energy of electrons being considerably greater (10–100 times) than the energy of ions, molecules, and radicals.

The selection of working gas is an important aspect of the dry etching process. The gases of choice should

- be nontoxic, inexplosive compounds that are easy to feed into the reactor in the gas or vapor phase;
- produce a maximal output of energy and chemically active, plasma-decomposed particles that form stable volatile compounds during etching;
- produce no corrosion and pollution of working volumes and pumps.

In plasmo-chemical etching, one uses a mixture of halogen compounds with oxygen, hydrogen, nitrogen, and inert gases. Organic materials are removed using oxygen.

4.5.1 Use of the Plasma-Etching Technology in the Microrelief Fabrication

Plasma etching allows the microrelief to be generated in any material with the accuracy and surface quality unachievable with the conventional liquid etching. These advantages are conditioned by the capabilities of the anisotropic etching, high-level controllability, and stability of the technological processes. Because of this, it appears to be most expedient to employ the plasmo-chemical etching for generating the microrelief of visible and near-IR DOEs.

With a plasma-etching unit used at IPSI RAS, 0.1-μm wide lines can be etched in the atmosphere of high-frequency discharge. The unit is capable of adjusting the pressure in the working chamber within the range 0.065–1.3 Pa, varying the incident high-frequency power in the range from 100 to 700 W with a 10 percent accuracy, four-channel puffing the gas into the chamber within a wide range, and accurately keeping the gas mixture consumption on a constant level.

The unit is provided with a system for conveying a portion of high-frequency power onto the operating table and with a magnetic plasma stabilization system.

The sequence of technological operations for material processing (polymers, chromium, as well as silicon, glass and quartz substrates) is as follows:

1. Bringing the unit to stable operating conditions (i.e., the warming-up of the vacuum pumps, evacuation of the working volume to 0.001 Pa, and the warming-up of the high-frequency generator).

2. Puffing the working gas (or gases) and adjustment of the gas (gas mixture) working pressure. Note that because of inertia it takes some time to stabilize the pressure.

3. Switching-on the high-frequency (HF) discharge, HF generator's load matching. The matching depends on the gas pressure in the chamber and on the type of the gas used (generally speaking, a variety of other factors may exert their influence). If necessary, the HF bias relative to the substrate or a constant reverse bias as well as the magnetic field is adjusted.

4. Switching-off the HF power from the inductor (extinction of plasma).

5. Loading the material (plate) to be processed into the chamber and onto the holder, evacuation of gases from the chamber, input of the plate to be processed into the working volume followed by its fixation on a water-cooled table.

6. Feeding the HF power with preestablished parameters into the working volume (reaction chamber).

In the following example, we discuss specific features and techniques for the plasma etching of some materials that have found use in DOE fabrication.

Example 4.6 Etching of chromium. A chromium layer of thickness 0.1 to 0.5 μm is used as a protective mask in the course of substrate etching [66]. Chromium layers are exposed to plasma etching in the vapors of tetrachloride carbon (CCl_4). Chromium is unable to form volatile two-component compounds. For example, for all halogens, the boiling temperature is more than 1,000 °C, but the oxychloride chromium boils at 118 °C. Because of this, molecular oxygen is added to the vapors of CCl_4 to increase the rate of chromium etching. On the other hand, rich content of oxygen leads to a heavy degradation of hardened photoresist mask; thus the rate of photoresist etching may become greater than that of chromium.

Chromium layers of thickness 0.3 μm on the glass substrates possess sufficient optical density. A typical thickness of the photoresist being hardened at 90 °C during three hours is 1.5 to 2 μm. The etching rate of chromium in the $CCl_4 + O_2$ vapors (in proportion 10:1) is on average 0.0003 μm/s, whereas the etching rate of a hardened photoresist is 0.0002 μm/s. With this etching mode, one manages to generate one metallized DOE photomask within 20–30 minutes of plasma etching.

Properly chosen etching modes for the photoresist and chromium allow one to generate metallized photomasks of higher quality (cf. a metallized photomask in Fig. 4.7 and the initial photomask on a photofilm in Fig. 4.6).

Example 4.7 Fabrication of high-resolution diffraction gratings. To fabricate a reflection diffraction grating capable of splitting the incident light of wavelength $\lambda = 0.59$ μm into beams of varying intensity deflected by large angles, one needs to generate a microrelief with the following parameters: the grating period is 0.6 μm, the height is

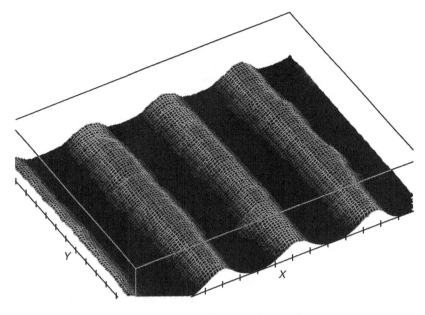

Scale - *X*:1000Å *Y*:1000Å *Z*:500Å

Figure 4.46. A microrelief fragment of the silicon-based diffraction grating.

0.1 μm, and the angle of deflection from the main beam is 45° (upon reflection in the medium with reflective index $n = 1.5$).

Silicon polished wafers (100 mm in diameter) featured by high rate of plasma etching turned out to be suitable for fabricating such an element. The unit allows one to etch the silicon wafers to a diameter of 150 mm, while ensuring the uniform etching across the entire surface within ±5 percent. The initial pattern of the diffraction grating was generated using the e-beam lithographer in 1-μm photoresist layers applied directly onto polished silicon wafers.

The silicon was etched in a gas-etching agent composed of the $CCl_2F_2 + O_2$ mixture taken in the 5:1 ratio. Oxygen was added to increase the number of chemically active atoms of fluorine and chlorine and suppress organic contaminants on the surface under etching. To enhance the rate of etching the silicon wafer coated with photoresist, the content of oxygen added to the main gas was increased to 25 percent. Figure 4.46 shows the pattern of grating profile produced by a scanning probe microscope P4-SPM-MDT manufactured by Nanotechnologies-MDT (Zelenograd, Russia) [67].

Analysis of the shown fragment testifies to the high reproducibility of linear measures of the grating profile. Absence of waviness on the grating bottom complies with high-quality and properly fitted etching conditions.

4.6 GENERATION OF DIFFRACTIVE MICRORELIEF BY LASER-AIDED STRUCTURING OF DIAMOND FILMS

While being multistage and costly, the widely used methods for generating diffractive microreliefs mentioned earlier sometimes fail to produce the desired result. Problems arise, for example, when one needs to generate the microrelief on a nonplanar (heavily concave or convex) surface made of an intractable material. The method of the DLW of microrelief [68–70] proposes an alternative and relatively inexpensive technique for generating the diffractive microrelief on various materials. The use of high-power light of the excimer laser for the direct laser etching of the diffractive microrelief by means of selective removal (ablation) of the substrate material proves to be up-to-date, highly efficient, and heavy-duty technology for DOE fabrication [69,70]. At present, it has been demonstrated that this method is suitable for generating submicron structures, with PMMA, polycarbonate, aluminum, and stainless steel used as a substrate [70]. An experimental setup for directly writing the microrelief using the excimer laser [70] is shown in Figure 4.47. In the device, the substrate experiences a high-precision piezoelectric displacement (accurate within 0.05 μm) along the X-Y axes across the area of 25 mm × 25 mm. Both the laser and the operating table are computer-controlled, whereas the working field is examined using a microscope and CCD-camera. The substrate of the element under fabrication is displaced by piezoelectric microengines over the X-Y plane so that the diffractive microrelief is generated in a stepwise mode using laser impulses.

The mode of the substrate microetching is shown in Figure 4.47a, with Figure 4.47b, and c showing the modes for microcopying the material onto (b) a substrate and (c) a fiber, respectively. Currently elaborated techniques for copying the layers of chromium, indium oxide [70], copper [71], and superconducting films [72] are able to transfer submicron structures either onto a plane substrate or onto a curvilinear optical fiber surface [70], thus testifying to unique potentialities of the new method.

The method of laser microrelief etching opens new possibilities of employing intractable materials, such as diamond, for developing the transmission optics of medium IR range ($\lambda = 10.6$ μm). Achievements in gas-phase synthesis [73] allow the generation of polycrystal diamond films (DF), with their optical and thermophysical properties similar to those of diamond monocrystals (thermo-conductivity is $\cong 18$–20 KW/cm, absorption coefficient is $\cong 5 \cdot 10^{-2}$ cm, and refractive index is $n = 2.38$–2.42 for $\lambda = 10.6$ μm). Interest in use of such DF of thickness 1–2 mm

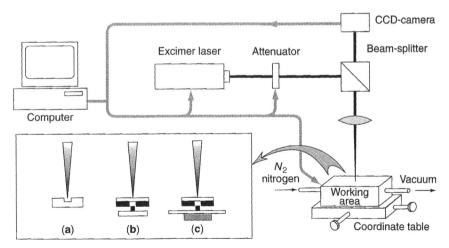

Figure 4.47. Experimental setup for excimer-laser-aided structuring (**a**) microetching, (**b**) microcopying, and (**c**) microcopying onto an optical fiber.

and area up to 100 cm^2 as output windows of CO_2 lasers of power 10–20 kW [74] is because of higher thermal stability and damage thresholds, as compared with the conventional IR optics materials (ZnSe, KCl and others). However, more complicated optical elements could not be generated because of two basic hindrances. First, the diamond hardness makes difficult the mechanical treatment designed to generate the desired profile. Second, a relatively small thickness of diamond wafers does not allow optical elements of fairly large aperture to be fabricated through conventional techniques. As an alternative, in Ref. [75,76] they proposed that DFs should be used as substrates for the DOEs, with their phase relief generated by selective laser etching.*

Another problem of diamond-based optics arises from relatively high energy losses caused by Fresnel reflection, which is essential when focusing the high-power industrial laser light. Note that because of a comparatively large refractive index of diamond resulting in high reflection losses, the transmission of a diamond wafer does not exceed 71 percent at a wavelength of 10.6 μm. Therefore, application of antireflection coating on the DF is very important. Being inferior to DFs in their properties, conventional film antireflection coatings do not allow one to use the unique properties of the DFs to a full extent. In Refs. [77,78], they have conducted real experiments to demonstrate the efficiency of antireflection subwavelength periodic diffractive microstructures generated on the surface of DFs through selective laser etching. Figure 4.48 depicts the results of studies of the antireflection structures implemented at the Institute of General Physics of the Russian Academy of Sciences. The analysis of numerical simulation and real experiments has shown [77,78] that application of antireflection subwavelength structures on each side of the DF allows the transmission to be increased by more than 10 percent.

In Refs. [77,78], they conducted the numerical simulation of the operation of antireflection structures using the theory of effective media [79]. Meanwhile, the approximation of the theory of effective media fails to take full consideration

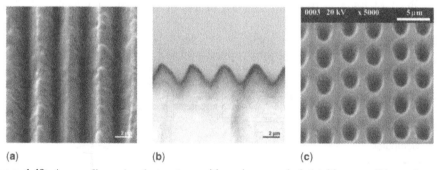

(a)   (b)   (c)

Figure 4.48. A one-dimensional structure with a 4-μm period (etching conditions: impulse energy is $E = 12$ J/cm^2, 15 impulses per pixel): (**a**) top view, (**b**) cross section; (**c**) a 2D structure with a 4-μm period implemented using a Nd:YAP laser: surface photo ($E = 5$ J/cm^2, 10 impulses per pixel).

* The authors wish to thank the Institute of General Physics of RAS's researchers, Prof. V.I. Konov and V.V. Kononenko, for the materials they have kindly supplied for this study.

TABLE 4.5. Comparison of Energy of the Reflection Wave for Various Shapes of Diffractive Microrelief

Number of the Numerical Simulation	Diffractive Microrelief Shape	Permittivity of Wafer (P/w)	Fraction of Reflected Energy (%)
1	without diffractive microrelief	5.6644	17.2
2	triangle of base 4 μm and height 2.5 μm	5.6644	12.5
3	triangle of base 3 μm and height 2.5 μm	5.76	9.8
4	triangle of base 2 μm and height 2.5 μm	5.76	9.37

of electromagnetic effects emerging when IR light passes through the diamond subwavelength structure. To provide a more accurate evaluation of the performance of antireflection coating, the simulation needs to be conducted using the rigorous electromagnetic theory [80–81]. The analysis of how the electromagnetic wave propagates through a surface coated with a diffractive subwavelength microrelief that has been conducted by solving the Maxwell equations using difference schemes is given in Chapter 3.5. Numerical simulation (for their results see Table 4.5) involved the formation of H_{01} waves ($\lambda = 10.6$ μm, with a one-wavelength tandem) illuminating the wafer–air interface, followed by modeling the subsequent propagation of reflected and transmitted waves. In Ref. [78], the results of experimental studies of a real antireflection structure with a period of 3 μm and a depth of about 1.8 to 2.0 μm, implemented on a diamond wafer has been presented. The maximal increase of transmission for a diamond wafer having one-side subwavelength microrelief amounted to about 6 to 7% that is in good agreement with the results of Table 4.5. Parameters of the difference scheme were as follows: the size of the domain under study is 500 μm × 180 μm along the Y-axes and Z-axes, respectively, time interval is 8.1×10^{-14} s, the size of discretization cell is 1/3 μm × 0.2 μm, and time span is 3.5×10^{-18} s.

Figure 4.49 shows how the incident wave (experiment 4) is divided into the wave transmitted through the diamond-air interface and that reflected from the interface.

The results of numerical simulation are in good agreement with the real experiments reported in Refs. [77,78] and with the results of numerical analysis conducted using the theory of effective media of second order [78,79]. Difference scheme for solving the Maxwell equations for the first time allowed diamond antireflection structures to be simulated (Chapter 3), their efficiency to be evaluated on the basis of the electromagnetic theory, and the fine structure of the reflected electromagnetic wave to be analyzed. Thus, the results arrived at in Refs. [77,78] and Section 3.5 testify to the fact that subwavelength antireflection structures can be effectively implemented on DF. Note that in the general case the implementation of antireflection diamond structures imposes more rigid requirements on the relief accuracy, as compared with the DOE relief calculated using the scalar approximation.

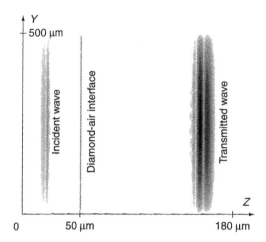

Figure 4.49. The amplitude module distribution of the electric component of the electromagnetic field for the transmitted and reflected waves.

Example 4.8 Cylindrical diamond diffraction lens. To demonstrate the capabilities of laser-aided generation of diamond-based relief for medium IR DOEs ($\lambda = 10.6$ μm), we shall analyze the results of fabrication of a four-level cylindrical lens [75,76] of focal length $f = 25$ mm and aperture $S = 4 \times 4$ mm^2, calculated using the diffractive optics software [3]. The equation of the phase function of a cylindrical lens in the paraxial approximation takes the form of Eq. (1.15), whereas the maximal relief height given by Eq. (4.3) takes the value of $h_{max} = 7.68$ μm for the refractive index $n_{max} = 2.38$. The width of Fresnel zones can be derived from Eq. (1.12). The number of complete zones satisfies Eq. (1.13). The characteristic parameter Z is the width of the narrowest—in this case most peripheral—zone that determines the requirements to the technological equipment. In our case, the minimal zone width was about $Z = 140$ μm. The derived values of the phase function in Eq. (1.13) reduced to the interval $[0, 2\pi)$, were quantized in four levels, as shown in Figure 1.19. The calculated diffractive microrelief of the four-level lens (Fig. 4.50) was reproduced on the surface of a DF.

The technology of fabricating diamond plates [82] involves the following stages: *(1)* gas-phase deposition of a diamond film on silicon substrates in a plasma microwave reactor, *(2)* separation of the DF from the substrate by etching the silicon in a mixture of acids, *(3)* laser cutting, and *(4)* mechanical polishing of the DF growth surface. The plates were of size 0.5 to 1 cm^2 and thickness 300 to 400 μm. The diamond surface was microprocessed by an excimer KrF laser (model 1701, wavelength $\lambda = 0.248$ μm, impulse energy is about 150 mJ). The one-side DOE relief on the plate surface was composed of an array of grooves 40 μm in width and varying depth. Note that the groove's width was chosen, taking into account both the minimal zone width of the lens and the technological considerations.

The depth of etching was controlled by the energy and the number of impulses per surface spot. The parameters of laser microstructuring of the DF surface were selected in test experiments aimed at implementing desired etching depths at a maximal achievable steepness of the DOE zone edge. Some results of such experiments are shown in Figure 4.51.

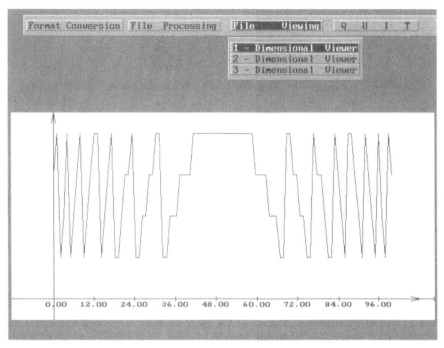

Figure 4.50. The software display shows the profile of the calculated four-level microrelief of a cylindrical lens (one pixel on the X-axis corresponds to 40 µm).

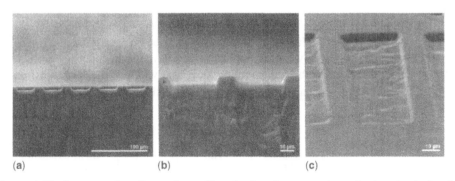

Figure 4.51. Some results of experimentally selecting the parameters of microstructuring the DF surface.

Figure 4.52 shows a fragment of the profile of the fabricated diamond cylindrical lens. The root-mean-square deviation of the relief depth from the desired value is about $\delta \approx 10$ percent.

The absorbing graphite layer on the diamond surface, generated as a result of laser ablation [83] was eliminated by annealing in arc-discharge plasma in hydrogen atmosphere. In Ref. [84] a report on the numerical simulation of a diffraction cylindrical lens operation is given. The DOE diffraction efficiency was defined as a portion of the transmitted energy concentrated in the main maximum [84]. The intensity in various planes

Figure 4.52. A fragment of the profile of the fabricated diamond cylindrical lens.

Figure 4.53. The result of interaction of the CO_2 laser beam and a paper. Left: the initial defocused Gaussian beam of square aperture illuminates the paper; right: the cylindrical lens has its focus on the paper.

of the lens focal domain was calculated on the computer using numerical methods described in Ref. [84] for the main mode of the TEM_{00} beam illuminating the optical element. Numerical simulation was conducted using the dedicated diffractive optics software [3]. The diffraction efficiency of the element derived through numerical simulation is in good agreement with that reported in Ref. [84]. The fabricated DOE was tested using a continuous CO_2 laser of power 20 W. After modulation by the optical chopper, the laser light was registered by a pyrometer. The energy distribution over the laser beam cross section was Gaussian, of radius $\sigma_0 = 1.55$ mm. Figure 4.53 (right) depicts the result of interaction between the CO_2 laser beam and a paper found in the focus of the fabricated lens.

In the DOE focal domain, the intensity distribution $I(x)$ remains quasi-Gaussian in shape (Fig. 4.54). The width σ_X of the transformed beam was defined as half the distance along the X-axis between two points at which the light intensity drops by a factor of e^2, as compared with its maximum value. The width of the lens-transformed beam, $\sigma_X^{exp} = 70.8$ μm is greater than the theoretical estimate, $\sigma_X^{theory} = 65.8$ μm, for

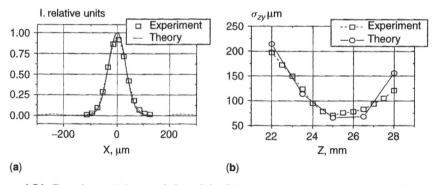

Figure 4.54. Experimental characteristics of the fabricated DOE and the corresponding results of numerical simulation: (a) intensity distribution $I(x)$ of the CO_2 laser light in the lens focal plane (the X-axis is perpendicular to the symmetry axis of the cylindrical lens); (b) the beam width σ_X vs the distance Z to the element plane. Focal length is $f = 25$ mm.

several reasons. First, the lens profile is somewhat different from the calculated value, and the light is scattered by the film polycrystalline structure. Second, in the laser beam there are higher-order modes with greater angular divergence, as compared with the main mode. The experimentally measured diffraction efficiency of the DOE was 78 percent and close to the theoretical estimate of 79 to 80%. Figure 4.54b shows the values of σ_X^{exp} and σ_X^{theory} versus the distance to the element plane. The focal depth of $\Delta f = 5$ mm was defined as the distance between points on the optical axis at which the light intensity is halved, as compared with the maximal value.

Thus, the analysis of the technology of fabricating the diffractive microrelief through the laser etching of synthetic diamond plates illustrated by the fabrication of a cylindrical diffraction lens has shown the efficiency and potentialities of the new technique. Good correlation between the experimental and numerically simulated results suggests that the laser treatment provides the desired accuracy in the formation of phase microreliefs for multilevel ($M \geq 4$) diamond-based DOEs and subwavelength antireflection structures for medium IR spectral region.

Example 4.9 Diamond DOEs for CO_2 laser beam focusing into complex focal domains. It would be very attractive to use CVD (chemical vapor deposition) diamond material not only for windows and lenses but also for elements with advanced optical functions. Main goal of the present example is to show that DOEs with complex relief topology can be produced from CVD diamond plates using the laser ablation process as well. For instance, DOEs capable of focusing the beam of high-power CO_2 lasers into pregiven complex focal domains (so called *focusers* or *focusators*, See Chapter 5 of the present book) are of actual practical interest. The task of DOE design for focusing an input laser beam into a pregiven 2D domain is considered in Chapter 5 of the present book. In Ref [85] the design, fabrication, and testing of two different types of CVD diamond DOEs focusing a laser beam into different pregiven domains are considered. Firstly, a DOE focusing a Gaussian beam into a homogeneously filled focal rectangle ("Gauss-to-rectangle" focuser) was calculated by a ray-tracing approach discussed in Chapter 5 of the present book. Secondly, a DOE focusing a Gaussian beam into a focal square contour ("Gauss-to-square contour" focuser) was calculated, exploiting an adaptive iterative procedure described in detail in Chapter 2 of the present book. Both elements were designed and fabricated to operate at the CO_2 laser wavelength ($\lambda = 10.6$ μm). All numerical calculations of the diffractive surface profile were made for an illuminating beam described by a Gaussian intensity distribution $I_0(\mathbf{u}) = C \exp(-2\mathbf{u}^2/\sigma^2)$, $\mathbf{u} = (u, v)$ and an initial phase distribution according to $\varphi_0(u, v) = $ const. Relevant parameters of both designed diffractive elements are presented in Table 4.6.

The lateral discretization step was chosen as $\Delta u = \Delta v = 40$ μm (which is nearly 4λ) as a compromise between diffractive scalar theory demands and technological considerations. The number of phase quantization levels M $= 8$ was selected from technological considerations and from the intention to approximate the designed continuous-phase function of DOEs as well as possible. Calculated eight-level phase distributions for the two investigated elements are displayed in Figures 4.55a and 4.55b.

Both DOEs are "Fresnel elements," which means that a lenslike phase function has been included into the focusers' phase function. Intensity distributions obtained by "simulated illumination" of the calculated elements, on the basis of a 2D fast Fourier

TABLE 4.6. Parameters of Diamond DOEs

	"Gauss-to-Rectangle" Focuser	"Gauss-to-Square Contour" Focuser
Focal length, f	100 mm	100 mm
Operating wavelength, λ	10.6 μm	10.6 μm
Number of phase quantization levels, M	8	8
Aperture, G	6.64 mm × 6.64 mm	6.64 mm × 6.64 mm
Pixel size	40 μm × 40 μm	40 μm × 40 μm
Focal domain, D	Homogeneously filled rectangle, 1.75 mm × 3.5 mm	Square like line contour, 4.2 mm × 4.2 mm, line thickness 0.4 mm.
Illuminating laser beam radius, σ	1.85 mm	1.85 mm
Refractive index of CVD diamond substrate, n	2.4	2.4
Maximum depth of microrelief, $h_{max} = \lambda/(n-1)$	7.57 μm	7.57 μm
Calculated efficiency*, E	68.7%	51.8%
Method of calculation	Ray-tracing	Adaptive iterative procedure (35 iterations)

*including Fresnel losses, which are about 30% for two diamond–air interfaces

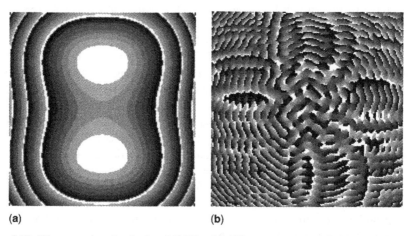

(a) **(b)**

Figure 4.55. Phase masks of calculated DOEs: (a) "Gauss-to-rectangle" focuser, (b) "Gauss-to-square contour" focuser.

transform (FFT) algorithm with 256 × 256 pixels, are displayed in Figures 4.56a and 4.56b.

To estimate the focusing quality, the energy efficiency $E = \int_D I(\mathbf{x})d^2\mathbf{x} / \int_G I_0(\mathbf{u})d^2\mathbf{u}$, was used; this characterizes the portion of illuminating beam's energy focused into the desired focal domain D, where $I(\mathbf{x})$ is the focal intensity distribution and $I_0(\mathbf{u})$ is the illuminating beam's intensity distribution. To manufacture the calculated elements,

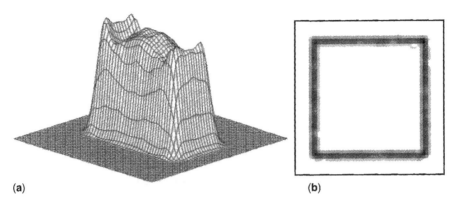

(a)   (b)

Figure 4.56. Computer-simulated intensity distribution in the focal plane: (**a**) "Gauss-to-rectangle" focusator, (**b**) "Gauss-to-square contour" focuser.

achieved eight-level phase distributions had to be transferred into corresponding etching-depth profiles. DF with a thickness of 300 to 400 μm were grown on polished Si substrates by a microwave plasma CVD technique using an ASTeX CVD diamond reactor (Model ASTeX-PDS19, 5 kW power, 2.45 GHz frequency). After separation from the substrates, resulting free-standing DF were cut into pieces of about 1 cm^2 size by laser cutting, polished, and then used for laser patterning experiments. Micro patterning of the surface was performed with a KrF excimer laser (model EMG 1003i "Lambda Physik," 248-nm wavelength, 15-ns pulse duration, energy per pulse ~200 mJ) in an optical projection scheme with a linear demagnification of 1:10. This setup is shown in Figure 4.57 schematically.

Resulting profile depth could be modified by variation of energy density and number of laser pulses. As an example, in Figure 4.58, the achieved etching rate is depicted in dependence of the KrF laser's fluence effective for an image size of 40 μm × 40 μm at the sample's surface.

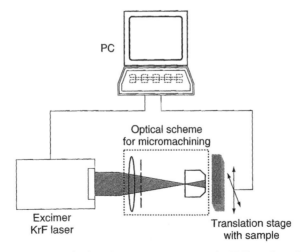

Figure 4.57. Optical projection scheme with the KrF excimer laser.

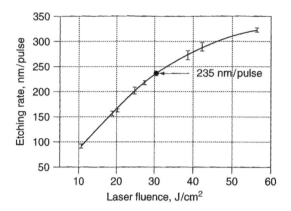

Figure 4.58. Etching rate as a function of the KrF laser's fluence, effective for an image size of 40 μm × 40 μm at the diamond sample surface.

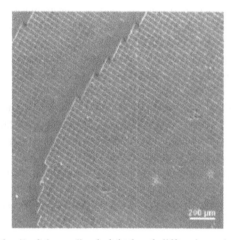

Figure 4.59. A typical detail of the realized eight-level diffractive microrelief (SEM measurement).

A typical detail of the manufactured diffractive microrelief, achieved by SEM investigation, is depicted in Figure 4.59. Note that specific "borders effects" occur between neighboring pixels as a result of different character of interaction of UV radiation with diamond material at the borders of illuminated squarelike spot and in its central part. It can be estimated that light diffracted at these structures will not give significant contributions to the focal image because the feature size is smaller than the wavelength. However, such effect will lead to certain decrease of DOEs' diffractive efficiency.

The setup used for experimental investigation of the field formed by fabricated diamond DOE and the applied input beam is schematically shown in Figure 4.60. The main components are a 5-W CO_2 laser (single-mode TEM_{00}) with a divergence of 3.84 mrad (full angle) and a beam-waist radius $\sigma = 1.85$ mm, and an IR camera with 120 × 120 pixels, a pixel size of 100 μm, and an eight-bit intensity resolution. The experimental determination of diffraction efficiency was realized in the same setup by evaluating the "integral" signals delivered by the camera for certain different focal

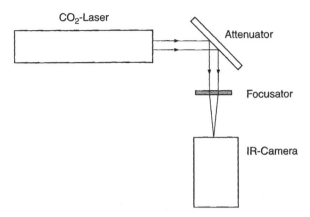

Figure 4.60. Experimental setup for the investigation of formed intensity distribution and of diffraction efficiency.

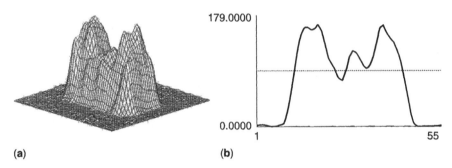

(a)   (b)

Figure 4.61. (a) Measured intensity in the focal plane of "Gauss-to-rectangle" focuser and (b) a corresponding sectional view through the center.

areas, normalized to the input beam, and was furthermore compared with results achieved by application of a conventional laser power meter.

The structure of the generated beams as seen by the IR camera in the focal plane or in different planes near focal plane for the two manufactured diamond focusers is illustrated in Figure 4.61 and Figure 4.62, respectively.

Comparing Figure 4.62 with corresponding simulation results in Figure 4.63 manifests a very good correspondence regarding the formed intensity distribution.

So, measured contour width for this square contour follows nearly exactly the predictions of computer simulation and especially the design value, which ties up with the fact that the iterative calculation of the phase mask for this element was done in the frame of diffraction theory.

Comparing measured intensity distribution formed by the "Gauss-to-rectangle" focuser in Figure 4.61a with related results of computer simulation (Fig. 4.56a), at least a qualitative correspondence becomes evident. The size (in both dimensions) of experimental and "simulated" rectangular intensity distribution is larger than the design value by approximately the size of an Airy disc. This is caused by the applied geometric ray-tracing algorithm used for the calculation of the diffractive profile, whereas in optical and in simulation experiment, diffraction theory is in force. Furthermore, such

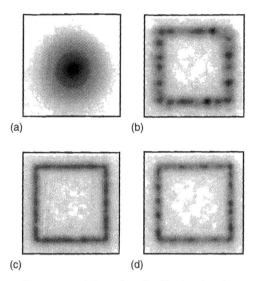

Figure 4.62. Experimentally measured intensity distribution in the cross section of illuminating beam (**a**) and for different cross sections of the formed beam ("Gauss-to-square contour" focuser): (**b**) $z = 90$ mm, (**c**) $z = f = 100$ mm, (**d**) $z = 110$ mm.

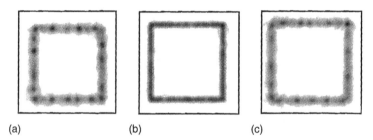

Figure 4.63. Computer-simulated intensity distribution in different cross sections of the focused beam: (**a**) $z = 90$ mm, (**b**) $z = f = 100$ mm, (**c**) $z = 110$ mm.

a qualitative correspondence between measured and "simulated" intensity distribution exists regarding the form of deviation from "flat" or "homogeneously filled-in" rectangle, whereas the measure of deviation in experiment is stronger than in computer simulation. This different behavior could be assigned to manufacturing imperfections caused by insufficient stability of applied UV laser ablation process. The measured power efficiency in these experiments was found to be $E = 50.5$ percent for the "Gauss-to-rectangle" focuser and $E = 38.0$ percent for "Gauss-to-square contour" focuser, which is somewhat less than the theoretical estimations presented in Table 4.6. This difference may be accounted for by scatter losses generated by small-size structures at the borders between neighboring pixels as mentioned earlier, by imperfections of the manufactured depths distribution representing the diffractive profile, and finally by absorption losses and scattering losses caused by intergrain boundaries inside the bulk CVD material used for these first test samples. This correspondence suggests that the applied laser ablation process provides an adequate accuracy for the formation of the calculated phase microrelief. Thus, our investigations have shown that such a UV laser ablation technique is a promising method for manufacturing of high-quality multilevel diamond DOEs for CO_2 laser optics.

4.7   REPLICATION OF THE DOE MICRORELIEF

Fabrication of the original relief matrix of the optical element is the most complicated and costly procedure. The next stage is the replication and manufacturing of intermediate copies. Of the available techniques for phase microrelief transfer, we can distinguish the following most popular ones: relief transfer through hot stamping onto a polymeric material of PMMA, making copies using photopolymerizable compositions and electroplating.

The fabrication technology of PMMA-based optical elements is as follows. A PMMA work-piece is gripped between two planes (with one of them being a reverse DOE matrix) and heated up to a temperature at which the PMMA transits from the solid to ductile state. On applying an adequate pressure, the PMMA spreads over the entire matrix surface, filling all free volume. On cooling, the PMMA undergoes the reverse transition from ductile to solid state, while preserving its optical properties. However, it should be noted that the cool-down is accompanied by shrinkage so that the resulting refractive surfaces have larger radius for lenses and lesser modulation depth of phase relief for the diffractive element. The shrinkage amounts to 3 to 5% on an average and should be taken into consideration when fabricating the initial matrix.

For replicating DOEs on photopolymerizable compositions, a variety of organic oligomers can be used. Depending on the chemical composition and a method by which the polymerization reaction is initiated, the number of technological operations aimed at generating the replica and their conditions are essentially varied. When copying the microrelief of zone plates and other DOEs, one can use the resin oligocarbonatemethacrylate — a nontoxic, inexpensive, industrially manufactured product. An enhanced sensitivity of oligocarbonatemethacrylates to UV light is probably due to peculiarities in the electronic composition of the carbonate group. An addition of photosensibilizer is made to the resin — the methylester of benzoin is capable of forming free radicals when illuminated by UV light. The photo-initiated polymerization of the resin lasts for 20 minutes. The refractive index of the resin is $n = 1.49$.

The technology of copying the microrelief onto the resin is as follows [86,87]. The surface of a glass substrate with etched microrelief is coated by antiadhesive. In the meantime, the surface of the other glass plate is coated with a substance with enhanced adhesion to the resin. After that, a drop of resin is applied on the working surface of the former substrate and accurately covered with the latter substrate, provided the resin spreads uniformly over the entire optical element without air bubbles. Then, this sandwich is exposed to the UV light for 15 to 30 minutes. Once the light exposure is completed, the sandwich is disassembled, with a microrelief copy found in the polymeric layer of one glass and with the other glass being clean and suitable for the subsequent replication procedure. With such copying on liquid, UV-sensibilized oligomers, there is a ripple ranging from 0.1 to 1.0 µm on the copy's surface, depending on the height of the microrelief under copying. The ripple size can be essentially reduced by use of complicated exposure technique. The original exposure is being done through a binary raster (e.g., for UV light of wavelength $\lambda = 0.365$ µm and power 1 mW/cm^2). Next, the sample is exposed to the same light source without raster. The resin layer separated from the glass substrate presents a transmission optical element, with its surface being a negative image of the microrelief found on the glass substrate. At the next stage, given that the generated relief corresponds to the desired relief of the optical element, an antireflection coating is applied. If the resulting relief is a negative image of the desired relief, the copying is conducted once again, usually by electroplating.

Electroplating is a chemical method for manufacturing a wide variety of products. In electroplating, the metal deposits at the surface, achieving significant thickness (3–5 mm) and reproducing the shape of the surface of deposition.

In the DOE-fabrication technologies, this process is employed for generating accurate, easily detachable metallic copies of the surface of a complex and precise relief. These are then used as reflection optical elements or matrices for replicating phase DOEs.

The basic benefits of the electroplating are as follows:

- Highly accurate reproduction of complex micro- and macrogeometric topology of the surface relief (matrix) onto which the electroplating is being conducted.
- Low-cost fittings and equipment.
- Recyclable matrices for electroplating.
- Microreliefs made from the same matrix are identical.
- For large-scale production, the quantity of simultaneously manufactured optical elements is determined by the size of electroplating bath.
- Properties of electroplated metals can be varied over a wide range by varying deposition modes and using various additions in electrolytes.
- Metal consumption is essentially less than that in resin-based copying.

In this connection, technological aspects, such as the design of electroplating matrices, the selection of methods for predeposition surface preparation, composition, and modes of metal (or alloy) electroplating to provide the generation of desired microreliefs should be given special emphasis.

The technological scheme of electroplating process consists of a number of subsequent operations:

1. Fabrication of the initial microrelief of an optical element (form).
2. Preparation of the form surface (cleaning, degreasing).
3. Application of a separating layer.
4. Application of a conducting layer onto the form surface.
5. Metal electroplating (growing).
6. Hardening of the electroplated layer.
7. Removal of mechanical tolerances.
8. Separation of the form (removal of the model, the matrix, and the mount).
9. Finishing of the product.

A glass substrate or polymeric layer with a coating of DOE microrelief are used as a form for generating optical elements through electroplating. The size of the surface under replication is determined by the size of the active part of the optical element.

When the form is made of nonmetal material, its surface is metallized. This operation is mainly intended to create a conducting layer, allowing the metal to be electroplated on the surface of the form. The conducting layers are applied in a mechanical or chemical way by high-vacuum metal deposition, cathode evaporation, and metal reduction from gaseous phase.

Conducting layers can be applied on nonmetal forms using a cost-effective and highly productive technique of vacuum metallization through condensation of metal vapor on a high-clean and dry surface [88]. A disadvantage of the method is the necessity of using costly equipment. Because, for generating the microrelief of optical elements through electroplating, one needs to produce thick layers, and low deposition rates sharply reduce the process productivity. To increase the deposition rate, electrolytes allowing the process to be conducted at high current densities are chosen. Copper deposition is in most common use. Copper has become the basic material for fabricating the focusing reflection phase DOEs because of the high reflection and heat conductivity coefficients, the inexpensiveness and availability of the reagents used, and highly developed techniques for copper electroplating. The entire process of copper electroplating lasts for 72 hours, producing a 3- to 4-mm thick DOE.

4.8 AUTOMATION OF EXPERIMENTAL STUDIES AND TECHNOLOGICAL TESTS OF DOEs

4.8.1 Operations and Equipment to Control the Process of DOE Fabrication

It is impossible to get an integral idea of the up-to-date state of fabrication technology of DOEs without knowing the means for automatically controlling the DOE parameters. Control operations are incorporated in all technological stages of DOE fabrication and involve the following:

1. *Input control of materials and prepared raw materials.* This involves controlling the quality of substrate materials, metals, inorganic products (solvents, alkalines, acids), controlling the parameters of the equipment, glasses, photo-emulsion-coated plates, and so on.

2. *Control of environment, energy carrying agents, equipment.* This involves controlling the temperature, moisture, pressure, and dust content of the medium; controlling the water pureness; controlling the pureness, content, pressure and rate of gas flux; controlling the temperature of reaction zones of units.

3. *Control of technological operations.* Examination of physical and chemical cleanness of substrate surfaces, control of photomask fabrication quality (at various fabrication stages), control of metal deposition modes and adhesion, and microrelief control.

4. *Experimental testing of fabricated DOEs.*

In DOE fabrication, it appears most important to control

- the original substrate on which the DOE microrelief is to be generated (control of the substrate physical and chemical cleanness)
- photomasks (the photo-plates should be plane, uniformly thick, comply with desired linear size, and mutually compatible)
- microrelief parameters (linear size, physical cleanness of etched surfaces, profile configuration);
- parameters of the fabricated DOE (energy efficiency, and according to the purpose of the optical element—the energy distribution in the focal plane, the accuracy of wave front generation, the compliance of the light directivity diagram with the desired pattern, or generation of the desired mode composition);

Let us briefly characterize the control equipment and automation means utilized in DOE fabrication.

Profilometer-profilograph is intended to measure in laboratory conditions the roughness and waviness of the product surface whose cross section in the measurement plane is a straight line. The profilometer-profiligraph feels the surface under examination with a diamond needle of the probe, with the resulting probe vibrations being transformed into proportional electrical signals. The device is used to control the microrelief quality of medium IR DOEs (Fig. 4.24 or Fig. 4.29) because its accuracy in terms of height is not very high (0.2–500 µm).

Microinterferometer is intended to visually estimate, measure and photograph the height of roughness of the processed surface and its interferogram. Linnic microinterferometers serially produced by the Russian LOMO Association (St. Petersburg) ensure the measurement of heights ranging from 0.1 µm to 8 µm with a deviation from the measurement limits of 37 percent and 14 percent, respectively. From the microinterferometer's field of view one can simultaneously observe interference fringes and the surface under measurement. If there is an asperity or dent on the surface under measurement, the interferogram fringes will be curved (e.g., Fig. 4.21). If the interference fringe is curved by a value equal to the distance between the neighboring light (dark) fringes (one period), the surface microrelief is changed by $\lambda/2$ (half the wavelength).

Microscope for controlling defects (MCD-P) is used to visually control defects found on the photomask and substrate surface and the DOE microrelief.

Refractometer is intended to measure the refractive index, spectral lines, and average dispersion of nonaggressive liquids and solids. The accurate determination of the refractive index n is a necessary condition for the transmission DOE microrelief height to be calculated correctly.

Universal photometer is intended to measure the transmission coefficients (or optical density) of solid and liquid transparent (nonscattering) media lacking the spectral selectivity. The photometer also measures a number of other parameters and is used to control the parameters of halftone, LPPC-based photomasks.

A unit intended to control the degree of cleanness of wafer surfaces [89 –91].

Automatic devices to control the wafer planeness [92–93].

A unit intended to control the height of a microrelief grown in LPPC layers.

E-beam and scanning probe microscopes.
Automatic means for DOE testing.

Leaving aside the conventional widely used equipment, let us take a detailed look at the latest tools for high accurate control of microrelief, based on advances of scanning probe microscopy, and means for automatic control of DOE parameters.

4.8.2 Scanning Probe Microscope

The scanning probe microscope (SPM) has found use in a wide range of techniques for surface examination. These techniques include the scanning tunnel (STM) and scanning force microscopy (SFM), scanning near-field microscopy, magnetic-power microscopy, and a number of other techniques having the scanning tunnel microscope as their predecessor. These techniques use a pinpoint probe (needle) moved with piezo-motors over the sample under examination at a distance of several angstroms without contact with the surface or providing a very delicate contact that excludes any damage to the surface.

To date, two generations of SPMs have come to light [94]. STM invented in 1981 are classed with the first generation. It is with these ultrahigh-vacuum devices that the atomic resolution in studies of crystalline surface was achieved. Liquid, air, vacuum, and ultra-vacuum versions of the STM were also developed and have found wide use.

The STMs depend on the registration of the tunnel current between the conducting sample and a microneedle for their operation. The microneedle produces the tunnel current localized on a small area. For example, if the microprobe is at some distance from the surface, the physical relief height at the point under scan will determine the tunnel current value. By keeping the microprobe tunnel displacement constant, the surface microrelief is being determined. The STM is suitable only for conducting surfaces, with studies being of purely academic interest. Besides, the STM data allow an equivocal interpretation, for the current is not only distance-dependant but also affected by the electron-state densities, electron binding energy, and the presence of absorption layers.

Invented in 1986, the scanning force microscopes (SFM) derive their name from the fact that they are able to register one of the interatomic interaction forces, so-called near-field force. The SFMs are designed similar to a gramophone: a sharp-tipped, spring-aided needle slides over the surface, with the spring deviation to be measured. Originally, the springs were manufactured of a thin platinum foil, with a sharp-tipped tiny needle (e.g. a sapphire monocrystal piece), called *cantilever*, pasted to it. A major requirement on the cantilever is that its tip should be extremely sharp, on the order of several atoms. The technology for the industrial production of the cantilevers was created in 1990, giving rise to the second generation of probe microscopes.

The SPM is a computer-controlled desktop device that is feeling the object with a microprobe (Fig. 4.64). Note that the "feeling" is possible both in vacuum and in air, and even under water. A microbeam with a cantilever fixed at its free end is used as a firm probe. A change in the beam tilt angle is registered using a sensitive detector (laser photodiode).

Displacement of the cantilever during the scan process can be measured in various ways: with the needle of an STM, interferometrically, using an optical position scheme,

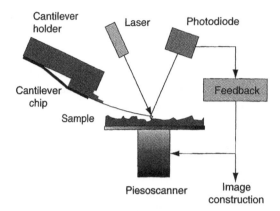

Figure 4.64. Scheme of the scanning probe microscope [94].

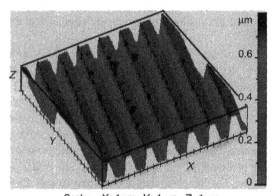

Scale – *X*: 1 μm, *Y*: 1 μm, *Z*: 1 μm.

Figure 4.65. A fragment of diffraction microrelief produced by SPM.

or with a pressure sensor (strain gauge). The optical position registration scheme is most popular.

As the needle approaches a sample, an exchange attractive interaction emerges between them. The cantilever is able to detect the attraction at a distance of tens of angstroms. By scanning the surface and keeping the attraction force constant, one can obtain information on the surface relief. Such a regime is called a *contact-free mode*. The stability is attained because of feedback.

With the SFM, the cantilever deviations with curvature radius ranging from 0.01 μm to 0.05 μm are easy to register, thus allowing subangstrom cantilever deviations to be detected.

The source is a semiconductor laser ($\lambda = 0.65$ μm, $P = 0.7$–4 mW), with its beam being focused on the cantilever mirror surface, in the tip region. The cantilever reflects the light sending it to a four-section photodiode, with the photodiode's amplified difference signal allowing the cantilever's angular deviation to be determined with the accuracy of up to $0.1''$, thus providing a 0.0001-μm resolution.

In the STM mode, one registers a current that flows through a dielectric span between the supersharp needle (the curvature radius is 0.003–0.005 μm) and a sample,

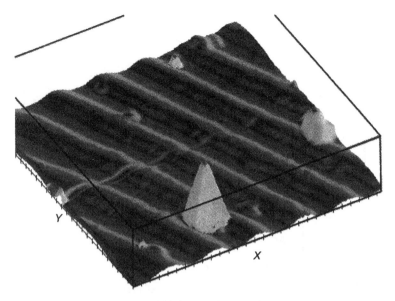

Scale X: 1000 A Y: 1000 A Z: 1000 A

Figure 4.66. Submicron microrelief of silicon with a conelike defect.

emerging when the needle is brought to the sample surface at a distance of about 10 angstroms. For the current to emerge, both the needle and the sample should be either conductors or semiconductors. The tunnel current is amplified in a preamplifier placed on the common adjustment table with the needle and then comes to the feedback circuit. Having passed through the ADC, the current turns into a signal registered by the program for processing and constructing the scanned surface image.

The data produced by the SPM is generally controlled and processed using a PC. The software available allows the microrelief fabricated to be conveniently and visually represented. Figure 4.65 shows an example of a microrelief fragment of an optical memory disk derived using the SPM. The image produced allows the fabricated microrelief quality to be evaluated and the factors that account for the occurrence of defects to be established and classified without cutting the optical element. Figure 4.66 depicts a microrelief fragment of a visible-range submicron diffraction grating with a characteristic, cone-shaped defect caused by the contamination of the original specimen by a dust particle. Computer-aided processing of the derived experimental data allows the scanned fragment to be magnified and presented in a greater detail (Fig. 4.67).

High accuracy and essentially lesser (by several orders of magnitude) cost of the SPM as compared with the e-beam microscopes makes them a highly effective control means when fabricating DOEs for near IR, visible range, and shorter wavelengths.

4.8.3 Automation Facilities for DOE Testing

At the final technological stage, the fabricated DOE is tested for the energy efficiency and compliance of the real parameters with the designed ones. According to their different functional purposes, various classes of DOEs are tested using different

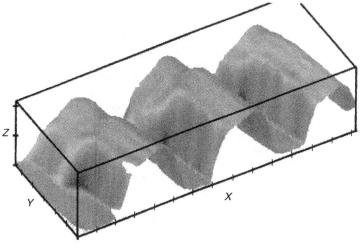

Scale X:1000 A Y:1000 A Z:500 A

Figure 4.67. A fragment of the diffractive microrelief presented with high resolution.

optical schemes, input devices, and software products. The compensators can be tested using any of the control schemes described in Section 8.2, with the optical surface under control replaced by the standard one, which will allow the deviation of the compensator-produced wave front from the desired one to be determined. By automatically processing the resulting interferograms, or shadow patterns, one will be able to evaluate the compensator's performance and direct the way to eliminating the drawbacks, if any (through the use of enhanced calculational techniques, more accurate technology of microrelief formation, and so on). Automation facilities to control the quality of the generated modal composition of light are discussed in Chapter 6, and the means for the automatic testing of lighting devices are dealt with in Section 9.7. In this section, we shall discuss the automation facilities for DOE testing using the focusing DOEs as an illustration (for the systematic theory of calculation of such DOEs, see Chapter 5).

Figure 4.68 depicts an optical setup for testing DOEs intended to focus near-IR laser light. When testing DOEs for a different light range, appropriate light sources, registration devices, and fittings are used. The general view of the testing unit is shown in Figure 4.69. The optical configuration for testing near-IR DOEs (Fig. 4.69) is composed of 1 = a continuous NdGR laser of wavelength 1.06 μm and maximum power 4 W, 2 = a quartz collimator, 3 = a separating glass, 4 = a focusing DOE, 5 = lenses, 6 = a pyrowattmeter sensor, and 7 = a TV camera + monitor. The information picked up from the pyrowattmeter and TV camera comes to the processing PC, which also controls the precision device for displacing sensors in the plane of focusing. The laser light passes through the glass-substrated collimator 2 and falls onto the focusing DOE 4, which focuses the laser light in the pyrowattmeter pick-up plane, with a light portion diverted by the dividing plate 3 focused with the TV camera objective.

The measurements are being taken in the following planes: *(1)* directly before the DOE, with mirror 3 and lens 5 used to measure the incident beam intensity; *(2)* directly after the DOE, where the degree of light absorption by the DOE substrate material is

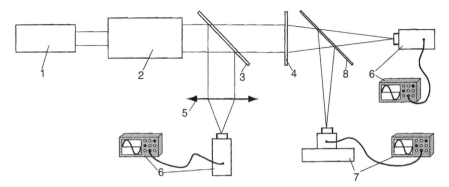

Figure 4.68. Optical setup for testing near-IR focusing DOEs.

Figure 4.69. The general view of the laser bench: measuring optical system includes a pyrowattmeter and a TV camera.

measured; and *(3)* in the plane of laser light focusing on the pyrowattmeter 6 sensor. The ratio of the focused light intensity to the light intensity found directly after the DOE characterizes the DOE performances in terms of microrelief fabrication quality. The ratio of intensities of the focused and incident beams defines the DOE general energy efficiency, with due account of light absorption by the substrate material and light reflection from the DOE surface. Automation facilities not only make it possible to take high accurate measurements of the laser beam intensity having passed through the DOE and compare it with the incident light intensity but also allow the intensity distribution in the focusing plane to be analyzed using the TV camera.

Example 4.10 Studies of near-IR DOEs intended to focus onto a ring and a twin spot. The use of the earlier-mentioned test bench is exemplified by studies on the operation of two near-IR DOEs with the following parameters: the working wavelength is $\lambda = 1.06$ μm, the working aperture diameter is $d = 20$ mm, and the focal length is $f = 150$ mm. The DOEs with an eight-level stepped microrelief were fabricated using photolithography. The first DOE was intended to focus light onto a 3-mm ring, whereas the second DOE focused the light into a pair of spots found at a 5-mm distance.

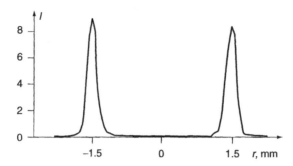

Figure 4.70. Intensity distribution in the cross section of the focal plane of the DOE focusing onto a ring.

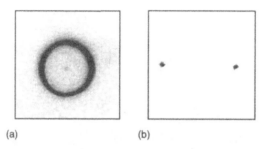

(a)   (b)

Figure 4.71. The results of focusing: (**a**) into a ring and (**b**) into a twin spot.

The profile of the intensity distribution in the focal plane of the DOE focusing onto a ring is shown in Figure 4.70.

The line diffraction width with respect to 0.3 level is 230 μm. The evaluation of the focusing DOE energy efficiency was based on the intensity distribution measurements. The experimental measurement data were computer-processed and showed that 82.5 percent of the entire energy having come to the focusing plane is found on the ring, with 85.7 percent of the entire energy being concentrated on the twin spot.

Shown in Figure 4.71 are the results of focusing the laser light, picked up by the TV camera and computer-processed.

The software-hardware facilities employed in DOE studies include original components allowing the intensity distribution along a complex contour of focusing (or over a desired plane domain) to be analyzed, thus evaluating the DOE energy efficiency. This is done by evaluating (with use of software or hardware capabilities) the energy fraction coming to a desired region of the focal plane corresponding to the tested DOE domain of focusing.

4.9 EXAMPLES OF DOE SYNTHESIS AND APPLICATION OF SOFTWARE COMPLEXES

4.9.1 Software in Diffractive Optics

Some examples of IPSI RAS outlined in the present Section (Image Processing Systems Institute of the Russian Academy of Sciences) are noteworthy for software product specialists working in diffractive optics.

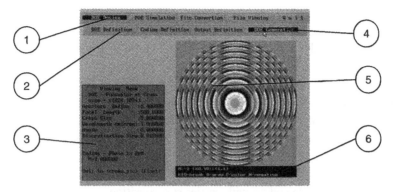

Figure 4.72. Display with a fragment of QUICK-DOE software with explanatory comments: *(1)* menu of DOE calculation functions; *(2)* menu of DOE simulation functions; *(3)* input parameters; *(4)* menu of DOE calculation functions; *(5)* visualization of the designed DOE phase function; *(6)* visualization parameters.

Figure 4.72 presents the display (with explanatory comments) of the QUICK-DOE software [3,95]. This software aims to implement analytical methods for calculating matrices describing the DOE phase functions, as well as methods for phase function coding. The software is also provided with tools for *(1)* file generation to support the output onto a raster photo-plotter, *(2)* digital hologram generation, and *(3)* execution of a variety of auxiliary functions. In particular, the auxiliary functions include file format conversion, file mask visualization, DOE operation simulation using the FFT, and definition and preparation of the composite image to be output on a photo-plotter. The QUICK-DOE software is intended for optical physicists, DOE designers, and programmers dealing with the DOE design software.

QUICK-DOE software comprises programs for calculating the following analytically defined DOEs:

- A variety of diffraction lenses (radial, bifocal, multifocus, cylindrical, and crossed cylindrical lenses, and those with enhanced focal depth — Chapter 1 and Refs. [96–98])
- Focusing DOEs (to focus into a ring, cross, square contour, focal segment, and a rectangular domain — Chapter 5)
- Compensators to transform the spherical wave front into a wave front with an axially symmetric quadric surface of revolution (including paraboloid, ellipsoid, and hyperboloid — Chapter 8)
- Optical filters (Karhunen-Loeve basis functions, Wiener filter, regularizing Tikhonov filter — Chapter 10)
- DOEs matched to coherent light modes (modans) (Gauss-Hermite and Gauss-Laguerre modes — Chapter 6)

The list of DOEs calculated using the QUICK-DOE software can be complemented with user-oriented DOEs. A simple technique for inclusion of new optical elements was developed and realized. To introduce a new element, one needs to edit the dialog program for entering the desired parameters and write a program for calculating the field (phase and amplitude) at a point.

The software includes different variants for coding the phase and the amplitude:

- Modulo 2π phase coding
- Phase-into-amplitude coding with carrier superposition
- Amplitude-into-phase coding in the $\{0, \pi\}$ interval
- Amplitude-into-phase coding with carrier superposition using the Kirk-Jones method [17]
- Coding with the Lohmann and Lee methods [17]
- Amplitude-amplitude coding with carrier superposition
- Amplitude transformation into intensity.

The DOE operation in the Fresnel approximation was simulated using a diffractive calculation technique based on the FFT [99,100], whereas more complicated optical configurations were implemented using a less demanding ray-tracing technique.

All the transformations can be implemented not only for the existing optical elements but also for the later included user elements. In the course of calculation, both halftone and binary photomasks can be generated. The photomask can be stored in a file as follows:

- Every pixel as a real number;
- Byte per pixel;
- Bit per pixel (only for binary photomasks).

For a set of binary photomasks (2–4) they can be calculated in sequence, one after the other, or derived from a single halftone photomask through appropriate transformations. Calculating the DOE photomask and changing the photomask format are accompanied by the synchronous visualization.

In operating QUICK-DOE, the internal, raster-type file format is supported, which is written linewise, with comments incorporated into the file heading and ending. The matching with other software is provided through recoding into the byte/pixel TIF-format and back, as well as into the byte/pixel field with linewise organization. A convenient user shell provides the simplicity of the software operation. If the QUICK-DOE simulation tools appear to be inadequate, the DOE characteristics can be estimated and analyzed using specialized software called *WAVE-DOE* [101].

If necessary, the DOE phase functions calculated using the QUICK-DOE can be optimized through the software implementing iterative procedures described in Chapter 2. Such software is also employed when one finds it impossible to derive and then program the analytical definition of the DOE phase function. In Figure 4.73, the PC display presents the *Iter-DOE software* for designing phase optical elements (kinoforms, focusing DOEs, multifocus lenses, axicons, and compensators) through the use of fast integral transforms. The multiwindow interface can be used to visualize all the changes in the phase function and the DOE performances during the course of DOE iterative design.

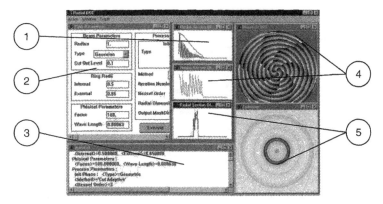

Figure 4.73. The PC display of the Iter-DOE software with explanatory comments (exemplified by the calculation of a phase DOE to focus into a ring): 1: the radial section of the incident light; 2: the parameter window (the incident light type, the wavelength, the ring radii, the initial phase type, the iterative technique type, etc.); 3: the protocol window (input parameters, deviation and efficiency at each iteration, and so on); 4: the calculated phase (2D photomask and its radial section); and 5: the intensity distribution in the plane of focusing (2D pattern and its radial section).

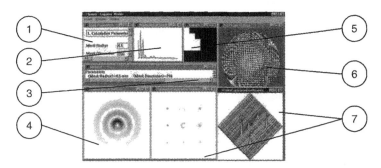

Figure 4.74. The PC display of the Iter-MODE software with explanatory comments (exemplified by designing a DOE to generate a multi-mode Gauss-Laguerre beam): 1: the parameter window (the mode composition of the beam and the filter, the initial phase type, the iterative technique, the number of iterations, etc.); 2: the amplitude radial section; 3: the protocol window (input parameters, deviation and efficiency in the course of iterations, etc.); 4: three-mode light beam; 5: table of the spatial filter mode composition; 6: phase photomask of the spatial filter; 7: the result of filter's operation (intensity peaks are found at points corresponding to the illuminating beam mode composition, 2D and 3D patterns).

In Figure 4.74, the PC display presents another example of the software for the iterative DOE design. This is Iter-MODE software for designing DOEs that can generate Gauss-Laguerre, Gauss-Hermite, and Bessel modes, on the basis of algorithms in which the complex function is approximated by a finite number of base functions. The multi-window interface allows one to visualize both the phase photomask of the calculated nine-mode spatial filter and the simulated effect the filter produces on the illuminating beam with the corresponding modal composition.

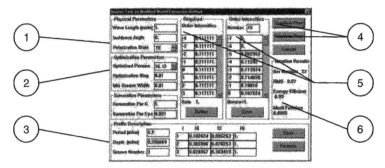

Figure 4.75. The "GRATING SOLVER" software PC display with explanatory comments (exemplified by designing a nine-order, three-groove grating): 1: physical parameters of the task; 2: profile optimization parameters; 3: parameter window of the calculated binary profile; 4: optimization type (gradient or stochastic search); 5: calculated and desired order intensities; and 6: the grating performance characteristics (energy efficiency, rms error, and the residual function).

During the course of iterative design, if it turns out that iterative Fresnel-Kirchhoff approximation is unable to produce the desired result, one has to resort to a more accurate electromagnetic approach dealt with in Chapter 3. The electromagnetic methods must also be applied when the Fresnel approximation conditions are violated. The software *GRATING SOLVER* (Fig. 4.75) is intended to design and simulate DOEs using the electromagnetic theory. This software covers the following:

- Simulation of reflection and transmission diffraction gratings with a continuous and binary relief profile
- Gradient methods and stochastic algorithms for solving the inverse problem of calculation of the binary profile on the assumption of generation of desired diffraction orders
- Gradient methods for solving the inverse problem of calculation of a continuous reflection profile in the Rayleigh approximation

Figure 4.75 shows the PC display of the software GRATING SOLVER with explanatory comments (exemplified by designing a nine-order, three-groove grating). With this calculational technique, the groove coordinates (x_i, c_i, h_i) are optimized through the minimization of the residual functional of the calculated and desired order intensities.

The *RAY-TRACING-DOE* software based on specially elaborated ray-tracing techniques was developed [102] to simulate and optimize DOE-based optical schemes (Chapter 9).

4.9.2 Examples of DOE Synthesis

Examples of DOE calculation and fabrication can be found throughout the entire text of the book, aimed to illustrate some features of a method, technology, or a technique

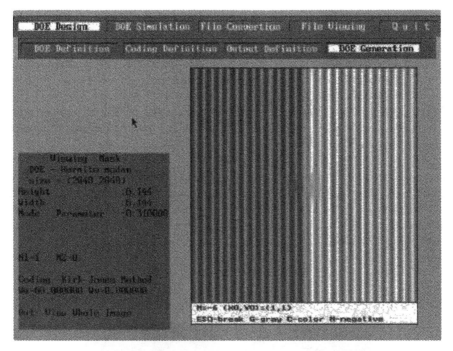

Figure 4.76. The "QUICK-DOE" software PC display with an example of a modan design.

for studying the optical element. Example 4.3 illustrates the technology of the stepwise etching of the microrelief of a DOE to focus into a ring. Example 4.4 describes the technology of LPPC-based fabrication of the quasi-diffractive microrelief for visible DOE, whereas Example 4.8 illustrates the fabrication of the diffraction microrelief on diamond substrates using direct laser etching. In the following example, we analyze the entire technological process — from the design stage to testing the DOE performance.

Example 4.11   Design, fabrication, and testing of a unibeam modan. Consider the synthesis of a unibeam modan to transform the zero Gaussian mode into the Gauss-Hermite mode (1,0). The following parameters are used: the wavelength is $\lambda = 0.6328$ μm, the input beam waist is $\sigma_{00} = 0.835$ mm, DOE diameter is 6.144 mm, and the number of the calculated phase function pixels is 2048×2048. Figure 4.76 shows the PC display of the "QUICK-DOE" software allowing such an element to be calculated using the Kirk-Jones method [103]. The central and most informative part of the modan can just scarcely be seen on the carrier background.

Note, however, that numerical simulation demonstrated that the DOE designed using the Kirk-Jones method has low energy efficiency. Because of this reason, in order to design a highly efficient modan, special iterative procedures were developed [42]. The designed modan was fabricated using the technology of uniform etching of a PMMA photoresist applied on a quartz substrate. With this technology, the e-beam coming from the ZBA-23 lithographer is scanning over the surface (Section 4.3 and Fig. 4.28). The fabricated phase microrelief of a one-beam modan was evaluated using a microinterferometer MICROMAP-512. The characteristic regions of distribution of the element phase function quantized in 16 levels were selected for examination. Then, the calculated phase distribution was compared with that of the real microrelief. Shown in Figure 4.77a, b are the central fragments of the calculated halftone photomask of modans composed of 50×50 and 200×200 pixels, respectively, whereas their central sections are shown in Figure 4.78.

Figure 4.79 depicts the measured profiles of the corresponding fragments of the fabricated element. The intensity "peaks" found at the microrelief height jumps are due to interference effects taking place in the course of measurements.

Figure 4.80 shows the intensity distribution produced by the fabricated element [40,42] that was measured using the SPIRICON camera (light wavelength is $0.6328 \, \mu m$). The resolution of the camera is $13 \, \mu m$. The studies conducted have demonstrated that a high-quality microrelief of iteratively calculated elements can be fabricated using the technology of uniform, 16-level etching of the PMMA photoresist applied on a quartz substrate.

Table 4.7 gives a number of DOEs produced using various technologies at IPSI RAS. The optical elements were implemented in various materials (copper, glass,

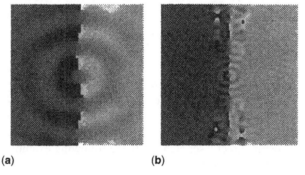

(a)   (b)

Figure 4.77. The central fragment of the calculated halftone photomask of the modan: (**a**) 50×50 pixels (**b**) 200×200 pixels.

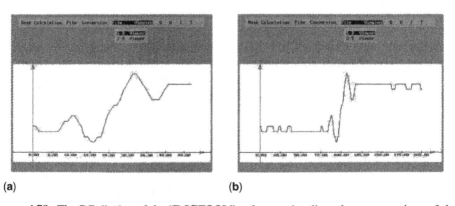

(a)   (b)

Figure 4.78. The PC display of the "DOETOOL" software visualizes the cross sections of the photomask fragments shown in Fig. 4.77a, b.

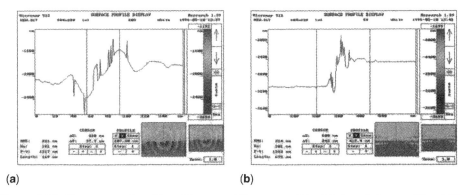

(a)   (b)

Figure 4.79. The measured profiles of the central fragments of the fabricated element (Fig. 4.78a and b).

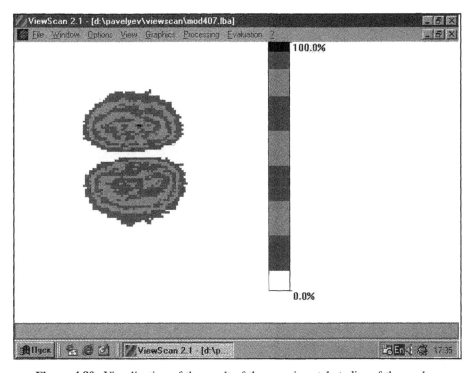

Figure 4.80. Visualization of the result of the experimental studies of the modan.

fused silica, silicon, PMMA, and a photoresist coated with aluminum or silver film) using the technologies such as liquid photopolymerizable compositions (LPPC), bichromated gelatin, plasmo-chemical etching, e-beam lithography, photolithography, uniform photoresist growth, and others. The earlier-listed DOEs were calculated and simulated using the "QUICK-DOE" software (LPPC:liquid photopolymerizable composition, BCG:bichromated gelatin, PCE:plasmo-chemical etching, EBL:e-beam lithography, UPG:uniform photoresist growth, UCE:uniform copper etching).

TABLE 4.7. Examples of DOEs Fabricated using Various Technologies

Focal Area Configuration	Wavelength, μm	Aperture, mm	Focal Length, mm	Focal Line Size, mm	Number of Phase Quantization Levels	Fabrication Technique Levels	Substrate Material
"Line-segment"	10.6	16	250	6	5	Photolithography	Copper
"Line-segment"	10.6	40	400	10	8	Photolithography	Copper
"Line-segment"	10.6	50	1200	20	Contin. microrelief	LPPC	Copper
"Line-segment"	10.6	40	500	10	8	PCE	Silicon
"Spot"	10.6	10	250	—	8	UCE	Copper
"Line-segment"	1.06	6	80	5	5	Photolithography	Glass
"Ring"	10.6	50	800	10	Contin. microrelief	BCG	Copper
"Ring"	10.6	12	400	12	8	UPG	Photoresist coated with Al/Ag film
"Ring"	1.06	20	100	4	8	Photolithography	Glass
"Ring"	1.06	35	150	3 × 1	2	PCE	Fused silica
"Twin spot"	1.06	20	100	3	8	Photolithography	Glass
"Twin spot"	1.06	35	150	2	2	PCE	Fused silica
"2D area"	1.06	35 × 35	150	1 × 3	2	PCE	Fused silica
Letter "A"	1.06	5	100	5	2	Photolithography	Glass
Letter $\langle\langle\pi\rangle\rangle$	10.6	18	250	10 × 10	Contin. microrel	BCG	Copper
Lens raster	0.55	5 × 5, 100 × 100	3	—	2	PCE	Glass
Diffuser (diffraction grating)	0.55	1,000 lines/mm	—	—	2	EBL, PCE	PMMA

CONCLUSION

The foregoing review of a variety of current technologies for generating the diffractive microrelief of optical elements is far from being complete. A keen interest is being taken all over the world in diffractive optics, and the wide range of DOE parameters and microrelief requirements have resulted in a great number of original technologies. However, the analysis conducted suggests that a great part of technologies, techniques, and process equipment have been borrowed from other fields of engineering (mostly, microelectronics), thus carrying typical traits of these, which are often extraneous to diffractive optics. It seems justified to do such forced borrowing when the costly precision equipment is mainly used for its direct purpose, whereas operations of the DOE microrelief generation are performed in idle time. As a result, the process of DOE studies and fabrication is essentially inexpensive. Note, however, that the recent years have seen a number of technologies (e.g., direct laser etching of microrelief) and technological equipment (last-generation laser writing machines) developed especially for the diffractive optics purposes. In this chapter best efforts have been made to maintain a balance between the widespread classical technologies, and latest technologies which, sometimes, have not yet left the research laboratories.

REFERENCES

1. V.A. Soifer and M.A. Golub, *Proc. SPIE* **1751**, 140–154 (1992).

2. O. Bryndahl, *J. Opt. Soc. Am.* **60**, 140–145 (1970).

3. S.G. Volotovsky et al., Software for computer optics, *Computer Optics*, **14–15**(2), 94–106 (1995).

4. L.L. Doskolovich, N.L. Kazansky, and V.A. Soifer, Design of two-order focusing DOEs, *Avtometriya* (1), 58–63 (1993).

5. M. Curcio, *Proc. SPIE* **306**, 105–113 (1981).

6. P.P. Clark and C. Londono, *Opt. News* **15**, 39–40 (1989).

7. Ye.D., Bulatov, S.A. Gridin, and A.A. Danilenko, Production of planar optics elements of millimeter and submillimeter range using mass-production, numerical control machines, *Computer Optics*, **1**, 167–173 (1987).

8. D.W. Sweeney and G.E. Sommargren, *Appl. Opt.* **34**(14), 2469–2475 (1995).

9. S.T. Bobrov and Yu.G. Turkevich, Use of lasers in systems for data transformation, *Transmission and Processing*, LDNT Publisher Leningrad, Saint Petersburg, 1978, pp. 73–77.

10. S.B. Gurevich, N.I. Ilyashenko, and B.T. Kolomietz, *Optical Methods for Data Processing*, LDNT Publisher Leningrad, Saint Petersburg, 1974, pp. 117–134.

11. G.I. Greisukh, I.M. Yefimenko, and S.A. Stepanov, *Optics of Gradient-Index and Diffractive Elements*, Radio i Svyaz Publishers, Moscow, Russia, 1990.

12. V.K. Grishchenko, A.F. Maslyuk, and S.S. Gundzera, *Liquid Photopolymerizable Compositions*, Naukova dumka Publishers, Kiev, Ukraine, 1985.

13. Yu.B. Boiko, V.S. Solovjev, S. Calixto, and D.J. Lougnot, *Appl. Opt.* **33**(5), 787–793 (1994).

14. V.P. Lavrishchev, ed., *Introduction into Photolithography*, Energiya Publishers, Moscow, Russia, 1997.

15. G.J. Swanson, Technical Report 854, Lincoln Laboratory, Massachusetts Institute of Technology, Cambridge; 1989.

16. G.J. Swanson and W.B. Veldkamp, *Opt. Eng.* **28**(6), 605–608 (1989).

17. L.P. Yaroslavsky and N.S. Merzlyakov, *Digital Holography*, Nauka Publishers, Moscow, Russia, 1982.

18. U. Krackhard, J. Schwider, M. Schrader, and N. Stiedl, *Opt. Eng.* **32**(4), 781–785 (1993).

19. M.A. Golub et al., *Opt. Laser Technol.* **27**(4), 215–218 (1995).

20. V.P. Korohkevich, V.P. Korolkov, and A.G. Poleshchuk, Laser technologies in diffractive optics, *Avtometriya* (6), 5–26 (1998).

21. V.V. Cherkashin, E.G. Churin, and J.H. Burge, *Proc. SPIE* **3010**, 168–179 (1997).

22. K.A. Valiyev, *Physics of Submicron Lithography*, Nauka Publishers, Moscow, Russia, 1990.

23. P. Rai-Choudhury, ed. *Handbook of microlithography, micromachining & microfabrication*, SPIE Optical Engineering Press, Bellingham, Washington, USA, 1997.

24. G.N. Beryezin, A.V. Nikitin, and R.A. Suris, *Optical Basics of Contact Photolithography*, Radio i Svyaz, Moscow, Russia, 1982.

25. M.P. Watts, *C. J. Vac. Sci. Tecnol.* **1**, 434–440 (1985).

26. D. Kyser and R. Pyle, *IBM J. Res. Dev.* **24**, 426–438 (1989).

27. W.S. Ruska, *Microelectronic processing*, McGraw-Hill, New York, 1987.

28. V.N. Cherniayev, *Technology of Integrated Microcircuit Production*, Energiya Publishers, Moscow, Russia, 1977.

29. I.Ye. Yefimov and I.Ya. Kozyr, *Basics of Microelectronics*, Visshaya Shkola Publishers, Moscow, Russia, 1983.

30. B.I. Spektor, A method for synthesizing a kinoform phase structure, *Avtometriya* (6), 34–38 (1985).

31. A.V. Volkov, N.L. Kazansky, O. Yu. Moiseyev, and V.A. Soifer, Generating a diffarction microrelief using a layer-wise photoresist growth, *Computer Opt.* **16**, 12–14 (1996).

32. Z.Yu. Gotra, *Technology of Microelectronic Devices*, *Reference book*, Radio i Svyaz Publishers, Moscow, Russia, 1991.

33. P. Perlo, S. Sinezi, M. Ripetto, and G.V. Uspleniev, Use of a circular laser writing system for fabrication of halftone photomasks of diffractive optical elements on DLW-glass, *Computer Opt.* **17**, 85–90 (1997).

34. V.P. Korolkov, A.I. Malyshev, V.G. Nikitin, and A.G. Poleshchuk, Halftone photomasks on DLW-glass, *Avtometriya* (6), 27–37 (1998).

35. V.P. Korolkov, A.I. Malyshev, V.G. Nikitin, and A.G. Poleshchuk, Fabrication of high-efficiency DOEs using halftone photomasks on DLW-glass, *Computer Opt.* **18**, 121–126 (1998).

36. J.R. Brewer, ed., *Use of e-beam Lithography in Fabrication of Microelectronic Devices*, translated from English, Radio i Svyaz Publishers, Moscow, Russia, 1984.

37. W. Moreau, *Semiconductor Lithography, Principles, Practices and Materials*, Plenum Press, New York, 1988.

38. E. Veber and G. Jurke, High-production scan e-beam systems in integrated circuit technology, *Elektronika*, **50**(23), 14–19 (1977).

39. H. Aagedal, S. Teiwes, and T. Beth, *Proc. SPIE* **2404**, 50–58 (1994).

40. M. Duparre et al., *Proc. SPIE* **3110**, 741–751 (1997).

41. M. Duparre et al., *Proc. SPIE* **3134**, 357–368 (1997).

42. M. Duparre et al., *Proc. SPIE* **3291**, 104–114 (1998).

43. M. Duparre et al., *Appl. Opt.* **34**(14), 2489–2497 (1995).

44. S.N. Khonina et al., Generation of Gauss-Hermite modes using binary DOEs, *Computer Opt.* **18**, 42–28 (1998).

45. Ye.B. Brui and S.N. Koreshev, Peculiarities of usage of thin photoemulsion layers for generating low-frequency holographic microreliefs, *Opt. Spectroscopy*, **67**(3), 685–688 (1989).

46. S.N. Koreshev and C.V. Geel, On the profile shape of low-frequency holographic structures generated on thin photoemulsion films, *Opt. Spectroscopy*, **68**(2), 422 (1990).

47. A.D. Galpern, V.P. Smayev, L.V. Selayvko, and N.S. Shelekhov, Phase-relief holograms on halide-silver materials and their replication using a thermo-polymerization technique, Transactions of Leningrad Physical & Technical Institute, High-Efficiency Techniques for Writing Holograms, Leningrad, Saint Petersburg, 1988.

48. K.S. Pennington and J.S. Harper, *Appl. Opt.* **9**(7), 1643–1650 (1970).

49. N.J. Phillips and D. Porter, *J. of Phys. Sci. Instrum.* **9**(8), 631–634 (1976).

50. A.M. Prokhorov, ed., *Handook of Lasers*, **2**, Sovetskoye Radio Publishers, Moscow, Russia, 1978.

51. L.V. Krasny-Admoni and Ya.Z. Zeidenberg, Studies into a photometric technique for measuring the height of a relief photo-image, *J. Sci. Appl. Photogr. Cinematogr.* **10**(1), 8–10 (1965).

52. L.V. Krasny-Admoni, *Low-Silver Photographic Materials and Processing Techniques*, Khimiya Publishers, Leningrad, Saint Petersburg, 1986, p. 168.

53. L.L. Doskolovich, N.L. Kazanskiy, S.I. Kharitonov, and G.V. Usplenjev *Opt. and Lasers in Eng.* **15**(5), 311–322 (1991).

54. M.A. Golub et al., *Optical Recording and Processing of Information*, *Transactions of KuAI*, KuAI Publishers, Kuibyshev, 1988, pp. 14–18.

55. Ye.Yu. Arefiev et al., Experimental studies of a planar optical element to focus into a ring, *Computer Opt.* **5**, 49–54 (1989).

56. V.A. Soifer et al., A Technique for Production of Phase-Relief Holographic Focusing Elements, Author's Certificate of the USSR No. 1624864.

57. S.V. Karpeyev and V.S. Solovjov, Methods for generating relief, continuous-profile images, *Computer Opt.* **4**, 60–61 (1989).

58. S.V. Solovjev, Studies into the Behavior of a layer of liquid photopolymerizable composition during the relief formation, *Computer Opt.* **10–11**, 145–149 (1989).

59. S.V. Solovjev, Generation of a DOE microrelief in LPPC layers, Thesis for Candidate's Degree, Samara, Russia 1991.

60. Y.B. Boiko et al., *Proc. SPIE* **1238**, 253–257 (1990).

61. A.A. Berlin, T.Ya. Kefeli, and G.V. Korolyev, *Polyetheracrylates*, Moscow, Russia, 1967.

62. Yu.S. Lipatov, V.K. Grishchenko, and S.S. Gudzera, Liquid oligomer compositions in quantum electronics and holography, *Messenger of the Academy of Sciences of the Ukraine SSR* **2**, 45–50 (1985).

63. S.N. Nikiforova-Denisova, Machining and chemical processing, *Technology of Semi-Conductor Devices and Microelectronics Products*, Visshaya Shkola Publishers, Moscow, Russia, 1989.

64. N. Einsprook and D. Brown, eds., *Plasma Technology in Production of VLIS*, Mir Publishers, Moscow, Russia, 1987, translated from English.

65. V.Yu. Kireyev, B.S. Danilin, and V.I. Kuznetzov, *Plasmo-Chemical and Ion-Chemical Etching of Microstructures*, Radio i Svyaz Publishers, Moscow, Russia, 1983.

66. A.V. Volkov, N.L. Kazansky, and O.Ye. Rybakov, Investigation into the technology of plasma etching to generate multi-level diffractive optical elements, *Computer Opt.* **18**, 127–130 (1989).

67. A.V. Volkov, N.L. Kazansky, and O. Ye. Rybakov, Development of a technique for generating a diffractive optical element with submicron microrelief on a silicon substrate, *Computer Opt.* **18**, 130–133 (1998).

68. N.A. Vainos et al., *Appl. Opt.* **35**, 6304–6319 (1996).

69. G.P. Behrmann and M.T. Duignan, *Appl. Opt.* **36**, 4666–4674 (1997).

70. S. Mailis et al., *Appl. Opt.* **38**(11), 2301–2308 (1999).

71. J. Bohandy, B.F. Kim, and F.J. Adrian, *J. Appl. Phys.* **60**, 1538–1539 (1986).

72. E. Fogarassy et al., *Mater. Manuf. Processes* **7**, 31–51 (1992).

73. V. Ralchenko et al., Spatial distribution of thermal conductivity of diamond wafers as measured by laser flash technique, Proceedings of SPIE: International Conference, Tashkent, Uzbekistan, 1998.

74. R.S. Sussmann et al., *Finer Points*, **10**(2), 6–10 (1998).

75. V.V. Kononenko et al., Diamond-based diffractive optics for high-power CO_2-lasers, *Quant. Electron.* **26**(1), 9–10 (1999).

76. V.V. Kononenko et al., Studies into a diamond diffractive cylindrical Lens, *Computer Opt.* **19**, 102–106 (1999).

77. T.V. Kononenko et al., *Appl. Phy. A* **68**(1), 99–102 (1999).

78. V.V. Kononenko et al., Generation of anti-reflecting microstructures on the diamond film using laser-writing, *Quant. Electron.* **26**(2), 158–162 (1999).

79. D.H. Raguin and G.M. Morris, *Appl. Opt.* **32**(7), 1154–1167 (1993).

80. D.L. Golovashkin, V.S. Pavelyev, and V.A. Soifer, Numerical simulation of light propagation through an anti-reflecting grating using the electromagnetic theory, *Computer Opt.* **19**, 44–47 (1999).

81. D.L. Golovashkin, A difference scheme for the Maxwell equation, Proceedings of 9-th Inter-University Conference, Samara, Russia, 1999, pp. 43–45.

82. V.G. Ralchenko et al., *Diam. and Rel. Mat.* **6**, 417–425 (1997).

83. M. Rothschild, C. Arnone, and D.J. Ehrlich, *J. Vac. Sci. Technol.* **B4**, 310–314 (1986).

84. M.A. Golub, N.L. Kazanskiy, and V.A. Soifer, A Mathematical Model of Light Focusing by Computer-Generated Optical Elements, vol. **3** Nauchnoye Proborostroyenie (Scientific Instrumentation) Publishers, 1993, pp. 9–23.

85. V.S. Pavelyev et al., *Diamond Focusators for Far IR lasers*, *Computer Optics*, ICNTI, Moscow, Russia, 2000, pp. 71–75.

86. A.V. Volkov et al., Experimental studies of mass-transfer in liquid photopolymerizable compositions, *J. Technical physics* **65**(9), 181–185 (1995).

87. V.S. Solovjev and P. Perlo, Studies into the mass-transfer to eliminate the shrinkage effect in replicating diffractive optical elements, *Computer Opt.* **18**, 130–133 (1998).

88. Sh. A. Furman, *Thin optical coatings*, Mashinostoyeniye (Machine-building) Publishers, Moscow, Russia, 1977.

89. S.A. Borodin, A.V. Volkov, A.I. Kolpakov, and L.L. Rafelson, A device to check the substrate surface cleanness, *Devices and Techniques of Experimentation*, No. 5, 1990, pp. 230–232.

90. L.L. Rafelson, A.V. Volkov, S.A. Borodin, and V.A. Ivanov, A device to check the substrate surface cleanness, Author's Certificate No. 1741032 February 15, 1992.

91. A.V. Volkov and A.I. Kolpakov, A technique to check the substrate surface cleanness, Author's Certificate No. 1784868 September 1, 1992.

92. V.V. Kotlyar, V.A. Soifer, and A.V. Khramov, An interferometer to check the planeness of reflecting surfaces, Author's Certificate No. 1744452 of 30 June, 1992, Bulletin 24, priority of December 7, 1990. G01B 11/24 class.

93. V.V. Kotlyar, V.A. Soifer, and A.V. Khramov, An interferometer to check the planeness of reflecting surfaces, Author's Certificate No. 1760312 of September 7, 1992, Bulletin 33, priority of December 7, 1990. G01B 11/24 class.

94. V.A. Bykov, M.I. Lazaryev, and A.V. Tavrov, Scan Probe Microscopy in Science and Industry, *Computerra* (41), 38–41 (1997).

95. M.A. Golub, N.L. Kazansky, M.V. Shinkaryev, Architecture of a program complex for synthesis of computer-generated optical elements, *Computer Optics*, **5**, 43–48 (1989).

96. V.P. Koronkevich and I.G. Palchikova, Modern zone plates, *Avtometriya* (1), 85–100, (1992).

97. L.L. Doskolovich, N.L. Kazanskiy, V.A. Soifer, and A. Ye. Tzaregorodtzev, *Opt.* **101**(2), 37–41 (1995).

98. M.A. Golub et al., *J. Mod. Opt.* **39**(6), 1245–1251 (1992).

99. E. Siklash and A. Siegman, *Proc. IEEE* Diffraction Computation Using The Fast Fourier Transform Techniques **62**(3), 161–162 (1974).

100. M.A. Vorontzov and V.I. Shmalgauzen, *Principles of Adaptive Optics*, Nauka Publishers, Moscow, 1985.

101. A.A. Bazarbayev et al., A Program Complex Analysis of Diffraction Characteristics of Planar Optics Elements, State Foundation of Algorithms and Programs, No. 50890001345.

102. N.L. Kazansky, V.A. Soifer, and S.I. Kharitonov, *Mathematical Modeling of DOE-aided Illuminating Devices, Computer Opt.* **14–15**(2), 107–116 (1995).

103. J.P. Kirk and A.L. Jones, *J. Opt. Soc. Am.* **61**(8), 1023–1028 (1971).

CHAPTER 5

DOE for Focusing the Laser Light

5.1 INTRODUCTION

The elements focusing the laser light represent one of the most interesting classes of DOEs. The focusing DOEs are designed using the geometric ray-tracing and featured by a regular structure that focuses the laser light onto thin lines and small spatial areas. For the first time, they were developed and studied in Russia, in 1981, by Golub and associates [1]. In the early 1980s, I. Sisakian and other Russian researchers obtained basic geometric optical solutions for the problem of focusing and designed a variety of focusing DOEs [2–8]. In the subsequent years, the methods for their design were theoretically substantiated and the theorems of existence and solvability of the problem of their synthesis were proved [9–13].

The focusing DOEs designed through iterative and geometric optics methods have a number of distinctions.

The geometric optical ray-tracing used when designing the DOE yields a regular zoned microrelief. Iterative algorithms are more accurate, but, as a rule, they result in an irregular microrelief. The regular character of the DOE's microrelief allows one to moderate the requirements for the photolithographic fabrication technology. The type of geometric DOE's microrelief makes it possible to utilize a wider range of fabrication technologies [14–18]. To take one example, as opposed to the stochastic microrelief of an iterative DOE, the regular DOE's microrelief can be generated using precision automatic cutting machines [14,15].

An urgent problem is the application of DOEs to high-power lasers for far-IR range, where the use of diffractive optical microreliefs with reduced weight and size allows one to rule out costly laser focusing lens components. The use of geometric DOEs turns out to be most promising in high-power lasers since the stochastic microrelief of iterative DOEs, as a rule, leads to the uncontrolled scattering of about 10 to 15 percent of incident light energy. Of particular interest are diamond-based DOEs with high heat resistance (up to 5 kW/cm^2) in the far-IR range.

When designing a focusing DOE, a key problem is that of attaining high energy efficiency (about 90 percent) while generating a desired intensity distribution in the focal plane. Since the ill-posed inverse problem of focusing results in a variety of solutions [19] and these are found using the geometric optical ray-tracing it is essential that the DOE characteristics be studied. This brings up the problems regarding the limits of the geometric optics validity for DOE design and the effect of the sampling and quantization inherent in the DOE design and fabrication techniques on their operation [20–24]. Another urgent problem is concerned with comparative analysis of different solutions of the inverse problem of focusing.

347

The characteristics that describe the processes of DOE design and operation may be divided into three classes. In the first class are the physical parameters used when computing the DOE phase function: focal length, the wavelength used, the size of the DOE and of the domain of focusing. The second class includes the sampling and quantization parameters of the DOE phase function, namely, the size and shape of the sampling elements (modules). These parameters are associated with the choice of a device for registering the DOE. The third class of parameters is concerned with the DOE diffraction characteristics: the energy efficiency, the focal line width, the rms deviation of the calculated intensity distribution in the focal plane from the desired one, and the like. In terms of DOE design, the first two classes of parameters are internal, whereas the diffraction parameters are external and appear as a result of operation of a DOE with the internal parameters chosen. When studying the DOE, it is important to bring out the relation between the internal and external design parameters. Taking into account that the DOE fabrication procedure is complex and multivariant, its characteristics should be studied at the design stage.

To date, using the geometric optical techniques as a base, a variety of diffraction methods for designing DOEs has been developed and aimed at extending their functional capabilities.

An example is the method of nonlinear transformation of the phase function of the DOE focusing onto a line by the law of a multiorder diffraction grating [25–30]. The nonlinear transformation of the phase of the DOE onto a curve enables one to design multifocus DOE that generate an array of axial lines (spots) of various (or the same) size located in different planes. Note that a DOE that corresponds to a common (linear) combination of a DOE focusing onto a curve and a multiorder diffraction grating makes possible the focusing only onto an equal-line array and only on a single plane.

Another interesting DOE class is represented by the spectral DOE designed using the method of nonlinear transformation of the DOE phase by the law of color separation diffraction grating [31,32]. For the first time, the color separation diffraction gratings were proposed by Dammann [31,33] and were intended for the separation of three different spectral components between the 0, +1st, and −1st diffraction orders. The spectral DOEs are a generalization of the color separation gratings and are intended for focusing different spectral components onto different focal domains.

In the author's opinion, this chapter adequately covers topics of geometric DOEs ranging from the design methods and detailed studies of operation characteristics to the design of new DOE classes with desired multifocus and spectral properties. Sections 5.2 and 5.4 are devoted to the theoretical basics of the methods for designing a DOE focusing onto a curve and onto a two-dimensional (2D) domain. Sections 5.3 and 5.4 deal with the studies of some most important focusing problems, which allow one to gain an insight into the DOE operation and the possibilities of their application in particular technological problems. The diffraction methods for designing multifocus and spectral DOEs that enhance the functional capabilities of the geometric optical DOE are covered in Sections 5.4 to 5.7.

5.2 GEOMETRIC OPTICAL CALCULATION OF DOEs FOCUSING ONTO A LINE

Assume that we need to compute the phase function of a DOE that focuses the plane light beam of intensity $I_o(\mathbf{u})$, where $\mathbf{u} = (u, v)$ are the Cartesian coordinates in the

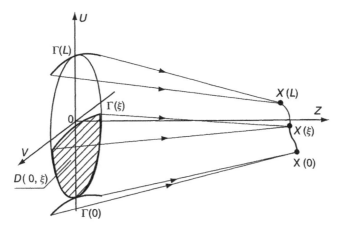

Figure 5.1. Geometry of focusing onto a spatial curve.

DOE plane ($z = 0$), onto a curve S specified by the parametric equation

$$\mathbf{X}(\xi) = [X(\xi), Y(\xi), Z(\xi)], \quad \xi \in [0, L]. \tag{5.1}$$

where ξ is a natural parameter (Fig. 5.1).

When designing a DOE, we seek for the ray correspondence $\xi = \xi(\mathbf{u})$ between points on the focal curve and those on the DOE aperture and then reconstruct the DOE phase function from the inclination equation

$$\frac{\partial \varphi(\mathbf{u})}{\partial u} = \frac{k\{X[\xi(\mathbf{u})] - u\}}{\sqrt{\{u - X[\xi(\mathbf{u})]\}^2 + \{v - Y[\xi(\mathbf{u})]\}^2 + Z^2[\xi(\mathbf{u})]}} \tag{5.2}$$

$$\frac{\partial \varphi(\mathbf{u})}{\partial v} = \frac{k(Y(\xi(\mathbf{u})) - v)}{\sqrt{\{u - X[\xi(\mathbf{u})]\}^2 + \{v - Y[\xi(\mathbf{u})]\}^2 + Z^2[\xi(\mathbf{u})]}}$$

Because the DOE is two-dimensional and the focal curve is one-dimensional (1D), on the DOE aperture there is an 1D set $\Gamma(\xi)$ of points (u, v) directing the light into the same point $\mathbf{X}(\xi)$ of the curve (Fig. 5.1). Following the terminology adopted, the aforementioned set will be referred to as the layer. The structure of the ray correspondence $\xi(\mathbf{u})$ and the form of the layers is determined by the following fundamental property: all the rays coming to a given point on the curve of focusing are found on the surface of the circular cone whose axis is tangent to the curve of focusing at that point. In this case, the set of layers on the DOE's aperture defining the ray correspondence $\xi(\mathbf{u})$ will correspond to a family of the quadric curves being the cross sections of the conic surfaces by the plane $z = 0$. For the rigorous proof of the foregoing statements the reader may refer to Ref. [12]. Solving a simpler problem of computing the phase function of a DOE that generates an array of N spots located on the spatial curve of Eq. (5.1) provides a simple and illustrative interpretation of the aforementioned property. Suppose that the coordinates (x_i, y_i, z_i) of focusing points on the curve in Eq. (5.1) correspond to the increasing values $\xi_i, i = 0, \ldots, N$ of the parameter ξ. To derive the phase function $\varphi(\mathbf{u})$ of a DOE focusing into N spots, its aperture D is divided into N domains (segments) D_i. The phase function $\varphi_i(\mathbf{u})$ within the limits of the segment D_i will be determined from the condition of focusing into the point (x_i, y_i, z_i) of the curve. Then, at $\mathbf{u} \in D_i$ the phase function of the DOE is the phase function of a lens with focus at point (x_i, y_i, z_i):

$$\varphi_i(u, v) = -k\sqrt{(u - x_i)^2 + (v - y_i)^2 + z_i^2}. \tag{5.3}$$

In the paraxial approximation,

$$\frac{(x_i - u)^2 + (y_i - v)^2}{z_i^2} \ll 1, \quad (u, v) \in D, \quad i = \overline{1, N},$$

Equation (5.3) changes to the familiar formula for the phase function of a spherical lens

$$\varphi_i(u, v) = -k\frac{(u - x_i)^2 + (v - y_i)^2}{2z_i}. \tag{5.4}$$

From physical considerations, the phase function of the segmented DOE should be continuous. To derive the continuous phase function, the boundaries of segments of the DOE aperture should be chosen in such a manner that when passing the boundary at any point the function is changed by the same constant. Thus, the boundary between the domains D_i and D_{i+1} should be sought for from the condition

$$\varphi_i(u, v) - \varphi_{i+1}(u, v) = C(\xi_i),$$

or in more detail

$$k\sqrt{(u - x_{i+1})^2 + (v - y_{i+1})^2 + z_{i+1}^2} - k\sqrt{(u - x_i)^2 + (v - y_i)^2 + z_i^2} = C(\xi_i). \tag{5.5}$$

It can be easily seen that Eq. (5.5) is the equation of a certain curve being a cross section of the two-sheeted hyperboloid of rotation

$$\sqrt{(x - x_{i+1})^2 + (y - y_{i+1})^2 + (z - z_{i+1})^2} - \sqrt{(x - x_i)^2 + (y - y_i)^2 + (z - z_i)^2}$$
$$= \frac{C(\xi_i)}{k} \tag{5.6}$$

by the plane of the optical element. The foci of this hyperboloid are found at points (x_i, y_i, z_i) and $(x_{i+1}, y_{i+1}, z_{i+1})$, whereas the axis of symmetry coincides with a line-segment connecting the points of focusing with indices i and $i + 1$. It is noteworthy that the constant

$$\Delta\Psi(\xi_i) = \frac{C(\xi_i)}{k} \tag{5.7}$$

in the right-hand side of Eq. (5.6) corresponds to the eikonal increment in passing from point (x_i, y_i, z_i) to point $(x_{i+1}, y_{i+1}, z_{i+1})$.

With the indicated technique of choosing the segment boundaries, the continuous phase function of a DOE focusing into N spots appears as a sum of the phase function

$\varphi_{i+1}(\mathbf{u})$ and a constant

$$\tilde{\varphi}_i = \sum_{n=0}^{n=i} C(\xi_n). \tag{5.8}$$

It can be shown that the aforementioned method for computing an optical element with the continuous phase function is unique and that other segmentation techniques produce a discontinuous phase function.

In the limit, as the number of spots of focusing tends to infinity so that the distance between the neighboring spots tends to zero, we obtain a DOE that generates a continuous curve S. In this case, the two-sheeted hyperboloid of rotation, Eq. (5.6), tends to a conic surface. Actually, replacing the difference in the right-hand side of Eq. (5.6) by the first term of the Taylor series gives the following equation of the cone

$$\frac{(x_{i+1} - x_i)(x - x_i) + (y_{i+1} - y_i)(y - y_i) + (z_{i+1} - z_i)(z - z_i)}{\sqrt{(x - x_i)^2 + (y - y_i)^2 + (z - z_i)^2}} = \Delta \Psi(\xi_i). \tag{5.9}$$

The axis of this cone coincides with a line-segment connecting two neighboring points of the focal curve and, in the limit, coincides with the direction of tangent to the focal curve at this point.

Substituting

$$(x_{i+1} - x_i) = \frac{dX(\xi_i)}{d\xi} \Delta \xi, \quad (y_{i+1} - y_i) = \frac{dY(\xi_i)}{d\xi} \Delta \xi, \quad (z_{i+1} - z_i) = \frac{dZ(\xi_i)}{d\xi} \Delta \xi,$$

Equation (5.9) will be given by:

$$\frac{\dfrac{dX(\xi_i)}{d\xi}[u - X(\xi_i)] + \dfrac{dY(\xi_i)}{d\xi}[v - Y(\xi_i)] + \dfrac{dZ(\xi_i)}{d\xi}[z - Z(\xi_i)]}{\sqrt{[u - X(\xi_i)]^2 + [v - Y(\xi_i)]^2 + [z - Z(\xi_i)]^2}} = c(\xi_i), \tag{5.10}$$

where $c(\xi_i) = \dfrac{\Delta \Psi(\xi_i)}{\Delta \xi}$ is the cone angle.

In this case, the area of the ith domain on the DOE aperture tends to zero and the domain itself is contracted to a layer, that is, to the quadric curve being the cross section of the cone of Eq. (5.10) by the optical element plane. Assuming $z = 0$ in Eq. (5.10), the layer equation takes the form

$$\frac{\dfrac{dX(\xi_i)}{d\xi}[u - X(\xi_i)] + \dfrac{dY(\xi_i)}{d\xi}[v - Y(\xi_i)] - \dfrac{dZ(\xi_i)}{d\xi}Z(\xi_i)}{\sqrt{[u - X(\xi_i)]^2 + [v - Y(\xi_i)]^2 + Z(\xi_i)^2}} = c(\xi_i). \tag{5.11}$$

Obtained by passage to the limit, the cone equation, Eq. (5.10), and the layer equation, Eq. (5.11), serve to prove the previously mentioned fact that all the rays coming to a given point of focusing are found on the surface of the circular cone whose axis is tangent to the curve of focusing on this point, with the cone angle being equal to the eikonal derivative along the curve. In the following text, we shall make use of the continuous analog of Eq. (5.11):

$$\frac{\dfrac{dX(\xi)}{d\xi}[u - X(\xi)] + \dfrac{dY(\xi)}{d\xi}[v - Y(\xi)] - \dfrac{dZ(\xi)}{d\xi}Z(\xi)}{\sqrt{[u - X(\xi)]^2 + [v - Y(\xi)]^2 + Z(\xi)^2}} = c(\xi) = \frac{d\Psi(\xi)}{d\xi}. \qquad (5.12)$$

The cone angle $c(\xi)$ in Eq. (5.12) determines the energy distribution $I(\xi)$, $\xi \in [0, L]$ along the curve of focusing. Following the adopted terminology, this function will be referred to as *linear density*. This name is related to the definition of the linear density as the integral quantity corresponding to the energy flux per unit length of the focal curve. The desired linear density distribution $I(\xi)$ may be obtained by the proper choice of the eikonal distribution $\Psi(\xi)$ on the curve. Actually, to generate a desired linear density $I(\xi)$ we shall derive the $c(\xi) = d\Psi(\xi)/d\xi$ function in Eq. (5.12) from the integral form of the law of energy conservation. To do this would require equaling the light flux coming to the DOE's aperture fragment $D(0, \xi)$ confined between the initial and the current layers $\Gamma(0)$ and $\Gamma(\xi)$ and the light flux passing through the focal curve fragment confined between the points $X(0)$ and $X(\xi)$ (Fig. 5.1):

$$\int_0^{\xi} I(t)\, dt = E[\xi, c(\xi)] = \int_{D(0,\xi)} I_0(\mathbf{u})\, d^2\mathbf{u}. \qquad (5.13)$$

Equations (5.12) and (5.13) make possible the formulation of the following technique for computation of the phase function of a DOE focusing onto a curve of pregiven linear density:

1. Derivation of the $c(\xi)$ function of Eq. (5.13) from the required linear density,
2. Derivation of the function of ray correspondence $\xi(\mathbf{u})$ from Eq. (5.12),
3. Reconstruction of the DOE phase function from the inclination equation, Eq. (5.2), using the potential theory methods

$$\varphi(\mathbf{u}) = \varphi(\mathbf{u}_0) + \int_{\mathbf{u}_0}^{\mathbf{u}} \nabla_{\perp}\varphi(\mathbf{u})\, d^2\mathbf{u}, \qquad (5.14)$$

where integration is along an arbitrary curve connecting the point $\mathbf{u}$ with some initial point $\mathbf{u}_0$ and

$$\nabla_{\perp} = \left(\frac{\partial}{\partial u}, \frac{\partial}{\partial v} \right).$$

A practically important case is focusing onto a plane curve $\mathbf{X}(\xi) = [X(\xi), Y(\xi), f]$ located in the plane $z = f$, in which case the layer of Eq. (5.11) is a hyperbola [9,10,12,13]

$$\frac{\dfrac{dX(\xi)}{d\xi}[u - X(\xi)] + \dfrac{dY(\xi)}{d\xi}[v - Y(\xi)]}{\sqrt{[u - X(\xi)]^2 + [v - Y(\xi)]^2 + f^2}} = c(\xi), \qquad (5.15)$$

The axis of symmetry for the hyperbola coincides with the projection of the cone axis onto the DOE's plane.

In the paraxial approximation

$$\sqrt{[u - X(\xi)]^2 + [v - Y(\xi)]^2 + f^2} \approx f,$$

the layers of Eq. (5.15) are degenerated into the straight lines perpendicular to the focal curve tangents

$$\frac{dX(\xi)}{d\xi}u + \frac{dY(\xi)}{d\xi}v = p(\xi), \tag{5.16}$$

where the function $p(\xi) = c(\xi)f + (dX(\xi)/d\xi)X(\xi) + (dY(\xi)/d\xi)X(\xi)$ denotes the distance from the layer to the origin of coordinates in the DOE's plane.

In the paraxial approximation, the DOE's phase function takes the form

$$\varphi(\mathbf{u}) = -\frac{k\mathbf{u}^2}{2f} + \varphi_D(\mathbf{u}), \tag{5.17}$$

where

$$\varphi_D(\mathbf{u}) = \frac{k}{f}\int_{u_0}^u X[\xi(u, v_0)]\, du + \frac{k}{f}\int_{v_0}^v Y[\xi(u, v)]\, dv. \tag{5.18}$$

As an illustration, let us consider the most practically important case of focusing onto a straight-line segment in the plane $\mathbf{X}(\xi) = (-d + \xi, 0, f)$, $\xi \in [0, 2d]$ with linear density $I(\xi)$, $\xi \in [0, 2d]$. When focusing onto a straight-line segment, the layers become the segments of the straight lines $u = p(\xi)$ perpendicular to the segment under focusing. Suppose that the DOE's D aperture is limited by the curves $v = g_1(u)$ and $v = g_2(u)$, and by the straight-line segments $u = a$ and $u = b$. Then, supposing in the law of light flux conservation, Eq. (5.13), $u = p(\xi)$, the ray correspondence function $\xi = \xi(u)$ is derived from the following relationship

$$\int_a^u \int_{g_1(u)}^{g_2(u)} I_0(\gamma, \chi)\, d\chi\, d\gamma = \int_0^\xi I(\chi)\, d\chi. \tag{5.19}$$

In the authors' opinion, the function $x(u) = \xi(u) - d$ specifying the point's position on the segment of focusing is more convenient to use, and the law of light flux energy conservation is most conveniently represented in the differential form:

$$\frac{dx(u)}{du} = \frac{1}{I[x(u)]}\int_{g_1(u)}^{g_2(u)} I_0(u, v)\, dv, \quad x(a) = -d, \quad x(b) = d. \tag{5.20}$$

In this case, the phase function of a DOE focusing onto a line-segment takes the form

$$\varphi(\mathbf{u}) = -\frac{k\mathbf{u}^2}{2f} + \frac{k}{f}\int_0^u x(\gamma)\, d\gamma. \tag{5.21}$$

One should note that even in the paraxial approximation it is possible to design only the DOE that would focus onto simple lines such as a line-segment, a ring, a semi-ring, and the like. It is a challenge to compute the phase of a DOE focusing onto more complex curves. Actually, in the general case, items 1 and 2 of the afore-mentioned method are the complicated computational tasks involving the solution of nonlinear equations. Item 2 requires solving the nonlinear Eq. (5.12) for every point **u** of the DOE's aperture. The realization of item 1 also involves a 2D numerical integration.

The geometric DOE design is essentially simplified with the use of the following curvilinear coordinates

$$\begin{cases} u(\xi,t) = p(\xi)\dfrac{dX(\xi)}{d\xi} - t \cdot \dfrac{dY(\xi)}{d\xi} \\ v(\xi,t) = p(\xi)\dfrac{dY(\xi)}{d\xi} + t \cdot \dfrac{dX(\xi)}{d\xi} \end{cases}. \tag{5.22}$$

The coordinate system in Eq. (5.22) is related to the DOE layers and expresses the coordinates (u, v) through the coordinate ξ defining a layer $\Gamma(\xi)$ comprising the given point and a coordinate t defining the point's position on the layer. Note that the coordinate t is the distance from the point $[u(0, t), v(0, t)]$, where the layer intersects its normal to the current point on the layer. Further, we shall confine our discussion to a practically important case of focusing the radial beams onto a curve:

$$I_0(\mathbf{u}) = I_0(u^2 + v^2), \ |\mathbf{u}| \le R, \tag{5.23}$$

where R is the DOE's aperture radius.

For radially symmetric beams, the law of light flux conservation in Eq. (5.13) may be written in the coordinates (ξ, t) in a compact differential form

$$dp(\xi) \int_{-\sqrt{R^2 - p^2(\xi)}}^{\sqrt{R^2 - p^2(\xi)}} I_0[p^2(\xi) + t^2] dt = I(\xi) d\xi. \tag{5.24}$$

Since the integral in Eq. (5.24) turns to zero at $p(0)$, $p(L) = \pm R$, Eq. (5.24) should be resolved relative to the function $\xi(p)$. According to Eq. (5.24), the function $\xi(p)$ can be derived by solving a first-order differential equation using a standard Ruhnge-Kutt method. Then, the $p(\xi)$ function is found using the inversion of a smooth one-valued function $\xi(p)$.

The special convenience of the coordinates (ξ, t) is that they make it possible to omit the computation of the function $\xi(\mathbf{u})$ by solving the nonlinear equation for every point **u** of the DOE's aperture and instead directly compute the DOE phase. Actually, from Eqs. (5.17) and (5.22) one can easily obtain the partial derivatives of the function $\varphi_D(\mathbf{u})$ in Eq. (5.17) with respect to (ξ, t) in the form

$$\begin{aligned} \frac{\partial \varphi_D(\xi, t)}{\partial \xi} = {} & \frac{k}{f} X(\xi) \cdot \left[\frac{dp(\xi)}{d\xi}\frac{dX(\xi)}{d\xi} + p(\xi) \right. \\ & \times \frac{d^2 X(\xi)}{d\xi^2} - t\frac{d^2 Y(\xi)}{d\xi^2} \Bigg] + \frac{k}{f} Y(\xi) \\ & \times \left[\frac{dp(\xi)}{d\xi}\frac{dY(\xi)}{d\xi} + p(\xi)\frac{d^2 Y(\xi)}{d\xi^2} + t\frac{d^2 X(\xi)}{d\xi^2} \right], \end{aligned} \tag{5.25}$$

$$\frac{\partial \varphi_D(\xi, t)}{\partial t} = \frac{k}{f} \left[\frac{dX(\xi)}{d\xi} Y(\xi) - X(\xi) \frac{dY(\xi)}{d\xi} \right]. \tag{5.26}$$

Equations (5.25) and (5.26) allow one to represent the DOE phase function in the variables (ξ, t) as

$$\varphi(\xi, t) = -\frac{k}{2f} [p^2(\xi) + t^2] + \varphi_D(\xi, t), \tag{5.27}$$

where

$$\varphi_D(\xi, t) = \frac{k}{f} \left[\frac{dX(\xi)}{d\xi} Y(\xi) - X(\xi) \frac{dY(\xi)}{d\xi} \right] \cdot t$$

$$+ \frac{k}{f} \left[\frac{dX(\xi)}{d\xi} X(\xi) + \frac{dY(\xi)}{d\xi} Y(\xi) \right] p(\xi) - \frac{k}{f} \int_0^\xi p(\eta) \, d\eta. \tag{5.28}$$

Equations (5.24) and (5.27) suggest that the DOE phase in the variables (ξ, t) can be computed by solving a first-order differential equation, the inversion of the solution derived, and a 1D integration of the function $p(\xi)$. It should be noted that the considered curvilinear coordinates of Eq. (5.22) are easily generalized onto a nonparaxial case. It stands to reason that the only distinction of the nonparaxial case is that the nonparaxial layers are hyperbolas, Eq. (5.15), rather than straight-line segments, Eq. (5.16). Therefore, in the nonparaxial case, the coordinates (u, v) should be specified by the coordinate ξ defining the hyperbola $\Gamma(\xi)$ that contains the given point and a coordinate t that determines the position of the point on the hyperbola with respect to its apex. In particular, when focusing onto a line-segment $X(\xi) = (-d + \xi, 0, f)$, $\xi \in [0, 2d]$ of linear density $I(\xi)$, the coordinates take the simplest form in the nonparaxial case:

$$\begin{cases} u(\xi, t) = \xi - d + \beta(\xi) \cdot \sqrt{f^2 + t^2} \\ v(\xi, t) = t \end{cases}, \tag{5.29}$$

where the function

$$\beta(\xi) = c(\xi) / \sqrt{1 - c^2(\xi)}$$

corresponds to the cotangent of the apex angle of the conic surface containing the rays coming to a given point on the line-segment.

Expressing the paraxial phase function in Eq. (5.27) of a DOE focusing onto a curve S specified by $\mathbf{X}(\xi) = (X(\xi), Y(\xi), f)$ in terms of the coordinates (ξ, t) Eq. (5.22) allows the following interesting property to be established: if in Eq. (5.27) the added function $\varphi_D(\xi, t)$ of Eq. (5.28) is multiplied by a constant p, the resulting phase function will produce a p-times-increased curve S_p defined by the equation

$$X_p(\xi_p) = [pX(\xi_p/p), pY(\xi_p/p), f], \quad \xi_p \in [0, pL]. \tag{5.31}$$

The linear energy density

$$I_p(\xi_p) = \frac{1}{p} I(\xi_p/p), \quad \xi_p \in [0, pL], \tag{5.32}$$

along the line S_p coincides with the $I(\xi)$ function for the line S up to a scale. The afore-mentioned property will be widely used in further discussion and can easily be checked by directly substituting the curve equation in Eq. (5.31) into the general equations for the phase function, Eqs. (5.27) and (5.28).

Fabrication of a DOE's photomask by a lithographer or a laser plotter implies the use of the Cartesian or polar coordinates. According to Eq. (5.27), for the fixed ξ, the phase function along the layer corresponds to a superposition of the phase functions of a lens and a prism, thus allowing one to interpret the DOE as a set of cylindrical lenses and prisms oriented along the layers $\Gamma(\xi)$. In this case, for the points $\mathbf{u} \in \Gamma(\xi)$, the phase function takes the form

$$\varphi(\mathbf{u}) = -\frac{k\mathbf{u}^2}{2f} + \frac{k}{f}[uX(\xi) + vY(\xi)] + c(\xi), \qquad (5.33)$$

where $c(\xi) = -\dfrac{k}{f}\displaystyle\int_0^\xi p(\eta)\,d\eta.$

According to Eq. (5.33), when deducing the phase function in Eq. (5.17), it will suffice to construct in the Cartesian coordinates (u, v) a set of N layers in Eq. (5.16) with respect to the function $p(\xi)$. The layer set $\Gamma(\xi_n)$ $n = 1, N$ determines the breakdown of the DOE's aperture into N segments D_i. Then, to determine the DOE's phase at point $\mathbf{u}$ it will suffice to find the segment D_i comprising the given point and make use of Eq. (5.33). Note that we seek the segment D_i comprising the given point $\mathbf{u}$ through the trivial determination of the point position relative to straight lines.

The analysis of the DOE's phase structure along the layers makes possible the following simple algorithm for the derivation of the DOE's phase function:

1. Derivation of the function $p(\xi)$ from Eq. (5.24)
2. Change to the Cartesian (or polar) coordinate system with the introduction of a discrete set of layers and the subsequent computation of the phase in the layers using Eq. (5.33).

By way of example, let us design a DOE focusing a plane circular beam of radius R onto a circumference arc of uniform linear density. The parametric equation of a circumference arc is given by

$$\begin{cases} X(\xi) = R_1 \cos[(\xi - R_1\alpha/2)/R_1] \\ Y(\xi) = R_1 \sin[(\xi - R_1\alpha/2)/R_1] \end{cases}, \quad \xi \in [0, R_1\alpha], \qquad (5.34)$$

where R_1 is the arc radius and α is the arc angular measure.

From the law of light flux conservation, Eq. (5.24), the $\xi(p)$ function is given by:

$$\xi(p) = \frac{R_1\alpha}{\pi}\left(\arcsin\left(\frac{p}{R}\right) + \frac{p}{R}\sqrt{1 - \left(\frac{p}{R}\right)^2}\right). \qquad (5.35)$$

Substituting Eq. (5.34) in (5.22) and (5.27) gives the phase function of the DOE focusing onto a curve

$$\varphi(\xi, t) = -\frac{k}{2f}(p^2(\xi) + t^2) - \frac{k}{f}\left(t \cdot R_1 + \int_0^\xi p(\eta)\, d\eta\right). \qquad (5.36)$$

The simple form of the derived phase in Eq. (5.36) testifies in favor of the curvilinear system in Eq. (5.22). The derivation of the phase in Eq. (5.36) involves only two simple numerical operations: inversion of the function in Eq. (5.35) and its 1D integration.

Shown in Figure 5.2a is a halftone image of the phase function of a DOE focusing onto a circumference arc, designed as an addition to a lens for the following parameters: $\lambda = 0.63$ μm, $f = 500$ mm, $R = 5$ mm, $R_1 = 1.25$ mm, $\alpha = \pi/2$. To compute the phase of Eq. (5.36) in the Cartesian coordinates, we constructed a set of 200 layers using the $p(\xi)$ function deduced from Eq. (5.35). The halftone intensity distribution generated by the DOE shown in Figure 5.2a is depicted in Figure 5.2b and demonstrates high robustness of the method proposed.

5.3 DESIGN AND STUDIES OF GEOMETRIC DOE

In this section, we study some most important standard problems of focusing. The discussed results of the DOE design and studies allow one to evaluate the applicability of geometric optical methods to the DOE design, to establish the connection between the physical and diffraction characteristics of focusing DOE, and evaluate the effects of technological errors (phase function sampling and quantization) on the DOE's operational ability. The results derived from the analysis of different approaches to solving a number of inverse standard problems of focusing are critical in terms of DOE potential applications, particularly, in technological units.

Through this section, all the results relating to the diffraction studies of DOE have been obtained by the numerical computation of the Fresnel-Kirhhoff integral. To find out how the errors of phase sampling and quantization affect the DOE's operational ability, the Fresnel-Kirhhoff integral was computed using the specially derived quadrature formulae [20,24] based on

1. the breakdown of the DOE's aperture onto rectangular (or ringlike, in the case of radial symmetry) modules (cells);

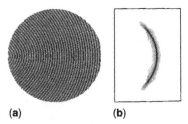

(a)   **(b)**

Figure 5.2. (a) Phase function of a DOE for focusing onto a circumference arc; and (b) intensity distribution in the plane of focusing.

2. the use within each module boundaries of a piecewise-constant approximation for the DOE's complex transmission function (CTF);

3. the use of basic analytical solutions for the problems of diffraction by rectangular and ringlike modules [20,24].

Note that for the DOE's CTF, the piecewise-constant approximation corresponds to the process of the phase realization by a photo-plotter with rectangular or circular raster, whereas the use of basic analytical solutions of the problem of diffraction by the rectangular and circular modules ensures high accuracy of the diffraction computation.

5.3.1 Diffraction Lens

The diffraction lens is the most important and popular diffractive element. The results of studying the diffraction lens, considered in this subsection are of great significance for evaluating the operation of DOE focusing onto a line. This is due to the fact that in Section 5.2 the DOE focusing onto a curve is interpreted as a set of lenses oriented along the layers.

The method and the computed three-dimensional (3D) distribution of light near the focus of a conventional refractive lens may be found in the classical work by Born and Wolf, *Principles of Optics* [34]. More accurate methods and results have been derived in a number of later works [35–41] and have made it possible to reveal the asymmetry in the intensity distribution with respect to the focal plane and evaluate the magnitude of the intensity maximum focal shift. Similar results have been obtained for focusing the Gaussian beams [42–47] and for cylindrical lenses [48,49]. The papers dealing with zone plates and planar diffraction lenses [21,23,50–58] are devoted to the analysis of focusing onto a spot. In particular, intensity distributions in the focal plane of a diffraction lens for different numbers of phase quantization levels have been obtained in Ref. [55]. In Refs. [21,57,58] one finds numerical simulations for the intensity distributions along the optical axis of the diffraction lens for various numbers of phase quantization levels. Plots for the light intensity distribution in the focal plane and in the optical axis vicinity have been obtained in Refs. [57,58], whereas it is the full investigation of the focused light structure in the entire focal domain which is of main interest [23].

In the paraxial approximation, the lens phase function is given by

$$\varphi(r) = -\frac{kr^2}{2f}, \quad r \leq a, \tag{5.37}$$

where f is the focal length, and $k = 2\pi/\lambda$, λ being the illuminating beam wavelength.

Figure 5.3 gives the stages of fabrication of a planar lens. The phase function shape of the conventional lens of Eq. (5.37) is depicted in Figure 5.3a. The phase function of an ideal planar lens, that is, the modulo 2π function in Eq. (5.37), is shown in Figure 5.3b. Figure 5.3c shows a real steplike relief of the planar lens, produced by a multistep DOE fabrication technology. The profile of the modulo 2π phase function may be approximated by a steplike profile composed either of equal-width steps (uniform sampling) or of equal-depth steps, the latter being the case in Figure 5.3c and referred to as nonuniform sampling. The nonuniform sampling is determined by

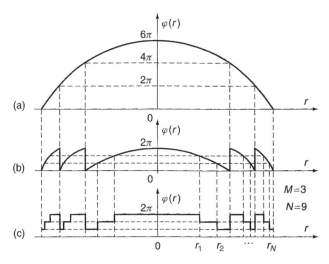

Figure 5.3. Stages of planar lens fabrication.

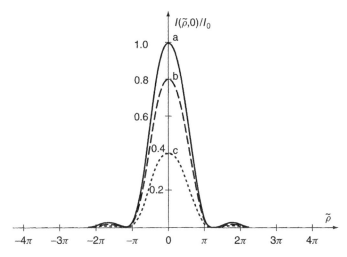

Figure 5.4. Normalized intensity in the focal plane of the planar lens with nonuniform sampling for various numbers M of quantization levels: (a) $M = 16$, (b) $M = 4$, and (c) $M = 2$.

the number M of phase quantization levels chosen. For the lens shown in Figure 5.3c and having three-phase quantization levels and three Fresnel zones present on the lens aperture ($r \leqslant a$) one obtains $N = 9$ circular modules. The outer radii of the circular zones for M phase quantization levels are given by

$$r_n = \sqrt{\frac{2nf \cdot \lambda}{M}}, \quad n = \overline{1, N}, \tag{5.38}$$

where

$$N = \left[\frac{Ma^2}{2\lambda f}\right] + 1,$$

[...] denotes the operation of taking the whole part. With uniform sampling, the phase function quantization within the circular module does not depend on the number of the sampling elements.

Figure 5.4 depicts the field intensity distributions $I(\tilde{\rho}, 0)/I_0$ in the focal plane of a focal lens with the sampling of Eq. (5.38) for 2, 4, and 16 phase quantization levels. Shown in Figure 5.5 are the similar distributions $I(0, \tilde{z})/I_0$ along the optical axis for large Fresnel numbers when one may neglect both the distribution asymmetry with respect to the optical axis and the focal shift value. Here, I_0 is the intensity in the focus of an aberration-free lens [34]:

$$I_0 = \left(k \frac{a^2}{2f} A \right)^2 , \tag{5.39}$$

where A is the plane illumination beam amplitude;

$$\begin{cases} \tilde{p} = k \left(\dfrac{a}{f} \right) \rho \\[2mm] \tilde{z} = k \left(\dfrac{a}{f} \right)^2 z \end{cases} , \tag{5.40}$$

are unitless coordinates in the focal plane of the planar lens, centered at the lens focus.

Figure 5.6 depicts isophotes [equal intensity lines $I(\tilde{\rho}, \tilde{z})/I_0$] in the meridian section of the focal domain of a planar lens with the large Fresnel number $F = a^2/(\lambda f) \gg 1$ for two- and four-phase quantization levels M. The isophotes in Figure 5.6 add to the results of the papers [55,56] in which only the intensity distributions equivalent to those shown in Figures 5.4 and 5.5 have been obtained.

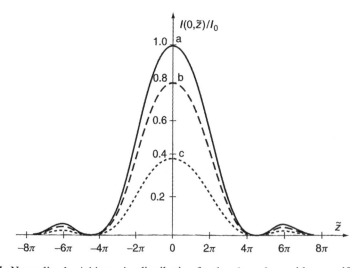

Figure 5.5. Normalized axial intensity distribution for the planar lens with nonuniform sampling for various numbers M of quantization levels: (a) $M = 16$, (b) $M = 4$, and (c) $M = 2$ for large Fresnel numbers.

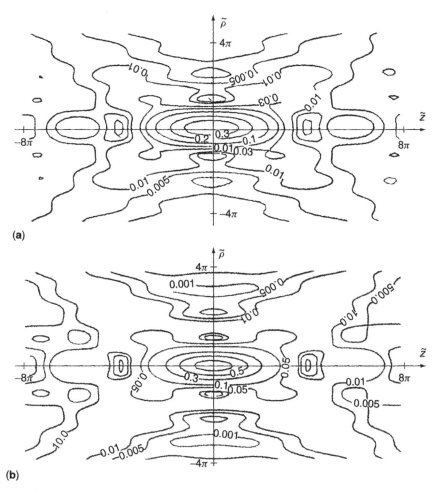

(a)

(b)

Figure 5.6. Isophotes of the normalized intensity distribution $I(\tilde{\rho}, \tilde{z})/I_0$ in the focal plane of the planar lens with nonuniform sampling: (**a**) for two phase quantization levels and (**b**) for four phase quantization levels.

Analysis of Figures 5.4–5.6 lends support to the deduction made in Ref. [59] that the wave front shape generated in the useful +1st diffraction order of a quantized lens is practically independent of the lens energy efficiency, that is, of the portion of illuminating beam energy diffracted in focus.

It would be interesting to study the axial intensity distribution for a planar lens with a small Fresnel number F. Shown in Figures 5.7 and 5.8 are normalized axial intensity distributions $i = I(0, \tilde{z})/I_0$ for a diffraction lens with the number of phase quantization levels $M = 2, 4, 16$. The plots in Figures 5.7 and 5.8 are derived for the uniform and Gaussian ($W_0(r) = \exp(-r^2/\sigma^2)$) beams for the following parameters: the radius is $a = 1$ mm, the wavelength is $\lambda = 10.6$ μm, the Fresnel number is $F = a^2/(\lambda f) = 4$, nonuniform sampling, and the Gaussian beam parameter is $\sigma = 0, 8$ mm. The intensities in Figures 5.7 and 5.8 were normalized to the intensity in the focus of a refractive lens.

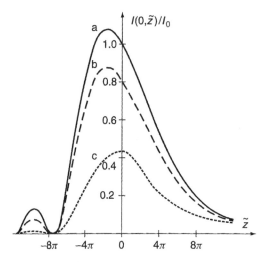

Figure 5.7. Normalized axial intensity distribution in the focal plane of the diffraction lens with the Fresnel number $F = 4$ for a uniform illuminating beam and various numbers of quantization levels M: (a) $M = 16$, (b) $M = 4$ and (c) $M = 2$.

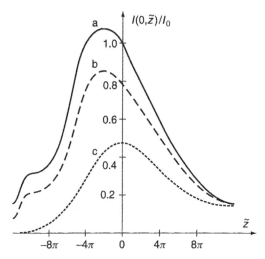

Figure 5.8. Normalized axial intensity distribution in the focal plane of the diffraction lens with the Fresnel number $F = 4$ for the Gaussian illuminating beam and various numbers of quantization levels M: (a) $M = 16$, (b) $M = 4$, and (c) $M = 2$.

The plots shown in Figure 5.7 correlate with Refs. [57,58], thus allowing the conclusion that the use of the aforementioned technique for computing the Fresnel-Kirhhoff integral for the radial case is justified. Figure 5.8 shows that for the Gaussian beam with the waist radius less than the lens radius the focal spot is blurred along the optical axis. As the number of quantization levels increases, the distribution asymptotically tends to the intensity distribution in the focal plane of a refractive lens illuminated by the Gaussian beam [42–47]. As the waist radius increases ($\sigma > a$), the focal intensity distribution tends to the intensity distribution for the uniform illuminating beam. With decreasing waist radius ($\sigma < a$), the focal shift and the asymmetry of intensity distribution with respect to the focal plane, peculiar to the decreasing Fresnel number, are increased.

The efficiency of a planar lens may be characterized by the ratio $I(0, 0)/I_0$ of the intensity in the focus of the planar lens to that in the focus of an ideal lens with the same parameters. The calculated values for the efficiency of a planar lens with nonuniform sampling are given in Table 5.1 and coincide with analogous data obtained through Fourier analysis [59].

The Refs. [55–59] do not provide data about what the behaviour of diffraction efficiency and light distribution in the planar lens focal plane will be when the sampling is different from the optimal nonuniform sampling. Here, the main difficulty is due to the fact that the planar lens efficiency and the generated light structure will be determined not only by the number of quantization levels but also by physical and quantization parameters. Table 5.2 gives the efficiency of a planar lens with uniform sampling versus the number of quantization levels M and the number of circular elements N of sampling for the following parameters: $f = 100$ mm, the lens diameter is $2a = 6.04$ mm; $\lambda = 0.633$ μm, and the Fresnel number is $F = a^2/(\lambda f) = 144$. The number of samplings for a planar lens with nonuniform sampling is $N = [MF/2] + 1$, with the circular module width δ decreasing to the lens edges and reaching the edge value δ_{min} given in Table 5.2. According to Eq. (5.38), the value of δ_{min} is found from

$$\delta_{min} = r_N - r_{N-1} = \sqrt{\frac{2Nf\lambda}{M}} - \sqrt{\frac{2(N-1)\lambda f}{M}} = \sqrt{\frac{2\lambda f}{M}}(\sqrt{N} - \sqrt{N-1}). \quad (5.41)$$

TABLE 5.1. Efficiency of a Planar Lens with Nonuniform Sampling, the Number of Quantization Levels Being M

M	2	4	5	8	16	32
$I(0, 0)/I_0(0, 0)$	0,405	0,811	0,875	0,9495	0,9871	0,9966

TABLE 5.2. Efficiency $I(0, 0)/I_0$ of a Planar Lens with Uniform Radius Sampling at N Points and M Quantization Levels. The Lens Parameters: $f = 100$ mm; $a = 3.02$ mm; $\lambda = 0.633$ μm

M N	∞	16	4	2	$\delta = a/N$ (μm)
128	0,094	0,093	0,076	0,038	23,6
256	0,585	0,577	0,476	0,263	11,8
512	0,877	0,866	0,711	0,356	5,9
1024	0,968	0,955	0,786	0,392	2,95
2048	0,992	0,979	0,804	0,402	1,47
δ_{min} (μm)	—	1,31	5,25	10,5	—

Comparative analysis of the data given in Tables 5.1 and 5.2 testifies in favor of high efficiency of nonuniform sampling. In order that the uniform sampling yield the efficiency identical with that of nonuniform sampling with M_0 quantization levels, the step δ of the uniform sampling should be approximately equal to $\delta_{min}(M_0)$, with δ_{min} determined from Eq. (5.41) and the number of quantization levels M within the module greater than M_0.

5.3.2 Diffraction Cylindrical Lens

The diffraction cylindrical lens is studied in the Fraunhofer approximation in Ref. [60], where the visibility of the computed Fraunhofer pattern is used to form the judgment on the diffraction cylindrical lens characteristics. However, it would be interesting not only to study the far-field visibility but also to analyze the focused light structure in the focal plane of a planar cylindrical lens.

In the paraxial approximation, the phase function of a cylindrical lens is given by

$$\varphi(u) = -\frac{ku^2}{2f}, \quad |u| \leq a, \tag{5.42}$$

where k is the wave number, f is the focal length, and $2a$ is the lens size.

The coordinates of linear zone boundaries with M phase quantization levels take the form

$$u_n = \pm\sqrt{2n\lambda f/M}, \tag{5.43}$$

with the total number of linear modules being equal to

$$N = \lceil Ma^2/\lambda f \rceil. \tag{5.44}$$

Shown in Figure 5.9 are normalized intensity distributions $I_M(\tilde{x}, 0)/I_0$ in the focal plane of a diffraction cylindrical lens with nonuniform sampling of Eq. (5.43) for $M = 2, 4, 16$ phase levels. Here, $\hat{x} = x/(\pi a)$ is the unitless coordinate in the focal plane and

$$I_0 = \frac{4a^2}{\lambda f}|A|^2 \tag{5.45}$$

is the intensity in the focus of a refractive cylindrical lens.

From the analysis of Figure 5.9, it can be seen that the decreased number of phase quantization levels for the planar cylindrical lens leads to the redistribution of the focused energy from the main peak to the neighboring ones.

The calculated efficiency $I_M(0, 0)/I_0$ of the diffraction cylindrical lens is in agreement with the known data [59,61] and coincides with the data given in Table 5.1.

Figure 5.10 shows normalized intensity distributions $I(0, z/f)/I_0$ along the "optical axis" of a diffraction cylindrical lens with nonuniform sampling of Eq. (5.43) for $M = 2, 4, 16$ phase quantization levels and for the following parameters: $a = 1$ mm; $f = 25$ mm and $\lambda = 10.6$ μm.

From the analysis of Figure 5.10, the focal shift value (the displacement of the point of maximum intensity from the focal plane) is seen to depend not only on physical parameters but also on the number of phase quantization levels, running for the lens under study: $\Delta z = -0.05 \cdot f = -1.25$ mm for $M = 16$, $\Delta z = 0$ for $M = 4$, and

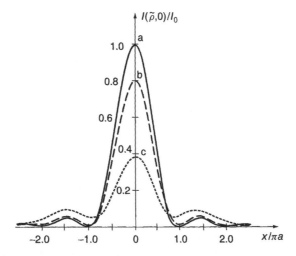

Figure 5.9. Normalized intensity distribution in the focal plane of the diffraction cylindrical lens for various numbers of quantization levels M: (a) $M = 16$, (b) $M = 4$, and (c) $M = 2$.

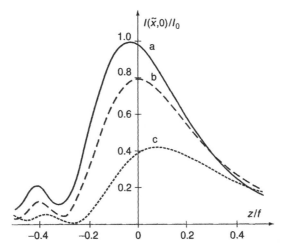

Figure 5.10. Normalized intensity distribution along the "optical axis" of the diffraction cylindrical lens for different numbers of quantization M: (a) $M = 16$, (b) $M = 4$, and (c) $M = 2$.

$\Delta z = 0.09 \cdot f = 2.25$ mm for $M = 2$. Note that as M increases, the general character of distribution and the focal shift value asymptotically tend to the light distribution produced by a refractive cylindrical lens [48,49]. Correlation between the obtained results and the data reported in the papers devoted to studies of refractive cylindrical lenses [48,49] favors the propriety of the used method for the computation of the Fresnel-Kirhhoff integral.

A previously unnoticed interesting energy redistribution takes place in the focal plane with decreasing M (Fig. 5.9). In accordance with the data given in Table 5.2, the main maximum is evidently decreased but the side lobes are also absolutely increased, whereas at the point of the first and second minima, the intensity ceases to tend to zero and for $M = 2$ at the point of the first minimum, it becomes greater than the maximum intensity in the side lobe for $M = 16$. It should be noted that for small M we observe not only a general smoothing of intensity distribution in the focal plane but also a decrease in the focal spot size (the main lobe of distribution). This is the main distinction of Figure 5.9 from analogous distributions for a radial planar lens (Fig. 5.4) where with increasing M the central spot and absolute maximum values remain unchanged, and the side intensities are also proportionally (in correspondence with the efficiency) decreased.

5.3.3 DOE Focusing onto a Ring

In Refs. [2,62–64], the solution of the inverse problem of focusing the laser light have formed the basis for several proposed types of the phase function of a DOE focusing onto a ring. Among others, an "axicon + lens" combination is also used to focus a plane light beam onto a ring [65,66].

The phase function of a DOE focusing onto a ring that functions as an "axicon + lens" combination can easily be obtained from the general Eqs. (5.12)–(5.14) in the form

$$\varphi(r) = -k\sqrt{f_0^2 + (r - r_0)^2}, \quad 0 \le r \le a, \tag{5.46}$$

where r is the polar radius; $k = 2\pi/\lambda$, λ being the light wavelength; f_0 is the focal length; a is the DOE's radius; and r_0 is the radius of the ring of focusing. Owing to the radial symmetry of the problem of focusing onto a ring, the layers take the form of straight lines passing through the center of the DOE. Because the phase along the layer corresponds to the lens phase, each narrow sector of the DOE in Eq. (5.46) (Fig. 5.11) is represented by a strip of a converging lens that focuses into a point displaced from the optical axis by the distance r_0. In the paraxial approximation, the phase function of Eq. (5.46) takes the form

$$\varphi(r) = -kR_0 - \frac{kr^2}{2R_0} + \frac{krr_0}{R_0}, \quad R_0 = \sqrt{f_0^2 + r_0^2} \tag{5.47}$$

corresponding to the combination of a converging lens of focus R_0 (phase is quadratic in r) and an axicon (phase is linear in r).

Because the focusing onto a ring has been widely used in laser technology and instrument making, obtaining the estimates of the ring width, the energy efficiency of focusing, and also the ring's focal depth that determines the accuracy of the focal plane axial adjustment would be of interest. The geometric optical approach used for designing the optical element of Eq. (5.46) does not allow the previously listed diffraction parameters to be evaluated.

There are several papers devoted to the focusing onto a ring [20,24,62–68]. In Ref. [65], the light distribution in the focal plane (in the vicinity of the ring) of an "axicon + lens" combination has been derived for a uniform plane illuminating beam and in Ref. [66] for the Gaussian illuminating beam. In Ref. [63], a converging spherical beam has been focused onto a ring with the aid of a DOE with the binary CTF sign$[J_0(krr_0/f_0)]$. In Refs. [62–64], several types of CTFs have been used to describe an optical element with the circular impulse response, and integral relationships for the light field intensity in the focal plane near the ring have been obtained.

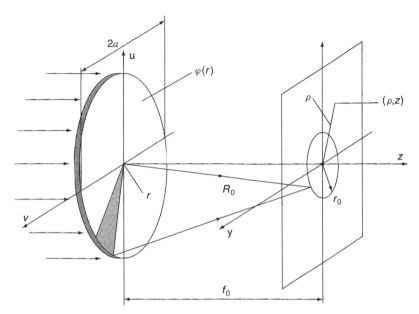

Figure 5.11. Geometry of focusing onto a ring.

At the same time, the problem of studying the light field spatial structure near the focal plane with due account for the resolution δ and the number of DOE's quantization levels M is still to be resolved. Note that for a DOE focusing onto a ring it becomes possible to elucidate which of the diffraction effects are due to imperfectness of the geometric optical phase function and which are due to the DOE-fabrication technology (i.e. the phase function sampling and quantization). Solving this problem requires the use of both analytical computation methods [64,68] and numerical simulation techniques [20,24].

Let us study the DOE of Eq. (5.46) whose paraxial approximation is given by the "axicon + lens" combination of Eq. (5.47). Using analytical techniques [68] and numerical simulation, we shall study a DOE focusing onto a ring for the following parameters: $f_0 = 750$ mm; $2a = 25.6$ mm; $\lambda = 0.6328$ μm. The DOE's energy efficiency will be determined by an energy fraction of illuminating beam that comes to the vicinity of the ring under focusing with the width taken with respect to the 0.1 level of the maximum intensity. Figure 5.12 and Table 5.3 make it possible to see how the ring width, energy efficiency, and intensity distribution in the ring plane vary with the ring radius (for $N = M = \infty$). Note that the numerically simulated plot in Figure 5.12b and the value for the energy efficiency at $r_0 = 1$ mm coincide with the corresponding theoretical data [68]. There is also good agreement with the results reported in Ref. [65]. According to the Ref. [65], 95 percent of the energy coming to the DOE falls to a ring of the diffraction width

$$\Delta = 2.28 \cdot \left(f_0 \cdot \frac{\lambda}{a} \right) = 84 \text{ μm}, \tag{5.48}$$

determined by the boundaries of the first minimum. According to our data, 90 percent of the energy falls to a ring of diffraction width 64 μm determined with respect to the 0.1 level of maximum intensity.

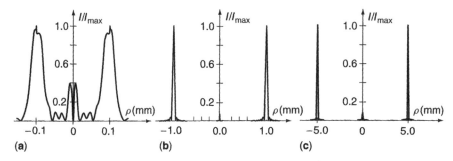

(a)   (b)   (c)

Figure 5.12. Intensity distributions in the focal plane of a DOE focusing ontoaringwiththe following parameters: $f_0 = 750$ mm; $2a = 25.6$ mm; $\lambda = 0.6328$ μm, for various radius r_0 of the ring under focusing: **(a)** $-r_0 = 0.1$ mm; **(b)** $-r_0 = 1$ mm; **(c)** $-r_0 = 5$ mm.

TABLE 5.3. Energy Efficiency E and the Ring Width $\Delta\rho$ Determined with Respect to the 0.1 Level of Maximum Intensity, as a Function of Radius r_0 of the Ring Under Focusing for a DOE with the Following Parameters: $f_0 = 750$ mm; $a = 12.8$ mm; $\lambda = 0.6328$ μm; $N = \infty, M = \infty$

r_0 (MM)	0,1	1,0	5,0
$\Delta\rho$ (MKM)	67	64	65
$\Delta\rho/r_0$	0.67	0.064	0.013
E	0.894	0.885	0.877

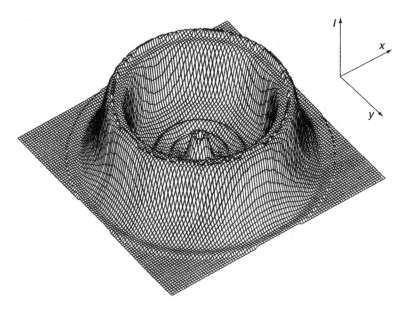

Figure 5.13. Intensity distribution in the focal plane of a DOE focusing onto a ring with the parameters: $f_0 = 750$ mm; $2a = 25.6$ mm; $\lambda = 0.6328$ μm; $r_0 = 0.1$ mm; $N = \infty, M = \infty$.

Analysis of Figures 5.12 and 5.13 makes it possible to reveal interesting peculiarities of diffraction when focusing onto a ring. As the ring radius decreases to $r_0 = 0.1$ mm, the ring diffraction width $\Delta\rho \sim 0.067$ mm (on the 0.1 level of maximum intensity, see Table 5.3) becomes comparable to the ring radius, thus marking the ring merge with the central spot. Thus, for a small-sized ring it becomes important to take into account diffraction phenomena, even in the absence of phase quantization.

The expediency of fabricating the axicon as a planar (diffractive) optical element is justified in Ref. [62]. Following the terminology adopted in Ref. [62], the planar axicon will be referred to as DOE focusing the converging spherical beam onto a ring. The phase function of such a DOE is given by

$$\varphi(r) = \frac{krr_0}{\sqrt{f_0^2 + r_0^2}}.$$

(5.49)

Numerical simulation for the DOE in Eq. (5.49) will be conducted for $r_0 = 0.1$ mm. Shown in Figure 5.14 are isophotes that characterize the intensity distribution as a

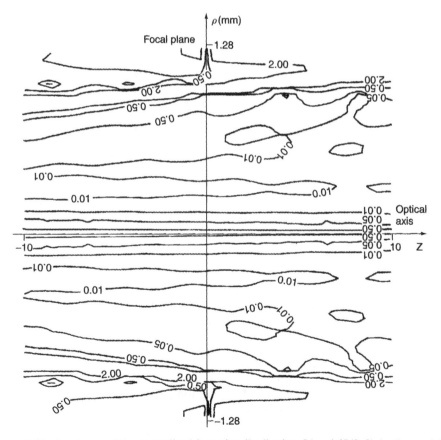

Figure 5.14. Isophotes of the normalized intensity distribution $I(\rho, z)/I(0, 0)$ in the meridian section of the focal plane of a DOE focusing onto a ring with the parameters: $f_0 = 750$ mm; $2a = 25.6$ mm; $\lambda = 0.6328$ μm; $r_0 = 1$ mm; $N = 128$; $M = \infty$.

function of the distance from the plane of focusing for a uniformly sampled ($N = 128$), unquantized DOE. As opposed to the isophotes of the lens in Figure 5.6, the energy is seen to pass not only through the focus but also through the ring domain as well.

With the aim of evaluating phase quantization effects of the DOE (5.49) with uniform sampling ($N = 128$), the intensity distributions in the ring plane for $M = 16$, 4, 2 (Fig. 5.15) were computed. The plots in Figure 5.15 are normalized to the intensity on a geometric ring for $M = \infty$.

For $M = 16$, the intensity distribution in the ring plane is almost indistinguishable from the corresponding plot for $M = \infty$. For $M = 4$, additional internal rings are found near the enhanced central spot. For $M = 2$, the central spot intensity exceeds half the maximum intensity. At the same time, the energy efficiency of focusing drops (Table 5.4). The values of the energy efficiency ε in Table 5.4 are given for $N = 128$ and for the ring width, $\Delta\rho = 0.064$ mm, corresponding to its real width with respect to the 0.1 level of the maximum intensity for $N = M = \infty$. From comparison of the value $E = 0.767$ for $M = \infty$ (Table 5.4) and the theoretical value $E = 0.885$ for $N = M = \infty$ (Table 5.3), the radial sampling with $N = 128$ pixels is seen to decrease the energy efficiency by approximately 10 percent.

The plots in Figure 5.15 and the data in Table 5.4 allow one to observe a highly interesting effect of how phase sampling and quantization errors mutually affect the

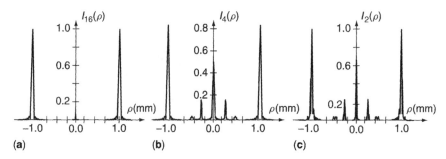

Figure 5.15. Normalized intensity distributions $I_M(\rho, 0)/I_\infty(r_0, 0)$ in the focalplane of a DOE focusing onto a ring for the parameters: $f_0 = 750$ mm; $2a = 25.6$ mm; $\lambda = 0.6328$ μm; $r_0 = 1$ mm; $N = 128$ for various numbers of phase quantization levels M: (**a**) $M = 16$; (**b**) $M = 4$; (**c**) $M = 2$.

TABLE 5.4. Energy Efficiency E as a Function of the Number M of Phase Quantization Levels for the DOE (5.49) for Uniform Radius Sampling with the Parameters: $f_0 = 750$ mm; $a = 12.8$ mm; $\lambda = 0.6328$ μm; $r_0 = 1$ mm; $N = 128$ and the Focusing Ring Width is $\Delta\rho = 64$ μm

M	∞	16	4	2
E	0,767	0,757	0,624	0,597

DOE's operation. Actually, in Figure 5.15b, c for $M = 16$, the internal spurious rings in Figure 5.15a are absent. At the same time, it is not only phase quantization, for (b) and (c) that can be responsible for the emergence of spurious rings in Figure 5.15 for $M = 2, 4$. According to subsection 2.8.10, for $N = \infty$, the phase quantization for the DOE in Eq. (5.49) results in the appearance of additional diffraction orders corresponding to the focusing onto rings with radii

$$R_p = |r_0 \cdot (1 + pM)|, \quad p = 0, \pm 1, \pm 2, \ldots \tag{5.50}$$

The spurious orders [$p \neq 0$ in Eq. (5.50)] enhance the central peak. However, since the radii in Eq. (5.50) at $p \neq 0$ are greater than the radius r_0 of the ring of focusing, the spurious orders cannot account for the emergence of the internal rings in Figure 5.15b and c. Thus, it is the joint effect of phase sampling and quantization errors that is responsible for the emergence of the internal rings. It is noteworthy that the DOE of Eq. (5.49) produces almost the same value of energy efficiency for $M = 2$ as it does for $M = 4$ (Table 5.4). This is due to the fact that for $M = 2$, apart from the main order, the -1st quantization order [$p = -1$ in Eq. (5.51)] contributes to the ring of radius r_0. According to Eq. (2.304), approximately the same portion of the illuminating beam energy is contained in the zero and -1st order at $M = 2$ as is contained in the main zero order at $M = 4$. Note that the interference between the zero and first order results in a "carved" form of the ring in Figure 5.15c.

Let us now study the quantized DOE, Eq. (5.47), focusing a plane beam. For the chosen number M of phase quantization levels, the paraxial phase of Eq. (5.47) yields the following sampling:

$$\frac{k}{2R_0}(r_n - r_0)^2 = \frac{2\pi}{M}n', \quad 0 \leq r_n \leq a, \tag{5.51}$$

whence

$$|r_n - r_0| = \sqrt{\frac{2\lambda R_0 n'}{M}}, \quad 0 \leq r_n \leq a. \tag{5.52}$$

Here, each value of $n' = 1, 2, \ldots, N_1$ may correspond to one or two values of the ring radius

$$r_n = r_0 \pm \sqrt{\frac{2\lambda R_0 n'}{M}}, \quad 0 \leq r_n \leq a, \quad n' = 1, 2, \ldots, N_1; \tag{5.53}$$

with the general number of circular modules determined by

$$N = \left[\frac{r_0^2 M}{2\lambda R_0} + \frac{(a - r_0)^2 M}{2\lambda R_0} \right] + 1. \tag{5.54}$$

In an effort not to increase the computation time, which is in direct proportion to N and in inverse proportion to the wavelength λ, we used a DOE for IR CO_2-laser with the parameters: $f_0 = 500$ mm; $\lambda = 10.6$ μm; $2a = 25.6$ mm. Table 5.5 and Figures 5.16 and 5.17 present the results of studying the DOE focusing into rings with radii $r_0 =$

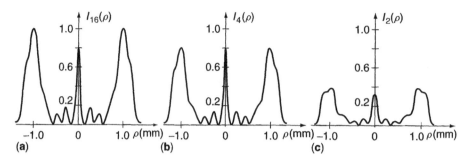

Figure 5.16. Normalized intensity distributions $I_M(\rho, 0)/I_\infty(r_0, 0)$ in the focal plane of a DOE focusing the plane beam onto a ring, for the parameters: $f_0 = 500$ mm; $2a = 25.6$ mm; $\lambda = 10.6$ μm; $r_0 = 1$ mm for various numbers of quantization levels M: (a) $M = 16$; (b) $M = 4$; (c) $M = 2$.

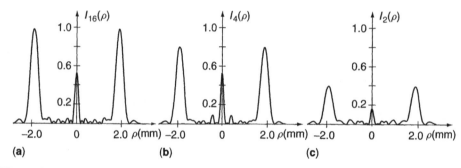

Figure 5.17. Normalized intensity distributions $I_M(\rho, 0)/I_\infty(r_0, 0)$ in the focal plane of a DOE focusing the plane beam onto a ring, for the parameters: $f_0=500$ mm; $2a=25.6$ mm; $\lambda=10.6$ μm; $r_0=2$ mm, for various numbers of quantization levels M: (a) $M = 16$; (b) $M = 4$; (c) $M = 2$.

1 mm (Fig. 5.16) and $r_0 = 2$ mm (Fig. 5.17) for various numbers of phase quantization levels.

Table 5.5 contains the following quantities:

Θ the intensity level used to determine the boundaries of the ring of focusing (ρ_-, ρ_+);

(ρ_-, ρ_+) the boundaries of the ring of focusing determined with respect to the level Θ;

$\Delta\rho = \rho_+ - \rho_-$ the width of the ring of focusing with respect to the level Θ;

E the DOE's energy efficiency (the energy portion coming to the vicinity of the ring of focusing of width $\Delta\rho$);

$\Delta\rho_\Theta$ theoretical estimate of the width of the ring of focusing for a nonquantized DOE ($M = N = \infty$) [68];

E_Θ theoretical estimate of the energy efficiency of focusing for a nonquantized DOE [68].

TABLE 5.5. Energy Efficiency E and Width of the Ring of Focusing $\Delta\rho$, with Respect to the Θ Level of Maximum Intensity, as a Function of the Number M of Phase Quantization Levels for the DOE Focusing the Plane Beam onto a Ring of Radius r_0 ($f_0 = 500$ mm; $\lambda = 10.6$ μm; $a = 12.8$ mm)

M	$\Theta = 0.5$ ($\Delta\rho_\Theta = 0.408$ mm)					$\Theta = 0.2$ ($\Delta\rho_\Theta = 0.613$ mm)					$\Theta = 0.1$ ($\Delta\rho_\Theta = 0.701$ mm)				
	E	ρ_- (mm)	ρ_+ (mm)	$\Delta\rho$ (mm)	E/E_Θ	E	ρ_- (mm)	ρ_+ (mm)	$\Delta\rho$ (mm)	E/E_Θ	E	ρ_- (mm)	ρ_+ (mm)	$\Delta\rho$ (mm)	E/E_Θ
						$r_0 = 1.0$ mm									
16	0.682	0.798	1.179	0.381	0.958	0.845	0.652	1.259	0.608	0.992	0.873	0.617	1.306	0.690	0.989
4	0.570	0.811	1.193	0.382	0.801	0.699	0.650	1.266	0.617	0.820	0.721	0.611	1.310	0.700	0.817
2	0.289	0.829	1.218	0.389	0.406	0.353	0.632	1.289	0.657	0.414	0.365	0.574	1.338	0.764	0.413
						$r_0 = 2.0$ mm									
16	0.686	1.797	2.189	0.392	0.963	0.844	1.684	2.282	0.588	0.991	0.872	1.643	2.328	0.658	0.988
4	0.578	1.803	2.220	0.417	0.812	0.695	1.687	2.305	0.618	0.816	0.717	1.644	2.348	0.704	0.812
2	0.282	1.863	2.242	0.379	0.396	0.345	1.729	2.330	0.601	0.405	0.364	1.615	2.382	0.767	0.412

Analysis of the aforementioned results of computation makes possible the following conclusions:

- The experimental radius of the ring of focusing increases with decreasing number of quantization levels;
- With decreasing number of quantization levels, the ring of focusing is blurred (the ring width is increased and the portion of the energy coming to the ring is decreased);
- The ring width and the energy efficiency are practically independent of the ring radius r_0;
- The relative value of the central peak decreases with increasing radius of the ring of focusing r_0;
- The theoretical estimate of the diffraction width $\Delta\rho_\Theta$ of the ring of focusing of a nonquantized focusing DOE is in a fairly good agreement with numerical simulation.

We also simulated operation of the DOE focusing onto a ring, Eqs. (5.47), (5.53), and (5.54) for the Gaussian illuminating beam of amplitude

$$A(r) = A_0 \exp(-r^2/2\sigma^2) \tag{5.55}$$

for the following parameters: $f_0 = 500$ mm; $a = 12.8$ mm; $\lambda = 10.6$ μm; $\sigma = 0.4 \cdot a$; $r_0 = 1$ mm; $M = 2, 4, 16$. Shown in Figure 5.18 are the results of computation for the DOE focusing the Gaussian beam onto a ring. When this result is compared with that shown in Figure 5.16, it is apparent that the width of the ring of focusing is greater for the Gaussian beam, and at the great number of quantization levels the central peak is suppressed and blends into the background. Another reason for an increase in the ring's width is the actual decrease of the DOE's active area for the σ chosen.

If a circular photo-plotter is unavailable, a DOE focusing onto a ring may be fabricated using a raster laser image generator. The results of an investigation into the DOE of Eq. (5.49) focusing the converging spherical beam onto a ring, with the DOE's aperture broken down into $N \cdot N$ square pixels, are shown in Figure 5.19 and Table 5.6. Recall that the quadratic relationships [19,20,45,47] used for the computation of the

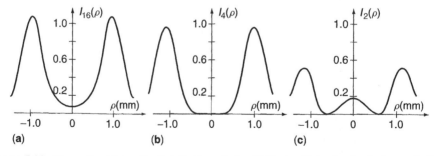

Figure 5.18. Normalized intensity distributions $I_M(\rho, 0)/I_\infty(r_0, 0)$ in the focal plane of a DOE focusing onto a ring for various numbers M of quantization levels when focusing the Gaussian beam. The parameters: $f_0 = 500$ mm; $2a = 25.6$ mm; $\sigma = 0.4 \cdot a$; $\lambda = 10.6$ μm; $r_0 = 1$ mm: (a) $M = 16$; $M = 4$; (b) $M = 2$.

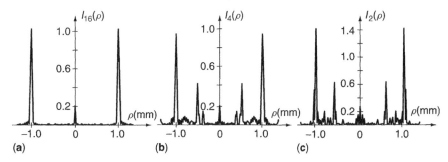

Figure 5.19. Normalized intensity distributions $I_M(\rho, 0)/I_\infty(r_0, 0)$ in the focal plane of a DOE focusing onto a ring for the rectangular raster sampling. The parameters: $f_0 = 750$ mm; $2a = 25.6$ mm; $\lambda = 0.6328$ μm; $r_0 = 1$ mm; $N_1 = N_2 = 128$ for various numbers M of phase quantization levels: (**a**) $M = 16$; (**b**) $M = 4$; (**c**) $M = 2$.

TABLE 5.6. Energy Efficiency E of the DOE (5.49) with a Rectangular Raster of Sampling Versus the Number M of Phase Quantization Levels, for the Parameters: $f_0 = 750$ mm; $\lambda = 0.6328$ μm; $2a = 25.6$ mm; $r_0 = 1$ mm; $N \cdot N$ is the Number of Sampling Pixels, E is the Energy Portion Coming to a Ring of Width $\Delta\rho = 64$ μm

M N	∞	16	4	2
128	0.472	0.470	0.378	0.327
256	0.758	0.741	0.602	0.584

Kirhhoff-Fresnel integral employ the piecewise-constant approximation for the DOE's complex transmission function on a network of $N \cdot N$ square pixels. A comparison between Figure 5.15 and Figure 5.19, and Tables 5.4 and 5.6 is indicative of the close similarity of the results.

Note, however, that for the energy equivalence the number of pixels N along each axis of the rectangular raster should be twice as great as the number of rings for the uniform sampling along the radius. This is supported by a large number and high intensity of spurious rings in Figure 5.19 as compared with Figure 5.15.

5.3.4 DOE Focusing onto a Semi-Ring

The phase function of a DOE that focuses the plane beam onto a semi-ring of radius r_0 can easily be derived from the phase function of a DOE focusing onto a ring. Actually, when focusing onto a ring, the layers take the form of straight lines, although the phase along the "radius layer" corresponds to the phase of a lens that focuses into a point on the ring. For focusing onto a semi-ring of radius r_0, it will suffice to define the phase of a lens focusing into the point r_0 not along the "radius layer" but along the "diameter layer." In this case, the phase function of a DOE focusing onto a semi-ring takes the form [69]:

$$\varphi(u, v) = \begin{cases} -k\sqrt{f_0^2 + (r - r_0)}^2, & u \geq 0 \\ -k\sqrt{f_0^2 + (r + r_0)}^2, & u < 0 \end{cases} \tag{5.56}$$

$$0 \leq r = \sqrt{u^2 + v^2} \leq a,$$

The phase function of a DOE that focuses the converging spherical beam onto a semi-ring at $z = f_0$ may be derived from Eq. (5.56) by introducing the phase of a diverging lens with focus f_0. In the paraxial approximation, the phase of a DOE focusing the converging spherical beam takes the form:

$$\varphi(u, v) = \begin{cases} \dfrac{krr_0}{\sqrt{f_0^2 + r_0^2}}, & u \geq 0 \\ \dfrac{-krr_0}{\sqrt{f_0^2 + r_0^2}}, & u < 0 \end{cases} \tag{5.57}$$

$$0 \leq r = \sqrt{u^2 + v^2} \leq a.$$

The results of studying the DOE of Eq. (5.57) with the parameters: $f_0 = 750$ mm; $\lambda = 0.6328$ μm; $r_0 = 1$ mm; $2a = 25.6$ mm; $N_1 = N_2 = 128$ are shown in Figures 5.20 and 5.21.

Shown in Figure 5.20 is the intensity distribution in the focal plane of a DOE focusing onto a semi-ring for the aforementioned parameters. It can be seen that the intensity peak on the optical axis, characteristic of a DOE focusing onto a ring, is preserved. In the course of numerical computation of the Fresnel-Kirchhoff integral, the DOE was supposed to consist of $N_1 \cdot N_2$ square modules, with the phase function determined in each module in accordance with its value (5.57) at the center of the cell. For the modules with their centers found beyond the limits of radius a, the amplitude transmittance is taken to be equal to zero. Figure 5.21 depicts in polar coordinates the intensity distributions over the semi-ring of focusing ($r = r_0$, $-2\pi/3 \leq \varphi \leq 2\pi/3$) for the DOE of Eq. (5.57) for various numbers of phase quantization levels. Intensity peaks on the periphery of the lines of focusing may be because of the DOE's phase

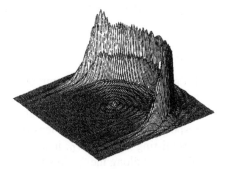

Figure 5.20. Intensity distribution in the focal plane of a DOE focusing onto a semi ring.

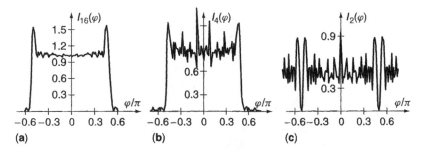

Figure 5.21. Normalized angular intensity distribution $I_M(r_0, \varphi)/I_{16}(r_0, 0)$ along the semi ring of for the parameters: $f_0 = 750$ mm; $\lambda = 0.6328$ μ m; $r_0 = 1$ mm; $2a = 25.6$ mm; $N_1 = N_2 = 128$: (a) $M = 16$; (b) $M = 4$; (c) $M = 2$.

break at $u = 0$. For four phase levels (Fig. 5.21b), a decrease in the average intensity along the line of focusing occurs in concurrence with an increase in the root-mean-square (rms) deviation of the intensity from a uniform distribution. Because a binary DOE allows only a centrally symmetric intensity distribution to be generated, with two phase quantization levels (Fig. 5.21c) the desired domain of focusing is entirely destroyed. Instead of focusing onto a semi-ring, the focusing onto a highly nonuniform ring takes place.

5.3.5 DOE Focusing onto a Transverse Line-Segment

Consider a square DOE that focuses the plane beam onto a line-segment $|x| \le d$ of uniform linear density. The DOE's phase function may be derived from the general equations (5.20) and (5.21) in the form

$$\varphi(u, v) = -k\frac{\left(1 - \dfrac{d}{a}\right)u^2 + v^2}{2f}, \quad |u| < a, \quad |v| < a, \qquad (5.58)$$

where $2a \cdot 2a$ is the DOE's aperture size.

The results of numerical simulation of the field produced by the DOE of Eq. (5.58) for the parameters $f = 500$ mm; $\lambda = 10.6$ μm; $2d = 2$ mm; $2a = 12.8$ mm and with $N_1 = N_2 = 128$ phase pixels are shown in Figures 5.22 and 5.23. Figure 5.22 illustrates a 3D intensity distribution in the focal plane of the DOE under study. In the course of numerical computation of the Fresnel-Kirhhof integral, the DOE was supposed to consist of $N_1 \cdot N_2$ square modules, with each phase function determined in accordance with its value in Eq. (5.58) at the center of the module.

The intensity distributions along the line under focusing for various numbers of quantization levels ($M = 2, 4, 16$) are shown in Figure 5.23 and demonstrate that for small M the focal domain shape is conserved, while the corresponding energy efficiencies are decreased: $E = 75.3\%(M = 16)$, $E = 61.8\%(M = 4)$, and $E = 31.3\%$ ($M = 2$). Note that the plot for $M = 256(E = 76.3\%)$, which is not shown in Figure 5.23, practically coincides with that for $M = 16$, thus demonstrating that it is no good using more than 16 phase quantization levels. The focal line width ε determined by the level of intensity drop $\Theta = 0, 1(M = 256, y = 0)$ is 0.62 mm. The

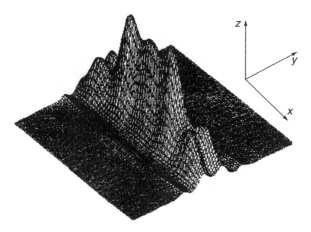

Figure 5.22. 3D intensity distribution in the focal plane of a DOE focusing onto a line-segment.

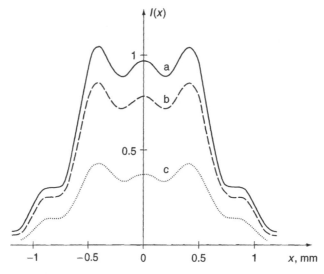

Figure 5.23. Normalized intensity distribution along the segment under focusing in the focal plane of the DOE (5.58) for various numbers of quantization levels M: (a) $M = 16$, (b) $M = 4$, (c) $M = 2$.

energy efficiency of focusing was defined as the energy portion coming to the rectangle of $2d \cdot \varepsilon$. The fact that the focal domain shape is preserved for a small number of phase quantization levels is due to the diffraction order structure, Eq. (2.306), of a quantized DOE. The diffraction orders resulting from the quantization of the phase in Eq. (5.58) correspond to the focusing onto line-segments in the planes

$$z = F_n = f/n, \quad n = 1 + pM, \quad p = 0, \pm 1, \pm 2, \ldots \quad (5.59)$$

with the images generated by the quantized DOE in the plane $z = f$ corresponding to defocused line-segments. The width of the defocused segments is several orders of magnitude greater than the diffraction width of the segment of focusing, thus making their effect on the useful line-segment [for $p = 0$ in Eq. (5.59)] negligibly small. It is noteworthy that the aforementioned variation of the energy efficiency E with decreasing number of quantization levels M is proportional to the variation of the squared module of the Fourier coefficient c_0 in Eq. (2.304) that describes the energy portion being focused onto the useful image for a quantized DOE.

The phase function of a square DOE focusing the converging spherical beam onto a line-segment with uniform intensity distribution is given by

$$\varphi(u, v) = \frac{kd}{2af} u^2, \quad |u| < a, \quad |v| < a. \tag{5.60}$$

The results of studying the DOE in Eq. (5.60) for the parameters $f = 500$ mm; $\lambda = 10.6$ μm; $2d = 10$ mm; $2a = 25.6$ mm; $N_1 = 128$, $N_2 = 1$ are shown in Figure 5.24 and in Table 5.7. In this case, pixels of the DOE sampling take the form of rectangles, with their large side equal to the DOE's width. Shown in Figure 5.23 are the intensity distributions $i = I_M(x, 0)/I_{256}(0, 0)$ in the DOE's focal plane for $M = 16, 4, 2$. Table 5.7 gives the energy efficiency $E(\varepsilon)$ and the rms deviation δ of the intensity over the segment from a constant value. The rms deviation of the generated intensity distribution over the segment of focusing from the desired one was determined by

$$\delta = \sqrt{\frac{\int_{-d}^{d} [I(x, 0) - I_c(x)]^2 \, dx}{\int_{-d}^{d} I_c^2(x) \, dx}}, \tag{5.61}$$

where $I_c(x)$ is the desired intensity distribution over the segment of focusing. For the DOE of Eq. (5.60), the value of intensity $I_c(x)$ at $|x| \le d$ is constant and equal to an average intensity value over the segment of focusing.

From the analysis of Figure 5.24 and Table 5.7 one can see that when the number M of phase levels is small (Fig. 5.24b, c) the shape of the focal domain is destroyed, although the values of the energy efficiency still remain fairly high (Table 5.7). The fact that the segment of focusing is disintegrated at small M is also due to the structure

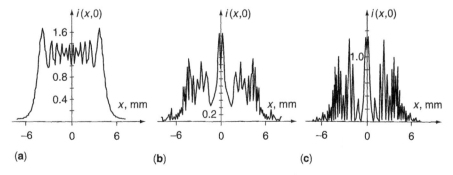

Figure 5.24. Intensity distribution along the segment of focusing in the focal plane of the DOE (5.60) for various numbers of quantization levels M: (**a**) $M = 16$, (**b**) $M = 4$, and (**c**) $M = 2$.

TABLE 5.7. Energy Efficiency $E(\varepsilon)$ and rms Deviation δ of the Intensity from a Constant Value for Various Numbers of Quantization Levels M and Pixels N_1 for the DOE (5.60). The DOE's Parameters are: $f = 500$ mm; $\lambda = 10.6$ μm; $2d = 10$ mm; $2a = 25.6$ mm; $N_2 = 1$; $\varepsilon_0 = \lambda f/a$

M			$E(\varepsilon)$, %			δ, %
	$\varepsilon = 0.25 \cdot \varepsilon_0$	$\varepsilon = 0.5 \cdot \varepsilon_0$	$\varepsilon = 0.75 \cdot \varepsilon_0$	$\varepsilon = 1.0 \cdot \varepsilon_0$	$\varepsilon = 1.5 \cdot \varepsilon_0$	
			$N_1 = 128$			
256	43.9	71.5	81.5	82.4	84.0	24.7
4	38.6	63.1	71.9	72.6	74.1	46.1
2	39.2	64.0	72.9	73.8	75.3	92.7
			$N_1 = 256$			
256	45.0	73.3	83.5	83.9	84.0	24.3
4	38.8	63.4	72.2	72.6	74.1	46.0
2	39.4	64.3	73.4	73.8	75.3	
						91.9

of the diffraction orders in Eq. (2.306) that emerge as the result of quantization. The diffraction orders caused by the quantization of the phase in Eq. (5.60) correspond to the focusing onto the segments of length $d_p = 2d \cdot (1 + pM)$, $p = 0, \pm1, \pm2, \ldots$ in the focal plane $z = f$. In this situation, if $p \neq 0$, spurious images of the segments are superimposed onto the useful segment $|x| \leq d$ and destroy it as a consequence of interference. The energy efficiency still remains fairly high (Table 5.7), because in this situation the energy is not dissipated between other diffraction planes. For small M, one proves to be unable to compensate for the disintegration of the segment of focusing through twice-as-frequent sampling (Table 5.7).

For the results of testing, the DOE focusing far-IR laser light onto a ring and a segment, the reader is directed to Ref. [70]. For various DOEs, the energy efficiency of focusing measured by the method of calibrated diagrams was 60 to 75 percent [70] and corresponded to the simulated data for the DOE focusing onto a segment, Eq. (5.58) with consideration for diffraction microrelief fabrication errors.

It would be interesting to study a DOE focusing onto a segment of nonconstant linear density. Shown in Figure 5.25 and Table 5.8 are the results of simulation of a DOE focusing onto a segment with the linear increase of linear density and with the parameters: $f = 500$ mm; $\lambda = 10.6$ μm; $2d = 10$ mm; $2a = 25.6$ mm; $N_1 = 256$, $N_2 = 1$. The DOE's phase function may be derived from Eqs. (5.20) and (5. 21) and, when focusing a converging spherical beam onto a segment with a twofold increase of linear density, takes the form:

$$\varphi(u, v) = -\frac{k}{f}\left[3\,du - \frac{ad}{9}\sqrt{\left(10 + 6\frac{u}{a}\right)^3}\right], \quad |u| < a, \quad |v| < a. \tag{5.62}$$

In general, the character of distribution in Figure 5.25a reflects a twofold linear increase of intensity along the segment of focusing, with the energy efficiency of the DOE in Eq. (5.62) being close to that of the DOE focusing onto a segment with uniform

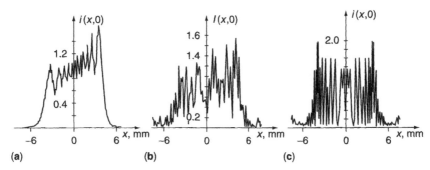

Figure 5.25. Intensity distribution along the segment of focusing in theDOE's focal plane, Eq. (5.62), for various numbers of quantization levels M: (**a**) $M = 16$, (**b**) $M = 4$, and (**c**) $M = 2$.

TABLE 5.8. Energy Efficiency $E(\varepsilon)$ and rms Deviation δ of the Intensity from the Linear Distribution for Various Numbers of Quantization Levels M and Pixels N for the DOE (5.62). The Parameters of the DOE are: $f = 500$ mm; $\lambda = 10.6$ μm; $2 \cdot d = 10$ mm; $2 \cdot a = 25.6$ mm; $N_2 = 1$, $\varepsilon_0 = \lambda \cdot f / a$

M	$E(\varepsilon)$, %					δ, %
	$\varepsilon = 0.25 \cdot \varepsilon_0$	$\varepsilon = 0.5 \cdot \varepsilon_0$	$\varepsilon = 0.75 \cdot \varepsilon_0$	$\varepsilon = 1.0 \cdot \varepsilon_0$	$\varepsilon = 1.5 \cdot \varepsilon_0$	
			$N_1 = 128$			
256	43.4	70.9	80.8	81.5	82.7	30.1
4	38.2	62.2	70.7	71.3	72.4	49.8
2	38.1	62.2	70.7	71.4	72.6	91.1
			$N_1 = 256$			
256	44.5	72.7	82.8	83.6	84.8	29.4
4	38.2	62.2	70.8	71.4	72.4	47.9
2	38.2	62.2	70.7	71.4	72.6	81.5

distribution. At the same time, with decreasing M an increase in the rms deviation of intensity δ from the linear distribution becomes more essential. Since the binary DOE allows only a centrally symmetric intensity distribution to be produced, the DOE becomes inoperative at $M = 2$. (Fig. 5.25c).

The rms deviation was found from Eq. (5.61), where $I_c(x) = c \cdot x + b$ while $c = b/3d$ and the constant b was determined by the least squares method from the calculated values of intensity $I(x, 0)$ along the segment of focusing.

Earlier, we analyzed how the sampling and quantization of the phase function affect the operation of simplest geometric optical DOE focusing onto a segment.

For the considered DOE with square aperture, the layer's length was constant, thus preventing us from evaluating the effects of nonuniform diffractive widening of lines when focusing a nonsquare illuminating beam, and directing the way to their correction. In this connection, it would be pertinent to consider a more general problem of focusing a beam with complex amplitude $w_0(\mathbf{u}) = \sqrt{I_0(\mathbf{u})} \exp(i\varphi_0(\mathbf{u}))$, where $I_0(\mathbf{u})$

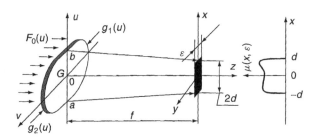

Figure 5.26. Geometry of focusing onto a segment.

is the illuminating beam intensity and $\varphi_0(u)$ is the beam phase, onto a segment $|x| \leq d$ in the plane $z = f$ (Fig. 5.26). The DOE's aperture is supposed to be limited by the curves $v = g_1(u)$ and $v = g_2(u)$, and by the straight-line segments $u = a$ and $u = b$.

The phase function of a DOE focusing onto a segment with the linear density distribution $\theta(x)$, $|x| \leq d$ takes the form of Eqs. (5.20) and (5.21). The essence of the geometric optical solution can be made clear if we conduct the diffraction analysis of the field in the DOE's focal plane, Eq. (5.20) and (5.21).

In the Fresnel-Kirhhoff approximation, the complex amplitude $w(x)$ in the plane of focusing takes the form

$$w(\mathbf{x}) = \frac{k \exp(ikf)}{2\pi i f} \int_G w_0(\mathbf{u}) \exp[i\varphi(u)] \exp\left(\frac{ik}{2f}(\mathbf{x} - \mathbf{u})^2\right) d^2\mathbf{u}. \qquad (5.63)$$

Substituting Eq. (5.21) into (5.63) gives

$$w(\mathbf{x}) = \frac{k \exp(ikf)}{2\pi i f} \int_G \sqrt{I_0(\mathbf{u})} \exp\left(\frac{ik}{f}\int_{u_0}^u x(\xi)\,d\xi\right) \exp\left(-\frac{ik}{f}\mathbf{xu}\right) d^2\mathbf{u}, \qquad (5.64)$$

where the function $x(\xi)$ describes the ray correspondence between the points on the segment of focusing and the layers on the DOE's aperture. Using the diffraction design techniques [71–73] we can obtain a diffraction approximation of the integral (5.64) based on the use of the stationary-phase method [12], with the integration performed across the layer, that is, with respect to u and

$$I(\mathbf{x}) = \left|\sqrt{\frac{k}{2\pi f}} \int_{g_1(u_x)}^{g_2(u_x)} \sqrt{I_0(u_x, v)} \left(\frac{dx}{du}\bigg|_{u=u_x}\right)^{-1/2} \exp\left(-\frac{ikyv}{f}\right) dv\right|^2, \qquad (5.65)$$

where u_x is the solution to the equation $x = x(u)$ in u.

The approximation in Eq. (5.65) is fairly good in describing the diffraction effects in the cross section of the focal segment, but it will never do for the segment's edges. Let us introduce the function

$$\mu(x, \varepsilon) = \int_{-\varepsilon/2}^{\varepsilon/2} I(x, y)\,dy$$

that characterizes the energy distribution in the ε-vicinity of the segment under focusing. Substituting Eq. (5.65) in (5.66) gives

$$\mu(x, \varepsilon) = \int_{-\varepsilon/2}^{\varepsilon/2} \left| \sqrt{\frac{k}{2\pi f}} \int_{g_1(u_x)}^{g_2(u_x)} \sqrt{I_0(u_x, v)} \left(\frac{dx}{du} \bigg|_{u=u_x} \right)^{-1/2} \exp\left(-\frac{ikyv}{f}\right) dv \right|^2 dy.$$

(5.67)

Given $\varepsilon_0 \ll \varepsilon$, where ε_0 is the segment's diffraction width, we shall replace the limits in the outer integral by infinity and apply the Parseval equation. In view of the preceding replacement and Eq. (5.20), Eq. (5.67) takes the form

$$\mu(x, \varepsilon) = \theta(x), \quad \varepsilon \gg \varepsilon_0.$$

(5.68)

According to Eq. (5.68), by the linear density one should imply the integral of the intensity taken over the direction perpendicular to the segment. Thus, the geometric optical approach of Eqs. (5.20) and (5.21) is seen to be limited to the case $\varepsilon_0 \gg \varepsilon$, not allowing the desired intensity distribution to be produced along the focal segment. Let us make use of the diffraction relationship in Eq. (5.67) to design a DOE with diffraction corrections that generates the desired energy distribution along the focal segment for arbitrary ε [72,73]. To do this, the phase function of the DOE with diffraction corrections will also be specified in the form of Eq. (5.21) and the differential equation for the determination of $x(u)$ in Eq. (5.21) will be deduced from Eq. (5.67) in the form

$$\frac{dx(u)}{du} = \frac{1}{\mu(x(u), \varepsilon)} \int_{-\varepsilon/2}^{\varepsilon/2} \left| \sqrt{\frac{k}{2\pi f}} \int_{g_1(u)}^{g_2(u)} \sqrt{I_0(u, v)} \exp\left(-\frac{ikyv}{f}\right) dv \right|^2 dy$$

$$x(a) = -d, x(b) = d$$

(5.69)

For the uniform intensity of the illuminating beam, Eq. (5.69) takes the form

$$\frac{dx}{du} = \frac{c}{\mu(x(u), \varepsilon)} \cdot \Phi\left(\frac{k\varepsilon}{4f}[g_2(u) - g_1(u)]\right) \cdot [g_2(u) - g_1(u)],$$

(5.70)

$$x(a) = -d, \quad x(b) = d,$$

where c is constant, $\Phi(\beta) = Si(2\beta) - \beta \operatorname{sinc}^2(\beta)$ and

$$Si(\beta) = \int_0^\beta \frac{\sin(x)}{x} \, dx, \quad \operatorname{sinc}(\beta) = \frac{\sin(\beta)}{\beta}.$$

For $\varepsilon \ll \varepsilon_0$, we shall decompose both sides of Eq. (5.69) into a series in terms of powers ε and take into account only the linear terms of the decomposition. In this case, the equation in $x(u)$ takes the form

$$\frac{dx}{du} = \frac{1}{I[\kappa(u), 0]} \left| \sqrt{\frac{k}{2\pi f}} \int_{g_1(u)}^{g_2(u)} \sqrt{I_0(u, v)} \, dv \right|^2,$$

$$x(a) = -d, \quad x(b) = d,$$

where $I(x, 0)$ is the desired intensity along the segment $y = 0$ for $|x| \leq d$.

It would be interesting to compare the robustness of the geometric optical DOE of Eqs. (5.20) and (5.21) and the DOE with diffraction corrections of Eqs. (5.21) and (5.69). We shall make the comparison by the example of focusing a circular and a ringlike beam onto a segment with uniform intensity distribution. For the DOE with diffraction corrections and with uniform circular illuminating beam of radius R, the function $x(u)$ is sought for from Eq. (5.70) at $g_1(u) = -(R^2 - u^2)^{1/2}$ and $g_2(u) = (R^2 - u^2)^{1/2}$. For the ringlike illuminating beam, the function $x(u)$ is soughtfor from the solution of the following differential equation

$$\frac{dx(u)}{du} = \begin{cases} c \int_{-\varepsilon/2}^{\varepsilon/2} \left[\sqrt{R_2^2 - u^2} \operatorname{sinc}\left(\frac{k}{f}y\sqrt{R_2^2 - u^2}\right) \right. \\ \left. - \sqrt{R_1^2 - u^2} \operatorname{sinc}\left(\frac{k}{f}y\sqrt{R_1^2 - u^2}\right) \right]^2 dy, & |u| < R_1, \\ c \int_{-\varepsilon/2}^{\varepsilon/2} (R_2^2 - u^2) \operatorname{sinc}^2\left(\frac{k}{f}y\sqrt{R_2^2 - u^2}\right) dy, & R_1 \le |u| \le R_2, \end{cases}$$

$$x(-R_2) = -d; \quad X(R_2) = d, \tag{5.72}$$

where c is constant, and R_1 and R_2 are the inner and outer radii of the ringlike illuminating beam.

It should be noted that the differential equations for the function $x(u)$ of geometric optical DOEs take an essentially different form

$$\frac{dx(u)}{du} = c(R^2 - u^2)^{1/2}, \quad x(-R) = -d, \quad x(R) = d, \tag{5.73}$$

for the circular illuminating beam, and

$$\frac{dx(u)}{du} = \begin{cases} c\left(\sqrt{R_2^2 - u^2} - \sqrt{R_1^2 - u^2}\right), & |u| < R_1 \\ c\sqrt{R_2^2 - u^2}, & R_1 \le |u| \le R_2 \end{cases} \tag{5.74}$$

for the ringlike illuminating beam.

To characterize the operational quality of the DOEs, we shall introduce the energy efficiency E and the rms deviation δ. The quantity

$$E(\varepsilon) = \int_{-d}^{d} \mu(x, \varepsilon)dx \bigg/ \iint_G I_0(\mathbf{u}) \, d^2\mathbf{u} \tag{5.75}$$

defines the portion of the illuminating beam energy focused onto the ε-vicinity of the focal segment. The quantity

$$\delta(\varepsilon) = \frac{1}{\overline{I}} \left[\int_{-d}^{d} [\mu(x, \varepsilon) - \overline{I}]^2 \, dx \right]^{1/2} \tag{5.76}$$

defines the rms deviation of the energy distribution $\mu(x, \varepsilon)$ along the focal segment from an average value

$$\overline{I} = \frac{1}{2d} \int_{-d}^{d} \mu(x, \varepsilon) \, dx.$$

TABLE 5.9. Characteristics of the Quality of Focusing for the Geometric Optical DOE and the DOE with Diffraction Corrections with a Circular Incident Beam

ε	Geometric Optical DOE		DOE with Diffraction Corrections	
	$E(\varepsilon)$, %	$\delta(\varepsilon)$, %	$E(\varepsilon)$, %	$\delta(\varepsilon)$, %
$\varepsilon \ll \varepsilon_0$	—	24.3	—	14.6
$\varepsilon_0/2$	65.6	27.1	65.2	13.4
ε_0	85.9	18.1	85.6	14.5
$3 \cdot \varepsilon_0/2$	88.5	17.6	88.2	16.1
$2 \cdot \varepsilon_0$	95.1	15.8	93.1	14.9

For $\varepsilon \ll \varepsilon_0$, the value of $\delta(\varepsilon)$ corresponds to the rms deviation of intensity distribution along the geometric segment from a constant value.

Table 5.9 gives in its left the calculated values of $E(\varepsilon)$ and $\delta(\varepsilon)$ for a geometric optical DOE focusing onto a segment for the circular illuminating beam and different values of ε. The analogous values for a DOE with diffraction corrections are in the right of Table 5.9. The data given in Table 5.9 were obtained for the following parameters: $\lambda = 1.06$ µm, $f = 100$ mm, $2d = 0.68$ mm, $R = 5$ mm is the illuminating beam radius, and $\varepsilon_0 = \lambda \cdot f/R$ is the diffraction width at the center of the segment under focusing. From the analysis of the data given in Table 5.9 it can be seen that while the energy efficiency $E(\varepsilon)$ is almost the same for both the DOEs, the DOE with diffraction corrections allows a more uniform energy distribution to be formed in the ε-vicinity of the focal segment. For $\varepsilon \ll \varepsilon_0$, $\varepsilon = \varepsilon_0/2$, and $\varepsilon = \varepsilon_0$ the rms deviation $\delta(\varepsilon)$ for the DOE with diffraction corrections is, respectively, 1.7, 2, and 1.25 times smaller than that for the geometric optical DOE. The plots for the functions $\mu(x, \varepsilon)$ for $\varepsilon \ll \varepsilon_0$, $\varepsilon = \varepsilon_0/2$ and $\varepsilon = \varepsilon_0$ are shown in Figure 5.27 for the geometric DOE and in Figure 5.28 for the DOE with diffraction corrections.

As ε increases relative to ε_0, the DOE with diffraction corrections does not allow one to attain an essentially decreased rms deviation $\delta(\varepsilon)$ as compared with the geometric optical DOE.

Table 5.10 gives the values of $E(\varepsilon)$ and $\delta(\varepsilon)$ for the geometric optical DOE and for the DOE with diffraction corrections for a ringlike illuminating beam, the diffraction width in the center of the focal segment being $\varepsilon_0 = 2\lambda f/(R_2 - R_1)$. The computation was conducted for the following parameters: $\lambda = 1.06$ µm, $f = 100$ mm, $2 \cdot d =$

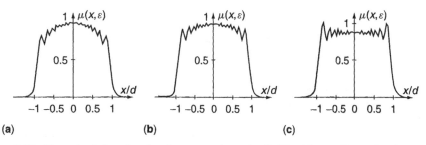

Figure 5.27. The $\mu(x,\varepsilon)$ function for the geometric optics DOE with a uniform circular illuminating beam: (**a**) $-\varepsilon \ll \varepsilon_0$, (**b**) $-\varepsilon = \varepsilon_0/2$, (**c**) $-\varepsilon = \varepsilon_0$.

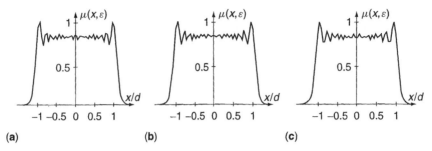

Figure 5.28. The $\mu(x,\varepsilon)$ function for the DOE with diffraction corrections for a uniform circular illuminating beam: (a) $-\varepsilon \ll \varepsilon_0$, (b) $-\varepsilon = \varepsilon_0/2$, (c) $-\varepsilon = \varepsilon_0$.

TABLE 5.10. Characteristics of the Quality of Focusing for the Geometric optical DOE and the DOE with Diffraction Parameters with a Ringlike Illuminating Beam

ε	Geometric Optical DOE		DOE with Diffraction Corrections	
	$E(\varepsilon)$, %	$\delta(\varepsilon)$, %	$E(\varepsilon)$, %	$\delta(\varepsilon)$, %
$\varepsilon \ll \varepsilon_0$	—	28.3	—	13.3
$\varepsilon_0/4$	62.3	36.3	62.2	16.2
$\varepsilon_0/2$	83.7	18.6	83.6	14.8
$3 \cdot \varepsilon_0/4$	89.7	18.2	89.5	15.0
ε_0	90.9	15.6	90.8	15.2

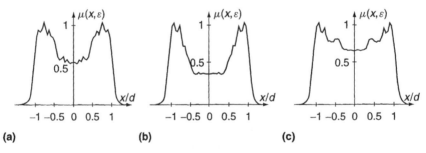

Figure 5.29. The $\mu(x, \varepsilon)$ function for the geometric optics DOE when illuminated by a uniform ringlike beam: (a) $-\varepsilon \ll \varepsilon_0$, (b) $-\varepsilon = \varepsilon_0/4$, and (c) $-\varepsilon = \varepsilon_0/2$.

1 mm, and $R_1 = 3$ mm and $R_2 = 5$ mm are the radii of the illuminating beam. From Table 5.10, the energy distribution $\mu(x, \varepsilon)$ for the geometric optical DOE is seen to be most nonuniform for $\varepsilon \ll \varepsilon_0$ and $\varepsilon = \varepsilon_0/4 : \delta(\varepsilon \ll \varepsilon_0) = 28.7$ percent and $\delta(\varepsilon_0/4) = 36$ percent (Fig. 5.29a and 5.29b).

For the aforementioned parameters, the DOE with diffraction corrections provides a more than twice decreased rms deviation (Figs. 5.30a and 5.30b). When $\varepsilon = \varepsilon_0/2$, the DOE with diffraction corrections allows the deviation $\delta(\varepsilon)$ to be decreased by a factor of only 1.26 (Figs. 5.29c and 5.30c), and for $\varepsilon = \varepsilon_0$ the geometric optical DOE and the DOE with diffraction parameters offer almost the same rms deviations.

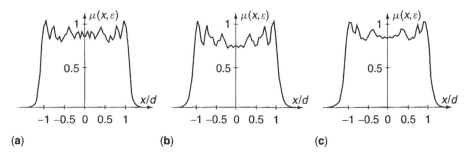

Figure 5.30. The $\mu(x, \varepsilon)$ function for the DOE with diffraction corrections when illuminated by a uniform ringlike beam: (**a**) $-\varepsilon \ll \varepsilon_0$, (**b**) $-\varepsilon = \varepsilon_0/4$, and (**c**) $-\varepsilon = \varepsilon_0/2$.

The studies pursued have demonstrated that the DOEs with diffraction corrections, when illuminated by a uniform circular or ringlike beam, allow one to generate a desired intensity distribution $\mu(x, \varepsilon)$ along the focal segment for the arbitrary ε with a 13 to 16 percent error. The geometric optical DOE is a special case of the DOE with diffraction corrections and, for the value of ε equal to the diffraction width of focused segment, is able to produce the desired intensity distribution $\mu(x, \varepsilon)$ with the error of about 15 percent.

5.3.6 Composite DOE to Focus onto a Cross

The term, *composite* or *segmented DOE*, is used in reference to a DOE whose aperture is divided into several domains (segments) capable of focusing the light independently onto separate domains. The DOE focusing onto a semi-ring dealt with in subsection 5.3.4 is intermediate between a conventional geometric optical DOE represented as a continuous set of focusing layers and a composite DOE, because despite the presence of a characteristic phase jump at $u = 0$, either fragment of the DOE focusing onto a semi-ring focuses the light onto the same focal line. The composite DOEs are of special interest in laser marking [74–77], in particular, in laser-aided marking of alphabetical-digital symbols. Taking into account that the phase functions of such DOEs are extremely complex, it would be interesting to pursue the diffraction studies of the composite DOE's efficiency.

As an example of a composite DOE, we shall consider a DOE focusing onto a cross when illuminated by the converging spherical beam (Fig. 5.31). The DOE's aperture $2a \times 2a$ is supposed to be composed of four segments $a \times a$, with each of them focusing onto a cross fragment. In this case, the phase function of the composite DOE is given by

$$
\varphi(u, v) = \begin{cases} \dfrac{kd}{4af_0}u^2, & u \cdot v \geq 0, \\[2mm] \dfrac{kd}{4af_0}v^2, & u \cdot v < 0, \end{cases}
\tag{5.77}
$$

$$
-a \leq u \leq a, \qquad -a \leq v \leq a.
$$

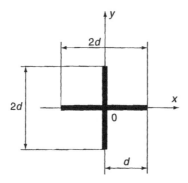

Figure 5.31. Domain of focusing for the DOE focusing onto a cross.

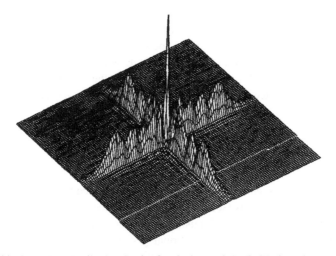

Figure 5.32. Intensity distribution in the focal plane of the DOE focusing onto a cross.

The intensity distribution in the focal domain of the DOE (5.77) with the $f_0 = 750$ mm; $\lambda = 0.6328$ μm; $d = 2$ mm; $2a = 25.6$ mm; $N_1 = N_2 = 128$, is shown in Figure 5.32 and clearly demonstrates the cross-shaped structure of the light focused.

Analysis of Figure 5.32 makes it possible to direct the way to improvements in the DOE's phase function of Eq. (5.77). Owing to uniqueness of the intersection point of the cross-focal lines (optical axis), the interference effects typical of such caustics are practically absent. However, there is an essential intensity peak on the optical axis to be eliminated in the course of the DOE's design. For this purpose, one should utilize a composite DOE focusing onto a centerless cross (Fig. 5.33), with the phase function given by

$$\varphi(u, v) = \begin{cases} \dfrac{k}{2f_0}\left[\dfrac{d - \beta}{2a}u^2 + \beta u\right], & u \cdot v \geq 0, \\[4mm] \dfrac{k}{2f_0}\left[\dfrac{d - \beta}{2a}v^2 + \beta v\right], & u \cdot v < 0, \end{cases} \tag{5.78}$$

$$-a \leq u \leq a, \qquad -a \leq v \leq a.$$

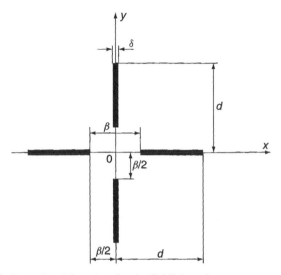

Figure 5.33. Domain of focusing for the DOE focusing onto a centerless cross.

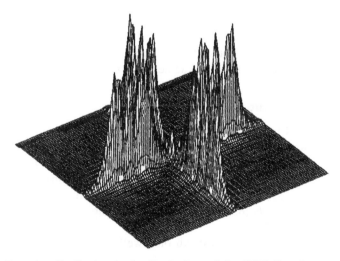

Figure 5.34. Intensity distribution in the focal plane of the DOE focusing onto a centerless cross.

The intensity distribution in the focal plane of the DOE of Eq. (5.78), with $f_0 = 750$ mm; $\lambda = 0.6328$ µm; $d = 2$ mm; $\beta = 0.2$ mm; $2a = 25.6$ mm; $N_1 = N_2 = 128$, is shown in Figure 5.34. Comparison of Figure 5.32 and Figure 5.34 suggests that for the given parameters of the DOE focusing onto a cross, the central peak is possible to eliminate by optimization of the value of β.

The energy efficiency values, E_ε, of the DOE in Eq. (5.78) with the aforementioned parameters for various numbers of phase function quantization levels are given in Table 5.11.

TABLE 5.11. Energy Efficiency $E(\varepsilon)$ of the DOE (5.78) with the Parameters $f_0 = 750$ mm: $\lambda = 0.6328$ μm; $d = 2$ mm; $\beta = 0.2$ mm; $2a = 25.6$ mm; $N_1 = N_2 = 128$ for Various Numbers M of Phase Quantization Levels

ε (mm) M	0.02	0.04	0.06	0.08	0.1	0.12	0.14
256	0.452	0.712	0.788	0.792	0.805	0.825	0.832
16	0.450	0.709	0.875	0.789	0.802	0.823	0.830
4	0.385	0.608	0.674	0.677	0.688	0.706	0.712
2	0.369	0.593	0.657	0.661	0.671	0.689	0.695

Here, $E(\varepsilon)$ is the illuminating energy portion coming to the domain of focusing D [a centerless cross of diffraction line width ε (Fig. 5.33)]

$$D = \{(x, y) : [(\beta/2 \leq |x| \leq d)\&|y| \leq \varepsilon] \cup [(\beta/2 \leq |y| \leq d)\&|x| \leq \varepsilon]\}.$$

Table 5.11 gives the energy efficiency values, $E(\varepsilon)$, for a set of values of diffraction width, ε, within the range from 0.02 mm to 0.14 mm. It should be noted that for a conventional lens with identical parameters: $f_0 = 750$ mm; $\lambda = 0.6328$ μm; $2a = 25.6$ mm, the focal spot width with respect to the intensity drop of $\Theta = 0.1$ is derived from the relation $\varepsilon_0 = 2 \cdot 2{,}73(f_0/ka) \approx 0.032$ mm [34]. Considering the results of studying the DOE focusing onto a segment and the fact that only a quarter of the composed DOE's aperture contributes to each cross segment, the expected expansion of the focal spot is at least fourfold and agrees with the data in Table 5.11.

5.3.7 DOE Focusing onto an Axial Segment

A DOE with enhanced focal depth, or a DOE focusing onto an axial segment has first been proposed in Ref. [1]. In later references, several techniques for computing the phase functions of such DOEs have been proposed [20, 78–83]. The use of DOEs with enhanced focal depth is topical in optical playback systems [84], in producing optical gas discharge [85], in producing a reference light channel in metrology [79], in noncontact measurements [82], in computer image input-output units [79], and in laser technological units [86].

It has been known that the focal depth of a well-corrected lens is estimated [34] by the formula $L \sim \lambda f_0^2/a^2$ and amounts to $L \sim 10^{-1}$ mm for a lens with the relative pinhole of 1:10. Enhancing the focal depth requires a purposeful introduction of spherical aberration.

The phase function of a DOE focusing onto an axial segment may be derived from the general equations, (5.13)–(5.15). According to Eq. (5.15), when producing a light segment on an optical axis, the layers are represented by circumferences. Considering the radial symmetry of the problem, the DOE's phase function is derived from the following set of equations:

$$\begin{cases} \phi(r) = -k \int_0^r \dfrac{\rho}{\sqrt{\rho^2 + (f_0 + z(\rho))^2}} \, d\rho - \varphi_0(r), \\ \theta(z)\dfrac{dz(\rho)}{d\rho} = I_0(\rho) \cdot 2\pi\rho, \quad z(0) = 0, \quad z(a) = L. \end{cases} \quad (5.79)$$

Here, r is the radial coordinate in the DOE's plane, $\theta(z)$ is the linear density along the segment of focusing $[0, L]$, $I_0(r)$ and $\varphi_0(r)$ are, respectively, the intensity and phase of the illuminating beam, and a is the DOE radius. The first equation in (5.79) corresponds to Eq. (5.14) and has been derived from the inclinations equation, Eq. (5.2), in polar coordinates. The second equation in (5.79) corresponds to the differential form of the law of light flux conservation, Eq. (5.13).

For $f_0 \gg a$ and constant linear density, $\theta(z) = \text{const}$, from Eq. (5.79) we get that the phase function for focusing onto an axial segment is given by

$$\varphi(r) = \varphi_0 - \left(\frac{k}{2c}\right) \ln[1 + 2c\sqrt{r^2 + (f_0 - cr^2)^2} - 2cf_0 + 2c^2r^2],$$

$$c = \frac{L}{a^2}, \quad 0 \le r \le a, \tag{5.80}$$

for the plane illuminating beam, and

$$\varphi(r) = \varphi_0 - \left(\frac{k}{2c}\right) \ln\left[1 + 2c\sqrt{r^2 + (f_0 - cr^2)^2} - 2cf_0 + 2c^2r^2\right]$$

$$+ k\sqrt{r^2 + f_0^2}, \tag{5.81}$$

$$c = \frac{L}{a^2}, \quad 0 \le r \le a,$$

for the converging illuminating beam. Let us investigate the DOE in Eq. (5.81) with uniform sampling.

In an effort to determine the real focal depth and the scattering spot size provided by the DOE at different quantization parameters, the numerical simulation was conducted for the following parameters: $f_0 = 300$ mm; $2a = 25.6$ mm; $L = 15$ mm; $\lambda = 0.6328$ μm, and the number of annular sampling modules is $N = 128$. The intensity isophotes obtained in the meridian section of the focal plane (Fig. 5.35) and the corresponding 3D images (Fig. 5.36) for various numbers of quantization levels $M = \infty, 4, 2$ give a good idea of the operation of the element in Eq. (5.81).

The plot for the intensity distribution along the optical axis for the same DOE parameters and for $M = \infty$ is shown in Figure 5.37, the intensity being normalized to the intensity at $z = f_0$. The rms deviation of the intensity along the segment under focusing from a constant value is 37.4 percent. The intensity is seen to drop toward the segment edges and show considerable variations in value along the segment. When the number of phase quantization levels is large ($M = \infty$, Figs. 5.35a and 5.36a), one observes an extended focal domain of depth ~ 10–15 mm enclosed by the surfaces corresponding to higher-order diffraction rings. When $M = 4$ and, particularly, $M = 2$, the focal domain is disintegrated into two to three subdomains of depth 2–5 mm, the number of higher-order rings being increased. Analysis of Figure 5.35a shows that the focal spot size of $\Delta \sim 0.06$ mm is preserved through a distance of ~ 15 mm, thus ensuring a considerable focal depth.

The energy efficiency $E(z)$ may be estimated by the ratio of the energy portion passing through a circle of diameter $\Delta \sim 0,06$ mm, located at the depth of z in the

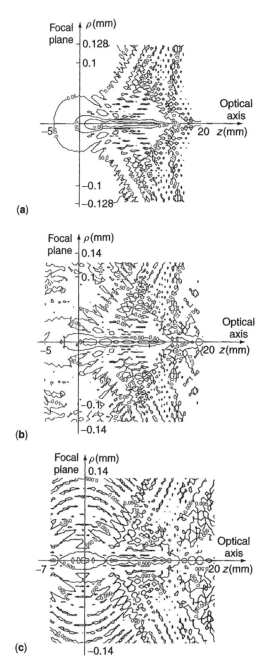

Figure 5.35. Isophotes of normalized intensity distribution $I_M(\rho, z)/I_\infty(0, 0)$ in the meridian section of the focal domain of a DOE with enhanced focal depth. The DOE parameters are: $f_0 = 300$ mm; $\lambda = 0.6328$ μm; $2a = 25.6$ mm; $L = 15$ mm; $N = 128$; (**a**) $M = \infty$; (**b**) $M = 4$; (**c**) $M = 2$.

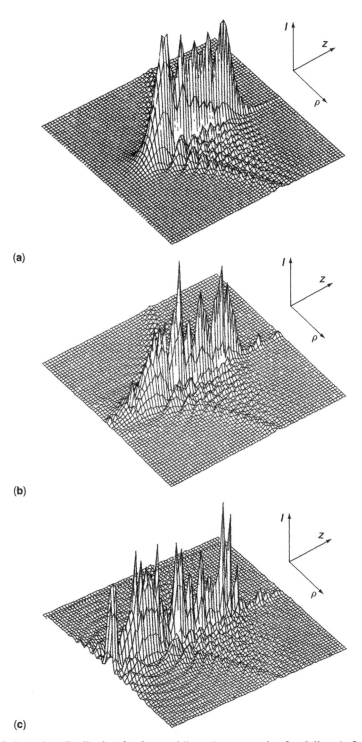

Figure 5.36. Intensity distribution in the meridian plane near the focal line (-5 mm $< z <$ 20 mm; $0 < \rho < 128$ μm) of the DOE with enhanced focal depth. The DOE parameters are: $f_0 = 300$ mm; $\lambda = 0.6328$ μm; $2a = 25.6$ mm; $L = 15$ mm; $N = 128$; (**a**) $M = \infty$; (**b**) $M = 4$; (**c**) $M = 2$.

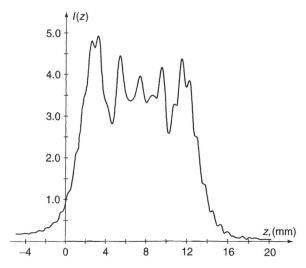

Figure 5.37. Intensity distribution $I(z) = I(0, z)/I_\infty(0, 0)$ along the optical axis of a DOE with enhanced focal depth.

focal domain, to the total energy illuminating the optical element:

$$E(z) = \frac{\displaystyle\int_0^{\Delta/2} I(\rho, z) \cdot 2\pi\rho \, d\rho}{\displaystyle\int_0^{\infty} I(\rho, z) \cdot 2\pi\rho \, d\rho}. \tag{5.82}$$

From the plot of the $E(z)$ function in Figure 5.37 one can see that the value of $E(z)$ does not drop below 10 percent over a length of 15 mm and that there is a peak of more than 15 percent over a length of 4 mm. For $M = 2$, the average value of $E(z)$ along the segment of focusing essentially reduces, whereas the peak is displaced toward the lens focus. Note for comparison that the energy efficiency of an ordinary-depth lens is about $\sim$78 percent.

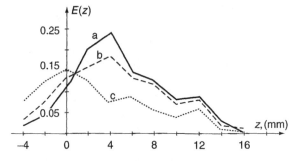

Figure 5.38. Energy efficiency of the DOE with enhanced focal depth: $f_0 = 300$ mm; $\lambda = 0.6328$ μm; $2a = 25.6$ mm; $\Delta/2 = 30$ μm; $L = 15$ mm; $N = 128$; (**a**) $M = \infty$; (**b**) $M = 4$; (**c**) $M = 2$.

5.4 DOE FOCUSING ONTO A 2D DOMAIN: A METHOD OF COORDINATED RECTANGLES

Although there are quite a lot of papers dealing with DOEs that can focus onto a curve, the DOEs focusing onto a plane domain are scantily studied. Solving the inverse task of focusing onto a plane domain in terms of geometric optics, as a rule, presents a very complicated problem [12]. Perhaps, the only exception is focusing the rectangular beam onto a rectangular domain [12,87–89]. This problem may be decomposed into two 1D problems and resolved analytically [12,87–89]. In this subsection, we consider a simple numerical technique to design DOE focusing onto 2D domains, in which the analytically solved problem of focusing onto a rectangle is used as a basis.

Consider the problem of focusing onto an arbitrary 2D domain. Let a DOE of aperture G in the plane $\mathbf{u} = (u, v)$, $z = 0$, be illuminated by a light beam of wavelength λ and complex amplitude given by

$$W_0(\mathbf{u}) = \sqrt{I_0(u)} \exp[i\varphi_0(\mathbf{u})],$$

where $I_0(\mathbf{u})$ is the beam intensity and $\varphi_0(\mathbf{u})$ is the beam phase.

It is required to compute the DOE's phase function $\varphi(\mathbf{u})$ if the illuminating beam is focused onto the domain D at $z = \mathrm{f}$ and produces a desired intensity distribution $I(\mathbf{x})$, where $\mathbf{x} = (x, y)$ are the coordinates in the plane of focusing.

In the paraxial approximation, the DOE's geometric optical phase function, $\varphi(\mathbf{u})$, may be derived from solving the following set of equations

$$
\begin{cases}
\mathbf{x}(\mathbf{u}) = \mathbf{u} + f \nabla_\perp \varphi(\mathbf{u})/k, \\[2mm]
\dfrac{I_0(\mathbf{u})}{I(\mathbf{x}(\mathbf{u}))} = \dfrac{d\mathbf{x}(\mathbf{u})}{d\mathbf{u}} = |x_u'(\mathbf{u})y_v'(\mathbf{u}) - x_v'(\mathbf{u})y_u'(\mathbf{u})|, \; x_u'(\mathbf{u}) = y_v'(\mathbf{u}), \\[2mm]
\varphi(\mathbf{u}) = \int_{\mathbf{u}_0}^{\mathbf{u}} \nabla_\perp \varphi(\mathbf{u}) \, d\mathbf{u} - \varphi_0(\mathbf{u}) = -\dfrac{k\mathbf{u}^2}{2f} + \dfrac{k}{f} \int_{\mathbf{u}_0}^{\mathbf{u}} \mathbf{x}(\mathbf{u}) \, d\mathbf{u} - \varphi_0(\mathbf{u})
\end{cases}
\tag{5.83}
$$

where $k = 2\pi/\lambda$. The first equation in (5.83) defines the ray equation and determines the ray correspondence between the points $\mathbf{u}$ of the DOE's aperture and the points $\mathbf{x}$ of the domain of focusing D. The second equation in (5.83) corresponds to the differential form of the law of light flux conservation along the ray pipes and allows one to deduce the function $\mathbf{x}(\mathbf{u})$, supposing the formation of the desired intensity distribution $I(\mathbf{x})$ at $\mathbf{x} \in D$. At last, the third equation in (5.83) corresponds to reconstructing the phase from the total differential, with the term $\varphi_0(\mathbf{u})$ introduced to compensate for the illuminating beam phase.

In the general case, solving the set (5.83) presents a very complicated problem, but it may be essentially simplified for the rectangular DOE's aperture G and rectangular domain of focusing, D, on the condition of factorization of the functions

$$W_0(\mathbf{u}) = W_1(u)W_2(v), \quad I(\mathbf{x}) = I_1(x)I_2(y), \tag{5.84}$$

that is, for

$$I_0(\mathbf{u}) = I_{01}(u)I_{02}(v), \quad \varphi_0(\mathbf{u}) = \varphi_{01}(u) + \varphi_{02}(v). \tag{5.85}$$

In this case, solving two 1D problems of focusing onto a line-segment allows one to determine the 2D phase function of the DOE:

$$\varphi(\mathbf{u}) = \varphi_1(u) + \varphi_2(v). \tag{5.86}$$

The phase function $\varphi_1(u)$ of a 1D (cylindrical) DOE that can perform the desired transformation of the light beam is found from the following set of equations

$$\begin{cases} x(u) = u + f\dfrac{d\varphi_1(u)}{du}\Big/k, \\[2mm] \dfrac{I_{01}(u)}{I_1(x)} = \dfrac{dx(u)}{du}, \quad u_0 \le u \le u_1, \quad x_0 \le x \le x_1, \\[2mm] \varphi_1(u) = -\dfrac{ku^2}{2f} + \dfrac{k}{f}\displaystyle\int_{u_0}^{u} x(\xi)\,d\xi - \varphi_{01}(u). \end{cases} \tag{5.87}$$

The equations in the set (5.87) are, respectively, the ray equation, the law of light flux conservation along the ray pipes, and the equation for phase retrieval. The solution to the set (5.87) is essentially simpler than that to the set (5.83). For instance, if

$$I_0(x) = \begin{cases} I_1, & x_0 \le x \le x_1 \\ 0, & x < x_0, x > x_1 \end{cases},$$

the solution to the set (5.87) takes the form

$$\varphi_1(u) = -\frac{ku^2}{2f} + \frac{k}{f}\int_{u_0}^{u}\left[\frac{1}{I_1}\int_{u_0}^{\xi} I_{01}(\eta)\,d\eta - x_0\right]d\xi - \varphi_{01}(u), \tag{5.88}$$

and, hence, the 2D phase function of the DOE with rectangular aperture that can produce a rectangular domain of uniform intensity is given by

$$\varphi(\mathbf{u}) = -\frac{u^2 + v^2}{2f} + \frac{k}{f}\int_{u_0}^{u}\left[\frac{1}{I_1}\int_{u_0}^{\xi} I_{01}(\eta)\,d\eta - x_0\right]d\xi$$

$$+ \frac{k}{f}\int_{v_0}^{v}\left[\frac{1}{I_1}\int_{v_0}^{\xi} I_{02}(\eta)\,d\eta - y_0\right]d\xi - \varphi_0(\mathbf{u}), \tag{5.89}$$

where (x_0, y_0) are the coordinates of the bottom-left corner of the rectangle under focusing.

If at least one of the domains, G or D, is not rectangular, the DOE's phase function is no longer factorable, even with factorable functions $W_0(\mathbf{u})$, $I(\mathbf{x})$, and assumes a much more complicated form. Eqs. (5.87)–(5.89) make possible the formulation of a coordinated rectangles method for designing DOEs with arbitrary domains G and D and factorable functions in Eqs. (5.84) and (5.85). With this method, the DOE's aperture (domain G) and the domain under focusing (domain D) are approximated by the sets of aperture rectangles, G_i, and focal rectangles, D_i, $i = 1, N$. Then, the phase function $\varphi_i(\mathbf{u})$ is computed for each aperture rectangle G_i from Eqs. (5.86) and (5.87) on the condition of focusing onto the corresponding focal rectangle D_i. Consider the described method in more detail. Let the DOE's aperture G be limited by the curves $v = g_1(u)$ and $v = g_2(u)$ and by the line-segments $u = u_{\min}$ and $u = u_{\max}$ (Fig. 5.39), and let the domain of focusing D be limited by the curves $y = f_1(x)$ and $y = f_2(x)$ and by the straight lines $x = x_{\min}$ and $x = x_{\max}$ (Fig. 5.40).

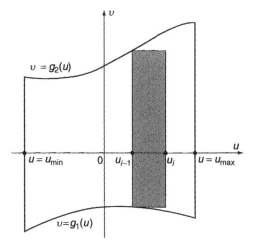

Figure 5.39. DOE's aperture.

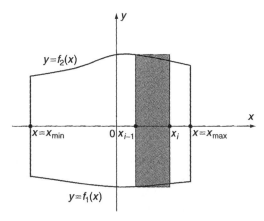

Figure 5.40. Domain of focusing.

Introduce the breakdown u_i, $i = 0, N$, $u_0 = u_{min}$, $u_N = u_{max}$ of the line-segment $[u_{min}, u_{max}]$ and the aperture's rectangles $G_i = [u_{i-1}, u_i] \times [g_1(u_{i-1}), g_2(u_{i-1})]$. The breakdown x_i, $i = 0, N$, $x_0 = x_{min}$, $x_N = x_{max}$ of the line-segment $[x_{min}, x_{max}]$ is determined from the solution of the following nonlinear recurrent equation

$$\int_{u_{i-1}}^{u_i} \int_{g_1(u_{i-1})}^{g_2(u_{i-1})} I_0(\mathbf{u}) \, d^2\mathbf{u} = \int_{x_{i-1}}^{x_i} \int_{f_1(x_{i-1})}^{f_2(x_{i-1})} I(\mathbf{x}) \, d^2\mathbf{x}, \quad i = \overline{1, N}. \tag{5.90}$$

Equation (5.90) defines the law of light flux conservation as the light propagates from the aperture rectangle G_i to the focal rectangle D_i.

Having solved Eq. (5.90), we obtain the approximation of the domain D by the set of rectangles

$$D_i = [x_{i-1}, x_i] \times [f_1(x_{i-1}), f_2(x_{i-1})], \quad i = \overline{1, N}.$$

To determine the phase function $\varphi_i(\mathbf{u}) = \varphi_{i1}(u) + \varphi_{i2}(v)$ in the aperture rectangle, one needs to solve the set (5.87) twice. The obtained DOE's phase function is

$$\varphi(u) = \sum_{i=1}^{N} \varphi_i(u, v) \, \text{rect}\left(\frac{2u - (u_{i-1} + u_i)}{2(u_i - u_{i-1})}\right)$$

$$\text{rect}\left(\frac{2v - [g_1(u_{i-1}) + g_2(u_{i-1})]}{2[g_2(u_{i-1}) - g_1(u_{i-1})]}\right) - \varphi_0(u, v), \qquad (5.91)$$

where

$$\text{rect}\,(u) = \begin{cases} 1, & |u| < 0,5 \\ 0, & |u| \geq 0,5, \end{cases}$$

suffers breaks along the straight lines $u = u_i$, $i = 1, N-1$, which results in the interference on the junctions of the rectangles of focusing. The interference effects may be decreased if the phase function $\varphi(\mathbf{u})$ is made continuous along some curve $v = f(u)$. For this to happen, we put

$$\varphi_i(\mathbf{u}) = \varphi_i(\mathbf{u}) + \tilde{\varphi}_i, \qquad (5.92)$$

where

$$\tilde{\varphi} = \begin{cases} 0, & i = 0 \\ \displaystyle\sum_{j=1}^{i-1}\{\varphi_j[u_j, f(u_j)] - \varphi_{j+1}[u_j, f(u_j)]\}, & 2 \leq i \leq N. \end{cases} \qquad (5.93)$$

By way of illustration, let us consider the synthesis of a DOE with circular aperture $G = \{(u, v)\, u^2 + v^2 \leq R^2\}$ that focuses the plane circular beam onto a rectangle $D = [-b, b] \times [-a, a]$ of uniform intensity ("circular DOE focusing onto a rectangle").

In this case, the aperture G is approximated by the set of rectangles

$$G_i = [u_{i-1}, u_i] \times \left[\sqrt{R^2 - u_{i-1}^2}, -\sqrt{R^2 - u_{i-1}^2}\right], \quad i = 1, N, \quad u_0 = -R, \quad u_N = R, \qquad (5.94)$$

and the domain D by the set of rectangles

$$D_i = [x_{i-1}, x_i] \times [-a, a], \quad i = 1, N, \quad x_0 = -b, \quad x_N = b. \qquad (5.95)$$

The solution to Eq. (5.90) that determines the breakdown of the focal domain takes the form

$$x_i = x_{i-1} + \frac{4b(u_i - u_{i-1})\sqrt{R^2 - u_{i-1}^2}}{\pi R^2}, \quad i = \overline{1, N-1}. \qquad (5.96)$$

The phase function $\varphi_i(\mathbf{u})$ that represents the geometric optical solution to the problem of focusing from the rectangle G_i onto the rectangle D_i is determined from Eq. (5.89). The phase addition $\tilde{\varphi}_i$ in Eq. (5.92) is chosen from the condition that the phase function is continuous along the u-axis:

$$\tilde{\varphi}_i = \begin{cases} 0, & i = 1 \\ \displaystyle\sum_{j=1}^{i-1}[\varphi_j(u_j, 0) - \varphi_{j+1}(u_j, 0)], & 2 \le i \le N. \end{cases} \tag{5.97}$$

The DOE's operation may be characterized by the energy efficiency, E, and the rms deviation, δ. The quantity

$$E = \iint_D I(\mathbf{x}) \, d^2\mathbf{x} / \iint_G I_0(\mathbf{u}) \, d^2\mathbf{u} \tag{5.98}$$

characterizes the energy portion of the illuminating beam that has come to the domain of focusing. The quantity

$$\delta = \frac{1}{\overline{I}} \left(\frac{1}{\|D\|} \iint_D [I(\mathbf{x}) - \overline{I}]^2 \, d^2\mathbf{x} \right) \tag{5.99}$$

characterizes the deviation of the intensity distribution $I(\mathbf{x})$ from an average intensity, $\overline{I} = (1/\|D\|) \iint_D I(\mathbf{x}) \, d^2\mathbf{x}$, in the domain of focusing. The field produced by the "circular DOE focusing onto a rectangle" was computed for the following parameters: $\lambda = 10.6$ μm, $f = 800$ mm, the illuminating beam radius is $R = 20.5$ mm, and the rectangle of focusing size is 8×4 mm. The initial DOE was approximated by a set of 60 rectangles constructed on the uniformly divided segment $[-R, R]$. The energy efficiency of focusing onto a rectangle was 85.4 percent and the rms deviation of intensity was 34.4 percent. The 3D intensity distribution in the focal plane is shown in Figure 5.41 and the isophotes of the 3D distribution are depicted in Figure 5.42. The analysis of the results obtained testifies in favor of high-quality focusing. The

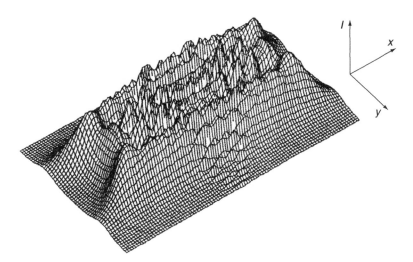

Figure 5.41. Intensity distribution in the focal plane of a DOE focusing onto a rectangle.

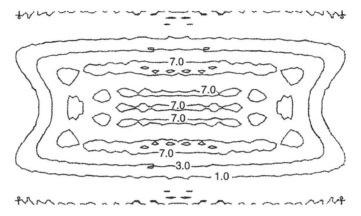

Figure 5.42. Isophotes of the intensity distribution in the focal plane of the DOE focusing onto a rectangle.

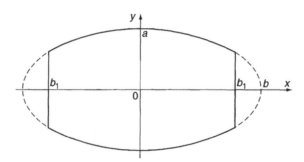

Figure 5.43. "A frustum of an ellipse".

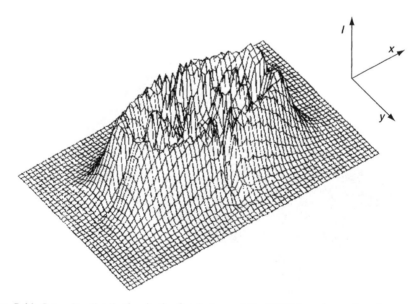

Figure 5.44. Intensity distribution in the focal plane of the DOE focusing onto a frustum of an ellipse.

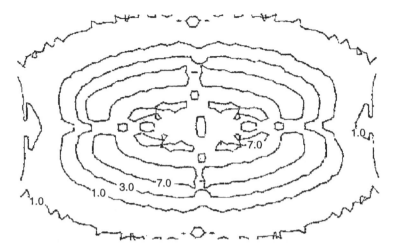

Figure 5.45. Isophotes of the intensity distribution in the focal plane of the DOE focusing onto a frustum of an ellipse.

method of coordinated rectangles was also used to synthesize a circular-aperture DOE that focuses a plane circular beam onto a frustum of an ellipse (Fig. 5.43) of uniform intensity distribution ("DOE focusing onto a frustum of an ellipse").

The "DOE focusing onto a frustum of an ellipse" was studied with the following parameters: $\lambda = 10.6$ μm; $f = 800$ mm, the illuminating beam radius is $R = 20.5$ mm, the characteristic parameters of the ellipse being $a = 2$ mm, $b = 4$ mm, $b_1 = 3.5$ mm. The energy efficiency of focusing onto a frustum of an ellipse was 87.6 percent and the rms deviation was 38.2 percent. Shown in Figure 5.44 is a 3D intensity distribution in the focal plane of the DOE focusing onto a frustum of an ellipse, whereas Figure 5.45 depicts the isophotes of the 3D intensity distribution when focusing onto a frustum of an ellipse. The results of numerical simulation confirm that the method of "coordinated rectangles" can be successfully applied to designing DOEs that focus onto complex 2D domains.

5.5 MULTIFOCUS DOEs

The focusing onto an array of identical, mutually displaced focal curves may be implemented using a DOE whose phase function is represented as a superposition of the phase functions of a DOE focusing onto a curve and a multiorder diffraction grating. Such DOEs multiplicate (replicate) a desired focal line in the same plane. In this subsection we deal with multifocus DOE, that is, DOEs aimed to focus the illuminating beam onto N lines of various length, located in different planes along the optical axis, with the desired energy distribution, $I_1, \ldots, I_N$, $\left(\sum_{i=1}^{N} I_i = 1 \right)$ produced between the lines (Fig. 5.46).

The introduction of nonlinearity into the DOE phase function is known to result in the emergence of additional diffraction orders [25–30,90–92]. When designing multifocus DOEs, the main idea lies in the use of the diffraction orders emerging as the result of nonlinear transformation of the paraxial phase function, Eqs. (5.17) and (5.18), of a

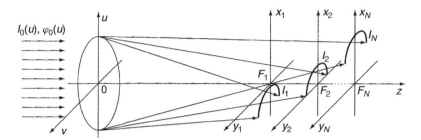

Figure 5.46. The process of focusing implemented by a multifocus DOE.

DOE focusing onto a curve. In this case, the images produced in the diffraction orders correspond to an array of scaled lines located in different planes perpendicular to the optical axis. The type of nonlinear transformation of the phase of a DOE focusing onto a curve affects the energy distribution between the lines and can be chosen in accordance with the desired energy distribution between the lines of focusing.

From the preceding text, it is found that the phase function of a multifocus DOE may be represented as follows [25–30]:

$$\varphi_{mf}(\mathbf{u}) = \varphi_1(\mathbf{u}) + \varphi_{11}(\mathbf{u}) + \Phi[\varphi_d(\mathbf{u})] - \varphi_0(\mathbf{u}), \quad \mathbf{u} \in G, \tag{5.100}$$

where

$$\varphi_d(\mathbf{u}) = \mathrm{mod}_{2\pi}[\varphi_2(\mathbf{u}) + \varphi_{22}(\mathbf{u}) + \varphi_{23}(\mathbf{u})]. \tag{5.101}$$

Here, $\varphi_0(\mathbf{u})$ is the phase of a beam that illuminates a DOE of aperture G, whereas $\varphi_1(\mathbf{u})$ and $\varphi_2(\mathbf{u})$ are the paraxial phase functions for focusing onto the lines L defined by the parametrical equation

$$\mathbf{X}(\xi) = [X(\xi), Y(\xi)], \quad \xi \in [0, S], \tag{5.102}$$

and located in the focal planes $z = f_1$ and $z = f_2$. From the general formulae (5.17) and (5.18) for the phase function of a DOE focusing onto a curve, the functions $\varphi_1(\mathbf{u})$ and $\varphi_2(\mathbf{u})$ are given by

$$\varphi_i(\mathbf{u}) = -\frac{k\mathbf{u}^2}{2f_i} + \tilde{\varphi}_i(\mathbf{u}), \quad i = 1, 2, \tag{5.103}$$

where

$$\tilde{\varphi}_i(\mathbf{u}) = \frac{k}{f_i} \int_{u_0}^{u} X[\xi(u, v_0)] \, du + \frac{k}{f_i} \int_{v_0}^{v} Y[\xi(u, v)] \, dv. \tag{5.104}$$

Finally, the functions

$$\varphi_{11}(\mathbf{u}) = \frac{k}{f_1}\mathbf{x}_1\mathbf{u}, \quad \varphi_{22}(\mathbf{u}) = \frac{k}{f_2}\mathbf{x}_2\mathbf{u}, \quad \varphi_{23}(\mathbf{u}) = -\frac{k}{2f_3}\mathbf{u}^2 \tag{5.105}$$

in Eq. (5.100) are the paraxial phase functions of prisms and a lens, respectively.

The term $\varphi_0(\mathbf{u})$ in Eq. (5.100) is introduced to compensate for the illuminating beam phase. Note that the DOE's phase, $\varphi_1(\mathbf{u})$, the prisms' phases, $\varphi_{11}(\mathbf{u})$, $\varphi_{22}(\mathbf{u})$,

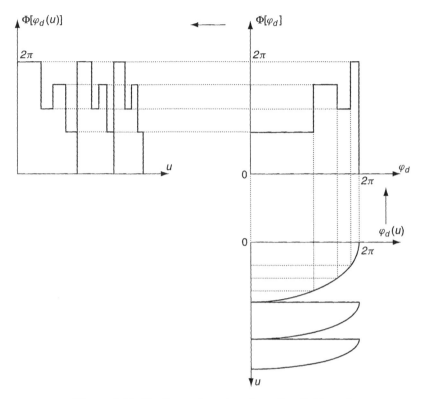

Figure 5.47. Nonlinear phase transformation (1-D case).

and the lens's phase, $\varphi_{23}(\mathbf{u})$, in Eq. (5.100) do not contribute directly to the generation of diffraction orders, but only provide additional degrees of freedom when choosing the coordinates of focal planes, the location of lines in those planes, and a scaling factor used to define how the size of the lines of focusing should be changed. The $\Phi[\varphi_d(\mathbf{u})] \in [0, 2\pi)$ function describes a nonlinear transformation of the phase $\varphi_d(\mathbf{u}) \in [0, 2\pi)$. The mechanism of the nonlinear transformation is depicted in Figure 5.47. The $\Phi[\varphi_d(\mathbf{u})]$ function serves as an analog of a zone plate with a binary, stepwise, or a continuous relief.

Let us consider the operation of a multifocus DOE illuminated by the following beam

$$W_0(\mathbf{u}) = \sqrt{I_0(\mathbf{u})}\,\exp[i\varphi_0(\mathbf{u})].$$

In this case, the field directly behind the DOE's plane takes the form

$$W(\mathbf{u}) = \sqrt{I_0(\mathbf{u})}\,\exp\{i\varphi_1(\mathbf{u}) + i\varphi_{11}(\mathbf{u}) + i\,\Phi[\varphi_d(\mathbf{u})]\}. \tag{5.106}$$

To describe the way an array of lines is produced, we shall decompose the function $\exp[i\Phi(\varphi)]$ into the Fourier series on the interval $[0, 2\pi)$ [25–30,90–92]

$$\exp[i\Phi(\xi)] = \sum_{j=-\infty}^{\infty} c_j \exp(ij\xi), \tag{5.107}$$

where

$$c_j = \frac{1}{2\pi} \int_0^{2\pi} \exp(i\Phi[\xi] - ij\xi)\,d\xi \tag{5.108}$$

are the Fourier coefficients; $\sum_{j=-\infty}^{\infty} |c_j|^2 = 1$.

Substituting $\xi = \varphi_d(\mathbf{u})$ in Eq. (5.107) and taking account of the 2π-periodicity, Eq. (5.106) takes the form

$$W(\mathbf{u}) = \sqrt{I_0(\mathbf{u})}\,\exp[i\varphi_1(\mathbf{u}) + i\varphi_{11}(\mathbf{u})] \sum_{j=-\infty}^{\infty} c_j \exp\{ij[\varphi_2(\mathbf{u}) + \varphi_{22}(\mathbf{u}) + \varphi_{23}(\mathbf{u})]\}. \tag{5.109}$$

Equation (5.109) corresponds to a superposition of the beams with the following phase functions

$$\varphi_j(\mathbf{u}) = -\frac{k\mathbf{u}^2}{2F_j} + p_j\tilde{\varphi}_j(\mathbf{u}) + \frac{k}{F_j}\mathbf{X}_j\mathbf{u}, \tag{5.110}$$

where

$$\tilde{\varphi}_j(\mathbf{u}) = \frac{k}{F_j} \int_{u_0}^{u} X[\xi(u, v_0)]\,du + \frac{k}{F_j} \int_{v_0}^{v} Y[\xi(u, v)]\,dv, \tag{5.111}$$

$$F_j = \frac{f_1 f_2}{f_2 + jf_1(1 + f_2/f_3)}, \tag{5.112}$$

$$p_j = \frac{f_2 + jf_1}{f_2 + jf_1(1 + f_2/f_3)}, \tag{5.113}$$

$$\mathbf{X}_j = \frac{\mathbf{x}_1 f_2 + j\mathbf{x}_2 f_1}{f_2 + jf_1(1 + f_2/f_3)}. \tag{5.114}$$

Squared modules of the Fourier coefficients in Eq. (5.108) specify the energy distribution between the beams, while the function in Eq. (5.111) defines the structure of the images produced in the diffraction orders of the multifocus DOE.

In Section 5.2, it has been shown that when a lens addition in the phase function of a DOE focusing onto a curve is multiplied by a constant p, the line under focusing is scaled by a factor of p. According to the above property and the general form of the phase function of a DOE focusing onto a curve, the phase function $\varphi_j(\mathbf{u})$ in Eq. (5.110) will produce in the plane $z = F_j$ a line L_{p_j} described by the equation

$$\mathbf{X}_{p_j}(\xi) = [p_j X(\xi/p_j), p_j Y(\xi/p_j)], \quad \xi \in \lfloor 0, p_j S \rfloor. \tag{5.115}$$

The line L_{p_j} is the line L scaled by the factor of p_j. The last term in Eq. (5.110) corresponds to the phase function of the prism that provides the shift $\mathbf{X}_j$ of the line L_{p_j} in the plane $z = F_j$. It should be noted that the process of generation of the line L_{p_j} is not entirely independent of the other diffraction orders. Actually, the images produced by the beams with the phase functions $\varphi_k(\mathbf{u})$, $k \neq j$ in the plane $z = F_j$, correspond to defocused lines. In the general case, the width of the defocused lines is by the order of magnitude higher than the diffraction width of the line L_{p_j}, thus making their interference negligibly small. In some rare cases, when the interference between the orders is impossible to neglect, by properly fitting the vectors $\mathbf{x}_1$ and $\mathbf{x}_2$ in Eq. (5.114), the spurious defocused lines can be separated from the useful ones, thus providing the independent generation of the focal lines. In view of the aforementioned reasons the interference between the images produced in different diffraction orders will be disregarded in further discussion.

Denote $j_1, \ldots, j_N$ the indices corresponding to pregiven focal planes. Then, the desired energy distribution $I_1, \ldots, I_N$, between the lines under focusing may be provided if the Fourier coefficients, Eq. (5.108), of the $\exp(i\Phi[\xi])$, $\xi \in [0, 2\pi)$ function satisfy the equation

$$|c_{j_i}|^2 = I_i, i = 1, \ldots, N. \tag{5.116}$$

According to Eq. (5.116), we shall interpret the nonlinear transform $\Phi[\varphi]$ as the phase function of an N-order diffraction grating of period 2π and the intensities $I_1, \ldots, I_N$ in the orders $j_1, \ldots, j_N$ [25–30]. Such an interpretation allows the problem of computation of the nonlinear transform $\Phi[\xi]$ to be reduced to the well-known problem of synthesis of a phase diffraction grating with a desired intensity distribution between the diffraction orders. The energy efficiency of the grating

$$E = \sum_{i=1}^{N} |c_{j_i}|^2$$

determines the energy portion of the illuminating beam that will be focused on the desired focal lines, whereas the deviations of the intensity values in the orders $j_1, \ldots, j_N$ from the desired values $I_1, \ldots, I_N$ define the error in the generation of the desired intensity distribution between the lines under focusing.

Let us consider some special cases of multifocus DOEs. For

$$f_3 = \infty[\varphi_{23}(\mathbf{u}) \equiv 0] \tag{5.117}$$

in Eqs. (5.100) and (5.101), the scale coefficients p_j in Eq. (5.113) describing the change in the size of focal lines are equal to one. Accordingly, the focal lines are of the same size in all planes. For

$$f_3 = -f_2 \tag{5.118}$$

in Eqs. (5.100) and (5.101), the functions in Eqs. (5.110) and (5.111) that define the structure of images generated in the diffraction orders of a multifocus DOE take the form

$$\varphi_j(\mathbf{u}) = -\frac{k\mathbf{u}^2}{2f_1} + p_j \left[\frac{k}{f_1} \int_{u_0}^{u} X[\xi(\mathbf{u})] \, du + \frac{k}{f_1} \int_{v_0}^{v} Y[\xi(\mathbf{u})] \, dv \right] + \frac{k}{f_1} \mathbf{X}_j \mathbf{u}, \tag{5.119}$$

where

$$p_j = 1 + j\frac{f_1}{f_2}, \tag{5.120}$$

$$\mathbf{X}_j = \frac{\mathbf{x}_1 f_2 + j\mathbf{x}_2 f_1}{f_2}. \tag{5.121}$$

Thus, if the condition in Eq. (5.118) is fulfilled, the multifocus DOE produces N lines in the same focal plane $z = f_1$, with the scale of the focal lines described by the linear function in Eq. (5.120). The method considered may be illustrated by the following examples.

Example 5.1 Consider the design of a multifocus DOE of Eqs. (5.100)–(5.105), (5.117) intended to produce three equal-length line-segments located in different focal planes, the energy equally distributed between them. To calculate the phase of the multifocus DOE, we shall define the functions $\varphi_1(\mathbf{u})$ and $\varphi_2(\mathbf{u})$ in Eqs. (5.100) and (5.101) as the phase functions of DOE focusing onto the line-segments $|x| \le d$ found in the planes $z = f_1$ and $z = f_2$. For the square aperture $G(2a \times 2a)$ and uniform illuminating beam intensity, the functions $\varphi_1(\mathbf{u})$ and $\varphi_2(\mathbf{u})$ can easily be derived from Eqs. (5.20) and (5.21) in the form

$$
\begin{cases}
\varphi_1(\mathbf{u}) = -\dfrac{k\mathbf{u}^2}{2f_1} + \dfrac{kd}{2f_1 a}u^2 \\
\varphi_2(\mathbf{u}) = -\dfrac{k\mathbf{u}^2}{2f_2} + \dfrac{kd}{2f_2 a}u^2.
\end{cases}
\tag{5.122}
$$

Then, the nonlinear transformation function, $\Phi[\xi]$, will be defined as the phase function of a three-order diffraction grating

$$
\Phi[\xi] = \begin{cases}
0, & \xi \in [0, \pi) \\
2\tan^{-1}(\pi/2), & \xi \in [\pi, 2\pi)
\end{cases}.
\tag{5.123}
$$

The Fourier coefficients of the function $\exp(i\,\Phi[\xi])$ are given by

$$
c_j = \begin{cases}
\dfrac{1-(-1)^j}{2\pi i j}\left[1 - \exp\left(2i\tan^{-1}\dfrac{\pi}{2}\right)\right], & j \ne 0,\ j = \pm 1,\ \pm 2, \ldots \\
\dfrac{1}{2}\left[1 + \exp\left(2i\tan^{-1}\dfrac{\pi}{2}\right)\right], & j = 0
\end{cases},
\tag{5.124}
$$

According to Eq. (5.124), $|c_{-1}|^2 = |c_0|^2 = |c_1|^2 = 0.2884$, which means that the grating in Eq. (5.123) concentrates more than 86 percent of energy in the three main orders. In view of the three main diffraction orders, substituting Eqs. (5.122) and (5.124) in (5.109) gives the focusing onto three line-segments in the planes $z = F_j$, $j = -1, 0, 1$. The centers of the segments in these planes are found at points $\mathbf{X}_j$, $j = -1, 0, 1$, with their coordinates defined by Eq. (5.114).

To estimate the efficiency of the multifocus DOE of Eqs. (5.100)–(5.102), (5.117), (5.122), and (5.123), the field intensity produced by the multifocus DOE was computed for the following parameters: $\lambda = 1.06$ μm, $2d = 8$ mm, $2a = 9$ mm, $f_1 = 100$ mm, $f_2 = 3000$ mm, $\mathbf{x}_1 = (0, 0)$ mm, $\mathbf{x}_2 = (-145, 0)$ mm. For the aforementioned parameters, the coordinates of the focal planes are 96.774 mm ($j = 1$), 100 mm ($j = 0$), and 103.448 mm ($j = -1$), whereas the segment centers are displaced with respect to the optical axis to the points $\mathbf{X}_1 = (-4.68, 0)$ mm, $\mathbf{X}_0 = (0, 0)$ mm, and $\mathbf{X}_{-1} = (+5, 0)$ mm. Figure 5.48 depicts a fragment of the zone plate $\Phi[\varphi_d(\mathbf{u})]$ and Figure 5.49 shows the intensity distributions produced by the multifocus DOE. The intensity distributions in Figure 5.49 are obtained through the

Figure 5.48. A fragment of the zone plate $\Phi[\varphi_d(u)]$.

numerical computation of the Fresnel-Kirhhoff integral by the methods described in Refs. [20–24]. Shown in Figure 5.49a is the halftone intensity distribution in the plane *XOZ* containing the focal lines, and in Figure 5.49 b,c,d are the halftone intensity distributions produced in the planes $z = F_j$, $j = -1,0,1$. The results of numerical simulation confirm the efficiency of the method proposed.

Example 5.2 Consider the design of a multifocus DOE of Eqs. (5.100)–(5.105), (5.118) of square aperture that focuses a uniform beam onto five different-length line-segments in the same plane $z = f_1$. Let 1:2:3:4:5 be the desired ratios between the segment lengths and x_0 be the desired distance between them (Fig. 5.50a). These length ratios and the distance between the segments are obtained if we put $f_2 = 3f_1$, $j = \overline{-2,2}$ in Eq. (5.120) and $\mathbf{x}_1 = (0,0)$ and $\mathbf{x}_2 = (3x_0,0)$ in Eq. (5.121). Note that the functions $\varphi_1(\mathbf{u})$ and $\varphi_2(\mathbf{u})$ in Eqs. (5.100) and (5.101) take the form

$$\begin{cases} \varphi_1(\mathbf{u}) = -\dfrac{k\mathbf{u}^2}{2f_1} + \dfrac{kd}{2f_1 a}v^2 \\[3mm] \varphi_2(\mathbf{u}) = -\dfrac{k\mathbf{u}^2}{6f_1} + \dfrac{kd}{6f_1 a}v^2 \end{cases}. \qquad (5.125)$$

The eventual formula for the phase function of a multifocus DOE may be derived if the function of the nonlinear transform $\Phi[\xi]$ in Eq. (5.100) is defined as the phase function of a five-order diffraction grating. To produce equal intensities on the lines under focusing the diffraction order intensities should be assumed to be proportional to the lengths of the segments

$$I_j/I_0 = 1 + j/3, \quad j = \overline{-2,2}. \qquad (5.126)$$

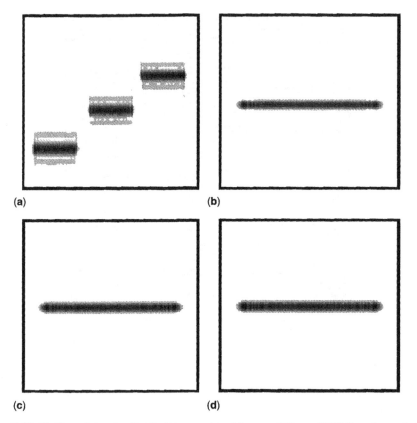

Figure 5.49. Halftone intensity distributions produced by a multifocus DOE focusing onto three line-segments located in three different focal planes: (**a**) in the plane **XOZ** comprising the focal lines, (**b**), (**c**), and (**d**) in the planes $z = F_j$, $j = -1, 0, 1$.

The required diffraction grating, Eq. (5.126), was designed using the AA algorithm described in Chapter 2. The energy efficiency of the grating was found to be 88.8 percent, whereas the rms error of formation of the desired intensity distribution, Eq. (5.126), was 1.4 percent. The phase function of the computed grating on period and the intensities of the grating diffraction orders are shown in Figures 5.50b and 5.50c, respectively. To estimate the operational efficiency of the multifocus DOE in Eqs. (5.100)–(5.105), (5.118), (5.125) with the $\Phi[\xi]$ function depicted in Figure 5.50b, the field intensity produced by the DOE was numerically simulated for the following parameters: $\lambda = 1.06$ mkm, $2d = 0.6$ mm, $2a = 10$ mm, $f_1 = 100$ mm, $f_2 = 3f_1 = 300$ mm, $x_1 = (0, 0)$ mm, and $x_2 = (0.75, 0)$ mm. The calculated intensity distribution is shown in Figure 5.51 and demonstrates high-quality focusing.

5.5.1 Multifocus Binary Zone Plates

If the nonlinear transform function, $\Phi[\xi]$, in Eq. (5.100) corresponds to a multiorder binary grating, the phase function

$$\varphi_{zp}(\mathbf{u}) = \Phi[\varphi_d(\mathbf{u})] \qquad (5.127)$$

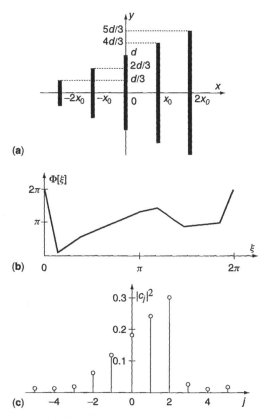

Figure 5.50. (a) Geometry of the lines to be focused; (b) the nonlinear transform function under focusing onto the array of segments shown in Figure 5.50a; (c) squared modules of the Fourier coefficients for the function $\exp[i\,\Phi(\xi)]$.

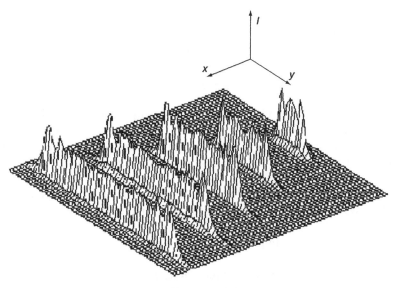

Figure 5.51. Intensity distribution produced by the multifocus DOE in the plane $\mathbf{z} = \mathbf{f}_1$ when focusing onto the array of segments in Figure 5.50a.

describes a binary zone plate. The zone plate in Eqs. (5.127) and (5.101) is a particular case of the multifocus DOE of Eqs. (5.100) and (5.101). Because the binary elements are of particular interest due to simplicity of their fabrication, we shall specially dwell upon the multifocus properties of the zone plate $\varphi_{zp}(\mathbf{u})$. Assume that the zone plate of Eqs. (5.127) and (5.101) is illuminated by a spherical converging beam of complex amplitude

$$W_0(\mathbf{u}) = \sqrt{I_0(\mathbf{u})} \exp\left(-\frac{ik\mathbf{u}^2}{2f_1}\right). \tag{5.128}$$

On the basis of Eqs (5.106)–(5.109), the field directly behind the plate $\varphi_{zp}(\mathbf{u})$ may be represented as

$$
\begin{aligned}
W(\mathbf{u}) &= \sqrt{I_0(\mathbf{u})} \exp\left(-\frac{ik\mathbf{u}^2}{2f_1}\right) \sum_{j=-\infty}^{\infty} c_j \exp[ij\varphi_d(\mathbf{u})] \\
&= \sqrt{I_0(\mathbf{u})} \sum_{j=-\infty}^{\infty} c_j \exp[i\varphi_j(\mathbf{u})]
\end{aligned}
\tag{5.129}
$$

where c_j are the Fourier coefficients of Eq. (5.108). The $\varphi_j(\mathbf{u})$ functions in Eq. (5.129) that determine the structure of the images produced in the diffraction orders of the zone plate $\varphi_{zp}(\mathbf{u})$ take the form of Eq. (5.110) and correspond to the phase function of DOEs focusing onto scaled lines. The parameters p_j, F_j, and $\mathbf{X}_j$ that determine the scale and location of the focal line produced in the jth diffraction order are specified by the relations

$$F_j = \frac{f_1 f_2}{f_2 + jf_1(1 + f_2/f_3)}, \tag{5.130}$$

$$p_j = \frac{jf_1}{f_2 + jf_1(1 + f_2/f_3)}, \tag{5.131}$$

$$\mathbf{X}_j = p_j \mathbf{x}_2. \tag{5.132}$$

If $f_3 = -f_2$, the focal lines are found in the same focal plane $z = f_1$, and the change in the line length is given by the linear function

$$p_j = jf_1/f_2. \tag{5.133}$$

Thus, the zone plate of Eqs. (5.127) and (5.101) with the $\Phi[\xi]$ function defined as the phase function of an N-order grating with intensities $I_1, \ldots, I_N$ in the orders $j_1, \ldots, j_N$ produces the focusing of the converging spherical beam, Eq. (5.128), on N scaled lines in the planes $z = F_{j_i}$, $i = 1, N$, with the energy ratios between the lines given by $I_1, \ldots, I_N$.

Because the $\Phi[\xi]$ function is defined as the phase function of an N-order binary grating, the modules of its Fourier coefficients are symmetric:

$$|c_j| = |c_{-j}|, \quad j = -\infty, \infty. \tag{5.134}$$

Owing to symmetry, the multifocus binary zone plate may be designed only for a symmetric set of indices j_i and a symmetric ratio of the energies $I_1, \ldots, I_N$.

In conclusion, let us consider the design of a binary zone plate intended to focus onto a centrally symmetric contour C in the plane $z = f_1$. The contour may be represented as a combination of two centrally symmetric lines. Assume that $f_3 = -f_2$ and the function $\varphi_d(\mathbf{u})$ in Eq. (5.127) is the phase function of a DOE focusing onto a line L corresponding to one-half the focal contour C. This being the case, the focal lines $L_{p_1} \equiv L$ and L_{p-1} produced in the 1st and -1st diffraction orders of the zone plate $\varphi_{zp}(\mathbf{u})$ are centrally symmetric and generate the desired contour C in the plane $z = f_1$. To design the binary zone plate $\varphi_{zp}(\mathbf{u})$, we shall define the function $\Phi[\xi]$ as the phase function of a binary two-order grating

$$\Phi[\xi] = \begin{cases} 0, & \xi \in [0, \pi) \\ \pi, & \xi \in [\pi, 2\pi) \end{cases}. \tag{5.135}$$

The Fourier coefficients, c_j, in the decomposition of the function $\exp(i\Phi[\xi])$ take the form

$$c_j = \begin{cases} \dfrac{1 - (-1)^j}{\pi i j}, & j = \pm 1, \pm 2, \ldots \\ 0, & j = 0 \end{cases}, \tag{5.136}$$

Because $|c_1|^2 = |c_{-1}|^2 = 0.405$, the main, 1st and -1st diffraction orders in Eq. (5.129) of the binary zone plate in Eqs. (5.127) and (5.135) contribute 81 percent of the illuminating beam energy to the lines L_{p_1} and $L_{p_{-1}}$ that produce the desired contour C.

Let us consider some examples of designing multifocus binary plates.

Example 5.3   Consider the design of the binary plate of Eqs. (5.127) and (5.101) to focus the converging spherical beam of Eq. (5.128) onto an array of six line-segments with the length ratio of 3:2:1:1:2:3 in the plane $z = f_1$ (Fig. 5.52 a)). According to Eqs. (5.130)–(5.132), the focusing onto a preset array of line-segments takes place under the following parameters: $f_1 = f_2$, $f_3 = -f_2$, and $\mathbf{x}_2 = (x_2, 0)$. The function $\varphi_2(\mathbf{u})$ in Eq. (5.101) is the phase of a DOE focusing onto a line-segment $|y| \leq d$ in the plane $z = f_1$. With the square-shape illuminating beam ($2a \times 2a$) of uniform intensity, the $\varphi_2(\mathbf{u})$ function is given by

$$\varphi_2(\mathbf{u}) = -\frac{k\mathbf{u}^2}{2f_1} + \frac{kd}{2f_1 a} v^2. \tag{5.137}$$

To produce equal-intensity line-segments, the function $\Phi[\xi]$ will be defined as the phase of a binary six-order grating with order intensities proportional to the length of the segments of focusing

$$I_j / I_0 = |j|, \quad j = \overline{-3, 3} \quad j \neq 0. \tag{5.138}$$

The binary grating with order intensities in Eq. (5.138) was designed using the gradient algorithm described in Chapter 2. The calculated binary profile and the intensities in diffraction orders are shown in Figures 5.52b and 5.52c, respectively. The energy efficiency of the grating in Figure 5.52b is 74.5 percent, whereas the rms error of formation of the desired linear intensity distribution, Eq. (5.138), is 1.6 percent. Shown

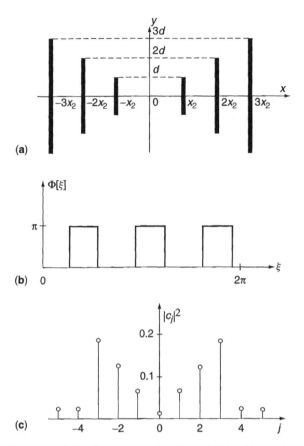

Figure 5.52. (a) Geometry of the lines under focusing; (b) the binary function $\Phi[\xi]$ of the nonlinear transform when focusing onto the array of line-segments shown in Figure 5.52a; (c) squared modules of the Fourier coefficients for the function $\exp[i\Phi(\xi)]$.

in Figure 5.53 is the calculated intensity distribution produced by the zone plate of Eqs. (5.127), (5.101), (5.137) with the $\Phi[\xi]$ function depicted in Figure 5.52b, the simulation parameters being: $\lambda = 1.06$ μm, $2d = 0.5$ mm, $2a = 10$ mm, $f_1 = f_2 = -f_3 = 100$ mm, $x_2 = (0.25, 0)$ mm. Figure 5.53 demonstrates high-quality focusing, however, there is an intensity peak at the center. This intensity peak is due to the error in calculating the $\Phi[\xi]$ function: the Fourier coefficient c_0 in the decomposition of the function $\exp(i\Phi[\xi])$ is not equal to zero, $|c_0|^2 \approx 0.01$. According to Eq. (5.131), the image produced in the zero order corresponds to a point. Since in the desired orders $j = \overline{-3, 3}$, $j \neq 0$, the energy is distributed uniformly over the length of the segment under focusing, the central peak appears to be fairly large. At the same time, it is only 1 percent of the illuminating beam energy that is concentrated in the central peak.

Example 5.4   Let us consider the design of the binary zone plate of Eqs. (5.127) and (5.135) intended to focus the light onto the letter "x" in the plane $z = f_1$. Assume that the letter "x" is composed of two centrally symmetric semi-rings of radius R_0. In this case, the $\varphi_d(\mathbf{u})$ function in Eq. (5.127) is the phase function of a DOE focusing the converging spherical beam onto the semi-ring centered at point $(-x_0, 0)$ at $z = f_1$,

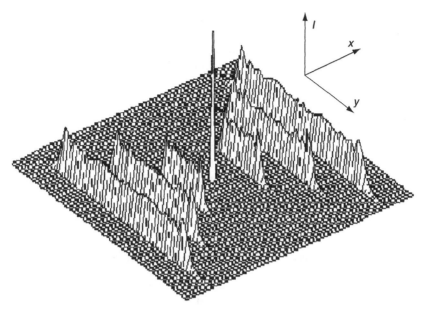

Figure 5.53. Intensity distribution produced by the multifocus binary zone plate in the plane $z = f_1$ when focusing onto the array of segments in Figure 5.52a.

with the x_0 parameter specifying the distance between the semi-rings. For the circular shape illuminating beam of uniform intensity, the function $\varphi_d(\mathbf{u})$ may be derived from Eqs. (5.17) and (5.18) in the form

$$\varphi_d(\mathbf{u}) = \text{mod}_{2\pi} \left[\frac{k}{f_1} R_0 \, \text{sign}(u)|\mathbf{u}| - \frac{k}{f_1} x_0 u \right], \qquad (5.139)$$

where $\text{sign}(u) = \begin{cases} 1, & u \geq 0 \\ -1, & u < 0 \end{cases}$.

Figure 5.54a depicts a photomask of the zone plate in Eqs. (5.127), (5.135), and (5.139), computed for the following parameters: $\lambda = 10.6$ μm, $R_0 = 5$ mm, $f_1 = 500$ mm, $x_0 = 5.5$ mm, and the illuminating beam radius is $R = 4$ mm. The

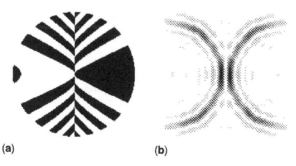

(a)   (b)

Figure 5.54. (a) Binary zone plate to focus onto the letter "x", (b) halftone intensity distribution produced by the zone plate in Figure 5.54a at $z = f_1$.

replacement $x_0 = 5.5$ mm, greater than the semi-ring radius, $R_0 = 5$ mm, was utilized in order to avoid interference between the fields generated in the 1st and -1st orders. The simulated halftone intensity distribution produced by the zone plate in Figure 5.54a is shown in Figure 5.54b and corroborates the robustness of the developed design technique.

5.5.2   DOEs with Nonlinearly Combined Phases

One can achieve a combined effect of a lens and a diffraction grating using a single DOE whose phase function corresponds to the sum of the phase functions of the lens and the diffraction grating. The superposition of the CTFs of any two binary elements, given by

$$T(\mathbf{u}) = \frac{1}{\sqrt{2}}\{\exp[i\varphi_{b1}(\mathbf{u})] + i\,\exp[i\varphi_{b2}(\mathbf{u})]\} \tag{5.140}$$

corresponds to a purely phase element with the phase function

$$\varphi[\varphi_{b1}(\mathbf{u}), \varphi_{b2}(\mathbf{u})] = \begin{cases} \pi/4, & \varphi_{b1}(\mathbf{u}) = 0, \varphi_{b2}(\mathbf{u}) = 0 \\ 3\pi/4, & \varphi_{b1}(\mathbf{u}) = \pi, \varphi_{b2}(\mathbf{u}) = 0 \\ 5\pi/4, & \varphi_{b1}(\mathbf{u}) = \pi, \varphi_{b2}(\mathbf{u}) = \pi \\ 7\pi/4, & \varphi_{b1}(\mathbf{u}) = 0, \varphi_{b2}(\mathbf{u}) = \pi \end{cases}. \tag{5.141}$$

Let us make use of Eqs. (5.140) and (5.141) to design a "DOE with combined effect", which means the DOE intended to simultaneously produce two line arrays. For this purpose, we introduce the $\varphi[\varphi_{zp1}(\mathbf{u}), \varphi_{zp2}(\mathbf{u})]$ function of Eq. (5.141) that corresponds to the superposition (5.140) of binary multifocus zone plates $\varphi_{zp1}(\mathbf{u})$ and $\varphi_{zp2}(\mathbf{u})$ focusing the converging spherical beam in Eq. (5.128) onto the line arrays S_1 and S_2, respectively. Then, define the phase function of a DOE with combined effect in the form

$$\varphi_{com}(\mathbf{u}) = \varphi_l(\mathbf{u}) + \varphi[\varphi_{zp1}(\mathbf{u}), \varphi_{zp2}(\mathbf{u})] - \varphi_0(\mathbf{u}), \quad \mathbf{u} \in G, \tag{5.142}$$

where $\varphi_0(\mathbf{u})$ is the illuminating beam phase and $\varphi_l(\mathbf{u}) = -(k\mathbf{u}^2/2f_1)$ is the lens paraxial phase.

According to Eqs. (5.142) and (5.141), if the "combined-effect DOE" is illuminated by the beam of complex amplitude

$$W_0(\mathbf{u}) = \sqrt{I_0(\mathbf{u})}\,\exp[i\varphi_0(\mathbf{u})],$$

the field just behind it takes the form

$$W(\mathbf{u}) = \sqrt{\frac{I_0(\mathbf{u})}{2}}\exp\left(-\frac{ik\mathbf{u}^2}{2f_1} + i\varphi_{zp1}(\mathbf{u})\right)$$

$$+ i\sqrt{\frac{I_0(\mathbf{u})}{2}}\exp\left(-\frac{ik\mathbf{u}^2}{2f_1} + i\varphi_{zp2}(\mathbf{u})\right). \tag{5.143}$$

The terms of Eq. (5.143) correspond, up to a constant, to the fields generated by the binary zone plates $\varphi_{zp1}(\mathbf{u})$ and $\varphi_{zp2}(\mathbf{u})$, if the converging spherical illuminating beam is given by Eq. (5.128). In view of the linear character of the light-propagation operator, the combined-effect DOE in Eq. (5.142) produces simultaneously two line arrays, S_1 and S_2.

Example 5.5 Let us consider the design of a "combined-effect DOE" aimed to focus the circular beam of uniform intensity onto a square contour of side $2d$. We shall represent the square contour as two sets of line-segments, S_1 and S_2. The set S_1 is composed of two centrally symmetric line-segments $x = d$, $|y| \leq d$ and $x = -d$, $|y| \leq d$ parallel to the axis Oy, and the set S_2 is composed of two centrally symmetric line-segments $y = d$, $|x| \leq d$ and $y = -d$, $|x| \leq d$ parallel to the axis Ox. Note that because of symmetry of the task of focusing, the following relation will hold:

$$\varphi_{zp1}(u, v) = \varphi_{zp2}(v, -u). \tag{5.144}$$

The phase function of the zone plate producing the line-segment array S_1 takes the form of Eqs. (5.127) and (5.135). The function $\varphi_d(\mathbf{u})$ in Eq. (5.127) takes the form of Eq. (5.101), where $f_1 = f_2 = -f_3$, $\mathbf{x}_2 = (d, 0)$, and the $\varphi_2(\mathbf{u})$ function is the phase function of a DOE focusing onto a line-segment $|y| \leq d$, in the plane $z = f_1$. With circular uniform illuminating beam of radius R, the phase function $\varphi_2(\mathbf{u})$ may be derived from Eqs. (5.20) and (5.21) in the form

$$\varphi_2(\mathbf{u}) = -\frac{k\mathbf{u}^2}{2f} + \frac{2kd}{\pi f}\left\{ v \arcsin\left(\frac{v}{R}\right) - R\left[1 - \left(\frac{v}{R}\right)^2\right]^{1/2} + \frac{R}{3}\left[1 - \left(\frac{v}{R}\right)^2\right]^{3/2} \right\}. \tag{5.145}$$

Because we have $|c_1|^2 = |c_{-1}|^2 = 0.405$ for the binary grating of Eq. (5.135), it follows from the expansion in Eqs. (5.129)–(5.132), that the zone plate of Eqs. (5.127), (5.101), (5.135), and (5.145) focuses 81 percent of the illuminating beam energy onto the desired line-segment array, S_1. To evaluate the efficiency of the combined-effect DOE, the intensity distribution in the plane of focusing was computed for the following parameters: $\lambda = 10.6$ μm, $2d = 8$ mm, $R = 5$ mm, and $f_1 = f_2 = -f_3 = 350$ mm.

(a)   **(b)**

Figure 5.55. (a) Photomask of the zone plate $\varphi[\varphi_{zp1}(u), \varphi_{zp2}(u)]$ when focusing onto a square contour; (b) halftone intensity distribution at $z = f_1$, produced by the combined-effect DOE.

Figure 5.55a depicts the amplitude mask of the designed zone plate $\varphi[\varphi_{zp1}(\mathbf{u})$, $\varphi_{zp2}(\mathbf{u})]$ in Eq. (5.142). The halftone distribution in Figure 5.55b produced by the combined-effect DOE testifies in favor of the robustness of the approach developed.

5.6   DIFFRACTIVE MULTIFOCUS LENSES

As a special case of the method for designing multifocus DOE we shall consider the design of a multifocus DOE that can produce an array of N spots on an optical axis with energy distribution given by $I_1, \ldots, I_N$ between the spots (foci). In the following text, such DOEs will be referred to as a *diffractive-multifocus lens*. Because the spot is a special case of the focal line, we can design the phase of the multifocus lens if we replace the phase functions $\varphi_1(\mathbf{u})$ and $\varphi_2(\mathbf{u})$ of the DOE focusing onto the line by the phase functions of the lens in the general formula for the multifocus DOE phase, Eq. (5.100). Then, the phase function of the multifocus lens takes the form [28–30]

$$\varphi_{ml}(\mathbf{u}) = \varphi_1(\mathbf{u}) + \Phi[\varphi_2(\mathbf{u})] - \varphi_0(\mathbf{u}), \quad \mathbf{u} \in G, \tag{5.146}$$

where

$$\varphi_1(\mathbf{u}) = -\frac{k\mathbf{u}^2}{2f_1}, \quad \varphi_2(\mathbf{u}) = \text{mod}_{2\pi}\left(-\frac{k\mathbf{u}^2}{2f_2}\right) \tag{5.147}$$

are the paraxial phase functions of the lenses with foci f_1 and f_2. The $\Phi[\varphi_2(\mathbf{u})]$ function in Eq. (5.146) describes a nonlinear transformation of the lens phase $\varphi_2(\mathbf{u})$. Thus, the multifocus lens is represented as a superposition of the conventional lens $\varphi_1(\mathbf{u})$ and the zone plate $\Phi[\varphi_2(\mathbf{u})]$.

According to the general formula (5.109), the field just behind the plane of the multifocus lens illuminated by a beam of complex amplitude

$$W_0(\mathbf{u}) = \sqrt{I_0(\mathbf{u})} \exp[i\varphi_0(\mathbf{u})]$$

takes the form

$$W(\mathbf{u}) = \sqrt{I_0(\mathbf{u})} \exp = \left(-\frac{ik\mathbf{u}^2}{2f_1}\right) \sum_{j=-\infty}^{\infty} c_j \exp\left[ij\left(-\frac{k\mathbf{u}^2}{2f_2}\right)\right]. \tag{5.148}$$

In paraxial approximation, the expression (5.148) corresponds to a superposition of spherical beams with foci

$$F_j = \frac{f_1 f_2}{f_2 + j f_1} \tag{5.149}$$

and the energy distribution between the beams given by $|c_j|^2$, $j = -\infty, \infty$. The Fourier coefficients c_j of the $\exp[i\,\Phi[\xi]]$ function are derived from Eq. (5.108). Assume that $j_1, \ldots, j_N$ are indices corresponding to the desired focal distances in Eq. (5.149). Then, an array of spots F_{j_i}, $i = \overline{1, N}$, with desired intensity distribution $I_1, \ldots, I_N$ between foci may be produced if the nonlinear transformation function $\Phi[\xi]$ is defined as a phase function of an N-order diffraction grating with intensities $I_1, \ldots, I_N$ in the orders $j_1, \ldots, j_N$.

As a rule, the computation of the diffraction grating $\Phi[\xi]$ calls for the application of numerical iterative algorithms. Note that in a number of cases the function $\Phi[\xi]$ may be calculated using an analytical method for designing 1D DOEs [Eq. (5.87)]. Let $\tilde{\varphi}(\xi)$, $0 < \xi < d$ be the phase function of a 1D DOE focusing a converging cylindrical beam onto a line-segment with intensity distribution $I(x)$, $n_1\Delta < x < n_2\Delta$, where $\Delta = \lambda f/d$ is the diffraction spot size. The phase function $\tilde{\varphi}(\xi)$ may be derived from Eq. (5.87) in the form

$$\tilde{\varphi}(\xi) = \frac{k}{f} \int_0^{\xi} \chi(\eta)\, d\eta, \tag{5.150}$$

where the $\chi(\eta)$ function is sought from the solution of the following differential equation:

$$\frac{d\chi(\xi)}{d\xi} = \frac{1}{I[\chi(\xi)]} \tag{5.151}$$

with the boundary conditions $\chi(0) = n_1\Delta$, $\chi(\eta) = n_2\Delta$.

As is shown in Chapter 2, the $\tilde{\varphi}(\xi)$ function may be treated as the phase function of a diffraction grating with period d and diffraction order intensities given by

$$I_j = \begin{cases} I(j\Delta), & j = \overline{n_1, n_2} \\ 0, & \text{else} \end{cases}. \tag{5.152}$$

As a consequence, the nonlinear transform function $\Phi[\xi] = \tilde{\varphi}(\xi)$ may be derived from Eqs. (5.150) and (5.151). However, during computation it has been found that the geometric optical computation of the $\Phi[\xi] = \tilde{\varphi}(\xi)$ function is only practical when designing the grating with a large number of orders (30–40, or more).

In conclusion, let us discuss the computation of "multifocus lenses with combined effect" intended to focus simultaneously onto two spot arrays. The first array is composed of spots found in the same plane, whereas the second one is composed of spots found on the optical axis. Such lenses are a specific case of the combined-effect DOE.

If the nonlinear transform function in Eq. (5.146) is defined as a multiorder binary grating, the function $\Phi[\xi]$ is binary. The superposition in Eq. (5.141) of the complex transmission functions of binary zone plate, $\Phi[\varphi_2(\mathbf{u})]$, and multiorder binary grating, $\varphi_{\mathrm{gr}}(\mathbf{u})$, corresponds to a pure-phase element with the phase function $\varphi\{\Phi[\varphi_2(\mathbf{u})], \varphi_{\mathrm{gr}}(u)\}$, in Eq. (5.141). Then, the phase function of a multifocus lens with combined effect may be defined as

$$\varphi_{\mathrm{cml}}(\mathbf{u}) = \varphi_1(\mathbf{u}) + \varphi\{\Phi[\varphi_2(\mathbf{u})], \varphi_{\mathrm{gr}}(\mathbf{u})\} - \varphi_0(\mathbf{u}), \quad \mathbf{u} \in G, \tag{5.153}$$

where $\varphi_0(\mathbf{u})$ is the illuminating beam phase and $\varphi_1(\mathbf{u})$ is the phase function of the lens in Eq. (5.146).

According to Eq. (5.140), the lens CTF, Eq. (5.153), may be represented as

$$\exp[i\varphi_{\mathrm{cml}}(\mathbf{u})] = \frac{1}{\sqrt{2}} \exp[i\varphi_{\mathrm{ml}}(\mathbf{u})] + \frac{i}{\sqrt{2}} \exp[i\varphi_1(\mathbf{u}) + i\varphi_{\mathrm{gr}}(\mathbf{u}) - i\varphi_0(\mathbf{u})]. \tag{5.154}$$

The first term in Eq. (5.154) describes the multifocus lens of Eq. (5.146), with the function $\Phi[\xi]$ corresponding to a multiorder binary grating. The second term contains the phase functions of a lens and a binary grating, thus providing the focusing onto a spot array in the plane $z = f_1$. Note that the phase $-\varphi_0(\mathbf{u})$ in the second term compensates for the illuminating beam phase. Because the operator of light propagation is linear, the lens in Eq. (5.153) simultaneously implements the focusing onto the spot arrays on the optical axis and in a single fixed plane.

Consider some examples of designing multifocus lenses.

Example 5.6   Let us design a bifocal lens of foci f_a and f_b, with the energy equally distributed between the foci. Putting $F_1 = f_a$, $F_{-1} = f_b$ in the general expression (5.149) for the foci of a multifocus lens, we get

$$f_1 = \frac{2f_a f_b}{f_a + f_b}, \quad f_2 = \frac{2f_a f_b}{f_a - f_b}. \tag{5.155}$$

Next, we shall define the nonlinear transform function, $\Phi[\xi]$, as the phase function of the two-order diffraction grating in Eqs. (5.135) and (5.136). Substituting Eqs. (5.155) and (5.136) into Eq. (5.148) and taking account of the main nonzero orders, $j = \pm 1$, yields the following expression for the field immediately behind the bifocal lens plane

$$W(\mathbf{u}) = c_1 \exp\left(-\frac{ik\mathbf{u}^2}{2f_a}\right) + c_{-1} \exp\left(-\frac{ik\mathbf{u}^2}{2f_b}\right). \tag{5.156}$$

where $c_{\pm 1}$ are the Fourier coefficients of Eq. (5.136). The expression (5.156) describes the required process of focusing onto two spots in the paraxial approximation. According to Eq. (5.136), we have $|c_1|^2 = |c_{-1}|^2 = 0.405$, which means that 81 percent of the illuminating beam energy is concentrated in the desired foci f_a and f_b. It would be interesting to compare the discussed diffractive lens of Eqs. (5.146), (5.155), and (5.135) with a segmented bifocal lens whose aperture is composed of two equal-area segments. The phase function of the segmented lens is given by

$$\varphi_s(\mathbf{u}) = \begin{cases} -\dfrac{k\mathbf{u}^2}{2f_a}, & |\mathbf{u}| \leq \dfrac{R}{\sqrt{2}} \\[2mm] -\dfrac{k\mathbf{u}^2}{2f_b}, & \dfrac{R}{\sqrt{2}} < |\mathbf{u}| \leq R \end{cases}. \tag{5.157}$$

Shown in Figure 5.56a are the plots of the intensity distribution I (in relative units) along the z-axis for the diffractive bifocal lens (solid line) and segmented lens of Eq. (5.157) (dotted line). The plots were obtained using the numerical computation of the Fresnel-Kirhhoff integral for the following parameters: $\lambda = 0.555$ μm, $f_a = 30$ mm, $f_b = 34$ mm, and $R = 1.5$ mm. From Figure 5.56a, the focal depth of the bifocal diffractive lens is seen to be less than that of the segmented lens, because the entire aperture contributes to each focus of the diffractive lens. The computed function of spot scattering in the two focal planes is depicted in Figure 5.56b and c. We shall introduce the energy efficiency E as the illuminating beam energy portion focused within the spot of radius $\Delta = 0.61\lambda z/R$. In the first focal plane ($z = 30$ mm), the value of E is 32.8 percent and 32.6 percent for the diffractive and segmented lens, respectively. In the second focal plane ($z = 34$ mm), E is equal to 34.2 percent and 14.5 percent, respectively. Because only the central segment contributes to the first

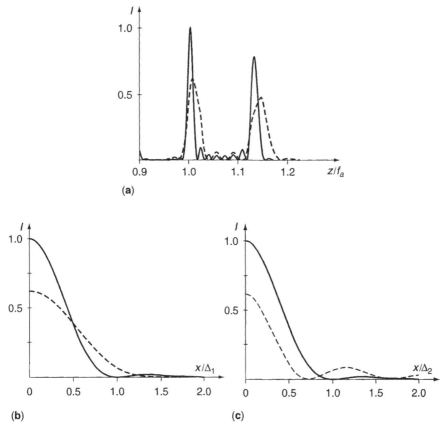

Figure 5.56. Intensity distribution for the diffractive (solid line) and segmented (dotted line) bifocal lenses: **(a)** along the optical axis; **(b)**, **(c)** in the focal planes $z = f_a$ and $z = f_b$, where $\Delta_1 = 0.61\lambda f_a/R$ and $\Delta_2 = 0.61\lambda f_b/R$.

focal plane in the segmented lens, its diffraction width is 1.5 times greater than that of the diffractive bifocal lens (Fig. 5.56b). A similar effect takes place in the second focal plane, considering the two-petal function of spot scattering for the annular pupil (Fig. 5.56c). Thus, the studies pursued have shown that the diffractive bifocal lens works similar to the conventional (nonsegmented) lens at each of the two foci.

Example 5.7 To design the diffraction lens of Eq. (5.146) with more than two foci will not present a particular problem. Consider the computation of a seven-focus lens. The phase of the seven-focus lens is specified by the superposition of the phase functions of a conventional lens, $\varphi_1(\mathbf{u})$, and a zone plate $\Phi[\varphi_2(\mathbf{u})]$ corresponding to the transformation of the lens $\varphi_2(\mathbf{u})$ by the law of a seven-order grating. Shown in Figure 5.57a is a profile of the binary zone plate $\Phi[\varphi_2(\mathbf{u})]$ derived by the transformation of the phase $\varphi_2(\mathbf{u})$ by the law of the seven-order binary grating concentrating the light into the orders $-3, -2, -1, 0, 1, 2, 3$ for the parameters: $\lambda = 1.06$ μm, $f_1 = 34$ mm, $f_2 = 1000$ mm, and $R = 4$ mm. The plot for the intensity distribution I along the z-axis for the seven-focus lens is depicted in Figure 5.57b. Note that over 80 percent of the illuminating beam energy is directed to the desired foci. The illuminating beam energy portions

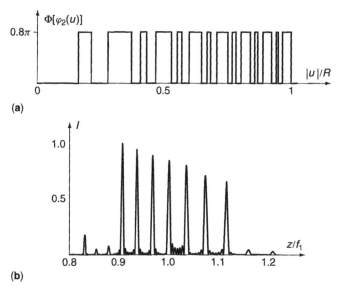

(a)

(b)

Figure 5.57. (a) The $\Phi[\varphi_2(\mathbf{u})]$ function for the seven-focus lens; (b) intensity distribution along the optical axis for the seven-focus lens.

focused in the diffraction vicinity of radius $\Delta = 0.61\lambda F_j/R$, $j = \overline{-3,3}$, are practically constant for the required planes $z = F_j$, $j = \overline{-3,3}$, whereas an insignificant decrease in the focal peaks intensity which takes place with increasing focal length, is due to the increased diffraction blurring (the intensity in the geometric focus is in inverse proportion to the focal length).

Example 5.8 Consider the analytical computation of a multifocus lens, with the phase function of Eqs. (5.150) and (5.151) of a geometric optical DOE used as the nonlinear transform function $\Phi[\xi]$. It is recalled that the geometric optical approach allows one to design a multifocus lens only for a great number of foci (30–40 or more) taken in succession. From Eqs. (5.146), (5.147), (5.150), and (5.151), one can easily obtain the phase function of a lens with $N = n_2 - n_1$ foci of equal intensity in the form

$$\varphi_{mf}(\mathbf{u}) = \varphi_1(\mathbf{u}) + \varphi_2(\mathbf{u}) \left[n_1 + \frac{n_2 - n_1}{4\pi} \varphi_2(\mathbf{u}) \right] - \varphi_0(\mathbf{u}). \qquad (5.158)$$

The coordinates of foci of the lens in Eq. (5.158) are described by the general relation (5.149) at $j = \overline{n_1, n_2}$. Shown in Figure 5.58 is the intensity distribution along the optical axis of the lens in Eq. (5.158) for the following parameters: the number of foci is $N = 40$ ($n_1 = 20$, $n_2 = 60$), $\lambda = 1.06$ μm, $f_1 = 30$ mm, $f_2 = 4000$ mm and $R = 4$ mm. Nonuniformity of the focal peaks in Figure 5.58 is due to both the geometric optical approach used for computing of the function $\Phi[\xi]$ and the enhanced blurring taking place with increased focal length. The rms deviation δ of the energy distribution between the focal planes of the lens of Eq. (5.158) from a constant value is determined by nonuniform intensity distribution generated by the geometric optical DOE focusing onto a segment $[n_1\Delta, n_2\Delta]$. For the aforementioned example (Fig. 5.58), the value of δ is 25.2 percent.

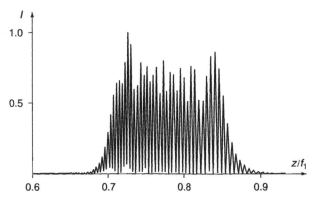

Figure 5.58. The axial intensity distribution for the analytically computed 40-focus lens in Eq. (5.158).

According to Eq. (5.148), the multifocus lens in Eq. (5.146) works in each focus as a conventional lens. If

$$f_2 = \frac{R^2}{2\lambda}, \tag{5.159}$$

the lens $\varphi_2(\mathbf{u})$ in Eq. (5.146) has a single central zone. For the multifocus lens of Eqs. (5.146) and (5.159), the distance between the neighboring foci

$$l_j = F_{j-1} - F_j \approx 2\lambda \left(\frac{F_j}{R}\right)^2 \tag{5.160}$$

is equal to half the Fresnel length, $l_f = 4\lambda f^2/R^2$, that determines the diffraction spot size along the optical axis for a lens of focal length f. In this case, the multifocus lens of Eqs. (5.146), (5.147), and (5.159) produces no separate foci but generates a continuous intensity distribution along the optical axis. This effect is analogous to the fact that a single period of the diffraction grating does not provide the disintegration of the focal pattern onto an array of spots.

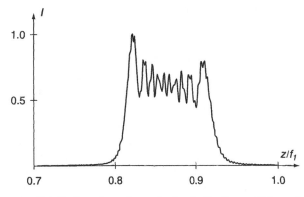

Figure 5.59. Intensity distribution along the optical axis for the multifocus lens of Eq. (5.158) at $f_2 = R^2/2\lambda$.

Shown in Figure 5.59 is the calculated intensity distribution along the optical axis of the lens in Eqs. (5.158) and (5.159) for the parameters: $N = 40(n_1 = 20, n_2 = 60)$, $\lambda = 1.06$ μm, $R = 4$ mm, $f_1 = 30$ mm, $f_2 = R^2/2\lambda = 7547.17$ mm. As expected, the intensity distribution in Figure 5.59 is continuous.

5.7 TWO-ORDER DOEs

Multifocus DOEs make it possible to generate an array of lines, which are of different scale but of equal shape. In this section we consider the design of two-order DOEs intended to generate two different focal lines, L_1 and L_2. The phase functions $\varphi_a(\mathbf{u})$ and $\varphi_b(\mathbf{u})$ of DOE focusing onto the lines L_1 and L_2, respectively, are taken as the initial data for designing the two-order DOE.

Let the phase function of the two-order DOE be specified in the form [26]

$$\varphi(\mathbf{u}) = \tfrac{1}{2}[\varphi_a(\mathbf{u}) + \varphi_b(\mathbf{u})] + \Phi[h(\mathbf{u})], \tag{5.161}$$

where $h(\mathbf{u}) = \mathrm{mod}_{2\pi} \tfrac{1}{2}\{\varphi_a(\mathbf{u}) - \varphi_b(\mathbf{u})\}.$

As earlier, the $\Phi[h(\mathbf{u})]$ function in Eq. (5.161) describes a specially fitted nonlinear transform of the continuous function $h(\mathbf{u}) \in [0, 2\pi)$.

To determine the form of the nonlinear transform $\Phi[\xi]$, we shall analyze how the DOE of Eq. (5.161) operates. Decomposing the $\exp(i\Phi[\xi])$ function into the Fourier series on the interval $[0, 2\pi)$ and putting $\xi = h(\mathbf{u})$, in view of the 2π-periodicity, the DOE's CTF will be given by

$$\exp[i\varphi(\mathbf{u})] = \sum_{j=-\infty}^{\infty} c_j \exp\left\{\frac{i}{2}[\varphi_a(\mathbf{u})(1 + j) + \varphi_b(\mathbf{u})(1 - j)]\right\}, \tag{5.162}$$

where c_j are the Fourier coefficients of the function $\exp(i\Phi[\xi])$, Eq. (5.108).

According to Eq. (5.162), the diffraction of the illuminating beam by the two-order DOE of Eq. (5.161) produces a number of orders. The image generated in the jth diffraction order corresponds to the transformation of the illuminating beam by an element with the phase function

$$\varphi_j(\mathbf{u}) = \tfrac{1}{2}[\varphi_a(\mathbf{u})(1 + j) + \varphi_b(\mathbf{u})(1 - j)]. \tag{5.163}$$

The focusing onto the desired focal lines L_1 and L_2 takes place in the 1st and -1st diffraction orders: $\varphi_1(\mathbf{u}) = \varphi_a(\mathbf{u})$ and $\varphi_{-1}(\mathbf{u}) = \varphi_b(\mathbf{u})$. The illuminating beam energy portion focused in the jth order is proportional to the squared modules of the Fourier coefficients c_j, which implies that the nonlinear transform function, $\Phi[\xi]$, should be chosen in such a manner that the Fourier coefficients c_j are equal to zero at $j \neq \pm 1$. The phase function of a two-order diffraction grating concentrating the light in the $+1$st and -1st orders will conform with such a nonlinearity. To produce uniform intensity along the focal lines L_1 and L_2, the values of $|c_1|^2$ and $|c_{-1}|^2$ should be chosen proportional to the geometric sizes of those lines. At $|c_1|^2 \neq |c_{-1}|^2$, the two-order grating $\Phi[\xi]$ is designed using iterative procedures. At $|c_1|^2 = |c_{-1}|^2$, the $\Phi[\xi]$ function corresponds to the phase function of the two-order binary grating of Eqs. (5.135) and (5.136). For the grating in Eq. (5.135), we have $|c_1|^2 = |c_{-1}|^2 = 0.405$ and the two-order DOE of

Eqs. (5.161) and (5.135) will focus 81 percent of the illuminating beam energy in the 1st and -1st diffraction orders.

The two-order phase gratings with the 100 percent energy efficiency are simply not there, which means that alongside the desired focal lines L_1 and L_2, the two-order DOE of Eq. (5.161) produces spurious images corresponding to nonzero Fourier coefficients c_j at $j \neq \pm 1$. The extent to which the useful image is affected by the spurious images is evaluated individually for each particular task and may be reduced by the "off-axis" focusing, if necessary. The off-axis focusing involves the introduction of the prism phases in the functions $\varphi_a(\mathbf{u})$ and $\varphi_b(\mathbf{u})$. The prisms play the part of the carriers and allow the spurious images to be displaced relative to the useful ones.

The considered method for designing two-order DOEs imposes no limitations on the structure of the functions $\varphi_a(\mathbf{u})$ and $\varphi_b(\mathbf{u})$. By way of illustration, the functions $\varphi_a(\mathbf{u})$ and $\varphi_b(\mathbf{u})$ may be computed using iterative procedures. If the functions $\varphi_a(\mathbf{u})$ and $\varphi_b(\mathbf{u})$ are the phase functions of multifocus DOEs that generate the line arrays S_1 and S_2, the two-order DOE will produce the line arrays S_1 and S_2 in the 1st and -1st orders.

In the subsequent examples we shall discuss the most practical cases of focusing onto two spots and onto two differently oriented line-segments.

Example 5.9 Consider the design of a two-order lens focusing the plane beam onto two spots, $z = f_a$ and $z = f_b$ on the optical axis. The phase function of a two-order lens takes the form of Eq. (5.161), where $\Phi[\xi]$ is the phase function of the two-order grating in Eq. (5.135), while the functions $\varphi_a(\mathbf{u})$ and $\varphi_b(\mathbf{u})$ correspond to the phase functions of lenses with foci f_a and f_b. In the nonparaxial approximation, the functions $\varphi_a(\mathbf{u})$ and $\varphi_b(\mathbf{u})$ are given by

$$\begin{cases} \varphi_a(\mathbf{u}) = -k\sqrt{f_a^2 + \mathbf{u}^2} \\ \varphi_b(\mathbf{u}) = -k\sqrt{f_b^2 + \mathbf{u}^2}. \end{cases} \tag{5.164}$$

As distinct to the bifocal lens of Eqs. (5.135), (5.146), (5.147), and (5.155), the two-order lens of Eqs. (5.135), (5.161), and (5.164) presents a generalization onto the case of nonparaxial approximation.

Example 5.10 Consider the design of a two-order DOE focusing onto a cross composed of two perpendicular line-segments of length $2b$. In this case, the $\Phi[\xi]$ function also takes the form of Eq. (5.135), whereas the functions $\varphi_a(\mathbf{u})$ and $\varphi_b(\mathbf{u})$ in Eq. (5.161) are the phase functions of the DOE focusing onto the line-segments forming the cross. With the square aperture $G(2a \times 2a)$ of the DOE and plane illuminating beam, the functions $\varphi_a(\mathbf{u})$ and $\varphi_b(\mathbf{u})$ may be derived from Eqs. (5.20) and (5.21) in the form

$$\begin{cases} \varphi_a(\mathbf{u}) = -\dfrac{k\mathbf{u}^2}{2f} + \dfrac{kd}{2fa}u^2 \\ \varphi_b(\mathbf{u}) = -\dfrac{k\mathbf{u}^2}{2f} + \dfrac{kd}{2fa}v^2 \end{cases}, \tag{5.165}$$

where f is the distance from the two-order DOE to the focal plane.

Let us analyze spurious images emerging when focusing onto a cross. According to Eq. (5.163), the spurious image structure is determined by the phase functions

$$\varphi_j(\mathbf{u}) = -\frac{k\mathbf{u}^2}{2f} + \frac{kd}{4fa}[(1+j)u^2 + (1-j)v^2]. \qquad (5.166)$$

The function in Eq. (5.166) is the phase function of a DOE that focuses the plane beam onto a rectangle with sides $|d(1+j)|$ and $|d(1-j)|$ [87–89]. Because the energy is distributed uniformly over the rectangle area, the spurious order intensity will be significantly less than that of the focal lines composing the cross. This suggests the conclusion that the spurious orders should not exert an essential effect on the quality of the useful image to be produced. To evaluate the approach developed, we conducted the diffraction computation of intensities in the focal plane of the two-order DOE focusing onto a cross in Eqs. (5.161), (5.135), and (5.165) for the following parameters: $\lambda = 1.06$ μm, $f = 100$ mm, $2d = 1.2$ mm, and $2a = 5$ mm (Fig. 5.60a).

In Figure 5.60a the cross-shaped structure of focused light is clearly seen. Although spurious images are not seen, there is, however, a pronounced central intensity drop, caused by the opposite signs of the Fourier coefficients c_1 and c_{-1} in Eq. (5.136). According to Eq. (5.162), this leads to the subtraction of the fields producing the elements of the cross. The central intensity drop may be compensated through the cyclic shift of profile of the grating in Eq. (5.135). If the profile of the grating in Eq. (5.135) undergoes a cyclic shift of φ_0, the Fourier coefficients in Eq. (5.136) take the form

$$c_j^{\varphi_0} = c_j \exp(ij\varphi_0). \qquad (5.167)$$

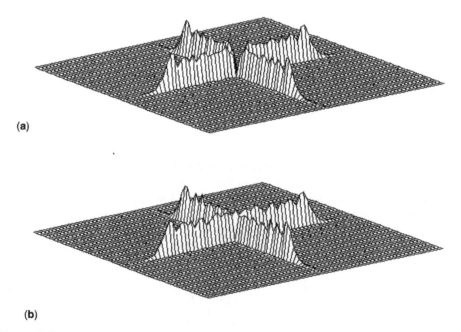

(a)

(b)

Figure 5.60. Intensity distribution in the focal plane of two-order DOEs focusing onto a cross: (a) for the function $\Phi[\xi]$ in Eq. (5.135) and (b) for the cyclic shift of the profile $\Phi[\xi]$ by $\pi/6$.

As the field amplitude at the cross center is in direct proportion to the value of $\eta = c_1 \exp(i\varphi_0) + c_{-1} \exp(-i\varphi_0) = 2ic_1 \sin(\varphi_0)$, putting $\varphi_0 = \pi/6$ and $\eta = ic_1$ should eliminate the central intensity drop. The intensity distribution in the focal plane of the two-order DOE in Figure 5.60b produced by the grating in Eq. (5.135), whose profile is cyclically shifted by $\pi/6$, confirms the absence of intensity drop at the cross center.

It makes sense to compare the two-order DOE focusing onto a cross and the segmented DOE focusing onto a cross treated in subsection 5.3.6. The aperture $2a \times 2a$ of the segmented DOE in subsection 5.3.6 is composed of four square segments, $a \times a$, focusing onto four line-segments of length d, which make up the cross. When focusing onto a cross, the aperture segmentation results in a twofold reduction of the layer length and, as a consequence, a twofold increase in the diffraction width of the cross elements. Because of this, despite the fact that the two-order DOE loses 19 percent of the illuminating beam energy in the spurious orders, it should generate a cross of greater intensity because of a two-times smaller diffraction width of lines. The computation of the field average intensity over the geometric cross conducted for the aforementioned parameters has shown that the intensity produced by the two-order DOE is 1.8 times higher than that produced by the segmented DOE. Also, we have managed to analytically compensate for the interference effects generated by the two-order DOE at the cross center, whereas for the segmented DOE such a correction can only be made by fitting the shift parameters of the cross elements.

5.8 DESIGN OF SPECTRAL DOEs

To handle different spectral components, one uses the familiar color separation gratings, making it possible to separate three different spectral components of the illuminating beam onto the -1st, 0, and -1st diffraction orders [31–33].

In the present section, we discuss the design of "spectral" DOEs that generalize the color separation gratings. The main idea of the design technique is in the nonlinear transformation of the DOE's phase function by the law of the color-separation grating. The proposed spectral DOEs make it possible *(1)* to focus three different spectral components of the illuminating beam onto three identical focal domains, *(2)* to change, in response to the wavelength change, the pattern to be focused for three different wavelengths.

5.8.1 Color-Separation Gratings

Before to describing the way the "spectral" DOEs work, let us consider the principles of operation of color-separation gratings. The grating that can separate three spectral components of wavelengths

$$\lambda_0, \quad \lambda_{+1} = \frac{\lambda_0 N}{(N+1)}, \quad \lambda_{-1} = \frac{\lambda_0 N}{(N-1)} \tag{5.168}$$

onto 0, +1s t, and -1st diffraction orders has N equal-width steps per period [31–33].

The step height is found from

$$d_i = \frac{\lambda_0 \cdot i}{(n_0 - 1)}, \quad i = \overline{0, N-1}, \tag{5.169}$$

where n_0 is the refractive index of the grating material for the wavelength λ_0.

Neglecting the grating material dispersion [31–33], it is found that the grating of Eq. (5.169) illuminated by the plane beams of wavelengths in Eq. (5.168) will produce the following phase delays:

$$\varphi_0 = 2\pi \cdot i,$$

$$\varphi_{-1} = 2\pi \cdot i \frac{\lambda_0}{\lambda_{-1}} = 2\pi \cdot i - \frac{2\pi \cdot i}{N},$$

$$\varphi_{+1} = 2\pi \cdot i \frac{\lambda_0}{\lambda_{+1}} = 2\pi \cdot i + \frac{2\pi \cdot i}{N}$$

$$(5.170)$$

Considering the 2π-periodicity of phase, the phase distribution in Eq. (5.170) will be given by

$$\varphi_0 = 0, \quad \varphi_{-1} = -\frac{2\pi \cdot i}{N}, \quad \varphi_{+1} = \frac{2\pi \cdot i}{N}, \quad i = \overline{0, N-1}. \qquad (5.171)$$

According to Eq. (5.171), for the wavelength λ_0, the phase delay is equal to zero; hence, this spectral component is diffracted onto the zero diffraction order. For the wavelengths λ_{+1} and λ_{-1}, the phase delays in Eq. (5.171) correspond to an N-step approximation of the linear phase functions implementing the focusing onto the -1st and $+1$st orders, respectively. The energy portion of these spectral components focused in the 1st and -1st orders determines the efficiency of the N-level linear grating:

$$E(N) = \sin c^2(\pi/N). \qquad (5.172)$$

The function $E(N)$ is plotted in Figure 5.61. For instance, if $N = 4$, the grating in Eq. (5.169) directs 100 percent of the energy of the spectral component λ_0 to the zero order, and 81 percent of the energy of the spectral components $\lambda_{+1} = 0.8\lambda_0$ and $\lambda_{-1} = 1.33\lambda_0$ to the $+1$st and -1st orders.

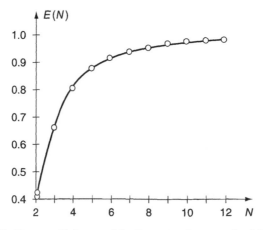

Figure 5.61. Energy efficiency of the linear grating quantized in N levels.

5.8.2 Spectral DOE Focusing onto an Array of Identical Focal Domains

The use of a "color-separation grating + lens" combination allows three spectral components to be focused onto three spots in the lens focal plane. Consider the designing of a spectral phase DOE that can separate and focus three spectral components in Eq. (5.168) onto three identical focal domains of desired shape, located in the same plane or in different planes along the optical axis (Fig. 5.62).

The microrelief of the spectral DOE will be given by

$$H(\mathbf{u}) = \frac{\lambda_0}{2\pi \cdot (n_0 - 1)} \Phi(\mathbf{u}; \lambda_0) = \frac{\lambda_0}{2\pi(n_0 - 1)} \{\varphi(\mathbf{u}) + G[\tilde{\varphi}(\mathbf{u})]\}, \qquad (5.173)$$

where $\varphi(\mathbf{u}) \in [0, 2\pi)$ is the DOE's phase function found from the condition of focusing the plane monochromatic beam of wavelength λ_0 onto the domain D in the plane $z = f$.

To make subsequent manipulation more convenient, the lens phase function is separated from the function $\varphi(\mathbf{u})$ in an explicit form

$$\varphi(\mathbf{u}) = \mathrm{mod}_{2\pi}\left(-\frac{\pi \cdot u^2}{\lambda_0 f} + \varphi_D(\mathbf{u})\right), \qquad (5.174)$$

where the addition to the lens $\varphi_D(\mathbf{u})$ provides the focusing of the converging spherical beam of focus f onto the domain D at $z = f$.

The G function in Eq. (5.173) describes the nonlinear transformation of the phase:

$$\tilde{\varphi}(\mathbf{u}) = \mathrm{mod}_{2\pi}\left(-\frac{1}{N}\varphi(\mathbf{u}) + \varphi_{pr}(\mathbf{u}) + \varphi_l(\mathbf{u})\right) \qquad (5.175)$$

by the law of phase delay of a color-separation grating for the wavelength λ_0:

$$G(\xi) = 2\pi \cdot \mathrm{int}\left[\frac{N\xi}{2\pi}\right], \quad \xi \in [0, 2\pi). \qquad (5.176)$$

The functions

$$\varphi_{pr}(\mathbf{u}) = \frac{2\pi}{\lambda_0 f}\mathbf{x}_0\mathbf{u}, \quad \varphi_l(\mathbf{u}) = -\frac{\pi}{\lambda_0 f_l}\mathbf{u}^2 \qquad (5.177)$$

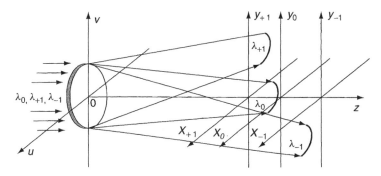

Figure 5.62. DOE focusing three spectral components onto three identical focal domains of desired shape.

in Eq. (5.175) specify the phase functions of a lens and a prism and are intended to separate the domains of focusing for different spectral components.

Note that the $\Phi(\mathbf{u}; \lambda_0)$ function in Eq. (5.173) describes the phase delay produced by the spectral DOE for the wavelength λ_0, while for the beam of wavelength $\lambda \neq \lambda_0$, the phase delay is given by

$$\Phi(\mathbf{u}; \lambda) = \frac{\lambda_0}{\lambda} \Phi(\mathbf{u}; \lambda_0). \tag{5.178}$$

Let us analyze the operation of the spectral DOE of Eqs. (5.173)–(5.177) if the illuminating beam is composed of three mutually incoherent plane beams of the wavelengths in Eq. (5.168). To describe the relationship between the field intensity distribution and the phase delay $\Phi(\mathbf{u}; \lambda)$ we shall make use of the Kirhhoff integral in the Fresnel approximation:

$$I(\mathbf{x}; z, \lambda) = \left| \frac{1}{\lambda z} \int \exp\left[i \frac{\lambda_0}{\lambda} \Phi(\mathbf{u}; \lambda_0) \right] \times \exp\left(\frac{i\pi}{\lambda z} (\mathbf{x} - \mathbf{u})^2 \right) d^2\mathbf{u} \right|^2. \tag{5.179}$$

For $\lambda = \lambda_0$, the phase delay introduced by the spectral DOE corresponds to the phase function $\varphi(\mathbf{u})$, hence providing the focusing onto the domain D in the plane $z = f$.

For the beams with the wavelengths λ_{+1} and λ_{-1}, the phase delays, when taking into account the phase 2π-periodicity, are given by

$$\Phi(\mathbf{u}; \lambda_{+1}) = \frac{N+1}{N}\{\varphi(\mathbf{u}) + G[\tilde{\varphi}(\mathbf{u})]\} = \frac{N+1}{N}\varphi(\mathbf{u}) + F_N[\tilde{\varphi}(\mathbf{u})],$$
$$\Phi(\mathbf{u}; \lambda_{-1}) = \frac{N-1}{N}\{\varphi(\mathbf{u}) + G[\tilde{\varphi}(\mathbf{u})]\} = \frac{N-1}{N}\varphi(\mathbf{u}) - F_N[\tilde{\varphi}(\mathbf{u})]. \tag{5.180}$$

The function

$$F_N(\xi) = \frac{2\pi}{N}\text{int}\left(\frac{\xi N}{2\pi} \right) \tag{5.181}$$

in Eq. (5.180) describes the quantization of the phase $\tilde{\varphi} \in [0, 2\pi)$ in N levels, which results in the emergence of additional diffraction orders [25–30,90–92]. Let us see how the spectral DOE works at the wavelength λ_{+1}. Decompose the field complex amplitude $w(\mathbf{u}; \lambda_{+1}) = \exp[i\Phi(\mathbf{u}; \lambda_{+1})]$ directly behind the DOE plane into a series in terms of diffraction orders [25–30]:

$$\exp[i\Phi(\mathbf{u}; \lambda_{+1})] = \sum_{n=-\infty}^{n=\infty} c_n \exp\left[i\frac{N+1}{N}\varphi(\mathbf{u}) + i \cdot n \cdot \left(-\frac{1}{N}\varphi(\mathbf{u}) + \varphi_{pr}(\mathbf{u}) \right. \right.$$
$$\left. \left. + \varphi_l(\mathbf{u}) \right) \right], \tag{5.182}$$

$$\text{where } c_n = \begin{cases} \text{sin } c\left(\dfrac{\pi n}{N} \right) \exp\left(i\dfrac{-\pi}{N} \right), & n = 1 + pN, \quad p = 0, \pm 1, \pm 2, \ldots - \\ 0, & n \neq 1 + pN. \end{cases} \tag{5.183}$$

are the Fourier coefficients of the function $\exp[i F_N(\xi)]$.

According to Eq. (5.182), in the first diffraction order [at $n=1$ in Eq. (5.182)], a beam with the phase function given by

$$\Phi_{+1}(\mathbf{u};\lambda_{+1}) = \varphi(\mathbf{u}) + \varphi_{pr}(\mathbf{u}) + \varphi_l(\mathbf{u}) \qquad (5.184)$$

will be generated. To evaluate the structure of the field generated by the beam with the phase front $\Phi_{+1}(\mathbf{u};\lambda_{+1})$, we shall substitute the phase function of Eq. (5.184) in the Fresnel-Kirhhoff integral in Eq. (5.179). After simple mathematical treatment, the intensity distribution produced in the first diffraction order at

$$z = z_{+1} = \frac{N+1}{N} \frac{f \cdot f_l}{f + f_l} \qquad (5.185)$$

will be represented by

$$I(\mathbf{x};z,\lambda_{+1}) = \left| \frac{1}{\lambda_{+1}z_{+1}} \int_G \exp[i\varphi_D(\mathbf{u}) - \varphi_{pr}(\mathbf{u})] \exp\left(\frac{i\pi}{\lambda_{+1}z_{+1}}\mathbf{x}\mathbf{u}\right) d^2\mathbf{u} \right|^2 \qquad (5.186)$$
$$= p_{+1}^2 \cdot I[(\mathbf{x} \cdot p_{+1} - \mathbf{x}_0); f, \lambda_0]$$

where

$$I(\mathbf{x};f,\lambda_0) = \left| \frac{1}{\lambda_0 f} \int_G \exp[i\varphi_D(\mathbf{u})] \exp\left(\frac{-i\pi}{\lambda_0 f}\mathbf{x}\mathbf{u}\right) d^2\mathbf{u} \right|^2 \qquad (5.187)$$

is the intensity distribution produced by the phase front $\varphi_D(\mathbf{u})$ for the beam of wavelength λ_0 at $z = f$. By the definition of the $\varphi_D(\mathbf{u})$ function, the intensity distribution in Eq. (5.187) corresponds to the focusing onto the domain D. According to Eqs. (5.186) and (5.187), the intensity distribution produced by the spectral DOE in the first order for the wavelength λ_{+1} corresponds to the focusing onto the domain D displaced by the vector $\mathbf{x}_0$ in the plane $z = z_{+1}$. The domain D size in terms of diffraction spots remains unchanged. The scale factor

$$p_{+1} = 1 + \frac{f}{f_l} \qquad (5.188)$$

in Eq. (5.186) describes the change in the domain D size caused by the decreased size of the diffraction spot

$$\Delta(z_{+1},\lambda_{+1}) = \lambda_{+1}z_{+1}/a = \frac{1}{p_{+1}}(\lambda_0 f/a), \qquad (5.189)$$

where a is the characteristic size of the DOE aperture.

The energy portion E of the spectral component λ_{+1}, focused in the +1st order is equal to the squared module of the Fourier coefficient c_1 [Eq. (5.172)] and amounts to over 80 percent for $N > 3$.

When applied to the wavelength λ_{-1}, the foregoing reasoning leads us to the conclusion that the phase front produced by the DOE of Eqs. (5.173)–(5.177) in the main, −1st diffraction order corresponds to focusing onto the domain D displaced by the vector $-\mathbf{x}_0$ at

$$z = z_{-1} = \frac{N-1}{N}\frac{f \cdot f_l}{f_l - f}. \tag{5.190}$$

The change in the physical size of the domain D is described by the factor

$$p_{-1} = 1 - \frac{f}{f_l}. \tag{5.191}$$

The f_l parameter in Eqs. (5.177), (5.185), and (5.190) allows the position of the planes of focusing to be varied. In particular, putting $f_l = Nf$ in Eqs. (5.185) and (5.190), we get $z_{+1} = z_{-1} = f$. In this case, the spectral DOE focuses three spectral components of Eq. (5.168) onto three domains D located in the same plane at $z = f$ and spaced by the vector $\mathbf{x}_0$.

Note in conclusion that to reduce requirements imposed on the photolithographic technology resolution, the spectral DOE is expedient to design as an addition to a thin lens of focus f. In this case, instead of the function $\varphi(\mathbf{u})$ in Eq. (5.173), one should use the $\varphi_D(\mathbf{u})$ function computed for focusing the converging spherical beam of focus f onto the domain D at $z = f$.

5.8.3 Spectral DOE Focusing onto Various Focal Domains

The design technique dealt with in subsection 5.8.2. allows one to separate and focus the spectral components of Eq. (5.168) onto three equal-shape domains either in the same desired plane or in three different planes along the optical axis. Let us consider how to design spectral DOEs that can, in response to the change of wavelength by the law of Eq. (5.168), change the focal domain pattern.

The wavelengths in Eq. (5.168) and the phase delays in Eq. (5.171) for the color-separation grating in Eq. (5.169) are not mutually independent. Therefore, in the general case, the design technique in Eqs. (5.173)–(5.177) may be modified for the case of focusing of two different wavelengths in Eq. (5.168) onto two different domains D_0 and D_1. Denote $\varphi(\mathbf{u})$, $\varphi_1(\mathbf{u})$ the phase functions of DOEs that would focus the beams of wavelengths λ_0 and λ_{+1} onto the domains D_0 and D_1. The $\tilde{\varphi}(\mathbf{u})$ function in the general expression for the microrelief structure of the spectral DOE in Eq. (5.173) will be rewritten as

$$\tilde{\varphi}(\mathbf{u}) = \mathrm{mod}_{2\pi}\left(-\frac{N+1}{N}\varphi(\mathbf{u}) + \varphi_1(\mathbf{u})\right). \tag{5.192}$$

For $\tilde{\varphi}(\mathbf{u})$ taking the form of Eq. (5.192), the spectral DOE for the beams of wavelengths λ_0 and λ_{+1} will generate in the zero and +1st diffraction orders beams with the following phase functions:

$$\Phi_0(\mathbf{u};\lambda_0) = \varphi(\mathbf{u}), \tag{5.193}$$

$$\Phi_{+1}(\mathbf{u};\lambda_{+1}) = \varphi_1(\mathbf{u}), \tag{5.194}$$

thus providing the focusing onto the domains D_0 and D_1, respectively.

For the wavelength λ_{-1}, the DOE of Eqs. (5.173), (5.176), and (5.192) produces in the main -1st order a beam with the phase function

$$\Phi_{-1}(\mathbf{u};\lambda_{-1}) = 2\varphi(\mathbf{u}) - \varphi_1(\mathbf{u}) \qquad (5.195)$$

To analyze the domain structure produced at $\lambda = \lambda_{-1}$ we shall, for simplicity, suppose that the spectral DOE is designed as an addition to a thin lens of focus f. In this case, the functions $\varphi_0(\mathbf{u})$, $\varphi_1(\mathbf{u})$ correspond to the phase functions of DOE focusing converging spherical beams of wavelengths λ_0 and λ_{+1} onto the domains D_0 and D_1 at $z = f$. It is recalled that the DOEs calculated within the geometric optical approach possess an interesting property: if the phase of a DOE intended for focusing a converging spherical beam is multiplied by a constant p, the domain of focusing experiences a p-fold scaling. On the basis of this property, consider three examples of choosing the functions $\varphi(\mathbf{u})$ and $\varphi_1(\mathbf{u})$ allowing three wavelengths, λ_0, λ_{+1}, and λ_{-1}, to be operated.

Example 5.11   Let $\varphi(\mathbf{u})$ be the phase function of a DOE calculated within the geometric optical approach and $\varphi_1(\mathbf{u})$ be the phase function of an N-order diffraction grating. Then, for $\lambda = \lambda_{-1}$ the phase function $2\varphi(\mathbf{u})$ in Eq. (5.195) will implement the focusing onto the domain $2 \times D$, whereas the function $\varphi_1(\mathbf{u})$ will multiply the domain $2 \times D$ onto N orders. In this case, the element represented by a "spectral DOE + thin lens" combination will implement the focusing onto the domain D for $\lambda = \lambda_0$ onto an array of N spots for $\lambda = \lambda_{+1}$ and onto an array of N domains of size 2D for $\lambda = \lambda_{-1}$.

Example 5.12.   Let $\varphi(\mathbf{u})$ be the phase function of a DOE calculated within the geometric optical approach and $\varphi_1(\mathbf{u})$ be the phase function of an N-focus lens treated in section 5.6. Then, at $\lambda = \lambda_{-1}$, the phase function $2\varphi(\mathbf{u})$ in Eq. (5.195) will implement the focusing onto the domain $2 \times D$, while the function $\varphi_1(\mathbf{u})$ will scale and multiply the $2 \times D$ domain onto N different focal planes of the multifocus lens $\varphi_1(\mathbf{u})$. In this case, the element corresponding to the "spectral DOE + thin lens" superposition will focus onto the domain D for $\lambda = \lambda_0$ onto an array of N spots on an optical axis for $\lambda = \lambda_{+1}$ and onto an array of N-scaled domains D in different focal planes for $\lambda = \lambda_{-1}$.

Example 5.13   Let $\varphi(\mathbf{u})$ and $\varphi_1(\mathbf{u})$ be the phase functions of geometric optical DOEs focusing rectangular beams onto the line-segments $|x| \leq d$, $y = 0$ and $|y| \leq d_1$, $x = 0$. Then, at $\lambda = \lambda_{-1}$, the phase function in Eq. (5.195) will correspond to the focusing onto a rectangle of size $(4d) \times (2d_1)$ [87–89]. With the aforementioned choice of the functions $\varphi(\mathbf{u})$ and $\varphi_1(\mathbf{u})$, the spectral DOE will focus onto a line-segment on the Ox-axis for $\lambda = \lambda_0$, onto a line-segment on the Oy-axis for $\lambda = \lambda_{+1}$, and onto a rectangle for $\lambda = \lambda_{-1}$.

5.8.4 Design of Quantized Spectral DOEs

The traditional photolithographic technology of DOE fabrication provides the quantization of diffraction microrelief in M levels. The microrelief of the spectral DOE in Eq. (5.173) contains a component corresponding to the $\varphi(\mathbf{u})$ function and an N-level stepwise function $G[\tilde{\varphi}(\mathbf{u})]$. When quantizing the $\varphi(\mathbf{u})$ function in L levels, the microrelief of Eq. (5.173) becomes quantized in $M = N \times L$ levels.

The quantization results in a reduced efficiency of focusing and the deteriorated quality of the images under focusing owing to the emergence of additional diffraction orders. To remedy the quantization errors at the stage of designing the spectral DOE, the $\varphi(\mathbf{u})$ function in Eq. (5.173) for focusing the beam of wavelength λ_0 is expedient to compute using the iterative algorithms for computing the quantized phase functions, dealt with in subsection 2.8.10. We are reminded that the algorithms discussed in subsection 2.8.10 are based on the gradient optimization of the continuous function being a truncated series expanded in terms of the diffraction orders of the quantized CTF.

The spectral DOE for the beams of wavelengths $\lambda_{\pm 1}$ produces the desired images in the main, $+1$st, and -1st diffraction orders. In the general case, the useful images are diversely affected by the spurious-order images at $n \neq \pm 1$. The spectral DOEs in Eqs. (5.173) and (5.192) intended to focus two wavelengths, λ_0 and λ_{+1} onto two different domains D_0 and D_1 will be referred to as *two-wavelength DOEs*.

For the two-wavelength DOEs, the functions $\varphi_1(\mathbf{u})$ in Eq. (5.192) may also be computed with regard for the influence of spurious diffraction orders. Actually, at $\lambda = \lambda_{+1}$, the DOE of Eqs. (5.173) and (5.192) will produce in diffraction orders beams with the phase functions given by

$$\Phi_n(\mathbf{u};\lambda_{+1}) = \frac{N+1}{N}\varphi(\mathbf{u}) + n\left(-\frac{N+1}{N}\varphi(\mathbf{u}) + \varphi_1(\mathbf{u})\right), \quad n = (1 + pN),$$

$$p = 0, \pm 1, \pm 2, \ldots \tag{5.196}$$

For $n = 1$ ($p = 0$), in Eq. (5.196) we have $\Phi_1(\mathbf{u};\lambda_{+1}) = \varphi_1(\mathbf{u})$, the result being the focusing onto the domain D_1 in the main, 1st diffraction order. Assume that the function $\varphi(\mathbf{u})$ is quantized in $(N + 1)$ levels. In this case, the phase distributions in Eq. (5.196) take the form

$$\Phi_n(\boldsymbol{u};\lambda_{+1}) = n\varphi_1(\boldsymbol{u}), \quad n = (1 + pN), \quad p = 0, \pm 1, \pm 2, \ldots \tag{5.197}$$

According to Eq. (5.197), the phase delay $\Phi(\mathbf{u};\lambda_{+1})$ does not depend on the phase $\varphi(\mathbf{u})$ and can be substituted by those corresponding to the $\varphi_1(\mathbf{u})$ function quantized in N levels:

$$\Phi(\mathbf{u};\lambda_{+1}) = F_N[\varphi_1(\mathbf{u})]. \tag{5.198}$$

Thus, when quantizing the phase $\varphi(\mathbf{u})$ in $N + 1$ levels, the design of the two-order DOE may be brought to two independent tasks of deriving quantized functions $F_{N+1}[\varphi(\mathbf{u})]$ and $F_N[\varphi_1(\mathbf{u})]$ on the condition that the beams of wavelengths λ_0 and λ_{+1} are focused onto the domains D_0 and D_1, respectively, the number of quantization levels for the two-wavelength DOE being $M = N \cdot (N + 1)$. Interestingly, the relief of the two-wavelength DOE of Eqs. (5.173) and (5.192) may be determined directly through the discrete values

$$\varphi(i) = \frac{2\pi}{N+1}i, \quad i = 0, N, \quad \varphi_1(j) = \frac{2\pi}{N}j, \quad j = 0, N - 1,$$

taken by the quantized functions $F_{N+1}[\varphi(\mathbf{u})]$ and $F_N[\varphi_1(\mathbf{u})]$. Actually, if in Eqs (5.192) and (5.173) we substitute the function $\varphi(i)$ and $\varphi_1(j)$ instead of the functions $\varphi(\mathbf{u})$

and $\varphi_1(\mathbf{u})$, the discrete analogs of the functions $\tilde{\varphi}(\mathbf{u})$ and $G[\tilde{\varphi}(\mathbf{u})]$ will be given by

$$\tilde{\varphi}(i, j) = \mathrm{mod}_{2\pi}\left(\frac{2\pi}{N}(j - i)\right), \tag{5.199}$$

$$G(i, j) = 2\pi \cdot \mathrm{mod}_N(j - i). \tag{5.200}$$

Relationships (5.199) and (5.200) allow the relief height of the two-wavelength DOE to be represented at each point of aperture through the indices (i, j) corresponding to the values of the quantized functions $F_{N+1}[\varphi(\mathbf{u})]$ and $F_N[\varphi_1(\mathbf{u})]$ in the form:

$$H(i, j) = \frac{\lambda_0}{2\pi(n_0 - 1)}\left[\frac{2\pi}{N + 1}i + 2\pi \cdot \mathrm{mod}_N(j - i)\right], \quad i = \overline{0, N}, \quad j = \overline{0, N - 1} \tag{5.201}$$

The number of levels, $L = N \cdot (N + 1)$, of the microrelief in Eq. (5.201) may be reduced. Let d_1 and d_2 be the greatest common divisors of the numbers N and $N + 1$, such that $N = p_1 d_1$, $p_1 > 1$, $N + 1 = p_2 d_2$, $p_2 > 1$. In that case, using the quantized functions $F_{p_2}[\varphi(\mathbf{u})]$ and $F_{p_1}[\varphi_1(\mathbf{u})]$ satisfying the condition of focusing the beams of wavelengths λ_0 and λ_{+1} onto the domains D_0 and D_1, one can construct a two-wavelength DOE with $L = p_1 p_2$ relief levels by the rule

$$H(i, j) = \frac{\lambda_0}{2\pi(n_0 - 1)}\left[\frac{2\pi}{p_2}i + 2\pi \cdot \mathrm{mod}_N(d_1 j - d_2 i)\right],$$
$$i = \overline{0, p_2 - 1}, \quad j = \overline{0, p_1 - 1}. \tag{5.202}$$

At $\lambda = \lambda_0$, the DOE in Eq. (5.202) generates the phase delay corresponding to the pixels of the phase function $F_{p_2}[\varphi(\mathbf{u})]$, thus providing the focusing onto the domain D.

For $\lambda = \lambda_{+1}$, the phase delay produced by the DOE in Eq. (5.202) takes the form

$$\Phi(i, j; \lambda_{+1}) = 2\pi \frac{N + 1}{N}\left[\frac{i}{p_2} + \mathrm{mod}_N(d_1 j - d_2 i)\right]$$
$$= \frac{2\pi}{p_1}j + 2\pi \cdot \mathrm{mod}_{N+1}(d_1 j - d_2 i), \quad i = \overline{0, p_2 - 1}, \quad j = \overline{0, p_1 - 1}. \tag{5.203}$$

Considering the 2π-periodicity, the $\Phi(i, j; \lambda_{+1})$ function is given by

$$\Phi(i, j; \lambda_{+1}) = \frac{2\pi}{p_1}j, \quad j = \overline{0, p_1 - 1} \tag{5.204}$$

and corresponds to the pixels of the phase $F_{p_2}[\varphi(\mathbf{u})]$, thus providing the focusing of the beam of wavelength λ_{+1} onto the domain D_1.

Note that because one of the numbers N and $N + 1$ is even, the number of relief levels of a two-wavelength DOE can always be reduced to at least $N(N + 1)/2$.

The quantized DOEs for focusing onto the domains D_0 and D_1 may be designed not only for the wavelengths λ_0 and λ_{+1} in Eq. (5.168), but also for two wavelengths, λ_0 and λ_1, related in a more general manner:

$$\frac{\lambda_0}{\lambda_1} = \frac{M}{N} \tag{5.205}$$

where M and N are relatively prime numbers.

Equation (5.201) suggests constructing a two-wavelength DOE from the functions $F_M[\varphi(\mathbf{u})]$ and $F_N[\varphi_1(\mathbf{u})]$ quantized in M and N levels. Let us define the relief of the two-wavelength DOE through the values of the quantized functions $F_M[\varphi(\mathbf{u})]$ and $F_N[\varphi_1(\mathbf{u})]$ in the form

$$H(i, j) = \frac{\lambda_0}{2\pi(n_0 - 1)} \left[\frac{2\pi}{M} i + 2\pi \cdot M_0(i, j) \right], \quad i = \overline{0, M-1}, \quad j = \overline{0, N-1},$$
(5.206)

where $M_0(i, j)$ is some unknown function taking integer nonnegative values. At $\lambda = \lambda_0$, the phase delay

$$\Phi(i, j; \lambda) = \frac{2\pi i}{M} + 2\pi M_0(i, j), \quad i = \overline{0, M-1}, \quad j = \overline{0, N-1},$$
(5.207)

produced by the DOE in Eq. (5.206) corresponds, in view of phase 2π-periodicity, to the pixels of the phase function $F_M[\varphi(\mathbf{u})]$ and provides the focusing onto the domain D. At $\lambda = \lambda_1$, the phase delay produced by the DOE of Eq. (5.206) takes the form

$$\Phi(i, j; \lambda_1) = 2\pi \frac{M}{N} \left[\frac{i}{M} + M_0(i, j) \right], \quad i = \overline{0, M-1}, \quad j = \overline{0, N-1}.$$
(5.208)

To provide the focusing of the beam of wavelength λ_1 onto the domain D_1, the function $M_0(i,j)$ in Eq. (5.206) should be chosen from the condition that the expression in Eq. (5.208) equals, with respect to modulo 2π, the pixels of the quantized function $F_N[\varphi_1(\mathbf{u})]$. As a result, we get the following equation for the computation of the function $M_0(i,j)$:

$$2\pi \frac{M}{N} \left[\frac{i}{M} + M_0(i, j) \right] = 2\pi \left[\frac{j}{N} + M_1(i, j) \right], \quad i = \overline{0, M-1}, \quad j = \overline{0, N-1}.$$
(5.209)

where $M_1(i, j)$ is an arbitrary function taking integer values.

By direct substitution, one can make sure that the solution to Eq. (5.209) takes the form

$$\begin{cases} M_0(i, j) = \alpha_1(j - i) + Nz \\ M_1(i, j) = \alpha_2(j - i) + Mz \end{cases} \quad i = \overline{0, M-1}, \quad j = \overline{0, N-1}.$$
(5.210)

where α_1 and α_2 are integer numbers derived from the solution of the equation

$$M \cdot \alpha_1 - N \cdot \alpha_2 = 1$$
(5.211)

and z is the least integer number chosen from the condition that the function $M_0(i,j)$ is nonnegative. Note that since the numbers M and N are supposed to be relatively prime, owing to the greatest common divisor theorem, Eq. (5.211) always has solutions in integer numbers.

According to the definition of z, Eq. (5.209) may be written in the form

$$\begin{cases} M_0(i, j) = \mathrm{mod}_N(\alpha_1(j - i)) \\ M_1(i, j) = \alpha_2(j - i) + Mz \end{cases} \quad i = \overline{0, M-1}, \quad j = \overline{0, N-1}.$$
(5.212)

The microrelief height for the two-wavelength DOE will be derived from

$$H(i, j) = \frac{\lambda_0}{2\pi(n_0 - 1)} \left[\frac{2\pi}{M} i + 2\pi \cdot \text{mod}_N(\alpha_1(j - i)) \right], \quad i = \overline{0, N}, \quad j = \overline{0, N - 1}$$

(5.213)

Comparison between Eqs. (5.201) and (5.213) suggests that the use of the more general relation (5.205) for the wavelengths λ_0 and λ_1 does not result in an increase in the DOE microrelief height in Eq. (5.213), as compared with the earlier computed DOE of Eq. (5.201). It should also be noted that for $N = p_1 d_1$, $p_1 > 1$, $M = p_2 d_2$, $p_2 > 1$, the number of levels $L = NM$ of the microrelief in Eq. (5.213) can be reduced to $p_1 p_2$.

From Eq. (5.213), one can easily produce the equation for a color-separation grating that can separate the spectral components onto the 0 and +1st orders. Such a grating has per period N equal-width steps of height

$$d_i = \frac{\lambda_0}{(n_0 - 1)} \text{mod}_N(\alpha_1 i), \quad i = \overline{0, N - 1},$$

(5.214)

where α_1 is found from solving Eq. (5.211).

The grating in Eq. (5.214) may be used for the analytical computation of the spectral DOEs with the wavelengths in Eq. (5.205) focusing onto the domains D_0 and D_1. In this case, it will suffice to rearrange in the general relation (5.173) the $G(\xi)$ and $\tilde{\varphi}(\mathbf{u})$ function as

$$G(\xi) = 2\pi \cdot \text{mod}_N \left(\alpha_1 \cdot \text{int} \left[\frac{N\xi}{2\pi} \right] \right), \quad \xi \in [0, 2\pi),$$

(5.215)

$$\tilde{\varphi}(\mathbf{u}) = \text{mod}_{2\pi} \left(-\frac{M}{N} \varphi(\mathbf{u}) + \varphi_1(\mathbf{u}) \right).$$

(5.216)

It can easily be seen that the spectral DOE of Eqs. (5.173), (5.215), and (5.216) for the beams of wavelengths in Eq. (5.205) will produce in the 0 and +1st diffraction orders the beams with the phase functions $\varphi(\mathbf{u})$ and $\varphi_1(\mathbf{u})$, thus providing the focusing onto the domains D_0 and D_1, respectively.

To evaluate the robustness of the method proposed, we shall consider some examples of designing spectral DOEs.

Example 5.14 The DOE in Eqs. (5.173)–(5.177) was designed as an addition to a thin lens of focus f and was intended for the separation and focusing of the spectral components in Eq. (5.168) onto three line-segments in the plane $z = f$. As the $\varphi(\mathbf{u})$ function in Eqs. (5.173)–(5.177), we took the phase function of the DOE with diffraction corrections in Eqs. (5.21) and (5.71) that can focus the converging spherical beam of focus f onto a uniform line-segment

$$\varphi(\boldsymbol{u}) = \text{mod}_{2\pi} \left[\frac{3\pi d}{\lambda_0 f R^3} \left(R \frac{u^2}{2} - \frac{u^4}{12} \right) \right],$$

(5.217)

where R is the aperture radius and d is the length of the segment under focusing.

The DOE of Eqs. (5.173)–(5.177) and (5.217) was designed for the following parameters: the wavelengths are $\lambda_0 = 0.525 \ \mu\text{m}$, $\lambda_{+1} = 0.42 \ \mu\text{m}$, and $\lambda_{-1} = 0.7 \ \mu\text{m}$

($N = 4$ in Eq. (5.168)), the length of the segments under focusing is $d = 30\Delta(\lambda)$, ($\Delta(\lambda) = \lambda f/R$), the aperture radius is $R = 2.5$ mm, the lens focal length is $f = 500$ mm, the lens and prism parameters in Eq. (5.177) are $\mathbf{x}_0 = [0, 10\Delta(\lambda_0)]$ and $f_l = Nf = 2000$ mm.

The halftone image of the computed microrelief for the spectral DOE is shown in Figure 5.63a. The intensity distribution produced by the spectral DOE of Eqs. (5.173)–(5.177) and (5.217) for the illuminating beam composed of three plane beams of wavelengths indicated earlier is depicted in Figure 5.63b and demonstrates the high accurate focusing onto three line-segments.

Different lengths and intensities of the segments in Figure 5.63b are due to different diffraction spot sizes $\Delta(\lambda)$ for different wavelengths. The left, central, and right segments in Figure 5.63b, correspond to the components $\lambda_{-1} = 0.7$ µm, $\lambda_0 = 0.525$ µm and $\lambda_{+1} = 0.42$ µm respectively.

Example 5.15   We designed the spectral DOE of Eqs. (5.173) and (5.192) that can, in response to the changed wavelength, change the focal domain pattern. This DOE designed as an addition to a lens was intended for focusing the component $\lambda_0 = 0.525$ µm onto the line-segment of length $20\Delta(\lambda_0)$, the component $\lambda_{+1} = 0.42$ µm, onto four spots, and the component $\lambda_{-1} = 0.7$ µm onto four line-segments of length $40\Delta(\lambda_{-1})$. As the $\varphi(\mathbf{u})$ function in Eqs. (5.173) and (5.192), we took the phase function of a DOE focusing onto a line-segment, Eq. (5.217). The additional prism phase function $\varphi_{\mathrm{pr}}(\boldsymbol{v}) = (2\pi/\lambda_0 f)y_0 v$ at $y_0 = 2\Delta(\lambda_0)$ was introduced into the phase in Eq. (5.217) to compensate for the adverse effects of spurious diffraction orders when focusing the components λ_{+1} and λ_{-1}. As the function $\varphi_1(\mathbf{u})$ in Eqs. (5.173) and (5.192), we used the phase function of a four-order diffraction grating described on the period p ($p = 0, 3571$ mm) by the following relations:

$$\varphi_1(\boldsymbol{u}) = \begin{cases} 0, & u \in [0, p/4) \\ \pi, & u \in [p/4, p/2) \\ \pi/2, & u \in [p/2, 3p/4) \\ 3\pi/2, & u \in [3p/4, p) \end{cases} . \tag{5.218}$$

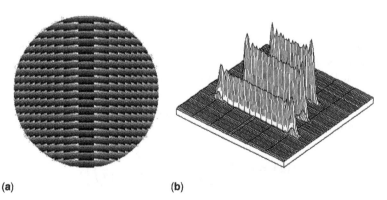

(a)   **(b)**

Figure 5.63. (a) Halftone microrelief of a spectral DOE for separating and focusing the spectral components $\lambda_0 = 0.525$ µm, $\lambda_{+1} = 0.42$µm, and $\lambda_{-1} = 0.7$ µm onto three line-segments; (b) Intensity distribution in the plane of focusing.

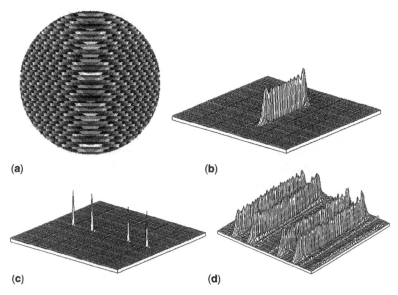

Figure 5.64. (a) Halftone relief of a spectral DOE to focus the spectral components of Eq. (5.168) onto a line-segment, four spots, and four line-segments, (b) Intensity distributions in the plane of focusing for $\lambda_0 = 0.525$ μm (c) $\lambda_{+1} = 0.42$ μm, (d) $\lambda_{-1} = 0.7$ μm.

The four-order grating of Eq. (5.218) focuses 81 percent of the illuminating beam energy onto the orders -2, -1, $+1$, and $+2$. The halftone image of the calculated relief for the spectral DOE is depicted in Figure 5.64a. The intensity distributions generated by the spectral DOE for the plane beams of wavelengths $\lambda_0 = 0.525$ μm, $\lambda_{+1} = 0.42$ μm, and $\lambda_{-1} = 0.7$ μm are depicted in Figure 5.64b–d and clearly show the light structure having been focused onto a line-segment, four spots and four line-segments.

Example 5.16   We designed the spectral DOE of Eqs. (5.173) and (5.192) with a square aperture of 2.5×2.5 mm to focus the component $\lambda_0 = 0.525$ μm onto a square of $20\Delta(\lambda_0) \times 20\Delta(\lambda_0)$ and the components $\lambda_{+1} = 0.42$ μm and $\lambda_{-1} = 0.7$ μm onto the line-segments of lengths $40\Delta(\lambda_{+1})$ and $40\Delta(\lambda_{-1})$ on the axes Ox and Oy. As the functions $\varphi(\boldsymbol{u})$ and $\varphi_1(\boldsymbol{u})$ in Eqs. (5.173) and (5.192), we took the phase functions of a DOE focusing the converging spherical beam of focus f onto a square of size $K\Delta(\lambda_0)$:

$$\varphi(\boldsymbol{u}) = \mathrm{mod}_{2\pi}\left(\frac{\pi K}{a^2}(u^2 + v^2) \right) \tag{5.219}$$

and onto a line-segment of length $2K\Delta(\lambda_{+1})$ on the Ox-axis:

$$\varphi_1(u) = \frac{2\pi K}{a^2}u^2, \tag{5.220}$$

where a is the DOE aperture size.

For the wavelength λ_{-1}, the DOE of Eqs. (5.173), (5.192), (5.219), and (5.220) will produce in the main and -1st order, a beam with the phase function

$$\Phi_{-1}(\mathbf{u};\lambda_{-1}) = 2\varphi(\mathbf{u}) - \varphi_1(\mathbf{u}) = \frac{2\pi K}{a^2}v^2. \tag{5.221}$$

The phase in Eq. (5.221) corresponds to the phase function of a DOE focusing the converging spherical beam onto a line-segment of length $2K\Delta(\lambda_{-1})$ on the Oy-axis.

The halftone image of the spectral DOE in Eqs. (5.173), (5.192), (5.219), and (5.220) is depicted in Figure 5.65a. The intensity distributions produced by the spectral DOE for the beams of wavelengths $\lambda_0 = 0.525$ μm, $\lambda_{+1} = 0.393$ μm, and $\lambda_{-1} = 0.656$ μm are shown in Figure 5.65b–d and clearly demonstrate the light structure focused onto a square and onto line-segments.

Example 5.17   We designed two quantized spectral diffraction gratings intended for the generation of four orders: -2, -1, $+1$, and $+2$ for the wavelength λ_0, and three orders: $-1, 0$, and $+1$ for the wavelengths $\lambda_{+1} = 3\lambda_0/4$ and $\lambda_{+1} = 9\lambda_0/4$. The quantized spectral gratings (period of p) were designed using Eqs. (5.202) and (5.213) and based on the quantized phase functions of the four-order grating in Eq. (5.218) and the three-order grating given by

$$\varphi_1(u) = \begin{cases} 2\pi/3, & u \in [0, p/2) \\ 0, & u \in [p/2, p) \end{cases}. \tag{5.222}$$

The intensities in orders, corresponding to the squared modules of the Fourier coefficients in the decomposition of the function $\exp[i\varphi(u)]$ for the grating of Eq. (5.222) are equal to $I_{-1} = 0.304$, $I_0 = 0.25$, and $I_{+1} = 0.304$.

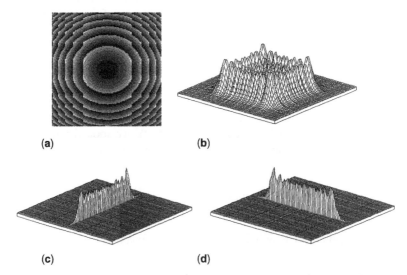

(a)   (b)

(c)   (d)

Figure 5.65. (a) Halftone microrelief of a spectral DOE to focus the spectral components of Eq. (5.168) onto a square, a line-segment on the Ox-axis, and a line-segment on the Oy-axis. Intensity distributions in the plane of focusing for (b) $\lambda_0 = 0.525$ μm, (c) $\lambda_{+1} = 0.42$ μm, and (d) $\lambda_{-1} = 0.7$ μm.

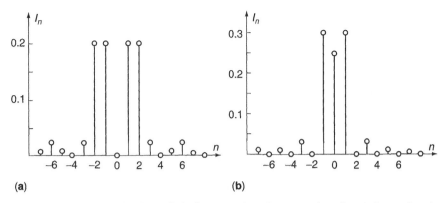

Figure 5.66. (a) The profile of a period of a spectral grating to produce four orders: $-2, -1, +1,$ $+2$ for the wavelength $\lambda = \lambda_0$, and three orders: $-1, 0, +1$ for the wavelength $\lambda = \lambda_{+1} = 3\lambda_0/4$; Intensities in the orders of the diffraction gratings of equations for the wavelength (**b**) λ_0 and (**b**) λ_{+1}.

Hence, the grating in Eq. (5.222) concentrates 85 percent of the illuminating beam energy in the orders -1, 0, and $+1$. The relief of the quantized spectral grating in Eqs. (5.202), (5.218), and (5.222) intended to focus the components λ_0 and $\lambda_{+1} = 3\lambda_0/4$ is given by

$$h(n) = \frac{\pi_0}{2\pi(n_0 - 1)} \begin{cases} 0, & u \in [0, p/4) \\ 3\pi, & u \in [p/4, p/2) \\ 0.5\pi, & u \in [p/2, 3p/4) \\ 3\pi, & u \in [3p/4, p) \end{cases} \tag{5.223}$$

whereas the relief of the spectral grating in Eqs. (5.213), (5.218), and (5.222) to focus the components λ_0 and $\lambda_{+1} = 9\lambda_0/4$ has the form.

$$h(n) = \frac{\pi_0}{2\pi(n_0 - 1)} \begin{cases} 0, & u \in [0, p/4) \\ 9\pi, & u \in [p/4, p/2) \\ 10.5\pi, & u \in [p/2, 3p/4) \\ 1.5\pi, & u \in [3p/4, p) \end{cases} \tag{5.224}$$

The diffraction order intensities produced by the gratings of Eqs. (5.223) and (5.224), illuminated by the plane beams of wavelengths λ_0, $\lambda_{+1} = 3\lambda_0/4$, and λ_0, $\lambda_{+1} = 9\lambda_0/4$ are the same and are depicted in Figures 5.66a and 5.66b.

REFERENCES

1. M.A. Golub et al., Focusing of coherent light onto a desired spatial domain using computer-generated holograms, *Lett. J. Tech. Phys.* **7**(10), 618–623 (1981).

2. M.A. Golub et al., Computer-aided synthesis of focusing elements for the CO2-laser, *Lett. J. Tech. Phys.* **8**(13), 449–451 (1982).

3. V.A. Danilov et al., Optical elements to focus the coherent light onto an arbitrary focal line, Pre-print No. 69, Lebedev Physical Institute, Moscow, 1983, p. 41.

4. A.V. Goncharsky et al., Planar focusing elements of visible range, *J. Quant. Electron.* (Moscow), **13**(3), 660–662 (1986).

5. A.G. Vasin et al., Computation and studies of the coherent light field in the focal domain of radially symmetric optical elements, Pre-print No. 304, Lebedev Physical Institute, Moscow, 1983, p. 38.

6. A.V. Goncharsky et al., Solving the inverse problem of focusing the laser light onto an arbitrary curve, *Dokl. USSR Acad Sci.* **273**(3), 605–608 (1983).

7. V.A. Danilov et al., Synthesis of optical elements to produce an arbitrary focal line, *Lett. J. Tech. Phys.* **8**(13), 810–815 (1982).

8. A.V. Goncharsky et al., Focusators of grazing-incidence laser light, *J. Quant. Electron.* (Moscow) **11**(1), 166–168 (1984).

9. A.V. Goncharsky and V.V. Stepanov, On the existence of smooth solutions of the problems on focusing the electromagnetic radiation, *Dokl. USSR Acad. Sci.* **279**(4), 788–792 (1984).

10. A.V. Goncharsky and V.V. Stepanov, Inverse problems of coherent optics, Focusing onto a line, *J. Calculat. Math. and Math. Phy.* **26**(1), 80–91 (1986).

11. A.V. Goncharsky, Mathematical models in the problems of synthesis of planar optical elements, *Comput. Opt.* (Moscow) **1**, 19–31 (1987).

12. A.V. Goncharsky, V.V. Popov, and V.V. Stepanov, *Introduction into Computer Optics*, Moscow University Publishers, 1991, 309 pages.

13. V.A. Danilov, B.E. Kinber, and A.E. Shilov, Theory of coherent focusators, *Comput. Opt.* (Moscow), **1**, 40–52 (1987).

14. M. Curcio, Diamond machining of infrared optics utilizing two-axis machine technology, *Proc. SPIE* **306**, 105–113 (1981).

15. E.D. Bulatov, S.A. Gridin, and A.A. Danilenko, Fabrication of planar optics elements of millimeter and submillimeter range using commercial computer-controlled lathes, *Comput. Opt.* (Moscow) **1**, 167–173 (1987).

16. Yu.B. Boiko, V.S. Solovjev, S. Calixto, and D.-J. Lougnot, Dry photopolymer films for computer-generated infrared radiation focusing elements, *Appl. Opt.* **33**(5), 787–793 (1994).

17. V.S. Solovjov, Studying the behavior of the LPPC layer in the course of relief formation, *Comput. Opt.* (Moscow) **10–11**, 145–149 (1992).

18. A.V. Volkov et al., Experimental studies of mass-transfer in liquid photopolymerizable compositions, *J. Tech. Phys.* **65**(9), 181–185 (1995).

19. I.N. Sisakian and V.A. Soifer, Computer-Optics: achievements and problems, *J. Comput. Opt.* (Moscow) **1**, 5–19 (1987).

20. M.A. Golub, N.L. Kazansky, I.N. Sisakian, and V.A. Soifer, Numerical simulation of computer optics elements, *Avtometriya*, **1**, 70–82 (1988).

21. M.A. Golub, N.L. Kazansky, and V.A. Soifer, Mathematically modeled focusing of light using computer-synthesized optics, *Sci. Instrum.* **3**(1), 9–23 (1993).

22. M.A. Golub, N.L. Kazansky, and M.V. Shinkaryev, Structure of a program complex for synthesizing computer optics elements, *Comput. Opt.* (Moscow) **5**, 43–48 (1989).

23. N.L. Kazansky, Numerical simulation of the Fresnel lens, *Comput. Opt.* (Moscow) **3**, 22–28 (1988).

24. N.L. Kazansky, Studies of diffraction characteristics of a focusator onto a ring using numerical simulation, *Comput. Opt.* (Moscow) **10–11**, 128–144 (1992).

25. M.A. Golub et al., Synthesis of multi-functional phase elements using the diffraction approach, *Opt. Spectrosc.* **73**(1), 191–195 (1992).

26. L.L. Doskolovich, N.L. Kazansky, and V.A. Soifer, Design of two-order focusators, *Avtometriya* **1**, 58–63 (1993).

27. L.L. Doskolovich, N.L. Kazansky, V.A. Soifer, and I.S. Kharitonov, Nonlinear phase predistortion for focusing onto an array of focal lines, *Sci. Instrum.* **3**(1), 24–37 (1993).

28. M.A. Golub et al., Computer generated diffractive multi-focal lens, *J. Mod. Opt.* **39**(6), 1245–1251 (1992).

29. V.A. Soifer et al., Multifocal and combined diffractive elements (Invited Paper), *Proceedings SPIE* 1992 "Miniature and Micro-Optics and Micromechanics" 226–234 (1993).

30. V.A. Soifer, L.L. Doskolovich, and N.L. Kazanskiy, Multifocal diffractive elements. *Opt. Eng.* **33**(11), 3610–3615 (1994).

31. H. Dammann, Color separation gratings, *Appl. Opt.* **17**(15), 2273–2279 (1978).

32. H. Dammann, Spectral Characteristics of Stepped-phase Gratings, *Optik* **53**, 409–417 (1979).

33. M.W. Farn and M.B. Stern, Color separation by use of binary optics, *Opt. Lett.* **18**, 1214–1216 (1993).

34. M. Born and E. Wolf, *Principles of Optics*, Pergamon press, Oxford, 1968.

35. Y. Li and E. Wolf, Focal shifts in diffracted converging spherical waves, *Opt. Commun.* **39**(4), 211–215 (1981).

36. J. H. Erkkila, On the maximum wave intensity in the focal volume, *Opt. Commun.* **43**(5), 313–314 (1982).

37. M.P. Givens, Focal shifts in diffracted converging spherical waves, *Opt. Commun.* **41**(3), 145–148 (1982).

38. Y. Li and E. Wolf, Three-dimensional intensity distribution near the focus in systems of different Fresnel numbers, *J. Opt. Soc. Am. A.* **1**(8), 801–808 (1984).

39. A.S. Dementyev and D.P. Domarkene, On diffraction of converging spherical waves by circular apertures, *Opt. Spectrosc.* **56**(5), 869–872 (1984).

40. B.E. Kinber and S.V. Novosyelov, Field in the focal vicinity, *Radio Eng. Electron.* **30**(8), 1469–1482 (1985).

41. R.G. Wenzel, Effect of the aperture-lens separation on the focal shift in large-F-number systems, *J. Opt. Soc. Am. A.* **4**(2), 340–345 (1987).

42. W.H. Carter, Focal shift and concept of effective Fresnel number for a Gaussian laser beam, *Appl. Opt.* **21**(11), 1989–1994 (1982).

43. Y. Li and E. Wolf, Focal shift in focused truncated Gaussian beams, *Opt. Commun.* **42**(3), 151–156 (1982).

44. V.B. Fyodorov and V.G. Mityakov, Comparing the characteristics of focusing truncated Gaussian, uniform and optimal light beams, *Opt. Spectroc.* **56**(5), 878–883 (1984).

45. K. Tanaka, N. Saga, and K. Hauchi, Focusing of a Gaussian beam through a finite aperture lens, *Appl. Opt.* **24**(8), 1098–1101 (1985).

46. R.M. Herman, J. Pardo, and T.A. Wiggins, Diffraction and focusing of Gaussian beams, *Appl. Opt.* **24**(9), 1346–1354 (1985).

47. Ch. Campbell, Fresnel diffraction of Gaussian laser beams by circular apertures, *Opt. Eng.* **26**(3), 270–275 (1987).

48. J.J. Stamnes, Focusing of two-dimensional waves, *J. Opt. Soc. Am.* **71**(1), 15–31 (1981).

49. A.S. Dementyev and D.P. Domarkene, Focal shift in the focused waves diffracted by a small rectangular pin-hole, *Phys. collect.* (Lithuania) **24**(3), 59–68 (1984).

50. M. Bottema, Fresnel zone-plate diffraction patterns. *J. Opt. Soc. Am.* **59**(12), 1632–1638 (1969).

51. J. Mozer, Lj. Janicijevic, and R. Bejtulahu, Fresnel diffraction of a circular Gaussian wave due to a wood zone plate, *J. Opt.* (Paris) **12**(5), 309–316 (1981).

52. Lj. Janicijevic, Diffraction characteristics of square zone plates. *J. Opt.* (Paris) **13**(4), 199–206 (1982).

53. Lj. Janicijevic, Diffraction of Gaussian beams through different types of zone plates, *J. Opt.* (Paris) **18**(1), 23–42 (1987).

54. P.Kh. Baibulatov, I.V. Minin, and O.V. Minin, Investigation into focusing properties of the Fresnel zone plate, *Radioeng. and Electron.* **30**(9), 1681–1688 (1985).

55a. J.J. Stamnes, T. Gravelsaeter, and O. Bentsen, Image quality and diffraction efficiency of holographic lens for sound waves, Acoustical Imaging 10, Proceedings of 10th International Symposium, Cannes, October 12–16, 1980.

55b. J.J. Stamnes, T. Gravelsaeter, and O. Bentsen, Image quality and diffraction efficiency of holographic lens for sound waves, Acoustical Imaging 10, *Proc. of 10th Int. Symposium*, Cannes, Oct. 12–16, 1982, pp. 587–606.

56a. J.J. Stamnes and T. Gravelsaeter, Methods for efficient computation of the image field of holographic lenses for sound waves, Acoustical Imaging 10, Proceedings of 10th International Symposium Cannes, October 12–16, 1980.

56b. J.J. Stamnes and T. Gravelsaeter, Methods for efficient computation of the image field of holographic lenses for sound waves, Acoustical Imaging 10, *Proc. of 10th Int. Symposium*, Cannes, Oct. 12–16, 1982, pp. 575–585.

57. I.G. Palchikova, Mathematical simulation of light wave diffraction by phase zone plates, Pre-print No. 433, Siberian chapter of the USSR Academy of Sciences, Novosibirsk, 1989, 27 pages.

58. V.P. Koronkevich and I.G. Palchikova, Modern zone plates, *Avtometriya*, **1**, 85–100 (1992).

59. S.T. Bobrov, G.I. Greisukh, and G.Yu. Turkevich, *Optics of diffractive elements and systems*, Leningrad, Mashinostroyeniye Publishers, 1986, 224 pages.

60. N.A. Mescheryakov and E.A. Tomolina, Simulation of the far-field diffraction using the cylindrical lens kinoform, the manuscript is deposited in AISTI, No. 4784–87, Tomsk, 1987, 8 pages.

61. H. Dammann, Blazed synthetic phase-only holograms, *Optik.* **31**(1), 95–104 (1970).

62. V.P. Koronkevich et al., Kinoform optical elements: design techniques, fabrication technologies and application, *Avtometriya*, **1**, 4–25 (1985).

63. A. Fedotowsky and K. Lehovec, Optimal filter design for annular imaging, *Appl. Opt.* **13**(12), 2919–2923 (1974).

64. L.L. Doskolovich et al., Uspleniev G.V. Focusators into a ring, *Opt. Quant. Electron.* **25**, 801–814 (1993).

65. P.A. Belanger and M. Rioux, Diffraction ring pattern at the focal plane of a spherical lens-axicon doublet, *Journ. Canadien de Physique.* **54**, 1774–1780 (1976).

66. P.A. Belanger and M. Rioux, Ring pattern of a lens-axicon doublet illuminated by a Gaussian beam, *Appl. Opt.* **17**(7), 1080–1086 (1978).

67. M.W. Farn and J.W. Goodman, Effect of VLSI fabrication errors on kinoform efficiency, *Proc. SPIE* **1211**, 1256–1266 (1990).

68. M.A. Golub et al., Diffraction-based design of an optical element focusing onto a ring, *Avtometriya* **6**, 6–15 (1987).

69. M.A. Golub et al., Computational experiment for computer generated optical elements, *Proc. SPIE* **1500**, 194–206 (1991).

70. V.A. Danilov et al., Diffractive beam focusators for high-power CO2-lasers, *Sci. Instrum.* **3**(1), 64–71 (1993).

71. M.A. Golub et al., Diffraction-based calculation of the field intensity near the focusator's focal line, *Opt. Spectrosc.* **67**(6), 1387–1389 (1989).

72. M.A. Golub et al., Focusing the laser light onto a line-segment using diffraction corrections, *Opt. Spectrosc.* **6**, 1069–1073 (1991).

73. V.A. Soifer, L.L. Doskolovich, M.A. Golub, and N.L. Kazanskiy, Diffraction investigation of focusators into straight-line segment, *Proc. SPIE* **1718** "Workshop on Digital Holography" 33–44 (1992).

74. M.A. Golub et al., Focusators at letters diffraction design, *Proc. SPIE* **1500**, 211–221 (1991).

75. L.L. Doskolovich, N.L. Kazanskiy, S.I. Kharitonov, and G.V. Usplenjev, Focusators for laser-branding, *Opt. Lasers Eng.* **15**(5), 311–322 (1991).

76. M.A. Golub, L.L. Doskolovich, N.L. Kazansky, and S.I. Kharitonov, Focusing of laser light onto rectangular-round-off patterns, *Comput. Opt.* (Moscow) **12**, 3–8 (1992).

77. L.L. Doskolovich et al., Diffractive optical elements for laser processing, *Proc. SPIE* **1983**, "ICO-16" Part 2. 647–648 (1993).

78. N.L. Kazansky, Correcting the focusator's phase function from the results of numerical simulation, *Comput. Opt.* (Moscow), **1**, 90–96 (1987).

79. I.G. Palchikova, kinoform optical elements with enhanced focal depth, *Comput. Opt.* (Moscow) **6**, 9–19 (1989).

80. L.L. Doskolovich, N.L. Kazanskiy, V.A. Soifer, and A. Ye, Tzaregorodtzev Analysis of quasiperiodic and geometric optical solutions of the problem of focusing into an axial segment, *Optik.* **101**(2), 37–41 (1995).

81. S.N. Khonina, V.V. Kotlyar, and V.A. Soifer, Calculation of the focusators into a longitudinal line-segment and study of a focal area, *J. Mod. Opt.* **40**, 761–769 (1993).

82. I.A. Michaltsova, V.I. Nalivaiko, and I.S. Soldatenkov, Kinoform axicon, *Optik.* **67**(3), 267–270 (1984).

83. A. Kolodziejczyk, S. Bara, Z. Jaroszewicz, and M. Sypek, The light sword optical element-a new diffraction structure with extended depth of focus, *J. Mod. Opt.* **37**(8), 1283–1286 (1990).

84. B.B. Brenden and J.T. Russel, Optical playback apparatus focusing system for producing a prescribed energy distribution along an axial focal zone, *Appl. Opt.* **23**(19), 3250–3253 (1984).

85. R. Tremblay, Y. D'Astons, G. Roy, and M. Blanshard, Laser plasmasoptically pumped by focusing with axicon a CO_2-TEA laser beam in a high-pressure gas, *Opt. Commun.* **28**(2), 193–196 (1979).

86. M. Rioux, R. Tremblay, and P.A. Belanger, Linear, annular and radial focusing with axicons and applications to laser machining, *Appl. Opt.* **17**(10), 1532–1536 (1978).

87. M.A. Golub et al., Numerical simulation of focusing a Gaussian beam onto a uniform rectangle, *Comput. Opt.*, **7**, 42–49 (1990).

88. M.A. Golub et al., Studies of a focusator onto a rectangle using numerical simulation, *Comput. Opt.* (Moscow) **10–11**, 110–1122 (1992).

89. M.A. Golub et al., Designing focusators onto a plane domain using a method of coordinated rectangles, *Comput. Opt.* (Moscow) **10–11**, 100–110 (1991).

90. J.W. Goodman and A.M. Silvestri, Some effects of Fourier-domain phase quantization, *IBM Journ. Res. Develop.* **14**(9), 478–484 (1969).

91. W.J. Dallas and A.W. Lohmann, Quantization and other nonlinear distortions of the hologram transmittance, *Opt. Commun.* **5**(2), 78–81 (1972).

92. J.M. Dallas, Phase quantization—a compact derivation, *Appl. Opt.* **10**, 674–676 (1971).

CHAPTER 6

Selection of Laser Light Modes

6.1 LASER LIGHT MODES

The concept of waveguide modes, or simply modes, is of great importance in laser optics. In particular, the propagation of coherent light beams in waveguides with quantized propagation constant is described in terms of modes [1]. We shall define the mode as a light beam that is capable of self-reproducing as it propagates in a corresponding wave medium. We shall call the beam self-reproducing if the transverse structure of its amplitude-phase distribution in the Cartesian or cylindrical coordinates is preserved up to a scale. This definition will allow us not to be restricted to the exact solutions of the Helmholtz equation for various media but also to describe, in the same terms, for example, the behavior of Gaussian beams (Gaussian modes) in free space. Each mode is characterized by its own attenuation coefficient and a phase delay proportional to the optical path and the propagation constant. The phase delay is continuously accumulated as the mode propagates in a medium. Note that, as far as waveguides are concerned, we are only interested in modes that preserve their energy as they travel through any distance in a waveguide with zero absorption, so-called *channeled* or *directed modes* [1]. The channeled mode self-reproduces its structure after travelling through an arbitrary distance in a fiber, whereas the mode propagated in a resonator is capable of self-reproducing every time only after passing through the complete distance from the first mirror to the second and back [2,3].

This section is devoted to a detailed review of the concept of coherent light modes. We also consider the modal properties that appear to be essential for computer-aided synthesis of diffractive optical elements (DOEs) matched to the complex amplitudes of mode functions. It will be demonstrated that the use of laser mode properties in combination with diffractive optical methods allows one to solve both important fundamental physical problems and applied problems such as an increase in the transmission capacity of optical communication lines.

6.1.1 Mode Beams in the Scalar Approximation

We begin with some mathematical equations describing the modes as eigenfunctions of the propagation operator. Let us introduce the Cartesian coordinates $(x, y, z) = (\mathbf{x}, z)$ in the medium of the beam propagation. The two-dimensional (2D) vector $\mathbf{x} = (x, y)$ represents transverse coordinates, whereas z is a longitudinal coordinate along the optical axis. Introduce different designations for the transverse coordinates in parallel planes $\mathbf{u} = (u, v)$, $\mathbf{x}' = (x', y')$, and so on. Assume that the modes considered are localized within a domain $\mathbf{x} \in G$ in the beam cross section. Apply the scalar representation of the light field and the scalar diffraction theory without regard for polarization effects. Thus, we shall describe the monochromatic or quasi-monochromatic field by a complex amplitude $F(\mathbf{x}, z)$ corresponding to the wavelength λ. In the following section, we shall discuss to what extent the scalar diffraction theory can apply to the description of waveguide media. It should be noted that the complex mode amplitude $\psi_{\mathbf{p}}(\mathbf{x})$ with the number $\mathbf{p} = (p, l)$ is considered on the wave front surface and $\mathbf{x}$ is the coordinate of the wave front point projection onto the nearest plane perpendicular to the direction of mode propagation. For the linear medium, we can introduce a linear propagation operator, $\hat{P}$, relating the complex distributions F and F_1 on two wave fronts separated by some distance

$$\hat{P}F(\mathbf{x}) = F_1(\mathbf{x}').$$
(6.1)

Modes of a particular linear medium, $\psi_{\mathbf{p}}(\mathbf{x})$ do not change their transverse configuration as they propagate thus satisfying the eigenvalues equation

$$\hat{P}\psi_{\mathbf{p}} = \gamma_{\mathbf{p}}\psi_{\mathbf{p}},$$
(6.2)

where $\gamma_{\mathbf{p}}$ are the complex-valued eigenvalues. Note that the operator $\hat{P}$ and its eigenvalues $\gamma_{\mathbf{p}}$ depend on the distance between the wave fronts considered. Thus, the modes $\psi_{\mathbf{p}}$ are the eigenfunctions of the propagation operator $\hat{P}$. It has been known that if the mathematical properties of normalization and compactness are satisfied,

$$\hat{P}\hat{P}^* = \hat{P}^*\hat{P} \equiv \hat{Q},$$
(6.3)

where * denotes the operator conjugated in the Hermitean sense, the operator $\hat{P}$ has a complete and denumerable set of orthogonal eigenfunctions [4]. In further discussion, the orthogonality property is assumed to be fulfilled with regard to some weight function, $\rho_0(\mathbf{x}) \geq 0$, $\mathbf{x} \in G$, depending on various inclination of the mode wave front plane. Obviously, using an adequate normalization, we can choose the orthonormalized modes $\psi_{\mathbf{p}}$

$$\iint\limits_{G} \psi_{\mathbf{p}}(\mathbf{x})\psi_{\mathbf{p}'}^*(\mathbf{x})\rho_0(\mathbf{x})d^2\mathbf{x} = \delta_{\mathbf{p}\mathbf{p}'},$$
(6.4)

where * denotes complex conjugation and

$$\delta_{\mathbf{p}\mathbf{p}'} = \delta_{pp'}\delta_{ll'} = \begin{cases} 1, & \mathbf{p} = \mathbf{p}' \\ 0, & \mathbf{p} \neq \mathbf{p}' \end{cases}$$
(6.5)

is the Kronecker delta. Note that the ρ_0 function changes its form along the $\mathbf{x}$-coordinate. The powers $\hat{P}^{m_0}$ of the operator $\hat{P}$ correspond to the number m_0 of full passages of the beam. The operators $\hat{P}^*$ and $\hat{P}^{m_0}$ commute with the operator $\hat{P}$, thus having the same eigenfunctions $\psi_{\mathbf{p}}$ and eigen-numbers related by the equations

$$\hat{P}^*\psi_{\mathbf{p}} = \gamma_{\mathbf{p}}^*\psi_{\mathbf{p}},$$

$$\hat{P}^{m_0}\psi_{\mathbf{p}} = (\gamma_{\mathbf{p}})^{m_0}\psi_{\mathbf{p}}.$$
(6.6)

The operator $\hat{Q}$ in Eq. (6.3) has nonnegative eigennumbers

$$\lambda_{\mathbf{p}} = |\gamma_{\mathbf{p}}|^2, \quad \hat{Q}\psi_{\mathbf{p}} = \lambda_{\mathbf{p}}\psi_{\mathbf{p}}, \tag{6.7}$$

and may be referred to as the *energy operator*. The values of $\lambda_{\mathbf{p}}$ in Eq. (6.7) characterize the attenuation of mode powers during one complete passage, whereas the values of $\arg \gamma_{\mathbf{p}}$ characterize the phase delay during one passage. In a passive waveguide we have

$$0 \leq \gamma_{\mathbf{p}} \leq 1, \tag{6.8}$$

with the magnitude

$$\alpha_{\mathbf{p}} = 1 - \lambda_{\mathbf{p}} \tag{6.9}$$

characterizing the power losses of the $\psi_{\mathbf{p}}$ mode (including diffraction losses) during one waveguide passage. A mode that has a maximal value of $\lambda_{\mathbf{p}}$ (and, thus, minimal losses) is called the *dominant* or *principal mode*. It is common to denote it by zero index, $\mathbf{0} = (0, \; 0)$.

$$\lambda_0 = \max_{\mathbf{p}}\lambda_{\mathbf{p}}. \tag{6.10}$$

In accordance with Eq. (6.6), the mode power attenuation, $\psi_{\mathbf{p}}$, for m_0 passages is equal to $|\gamma_{\mathbf{p}}|^{2m_0}$ and the phase delay is $m_0 \arg \gamma_{\mathbf{p}}$. The losses of the **p**th mode cumulating during m_0 passages are defined by

$$\alpha_{\mathbf{p}}^{m_0} = 1 - \lambda_{\mathbf{p}}^{m_0} \tag{6.11}$$

and are ordered in a manner similar to the one-passage losses. Consider the $\psi_{\mathbf{p}}$ mode of a higher order as compared with the $\psi_{\mathbf{p}'}$-mode. The $\psi_{\mathbf{p}'}$-mode is characterized by higher diffraction losses, that is, $\alpha_{\mathbf{p}} > \alpha_{\mathbf{p}'}$, or $\lambda_{\mathbf{p}} < \lambda_{\mathbf{p}'}$. The $\psi_{\mathbf{p}}$ and $\psi_{\mathbf{p}'}$ modes, with equal $\lambda_{\mathbf{p}} = \lambda_{\mathbf{p}'}$ for $p \neq \mathbf{p}'$, correspond to degenerate eigenvalues of the $\hat{Q}$-operator and can be ordered, for example, according to the increased value of the propagation constant, which is proportional to $|\arg \gamma_{\mathbf{p}}|$. Being free oscillations of the waveguide, the modes can be characterized by the following invariant and extreme properties, which account for the wide use of modes, rather than other bases, when describing the coherent light propagation:

1. The modes are a unique 2D basis of the functions that preserve mutual orthogonality while propogating in their own waveguide medium.
2. A unimode beam is characterized by least power losses as compared with any other beams composed of higher-order modes.

The property of the mode to self-reproduce the cross section structure during propagation was formulated earlier in this section and can be added to the aforesaid properties. Having defined the mode notion by Eq. (6.2), the total field $F(\mathbf{x}, z)$ in a waveguide medium is represented as a superposition of modes:

$$F(\mathbf{x}, z) = \sum_{\mathbf{p}} F_{\mathbf{p}}\gamma_{\mathbf{p}}(z)\psi_{\mathbf{p}}(\mathbf{x}), \quad \gamma_{\mathbf{p}}(0) = 1. \tag{6.12}$$

The coefficients $F_{\mathbf{p}}$ of the orthogonal decomposition are said to define the mode composition of the field

$$F_{\mathbf{p}} = \iint\limits_{G} F(\mathbf{x}, 0)\psi_{\mathbf{p}}(\mathbf{x})\rho_0(\mathbf{x})d^2\mathbf{x} \tag{6.13}$$

Because the Fourier expansion satisfies the Parseval theorem condition, the total energy of the field F composed of the partial powers, $|F_{\mathbf{p}}|^2$, of separate modes is given by

$$\iint\limits_{G} |F(\mathbf{x}, 0)|^2\rho_0(\mathbf{x})\, d^2\mathbf{x} = \sum_{\mathbf{p}} |F_{\mathbf{p}}|^2 \tag{6.14}$$

The field power distribution between modes will be defined as a normalized magnitude given by

$$\frac{|F_{\mathbf{p}}|^2}{\iint\limits_{G} |F(\mathbf{x}, 0)|^2\rho_0(\mathbf{x})\, d^2\mathbf{x}} \tag{6.15}$$

Being determined by the state of the excited waveguide medium, the variations of the coefficients $F_{\mathbf{p}}$, in accordance with the value of $\mathbf{p}$ determine the field mode composition.

6.1.2   Mode Excitation in Optical Fibers and Cavities

The mode function type is known to be determined by the type of distribution of the refractive index of the waveguide or optical fiber cross section (optical fiber profile) or by the configuration and shape of laser cavity mirrors. The excitation of definite-number modes is heavily dependent on a variety of factors that include excitation conditions, optical fiber core geometry, the light wavelength, the active-medium type, and diffraction losses in the cavity. Classical equations to define modes and the excitation conditions are given in this subsection. For passive cavity modes, the $\hat{P}$ operator is some integral operator that describes how the light propagates in the cavity from the first to the second mirror and back, that is, over the distance $2l_0$, where l_0 is the cavity length (Fig. 6.1). The mode complex amplitudes, $\psi_{\mathbf{p}}(\mathbf{x}_2)$, found at the output mirror of the open passive cavity satisfy the integral equation of Fox and Lee type [3]

$$\iint\limits_{D_2} K(\mathbf{x}_2, \mathbf{x}'_2)\psi_{\mathbf{p}}(\mathbf{x}'_2)\, d^2\mathbf{x}'_2 = \gamma_{\mathbf{p}}\psi_{\mathbf{p}}(\mathbf{x}_2), \tag{6.16}$$

where

$$K(\mathbf{x}_2, \mathbf{x}'_2) = \left(\frac{k}{2\pi i}\right)^2 \iint\limits_{D_1} \frac{\exp[ik(L + L')]}{LL'} \cdot \frac{(1 + \cos\alpha)}{2} \cdot \frac{(1 + \cos\alpha')}{2}$$

$$\times \cos\alpha \cdot \cos\alpha'd^2\mathbf{x}_1, \tag{6.17}$$

where $\mathbf{x}_2, \mathbf{x}'_2$ are the 2D Cartesian coordinates of the projection onto a plane perpendicular to the optical axis of a point taken, respectively, in the first or second mirror; D_1, D_2 are domains corresponding to the mirrors' light pinholes; L, α are the length and the angle between the optical axis, and a segment connecting point $\mathbf{x}_1$ of the first mirror with point $\mathbf{x}_2$ of the second mirror, respectively (Fig. 6.1); L', α' are analogous magnitudes for the points $\mathbf{x}_1$ and $\mathbf{x}'_2$, and k is the wave number.

For example, in the paraxial approximation we can put

$$L \cong l_0 + \frac{g_1}{2l_0}\mathbf{x}_1^2 + \frac{g_2}{2l_0}\mathbf{x}_2^2 - \frac{1}{l_0}\mathbf{x}_1\mathbf{x}_2, \quad \cos\alpha \cong 1, \qquad (6.18)$$

where $g_1 = 1 - (l_0/R_1)$, $g_2 = 1 - (l_0/R_2)$, and R_1 and R_2 are the radii of curvature at the mirrors' apexes. For a gradient fiber waveguide with the cross-sectional non-homogeneous refractive index $n(\mathbf{x})$, the wave fronts of the directed modes are plane [1]. In this case, the $\hat{P}$ operator relates the solution $F(\mathbf{x}, z)$ of the Helmholtz equation

$$\nabla_\perp^2 F(\mathbf{x}, z) + \frac{\partial^2 F(\mathbf{x}, z)}{\partial^2 z} + n^2(\mathbf{x})k^2 F(\mathbf{x}, z) = 0 \qquad (6.19)$$

to the boundary value of complex amplitude, $F|_{z=0} = F(\mathbf{x}, 0)$, where $\nabla_\perp = (\partial/\partial x, \partial/\partial y)$ is the transverse differential Hamilton operator (Fig. 6.2).

Considering a finite waveguide diameter, additional boundary conditions will appear at the core boundary. The gradient fiber modes have a plane wave front and satisfy the equation [5]

$$\nabla_\perp^2 \psi_{\mathbf{p}}(\mathbf{x}) + [k^2 n^2(\mathbf{x}) - \beta_{\mathbf{p}}^2]\psi_{\mathbf{p}}(\mathbf{x}) = 0. \qquad (6.20)$$

For an arbitrary value of z, we have

$$F(\mathbf{x}, z) = \gamma_{\mathbf{p}}\psi_{\mathbf{p}}(\mathbf{x}), \qquad (6.21)$$

$$\gamma_{\mathbf{p}} = \exp(i K_{\mathbf{p}}z), \qquad (6.22)$$

$$K_{\mathbf{p}} = \beta_{\mathbf{p}} + i q_{\mathbf{p}}, \qquad (6.23)$$

where $\beta_{\mathbf{p}}$ is the propagation constant $q_{\mathbf{p}}$ is the attenuation coefficient for the mode $\psi_{\mathbf{p}}$ (Fig. 6.2). Thus, the gradient fiber modes satisfy the equation for eigenvalues, Eq. (6.2)

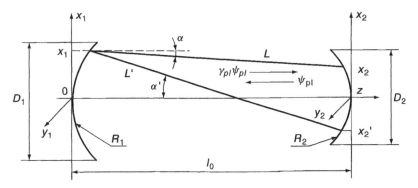

Figure 6.1. Geometry of calculating the modes of an open passive cavity.

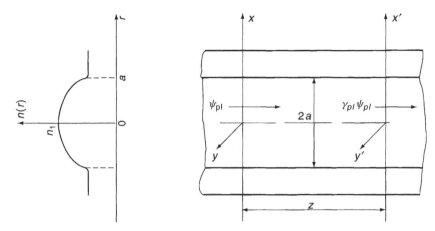

Figure 6.2. The modes in an optical fiber with gradient profile $r = \sqrt{x^2 + y^2} \le a$.

for any distance z, the eigenvalues being defined by Eq. (6.22). It should be noted that, in this case, the modes are self-reproduced with a constant scale along the Cartesian coordinates $\mathbf{x} = (x, y)$.

6.1.3 A Complex Eikonal Method

Note that the mechanism of propagation of a mode beam in free space is purely diffractive and hence it cannot be described in terms of the traditional interpretation of the eikonal. At the same time, the diffraction light fields that appear within caustics and upon total internal reflection, are described in terms of a complex eikonal that defines a field with damping amplitude. In Ref. [6], it has been shown that the principal mode of the Gaussian beam can be described in terms of the complex eikonal method in the paraxial approximation. More general solutions to the Helmholtz equation were derived in Refs. [7,8]. In this section, we study the mode solutions of the Helmholtz equation that exist for the desired-shape wave fronts that are general for the entire set of modes. The complex eikonal, just as the complex transfer equation, is used as a basis for constructing higher-order modes in curvilinear coordinates. Such an approach yields, in particular, nonparaxial beams with their paraxial approximation coinciding with the Gauss-Hermite and Gauss-Laguerre modes. The complex eikonal method is the direct generalization of the geometric optical approximation [9] for a medium with an arbitrary distribution of the refractive index $n = n(\mathbf{r})$, in particular, for a homogeneous medium $n = n_0 \equiv$ const. The desired wave fronts will be chosen from a certain set generated by a real function $S(\mathbf{r})$ of the three-dimensional (3D) coordinate $\mathbf{r}$ according to the equation $S =$ const. From Ref. [10] it follows that an additional function $B(\mathbf{r})$ should be introduced in such a way that the equation $B(\mathbf{r}) =$ const defines the surface of a desired intensity drop. These surfaces resemble the hyperboloid of the Gaussian beam (Fig. 6.3). The complex eikonal is defined by the equation

$$V(\mathbf{r}) = S(\mathbf{r}) + i B(\mathbf{r}) \tag{6.24}$$

It should be noted that each of the functions $V(\mathbf{r})$, $S(\mathbf{r})$, $B(\mathbf{r})$ is independent of both the wavelength and the number of the mode. With the complex eikonal method,

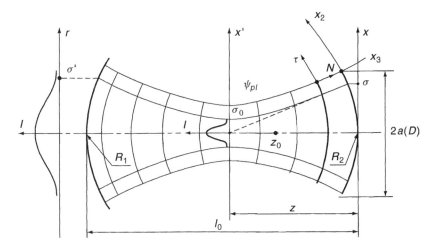

Figure 6.3. Gaussian beams in free space. σ_0 is the principal mode waist radius, σ, σ' are the radii of the principal mode on the mirrors' surfaces, $2z_0$ is a confocal parameter, I is the Gaussian beam intensity, l_0 is the cavity length, R_1, R_2 are the radii of curvature of the mirrors, and $2a$ is the aperture size of the outlet mirror.

the complex amplitude can be represented in a manner equivalent to the geometric optics:

$$F(\mathbf{r}) = A_0(\mathbf{r})\tilde{F}(\mathbf{r})\exp[ikV(\mathbf{r})], \quad k = 2\pi\lambda, \tag{6.25}$$

where $A_0(\mathbf{r})$ the λ-independent major term of the asymptotic series with respect to the powers $1/k$ [9] and $\tilde{F}(\mathbf{r})$ is some multiplicative component that takes of account the remaining terms of the asymptotic series and is given by

$$\tilde{F}(\mathbf{r}) = 1 + O(1/k), \quad \nabla\tilde{F}(\mathbf{r}) = O(1/k), \tag{6.26}$$

where the magnitude $O(1/k)$ is of the same order of infinity as $1/k$ is, for $\lambda \to 0$, and ∇ is the operator of the 3D gradient with respect to $\mathbf{r}$. The imaginary part B of the eikonal V corresponds to the damping variation of the field amplitude by the law $\exp(-kB)$, which is due to the beam diffraction spreading. It is essential that the functions A_0, F and all constituent components are assumed to be slowly varied, as compared with the quickly oscillating factor $\exp(ikS)$. Substituting Eq. (6.25) into the Helmholtz equation

$$\nabla^2 F + k^2 n^2 F = 0 \tag{6.27}$$

yields the following equation

$$\nabla^2(A_0\tilde{F}) + 2ikA_0\nabla\tilde{F}\nabla V + ik\tilde{F}[2\nabla A_0\nabla V + A_0\nabla^2 V] + k^2 A_0\tilde{F}[n^2 - (\nabla V)^2] = 0. \tag{6.28}$$

In view of Eq. (6.26), the first two terms in Eq. (6.28) have the order of $O(k^0)$, the second two terms have the order of $O(k^1)$, and the last two terms have the order of $O(k^2)$. Let the V function satisfy the complex eikonal equation

$$(\nabla V)^2 = n^2, \tag{6.29}$$

while the major term A_0 of the asymptotic expansion satisfies the transfer equation

$$2\nabla A_0 \nabla V + A_0 \nabla^2 V = 0 \tag{6.30}$$

Given Eqs. (6.29) and (6.30), Eq. (6.28) for $\tilde{F}$ takes the form

$$\nabla^2(A_0 \tilde{F}) + 2ikA_0 \nabla \tilde{F} \nabla V = 0. \tag{6.31}$$

Equation (6.31) characterizes the diffraction spreading of the light beam in the process of propagation. The form of Eqs. (6.29) and (6.30) is equivalent to the case of geometric optics for the real eikonal V. Taking into account Eq. (6.24) for the complex eikonal, we get a specific equation that takes account of the diffraction spreading

$$(\nabla S)^2 - (\nabla B)^2 = n^2, \tag{6.32}$$

$$\nabla S \cdot \nabla B = 0, \tag{6.33}$$

$$2\nabla \ln A_0 \nabla B + \nabla^2 B - 2i\nabla \ln A_0 \cdot \nabla S - i\nabla^2 S = 0, \tag{6.34}$$

$$\nabla^2(A_0 \tilde{F}) - 2ikA_0 \nabla \tilde{F} \nabla B + 2ikA_0 \nabla \tilde{F} \nabla S = 0. \tag{6.35}$$

Note that, as distinct from the corresponding equations discussed in Ref. [10], we do not separate the real and imaginary part of the magnitude $\ln A_0$ for the sake of convenience of the subsequent manipulation. Equations (6.32)–(6.35) define the amplitude-phase relations of the beam. Surfaces given by $S(\mathbf{r}) = $ const will be called the *wave fronts* S. These are different from the wave fronts dealt with in geometric optics. A set of curves orthogonal to the wave fronts differs from the straight-line segments of geometric optical rays (even in free space) and can be referred to as *generalized rays*. The generalized rays have, at each point, a unique tangent vector

$$\mathbf{N} = \frac{\nabla S}{|\nabla S|}, \tag{6.36}$$

directed along the gradient S. The direction of amplitude attenuation at each point is characterized by a unit vector

$$\tau = \frac{\nabla B}{|\nabla B|}, \tag{6.37}$$

which is directed along the function gradient B and orthogonal to the $\mathbf{N}$ vector (owing to Eq. (6.33)) and, thus, found in a plane tangent to the wave front S. The field of Eq. (6.25), with a slowly varied function $A_0 \tilde{F}$, has a surface of constant phase $kS + \arg(A_0 \tilde{F}) = $ const, which is little different from the wave front $S(\mathbf{r}) = $ const as $k \to \infty$. It is essential that, similar to the conventional eikonal method, the complex eikonal method makes it feasible to replace the light beam in the vicinity of a point by a local plane wave. Actually, let us expand the slowly varied functions $S(\mathbf{r}')$ and $B(\mathbf{r}')$ into 3D series in terms of powers $(\mathbf{r}' - \mathbf{r})$ up to linear terms. In view of Eq. (6.25) and the condition $n = $ const, we get

$$F(\mathbf{r}') = A_0 \tilde{F} \exp(ikS - kB) \exp[-kn\alpha\tau(\mathbf{r}' - \mathbf{r})] \exp[ikn\beta N(\mathbf{r}' - \mathbf{r})], \tag{6.38}$$

where

$$\alpha = \frac{1}{n}|\nabla B|, \quad \beta = \frac{1}{n}|\nabla S|.$$

Equation (6.38) characterizes a plane, attenuated wave in the vicinity of point $\mathbf{r}(\mathbf{r}' \cong \mathbf{r})$ that propagates in the direction $\mathbf{N}$ and possesses the attenuation τ along the wave front. Note that, such a plane wave is not geometric optical, because the modulus $kn\beta$ of its wave vector

$$\mathbf{k} = kn\beta \; \mathbf{N} \tag{6.39}$$

is not equal to the wave number kn in the given medium. In this case, instead of the geometric optical equality, we have $\beta \neq 1$, and owing to Eq. (6.32), the magnitude β along with the function α satisfy the equation

$$\beta^2(\mathbf{r}) - \alpha^2(\mathbf{r}) = 1. \tag{6.40}$$

It is important to emphasize that the phase of the transversally attenuated wave in Eq. (6.38) linearly depends on the coordinates

$$kS = kn\beta \mathbf{N} \mathbf{r}'. \tag{6.41}$$

Changing to the conventional geometric optics yields $\beta \to 1$ and $kS = kn\mathbf{N}\mathbf{r}'$

6.1.4 Amplitude-Phase Relations for Mode Beams in Free Space

6.1.4.1 *Free Space Modes in the Generalized Coordinates*   In Refs. [11, 12] two well-known types of Gaussian beams–Gauss-Laguerre and Gauss-Hermite beams–resting only on the paraxial approximation and thus employing the changeover from the Helmholtz equation (6.19) to the parabolic equation have been described. In this subsection, we shall consider a more general class of beams that have more general aspheric wave fronts but nevertheless are capable of self-reproduction during propagation. Having set ourselves the task of selecting the light modes by use of optical elements (modans), we must take into account that the mode beam is changed in size as it propagates in free space between the optical element's plane and the optical fiber or the laser. For example, if a beam with plane wave front is diverged from the outlet end of an optical fiber with high numerical aperture, it will acquire a complex aspheric wave front in the course of propagation in free space. Also, similar beams are propagated both within and outside the open laser cavities. Of particular interest are beams that change only their wave front scale and shape as they propagate but do not change the amplitude distribution over their cross section. The self-reproducing beams allow one to operate in the modan plane the same modes as in an optical fiber with ideal parabolic profile. At the same time, we described the ability of the mode to self-reproduce its cross section as it propagates in a waveguide medium as a fundamental property of the modes. For example, in optical fibers this property manifests itself as a continuous self-reproduction of the spatial structure along the z-axis (Eqs. (6.21) and (6.22)). In laser cavities, the transverse structure is self-reproduced up to a scale, being periodic and discrete in character. The well-known Gauss-Laguerre and Gauss-Hermite modes are capable of self-reproducing their transverse structure in free space up to a scaling factor. However, introducing the generalized coordinates will enable

us to claim that they exactly self-reproduce their structure. The Gaussian modes are the solutions of Eqs. (6.2) and (6.20) in the paraxial approximation with parameters σ and R, which are the radius of the principal mode, taken with respect to the intensity drop of $\exp(-2) \cong 0.14$ and the radius of curvature of the wave front, respectively. The Gaussian mode in a graded-index waveguide has a constant radius of $\sigma \equiv \sigma_0$, the plane wave front ($R = \infty$), and is continuously self-reproduced in accordance with Eq. (6.21) as it propagates (Fig. 6.4). The Gaussian modes propagated in a passive cavity or in free space change their size $\sigma = \sigma(z)$ and the radius of the wave front $R = R(z)$ (Fig. 6.3).

Note, however, that the amplitude of the Gaussian mode, taken on the wave front surface, can be considered to be self-reproducing up to a varied scale of the coordinates of $\sigma(z)$, that is, for the modes defined in novel normalized coordinates

$$x_1 = \frac{x}{\sigma(z)}, \quad x_2 = \frac{y}{\sigma(z)}, \quad x_3 = z, \qquad (6.42)$$

with a scale varying along the z-axis. Thus, in free space the Gaussian beams are not self-reproduced in the form of a simple repetition of their transverse structure as is the case with the gradient-index fibers, but show this property in a specially scaled coordinate system. The problem of generating wave fronts with desired intensity distribution has been discussed, for example, in Ref. [13]. The generation of the self-reproducing light mode beams in free space may also be treated as a particular case of this problem. We will generate the free space modes in the following section, on the basis of a desired set of wave fronts corresponding to arbitrary orthogonal coordinates (x_1, x_2, x_3) that generalize the normalized coordinates in Eq. (6.42). The "longitudinal" coordinate x_3 corresponds to the direction of beam propagation, whereas the "transverse" coordinates (x_1, x_2) characterize the position of point on the surface $x_3 = $ const. The equation for the derivation of continuously self-reproduced modes can be written in curvilinear coordinates (x_1, x_2, x_3) in the eigenvalues of Eq. (6.2). In our

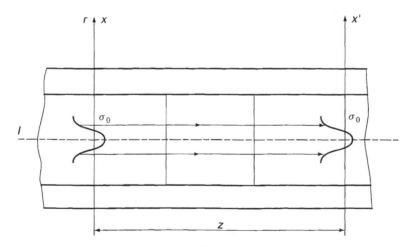

Figure 6.4. Gaussian modes in a fiber: σ_0 is the principal mode radius, z is the distance.

case, Eq. (6.2) on the wave front $x_3 = $ const takes the form

$$F_{\mathbf{p}}(x_1, x_2, x_3) = \psi_{\mathbf{p}}(x_1, x_2) \cdot \gamma_{\mathbf{p}}(x_3); \quad \gamma_{\mathbf{p}}(0) = 1. \tag{6.43}$$

The mode complex amplitude taken at an arbitrary point depends on both Eq. (6.43) and the wave front shape determining the phase. Thus, for the modes with preset wave front, the relationship between the amplitude and the phase is specific and stable owing to the self-reproduction property.

6.1.4.2 Equations for Modes with Preset General Wave Front   Let us find
the modes with desired set of wave fronts, $S(\mathbf{r}) = $ const, in a homogeneous medium by use of the complex eikonal method. To this end, let us change to the orthogonal curvilinear coordinates (x_1, x_2, x_3), related to the Cartesian coordinates (x, y, z) by $\mathbf{r} = \mathbf{r}(x_1, x_2, x_3)$, that is,

$$\begin{cases} x = x & (x_1, x_2, x_3), \\ y = y & (x_1, x_2, x_3), \\ z = z & (x_1, x_2, x_3). \end{cases} \tag{6.44}$$

We choose the curvilinear coordinates in such a manner that the coordinate planes $x_3 = $ const correspond to the wave fronts $S(\mathbf{r}) = $ const, whereas the coordinate planes $x_1 = $ const correspond to a definite intensity drop. Thus, we can write

$$S = S(x_3), \quad B = B(x_1). \tag{6.45}$$

Note that the curvilinear coordinate lines of the longitudinal coordinate x_3 are orthogonal to the wave fronts $S = $ const and characterize the propagation of the mode beam. At the same time, the coordinate lines along x_1 characterize the direction of the intensity drop in the beam cross section. Comparison of Eqs. (6.43), (6.25), and (6.24) yields

$$F(x_1, x_2, x_3) = \psi_{\mathbf{p}}(x_1, x_2)\gamma_{\mathbf{p}}(x_3) \exp[ikS(x_3)], \tag{6.46}$$

$$\psi_{\mathbf{p}}(x_1, x_2)\gamma_{\mathbf{p}}(x_3) = A_0(x_1, x_2, x_3)\tilde{F}(x_1, x_2, x_3) \exp[-ikB(x_1)], \tag{6.47}$$

where $\psi_{\mathbf{p}}$ are the eigenfunctions with the number $\mathbf{p}$, $\gamma_{\mathbf{p}}$ are the corresponding eigenvalues in Eq. (6.2), and S is the function characterizing the wave front shape that is general for all modes. Owing to the separation of the transverse variables (x_1, x_2) and the longitudinal variable x_3 in Eqs. (6.46) and (6.47), the $\tilde{F}$ and A_0 functions should also be separable in variables, assuming the following form:

$$A_0(x_1, x_2, x_3) = A_0(x_1, x_2) \cdot \gamma_0(x_3), \tag{6.48}$$

$$\tilde{F}(x_1, x_2, x_3) = \tilde{F}_{\mathbf{p}}(x_1, x_2) \cdot f_{\mathbf{p}}(x_3), \tag{6.49}$$

where $A_0(x_1, x_2)$, $\tilde{F}_{\mathbf{p}}(x_1, x_2)$, $\gamma_0(x_3)$, and $f_{\mathbf{p}}(x_3)$ are some introduced functions. As $k \to \infty$, the term $A_0(x_1, x_2)$ becomes the major one and can be interpreted as corresponding to the principal mode. Then, from Eqs. (6.47) and (6.26) we can obtain

$$\psi_0(x_1, x_2) = A_0(x_1, x_2) \exp[-kB(x_1)]. \tag{6.50}$$

In this case, the factor $\tilde{F}$ defined in Eq. (6.26) and applied to Eq. (6.47) defines the difference between higher-order modes and the principal mode. From Eqs. (6.47) and (6.50) we have

$$\psi_{\mathbf{p}}(x_1, x_2) = \psi_0(x_1, x_2) \cdot \tilde{F}_{\mathbf{p}}(x_1, x_2), \tag{6.51}$$

$$\gamma_{\mathbf{p}}(x_3) = \gamma_0(x_3) \cdot f_{\mathbf{p}}(x_3). \tag{6.52}$$

We shall use Eq. (6.35) and the relevant formula for the operators ∇, ∇^2 from Ref. [14] to recast Eq. (6.32) in the curvilinear coordinates. On the basis of the separation of variables in Eqs. (6.48) and (6.49), we obtain

$$\left(\frac{1}{H_3} S'\right)^2 - \left(\frac{1}{H_1} B'\right)^2 = n^2, \tag{6.53}$$

$$\frac{1}{A_0 \tilde{F}_{\mathbf{p}}} \frac{\partial}{\partial x_1} \left(\rho_1 \frac{\partial(A_0 \tilde{F}_{\mathbf{p}})}{\partial x_1}\right) - 2k\rho_1 B' \frac{1}{\tilde{F}_{\mathbf{p}}} \frac{\partial \tilde{F}_{\mathbf{p}}}{\partial x_1} + \frac{1}{A_0 \tilde{F}_{\mathbf{p}}} \frac{\partial}{\partial x_2} \left(\rho_2 \frac{\partial(A_0 \tilde{F}_{\mathbf{p}})}{\partial x_2}\right)$$
$$+ \frac{1}{\gamma_0 f_{\mathbf{p}}} \frac{\partial}{\partial x_3} \left(\rho_3 \frac{\partial(\gamma_0 f_{\mathbf{p}})}{\partial x_3}\right) + 2ik\rho_3 \frac{1}{f_{\mathbf{p}}} \frac{\partial f_{\mathbf{p}}}{\partial x_3} = 0, \tag{6.54}$$

$$2\rho_1 B' \frac{\partial \ln A_0}{\partial x_1} + \frac{\partial}{\partial x_1}(\rho_1 B') - 2i\rho_3 S' \frac{\partial \ln \gamma_0}{\partial x_3} - i \frac{\partial}{\partial x_3}(\rho_3 S') = 0, \tag{6.55}$$

$$\rho_1 = \frac{H_2 H_3}{H_1}, \quad \rho_2 = \frac{H_1 H_3}{H_2}, \quad \rho_3 = \frac{H_2 H_1}{H_3}, \tag{6.56}$$

where H_1, H_2, H_3 are the Lame coefficients in the Cartesian coordinates and B', S' correspond to the derivatives of the functions B and S of Eq. (6.45) with respect to the variables x_1 and x_3, respectively. Equation (6.54) suggests that the A_0 function can be chosen to be independent of the variable x_2. Having derived the functions S, B, A_0, γ_0, $F_{\mathbf{p}}$, and $f_{\mathbf{p}}$ from Eq. (6.53) and using Eq. (6.55), we can write down the modes in Eqs. (6.50) and (6.51) and the eigenvalues in Eq. (6.52).

Of particular interest are the paraxial beams propagating in the vicinity of the z-axis. The formal conditions are given by

$$\frac{|x|}{z} \ll 1, \quad \frac{|y|}{z} \ll 1. \tag{6.57}$$

For these beams, we can put down

$$A_0 \cong \text{const}, \tag{6.58}$$

$$\left|\frac{\partial}{\partial x_3} \left(\rho_3 \frac{\partial(\gamma_0 f_{\mathbf{p}})}{\partial x_3}\right)\right| \ll k\rho_3 \left|S' \gamma_0 \frac{\partial f_{\mathbf{p}}}{\partial x_3}\right|, \tag{6.59}$$

with the paraxial relations

$$\frac{\partial}{\partial x_1}(\rho_1 B') - 2i\rho_3 S' \frac{\partial \ln \gamma_0}{\partial x_3} - i \frac{\partial}{\partial x_3}(\rho_3 S') = 0 \tag{6.60}$$

$$\frac{1}{\tilde{F}_{\mathbf{p}}}\frac{\partial}{\partial x_1}\left(\rho_1\frac{\partial \tilde{F}_{\mathbf{p}}}{\partial x_1}\right) - 2k\rho_1 B'\frac{1}{\tilde{F}_{\mathbf{p}}}\frac{\partial \tilde{F}_{\mathbf{p}}}{\partial x_1} + \frac{1}{\tilde{F}_{\mathbf{p}}}\frac{\partial}{\partial x_2}\left(\rho_2\frac{\partial \tilde{F}_{\mathbf{p}}}{\partial x_2}\right) + 2ik\rho_3 S'\frac{1}{f_{\mathbf{p}}}\frac{\partial f_{\mathbf{p}}}{\partial x_3} = 0 \quad (6.61)$$

taken instead of Eqs. (6.54) and (6.55).

6.1.4.3 One-Dimensional (1D) Mode Beams

Consider 1D beams with x_2-independent complex amplitude distributions generated by the curvilinear cylindrical coordinates

$$\begin{cases} x = x(x_1, x_3), \\ y = x_2, \\ z = z(x_1, x_3), \end{cases} \quad (6.62)$$

that satisfy the Couchy-Riemann-type conditions [14]:

$$\begin{cases} \dfrac{\partial x}{\partial x_1} = \dfrac{\partial z}{\partial x_3} \\[2mm] \dfrac{\partial x}{\partial x_3} = -\dfrac{\partial z}{\partial x_1} \end{cases} \quad (6.63)$$

For the beams in Eq. (6.62) we have

$$H_1^2 = H_3^2 = \left(\frac{\partial x}{\partial x_1}\right)^2 + \left(\frac{\partial z}{\partial x_1}\right)^2; \quad H_2^2 = 1. \quad (6.64)$$

$\rho_1 = \rho_3 = 1$; $\rho_2 = H_1^2$, where ρ_2 is x_2-independent. The eikonal equation for 1D modes takes the form

$$[S'(x_3)]^2 - [B'(x_1)]^2 = H_1^2 \quad (6.65)$$

and imposes several restrictions onto admissible coordinate transformations in Eq. (6.62). Because the variable H_1^2 introduced in Eq. (6.65) is to be a sum of the functions x_1 and x_3, it should satisfy the equation

$$\frac{\partial^2 H_1^2}{\partial x_1 \partial x_3} = 0. \quad (6.66)$$

The transformation in Eq. (6.62) in the complex plane is convenient to write down as $X = x + iz$, $U = x_1 + ix_3$. Owing to Eq. (6.63), the complex function $X = X(U)$ should satisfy the Couchy-Riemann conditions given in Ref. [14]. Thus, $X(U)$ is an analytical function, whereas the transformation $X(U)$ is conformal ($H_1 \neq 0$). Note that $H_1^2 = |X'(U)|^2 = X' \cdot X'^*$, where X' is the derivative of X with respect to the complex variable U. Equation (6.66) can be recast as

$$\frac{\partial^2}{\partial x_1 \partial x_3}(X' \cdot X'^*) = i(X'^* \cdot X''' - X' \cdot X'''^*) = 0 \quad (6.67)$$

or

$$\frac{X'}{X'''} = \frac{X'^*}{X'''^*}. \quad (6.68)$$

The condition in Eq. (6.68) means that the function X'/X''' is real. Thus, the analytical function $X'(U)$ satisfies the equation

$$(X')'' + \omega_0^2(U)X' = 0 \tag{6.69}$$

with the real coefficient ω_0^2. The condition in Eq. (6.69) defines the class of admissible coordinate transformations. The entire class of admissible coordinate transformations for the cylindrical wave fronts can be derived by varying the smooth real function $\omega_0(U)$ while solving Eq. (6.69). Equation (6.69) produces such Lame coefficients H_1^2, which can be represented as a sum of functions of the variables x_1 and x_3. In order to find the eikonals B and S, while H_1^2 is known, make use of the arbitrariness in the choice of the functions $\theta(x_1, x_3) > 1$ and $\chi(x_1, x_3)$ in the equality

$$H_1^2 = \left(\frac{\theta^2}{\theta^2 - 1} H_1^2 + \chi \right) - \left(\frac{1}{\theta^2 - 1} H_1^2 + \chi \right). \tag{6.70}$$

We shall choose these functions so that the first bracket depends on the variable x_1 and the second bracket depends on the variable x_3. Then, assuming the derivatives of the expressions in the brackets to be equal to zero, we get the following equations

$$\begin{cases} \dfrac{\partial \chi}{\partial x_1} = -\dfrac{\partial}{\partial x_1} \left(\dfrac{\theta^2}{\theta^2 - 1} H_1^2 \right) \\[4mm] \dfrac{\partial \chi}{\partial x_3} = -\dfrac{\partial}{\partial x_3} \left(\dfrac{1}{\theta^2 - 1} H_1^2 \right) \end{cases}. \tag{6.71}$$

Because for the arbitrary θ the condition

$$\frac{\partial}{\partial x_3} \frac{\partial \chi}{\partial x_1} - \frac{\partial}{\partial x_1} \frac{\partial \chi}{\partial x_3} = \frac{\partial^2}{\partial x_1 \partial x_3} H_1^2 = 0 \tag{6.72}$$

is satisfied owing to Eq. (6.65), we can reconstruct the function $\chi(x_1, x_3)$ up to some constant χ_0, knowing its derivative for any θ, in particular, $\theta = \mathrm{const}(\theta > 1)$. Then, the components of the eikonals B and S can be derived from the equations

$$\frac{\partial S}{\partial x_3} = \left(\frac{\theta^2}{\theta^2 - 1} H_1^2 + \chi \right)^{1/2}, \quad \frac{\partial B}{\partial x_1} = \left(\frac{H_1^2}{\theta^2 - 1} + \chi \right)^{1/2} \tag{6.73}$$

represented in a form that allows the derivation of the complex eikonal. Here, the arbitrary constant χ_0 of the χ function is chosen in such a way as to provide the positive value of the expression in the brackets in the previous equation. Owing to Eq. (6.64), the transfer equation in Eq. (6.54) and the field equation in Eq. (6.55) admit the separation of variables, producing the equations

$$2B' \frac{\partial \ln A_0(x_1)}{\partial x_1} + B'' - C = 0, \tag{6.74}$$

$$2S' \frac{\partial \ln \gamma_0}{\partial x_3} + S'' + iC = 0, \tag{6.75}$$

$$\frac{1}{A_0}\frac{d^2(A_0 \tilde{F}_p)}{dx_1^2} - 2kB'\frac{d\tilde{F}_p}{dx_1} + 2kn_0\beta_p\tilde{F}_p = 0, \tag{6.76}$$

$$\frac{1}{\gamma_0}\frac{d^2}{dx_3^2}(\gamma_0 f_p) + 2ikS'\frac{df_p}{dx_3} - 2kn_0\beta_p f_p = 0, \tag{6.77}$$

with the separation constant for Eq. (6.55) denoted by $2kn_0\beta_0$. In this case, the transfer equations in Eqs. (6.74) and (6.75) can be integrated in the general form

$$A_0(x_1) = \exp\left[\frac{1}{2}\int_0^{x_1}\frac{C - B''}{B'}\,dx_1\right], \tag{6.78}$$

$$\gamma_0(x_3) = \exp\left[-\frac{1}{2}\int_0^{x_3}\frac{iC - S''}{S'}\,dx_3\right]. \tag{6.79}$$

At the same time, Eq. (6.76) can only be integrated for some specific eikonal types. In particular, in the paraxial approximation, Eqs. (6.76), (6.77), (6.78), and (6.79) take the following form

$$A_0(x_1) \cong \text{const}, \tag{6.80}$$

$$B'' - C = 0,\ B(x_1) = C(x_1 - x_{10})^2,\ C = \frac{1}{2}B''(0), \tag{6.81}$$

$$f_p(x_3) = \exp\left[-i\beta_p n_0 \int_0^{x_3}\frac{dx_3}{S'(x_3)}\right], \tag{6.82}$$

$$\frac{d^2\tilde{F}_p}{dx_1^2} - 2kB' \cdot \frac{d\tilde{F}_p}{dx_1} + 2kn_0\beta_p\tilde{F}_p = 0. \tag{6.83}$$

Knowing the functions B, S, A_0, f_p, and $\tilde{F}_p$, we can derive the formulae for the 1D modes and eigenfunctions from Eqs. (6.50) to (6.52):

$$\psi_0(x_1) = A_0(x_1)\exp[-kB(x_1)], \tag{6.84}$$

$$\psi_p(x_1) = \psi_0(x_1)\tilde{F}_p(x_1), \tag{6.85}$$

$$\gamma_p(x_3) = \gamma_0(x_3)f_p(x_3). \tag{6.86}$$

Previously, it has been shown that the 1D beams are capable of generating 2D beams with separated transverse coordinates. Let us consider the separation of variables in the Cartesian coordinates using the paraxial approximation. Assume that we have already derived the 1D mode complex amplitude

$$F_p(x, z) = \exp[ikS(x, z)]\psi_p(x, z)\gamma_p(z) \tag{6.87}$$

that describes the complex amplitude of a function satisfying the Helmholtz equation and is expressed in the Cartesian coordinate system instead of the curvilinear coordinates x_1, x_3. Similarly, we can derive the functions $F_l(y, z)$ for the y-axis. The Helmholtz equation taken in the paraxial form changes to the parabolic equation, with the variable separated as

$$F_p(\mathbf{x}, z) = F_p(\mathbf{x}, z) F_l(\mathbf{x}, z) \exp(-i k n_0 z). \tag{6.88}$$

Moreover, all the methods discussed in this subsection apply to 2D modes. However, it should be noted that the 2D modes are expected to have a more complicated wave front defined by

$$S = S(x, z) + \tilde{S}(y, z) - n_0 z = \text{const}, \tag{6.89}$$

where $S(x, z)$, $\tilde{S}(y, z)$ are the eikonals S for the corresponding 1D cases. The 2D modes and their eigenvalues $\gamma_\mathbf{p}(z)$ are constructed on the basis of the 1D modes using the formulae

$$\psi_\mathbf{p}(\mathbf{x}, z) = \psi_p(x, z) \psi_l(y, z), \tag{6.90}$$

$$\gamma_\mathbf{p}(z) = \gamma_p(z) \gamma_l(z), \tag{6.91}$$

which follows from Eqs. (6.88), (6.89), and (6.46). Thus, the strategy of separating the transverse variables provides us with a convenient technique for constructing mode beams of various orders, which are capable of self-reproducing as they propagate. It should be noted that the transverse structure of the mode separable in x, y can be self-reproduced not only in the 2D case of Eq. (6.43) but for any 1D beam generated in a plane parallel to the plane (x, z) or (y, z).

6.1.5 Gaussian and Bessel Modes

6.1.5.1 *Generalized Gauss-Laguerre Modes* In Ref. [10] it has been demonstrated that in a homogeneous medium with refractive index $n_0 = \text{const}$ there exists an important class of light beams with wave fronts in the form of revolution ellipsoids. In Ref. [10] they also introduce a system of degenerated ellipsoid coordinates of an oblate ellipsoid of revolution:

$$\begin{cases} x = b \sin x_1 \, \mathrm{ch} x_3 \cos x_2 \\ y = b \sin x_1 \, \mathrm{ch} x_3 \sin x_2, \\ z = b \cos x_1 \, \mathrm{sh} x_3 \end{cases} \tag{6.92}$$

where

$$0 \le x_1 \le \frac{\pi}{2}, \quad 0 \le x_2 \le 2\pi, \quad 0 \le x_3 < \infty. \tag{6.93}$$

The surfaces of constant intensity drop, $x_1 = \text{const}$, are represented in this case by one-sheeted hyperboloids of revolution. According to Ref. [14], the Lame coefficients can be derived from the equations

$$\begin{cases} H_1 = b(\mathrm{ch}^2 x_1 - \sin^2 x_3)^{1/2} \\ H_2 = b \sin x_1 \, \mathrm{ch} x_3 \\ H_3 = H_1 \end{cases} \tag{6.94}$$

In Ref. [10] they describe the eikonal components, S and B, corresponding to Eq. (6.92):

$$\begin{cases} S = n_0 b \, \text{sh} x_3 \\ B = n_0 b (1 - \cos x_1) \end{cases} . \tag{6.95}$$

In the paraxial approximation, the solutions to Eqs. (6.58)–(6.61), (6.46), and (6.50)–(6.52) can be found in an analytical form and correspond to the well-known Gauss-Laguerre modes. The modes can be derived from solving the general equations, Eqs. (6.60) and (6.61), taken in the coordinate system of Eq. (6.92). Recasting Eq. (6.92) as

$$\begin{cases} r = b \sin x_1 \, \text{ch} x_3 \\ z = b \cos x_1 \, \text{sh} x_3 \end{cases} , \tag{6.96}$$

where $r = \sqrt{x^2 + y^2}$, makes it possible to infer that the coordinates are transformed in the plane r, z about the z-axis. In view of Eqs. (6.56) and (6.94), we have

$$\rho_1 = \rho_3 = b \sin x_1 \, \text{ch} x_3, \qquad \rho_2 = \frac{b(\text{ch}^2 x_3 - \sin^2 x_1)}{\sin x_1 \, \text{ch} x_3}. \tag{6.97}$$

Note that the functions ρ_1 and ρ_3 have the separable variables x_1, x_3 and the function ρ_2 is independent of the variable x_2. The eikonal can be defined in a rigorous form of Eq. (6.95). Let us describe a $\tilde{F}_p$ factor that serves to normalize the constant for the ψ_p function. The transfer equation is considered in the form

$$\frac{\partial \ln A_0}{\partial x_1} = \frac{C - \cos x_1}{\sin x_1} \equiv \frac{\sin(0, \, 5 x_1)}{\cos(0, \, 5 x_1)}, \frac{\partial \ln \gamma_0}{\partial x_3} = \frac{iC + \text{sh} x_3}{\text{ch} x_3} = -\frac{i \text{ch} x_3}{1 + i \text{sh} x_3} \tag{6.98}$$

and easily integrated in elementary functions

$$A_0(x_1) = \frac{1}{\cos^2(0, \, 5 x_1)}, \tag{6.99}$$

$$\gamma_0(x_3) = \frac{1}{1 + i \text{sh} x_3} = \frac{1}{\text{ch} x_3} \exp\{i \cdot \text{arctg}[\text{sh}(x_3)]\}. \tag{6.100}$$

Dividing both sides of Eq. (6.55) by ρ_2 easily separates the coordinate x_2 from the coordinates (x_1, x_3). Subsequently, we can separate the coordinates x_1 and x_2

$$\tilde{F}_p(x_1, x_2) = \tilde{F}_p(x_1) \tilde{F}_l(x_2) \tag{6.101}$$

and derive the oscillator equation for $\tilde{F}_l$ with respect to x_2:

$$\frac{d^2 \tilde{F}_l}{d x_2^2} + l^2 \tilde{F}_l = 0, \quad \tilde{F}_l(x_2) = \exp(\pm l x_2), \tag{6.102}$$

where l^2 denotes the separation constant. The requirement that the $\tilde{F}_l(x_2)$ function should have a unique value at each point x_2 leads to the requirement of the integral number l, where $l = 1, 2, 3, \ldots$. Next, separating the variables x_1 and x_3 from the constant denoted by $-2kbn_0(2p + l)$, where p is some ordinary number, yields

$$\frac{1}{A_0 \sin x_1} \cdot \frac{\partial}{\partial x_1} \left[\sin x_1 \frac{\partial (A_0 \tilde{F}_{\mathbf{p}})}{\partial x_1} \right] - 2kbn_0 \sin x_1 \frac{\partial \tilde{F}_{\mathbf{p}}}{\partial x_1}$$

$$+ \left[2kbn_0(2p + l) - \frac{l^2}{\sin^2 x_1} \right] \tilde{F}_{\mathbf{p}} = 0, \tag{6.103}$$

$$\frac{1}{\gamma_0 \mathrm{ch} x_3} \cdot \frac{\partial}{\partial x_3} \left(\mathrm{ch} x_3 \frac{\partial (\gamma_0 f_{\mathbf{p}})}{\partial x_3} \right) + 2ikbn_0 \mathrm{ch} x_3 \frac{\partial f_{\mathbf{p}}}{\partial x_3}$$

$$- \left[2kbn_0(2p + l) - \frac{l^2}{\mathrm{ch} x_3} \right] f_{\mathbf{p}} = 0, \tag{6.104}$$

where A_0, γ_0 are defined by Eqs. (6.99) and (6.100). Equations (6.99), (6.100), (6.102) to (6.104) define the nonparaxial Gauss-Laguerre beams propagating in a homogeneous medium, similar to the solutions discussed in Ref. [7]. Equations (6.58) to (6.61) considered in the paraxial approximation lead to the conventional Gauss-Laguerre modes. In fact, for the considered paraxial approximation, the functions B and S in Eq. (6.95) and the relations for the coordinate transformation can be expanded in a in power series of x_1. Thus, we can write down the following relationships:

$$r \cong bx_1 \, \mathrm{ch} x_3 \cong bx_1 \sqrt{1 + \mathrm{sh}^2 x_3}, \tag{6.105}$$

$$z \cong b\mathrm{sh} x_3 \left(1 - \frac{x_1^2}{2} \right) \cong b\mathrm{sh} x_3, \tag{6.106}$$

$$\mathrm{sh} x_3 \cong \frac{z}{b} \left(1 + \frac{x_1^2}{2} \right) \cong \frac{z}{b}, \quad x_1 = r \left/ \left(b \sqrt{1 + \frac{z^2}{b^2}} \right) \right., \tag{6.107}$$

$$B \cong n_0 b \frac{x_1^2}{2} = \frac{n_0 r^2}{2b \left(1 + \frac{z^2}{b^2} \right)} = \frac{r^2}{k\sigma^2}, \tag{6.108}$$

$$S \cong n_0 z \left(1 + \frac{r^2}{2b^2 \left(1 + \frac{z^2}{b^2} \right)} \right) = n_0 z + \frac{n_0 r^2}{2R}, \tag{6.109}$$

$$R = z \left(1 + \frac{b^2}{z^2} \right), \quad \sigma^2 = \sigma_0^2 \left(1 + \frac{z^2}{b^2} \right), \quad \sigma_0^2 = \frac{2b}{kn_0}, \tag{6.110}$$

$$A_0(x_1) \cong 1, \quad \gamma_0(x_3) = \frac{\sigma_0}{\sigma} \exp[-i\eta_0(z)], \tag{6.111}$$

$$f_{pe}(x_3) = \exp[-i(2p + l)\eta_0(z)], \tag{6.112}$$

where

$$\eta_0(z) = \mathrm{arctg} \frac{z}{b}. \tag{6.113}$$

It should be noted that in the paraxial approximation, the x_3-dependent coefficients γ_0, $f_{\mathbf{p}}$, become dependent only on z and are independent of x. Equation (6.103) takes the form

$$\frac{1}{x_1} \cdot \frac{\partial}{\partial x_1}\left(x_1 \frac{\partial \tilde{F}_{\mathbf{p}}}{\partial x_1}\right) - 2kbn_0 x_1 \frac{\partial \tilde{F}_{\mathbf{p}}}{\partial x_1} + \left[2kbn_0(2p+l) - \frac{l_2}{x_1^2}\right] = 0. \qquad (6.114)$$

Using the conventional substitution

$$\tilde{F}_{\mathbf{p}} = t^{1/2} \cdot L_p^l(t), \quad t = kn_0 x_1^2 \qquad (6.115)$$

reduces Eq. (6.114) to a canonical equation for the Laguerre polynomials

$$t\frac{d^2 L_p^l}{dt^2} + (l+1-t)\frac{dL_p^l}{dt} + pL_p^l = 0, \qquad (6.116)$$

which has finite solutions at zero and infinite solutions only for integral values of $p = 0, 1, 2, 3\ldots$. In view of Eq. (6.107), substituting the derived Eqs. (6.108), (6.109) and (6.111) to (6.115) into Eqs. (6.46) and (6.50) to (6.52) yields a well-known formula for the complex amplitudes of the Gauss-Laguerre modes discussed in Ref. [15]

$$F_{\mathbf{p}}(\mathbf{x}, z) = \psi_{\mathbf{p}}(\mathbf{x})\gamma_{\mathbf{p}}(z) \exp\left[ikn_0\left(z + \frac{\mathbf{x}^2}{2R}\right)\right], \qquad (6.117)$$

$$\gamma_{\mathbf{p}}(z) = \exp[-i(r_{\mathbf{p}}+1)\eta_0(z)], \qquad (6.118)$$

$$\psi_{\mathbf{p}}(\mathbf{x}) = E_{pl}\left(\frac{\sqrt{2}|\mathbf{x}|}{\sigma}\right)^l L_p^l\left(\frac{2\mathbf{x}^2}{\sigma^2}\right)\exp\left(-\frac{\mathbf{x}^2}{\sigma^2}\right)\exp(\pm il\alpha), \qquad (6.119)$$

where α is the polar angle of the x vector, L_p^l is the generalized Laguerre polynomial [14] with the numbers $p, l = 0, 1, 2\ldots$ and

$$r_{\mathbf{p}} = 2p + l, \quad E_{pl} = \frac{2}{\sigma\sqrt{2\pi C_{p+l}^l l!}} \qquad (6.120)$$

is the normalizing constant. In some cases, the modes in Eq. (6.119) are represented in a real form, using $\sin(l\alpha)$ and $\cos(l\alpha)$ instead of $\exp(\pm il\alpha)$. The value of $z = 0$ corresponds to the beam waist point, $2b$ is the confocal parameter of the Gaussian beam, and the parameters σ, R, and η are defined by Eqs. (6.110) and (6.113). Thus, with the introduced elliptic coordinate system, the complex eikonal method in the paraxial approximation makes it possible to derive the classical Gauss-Laguerre modes. On the basis of the quasi-classical approximation [16], we can easily estimate the diameter $2a = 2\sigma\sqrt{(2p+l)_{\max} + 1}$ for the Gauss-Laguerre modes that are numbered in such a way that $2p+l \leq (2p+l)_{\max}$ for large numbers p and l.

6.1.5.2 Generalized Gauss-Hermite Modes

For $\omega_0 = $ const, a solution of Eq. (6.69) can be written as

$$X(U) = b\sin U. \qquad (6.121)$$

Changing to the real and imaginary parts yields

$$\begin{cases} x = b \sin x_1 \mathrm{ch} x_3 \\ z = b \cos x_1 \mathrm{sh} x_3 \end{cases},$$ (6.122)

$$H_1^2 = b^2(\mathrm{ch}^2 x_3 - \sin^2 x_1) = H_3^2.$$ (6.123)

In this case, the eikonal is described similarly, Eq. (6.95), to the Gauss-Laguerre modes. In the following section, we shall demonstrate that, considering Eq. (6.88), the paraxial equations for the Gauss-Hermite modes give the solutions presented in Ref. [15]. Other generalizations of the 1D modes can rest on the conformal coordinate transformations, different from Eq. (6.121). Owing to Eq. (6.69), such transformations are induced by real-valued functions ω_0^2, varying along x_1 and x_2. 1D Gauss-Hermite modes can be derived from Eqs. (6.84) to (6.88) and (6.90), which utilize the functions S, B, $A_0(x_1)$, $\gamma_0(x_3)$, $f_p(x_3)$, $\tilde{F}_\mathbf{p}(x_1)$.

From Eqs. (6.76), (6.77), (6.78), and (6.79), respectively, it follows that

$$A_0(x_1) = \frac{1}{\cos \dfrac{x_1}{2}},$$ (6.124)

$$\gamma_0(x_3) = \frac{1}{\sqrt{1 + i \ \mathrm{sh} x_3}} = \frac{1}{\sqrt{\mathrm{ch} x_3}} \exp\left(-\frac{1}{2} i \arctg(\mathrm{sh} x_3)\right),$$ (6.125)

$$f_p(x_3) = \exp[-i p \ \arctg(\mathrm{sh} x_3)],$$ (6.126)

where

$$p = \frac{\beta l}{b}.$$ (6.127)

The $\tilde{F}_p$ function was derived by solving an ordinary differential equation of second order with varying coefficients; thus Eq. (6.76) becomes

$$\cos \frac{x_1}{2} \cdot \frac{d^2}{dx_1^2}\left(\frac{\tilde{F}_p}{\cos \dfrac{x_1}{2}}\right) - 2kbn_0 \sin x_1 \frac{d\tilde{F}_p}{dx_1} + 2kn_0 b_p \tilde{F}_p = 0.$$ (6.128)

In the paraxial approximation,

$$\frac{|x|}{z} \ll 1, \quad \cos \frac{x_1}{2} \cong 1; \quad \sin x_1 \cong x_1, \quad A_0 \cong 1.$$ (6.129)

In this case, the expression for $\tilde{F}_p$ in Eq. (6.128) is reduced (through the replacement of variables given by $t = \sqrt{kbn_0 x_1}$) to standard Hermite polynomials [14]

$$\frac{d^2 \tilde{F}_p}{dt^2} - 2t \frac{d\tilde{F}_p}{dt} = -2p\tilde{F}_p.$$ (6.130)

This equation has solutions for $t = 0$ and $t \to \infty$ only for integral values of $p = 0, 1, 2, \ldots$. Thus, the solutions for $\tilde{F}_p$ can be written as follows

$$\tilde{F}_p = \text{const } H_p(\sqrt{bkn_0 x_1}). \tag{6.131}$$

Then, using Eqs. (6.124) to (6.128) and (6.129) yields Eqs. (6.107) to (6.110), where σ^2 and R are defined by Eqs. (6.110) and (6.113), similarly to the Gauss-Laguerre modes. For γ_0 and f_p, we have

$$\gamma_0(x_3) = \sqrt{\frac{\sigma_0}{\sigma}} \exp\left(-i\frac{1}{2}\arctan\frac{z}{b}\right), \tag{6.132}$$

$$f_p(x_3) = \exp\left(-i\, p \arctan\frac{z}{b}\right). \tag{6.133}$$

Note that in the paraxial approximation the values of γ_0 and f_p depend only on z and not on x. Thus, we can make the conclusion that the 2D modes and the corresponding eigenvalues can be derived from the corresponding known 1D modes. Using Eqs. (6.131) and (6.132), the 2D modes can be represented as follows [15]:

$$\psi_{\mathbf{p}}(\mathbf{x}) = E_{pl} H_p\left(\frac{\sqrt{2}x}{\sigma}\right) H_l\left(\frac{\sqrt{2}y}{\sigma}\right) \exp\left(-\frac{\mathbf{x}^2}{\sigma^2}\right), \tag{6.134}$$

$$r_{\mathbf{p}} = p + l, \tag{6.135}$$

and

$$E_{pl} = \frac{1}{\sigma}\sqrt{\frac{2}{\pi 2^{p+l} p!l!}}, \tag{6.136}$$

where $H_p(\cdot)$ is the Hermite polynomial of pth order. Making use of the quasi-classical approximation of Ref. [16] for large p and l, we can easily determine the size of a domain $2a \times 2b$ comprising the modes with the numbers up to (p, l):

$$2a = 2\sigma\sqrt{p_{\max} + 1/2}, \quad 2b = 2\sigma\sqrt{l_{\max} + 1/2}, \tag{6.137}$$

where $p_{\max}$ and $l_{\max}$ are the maximum values of the mode numbers p or l, respectively.

6.1.5.3 Gaussian Modes in Passive Cavities and Graded-Index Fibers

The Gaussian modes are mode functions constructed using the Gauss-Hermite and Gauss-Laguerre bases, showing a number of general properties. Strictly speaking, the Gaussian modes are orthogonal at an indefinite domain. However, because of quickly decreased amplitude, they can be treated as an orthogonal basis on a certain finite domain G. These mode functions describe average-order modes in open passive cavities with spherical-profile mirrors. Besides, it is the Gaussian modes that are found in graded-index fibers with parabolic profile and in other lenslike media. The Gauss-Laguerre modes are found in systems with circular mirrors and graded-index fibers with cylindrical core, whereas square-shaped mirrors and graded-index fibers with square-shaped core are capable of producing the Gauss-Hermite modes. To generate the Gauss modes in cavities, the paraxial approximation condition should be met:

$$\frac{2a2b}{R_1 R_2} \ll 1 \text{ or } \frac{(2a)^2}{R_1 R_2} \ll 1, \tag{6.138}$$

where $2a \times 2b$ is the aperture size of the largest spherical mirror, R_1, R_2 are the radii of curvature of the spherical mirrors. For the cavities, the σ_0 parameter can be derived from [17]

$$\sigma_0 = \left(\frac{\lambda}{\pi}\right) \frac{[l(R_1 - l)(R_2 - l)(R_1 + R_2 - l)]^{1/2}}{(R_1 + R_2 - 2l)}. \tag{6.139}$$

The waist is found in the cavity at the distance

$$z_2 = \frac{l(R_1 - l)}{R_1 + R_2 - 2l} \tag{6.140}$$

from the outlet mirror. For the mode propagated in a fiber with quadratic refractive index

$$n^2(r) = n_1^2 \left(1 - 2\Delta \frac{r^2}{a^2}\right), \tag{6.141}$$

we have

$$\gamma_{\mathbf{p}}(z) = \exp(i\beta_{\mathbf{p}} z), \tag{6.142}$$

with $\beta_{\mathbf{p}}$ and σ_0 derived from [15]

$$\beta_{\mathbf{p}} = \left[k^2 n_0^2 - \frac{4}{\sigma_0^2}(r_{\mathbf{p}} + 1)\right]^{1/2} \tag{6.143}$$

$$\sigma_0 = \left(\frac{\lambda a}{\pi n_1}\right)^{1/2} \left(\frac{1}{2\Delta}\right)^{1/4} = \text{const}; \quad R = \infty. \tag{6.144}$$

The Gauss modes preserve their structure during propagation not only in free space but also in lenses and lens like media. When passing through a Fourier stage [15] with a lens of focal length f, the Gauss mode changes its parameters σ and $R = \infty$, by σ_F and R_F, respectively, where

$$\sigma_F = \frac{\lambda f}{\pi \sigma}, \quad R_F = \infty. \tag{6.145}$$

In this case, the beam phase is changed by

$$kf + \arg(i^{2p+l}) = kf + r_{\mathbf{p}} \frac{\pi}{2}. \tag{6.146}$$

Because the Gauss modes are invariant to passing through the Fourier stage, the latter can be used as an optical projection system to project a beam with a desired mode composition from the outlet fiber end into the DOE plane, or vice versa.

6.1.5.4 Bessel Modes   The amplitude-phase distribution in the cross section of a Bessel mode is described as follows [5]:

$$\psi_{\mathbf{p}}(\mathbf{x}) = E_{pl} J_l \left(\rho_{pl} \frac{|\mathbf{x}|}{a} \right) \exp(\pm i l \alpha), |\mathbf{x}| \leq a; \quad p, l = 0, 1, 2 \ldots \quad (6.147)$$

$$E_{p,l} = \frac{1}{a \sqrt{\pi} J_l'(\rho_{pl})}, \quad (6.148)$$

where J_l is the integral-order Bessel function and ρ_{pl} is the pth zero of the J_l function. The Bessel modes are eigenfunctions of the light-propagation operator in a step-index fiber and in free space.

6.1.5.5 Cosine Modes   The cosine modes comprise a trigonometric basis that is orthogonal of a rectangle G with a characteristic size of $[-R_x, R_x] \times [-R_y, R_y]$:

$$\psi_{\mathbf{p}}(\mathbf{x}) = \cos\left(\frac{\pi p}{2R_x} x\right) \cdot \cos\left(\frac{\pi l}{2R_y} y\right) \cdot \exp\left\{ -\frac{\pi \lambda}{16} \left[\left(\frac{p}{R_x}\right)^2 + \left(\frac{l}{R_y}\right)^2 \right] z \right\}$$

$$\times \exp\left(i \frac{2\pi}{\lambda} z \right) \quad (6.149)$$

Such functions, for example, are used to describe the modes in a hollow rectangular waveguide with perfectly conducting walls of size $[-R_x, R_x] \times [-R_y, R_y]$.

6.2 GENERATION AND SELECTION OF LASER LIGHT MODES USING DOEs

6.2.1 Formulation of the Problem of Synthesizing DOEs Matched to the Laser Modes

In the previous section, we noted that in the laser cavities, lenslike media, fiber light guides, and beams with various energy distribution between modes are found and required [7,15,18]. At the same time, there are problems that require selectively operating a single mode or a definite mode group, for example, a mode group with a desired propagation constant distribution between modes [19,20]. When designing fiber-optical communication systems, we need to deal with a topical problem of measuring or correcting the mode differential attenuation and their differential mode delays that cause the impulse widening [18,19]. Formally speaking, in every such case, the amplitude and phase of the light-beam expansion coefficients are to be measured or corrected, that is, the modes are to be *analyzed* or *filtered*. Similar problems are solved while operating a time-varying light beam used to construct a fiber-optical communication line with mode channel multiplexing [19]. In this case, one has to be able to change mode powers independently with time to conduct real-time summation of modes and analyze the mode composition at the communication line output (the problem of real-time light field analysis).

Let us formulate three main types of mode selection problems:

The *mode analysis problem* involves separating a multimode beam into separate mode components and measuring the between-mode power distribution and between-mode phase shifts (Fig. 6.5).

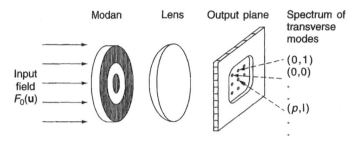

Figure 6.5. Formulation of the problem of designing a modan—a DOE to measure the generalized mode spectrum.

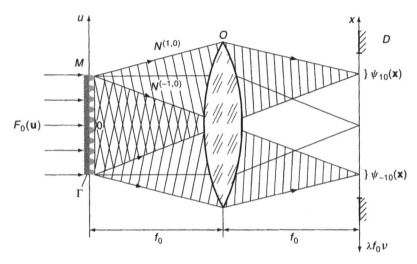

Figure 6.6. Formulation of the problem of designing a DOE to generate mode patterns from the illuminating beam $F_0(\mathbf{u})$ (M is the phase modan and f_0 is the focal length of the thin lens).

The *mode synthesis problem* involves exciting standards of the required modes or multimode beams with required power and phase distribution between modes (Fig. 6.6).

Mode transform–based *mode filtration* involves changing the beam mode composition in terms of both the power and between-mode phase shifts (Fig. 6.7). In Ref. [19] they discuss the following optically meaningful problem: would it be justified to assert that the modes exist independently as some reference beams or that they are only an abstract notion that represents one of multiple orthogonal mathematical bases introduced for a convenient description of coherent light beams? Some time ago, a similar problem was discussed related to the "longitudinal" (chromatic) spectrum of light: if there are *physically* existing monochromatic light components or they are only a convenient mathematical form to represent light oscillations as a decomposition of light field in longitudinal sine harmonics? From the modern point of view, we can justly answer this question as follows: monochromatic harmonics do exist because (*1*) they are able to propagate in free space without changing their structure and wavelength; (*2*) there are spectral devices allowing the harmonics to be selected, excited, observed, and measured as a spectrum.

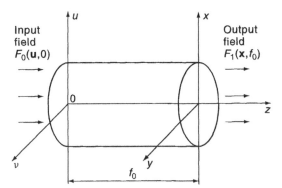

Figure 6.7. Formulation of the problem of changing the mode composition of the beam.

Note that, because the monochromatic plane and spherical waves are not blurred in color spectrum and retain their spatial shape when propagated in free space, acquiring only a phase lead, it is possible to introduce the notion of a spatial ("longitudinal") spectrum represented as an expansion in plane waves [21]. The property (2) is implemented using spectrographs that perform the spectral analysis of light, monochromators, light filters, and laser sources, allowing the spectral synthesis to be conducted, that is, selectively to excite separate monochromatic components or their groups. Thus, showing the properties (1) and (2), the spectral harmonics do exist physically as reference longitudinal modes. Similar to monochromatic harmonics, the eigenfunctions of the propagation operator — transverse modes of coherent light — may be treated as "generalized spectral" components because, by analogy with the property (1) of the longitudinal spectrum, they are able to propagate in a corresponding medium, retaining their individual shape and acquiring only a phase lead. Thus, the solution to the problem of physical existence of modes appears entirely to depend on the feasibility to develop devices that can generate reference mode beams and devices to measure beam mode composition [property (2)]. Such devices will be able to perform individual excitation, measurement, and detection of definite coherent light modes. The classical optical elements are unable to generate reference unimode beams and desired groups of coherent light modes (mode packages). In Refs. [19,22], a new-type phase DOE, called *modan*, was proposed for generating and analyzing light beams with desired transverse-mode structure. In Refs. [19,20,22–36], they describe the application of various diffractive optics and digital holography techniques to synthesize phase modans, discuss the results of numerical simulation of the modans and the results of physical experiments concerned with mode selection and analysis of the light transverse-mode composition. Note that most works on the subject are devoted to the Gaussian modes-Gauss-Hermite and Gauss-Laguerre modes. One reason for this lies in the "universality" of this mode type-being characteristic of the gradient media with parabolic profile, the Gaussian beams retain their structure up to a scale as they propagate in free space or through a Fourier stage [15]. On the other hand, great attention focused on this type of modes is due to a growing interest in so-called "lenslike" media and their applications in image processing systems and integrated and waveguide optics [5,15]. Latest technological advances in fabrication of graded-index optical fibers allow the multimoded fibers with nearly perfect parabolic profile to be fabricated. Note, however, that a considerable portion of approaches aimed at design and study modans, matched to Gaussian modes, can be easily adapted to design modans intended to operate modes of graded-index waveguides of arbitrary nonparabolic profile in cases in which the polarization effects can be neglected. For the detailed analysis of applicability of the scalar theory of diffraction to describe graded-index waveguides, see, for example, Ref. [18]. However, one should bear in mind that the modes in graded-index waveguides with arbitrary nonparabolic profile do not retain their structure in free space. Therefore, in the general case, complex-valued transmission function of the DOE should be calculated using the exactly calculated Fresnel-Kirchhoff integral. For the results of designing Bessel-mode-matched modans, see Refs. [23,36] and Chapter 7 of this book.

6.2.2 Methods to Design Phase Modans

In terms of the effective use of the light source power, the modan is best to be implemented as a transparent or well-reflecting, that is, pure-phase optical element. In Ref. [19] it has been demonstrated that, for a complex-valued transmission function, the energy efficiency of an amplitude DOE is, by more than order, less than that of a phase DOE with the same complex transmission function. A thin, pure-phase, optical element has been known [22] to be characterized by the phase function $\varphi(\mathbf{u})$, where $\mathbf{u} = (u, v)$ are the transverse coordinates of a point found on the substrate surface of the optical element. When illuminated by a beam of complex amplitude $F_0(\mathbf{u})$, the thin optical element is assumed to generate, immediately behind its plane, a field with the complex amplitude given by

$$F(\mathbf{u}) = F_0(\mathbf{u}) \exp[i\varphi(\mathbf{u})]. \tag{6.150}$$

6.2.3 Designing Unimode Modans

Note that, in the general case, it is an ill-defined problem trying to generate a desired unimode complex distribution using a phase DOE that is modifying only the illuminating beam phase. The problem appears to be ill-defined because of the properties of the light-propagation operator [9]: the phase of the signal spectrum alone is not able to define the signal uniquely. Because of this, two approaches are used to design a thin phase DOE intended to generate a desired unimode distribution. With the first approach, one calculates the phase function of an element that converts the illuminating beam into a certain light distribution in which the desired mode is present in a maximum possible proportion [37].

Subsequently, the same approach was taken to design modans capable of generating the unimode Gauss-Laguerre and Gauss-Hermite distribution [25,26]. In Ref. [25], they have demonstrated that choosing the signum function of the desired Gauss-Laguerre mode as a modan phase function makes it possible to generate the mode with a 77–81 percent efficiency, depending on the desired mode number. In Ref. [26] they have also shown that the use of the signum function of the desired mode as a phase function allows one to design the Gauss-Hermite modan. This method is covered comprehensively in Chapter 7 of this book. However, notwithstanding all the benefits such as simplicity, little computational efforts, and feasibility to design a binary element, the earlier-described approach, which is based on fitting the element phase to maximize the desired mode in the beam, inevitably results in the impulse widening if the generated quasi-unimode beam is intended for waveguide excitation. This is because, in the general case, the propagation constant of spurious modes found in the beam is different from that of the useful modes. Besides, the presence of spurious modes is inadmissible by definition when generating reference-mode beams. Because of this reason, in the core of the other approach to the problem of generating a unimode distribution is the idea of introducing auxiliary elements in order to bring the element complex transmission function to a pure-phase form [19]. Being spatially separated from the useful image, the auxiliary elements do not adversely affect the reconstructed image quality; they only reduce the energy portion that is going to form the useful image (Fig. 6.8).

It has been well known that the (parity) auxiliary elements can be generated as spurious diffraction orders by introducing a modulated carrier into the element phase [19,38]. The carrier's shape is determined by the specific encoding technique — the rectangular-impulse carrier corresponds to the synthetic coefficients method [39], whereas the cosine carrier is found in the Kirk-Jones method [38]. The carrier amplitude is chosen to be locally dependent on the transmission function — at points of the maximum complex transmission function it is equal to zero, whereas at points of the minimal complex transmission function the carrier amplitude is maximum. Equations that specify the nonlinear relation between the modulus of the complex transmission function and the carrier amplitude for various carrier shapes such as rectangular-impulse, sinusoidal, and saw-tooth, are presented in Ref. [19]. Shown in Figure 6.9 is a halftone photomask of a modan intended to generate the Gauss-Hermite mode (1, 0) in the zero diffraction order. The encoding was implemented using the generalized Kirk-Jones method [19]. The halftone mask in Figure 6.9 gives a general idea of the elements designed by the method of Ref. [19], which are diffraction gratings of a special form. Somewhat anticipating, note that modans designed by introducing the carrier can be employed to generate the desired mode beams and to analyze the beam mode composition [19].

An undoubted advantage of this method for modan design is the feasibility to calculate the element transmission function analytically. However, introducing auxiliary (parity) elements in the form of spurious diffraction orders does not necessarily produce an optimal result in terms of the relation between the mode-generation quality (proportion of the reference mode of Eq. (6.13) in the generated beam) and the DOE energy efficiency, that is, the relation between the energies going to the mode image and the spurious diffraction orders.

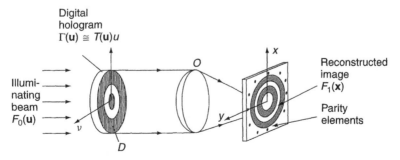

Figure 6.8. Reducing the DOE transmission function to the phase-only by introducing auxiliary (parity) elements in the DOE output plane.

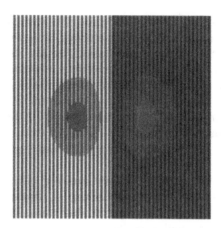

Figure 6.9. The halftone photomask of a modan intended to generate the Gauss-Hermite mode (1, 0).

Figure 6.10. The output amplitude (central part) generated by the modan whose phase photomask is depicted in Figure 6.9.

The use of the method proposed in Ref. [19] allows the desired unimode distribution to be generated with high accuracy. In essence, the error in generating the desired complex distribution is determined in this situation only by phase quantization errors and technological errors of DOE fabrication. However, the spurious diffraction orders caused by introducing the reference wave into the phase result in low energy efficiency of the DOE. This is because the structure of the amplitude distribution of the generated mode differs greatly from that of the illuminating beam, namely, the Gaussian or plane beam. Figure 6.10 shows the simulated result of the modan operation, with the modan phase photomask shown in Figure 6.9. One can easily see the working diffraction order (at the center) and spurious diffraction orders. Analysis of Figure 6.10 suggests that the energy portion going to the spurious orders is greater than that going to form the useful image.

For a phase modan intended to generate the Gauss-Hermite mode (1, 0) from the Gaussian beam, the upper boundary of the energy efficiency offered by the generalized Kirk-Jones method is as low as 33 percent. The low diffraction efficiency of the elements designed by introducing a carrier into the phase is the main hindrance to their practical application. Obviously, each particular choice between the accurate generation of the mode and the modan energy efficiency is based on a specific problem. Here, we arrive at the idea that there should be numerical method tools that would allow the necessary compromise to be found in every particular case.

6.2.4 Constructing an Iterative Procedure to Design a Unimode Modan

In Refs. [27–31], has been discussed the use of iterative procedures to design phase DOEs capable of generating a unimode distribution. In this case, the iterative procedure is used to find the auxiliary elements intended to ensure a minimal difference between the amplitude of the generated image spectrum and that of the illuminating beam. The iterative procedures are built using various approaches: the projection [27,28] and the gradient [31] approaches. Obviously, other techniques of the optimization theory can also be utilized in solving the problem.

The iterative procedure to design a unimode modan, as described in Refs. [27,28], was built using a mathematical method of generalized projections. The generalized projections method was developed and rigorously substantiated for reconstructing the functions from available a priori information [40]. The core of the method is in successively constructing the mathematical projections onto closed sets, corresponding to limitations imposed on the function and its spectrum. Let us introduce several key notions. For any closed set G_j, a certain function $p_j = \hat{P}_j q$ can be called the projection of q onto G_j if $p_j \in G_j$ and

$$\|p_j - q\| = \min_{f \in G_j} \|f - q\|. \tag{6.151}$$

A norm in space $L_{2,2}$

$$\|F_1(\mathbf{x})\|^2 L_{2,2} = \iint\limits_{\infty} F_1(\mathbf{x}) F_1^*(\mathbf{x}) d^2\mathbf{x} \tag{6.152}$$

is usually used as the norm $\|\cdot\|$ [40]. The $\hat{P}_j$ operator will be called a *projection operator* (or projector) onto the set G_j. We shall assume that m a priori properties of the F function are known, each of them assigning it to one of m closed sets $G_1, \ldots, G_m$. Then, the solution of the reconstruction problem will be given by the $F_1 \in G_0$ function, where

$$G_0 = \cap_{j=0}^{m} G_j. \tag{6.153}$$

We shall call G_0, a set of admissible solutions. Note that if G_0 is an empty set there will be no solution; if G_0 comprises a single element the solution is unique; and if G_0 comprises more than one element, any of those elements can be chosen as the solution of the formulated reconstruction problem. In Ref. [40], it is proposed that the function F_1 should be sought for using a recursive procedure given by

$$F_{1,n+1} = \hat{T}_{1,n} \hat{T}_{2,n}, \ldots \hat{T}_{m,n} F_{1,n}, \tag{6.154}$$

where $F_{1,0}$ is the chosen initial solution;

$$\hat{T}_{j,n} = \hat{E} + \alpha_{j,n}(\hat{P}_j - \hat{E}), j = 1, 2, \ldots m \tag{6.155}$$

$\hat{E}$ is the unity operator, and $\alpha_{j,n}$, $(0 \leq \alpha_{j,n} \leq 1)$ are some parameters generally introduced to speed up the search for point F_1 and called the *relaxation parameters*. In the general case, for $m = 2$, the algorithm of Eq. (6.154) only shows the property of reducing the total distance error (TDE) [40], which means that the functional

$$J(F_{1,n}) = \|\hat{P}_1 F_{1,n} - F_{1,n}\| + \|\hat{P}_2 F_{1,n} - F_{1,n}\| \tag{6.156}$$

possesses the following property:

$$J(F_{1,n+1}) \leq J(F_{1,n}). \tag{6.157}$$

The geometric interpretation of the projection-based approach with which the function is reconstructed using two imposed limitations implying the membership in the closed sets, is depicted in Figure 6.11.

In an effort to build the iterative procedure for designing phase DOEs using the generalized projection method, we need to define the sets G_1 and G_2, and respectively construct the projection operators $\hat{P}_1$ and $\hat{P}_2$. As a rule, closed sets corresponding to the limitations imposed on the distribution $F_1(\mathbf{x})$ that the DOE generates in the observation plane and on its spectrum $F(\mathbf{u})$ are chosen as the sets G_1 and G_2. The construction of the projection operators generally presents no problem [27,28]. Consider the construction of an iterative procedure for designing a unimode modan. Given the paraxial approximation and the far-field diffraction, the Fresnel-Kirchhoff transform is reduced to the Fourier transform [9]

$$\begin{cases} F_1(\mathbf{x}) = \mathcal{F}[F(\mathbf{u})] \\ F(\mathbf{u}) = \mathcal{F}^{-1}[F_1(\mathbf{x})] \end{cases}. \tag{6.158}$$

Given the preceding conditions, we can formulate the problem of synthesizing a phase DOE intended to generate a desired complex unimode distribution $\psi_{\mathbf{p}}(\mathbf{x})$ in the observation plane domain M, as a problem of seeking for such function $F_1(\mathbf{x})$ that, while satisfying the condition $\iint_M |F_1(\mathbf{x}) - \psi_{\mathbf{p}}(\mathbf{x})|^2 d^2\mathbf{x} = 0$, would have the Fourier-spectrum amplitude, $C\sqrt{I_0(\mathbf{u})}$, where $I_0(\mathbf{u})$ is the illuminating beam intensity distribution and C is a constant chosen from the condition of energy conservation. The limitation on the Fourier-spectrum amplitude of the sought-for function is described by a set G_1 of functions $F_1(\mathbf{x})$ with the Fourier-spectrum amplitude

$$|F(\mathbf{u})| = \begin{cases} C\sqrt{I_0(\mathbf{u})} & (\mathbf{u}) \in D \\ 0 & (\mathbf{u}) \notin D \end{cases}. \tag{6.159}$$

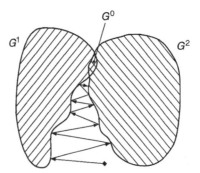

Figure 6.11. Projection-based function reconstruction.

and the corresponding projector [41]

$$\hat{P}_1 F_1 = \mathscr{F}\left(C\sqrt{I_0(\mathbf{u})}\exp i \cdot \arg[F(\mathbf{u})]\right). \tag{6.160}$$

It seems natural to define the closed set

$$G_2 = \left\{ F_1 : \iint_{\mathbf{x}\in M} |F_1(\mathbf{x}) - \psi_{\mathbf{p}}(\mathbf{x})|^2 \, d^2\mathbf{x} = 0; \iint_{\mathbf{x}\notin M} |F_1(\mathbf{x})|^2 \, d^2\mathbf{x} = 0 \right\} \tag{6.161}$$

as a set that describes the limitation imposed on the distribution in the focal plane.
The operator

$$\hat{P}_2 F_1 = \begin{cases} \psi_{\mathbf{p}}(\mathbf{x}), & (\mathbf{x}) \in M, \\ 0, & (\mathbf{x}) \notin M \end{cases} \tag{6.162}$$

is a projector onto the set G_2. If, however, the illuminating beam amplitude is different from the Fourier-image amplitude of the mode under reconstruction, the set of admissible solutions will be empty. Thus, the corresponding iterative procedure becomes stagnated as early as in the first iterations. Because of this, in Refs. [27,28], it is proposed that the projection should be constructed onto the set G_2', instead of the set G_2:

$$G_2' = \left[F_1 : \iint_{\mathbf{x}\in M} |\psi_{\mathbf{p}}(\mathbf{x}) - F_1(\mathbf{x})|^2 \, d^2\mathbf{x} = 0; \iint_{r \geq R_2} |F_1(\mathbf{x})|^2 \, d^2\mathbf{x} = 0 \right], \tag{6.163}$$

where $r = \sqrt{x^2 + y^2}$, $\mathbf{x} = (x, y)$, R_2 is the radius of a certain domain M', such that for any $\mathbf{x} \in M$, we have $\mathbf{x} \in M'$. Obviously, $G_2 \subset G_2'$. The operator

$$\hat{P}_2' F_1(\mathbf{x}) = \begin{cases} \psi_{\mathbf{p}}(\mathbf{x}) & (\mathbf{x}) \in M \\ F_1(\mathbf{x}) & (\mathbf{x}) \in M'/M \\ 0 & r \geq R_2 \end{cases} \tag{6.164}$$

is a projector onto the set G_2'. The complex amplitude values at points within an auxiliary domain M'/M are free parameters necessary for the operation of the iterative procedure. A portion of the illuminating beam energy diffracted into the auxiliary-domain points is a penalty to be paid for the reduction of the Fourier-image amplitude of the mode to be generated to the illuminating beam amplitude. Interestingly, the size of the domain M' determines the degree of "blurring" of the set G_2. The iterative procedure, making use of the operators in Eqs. (6.160) and (6.164) has the property of reducing the TDE to the sets G_1 and G_2'. In this case, the second term in the functional of Eq. (6.156) describes the deviation of the complex distribution $F_1(\mathbf{x})$ under generation from a reference unimode distribution $\psi_{\mathbf{p}}(\mathbf{x})$ at $(x, y) \in M$, with the first term characterizing the deviation of the amplitude $|F(\mathbf{u})|$ of the Fourier spectrum from the illuminating beam amplitude distribution, $C\sqrt{I_0(\mathbf{u})}$, on the aperture D of the element under design at a given iteration step. The algorithm constructed can straightforwardly be applied to design a DOE capable of generating in a given domain M, a desired, arbitrary-shaped, complex amplitude distribution. Note that it is the size of the domain M' that determines the necessary trade-off between the energy efficiency and the accuracy of generation of the desired unimode distribution. As a result, the designed DOE generates, with a desired efficiency, a beam composed of the useful mode, with an admissible contribution of "spurious" modes. If the set of points of the domain M'/M is empty, the derived DOE phase function will be in the form of the mode signum function, coinciding with the solution arrived at in Refs. [25,26]. The approach proposed can be advantageously employed to generate a unimode distribution with radial symmetry [42] by constructing highly effective iterative procedures because, in this case, the 2D translation of the field from the DOE plane into the image plane can be reduced to the 1D case. This can be exemplified by the problem of forming Gauss-Laguerre modes dealt with in Ref. [42] or that of forming Bessel modes covered in Chapter 7 of this book.

6.2.5 Fast Design of DOEs to Form a Desired Unimode Distribution of Radial Modes

In Ref. [43] it has been demonstrated that if both the image $F_1(\mathbf{x}) = F_1(r)$ to be generated and the illuminating beam $I_0(\mathbf{u}) = I_0(\rho)$, $r = \sqrt{x^2 + y^2}$, $\rho = \sqrt{u^2 + v^2}$, $\mathbf{u} = (u, v)$, $\mathbf{x} = (x, y)$ possess radial symmetry, the transform in Eq. (6.158) can be reduced to the zero-order Hankel transform

$$\begin{cases} F_1(r) = \mathcal{H}_0[F(\rho)] \\ F(\rho) = \mathcal{H}_0[F_1(r)] \end{cases}.$$

(6.165)

In this situation, the problem of designing a DOE is formulated as follows (Fig. 6.12): we need to find a function $F(r)$ that under the condition $\iint_{r < R_1} |F_1(r) - \psi_{\mathbf{p}}(r)|^2 r\, dr = 0$ will have the Fourier-spectrum amplitude, $C\sqrt{I_0(\rho)}$, where R_1 is the radius of the useful domain (e.g., the core radius of an optical graded-index fiber). In Ref. [43] it has been shown that taking the Hankel transform is easily reduced to taking three 1D Fourier transforms.

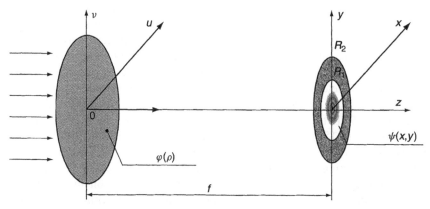

Figure 6.12. Formulation of the problem of designing a modan to generate the Gauss-Laguerre mode.

Thus, assuming that the "auxiliary" domain is also radially symmetric, the iterative procedure [27] can be essentially simplified, requiring only three 1D Fourier transforms per iteration. Note that on the basis of the effective procedure of designing radially symmetric modans, we can get a distribution described by any generalized Gauss-Laguerre mode, forming a helical "addition" by a corresponding phase filter selected from the following considerations. To form in the far-field Fraunhofer zone a generalized Gauss-Laguerre mode [19]

$$\psi_{\mathbf{p}}^{\pm}(r, \theta) = E_{pl} \left(\frac{\sqrt{2}r}{\sigma} \right)^l L_p^l \left(\frac{2r^2}{\sigma^2} \right) \exp \left(-\frac{r^2}{\sigma^2} \right) \exp(\pm il\theta)$$

$$= \tilde{\psi}_{\mathbf{p}}(r) \exp(\pm il\theta), \tag{6.166}$$

where σ is the principal mode radius, θ is the polar angle, L_p^l is the Laguerre polynomial, and $\mathbf{p} = (p, l)$ are the mode ordinal numbers, we need to form the following input distribution of complex amplitude

$$\Psi(\rho, \nu) = \int_0^{2\pi} \int_0^{\infty} \psi_{\mathbf{p}}^{\pm}(r, \theta) \exp[-i \cdot 2pr \cos(\theta - \nu)] r \, dr \, d\theta$$

$$= \exp(\pm il\nu) \int_0^{\infty} \tilde{\psi}_{\mathbf{p}}(r) \left\{ \int_0^{2\pi} \exp(\pm ilt) \exp[-i2\pi r\rho \cos(t)] dt \right\} r \, dr. \tag{6.167}$$

Using the reference integral [14]

$$J_l(\mathrm{x}) = \frac{i^l}{2\pi} \int_0^{2\pi} \exp(\pm ilt) \exp[-ix \cos(t)] dt, \tag{6.168}$$

Eq. (6.167) is easily reduced to the following form

$$\Psi(\rho, \nu) = \exp(\pm il\nu) \frac{2\pi}{i^l} \int_0^{\infty} \tilde{\psi}_{\mathbf{p}}(r) J_l(r\rho) r \, dr = \tilde{\Psi}(\rho) \exp(\pm il\nu). \tag{6.169}$$

Thus, to form the function in Eq. (6.167), we only need to calculate the radial coefficient of the sought-for function

$$\tilde{\Psi}(\rho) = \frac{2\pi}{i^l} \int_0^{\infty} \tilde{\psi}_{\mathbf{p}}(r) J_l(r\rho) r \, dr, \tag{6.170}$$

which is the first-order Hankel transform. Note also that if the image under generation contains only zero values at points in the vicinity of the optical axis, we can translate the field from the aperture to the focal plane and back by taking only two 1D Fourier transforms per iteration [44]. Such a distribution may be exemplified by the generalized Gauss-Laguerre modes with equal values of the first and second mode numbers.

Example 6.1. Iterative design of a unimode modan. In Ref. [45], studies regarding how the iterative procedure with the projectors in Eqs. (6.164) and (6.160) can be used to design a DOE capable of generating from the Gaussian beam with intensity distribution

$$I_0(\mathbf{u}) = \exp\left(-\frac{2\mathbf{u}^2}{{\sigma_{00}}^2}\right) \qquad (6.171)$$

a reference distribution described by the laser light mode $\psi_\mathbf{p}(\mathbf{x})$ within a domain M of radius R_1 has been done. The distribution described by the Gauss-Hermite, (1, 0), and Gauss-Laguerre, (1, 0) mode functions is taken as a reference distribution. The initial approximation was chosen in the form

$$F_{1,0}(\mathbf{x}) = \begin{cases} \psi_\mathbf{p}(\mathbf{x}), & \mathbf{x} \in M, \\ \tilde{\mu}\chi(\mathbf{x}), & \mathbf{x} \in M'/M, \\ 0, & r \geqslant R_2, \end{cases} \qquad (6.172)$$

where $\chi(\mathbf{x})$ is a random, real-valued function uniformly distributed on the interval $\left[0, \max\limits_{\mathbf{x} \in M} |\psi_\mathbf{p}(\mathbf{x})|\right]$, the parameter $\tilde{\mu}$ determines the relation between the energy portions going to form the useful and auxiliary domains of the initial approximation. The introduction of the random predistortion into the auxiliary domain results in the emergence of free parameters, which are necessary for the operation of the iterative procedure. Shown in Figure 6.13 is the amplitude of the initial distribution, $F_{1,0}(\mathbf{x})$, containing the reference distribution in the useful domain and the random predistortion in the auxiliary domain. Figure 6.14 shows the phase photomask of the iteratively designed Gauss-Hermite modan (1, 0). Figure 6.15 depicts the computer-simulated amplitude of an image generated by the designed element.

The quality of the mode formation was estimated by the following criteria [27]: the energy efficiency

$$E_m = \frac{\displaystyle\iint\limits_{M} |F_{1,m}(\mathbf{x})|^2 \, d^2\mathbf{x}}{\displaystyle\iint\limits_{D} I_0(\mathbf{u}) \, d^2\mathbf{u}}, \qquad (6.173)$$

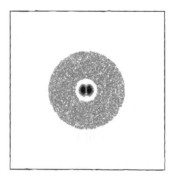

Figure 6.13. The amplitude of the initial distribution.

Figure 6.14. The phase photomask of the designed modan.

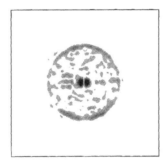

Figure 6.15. The result of simulation of the modan operation.

where $F_{1,m}(\mathbf{x})$ is the complex distribution that the designed element generates in the mth iteration, and the specific power of the desired mode in the domain M

$$\zeta_m = \left| C_0 \iint\limits_{M} F_{1,m}(\mathbf{x}) \psi_{\mathbf{p}}^*(\mathbf{x}) \, d^2\mathbf{x} \right|^2 \qquad (6.174)$$

that characterizes the energy portion accounted for by the generated mode in the useful domain M. Given the orthonormalized basis of the mode functions $\iint_{\infty} \psi_{\mathbf{p}}(\mathbf{x}) \psi_{\mathbf{p}}^*(\mathbf{x}) \, d^2\mathbf{x} = 1$, we have

$$C_0 = \frac{1}{\sqrt{\iint\limits_{M} |F_{1,m}(\mathbf{x})|^2 \, d^2\mathbf{x}}}. \qquad (6.175)$$

Because the mode function amplitude is decreased fairly quickly with the distance from point $(0, 0)$, with the adequate choice of size of the useful domain M, we can change to the integration over M in Eq. (6.174). Because of orthogonality, the modes interact in such a manner that, upon integrating Eq. (6.174), the spurious modes are eliminated, with the magnitude ζ determining the energy portion in the domain M accounted for by the generated mode $\psi_{\mathbf{p}}(\mathbf{x})$. In the computer simulation, the following parameters were used: the element aperture radius $a = 10$ mm, the Gaussian parameter of the illuminating beam $\sigma_{00} = 3.5$ mm, the illuminating light wavelength $\lambda = 0.6328$ μm, the focal length of the Fourier lens $f = 50$ mm, the outer radius of the useful domain $R_1 = 30$ μm, the outer radius of the auxiliary domain $R_2 = 95$ μm, the fundamental radius of the generated mode in the output focal plane of the lens $\sigma = 5.6$ μm, and the matrix is 128×128 pixels. In Ref. [45], the characteristics of modans designed using the proposed iterative procedure were compared with those designed using the Kirk-Jones method. It has been demonstrated in Ref. [19] that the energy efficiency of a unimode modan designed using the generalized Kirk-Jones method is given by

$$E_k = g\tilde{C}^2, \tag{6.176}$$

where $g \leq 1$ is determined by the type of the base diffraction grating. With the sine or rectangular carrier and zero diffraction order taken as the working order, we have $g = 1$,

$$\tilde{C}^{-1} = \max_{u \in D} \left| \frac{\Psi_{\mathbf{p}}(\mathbf{u})/\sqrt{E_1}}{\sqrt{I_0(\mathbf{u})}/\sqrt{E_0}} \right|, \tag{6.177}$$

$$E_0 = \iint\limits_G I_0(\mathbf{u}) \, d^2\mathbf{u}, \tag{6.178}$$

$$E_1 = \iint\limits_G |\Psi_{\mathbf{p}}(\mathbf{u})|^2 \, d^2\mathbf{u}, \tag{6.179}$$

and $\Psi_{\mathbf{p}}(\mathbf{u}) = \mathscr{F}^{-1}[\psi_{\mathbf{p}}(\mathbf{x})]$ is the generated unimode distribution in the element's plane. The results of computer simulation are given in Table 6.1.

From Table 6.1, it can be seen that the proposed method allows the unimode modans to be designed with the energy efficiency more than twice greater than that of the generalized Kirk-Jones method. Note that 95-98 percent of the generated quasi-unimode distribution is accounted for by the desired mode.

TABLE 6.1. The Results of Computer-Simulated Iterative Design of the Unimode Modans (the Energy Efficiency for the Kirk-Jones Method is Given in the Brackets)

Criterion	Gauss-Hermite Mode (1, 0)	Gauss-Laguerre Mode (1, 0)
Efficiency E,%	53.3 (26.3)	59.4 (26.4)
Specific power of the desired mode, ζ,%	95.2	98.6

Example 6.2. Designing a Unimode Modan Capable of Generating the Gauss-Laguerre mode. In Ref. [42], the iterative design of a DOE, capable of transforming the Gaussian beam of intensity distribution $I_0(\rho) = \exp[-2\rho^2/\sigma_{00}^2]$ into a reference distribution described by a laser mode $\psi_\mathbf{p}(r)$ within a domain M of radius R_1 has been discussed. The generalized Gauss-Laguerre modes (1, 0), (4, 0), and (2, 2) were chosen as the reference distributions. The function

$$F_{1,0}(r) = \begin{cases} \psi_\mathbf{p}(r), & r \leq R_1, \\ \tilde{\mu}\chi(r), & R_1 < r < R_2, \\ 0, & r \geq R_2. \end{cases} \qquad (6.180)$$

was chosen as the initial approximation. A random real-valued function uniformly distributed on the interval $[0, \max|\psi_\mathbf{p}(r)|]$ was chosen as $\chi(r)$, with the $\tilde{\mu}$ parameter defining the relation between the energy portions accounted for by the "useful" and "auxiliary" domains of the initial approximation. To translate the field from the element's plane into the focal plane and back, the procedure of fast Hankel transform was employed. The elements were calculated as an addition to a lens with the following physical parameters: the focal length $f = 50$ mm, the wavelength $\lambda = 0.6328$ µm, the DOE aperture radius $R_{ap} = 10$ mm, the fundamental radius of the generated mode $\sigma = 5.6$ µm, the radius of the illuminating Gaussian beam $\sigma_0 = 3.0{-}3.5$ mm, and the number of iterations $N = 10$. The results of calculation and computer-simulated operation of the DOE are given in Table 6.2, Figures 6.16, and 6.17. The computer simulation conducted suggests that the proposed iterative procedure allows the modans capable of generating the Gauss-Laguerre modes to be calculated with the energy efficiency 2 to 3 times that of the modans, calculated using the Kirk-Jones method. Note that more than 95 percent of the generated beam is accounted for by the desired mode (Table 6.2).

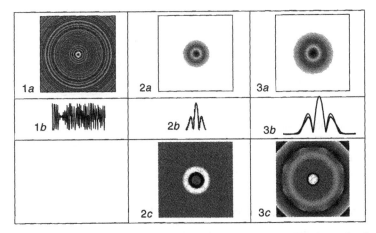

Figure 6.16. Generation of the Gauss-Laguerre mode (1, 0): (1a) DOE phase distribution; (1b) phase radial section; (2a) generated amplitude distribution in the effective domain; (2b) its cross section (reference mode's cross section is shown by dotted line); (2c) generated phase distribution in the effective domain (the range of values is $[0, 2\pi]$), column 3 depicts computer-simulated propagation of the generated mode through a Fourier stage.

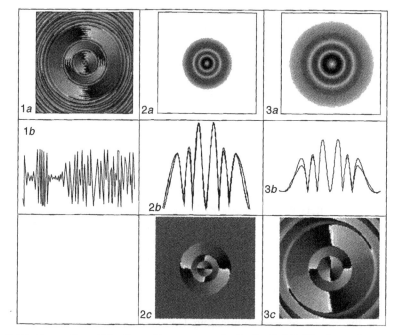

Figure 6.17. Generation of the Gauss-Laguerre mode (2, 2): (1a) DOE phase distribution; (1b) phase radial section; (2a) generated amplitude distribution in the effective domain; (2b) its cross section (reference mode's cross section is shown by dotted line); (2c) generated phase distribution in the effective domain (the range of values is $[0, 2\pi]$), column 3 depicts computer-simulated propagation of the generated mode through a Fourier stage.

TABLE 6.2. The Results of Computer-Simulated Design of Gauss-Laguerre Modans

% Mode numbers	σ, mm	E, %	ζ, %
$(p, l) = (1, 0)$	3	40.1	97.5
$(p, l) = (2, 0)$	3.3	35.4	96.4
$(p, l) = (2, 2)$	3.5	62.8	96.7
$(p, l) = (4, 0)$	3.5	33.7	96.4

An interesting phenomenon is the "rotation" of the (2, 2) mode (Fig. 6.17) as it passes through the Fourier-stage, which is due to the presence of an additional helical phase component. The remarkable properties of the rotating or self-reproducing beams are comprehensively covered in Ref. [46] and in Chapter 7 of this book.

6.2.6 Designing a DOE to Form an Array of Laser Modes

Because the cross section of a beam comprising an array of laser modes with required weights is also described by a corresponding complex-valued function, a phase DOE intended to form an array of modes can be designed using encoding techniques based on the introduction of a carrier into the element's phase [19]. As is the case with the design of a DOE intended to form a desired unimode distribution (subsection 6.2.3), the use of analytical coding methods, with a carrier introduced into the element's phase, to design a modan capable of forming a required mode array generally results in a low energy efficiency of the element. Note, however, that when one aims to generate several mode beams using a single element simultaneously, the ratio of the initial phase delays being of no importance, the arbitrary choice of those delays offers an additional freedom for calculating the element's phase function, doing without auxiliary elements and, hence, without considerable energy losses. This suggests an alluring idea of building an iterative procedure for designing a multimode modan, with the modan phase function pixels in the element plane and mutual phase shifts of the modes under generation in the output plane used as free parameters [24]. Here, we can draw the analogy with iteratively designing a DOE intended to form a desired intensity distribution through a Fienup-type procedure [47]. The task of designing a modan differs from that of designing a DOE generating a desired intensity distribution in that the phase pixels of the generated light distribution are taken in the latter case as free parameters in the output plane. In Refs. [23,24], the design of phase modans matched to the Gaussian laser modes and capable of generating light beams in the form of a superposition of Gauss-Hermite or Gauss-Laguerre modes with desired amplitudes of the mode coefficients has been discussed. Consider the construction of the iterative procedure for designing multibeam Gauss-Hermite modans. We can easily show [19,23] that there is a partial solution of the 1D paraxial equation (Section 6.1)

$$2ik\frac{\partial F(u,z)}{\partial z} + \frac{\partial^2 F(u,z)}{\partial^2 u} = 0, \tag{6.181}$$

where z is the axis of beam propagation, with the beam represented by

$$F_n(u,z) = a^{-n-1}\exp[-(u/a)^2]H_n(u/a), \tag{6.182}$$

where $a^2(z) = a_0^2 + 2iz/k$, (a_0^2 is the beam radius at $z = 0$) and $H_n(u)$ is the Hermite polynomial. Hence, the general solution of Eq. (6.181) can be written as a linear combination of its partial solutions in Eq. (6.182):

$$F(u,z) = \exp[-(u/a)^2]\sum_{n=0}^{\infty} C_n a^{-n-1}H_n(u/a). \tag{6.183}$$

In order for the light field of amplitude in Eq. (6.183) to propagate along the z-axis, we should form the following complex amplitude in the plane $z = 0$:

$$F_0(u) = \exp[-(u/a_0)^2]\sum_{n=0}^{\infty} C_n a_0^{-n-1}H_n(u/a_0). \tag{6.184}$$

Thus, the problem of designing phase optical elements intended to generate Hermite beams with an arbitrary mode composition can be formulated as follows [23]. We need to find a phase $\varphi(u)$ that satisfies the following set of $N + 1$ algebraic equations

$$|C_n| = \left|\int_{-\infty}^{\infty} \sqrt{I_0(u)}\exp[i\varphi(u)]P_n(u)\,du\right|, \qquad n = \overline{0, N}, \tag{6.185}$$

where

$$\sqrt{I_0(u)} \exp[i\varphi(u)] = \sum_{n=0}^{N} C_n P_n(u) \tag{6.186}$$

and

$$P_n(u) = \left(2^n n! \sqrt{n}\right)^{-1/2} \exp\left(-\frac{u^2}{2}\right) H_n(u), \tag{6.187}$$

where $P_n(u)$ is the Hermite function and $\sqrt{I_0(u)}$ is the illuminating beam amplitude. The coefficient modules, $|C_n|$, are specified and determine the energy contribution of each Hermite mode into the total light beam. The Hermite functions in Eq. (6.187) satisfy the orthogonality relationships

$$\int_{-\infty}^{\infty} P_n(u) P_m(u) \, du = \delta_{mn}, \tag{6.188}$$

where δ_{mn} is the Kronecker delta. The initial phase guess, $\varphi_0(u)$, is chosen at random [23]. Then, $N+1$ of the C_n coefficients are derived from Eq. (6.185). The coefficients derived in the kth iteration step are replaced by

$$\overline{C}_n^{(k)} = B_n \frac{C_n^{(k)}}{|C_n^{(k)}|}, \tag{6.189}$$

where $B_n \geq 0$ are specified real numbers that characterize the light energy distribution between the modes. Then, we find the sum in Eq. (6.186), with its argument taken as a new guess $\varphi_{k+1}(u)$ of the sought-for phase, and so on. Note that all foregoing reasoning can be extended onto a 2D case in full measure if we need to get the phase $\varphi(\mathbf{u})$ of an optical element to form a light beam composed of a desired array of Hermite beams with specified energy weights

$$\sqrt{I_0(\mathbf{u})} \exp[i\varphi(\mathbf{u})] = \sum_{n=0}^{N} \sum_{m=0}^{M} C_{mn} P_n(u) P_m(v). \tag{6.190}$$

Note also that a procedure similar to that of Eqs. (6.185) to (6.189) can be built using the generalized projections technique of Eq. (6.154). Actually, the amplitude of the complex function F that we are looking for should satisfy the following condition

$$|F(\mathbf{u})| = \sqrt{I_0(\mathbf{u})} \tag{6.191}$$

defined by the shape of the illuminating beam, with the modules of complex coefficients of the function expansion in terms of a mode basis defined as

$$\begin{cases} B_1 = \left| \iint_G F(\mathbf{u}) \psi_{\mathbf{p}_1}^*(\mathbf{u}) \, d^2\mathbf{u} \right| \\ B_2 = \left| \iint_G F(\mathbf{u}) \psi_{\mathbf{p}_2}^*(\mathbf{u}) \, d^2\mathbf{u} \right| \\ \quad \cdots \end{cases}, \tag{6.192}$$

where $B_n \geq 0$ are the given numbers that characterize the light energy distribution between the modes. The argument $\varphi(\mathbf{u}) = \arg[F(\mathbf{u})]$ of the sought-for function $F(\mathbf{u})$

is the phase function of the modan under design. Thus, we need to reconstruct a complex-valued function from its amplitude and the amplitude of the transverse mode spectrum. The only difference of this task from that of designing a DOE to focus the laser light into a desired domain is using a fixed amplitude of the transverse-mode spectrum instead of the Fourier-spectrum amplitude. Constructing the iterative procedure to reconstruct the complex-valued function from its own amplitude and its Fourier-spectrum amplitude using the generalized projections method is discussed in Refs. [40,41]. We shall construct the iterative procedure for reconstructing the phase from the amplitude and the transverse-mode-spectrum amplitude, Eq. (6.13).

Example 6.3. Designing a DOE to form several Gauss-Hermite modes simultaneously. In the course of computer simulation, the pixels on the u variable were taken at 0.02 mm intervals. Taking an indefinite integral over infinite interval, Eq. (6.185) was replaced by taking the integral over the interval $[-a, a]$, $a = 6$ mm. As a increased, the coefficients were changed by a tenth fraction of a percent. The number of terms in the sum in Eq. (6.186) was equal to 20. Shown in Figure 6.18b is the phase of an optical element illuminated by a plane Gaussian beam that produces a Hermite beam effectively composed of five Gauss-Hermite modes with constant modules of the C_k coefficients.

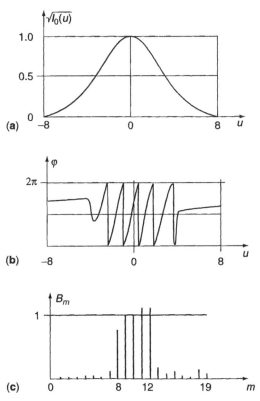

Figure 6.18. Calculation of the Hermite beam: (**a**) the illuminating beam amplitude, (**b**) the DOE phase, and (**c**) the modules of the coefficients C_k.

The modules of the coefficients are shown in Figure 6.18c. Note that the general slope of the optical element's phase, (Fig. 6.18b) causing the axial displacement of the Hermite beam as this propagates results from the presence of odd-number modes in the sum in Eq. (6.186). Figure 6.19 depicts the root-mean-square deviations for the amplitude in the optical element's plane (curve 1):

$$\delta_A = \left[\int_{-a}^{a} \left| |F_{k+1}(u)| - \sqrt{I_0(u)} \right|^2 du \right]^{1/2} \left[\int_{-a}^{a} I_0(u)\, du \right]^{-1/2} \qquad (6.193)$$

and for the coefficients of the series in Eq. (6.186) (curve 2):

$$\delta_C = \left[\sum_{n=0}^{N} \left(|C_n^{(k)}| - B_n \right)^2 \right]^{1/2} \left[\sum_{n=0}^{N} B_n^2 \right]^{-1/2} \qquad (6.194)$$

as a function of the number of iterations.

From Figure 6.19, the deviations are seen to monotonically decrease as the number of iterations increases. Note that the Hermite beam can be represented as five modes with a 90 percent efficiency (Fig. 6.18c). The efficiency is derived from the following relationship

$$E = \left[\sum_{\Omega} |C_n^{(k)}|^2 \right] \left[\sum_{n=0}^{N} |C_n^{(k)}|^2 \right]^{-1}, \qquad (6.195)$$

where k is the number of the iteration and Ω is a set of the mode numbers specified by nonzero coefficients. The next task somewhat differs from the previous one, for it involves the design of a phase optical element intended to form Gauss-Hermite beams in desired diffraction orders and with desired light energy distribution between the orders. Thus, in this situation, every light mode is propagated at its own angle to the optical axis. Hence, in order to find the DOE phase $\varphi(u)$ we need to use the following relationship instead of Eq. (6.186):

$$\sqrt{I_0(u)} \exp[\, i\varphi(u)] = \sum_{n=0}^{N} C_n P_n(u) \exp(-i\nu_n u), \qquad (6.196)$$

where $P_n(u)$ is the Hermite function specified in Eq. (6.187) and ν_n is the carrier spatial frequency, where, $\nu_1 < \nu_2 < \cdots < \nu_N$. As described earlier, the modules of the

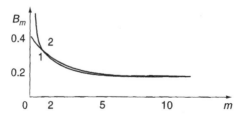

Figure 6.19. Root-mean-square deviations.

coefficients C_n are fixed, whereas their arguments are free parameters of the task. The Hermite functions are eigenfunctions of the Fourier transform

$$\int_{-\infty}^{\infty} P_n(u) \exp(-ivu) \, du = (-i)^n P_n(v).$$ (6.197)

Using Eq. (6.197) yields

$$\int_{-\infty}^{\infty} P_n(u) P_m(u) \exp[-i(v_n - v_m)u] \, du = i^{n+m} \int_{-\infty}^{\infty} P_n(\zeta) P_m(\zeta + v_n - v_m) \, d\zeta.$$ (6.198)

The function on the right-hand side of Eq. (6.198) is a correlation of two Hermite functions. Therefore, making the difference between two consecutive carrier spatial frequencies, $|v_{n+1} - v_n|$, fairly large (which practically means that the generated Hermite beams are to be separated by a certain threshold), the functions $P_n(u) \exp[-iv_n u]$ can be treated as being approximately orthogonal, and the coefficients in the sum of Eq. (6.196) are derived from

$$C_n = \int_{-\infty}^{\infty} \sqrt{I_0(u)} \exp[i\varphi(u) + iv_n u] P_n(u) \, du, \, n = \overline{0, N}.$$ (6.199)

Using Eqs. (6.196) and (6.199), we can build an iterative procedure for searching for the phase $\varphi(u)$ of the optical element, similar to the algorithm described by Eqs. (6.185) to (6.187). The coefficients C_n derived from Eq. (6.199) in the kth iteration step are subjected to the following replacement: their modules are replaced by specified numbers B_n, while their phases (arguments) remain unchanged. Then, the sum in Eq. (6.196) is derived and the resulting function, is subjected to a similar replacement: its modulus is replaced by the illuminating beam amplitude, $\sqrt{I_0(\mathbf{u})}$, with the phase remaining unchanged and being a new estimate of the sought-for phase. Obviously, the foregoing considerations apply to a 2D case if we employ the following relationship instead of Eq. (196):

$$\sqrt{I_0(\mathbf{u})} \exp[i\varphi(\mathbf{u})] = \sum_{n=0}^{N} \sum_{m=0}^{M} C_{nm} P_n(u) P_m(v) \exp[-i(v_1^n u + v_2^m v)].$$ (6.200)

Example 6.4. Designing a Four-channel Gauss-Hermite Modan (2D case) For a particular calculation, we have chosen the following parameters: the variables x and y are changed over the interval $[-10, 10]$ with a 0.02 step. The total number of pixels is 128×128. The number of terms in the sum of Eq. (6.200) is M = N = 9. The illuminating beam amplitude is constant: $\sqrt{I_0(\mathbf{u})} = $ const. Figure 6.20a depicts the phase of a four-channel optical element calculated during eight iterations, which is capable of forming the intensity distribution (a) and the phase distribution (b) in the focal plane of the lens. Figure 6.20b depicts the (0, 1) mode at the top left, the (1, 1) mode at the top right, the (1, 2) mode at the bottom left, and the (2, 0) mode at the bottom right. About 95 percent of the illuminating beam energy is spent for forming these four modes, the energy being distributed between them in nearly equal proportions with an average error of 2 percent. The mean intensity deviation of the formed modes from ideal values amounts to 21 percent. Shown in Figure 6.20c

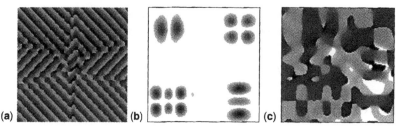

Figure 6.20. Designing a four-channel Hermite mode former: (**a**) DOE phase, (**b**) intensity, (**c**) phase distribution in the focal plane.

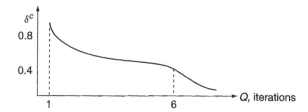

Figure 6.21. The error (6.165) vs the number of iterations.

is the phase in the frequency plane. It can be seen that there are characteristic phase jumps by π at the location of the four modes while passing through the zero intensity line. Figure 6.21 shows how the error changes with iterations. The error is seen to decrease monotonically. An increase in the rate of convergence after the 6th iteration (Fig. 6.21) is due to the use of an adaptive-additive technique [48].

An optical element with the phase in Figure 6.20a can be used not only to generate spatially separated Gauss-Hermite modes but also as a spatial filter matched to four aforementioned filters (subsection 6.2.8).

In fact, when illuminated by the light beam of an amplitude proportional to a mode amplitude, $T_{mn} = P_n(u) P_m(v)$, such an optical element produces a correlation intensity peak in the frequency plane at point (v_n^1, v_m^2). Figure 6.22 depicts the intensity distribution in the frequency plane a DOE in Figure 6.20a that is produced when illuminated by (a) T_{01}-mode, (b) T_{20}-mode, (c) $T_{11} + T_{12} + T_{20}$-mode, and (d) T_{02}-mode. Note that the last mode was not spotted in the design procedure. The iterative procedure and the corresponding results of designing DOEs matched to a group of the Gauss-Laguerre modes may be found in Chapter 7 of this book. Note that trying to design a unimodal modan by the use of the procedure in Eqs. (6.185) to (6.189) results in stagnation just after the first iteration, the signum function of the mode under generation appearing as the derived solution, similar to Refs. [25,26].

6.2.7 Setting up a Multichannel Communication Line in a Perfect Lenslike Medium with Minimal Energy Losses

Although the methods for modan design based on introducing a carrier into the element's phase [19] result in a low energy efficiency of the elements, the procedures for designing phase DOEs by consecutively constructing projections onto closed sets [27–30] are absolutely devoid of convergence [40]. After several iterations, we

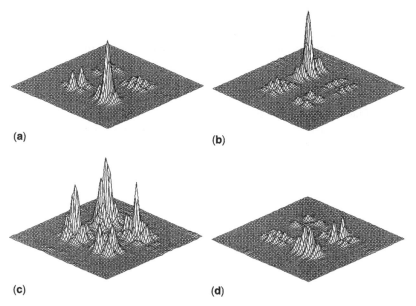

Figure 6.22. Intensity distribution in the frequency plane than a DOE produces when it is illuminated by (a) T_{01}-mode, (b) T_{20}-mode, (c) $T_{11} + T_{12} + T_{20}$-mode, and (d) T_{02}-mode.

are to face with the algorithm stagnation in which further iterations do not result in appreciably improved characteristics of the element under design [23,45]. Note that the iterative procedure stagnation does not necessarily mean that the best solution has been found. A variety of reasons for the stagnation and approaches being taken to solve it are comprehensively covered in Chapter 2 of this book and in Refs. [23,40,45]. If powerful computers are available, stochastic optimization procedures that have recently become more popular in the DOE design [49] may offer an alternative to the gradient and projection techniques. In any case, the outcome of the iterative procedure is directly linked to the presence of free parameters that can be varied in order for the complex transmission function to be reduced to a pure-phase form. As a rule, with the algorithm of Eqs. (6.185) to (6.189), the mode beams can be generated with high quality if they consist of more than four to five modes [23]. Otherwise, the proportion of spurious modes in the generated quasi-mode beams will be extremely large, leading to a significantly widened impulse in the communication channel of a DOE-aided optical telecommunication system. The number of the modes to be generated is determined by the specific job to be performed. For example, the number of modes may be equal to the number of independent channels in a fiber-optical communication system. Implementing a single communication channel as an arbitrary group of several modes will widen the channel impulse [18]. To increase the number of free parameters required to make the iteration procedure operate, it has been proposed in Ref. [20] that every communication channel in a parabolic fiber should be set up through the use of a packet of 2D Gaussian modes with the same propagation constant, β. We shall remember that from Eqs. (6.117), (6.118), and (6.120) it follows that the 2D Gauss-Laguerre modes, with their numbers satisfying the relation $r_p = 2p + l = \text{const}$, possess the same propagation constant β_{r_p} in a lenslike medium. Similarly, from Eqs. (6.117), (6.118), and (6.135), we follow the condition for the Gauss-Hermite modes $r_p = p + l = \text{const}$.

Thus, it is possible to increase the number of free parameters without facing the problem of impulse widening if a single information channel in a perfect lenslike medium is implemented as a superposition of the Gaussian modes with the same propagation constant. Figure 6.23 depicts a 3D amplitude distribution for four Gauss-Hermite mode packets characterized by the same propagation constant within each packet and generated by the DOE in different diffraction orders [20]. Figure 6.24 depicts the analogous result for the Gauss-Laguerre modes [20].

Beams composed of Gaussian modes with the same propagation constant feature an interesting peculiarity. The complex amplitude in their cross section is given by

$$\chi_{r_p}(\mathbf{x}) = \sum_{r_p = \text{const}} \tilde{C}_{\mathbf{p}} \psi_{\mathbf{p}}(\mathbf{x}). \tag{6.201}$$

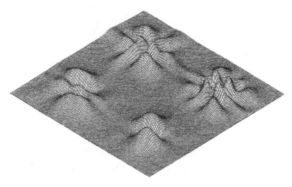

Figure 6.23. Amplitude distribution for four mode packets composed of the Gauss-Hermite modes with the same propagation constant.

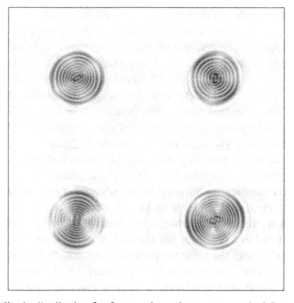

Figure 6.24. Amplitude distribution for four mode packets composed of Gauss-Laguerre modes with the same propagation constant.

The beam of Eq. (6.201) will propagate similar to the separate modes $\psi_\mathbf{p}(\mathbf{x})$. Actually, a coherent light beam of cross section in Eq. (6.201) will self-reproduce its amplitude-phase structure as it propagates in a corresponding medium. Such beams are called *invariant mode packets* [20] (or *multimode dispersion-free impulses*). The fundamental properties of invariant mode packets are as follows:

1. A discrete set of waveguide modes, $[\psi_\mathbf{p}(\mathbf{x})]$, induces a continual set of invariant mode packets because of arbitrary choice of the coefficients $\tilde{C}_\mathbf{p}$ in Eq. (6.201).

2. Self-reproduction: the invariant mode packets of Eq. (6.201) do not change their amplitude-phase structure while propagating in a corresponding waveguide medium in view of Eqs. (6.117), (6.118), (6.120).

3. The Gaussian invariant mode packets do not change their amplitude-phase structure while propagating in lenslike media, in free space, travelling through a Fourier stage, changing only the principal modal radius according to Eq. (6.144).

4. The invariant mode packets travel in a waveguide without the impulse widening that can be caused by intermode dispersion discussed, for example, in Ref. [5].

Figures 6.25 and 6.26 show the computer-simulated result of propagation through a Fourier stage of a sum of two Gauss-Hermite modes, (2, 2) and (4, 0), taken with unit weights, $\tilde{C}_{22} = 1$, $\tilde{C}_{40} = 1$. The two-mode beam amplitude before passing through the Fourier stage is shown in Figure 6.25 and the same after passing through the Fourier stage is shown in Figure 6.26. The simulation result proves that similar to a single mode, a beam composed of two modes with the same propagation constant preserves its structure as it propagates.

Figures 6.27 to 6.30 show the results of the experimental studies of an element that generates the amplitude-phase distribution as a sum of two Gauss-Hermite modes, (2, 2) and (4, 0), taken with unit weights $\tilde{C}_{2,2} = 1$, $\tilde{C}_{4,0} = 1$. The DOE under study was fabricated using the technology described in Ref. [29]. The DOE complex transmission function was encoded using the generalized Kirk-Jones technique discussed in Ref. [19]. The results of physical experiments obviously testify in favor of the feasibility of generating invariant mode packets using DOEs.

Later we realized a more sophisticated experiment. Discussed in the following section are new results, relating to the synthesis and investigation of beams consisting

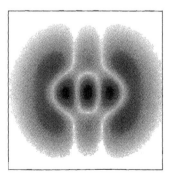

Figure 6.25. Amplitude of a beam composed of two Gauss-Hermite modes, (2, 2) and (4, 0) which the DOE produces.

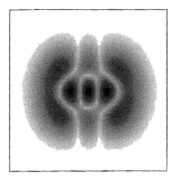

Figure 6.26. The computer-simulated result of propagation through a Fourier stage of the beam with the amplitude in Figure 6.25.

Figure 6.27. The amplitude distribution produced by the DOE in the focal plane as a sum of two Gauss-Hermite modes, $(2, 2) + (4, 0)$ (reconstructed from intensity measurements).

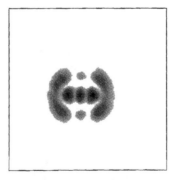

Figure 6.28. The experimental pattern produced after the sum of two Gauss-Hermite modes, $(2, 2) + (4, 0)$, have passed through a Fourier stage.

of two modes with the same propagation constant (*multimode dispersionless beams*) with the possibility of changing the intermode phase shift during the experiment. In order to demonstrate the fundamental properties of multimode dispersionless beams, we designed a modan that should be able to transform a single transverse mode

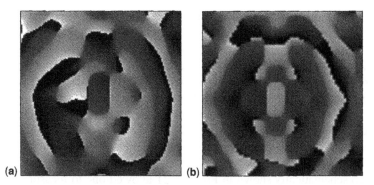

(a)   **(b)**

Figure 6.29. The phase of the beam is reconstructed through computer simulation from the amplitude distributions in the input and output planes of the Fourier stage shown in Figures 6.27 and 6.28.

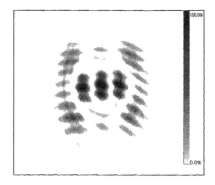

Figure 6.30. The interferometric studies of the phase of the beam composed of the sum of two Gauss-Hermite modes, $(2, 2) + (4, 0)$.

into two different modes having the same propagation constant in different diffraction orders. For the input beam, we selected the Gaussian $(0, 0)$-mode of He-Ne laser (wavelength $\lambda = 0.63$ μm), with the intensity distribution in the modan plane given by

$$I_0(u, v) = \exp\left[-\frac{2(u^2 + v^2)}{\sigma_{00}^2} \right] \tag{6.202}$$

and the phase distribution assumed to be constant, which is a good approximation in the vicinity of the beam waist. The modan was calculated to be able to form Gauss-Hermite modes $(2, 2)$ and $(4, 0)$ $(r_p = 4)$ in different diffraction orders in the output planes. The complex transmission function of modan $T(u, v)$ can be written as follows

$$T(u, v) = \frac{1}{\sqrt{I_0(u, v)}} \left[\psi_{22}(u, v) \exp(i2\pi \nu_{22} u) + \psi_{40}(u, v) \exp(i2\pi \nu_{40} u) \right], \tag{6.203}$$

where ν_{22}, ν_{40} are the carriers introduced for the spatial separation of unimode beams. The well-known Kirk-Jones [38] method was used for coding the complex transmission function $T(u, v)$ of the modan into a pure-phase function of the modan $\varphi(u, v)$.

The calculated element was manufactured, as a multilevel surface profile, by (variable dose) e-beam direct-writing into a polymethylmethacrylate (PMMA) resist film and a subsequent development procedure of the resist. The final element consists of a fused silica substrate coated with the structured PMMA film. The continuous-phase profile had to be transferred into a corresponding surface profile, which in turn had to be approximated by a steplike structure. For the element under discussion, we used a 15-step to 16-level approximation of the continuous profile. The 15 dose levels, each corresponding to one of the final surface levels, were realized by a 15-times repeated, binary e-beam-writing process, using a commercial ZBA 23 system (Carl Zeiss, Jena, Germany).

The setup schematically shown in Figure 6.31 allowed one to measure the intensity distribution in the cross section of the beam combined of two different modes taken with different phase shifts. To demonstrate the "invariant" character of the complex amplitude distribution, further experiments were needed: one possibility was to use an additional Fourier transform (lens L2 was used). A complex amplitude distribution, representing any multimode dispersionless beam, should retain its spatial structure during this procedure, while changing its fundamental radius. Camera 1 and Camera 2 were synchronized by computer. Positions of Camera 1 and Camera 2 corresponded exactly to both focal planes of the lens L2.

For both the cameras applied, pixel size was $11.0 \ \mu m \times 11.0 \ \mu m$. System of mirrors M was used for fine control of intermode phase shift. The focal length of the lens L2 was $f = 300$ mm. The measured fundamental radius of modes in the plane of Camera 1 was $\sigma_1 = 0.61$ mm, which is in good agreement with a theoretical estimate of $\sigma_1 = 0.62$ mm. The measured radius of modes in the plane of Camera 2 was $\sigma_2 = 0.33$ mm.

Typical results of this investigation are depicted in Figure 6.32 (corresponding to $\Delta\varphi = \arg\lfloor \tilde{C}_{22} \rfloor - \arg\lfloor \tilde{C}_{40} \rfloor \approx 0$) and Figure 6.33 (corresponding to $\Delta\varphi = \arg\lfloor \tilde{C}_{22} \rfloor - \arg\lfloor \tilde{C}_{22} \rfloor \approx \pi$).

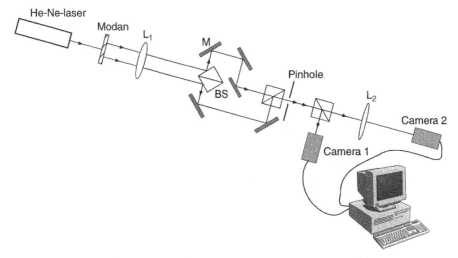

Figure 6.31. Setup for experimental investigation of multimode dispersionless beams. BS = beam splitter, L_1, L_2 = lenses, M = mirrors, Camera 1, Camera 2 = CCD cameras synchronized by computer.

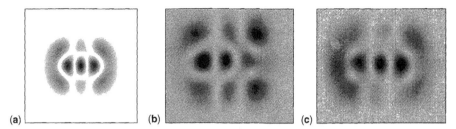

Figure 6.32. The intensity distribution in the cross section of two-mode beam Gauss-Hermite modes (4, 0) and (2, 2) with intermode phase shift value $\Delta\varphi = 0$: (**a**) the result of computer simulation, (**b**), (**c**) intensity distributions measured in different focal planes of the lens L2.

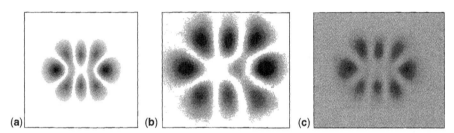

Figure 6.33. The Gauss-Hermite (4, 0) and (2, 2) two-modal beam intensity distribution with intermodal phase shift value $\Delta\varphi = \pi$: (**a**) the result of computer simulation, (**b**), (**c**) intensity distributions measured in different focal planes of the lens L2.

All results of measurement here and further are given without taking account of the scale of picture.

So, the conservation feature of amplitude structure of the multimode dispersionless beam was investigated by intensity distribution measurements in the input and output planes of the Fourier stage. Intensity investigation results showed good stability of the intensity structure of the multimode dispersionless beam during propagation.

Fundamental properties of the multimode dispersionless beams were investigated (self-reproduction, intensity structure stability), and they show good promise for future high-efficient telecommunication systems.

Fundamental properties of multimode dispersionless beams were investigated through computer simulation and optical experiment.

There is a good agreement between theory and experimental results. Using a mode packet with the same propagation constant to set up independent information channels makes it possible to ensure the iterative procedure operation not only through the choice of intermode shifts, $\arg(\tilde{C}_{\mathbf{p}})$, but also through intermode energy distribution, $|\tilde{C}_{\mathbf{p}}|^2$, within a single packet as free parameters, provided a fixed energy of each packet: $\sum_{r_{\mathbf{p}}} |\tilde{C}_{\mathbf{p}}|^2 = B_m$, where m is the information channel number and B is a pregiven nonnegative constant. Note that $r_{\mathbf{p}} = p + l$ for the Gauss-Hermite modes and $r_{\mathbf{p}} = 2p + l$ for the Gauss-Laguerre modes.

Example 6.5. Setting up an Effective Multichannel Communication System in an Ideal Lenslike Medium   Suppose we have to construct a system consisting of N_k independent digital information channels (Fig. 6.34) transferred through an ideal lenslike medium without *mode dispersion* and with *energy efficiency* as high as possible. Let us try to use different multimode dispersionless Gauss-Hermite beams for the representation of different channels. Assume also a "homogeneous" energy distribution between the N_k channels $B_0 = B_1 = \cdots = B_{N_k-1}$, with

$$B_i = \sum_{p=0}^{i} |\tilde{F}_{p(i-p)}|^2, \tag{6.204}$$

and

$$\sum_{i=0}^{N_k-1} B_i = E_0, \tag{6.205}$$

where $\tilde{F}_{p(i-p)}$ are the mode coefficients of the corresponding ith multimode dispersionless beam of Eq. (6.201), and E_0 is the energy of the collimated laser source L. We will not take into account the energy losses connected with absorption and Fresnel reflection. For spatial separation and subsequent time modulation we realize the following decomposition, which is a modification of the one proposed in Ref. [23]:

$$\sqrt{I_0(u,v)} \exp[i\varphi(u,v)] = \sum_{j=0}^{N_k-1} \exp(i2\pi v_j u) \sum_{p=0}^{j} \tilde{F}_{p(j-p)} \psi_{p(j-p)}(u,v) \tag{6.206}$$

where $\sqrt{I_0(u,v)}$ is the amplitude distribution in the cross section of the illuminating collimated beam, $\varphi(u,v)$ is the phase function of the modan M and v_j is the carrier frequency introduced for spatial beam separation (Fig. 6.34).

To find the coefficients $\tilde{F}_{p(j-p)}$ in Eq. (6.206), we can use any recursive optimization procedure minimizing the functional

$$\delta_m = \sum_{j=0}^{N_k-1} \left| \frac{E_0}{N_k} - \sum_{p=0}^{j} |\tilde{F}_{p(j-p)}|^2 \right| \tag{6.207}$$

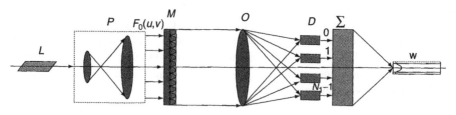

Figure 6.34. General scheme of a multichannel waveguide telecommunication system. L-laser light source, P-collimator, M-modan, O-Fourier stage, D-a set of modulators, W-ideal parabolic index waveguide.

with the coefficient estimate after mth iteration step given by procedure

$$\tilde{F}_{p(j-p)} = \iint\limits_{G} \sqrt{I_0(u, v)} \exp[i\varphi_m(u, v)] \times \psi_{p(j-p)}(u, v) \exp(i2\pi v_j u) \, du \, dv, \quad (6.208)$$

where $\varphi_m(u, v)$ is the DOE's phase distribution after mth iteration.

6.2.8 Design of a DOE Intended to Analyze the Transverse-Mode Composition of Coherent Light Beams

We have already mentioned (subsection 6.2.1) that analyzing the beam transverse-mode composition involves measuring the between-mode energy distribution (i.e., the values of squared modules of the coefficients in Eq. (6.13)) and the intermode phase shifts [the arguments of the coefficients in Eq. (6.13)]. Leaning upon the theoretical treatment discussed earlier, we shall consider the calculation of the complex transmission function of a DOE intended to analyze the transverse-mode composition of coherent light beams. Assume that $[\psi_\mathbf{p}(\mathbf{u})]$ are complex mode amplitudes in the illuminating beam cross section that obey the orthogonality condition (Section 6.1)

$$\int_G \psi_\mathbf{p}(\mathbf{u})\psi_{\mathbf{p}'}^*(\mathbf{u})d^2\mathbf{u} = \delta_{\mathbf{p}'\mathbf{p}}, \quad (6.209)$$

where $\mathbf{u} = (u, v)$ are the 2D Cartesian coordinates at the beam cross section, G is the light aperture, * denotes the complex conjugation, and

$$\delta_{\mathbf{pp}'} = \delta_{pp'}\delta_{ll'} = \begin{cases} 1, & \mathbf{p} = \mathbf{p}' \\ 0, & \mathbf{p} \neq \mathbf{p}' \end{cases} \quad (6.210)$$

is the Kronecker delta. Having expanded the complex amplitude of the beam as a series in terms of modal functions, the problem reduces to the derivation of the complex-valued coefficients $F_\mathbf{p}$ in Eq. (6.13). The squared modules of the coefficients, $|F_\mathbf{p}|^2$, define the between-mode energy distribution in the beam, whereas the coefficient arguments, $\arg(F_\mathbf{p})$, define the beam intermode phase shifts. In Ref. [19], it is proposed that the problem of measuring the mode composition, $[\psi_\mathbf{p}(\mathbf{u})]$, of a field with the complex amplitude given by

$$F(\mathbf{u}) = \sum_\mathbf{p} F_\mathbf{p}\psi_\mathbf{p}(\mathbf{u}), \mathbf{u} \in G, \quad (6.211)$$

should be solved in two stages.

First stage. The modes are optically selected using their orthogonality property, with the between-mode energy distribution being transformed into the light distribution between desired points on the focal plane or an array of corresponding correlation peaks.

Second stage. For every mode, the power $|F_\mathbf{p}|^2$ is measured by conventional photo-receivers found at the correlation-peak centers corresponding to the desired modes.

We shall demonstrate that with a spatial filter of complex transmittance $T(\mathbf{u}) = \psi_\mathbf{p}^*(\mathbf{x})$ found at the Fourier-stage input and illuminated by a beam of transverse complex amplitude distribution $F(\mathbf{u})$, the complex amplitude at the output plane center will be uniquely defined by the coefficient F_p in Eq. (6.211). Actually, multiplying the beam complex amplitude, $F(\mathbf{u})$ by the element complex transmittance, $T(\mathbf{u})$, where $T(\mathbf{u}) = \psi_p^*(\mathbf{u})$ is complex-conjugated with $\psi_p(\mathbf{u})$, yields

$$F(\mathbf{u})\psi_p^*(\mathbf{u}) = \sum_{p'} F_{p'}\psi_{p'}(\mathbf{u})\psi_p^*(\mathbf{u}). \tag{6.212}$$

The Fourier transform taken at the center $\mathbf{x} = \mathbf{0}$ of the output plane of spatial frequencies, $\mathbf{x} = (x, y)$, amounts to the integration of the complex amplitude.

The 2D integration over the aperture G yields

$$F_1(\mathbf{0}) = \int_G F(\mathbf{u})\psi_p^*(\mathbf{u})\, d^2\mathbf{u}. \tag{6.213}$$

Owing to the orthogonality, the modes interact in such a manner that the complex amplitude integration in Eq. (6.213) at point $\mathbf{x} = \mathbf{0}$ results in cancelled background, with the field given by

$$F_p = \int_G F(\mathbf{u})\psi_p^*(\mathbf{u})\, d^2\mathbf{u}. \tag{6.214}$$

The power $|F_p|^2$ of the mode $\psi_p(\mathbf{u})$ will be measured by a conventional point-aperture photo-receiver. By successively changing the filters $\psi_p(\mathbf{u})$, the power distribution can be measured over the entire transverse-mode spectrum. However, in practical tasks one need to measure the transverse-mode power distribution in real time [19]. An adequate "multichannel" implementation must ensure the parallel formation of the coefficients F_p to produce the desired complex amplitude values at a set of points in the plane $\mathbf{x} = (x, y)$. With this approach, measuring the intensity $|F_1(\mathbf{x})|^2$ in the corresponding point of the Fourier plane with a small-aperture detector or a CCD-camera array allows the determination of the required values $|F_p|^2$. In doing so, the aperture G may be interpreted as a sum of two (or more) linked "virtual" apertures, each of which are described by the complex transmission function $T_p(\mathbf{u}) = \xi_p \psi_p^*(\mathbf{u}) \exp(i2\pi \mathbf{v}_p\mathbf{u})$. This is matched to the corresponding mode $\psi_p(\mathbf{x})$ and related to a carrier $\mathbf{v}_p$ introduced in order to separate, by angles, the partial beams that produce the complex amplitudes F_p at the corresponding points (ξ_p are nonnegative weight coefficients, in the simplest case, $\xi_p = 1$).

In this case, the DOE complex transmission function takes the form:

$$T(\mathbf{u}) = \sum_p \xi_p \psi_p^*(\mathbf{u}) \exp(i2\pi \mathbf{v}_p\mathbf{u}). \tag{6.215}$$

With a transverse-mode analyzer inserted into the optical scheme, the modan simultaneously generates a set of mode beams that are separated by angles in the modan plane and separated by coordinate in the Fourier-conjugated plane. At the Fourier plane points, with the coordinates

$$\mathbf{x}_p = f\lambda\mathbf{v}_p, \tag{6.216}$$

assigned to the spatial frequencies [19], the complex amplitude will be proportional to

$$F_{\mathbf{p}} = \int_G F(\mathbf{u}) \xi_{\mathbf{p}} \psi_{\mathbf{p}}^*(\mathbf{u}) \exp(-i 2\pi \mathbf{v_p} \mathbf{u}) \, d^2\mathbf{u}. \tag{6.217}$$

Thus, assuming $\xi_{\mathbf{p}}^{(k)} = \delta_{\mathbf{pk}}$ for the weight coefficient of the **k**th channel in the multi-channel modan amounts to the feasibility, Eqs. (6.212) to (6.217), of generating in each channel a complex amplitude proportional to the mode coefficient $F_{\mathbf{p}}$ whose squared modulus $(\sim |F_{\mathbf{p}}|^2)$ can be measured by a photo-receiver. Measuring the intermode phase shifts, $\arg F_{\mathbf{p}}$, requires the use of a more complex weight coefficient. Consider a multichannel analyzing modan with the coefficients $\zeta_{\mathbf{p}}^{(\mathbf{k_c})}$ and $\zeta_{\mathbf{p}}^{(\mathbf{k_s})}$, corresponding to the channels $\mathbf{k_c}$ and $\mathbf{k_s}$:

$$\left. \begin{aligned} \zeta_{\mathbf{p}}^{(\mathbf{k_c})} &= \delta_{\mathbf{p_1 k_c}} + \delta_{\mathbf{p_2 k_c}} \\ \zeta_{\mathbf{p}}^{(\mathbf{k_s})} &= \delta_{\mathbf{p_1 k_s}} + \exp(i\,\Delta\varphi)\delta_{\mathbf{p_2 k_s}}, \quad \Delta\varphi = \text{const} \end{aligned} \right\} \tag{6.218}$$

When illuminated by a beam with the transverse complex amplitude distribution of $F(\mathbf{u})$, such a modan generates the following complex coefficients

$$\left. \begin{aligned} F^{(\mathbf{k_c})} &= F_{\mathbf{p_1}} + F_{\mathbf{p_2}} \\ F^{(\mathbf{k_s})} &= F_{\mathbf{p_1}} + \exp(i\,\Delta\varphi) F_{\mathbf{p_2}} \end{aligned} \right\} \tag{6.219}$$

in the channels $\mathbf{k_c}$ and $\mathbf{k_s}$, respectively. With a point-aperture photo-receiver that measures the interference of the coefficients $F_{\mathbf{p_1}}$ and $F_{\mathbf{p_2}}$ at points $\lambda f \mathbf{v}^{(\mathbf{k_s})}$ and $\lambda f \mathbf{v}^{(\mathbf{k_c})}$, the phases $\varphi_{\mathbf{p}} = \arg F_{\mathbf{p}}$ of the coefficients $F_{\mathbf{p}}$ cannot be reconstructed directly. In order to reconstruct the phases $\arg F_{\mathbf{p}}$ similar to processing the quadratic interferograms, we need to solve a set of equations. To derive the required equations, we shall recast Eq. (6.218) as follows:

$$\left. \begin{aligned} |F^{(\mathbf{k_c})}|^2 &\cong |F_{\mathbf{p_1}}|^2 + |F_{\mathbf{p_2}}|^2 + 2 \cdot |F_{\mathbf{p_1}}| \cdot |F_{\mathbf{p_2}}| \cos(\varphi_{\mathbf{p_1}} - \varphi_{\mathbf{p_2}}) \\ |F^{(\mathbf{k_s})}|^2 &\cong |F_{\mathbf{p_1}}|^2 + |F_{\mathbf{p_2}}|^2 + 2 \cdot |F_{\mathbf{p_1}}| \cdot |F_{\mathbf{p_2}}| \times \\ &\quad [\cos(\varphi_{\mathbf{p_1}} - \varphi_{\mathbf{p_2}}) \cos \Delta\varphi - \sin(\varphi_{\mathbf{p_1}} - \varphi_{\mathbf{p_2}}) \sin \Delta\varphi] \end{aligned} \right\} \tag{6.220}$$

Let the power $|F_{\mathbf{p_1}}|^2$ be measured in the channel $\mathbf{k_1}$ and the power $|F_{\mathbf{p_2}}|^2$ in the channel $\mathbf{k_2}$, so that

$$|F^{(\mathbf{k_1})}|^2 \approx |F_{\mathbf{p_1}}|^2, \ |F^{(\mathbf{k_2})}|^2 \approx |F_{\mathbf{p_2}}|^2. \tag{6.221}$$

In this case, the powers of the modes $\mathbf{p_1}$ and $\mathbf{p_2}$ can be derived from Eq. (6.214). Next, to reconstruct the phase shift $\varphi_{\mathbf{p_1}} - \varphi_{\mathbf{p_2}}$ we need to find the sine and cosine function of the shift:

$$\cos(\varphi_{\mathbf{p_1}} - \varphi_{\mathbf{p_2}}) = \frac{|F^{(\mathbf{k_c})}|^2 - |F^{(\mathbf{k_1})}|^2 - |F^{(\mathbf{k_2})}|^2}{2[|F^{(\mathbf{k_1})}|^2 \cdot |F^{(\mathbf{k_2})}|^2]^{1/2}} \tag{6.222}$$

$$\sin(\varphi_{\mathbf{p_1}} - \varphi_{\mathbf{p_2}}) = \frac{\cos(\varphi_{\mathbf{p_1}} - \varphi_{\mathbf{p_2}})}{\text{tg}\Delta\varphi} - \frac{|F^{(\mathbf{k_s})}|^2 - |F^{(\mathbf{k_1})}|^2 - |F^{(\mathbf{k_2})}|^2}{2 \sin \Delta\varphi [|F^{(\mathbf{k_1})}|^2 \cdot |F^{(\mathbf{k_2})}|^2]^{1/2}}. \tag{6.223}$$

Then, taking account of the sign of the function $\cos(\varphi_{\mathbf{p}_1} - \varphi_{\mathbf{p}_2})$, the phase shift can be derived from

$$\operatorname{tg}(\varphi_{\mathbf{p}_1} - \varphi_{\mathbf{p}_2}) = \frac{1}{\operatorname{tg}\Delta\varphi} - \frac{1}{\sin\Delta\varphi} \cdot \frac{|F^{(\mathbf{k}_s)}|^2 - |F^{(\mathbf{k}_1)}|^2 - |F^{(\mathbf{k}_2)}|^2}{|F^{(\mathbf{k}_c)}|^2 - |F^{(\mathbf{k}_1)}|^2 - |F^{(\mathbf{k}_2)}|^2}. \qquad (6.224)$$

The corresponding phase values, $\varphi_{\mathbf{p}}$, can be found either from the recurrent relationships $\varphi_{\mathbf{p}_1} - \varphi_{\mathbf{p}_2}$ or by using a reference beam. The calculated complex transmission function of a modan intended to analyze the beam mode composition can be encoded into the pure-phase [19] using a generalized Kirk-Jones method that has also been used for encoding modans intended to generate a desired mode distribution. It can easily be seen that the phase transmission function of a modan intended only to measure the Gaussian-mode power in the beam under study, can be calculated using the iterative procedure of Eqs. (6.196) to (6.199), if the illuminating beam $\sqrt{I_0(\mathbf{u})}$ is a plane beam with uniform intensity distribution $\sqrt{I_0(\mathbf{u})} = \text{const}$.

Knowing the maximal admissible mode number in the beam under analysis, we can write the relation for the complex transmission function of a filter intended for the analysis of the beam amplitude-phase composition:

$$T(\mathbf{u}) = \sum_{n'=1}^{N_{\text{mod}}} \zeta_{n'}\psi_{n'}^*(\mathbf{u})\exp(i2\pi v_{n'}\mathbf{u}) + \sum_{k=1}^{N_{\text{mod}}-1} \overline{\zeta}_k[\psi_k^*(\mathbf{u}) + \psi_{k+1}^*(\mathbf{u})]\exp(i2\pi v_k\mathbf{u})$$

$$+ \sum_{s=1}^{N_{\text{mod}}-1} \tilde{\zeta}_s[\psi_s^*(\mathbf{u})\exp(i\Delta\varphi) + \psi_{s+1}^*(\mathbf{u})] \times \exp(i2\pi v_s\mathbf{u}). \qquad (6.225)$$

Taking into account that certain mode(s) $\psi_k(\mathbf{u})$ can have zero-valued coefficient $F_k = 0$, the relation for the complex transmission function should be changed to

$$T(\mathbf{u}) = \sum_{n'=1}^{N_{\text{mod}}} \zeta_{n'}\psi_{n'}^*(\mathbf{u})\exp(i2\pi v_{n'}\mathbf{u}) + \sum_{k=0,k\neq r-1}^{N_{\text{mod}}-1} \overline{\zeta}_k[\psi_r^*(\mathbf{u}) + \psi_{k+1}^*(\mathbf{u})]\exp(i2\pi v_k\mathbf{u})$$

$$+ \sum_{s=0,s\neq r-1}^{N_{\text{mod}}-1} \tilde{\zeta}_s[\psi_r^*(\mathbf{u})\exp(i\Delta\varphi) + \psi_{s+1}^*(\mathbf{u})\cdot] \times \exp(i2\pi v_s\mathbf{u}), \qquad (6.226)$$

where r is the number of the "reference" mode, which always has nonzero-valued coefficient $F_r \neq 0$ (for most real laser resonators this can be the fundamental mode $\mathbf{n} = (0, 0)$). Now, on the basis of the measurements taken for N_{mod} modes, we can estimate the initial amplitude-phase distribution, except for a constant phase shift of $\arg F_r = \varphi_r$; as

$$F(\mathbf{u}) \cong |F_r|\exp(i \cdot \varphi_r)\psi_r(\mathbf{u}) + \sum_{n'=1,n'\neq r}^{N_{\text{mod}}} |F_{n'}|\psi_{n'}(\mathbf{u})\exp[i(\Delta\overline{\varphi}_{n'} + \varphi_r)], \qquad (6.227)$$

$$\Delta\overline{\varphi}_{n'} = \arg F_{n'} - \varphi_r. \qquad (6.228)$$

Example 6.6. Design and manufacture of a DOE for mode power distribution measurement. The derived complex transmission function in Eq. (6.215) (which is certainly not phase-only in general case) can be reduced to the pure-phase function using well-known encoding techniques based on the introduction of a carrier into the phase function, for example, by generalization of well-known Kirk-Jones method described in Ref. [19]. Thus, the modan for measurement of the mode power distribution for 10 Gaussian-Laguerre modes was calculated by Eq. (6.215) and then manufactured and investigated. The analyzing modan used for studies pursued in this example was designed to detect 10 Gauss-Laguerre(GH)modes, with their numbers chosen below the cut-off condition $2n + |m| \leq 3$: $(n, m) = (0, 0), (1, 0), (0, 1), (1, 1), (0, 2), (0, 3),$ $(0, -1), (1, -1), (0, -2), (0, -3)$. In accordance with the experimental conditions, the design value of the beam-size parameter for these 10 modes was selected as $\sigma = 0.8$ mm. The element was calculated for a wavelength of $\lambda = 632.8$ nm and was intended to work together with a Fourier lens of $f = 452$ mm. The corresponding "correlation points" for each mode, respectively, should develop in the focal plane of this lens at a distance of 1.5 mm from each other (see Fig. 6.36). The element was coded as a grating with 55.5 lines/mm, with a rectangular carrier function "slowly" modulated across the aperture ("synthetic coefficients' method"). The grating was calculated with a resolution of 2048×2048 pixels, with a pixel size of 3.0 μm × 3.0 μm. Figure 6.35 depicts the calculated phase distribution at the aperture of modan. Figure 6.36 depicts the amplitude distribution in the used (zeroth) diffraction order of the element under the suggestion that it was illuminated by a pure (0, 0) Gaussian mode with $\sigma = 0.8$ mm.

The calculated phase would have to be transferred into a corresponding surface depth, taking into consideration the intended transmission mode of the element and the refractive index of the resist. In the next step, this 2D "continuous" surface pixel map should be copied out into a corresponding electron dose map, which in turn could have been written subsequently by the e-beam lithograph. However, thermal load resulting from such a one-shot-per-pixel procedure negatively influences the final resist and surface quality. As a consequence, the "continuous" surface pixel map was approximated by a staircase structure with 16 permitted levels in depth (=15 steps of equal height in the staircase). Each of these 15 steps had to be generated by an

Figure 6.35. Calculated phase distribution at the aperture of the modan (white color corresponds to the phase 2π and black color to the phase 0).

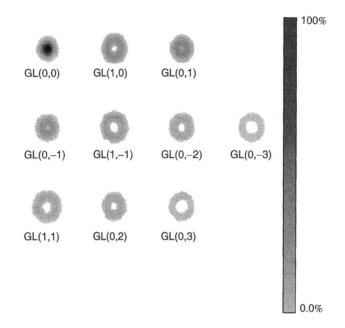

Figure 6.36. Computer-simulated detection of the (0, 0) mode by the designed DOE.

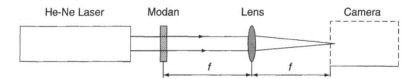

Figure 6.37. Optical setup for modan investigation.

individual "etching" process. Therefore, 15 single binary masks had to be generated (as data fields) by software, starting from the "continuous" surface pixel map. At the first stage of manufacturing, a substrate made of quartz glass, and covered with a thin film of PMMA (thickness nearly 2.5 μm), was implanted with a spatially varying dose of electrons. The 15 dose levels, each corresponding to one of the future new surface levels were realized through a 15-times repeated, binary e-beam writing process, using a commercial ZBA 23H system. After finishing the development procedure of the PMMA film, the profile depth over all 15 steps should be 1200 nm.

The manufactured modan under analysis had to demonstrate its performance in a series of optical experiments. For this purpose, the setup schematically shown in Figure 6.37 was used. The 10-channel modan ($\sigma = 0.8$ mm) was illuminated by the Gaussian beam with $\sigma = 0.525$ mm (Figs. 6.38, 6.39). The decomposition of the Gaussian distribution with $\sigma = 0.525$ mm into the basis of the Gaussian-Laguerre modes with $\sigma = 0.8$ mm gives two nonzero values of the (0, 0)-mode coefficient and (1, 0)-mode coefficient (nearly 25 percent of (0, 0)-mode coefficient).

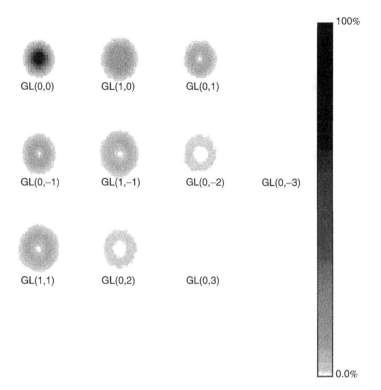

Figure 6.38. Computer-simulated illumination of modan by the $(0, 0)$ mode with $\sigma = 0.525$ mm.

Note that there is good agreement between the results of computational and physical experiments. Note also, a spurious intensity peak in the central diffractive order (at the place of $(1, -1)$ mode correlation peak), which is connected with technological problem—the calculated surface profile-was not perfectly achieved.

Thus, the remarkable properties of the Gaussian modes make it possible to employ the aforementioned approaches that were developed to design modans capable of generating the desired mode distribution and also to design modans for analysis of the transverse-mode composition of light. The computer-simulated results of measuring the Gauss-Hermite mode power in the illuminating beam are shown in Figure 6.22.

6.2.9 The Results of the DOE-Aided Experimental Studies of Fundamental Properties of the Gaussian Modes

The first work on computer-synthesized optical elements intended to analyze and generate a transverse-mode composition of light was published in 1982 [50]. At that time, DOEs matched to transverse modes represented computer-synthesized binary-amplitude (later, binary-phase) irregular gratings. In Ref. [51] published in 1983, a problem formulation similar to that in Ref. [50] was proposed. Before the advent of the DOEs, there was an attempt to attack the problem using complex diaphragms with gas cells, reproducing mode zeros in shape [52]. However, the images those diaphragms

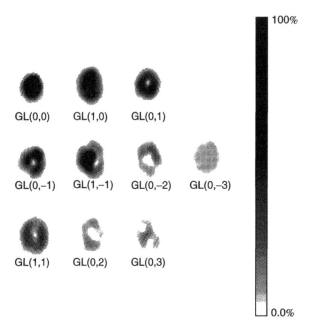

Figure 6.39. Result of measurement of intensity in the output plane of modan illuminated by the (0, 0) mode with $\sigma = 0.525$ mm.

were producing contained a lot of spurious modes. Later, phase modans designed by introducing a carrier into the element phase were fabricated [19]. In Ref. [53] the results of mode excitation in a graded-index optical fiber using a DOE are reported. The results of the experimental studies of the phase modans generating the Gaussian modes and the fundamental properties of the generated modes are discussed in Refs. [19,27–30,33–35].

6.2.9.1 Experimental Studies of the Phase Gauss-Hermite Modans
To conduct the experimental studies of the properties of the elements designed by the iterative procedures of Eqs. (6.154), (6.155) with the operators in Eqs. (6.160) and (6.164), a modan generating the Gauss-Hermite mode (1, 0) was fabricated and tested [27–30]. An interesting peculiarity of the Gauss-Hermite modes is that by turning the modan by 90 degrees the first and second numbers of the mode under formation are mutually changed. Thus, using a single kit of technological binary masks we can synthesize two Gauss-Hermite modans (1, 0) and generate two Gauss-Hermite modes–(1, 0) and (0, 1)–with the same fundamental mode radius, which was demonstrated in Ref. [29]. The element was designed as an addition to a lens. On the basis of specific conditions of the physical experiment, the physical parameters were as follows: the illuminating beam wavelength $\lambda = 0.6328$ μm, the element's aperture radius $a = 3.072$ mm, the illuminating Gaussian beam radius $\sigma_{00} = 0.835$ mm, the outer radius of the working domain $R_1 = 2$ mm, the outer radius of the auxiliary domain $R_2 = 10$ mm, focal length of the lens $f = 452$ mm, the number of pixels of the element's phase function $N = 2048 \times 2048$, and the number of iterations [27] $n = 10$. Figure 6.40 depicts the calculated phase function distribution over the modan aperture reduced to the interval $[0,2\pi]$. The fast Fourier transform procedure was used to computer-simulate

Figure 6.40. The phase function of the fabricated modan (central part) (white color corresponds to the phase 2π and black color corresponds to the phase 0).

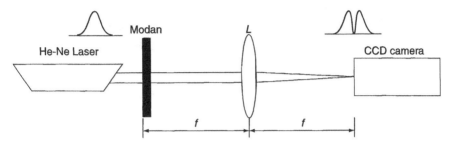

Figure 6.41. Experimental optical setup for mode intensity measurement.

the operation of the designed element. The simulation produced the following quality criteria: energy efficiency $E = 0.455$, specific power $\zeta = 0.88$.

For the aforementioned set of parameters, the estimate of the modan energy efficiency in Eq. (6.176) calculated using the Kirk-Jones method was $E_K = 0.16$. The designed modan was technologically implemented by a uniform 16-level etching of the photoresist PMMA coated on a quartz glass at the Applied Physics Institute of the Friedrich Schiller University, Jena, Germany. The ability of the fabricated element to generate a desired quasi-mode distribution was studied on a unit schematically shown in Figure 6.41. The element was illuminated by a light beam from laser HNA-180 (by "Carl-Zeiss Jena", Germany). The SPIRICON camera was used to study the intensity distribution generated behind the focal plane of the converging lens L and to measure the energy efficiency of the element. To measure the energy efficiency, the auxiliary domain in the focal plane of the converging lens was masked by an opaque screen with a pinhole at the center. The experimental energy efficiency was found to be $E = 0.377$, being somewhat less than the computer-simulated energy efficiency $E = 0.455$. This difference may be assigned to both errors in the DOE fabrication and quantization and discretization errors.

Shown in Figure 6.42 is the experimentally measured intensity of the generated quasi-modal beam.

The ability of the generated quasi-mode beam to retain a structure similar to that of the Gauss–Hermite mode (1, 0) while propagating through a Fourier stage was studied in the course of the experiment schematically shown in Figure 6.43.

The auxiliary domain in the focal plane of the converging lens $L1$ was masked with an opaque screen with the pinhole at the center. The pinhole radius was chosen to be somewhat less than the outer radius of the working domain — 1.7 mm. The beam was formed at the Fourier-stage input with a lens $L2$, thus making it possible to estimate the mode properties by estimating changes in the beam structure after passing the Fourier

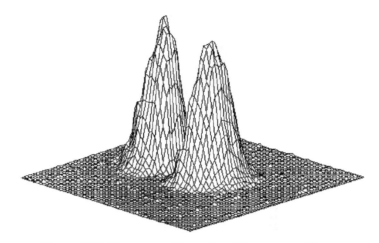

Figure 6.42. The measured intensity of the generated beam.

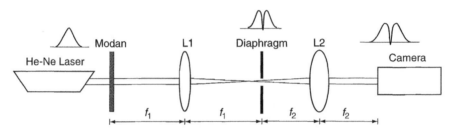

Figure 6.43. Experimental optical setup for intensity structure stability investigation.

stage. The energy efficiency was found to be $E = 0.362$, which is in good agreement with the previous results. Figure 6.44 depicts the 2D intensity distribution measured in the focal plane of lens $L2$.

We can note that the stability of the produced quasi-mode beam to the Fourier transform is fairly good. The mode structure was also studied at a plane found at a distance $z = 240$ mm from the focal plane of lens $L2$. Figure 6.45 depicts the intensity distribution measured in this plane.

The comparison of patterns in Figures 6.44 and 6.45 visually confirms the stability of the generated quasi-mode beam as it propagates in free space. The phase structure of the generated distribution was studied using an optical experimental unit schematically shown in Figure 6.46, with the resulting pattern shown in Figure 6.47.

A shift between the interference fringes suggests that the phase difference on the fragments of the quasi-mode distribution amounts to a value close to π rad. This fact testifies in favor of the ability of the fabricated modan to generate a distribution of desired phase structure. The phase structure of a quasi-mode distribution after passing through a Fourier stage was studied using an optical experimental setup schematically shown in Figure 6.48. Shown in Figure 6.49 is the experimental intensity distribution measured using the setup in Figure 6.48. The experimental results show that the phase structure of the generated beam is stable to the optical analog of the Fourier transform.

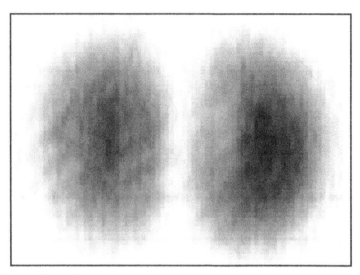

Figure 6.44. The beam intensity after passing through the Fourier stage.

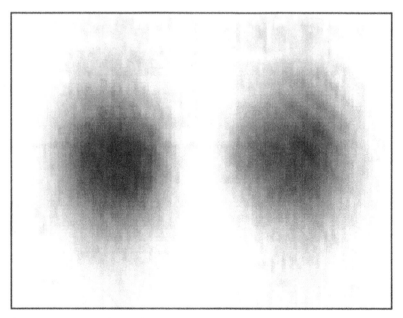

Figure 6.45. The intensity distribution of the beam is measured in a plane found at a distance $z = 240$ mm.

Physical experimental studies of the phase structure were conducted in parallel with numerically simulated reconstruction of the beam phase in the focal plane of the first Fourier lens: the phase distribution was reconstructed from the measured intensity distribution at the input and output planes of the Fourier lens $L2$ during 30 iteration steps of the procedure discussed in Ref. [47]. The experimental setup for measuring two distributions is shown in Figure 6.43. After 30 iterations, the root-mean-square

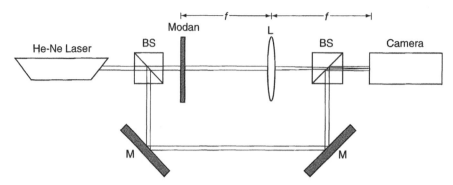

Figure 6.46. Experimental optical setup for phase structure investigation.

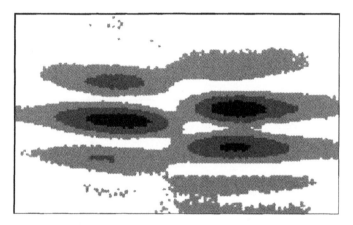

Figure 6.47. Intensity distribution measured in the course of experiment schematically shown in Figure 6.46.

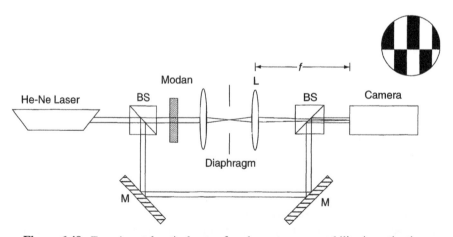

Figure 6.48. Experimental optical setup for phase structure stability investigation.

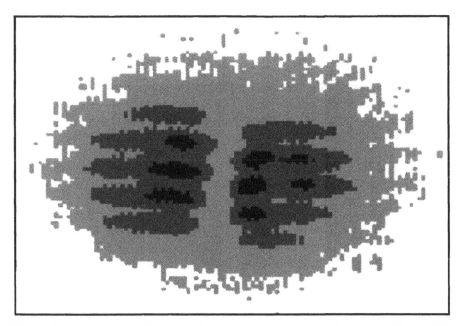

Figure 6.49. Experimental intensity distribution measured using the setup in Figure 6.48.

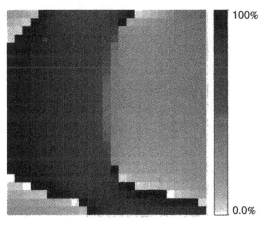

Figure 6.50. Iteratively reconstructed phase of the Gauss-Hermite mode (0, 1) (white color corresponds to the phase π and black color corresponds to the phase 0).

deviation of the experimental amplitude distribution from its last-iteration estimate was less than 17 percent. The reconstructed phase distribution in the Fourier lens input plane is shown in Figure 6.50. The phase shift between the mode halves is about 0.85π, which is in good agreement with the results of interferometry and a theoretical estimation of π. The stability of the amplitude-phase structure of the Gauss-Hermite modes to the Fourier transform allows the iterative procedure [47] based on taking the direct and inverse Fourier transform to be used for verifying the results of interferometric studies of the phase structure of the generated mode beam (Figures 6.47, 6.49, and 6.50). Thus, full agreement between the experimental and computer-simulated results corroborates the potential of the approach taken in Refs. [27,28] for solving the problem of high effective generation of unimode beams.

6.2.9.2 Experimental Studies of the Phase Gauss-Laguerre Modans

The results of the experimental studies of the Gauss-Laguerre modans designed using a generalized Kirk-Jones method [19] are discussed in Ref. [33]. Figure 6.51 shows the interferograms of the generated Gauss-Laguerre mode beams, (1, 0) and (2, 0) [33]. Notice a phase change by π at places where the modal function is negative. Shown in Figure 6.52 is the oscillogram of a signal taken from a CCD array while studying the intensity distribution of the Gauss-Laguerre mode (2, 0) [33]. Owing to radial symmetry at $l = 0$, it will suffice to use a single cross section passing through the symmetry center. The symmetry of the curve in Figure 6.52 is somewhat disturbed because of noise. On the whole, the result in Figure 6.52 shows good agreement between the theory and experiment. The root-mean-square deviation is about 12 percent. In Ref. [34], the interferometric studies of the phase structure [33] were

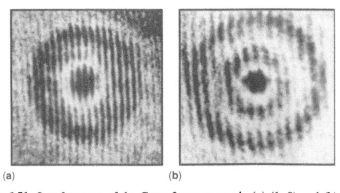

(a)   (b)

Figure 6.51. Interferogram of the Gauss-Laguerre mode (**a**) (1, 0) and (**b**) (2, 0).

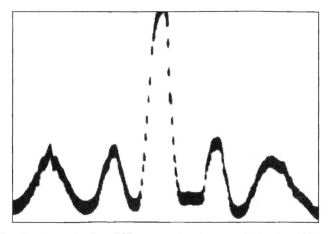

Figure 6.52. Oscillogram of the CCD-array signal was derived while measuring the Gauss-Laguerre mode (2, 0).

Figure 6.53. The phase of the Gauss-Laguerre mode (2, 0) was iteratively reconstructed from two intensity measurements (white color corresponds to the phase 2π and black color corresponds to the phase 0).

supplemented by a computer-simulated beam phase reconstruction [47] in the focal plane of the first Fourier lens. Here, the phase distribution was reconstructed from the results of measuring the intensity distribution at the input and output planes of the Fourier lens. The reconstructed phase distribution at the input plane of the Fourier lens is shown in Figure 6.53.

6.2.10   Experimental Studies of the Feasibility of Multiplexing Optical Communication Channels Using Selective Gauss-Hermite Mode Excitation

In Refs. [29,34] the experimental results concerned with building and studying a prototype of the two-channel communication line, with two information channels independently transmitted using the Gauss-Hermite modes (1, 0) and (0, 1) are discussed. These were generated by unimode modans designed using the iterative procedure in Eqs. (6.154) and (6.155) with the operators in Eqs. (6.160) and (6.164). The physical parameters of the experimental setup shown in Figure 6.54 were as follows: $f_1 = 452$ mm, $f_2 = 840$ mm, $f_3 = 300$ mm, the diameter of the circular aperture = 2.7 mm, the beam-mode parameter $\sigma_{10} = \sigma_{01} = 0.58$ mm in the plane of the analyzing Modan 3 was chosen in relation with the size of the effective diffraction domain 4.096 mm × 4.096 mm, and the CCD-camera pixel size = 13 µm. The correlation peaks corresponding to the Gauss-Hermite modes (1, 0) and (0, 1) were spatially separated by introducing into the phase function of Modan 3 a spatial carrier that ensured a 30-mm between-peak distance in the focal plane of lens $L3$. It should be mentioned that lens $L2$ in this configuration serves as a "model" of a lenslike medium in which the generated modes are propagated. On the other hand, in the output plane of lens $L2$ the beam produces the pattern of a far-field diffraction taking place, for example, while

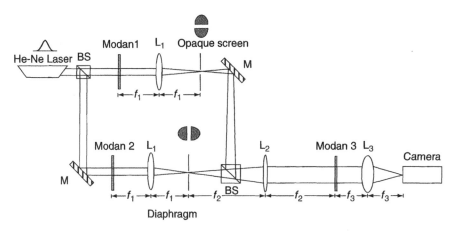

Figure 6.54. The experimental optical setup for studying DOE-aided mode selection: BS is a beam splitter, M is a mirror, $L1$, $L2$, and $L3$ are the lenses.

implementing optical communication in free space. Lenslike media and lens waveguides are covered comprehensively in Ref. [15]. The analyzing Modan 3, matched to the modes (1, 0) and (0, 1) was designed using the Kirk-Jones method [19] and fabricated by the technology analogous to that used for fabricating mode-generating modans [27–29]. The complex transmission function of Modan 3 was brought to pure-phase by introducing a rectangular impulse carrier of frequency 41.7 lines/mm into the DOE phase.

At the first stage, the operation of the analyzing Modan 3 illuminated by a unimode Gauss-Hermite beam (1, 0) or (0, 1) of radius $\sigma_{10} = 0.58$ mm was computer-simulated. The amplitude-phase distribution in the focal plane of the Fourier lens $L3$ was estimated using the fast Fourier transform. The calculated amplitude, phase and intensity distributions in the focal plane of the Fourier lens $L3$ are shown in Figure 6.55. Numerical simulation was conducted disregarding the quantized character of the DOE phase. Note that in Figure 6.55b, d there is a correlation peak produced by the illuminating mode, whereas in Figures 6.55a, c the peak is not found, corresponding to the absence of the (0, 1) mode under detection. What is seen in Figure 6.55 are four spurious spots around the point corresponding to the correlation peak position. The distance between the points corresponding to the correlation peak and the spurious spot centers is 150 μm.

The approximate ratio of the maximum intensity of the correlation peak found if the detected mode is present and maximum intensities of the spurious peak if the detected mode is absent at the center was 3:1. Because of microlithography technological requirements, the fabricated element had 15 phase quantization levels, which theoretically corresponded to 1200 nm [29,30]. However, because of the problems in controlling the etching depth, the maximum etching depth was only 70 percent of the calculated value of 1200 nm. Because of this reason, the fast Fourier transform was used to simulate operation of an element with a maximum 70 percent etching depth illuminated by a unimode beam (1, 0) or (0, 1) and a beam composed of the two modes with equal energies. The computer-simulated intensity distributions are shown in Figure 6.56.

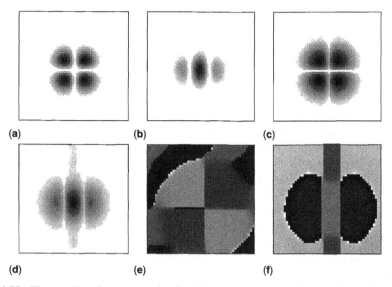

Figure 6.55. The results of computer-simulated input beam analysis using the designed DOE (without regard for quantization): estimated distributions of (**a**), (**b**) intensity, (**c**), (**d**) amplitude, and (**e**), (**f**) phase in the vicinities of points of generation of correlation peaks, corresponding to the Gauss-Hermite modes (0, 1) and (1, 0).

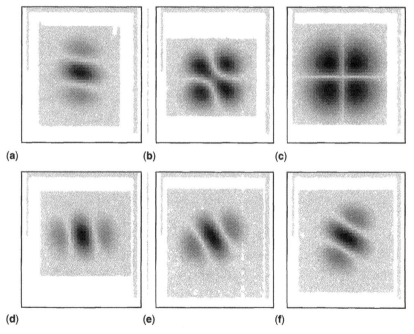

Figure 6.56. Computer-simulated results of analyzing the input beam using the designed DOE: the calculated intensity distributions in the vicinity of correlation peaks corresponding to the Gauss-Hermite modes (0, 1) and (1, 0) when the modan is illuminated by (**a**), (**b**) a Gauss-Hermite mode beam (0, 1), (**c**), (**d**) a Gauss-Hermite beam (1, 0) and (**e**), (**f**) by a combination of the two beams. In the computer simulation, we took into consideration that the element phase was quantized into 16 levels and the relief depth was only 70 percent of the calculated depth.

In Figures 6.56a, b, c, and d, the element is illuminated by a unimode Gauss-Hermite beam and in Figures 6.56e, f it is illuminated by a superposition of two equal-energy modes.

Finally, Figure 6.57 shows the experimental results produced on the experimental setup in Figure 6.54, with the set of physical parameters corresponding to those used in the computer simulation in Figure 6.56.

Note that there is good agreement between the experimental and computer-simulated results for the element with a 70 percent microrelief depth. Considering the physical size of the CCD-camera cell and the simulation results, we can infer that there is a qualitative correspondence between the experimental distributions in the focal plane of lens L3 and the simulated results, notwithstanding minor differences in correlation peak shapes. Thus, in Ref. [29] it has been demonstrated by computer-simulation and experiments that it is feasible to use the transverse laser light modes to carry information over independent channels of a telecommunication system discussed in Ref. [19]. It has also been shown that for this purpose it is appropriate to employ modans designed using the iterative procedure discussed in Ref. [27] and a synthetic-elements method [39] and fabricated by e-beam lithography. Similar results for the Gauss-Laguerre modes are considered in Ref. [33]. The transverse-mode composition of a reference multimode beam was measured using a spatial filter designed by the Kirk-Jones method [19], with the complex transmission function represented by a superposition of desired Gauss-Laguerre modes. A CCD array was placed in the output

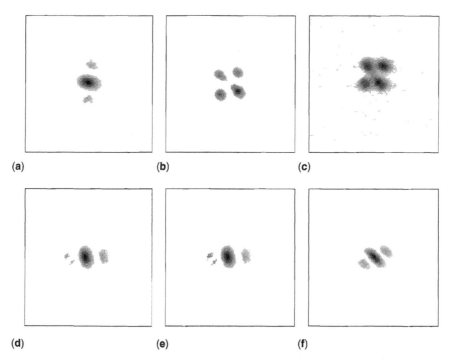

(a)   (b)   (c)

(d)   (e)   (f)

Figure 6.57. Measured intensity in the vicinity of the correlation peak centers for the Gauss-Hermite modes (0, 1) and (1, 0) when the modan was illuminated by (**a**), (**b**) the Gauss-Hermite beam (0, 1), (**c**), (**d**) the Gauss-Hermite beam (1, 0), and (**e**), (**f**) a combination of the two beams.

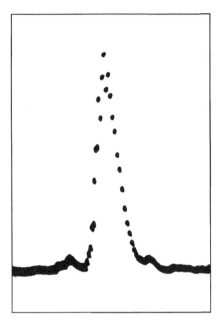

Figure 6.58. Oscillogram of the CCD-array signal derived while detecting the DOE-excited Gauss-Laguerre mode (1, 0).

plane at points where the correlation peaks of the modes measured were to be found. In accordance with Eq. (6.209), the power of the mode measured is equal to the light intensity at the center of the corresponding diffraction order up to a constant factor. Figure 6.58 shows the oscillogram of the CCD-array signal derived from measurements of the intensity distribution in the first diffraction order of the modan matched to the Gauss-Laguerre mode (1, 0) at the moment the mode is detected. Note that the difference between the measured and theoretical coefficients was not more than 5 percent of the maximum value [33].

6.2.11 Designing DOEs Matched to the Modes of Graded-Index Fibers with Nonparabolic Profile

Note that modern technologies for manufacturing graded-index optical fibers do not necessarily ensure the desired profile with high accuracy [18]. Figure 6.59 depicts the typical refractive index distribution across the industrially manufactured optical fiber.

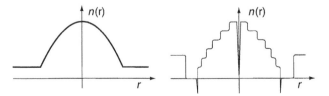

Figure 6.59. (Left) Ideal parabolic profile, (right) typical profile of industrially manufactured quartz fiber.

The central refractive index drop schematically shown in Figure 6.59 results from the technology of paraphase deposition used in optical fiber production [18].

Apart from technological deviations from the desired parabolic profile, there are waveguides intentionally manufactured with the other-than-parabolic profile [18]. Because of this, it seems appropriate to pose the problem of designing DOEs matched to nonparabolic gradient fibers. In Ref. [18], it has been demonstrated that the scalar diffraction theory disregarding polarization effects is fairly suitable for describing the light propagation in weakly directing gradient fibers. They also seek the eigenfunctions of the light-propagation operator in graded-index fibers with various desired profile shapes [18]. If there are minor deviations of the real profile from the desired one, the perturbation theory may be used. The theory of first-order perturbations was employed to find the propagation constants and solutions of the scalar wave equation. In Ref. [18], it has been shown that for gradient fibers with radially symmetric perturbed refractive index the first-order approximations of the propagation constant and mode distributions are given by

$$\beta_{\mathbf{p}}'^2 = \beta_{\mathbf{p}}^2 + k^2 \int_0^\infty \psi_{\mathbf{p}}^2(r)\delta n^2(r) r \, dr, \tag{6.229}$$

$$\psi_{\mathbf{p}}'(r) = \psi_{\mathbf{p}}(r) + \sum_{\substack{k \\ (p \neq k)}} \frac{\psi_{\mathbf{p}}(r) \int_0^\infty \psi_{\mathbf{p}}(r)\psi_{kl}(r)\delta n^2(r) r \, dr}{(\beta_{\mathbf{p}}^2 - \beta_{kl}^2)}, \tag{6.230}$$

where $\beta_{\mathbf{p}}'$ and $\psi_{\mathbf{p}}'(r)$ are the propagation constants and the field of the mode $p = (p, l)$ for the perturbed profile, whereas β_{pl} and ψ_{pl} are the corresponding magnitudes for the nonperturbed profile $n(r)$, $\delta n^2(r)$ is the profile perturbation. Thus, it becomes feasible to calculate the complex fields of modes in gradient-index fibers with nonideal profile and design DOEs matched to such modes. However, one should bear in mind that the modes in nonparabolic graded-index fibers are devoid of the property of self-reproduction in space, as distinct from the Gaussian modes. Because of this reason, the translation of the field at the end of such a fiber to the plane of a modan matched to a desired mode distribution should be carried out using the rigorous calculation of the Kirchhoff-Fresnel integral [9]. But for this factor, all the approaches developed previously to design DOEs matched to the Gaussian modes may easily be applied to design DOEs matched to real graded-index, nonparaxial fibers. A DOE that generates a desired mode in the nonparabolic fiber can be designed, both by introducing a carrier into the element's phase, like in Ref. [19], and through iterative procedures similar to those discussed in Ref. [27]. If the relation of phase intermode delays in a generated multimode fiber is of no importance, the desired DOE can be designed iteratively, on the basis of the orthogonality of a set of mode functions in Eq. (6.4), similar to the procedure of Eqs. (6.185) to (6.187) constructed to generate an array of Gaussian modes. However, it should be noted that, for the non-Gaussian modes, the decomposition analogous to Eq. (6.196) needs to be conducted using the Kirchhoff-Fresnel integral to derive the complex amplitude [9]. Note also that the diffraction analysis is based on solving (in a variety of ways) the wave equation that is able to adequately describe the light propagation (in particular, diffraction) only for one of polarization states, TE or TM. This is because the electromagnetic wave can be uniquely specified through its two longitudinal components—the electric (TE-wave) and the magnetic

(TM-wave) components. Constructing and solving the wave equation for a single longitudinal component is justified for a homogeneous medium or a medium with cylindrical inhomogeneities. Otherwise, modes with different polarization appear inevitably. In this situation, solving the wave equation will yield a distorted mode composition, with nonexistent higher-order modes being present and the real but differently polarized modes being absent. Hence, the diffraction theory ceases to be satisfactory when applied for calculating the light propagation in a waveguide with cylindrical inhomogeneities, greater than the wavelength quarter in size. Thus, when a gradient multimode optical fiber can be described in terms of the scalar diffraction theory, the waveguide modes can be generated and selected using DOEs designed by the methods described in Sections 6.2.3. to 6.2.6.

6.3 APPLICATION OF DOEs IN SYSTEMS FOR ACQUISITION, TRANSMISSION, AND STORAGE OF DATA

Possessing unique qualitative capabilities [23], as compared with conventional optical elements, computer-synthesized optical elements have become widely used in tackling various problems, having to do with building systems for acquisition, transmission, and storage of data. These include optical telecommunication systems [19], parallel signal-processing systems, neural optical networks [54–56], development of coherent optics computers [57,58], highly sensitive optic fiber sensors [59,60], reading heads for CD players [61], and others. In this section, we shall look into more details about the use of DOEs for solving some of these problems. Design and implementation using diffractive optical techniques of optical spatial filters widely used in optical information systems is addressed in Chapter 10 of this book and in Refs. [19,57,58].

6.3.1 Enhancement of Data-Carrying Abilities of Optical Communication Lines

An increase in the data-carrying abilities of modern communication systems is a most important scientific and technical challenge, requiring further studies of the physical (including optical) effects involved. One of most attractive approaches for solving the problem is looking into the feasibility of increasing the number of information channels without setting up extra communication lines. With a coherent light beam used as the data carrier and a linear waveguide medium (e.g., optical waveguide) used as a communication line, the simultaneous use of different laser modes (both longitudinal and transverse) to implement separate channels holds promise. In modern telecommunication systems, different information channels have often been implemented by different longitudinal modes, that is, by different wavelengths of the light propagated in a waveguide [62–64]. Such systems called wavelength division multiplexing (WDM) systems use optical filters separating different wavelengths as demultiplexers (Fig. 6.60). Latest advances in the development of dielectric bandwidth filters with a transmission bandwidth of $\Delta\lambda < 1$ nm and suitable for mass production have already made a considerable degree of channel multiplexing in such systems feasible.

In Ref. [64] the implementation of a two-channel, fiber-optic communication line in which two independent channels of wavelength 1.3 μm and 1.55 μm are transmitted over a unimode fiber has been discussed. A holographic diffraction grating was used to select the channels at the fiber output. To these ends, apart from the diffraction grating,

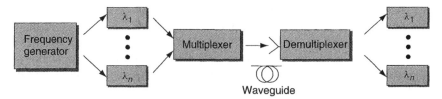

Figure 6.60. Block diagram of a telecommunication WDM system.

one can utilize spectral diffractive elements matched to several wavelengths [65,66]. A system for direct image transmission over the optical fiber developed in Ref. [64] uses the decomposition of white light into spectral components. In Ref. [64], the components are selected using a segmented holographic optical element, each segment being matched to a definite spectrum region. It would also be of interest to study transverse modes as independent carriers of information channels instead of, or probably, in combination with the longitudinal modes. We have already defined the transverse modes as light beams whose cross section complex amplitude distribution is described by the eigenfunctions of the light-propagation operator in a corresponding medium. A fundamental property of the transverse modes to conserve their structure and mutual orthogonality as they propagate in a medium may form a basis for implementing communication systems with mode channel multiplexing. An interest in the transverse modes as the carriers of independent channels for data transmission is due first to the ever-enhanced quality of manufactured multimode fibers [Ref. 67] and, second to the development of techniques for synthesizing high-quality DOEs — modans [19,27–30] capable of effectively generating and selecting the transverse laser modes (see also Section 6.2 of this book). The general theory for building telecommunication systems with transverse-mode-based channel multiplexing is comprehensively covered in Ref. [19]. Note that the selective excitation of transverse modes in an optical fiber will increase the data-carrying ability of communication lines not only owing to the parallel transmission of several channels over a single fiber but also owing to solving the widened impulse problem caused by the between-mode dispersion (Refs. [18–20] and Section 6.2.7). Figure 6.61 presents one of the proposed engineering implementations of fiber-optic communication line based on selectively exciting transverse modes [19]. The spatial filter MA is an array of electro-optical modulators illuminated by a plane coherent wave $F_0(\mathbf{u})$, with time-modulated signals (S_i) directly fed to the array. The Fourier lens O_1 transforms a set of point sources into a set of plane waves illuminating the modan M_1.

The modan M_1 is a spatial filter matched to a number of modes coded using various spatial frequencies (Ref. [19] and Section 6.2). The values of the spatial carrier frequencies of modan M_1 are matched to the coordinates of the modulator cells and their distances to the objective O_1. At the modan M_1, the output is found as a superposition of modes, with their energies proportional to the intensity of light passing through the corresponding cells of the modulator MA. The microobjective O_2 serves to bring the radius of the generated modes to that of the principal mode of an "ideal" optical fiber W. A multimode beam entering into the fiber is analyzed at the output of the fiber-optic line. The microobjective O_3 couples the optic-fiber principal mode radius with the radius of modes found in the plane of the modan M_2. The modan M_2 is matched to conjugated modes coded using different carrier frequencies. The light

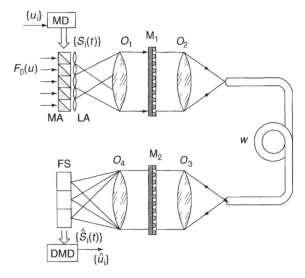

Figure 6.61. Implementation of a fiber-optic-communication line based on mode selection; $F_0(u)$ the illuminating beams; $\{u_i\}$ — the input signal vector; $\{S_i(t)\}$ = the time-modulated signal-vector; MD = the electric signal modulator; MA the array of acousto-optical or electro-optical modulators; LA = a microlens array; O_1, O_2, O_3, O_4 = objectives; M_1, M_2 = multimodal modans; FS = a photo-receiver matrix; DMD = an electric signal demodulator; and $[\hat{S}_i(t)]$ = the time-modulated electric signal vector.

intensity in different cells of the photo-receiver FS are proportional to the power of the corresponding modes. Note that because of the different phase velocities of different modes, their powers are to be measured with time delays proportional to the propagation constants. To compensate for different mode delay and attenuation values, it is expedient to introduce compensating phase additions in the channels of the modan M_2, given by

$$\alpha^{(\mathbf{p})} = (\beta_{\max} - \beta_{\mathbf{p}})z, \qquad (6.231)$$

where $\beta_{\mathbf{p}}$ is the propagation constant for the mode with index $\mathbf{p}$,

$$\beta_{\max} = \max_{\mathbf{p}} \beta_{\mathbf{p}}, \qquad (6.232)$$

and z is the optical fiber length. The values of the power coefficients in the channels are chosen as follows;

$$\mathrm{P}^{(\mathbf{p})} = \frac{1}{\rho_{\mathbf{p}}}, \qquad (6.233)$$

where $\rho_{\mathbf{p}}$ are various values of mode attenuation. To perform filtration, the filtration coefficients are chosen in the form

$$\mathrm{P}^{(\mathbf{p})} = \frac{1}{\rho_{\mathbf{p}}} \cdot \frac{1}{1 + \dfrac{S_{\mathbf{p}}}{N_{\mathbf{p}}}}, \qquad (6.234)$$

where $S_\mathbf{p}$ is the mathematical expectation of the power of a signal corresponding to the input mode $\mathbf{p}$, and $N_\mathbf{p}$ is the mathematical expectation of noise in the channel for the mode $\mathbf{p}$. Note that this reasoning applies to the case of the linear propagation of the light beam in a waveguide (optical fiber). At present, the potential of nonlinear optical effects for increasing the data-carrying ability of fiber-optic communication lines arouses considerable interest [68,69]. In Ref. [70], they look into the possibility of selectively exciting transverse modes in a graded-index, multimode fiber with nonlinear effects for getting the enhanced data-carrying ability. The results of computer-simulated operation of such communication channel are also given in Ref. [70]. Generating a desired mode composition may be useful for getting a higher-quality optical communication line not only in a fiber but also in free space. In Ref. [71], they discuss the result of comparative studies of the use of the Gaussian mode (0, 0) and the Bessel mode (0, 0), being a free-space mode [23], for optical data transmission in free space. Note also that, measuring beam mode composition with a modan treated in Section 6.2.8. of this book can be used not only for implementing a multichannel optical communication system (Fig. 6.61) but also for examining the mode composition of the output laser light. In Refs. [72,73], the computer-simulated reconstruction of the complex transverse structure of the laser under study from the results of measuring the intensity in the far- and near-field diffraction are described. However, as distinct from the technique discussed in Section 6.2.8, such an approach does not allow the mode composition to be analyzed in real time.

6.3.2   Fiber-Optic Sensors

Fiber-optic sensors of microdisplacement, based on measuring the total energy of the light beam having passed through a deformed optical fiber have gained wide popularity [74,75]. However, with this approach the aggregate energy of all output modes is measured. Because in this case the summarized energy modes are averaged, the total energy changes fairly slowly as compared with changes in the energy of separate modes. An alternative approach taken in Refs. [19,59] involves selectively exciting modes in an optical fiber and measuring the mode energy at the output of the deformed fiber. In Refs. [76,77], it has been shown that the changes in power are much more sensitive to fiber deformations for a separate mode than for the entire beam. This idea has formed the basis for the development of a highly sensitive fiber-optic displacement sensor. The major challenge to be addressed while solving this task is to implement the selective excitation of desired modes in an optical fiber and to measure their selective output power. This problem can be effectively tackled by the use of modans, which we designed and studied in Section 6.2. Consider a sensor that uses an optical fiber with directed modes with the numbers $\mathbf{p} = (p, l)$ defined in the scalar approximation by the complex amplitudes $\{\psi_\mathbf{p}(\mathbf{x})\}$. The Cartesian coordinates $\mathbf{x} = (x, y)$ are introduced in the fiber cross section. The mode orthogonality condition in Eq. (6.4) is satisfied on the domain $G(\rho_0 \equiv 1)$. Exciting an optical fiber implies illuminating by a beam with the complex amplitude

$$F(\mathbf{x}) = \sum_\mathbf{p} F_\mathbf{p} \psi_\mathbf{p}(\mathbf{x}) \tag{6.235}$$

with the coefficients $\{F_\mathbf{p}\}$. To describe the light-beam propagation in an optical fiber, we shall make use of the linear operator $\hat{T}$ acting on the function $F(\mathbf{x})$. The beam complex amplitude $F_1(\mathbf{x})$ at the optical fiber output is defined by

$$F_1 = \hat{T}F. \tag{6.236}$$

The mode spectrum $\{F_1\}$ of the output beam

$$F_1(\mathbf{x}) = \sum_{\mathbf{p'}} F_{\mathbf{p'}}^1 \psi_{\mathbf{p'}}(\mathbf{x}) = \sum_{\mathbf{p}} F_{\mathbf{p}} \hat{T} \psi_{\mathbf{p}}(\mathbf{x}) \tag{6.237}$$

is defined by the mode composition $\{F_{\mathbf{p}}\}$ of the input beam and the fiber properties specified by the operator $\hat{T}$. The form of the operator $\hat{T}$ depends on the fiber state, which depends on perturbations of the physical parameters of the fiber, characterized by the measured parameters $\mathbf{V} = (V_1, V_2 \ldots V_n)$. Thus, we can write

$$\hat{T} = \hat{T}(\mathbf{V}), \; F_{\mathbf{p}}^1 = F_{\mathbf{p}}^1(\mathbf{V}). \tag{6.238}$$

In the absence of fiber perturbations we have $\mathbf{V} = \mathbf{0}$, $\hat{T} = \hat{T}(\mathbf{0})$, where $\hat{T}(\mathbf{0})$ is the operator describing the mode propagation in the proper medium. Making use of the propagation constant definition $\beta_{\mathbf{p}}$ we can write

$$\hat{T}(\mathbf{0}) \psi_{\mathbf{p}}(\mathbf{x}) = \exp(i\beta_{\mathbf{p}}z) \psi_{\mathbf{p}}(\mathbf{x}), \tag{6.239}$$

where z is the distance the mode has passed in the fiber. Note that there is no intermode interaction if there are no perturbations:

$$F_{\mathbf{p'}}^1 = \exp(i\beta_{\mathbf{p'}}z) F_{\mathbf{p'}}, \; |F_{\mathbf{p'}}^1|^2 = |F_{\mathbf{p'}}|^2, \tag{6.240}$$

because the modes are eigenfunctions of the light propagation operator in a nonperturbed fiber. The values of $\mathbf{p}$ correspond to the numbers of the directed optical fiber modes. With a nonzero optical fiber perturbation, $\mathbf{V}$, instead of Eq. (6.237) we shall introduce the $T_{\mathbf{pp'}}$ coefficients, so that

$$\hat{T}(\mathbf{V}) \psi_{\mathbf{p}}(\mathbf{x}) = \sum_{\mathbf{p'}} T_{\mathbf{pp'}}(\mathbf{V}) \psi_{\mathbf{p'}}(\mathbf{x}). \tag{6.241}$$

The $T_{\mathbf{pp'}}(\mathbf{V})$ coefficients represent an array of elements of the operator $\hat{T}$ and correspond to the values of mode overlapping integrals. The orthogonality property in Eq. (6.4) for the mode basis $\psi_{\mathbf{p}}$ yields

$$T_{\mathbf{pp'}}(\mathbf{V}) = \int_G \psi_{\mathbf{p'}}^*(\mathbf{x}) \hat{T} \psi_{\mathbf{p}}(\mathbf{x}) \, d^2\mathbf{x} \tag{6.242}$$

The coefficients $F_{\mathbf{p'}}^1$ can be defined by

$$F_{\mathbf{p'}}^1(\mathbf{V}) = \int_G F_1(\mathbf{x}) \psi_{\mathbf{p'}}(\mathbf{x}) \, d^2\mathbf{x}, \tag{6.243}$$

$$F_{\mathbf{p'}}^1(\mathbf{V}) = \sum_{\mathbf{p}} T_{\mathbf{pp'}}(\mathbf{V}) F_{\mathbf{p}}. \tag{6.244}$$

Because the Parseval equality holds for the orthogonal bases, the input and output beam powers in a fiber are defined by the corresponding series

$$E = \sum_{\mathbf{p}} |F_{\mathbf{p}}|^2, \ E'(\mathbf{V}) = \sum_{\mathbf{p'}} |F_{\mathbf{p'}}^1(\mathbf{V})|^2. \tag{6.245}$$

Most available fiber-optic sensors work by measuring the total output beam energy $E'(\mathbf{V})$ as a function of the perturbation $\mathbf{V}$. As is seen from Eq. (6.245), the value of $E'(\mathbf{V})$ is ensemble-averaged over the powers of separate excited modes $|F_{\mathbf{p'}}(\mathbf{V})|^2$ with the numbers $\mathbf{p'}$. The sensor that is proposed in Ref. [59] is able to measure the separate mode powers, $|F_{\mathbf{p'}}^1(\mathbf{V})|^2$, selectively. Note that in a special case of exciting a single mode the coefficient $F_{\mathbf{p}}$ will be nonzero only for one value of $\mathbf{p}$. The magnitude $|T_{\mathbf{p'p}}(\mathbf{V})|^2$ will be called the *mode excitation coefficient* as it defines the power of the mode $\mathbf{p'}$ in the case when the fiber is excited by the mode $\mathbf{p}$. In Refs. [78,79] they studied how the excitation coefficients depend on the various mode excited and on the excitation conditions.

6.3.3 Experimental Studies of a Modan-Aided Microdisplacement Sensor

The development of a modan has made it possible to construct a family of microdisplacement sensors with high and controllable sensitivity [59]. An enhanced sensitivity of the microdisplacement sensor in Figure 6.62 is due to the fact that the intensity of a separate mode is more sensitive to microdisplacements than the total intensity of the beam. This comprises the difference between the scheme in Figure 6.62 and the

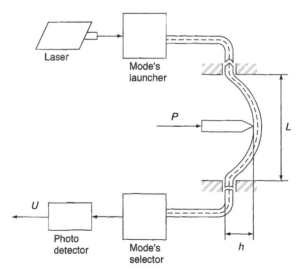

Figure 6.62. The blockdiagram of a fiber-optic microdisplacement sensor. P: the mechanical microshift, h: the amplitude of the fiber microsag, L: the distance between the contact points and U: the output electric voltage.

conventional configuration of the displacement sensor. The highly sensitive microdisplacement sensor was experimentally studied using a graded-index optic fiber with parabolic profile of length 1200 μm. The fiber experienced a single quasi-sine sag of a varied amplitude h (Fig. 6.62). The sag was implemented using a working membrane 4 having a single point of contact with the fiber and a reference membrane with two points of contact (Fig. 6.63). The distance of $L = 1.0$ mm between the contact points was chosen to ensure the mode resonance [5]. Both the membranes were fixed between frame 3 and lids 5 and 8. The screw 9 serves to perform the initial fiber deformation. The displacement of the working membrane was measured by indicator 1. Fiber F was passed through two metallic microtubes 2 embedded into frame 3 and filled with silicon hermetic filter 7. The selective excitation of separate transverse modes in the optical fiber takes place in a mode former that includes a laser L, a collimator O_1–O_2, a modan M_1, and an objective O_3. The complex transmission function of modan M_1 is matched to one of the fiber transverse modes. The selective extraction of a desired mode at the fiber output takes place in an analyzer composed of an objective O_4, second modan M_2, an objective O_5, and a photo-receiver FS with diaphragm D. The complex transmission function of modan M_2 is also matched to the desired fiber mode. The selective excitation and detection of the mode is ensured by a multimode filter performing a unimodal operation. The number of modes is determined by the number of channels of the multichannel modan. Thus, a single filter can be used to excite different modes.

By adjusting the mode beam about the fiber axis in terms of the scale, angle, and shift, the desired mode can be excited with a maximum accuracy. Figure 6.64 shows the

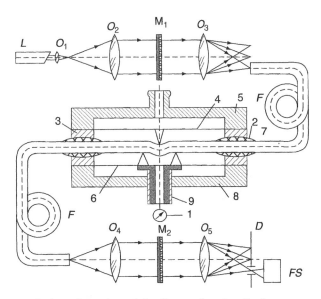

Figure 6.63. The optical configuration of the fiber-optic microdisplacement sensor. L: a laser; O_1, O_2, O_5: objectives; O_3, O_4: microobjectives; M_1, M_2: multibeam modans; F: an optical fiber; D: a diaphragm; FS: a photoreceiver; 1: an indicator of membrane displacement; 2: metallic microtubes; 3: sensor frame; 4: working membrane; 5: upper lid; 6: reference membrane; 7: hermetic silicon filter; 8: lower lid; 9: microscrew for implementing the optical fiber deformation h.

output signal (experimental results and theoretical estimation) versus the value of the fiber sag h. The output signal represents the power of a single mode normalized with respect to the maximum value corresponding to the zero sag. Figure 6.64 also depicts a change in the total light flux for the Gaussian input beam. From the experimentally derived curves in Figure 6.64, it is seen that modan-measured changes in the normalized mode powers are found in the interval 0.4–1, whereas changes in the total light flux E are found in a significantly narrower interval of 0.85–1, with the values of sag found in the same interval 0–80 μm for both the cases.

Note, however, that some experimental results shown in Figure 6.64 are different from the theoretical estimations [15], which may be caused by inaccurate adjustment of the unit and technological distortions of the calculated modan transmission function. Figure 6.65 shows the sensor sensitivity

$$S_{\mathbf{p}} = \frac{\partial |F_{\mathbf{p}}|^2}{\partial h} \tag{6.246}$$

as a function of the microsag value h normalized to the maximum sensitivity of the principal mode, (0, 0). From Figures 6.64 and 6.65, the maximum sensitivity of the mode as a function of the optical fiber sag is seen to fall on the output signal interval of 0.4–0.6. Let us estimate the benefit in sensitivity a sensor, working by use of selectively excited modes, ensures over the conventional fiber-optic sensor, working by measuring the total light flux. For making comparison, a sag of 175 μm was chosen. For the conventional sensor, such a sag produces a 0.85 signal. From the analysis of the curves in Figure 6.65 and data in Table 6.3, the principal mode sensitivity (0, 0) is seen to be 3.9 times higher than that of the total light beam. With the same sag, the sensitivity of the mode (1, 0) is 2.1 times higher, and that of the mode (2, 0) is 2.4 times higher than the principal mode sensitivity (Table 6.3).

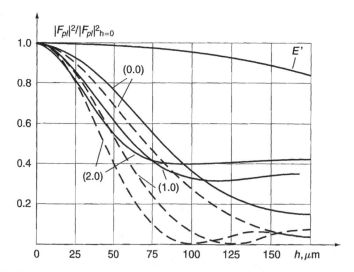

Figure 6.64. The output signal of the sensor versus the shift h of the working diaphragm, $E' =$ the total light beam having passed through the fiber; the (0, 0), (1, 0), (2, 0) denote the curves corresponding to the selected Gauss-Laguerre mode.

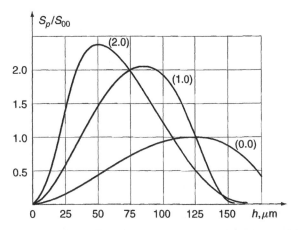

Figure 6.65. The sensor sensitivity as a function of the working diaphragm shift h. (0, 0), (1, 0), and (2, 0) denote the curves corresponding to the modes selected.

TABLE 6.3. The Experimental Results of Studying the Sensor

Mode Numbers (p, l),	(0, 0)	(1, 0)	(2, 0)
S_{pl} Theoretical Estimate	1.0	1.9	2.3
S_{pl}, Experimental Result	1.0	1.8	2.1

Thus, the use of a fiber-optic displacement sensor based on selectively exciting the transverse modes of laser light allows the sensitivity to be 4 to 8 times increased as compared with the conventional fiber-optic sensors.

6.3.4 Application of a DOE for Collimating the Semiconductor Laser Light

Wide use of semiconductor lasers in optical communication, write–read CD heads, laser guidance, and the like has made the task of improving dedicated optics the issue of the day. The optical properties of the semiconductor laser have been known to feature an essential asymmetry of the light-directivity diagram and a fairly high numerical aperture over one of the beam cross sections. These peculiarities become most essential when implementing communication lines based on unimode fibers. As a rule, laser diodes or laser diode arrays working in the visible and infra red (IR) range are employed as the light source in fiber-optic communication lines. Figure 6.66 depicts the measured intensity distribution produced by a laser diode of power 5 mW and wavelength 0.67 μm.

The peculiarities of the laser diode light mentioned in the preceding section commonly result in light-energy losses that can sometimes amount to 80 percent. Thus, a narrow spectral range ($\Delta\lambda < 1$ nm) in combination with a complex asymmetric intensity-distribution pattern resulting in high energy losses of the conventional optical elements make the DOEs fairly competitive. In Ref. [80] they discuss a diffractive microobjective for a laser player based on a binary microlens, but such a lens fails to eliminate the beam asymmetry, features low efficiency, and has rather limited

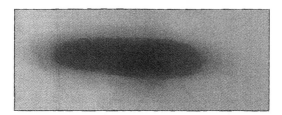

Figure 6.66. The intensity distribution produced by a visible-range laser diode.

application. A more perfect Fresnel lens used to collimate the semiconductor laser light [81] features the continuous profile and takes account of the variations in the DOE temperature. With the Fresnel lens, the output-beam asymmetry is considerably reduced, although not eliminated, by fitting parameters in the course of the ray-tracing design. Another possible application of the DOE [82] is as an array of anamorphic microlenses with elliptic zones to change the divergence ratio along the X- and Y-axes. Such microlenses are able to produce, at a definite distance, a circular-shaped beam, owing to the fact that for small waist radii (tens of microns) the beam divergences are great and can be fitted in such a manner that the beam becomes circular-shaped at a small distance of $1.5-2$ mm from the lens. However, this plane is unique and the beam becomes asymmetric once again as it propagates further. Because of this peculiarity, such elements are mainly used to make the light beam enter into fiber-optic waveguides.

6.3.5 Diffractive Beam Splitters

In the preceding sections we discussed approaches to parallel data transmission and processing by the use of longitudinal and transverse laser modes. At the same time, the optical communication channels can be implemented through the straightforward space separation of beams responsible for different data channels. Such an approach has become widely used in parallel signal processing [54,56,83]. For this purpose, diffractive beam splitters made up of the multiorder diffraction gratings [83] are used. The monograph [23] treats a variety of approaches to design beam splitters, including those with quantized phase. Being phase elements intended to generate a desired intensity distribution, beam splitters can be designed using an iterative gradient procedure [83] or a Gerchberg-Saxton-type procedure [55,56]. Sections 2.8.4 and 2.8.5 of this book cover the results of designing multiorder diffractive beam splitters using various iterative procedures. Note, however that we often need not only to generate a set of diffraction orders from the illuminating beam with desired intensity distribution between them but also to control the complex amplitude distribution in each order. Such a task may appear if we need to simultaneously excite several optical fibers (Fig. 6.67).

Actually, if in place of the element M we employ a conventional diffraction grating that generates complex-valued distributions of arbitrary modal composition at the fibers' end, it will result in inevitable energy losses caused by the "leakage" of unchannelled modes [18]. In Ref. [19] it was proposed that the problem should be solved by use of a modan, with its calculated transmission function being coded as the phase-only function by introducing a reference carrier into the phase. It can easily be seen that in this way, for example, one can design an element capable of generating from the

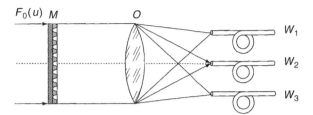

Figure 6.67. Parallel excitation of several optical fibers by a single beam. W_1, W_2, and W_3 are optical waveguides, M is a DOE, and O is a lens.

illuminating Gaussian laser beam the fundamental modes, $(0, 0)$, at the ends of the fibers W_1, W_2, and W_3.

Note that, in the general case, the feasibility of implementing the DOE phase function, as a sum of phases corresponding to several subapertures as is the case in Section 6.2.8 allows several transformations of the light beam to be performed in parallel. Consider the following example.

Example 6.7 On-line Analysis of the Mode Content of the Laser Beam by DOE.   Analyzing the amplitude-phase characteristics of the laser beam in real-time mode is topical in experimental physics and in a great number of laser applications, such as laser material treatment. The task of analyzing the amplitude-phase beam structure of the beam may be treated as that of analyzing the mode composition if this is thought of as both analyzing individual mode powers and intermodal phase shifts. In this Chapter the problem is tackled using a special diffractive element (DOE), called modan, matched to a group of laser radiation modes. Rapid progress in technologies for DOE fabrication, including those for high-power lasers, open wide prospects for the use of such elements in the studies of the laser beam cross section structure. However, to use such elements for the on-line beam analysis, one needs to use extra optical components capable of splitting the laser beam into two beams at least, each of them retaining the initial amplitude-phase structure and having a desired energy distribution. Energy losses relating to the beam splitting and Fresnel reflection on each interface (air-optical medium) may lead to essential problems, especially when analyzing the beam of a high-power laser. As a solution to this problem, we may consider the synthesis of an element that combines the functions of a beam splitter and that of a mode-correlation filter, decreasing the number of interfaces (air-optical medium) and making the system much more compact. Thus, it is expedient to consider the synthesis of an optical element that would allow one to measure the individual mode powers and intermode phase shifts using just a minor part of the illuminating beam energy; in the meantime the major part of the beam is allowed to pass through the element without any essential change in the amplitude-phase structure. By way of illustration, such an optical element may be implemented as a microrelief applied directly onto an optical material of the laser output window.

In this Chapter we report on the designing of phase modans intended for the analysis of the coherent beam transverse-mode spectrum. To change from the complex-valued transmission function (in the general case) to the pure-phase function, both analytical coding methods (with a coding carrier entered into the element's phase) and highly efficient, iterative coding methods have been developed. However, the elements described earlier prohibit the on-line measuring of the mode composition when doing without an extra beam splitter.

It was suggested that the beam may be split into the "basic" one (retaining the amplitude-phase structure of the initial beam) and the "auxiliary" or "informative" ones (i.e., intended for measuring the mode composition) by a single element using a strategy of "linked" or "virtual" subapertures (Fig. 6.68).

To this end, we need to seek the DOE complex transmission function as a superposition of the complex transmission functions of "virtual" subapertures with corresponding weight coefficients.

One of such "virtual" apertures corresponds to the transmission of the basic beam without a change in the amplitude-phase structure $F(\mathbf{u})$ up to a certain coefficient $C < 1$ that describes a decrease in energy, while the others correspond to optical filters matched to the modes and intended for deriving information about the mode powers, $|C_{n'}|^2$, and intermode phase shifts $\Delta\varphi_{n'}$. Let us consider the calculation of the complex transmission function for such an element in more detail. Earlier, we have shown that if a beam cross section of complex-valued distribution $F(\mathbf{u})$ interacts with a filter of complex transmission function $\psi_{\mathbf{n}}^*(\mathbf{u})$ (where $\psi_{\mathbf{n}}(\mathbf{u})$ is the mode numbered $\mathbf{n}$, and $*$ denotes complex conjugation) at the Fourier-stage input, the resulting complex distribution at the center of the Fourier-stage output plane will be given by Eq. (6.217), where $F_{\mathbf{n}}$ is the mode coefficient of the nth mode in the decomposition in Eq. (6.211) and D is the element aperture. Measuring the intensity $|F_{\mathbf{n}}|^2$ at the output plane center using a point sensor allows one to derive information about the energy contribution of the mode number $\mathbf{n}$ to the beam $F(\mathbf{u})$. To measure the N_{mod} mode powers simultaneously, we considered this element with the complex transmission function in the form

$$T(\mathbf{u}) = \sum_{n'=1}^{N\,\text{mod}} \zeta_{n'}\,\psi_{n'}^*(\mathbf{u})\,\exp(i2\pi\boldsymbol{\nu}_{\mathbf{n}'}\mathbf{u}). \tag{6.247}$$

The interaction of the beam with a filter of complex transmission function in (Eq. 6.247) at the input of a Fourier stage of focal length f will result in the emergence of complex distributions $F_{n'}$ at point $\lambda f \boldsymbol{\nu}_{n'}$ of the output plane. Let us derive the relation for the complex transmission function of the element that analyzes the individual power

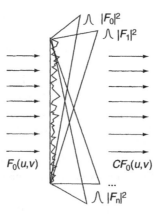

Figure 6.68. Formulation of the problem: on-line analysis of the mode composition of the beam.

distribution between modes using only part of the illuminating beam energy. In this case, it is necessary to introduce into Eq. (6.247) an additional term corresponding to the illuminating beam transmission function without changing its amplitude-phase distribution:

$$T(\mathbf{u}) = \zeta_0 + \sum_{n'=1}^{N\text{mod}} \zeta_{n'} \psi_{n'}^*(\mathbf{u}) \exp(i 2\pi \mathbf{v_{n'}u}). \tag{6.248}$$

The ratio of weight modules, $|\zeta_0|$ and $|\zeta_{n'}|$, determines the ratio of energy fractions accounted for by the beam propagated with no changes in the amplitude-phase distribution and the "informative" beams $\zeta_{n'} \psi_{n'}^*(\mathbf{u}) \exp(i 2\pi \mathbf{v_{n'}u})$. When such an element found at the input of a Fourier stage of focal length f is illuminated by a beam with transverse complex-valued distribution $F(\mathbf{u})$, a beam with transverse distribution $CF(\mathbf{u})$ will appear in a plane directly behind the element and with complex distributions $F_1(\lambda f v_{n'}) \cong \zeta_{n'} F_{n'}$ at the output plane, where the values proportional to individual mode powers $|\zeta_{n'} F_{n'}|^2$ can be measured using point sensors. The derived complex transmission function in Eq. (6.247) (which is certainly not phase-only in the general case) can be reduced to the pure-phase function using well-known encoding techniques based on the introduction into the beam phase of a carrier, for example, by the Kirk-Jones method. Figure 6.69 depicts the cross section of the calculated amplitude distribution in the working (zero) diffraction order of the element intended to determine in real-time mode whether the Gauss-Hermite modes (1, 0) and (0, 1) are present in the illuminating beam. The element was designed using the Kirk-Jones method. In the computer simulation, the element was illuminated by the Gauss-Hermite mode (1, 0). At the center, there is a "basic" beam Gauss-Hermite mode (1, 0) having passed through the DOE, and at the right is a correlation peak corresponding to the presence of the Gauss-Hermite mode (1, 0). At the left of basic beam there is a region of formation of a correlation spot corresponding to the Gauss-Hermite mode (0, 1). At the center of the region there is the zero-amplitude value corresponding to the absence of the Gauss-Hermite mode (0, 1) in the illuminating beam. Note that the greater the energy fraction accounted for by the basic beam, the greater is the diffractive efficiency of coding because the diffraction efficiency of the synthetic Kirk-Jones hologram is the greatest when the amplitude of its complex transmission function is

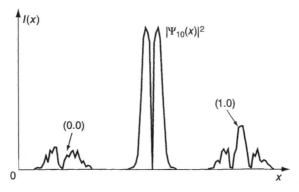

Figure 6.69. The result of the computer simulation of the designed DOE (cross section of the focal-intensity distribution).

closer to a constant. In the computer simulations conducted by the present authors, the energy fraction accounted for by the unperturbed beam amounted to more than 85 percent.

CONCLUSION

In this chapter we have looked into the feasibility of generating and selecting laser modes using dedicated DOEs called modans and have treated problems related to the use of DOEs in systems for acquisition, transmission, and storage of data. It has been demonstrated that the development and implementation of new-type DOEs, modans, has made the solution to the fundamental problems possible, which could not be resolved using conventional optical elements. These are the problems of generating laser beams with desired transverse-mode composition and detecting the transverse-mode composition in real time. Potential applications of the DOE in systems for acquisition, transmission, and storage of data include an increase in the data-carrying ability of fiber-optic communication systems, development of highly sensitive displacement sensors, and real-time analysis of amplitude-phase characteristics of laser light. It should be noted that until now an increase in the data-carrying ability of fiber-optic communication lines through the selective excitation of transverse laser modes has not been practically implemented. There are several reasons for this:

- implementing high-quality profile of gradient fibers that would allow the beams to be transmitted without essential changes in the modal composition is much more expensive than well-established manufacturing of conventional quartz multimodal fibers;
- availability of alternative approaches to multiplexing fiber-optic communication lines — WDM approach that imposes no special requirements on the fiber quality and nonlinear techniques for multiplexing data-transmission channels in unimodal fibers allowing high-speed data transmission;
- the technology for synthesizing modans is as yet imperfect because it is at the stage of conception.

However, in the authors' opinion, with advances in fiber and integrated optics as well as with enhanced requirements imposed on the optical communication lines developed, the modan-based approach will be able to find its niche in future telecommunication systems. Note also that with the development of novel technologies such as the technology for fabricating transmission DOEs for high-power lasers, (section 4.6), the DOEs matched to transverse mode composition of laser light are likely to be used to measure the transverse mode composition of light and reconstruct the amplitude-phase distribution in the beam cross section. Besides, the development of methods for synthesizing the modans provides valuable information pertaining to possible solutions of the problem of synthesizing DOEs intended to generate arbitrary amplitude-phase distributions. In this connection, it would be interesting to note that the choice between the accurate generation of the mode and the modan energy efficiency was made every time, considering the specific task to be solved, whether it be the implementation of a fiber-optic communication line or the development of a fiber-optic displacement sensor. That is the reason why dedicated tools of numerical methods that would allow the necessary compromise to be found in every particular case were developed. Obviously, this approach may as well be extended to design a DOE, capable of generating arbitrary amplitude-phase distributions. To sum up, owing to their unique capabilities, the DOEs, together with waveguide and integrated optics components, have their part to play in highly effective optical and electro-optical systems for acquisition, transmission, and storage of data.

REFERENCES

1. A.W. Snyder and J.D. Love, *Optical Waveguide Theory*, Chapman Hall, New York, 1983.

2. Yu.A. Ananiev, *Optical Cavities and Laser Beams*, Nauka Publishers, Moscow 1990 (in Russian).

3. O. Svelto, *Principles of Lasers,* Plenum Press, New York, 1982.

4. W. Rudin, *Functional Analysis*, McGraw-Hill, New York, 1973.

5. H.G. Unger, *Planar Optical Waveguides and Fibers*, Oxford University Press, New York, 1977.

6. L.B. Felsen and M. Marawitz, *Radiation and Scattering of Waves*, Prentice-Hall, Englewood Cliffs, New Jersey, 1973.

7. B.T. Landesman and H.H. Barrett, *J. Opt. Soc. Am. A* **5**, 1610 (1988).

8. S. Nemoto, *Appl. Opt.* **29**, 1940 (1990).

9. M. Born and E. Wolf, *Principles of Optics*, Pergamon Press, Oxford, London, 1980.

10. S. Solimeno, B. Crosignani, and P. DiPorto, *Guiding, Diffraction, and Confinement of Optical Radiation*, Academic Press, Orlando, San Diego, 1986.

11. H.A. Haus, *Waves and Fields in Optoelectronics*, Prentice Hall, Englewood Cliffs, New Jersey, 1984.

12. D. Marcuse, *Light Transmission Optics*, Van Nostrand Reinhold, New York, 1982.

13. M.A. Golub, I.N. Sisakyan, and V.A. Soifer, *Modern Opt.* **38**, 1067 (1991).

14. G.A. Korn and T.A. Korn, *Mathematical Handbook*, McGraw-Hill, New York, 1968.

15. A. Yariv, *Optical Electronics*, Holt, Rinehart, and Winston, New York, 1985.

16. L.D. Landau and E.M. Lifshitz, *Quantum Mechanics*, Nauka Publishers, Moscow, 1974.

17. R.I. Pressley, *Handbook of Lasers with Selected Data on Optical Technology*, Chemical Rubber Co., Cleveland, 1971.

18. M.J. Adams, *An Introduction to Optical Waveguides*, Wiley & Sons, Chichester, 1981.

19. V.A. Soifer and M.A. Golub, *Laser Beam Mode Selection by Computer Generated Holograms*, CRC Press, Boca Raton, Fla. 1994.

20. M.A. Bakharyev et al., *Comput. Opt., ICNTI* **17**, 21–25 (1997) (in Russian).

21. J.W. Goodman, *Introduction to Fourier Optics*, McGraw-Hill, New York, 1968.

22. M.A. Golub, I.N. Sisakian, and V.A. Soifer, *Comput. Opti. ICNTI* **8**, 3–64 (1990) (in Russian).

23. V.A. Soifer, V.V. Kotlyar, and L.L. Doskolovich, *Iterative Methods for Diffractive Optical Elements Computation*, Taylor & Francis Ltd., London, 1997.

24. V.V. Kotlyar, I.V. Nikolsky, and V.A. Soifer, *Optik* **98**, (1) 26–30 (1994).

25. S.N. Khonina, V.V. Kotlyar, and V.A. Soifer, *Comput. Opt. ICNTI* **17**, 25–31 (1997) (in Russian).

26. V.V. Kotlyar, V.A. Soifer, and S.N. Khonina, *Comput. Opt. ICNTI* **17**, 31–36 (1997) (in Russian).

27. M. Duparre et al., *Proc. SPIE* **3110**, 741–752 (1997).

28. M. Duparre et al., *Proc. SPIE* **3134**, 357–368 (1997).

29. M. Duparre et al., *Proc. SPIE* **3291**, 104–113 (1998).

30. V.S. Pavelyev et al., *Opt. Lasers Eng.* **29**, 269–279 (1998).

31. L.L. Doskolovich et al., *Proc. SPIE* **3348**, 37–47 (1998).

32. V.A. Soifer, M.A. Golub, and V.S. Pavelyev, *OSA: Diffract. Opt.: Design, Fabrication and Applications Tech. Digest Ser.* **11**, 209–212 (1994).

33. S.V. Karpeyev, Spatial filters for analysis and synthesis of transverse-modal composition of coherent light in fiber-optic waveguides, Thesis for candidate degree in Physics and mathematics, Kuybyshev, Russia 1985.

34. V.S. Pavelyev et al., *Comput. Opt. ICNTI* **18**, 115–120 (1998) (in Russian).

35. A.E. Berezny, S.V. Karpeev, and G.V. Uspleniev, *Opt. Lasers Eng.* **15**, 331–340 (1991).

36. S.N. Khonina and V.V. Kotlyar, *Proc. SPIE* **2363**, 184–190 (1994).

37. W.Q. Thornburg, B.J. Corrado, and X.D. Zhu, *Opt. Lett.* **19**(7), 454–456 (1994).

38. J.P. Kirk and A.L. Jones, *J.Opt. Soc. Am.* **61**(8), 1023 (1971).

39. D.C. Chu and J.R. Fienup, *Opt. Eng.* **13**(3), 189 (1974).

40. H. Stark, *Image Recovery: Theory and Application*, Academic Press, San Diego, 1987.

41. A. Levi and H. Stark *J. Opt. Soc. Am.* **1**(2), 932–943 (1984).

42. V.S. Pavelyev and S.N. Khonina, *Comput. Opt. ICNTI* **17**, 15–20 (1997) (in Russian).

43. S.N. Khonina, V.V. Kotlyar, and V.A. Soifer, *Optik* **88**(4), 182–184 (1991).

44. V.A. Soifer, L.L. Doskolovich, N.L. Kazanskiy, and V.S. Pavelyev, *Proc. SPIE* **2426**, 358–365.

45. V.S. Pavelyev, Designing diffractive optical elements using a generalized projection method thesis for candidate degree in Physics and Mathematics, Samara, Russia (1996).

46. V. Bagini et al., *Laser Beam Characterization SEDO*, Madrid, Spain, 31–40 (1993).

47. J.R. Fienup, *Appl. Opt.* **21**(15), 2758–2769 (1982).

48. V.V. Kotlyar, I.V. Nikolski, and V.A. Soifer, *Optik* **88**(1), 17–19 (1991).

49. C.Y. Lu, H.Z. Liao, C.K. Lee, and J.S. Wang, *Appl. Opt.* **36**(20) (1997).

50. M.A. Golub, A.M. Prokhorov, I.N. Sisakian, and V.A. Soifer, *Quant. Electron.* **9**(9), 1866–1868 (1982).

51. H.O. Bartelt, A.W. Lohmann, W. Freude, and G.K. Grau, *Electron. lett.* **19**(7), 247–249 (1983).

52. S. Berdague and P. Facq, *Ap. Opt.* **21**(11), 1950–1955 (1982).

53. F. Dubois, Ph. Emplit, and O. Hugon, *Opt. Lett.* **19**(7), 433–435 (1994).

54. Ph. Lalanne and P. Chavel, *Perspectives for parallel optical interconnects. DG 3 Comiss. of the Europ. Communities*; Springer-Verlag, Berlin 1993.

55. S.A. Prokopenko et al., *Proc. SPIE* **3348**, 22–29 (1998).

56. S.A. Prokopenko et al., *Proc. SPIE* **3348**, 83–93 (1998).

57. A.A. Akayev and S.A. Mayorov, *Coherent Opt. Comput.*, Mashinostroyeniye Publishers, Leningrad, 1977 (in Russian).

58. A.A. Akayev and S.A. Mayorov, *Optical Methods for Data Processing*, Vishaya Shkola Publishers, Moscow, 1988 (in Russian).

59. G.V. Uvarov, Fiber-Optic Transducers Based on Transverse Mode Separation, Thesis for candidate degree in Engineering, Kuybyshev Russia (1988).

60. M.A. Golub, I.N. Sisakyan, V.A. Soifer, and G.V. Uvarov, *Proc. SPIE* **1572**, 101 (1991).

61. Yu. Bazhanov, S.N. Shaposhnikov, and S.N. Adrianov, *Proc. SPIE* **3348**, 130–139 (1998).

62. J.T. Chang, D.C. Su, and Y.T. Huang, *Appl. Opt.* **33**(35), 8143–8145 (1994).

63. Y. Fainman et al., *Proc. SPIE* **3348**, 152–162.

64. V.I. Bobrinyev, J.Ya. Son, and H.V. Chon, *Quant. Electron.* Vol. **22** (1995).

65. L.L. Doskolovich, *Comput. Opt. ICNTI* **18**, 16–24 (1998) (in Russian).

66. V.A. Soifer, *Introduction into Diffractive Microoptics*, SSAU Publishers, Samara, Russia (1996) (in Russian).

67. C. Koeppen, R.F. Shi, W.D. Chen, and W.D. Garito, *J. Opt. Soc. Am.* B **15**(2), 727–739 (1998).

68. A. Hasegawa and Yu. Kodama, *TIIER* **69**(9), 57–63 (1981).

69. S.A. Akhmanov, V.A. Vysloukh, and A.S. Chirkin, *Adv. Phys. Sci.* **149**(3), 450–509 (in Russian).

70. A.Yu. Sherman, *Comput. Opt. ICNTI* **6**, 32–37 (in Russian).

71. R.M. Gagliardi, *Optical Communications*, Wiley Series in Telecommunications and Signal Processing; Wiley & Sons, New York, 1995.

72. A. Cutolo, T. Pierri, L. Zeni, *Laser Beam Characterization*, SEDO, Madrid, Spain 263–273 (1993).

73. K.-M. Du, G. Herziger, P. Loosen, and F. Ruhl, *Opt. Quant. Electron.* **24**, 1119–1127 (1992).

74. J.N. Fields, *Appl. Opt. Phys. Lett.* **36**, 799–801 (1980).

75. J.N. Fields, C.K. Asawa, O.G. Ramer, and M.K. Barnoski, *J. Acoust. Soc. Am.* **67**, 816–818 (1980).

76. G.K. Grau, O.G. Leminger, and E.G. Sauter, *Archiv fur Electronik und Ubertragungstechnik, Electronics and Communication* **34**, 259 (1980).

77. S.G. Krivoshlykov, N.I. Petrov, and I.N. Sisakyan, *Opt. Quant. Electron.* **15**, 193 (1983).

78. S.G. Krivoshlykov and E. Sauter *J. Phys. A* **20**, 3805 (1987).

79. V.P. Garichev, *Comput. Opt. ICNTI* **3**, 103–109 (1988) (in Russian).

80. S. Ogata and Y. Ito, *Opt. Eng.* **33**(11), 3656–3661 (1994).

81. W. Chen, C.S. Roychoudhuri, and C.M. Banas, *Opt. Eng.* **33**(11), 3662 (1994).

82. M. Rossi, G.L. Bona, and R.E. Kunz, *Appl.Opt.* **34**(14), 2483–2488 (1995).

83. L.L. Doscolovich et al., *Pure Appl. Optics (JEOS)* **3**, 921–930 (1994).

CHAPTER 7

Light Beams with Periodic Properties

7.1 INTRODUCTION

Periodic self-reproducing images have been known in optics since 1836, when Talbot studied light beams produced by the binary masks with a transverse periodic transmission function (linear and crossed gratings) [1]. It is since then that the self-reproduction of coherent light field that shows up as a transverse periodicity at definite intervals while propagating (axial periodicity) is referred to as *Talbot effect*. For incoherent light, this effect is called the *Lau effect* [2].

In 1881, Rayleigh showed that for the grating self-reproduction to be easily observable, it should be illuminated by a monochromatic collimated beam, and derived the relation for the distance (received the name Talbot period) at which the grating will be self-reproduced for the first time [3]:

$$d = \frac{2a^2}{\lambda},\qquad(7.1)$$

where a is the grating period and λ is the illuminating beam wavelength. The subsequent papers mainly dealt with variations in the grating's properties (phase, rectangular gratings, and the like).

Thus, it was periodic properties of the light fields composed of a finite number of plane waves that were pointed out first.

In Ref. [4], it has been intimated that linear gratings can produce periodically reproducible images different from the object itself. Formulae for the light field distribution on the fragments of Talbot period in Eq. (7.1) have been derived in Refs. [5–7]. For instance, a rectangular grating of period $a \times a$ and with transmission function

$$f(x, y, 0) = f(x + pa, y + qa, 0) = \sum_{n,m} F_{nm} \exp\left[i2\pi\frac{nx + my}{a}\right],\qquad(7.2)$$

where F_{nm} is the spatial spectrum of $f(x, y)$ will generate, in the Fresnel approximation, the light field

$$f(x, y, z) = \exp(ikz) \sum_{n,m} F_{nm} \exp\left[i2\pi\frac{nx + my}{a}\right]$$

$$\times \exp\left[-i2\pi\frac{(n^2 + m^2)z}{d}\right],\qquad(7.3)$$

535

where d is the Talbot period of Eq. (7.1). It stands to reason that at the distances multiple to the period, $z = ld$, we have $\exp[-i2\pi(n^2 + m^2)l] = 1$ and

$$|f(x, y, z)|_{z=ld}|^2 = \left|\exp(ikld)\sum_{n,m} F_{nm} \exp\left[i2\pi\frac{nx + my}{a}\right]\right|^2 = |f(x, y, 0)|^2, \quad (7.4)$$

which means that the grating is self-reproduced. At a distance of half the period d (at $l = 1/2$), we get a grating copy shifted by half the transverse period a

$$f(x, y, z)|_{z=d/2} = \exp(ikd/2)\sum_{n,m} F_{nm} \exp\left[i2\pi\frac{nx + my}{a}\right]\exp[-i\pi(n^2 + m^2)]$$

$$= \exp(ikd/2)f(x + a/2, y + a/2, 0), \quad (7.5)$$

whereas at a distance of $4q$ fractions of period d we get

$$f(x, y, z)|_{z=d/4q} = \exp(ikd/4q)\frac{\exp(-i\pi/2)}{2q}\sum_{s,r}^{2q-1} \exp\left[i\pi\frac{(s^2 + r^2)}{2q}\right]$$

$$\times f(x + sa/2q, y + ra/2q, 0). \quad (7.6)$$

Generally speaking, at the distances composed of Talbot period fractions, a superposition of shifted copies of the initial image takes place.

In 1967, Montgomery showed that an object with infinite aperture would be self-reproduced while propagating, if its spectrum is found on the rings of a zone plate [8]. In his work, based on the integral representation of the Helmholtz equation solution:

$$f(\mathbf{x}, z) = \int_{R^2} F(\boldsymbol{\xi}) \exp[iK(\boldsymbol{\xi})z] \exp(i2\pi\mathbf{x}\boldsymbol{\xi}) \, d\boldsymbol{\xi}, \quad (7.7)$$

where $F(\boldsymbol{\xi})$ is the Fourier image of the function $f(\mathbf{x})$, $K(\boldsymbol{\xi}) = k\sqrt{[1 - (\lambda\boldsymbol{\xi})^2]}$, $\boldsymbol{\xi} = (\xi, \eta)$ is the vector of spatial frequencies, and k is the wave number, and imposing the condition of self-reproduction at distance d up to a complex constant

$$f(\mathbf{x}, d) = wf(\mathbf{x}, 0) \; \forall \mathbf{x}, \quad w = \text{const}, \quad \mathbf{x} = (x, y), \quad (7.8)$$

Montgomery arrived at the following expression for spatial frequencies:

$$\frac{d}{\lambda}\left[1 - \sqrt{1 - (\lambda\boldsymbol{\xi})^2}\right] = m(\boldsymbol{\xi}), \quad (7.9)$$

where $m(\boldsymbol{\xi})$ is the integer $\boldsymbol{\xi}$-dependent number.

Dividing the spectrum $F(\boldsymbol{\xi})$ into two types, one can single out two types of self-reproduction:

(1) "Weak" self-reproduction: the spatial frequencies $\boldsymbol{\xi}$ of object $f(\mathbf{x})$, for which the values $F(\boldsymbol{\xi}) \neq 0$ are found within a circle of radius $R \ll 1/\lambda$. In this case,

the self-reproduction at distance d takes place if

$$|\xi| = \sqrt{\frac{2}{\lambda d}}\sqrt{m(\xi)}, \tag{7.10}$$

that is, the spatial frequencies are found on the rings of a zone plate with radii $R_m = \sqrt{(2\lambda d m)}$. For transverse periodic objects, $f(\mathbf{x} + \mathbf{a}_n) = f(\mathbf{x})$, the spatial frequencies are discrete:

$$|\mathbf{b}_n| = \sqrt{\frac{2}{\lambda d}}\sqrt{m(\mathbf{n})}, \tag{7.11}$$

with the Rayleigh formula of Eq. (7.1) being the particular case of Eq. (7.11) for the object periodic in one coordinate: $f(x + na, y) = f(x, y), m(n) = n^2$.

(2) "Strong" self-reproduction: the spatial frequencies ξ of object $f(\mathbf{x})$, for which the values $F(\xi) \neq 0$ are found within a circle of radius up to $1/\lambda$. In this case, the self-reproduction at distance d takes place if

$$|\xi|^2 + \left(\frac{m(\xi)}{d} - \frac{1}{\lambda}\right)^2 = \left(\frac{1}{\lambda}\right)^2, \tag{7.12}$$

with the last relation defining the equation of a circumference of radius $1/\lambda$ with the center at point $(0, 1/\lambda)$. For $d \gg \lambda$, we get a circumference array

$$|\xi|^2 = \frac{2m(\xi)}{\lambda d}, \tag{7.13}$$

of radii $\rho_m = \sqrt{\dfrac{2m(\xi-)}{\lambda d}}$.

Considering that $\mathbf{x} = (x, y)$, $\xi = (\xi, \eta)$, and $|\xi| = \sqrt{(\xi^2 + \eta^2)}$, rewrite Eq. (7.7) in the scalar form:

$$f(x, y, z) = \int_{-\infty}^{\infty}\int_{-\infty}^{\infty} F(\xi, \eta)\exp[ikz\sqrt{1 - \lambda^2(\xi^2 + \eta^2)}]\exp[i2\pi(x\xi + y\eta)]\,d\xi\,d\eta, \tag{7.14}$$

The self-reproduction at distance d will take place if the condition in Eq. (7.10) or (7.13) is met:

$$\xi^2 + \eta^2 = \frac{2m}{\lambda d}. \tag{7.15}$$

Substituting Eq. (7.15) into Eq. (7.14) yields

$$f(x, y, z) = \exp\left[ikz\sqrt{1 - \frac{2m\lambda}{d}}\right]\int_{-\infty}^{\infty}\int_{-\infty}^{\infty} F(\xi_m, \eta_m)\exp[i2\pi(x\xi_m + y\eta_m)]\,d\xi_m\,d\eta_m$$

$$= \exp(i\beta_m z)f(x, y), \tag{7.16}$$

where $\beta_m = k\sqrt{(1 - 2m\lambda/d)}$ and $f(x, y)$ is the transverse periodic function.

Assume that in polar coordinates, $\mathbf{x} = (r, \varphi)$ and $\boldsymbol{\xi} = (\rho, \theta)$, the spectrum has frequencies only on a single ring, $F(\rho, \theta) = A_m(\theta)\delta(\rho - \sqrt{(2m/\lambda d)})$, then, instead of Eq. (7.16), we get the relation for the complex amplitude of beams with axial periodicity:

$$f(r, \varphi, z) = \exp(i\beta_m z) \int_0^{2\pi} A_m(\theta) \exp\left[i 2\pi r \sqrt{\frac{2m}{\lambda d}} \cos(\varphi - \theta)\right] d\theta$$

$$= \exp(i\beta_m z) \int_0^{2\pi} A_m(\theta) \exp[i r \alpha_m \cos(\varphi - \theta)] d\theta, \tag{7.17}$$

where $A_m(\theta)$ is some complex function and $\alpha_m = 2\pi\sqrt{(2m/\lambda d)}$. It can easily be seen that $\alpha_m^2 + \beta_m^2 = k^2$. For $A_m(\theta) = \exp(im\theta)$, it follows from Eq. (7.17) that the function $f(r, \varphi) = 2\pi(i)^m J_m(\alpha_m r) \exp(im\varphi)$ is no more transverse periodic [$J_m(x)$ is the Bessel function of the m-th order].

Thus, we defined one more type of self-reproducing functions, namely, the *Bessel modes*. The methods for generating such modes are dealt with in Sections 7.2 to 7.4.

In Ref. [9], Montgomery generalized the results arrived at in Ref. [8]. Considering the eigenfunctions of the propagation operator

$$D_z f = wf, \tag{7.18}$$

where $$D_z f = \int f(\mathbf{u}) D_z(\mathbf{x} - \mathbf{u}) \, d\mathbf{u}, \tag{7.19}$$

$$D_z(\mathbf{x}) = \int \exp[i K(\boldsymbol{\xi}) z] \exp(i 2\pi \mathbf{x}\boldsymbol{\xi}) \, d\boldsymbol{\xi}, \tag{7.20}$$

he managed to demonstrate that if the aperture is infinite, the discrete spectrum of these functions is empty. Only the fields with continuous spectrum can exist. For such fields to be self-reproduced the spectrum energy should be concentrated on a ring or a ring array:

$$\exp[i K(\boldsymbol{\xi})] = w. \tag{7.21}$$

If, however, the aperture is finite (which corresponds to the introduction of a black screen with pinhole shaped as Σ), the discrete spectrum is not empty and there are eigenfunctions of the operator

$$B_z A f = wf, \quad |w| < 1, \tag{7.22}$$

where $$B_z A f = \int_\Sigma f(\mathbf{u}) B_z(\mathbf{x} - \mathbf{u}) \, d\mathbf{u}, \tag{7.23}$$

$$B_z(\mathbf{x}) = \int_{|\boldsymbol{\xi}| \leq 1/\lambda} \exp[i K(\boldsymbol{\xi}) z] \exp(i 2\pi \mathbf{x}\boldsymbol{\xi}) \, d\boldsymbol{\xi}. \tag{7.24}$$

It is proposed that the self-reproducing function f should be sought for through the functions ϕ_n:

$$f = \sum_n C_n \phi_n, \tag{7.25}$$

$$B_0 A \phi_n = \lambda_n \phi_n, \quad (\phi_n, \phi_k) = \delta_{nk}, \tag{7.26}$$

from the solution of the matrix equation

$$\mathbf{M}_z \Lambda \mathbf{C} = w \mathbf{C}, \tag{7.27}$$

where $\mathbf{M}_z$ is the element matrix, $m_{nk} = (B_z \phi_n, \phi_k)$, Λ is the diagonal matrix of eigen-values λ_n, and $\mathbf{C}$ is the vector of the coefficients C_n.

From Ref. [10], it is known that in the case of square aperture, prolate spheroidal functions possess the properties of ϕ_n.

The relation between the transverse and axial periodicity of light fields has been demonstrated in Ref. [11]. For instance, the light field generated by the Fabry-Perot etalon with the spacing between mirrors of Δ is self-reproduced at a period of $d = 2\Delta$, with its spectrum made up of rings. If Δ is equal to the integer number of half-wavelengths

$$\Delta = N \frac{\lambda}{2}, \tag{7.28}$$

where N is integer, we get the spectrum with the rings of radii

$$\rho_m = \sqrt{\frac{m}{\lambda \Delta}} = \sqrt{\frac{2m}{\lambda d}}, \quad m = 0, 1, 2, \ldots \tag{7.29}$$

Choosing only the first two rings yields the spectrum $\delta(\rho) + \delta(\rho - \rho_1)$ and corresponds (at $z = 0$) to the amplitude $1 + J_0(2\pi \rho_1 r)$, where $J_0(x)$ is the Bessel function of zero order.

The results Montgomery had obtained were generalized onto the case of partially coherent fields in Ref. [8]. Considering that the cross-correlation function of the partially coherent field satisfies a pair of Helmholtz equations:

$$(\nabla_1^2 + k^2) W(x_1, y_1, x_2, y_2, z) = 0,$$
$$(\nabla_2^2 + k^2) W(x_1, y_1, x_2, y_2, z) = 0, \tag{7.30}$$

and imposing the condition that the partially coherent field is invariant while propagating

$$W(x_1, y_1, x_2, y_2, z) = W(x_1, y_1, x_2, y_2, 0), z \geq 0, \tag{7.31}$$

it has been found that in this case the spectrum of the cross-correlation function of the partially coherent light field at $z = 0$ (in polar coordinates)

$$\Im[W(x_1, y_1, x_2, y_2, 0)] = A(r_1, \varphi_1, r_2, \varphi_2) = S(r_1, \varphi_1, \varphi_2)\delta(r_1 - r_2) \tag{7.32}$$

is not correlated along the radial component.

The light fields rotating during propagation may be considered to be invariant up to a turn, or invariant in a rotating coordinate system. In Ref. [12], the rotating waves are defined as travelling waves propagated in circles, but having the mode structure (or discrete spectrum) of standing waves. In Refs. [12,13], two types of rotating waves are separated:

$$\text{cylindrical: } f(r, \varphi, z, t) = H_m^{(\pm)}(\alpha r) \exp(i\beta z + im\varphi - i\omega t), \tag{7.33}$$

where $H_m^{(\pm)}(x) = J_m(x) \pm i N_m(x)$, $H_m^{(\pm)}(x)$ is the Hankel function, $J_m(x)$ is the Bessel function, and $N_m(x)$ is the Neumann function, and

$$\text{spherical : } f(R, \theta, \varphi, t) = P_l^m(\cos\theta)h_l^{(\pm)}(\alpha R) \exp(im\phi - i\omega t), \tag{7.34}$$

where $h_l^{(\pm)}(x) = j_l(x) \pm i n_l(x)$, $h_l^{(\pm)}(x)$ is the spherical Hankel function, $j_l(x)$ is the spherical Bessel function, $n_l(x)$ is the spherical Neumann function, and $P(x)$ is the Legendre function.

Although the described functions include the angular momentum $\exp(im\varphi)$, their revolution is not observable because the intensity of such functions is radially symmetric. To produce a visually observable rotating beam, one needs to use a composition of at least two such functions. In Refs. [13,14], a composition of two functions, $J_n(\alpha r) \exp(in\varphi)$ and $J_m(\beta r) \exp(im\varphi)$, is treated and rotates (at $n \neq m$) as a whole, making one revolution at distance

$$\Delta z_{2\pi} \approx 4\pi k \frac{n - m}{\alpha^2 - \beta^2}, \quad k = \frac{2\pi}{\lambda} \tag{7.35}$$

and having the period of transverse intensity pattern self-reproduction given by

$$\Delta z \approx \frac{4\pi k}{\alpha^2 - \beta^2}, \tag{7.36}$$

resulting from the intensity symmetry of the order $(n - m)$.

The general condition for the periodicity of Bessel beams and their rotation as a whole for the composition of more than two components is dealt with in Sections 7.2 and 7.3.

In Refs. [15,16], another type of function with angular momentum represented by Gaussian beams is discussed:

$$f(x, y) = \exp\left[-\frac{x^2 + y^2}{\sigma^2}\right] \prod_{m=0}^{M} \prod_{n_m=1}^{K_m} [(x - x_{n_m}) + i(y - y_{n_m})]^m$$

$$\times \prod_{l_m=1}^{L_m} [(x - x_{l_m}) - i(y - y_{l_m})]^m, \tag{7.37}$$

where K_m is the number of positive angular momentums:

$$(x - x_{n_m}) + i(y - y_{n_m}) = r \exp(i\varphi) - r_{n_m} \exp(i\varphi_{n_m}),$$

$$r = \sqrt{x^2 + y^2}, \quad \varphi = \tan^{-1}\left(\frac{y}{x}\right), \quad r_{n_m} = \sqrt{x_{n_m}^2 + y_{n_m}^2}, \varphi_{n_m} = \tan^{-1}\left(\frac{y_{n_m}}{x_{n_m}}\right),$$

$$\tag{7.38}$$

and L_m is the number of negative angular momentums,

$$(x - x_{l_m}) - i(y - y_{l_m}) = r \exp(-i\varphi) - r_{l_m} \exp(-i\varphi_{l_m}), \qquad (7.39)$$

(x_{n_m}, y_{n_m}) and (x_{l_m}, y_{l_m}) are the centers of the corresponding whirlpools.

In Ref. [17], the condition under which the structure of a multimode Gauss-Laguerre (GL) beam is preserved up to a scale and a turn in the course of light propagation in free space has been derived. The composition

$$f(x, y) = \sum_{n,m} C_{nm} \Psi_{nm}(x, y), \qquad (7.40)$$

where

$$\Psi_{nm}(x, y) = \exp(-x^2 - y^2)(x + imy)^{|m|} L_n^{|m|}(2x^2 + 2y^2) \qquad (7.41)$$

and $L_n^m(x)$ is the Laguerre polynomial, will rotate if

$$2n + |m| + \mu m = \gamma - 1, \qquad (7.42)$$

where μ and γ are constant.

It is interesting that all the light modes of free space mentioned earlier, may be derived as the solution to an isoperimetrical problem [18], that is, from the condition that some functional proportional to the parameter of the light beam divergence is minimal. In such a case, the modes are represented by such light states that ensure the minimal divergence and the maximal intensity in the lens focal plane, other conditions being equal (the desired beam energy and radius).

The variation problem of searching for the beams with minimal divergence, the preset values of the beam (or diaphragm) energy and radius being given, leads to the explicit expressions for the four known types of light modes in free space: Gauss-Hermite (GH), GL, Bessel, and cosine modes [19]. These are described by the amplitude-phase functions. Methods for deriving the phase-only transmission function of the DOEs matched to the free-space modes is covered in the subsequent sections.

7.2 PHASE FORMERS OF LIGHT FIELDS WITH LONGITUDINAL PERIODICITY

Of the light modes pointed out in Section 7.1, the Bessel beams are of particular interest owing to their ability of diffraction-free propagation in free space. There are numerous papers dealing with the generation of such modes.

The light beams described by the Bessel function of zero order and of the first kind have been treated in Refs. [20,21], and the light beam whose amplitude is proportional to the product of the Bessel function by the Gaussian function has been given consideration in Ref. [22]. Diffraction-free beams of higher orders described by the Bessel functions of arbitrary order have been covered in Refs. [23,24] and have come to be known as *Bessel modes*. Such modes, for instance, propagate within a circular gradient-index optical fiber and are found at the output of a cavity with circular plane mirrors of the same diameter.

The general expression for the complex amplitude of diffraction-free beams that do not change while propagating has been derived in Ref. [25]. An iterative algorithm has been developed for designing phase diffractive optical elements (DOEs) that can generate light beams with the arbitrary composition of Bessel modes [26]. Such DOEs operate like a helical axicon [14], thus providing invariant properties of the beam at a distance that is in direct proportion to the DOE radius and in inverse proportion to the angle of inclination of plane waves included into the field spatial spectrum. The diffraction divergence of the beam diameter is compensated by the energy coming from DOE peripheral domains. In other words, with increasing distance z from the DOE to the plane of interest, it is found that the DOE zone (ring) that contributes to the generation of the light field in this plane is also increased in radius.

Axially periodic beams occur when several (not less than two) conic light waves with different apex angles propagate along the optical axis. Their interference produces an interference pattern along the optical axis, with the modulation amplitude being approximately the same on the optical axis segment from the DOE up to the invariance distance spoken of earlier. The light wave propagated along the optical axis shows periodic variations in its cross section. The minimal period of the interference pattern is determined by the maximal difference between the inclination angles of different conic waves.

Topics related to the synthesis of phase optical elements capable of generating light fields with a desired longitudinal (axial), in particular, longitudinally periodic, intensity distribution have been covered in Refs. [27–29]. Note, however, that the algorithms developed in the works mentioned earlier, allow one to design the phase DOEs capable of generating a desired axial intensity distribution only on a small length of the optical axis.

In this section, we develop an iterative algorithm for designing DOEs that can generate the axially periodic light fields of mode character, which, in fact, conserve their periodicity along the entire optical axis.

Assume that the complex amplitude of monochromatic light field, $U(x, y, z)$, satisfies the Helmholtz equation [see Eq. (6.13) at $n = 1$]:

$$(\nabla^2 + k^2)U(x, y, z) = 0, \tag{7.43}$$

where ∇^2 is the differential operator and k is the light wave number. If the complex amplitude can be specified in cylindrical coordinates

$$U(x, y, z) = U_1(r)U_2(\varphi)U_3(z), \tag{7.44}$$

the partial solution of Eq. (7.43) may be written in the form [30]:

$$U_{qm}(r, \varphi, z) = e^{qz} J_m(r\sqrt{k^2 + q^2})e^{im\varphi}, \tag{7.45}$$

where (r, φ) are the transverse polar coordinates of the light field, q is the separation constant, and $J_m(x)$ is the Bessel function of the mth order. The separation constant q can be derived from the requirement that the field should be periodic along the z-axis:

$$U(r, \varphi, z + z_0) = U(r, \varphi, z), \tag{7.46}$$

where z_0 is the period. From Eq. (7.46), it follows that the light field can be represented through the functional Fourier series:

$$U(r, \varphi, z) = \sum_{n=-\infty}^{\infty} U_n(r, \varphi) \exp\left(\frac{2\pi i n z}{z_0}\right), \tag{7.47}$$

where

$$U_n(r, \varphi) = \frac{1}{z_0} \int_0^{z_0} U(r, \varphi, z) \exp\left(-\frac{2\pi i n z}{z_0}\right) dz. \tag{7.48}$$

From comparison of Eqs. (7.45) and (7.47), we can get the function $U_n(r, \varphi)$ in the explicit form:

$$U_n(r, \varphi) = \sum_{m=-\infty}^{\infty} C_m J_m\left(r\sqrt{k^2 + q_n^2}\right) e^{im\varphi}, \tag{7.49}$$

where $q_n = 2\pi i n / z_0$.

Thus, the general expression for the light field possessing the axial periodicity in Eq. (7.46), should be as follows:

$$U(r, \varphi, z) = \sum_{n,m=-\infty}^{\infty} C_m J_m(kr\overline{\rho}_n) \exp\left\{\frac{2\pi i n z}{z_0} + im\varphi\right\}, \tag{7.50}$$

where $\overline{\rho}_n = \sqrt{[1 - (n\lambda/z_0)^2]}$ and $\lambda = 2\pi/k$ is the wavelength. The requirement that the subradical expression for $\overline{\rho}_n$ should be positive restricts the number of terms in the sum of Eq. (7.50) on the index n:

$$|n| \leq z_0/\lambda \tag{7.51}$$

If $|n| > z_0/\lambda$, the terms in Eq. (7.50) will be proportional to the modified Bessel functions, $I_m(kr\overline{\rho}_n)$, which diverge when r tends to infinity. As they have no physical meaning, these terms are excluded from consideration.

According to Ref. [25], from the condition that the light field is axially periodic in magnitude

$$|U(r, \varphi, z + z_0)| = |U(r, \varphi, z)|, \tag{7.52}$$

one can derive an expression different from Eq. (7.50):

$$U(r, \varphi, z) = \sum_{n=n_1}^{n_2} U_n(r, \varphi) \exp\left[2\pi i z\left(\frac{\sigma_0}{\lambda} + \frac{n}{z_0}\right)\right], \tag{7.53}$$

where

$$U_n(r, \varphi) = \frac{1}{2\pi} \int_0^{2\pi} F_n(\theta) \exp[-ikr\rho_n \cos(\varphi - \theta)] \, d\theta, \tag{7.54}$$

$$\rho_n = \sqrt{1 - (\sigma_0 + n\lambda/z_0)^2}, \tag{7.55}$$

where $\sigma_0 = \cos\alpha_0$, α_0 is the minimal inclination angle for the plane waves of spatial spectrum for the given field, and n_1 and n_2 are found from the requirement that the subradical expression in Eq. (7.55) should be positive:

$$n_1 = -\left[\sigma_0 \frac{z_0}{\lambda}\right], \quad n_2 = \left[(1 - \sigma_0)\frac{z_0}{\lambda}\right], \tag{7.56}$$

where $[\ldots]$ denotes the integer part of number.

In Eq. (7.54), the arbitrary function $F_n(\theta)$ describes the angular dependence of the plane wave spectrum for a self-reproducing beam. Substituting in Eq. (7.54), the expression for the expansion of this periodic function into the Fourier series

$$F_n(\theta) = \sum_{m=-\infty}^{\infty} C_{mn} \exp(im\theta) \tag{7.57}$$

and making use of the integral form of the Bessel function, we get

$$U(r, \varphi, z) = \exp(ik\sigma_0 z) \sum_{n=n_1}^{n_2} \sum_{m=-\infty}^{\infty} C_{mn} J_m(kr\rho_n) \exp\left(\frac{2\pi i n z}{z_0} + im\varphi\right). \tag{7.58}$$

It can be seen from comparison of Eqs. (7.50) and (7.58) that at $\sigma_0 = 0$ they are functionally identical. The light fields specified by Eq. (7.58) present a wider family of fields as compared those described by Eq. (7.50) because the condition in Eq. (7.52) is weaker than that in Eq. (7.46).

It can also be seen from Eq. (7.58) that the nonzero contribution into the axially periodic light field $U(r, \varphi, z)$ comes from the plane waves whose wave vectors are found on conic surfaces with their generatrixes inclined to the z-axis at the angles given by

$$\cos \alpha_n^{\cdot} = \cos \alpha_0 + n\lambda/z_0, \quad n \in (n_1, n_2). \tag{7.59}$$

In what follows, the algorithms of designing phase DOEs are based on Eq. (7.58).

Consider the complete set of orthogonal functions within a circle of radius R [31]:

$$\Omega_{mn}(r, \varphi) = A_{mn} J_m\left(\frac{r}{R}\gamma_{mn}\right) \exp(im\varphi), \tag{7.60}$$

where $\qquad A_{mn} = [\sqrt{\pi} R J_m'(\gamma_{mn})]^{-1}, \tag{7.61}$

$J_m'(x)$ is the arbitrary Bessel function and γ_{mn} are the roots of the Bessel function $J_m(\gamma_{mn}) = 0$, $\gamma_{-m,n} = \gamma_{m,-n} = \gamma_{-m,-n} = \gamma_{m,n}$.

The condition of orthogonality of the functions in Eq. (7.60) takes the form

$$\int_0^R \int_0^{2\pi} \Omega_{mn}(r, \varphi) \cdot \Omega_{pq}^*(r, \varphi) \cdot r \, dr \, d\varphi = \delta_{mp}\delta_{nq}. \tag{7.62}$$

Any continuous and limited-in-the-circle function $U(r, \varphi)$ can be expanded in terms of the basis of Eq. (7.60):

$$U(r, \varphi) = \sum_{m,n=-\infty}^{\infty} C_{mn}\Omega_{mn}(r, \varphi). \tag{7.63}$$

To generate the light field $U(r, \varphi, z)$ of Eq. (7.58), one should generate, at $z = 0$, the light field with the complex amplitude given by

$$U_0(r, \varphi) = \sum_{n=n_1}^{n_2} \sum_{m=-\infty}^{\infty} \overline{C}_{mn} J_m(kr\rho_n) \exp(im\varphi). \tag{7.64}$$

From comparison of Eqs. (7.63) and (7.64), it can be seen that in the series in Eq. (7.64) only the coefficients $\overline{C}_{mn}$ that obey the condition

$$kR\rho_n = \gamma_{mn} \tag{7.65}$$

are not equal to zero. Note that the roots of the Bessel function alternate according to the inequalities

$$0 < \gamma_{m,1} < \gamma_{m+1,1} < \gamma_{m,2} < \gamma_{m+1,2} < \gamma_{m,3} \cdots.$$

Considering the condition in Eq. (7.65), the expansion in Eq. (7.63) makes it possible to construct an iterative procedure for designing a phase DOE that can generate the light field with axial periodicity. Once the values of period z_0 and parameters σ_0, λ, and R are chosen, the values of ρ_n, n_1, and n_2 are determined from Eqs. (7.55) and (7.56). Then, introducing the designation for the pth estimate of the desired phase of the DOE complex transmission function

$$S_p(r, \varphi) = \arg U_0^{(p)}(r, \varphi), \quad p = 0, 1, 2, \ldots, \tag{7.66}$$

we get an iterative algorithm for calculating the phase

$$S_{p+1}(r, \varphi) = \arg \left\{ \sum_{m,n=-\infty}^{\infty} B_{mn} \exp[i \arg C_{mn}^{(p)}] \Omega_{mn}(r, \varphi) \right\}, \tag{7.67}$$

$$C_{mn}^{(p)} = \int_0^R \int_0^{2\pi} \exp[i S_p(r, \varphi)] \cdot \Omega_{mn}^*(r, \varphi) \cdot r \, dr \, d\varphi, \tag{7.68}$$

$$B_{mn} \neq 0 \text{ at } Rk\rho_n = \gamma_{mn}, \tag{7.69}$$

where B_{mn} are nonnegative, arbitrarily specified numbers that determine the form of the light field transverse intensity distribution. The algorithm in Eqs. (7.67) to (7.69) shows a property of error relaxation implying the fulfilment of the following inequality for any p:

$$\sum_{m,n=-\infty}^{\infty} \left(|C_{mn}^{(p+1)}| - B_{mn} \right)^2 \leq \sum_{m,n=-\infty}^{\infty} \left(|C_{mn}^{(p)}| - B_{mn} \right)^2. \tag{7.70}$$

Note, however, that the algorithm of Eqs. (7.67) to (7.69) gives no way of designing the phase DOEs intended for the generation of axially periodic light fields with a desired transverse intensity distribution. For this algorithm the profile of the transverse intensity distribution is not the input but the output function.

Consider an algorithm for designing DOEs intended to generate radially symmetric light fields with axial periodicity and desired transverse intensity distribution along the axis. The algorithm is based on the expansion of the radial field into a series in terms of orthogonal basis functions:

$$Q_{mn}(r, z) = D_{mn} J_m \left(\frac{r}{R} \gamma_{mn} \right) \exp \left[i2\pi \left(\frac{n}{z_0} + \frac{\sigma}{\lambda} \right) z \right], \tag{7.71}$$

where
$$D_{mn} = \left[\sqrt{z_0} R J'_m (\gamma_{mn}) \right]^{-1},$$

$$U(r, z) = \sum_{m,n=-\infty}^{\infty} \overline{C}_{mn} Q_{mn}(r, z). \tag{7.72}$$

Instead of Eqs. (7.67) and (7.68), with Eq. (7.69) retained, let us put down similar equations for an iterative search of the light field phase $T_p(r, z) = \arg U^{(p)}(r, z)$:

$$T_{p+1}(r, z) = \arg \left\{ \sum_{m,n=-\infty}^{\infty} B_{mn} \exp[i \arg \overline{C}_{mn}^{(p)}] Q_{mn}(r, z) \right\}, \tag{7.73}$$

$$\overline{C}_{mn}^{(p)} = \int_0^R \int_0^{z_0} \sqrt{I_0(r, z)} \exp[i T_p(r, z)] \cdot Q_{mn}^*(r, z) \cdot r \, dr \, dz, \tag{7.74}$$

where $I_0(r, z)$ is a desired periodic (of period z_0) radial intensity distribution along the z-axis, with the $I_0(r)$ function describing the illuminating beam intensity for $z = 0$, B_{mn} are arbitrary nonnegative numbers that determine the phase form and the algorithm's convergence rate. The phase of a radial DOE computed after p steps of the algorithm in Eqs. (7.69), (7.73) to (7.74) is equal to the function $T_p(r, z = 0)$.

Example 7.1   The DOEs intended to generate axially periodic fields were designed using the algorithm in Eqs. (7.67) to (7.69) [32]. The parameters of calculation were as follows: $R = 6$ mm, $\lambda = 1.06$ μm, $z_0 = 20$ mm, and $\sigma_0 = 0.01$ mm. For the parameters mentioned earlier, the mode character of the light field having passed through the DOE is retained at an approximate distance of

$$z_1 = R\rho_0^{-1}, \tag{7.75}$$

where ρ_0 is the maximal value of the parameter ρ_n in Eq. (7.55), which is the lesser, the greater is the number of nonnegative terms in the sum in Eq. (7.63) [14,20].

Shown in Figure 7.1 are the normalized intensity distributions on the optical axis for a DOE computed on the assumption that in the sum of Eq. (7.63) only the first term was nonzero. This single term is proportional to the Bessel function of zero order $J_0 (kr\rho_0)$.

The propagation of such a field along the z-axis was calculated using a Fresnel transform which, in turn, was taken using an algorithm of fast Fourier transform. Shown in Figure 7.1a is the plot for the intensity along the axis within the range from 100 mm to 700 mm, and in Figure 7.2a is a halftone transverse intensity distribution in the (ρ, z)-coordinates on the z-axis within the range from 300 mm to 380 mm, with black color corresponding to the maximal value of intensity. The halftone normalized intensity distributions in the (ρ, z)-coordinates are depicted for the amplitude-phase (Fig. 7.2a) and phase (Fig. 7.2b) DOE designed using the iterative algorithm with one

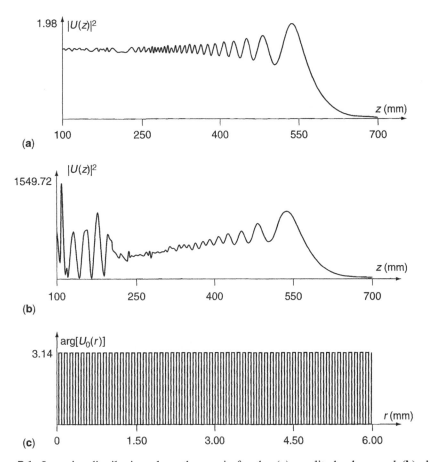

Figure 7.1. Intensity distribution along the z-axis for the (**a**) amplitude-phase and (**b**) phase DOE designed using the iterative algorithm with one term in the sum (7.63), and (**c**) the radial section of phase for such a DOE.

term taken in the sum of Eq. (7.63). The radial section of phase for such a DOE is shown in Figure 7.1c.

From Figures 7.1 and 7.2, it can be seen that the Bessel beam retains its shape, showing intensity variations with constant amplitude on the optical axis up to a distance of $z = 300$ mm, as estimated by Eq. (7.75). Then, as the beam propagates, the oscillation of amplitude increases because of the finite DOE aperture, and at $z > 550$ mm, the beam axial intensity monotonically drops, indicating the beginning of the beam diffractive divergence. The Bessel beam radius was near 0.02 mm.

Shown in Figures 7.1b and 7.2b are analogous plots for the intensity distribution for an optical element derived from the previous DOE with the amplitude replaced by the unit amplitude and without changing the phase. In effect, such a DOE represents a binary-phase axicon. From Figures 7.1b and 7.2b, it can be seen that although the amplitude of the axial intensity oscillations is increased, the beam mode character is retained, that is, the propagation occurs without changes. It stands to reason that it is impossible to obtain an axially periodic field by choosing only one term in the sum (7.63). To do this requires at least two nonzero terms.

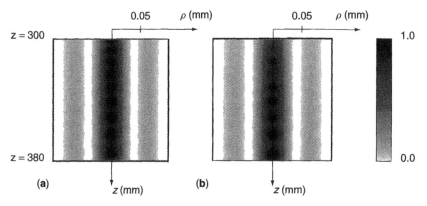

Figure 7.2. Halftone normalized intensity distributions in the (ρ, z)-coordinates for the (**a**) amplitude-phase and (**b**) phase-only DOE designed using the iterative algorithm with one term in the sum (7.63).

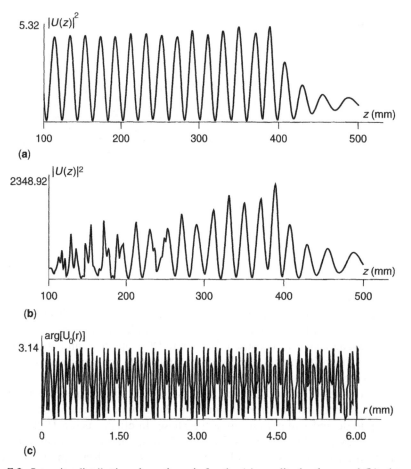

Figure 7.3. Intensity distribution along the axis for the (**a**) amplitude-phase and (**b**) phase-only DOEs designed using the iterative algorithm with two first terms in the sum (7.63), and (**c**) the radial section of the DOE phase.

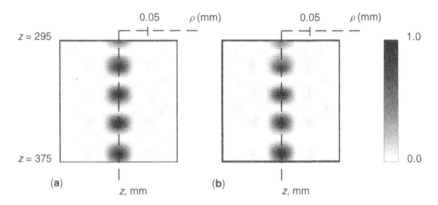

Figure 7.4. Halftone normalized intensity distributions in the (ρ, z)-coordinates for the (a) amplitude-phase and (b) phase-only DOEs designed using the iterative algorithm with two first terms in the sum (7.63).

Example 7.2 Figure 7.3 depicts the normalized axial intensity distributions for the amplitude-phase and phase-only DOEs designed using the method of Eqs. (7.67)–(7.69), if the coefficients numbered $m = 0$ and $n = 0$, 1 are not equal to zero and also the radial section of the DOE phase. The light field is seen to possess a periodicity with a period of $z_0 = 20$ mm at a distance of about 400 mm ($R = 6$ mm, $\lambda = 1.06$ μm). From Figure 7.3b, the phase-only DOE also shows the alternation of intensity maxima and minima along the optical axis every 20 mm, although the amplitude of light modulation is changed (increased) in every period. Shown in Figure 7.4 are the halftone normalized intensity distributions in the (ρ, z)-coordinates within the range $|\rho| < 0.1$ mm, 295 mm $< z < 375$ mm, produced by the amplitude-phase and phase-only DOE. Note that in both the cases the DOE phase was taken to be radially symmetric: $m = 0$ (Figs. 7.1c and 7.3c).

Example 7.3 In this example, the DOE phase is no longer radial (Fig. 7.5c). This time, the coefficients numbered $m = 1$, $n = 0$, 1, 2, 3 were taken to be not equal to zero. From Figures 7.5 and 7.6, the field character is seen to become more complicated and the distance at which the mode character is observable is seen to shorten from 400 mm (Fig. 7.3a) to 300 mm (Fig. 7.5a). In this case, the transverse intensity distribution of light field is circular (Fig. 7.6a,b): on the optical axis, the intensity is equal to zero. The intensity curves for $\rho = 0.02$ mm are shown in Figure 7.5.

The number of iterations after which the algorithm stagnates, that is, when the error shows no significant increase with increasing iterations, is proportional to the number of nonzero terms in the series in Eq. (7.63). So, when choosing one or two nonzero coefficients in Eq. (7.63), the error in Eq. (7.70) stabilizes after one or two iterations, whereas with four nonzero coefficients, it stabilizes after five to six iterations.

7.3 AN ALGORITHM FOR DESIGNING A DOE GENERATING ROTATING MULTIMODE BESSEL BEAMS

In the preceding section we dealt with a subclass of axially periodic light fields with a conic plane wave spectrum, referred to as *multimode Bessel beams*.

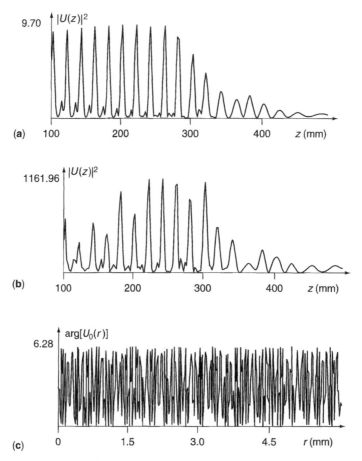

Figure 7.5. The axial intensity distribution for the (**a**) amplitude-phase and (**b**) pure-phase DOE designed using the iterative algorithm with four nonzero first terms in Eq. (7.63), and (**c**) the radial section of the DOE phase.

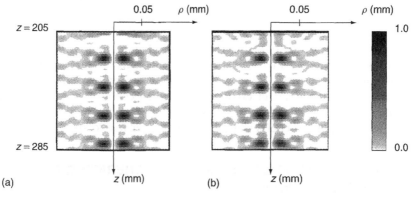

Figure 7.6. Halftone normalized intensity distributions in the (ρ, z)-coordinates for the (**a**) amplitude-phase and (**b**) pure-phase DOEs designed using the iterative algorithm with four first terms of the sum (7.63).

In this section, those conditions are specified under which the cross section of Bessel beams is rotated and a gradient algorithm is proposed to design DOEs that can generate such light fields. The Bessel beam cross section shows rotation because two conic waves propagating at different apex angles and with different "helical" components produce an interference pattern rotating about the optical axis.

When the propagating waves are more than two, the interference pattern is complicated, so for the cross section to be rotating as an integrity, certain conditions need to be imposed on the conic wave parameters.

It follows from Eq. (7.58) that if the nonzero coefficients C_{mn} have the same number $n = n_0$, the light field propagates as a diffraction-free Bessel mode without changing its shape:

$$U(r, \varphi, z) = \exp\left(ik\sigma_0 z + i\frac{2\pi n_0 z}{z_0}\right) \sum_{m=-\infty}^{\infty} C_m J_m(kr\rho_0)e^{im\varphi}, \qquad (7.76)$$

where $C_m = C_{mn_0}$, $\rho_0 = \rho_{n_0}$.

The axial periodicity of the light field in Eq. (7.58) takes place if at least two terms with different numbers n_1 and n_2 are not equal to zero.

The rotation of the cross section of the light beam in Eq. (7.58) is a particular case of the axial periodicity and can be provided by an agreed-upon choice of nonzero terms with different numbers n and m. To derive the condition of the beam rotation, let us, instead of Eq. (7.58), write down the relation for intensity:

$$I(r, \varphi, z) = \sum_{n,m=-\infty}^{\infty} |C_{mn} J_m(kr\rho_n)|^2 + 2 \sum_{m,n=-\infty}^{\infty} \sum_{m',n'=-\infty}^{\infty} |C_{mn} C_{m'n'}|$$

$$\times J_m(kr\rho_n) J_{m'}(kr\rho_{n'}) \cos \Phi_{mn}^{m'n'}(r, \varphi) \qquad (7.77)$$

$$\Phi_{mn}^{m'n'}(r, \varphi) = \arg C_{mn} - \arg C_{m'n'} + \frac{2\pi(n - n')z}{z_0} + (m - m')\varphi. \qquad (7.78)$$

From Eq. (7.78), it follows that the form of the function $I(r, \varphi + \Delta\varphi, z + \Delta z)$ does not change if

$$\frac{m - m'}{n - n'} = A, \quad n \neq n', \ m \neq m', \qquad (7.79)$$

where A is constant. From Eq. (7.79), it follows that if in Eq. (7.58) only two terms are not equal to zero, the light field will experience rotation around the propagation axis at any values of their numbers such that $n \neq n'$, $m \neq m'$. Equation (7.79) may also lead to less common but more convenient-to-use conditions of the beam rotation:

$$\frac{m}{n} = A, \qquad (7.80)$$

$$m - n = A. \qquad (7.81)$$

If the condition in Eqs. (7.79), (7.80), or (7.81) is fulfilled, with distance changing by Δz, the intensity $I(r, \varphi, z)$ in Eq. (7.77) will not change, provided the angle is equal to $\varphi + \Delta\varphi$, where

$$\Delta\varphi = -2\pi \frac{\Delta z}{A z_0}. \tag{7.82}$$

Because Δz and φ are arbitrary, the beam will rotate while propagating. From Eq. (7.82), it can be seen that if A^{-1} is the integer number, the rotating beam will make a whole number of revolutions on the period length z_0, with the rotation direction (left or right) being determined by the sign of the constant A.

Let us consider the orthogonal basis of the eigenfunctions of oscillations of a thin circular membrane of radius R, which is described by Eqs. (7.60) and (7.61) [33].

We may seek the DOE transmission function, $U_0(r,\varphi)$, as a linear combination of the functions in Eq. (7.60), with the coefficient modules considered as being pregiven and their arguments being free parameters. The modulus of the transmission function itself, $|U_0(r,\varphi)|$, is also given and has the meaning of the DOE illuminating beam amplitude. This linear combination is given by

$$U_0(r,\varphi) = \sum_{m,n=-\infty}^{\infty} C_{mn}\Omega_{mn}(r,\varphi), \tag{7.83}$$

considering that

$$k R_{\rho_n} = \gamma_{mn}. \tag{7.84}$$

The phase of the function $U_0(r,\varphi)$ and the corresponding coefficients C_{mn} in Eq. (7.83) may be derived by minimizing the following quadratic criterion:

$$K = \int_0^\infty \int_0^{2\pi} \left[|U_0(r,\varphi)| - \left| \sum_{m,n=-\infty}^{\infty} C_{mn}\Omega_{mn}(r,\varphi) \right| \right]^2 r \, dr \, d\varphi. \tag{7.85}$$

The gradient method for minimizing the criterion in Eq. (7.85) can easily be constructed using the results arrived at in Ref. [34]. The iterative procedure of searching for the coefficient arguments, $v_{mn} = \arg C_{mn}$, will be given by

$$v_{mn}^{(p+1)} = v_{mn}^{(p)} + \tau_p \frac{\partial K}{\partial V_{mn}^{(p)}}, \tag{7.86}$$

$$\frac{\partial K}{\partial v_{mn}^{(p)}} = 2|C_{mn}\overline{C}_{mn}^{(p)}| \sin\left(v_{mn}^{(p)} - \overline{v}_{mn}^{(p)}\right), \tag{7.87}$$

$$\overline{C}_{mn} = \int_0^\infty \int_0^{2\rho} F(r,\varphi)\Omega_{mn}^*(r,\varphi) r \, dr \, d\varphi, \tag{7.88}$$

$$F(r,\varphi) = |U_0(r,\varphi)| \frac{U(r,\varphi)}{|U(r,\varphi)|} - U(r,\varphi), \tag{7.89}$$

$$U(r,\varphi) = \sum_{m,n=-\infty}^{\infty} C_{mn}\Omega_{mn}(r,\varphi), \tag{7.90}$$

where $\bar{v}_{mn} = \arg \overline{C}_{mn}$, and p is the iteration number. The modules $|C_{mn}|$ are specified arbitrarily and are the task parameters that determine the shape of the cross section of the beam to be generated.

According to Ref. [34], the step τ_p in Eq. (7.86) may be represented in the form

$$\tau_p = \frac{K}{\overline{K}_p}, \tag{7.91}$$

$$\overline{K}_p = - \sum_{m,n=-\infty}^{\infty} \left| \frac{\partial K}{\partial v_{mn}^{(p)}} \right|^2. \tag{7.92}$$

This iterative algorithm is different from the algorithms in Eqs. (7.67) to (7.69) and (7.73) to (7.75).

This iterative algorithm was used for designing the phase optical elements intended to generate the light fields effectively composed (by 80–90%) of two-to-three Bessel modes.

Example 7.4   An example of a diffraction-free beam, or the stable Bessel mode, is shown in the left column of Figure 7.7. The calculation parameters are as follows: $\lambda = 1.06$ µm, $z_0 = 20$ mm, $R = 1$ mm, and $\sigma_0 = 0.01$. Shown in Figure 7.7 in the left column are: (a1) the binary phase of a DOE that generates the light beam effectively composed of two terms in Eq. (7.58) with numbers (m, n): $(-3,3)$ and $(3,-3)$. Because both the terms have the same number $n = -3$, it follows from Eq. (7.76) that the light field does not change its structure while propagating. This can be seen from Figure 7.7, which depicts in the left column the transverse intensity distributions of the beam (negative) at distances z: (b1) 25 mm, (c1) 30 mm, (d1) 35 mm, (e1) 40 mm, and (f1) 45 mm.

An example of the light field showing periodic changes while propagating is depicted in the middle column in Figure 7.7. The calculation parameters are: $\lambda = 1.06$ µm, $z_0 = 20$ mm, $R = 3$ mm, and $\sigma_0 = 0.02$. In Eq. (7.58), only three terms with the numbers (m, n): $(-2,-3)$, $(0,-1)$, and $(2,-2)$ were kept not equal to zero. Note that in this case the rotation conditions in Eqs. (7.79) and (7.80) were not observed. Shown in Figure 7.7 are: (a2) the halftone phase of such a DOE (black color is 2π and white color is 0), (b2–f2) the transverse intensity distributions (negative) generated at the distances z: (b2) 90 mm, (c2) 95 mm, (d2) 100 mm, (e2) 105 mm, and (f2) 110 mm.

An example of the rotating multimode Bessel beam is shown in the right column of Figure 7.7. The calculation parameters are: $\lambda = 1.06$ µm, $z_0 = 20$ mm, $R = 2$ mm, and $\sigma_0 = 0.015$. In Eq. (7.58), the following three terms were chosen to be not equal to zero, (m,n): $(-3,3)$, $(-1,-1)$, and $(1,1)$. The rotation conditions in Eqs. (7.79) and (7.80) are observed for these numbers. Shown in the right column in Figure 7.7 are (a3) the halftone DOE phase that generates the light beam effectively containing three Bessel modes, with the transverse intensity distributions (negative) shown at distances z: (b3) 70 mm, (c3) 75 mm, (d3) 80 mm, (e3) 85 mm, and (f3) 90 mm. In Figure 7.7, the beam is seen to be rotating, but with some changes of the beam cross section pattern taking place because of interference of three main modes (with 90% energy) and higher-order modes.

The transverse diffraction patterns in Figure 7.7 were computed using the Fresnel transform that, in turn, were taken using the fast Fourier transform algorithm.

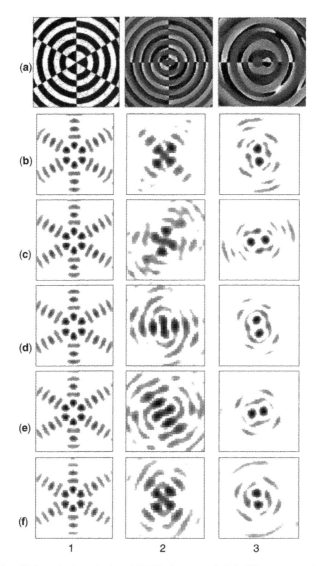

Figure 7.7. (a1–a3) Iteratively calculated DOE phases and (b1–f3) cross sections of the multi-mode Bessel beams generated by these DOEs.

7.4 GENERATION OF A COUPLE OF ROTATING DIFFRACTION-FREE BEAMS USING A BINARY-PHASE DOE

From the previous sections it is evident that if the spatial spectrum of a coherent light beam is composed of a finite number of narrow concentric rings, such a field will be self-reproduced at equal intervals along the propagation axis [8]. Diffraction-free Bessel beams with the complex amplitude represented by a superposition of Bessel functions of the first kind with angular harmonics, is a particular case of the aforementioned light fields [20,35,36]. Note that such diffraction-free light fields can also be generated for the partially coherent light [37,38]. Because the ideal self-reproducing light fields have the infinite size and energy, their practical implementation calls for the apodization, for example, by the Gaussian aperture [22,39]. To generate stable (the self-reproduction period is equal to zero) diffraction-free Bessel beams, one can use a Fabry-Perot interferometer [11,40], a narrow circular slit in the screen placed at the focal length before a spherical lens [21], binary-amplitude holograms with the spatial carrier frequency [24,41], and amplitude [42] and phase [43,44] diffraction axicons.

To generate a stable multimode Bessel beam with a desired contribution of every separate mode, one may iteratively design an appropriate phase diffractive optical element in the manner indicated in the previous sections [26]. Other types of light beams, whose amplitude is described by the Bessel functions of the second kind [45] or by the Neumann functions [13], possess the properties similar to those of diffraction-free beams. Near-diffraction-free beams may be generated by the amplitude diffractive elements that are designed using some special iterative procedures [46].

The light fields that can rotate about the propagation axis are a particular case of self-reproducing beams. The simplest of such fields are represented by a superposition of two Bessel functions [12] of different order and scale [13,14]. The general condition for the generation of rotating diffraction-free beams has been derived in Refs. [47,48]. Such beams can be produced using phase trochosons [43], binary helicons [14], or binary-phase helical axicons [14,44].

In this section, we deal with rotating Bessel beams produced by binary-phase DOEs with spatial carrier frequency. As is the case with helical axicons discussed in Ref. [14], these have about 40 percent efficiency, but are able to produce two identical beams simultaneously (each having 40% of energy), with opposite sense of rotation. As distinct from the beams in Ref. [14], each of the two identical beams may be described as a linear combination of the Bessel functions with angular harmonics, with their weight contribution set arbitrarily.

In Ref. [14], it has been proposed that multimode Bessel beams should be produced with the help of a DOE, whose transmission function $U(r, \theta)$ is a linear combination of axicons with angular harmonics. In this case, instead of Eq. (7.58), one should put at $z = 0$:

$$U(r, \varphi) = \sum_{m=-\infty}^{\infty} \sum_{n=0}^{N} C_{mn} \exp(-ik\rho_n r + im\varphi). \tag{7.93}$$

The axicon with transmittance $\exp(-ik\rho_n r + im\varphi)$ will effectively generate a light field near the optical axis on the line-segment $0 < z < R/\rho_n$, with the amplitude proportional to the Bessel function [42]: $J_m(k\rho_n r) \exp(im\varphi)$. According to Ref. [14], binary axicons with angular harmonics are suited to the generation of rotating Bessel beams. In this case, expanding the binary axicon transmission function into the functional Goodman-Silvester series yields [49]

$$\exp[i(-k\rho_0 r + m\varphi)_2] = \sum_{p=-\infty}^{\infty} \mathrm{sinc}\left[\pi\left(p + \frac{1}{2}\right)\right] \exp[i(2p+1)(-k\rho_0 r + m\varphi)],$$

$$\tag{7.94}$$

where $(\ldots)_2$ denotes the operation of quantization in two levels: 0 and π. In Eq. (7.94), the first two terms at $p = 0,1$ take the form

$$\frac{2}{\pi} \exp(-ik\rho_0 r + im\varphi) + \frac{2}{3\pi} \exp(-3ik\rho_0 r + 3im\varphi). \tag{7.95}$$

Near the optical axis on the line-segment $0 < z < R/3\rho_0$, these two terms will effectively produce the following light beam as a result of interference:

$$\frac{2}{\pi} J_1(k\rho_0 r) \exp\left(im\varphi + i\frac{kz\rho_0^2}{2}\right) + \frac{2}{3\pi} J_1(3k\rho_0 r) \exp\left(3im\varphi + i\frac{9kz\rho_0^2}{2}\right). \qquad (7.96)$$

The efficiency of this field is a little greater than $(2/\pi)^2 = 40.5$ percent. From Eq. (7.94), it follows that the binary axicon is only suited to the generation of a special type of rotating Bessel beams, whereas the phase DOE designed according to Eq. (7.64) allows one to generate the rotating diffraction-free beams of a more general form.

A binary DOE version based on the phase of the function in Eq. (7.64) may be derived by adding a linear phase in the $x = r \cos \varphi$ coordinate and quantizing with respect to two levels, 0 and π:

$$S_2(r, \varphi) = [S(r, \varphi) + 2\pi \nu r \cos \varphi]_2, \qquad (7.97)$$

where ν is the spatial carrier frequency, the symbol $[\ldots]_2$ has the same meaning as in Eq. (7.94), and $S(r, \varphi)$ is the argument of the $U_0(r, \varphi)$ function in Eq. (7.58) after a sufficient number of iterations.

Once again, make use of the expansion into the functional series [49] and derive the following expression for the binary phase of Eq. (7.97):

$$\exp[i S_2(r, \varphi)] = \sum_{p=-\infty}^{\infty} \text{sinc}\left[\pi\left(p + \frac{1}{2}\right)\right] \exp\{i(2p + 1)[S(r, \varphi) + 2\pi \nu r \cos \varphi]\}. \qquad (7.98)$$

Only the first two terms, at $p = 0, -1$, in the sum in Eq. (7.98) will describe two identical, but oppositely rotating and propagating at an angle to each other Bessel beams, each having the efficiency of about 40 percent:

$$\frac{2}{\pi} \exp[i S(r, \varphi) + 2\pi i \nu r \cos \varphi] + \frac{2}{\pi} \exp[-i S(r, \varphi) - 2\pi i \nu r \cos \varphi]. \qquad (7.99)$$

Example 7.5 Shown in Figure 7.8a is the halftone DOE phase [255 quantization levels within the range $(-\pi, \pi)$], calculated as the argument of Eq. (7.58), with two nonzero terms with numbers (m, n): $(-1,0)$ and $(1,1)$, in Eq. (7.58). The rotation condition in Eq. (7.79) is fulfilled. The period of revolution is $z_0 = 20$ mm. The phase function size in Figure 7.8a is 4×4 mm^2 (256×256 pixels).

Shown in Figure 7.8b–f are the halftone distributions of the light field transverse intensity (negative) produced by the DOE (Fig. 7.8a) and calculated using the Fresnel transform at distances: (7.8b) $z = 115$ mm, (7.8c) $z = 120$ mm, (7.8d) $z = 125$ mm, (7.8e) $z = 130$ mm, and (7.8f) $z = 135$ mm. Thus, the whole period is seen to be covered. The phase DOE designed by eliminating the amplitude information is able to successfully produce a rotating diffraction-free beam.

Shown in Figure 7.9a is the binary phase derived from the halftone phase (Fig. 7.8a) by adding a spatial frequency $\nu = 10$ mm^{-1}, according to Eq. (7.97). Shown in Figure 7.9b–f are the halftone transverse intensity distributions of the light field (negative) produced by the binary DOE (Fig. 7.9a) and calculated for the same

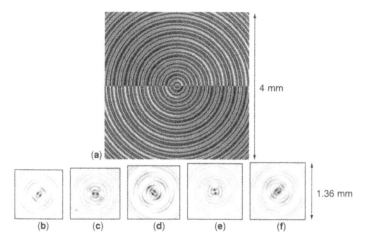

(a)

(b)   (c)   (d)   (e)   (f)

1.36 mm

Figure 7.8. The result of simulation: (**a**) the DOE phase, and the transverse intensity distribution for the Bessel beam with the numbers $(-1,0)$ and $(1,1)$ at distances: (**b**) 115 mm, (**c**) 120 mm, (**d**) 125 mm, (**e**) 130 mm, and (**f**) 135 mm.

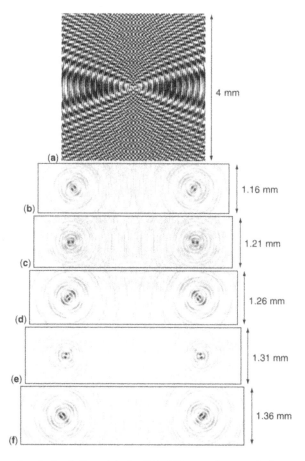

Figure 7.9. The result of simulation: (**a**) the DOE binary phase and the transverse intensity distribution of the Bessel beams with the numbers $(-1,0)$, $(1,1)$, and $(1,0)$, $(-1,1)$ at the distances z: (**b**) 115 mm, (**c**) 120 mm, (**d**) 125 mm, (**e**) 130 mm, and (**f**) 135 mm.

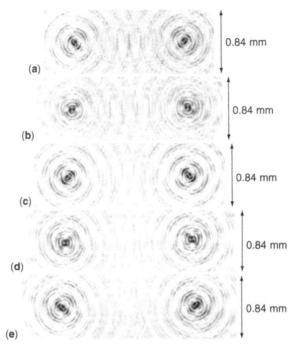

Figure 7.10. Experimentally measured transverse intensity distributions (negative) after the DOE with the phase shown in Figure 7.9a at the distances z: (**a**) 115 mm, (**b**) 120 mm, (**c**) 125 mm, (**d**) 130 mm, and (**e**) 135 mm.

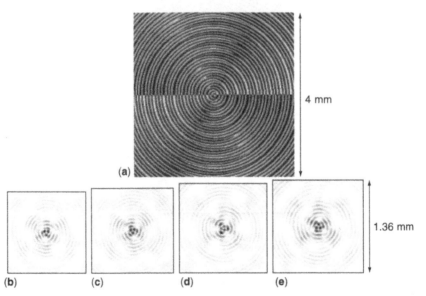

Figure 7.11. The result of simulation: (**a**) the DOE phase and the transverse intensity distribution for the Bessel beam with the mode numbers $(-1,0)$ and $(2,1)$ at the distances z: (**b**) 170 mm, (**c**) 175 mm, (**d**) 180 mm, and (**e**) 185 mm.

distances z: (7.9b) 115 mm, (7.9c) 120 mm, (7.9d) 125 mm, (7.9e) 130 mm, and (7.9f) 135 mm. In accordance with Eq. (7.99), the binary DOE produces two identical diffraction-free beams with the opposite sense of rotation. From comparison of the patterns in Figures 7.8b–f and 7.9b–f, both the elements are seen to generate fairly similar light fields.

The binary-phase DOE (Fig. 7.9a) was fabricated using a low-voltage e-beam image generator Leica LION LV1 at Joensuu University, Finland (see Chapter 4).

The ultimate resolution of this e-beam lithographer is about 0.04 μm, the DOE size is 4×4 mm^2 (1000×1000 pixels), with the binary relief depth intended for the He-Ne laser of wavelength $\lambda = 0.633$ μm. The resulting intensity distribution at various distances after the DOE was registered by a CCD camera with a 6.6×4.78 mm^2 window (768×567 pixels). Shown in Figure 7.10 is the experimentally measured light intensity distribution after the DOE at various distances within the limits of one period: (7.10a) $z = 115$ mm, (7.10b) $z = 120$ mm, (7.10c) $z = 125$ mm, (7.10d) $z = 130$ mm, and (7.10f) $z = 135$ mm. What we can see is that (*1*) there is no zero order, (*2*) there is the rotation effect, and (*3*) there is good agreement with theory (Fig. 7.9b–f).

Example 7.6 Shown in Figures 7.11 to 7.13 are the results of numerical simulation (Figs. 7.11 and 7.12) and physical experiment (Fig. 7.13) for the propagation of another two-mode Bessel beam with the mode numbers (m, n): $(-1,0)$ and $(2,1)$. The period of revolution is $z_0 = 30$ mm.

Figure 7.11a depicts the halftone DOE phase obtained as the argument of Eq. (7.58). Shown in Figure 7.11b–e are the estimated intensity distributions of the generated beam at half the period of revolution: (7.11b) $z = 170$ mm, (7.11c) $z = 175$ mm, (7.11d) $z = 180$ mm, and (7.11e) $z = 185$ mm.

Figure 7.12a depicts the binary phase derived using Eq. (7.97) from the phase shown in Figure 7.11a by means of adding the spatial frequency $\nu = 20$ mm^{-1}. Shown in Figure 7.12b–e are the estimated intensity distributions of the light field generated by the phase DOE (Fig. 7.12a) at the same distances.

Figure 7.13 depicts the experimental intensity distributions obtained at the distances z: (7.13a) 170 mm, (7.13b) 175 mm, (7.13c) 180 mm, and (7.13d) 185 mm.

From comparison, the theory and experiment are seen to be in good agreement. Noncomplete conservation of the rotating beam cross-section pattern is due to the fact that the amplitude information was disregarded while calculating the phase as the argument of Eq. (7.58).

7.5   A DOE TO GENERATE MULTIMODE GAUSS–LAGUERRE BEAMS

In Chapter 6, laser light modes are dealt with, and they show the properties of retaining the spatial structure and not spreading while propagating in their medium, although attaining a phase delay. The Gaussian modes are also able to retain their structure, changing only their scale while they are propagated in free space.

The DOEs intended to generate multimode GL beams and designed using diffractive optics methods are discussed in Refs. [50–52]. Of particular interest are the phase DOEs characterized by the enhanced energy efficiency and multichannel operation mode, allowing several mode beams to be produced.

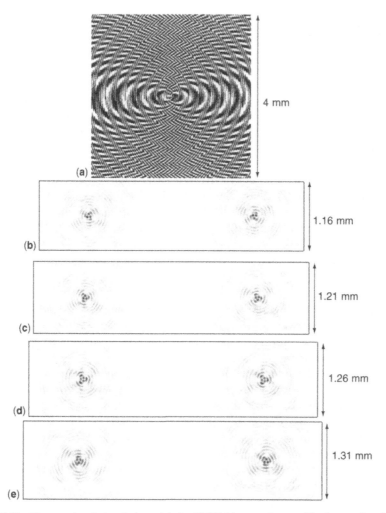

Figure 7.12. The result of simulation: (**a**) the DOE binary phase with the carrier frequency and the transverse intensity distribution for the two-mode Bessel beam at the distances z: (**b**) 170 mm, (**c**) 175 mm, (**d**) 180 mm, and (**e**) 185 mm.

As distinct from the method of coding with spatial carrier frequency treated in Ref. [50] and the iterative method involving the use of an auxiliary domain discussed in Ref. [51], in this section, we rely upon the technique developed in Ref. [52]. It implies an iterative approximation of the DOE-transmission function by a finite sum of Gaussian modes. It is only radially symmetric GL modes that have been treated in Refs. [52,53]. In the present section, the method is applied to the generalized GL modes, thus making it possible to attain high efficiency in generating the mode beams, with the desired image found in their cross section.

Besides, although the method under consideration works better when the number of modes in a beam is greater, it is still effective when producing a unimode beam. In this case, a DOE with the phase function proportional to the mode's signum function is obtained after one iteration. It has been shown that separate GL modes can effectively

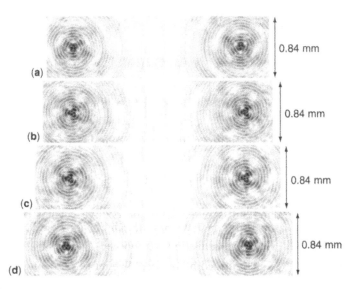

Figure 7.13. The experimental beam intensity distributions produced by the DOE with the phase shown in Figure 7.12a at the distance: (**a**) 170 mm, (**b**) 175 mm, (**c**) 180 mm, and (**d**) 185 mm.

be generated using the phase elements with the transmission function described as a signum function of the corresponding Laguerre polynomial.

In the case of generalized GL modes, the algorithm dealt with in Refs. [52,53] will look as follows: we need to calculate the phase $S(r, \varphi)$ of a DOE in polar coordinates (r, φ), satisfying the following relationship.

$$f(r, \varphi) = A_0(r, \varphi) \exp[i S(r, \varphi)] = \sum_{n=0}^{N} \sum_{|m| \leq n} C_{nm} \Psi_{nm}(r, \varphi), \qquad (7.100)$$

where $\Psi_{nm}(r, \varphi)$ is the generalized GL function in polar coordinates for its form in the Cartesian coordinates [see Eqs. (6.119) and (6.120)] given by:

$$\Psi_{nm}(r, \varphi) = \frac{\sqrt{n!}}{a\sqrt{\pi(n + |m|)!}} \left(\frac{r}{a}\right)^{|m|} \exp\left[-\left(\frac{r}{\sqrt{2}a}\right)^2\right] L_n^{|m|}\left[\left(\frac{r}{a}\right)^2\right] \exp(im\varphi),$$

$$r^2 = x^2 + y^2, \varphi = \text{arctg}\frac{y}{x}, \qquad (7.101)$$

where $L_n^m(x) = (-1)^m d^m/dx^m[L_{m+n}(x)]$ is the generalized Laguerre polynomial, $a = \dfrac{\sigma_0}{\sqrt{2}}$, σ_0 is the waist radius, $A_0(r, \varphi)$ is the known amplitude of the illuminating beam. The coefficients' modules, $|C_{nm}|$, are specified arbitrarily, and the arguments C_{nm} are free parameters.

The squared modules of the coefficients, $|C_{nm}|^2$, characterize the contribution of each mode into the beam.

The GL functions are orthogonal:

$$\int_0^{2\pi} \int_0^{\infty} \Psi_{nm}^{\infty}(r, \varphi)\Psi_{kl}(r, \varphi)r \, dr \, d\varphi = \delta_{nk}\delta_{ml}, \tag{7.102}$$

where $\delta_{nm} = \begin{cases} 1, & n = m, \\ 0, & n \neq m. \end{cases}$ is the Kronecker symbol.

Then, the coefficients in Eq. (7.100) can be derived from the formula

$$C_{nm} = \int_0^{2\pi} \int_0^{\infty} A_0(r, \varphi) \exp[iS(r, \varphi)]\Psi_{nm}^*(r, \varphi)r \, dr \, d\varphi. \tag{7.103}$$

The proposed iterative algorithm is relied on a consecutive calculation of the sums in Eq. (7.100) and integrals in Eq. (7.103), with the aid of the fast Fourier transform algorithm and with the corresponding restrictions imposed. So, in the fifth iteration the estimated coefficients $C_{nm}^{(k)}$ are replaced by the coefficients $\overline{C}_{nm}^{(k)}$ as follows:

$$\overline{C}_{nm}^{(k)} = D_{nm} C_{nm}^{(k)} |C_{nm}^{(k)}|^{-1}, \tag{7.104}$$

where D_{nm} are nonnegative numbers describing the energy distribution between the modes. The restrictions of type (7.104) are characteristic of the iterative Gerchberg-Saxton algorithm [34]. Note, however, that one can enhance the algorithm convergence if the replacement in Eq. (7.104) is modified by introducing some adaptivity coefficient $0 < \alpha \leq 1$, similar to that discussed in Chapter 2 (2.40):

$$\overline{C}_{nm}^{(k)} = \begin{cases} [D_{nm} - \alpha(|C_{nm}^{(k)}| - D_{nm})]C_{nm}^{(k)}|C_{nm}^{(k)}|^{-1}, & (n, m) \in \Omega \\ 0, & (n, m) \notin \Omega \end{cases} \tag{7.105}$$

or

$$\overline{C}_{nm}^{(k)} = \begin{cases} [D_{nm} - \alpha(|C_{nm}^{(k)}| - D_{nm})]C_{nm}^{(k)}|C_{nm}^{(k)}|^{-1}, & (n, m) \in \Omega \\ C_{nm}^{(k)}, & (n, m) \notin \Omega \end{cases} \tag{7.106}$$

where Ω is a set of index pairs, for which the numbers D_{nm} are not equal to zero.

Thus, the optical element phase, $S(r, \varphi)$, may be found through the following algorithm:

1. The initial phase is chosen as a stochastic value $S_0(r, \varphi)$.
2. Supposing that the kth phase estimate, $S_k(r, \varphi)$, is derived from Eq. (7.100) in the kth step, the coefficients $C_{nm}^{(k)}$ are found from Eq. (7.103) using $S_k(r, \varphi)$.
3. These are then replaced by the coefficients $\overline{C}_{nm}^{(k)}$, based on the rules in Eqs. (7.104), (7.105), or (7.106).
4. The coefficients $\overline{C}_{nm}^{(k)}$ are substituted in Eq. (7.100) to produce the $f_k(r, \varphi)$ function whose argument serves as a subsequent phase estimate

$$f_k(r, \varphi) = \sum_{n=0}^{N} \sum_{|m| \leq n} \overline{C}_{nm}^{(k)} \Psi_{nm}(r, \varphi), \quad S_{k+1}(r, \varphi) = \arg[f_k(r, \varphi)]. \tag{7.107}$$

Pass to step 2, and so on.

The algorithm's convergence is checked by the average deviations

$$\delta_A = \left\{ \int_0^{2\pi} \int_0^\infty [A_0(r,\theta) - |f_k(r,\varphi)|]^2 r \, dr \, d\varphi \right\}^{1/2}$$

$$\times \left\{ \int_0^{2\pi} \int_0^\infty A_0^2(r,\varphi) r \, dr \, d\varphi \right\}^{-1/2}, \tag{7.108}$$

$$\delta_C = \left\{ \sum_{n=0}^N \sum_{|m|\leq n} [D_{nm} - |C_{nm}^{(k)}|]^2 \right\}^{1/2} \left\{ \sum_{n=0}^N \sum_{|m|\leq n} D_{nm}^2 \right\}^{-1/2}. \tag{7.109}$$

Just like it was accomplished in Ref. [53], the errors in Eqs. (7.108) and (7.109) can be shown not to increase:

$$\delta_A^{(k+1)} \leq \delta_A^{(k)}, \quad \delta_C^{(k+1)} \leq \delta_C^{(k)}. \tag{7.110}$$

The GL functions are the eigenfunctions of the Fourier transform:

$$\frac{1}{2\pi} \int_0^{2\pi} \int_0^\infty \Psi_{nm}(r,\varphi) \exp[-ir\rho\cos(\varphi - \theta)] r \, dr \, d\varphi = (-1)^n(-i)^m \Psi_{nm}(\rho,\theta), \tag{7.111}$$

and, thus, may be effectively employed for entering the light into optical fibers [50]. By way of illustration, if the desired image is found in the cross section of a generated light beam being a superposition of GL modes

$$g(r,\varphi) = \sum_{n=0}^N \sum_{|m|\leq n} C_{nm}^g \Psi_{nm}(r,\varphi) \tag{7.112}$$

in the Fraunhofer diffraction zone or in the lens focal plane, we shall get the following image

$$\Im[g(r,\varphi)] = G(\rho,\theta) = \sum_{n=0}^N \sum_{|m|\leq n} \mu_{nm} C_{nm}^g \Psi_{nm}(\rho,\theta), \tag{7.113}$$

where $\Im$ denotes the Fourier transform and (ρ,θ) are the polar coordinates in the Fourier plane.

Hence, if it is only the modes with the same values of eigennumbers that contribute to the superposition

$$\mu_{nm} = (-1)^n(-i)^{|m|} = \mu_0, \tag{7.114}$$

the image pattern in the beam cross section does not change.

From Eq. (7.114), the eigennumbers of the GL functions are seen to take only four values:

$$\mu_{nm} = 1 : (n = 2k, m = 4l), (n = 2k + 1, m = 4l + 2),$$

$$\mu_{nm} = -1 : (n = 2k, m = 4l + 2), (n = 2k + 1, m = 4l),$$

TABLE 7.1. Eigenvalues for the Gauss-Laguerre Eigenfunctions

n	m									
	0	1	2	3	4	5	6	7	8	9
0	1									
1	-1	i								
2	1	$-i$	-1							
3	-1	i	1	$-i$						
4	1	$-i$	-1	i	1					
5	-1	i	1	$-i$	-1	i				
6	1	$-i$	-1	i	1	$-i$	-1			
7	-1	i	1	$-i$	-1	i	1	$-i$		
8	1	$-i$	-1	i	1	$-i$	-1	i	1	
9	-1	i	1	$-i$	-1	i	1	$-i$	-1	i

$$\mu_{nm} = i : (n = 2k, m = 4l + 3), (n = 2k + 1, m = 4l + 1),$$

$$\mu_{nm} = -i : (n = 2k, m = 4l + 1), (n = 2k + 1, m = 4l + 3),$$

$$k, l = 0, 1, 2, \ldots \tag{7.115}$$

Table 7.1 gives a more descriptive distribution of eigen-number values versus the number of the GL function.

Thus, it turns out quite realistic an undertaking to fit a superposition of GL modes with the same eigenvalues such that an image not changing its structure while passing through the Fourier-stage be produced.

Note that the GL functions with mutually opposite "curling" $\exp(\pm i|m|\varphi)$ have the same eigenvalues.

A set of GL modes with the same eigenvalues may be treated as a mode group, for this also represents an eigenfunction of the Fourier transform.

Obviously, the method under consideration will work better, when the number of terms taken into consideration in Eq. (7.100) and, hence, the number of modes in the beam is larger. The greater is the number of degrees of freedom, which are the phases of the coefficients C_{nm}, the more accurate is the approximation of the desired function $f(r, \varphi)$, in particular, the amplitude $A_0(x, y)$ from Eq. (7.100).

However, this method also applies to the generation of a unimode beam, in which case, after one iteration (with the subsequent stagnation) a DOE with the phase proportional to the signum function of the Laguerre polynomial is calculated:

$$\tau(r, \varphi) = \arg[\Psi_{nm}(r, \varphi)] = \frac{\pi}{2}(1 - \text{sgn}\{L_n^{|m|}[(r/a)^2]\}) + im\varphi. \tag{7.116}$$

Let us show such an approximation of the GL function to be effective.

Equation (7.116) for the phase function is equivalent to the following relation for the amplitude on the interval $[-R, R]$, where R is the aperture size, $t = (r/a)^2$:

$$\tau_{nm}(t, \varphi) = \text{sgn}[L_n^{|m|}(t)] \exp(im\varphi). \tag{7.117}$$

Let us expand the function in Eq. (7.117) in terms of Laguerre polynomials with "curling":

$$\tau_{nm}(t, \varphi) = \sum_{p=0}^{\infty} \sum_{|q| \leq p} C_{pq}^{(n,m)} L_p^{|q|}(t) \exp(iq\varphi) \tag{7.118}$$

and find the expansion coefficients:

$$C_{pq}^{(n,m)} = \sqrt{\frac{p!}{(p + |q|)!}} \int_0^{2\pi} \int_0^{\infty} \mathrm{sgn}[L_n^{|m|}(t)] e^{im\theta} L_p^{|q|}(t) e^{iq\theta} t^{|q|} e^{-t} \, dt \, d\varphi$$

$$= \sqrt{\frac{p!}{(p + |q|)!}} \int_0^{\infty} \mathrm{sgn}[L_n^{|m|}(t)] L_p^{|q|}(t) \cdot t^{|q|} e^{-t} \, dt \underbrace{\int_0^{2\pi} e^{im\theta} e^{iq\theta} \, d\varphi}_{\delta_{mq}}$$

$$= \sqrt{\frac{p!}{(p + |m|)!}} \int_0^{\infty} \mathrm{sgn}[L_n^{|m|}(t)] L_n^{|m|}(t) \cdot t^{|m|} e^{-t} \, dt = C_{pm}^{(n,m)} \tag{7.119}$$

Thus, only the coefficients with the same second indices as those of the function under expansion, $\tau_{nm}(t, \varphi)$, are nonzero.

Designating the polynomial zeros, $L_n^m(t_{k,n}) = 0$, as $t_{k,n}$ and putting $t_{0,n} = 0$, the expression in Eq. (7.119) can be represented as a sum of integrals:

$$C_{pm}^{(n,m)} = \sqrt{\frac{p!}{(p + |m|)!}} \sum_{k=0}^{n-1} \left[(-1)^k \int_{t_{k,n}}^{t_{k+1,n}} t^{|m|} e^{-t} L_p^{|m|}(t) \, dt \right]. \tag{7.120}$$

Substituting the reference integral [54]:

$$\int x^\alpha e^{-x} L_n^\alpha(x) dx = \frac{1}{n} x^{\alpha+1} e^{-x} L_{n-1}^{\alpha+1}(x) \tag{7.121}$$

in Eq. (7.120) yields the following expression for the coefficients in the expansion (7.117):

$$C_{pm}^{(n,m)} = \frac{2}{p} \sqrt{\frac{p!}{(p + |m|)!}} \sum_{k=1}^{n} [(-1)^{k-1} (t_{k,n})^{|m|+1} e^{-t_{k,n}} L_{p-1}^{|m|+1}(t_{k,n})]. \tag{7.122}$$

Note that the coefficients $C_{pq}^{(n,m)}$ with $q \neq m$ are equal to zero.

Example 7.7   Assume that we should generate a GL mode $\Psi_{10}(t, \varphi)$. For this purpose, we shall place in the plane $z = 0$, a phase element with transmittance $\tau_{10}(t) = \mathrm{sgn}[L_1^0(t)]$. Then, according to Eq. (7.122), in the space behind the filter, a superposition of light modes will be formed:

$$\tau_{10}(t) = \sum_{p=1}^{\infty} C_{p0}^{(1,0)} L_p^0(t) = 0.736 L_1^0(t) - 0.184 L_2^0(t) + 0.020 L_3^0(t) - 0.001 L_4^0(t) + \cdots .$$

$$\tag{7.123}$$

If illuminated by a collimated Gaussian beam, such a phase element will generate in the frequency plane, according to Eq. (7.111), a light field whose amplitude is proportional to the expression ($a = 1$ mm):

$$\int_0^\infty e^{-r^2/2} \, \mathrm{sgn}[L_1^0(r^2)] J_0(r\rho) \cdot r \, dr = \sum_{p=1}^\infty (-1)^p C_{p0}^{(1,0)} e^{-\rho^2/2} L_p^0(\rho^2) = -e^{-\rho^2/2}$$

$$\times \, [0.736 L_1^0(\rho^2) + 0.184 L_2^0(\rho^2) + 0.020 L_3^0(\rho^2) + 0.001 L_4^0(\rho^2) + \cdots], \qquad (7.124)$$

where $J_0(x)$ is the Bessel function.

The energy ratio for the light beams described by the first and second terms in Eq. (7.124) is given by

$$\frac{(0.184)^2 \int_0^\infty e^{-\rho^2} [L_2^0(\rho^2)]^2 \rho \, d\rho}{(0.736)^2 \int_0^\infty e^{-\rho^2} [L_1^0(\rho^2)]^2 \rho \, d\rho} = \frac{(0.184)^2 (2!)^2}{(0.736)^2 (1!)^2} \approx 0.25. \qquad (7.125)$$

Thus, more than 70 percent of the entire light beam energy is contained in the first term of the sum (7.124) describing the GL mode $\Psi_{10}(t, \varphi)$.

Example 7.8   Still more effective technique for generating the GL mode $\Psi_{nm}(r, \varphi)$, is to illuminate a phase DOE with the transmittance ($a = 1$ mm)

$$\tilde{\tau}_{nm}(r, \varphi) = \mathrm{circ}\left(\frac{r}{R}\right) \mathrm{sgn}[L_n^{|m|}(r^2)] \exp(im\varphi), \qquad (7.126)$$

not by the Gaussian but by a plane light beam, here $\mathrm{circ}\left(\dfrac{t}{t_0}\right) = \begin{cases} 1, & t \le t_0, \\ 0, & t > t_0. \end{cases}$

In this case, the value of R should be chosen in such a manner that the expression that determines the efficiency of a separate mode generation

$$\eta = \frac{\left| \int_0^{2\pi} \int_0^R \tilde{\tau}_{nm}(r, \varphi) \cdot \Psi_{nm}^*(r, \varphi) r \, dr \, d\varphi \right|^2}{\int_0^{2\pi} \int_0^R |\tilde{\tau}_{nm}(r, \varphi)|^2 r \, dr \, d\varphi \cdot \int_0^{2\pi} \int_0^\infty |\Psi_{nm}(r, \varphi)|^2 r \, dr \, d\varphi} \qquad (7.127)$$

will be maximal.

Let us consider an example with the GL mode $\Psi_{10}(r, \varphi)$. In this case, Eq. (7.127) takes the form

$$\eta = \frac{\left| 2 \cdot \left[\int_0^1 e^{-r^2/2}(1 - r^2) r \, dr - \int_1^R e^{-r^2/2}(1 - r^2) r \, dr \right] \right|^2}{R^2}$$

$$= \frac{4 \cdot [1,426 - e^{-R^2/2}(R^2 + 1)]^2}{R^2} \qquad (7.128)$$

and attains its maximum of $\eta = 0.786$ at $R = 2.5$ mm, which implies that the light field in Eq. (7.126) generates the GL mode $\Psi_{10}(r, \varphi)$ with an efficiency of about 79 percent.

Example 7.9   The numerical simulation parameters are 128 pixels along the radius r and 128 pixels on the angular component φ, the range of arguments is $r \in [0, 7 \text{ mm}]$ and $\varphi \in [0, 2\pi]$, the wavelength is $\lambda = 0.63$ μm, the focal length is $f = 100$ mm, and the Gaussian beam waist radius is $a = 1$ mm. In Eq. (7.100), the series terms with the numbers $n, m \leq N = 7$ were taken into account.

Operation of the designed DOEs was numerically simulated using the Fourier transform in Eq. (7.111)[55]. The results of generation of the GL mode are shown in Figure 7.14. The beam generated by such a DOE is shown in Figure 7.14b and, by comparison, the reference GL mode (3,2) is depicted in Figure 7.14c, with their radial sections shown in Figure 7.14d (solid line: the calculated mode; dashed line: the reference mode).

The maximal aperture radius R was determined from the condition of maximal efficiency of the generated beam η, in Eq. (7.127). The value of η as a function of R for the GL mode (3,2) is shown in Figure 7.15 and suggests that the optimal size of the DOE aperture for the generation of this mode is equal to $R = 4.5$ mm. The efficiency attains the value of 81 percent.

An optimal DOE radius can be fitted through similar studies for any other mode. Through numerical simulation it has been demonstrated that the phase DOEs designed using Eq. (7.126) enable one to produce unimode beams with the efficiency ranging from 77 to 81 percent, depending on the mode number. Table 7.2 gives the values of R and η for several modes.

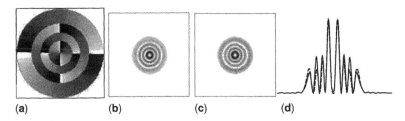

(a)   **(b)**   **(c)**   **(d)**

Figure 7.14. Unimode beam: (**a**) the DOE phase; the intensity distributions (negative) in the Fourier-spectrum for (**b**) the calculated and (**c**) reference Gauss-Laguerre mode (3,2); and (**d**) the intensity profile (solid line: estimation; dashed line: reference mode).

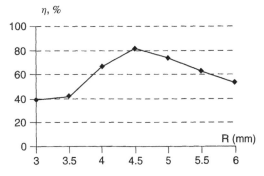

Figure 7.15. The efficiency η of mode generation as a function of the aperture radius R for a DOE that generates the Gauss-Laguerre mode (3,2).

TABLE 7.2. The DOE Optimal Radius R and Efficiency η ($a = 1$ mm)

GL Mode Number	(1,0)	(2,1)	(3,2)	(4,2)	(5,1)
Optimal Radius R (mm)	2.5	4	4.5	4.7	5
Efficiency η, (%)	79	77	81	78	77

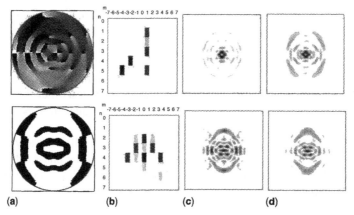

(a)   (b)   (c)   (d)

Figure 7.16. Multimode beams: (**a**) the DOE phase; (**b**) the squared modules of the coefficients in the expansion in Eq. (7.100); the intensity distributions in the focal plane for the (**c**) calculated, and (**d**) reference composition of Gauss-Laguerre modes (the upper row for the five-mode beam and the bottom row for the six-mode beam).

As one can expect, for a superposition of modes, the optimal radius will be found as an average radius of optimal radii of the modes incorporated into the superposition.

Example 7.10 Shown in Figure 7.16 are the examples of phase DOEs (Fig. 7.16a) intended to generate multimode GL beams in the spatial spectrum plane (Fig. 7.16c). The upper row in Figure 7.16 depicts a group of 5 modes: (1,1), (3,1), (4,−3), (5,1), and (5,−5), with eigen-numbers equal to i. The squared modules of the beam expansion coefficients are shown to be halftonic in Figure 7.16b. The bottom row in Figure 7.16 has to do with a group of six modes: (2,0), (3,−2), (3,2), (4,−4), (4,0), and (4,4), with eigen-numbers equal to 1. Both the beams are the eigenfunctions of the Fourier transform. For comparison, Figure 7.16d depicts the reference intensity distributions for the foregoing mode compositions.

7.6 ROTATION OF MULTIMODE GL LIGHT BEAMS IN FREE SPACE AND IN A FIBER

7.6.1 Free Space

In this section, the conditions under which a multimode GL beam will rotate about the propagation axis are derived in a way independent of that described in Ref. [17], and an expression for the complete number of revolutions is obtained.

It is known that it is light fields represented as a superposition of GL modes that satisfy the Helmholtz equation [56]. The complex amplitude of such fields in free space can be put down in the cylindrical coordinates (r, φ, z) as follows:

$$U(r, \varphi, z) = \exp\left[ikz + \frac{ikr^2}{2R} - \frac{r^2}{\sigma^2}\right] \sum_{n=0}^{\infty} \sum_{|m|\leq n} C_{nm} \left(\frac{\sqrt{2}r}{\sigma}\right)^{|m|}$$

$$\times L_n^{|m|}\left(\frac{2r^2}{\sigma^2}\right) \exp[-i\beta_{nm}(z) + im\varphi], \tag{7.129}$$

where
$$\beta_{nm}(z) = (2n + |m| + 1) \operatorname{arctg}(z/z_0), \tag{7.130}$$

$R = z(1 + z_0^2/z^2)$ is the curvature radius of a parabolic light field front, $\sigma^2 = \sigma_0^2(1 + z^2/z_0^2)$ is the effective beam radius, $2z_0 = 2\pi\sigma_0^2/\lambda$ is a confocal parameter, σ_0 is the waist radius, C_{nm} are constant coefficients, and k is the light wave number for the wavelength λ.

What we shall do is derive conditions for the rotation of the multimode beam's cross section. On the basis of Eq. (7.129), write down an expression for the intensity $I(r, \varphi, z) = |U(r, \varphi, z)|^2$:

$$I(r, \varphi, z) = \exp\left[-\frac{2r^2}{\sigma^2}\right] \left\{ \sum_{n=0}^{\infty} \sum_{|m|\leq n} |C_{nm}|^2 \left(\frac{\sqrt{2}r}{\sigma}\right)^{2|m|} \left| L_n^{|m|}\left(\frac{2r^2}{\sigma^2}\right)\right|^2 \right.$$

$$+ 2 \sum_{n\neq n'} \sum_{m\neq m'} |C_{nm}C_{n'm'}| \left(\frac{\sqrt{2}r}{\sigma}\right)^{|m|+|m'|} \left| L_n^{|m|}\left(\frac{2r^2}{\sigma^2}\right)\right.$$

$$\left. \times L_{n'}^{|m'|}\left(\frac{2r^2}{\sigma^2}\right)\right| \cos \Phi_{n'm'}^{nm}(r, \varphi) \right\}, \tag{7.131}$$

where
$$\Phi_{n'm'}^{nm}(r, \varphi) = \arg C_{nm} - \arg C_{n'm'} + [2(n - n') + (|m| - |m'|)]$$

$$\times \operatorname{arctg}\frac{z}{z_0} + (m - m')\varphi. \tag{7.132}$$

It can be seen from Eq. (7.132) that the $I(r, \varphi + \Delta\varphi, z + \Delta z)$ function will not change its form if in the relation

$$\varphi + \Delta\varphi = B \operatorname{arctg}\frac{z + \Delta z}{z_0} \tag{7.133}$$

the value of B is constant:

$$B = \frac{2(n - n') + (|m| - |m'|)}{m - m'} = \text{const}, \quad n, n', m, m' = 0, 1, 2, \ldots \tag{7.134}$$

Or more strictly, if in Eqs. (7.131) and (7.132) we produce the replacement of variables:

$$r' = \frac{r}{\sigma}, \quad \varphi' = \varphi - B \operatorname{arctg}\frac{z}{z_0}, \quad z' = z,$$

the intensity function $I(r', \varphi')$ will be z'-independent in this new expanded and rotating coordinate system.

The condition for the rotation of a multimode GL beam as a whole in free space, Eq. (7.134), is similar to the condition in Eq. (7.42), derived in Ref. [17] and can be reduced to the latter.

From Eq. (7.133), the length z_p, at which the beam will make p revolutions is given by

$$z_p = z_0 \, \text{tg} \, \left(\frac{2\pi p}{B} \right), \quad p = 1, 2, \ldots, N, \tag{7.135}$$

where $N = B/4$ is the maximal number of revolutions the beam is able to make at the length from $z = 0$ to $z = \infty (z \gg z_0)$. The rate of rotation v of the multimode beam's cross section depends on the length as follows:

$$v = \frac{d\varphi}{dz} = B \left[1 + \left(\frac{z}{z_0} \right)^2 \right]^{-1}. \tag{7.136}$$

As stated earlier, it follows that by fitting nonzero terms in Eq. (7.129), with their numbers satisfying Eq. (7.134) and relying on Eqs. (7.103) to (7.107), one can design phase optical elements that transform the illuminating laser light into multimode nonradially symmetric GL beams with high efficiency, with the transverse intensity distribution rotating about the propagation axis.

Example 7.11   The numerical simulation parameters are as follows: the number of pixels is 256×256, the waist radius is $\sigma_0 = 0.01$ mm, the wavelength is $\lambda = 0.63$ μm, the DOE radius is $R_0 = 0.5$ mm, and the confocal parameter is $z_0 = 49.86$ mm.

The numerical examples are depicted in Figure 7.17. In the first column is the DOE phase (a1) derived from Eqs. (7.103) to (7.107) with two nonzero terms in the sum in Eq. (7.129), with the coefficients $C_{1,-1}$ and $C_{11,2}$. Obviously, the condition in Eq. (7.134) for the two terms is satisfied: $B = 7$. The maximal number of revolutions is $N = 1.75$. It follows from Eq. (7.135) that at the distance $z = 62.53$ mm, the beam will make a complete revolution, and at the distance $z = 217.76$ mm, it will make another half revolution. Figure 7.17 depicts halftone normalized transverse intensity distributions (negative) produced by the phase DOE (a1) and computed using the Fresnel transform at the distances z: (b1) 62.53 mm, (c1) 101.34 mm, (d1) 140.15 mm, (e1) 178.95 mm, and (f1) 217.76 mm. The pattern is rotated in anticlockwise direction.

In the second column, there are similar results for the rotating beam composed of three modes with the coefficients: $C_{1,-1}$, $C_{5,0}$, and $C_{11,2}$. The condition in Eq. (7.134) is fulfilled: $B = 7, 7, 7$. The phase function of such an element (a2) is shown halftonic (black color–2π, white color–0). The transverse intensity distributions for such a beam (b2–f2) are shown at the same distances as in the first column (negative).

Shown in the third column is the phase (a3) and the intensity distributions (b3–f3) for a three-mode beam with the coefficients: $C_{2,-2}$, $C_{5,0}$, and $C_{15,2}$. In this case, the condition in Eq. (7.134) is not obeyed: $B = 2, 6, 11$, so different beam components are rotating at different rates, thus resulting in the distorted pattern.

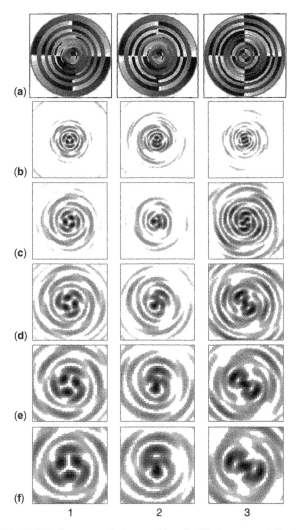

Figure 7.17. (a) The DOE phases producing multimode GL beams and (b–f) transverse intensity distributions at different distances from the DOEs.

7.6.2 Graded-Index Fiber

In what follows, we derive the condition for the beam rotation in a graded-index fiber.
Assume that the light field represented as a superposition of GL modes [57]

$$U(r, \varphi, z) = \sum_{n=0}^{\infty} \sum_{|m| \leq n} C_{nm} \left(\frac{r\sqrt{2}}{\sigma} \right)^{|m|} L_n^{|m|} \left(\frac{2r^2}{\sigma^2} \right) \exp \left[i\alpha_{nm} z - \frac{r^2}{\sigma^2} + im\varphi \right],$$

(7.137)

where $\sigma = (\lambda r_0 / \pi n_0)^{1/2} (2\Delta)^{-1/4}$, $\alpha_{nm} = [k^2 n_0^2 - 4\sigma^{-2}(2n + |m| + 1)]^{1/2}$, σ is the effective radius of the first mode, and α_{nm} is the coefficient proportional to the phase velocity of the corresponding mode, is propagated in a multimode round-shaped optical fiber with quadratic refractive index

$$n^2(r) = n_0^2 \left(1 - 2\Delta \frac{r^2}{r_0^2}\right), \tag{7.138}$$

where n_0 is the maximal value of the refractive index on the fiber axis, r_0 is the fiber radius, and Δ is the refractive index variance parameter.

Because of variance of the GL mode phase velocities, the input image $U(r, \varphi, z = 0)$ will be degraded as it propagates in the fiber. For the mode phase velocities to be partially compensated, one should select in the sum of Eq. (7.137), the terms for which phase velocities are in some manner agreed. For example, the DOE-generated light beam may be made rotating around the axis on a spiral path. The rotation conditions for the beam in Eq. (7.137) are similar to those in Eqs. (7.79) and (7.80) for multimode Bessel beams and take the form

$$\frac{\alpha_{nm} - \alpha_{n'm'}}{m - m'} = B, \quad m \neq m', \ n \neq n', \tag{7.139}$$

$$\frac{\alpha_{nm}}{m} = B, \tag{7.140}$$

where B is constant. In Eq. (7.139), the values α_{nm} may be approximated by

$$\alpha_{nm} \cong kn_0 - \alpha_0(2n + |m| + 1), \tag{7.141}$$

since $kn_0 \gg \alpha_0$ and $\alpha_0 = 2(kn_0\sigma^2)^{-1}$. For instance, for the characteristic fiber parameters: $r_0 = 10$ μm, $\Delta = 0.01$, $n_0 = 1.5$, and the visible light: $k = 10^4$ mm^{-1}, we get the following values: $kn_0 = 1.5 \times 10^4$ mm^{-1} and $\alpha_0 = 15$ mm^{-1}.

Considering Eq. (7.141), the condition in Eq. (7.139) takes a simpler form:

$$\alpha_0 \left[\frac{2(n - n') + (|m| - |m'|)}{m - m'}\right] = B, \quad n, n', m, m', = 0, 1, 2, \ldots \tag{7.142}$$

Here, the condition in Eq. (7.142) is seen to be analogous to Eq. (7.79) for Bessel modes and to Eq. (7.134) for GL modes in free space. For small mode numbers ($n < 10$), the approximate equality in (7.141) is held for the selected fiber parameters up to above 2 percent.

The period z_0, at which the beam makes a complete revolution is derived from

$$z_0 = \frac{2\pi}{|B|} \tag{7.143}$$

and, for the parameters chosen, is equal to tens and hundreds of microns.

Similar to the Bessel modes, an iterative approach was adopted when designing phase DOEs intended to produce light fields effectively composed (by 80–90 percent) of two to four GL modes and propagating in a multimode fiber with quadratic dependence of refractive index, Eq. (7.138).

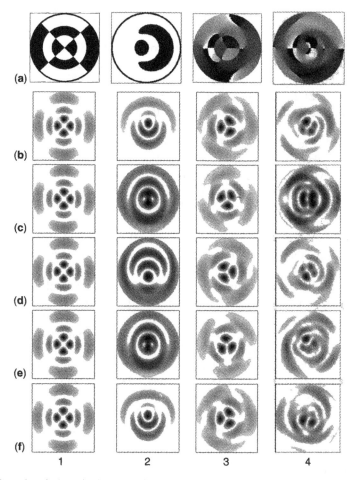

Figure 7.18. (**a1–a4**) Iteratively derived DOE phases and (**b1–f4**) the cross-section patterns of the multimode GL beams produced by such DOEs.

Example 7.12 Some examples are depicted in Figure 7.18. The calculation parameters are $r_0 = 10$ mkm, $\Delta = 0.01$, $n_0 = 1.5$, $\lambda = 0.63$ mkm, $R = 0.01$ mm, and $\alpha_0 = 15$ mm^{-1}.

The left column in Figure 7.18 illustrates an almost diffraction-free propagation of the GL mode in a fiber. In Eq. (7.137), only two terms with the numbers (n, m): $(2, -2)$ and $(2, 2)$, were taken to be nonzero. Note that Eqs. (7.141) to (7.143) give an infinite period of revolution: $z_0 = \infty$, $B = 0$. Shown in Figure 7.18 are (a1) the binary phase of such a DOE and the cross-section patterns of the beam (negative) at different distances z: (b1) 1 mm, (c1) 2 mm, (d1) 3 mm, (e1) 4 mm, and (f1) 5 mm. It can be seen that as this beam propagates, an insignificant intensity modulation caused by periodically varying influence of higher GL modes takes place. In the course of calculation, 25 modes with neighboring numbers were taken into consideration.

An example of the periodically varying multimode GL beam is shown in the second left column in Figure 7.18. In this case in Eq. (7.137), the terms with the numbers

(n, m): $(1,-1)$, $(3,0)$, and $(1,1)$ were taken to be nonzero. Although the rotation conditions in Eqs. (7.139) and (7.140) are not obeyed, the derived values of B are found out to be multiple, thus allowing a general period of $z_0 = 0.2087$ mm to be selected. In the second left column in Figure 7.18 are shown (a1) the DOE binary phase and the beam cross sections (negative) at different distances z: (b2) 2.087 mm, (c2) 2.139 mm, (d2) 2.191 mm, (e2) 2.243 mm, and (f2) 2.295 mm. The diffraction pattern is seen to periodically change as the beam propagates in the fiber.

An example of the rotating multimode GL beam is depicted in the third left column in Figure 7.18. In the sum in Eq. (7.137), two terms with the numbers (n, m): $(1,-1)$ and $(2,2)$ were taken to be nonzero. The rotation condition, Eq. (7.139) is obeyed, the period of revolution being $z_0 = 0.626$ mm. Shown in the third left column in Figure 7.18 are (a3) the halftonic phase for such a DOE and the beam cross sections for different distances z: (b3) 1 mm, (c3) 1.156 mm, (d3) 1.313 mm, (e3) 1.469 mm, and (f3) 1.626 mm.

By way of illustration, note that the three-mode GL beams with the numbers $(1,-1)$, $(5,0)$, and $(11,2)$ and the numbers $(2,-2)$, $(8,0)$, and $(14,3)$, satisfy the rotation condition in Eq. (7.139).

Shown in the first right column in Figure 7.18, is an example of a four-mode GL beam for which the rotation condition in Eq. (7.139) is not true, the result being a distorted profile of the beam pattern. In the first right column, Figure 7.18 depicts (a4) the DOE half-tonic phase derived iteratively with four nonzero terms in Eq. (7.137) with the numbers (n, m): $(2,-2)$, $(1,-1)$, $(2,1)$, and $(3,2)$. The cross-section patterns of such a beam are shown in the right column at different distances z: (b4) 1 mm, (c4) 1.094 mm, (d4) 1.187 mm, (e4) 1.281 mm, and (f4) 1.375 mm. The distortion of the beam cross section patterns is due to the fact that separate modes rotate at different rates and propagate at different phase velocities not matched to each other, in contrast to the previous cases depicted in Figure 7.18.

7.7 GENERATION OF ROTATING GL BEAMS USING BINARY-PHASE DIFFRACTIVE OPTICS

The results of experiments aimed at obtaining a rotating laser beam composed of two GL modes may be found, for example, in Ref. [58]. The beam was generated using an amplitude hologram with phase information encoded by the Lie method, thus giving a beam of fairly small efficiency.

In Ref. [59], one can find the numerically simulated rotation of GL beams. This section presents comparative discussion of the experiments and numerical simulation concerned with the generation of two identical oppositely rotating laser beams, each composed of two GL modes. These rotating beams are produced using a binary-phase DOE, each possessing the energy efficiency of about 40 percent. The theory and experiment are in good agreement.

Example 7.13 Figure 7.19a depicts a halftone DOE phase (255 gradation levels in the range $[-\pi, \pi]$) derived during two iterations by the method of Eqs. (7.103) to (7.107). In the sum in Eq. (7.129), only the terms numbered (n, m): $(1,-1)$ and $(15,1)$ were nonzero. Obviously, the rotation condition in Eq. (7.134) for the two terms is met: $B = 14$. The beam makes a complete revolution at the length $z_1 = 78$ mm, with the total number of revolutions being equal to $N = B/4 = 3.5$

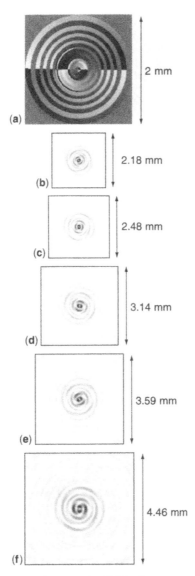

Figure 7.19. The result of simulation: (**a**) the DOE phase to generate a two-mode GL beam and the transverse intensity distributions at different distances z: (**b**) 215 mm, (**c**) 245 mm, (**d**) 310 mm, (**e**) 355 mm, and (**f**) 440 mm.

Figure 7.19b–f depicts halftone distributions of the transverse intensity for the light field (negative) produced by the DOE (Fig. 7.19a) and computed using the Fresnel transform at the distances $z = 215$ mm (7.19b), $z = 245$ mm (7.19c), $z = 310$ mm (7.19d), $z = 355$ mm (7.19e), and $z = 440$ mm (7.19f). The DOE radius is $R = 1$ mm, the number of pixels along the radius is 256. The Gaussian beam waist at $z = 0$, is $\sigma_0 = 0.18$ mm.

However, the halftone DOE is difficult to fabricate using lithographic methods. This suggests a simpler technique, namely, fabrication of a binary-phase DOE. If the phase

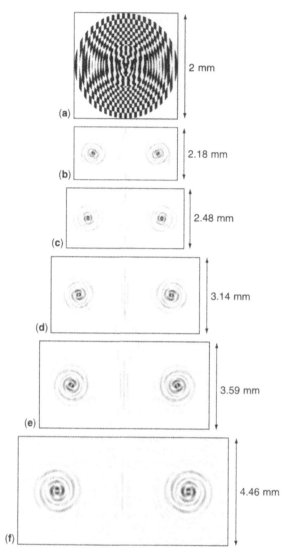

Figure 7.20. The result of simulation: (**a**) the DOE phase and the transverse intensity distributions at different distances z: (**b**) 215 mm, (**c**) 245 mm, (**d**) 310 mm, (**e**) 355 mm, and (**f**) 440 mm.

$S(r, \varphi)$ derived by the algorithm (7.103) to (7.107) is quantized in two levels, 0 and π, the resulting binary-phase DOE would not produce a rotating beam. For the rotation effect to be preserved, before quantizing, a linear prism term should be added to the phase $S(r, \varphi)$:

$$\hat{S}(r, \varphi) = S(r, \varphi) + 2\pi v r \cos \varphi. \tag{7.144}$$

Shown in Figure 7.20a is the binary phase derived from the halftonic phase (Fig. 7.19a) by adding the prism term [Eq. (7.144)] and subsequent quantizing in two levels: 0 and π, the carrier frequency being $v = 10$ mm^{-1}.

Figure 7.20b–f illustrates the halftonic transverse intensity distributions (negative) produced by the binary-phase DOE (Fig. 7.20a) and calculated using the Fresnel transform on the planes: (7.20b) $z = 215$ mm, (7.20c) $z = 245$ mm, (7.20d) $z = 310$ mm, (7.20e) $z = 355$ mm, and (7.20f) $z = 440$ mm.

It can be seen from Figure 7.20 that of the two beams produced, one is rotating in the same direction as the beam in Figure 7.19, and the other is rotating in the opposite direction. If in Eq. (7.144), the prism term was added with a negative sign, the rotation direction of the beams would alternate. More than 80 percent of the entire light energy goes to the formation of these two beams. Also, with this phase coding technique, the $\pm$1st diffraction orders appear, but not the zero order, as may be seen from the functional Goodman-Silvestri series [49]:

$$\exp[i\hat{S}_M(r, \varphi)] = \sum_{m=-\infty}^{\infty} \text{sinc}\left[\pi\left(m + \frac{1}{M}\right)\right] \exp[i(Mm + 1) \cdot \hat{S}(r, \varphi)], \quad (7.145)$$

where $\hat{S}(r, \varphi)$ is the halftone phase from Eq. (7.144) and $\hat{S}_M(r, \varphi)$ is the DOE phase quantized in M levels.

In our example, $M = 2$. Thus, instead of Eq. (7.145), we get

$$\exp[i\hat{S}_2(r, \varphi)] = \sum_{m=0}^{\infty} \text{sinc}\left[\pi\left(m + \frac{1}{2}\right)\right] \exp[i(2m + 1) \cdot \hat{S}(r, \varphi)]$$

$$= \left(\frac{2}{\pi}\right) \exp[iS(r, \varphi) + i2\pi vr \cos\varphi] + \left(\frac{2}{\pi}\right) \exp[-iS(r, \varphi)$$

$$- i2\pi vr \cos\varphi] - \left(\frac{2}{3\pi}\right) \exp[3iS(r, \varphi) + i6\pi vr \cos\varphi]$$

$$- \left(\frac{2}{3\pi}\right) \exp[-3iS(r, \varphi) - i6\pi vr \cos\varphi] + \cdots \quad (7.146)$$

Additional diffraction orders appearing as a result of diffraction of the plane wave by the binary-phase DOE according to Eq. (7.146), are not indicated in Figure 7.20b–f. What is indicated is only $\pm$1st orders corresponding to the first two terms in Eq. (7.146), each having the $4/\pi^2 = 40.5$ percent efficiency.

A DOE with the binary phase similar to that shown in Figure 7.20a was fabricated using a procedure described in Section 7.4 and illuminated by the collimated circular beam from a He-Ne laser. The transverse intensity distribution was registered by a CCD camera at different distances, with a 6.6 mm $\times$ 4.78 mm window and 768 $\times$ 567 pixels.

The experimentally measured intensity distribution at a distance of $z = 110$ mm from the DOE is shown in Figure 7.21a. One can observe the absence of zero order and the presence of the $\pm$1st diffraction orders. Next, the camera registered only the left diffraction order. Shown in Figure 7.21b–f are the measured intensity distributions for the $-$1st diffraction order at the distances: (b) $z = 215$ mm, (c) $z = 245$ mm, (d) $z = 310$ mm, (e) $z = 355$ mm, and (f) $z = 440$ mm.

From comparison of Figures 7.19b–f, 7.20b–f, and 7.21b–f, one can see the rotation of the laser beam cross-section pattern and good agreement between theory and experiment.

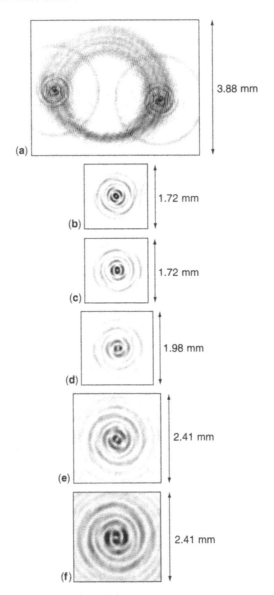

Figure 7.21. Experiment: intensity distributions in the beam cross section at the distances z: (**a**) 110 mm, (**b**) 215 mm, (**c**) 245 mm, (**d**) 310 mm, (**e**) 355 mm, and (**f**) 440 mm.

Example 7.14 Figures 7.22 and 7.23 illustrate the results of numerical simulation and the real experiment on propagating a two-mode GL beam with the numbers (n,m): (1,1) and (16, 2). The halftonic DOE phase derived after two iterations of the algorithm (7.164) and (7.165) is shown in Figure 7.22a. Shown in Figure 7.22b is a binary phase derived from the halftone phase (Fig. 7.22a) by adding the prism term of Eq. (7.144) and quantizing in two levels: 0 and π. The transverse intensity distributions (negative) derived through the Fresnel transform and produced by the binary-phase DOE (Fig. 7.22b) are depicted in Figure 7.22c–g at the distances (c) $z = 190$ mm,

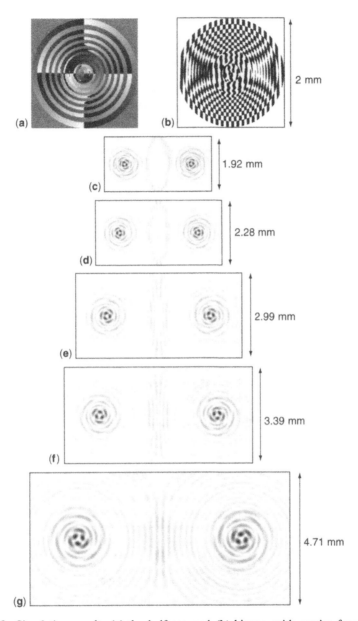

Figure 7.22. Simulation result: (**a**) the halftone and (**b**) binary, with carrier frequency DOE phases intended to generate two-mode GL beams; transverse intensity distributions at different distances z: (**c**) 190 mm, (**d**) 225 mm, (**e**) 295 mm, (**f**) 335 mm, and (**g**) 465 mm.

(d) $z = 225$ mm, (e) $z = 295$ mm, (f) $z = 335$ mm, and (g) $z = 465$ mm. The DOE radius is $R = 1$ mm and the number of pixels along the radius is 256. The Gaussian beam waist at $z = 0$, is $\sigma_0 = 0.17$ mm.

Figure 7.23a depicts the light field intensity distribution produced by a binary-phase DOE fabricated by the technology described earlier and registered by a CCD

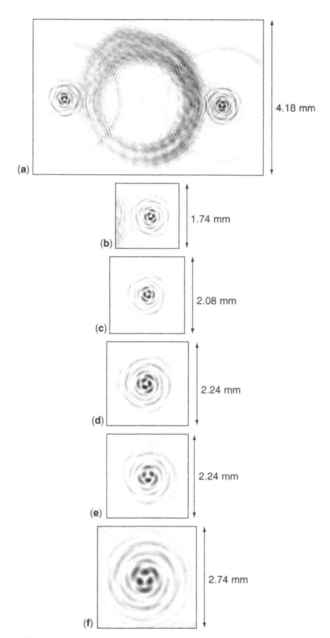

Figure 7.23. Experiment: transverse intensity distributions in the beam cross section at different distances z: (**a**) 167 mm, (**b**) 190 mm, (**c**) 225 mm, (**d**) 295 mm, (**e**) 335 mm, and (**f**) 465 mm.

camera at the distance $z = 167$ mm. Figure 7.23b–f illustrates the transverse intensity distribution only in the right beam (Fig. 7.23a) at the distances (b) $z = 190$ mm, (c) $z = 225$ mm, (d) $z = 295$ mm, (e) $z = 335$ mm, and (f) $z = 465$ mm.

Comparison of Figures 7.22 and 7.23 shows that there is a beam rotation effect and that theory and experiment are in good agreement. The light ring seen in Figures 7.21a and 7.23a is due to the fact that the diameter of the illuminating laser beam is greater than that of the DOE: the DOE diameter is 2 mm and the beam diameter is 3 mm. In Figures 7.21a and 7.23a, one can also observe interference between the nondiffracted beam portion and the ±1st diffraction orders: when passing from ring to ring, the fringes in the mode beam cross section are seen to be shifted by half the period.

7.8   GENERALIZED HERMITE BEAMS IN FREE SPACE

An interest shown in the Hermite beams or, in particular, the GH modes is because of the fact that they can propagate in free space without changing their structure and changing only their scale, whereas, while propagating in parabolic-index light fibers, they preserve even their scale.

Different analytical expressions for the GL modes proposed in Refs. [60, 61] gave an impetus for elucidating the similarities and dissimilarities between the two different types of Hermite beams, which eventually turned out to be a particular case of more general mode Hermite beams.

There are iterative algorithms [50,51,53] for designing an optical element intended to generate a unimode beam based on the auxiliary domain or the approximation of the transmission function by a finite sum of orthogonal modes.

In the present section, it is demonstrated that in terms of energy an optimal diffractive element to generate a unimode Hermite beam is a transparency with the signum function of the corresponding Hermite polynomial taken as a transmission function.

Analytical expressions describing the Fraunhofer diffraction by such phase elements are also given.

In a particular solution of the parabolic propagation equation

$$\left(2ik\frac{\partial}{\partial z} + \frac{\partial^2}{\partial x^2} + \frac{\partial^2}{\partial y^2} \right) E(x, y, z) = 0, \tag{7.147}$$

where k is the wave number of light, (x, y) are the transverse and z is the longitudinal coordinate in space, and $E(x, y, z)$ is the complex light field amplitude slowly varying along the z-axis, is the mode function given by [60]

$$E_{mn}^{(1)}(x, y, z) = \left[\frac{\omega_0}{\omega(z)} \right]^{m+n+2} \exp\left[-\frac{x^2 + y^2}{\omega^2(z)} \right] H_n\left(\frac{x}{\omega(z)} \right) H_m\left(\frac{y}{\omega(z)} \right), \tag{7.148}$$

where
$$\omega(z) = \omega_0 \left(1 + \frac{iz}{z_0} \right)^{1/2}, \tag{7.149}$$

$$z_0 = \frac{k\omega_0^2}{2}, \tag{7.150}$$

where $H_n(x)$ is the Hermite polynomial, 0 is the beam minimal radius at $z = 0$, and z_0 is referred to as confocal parameter.

With changing distance z, the $E_{mn}^{(1)}$ function changes only in scale but preserves its shape; therefore, the solution in Eq. (7.148) to Eq. (7.147) may be called the *light Hermite mode*. Note that according to the reference integral [54], the modes in

Eq. (7.148) are mutually not orthogonal:

$$\int_{-\infty}^{\infty} e^{-2x^2} H_n(x) H_m(x)\, dx = (-1)^{m+n/2} 2^{m+n-1/2} \Gamma\left(\frac{m+n+1}{2}\right), \qquad (7.151)$$

where $\Gamma(x)$ is the γ-function.

On the other hand, there are mutually orthogonal GH functions that are also known as particular solutions of Eq. (7.147) [61]:

$$E_{mn}^{(2)}(x, y, z) = \frac{\omega_0}{a(z)} \exp\left[i(n+m+1)\eta(z)\right] \exp\left[\frac{-ik(x^2+y^2)}{2R(z)}\right]$$

$$\times \exp\left[-\frac{x^2+y^2}{a^2(z)}\right] H_n\left[\frac{\sqrt{2}x}{a(z)}\right] H_m\left[\frac{\sqrt{2}y}{a(z)}\right], \qquad (7.152)$$

where

$$a(z) = \omega_0\left(1 + \frac{z^2}{z_0^2}\right)^{1/2}, \qquad (7.153)$$

$$\eta(z) = \text{arctg}\left(\frac{z}{z_0}\right), \qquad (7.154)$$

$$R(z) = z\left(1 + \frac{z_0^2}{z^2}\right), \qquad (7.155)$$

where $R(z)$ is the mode beam curvature radius.

The functions $E_{mn}^{(1)}$ and $E_{mn}^{(2)}$ describe different light beams because they are generated by different boundary conditions. At $z = 0$, instead of Eqs. (7.148) and (7.152), we get

$$E_{mn}^{(j)}(x, y, 0) = \exp\left(-\frac{x^2+y^2}{\omega_0}\right) H_n\left(\frac{\theta_j x}{\omega_0}\right) H_m\left(\frac{\theta_j y}{\omega_0}\right), \qquad j = 1, 2, \quad (7.156)$$

where

$$\theta_j = \begin{cases} 1, & j = 1 \\ \sqrt{2}, & j = 2 \end{cases}.$$

These two types of Hermite mode beams also differ by the type of the Fraunhofer diffraction. The light field $E_{mn}^{(2)}$ is the eigenfunction of a Fourier operator [18]:

$$\int_{-\infty}^{\infty} e^{-x^2} H_n\left(\sqrt{2}x\right) e^{-i2x\xi}\, dx = \sqrt{\pi}(-i)^n e^{-\xi^2} H_n\left(\sqrt{2}\xi\right). \qquad (7.157)$$

This property of GH modes to preserve their structure not only for the near-field Fresnel diffraction but also for the far-field Fraunhofer diffraction (or in the lens focal plane) is used for the highly effective input of laser light into optical fibers [50].

As will be seen from the expression

$$\int_{-\infty}^{\infty} e^{-x^2} H_n(x) e^{-i2x\xi}\, dx = \sqrt{\pi}(-i)^n e^{-\xi^2}(2\xi)^n, \qquad (7.158)$$

the light field $E_{mn}^{(1)}$ preserves its structure for the near-field Fresnel diffraction but degenerates into the field with zero central intensity for the far-field diffraction.

One can demonstrate that the $E_{mn}^{(1)}$ and $E_{mn}^{(2)}$ functions in Eqs. (7.148) and (7.152) are the particular case of a more general Eq. (7.147) that takes the form

$$E_{mn}^{(3)}(x, y, z) = A_{mn}(z) \exp[-B(z)(x^2 + y^2)] H_n \left[\frac{x}{C(z)} \right] H_m \left[\frac{y}{C(z)} \right], \quad (7.159)$$

where $\qquad A_{mn}(z) = \left(1 + \frac{i\gamma z}{z_0}\right)^{(m+n)/2} \left(1 + \frac{iz}{z_0}\right)^{[-(m+n)/2]-1}, \quad (7.160)$

$$B(z) = \left[\omega_0^2 \varepsilon^2 \left(1 + \frac{iz}{z_0}\right) \left(1 + \frac{i\gamma z}{z_0}\right) \right]^{-1} + k\gamma \left[2z_0 \left(1 + \frac{i\gamma z}{z_0}\right) \right]^{-1}, \quad (7.161)$$

$$C(z) = \omega_0 \varepsilon \left[\left(1 + \frac{iz}{z_0}\right) \left(1 + \frac{i\gamma z}{z_0}\right) \right]^{1/2}, \quad (7.162)$$

where $\gamma = 1 - \varepsilon^{-2}$ and ε is the mode parameter. At $\varepsilon = 1$, the solution in Eq. (7.159) changes to the solution $E_{mn}^{(1)}$, whereas at $\varepsilon = (\sqrt{2})^{-1}$ the solution $E_{mn}^{(3)}$ changes to the solution $E_{mn}^{(2)}$.

The generalized Hermite beams in Eq. (7.159) are generated at $z = 0$ with the aid of the complex amplitude

$$E_{mn}^{(3)}(x, y, 0) = \exp\left(-\frac{x^2 + y^2}{\omega_0^2}\right) H_n \left(\frac{x}{\omega_0 \varepsilon}\right) H_m \left(\frac{y}{\omega_0 \varepsilon}\right). \quad (7.163)$$

The expression for the complex amplitude of the light beam in Eq. (7.159) for the far-field diffraction follows from the relationship

$$\int_{-\infty}^{\infty} e^{-x^2} H_n \left(\frac{x}{\varepsilon}\right) e^{-i2x\xi} dx = \sqrt{\pi} (-i)^n (-\gamma)^{n/2} e^{-\xi^2} H_n \left(\frac{\xi}{\sqrt{1 - \varepsilon^2}}\right), \quad (7.164)$$

where $\varepsilon < 1$. At $\varepsilon = (\sqrt{2})^{-1}$, Eq. (7.164) changes to Eq. (7.157). At $\varepsilon = 1$, using the asymptotic property $H_n(\omega\xi) \xrightarrow{\omega \to \infty} 2^n (\omega\xi)^n$, we get $(-\gamma)^{n/2} H_n[\xi/\sqrt{(1 - \varepsilon^2)}] = (2\xi)^n$, which means that Eq. (7.164) changes to Eq. (7.158).

For both types of Hermite beams to be energy effective, the phase optical element with the transmission function

$$\tau_{mn}(x, y) = \text{sgn}[H_n(x) H_m(y)] = \text{sgn} \, H_n(x) \, \text{sgn} \, H_m(y), \quad (7.165)$$

should be placed in the plane $z = 0$, where $\text{sgn}(x)$ is the signum function.

The problem of searching for an optimal filter capable of generating the Hermite beams is similar to that for the Bessel beams [62].

Let us show in the one-dimensional (1D) case that the transparency in Eq. (7.165) can effectively form the Hermite beam of the nth order. Expand the $\tau_n(x)$ function in terms of orthogonal polynomials:

$$\operatorname{sgn} H_n(x) = \sum_{p=0}^{\infty} C_p^{(n)} H_p(x), \tag{7.166}$$

where

$$C_p^{(n)} = A \int_{\infty}^{\infty} \operatorname{sgn}[H_n(x)]e^{-x^2} H_p(x)\, dx, \tag{7.167}$$

and $A = \left(2^n n! \sqrt{\pi}\right)^{-1}$. For the even numbers $n = 2l$, the polynomial zeros $x_{k,l}$: $H_{2l}(x_{k,l}) = 0$ will be symmetrical, relative to the point $x = 0$: $x_{-k,l} = -x_{k,l}$. Then the integral in Eq. (7.167) can be represented as a sum of integrals

$$\int_{-\infty}^{\infty} \operatorname{sgn}[H_{2l}(x)]e^{-x^2} H_p(x)\, dx = \int_{-\infty}^{\infty} e^{-x^2} H_p(x)\, dx$$

$$+ 2(-1)^l \sum_{k=1}^{l} (-1)^{k-1} \int_{-x_{k,l}}^{x_{k,l}} e^{-x^2} H_p(x)\, dx, \tag{7.168}$$

Considering the reference integral [54]:

$$\int_0^{\xi} e^{-x^2} H_n(x)\, dx = H_{n-1}(0) - e^{-\xi^2} H_{n-1}(\xi), \tag{7.169}$$

instead of Eq. (7.168), we get the following relation for the expansion coefficients, Eq. (7.167):

$$C_{2s}^{(2l)} = [2^{2s-1}(2s)! \sqrt{\pi}]^{-1}(-1)^l \sum_{k=1}^{l} (-1)^k e^{-x_{k,l}^2} H_{2s-1}(x_{k,l}). \tag{7.170}$$

with the odd coefficients being equal to zero.

In a similar way, one can demonstrate that for the odd Hermite polynomials, $n = 2l + 1$, the expansion coefficients in Eq. (7.167) may be given by

$$C_{2s+1}^{(2l+1)} = \left[2^{2s}(2s+1)! \sqrt{\pi}\right]^{-1}(-1)^l \left[H_{2s}(0) \right.$$

$$\left. + 2 \sum_{k=1}^{l} (-1)^k e^{-x_{k,l}^2} H_{2s}(x_{k,l}) \right], \tag{7.171}$$

where $H_{2l+1}(x_{k,l}) = 0$, $H_{2s}(0) = (-1)^s \cdot 2^s \cdot 3 \cdot 5 \cdot 7 \ldots$,

with the even coefficients being equal to zero.

Thus, illuminating the optical element with transmission in Eq. (7.165) by a colli-mated Gaussian beam of amplitude $\exp[-(x^2 + y^2)/2]$ produces behind the element a field in the form of a superposition of Hermite beams, with one of them dominating in terms of energy over the others and possessing some 70 percent efficiency:

$$e^{-x^2/2} \operatorname{sgn}[H_n(x)] = \sum_{p=0}^{\infty} C_p^{(n)} [e^{-x^2/2} H_p(x)]. \tag{7.172}$$

The Fraunhofer diffraction of the plane wave by a $[-a, a]$ fragment of an optical element with transmission $\operatorname{sgn}[H_n(x)]$ [where a is supposed to be greater than the maximal root of the polynomial $H_n(x)$] can be conveniently determined from the following relation at $n = 2l$ [63]:

$$\operatorname{sgn}[H_{2l}(x)] = \operatorname{rect}\left(\frac{x}{a}\right) + 2(-1)^l \sum_{k=1}^{l} (-1)^{k-1} \operatorname{rect}\left(\frac{x}{x_{k,l}}\right), \tag{7.173}$$

where $\qquad H_{2l}(x_{k,l}) = 0, \quad \operatorname{rect}\left(\dfrac{x}{x_0}\right) = \begin{cases} 1, & |x| \le x_0, \\ 0, & |x| > x_0. \end{cases}$

In this case, the Fourier transform of Eq. (7.173) takes the form:

$$P_{2l}(\xi) = \Im\{\operatorname{sgn}[H_{2l}(x)]\} = 2a \operatorname{sinc}(a\xi) + 2(-1)^l \sum_{k=1}^{l} (-1)^k 2x_{k,l} \operatorname{sinc}(x_{k,l}\xi), \tag{7.174}$$

where $\quad \Im\{f(x)\} = \displaystyle\int_{-\infty}^{\infty} f(x) \exp(-ix\xi)\, dx, \quad \operatorname{sinc}(x) = \sin(x)/x. \tag{7.175}$

The diaphragm parameter a is chosen from energy considerations.

In a similar way, we can obtain the relationships for the odd Hermite polynomials:

$$\operatorname{sgn}[H_{2l+1}(x)] = \left[\operatorname{rect}\left(\frac{x}{a}\right) + 2(-1)^l \sum_{k=1}^{l} (-1)^{k-1} \operatorname{rect}\left(\frac{x}{x_{k,l}}\right) \right] \operatorname{sgn} x, \tag{7.176}$$

$$P_{2l+1}(\xi) = \Im\{\operatorname{sgn}[H_{2l+1}(x)]\} = -i \left[2a \operatorname{cosc}(a\xi) \right.$$

$$\left. + 2(-1)^l \sum_{k=1}^{l} (-1)^k 2x_{k,l} \operatorname{cosc}(x_{k,l}\xi) \right], \tag{7.177}$$

where $\qquad \operatorname{cosc}(x) = \dfrac{1 - \cos x}{x}.$

Example 7.15 Let it be required to produce the first Gauss-Hermite mode at $n = 1$, $m = 0$. This requires placing a transparency of transmittance $H_1(x) \exp(-x^2/2)$ in the plane $z = 0$. According to Eq. (7.157), a light field of complex amplitude proportional to

$$-i\sqrt{\pi} H_1(\xi) \exp(-\xi^2/2)$$

will be formed in the lens focal plane, where $H_1(\xi) = 2\xi$.

According to Eq. (7.171), if in the plane $z = 0$, one places a more efficient phase element of transmittance $\text{sgn}[H_1(x)] = \text{sgn}(x)$, the following superposition of light modes will be generated in the space behind the filter

$$\text{sgn}\, x = \sum_{s=0}^{\infty} C_{2s+1}^{(1)} H_{2s+1}(x) = \frac{1}{\sqrt{\pi}} \left[H_1(x) - \frac{1}{12} H_3(x) + \frac{1}{160} H_5(x) - \cdots \right]. \quad (7.178)$$

Illuminating such a phase element by a collimated Gaussian beam, we obtain that according to Eq. (7.178), a light field will be generated in the frequency plane with the amplitude proportional to

$$\int_{-\infty}^{\infty} \text{sgn}(x) e^{-x^2/2} e^{-ix\xi}\, dx = \sqrt{\pi} \sum_{s=0}^{\infty} C_{2s+1}^{(1)} (-i)^{2s+1} e^{-\xi^2/2} H_{2s+1}(\xi)$$

$$= -i e^{-\xi^2/2} \left[H_1(\xi) - \frac{1}{12} H_3(\xi) + \frac{i}{160} H_5(\xi) - \cdots \right]. \quad (7.179)$$

The energy ratio for the light beams described by the second and first terms in Eq. (7.179) is

$$\frac{\displaystyle\int_{-\infty}^{\infty} H_3^2(\xi) e^{-\xi^2}\, d\xi}{(12)^2 \displaystyle\int_{-\infty}^{\infty} H_1^2(\xi) e^{-\xi^2}\, d\xi} \approx 0.167. \quad (7.180)$$

Thus, the first term in Eq. (7.179), describing the first GH mode contains over 80 percent of the total light beam energy.

The first Hermite mode will be generated still more effectively if the phase filter with transmittance

$$\text{sgn}[H_1(x)] \, \text{rect}\left(\frac{x}{a}\right) \quad (7.181)$$

is illuminated, not by the Gaussian beam but by a plane wave. In this case, the light field produced in the lens focal plane will be described by the amplitude

$$\int_{-a}^{a} \text{sgn}(x) e^{-ix\xi}\, dx = -2ai \, \text{cosc}\,(a\xi), \quad (7.182)$$

with the $\text{cosc}(x)$ function defined in Eq. (7.177).

The mutual correlation of the light field in Eq. (7.182) and the first Hermite mode is evaluated by

$$\eta = \frac{\left| \displaystyle\int_{-\infty}^{\infty} [2a \, \text{cosc}\,(a\xi)] H_1(\xi) e^{-\xi^2/2}\, d\xi \right|^2}{\displaystyle\int_{-\infty}^{\infty} |2a \, \text{cosc}\,(a\xi)|^2\, d\xi \cdot \int_{-\infty}^{\infty} |H_1(\xi) e^{-\xi^2/2}|^2\, d\xi} = \frac{4}{a\sqrt{\pi}} (1 - e^{-a^2/2})^2. \quad (7.183)$$

Selection of the aperture size $[-a, a]$ of the phase element in Eq. (7.181) is based on the condition of maximum of the expression in Eq. (7.183), which is attained at

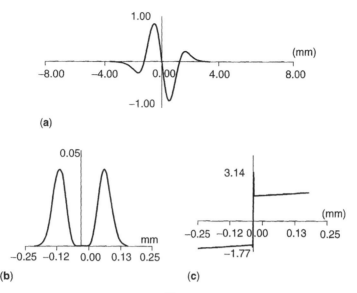

Figure 7.24. Results of simulation: (a) the $E_3^{(1)}(x)$ mode, (b) the squared modulus, and (c) the phase of its Fourier spectrum.

$a = 2.2$, with the mutual correlation in Eq. (7.183) being equal to $\eta = 0.85$. Thus, it is the first GH mode that accounts for some 85 percent of the light field energy.

The numerical simulation parameters are as follows: the array dimensionality is $N = 256$, the range of arguments is $x \in [-8, 8]$, the wavelength is $\lambda = 0.63$ μm, and the focal length is $f = 100$ mm.

Shown in Figure 7.24a is the Hermite beam

$$E_3^{(1)}(x) = H_3(x) \exp(-x^2). \tag{7.184}$$

The intensity (squared modulus) and phase (argument) of the Fourier transform of the function in Eq. (7.184) are shown, respectively, in Figure 7.24b and Figure 7.24c. For comparison purposes, Figure 7.25 depicts the Fraunhofer diffraction for the second type of Hermite beams. Shown in Figure 7.25a is the beam itself

$$E_3^{(2)}(x) = H_3(x) \exp(-x^2/2), \tag{7.185}$$

and in Figure 7.25b,c the intensity and the phase of its Fourier image are shown.

Figure 7.26a depicts the result of binarization of the Hermite beam in Eq. (7.185); curve 1 describes the function

$$\tau_3(x) = \text{sgn}[H_3(x)], \tag{7.186}$$

and curve 2 is the function in Eq. (7.185). Figure 7.26b,c illustrates the intensity and the phase of the Fourier transform of the binary function in Eq. (7.186) at $x \in [-3, 3]$.

The range of argument x of the function in Eq. (7.186) is chosen in such a manner that the correlation η, similar to that defined in Eq. (7.183) be maximal. In this case, the correlation between the intensity functions depicted in Figures 7.25b and 7.26b is 0.84, thus suggesting that 84 percent of energy of the plane beam illuminating the

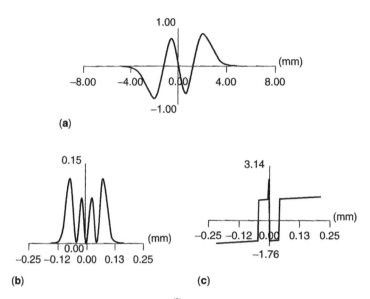

Figure 7.25. Results of simulation: (a) the $E_3^{(2)}(x)$ mode, (b) the squared modulus, and (c) the phase of its Fourier spectrum.

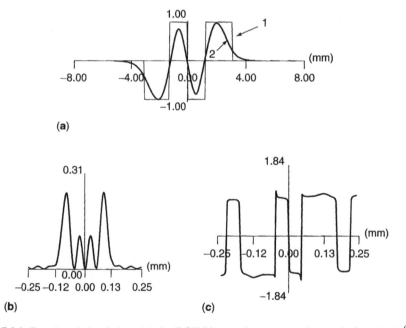

Figure 7.26. Results of simulation: (a) the DOE binary phase, curve 1, matched to the $E_3^{(2)}(x)$ mode, curve 2, (b) the intensity, and (c) the phase of the Fourier spectrum produced by the DOE.

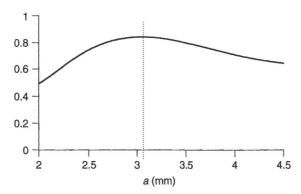

Figure 7.27. The mutual correlation in Eq. (7.183) vs the half-length of aperture for the Hermite beam of the third order.

TABLE 7.3. Optimal Aperture Sizes for the Signum Functions and Mutual Correlation Values

Mode Number, n	1	2	3	4	5	6	7
Optimal Aperture Size, a (mm)	2,1	2,6	3,0	3,4	3,7	4	4,2
Correlation, η	0,86	0,84	0,84	0,82	0,82	0,81	0,81

phase element in Eq. (7.186) will be spent to the formation of the Hermite beam in Eq. (7.185).

Shown in Figure 7.27 is the dependence of the mutual correlation η on the half-length of the segment $[-a, a]$ for the Hermite beam of the third order, $n = 3$. Table 7.3 gives optimal lengths for the segments $[-a, a]$, on which the binary functions $\mathrm{sgn}[H_n(x)]$, $n = \overline{1, 7}$, are specified and the values for the mutual correlation between the Fourier images of the function in Eq. (7.185) and the function in Eq. (7.186) at $n = \overline{1, 7}$.

From Table 7.3, it can be seen that as the number of the Hermite beam increases, the energy efficiency η slowly decreases from 86 percent to 81 percent.

7.9 GENERATION OF GAUSS-HERMITE MODES USING BINARY DOEs

There is a variety of methods for designing DOEs intended to generate unimode or multimode GH beams. Some of them are focused on the production of highly effective beams at the sacrifice of mode composition, while the others, although providing highly accurate mode formation, lose the desired intensity.

In Ref. [64], for the generation of the laser GL mode (1,0), a phase 16-level DOE was fabricated and experimentally studied. It was designed by the iterative procedure proposed in Ref. [51] and fabricated using the e-beam lithography, which involved the etching of the polymethylcrylate layer coated on a quartz glass substrate. The pixel dimensionality was 2048 × 2048 and the theoretical efficiency was 45.5 percent, whereas the measured efficiency amounted to 37.7 percent.

In Refs. [65,66], it has theoretically been shown that one can effectively generate 1D GH modes using binary-phase DOEs designed with the aid of the signum function of the corresponding Hermite polynomial. When such a DOE is illuminated by a plane light beam with an optimally selected aperture, the efficiency of the desired mode for the far-field diffraction is over 80 percent.

In the present section, we discuss the results of direct computation and experimental studies of two-level (binary) DOEs that can generate the modes (1,0), (1,1), and (1,2) with the theoretical efficiency of over 63.8 percent. Besides, the results presented in Refs. [65,66] are generalized onto the two-dimensional (2D) case of generation of GH modes.

Several binary-phase DOEs matched to the GH modes are fabricated using the e-beam lithography and their efficiency is experimentally evaluated.

It is proposed that a phase element with transmission function given by

$$\tau_{mn}(x, y) = \operatorname{sgn} H_m(x) \operatorname{sgn} H_n(y) \operatorname{rect}\left(\frac{x}{a}\right) \operatorname{rect}\left(\frac{y}{a}\right) \qquad (7.187)$$

be employed for the effective production of separate GH modes, where $H_m(x)$ and $H_n(y)$ are the Hermite polynomials of the mth and nth order,

$$\operatorname{sgn}(x) = \begin{cases} 1, & x \geq 0, \\ -1, & x < 0, \end{cases} \qquad (7.188)$$

$$\operatorname{rect}\left(\frac{x}{a}\right) = \begin{cases} 1, & |x| \leq a, \\ 0, & |x| > a. \end{cases} \qquad (7.189)$$

In the previous section, following the technique proposed in Ref. [65] and expanding the 1D signum function in Eq. (7.187) into a series, we expressed the expansion coefficients in Eqs. (7.170) and (7.171) as finite sums.

On the basis of Eq. (7.171), one can get specific values for the expansion coefficients in Eq. (7. 166) for each GH mode. For instance, for the GH mode (1,1)

$$\operatorname{sgn} H_{11}(x, y) = \operatorname{sgn}(x) \cdot \operatorname{sgn}(y) \qquad (7.190)$$

making use of the relation

$$\operatorname{sgn}(x) = \frac{1}{\sqrt{\pi}} \sum_{n=0}^{\infty} \frac{(-1)^n}{2^{2n}(2n+1)n!} H_{2n+1}(x), \qquad (7.191)$$

we can write down

$$\operatorname{sgn} H_{11}(x, y) = \frac{1}{\pi} \left(H_1(x) - \frac{1}{12} H_3(x) + \frac{1}{160} H_5(x) - \cdots \right) \left(H_1(y) - \frac{1}{12} H_3(y) \right.$$
$$\left. + \frac{1}{160} H_5(y) - \cdots \right) \qquad (7.192)$$

From Eq. (7.191) it follows that a binary DOE with transmittance $\operatorname{sgn} H_1(x)$ will produce the GH mode proportional to the polynomial $H_1(x)$ with the efficiency of about 86 percent.

TABLE 7.4. Estimated Average Errors and Efficiency (correlation) of Generation of GH Modes Using Binary Signum DOEs with Square, Optimal-Size Aperture

TEM (m, n)	$(1, 0)$	$(1, 1)$	$(1, 2)$	$(7, 0)$
δ, (%)	28.8	14.4	30.6	62.4
η, (%)	63.8	72.3	68.5	33.5

Obviously, for the 2D DOEs with transmittance of Eq. (7.187), the efficiency can be estimated as a product of the 1D efficiencies: $0.86 \times 0.86 \times 100\% = 73.96\%$. This estimate is confirmed by the results of simulation.

Table 7.4 gives the root-mean-square (rms) error δ and the efficiency η, derived using the following formulae:

$$\delta = \sqrt{\frac{\int_{-b}^{b}\int_{-b}^{b}\{\Im[\tau(x, y)]^2 - |\Psi_{mn}(x, y)|^2\}^2 \, dx \, dy}{\int_{-b}^{b}\int_{-b}^{b}\{|\Psi_{mn}(x, y)|^2\}^2 \, dx \, dy}}, \qquad (7.193)$$

$$\eta = \frac{\left|\int_{-b}^{b}\int_{-b}^{b}\Im[\tau(x, y)]\Psi_{mn}^{*}(x, y) \, dx \, dy\right|^2}{\int_{-b}^{b}\int_{-b}^{b}|\Im[\tau(x, y)]^2 \, dx \, dy \int_{-b}^{b}\int_{-b}^{b}|\Psi_{mn}(x, y)|^2 \, dx \, dy}, \qquad (7.194)$$

where $\Psi_{mn}(x, y) = \exp\left(-\frac{x^2 + y^2}{2}\right)H_m(x)H_n(y). \qquad (7.195)$

The domain of integration $[-b, b] \times [-b, b]$ in Eqs. (7.193) and (7.194) was chosen on the condition that $|\Psi_{mn}(x, y)|^2 \leq 10^{-4}$. In Eqs. (7.193) and (7.194), the designation

$$\Im[\tau(x, y)] = \int_{-\infty}^{\infty}\int_{-\infty}^{\infty}\tau(x, y)\exp\left[-\frac{ik}{f}(ux + vy)\right]dx \, dy. \qquad (7.196)$$

stands for the Fourier transform of the DOE transmission function.

However, it is not square but circular diaphragm that is used in practice, giving much the same result (maybe, a little worse or better), as can be seen in Table 7.5.

The binary-phase DOEs with the transmission function satisfying Eq. (7.187) were fabricated using a low-voltage image generator Leica LION LV1 at the University of Joensuu, Finland (see Chapter 4). Shown in Figure 7.28 is a microscopic view of a fragment of the obtained binary-phase DOE.

Lithographically fabricated binary-phase DOEs were tested using a unit schematically shown in Figure 7.29. The light beam from a small-power He-Ne laser was expanded by the microobjective and filtered by the small circular diaphragm. The diverging beam was then collimated by the lens, limited by another circular diaphragm of approximate radius 1.1 to 1.2 mm and passed to the binary DOE.

TABLE 7.5. Estimated rms Errors, δ, and Efficiency, η, (correlation) of Generation of GH Modes Using Binary Signum DOEs with Circular, Optimal-Size Diaphragm

TEM (m, n)	$(1, 0)$	$(1, 1)$	$(1, 2)$	$(7, 0)$
δ, (%)	26.9	15.6	31.8	66.9
η, (%)	70.1	69.5	65.4	40.7

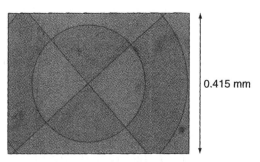

0.415 mm

Figure 7.28. A microscopic view of a fragment of the binary-phase DOE.

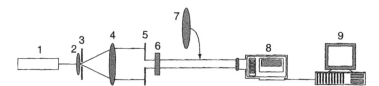

Figure 7.29. Experimental setup: a He-Ne Laser (1), a microobjective (2), a filtering diaphragm (3), a collimating lens (4), a limiting diaphragm (5), a binary DOE (6), an additional lens for taking the Fourier transform (7), a CCD camera (8), and a computer (9).

The far-field Fresnel diffraction of light by the DOE was studied using the light intensity distribution registered by the CCD camera. The camera input window was of size 6.6 mm × 4.78 mm with 768 × 567 photocells. The diffraction patterns registered were stored in the computer. For studying the Fraunhofer diffraction by the DOE, a lens of a 500 mm focal length was introduced into the space behind the element.

Example 7.16   The result of studies for the GH modes with the numbers (1,0), (1,1), (1,2), and (7,0), respectively, are shown in Figures 7.30 to 7.33. The binary-amplitude DOE photomasks limited by circular diaphragms 1.2 mm in diameter and computed according to Eq. (7.187) are shown in Figures 7.30a to 7.33a. However, the aperture being circular and a little larger than an optimal size reflected diversely on the performances (mainly, efficiency) compared with the optimal performance (Table 7.6).

Patterns of Fraunhofer diffraction by the corresponding binary-phase DOEs, derived from Eq. (7.195) are depicted in Figures 7.30b to 7.33b.

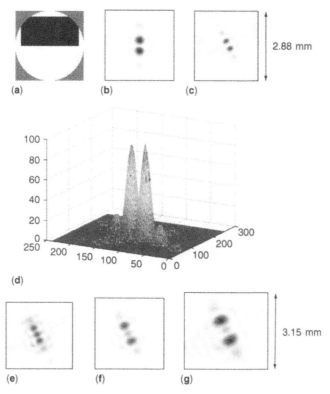

Figure 7.30. Results of simulation and experimentation for the GH mode (1,0): the photomask limited by a circular aperture; **(b)** the estimated far-field diffraction pattern; **(c)** the experimental far-field diffraction pattern; **(d)** its three-dimensional (3D) plot; and experimental intensity distributions at the distances **(e)** 370 mm, **(f)** 480 mm, **(g)** 620 mm from the DOE.

TABLE 7.6. Estimated rms Errors δ and Efficiency η when Generating the GH Modes Using Binary Signum DOEs with Circular, a Little Larger Than Optimal Aperture

TEM (m, n)	(1, 0)	(1, 1)	(1, 2)	(7, 0)
δ, (%)	24.7	42.7	31.5	64.2
η, (%)	55.6	62.2	59.4	31.7

Shown in Figures 7.30c to 7.33c are the far-field Fraunhofer diffraction patterns registered in the rear focal plane of an extra lens of focal length 500 mm introduced into the optical setup [Fig. 7.29, position (7)]. The 3D plots for the experimental Fraunhofer diffraction patterns (Figs. 7.30c–7.33c) are depicted in Figures 7.30d to 7.33d. Comparison between Figures 7.30b to 7.33b and 7.30c to 7.33c suggests that the theory and experiment are in good agreement.

Experimental near-field Fresnel diffraction patterns at different distances from the DOE in Figure 7.30e,f,g to 7.33e,f,g show that while propagating the laser beam manifests mode properties and preserves its structure.

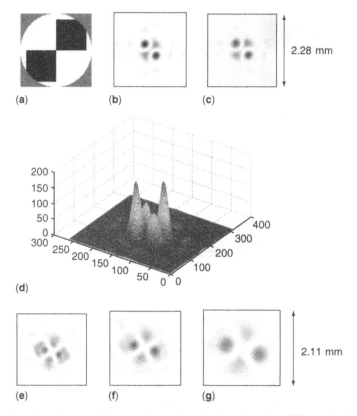

Figure 7.31. Results of simulation and experimentation for the GH mode (1,1): (**a**) the photomask limited by a circular aperture; (**b**) the estimated far-field diffraction pattern; (**c**) the experimental far-field diffraction pattern; (**d**) its 3D plot; and experimental intensity distributions at the distances (**e**) 340 mm, (**f**) 455 mm, and (**g**) 640 mm from the DOE.

7.10 SELF-REPRODUCTION OF MULTIMODE GH BEAMS

When propagated in free space, some types of coherent light field may produce the effect of self-reproduction, which is the reproduced cross-section intensity distribution at some periods. Unimode light beams are an example of self-reproducing beams with a zero period. In the previous sections, we derived the conditions for the rotation of model light beams being an example of axially periodic fields (up to a scale). A condition that provides the self-reproduction, in terms of intensity, of the multimode GL beam up to a scale at certain distances was derived in Ref. [67].

In this subsection, we deduce a similar condition for multimode GH beams. The numerical simulation is used to show the self-reproduction of some particular mode beams.

Let us consider a multimode GH beam that propagates in free space. The complex amplitude for such a beam may be written as follows:

$$E(x, y, z) = \sum_{m,n=0}^{N} C_{mn} \Psi_{mn}(x, y, z), \qquad (7.197)$$

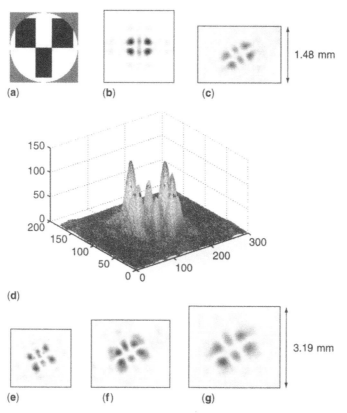

Figure 7.32. Results of simulation and experimentation for the GH mode (1,2): (**a**) the photo-mask limited by a circular aperture; (**b**) the estimated far-field diffraction pattern; (**c**) the experimental far-field diffraction pattern; (**d**) its 3D plot; and experimental intensity distributions at the distances (**e**) 260 mm, (**f**) 400 mm, and (**g**) 580 mm from the DOE.

where $\Psi_{mn}(x, y, z)$ are the functions of Eqs. (7.152) to (7.155), z is the axial and (x, y) is the transverse Cartesian coordinates, and C_{mn} are complex coefficients.

The light intensity distribution in the cross section of the GH beam is given by

$$
I(x, y, z) = \frac{\omega_0^2}{a^2(z)} \exp\left[-2\frac{x^2 + y^2}{a^2(z)}\right] \left\{ \sum_{m,n=0}^{N} |C_{mn}|^2 H_m^2\left(\frac{\sqrt{2}x}{a(z)}\right) \right.
$$

$$
\times H_n^2\left(\frac{\sqrt{2}y}{a(z)}\right) + \sum_{m,n}^{N} \sum_{m',n'}^{N} |C_{mn} C_{m'n'}| H_m\left(\frac{\sqrt{2}x}{a(z)}\right) H_{m'}\left(\frac{\sqrt{2}x}{a(z)}\right)
$$

$$
\left. \times H_n\left(\frac{\sqrt{2}y}{a(z)}\right) H_{n'}\left(\frac{\sqrt{2}y}{a(z)}\right) \cos \Phi_{m'n'}^{mn} \right\}, \tag{7.198}
$$

where

$$
\Phi_{m'n'}^{mn} = \arg C_{mn} - \arg C_{m'n'} + [(m - m') + (n - n')]\eta(z). \tag{7.199}
$$

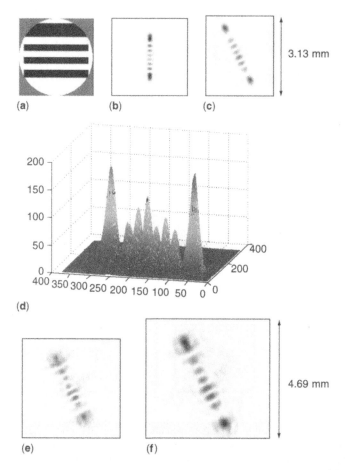

Figure 7.33. Results of simulation and experimentation for the GH mode (7,0): (**a**) the photomask limited by a circular aperture; (**b**) the estimated far-field diffraction pattern; (**c**) the experimental far-field diffraction pattern; (**d**) its 3D plot; and experimental intensity distributions at the distances (**e**) 360 mm and (**f**) 470 mm from the DOE.

For the intensity in Eq. (7.198) found at distance z_1 to be reproduced up to a scale at distance z_2, the functions in Eq. (7.199) in each term of Eq. (7.198) should satisfy the condition

$$\Phi_{m'n'}^{mm}(z_2) = \Phi_{m'n'}^{mn}(z_1) + 2\pi l, \quad l = 1, 2, 3, \ldots \tag{7.200}$$

Substituting the function in Eq. (7.199) in Eq. (7.200) gives the following expression for the distance z_2:

$$z_2 = \frac{z_1 + z_0 \operatorname{tg}\left(\dfrac{2\pi l}{p}\right)}{1 - \dfrac{z_1}{z_0} \operatorname{tg}\left(\dfrac{2\pi l}{p}\right)}, \tag{7.201}$$

where $\quad p = (m - m') + (n - n')$. $\tag{7.202}$

The presence of the parameter l in Eq. (7.201) shows that for the pair of modes with the numbers (m, n) and (m', n'), the transverse intensity distribution of their sum registered at some distance z may be reproduced at several distances:

$$z_{l,p}(z) = \frac{z + z_0 \, \text{tg}\left(\dfrac{2\pi l}{p}\right)}{1 - \dfrac{z}{z_0} \, \text{tg}\left(\dfrac{2\pi l}{p}\right)}, \quad l = 1, 2, 3, \ldots \tag{7.203}$$

Let us consider an example for a pair of modes with $p = 20$ and find the distances at which the intensity distribution registered for $z = 0$ will be reproduced:

$$z_{l,p}(0) = z_{l,p} = z_0 \, \text{tg}\left(\frac{2\pi l}{p}\right), \quad l = 1, 2, 3, \ldots \tag{7.204}$$

In this case, there are five points of self-reproduction with an increasing period:

$$z_{1,20} = 0.3249 \cdot z_0, \quad z_{2,20} = 0.7265 \cdot z_0, \quad z_{3,20} = 1.3764 \cdot z_0,$$

$$z_{4,20} = 3.0777 \cdot z_0, \quad z_{5,20} = \infty,$$

with one of them reproduced at infinity or in the lens focal plane. Obviously, all the changes taking place at the interval $[z, z_{1,p}(z)]$ will be reproduced at the subsequent periods $[z_{l,p}(z), z_{l+1,p}(z)]$, with the velocity decreased as the l increases.

Let us consider how we can select the mode numbers for the self-reproducing beam in Eq. (7.197) with more than two terms.

Once the pair of modes with the numbers (m, n), (m', n'), $p_0 = (m - m') + (n - n')$ is chosen, the addition of modes with the same velocities, namely, with the numbers (m'', n'') such that

$$m'' + n'' = m + n \quad \text{or} \quad m'' + n'' = m' + n' \tag{7.205}$$

makes it possible to generate a beam that is capable of self-reproduction at the same distances, Eq. (7.203), as is the case for the initial pair of modes. This is due to the fact that the additional modes will produce only two values $p' = p_0$ and $p' = 0$. For $p = 0$ in Eq. (7.199), the z-dependence is not there any more, which is typical of the stable beam. As an example of such a multimodal beam with $p_0 = 20$, we may take a composition of seven modes:

$$(0, 1) + (1, 0) + (10, 11) + (11, 10) + (9, 12) + (8, 13) + (0, 20).$$

Figure 7.34 depicts the result of numerical simulation for the four-mode GH beam $(0, 1) + (1, 0) + (10, 11) + (11, 10)$, with all modes incorporated into the beam with the same weights. The experimental parameters are as follows: the array size is 512×512 pixels, the range of arguments is $x, y \in [-0.5 \text{ mm}, 0.5 \text{ mm}]$, the wavelength is $\lambda = 0.63 \ \mu\text{m}$, the Gaussian beam radius is $\omega_0 = 0.1$ mm, and the Rayleigh parameter is

$$z_0 = \frac{k\omega_0^2}{2} = 49.63 \text{ mm}.$$

The transverse intensity distribution for such a beam registered at any distance within the interval $[0, z_{1,20}(0)] = [0, 16.24]$ must be self-reproduced four times before $z = \infty$. Actually, for $z = 12$ mm, Eq. (7.203) gives the following distances of self-reproduction:

$$z_{1,20}(12) = 30.63 \text{ mm}, \quad z_{2,20}(12) = 58.53 \text{ mm}, \quad z_{3,20}(12) = 120.69 \text{ mm},$$

$$z_{4,20}(12) = 634.72 \text{ mm}.$$

Figure 7.34 depicts (a) the binary phase and (b) the intensity in the plane $z = 0$, with the size corresponding to the aperture size of 1 mm for the four-mode GH beam $(0, 1) + (1, 0) + (10, 11) + (11, 10)$. The subsequent illustrations depict the intensity distributions at different distances: (c) $z = 12$ mm, (d) $z_{1,20}(0) = 16.24$ mm, (e) $z_{1,20}(12) = 30.63$ mm, (f) $z_{2,20}(0) = 36.33$ mm, and (g) $z_{2,20}(12) = 58.53$ mm, with every frame being of size 0.97 mm.

From Figure 7.34, the intensity patterns at (b) $z = 0$, (d) $z = 16.24$ mm, and (f) $z = 36.33$ mm are seen to coincide up to a scale. The same coincidence takes place at the distances (c) $z = 12$ mm, (e) $z = 30.63$ mm, and (g) $z = 58.53$ mm.

Another degree of freedom in choosing the numbers of additional modes appears if we consider the following condition for the expression in Eq. (7.203):

$$z_{l,p}(z) = z_{l',p'}(z). \tag{7.206}$$

Thus, once the pair with the numbers (m, n), (m', n'), $p_0 = (m - m') + (n - n')$ has been chosen, the difference between the numbers of the additional modes for the self-reproduction to take place at the same distances should be as follows:

$$p = |p_0|q, \quad q = 0, 1, 2, \ldots, \tag{7.207}$$

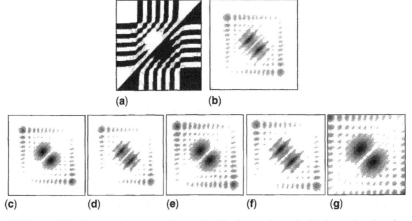

(a) (b)

(c) (d) (e) (f) (g)

Figure 7.34. (a) The binary phase (white -0, black $-\pi$) and (b) intensity in the plane $z = 0$, and the intensity distributions in the planes: (c) $z = 12$ mm, (d) $z = 16.24$ mm, (e) $z = 30.63$ mm, (f) $z = 36.33$ mm, and (g) $z = 58.53$ mm.

whereas their numbers should be given by

$$m'' + n'' = m + n + |p_0|q, \quad q = 0, 1, 2, \ldots \tag{7.208}$$

For example, if the beam $(1,1) + (5,5)$ reproduces its initial transverse intensity distribution (found at $z = 0$) at the distance [Eq. (7.204)]:

$$z_{1,8} = z_0 \, \text{tg}\left(\frac{\pi}{4}\right) = z_0, \tag{7.209}$$

the beam $(1, 1) + (0, 2) + (5, 5) + (4, 6) + (9, 9) + (8, 10)$ will also be self-reproduced at this distance:

$$z_{1,8} = z_{2,16} = z_0. \tag{7.210}$$

It is interesting to note that depending on the value of $|p_0|$ in Eq. (7.208), one may predict the location of points at which the initial intensity distribution (at $z = 0$) will be reproduced relative to z_0 (Table 7.7).

If the distances z_1 and z_2 in Eq. (7.201) are given, the numbers of the GH modes that must enter into the beam so that the beam has the intensity distributions at these distances aforementioned will satisfy the condition

$$\frac{2\pi l}{p} = \text{arctg}\left[\frac{z_0(z_2 - z_1)}{z_2 z_1 + z_0^2}\right], \quad |p| > 4l. \tag{7.211}$$

From Eq. (7.206), it follows that the distances z_1 and z_2 should not be specified arbitrarily.

Alongside the distance of self-reproduction of the intensity distribution registered at distance z, of interest may be the so-called "fractional" period distances in Eq. (7.198) (i.e. a fraction of the period). So, the relation

$$z_{l,p}^q(z) = \frac{z + z_0 \, \text{tg}\left(\dfrac{2\pi}{q} \cdot \dfrac{l}{p}\right)}{1 - \dfrac{z}{z_0} \, \text{tg}\left(\dfrac{2\pi}{q} \cdot \dfrac{l}{p}\right)}, \quad l = 1, 2, 3, \ldots \tag{7.212}$$

TABLE 7.7. Location of Points of Self-Reproduction

Value of $|p_0|$	Point of Self-Reproduction z_{l,p_0}
$|p_0| < 4$	No
$|p_0| = 4$	$z_{l,p_0} = \infty$
$4 < |p_0| < 8$	$z_0 < z_{1,p_0} < \infty$
$|p_0| = 8$	$z_{1,p_0} = z_0, z_{2,p_0} = \infty$
$8 < |p_0| < 12$	$0 < z_{l,p_0} < z_0 < z_{2,p_0} < \infty$
$|p_0| = 12^*$	$0 < z_{l,p_0} < z_0 < z_{2,p_0} < \infty, z_{3,p_0} = \infty$

*On subsequent propagation the pattern is self-reproduced with a multiple increase in the number of points.

allows the distances corresponding to the qth fraction of the self-reproduction period to be determined, thus making it possible to draw the analogy with the "fractional" Talbot plane for gratings [7]. The partial distances for the initial intensity distribution in Eq. (7.204) are as follows:

$$z_{l,p}^q = z_0 \, \text{tg} \left(\frac{2\pi}{q} \cdot \frac{l}{p} \right), \qquad l = 1, 2, 3, \ldots \tag{7.213}$$

The value of $q = 2$ corresponds to half the period. In this case, for the odd $l = 2s + 1$, $s = 0, 1, 2, \ldots$, the crossed terms in Eq. (7.198) are subtracted rather than added: $\cos(x \pm \pi l) = -\cos(x)$, which may be classified as quasi-contrasting. The analogous situation takes place on half the Talbot period for gratings when the shift of the initial image of the grating appears as its contrasting [7].

For the fractional periods, the cosine arguments in Eq. (7.198) are given by

$$\cos \left[x + p \, \text{arctg} \left(\frac{z_{l,p}^q}{z_0} \right) \right] = \cos \left[x + \frac{2\pi l}{q} \right], \tag{7.214}$$

where $x = \arg C_{mn} - \arg C_{m'n'}$.

Figure 7.35 depicts the results of numerical simulation for the three-mode GH beam $(1, 1) + (5, 5) + (9, 9)$ with identical weights.

Making use of Eq. (7.213), one can obtain the following distances for the self-reproduction (at $q = 2$ and with even l) and quasi-contrasting (at $q = 2$ and with odd l) of the initial intensity distribution:

$$z_{2,8}^2 = z_0 \, \text{tg} \left(\pi \frac{1}{4} \right) = z_0 \approx 49.63, \quad z_{4,8}^2 = z_0 \, \text{tg} \left(\pi \frac{1}{2} \right) = \infty,$$

$$z_{1,8}^2 = z_0 \, \text{tg} \left(\pi \frac{1}{8} \right) \approx 20.71, \quad z_{3,8}^2 = z_0 \, \text{tg} \left(\pi \frac{3}{8} \right) \approx 120.71. \tag{7.215}$$

For the quarters of the period, the distances are as follows (at $q = 4$, $l = 2s + 1$, $s = 0, 1, 2, \ldots$):

$$z_{1,8}^4 = z_0 \, \text{tg} \left(\frac{\pi}{2} \cdot \frac{1}{8} \right) \approx 9.87, \quad z_{3,8}^4 = z_0 \, \text{tg} \left(\frac{\pi}{2} \cdot \frac{3}{8} \right) \approx 33.16,$$

$$z_{5,8}^4 = z_0 \, \text{tg} \left(\frac{\pi}{2} \cdot \frac{5}{8} \right) \approx 74.27, \quad z_{7,8}^4 = z_0 \, \text{tg} \left(\frac{\pi}{2} \cdot \frac{7}{8} \right) \approx 249.51. \tag{7.216}$$

The binary phase is shown in Figure 7.35a and the intensity distribution in the plane $z = 0$ (with the size corresponding to the aperture of 1 mm) is in Figure 7.35b. The subsequent illustrations depict the intensity distributions at different distances: (c) $z_{1,8}^2 = 20.71$ mm, (d) $z_{3,8}^4 = 33.16$ mm, (e) $z_{2,8}^2 = z_0 = 49.63$ mm, (f) $z_{5,8}^4 = 74.27$ mm, and (g) $z_{3,8}^2 = 120.71$ mm, every exposure being 1.6 mm in size.

From Figure 7.35, the intensity patterns at distances $z = 0$, and $z = z_0$ are seen to coincide up to a scale. The same coincidence takes place for the half-period distances

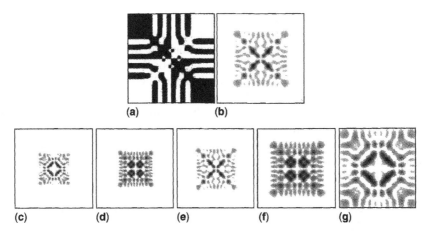

Figure 7.35. (a) The binary phase (white -0, black $-\pi$) and (b) the intensity in the plane $z = 0$, and the intensity distributions in the planes, (c) $z = 20.71$ mm, (d) $z = 33.16$ mm, (e) $z = 49.63$ mm, (f) $z = 74.27$ mm, and (g) $z = 120.71$ mm.

of $z = 20.71$ mm and $z = 120.71$ mm, which may be predicted from Eq. (7.212):

$$z_{1,8}^2(20.71) = 120.71 \tag{7.217}$$

For the quarter of the period in Eq. (7.214), we get $\cos\left[x + \dfrac{\pi l}{2}\right]$, $l = 2s + 1$, $s = 0, 1, 2, \ldots$, and the similarity of the intensity distributions in Figures 7.35d and 7.35g, is only possible if $x = \arg C_{mm} - \arg C_{m'n'} = 0$ (which is fulfilled in our case).

CONCLUSION

Studies conducted in this chapter allow the conclusion that it is possible to control the axially periodic properties of the main types of light modes propagated in free space. These include Bessel, GH, and GL modes. Despite the fact that these modes are described by the amplitude-phase functions, the methods dealt with in this chapter offer techniques for deriving a purely phase (which is most effective in terms of energy) transmission function of DOEs intended to generate multimode light beams. A series of tests conducted with the fabricated DOEs have shown good agreement between theory and experiment.

A subclass of light fields characterized by a conical spectrum of light waves and referred to as multimode Bessel beams exhibit the property of nearly diffraction-free propagation in free space. The DOEs we discuss in this chapter operate similar to helical axicons, thus providing the invariant properties of the beam generated at a distance, which is in direct proportion to the DOE radius and in inverse proportion to the inclination angle of plane waves of spatial spectrum of this field (or to the Bessel function scale). The diffraction spreading of the beam diameter is compensated by the energy supply from the DOE peripheral zones. In other words, as the distance z from the DOE to the plane of interest increases, the radius of the DOE zone (ring) contributing to the generation of the light field on the plane also increases.

Axially periodic beams emerge when several (no less than two) conical light waves with different apex angles are propagating along the optical axis. As the result of their interference, the interference pattern generated along the optical axis has an amplitude modulation that is approximately constant on the optical axis segment found between the DOE and the earlier specified invariance distance. The light wave propagated along the optical axis experiences periodic changes in its cross section. The minimal period of the interference pattern will be determined by the maximal difference of the inclination angles of different conical waves.

If a multimode beam is composed of a superposition of Bessel functions with different scales but with the same indices and, hence, the same helical components, this light field will propagate as a Bessel mode without diffraction and without changing its form. The pattern in the Bessel beam cross section is rotated if in the beam there are components differing both in scale (inclination angle of plane waves) and in indices. The rotation along the optical axis appears as a result of interference of two conical waves with different apex angles and different "helical" components. If more than two waves propagate in free space, the interference pattern becomes complicated and for the beam with its cross section rotating as a whole to be generated, one needs to impose the conditions deduced in this chapter.

The Gaussian modes of laser light do not spread and do not change their structure while propagated in a graded-index optical fiber, the only change being a phase delay acquired in the course of propagation. At the same time, the Gaussian modes retain their structure while propagated in free space, changing only in scale. A set of GL and GH modes with the same eigenvalues may be considered as a mode group, because this also represents an eigenfunction of the Fourier transform.

Unimode light beams are an example of self-reproducing beams of zero period. In this chapter, it has been shown that in terms of energy an optimal diffractive element capable of generating a unimode Gaussian beam is the phase transparency whose transmission function is equal to the signum function of the corresponding Laguerre or Hermite polynomial.

The studies conducted have made it possible to generate multimode GH beams capable of self-reproduction at certain distances.

The rotation conditions derived in this chapter allow one to generate GL beams rotating at different rates, both in a fiber and in free space. While propagating in free space, such beams rotate with decreasing rate, making a small number of revolutions at the distance form the DOE to infinity (for lower-order modes, one to three revolutions). In a graded-index optical fiber, the rotation occurs with a constant rate and the number of revolutions is great (for a fiber length of 1 mm, about 100 revolutions).

REFERENCES

1. H.F. Talbot, Facts relating to optical science, *Phil. Mag. J. Sci.* (London) **9**, 401–405 (1836).

2. E. Lau, *Annl. Phys.* **6**, 417–421 (1948).

3. Lord Rayleigh, *Phil. Mag.* **2**(5), 196–199 (1881).

4. John T. Winthrop and C.R. Worthington, *J. Opt. Soc. Am.* **55**, 373–381 (1965).

5. J.R. Leger and G.J. Swanson, Efficient array illuminator using binary-optics phase plates at Fractional-Talbot planes, *Opt. Lett.* **15**, 288–290 (1990).

6. Victor Arrizon and J. Ojeda-Castaneda, Irradiance at Fresnel planes of a phase gratings, *J. Opt. Soc. Am. A.* **9**(10), 1801–1806 (1992).

7. J. Westerholm, J. Turunen, and J. Huttunen, Fresnel diffraction in fractional Talbot planes: A new formulation, *J. Opt. Soc. Am. A.* **11**(4), 1283–1290 (1994).

8. W.D. Montgomery, Self-imaging objects of infinite aperture, *J. Opt. Soc. Am.* **57**(6), 772–778 (1967).

9. W.D. Montgomery, Algebraic formulation of diffraction applied to self imaging, *J. Opt. Soc. Am.* **58**(8), 1112–1124 (1968).

10. D. Slepian, *Bell Syst. Tech. J.* **43**, 3009–3057 (1964).

11. G. Indebetouw, Propagation of spatially periodic wavefields, *Opt. Acta.* **31**(5), 531–539 (1984).

12. P.H. Ceperley, Rotating waves, *Am. J. Phys.* **60**(10), 938–942 (1992).

13. S. Chavez-Cerda, G.S. McDonald, and G.H.C. New, Nondiffracting beams: travelling, standing, rotating and spiral waves, *Opt. Commun.* **123**, 225–233 (1996).

14. C. Paterson and R. Smith, Helicon waves: Propagation-invariant waves in a rotating co-ordinate system, *Opt. Commun.* **124**, 131–140 (1996).

15. I.V. Basistiy, V.Yu. Bazhenov, M.S. Soskin, and M.V. Vasnetsov, Optics of light beams with screw dislocations, *Opt. Commun.* **103**, 422–428 (1993).

16. G. Indebetouw, Optical vortices and their propagation, *J. Mod. Opt.* **40**(1), 73–87 (1993).

17. E. Abramochkin and V. Volostnikov, Spiral-type beams, *Opt. Commun.* **102**, 336–350 (1993).

18. V.I. Smirnov, *Handbook of Higher Mathematics*, vol. 4 Nauka Publishers, Moscow, 4, 1974.

19. V.V. Lebedev et al., Amplitude-Phase Characteristics of Light Beams with Minimal Divergence, Preprint of The Institute of Theoretical and Applied Mathematics, RAS, Siberian Branch, No. 16–89, 1989.

20. J. Durnin, Exact solution for nondiffracting beams I. The scalar theory, *J. Opt. Soc. Am.* **4**, 651–654 (1987).

21. J. Durnin, J.J. Miceli, and J.H. Eberby, Comparison of Bessel and Gaussian beams, *Opt. Lett.* **13**, 79–80 (1988).

22. F. Gori, G. Guattari, and C. Padovani, Bessel-Gauss beams, *Opt. Commun.* **64**(6), 491–495 (1987).

23. A.B. Valiyev and S.G. Krivoshlykov, Modal properties of Bessel beams, *J. Quant. Electron.* **16**, 1047–1049 (1989).

24. A. Vasara, J. Turunen, and A.T. Friberg, Realization of general nondiffracting beams with computer-generated holograms, *J. Opt. Soc. Am.* **6**, 1748–1754 (1989).

25. Kh. G. Unger, *Planar and Fiber Optical Waveguides*, Mir Publishers, Moscow, 1980.

26. A.M. Belsky, Self-reproducing beams and their relation to non-diffracting beams, *Opt. Spectrosc.* **73**(5), 947–951 (1992).

27. V.V. Kotlyar, S.N. Khonina, and V.A. Soifer, Algorithm for the generation of nondiffracting Bessel modes, *J. Mod. Opt.* **42**(6), 1231–1239 (1995).

28. M.A. Golub et al., Computer-generated diffractive multi-focal lens, *J. Mod. Opt.* **39**(6), 1245–1251 (1992).

29. S.N. Khonina, V.V. Kotlyar, and V.A. Soifer, Diffraction computation of a DOE focusing into a longitudinal segment and multifocal lens, *Proc. SPIE* **1780**, 263–272 (1993).

30. V.A. Soifer, L.L. Doskolovich, and N.L. Kazanskiy, Multifocal diffractive elements, *Opt. Eng.* **33**(11), 3611–3615 (1994).

31. G. Korn and T. Korn, *Handbook of Mathematics*, Nauka Publishers, Moscow, 1968.

32. V.V. Kotlyar, V.A. Soifer, and S.N. Khonina, Phase formers of axially periodic light fields, *J. Opt. Spectrosc.* **84**(50), 853–859 (1998).

33. D.S. Kuznetzov, *Special Functions*, Higher School Publishers, Moscow, 1962.

34. J.R. Fienup, Phase retrieval algorithms: A Comparison, *Appl. Opt.* **21**(15), 2758–2769 (1982).

35. P. Szwaykowski, Self-imaging in polar coordinates, *J. Opt. Soc. Am.* **5**(2), 185–191 (1988).

36. Yu.Yu. Ananev, Nondiffracting light waves, *Opt. Spectrosc.* (USSR) **64**, 722–723 (1988).

37. F. Gori, G. Guattari, and C. Padovani, Modal expansion for J0-correlated shell-model sources, *Opt. Commun.* **64**(4), 311–316 (1987).

38. J. Turunen, A. Vasara, and A.T. Friberg, Propagation invariance and self-imaging lin variable-coherence optics, *J. Opt. Soc. Am. A.* **8**(2), 282–289 (1991).

39. P.L. Overfelt and C.S. Kenney, Comparison of the propagation characteristics of Bessel, Bessel-Gauss, and Gaussian beams diffracted by a circular aperture, *J. Opt. Soc. Am. A.* **8**(5), 732–744 (1991).

40. G. Indebetouw, Nondiffracting optical fields: some remarks on their analysis and synthesis, *J. Opt. Soc. Am. A.* **6**(1), 150–152 (1988).

41. J. Turunen, A. Vasara, and A.T. Friberg, Holographic generation of diffraction-free beams, *Appl. Opt.* **27**(19), 3959–3962 (1988).

42. C. Paterson and R. Smith, Higher-order Bessel waves produced by Axicon-type computer-generated holograms, *Opt. Commun.* **124**, 123–130 (1996).

43. S.N. Khonina et al., *Opt. Commun.* **91**(3,4), 158–162 (1992).

44. N.E. Andreev et al., Formation of high-power hollow Bessel light beams, *Quant. Electron.* (Moscow) **23**(2), 130–134 (1996).

45. S. Ruschin, Modified Bessel nondiffracting beams, *J. Opt. Soc. Am. A.* **11**(12), 3224–3228 (1994).

46. B. Spektor, R. Piestun, and J. Shamir, Dark beams with a constant notch, *Opt. Lett.* **21**(7), 456–458 (1996).

47. V.V. Kotlyar, V.A. Soifer, and S.N. Khonina, An algorithm for the generation of laser beams with longitudinal periodicity: Rotating images, *J. Mod. Opt.* **44**(7), 1409–1416 (1997).

48. S.N. Khonina, V.V. Kotlyar, and V.A. Soifer, Design of optical elements for the generation of rotating beams, Technical Digest of EOS Topical meeting on Diffractive Optics, Savonlinna, 1997, p. 34.

49. J.W. Goodman and A.M. Silvestri, Some effects of Fourier-domain phase quantization, *IBM J. Res. Dev.* **9**, 478–484 (1970).

50. V.A. Soifer and M.A. Golub, *Laser Beam Mode Selection by Computer-Generated Holograms*, CRC Press: Boca Raton, Fla., 1994.

51. M.A. Golub, V.S. Pavelyev, and V.A. Soifer, Iteratively designing phase diffractive optical elements intended for generation of a desired unimodal distribution, using a generalized projections method, *J. Comput. Opt.* (Moscow) **14**(2), 85–93 (1995).

52. V.V. Kotlyar, I.V. Nikolsky, and V.A. Soifer, An algorithm for calculation of formers of Gaussian modes, *Optik* **98**(1), 26–30 (1994).

53. V.A. Soifer, V.V. Kotlyar, and L.L. Doskolovich, *Iterative Methods for Diffractive Optical Elements Computation*, Taylor & Francis, London, 1997.

54. A.P. Prudnikov, Yu.A. Brychkov, and O.I. Marychev, *Integrals and Series: Special Functions*, Nauka Publishers, Moscow, 1983.

55. S.N. Khonina, V.V. Kotlyar, and V.A. Soifer, Diffractive optical elements matched to Gauss–Laguerre modes, *J. Comput. Opt.* (Samara-Moscow) **17**, 25–31 (1997).

56. A. Yariv, *Optical Electronics*, Sovetskoye Radio Publishers, Moscow, 1986.

57. M.J. Adams, *An Introduction to Optical Waveguides*, Wiley & Sons, Chichester, U.K. 1981.

58. Y.V. Schechner, R. Piestun, and J. Shamir, Wave propagation with rotating intensity distributions, *Phys. Rev. E.* **54**(1), 50–53 (1996).

59. V.V. Kotlyar, V.A. Soifer, and S.N. Khonina, Rotation of multi-mode Gauss–Laguerre light beams in free space, *Lett. J. Tech. Phys.* **23**(17), 1–6, 1997.

60. M.B. Binogradova, O.V. Rudenko, and A.P. Sukhorukov, *Theory of Waves*, Nauka Publishers, Moscow, 1979.

61. A. Yariv, *Introduction into Optical Electronics*, Higher School Publishers, Moscow, 1983.

62. A. Fedotovsky and K. Lehovec, Optical filter design for annular imaging, *Appl. Opt.* **13**(12), 2919–2923 (1974).

63. J. Mait, Design of binary-phase and multiphase Fourier grating for array generation, *J. Opt. Soc. Am.* **A7**(8), 1514–1528 (1990).

64. V.V. Kotlyar, V.A. Soifer, and S.N. Khonina, Generalized Hermite beams in free space, *J. Comput. Opt.* (Samara-Moscow) **17**, 31–36 (1997).

65. M. Duparre et al., Forming of selected unimodal complex amplitude distributions by means of novel DOEs of MODAN-type, *Proc. SPIE* **3134**, 357–368 (1997).

66. V.V. Kotlyar, S.N. Khonina, and V.A. Soifer, Generalized Hermite beams in free space, *Optik* **108**(1), 20–26 (1998).

67. R. Piestun, Y.V. Schechner, and J. Shamir, Self-imaging with finite energy, *Opt. Lett.* **22**(4), 200–202 (1997).

CHAPTER 8

Wave Front Correction

8.1 PROBLEMS OF WAVE FRONT GENERATION

A wide range of problems dealt with in astronomy, optical instrumentation, and optical data processing call for the use of high-quality aspheric surfaces, for example, parabolic optics for large telescopes. The generation of high-quality aspheric surfaces hinges on the development of efficient certification techniques [1–4]. The aspheric surface certification techniques rely on the creation of reference wave fronts, with their shapes corresponding to the surface under control. Spherical and plane wave fronts are naturally generated by conventional optical systems composed of lenses, prisms, spherical mirrors, and test glasses. At the same time, the generation of complicated wave fronts can be a major challenge.

In conventional optics, desired wave fronts are generated using compensating lenses [1,2], making it possible to produce wave fronts in the form of the second-order surface of rotation. However, the development of a compensating objective is a unique problem for each type of wave front. It seems unlikely, in general, that one can generate higher-order aspheric wave fronts or wave fronts without circular symmetry using compensating objectives of practically acceptable complexity. Because of this reason, in the 1970s, the problem of generating complex wave fronts was tackled using digital holography methods [3–15]. In Refs. [3–7], axially symmetric aspheric wave fronts are generated by means of special circular diffraction gratings with the diffraction efficiency not greater than 40 percent. A feasibility of generating aspheric wave fronts by means of binary computer-generated holograms is shown in Ref. [8–15]. Note, however, that in this case only an insignificant fraction of the illuminating beam energy corresponding to the first diffraction order is diffracted into the desired wave front, whereas the major portion of the hologram resolution cells is spent for the transmission of the spatial carrier frequency, and the relative pinhole of the wave front is limited owing to the superposition of higher orders. This chapter deals with the analysis of the methods of diffractive optics used for the generation of complex-shaped wave fronts [16–24]. The underlying results concerned with the wave front correction using diffractive optical elements (DOEs) were reported by Soifer and coworkers in Ref. [16] and in succeeding years elaborated in Refs. [17–24]. In the present work, we omit specific problems of correcting optical system aberrations using diffractive and graded-index optical elements comprehensively covered in familiar monographs [25–26].

8.2 DOE-AIDED OPTICAL SYSTEMS FOR THE ANALYSIS OF ASPHERIC SURFACES

Consider certain optical configurations for control of optical surfaces, which contain computer-generated DOEs [3–30]. The functional purpose of a DOE is either to produce a reference aspheric wave front from the spherical or plane one, or to transform (compensate) one wave front into another. In the latter case, the DOE is referred to as an optical compensator. In control optical schemes, a wave front produced by the aspheric mirror or lens under study is analyzed. With interference techniques, such an analysis is conducted by comparing the wave front under study with the reference one. In the shadow method, one analyzes the shadow pattern of the wave front reflected from (or transmitted through) the element under control and transformed by an optical compensator. The shadow technique with the use of the Foucault knife is simplest in realization but shows low signal-to-noise ratio because the most high-energy zeroth spatial frequency is not used for the analysis.

Consider an optical configuration of an interferometer with spherical beams shown in Figure 8.1. In this configuration, the light beam from a laser L is transformed by a microlens ML into a diverging spherical light beam. This beam is then split by a semitranslucent mirror BS (beam splitter) into two beams. The reflected beam is directed onto a reference mirror RM, while the transmitted beam having passed through a DOE falls onto the aspheric mirror under control (AMC). Here, the compensator should be designed in such a manner as to transform the converging aspheric wave front having reflected from the reference aspheric mirror into a converging spherical wave front. Such a DOE will function as follows: According to Figure 8.1, the diverging wave front from the ML is transformed by the DOE into a diverging aspheric wave front, with its rays falling perpendicularly onto the aspheric mirror under control (AMC) and also reflected from it perpendicularly (if the mirror is ideal). On the return passage, the converging aspheric wave front reflected from the AMC is transformed by the DOE into the converging spherical wave front. In the reference arm of the interferometer, a reference spherical mirror RM is used for the generation of the reference converging spherical wave front. Two mutually coherent converging spherical wave fronts intersect

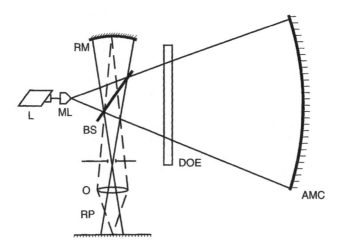

Figure 8.1. Optical configuration of interferometer with spherical beams.

in a registration plane RP to produce the interference pattern to be analyzed. Thus, the problem of manufacturing an aspheric mirror is reduced to a simpler problem of manufacturing a spherical reference mirror. However, strict requirements for the optical elements that they be stable both mutually and with respect to the AMC under microvibrations prohibits the use of the interferometer for the process control of mirrors.

When placed in the reference arm of the interferometer [28], the DOE compensator will serve a function inverse, in a sense, to that illustrated in Figure 8.1. In this case, the DOE will transform the diverging aspheric front into a spherical wave front and the converging spherical front into the converging aspheric front.

The aspheric mirrors are also checked using the Twyman-Green interferometer and a modified Mach-Zender interferometer [5,8,10–12,27–28], with the compensator acting in the same manner as in the aforementioned scheme (Fig. 8.1). However, the interference pattern is formed by plane and not by spherical waves, thus making the adjustment of the scheme much simpler and allowing the spherical reference mirror to be replaced by the plane one. However, the transformation of the spherical beam into the plane one calls for an extra lens, introducing additional errors.

Figure 8.2 depicts an optical configuration of the Twyman-Green interferometer comprising a compensator in the object arm. The interferometer operates as follows. The light beam from a laser L is expanded by a microlens M and is collimated by a lens O_1. Then, the plane light beam is split by a semitranslucent mirror into two beams. The reference beam is reflected from a reference mirror RM. The object beam is transformed by a lens O_3 into a converging spherical beam, which changes into a diverging spherical beam after passing through a diaphragm found in the focal plane. This beam is then transformed by a DOE into a diverging aspheric beam with its rays experiencing normal incidence on, and reflection from, the aspheric mirror under control (AMC). On the return passage, the two plane beams (the object and reference ones) intersect in the registration plane RP to produce the interference pattern in the form of an array of equidistant fringes. An objective O_2 produces the image of the mirrors' surfaces. Geometric defects in the AMC will be reflected in the distortion of the interference fringes.

The DOE compensator in the interferometer in Figure 8.2 can be placed in the reference arm to transform the plane wave front into a "quasi-plane" wave front that

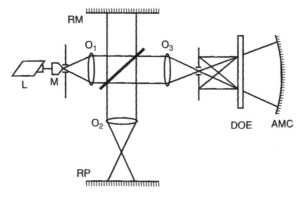

Figure 8.2. An optical configuration of the Twyman-Green interferometer with a compensator in the object arm.

would correspond to the spherical wave front in the same manner as the plane beam corresponds to the aspheric one.

There are optical configurations of an interferometer with a DOE found at the output [29]. A scheme of the Mach-Zehnder-type interferometer with the output compensator is shown in Figure 8.3. In this interferometer, the reference arm comprises two semitranslucent mirrors for splitting the beam and two plane reference perfectly reflecting mirrors for turning the light. In this situation, the DOE operates as follows. It transforms the incident plane reference beam into a "quasi-plane" beam and transforms the incident "quasi-plane" object beam having come from the AMC into a plane beam. Because both beams pass through the compensator, DOE fabrication flaws are mutually compensated and the control accuracy is enhanced.

Figure 8.4 shows an unconventional configuration of the interferometer with input compensator that has been proposed in Ref. [30]. The light beam from a laser L coupled with a collimator strikes a DOE that transforms it into a converging aspheric beam, with its rays falling on and reflected from an AMC perpendicularly. The optical scheme in Figure 8.4 combines the advantages of the schemes in Figures 8.2 and 8.3

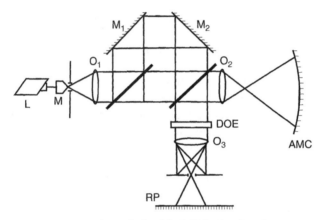

Figure 8.3. An optical configuration of the Mach-Zehnder interferometer with the output compensator.

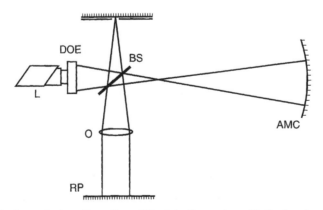

Figure 8.4. An optical configuration of the interferometer with the input compensator.

because the DOE fabrication errors are mutually compensated as the DOE generates both the reference and the object beams. In addition, the number of elements in the optical scheme in Figure 8.4 is minimal, as compared with those considered earlier. A plane reference mirror is not required because the reflection from the reference mirror takes place in a small area. A diaphragm near the reference mirror transmits only the zeroth spatial frequency. Unlike all the types of transformation (spherical-to-aspheric, plane-to-quasiplane) considered till now, the compensator in the present scheme should not only introduce desired aberrations into the wave front, but also have some positive resolution power. Thus, the DOE in Figure 8.4 is an analog of the aspheric lens, whereas the DOE in Figures 8.2 and 8.3 is an analog of the plate with the desired aberrations. Because of a significant difference in the ray paths for the plane and aspheric wave fronts, the corresponding compensator should be composed of several thousand structural zones (rings) whose fabrication presents a stubborn technological problem.

The interferometric optical schemes discussed previously are applicable to contact-free control of a wide range of optical surfaces (mirrors and lenses). Note that it is on the design stage that the specific features of the surface under control are taken into account, thus rendering the scheme modification unnecessary. The control scheme applies to both rotationally symmetric and asymmetric surfaces. Additional schemes of using DOEs for optical control are available in Ref. [18].

8.3 DESIGN OF A PLANAR COMPENSATOR

Let the reference wave front σ be generated from a light beam E by means of an optical setup (Fig. 8.5) whose base element is represented by a compensator C with zoned translucent computer-generated microrelief on the planar substrate.

The plane compensator C is intended to generate a uniform phase on the surface of the wave front σ, with its apex found at the distance l from the compensator C

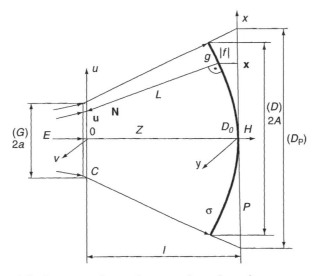

Figure 8.5. Geometry of wave front transformation using a compensator.

(Fig. 8.5). The wave front σ is specified by

$$H = f(\mathbf{x}), \quad \mathbf{x} \in D, \tag{8.1}$$

where f is the smooth, continuously differentiated function and $f(0) = 0$. Here, $\mathbf{x} = (x, y)$ are the Cartesian coordinates of the projection of point $Q \in \sigma$ on the plane P passing through the apex D_0 in parallel with the compensator, D is the range of values of $\mathbf{x}$ corresponding to the produced segment of the wave front σ, H is the algebraic distance from $Q \in \sigma$ to P, which is chosen negative if P is found behind Q along the ray path. The axis $z \perp C$ issues out of the center O along the ray path. The illuminating beam E is described by the wavelength λ, the intensity distribution $I_0(\mathbf{u})$, and the eikonal $\psi_0(\mathbf{u})$ in the working domain G of the compensator C, and $\mathbf{u} = (u, v)$ are the Cartesian coordinates in the compensator's plane. As a purely phase-planar optical element, the compensator C is described by the phase function $\varphi(\mathbf{u})$ [16,17]. In designing the compensator, the phase function $\varphi(\mathbf{u})$ is reduced to the interval $[0, 2\pi(m)]$ and realized as a phase microrelief ($m = $ const is a natural number, for kinoforms $m = 1$).

The geometric optical equation for the compensator takes the form

$$k\psi_0(\mathbf{u}) + \varphi(\mathbf{u}) + kL(\mathbf{x}) = \varphi_0 \equiv \text{const}; \ k = \frac{2\pi}{\lambda}, \tag{8.2}$$

where $L(\mathbf{x})$ is the distance from the compensator to the front σ along the ray, with the direction

$$\mathbf{N} = \frac{(-\nabla_x f, 1)}{\sqrt{1 + (\nabla_x f)^2}} \tag{8.3}$$

being normal to the surface in Eq. (8.1).

$L > 0$ if the ray passes through the front σ after the compensator C. Owing to Eq. (8.3), we have

$$L = [L + f]\sqrt{1 + (\nabla_x f)^2} \tag{8.4}$$

and the coordinates of point $\mathbf{u}$ on C and point $\mathbf{x}$ on σ are related by the equations of correspondence

$$\mathbf{u} = \mathbf{x} + [l + f(\mathbf{x})]\nabla_x f(\mathbf{x}). \tag{8.5}$$

Similar to $\mathbf{u}$ and $\mathbf{x}$, the domains G and D should also be related by a correspondence, and according to Eqs. (8.2) and (8.4), the compensator's phase function is defined by

$$\varphi(\mathbf{u}) = \varphi_0 - k\left\{[l + f(\mathbf{x})]\sqrt{1 + [\nabla_x f(\mathbf{x})]^2} + \psi_0(\mathbf{u})\right\} \tag{8.6}$$

where the coordinate $\mathbf{x}$ is found from the solution of Eq. (8.5) for a given coordinate $\mathbf{u}$.

8.4 SPECTRAL PROPERTIES OF COMPENSATORS

A computer-synthesized compensator is represented by a curvilinear phase diffraction grating of complex topology and grooves' profile.

Fix the wave front σ geometry and change the working wavelength from the estimated value λ_0 to the value $\lambda \neq \lambda_0$. Because the way in which the eikonal is affected by the compensator is independent of the wavelength λ, the compensator's phase function $\varphi(\lambda)$ required for the generation of the front σ on the wavelength λ is related to the phase function φ found at the wavelength λ_0 as follows:

$$\varphi(\lambda) = (\lambda_0/\lambda)\varphi$$

(in this section, the spatial argument $\mathbf{u}$ is omitted).

When a DOE compensator is illuminated by the light of wavelength $\lambda \neq \lambda_0$, the resulting wave front is different from the desired one. The errors come from the two main factors:

- The optical path difference in the compensator is changed because of the refractive index variance;
- The phase correspondence condition and the DOE zone equiphase conditions are violated.

The first-type errors are similar to chromatic aberrations of conventional transmitting optical elements. For a one-zone DOE, the refractive index variance is the only reason for aberration.

The latter factor is characteristic of DOEs in which the maximum value of the optical path difference should correspond to the phase $2\pi m$ for the estimated wavelength λ_0 ($m = 1, 2, \ldots$). By changing the wavelength, even a negligibly small refractive index variance results in the violation of the phase-correspondence condition. Obviously, the zones will again be in phase if the maximum value of phase difference for the working wavelength λ is close either to $2\pi m$ or to $4\pi m$, $6\pi m$, and so on.

For the quantitative studies of how the phase discrepancy affects the kinoform operation at $m = 1$, refer to Ref. [31]. Note, however, that in the cited work the kinoform performance was estimated on the basis of the accuracy of generating the desired intensity in the object plane. At the same time, in the studies of the compensator, the accuracy of generating the phase distribution defining the wave front shape counts.

Because according to Eqs. (8.6) and (8.5) the variation in the eikonal φ/k provided by the compensator does not depend on the wavelength, and the phase function is reduced to the interval $[0, 2\pi m)$ for the wavelength λ_0, the phase shift at $\lambda \neq \lambda_0$ at each point $\mathbf{u}$ is equal to

$$\Phi(\lambda) = c \; \mathrm{mod}_{2\pi m}\varphi, \tag{8.7}$$

where

$$c = \frac{\lambda_0}{\lambda} \cdot \frac{\Delta n(\lambda)}{\Delta n(\lambda_0)}; \quad \Delta n(\lambda) = n(\lambda) - 1, \tag{8.8}$$

where $n(\lambda)$ is the refractive index of the microrelief material of the compensator's zones and $\mathrm{mod}_{2\pi m}\varphi$ is the modulo $2\pi m$ phase φ.

The compensator's phase function

$$T(\lambda) = \exp[i\,\Phi(\lambda)] \tag{8.9}$$

is periodic in φ with a period of $2\pi m$ and, hence, can be decomposed into a Fourier series:

$$T(\lambda) = \sum_{l=-\infty}^{\infty} a_l \exp(i\frac{l}{m}\varphi), \tag{8.10}$$

$$a_l = \operatorname{sinc}(l - mc)(-1)^l \exp(i\pi mc). \tag{8.11}$$

corresponding to different diffraction orders [25,26]. According to the Parseval equality, we have

$$\sum_{l=-\infty}^{\infty} |a_l|^2 = 1. \tag{8.12}$$

According to Eq. (8.10), the lth diffraction order provides the phase function

$$\Phi^{(l)} = \frac{l}{m}\varphi = \frac{l\lambda}{m\lambda_0}\varphi(\lambda). \tag{8.13}$$

According to Eq. (8.11), the highest-intensity order is that with the number $l = v$, which is closest to mc, that is,

$$mc \equiv \frac{m\lambda_0}{\lambda} \cdot \frac{\Delta n(\lambda)}{\Delta n(\lambda_0)} = v \in \delta, \tag{8.14}$$

where $\delta \in [-1/2, 1/2]$ and v is λ-dependent. In the vth order, the phase function is

$$\Phi(v) = \frac{v}{m}\varphi = \mu\varphi(\lambda), \tag{8.15}$$

where

$$\mu = \frac{v\lambda}{m\lambda_0} = \frac{\Delta n(\lambda)}{\Delta n(\lambda_0)} \cdot \frac{1}{1 + \dfrac{\delta}{v}}. \tag{8.16}$$

Note that for any λ (any δ and v) we have

$$\mu \in \left[\frac{2}{3} \cdot \frac{\Delta n(\lambda)}{\Delta n(\lambda_0)}, 2\frac{\Delta n(\lambda)}{\Delta n(\lambda_0)}\right]. \tag{8.17}$$

Thus, if the wavelength λ is changed as compared with the estimated wavelength, the most intensive vth diffraction order is characterized, instead of $\varphi(\lambda)$, by a linearly distorted (by a factor of μ) phase transmittance that generates a deformed wave front shape.

8.5 ACCURACY CHARACTERISTIC OF THE REFERENCE WAVE FRONT

Owing to imperfections of microrelief fabrication technology, light diffraction and scattering effects in the compensator's medium, and the limited number of phase gradation levels and surface resolution, instead of the desired phase function of Eq. (8.6), the real phase function is $\hat{\varphi}$. Accordingly, instead of the reference wave front σ, the generated wave surface $\hat{\sigma}$ is somewhat distorted in shape in comparison with σ, thus determining the quality of the surface $\hat{\sigma}$. In the following text, quantitative characteristics of the difference between $\hat{\sigma}$ and σ, both in each point and in the whole, that are convenient to work with are defined.

Despite the fact that the compensator for the front σ was designed using geometric optics techniques, the wave surface is formed diffractively and may not be a geometric optics wave front. In the general case, the mechanism of the wave front $\hat{\sigma}$-formation is described by a superposition of many diffraction orders [25,32].

The compensator's quality is expedient to estimate through the direct comparison of the light fields corresponding to $\hat{\sigma}$ and σ in a virtual two-arm interferometer adjusted for infinite-width fringes with the between-arm phase difference being equal to π.

Introduce the designations w, I, and ψ for the complex amplitude, the intensity and the eikonal of the reference light field corresponding to the wave front σ and the analogous designations, $\hat{w}$, $\hat{I}$, and $\hat{\psi}$, corresponding to $\hat{\sigma}$:

$$I = |w|^2, \psi = \frac{1}{k}\arg w;$$

$$\hat{I} = |\hat{w}|^2, \hat{\psi} = \frac{1}{k}\arg \hat{w}.$$

With the light field intensities w and $\hat{w}$ input in the virtual interferometer's arms, the resulting difference light field will have the complex amplitude of $\hat{w} - w$ and the intensity

$$i = \left|\hat{w} - w\right|^2. \tag{8.18}$$

We shall use the coordinates of point in the Cartesian coordinate system centered at point 0 (Fig. 8.5) as the arguments for the functions w, I, $\hat{w}$, $\hat{I}$, $\hat{w} - w$, and i. Points on the compensator's C-plane have the coordinates $(u, v, 0) = (\mathbf{u}, 0)$, the wave front points — the coordinates $(x, y, l + f) = (\mathbf{x}, l + f(\mathbf{x}))$, and the plane P points — the coordinates $(x_P, y_P, l) = (\mathbf{x_P}, l)$. Note that by the data given, we can write

$$I(\mathbf{u}, 0) = I_0(\mathbf{u}), \psi(\mathbf{u}, 0) = \psi_0(\mathbf{u}) + \frac{1}{k}\varphi(\mathbf{u}), \tag{8.19}$$

$$\hat{I}(\mathbf{u}, 0) = I_0(\mathbf{u}), \hat{\psi}(\mathbf{u}, 0) = \psi_0(\mathbf{u}) + \frac{1}{k}\hat{\varphi}(\mathbf{u}), \tag{8.20}$$

$$i(\mathbf{u}, 0) = I(\mathbf{u}) \cdot 4\sin^2\left[\frac{\hat{\varphi}(\mathbf{u}) - \varphi(\mathbf{u})}{2}\right]. \tag{8.21}$$

Because $i(\mathbf{x_P}, l)$ become zero at $\hat{w} = w$, the normalized value

$$\aleph(\mathbf{x_P}) = \frac{i(\mathbf{x_P}, l)}{I(\mathbf{x_P}, l)} \in [0, 1] \tag{8.22}$$

can serve as the characteristic of difference between $\hat{\sigma}$ and σ at each point of the segment D of the wave front. For constructing the averaged characteristics of difference between $\hat{\sigma}$ and σ, on the whole, one can use the integral light fluxes of the difference field $\hat{w} - w$ and the field $\hat{w}$ passing through the segment D of the front σ:

$$\Phi_D = \int_{D_p} i(\mathbf{x_p}, l) \, d^2 \mathbf{x_p}, \tag{8.23}$$

$$E_D = \int_{D_p} I(\mathbf{x_p}, l) \, d^2 \mathbf{x_p}, \tag{8.24}$$

and the corresponding full light fluxes:

$$\Phi = \int_{-\infty}^{\infty} \int_{-\infty}^{\infty} i(\mathbf{x_p}, l) \, d^2 \mathbf{x_p}, \tag{8.25}$$

$$E = \int_{-\infty}^{\infty} \int_{-\infty}^{\infty} \hat{I}(\mathbf{x_p}, l) \, d^2 \mathbf{x_p} = \int_{-\infty}^{\infty} \int_{-\infty}^{\infty} I(\mathbf{x_p}, l) \, d^2 \mathbf{x_p}, \tag{8.26}$$

(D_P is the projection of D onto the plane P fulfilled by the rays).
Note that the complex amplitude w is close to zero outside the D_P domain of the segment σ. Therefore, $i(\mathbf{x_p}, l) = \hat{I}(\mathbf{x_p}, l)$ at $\mathbf{x_p} \in D_p$ and

$$\Phi = \Phi_D + E_{\bar{D}}, \tag{8.27}$$

where

$$E = E_D + E_{\bar{D}}, \tag{8.28}$$

whereas the quantity $E_{\bar{D}}$ yields the portion of the light flux E falling outside D_P and corresponding to higher diffraction orders. As averaged characteristics of quality of the reference wave front σ-formation, we may use the relative errors

$$\eta = \frac{\Phi}{E}; \quad \eta_D = \frac{\Phi_D}{E_D}, \tag{8.29}$$

derived from Eqs. (8.23), (8.25), (8.26), and (8.29) and varying in the interval [0,1].

The error η_D characterizes the error of formation of the segment D of the front σ exactly. The error η additionally includes the illuminating beam energy portion going to higher diffraction orders about σ.

Also, introduce the notion of wave front deviations. Note that in a particular case of the smooth geometric optical surface $\hat{\sigma}$ insignificantly different from σ, the following relations take place

$$|\hat{I}(\mathbf{x_p}, l) - I(\mathbf{x_p}, l)| \ll I(\mathbf{x_p}, l), \tag{8.30}$$

$$i(\mathbf{x_p}, l) = \hat{I}(\mathbf{x_p}, l) \cdot 4 \sin^2 \left[\frac{\pi}{\lambda} \varepsilon(\mathbf{x_p}) \right], \tag{8.31}$$

where the quantity

$$\varepsilon(\mathbf{x_p}) = \hat{\psi}(\mathbf{x_p}, l) - \psi(\mathbf{x_p}, l) \tag{8.32}$$

characterizes the deviation of $\hat{\sigma}$ from σ counted along the normal to σ passing through the point $(\mathbf{x_p}, l)$ (Fig. 8.6).

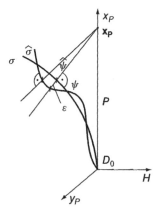

Figure 8.6. The computation of the wave front normal deviation.

In the general case, for the wavesurface $\hat{\sigma}$ we shall formally introduce a notion of the deviation $\varepsilon(\mathbf{x_p})$ $\hat{\sigma}$ from σ using Eqs. (8.31) and (8.18) at each point $\mathbf{x_P}$. By analogy, introduce an average deviation $\bar{\varepsilon}_D$ $\hat{\sigma}$ from σ within the D segment, replacing in Eq. (8.31) the intensities by the corresponding light fluxes:

$$\Phi_D = E_D \cdot 4 \sin^2 \left(\frac{\pi \bar{\varepsilon}_D}{\lambda} \right). \tag{8.33}$$

(If the geometric optical surface $\hat{\sigma}$ is only slightly different from σ, the quantity $\bar{\varepsilon}_D$ defines the normal deviation of $\hat{\sigma}$ from σ within the D-segment).

Owing to Eqs. (8.27) and (8.33), the following estimate takes place:

$$\bar{\varepsilon}_D \le \bar{\varepsilon}, \tag{8.34}$$

where $\bar{\varepsilon}$ is a characteristic averaged over the entire wave front

$$\Phi = E \cdot 4 \sin^2 \left(\frac{\pi \bar{\varepsilon}}{\lambda} \right). \tag{8.35}$$

For the light fluxes Φ and E, one can write down the conservation law that follows immediately from Helmholtz's equations

$$\Phi \equiv \int_{-\infty}^{\infty} \int_{-\infty}^{\infty} i(\mathbf{x_p}, l) \, d^2\mathbf{x_p} = \int_G i(\mathbf{u}, 0) \, d^2\mathbf{u}, \tag{8.36}$$

$$E \equiv \int_{-\infty}^{\infty} \int_{-\infty}^{\infty} \hat{I}(\mathbf{x_p}, l) \, d^2\mathbf{x_p} = \int_G \hat{I}(\mathbf{u}, 0) \, d^2\mathbf{u}. \tag{8.37}$$

Application of Eqs. (8.36) and (8.37) to Eq. (8.35) allows the deviation $\bar{\varepsilon}$ to be expressed directly through the compensator's phase function:

$$\bar{\varepsilon}_D \le \bar{\varepsilon} = \frac{\lambda}{\pi} \arcsin \left[\int_G \sin^2 \left(\frac{\hat{\varphi} - \varphi}{2} \right) \beta(\mathbf{u}) \, d^2\mathbf{u} \right]^{1/2}, \tag{8.38}$$

where

$$\beta(\mathbf{u}) = \frac{I_0(\mathbf{u})}{\int_G I_0(\mathbf{u})\, d^2\mathbf{u}}. \tag{8.39}$$

Equation (8.38) allows the upper bound of accuracy of the deviation $\bar{\varepsilon}_D$ of the wave front $\hat{\sigma}$ from the reference σ to be expressed directly through the residual of the compensator's phase function and holds for the compensator as a thin optical element any technique of fabricating. In the next section, the estimate in Eq. (8.38) is rendered concrete for the steplike microrelief with a limited spatial resolution characteristic of diffractive optics fabrication techniques [16,17].

8.6 THE IMPACT OF THE SAMPLING AND QUANTIZING OF THE COMPENSATOR'S PHASE FUNCTION ON THE REFERENCE WAVE FRONT ACCURACY

The presence of a finite number M of the microrelief height levels and a limited spatial resolution $\delta u \times \delta v$ of diffractive optics technologies [17] results in amplitude quantizing and sampling of the compensators' phase function reduced to the interval of values $[0, 2\pi m)$, $m = 1, 2, \ldots$.

Phase function quantizing effects are commonly studied using intensities of different diffraction orders [25,32]. Note, however, that the joint account of phase sampling and phase quantizing is possible [19,20] not only for off-axis binary holograms, as reported in the familiar papers [27,33].

Let us find out the combined effect of sampling and quantizing of the compensator with diffractive phase microrelief on the wave front quality using the previously defined deviation criterion, $\bar{\varepsilon}$, additionally averaged over the quantizing noise ensemble. A computer-generated compensator has a discrete structure made up of not more than $N_1 \times N_2$ resolution cells G_{jk}, $(j, k) \in J$ of size $\delta u \times \delta v$ each. Here, J is a set of numbers (j, k) of the resolution cells G_{jk} falling within the domain G. In each cell G_{jk}, the phase function $\hat{\varphi}$ takes a constant value, $\hat{\varphi}_{jk}$ being the result of quantizing in M levels of the pixel $\varphi(\vec{\xi}_{jk})$ of the function φ at the center $\vec{\xi}_{jk} = (\xi_i, \eta_k)$ of the cell G_{jk}. The values of $\hat{\varphi}_{jk}$ are chosen from a finite set

$$\left\{ \hat{\varphi} : \hat{\varphi} = j \cdot q;\ j = \overline{0, M-1} \right\}; \quad q = \frac{2\pi m}{M}. \tag{8.40}$$

We shall estimate the deviation $\bar{\varepsilon}$ in Eq. (8.38) on the understanding that the cell size is small in comparison with a characteristic range of phase variation and the quantization step q is small in comparison with $2\pi m$ so that the statistical quantization model can be applied [33].

For a fixed cell G_{jk}, the φ-function can be expanded into a series in terms of $(\mathbf{u} - \vec{\xi}_{jk})$

$$\varphi(\mathbf{u}) \cong \varphi(\vec{\xi}_{jk}) + (\mathbf{u} - \vec{\xi}_{jk})\nabla_u \varphi(\vec{\xi}_{jk}), \tag{8.41}$$

$$\mathbf{u} \in G_{jk}, \quad \nabla_u = \left(\frac{\partial}{\partial u}, \frac{\partial}{\partial v} \right), \quad \beta(\mathbf{u}) \cong \beta(\vec{\xi}_{jk}), \quad (\mathbf{u} \in G_{jk}), \tag{8.42}$$

whereas the quantizing noise values

$$\Theta_{jk} = \hat{\varphi}_{jk} - \varphi(\vec{\xi}_{jk}), \tag{8.43}$$

are not correlated, with their average equal to zero:

$$\left\langle |\Theta_{jk}|^2 \right\rangle = \frac{q^2}{12}, \tag{8.44}$$

where $\langle |\Theta_{jk}|^2 \rangle$ denotes the averaging over the quantizing noise ensemble.

Integrating with respect to $\mathbf{u}$ and taking the average $\langle |\Theta_{jk}|^2 \rangle$ in each cell G_{jk}, then changing from the derived integral sums to integrals and substituting the result into Eq. (8.38) yields

$$\langle \bar{\varepsilon} \rangle = \frac{\lambda}{\pi} \arcsin \left[\frac{\pi}{\lambda} \left(\varepsilon_q^2 + \varepsilon_d^2 \right)^{1/2} \right], \tag{8.45}$$

where

$$\varepsilon_q^2 = \frac{\lambda^2}{2\pi^2} \left(1 - \operatorname{sinc} \frac{m}{M} \right); \tag{8.46}$$

$$\varepsilon_d^2 = \frac{\lambda^2}{2\pi^2} \operatorname{sinc} \left(\frac{m}{M} \right) \int_G \left[1 - \operatorname{sinc} \left(\delta u \cdot \frac{\varphi_u(\mathbf{u})}{2\pi} \right) \cdot \operatorname{sinc} \left(\delta v \cdot \frac{\varphi_v(\mathbf{u})}{2\pi} \right) \right]$$

$$\times \beta(\mathbf{u}) \, d^2 \mathbf{u}; \quad \left(\varphi_u = \frac{\partial \varphi}{\partial u}; \ \varphi_v = \frac{\partial \varphi}{\partial v} \right). \tag{8.47}$$

The quantity ε_q becomes zero as $M \to \infty$ and is the component of the average deviation $\langle \bar{\varepsilon} \rangle$ caused by the phase amplitude quantization. The quantity ε_d becomes zero at δu, $\delta v \to 0$ and is the component of the deviation caused by the phase sampling in the compensator's plane.

Owing to the supposed smallness of δu, δv, and q, we can write down Eqs. (8.46) and (8.47) in a simpler form for $\delta u = \delta v = \delta$:

$$\left. \begin{array}{l} \langle \bar{\varepsilon} \rangle = (\varepsilon_q^2 + \varepsilon_d^2)^{1/2} \\[2mm] \varepsilon_q^2 = \dfrac{1}{12} \left(\dfrac{m\lambda}{M} \right)^2 \end{array} \right\}, \tag{8.48}$$

$$\varepsilon_d^2 = \frac{\delta^2}{12} \int_G \left[\frac{1}{k} \nabla_u \varphi(\mathbf{u}) \right]^2 \beta(\mathbf{u}) \, d^2 \mathbf{u} = \frac{\delta^2}{12} \int |\chi(\mathbf{x})|^2 \beta_0(\mathbf{x}) \, d^2 \mathbf{x}, \tag{8.49}$$

where according to Eqs. (8.6), (8.3), and (8.5) we have

$$\chi(\mathbf{x}) = \frac{1}{k} \nabla_u \varphi(\mathbf{u}) = - \left\{ \frac{\nabla_x f(\mathbf{x})}{\sqrt{1 + [\nabla_x f(\mathbf{x})]^2}} \right\} + \nabla_u \Psi_0(\mathbf{u}), \tag{8.50}$$

$$\beta_0(\mathbf{x}) = \beta(\mathbf{u}) \frac{\partial \mathbf{u}}{\partial \mathbf{x}}; \quad \nabla_u = \left(\frac{\partial}{\partial u}, \frac{\partial}{\partial v} \right), \tag{8.51}$$

Here $\partial \mathbf{u}/\partial \mathbf{x}$ is the Jacobean of the transform in Eq. (8.5), and the vector $\mathbf{u}$ is derived from the vector $\mathbf{x}$, Eq. (8.5).

It is useful to bear in mind that for a weakly aspheric surface σ with its major curvature centers found in the vicinity of the center of a nearest sphere, and for the uniform incident beam intensity I_0, the weight functions β and β_0 are approximated by the constants

$$\beta(\mathbf{u}) \cong \frac{1}{|G|}, \quad \beta(\mathbf{x}) \cong \frac{1}{|D|}, \tag{8.52}$$

where $|G|$ is the area of the domain G.

If we relate the wave front parameters to the compensator's characteristics, the estimates derived will allow us to find the accuracy $\bar{\varepsilon}$ of generation of the wave front by the compensator and to elucidate in advance, before trying to really fabricate the compensator, whether it is possible to get the desired accuracy $\bar{e} \leq \varepsilon_{adm}$. In addition, the estimates in Eqs. (8.45) to (8.49) allow us to choose the design parameters of the diffractive optics technology (δ, M, and others) on the basis of the desired accuracy ε_{adm} of the reference wave front generation.

8.7 GENERATION OF WAVE FRONTS WITH SMALL RELATIVE APERTURE

For the smooth wave fronts σ of Eq. (8.1) that satisfy the paraxial approximation condition

$$\frac{A}{R_1} \ll 1, \quad \frac{B}{R_2} \ll 1, \tag{8.53}$$

we can simplify the equations for the phase function φ and the accuracy ε by expanding them into a Taylor series. Here, $2A \times 2B$ is the size of a rectangular segment D of the σ-front along the axes x and y, respectively; R_1 and R_2 are the major curvature radii in the apex D_0. Also, introduce the size $2a \times 2b$ of the light aperture G of the compensator C, related to A and B by the equations similar to Eq. (8.5). In this section, we shall use a scalar notation for $(u, v) = \mathbf{u}$; $(x, y) = \mathbf{x}$ and the designations f_x, f_y, f_{xy} and so on for the derivatives of f.

For simplicity, direct the x-axis and y-axis from the apex 0 along the intersection of the major normal cross sections of σ, with a tangent plane to σ having the apex at D_0, that is, put

$$f(0, 0) = 0, \quad f_x(0, 0) = 0,$$

$$f_y(0, 0) = 0, \quad f_{xy}(0, 0) = 0. \tag{8.54}$$

If the function f has continuous derivatives at least up to order n_0, owing to Eq. (8.53), it seems expedient to expand the functions f and φ in a power series of x, y and u, v, respectively:

$$f(x, y) = \sum_{n=0}^{n_0} \frac{1}{n!} \sum_{i=0}^{n} c_n^i f_{i,n-i} x^i y^{n-i} + O\left[(x + y)^{n_0+1}\right], \tag{8.55}$$

$$\varphi(u, v) = \sum_{n=0}^{n_0} \frac{1}{n!} \sum_{i=0}^{n} c_n^i \varphi_{i,n-i} u^i v^{n-i} + O\left[(u + v)^{n_0+1}\right], \tag{8.56}$$

where c_n^i are the binomial coefficients; n_0 is the approximation order; and $O(\xi)$ symbolizes a quantity of the same order of smallness as ξ.

Owing to Eq. (8.54), we get

$$f_{00} = 0; \quad f_{01} = f_{10} = 0; \quad f_{11} = 0. \tag{8.57}$$

According to Eq. (8.57) and differential geometry relations, the major curvature radii at point $(x, y) = (0, 0)$ are equal to

$$R_1 = -\frac{1}{f_{20}}; \quad R_2 = -\frac{1}{f_{02}}. \tag{8.58}$$

If, in addition, the illuminating beam is expanded as

$$\psi_0(u, v) = \sum_{n=0}^{n_0} \frac{1}{n!} \sum_{i=0}^{n} c_n^i \psi_{i,n-i} u^i v^{n-i} + O\left[(u + v)^{n_0+1}\right], \tag{8.59}$$

Eqs. (8.5), (8.6), (8.57), and (8.58) allow one to establish the relation between the coefficients

$$\left.\begin{array}{l} \varphi_{00} = \varphi_0 - k(\psi_{00} + l) \\ \varphi_{01} = -k\psi_{01}; \varphi_{10} = -k\psi_{10} \end{array}\right\}, \tag{8.60}$$

$$\left.\begin{array}{l} \varphi_{20} = k\left(\dfrac{1}{R_1 - l} - \psi_{20}\right); \\[3mm] \varphi_{02} = k\left(\dfrac{1}{R_2 - l} - \psi_{02}\right); \end{array}\right\} \tag{8.61}$$

$$\varphi_{11} = -k\psi_{11};$$

$$\varphi_{21} = k\left[\frac{f_{21}}{(1 - l/R_1)^2(1 - l/R_2)} - \psi_{21}\right];$$

$$\varphi_{12} = k\left[\frac{f_{12}}{(1 - l/R_1)(1 - l/R_2)^2} - \psi_{12}\right]; \tag{8.62}$$

$$\varphi_{30} = k\left[\frac{f_{30}}{(1 - l/R_1)^3} - \psi_{30}\right]; \varphi_{03} = k\left[\frac{f_{03}}{(1 - l/R_2)^3} - \psi_{03}\right]. \tag{8.63}$$

Note that the solution to Eq. (8.5) can be represented as follows

$$\left.\begin{array}{l} x = \dfrac{u}{1 - \dfrac{l}{R_1}} + O((u + v)^3), \\[6mm] y = \dfrac{v}{1 - \dfrac{l}{R_2}} + O((u + v)^3). \end{array}\right\} \tag{8.64}$$

The wave front deviation $\bar{\varepsilon}$ can also be expressed through the coefficients of the paraxial phase function in Eq. (8.56). By way of illustration, Eqs. (8.46) and (8.49) in the approximation of Eq. (8.52) take the form

$$\bar{\varepsilon} = \left\{\frac{1}{12}\left(\frac{m\lambda}{M}\right)^2 + \frac{\delta^2}{48abk^2}\int_{-a}^{a}\int_{-b}^{b}(\varphi_u^2 + \varphi_v^2)\, du\, dv\right\}^{1/2}, \tag{8.65}$$

whereas the paraxial approximation in Eq. (8.53) produces the estimate (at $n_0 = 3$)

$$\bar{\varepsilon} = \left\{ \frac{1}{12} \left(\frac{m\lambda}{M} \right)^2 + \frac{\delta^2}{12k^2} \left[\varphi_{10}^2 + \varphi_{01}^2 + \frac{a^2}{3} (\varphi_{20}^2 + \varphi_{11}^2) + \frac{b^2}{3} (\varphi_{02}^2 + \varphi_{11}^2) \right] \right\}^{1/2},$$

(8.66)

where the coefficients φ_{01}, φ_0, φ_{10}, φ_{20}, φ_{02}, and φ_{11} are derived from Eqs. (8.60) to (8.61).

Note that with the approximation order used ($n_0 = 3$), we can substitute in Eqs. (8.65) and (8.66) [Fig. 8.5 and Eqs. (8.5) and (8.64)]

$$a \cong A \left(1 - \frac{l}{R_1} \right); \quad b \cong B \left(1 - \frac{l}{R_2} \right).$$

(8.67)

8.8   AXIALLY SYMMETRIC COMPENSATORS

Axially symmetric compensators that generate rotating wave fronts are the direct analogs of compensating objectives and have been covered in Refs. [16,18]. In this section, we derive the corresponding formulae as a particular case of the foregoing general theory. For radially symmetric functions of arguments $r = |\mathbf{u}| = \sqrt{(u^2 + v^2)}$ and $\rho = |\mathbf{x}| = \sqrt{(x^2 + y^2)}$, we shall employ the same designations as for the corresponding functions $\mathbf{u}$ and $\mathbf{x}$.

Assume that the wave front σ is a rotating surface of diameter D with the equation

$$z = f(\rho), \quad 0 \le \rho \le D/2,$$

(8.68)

and the incident beam has a radially symmetric intensity $I_0(r)$ and eikonal $\psi(r)$. Changing in Eqs. (8.5) and (8.6) to polar coordinates

$$x = \rho \cos\alpha, \quad y = \rho \sin\alpha,$$

(8.69)

$$u = r \cos\beta, \quad v = r \sin\beta,$$

(8.70)

easily yields [16,18]

$$\alpha = \beta,$$

(8.71)

$$r = \rho + [l + f(\rho) \cdot f'(\rho)],$$

(8.72)

$$\varphi(r) = \varphi_0 - k \left[[l + f(\rho)] \cdot \sqrt{1 + [f'(\rho)]^2} + \psi_0(r) \right],$$

(8.73)

where

$$f'(\rho) = \frac{df}{d\rho}.$$

Thus, to find the phase function at point r it will suffice to solve a nonlinear equation in ρ Eq. (8.72), and substitute the result in Eq. (8.73). Note that, according to Eq. (8.72), the compensator's diameter d and the wave front's diameter D are related to l:

$$l = -f \left(\frac{D}{2} \right) - \frac{D - d}{2 f'(d/2)}.$$

(8.74)

In the paraxial approximation with

$$\frac{D}{R} \ll 1 \tag{8.75}$$

and, respectively,

$$\frac{d}{R-l} \ll 1, \tag{8.76}$$

the functions f and ψ_0 can be expressed through the Taylor series coefficients

$$f(\rho) = -\frac{1}{2R}\rho^2 + \frac{1}{4!}f_4\rho^4 + \frac{1}{6!}f_6\rho^6 + O(\rho^8), \tag{8.77}$$

$$\psi_0(r) = \psi_0 + \frac{1}{2R}\psi_2 r^2 + \frac{1}{4!}\psi_4 r^4 + \frac{1}{6!}\psi_6 r^6 + O(r^8), \tag{8.78}$$

where R is the curvature radius at the wave front σ apex. In this case, the solution to Eq. (8.72) is given by

$$\rho = \rho(r) = \frac{1}{1 - \dfrac{l}{R}}r + \frac{1}{3!}\rho_3 r^3 + \frac{1}{5!}\rho_5 r^5 + O(r^7), \tag{8.79}$$

where

$$\rho_3 = -\frac{3}{R^2\left(1 - \dfrac{l}{R}\right)^4}\left(1 + \frac{1}{3}R^2 l f_4\right), \tag{8.80}$$

$$\rho_5 = \frac{90}{R^4\left(1 - \dfrac{l}{R}\right)^7}\left(1 + \frac{1}{3}R^2 l f_4\right) + \frac{90}{\left(1 - \dfrac{l}{R}\right)^6}\left(\frac{15 f_4}{R} - l f_6\right). \tag{8.81}$$

According to Eqs. (8.73)–(8.81), the expansion of the phase function

$$\varphi(r) = \varphi_0 + \frac{1}{2}\varphi_2 r^2 + \frac{1}{4!}\varphi_4 r^4 + \frac{1}{6!}\varphi_6 r^6 + O(r^8), \tag{8.82}$$

has the coefficients

$$\left.\begin{aligned}
\varphi_2 &= k\left[-\psi_2 + \frac{1}{R-l}\right]; \\
\varphi_4 &= k\left[-\psi_4 - \frac{3\left(2 - \frac{l}{R}\right)}{R^3\left(1 - \frac{l}{R}\right)^4} - \frac{f_4}{\left(1 - \frac{l}{R}\right)^4}\right]; \\
\varphi_6 &= k\left[-\psi_6 + \frac{45}{R\left(1 - \frac{l}{R}\right)^5} - \frac{90\left(2 - \frac{l}{R}\right)}{R^5\left(1 - \frac{l}{R}\right)^7}\right. \\
&\quad \left.+ \frac{15\left(5 - \frac{l}{R}\right)}{R^2\left(1 - \frac{l}{R}\right)^7}f_4 + \frac{10R\left(2 - \frac{l}{R}\right)}{\left(1 - \frac{l}{R}\right)^7}f_4^2 - \frac{f_6}{\left(1 - \frac{l}{R}\right)^6}\right].
\end{aligned}\right\} \tag{8.83}$$

The accuracy $\bar{\varepsilon}$ of generation of the rotating wave front is evaluated from Eqs. (8.49) and (8.82) and is expressed through the coefficients in Eq. (8.83). For instance, in the approximation in Eq. (8.52), we get a convenient-to-use formula

$$\bar{\varepsilon} = \left\{ \frac{1}{12} \left(\frac{m\lambda}{M} \right)^2 + \frac{\delta^2 d^2}{96k^2} \left(\varphi_2^2 + \frac{d^2}{18} \varphi_2 \varphi_4 + \frac{d^4}{9 \cdot 2^7} \varphi_4^2 + \frac{d^4}{15 \cdot 2^7} \varphi_2 \varphi_6 \right) \right\}^{1/2}. \quad (8.84)$$

Example 8.1 As an illustration, we shall consider a compensator that generates an aspheric rotating wave front of the second order, defined by

$$\rho^2 = -2Rf - (1 - e^2)f^2, \quad (8.85)$$

where e is the eccentricity. The incident beam E is generated by a point source found at point $(-S_0)$ on the optical axis. Here,

TABLE 8.1. Values of $\bar{\varepsilon}$ for the "Sphere-Paraboloid" Compensator ($e = 1$)

M \ N	256	512	1024	2048	4096
4	$\dfrac{\lambda}{8.5}$	$\dfrac{\lambda}{11.6}$	$\dfrac{\lambda}{13}$	$\dfrac{\lambda}{13.7}$	$\dfrac{\lambda}{14}$
8	$\dfrac{\lambda}{10}$	$\dfrac{\lambda}{17}$	$\dfrac{\lambda}{23}$	$\dfrac{\lambda}{26}$	$\dfrac{\lambda}{28}$
256	$\dfrac{\lambda}{11}$	$\dfrac{\lambda}{21}$	$\dfrac{\lambda}{43}$	$\dfrac{\lambda}{86}$	$\dfrac{\lambda}{173}$

TABLE 8.2. Values of $\bar{\varepsilon}$ for the "Sphere-Hyperboloid" Compensator ($e = 1.3$)

M \ N	256	512	1024	2048	4096
4	$\dfrac{\lambda}{6}$	$\dfrac{\lambda}{9,5}$	$\dfrac{\lambda}{12}$	$\dfrac{\lambda}{13}$	$\dfrac{\lambda}{14}$
8	$\dfrac{\lambda}{6.2}$	$\dfrac{\lambda}{12}$	$\dfrac{\lambda}{19}$	$\dfrac{\lambda}{25}$	$\dfrac{\lambda}{30}$
256	$\dfrac{\lambda}{6.4}$	$\dfrac{\lambda}{13}$	$\dfrac{\lambda}{26}$	$\dfrac{\lambda}{51}$	$\dfrac{\lambda}{102}$

TABLE 8.3. Values of $\bar{\varepsilon}$ for the "Sphere-Ellipsoid" Compensator ($e = 0.7$)

M \ N	256	512	1024	2048	4096
4	$\dfrac{\lambda}{11}$	$\dfrac{\lambda}{13}$	$\dfrac{\lambda}{13, 7}$	$\dfrac{\lambda}{14}$	$\dfrac{\lambda}{14}$
8	$\dfrac{\lambda}{17}$	$\dfrac{\lambda}{23}$	$\dfrac{\lambda}{26}$	$\dfrac{\lambda}{27}$	$\dfrac{\lambda}{28}$
256	$\dfrac{\lambda}{22}$	$\dfrac{\lambda}{44}$	$\dfrac{\lambda}{91}$	$\dfrac{\lambda}{182}$	$\dfrac{\lambda}{364}$

$$f_4 = -\frac{3(1 - e^2)}{R^3}, \quad f_6 = -\frac{45(1 - e^2)^2}{R^5}, \tag{8.86}$$

$$\psi_0 = 0; \quad \psi_2 = \frac{1}{S_0}; \quad \psi_4 = \frac{3}{S_0^3}; \quad \psi_6 = \frac{45}{S_0^5}, \tag{8.87}$$

and the phase function φ and deviation $\bar{\varepsilon}$ of the wave front can be derived from Eqs. (8.82) to (8.84). Of interest are two cases: the compensator "sphere-second-order surface" with a source characterized by $S_0 = R - l$, and the compensator "plane-second-order surface" with $S_0 = \infty$. Tables 8.1, 8.2, and 8.3 show how $\bar{\varepsilon}$ depends on M and $N = d/\delta$ for the compensator "sphere-paraboloid" (hyperboloid, ellipsoid), respectively, for $\lambda = 0.63$ μm, $D = 0.2$ mm, and $R = 1$ m.

Plots and isolines of the deviation $\bar{\varepsilon}$ are depicted in Figures 8.7 and 8.8 for $S_0 = R - l$ and in Figures 8.9 and 8.10 for a plane incident beam with $S_0 = \infty$. Domains wherein the desired accuracy is not attained are shaded in Figures 8.8 and 8.10.

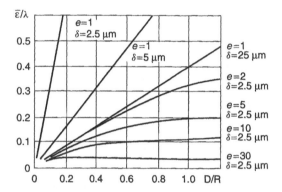

Figure 8.7. Sampling error for the "sphere-second-order surface of rotation" compensator ($D = 0.2$ m; $\lambda = 0.6328$ μm; $\delta = 25$ μm; $M = 256$).

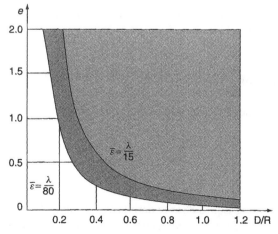

Figure 8.8. Range of values for the e and D/R parameters of the second-order wave fronts generated from a spherical wave front ($D = 0.2$ m; $\lambda = 0.6328$ μm; $M = 256$).

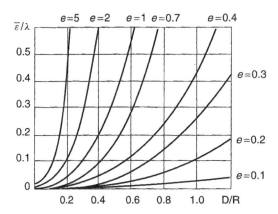

Figure 8.9. Sampling error for the "plane-second-order surface of rotation" ($D = 0.2$ m; $\lambda = 0.6328$ μm, $M = 256$).

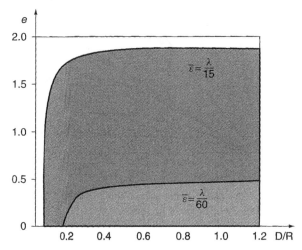

Figure 8.10. Deviation isolines for the second-order wave fronts generated from a plane wave front ($D = 0.2$ m; $\lambda = 0.6328$ μm; $\delta = 25$ μm; $M = 256$).

8.9 GENERATION OF HIGHER-ORDER WAVE FRONTS

The equation of nth order surfaces of rotation is given by

$$\rho^2 = -\sum_{p=1}^{n} a_p f^p. \tag{8.88}$$

Because by differentiating Eq. (8.88) the derivatives f' and f'' can easily be expressed as functions of f, Eq. (8.72) turns into a connection equation $r = r(f)$, and Eq. (8.73) gives the phase function φ of f. Thus, solving the equation $r = r(f)$ with respect to f enables the function $\varphi = \varphi[r(f)]$ to be derived from a given r.

TABLE 8.4. Values of $\bar{\varepsilon}$ for Various δ and M

M \ N	512	1024	2048	4096	8192
4	$\dfrac{\lambda}{3}$	$\dfrac{\lambda}{5.7}$	$\dfrac{\lambda}{9}$	$\dfrac{\lambda}{12}$	$\dfrac{\lambda}{13}$
8	$\dfrac{\lambda}{3.1}$	$\dfrac{\lambda}{6}$	$\dfrac{\lambda}{11}$	$\dfrac{\lambda}{18}$	$\dfrac{\lambda}{22}$
256	$\dfrac{\lambda}{3.1}$	$\dfrac{\lambda}{6.1}$	$\dfrac{\lambda}{12}$	$\dfrac{\lambda}{25}$	$\dfrac{\lambda}{33}$

Example 8.2. As an illustration of a nonalgebraic higher-order surface of rotation, let us consider the surface of a mirror whose peripheral circular zones are represented by fragments of purebloods of rotation with different foci. In Ref. [18] it has been demonstrated that the shape $z = f(\rho)$ of such a mirror focusing a plane axial light beam onto the thin axial cylinder of length $\aleph$, is specified by the equation

$$\frac{\rho}{\aleph \left(\dfrac{\rho}{D/2}\right)^2 + f(\rho) + \mathscr{F}_0} = \frac{-2f'(\rho)}{1 - [f'(\rho)]^2}, \tag{8.89}$$

where $\mathscr{F}_0$ is the paraxial focus and D is the mirror's diameter. It stands to reason that when the condition $D/\mathscr{F}_0 \ll 1$ is fulfilled, the solution to Eq. (8.89) is convenient to approximate by several terms of the expansion in Eq. (8.77), in which

$$f_4 = \frac{1}{2\mathscr{F}_0 D^2} \cdot \frac{\aleph}{\mathscr{F}_0}; \quad f_6 = \frac{1}{24\mathscr{F}_0^3 D^2} \cdot \frac{\aleph}{\mathscr{F}_0} - \frac{4}{3\mathscr{F}_0 D^4} \cdot \left(\frac{\aleph}{\mathscr{F}_0}\right)^2. \tag{8.90}$$

The phase function φ and the deviation $\bar{\varepsilon}$ may be evaluated using formulae of Eqs. (8.82) to (8.84). Table 8.4 gives values of $\bar{\varepsilon}$ for various δ and M (at $d = 25.6$ mm, $\aleph = 5$ mm, $D = 130$ mm, $\mathscr{F}_0 = 500$ mm, $\lambda = 0.6328$ μm, and for a spherical incident beam with $S_0 = R-l$).

8.10 GENERATION OF AXIAL-SYMMETRY-FREE WAVE FRONTS

General relations discussed in Sections 8.3 to 8.5 enable one to determine the compensator's phase function φ and the deviation $\bar{\varepsilon}$ of wave fronts not represented by surfaces of rotation.

Example 8.3. An elliptic paraboloid given by

$$f(x, y) = -\left(\frac{x^2}{2R_1} + \frac{y^2}{2R_2}\right) \tag{8.91}$$

may serve as an illustration of the wave front surface devoid of rotational symmetry.

For it, the relation between **x** and **u** is given by the equations

$$
\left.
\begin{array}{l}
u = x\dfrac{R_1 - l}{R_1} + \dfrac{x}{R_1}\left(\dfrac{x^2}{2R_1} + \dfrac{y^2}{2R_2}\right), \\[4mm]
v = y\dfrac{R_2 - l}{R_2} + \dfrac{y}{R_2}\left(\dfrac{x^2}{2R_1} + \dfrac{y^2}{2R_2}\right).
\end{array}
\right\}
\tag{8.92}
$$

For a spherical incident beam with

$$
\psi_0(u, v) = \sqrt{S_0^2 + u^2 + v^2} - S_0,
\tag{8.93}
$$

the phase function is given by

$$
\varphi(u, v, 0) = \varphi_0 - k\left[\left(l - \dfrac{x^2}{2R_1} - \dfrac{y^2}{2R_2}\right)\sqrt{1 + \dfrac{x^2}{R_1^2} + \dfrac{y^2}{R_2^2}} + \sqrt{S_0^2 + u^2 + v^2}\right],
\tag{8.94}
$$

where (x, y) is the solution to the set of algebraic equations in (8.92) and S_0 is the coordinate of the point source on the z-axis.

For the plane illuminating beam, we should put $\psi_0 = 0$.

Consider the estimate $\bar{\varepsilon}$ of the accuracy of generating from the plane wave an aspheric wave front represented by a segment of the elliptic paraboloid, Eq. (8.91), with domain

$$
D = \left\{(x, y) : \dfrac{x^2}{A^2} + \dfrac{y^2}{B^2} \leq 1\right\}.
\tag{8.95}
$$

The sizes A and B are matched to Eq. (8.91), that is,

$$
\dfrac{A}{R_1} = \dfrac{B}{R_2},
\tag{8.96}
$$

so that $\bar{\varepsilon}$ depends only on A/R_1.

According to Eqs. (8.50), (8.91), and (8.96), at $\varphi_0 = 0$, we get

$$
\chi(x, y) = \left(\dfrac{x}{R_1}, \dfrac{y}{R_2}\right)\Bigg/\sqrt{1 + \dfrac{x^2}{R_1^2} + \dfrac{y^2}{R_2^2}},
\tag{8.97}
$$

$$
\bar{\varepsilon} = \left\{\dfrac{1}{12}\left(\dfrac{m\lambda}{M}\right)^2 + \dfrac{\delta^2}{12}\left[1 - \dfrac{R_1^2}{A^2}\ln\left(1 + \dfrac{A^2}{R_1^2}\right)\right]\right\}^{1/2}.
\tag{8.98}
$$

Table 8.5 gives values of $\bar{\varepsilon}$ in accordance with Eq. (8.98).

Comparison of rows in Table 8.5 suggests that to fabricate a high-performance compensator of this type for visible light requires devices with a 2.5-μm resolution, whereas for the infrared (IR) light even a 25-μm resolution results in an acceptable quality of wave front.

TABLE 8.5. Values of $\bar{\varepsilon}$ ($2A = 0.2$; $R_1 = 2R_2 = 1$ m; $M = 256$; $m = 1$)

λ \ δ	50 μm	25 μm	12 μm	5 μm	2.5 μm	1 μm
0.6328 μm	—	$\dfrac{\lambda}{2}$	$\dfrac{\lambda}{3}$	$\dfrac{\lambda}{6}$	$\dfrac{\lambda}{13}$	$\dfrac{\lambda}{31}$
10.6 μm	$\dfrac{\lambda}{10}$	$\dfrac{\lambda}{21}$	$\dfrac{\lambda}{42}$	$\dfrac{\lambda}{100}$	$\dfrac{\lambda}{200}$	—

8.11 GENERATION OF OFF-AXIS SEGMENTS OF ROTATION WAVE FRONTS

Controlling the quality of off-axis parabolic and other mirrors calls for the generation of adequate reference wave fronts. The use of diffractive optics techniques is apparently the only way of producing compensators that are capable of forming the necessary segment without unneeded remaining part of the surface of rotation [21–23].

Assume that an aspheric surface of rotation σ_1 is defined by

$$\mathcal{H}_1 = \mathcal{F}(\rho_1), \quad \rho_1 = \sqrt{x_1^2 + y_1^2}, \tag{8.99}$$

in the Cartesian coordinate system $x_1 y_1 \mathcal{H}_1$ (or $\rho_1 \mathcal{H}_1$) centered at point $D_1 \in \sigma_1$ lying on the axis of rotation $D_1 \mathcal{H}_1$ (see Fig. 8.11), where $\mathcal{F}(\rho_1)$ is the smooth (continuously differentiable) function with $\mathcal{F}(0) = 0$ and with the second derivative of constant signs.

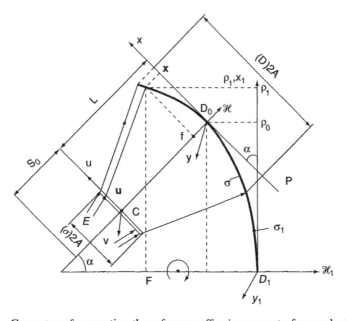

Figure 8.11. Geometry of generating the reference off-axis segment of an aspherical surface.

The off-axis segment σ of the surface σ_1 is characterized by its size $2A \times 2B$ and center D_0 with coordinates ρ_0, $\mathcal{F}(\rho_0)$ in the system $\rho_1 \mathcal{H}_1$. Direct a new individual optical axis $D_0 \mathcal{H}$ of the segment σ along the normal to the surface σ_1 at point D_0. Then, σ is characterized by the angle of inclination $\alpha \in [0, \pi/2]$ represented by the angle of normal to the axis of rotation $D_1 \mathcal{H}_1$ at point D_0, and related to ρ_0 through the formula (see Fig. 8.11)

$$\operatorname{tg}\alpha = -\mathcal{F}'(\rho_0), \quad \text{where } \mathcal{F}' = \frac{d\mathcal{F}}{d\rho_1}. \tag{8.100}$$

Viewing at the segment σ as an independent wave front (i.e. σ_1-independent), introduce a new Cartesian coordinate system x, y, $\mathcal{H}$ centered at point D_0, with its axis $\mathcal{H}$ directed along the optical axis $D_0 \mathcal{H}$ of the segment σ and the x-axis and y-axis found in plane P tangent to σ at point D_0 (the y-axis being parallel to the y_1-axis).

According to Eq. (8.99) and the construction of the coordinate system, the function

$$\mathcal{H} = f(x, y), \quad (x, y) \in D, \tag{8.101}$$

is smooth and satisfies the conditions

$$f(0, 0) = 0; \quad f_x(0, 0) = f_y(0, 0) = f_{xy}(0, 0) = 0 \tag{8.102}$$

and is implicitly defined by the equation

$$f \cos\alpha - x \sin\alpha - \mathcal{F}(\rho_0) = \mathcal{F}\{\sqrt{(f \sin\alpha + x \cos\alpha + \rho_0)^2 + y^2}\}, \quad (x, y) \in D \tag{8.103}$$

where

$$D = \{(x, y) : |x| \le A, |y| \le B\}, \tag{8.104}$$

f_x, f_y, f_{xy} are the derivatives of f.
Differentiating Eq. (8.103) yields

$$f_x(x, y) = \frac{\rho_1 \sin\alpha + \mathcal{F}'(\rho_1)x_1 \cos\alpha}{\rho_1 \cos\alpha - \mathcal{F}'(\rho_1)x_1 \sin\alpha}, \tag{8.105}$$

$$f_y(x, y) = \frac{y \cdot \mathcal{F}'(\rho_1)}{\rho_1 \cos\alpha - \mathcal{F}'(\rho_1) \cdot x_1 \cdot \sin\alpha}, \tag{8.106}$$

where
$$x_1 = f \sin\alpha + x \cos\alpha + \rho_0; \quad \rho_1 = \sqrt{x_1^2 + y_1^2}; \quad y_1 = y. \tag{8.107}$$

Place a planar phase compensator C perpendicularly to the optical axis $D_0 \mathcal{H}$ at the distance l from the plane P (see Fig. 8.11; $l > 0$ if the point D_0 lies behind C along the ray path). Introduce on the plane C the Cartesian coordinate system u, v, with its axes being parallel to the x-axis and y-axis. The compensator's pinhole will be shaped as a rectangle:

$$G = \{(u, v) : |u| \le a; |v| \le b\}. \tag{8.108}$$

Now we can apply the general formulas, Eq. (8.5) and (8.6), for designing a compensator, while taking into account that for the off-axis segment of the surface in Eq. (8.99), the f function is derived from the solution of Eq. (8.103), and f_x, f_y is derived from Eqs. (8.105) and (8.106). If the conditions of paraxial approximation in Eq. (8.53) is fulfilled and the function

$$\mathscr{F}(\rho_1) = \sum_{n=0}^{n_0} \frac{1}{n!} \mathscr{F}_n (\rho_1 - \rho_0)^n + O[(\rho_1 - \rho_0)^{n_0+1}] \tag{8.109}$$

is smooth, the expansion coefficients in Eq. (8.55) are derived from Eq. (8.57) and

$$f_{20} = \mathscr{F}_2 \cos^3 \alpha, \quad f_{02} = -\frac{1}{\rho_0} \operatorname{tg} \alpha, \tag{8.110}$$

$$\left. \begin{aligned} f_{30} &= (\mathscr{F}_3 + 3\mathscr{F}_2^2 \cos \alpha \cdot \sin \alpha) \cos^4 \alpha, \\ f_{21} &= 0; \quad f_{12} = \left(\frac{1}{\rho_0} \mathscr{F}_2 \cos^3 \alpha + \frac{1}{\rho_0^2} \sin \alpha \right) \cos \alpha, \\ f_{03} &= 0; \end{aligned} \right\} \tag{8.111}$$

$$\left. \begin{aligned} f_{40} &= (\mathscr{F}_4 - 10\mathscr{F}_3 \mathscr{F}_2 \cos \alpha \sin \alpha + 15\mathscr{F}_2^3 \cos^2 \alpha \sin^2 \alpha) \cos^5 \alpha, \\ f_{13} &= 0; \quad f_{31} = 0; \\ f_{22} &= -\left[\mathscr{F}_3 \cos^3 \alpha + \frac{1}{\rho_0} \mathscr{F}_2 \cos \alpha (3\sin^2 \alpha - 2) \right. \\ & \quad \left. +3\mathscr{F}_2^2 \cos^4 \alpha \sin \alpha - \frac{2}{\rho_0^2} \sin \alpha \right] \cdot \frac{1}{\rho_0} \cos^2 \alpha, \\ f_{04} &= 3\left[\mathscr{F}_2 \cos^5 \alpha + \frac{1}{\rho_0} \sin \alpha (\cos^2 \alpha - \sin^2 \alpha) \right] \cdot \frac{1}{\rho_0^2}. \end{aligned} \right\} \tag{8.112}$$

According to Eqs. (8.100) and (8.58), we have

$$f_{30} = \frac{3\sin \alpha \cos^5 \alpha}{R^2}; \quad f_{21} = 0; \quad f_{12} = \frac{\sin \alpha \cos^3 \alpha}{R^2}; \quad f_{03} = 0. \tag{8.113}$$

When focusing parallel light beams and optically processing information using Fourier-stages in Ref. [34], off-axis segments of the paraboloid of rotation

$$\mathscr{F}(\rho_1) = -\frac{\rho_1^2}{2R} \tag{8.114}$$

are of particular interest.

For the paraboloid, we have

$$\left\{ \begin{aligned} \mathscr{F}_0 &= -\frac{\rho_0^2}{2R}; \quad \mathscr{F}_1 = -\frac{\rho_0}{R}, \\ \mathscr{F}_2 &= -\frac{1}{R}; \quad \mathscr{F}_m = 0; \quad m \geq 3, \end{aligned} \right. \tag{8.115}$$

where R is the curvature radius of σ_1 at the apex D_1 on the axis of rotation.

According to Eq. (8.113),

$$R_1 = \frac{R}{\cos^3 \alpha}; \quad R_2 = \frac{R}{\cos \alpha}. \tag{8.116}$$

Equation (8.103) can be resolved analytically in f and

$$f(x, y) = \frac{\sqrt{R^2 + 2Rx \sin \alpha \cos^2 \alpha - y^2 \sin^2 \alpha \cos^2 \alpha}}{\sin^2 \alpha \cos \alpha} - \frac{x \sin \alpha \cos^2 \alpha + R}{\sin^2 \alpha \cos \alpha}, \tag{8.117}$$

while the segment center is given by the coordinates

$$\rho_0 = R \operatorname{tg} \alpha, \quad \mathscr{F}(\rho_0) = -\frac{R}{2} \operatorname{tg}^2 \alpha. \tag{8.118}$$

The phase function may be determined according to Eq. (8.5) and Eq. (8.6). Using Eqs. (8.110) to (8.112) and (8.115), we get

$$f_{20} = -\frac{\cos^3 \alpha}{R}; \quad f_{02} = -\frac{\cos \alpha}{R}; \tag{8.119}$$

$$f_{30} = \frac{3 \sin \alpha \cos^5 \alpha}{R^2}; \quad f_{21} = 0; \quad f_{12} = \frac{\sin \alpha \cos^3 \alpha}{R^2}; \quad f_{03} = 0; \tag{8.120}$$

$$f_{40} = -\frac{15 \sin^2 \alpha \cos^7 \alpha}{R^3}; \quad f_{31} = f_{13} = 0; \quad f_{22} = \frac{3 \sin^2 \alpha \cos^5 \alpha}{R^3};$$

$$f_{04} = \frac{3 \sin^2 \alpha \cos^3 \alpha}{R^3}. \tag{8.121}$$

Take a spherical illuminating beam E centered at $(-S_0)$ on the segment optical axis, for which in the paraxial approximation,

$$\psi_{00} = 0; \quad \psi_{10} = \psi_{01} = 0; \quad \psi_{20} = \psi_{02} = \frac{1}{S_0};$$

$$\psi_{30} = \psi_{03} = \psi_{12} = \psi_{21} = 0. \tag{8.122}$$

Substituting Eqs. (8.119) to (8.122) and (8.166) into Eqs. (8.60) to (8.63) gives the following phase function coefficients:

$$\varphi_{01} = \varphi_{10} = 0; \quad \varphi_{11} = 0;$$

$$\varphi_{20} = k \left(-\frac{1}{S_0} + \frac{1}{R_1 - l} \right); \quad \varphi_{02} = k \left(-\frac{1}{S_0} + \frac{1}{R_2 - l} \right); \tag{8.123}$$

$$\varphi_{21} = 0; \quad \varphi_{30} = k \frac{3R_1 \sin \alpha}{(R_1 - l)^3 \cos \alpha};$$

$$\varphi_{12} = k \frac{R_2 \sin \alpha}{(R_1 - l)(R_2 - l)^2 \cos \alpha}; \quad \varphi_{03} = 0. \tag{8.124}$$

According to Eqs. (8.66) and (8.123), in the paraxial approximation with $n_0 = 3$, the root-mean-square deviation is estimated by

$$\bar{\varepsilon} = \left\{ \frac{1}{12} \left(\frac{m\lambda}{M} \right)^2 + \frac{\delta^2}{36} \left[\left(\frac{1}{R_1 - l} - \frac{1}{S_0} \right)^2 a^2 + \left(\frac{1}{R_2 - l} - \frac{1}{S_0} \right)^2 b^2 \right] \right\}^{1/2}, \quad (8.125)$$

where a,b are derived from Eq. (8.67).

Example 8.4. As an example, consider a compensator that transforms a plane wave $((1/S_0) = 0)$ into an off-axis, square-shape segment $(B = A)$. Let us fix the compensator's size a. According to Eq. (8.67), we have

$$b = \frac{A}{\cos^2 \alpha} \left(\frac{a}{A} - \sin^2 \alpha \right); \quad l = R_1 \left(1 - \frac{a}{A} \right). \quad (8.126)$$

From Eqs. (8.125) and (8.126), we get the following calculational formula

$$\bar{\varepsilon} = \left\{ \frac{1}{12} \left(\frac{m\lambda}{M} \right)^2 + \frac{1}{2} \left(\frac{\delta^2}{12} \right) \cdot \left(\frac{4A}{R_1} \right)^2 \cdot \left(\frac{1}{2} + \frac{1}{2\cos^4 \alpha} \right) \right\}^{1/2}. \quad (8.127)$$

Expression (8.127) allows one to analyze how the $\bar{\varepsilon}$ variable depends on the wavelength λ, the segment angle of inclination α, and the segment relative diaphragm $4A/R_1$ in the process of focusing. Besides, Eq. (8.127) defines how $\bar{\varepsilon}$ depends on the number M of microrelief steps and on the resolution δ in the compensator's plane (Tables 8.6 and 8.7, Fig. 8.12). From Table 8.6 it can be seen that to generate a segment with $\alpha = 30°$, $4A/R_1 = 0.2$ at $\lambda = 0.63$ μm with a $\lambda/15$ accuracy one needs to provide a photomask resolution of $\delta \sim 2.5$ μm at $M = 8$. For great δ, the value of $\bar{\varepsilon}$ is practically independent of M. Simultaneously, for generating high-quality segments with $\bar{\varepsilon}$ ranging from $\lambda/20$ to $\lambda/40$, the choice of M becomes critical (see Table 8.6). From Table 8.7 and Figure 8.12 it is seen that as α increases, it becomes a more complicated task to attain a highly accurate segment generation.

TABLE 8.6. Values of $\bar{\varepsilon}$ ($\alpha = 30°$; $4A/R_1 = 0.2$; $\lambda = 0.63$ μm)

M \ δ, μm	0.2	0.5	1	2.5	5	10	25	50	100
4	$\frac{\lambda}{14}$	$\frac{\lambda}{14}$	$\frac{\lambda}{13}$	$\frac{\lambda}{11}$	$\frac{\lambda}{8}$	$\frac{\lambda}{4}$	$\frac{\lambda}{2}$	1.1λ	2.2λ
8	$\frac{\lambda}{28}$	$\frac{\lambda}{27}$	$\frac{\lambda}{24}$	$\frac{\lambda}{15}$	$\frac{\lambda}{9}$	$\frac{\lambda}{4.4}$	$\frac{\lambda}{2}$	1.1λ	2.2λ
16	$\frac{\lambda}{54}$	$\frac{\lambda}{47}$	$\frac{\lambda}{35}$	$\frac{\lambda}{17}$	$\frac{\lambda}{9}$	$\frac{\lambda}{4.5}$	$\frac{\lambda}{2}$	1.1λ	2.2λ
∞	$\frac{\lambda}{227}$	$\frac{\lambda}{91}$	$\frac{\lambda}{45}$	$\frac{\lambda}{18}$	$\frac{\lambda}{9}$	$\frac{\lambda}{4.5}$	$\frac{\lambda}{2}$	1.1λ	2.2λ

TABLE 8.7. Values of $\bar{\varepsilon}$ ($4A/R_1 = 0.2$; $\lambda = 0.63$ μm; $\delta = 2.5$ μm; $M = 8$)

α, degrees	0	10	20	30	40	50	60	70
$\bar{\varepsilon}$	$\dfrac{\lambda}{17}$	$\dfrac{\lambda}{16.7}$	$\dfrac{\lambda}{16}$	$\dfrac{\lambda}{15}$	$\dfrac{\lambda}{13}$	$\dfrac{\lambda}{11}$	$\dfrac{\lambda}{7}$	$\dfrac{\lambda}{3}$

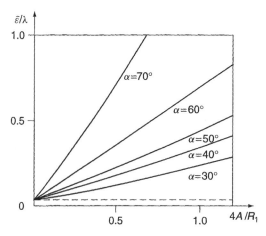

Figure 8.12. Root-mean-square deviation of the off-axis segment of a parabolic wave front ($\lambda = 0.63$ μm; $\delta = 2.5$ μm; $M = 8$).

8.12 GENERATION OF WAVE FRONTS WITH DESIRED INTENSITY DISTRIBUTION

A wide range of tasks of optical nondestructive control, nonlinear optics, and optical information processing pose the problem of generating a complex-shape wave front of an intensity distribution that varies over the surface. It will suffice to mention the problem of generation of light reference marks or a coordinate network on curvilinear mirrorlike or transparent surfaces, such as curved wind screens, eye cornea, and the like. Another important problem is generation of a pump wave when solving the problem of wave front inversion using either induced scattering effects or three- or four-wave interaction. Creation of a phase optical spatial filter matched to a nonplanar object in pattern recognition is also an interesting problem.

The compensators considered the preceding are capable of generating desired wave fronts. When designing a compensator, the intensity distribution does not play the part of a free parameter and is not controlled. The DOEs discussed in Chapter 5 have the phase distribution in the domain of focusing as uncontrolled parameter and allow a desired intensity distribution to be generated. DOEs that can generate both the desired amplitude and the desired phase can be designed using the coding methods traditionally used in digital holography [35]. The disadvantages of the coding methods such as high frequency of relief and low energy efficiency can be partially compensated by the use of more flexible iterative techniques. The iterative method for designing quantized DOE dealt with in Section 2.8.11 exemplifies such techniques. Low energy efficiency is a price to be paid for use of a single DOE for generating both the amplitude and the phase.

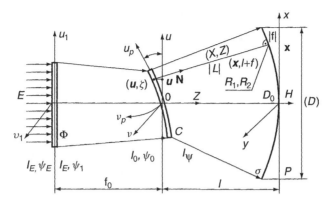

Figure 8.13. Two-stage optical configuration for generating a wave front with spatially modulated intensity.

This section is concerned with designing optical systems containing two DOE formers with smooth phase functions. These formers serve to (1) generate a wave front σ described by wavelength λ, apex D_0, optical axis $O D_0$, and a deviation function

$$H = f(\mathbf{x}), \quad \mathbf{x} \in D, \qquad (8.128)$$

from the nearest plane P passing through the apex D_0 perpendicularly to the optical axis, and (2) ensure the desired intensity distribution $I_\sigma, \mathbf{x} \in D$ over the surface σ (see Fig. 8.13). Here, $\mathbf{x} = (x, y)$ are the Cartesian coordinates of the projection of a point of the wave front σ onto the P plane. Note that $H < 0$ if the point is found before P as the beam propagates, the D domain for points $\mathbf{x}$ corresponds to the pinhole of the wave front σ, and the f function is continuous and smooth, $f(0,0) = 0$. In this task, the initial data are also given by the intensity distribution $I_E(\mathbf{u}_1)$ and the eikonal $\psi_E(\mathbf{u}_1)$ of the illuminating beam in the input plane found at distance $(f_0 + l)$ from the apex D_0 (Fig. 8.13).

The formulation of the task of generating a wave front former on the basis of f, I_σ, I_F, ψ_E is complete as it fully defines the light field within a volume of homogeneous medium including the wave front σ. Therefore, for the geometric optical light field, the eikonal and the intensity can be defined at any point of the volume. Choose a three-dimensional (3D) Cartesian system centered at point O on the optical axis at the distance Z from the apex D_0. Because the unit vector $\mathbf{N}$ of a ray passing through the point $[\mathbf{x}, l + f(\mathbf{x})] \in \sigma$ is defined by

$$\mathbf{N} = \frac{(-\nabla_\perp f, 1)}{(1 + |\nabla_\perp f|^2)^{1/2}}, \quad \nabla_\perp = \left(\frac{\partial}{\partial x}, \frac{\partial}{\partial y} \right),$$

the eikonal at $(\mathbf{X}, z) = [X, Y, z)$, an arbitrary point, is given by

$$\psi(\mathbf{X}, z) = -n_0 L(\mathbf{x}, z), \qquad (8.129)$$

where

$$L(\mathbf{x}, z) = [l + f(\mathbf{x}) - z] \cdot \sqrt{1 + |\nabla_\perp f(\mathbf{x})|^2}, \qquad (8.130)$$

whereas the two-dimensional (2D) vectors $\mathbf{x}$, $\mathbf{X}$ are related through the equation

$$\mathbf{X} = [l + f(\mathbf{x}) - z] \cdot \nabla_{\perp} f(\mathbf{x}). \tag{8.131}$$

In the geometric optical approximation, the intensity at the arbitrary point $(\mathbf{X}, z)$ is derived from the equation of energy conservation along the corresponding ray pipe:

$$I(\mathbf{X}, z) = I_{\sigma}(\mathbf{x}) \left| 1 - \frac{L(\mathbf{x}, z)}{R_1(\mathbf{x})} \right| \cdot \left| 1 - \frac{L(\mathbf{x}, z)}{R_2(\mathbf{x})} \right|,$$

where $R_1(\mathbf{x})$, $R_2(\mathbf{x})$ are major radii of curvature for the surface σ [Eq. (8.128)] at its point $[\mathbf{x}, l + f(\mathbf{x})]$, which are chosen positive if the corresponding center of curvature is found in front of the wave front along the ray path.

To simplify the computation, assume that the focusing element Φ of a two-stage optical system is implemented on a plane surface perpendicular to the optical axis (Fig. 8.13). The optical element C is performed on a curvilinear working surface that may be defined, for example, by the parametric equations

$$\mathbf{u} = u(\mathbf{u}_p), \quad \zeta = \zeta(\mathbf{u}_p),$$

where $(\mathbf{u}, \zeta)$ are the 3D Cartesian coordinates of a point on the compensator's C working surface, $\mathbf{u}_p = (u_p, v_p)$ are sets of curvilinear coordinates on the compensator's surface. We shall compute the generating system in two passages. The initial passage taken in the opposite direction to the ray path allows one to make the conclusion that the compensator C should generate immediately behind itself the eikonal

$$\Psi_{|C} = I_0(\mathbf{u}_p) = I[\mathbf{u}(\mathbf{u}_p), \zeta(\mathbf{u}_p)],$$

where ψ is derived from Eqs. (8.129) to (8.131). Besides, the focusing element Φ should produce on the compensator C, the intensity distribution given by

$$I_{|C} = I_0(\mathbf{u}_p) = I[\mathbf{u}(\mathbf{u}_p), \zeta(\mathbf{u}_p)]$$

The knowledge of $I_0(\mathbf{u}_p)$, $I_E(\mathbf{u}_1)$ and $\psi_E(\mathbf{u}_1)$ allows the eikonal $\psi_1(\mathbf{u}_1)$ to be derived directly behind the focusing element from its gradient

$$\nabla_{\perp} \psi_1(\mathbf{u}_1) = \frac{u[\mathbf{u}_p(\mathbf{u}_1)] - \mathbf{u}_1}{[f_0^2 + |\mathbf{u}[\mathbf{u}_p(\mathbf{u}_1)] - \mathbf{u}_1|^2]^{1/2}} n_0 \tag{8.132}$$

and a smooth ray mapping $\mathbf{u}_p = \mathbf{u}_p(\mathbf{u}_1)$ of points on the focusing element's Φ plane onto surface points of the compensator C. The definition of the smooth mapping with the desired Jacobean I_0/I_F and the solution to Eq. (8.132) is discussed in Chapter 5. The phase function of the focusing element is given by

$$\varphi_1(\mathbf{u}_1) = k[\psi_1(\mathbf{u}_1) - \psi_E(\mathbf{u}_1)].$$

The following direct passage through the optical configuration in Figure 8.13 allows the eikonal ψ_0 to be determined immediately in front of the surface of the compensator

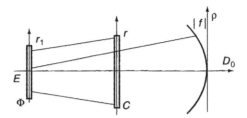

Figure 8.14. Radially symmetric forming system.

C in the form

$$\psi_0(\mathbf{u}_p) = \psi_1(\mathbf{u}_1) + [f_0^2 + |\mathbf{u}_1 - \mathbf{u}|^2]^{1/2} n_0,$$

and write down the compensator's phase function

$$\varphi(\mathbf{u}_p) = k\{\psi[\mathbf{u}(\mathbf{u}_p), \zeta(\mathbf{u}_p)] - \psi_0(\mathbf{u}_p)\},$$

where $\mathbf{u}_1$ is a point on the focusing element Φ corresponding to a compensator's point at a definite mapping $\mathbf{u}_p = \mathbf{u}_p(\mathbf{u}_1)$. The aforementioned functions φ_1 and φ define both the DOEs of the setup in Figure 8.13 for the known parameters f_0 and l.

Given the radially symmetric functions $f(\rho)$, $I_\sigma(\rho)$, $(\rho = |\mathbf{x}|)$, $\psi_E(r_1)$, $I_E(r_1)$, $(r_1 = |\mathbf{u}_1|)$, and a plane compensator's surface, one can make essential progress in geometric-optics-based designing of the wave front former shown in Figure 8.14. Using ringlike ray pipes, one can easily get the following design procedure being an immediate result of the foregoing general relations.

Using the specified wave front shape $\mathcal{H} = f(\rho)$ we find the eikonal

$$\psi(r) = -n_0[l + f(\rho)] \cdot \sqrt{1 + |f'(\rho)|^2}$$

and the equation of correspondence

$$r = \rho + [l + f(\rho)] \cdot f'(\rho), \tag{8.133}$$

where f' is the derivative of f with respect to ρ and $r = |\mathbf{u}|$.

The desired intensity $I_\sigma(\rho)$ and the illuminating beam intensity I_E related through the equation

$$\int_0^{r_1} I_E(r_1) \cdot 2\pi r_1 \, dr_1 = \int_{\rho(0)}^{\rho(r_1)} I_\sigma(\rho) \cdot 2\pi \rho \, d\rho$$

are used to find the correspondence $\rho = \rho(r_1)$, which is substituted into Eq. (8.133) to give the correspondence $r = r(r_1)$

Then, we reconstruct the focusing element's phase function

$$\varphi_1(r_1) = k[\psi_1(r_1) - \psi_E(r_1)],$$

where

$$\psi_1(r_1) = \psi_1(0) + n_0 \int_0^{r_1} \frac{[r(r_1) - r_1] \, dr_1}{[(r(r_1) - r_1)^2 + f_0^2]^{1/2}},$$

and the eikonal in front of the compensator's plane

$$\psi_0(r) = \psi_0(0) + n_0 \int_{r_0}^{r} \frac{[r - r_1(r)]\, dr}{[(r - r_1(r))^2 + f_0^2]^{1/2}},$$

where the correspondence $r_1 = r_1\,(r)$ is inverse to the correspondence $r = r\,(r_1)$

Finally, we can derive the compensator's phase function from the relation

$$\varphi(r) = k[\psi(r) - \psi_0(r)].$$

Example 8.5 By way of an illustration, we shall demonstrate the procedure of solving the task of generating a ring of radii a_1 and a_2 with a uniform intensity distribution over the parabolic wave front

$$f(\rho) = -\frac{\rho^2}{2R}$$

in the case of a plane wave of the illuminating beam of diameter $2a_0$. To simplify transformations, make use of the paraxial approximation and assume

$$\frac{r}{f_0} \ll 1, \quad \frac{r_1}{f_0} \ll 1, \quad \frac{\rho}{R} \ll 1, \quad \frac{|f(\rho)|}{l} \ll 1.$$

In this example, the desired intensity is given by

$$I_\sigma(\rho) = \begin{cases} I_\sigma, & a_1 \le \rho \le a_2, \\ 0, & \text{otherwise}; \ I_\sigma = \text{const}, n_0 = 1, \end{cases}$$

whereas the correspondence equations r_1, r, and S take the form

$$r = \rho - \left(1 - \frac{\rho^2}{2R}\right) \cdot \frac{\rho}{R} \cong \left(1 - \frac{l}{R}\right)\rho, \quad \frac{r_1^2}{a_0^2} = \frac{\rho^2 - a_1^2}{a_2^2 - a_1^2}.$$

The phase functions of the focusing element and the compensator are given here in the explicit form

$$\varphi_1(r_1) = k\left[\frac{a_3 a_4}{f_0} q_1\left(\frac{r_1}{a_3}\right) - \frac{r_1^2}{2f_0}\right], \quad 0 \le r_1 \le a_0,$$

$$\varphi(r) = k\left[-\frac{r^2}{2f_0} + \frac{r^2}{2(R - l)} + \frac{a_3 a_4}{f_0} q_2\left(\frac{r}{a_4}\right)\right],$$

at $a_4 \le r \le a_5$, where

$$a_2 = a_1 \frac{a_0}{\sqrt{a_2^2 - a_1^2}}, \quad a_4 = \left(1 - \frac{l}{R}\right) \cdot a_1, \quad a_5 = \left(1 - \frac{l}{R}\right) \cdot a_2,$$

$$q_1(t) = \frac{1}{2}\left[t\sqrt{t^2 + 1} + \ln\left(t + \sqrt{t^2 + 1}\right)\right],$$

$$q_2(t) = \frac{1}{2}\left[t\sqrt{t^2 + 1} - \ln\left(t + \sqrt{t^2 + 1}\right)\right].$$

8.13 ITERATIVE ALGORITHMS FOR DESIGNING DOEs TO GENERATE DESIRED PHASE DISTRIBUTIONS

When designing a compensator using geometric optical techniques, the light wave diffraction in free space is disregarded. Digital holography methods given in Refs. [3–15] allow one to synthesize a hologram that is capable of generating a desired wave front in the first diffraction order, thus reducing the optical element efficiency.

In this section, we deal with iterative procedures free from the disadvantages of the methods listed previously and allowing desired wave fronts to be generated.

Assume that we need to compute the phase $\varphi(u,v)$ of an optical element illuminated by a light beam of amplitude $A_0(u,v)$ and generating at the distance z the light field with a desired arbitrary phase distribution $\psi_0(\xi, \eta)$. The problem may be reduced to solving a nonlinear integral equation given by Refs. [36,37]

$$
\psi_0(\xi, \eta) = \arg \left\{ \int_{-\infty}^{\infty} \int_{-\infty}^{\infty} A_0(u, v) \exp[i\varphi(u, v)] \exp \left[\frac{ik}{2z} |(u - \xi)^2 \right. \right.
$$
$$
\left. \left. + (v - \eta)^2| \right] du\, dv \right\}, \tag{8.134}
$$

where $\arg(a + ib) = \mathrm{tg}^{-1}(b/a)$.

Obviously, the procedure of iteratively solving Eq. (8.134) will be only slightly different from the standard Gerchberg-Saxton (GS) algorithm [38]: instead of replacing the computed amplitude by a desired amplitude, we shall replace the computed phase by a desired phase. The steps of the algorithm are as follows:

(1) The initial guess of the desired phase $\varphi(u,v)$ is chosen at random.

(2) The Fresnel transform of the function $A_0(u, v) \exp[i\varphi(u, v)]$ (the expression within brackets in Eq. (8.134)) is taken using the fast Fourier transform algorithm.

(3) The derived function $F_n(\xi, \eta)$ (n is the number of iterations) is replaced by $\overline{F}_n(\xi, \eta)$ by the rule

$$
\overline{F}_n(\xi, \eta) = |F_n(\xi, \eta)| \exp[i\psi_0(\xi, \eta)]. \tag{8.135}
$$

(4) The inverse Fourier transform of the function in Eq. (8.135) is taken and the resulting function $W_n(u,v)$ in the DOE plane is replaced by $\overline{W}_n(u, v)$ using the common rule

$$
\overline{W}_n(u, v) = \begin{cases} A_0(u, v) W_n(u, v) |W_n(u, v)|^{-1}, & (u, v) \in Q, \\ 0, & (u, v) \notin Q. \end{cases} \tag{8.136}
$$

(5) Passage to step 2, and so on.

The rate of convergence of the computed phase $\psi_n(\xi, \eta) \in [0, 2\pi)$ to the desired phase $\psi_0(\xi, \eta) \in [0, 2\pi)$ is checked using the deviation

$$
\delta_\psi^2 = \left[\int_{-\infty}^{\infty} \int_{-\infty}^{\infty} |\psi_0 - \psi|^2 \, d\xi \, d\eta \right] \cdot \left[\int_{-\infty}^{\infty} \int_{-\infty}^{\infty} \psi_0^2 \, d\xi \, d\eta \right]^{-1}. \tag{8.137}
$$

The proof of convergence of the aforementioned algorithm is different from that used in the GS algorithm. The proof has been derived only "in the small," that is, under the condition of closeness of two consecutive light amplitudes in the observation plane, and discussed in Ref. [36]. From that proof follows the inequality

$$\int_{-\infty}^{\infty} \int_{-\infty}^{\infty} |A_{n+1} - A_0|^2 \, du \, dv \leq \int_{-\infty}^{\infty} \int_{-\infty}^{\infty} |A_n - A_0|^2 \, du \, dv, \tag{8.138}$$

where $A_{n+1}(u, v)$ and $A_n(u, v)$ are the light amplitudes in the DOE plane computed in the $(n+1)$th and nth iteration steps, and $A_0(u, v)$ is the desired light amplitude in the DOE plane.

From Eq. (8.138) it follows that in the course of iterations the root-mean-square deviation of the computed amplitude from the desired one in the DOE plane is reduced. We failed to prove the similar inequality for the phase $\psi_n(\xi, \eta)$, but all numerical simulations give evidence that the error in Eq. (8.137) is reduced from iteration to iteration.

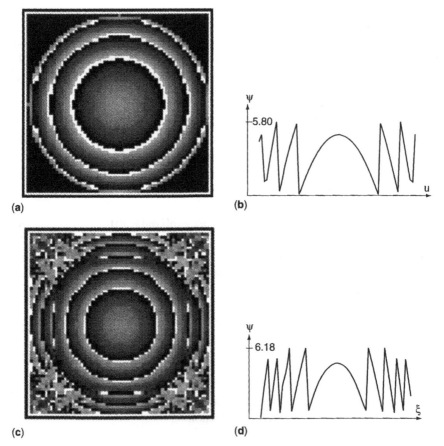

Figure 8.15. Design of a phase of wave front former: (**a**) DOE phase, (**b**) its horizontal profile, (**c**) generated phase, (**d**) its horizontal profile.

Example 8.6 To demonstrate the operation of the algorithm in Eqs. (8.134) to (8.136) we chose the following parameters: the number of pixels on the DOE and in the observation plane is 128×128, the DOE radius is 5.12 mm, the pixel step in those planes is 0.04 mm, $k = 10^4$ mm^{-1}, $z_0 = 325$ mm. The amplitude of the illuminating beam was given by

$$A_0(u, v) = \exp\left[-\frac{u^2 + v^2}{w^2}\right]. \tag{8.139}$$

Figure 8.15 depicts: (a) the phase of the wave front former derived after 10 iterations, (b) the profile section along the u-axis, (c) the phase generated at the distance z_0 from the DOE, (d) its profile along the $\frac{3}{4}$-axis

The desired phase was defined by

$$\psi_0(\xi, \eta) = -\alpha(\xi^4 + \eta^4), \tag{8.140}$$

where $\alpha = 0.8$.

The deviation of the computed phase $\psi_n(\xi, \eta)$ from the desired one, Eq. (8.140), specified by Eq. (8.137) is equal to 12 percent.

Example 8.7 This method can be applied to designing DOEs capable of generating the light field characterized by different curvature relative to the u-axis and v-axis. For example, shown in Figure 8.16 are (a) the DOE phase, (b) its profile along the u-axis, (c) phase generated at the distance z_0, (d) its profile along the ξ-axis (solid line corresponds to the desired phase, dashed line corresponds to the generated phase). The phase in Figure 8.16c is different from the desired phase specified by the relation

$$\psi_0(\xi, \eta) = -\beta(\xi^2 - \eta^4), \tag{8.141}$$

where $\beta = 0.46$, by 20 percent on an average.

Let us now consider a problem of designing an amplitude transparency (AT) that is capable of transforming the plane coherent wave into a desired phase distribution at some distance along the optical axis. In a particular case, such an AT may be considered as an amplitude lens that transforms the incident plane wave front into a converging wave front, thus providing the light energy concentration on the optical axis at some distance from the AT. The problem of focusing the laser light using an AT is addressed in Ref. [39].

When designing a DOE, the parameters, such as the amplitudes in the planes of the optical element and observation are considered to be pregiven, whereas the phase is sought for. In what follows, an "inverse problem" is discussed, with the light field phase in the AT plane and in the observation plane considered to be known and AT's amplitude transmission being sought for.

Formally speaking, this problem is equivalent to solving the following integral equation

$$\psi_0(\xi, \eta) = \arg\left\{\int_{-\infty}^{\infty}\int_{-\infty}^{\infty} A(u, v)\exp[i\varphi_0(u, v)]\exp\left[\frac{ik}{2z}|(u - \xi)^2\right.\right.$$
$$\left.\left. + (v - \eta)^2|\right] du\, dv\right\}, \tag{8.142}$$

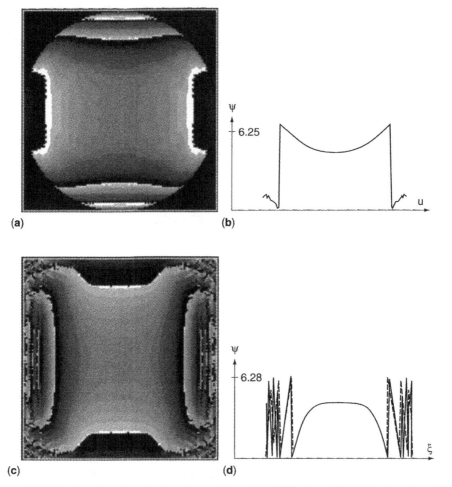

Figure 8.16. Design of a phase former of wave front: (**a**) DOE phase, (**b**) its horizontal profile, (**c**) resulting phase, (**d**) its horizontal profile.

where $\psi_0(\xi, \eta)$ and $\varphi_0(u, v)$ are the pregiven phases in the observation plane found at the distance z from the AT in the transparency plane, and $A(u, v)$ is the desired function of the transparency amplitude transmission.

The distinction between Eq. (8.142) and (8.134) implies that in the integrand in Eq. (8.134), it is the phase that is considered to be unknown, whereas in Eq. (8.142) the amplitude $A(u, v)$ is unknown. Thus, the algorithm for solving Eq. (8.142) involves the same steps as the algorithm for solving Eq. (8.134), but instead of the replacement in Eq. (8.136), one should use the following replacement given in Ref. [40]:

$$\overline{w}_n(u, v) = \begin{cases} |w_n(u, v)| \exp[i\varphi_0(u, v)], & (u, v) \in Q, \\ 0, & (u, v) \notin Q, \end{cases} \tag{8.143}$$

where Q is the shape of the AT aperture.

If the transparency is illuminated by a plane wave, $\varphi_0(u, v)$ is constant. For the case of such an iterative algorithm for solving Eq. (8.142), we can prove the convergence on average. Note that for any n (n is the number of the iterations) the following inequality is satisfied:

$$\int_{-\infty}^{\infty} \int_{-\infty}^{\infty} |A_{n+1}(u, v) - A_n(u, v)|^2 \, du \, dv \leq \int_{-\infty}^{\infty} \int_{-\infty}^{\infty} |A_n(u, v) - A_{n-1}(u, v)|^2 \, du \, dv.$$
(8.144)

The inequality (8.144) shows that in the course of iterations the root-mean-square deviation for two consecutive amplitudes in the AT plane is not increased.

Similarly, we can demonstrate that for the field amplitudes in the observation plane the following inequality holds:

$$\int_{-\infty}^{\infty} \int_{-\infty}^{\infty} |B_{n+1}(\xi, \eta) - B_n(\xi, \eta)|^2 \, d\xi \, d\eta \leq \int_{-\infty}^{\infty} \int_{-\infty}^{\infty} |B_n(\xi, \eta) - B_{n-1}(\xi, \eta)|^2 \, d\xi \, d\eta,$$
(8.145)

where B_{n+1}, B_n, B_{n-1} are the light field amplitudes in the observation plane in the corresponding iteration steps.

To prove the inequality (8.145), we shall introduce the designations

$$B_n \exp(i\psi_n) = \text{FR}[A_{n-1} \exp(i\varphi_0)],$$
(8.146)

$$A_n \exp(i\varphi_n) = \text{FR}^{-1}[B_n \exp(i\psi_0)],$$
(8.147)

where B, A are the amplitudes in the observation and transparency planes, ψ and φ are the phases in the observation and transparency planes, FR and FR^{-1} are the direct and inverse Fresnel transforms, and n is the number of the iterations.

From the condition of energy conservation, we can derive the Parseval equality. On the basis of this equality and on the statement that the modulus of difference of two complex numbers with different arguments is greater than the difference of two complex numbers with identical arguments, we get the following sequence of inequalities:

$$\int_{-\infty}^{\infty} \int_{-\infty}^{\infty} |B_{n+1} - B_n|^2 \, d\xi \, d\eta = \int_{-\infty}^{\infty} \int_{-\infty}^{\infty} |B_{n+1} \exp[i\psi_{n+1}] - B_n \exp[i\psi_{n+1}]|^2 \, d\xi \, d\eta$$

$$\leq \int_{-\infty}^{\infty} \int_{-\infty}^{\infty} |B_{n+1} \exp[i\psi_{n+1}] - B_n \exp[i\psi_n]|^2 \, d\xi \, d\eta$$

$$= \int_{-\infty}^{\infty} \int_{-\infty}^{\infty} |A_n \exp[i\varphi_0] - A_{n-1} \exp[i\varphi_0]|^2 \, du \, dv$$

$$\leq \int_{-\infty}^{\infty} \int_{-\infty}^{\infty} |A_n \exp[i\varphi_n] - A_{n-1} \exp[i\varphi_{n-1}]|^2 \, du \, dv$$

$$= \int_{-\infty}^{\infty} \int_{-\infty}^{\infty} |B_n \exp[i\psi_0] - B_{n-1} \exp[i\psi_0]|^2 \, d\xi \, d\eta$$

$$= \int_{-\infty}^{\infty} \int_{-\infty}^{\infty} |B_n - B_{n-1}|^2 \, d\xi \, d\eta.$$
(8.148)

Comparison of the first and the last expressions in this sequence produces the final inequality

$$\int_{-\infty}^{\infty} \int_{-\infty}^{\infty} |B_{n+1} - B_n|^2 \, d\xi \, d\eta \le \int_{-\infty}^{\infty} \int_{-\infty}^{\infty} |B_n - B_{n-1}|^2 \, d\xi \, d\eta. \tag{8.149}$$

Inequality (8.149) shows that the root-mean-square deviation for two consecutive estimates of the light field amplitude in the observation plane does not increase in the course of iterations.

It failed to demonstrate that in the course of iterations the root-mean-square deviation of phase in Eq. (8.137) reduces. However, numerical simulation has shown that at points (ξ, η) where the amplitude $B_n(\xi, \eta)$ is close to zero, the phase $\psi_n(\xi, \eta)$ may be essentially different from the desired phase $\psi_0(\xi, \eta)$. The amplitude convergence following from Eq. (8.145) leads to the convergence of phase, whereas the function to which the phase $\psi_n(\xi, \eta)$ converges may be essentially different from the desired phase at points where the light energy is close to zero.

Example 8.8   Figure 8.17 depicts (a) the AT transmission function derived using the iterative algorithm during 800 iterations, (b) the phase that the transparency generates at the distance $z_0 = 20$ mm (solid line), which is different from the desired phase (dashed line) at small intensity points, (c) the intensity distribution produced by the transparency at the distance $z = 900$ mm. The computational parameters are as follows: $k = 10^4$ mm^{-1}, the pixel step in the AT plane is 0.01 mm, and the number of pixels is 128.

The difference between the generated (Fig. 8.17b) and desired phase is of specific character: at those points where the intensity distribution is essentially not equal to zero (intensity distribution in the observation plane is just the same as in the plane of AT itself, see Fig. 8.17a), the agreement between the generated and desired phase is quite satisfactory, but at points where the intensity is close to zero the phases are essentially different.

The desired phase function is chosen in the form

$$\psi_0(\xi) = -\alpha \xi^2, \tag{8.150}$$

where $\alpha = 2$ mm^{-2}.

Note that we are able to understand, at least in general, the correlation between the intensity distribution on the transparency (Fig. 8.17a) and the field amplitude at a large

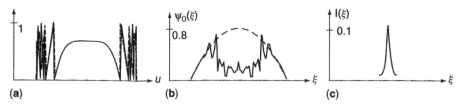

Figure 8.17. Design of an amplitude transparency: (a) the AT amplitude, (b) the generated phase (solid line) and desired phase (dashed line), (c) the far-field intensity.

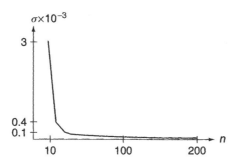

Figure 8.18. Error as a function of the number of iterations.

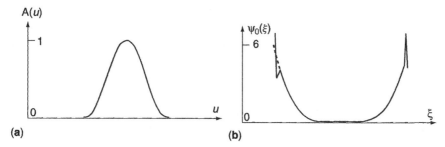

(a)   **(b)**

Figure 8.19. Designing an amplitude transparency: (**a**) the AT amplitude, (**b**) the generated phase.

distance from the transparency (Fig. 8.17c) from the following familiar integral:

$$\int_{-a}^{a} [a^2 - x^2]^{-1/2} \exp[ix\xi] \, dx = \pi J_0(a\xi), \tag{8.151}$$

where $J_0(x)$ is the Bessel function of zero order.

Shown in Figure 8.18 is the root-mean-square deviation, Eq. (8.145), as a function of the number of iterations for the light amplitude in the plane of the desired wave front generation. The error is seen not to increase with the increasing number of iterations, which agrees with the proof given.

Example 8.9   The iterative technique offers a much more evident advantage when applied to designing an AT that can produce diverging wave fronts. Figure 8.19 depicts (**a**) the AT transmission function derived after 100 iterations (with the same parameters of computation), (**b**) the phase generated by the transparency at the distance z_0 (solid line) and almost indistinguishable from the desired phase (dashed line):

$$\psi_0(\xi) = \beta\xi^4, \tag{8.152}$$

where $\beta = 17 \ \text{mm}^{-4}$.

Consider another example of retrofitting the iterative GS algorithm in Ref. [38] that appears to be better suited to designing amplitude lenses. By the amplitude lens, we mean an AT that ensures the concentration of light energy at a certain domain found in the observation plane

In this case, instead of Eq. (8.142), we need to iteratively solve the following equation:

$$I_0(\xi, \eta) = \left| \frac{k}{z} \int_{-\infty}^{\infty} \int_{-\infty}^{\infty} A(u, v) \exp\left[\frac{ik}{2z} |(u - \xi)^2 + (v - \eta)^2| \right] du\, dv \right|^2, \quad (8.153)$$

where $I_0(\xi, \eta)$ is a desired intensity distribution in the observation plane, $A(u, v)$ is the unknown amplitude transmission of the lens. To ensure the energy concentration in such a domain of the observation plane, the intensity is proposed to choose in the form

$$I_0(\xi, \eta) = p \operatorname{rect}\left(\frac{\xi}{T_1} \right) + q \operatorname{rect}\left(\frac{\xi}{T_2} \right), \quad (8.154)$$

where $T_1 = \lambda z/2a$ is the radius of a small diffraction spot in the observation plane, $T_2 = a$, $2a$ is the AT aperture size, $p \gg q$. In Eq. (8.154), the first term approximates the central intensity peak in the plane of focusing, whereas the second term approximates inevitable background noise.

We can solve Eq. (8.153) in the same manner as Eq. (2.5) was solved by using iterations of the GS algorithm, but instead of the replacement in Eq. (2.8) the following replacement should be used

$$\overline{W}_n(u, v) = \begin{cases} |W_n(u, v)|, & (u, v) \in Q, \\ 0, & (u, v) \notin Q, \end{cases} \quad (8.155)$$

where $W_n(u, v)$ is the complex light amplitude in the AT plane derived in the nth iteration step and Q is the shape of the AT aperture

Example 8.10   Shown in Figure 8.20 are (a) the function of the transparency amplitude transmittance derived during 20 iterations, (b) the intensity distribution generated by the transparency at the distance $z_0 = 20$ mm. By fitting the constants p and q we can attain in Eq. (8.154) a maximal possible energy density in the central peak for given parameters. In Figure 8.20, the central peak intensity is 5.6 times as great as the maximum relative efficiency of the field close to the transparency and 50

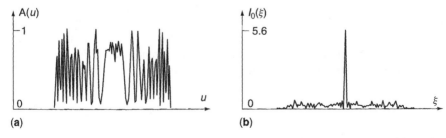

Figure 8.20. Designing an amplitude lens: (a) the AT amplitude, (b) generated intensity.

times as great as the average value of background noise intensity in the plane of focusing.

In this case, the efficiency of focusing is 5 percent. By efficiency is meant the illuminating-energy portion contributing to the generation of the central peak in the plane of focusing. The diffraction efficiency is the ratio of the light energy contributing to the central peak generation to the total energy having passed through the AT. In our case (Fig. 8.20), the diffraction efficiency is 17 percent.

8.14 PRACTICAL APPLICATION

The techniques and algorithms dealt with in this chapter have been realized in the software "QUICK-DOE" and "ITER-DOE" for the PC in the language C++ [41,42], with the analytical methods for geometric-optical DOE design implemented in "QUICK-DOE" and iterative methods in "ITER-DOE."

In particular, when designing off-axis compensators, the set (8.5) of two linear equations for coordinates (x, y) is solved numerically using the Newton-Rafson method on a network (u_j, v_k), $j = \overline{1, N_1}$, $k = \overline{1, N_2}$, with the step

$$\Delta u = u_{j+1} - u_j; \quad \Delta v = v_{k+1} - v_k. \tag{8.156}$$

To derive the next point (x, y) from point (x_j, y_k):

$$x = x_j + \Delta x; \quad y = y_k + \Delta y, \tag{8.157}$$

first, according to Eqs. (8.5), (8.103), (8.105), and (8.106), one finds the derivatives

$$v_x = u_y = (l + f)f_{xy} + f_x f_y, \tag{8.158}$$

$$u_x = 1 + (l + f)f_{xx} + f_x^2; \quad v_y = 1 + (l + f)f_{yy} + f_y^2, \tag{8.159}$$

where the function f and its derivatives are taken at point (x_j, y_k).

Then, the set of linear algebraic equations is solved:

$$\begin{cases} u_x \Delta x + u_y \Delta y = \Delta u \\ v_x \Delta x + v_y \Delta y = \Delta v, \end{cases} \tag{8.160}$$

and operations in Eqs. (8.157) to (8.160) are reiterated.

Once the points (u, v) and (x, y) have been derived, the compensator's phase function φ is determined using Eq. (8.6), which is transformed to a form that does not involve subtraction of great numbers.

Figure 8.21 shows the photomask of a compensator intended to generate from a spherical beam of the off-axis segment a paraboloid of rotation with parameters $R = 303$ mm, $\alpha = 15°$, $2A = 2B = 40$ mm, $\lambda = 0.63$ μm.

Recent advances in techniques for photomask-writing and DOE manufacturing has made it possible to fabricate optical components for large telescopes on the basis of super-precision DOE-aided testing [43].

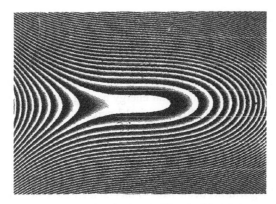

Figure 8.21. Photomask of the compensator "sphere-off-axis segment".

REFERENCES

1. D.T. Puryaev, *Methods for Testing Optical Aspheric Surfaces*, Mashinostroyeniye Publishers, Moscow, **1976**, 264 pages (in Russian).

2. A. Offner, *Appl. Opt.* **2**(2), 153–155 (1963).

3. N.P. Larionov, A.V. Lukin, and K.S. Mustafin, Artificial hologram as an optical compensator, *J. Opt. Spectrosc.* **32**, 396–399 (1972).

4. A.V. Lukin and K.S. Mustafin, *Optiko-Mehanicheskaya Promyshlennost* **4**, 53–59 (1979).

5. Y. Ichioka and A.W. Lohmann, *Appl. Opt.* **11**(11), 2597–2602 (1972).

6. J. Schwider and R. Burov, *Opt. Appl.* **6**(6), 83–88 (1976).

7. V.P. Koronkevich et al., Kinoform optical elements: computational techniques, fabrication technology, practical application, *J. Avtometriya* **1**, 4–25 (1985).

8. A.J. McGovern and J.C. Wyant, *Appl. Opt.* **10**(3), 619–624 (1971).

9. V.A. Soifer, M.A. Golub, and A.G. Khramov, Computer-aided synthesis and analysis of Fresnel holograms, *Proceedings of 10th All–Union Workshop on Holography*, Leningrad Nuclear Physics Institute Publishers, Leningrad, 1978, pp. 140–151.

10. K.G. Birch and F.J. Green, *Appl. Phys.* **5**(11), 1982–1992 (1972).

11. T. Takahashi, K. Konno, M. Kawai and M. Isshiki, *Appl. Opt.* **15**(2), 546–549 (1976).

12. T. Yatagai and H. Saito, *Opt. Acta* **26**(8), 985–993 (1979).

13. B. Prowe, *Optik* **63**(3), 203–212 (1982).

14. H.J. Tiziani, *Laser Optoelektron* **15**(4), 315–324 (1983).

15. A. Ono and J.C. Wayant, *Appl. Opt.* **24**(4), 560–563 (1925).

16. M.A. Golub et al., Generating Aspheric wave Fronts Using Computer-Synthesized Holograms, *USSR Academy of Sciences Reports* **253**(5), 1104–1108 (1980).

17. I.N. Sisakian and V.A. Soifer, Computer-synthesized fine optics, *Physical Principles And Applied Problems Of Holography*, Leningrad Nuclear Physics Institute Publishers, Leningrad, 1984, pp. 142–164.

18. M.A. Golub, A.M. Prokhorov, I.N. Sisakian, and V.A. Soifer, *Computer-Aided Synthesis Of Optical Compensators For Generating Aspheric Wave fronts*, vol. **29**, Lebedev Physical Institute Publishers, Moscow, 1981.

19. M.A. Golub, N.L. Kazanskiy, I.N. Sisakyan, and V.A. Soifer, *Proc. SPIE* **1183**, 727–750 (1990).

20. M.A. Golub, N.L. Kazansky, I.N. Sisakian, and V.A. Soifer, Generating reference wave fronts using computer optics elements, *J. Comput. Opt.* **7**, 3–26 (1990).

21. M.A. Golub, N.L. Kazansky, I.N. Sisakian, and V.A. Soifer, Synthesis of reference wave fronts for testing off-axis segments of aspheric surfaces, *J. Opt. Spectrosc.* **68**(2), 461–466 (1990).

22. M.A. Golub, N.L. Kazansky, I.N. Sisakian, and V.A. Soifer, *A Device for Testing Optical Aspheric Surfaces*, USSR Inventor's Certificate No. 1516767, Inventions Bulletin, No. 39, 1989.

23. M.A. Golub, N.L. Kazansky, I.N. Sisakian, and V.A. Soifer, *A Technique for Manufacturing Aspheric Mirrors*, USSR Inventor's Certificate 1675812, Inventions Bulletin, No. 33, 1991.

24. M.A. Golub, I.N. Sisakian, and V.A. Soifer, Designing diffractive optical elements for generation of wave fronts with spatially modulated intensity, *J. Opt. Spectrosc.* **69**(5), 151–1156 (1990).

25. S.T. Bobrov, G.I. Greisukh, and Yu .G. Turkevich, *Optics of Diffractive Elements and Systems*, Mashinostroyeniye Publishers, Leningrad, 1986.

26. G.I. Greisukh, S.T. Bobrov, and S.A. Stepanov, *Optics of Diffractive and Gradient-Index Elements and Systems*, SPIE PRESS, Bellingham, Washington, 1997.

27. J.C. Wyant and V.P. Bonnet, *Appl. Opt.* **11**(12), 2833–2839 (1972).

28. J.C. Wyant and P.K. O'Nelii, *Appl. Opt.* **13**(12), 2762–2765 (1974).

29. A. Handoro and J. de Fong, *Appl. Opt.* **16**(3), 546–547 (1977).

30. K. Biedermann, O. Holngren, *Appl. Opt.* **17**(8), 413–417 (1978).

31. I.N. Troitsky, A.N. Saphonov, and A.A Demin, *Kinoform: synthesis and application*, Foreign Radioelectronics, 1978, No. 9, pp. 3–28.

32. M.A. Gan, Computer-aided simulation of holographic correction of aberrations in optical systems, *J. Opt. Spectrosc.* **41**(4), 652–659 (1976).

33. R.A. Gabel and B. Lin, *Appl. Opt.* **9**(5), 1180–1191 (1970).

34. V.A. Soifer, M.A. Golub, *Laser Beam Mode Selection By Computer Generated Holograms*, CRC Press, Boca Raton, Fla. 1994.

35. G. Stark, ed., Application of Fourier-optics methods, Moscow, Radio i Svyaz Publishers, 1988, 536 pages, translated from English (edited by Kompanetz).

36. V.A. Soifer, V.V. Kotlyar, and L.L. Doskolovich, *Iterative Methods for Diffractive Optical Elements Computation*, Taylor and Francis, London, 1997.

37. V.V. Kotlyar and S.V. Philippov, *Opt. Las. Technol.* **27**(4), 229–234 (1995).

38. R.W. Gerchberg and W.D. Saxton, *Optik* **35**, 237–246 (1972).

39. Ya. A. Volynkin, Ye. A. Ibragimov and T. Usmanov, Determination of A Laser Beam Class With Desired Diffraction Divergence, *J. Optics Spectroscopy* **72**(6), 1457–1483 (1992).

40. V.V. Kotlyar, V.A. Soifer, and S.V. Philippov, Amplitude Wavefront Formers and Amplitude Lenses, *J. Opt. Spectrosc.* **75**(4), 923–927 (1993).

41. S.G. Volotovsky et al., Software For Diffractive Optics, *J. Comput. Opt.* **14–15**, 94–98 (1995).

42. S.G. Volotovsky, N.L. Kazansky, and V.S. Pavelyev, Software for iterative design and studies of DOE, *J. Comput. Opt.* **17**, 48–53 (1997).

43. V.V. Cherkashin et al., *Proc. SPIE* **3010**, 168–179 (1997).

DOE-Based Lighting Devices

9.1 PROSPECTS FOR USE OF DIFFRACTIVE OPTICS IN LIGHTING DEVICES

Designing lighting devices has always played an important part in human life, ranging from an optimal placement of candles in a ballroom to designing modern car headlamps with varying directivity diagram adaptable to environmental conditions and the speed of the car [1,2]. Leaving aside work methods for creating light sources, we shall enlarge upon the prospects of using diffractive optics in optical channels of lighting devices.

Wide functional capabilities, minimal weight and size, and low cost of mass production provide good prospects for the use of diffractive optical elements (DOE) in lighting devices. What we mean here is mainly devices that are capable of generating the coherent light. The advances made by modern technologies in generating "quasi-diffractive" (or "harmonic") [3,4] optical elements with microrelief heights proportional to a great number of wavelengths allows not only the advantages of diffractive optics to be retained but also DOE chromatic aberrations to be reduced.

The first paper to provide the theoretical substantiation for use of DOEs in lighting devices was the publication by Soifer and coworkers [5] and dealt with the theoretical background behind the design of DOEs capable of generating a desired light directivity diagram. This was followed by the papers by Soifer and coworkers [6,7], in which theoretical and software tools for the design of DOE-based optical devices have been developed. In Refs. [8–10], there are the results of the investigation of lighting devices based on DOEs.

As a convincing example in favor of the use of DOEs as a component of a lighting device, a variant of configuration of the car taillight scatterer shall be considered. The function of each section of a light scatterer in the car is to provide a diverging rectangular light beam differing in horizontal and vertical divergence angles. In some European car models, this is done through the use of a "sandwich" of two mutually perpendicular arrays of cylindrical lenses (Fig. 9.1).

Each of the sets is responsible for the generation of a desired beam divergence angle toward one of the directions (vertical or horizontal), whereas the whole system provides the generation of the required light directivity diagram. Note that the majority of the functions — taillamp, trafficator, and antifog functions — use the monochromatic light, with the exception of the reverse function. This makes it easier to implement the two arrays (and, respectively, of two optical plates) as a single optical element with diffractive microrelief that can provide the phase transmission equal to the sum of phase functions of the two cylindrical lens arrays. The design and fabrication of such an optical element presents no problem, whereas the taillight design and its assembly

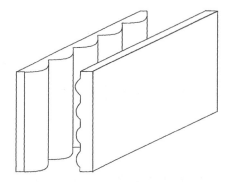

Figure 9.1. General view of crossed cylindrical lens arrays in a car taillight.

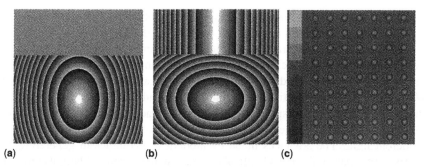

(a)   (b)   (c)

Figure 9.2. Photomasks of segments for (**a**) the taillamp function, (**b**) the trafficator function, and (**c**) the general view of the taillamp compartment.

techniques are obviously improved. When produced in large volumes using PMMA stamping, the production cost of the element is practically the same as that of only one of the two cylindrical lens arrays. Figure 9.2 depicts photomasks of segments of crossed cylindrical lenses for (a) the taillamp function, (b) the trafficator function, and (c) a general view of the photomask for the taillamp function with designer's drawing lines.

The results of testing of a prototype for the novel taillight are discussed in Section 9.7.

9.2 DESIGN TECHNIQUES FOR DOE-BASED LIGHTING DEVICES

Consider a sophisticated optical configuration made up of a point source, refractive surfaces, and DOEs. The optical setup may be represented as a set of media $S_1, \ldots, S_n$.

A refractive index and a boundary equation characterize each medium. The DOE microrelief causes a phase discontinuity along the element and brings into existence a surface of phase jumps. Further analysis indicate that the ideal reflecting surface corresponds to a medium with refractive index $n = -1$. To simulate the lighting device operation, we need to know the intensity distribution it produces on a three-dimensional (3D) surface described by the following equation:

$$\Phi(x_1, x_2, x_3) = 0,$$

where (x_1, x_2, x_3) are the coordinates on the 3D surface.

The scalar approximation for the field complex amplitude E obeys the Helmholtz equation [11]:

$$\nabla^2 E + k^2 n^2 E = \delta(\mathbf{r} - \mathbf{r}_0) \tag{9.1}$$

where $k = 2\pi/\lambda$ is the wave number, λ is the average wavelength, $n(x_1, x_2, x_3)$ is the refractive index in the optical system, and $\delta(\mathbf{r} - \mathbf{r}_0)$ is the Dirac function describing a point light source.

To solve the Helmholtz equation, we need to determine the boundary conditions for each medium. Besides, we should use information about the behavior of the light field complex amplitude in the DOE neighborhood.

Away from the light source, the light field can be approximated by simpler equations. This simplification relies upon the assumption that $kL \gg 1$, where L is a characteristic length describing the distance of observation, the size of obstacles, and medium nonhomogeneities.

Introduce the Debye approximation [11]:

$$E(\mathbf{x}) = \sqrt{I(\mathbf{x})} \exp\{ik\Psi(\mathbf{x})\}, \tag{9.2}$$

where $\mathbf{x} = (x_1, x_2, x_3)$ are the Cartesian coordinates, $I(\mathbf{x})$ is the light field intensity, and $\Psi(\mathbf{x})$ is the light field eikonal. Substituting Eq. (9.2) into the Helmholtz equation shows that the functions I and Ψ obey the set of equations

$$\begin{cases} (\nabla\Psi)^2 = n^2(\mathbf{x}), \\ \operatorname{div}[I(\mathbf{x})\nabla\Psi(\mathbf{x})] = 0. \end{cases} \tag{9.3}$$

The boundary conditions for the Helmholtz equation can be transformed for

1. the refractive surface

$$[\nabla\Psi_1, \mathbf{N}] = [\nabla\Psi_2, \mathbf{N}], \tag{9.4}$$

   where $\mathbf{N}$ is the normal to the boundary between two media with different refractive indices;

2. the reflecting surface

$$[\nabla\Psi_1, \mathbf{N}] = -[\nabla\Psi_2, \mathbf{N}], \tag{9.5}$$

3. the DOE

$$[(\nabla\Psi_2 - \nabla\Psi_1), \mathbf{N}] = [\nabla\varphi, \mathbf{N}]. \tag{9.6}$$

The light source being present in the optical setup is described by the boundary conditions on the initial surface.

Consider a point source enveloped by an initial surface that is described by the following set of equations

$$\begin{cases} x_1 = x_1(t_1, t_2), \\ x_2 = x_2(t_1, t_2), \\ x_3 = x_3(t_1, t_2), \end{cases} \tag{9.7}$$

where t_1, t_2 are the curvilinear coordinates on the initial surface.

Assume that $\Psi(t_1, t_2)$ and $I_0(t_1, t_2)$ are the eikonal and intensity distributions on the initial surface that are defined by the directivity diagram and the point source position. Instead of the eikonal distribution on the initial surface, it is possible to use the ray directions field. Although the Eq. (9.3) include partial derivatives, they can be brought to a set of ordinary differential equations by the use of ray coordinates. Introduce the ray coordinates:

$$\begin{cases} x_1 = x_1(t_1, t_2, l), \\ x_2 = x_2(t_1, t_2, l), \\ x_3 = x_3(t_1, t_2, l), \end{cases} \tag{9.8}$$

or in the vector form

$$\mathbf{r} = \mathbf{r}(t_1, t_2, l). \tag{9.9}$$

The $\mathbf{r}(t_1, t_2, l)$ function obeys the ray propagation equation

$$\frac{d}{dl}\left(n\frac{d\mathbf{r}}{dl}\right) = \nabla n. \tag{9.10}$$

For $l = 0$, the equation $\mathbf{r}_0 = \mathbf{r}(t_1, t_2, 0)$ describes the initial surface. The function $\mathbf{S}_0(t_1, t_2) = d\mathbf{r}/dl(t_1, t_2, 0)$ defines the ray direction on the initial surface. The solution to the transfer equation in the ray coordinates takes the form

$$I(t_1, t_2, l) = I_0(t_1, t_2)\frac{\partial(x_1, x_2, x_3)/\partial(t_1, t_2, 0)}{\partial(x_1, x_2, x_3)/\partial(t_1, t_2, l)}, \tag{9.11}$$

where $I_0(t_1, t_2)$ is the intensity distribution on the initial surface, $\partial(x_1, x_2, x_3)/\partial(t_1, t_2, l)$ is the Jacobean to transform the Cartesian to the ray coordinates. Recast Eq. (9.11) in a more convenient vector form

$$I(t_1, t_2, l) = I_0(t_1, t_2)\frac{[\mathbf{r}_{t_1}, \mathbf{r}_{t_2}]\mathbf{r}_l|_{l=0}}{[\mathbf{r}_{t_1}, \mathbf{r}_{t_2}]\mathbf{r}_l}, \tag{9.12}$$

and introduce a curvilinear coordinate system on the surface of registration

$$\mathbf{r} = \mathbf{r}[t_1, t_2, l(t_1, t_2)] = \mathbf{R}(t_1, t_2), \tag{9.13}$$

where $l(t_1, t_2)$ is the solution to the equation

$$\Phi[\mathbf{r}(t_1, t_2, l)] = 0. \tag{9.14}$$

Differentiating with respect to t_1 and t_2 gives expressions for the basis vectors:

$$\mathbf{R}_{t_1} = \mathbf{r}_{t_1} - \mathbf{r}_l \cdot \frac{\nabla\Phi \cdot \mathbf{r}_{t_1}}{\nabla\Phi \cdot \mathbf{r}_l},$$

$$\mathbf{R}_{t_2} = \mathbf{r}_{t_2} - \mathbf{r}_l \cdot \frac{\nabla\Phi \cdot \mathbf{r}_{t_1}}{\nabla\Phi \cdot \mathbf{r}_l}. \tag{9.15}$$

In view of the relations for the basis vectors on the initial surface and the registration surface, Eq. (9.12) takes the form

$$I(t_1, t_2, l) = I_0(t_1, t_2)\frac{[\mathbf{r}_{t_1}, \mathbf{r}_{t_2}]\mathbf{r}_l|_{l=0}}{[\mathbf{R}_{t_1}, \mathbf{R}_{t_2}]\mathbf{r}_l}. \tag{9.16}$$

As compared with Eq. (9.11), Eq. (9.16) comprises the intensity distribution on the initial surface and metrical characteristics of the initial and registration surfaces. A sphere of infinitely large radius may serve as the registration surface, the result being the normal incidence of rays on the registration surface:

$$[\mathbf{R}_{t_1}, \mathbf{R}_{t_2}]\mathbf{r}_l = |[\mathbf{R}_{t_1}, \mathbf{R}_{t_2}]|. \tag{9.17}$$

The same relation is possible on the initial surface:

$$[\mathbf{r}_{t_1}, \mathbf{r}_{t_2}]\mathbf{r}_l = |[\mathbf{r}_{t_1}, \mathbf{r}_{t_2}]|. \tag{9.18}$$

Using these equations may give a simpler expression for the intensity distribution on the registration surface. Note, however, that this expression is not suited for calculation. This inconvenience proceeds from the use of ray coordinates, for their choice depends upon the optical system.

Introduce a new curvilinear coordinate system (T_1, T_2) on the registration surface:

$$\mathbf{r} = \hat{\boldsymbol{\Phi}}(T_1, T_2). \tag{9.19}$$

Assume that the curvilinear coordinates (T_1, T_2) are related to the ray coordinates (t_1, t_2) as follows:

$$T_1 = F_1(t_1, t_2),$$
$$T_2 = F_2(t_1, t_2). \tag{9.20}$$

Substituting Eqs. (9.18) and (9.19) into Eq. (9.16) gives

$$I(t_1, t_2, l) = I_0(t_1, t_2) \frac{|[\mathbf{r}_{t_1}, \mathbf{r}_{t_2}]|}{|[\boldsymbol{\Phi}_{F_1}, \boldsymbol{\Phi}_{F_2}]| \partial(F_1, F_2)/\partial(t_1, t_2)}. \tag{9.21}$$

Using the properties of the Dirac function, it is possible to render Eq. (9.21) in the integral form:

$$I = \int I_0(t_1, t_2) \frac{|[\mathbf{r}_{t_1}, \mathbf{r}_{t_2}]|}{|[\boldsymbol{\Phi}_{F_1}, \boldsymbol{\Phi}_{F_2}]|} \delta[T_1 - F_1(t_1, t_2), T_2 - F_2(t_1, t_2)] \, dt_1 \, dt_2. \tag{9.22}$$

Equation (9.22) provides a basis for computer-aided simulation and optimization of operation of the optical configurations under design.

Assume that the initial and the registration surfaces are described by the equations

$$\mathbf{r}(t_1, t_2) = \varepsilon(\sin t_1 \cos t_2 \cdot \mathbf{e}_1 + \sin t_1 \sin t_2 \cdot \mathbf{e}_2 + \cos t_1 \cdot \mathbf{e}_3),$$

$$\boldsymbol{\Phi}(T_1, T_2) = R_0(\sin T_1 \cos T_2 \cdot \mathbf{e}_1 + \sin T_1 \sin T_2 \cdot \mathbf{e}_2 + \cos T_1 \cdot \mathbf{e}_3), \tag{9.23}$$

where ε is the initial surface radius, R_0 is the registration surface radius, and $(\mathbf{e}_1, \mathbf{e}_2, \mathbf{e}_3)$ are the basis vectors of a rectangular coordinate system. In that case, the intensity distribution on the initial surface is as follows

$$I(t_1, t_2) = \frac{I_0}{\varepsilon^2}, \tag{9.24}$$

and the intensity distribution on the registration surface is given by

$$I(T_1, T_2) = \int \frac{I_0}{R_0^2} \cdot \frac{\sin t_1}{\sin F_1(t_1, t_2)} \delta[T_1 - F_1(t_1, t_2), T_2 - F_2(t_1, t_2)] \, dt_1 \, dt_2. \quad (9.25)$$

9.3 DESIGNING DEVICES WITH MULTILEVEL DOEs

In the previous section we proposed a method for modeling DOE-based lighting devices. But this method is suitable for DOEs with continuous microrelief. Only a few types of technologies (see Section 4.4, or Refs. [3,4,12–16]) allow one to produce a microrelief of such form. However, most available fabrication processes and process equipment fail to provide the generation of DOEs with continuous phase function. In the meantime, there are a number of fabrication technologies that have been successfully employed for the generation of multilevel DOEs and given a substantial consideration in Chapter 4 or Refs. [17–18]. In this section, we deal with a method for computing the directivity diagram of multilevel, DOE-based lighting devices.

Analogous optical systems are modeled on the basis of a modified method for computing ray paths given in Refs. [5–8,19]. To provide a better understanding of the proposed method, consider how the light beam travels through a multilevel DOE.

The eikonal of a DOE with steplike microrelief profile can be given by

$$\tilde{\Psi} = \Phi[\mathrm{mod}_\lambda \Psi(t_1, t_2)], \quad (9.26)$$

where (t_1, t_2) are the Cartesian coordinates on the DOE and $\Phi(z)$ is the predistortion function [20,21]. The predistortion function describes how the eikonal function is transformed as the result of the use of a specific DOE fabrication technology and the accompanying microrelief fabrication errors.

The solution to the Helmholtz equation may be written as follows:

$$E(x_1, x_2, x_3) = \frac{i}{\lambda} \int E_0(t_1, t_2) \frac{z}{L} \cdot \frac{\exp\{ikL\}}{L} \exp\{ik\tilde{\Psi}(t_1, t_2)\} \, dt_1 \, dt_2. \quad (9.27)$$

To take the Kirchhoff integral, expand the function $\exp\{ik\tilde{\Psi}(t_1, t_2)\}$ into a Fourier series:

$$\exp\{ik\tilde{\Psi}(t_1, t_2)\} = \sum C_n \exp\{ikn\Psi(t_1, t_2)\}. \quad (9.28)$$

Substituting Eq. (9.28) into Eq. (9.27) and taking all the integrals by use of the stationary phase method [22] gives the light field complex amplitude in the form:

$$E = -\sum C_n E_0(t_1^n, t_2^n) \frac{\exp\{ikn\Psi(t_1^n, t_2^n)\}}{\sqrt{J_n(t_1^n, t_2^n, l^n)}}, \quad (9.29)$$

where

$$J_n(t_1^n, t_2^n, l^n) = \frac{\partial(x_1, x_2, x_3)/\partial(t_1^n, t_2^n, 0)}{\partial(x_1^n, x_2^n, x_3^n)/\partial(t_1^n, t_2^n, l^n)}$$

are the ray coordinates.

The function for translating the ray coordinates into the Cartesian ones obeys the set of differential equations:

$$\frac{d}{dl^n}\left(\frac{dx_i}{dl^n}(t_1^n, t_2^n, l^n)\right) = 0 \tag{9.30}$$

with the initial conditions

$$x_i(t_1^n, t_2^n, 0) = t_i, i = 1, 2; \quad x_3(t_1^n, t_2^n, 0) = 0;$$

$$\frac{dx_i}{dl}(t_1^n, t_2^n, 0) = \frac{\partial[n\Psi(t_1^n, t_2^n)]}{\partial t_i^n}, \quad i = 1, 2;$$

$$\frac{dx_3}{dl}(t_1, t_2, 0) = \sqrt{1 - \left(\frac{dx_1}{dl}\right)^2 - \left(\frac{dx_2}{dl}\right)^2}. \tag{9.31}$$

Using Eq. (9.29), the intensity distribution is given by

$$I(x_1, x_2, x_3) = \sum \frac{|C_n|^2 I_0(t_1^n, t_2^n)}{J_n(t_1^n, t_2^n, l)}$$
$$+ \sum_{m \neq n} \frac{C_n C_m E_0(t_1^n, t_2^n) E_0^*(t_1^m, t_2^m) \exp\{ik[n\Psi(t_1^n, t_2^n) - m\Psi(t_1^m, t_2^m)]\}}{\sqrt{J_n(t_1^n, t_2^n, l^n)}\sqrt{J_m(t_1^m, t_2^m, l^m)}}. \tag{9.32}$$

Let us analyze the relation that has been arrived at. The first term in Eq. (9.32) is the intensity of the light field produced by the DOE with the eikonal function $n\psi$, whereas the second term describes the interference between the light fields. As a rule, the light source in the lighting devices under study is incoherent, so that we can neglect the interference between different light beams.

9.4 THE RESULTS OF STUDYING A DOE-AIDED FOCUSING DEVICE

The mathematical relations arrived at in the previous Sections 9.2 and 9.3 have formed the basis of the software "RAY-TRACING DOE" developed at Image Processing Systems Institute of the Russian Academy of Sciences [6–8]. The software is IBM PC-compatible and intended for simulating sophisticated optical schemes composed of reflecting and refracting surfaces and DOEs, including gradient-index lenses and diffraction gratings. The software makes it possible to calculate, design, and investigate complex optical units with due regard for thermal effects.

The simplest focusing device schematically shown in Figure 9.3 exemplifies the simulation of an optical unit with the aid of the software developed. The device consists of a parabolic reflector, with an axial incandescent filament centered at its focus, and a DOE. Assume that the device under study is aimed at focusing the light into the Latin letter F. The result of focusing into the letter F can easily be generalized onto any desired domain of focusing.

To estimate the operational performances of the optical device at the design stage, we need to analyze the light field that the optical scheme under study produces in the desired space domain. The intensity distribution in the focal plane is numerically simulated and the relation between the parameters of the optical scheme and the quality of focusing is analyzed.

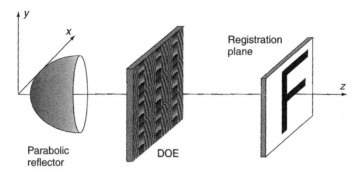

Figure 9.3. Optical configuration of the optical device to be simulated.

The quality of focusing is characterized by the following quantities:

$$\delta = \frac{\sqrt{\int [I(\overline{\mathbf{x}}) - I_0(\overline{\mathbf{x}})]^2 \, d\overline{\mathbf{x}}}}{\int I_0(\overline{\mathbf{x}}) \, d\overline{\mathbf{x}}} \tag{9.33}$$

$$\varepsilon = \frac{E_1}{E_0} \tag{9.34}$$

where ε is the energy efficiency of the device and δ is the root-mean-square deviation of $I_0(\overline{\mathbf{x}})$ from $I(\overline{\mathbf{x}})$; $I_0(\overline{\mathbf{x}})$ is an ideal (desired) intensity distribution, $I(\overline{\mathbf{x}})$ is the result of simulation; E_1 is the energy coming to the desired domain and E_0 is the light source energy; $\overline{\mathbf{x}}$ are the coordinates on the registration plane. The energy efficiency characterizes the energy portion coming to the desired space domain.

In the optical scheme under study (Fig. 9.3), the DOE was computed in the geometric optical approximation using a coordinated rectangles method [23], with the derived phase function being repeated along vertical and horizontal axes. When designing a DOE in such a device, the main problem is that a cone of rays from the extended source and the reflector comes to each point of the optical element. As a result, it turns out to be almost impracticable to design a DOE that is capable of optimally controlling the incoming heterogeneous beams, as evidenced from the simulation results (Fig. 9.4 and Table 9.1).

TABLE 9.1. The Results of Simulating an Optical Device

d/f	ε (%)	δ	Figure No.
2/3	69.00	1.485	9.4a
2/5	70.89	1.435	9.4b
4/15	59.63	1.357	9.4c
1/5	47.88	1.243	9.4d
2/15	30.44	1.009	9.4e
4/35	24.60	0.907	9.4f
1/10	20.22	0.837	9.4g

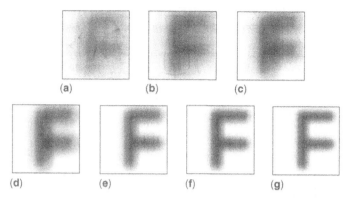

Figure 9.4. Intensity distribution in the registration plane for the parameters shown in Table 9.1.

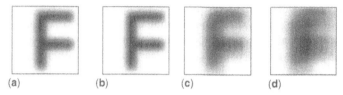

Figure 9.5. Changed intensity distribution for varied parameters of Table 9.2.

The numerical simulation has shown that the focusing quality can be enhanced by decreasing the ratio d/f, where d is the size of the source (filament length) and f is the focal length of the parabolic reflector (Table 9.1 and Fig. 9.4). This fact may as well be confirmed through analytical studies.

In the course of simulation, the reflector's depth and the source's size (filament length) were fixed, whereas the value of the parameter d/f was adjusted by increasing the reflector's focal length. With fixed depth, this resulted in the increased reflector's flare and, hence, the decreased energy efficiency of the focusing device (Table 9.1).

The other line of investigation involved the determination of the adjustment accuracy of the focusing device necessary for providing the desired intensity distribution. Figure 9.5 and Table 9.2 illustrate how the quality of focusing changes as the filament center moves along the reflector's axis of symmetry. The displacement is characterized by a relative value of shift, $\Delta z/f$, where f is the reflector's focal length. While insignificantly changing the energy efficiency of the incident (on the registration plane) light flux, this shift results in the significantly distorted intensity distribution.

A challenging task of designing focusing devices that are capable of generating a desired intensity distribution requires not only the use of unique potential of diffractive optics but also the obligatory simulation and optimization of operation of such optical systems at the design stage. The software developed allows one to simulate the sophisticated optical systems composed of reflecting and refractive optical components, including multilevel (quantized) DOEs. In the conducted studies of an optical device made up of a DOE, a parabolic reflector, and an extended light source, we have managed to demonstrate potentialities of the novel software and DOEs.

TABLE 9.2. Characteristics of Focusing Quality While Shifting the Filament Along the Optical Axis

d/f	Shift $\Delta z/f$	δ	Figure No.
1/10	1/60	0.876	9.5a
1/10	1/30	1.027	9.5b
1/10	1/20	1.273	9.5c
1/10	1/15	1.495	9.5d

9.5 DESIGNING A DOE-BASED CAR HEADLAMP

Example 9.1   As an exemplary study of the optical system, below we consider designing a car headlamp in the following text. According to the international standards, the headlamp optical system should produce the directivity diagram resulting in the remote intensity distribution schematically shown in Figure 9.6. The desired directivity diagram should not only illuminate the road in front of the car but also send the light sideways and prevent the oppositely moving car drivers from being dazzled.

In the modern automobile industry, the desired headlamp directivity diagram is produced, in particular, by the use of a complex-shaped reflector (e.g., vertically flattened ellipsoid), a diaphragm that is positioned in the front focal plane of a high-power lens and that reproduces the directivity diagram in shape (Fig. 9.7) and other tricks.

In this respect, the use of unique capabilities of DOEs in designing sophisticated lighting devices shows promise. The advantages are as follows: the simplified shape of the reflector, the enhanced energy efficiency and manufacturability, improved functional characteristics, and reduced fabrication cost. The studies conducted may be aimed, for

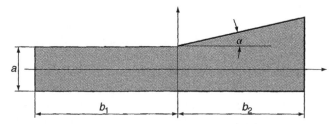

Figure 9.6. The desired directivity diagram of the car headlamp.

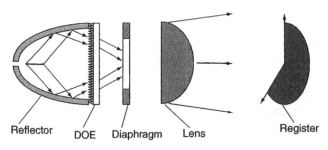

Figure 9.7. Optical setup of a car headlamp.

example, at replacing the high-cost reflector shaped as a vertically flattened ellipsoid by a much cheaper axially symmetric elliptical reflector.

Having this in mind, we can consider whether it is feasible to introduce into the headlamp optical system (Fig. 9.7) a DOE that would redistribute the radiation from the screening part of the diaphragm into its open (transmitting) part. The DOE shown in Figure 9.7 may be represented by a quasi-periodic diffractive element that focuses onto a light segment [24,25], with the focal segment found in the open part of the diaphragm near and along its bottom edge. The results of studying how such an optical scheme operates with and without the DOE are shown in Figure 9.8. The simulation parameters are as follows: the radiating filament length is 5 mm, the filament radius is 0.5 mm, the number of the filament coils is 14, the displacement of the filament center from the reflector's rear wall is 18 mm, the length of the semiaxes of the axially symmetric ellipsoid along the z-axis is 50 mm and along the x- and y-axes it is 40 mm, the diameter of a circular hole in the reflector's rear wall for mounting the light source is 10 mm, the reflector's depth is 50 mm, the DOE period is 1 mm, the segment length is 30 mm, the distance between the reflector's edge and the diaphragm is 20 mm, the inclination angle of half the diaphragm (which corresponds to the angle α on the directivity diagram being produced — Fig. 9.6) is 15 degrees, the lens diameter is 59 mm, the lens thickness is 14 mm, the refractive index of the lens material is 1.5, the lens-to-diaphragm distance is 52 mm, the distance to the registration plane is 25 m, the number of pixels per registrator's side is 201, and the number of the rays to be reckoned (in inverse proportion to the number of samplings on the radiator) is not less than 10,000 for Figure 9.8a and Figure 9.8c, and not less than 100,000 for Figure 9.8b. Taking a greater number of the reckoned rays requires much more time but produces a more accurate result (compare Fig. 9.8a and Fig. 9.8b). The distance to the registration point that we chose complies with standards adopted in motorcar industry tests.

Analysis of Figure 9.8 testifies in favor of the use of DOEs in lighting devices. The estimated intensity distributions in Figure 9.8a and Figure 9.8b produced by a DOE-aided reflector are much closer to the desired intensity distribution (Fig. 9.6) relative to those produced by an axially symmetric elliptical reflector without a DOE (Fig. 9.8c). The headlamp optical configuration (Fig. 9.7) may be further improved by use of more effective techniques for designing the proper DOEs. By way of illustration, an adequate application of the method of coordinated rectangles [23] intended to produce

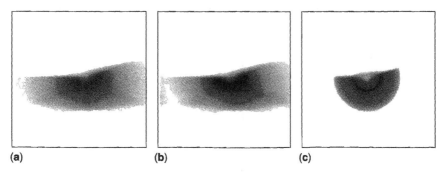

(a)   (b)   (c)

Figure 9.8. The intensity distribution in the plane of the headlamp light registration: (**a**) the number of the reckoned rays is not less than 10,000; (**b**) the number of the reckoned rays is not less than 1,000,00; (**c**) without a DOE.

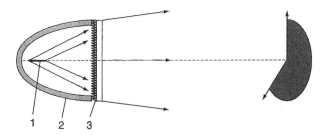

Figure 9.9. A simplest optical configuration of the DOE-based car headlamp: 1 — light source, 2 — parabolic reflector, 3 — DOE.

a DOE that focuses onto a domain cut out by the diaphragm makes the optical scheme in Figure 9.7 simpler because the diaphragm can be eliminated. High and efficient operation of such a DOE will only add to the headlamp quality and energy efficiency.

In its simplest variant, the headlamp optical scheme may include a parabolic reflector and a DOE that generates the desired directivity diagram (Fig. 9.9). With the aforementioned optical schemes, the main challenge lies with a great number of multidirectional rays coming to every point of the diffractive element from an extended source and a parabolic reflector. As a result, the use of a single optical element, however wide its functional capabilities may be, may prevent us from getting a highly efficient directivity diagram.

9.6 DESIGNING COPLANAR ILLUMINATORS

The approach developed makes it possible to advance and study original optical schemes based on the use of waveguide and diffractive structures. Coplanar illuminators belong to this new class of the optical systems studied. The coplanar systems are edge-illuminated, that is, the light fed from an edge is then distributed over the output plane, thus producing a uniform luminous front image. Consider several optical schemes realizing the aforementioned concept.

Example 9.2 Optical configuration 1 shown in Figure 9.10 is a plane parallel plate, with a diffraction microrelief found on its front (top — Fig. 9.10) side and a reflection diffraction grating found on the opposite (bottom) side. The optical system operates

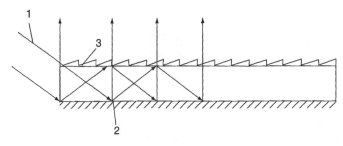

Figure 9.10. Optical scheme 1 of a coplanar illuminator: 1 — incident light, 2 — reflection diffractive microrelief, 3 — transmission diffractive microrelief.

as follows. A quasi-collimated light beam strikes the diffraction grating. The reflected flux is a superposition of several light beams propagated at different directions. The reflecting diffraction grating parameters are chosen so that only two reflected beams can exist, with the first beam propagating along the plate and the other outcoming perpendicularly from the diffractive microrelief.

Optical scheme 2 in Figure 9.11 is also represented by a plane parallel plate. One face of the plate presented to the observer is coated with a diffractive microrelief that serves to form a desired directivity diagram. The opposite face is coated with a triangle-profile relief to reflect the light. The optical system operates as follows. A quasi-collimated beam produced by the light source strikes the relief with the reflection coating. The reflected light passes through the diffractive microrelief coated on the front face of the plate, thus producing the desired directivity diagram.

Optical setup 3 shown in Figure 9.12 is composed of superposed prism plates with the refractive index n_1, separated by a saw-tooth slit filled with a medium of refractive index n_2. The bottom part of the plate is reflective and does not allow the light to go out, whereas on the top of the plate there is a transmission diffractive microrelief that produces the desired directivity diagram.

The relation between the refractive indices n_1 and n_2 in optical setup 3 is chosen in such a manner that the light flux is uniformly distributed over the plate depth, with the illuminator's width being chosen. As a result, the intensity is distributed uniformly over the front output surface owing to reflection of the desired light portion from the interface between the two media.

If necessary (e.g., for design purposes), the illuminator's plates can be made smoothly curved, following the shape of the car body or interior.

The simulation was aimed at finding fit-to-work optical schemes (studies were not limited to the schemes shown in Figures 9.10 to 9.12) and determining optimal

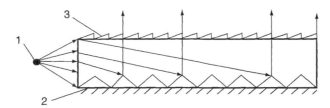

Figure 9.11. Optical scheme 2 of a coplanar illuminator: 1 — LED array, 2 — reflection relief, 3 — transmission diffractive microrelief.

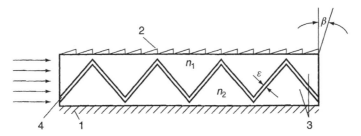

Figure 9.12. Optical scheme 3 of a coplanar illuminator; 1 — reflecting coating, 2 — transmission diffractive microrelief, 3 — optical medium of refractive index n_1, 4 — optical medium of refractive index n_2.

parameters of the optical scheme under study. Uniform intensity distribution of the output light flux was used as a criterion of the illuminator's quality. By way of illustration, the car taillamp should feature the uniform distribution. Some interesting results of the simulation are presented in Figures 9.13 to 9.15.

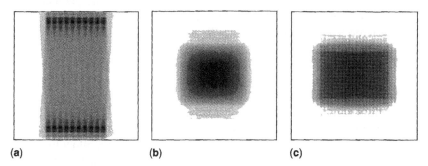

(a)   (b)   (c)

Figure 9.13. The intensity distribution in the registration plane produced by a coplanar illuminator shown in Figure 9.10: (**a**) at a distance of 1 mm, (**b**) at a distance of 1 m, and (**c**) at a distance of 10 m.

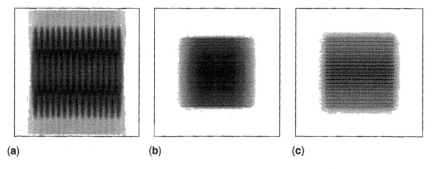

(a)   (b)   (c)

Figure 9.14. The intensity distribution in the registration plane produced by a coplanar illuminator shown in Figure 9.11: (**a**) at a distance of 1 mm, (**b**) at a distance of 1 m, and (**c**) at a distance of 10 m.

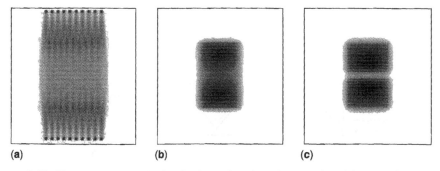

(a)   (b)   (c)

Figure 9.15. The intensity distribution in the registration plane produced by a coplanar illuminator shown in Figure 9.12: (**a**) at a distance of 1 mm, (**b**) at a distance of 1 m, and (**c**) at a distance of 5 m.

Figure 9.13 depicts the results of simulating the following version of optical scheme 1 (Fig. 9.10): the output diffractive microrelief is replaced at the input by a conventional binary transmission diffraction grating that forms two beams striking the reflection microrelief and the output plane at an angle, reflecting from which the light propagates further along the plate. The simulation parameters are as follows: the focal length of the light emitting diode (LED) lens is 5 mm, the LED lens diameter is 5 mm, the plate length is 100 mm, the plate thickness is 3 mm, the distance between the LED and the plate edge is 5 mm, the number of LEDs per side is 10 [10 LEDs on each (right and left) side of the plate], and the distance between the LEDs is 5 mm. The reflection grating microrelief was designed using techniques described in Chapter 3 or Ref. [26], so as to direct 95 percent of the incident light to the zeroth diffraction order, with 5 percent of the outcoming light going to the minus first diffraction order. The number of pixels per recorder's side is 100, the distance to the first recorder (Fig. 9.13a) is 1 mm, the distance to the second recorder (Fig. 9.13b) is 1 m, the distance to the third recorder (Fig. 9.13c) is 10 m, an angle with an outside edge of the recorder is $\beta = 10°$, and the number of reckoned rays is not less than 5,000. The LED model used in calculations was built on the assumption that in the first focal plane of the meniscus lens (the output LED lens) there is a luminous square-shaped area 1 mm × 1 mm in size. The intensity distribution at a distance of 1 mm from the illuminator's output plane is shown Figure 9.13a, at a distance of 1 m in Figure 9.13b, and at a distance of 10 m in Figure 9.13c. To provide the high-quality simulation of the illuminator's operation at larger distances, a substantially greater number of rays should be reckoned. Places where the LEDs are located clearly seen in Figure 9.13a; however, as the distance from the illuminator increases (Fig. 9.13b and 9.13c), the field produced by the illuminator is seen as a luminous rectangular area. Various light divergence angles result in the varying ratio of the luminous rectangle sides, as the observation distance increases (Fig. 9.13a–c).

Analysis of Figure 9.13 testifies that the proposed modification of optical scheme 1 (Fig. 9.10) is able to fulfill its function even without the output diffractive microrelief, provided the foregoing simulation parameters hold.

The results of simulation for optical scheme 2 (Fig. 9.11) are shown in Figure 9.14 for the following parameters: the focal length of the LED lens is 5 mm, the LED lens diameter is 1 mm, the number of the LEDs per side is 15 (15 diodes on each side of the plate), the distance between the diodes is 5 mm, the reflection microrelief height is 0.5 mm, the number of periods on the reflection microrelief is 100 (the plate length is, respectively, 100 mm), the plate thickness is 8 mm, the number of pixels per recorder's side is 100, the distance to the first recorder (Fig. 9.14a) is 1 mm, the distance to the second recorder (Fig. 9.14b) is 1 m, the distance to the third recorder (Fig. 9.14c) is 10 m, an angle with the outside edge of the recorder is $\beta = 10°$, and the number of the reckoned rays is no less than 5,000.

The intensity distribution at the distance of 1 mm is shown in Figure 9.14a, at the distance 1 m in Figure 9.14b, and at the distance 10 m in Figure 9.14c. As is the case in Figure 9.13, the places where the LEDs are located are clearly seen, but with increasing distance (Figs. 9.14b and 9.14c) the illuminator looks like a luminous rectangular area.

Analysis of Figure 9.14 shows that optical scheme 2 (Fig. 9.11) performs well at the aforementioned parameters.

The results of simulation of a simplified version of optical scheme 3 (Fig. 9.12) are depicted in Figure 9.15: there is no output diffractive microrelief, with the air used for the medium with refractive index n_1: $n_1 = 1$ and a Plexiglass ($n_2 = 1.5$) used for the medium with refractive index n_2. The simulation parameters are as follows: the focal length of the LED lens is 5 mm, the LED lens diameter is 5 mm, the distance between the LED and the comb edge is 5 mm, the number of LEDs on the side is 10 (10 diodes on each side of the plate), the distance between the diodes is 5 mm, the thickness of the layer with refractive index n_2 is $\varepsilon = 0.4$ mm, the plate length is 100 mm, the number of pixels per recorder side is 101, the distance to the first recorder (Fig. 9.15a) is 1 mm, the distance to the second recorder (Fig. 9.15b) is 1 m, the distance to the third recorder (Fig. 9.15c) is 5 m, the angle β with the recorder outside edge is 30°, and the number of the reckoned rays is no less than 5,000. The intensity distribution at the output plane at the distance of 1 mm is shown in Figure 9.15a, at the distance 1 m in Figure 9.15b, and at the distance 5 m in Figure 9.15c.

Analysis of Figure 9.15 confirms that optical scheme 3 (Fig. 9.12) is suitable for operation even in its simplified version. At the same time, the use a greater angle with the recorder's outside edge ($\beta = 30°$ instead of $\beta = 10°$ in Figs. 9.13 and 9.14) in the process of simulation results in a stronger divergence of the output light beam, whereas the attenuation of the output light at the output beam center (especially notable in Fig. 9.15c) shows that it is further necessary to optimize the parameters of optical scheme 3 so as to get a more uniform distribution of the LED light over the depth of the coplanar illuminator.

The studies pursued have demonstrated that the optical schemes proposed are able to perform well and have laid the basis for the development of a number of prototype coplanar illuminators. Among the schemes studied, an optimal choice may be made judging by different (not optical) criteria: manufacturability, inexpensiveness of production, minimal mass and weight, and so on. In the combination of merits and by the results of optical tests, optical scheme 1 (Fig. 9.10) seems to be most promising.

9.7 RESULTS OF TESTING DOE-BASED LIGHTING DEVICES

The quality of operation of the lighting devices described so far was tested on an automated unit schematically shown in Figure 9.16. The photograph of a unit for testing the car taillamp is shown in Figure 9.17.

Photometric data is expedient to enter not by a TV-camera, but by a high-precision calibrated luxmeter of class LX-02 (Fig. 9.17). The photometric pattern produced by the car lighting devices should comply with the EC standards in terms of the central pattern luminosity and percentage of the light intensity drop along the angle of sight at a definite distance. In particular, figures of the light intensity drop (in percents) for the trafficator function of the taillamp should be no worse than those shown in Table 9.3.

A taillamp prototype was realized as a single plate of crossed lenses peculiar for every lamp function, using the technique described in Section 9.1. The microrelief of maximal height 50 to 60 µm (proportional to 50 wavelengths) was fabricated using the technology for generating a harmonic ("quasi-diffractive") microrelief, which uses the dark-growth effect in the layers of liquid photopolymerizable (LPPC) compositions (see Section 4.4 or Refs. [3,12–14]). The results of testing one of the taillamp functions (trafficator) are shown in Table 9.4. In view of the fact that the central luminosity

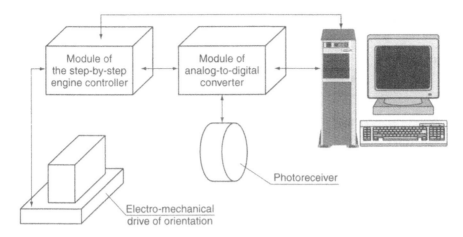

Figure 9.16. Block diagram of an automated system for photometric information processing.

Figure 9.17. The general view of the automated system for testing lighting devices.

TABLE 9.3. EC Requirements for the Standard Photometric Pattern of the Trafficator of the Car Taillamp

Horizontal Angle	Vertical Angle						
	−20°	−10°	−5°	0°	5°	10°	20°
10°			20		20		
5°	10	20		70		20	10
0°		35	90	100	90	35	
−5°	10	20		70		20	10
−10°			20		20		

TABLE 9.4. Testing Results for a Trafficator Function with an LPPC-Based Harmonic Scatterer

Vertical Angle	Horizontal Angle						
	−20°	−10°	−5°	0°	5°	10°	20°
10°			77.29	78.36	79.71		
5°	72.46	82.61	86.96	91.79	89.86	77.78	67.63
0°	72.46	88.89	97.10	100	94.20	82.13	69.08
−5°	73.43	82.13	91.79	93.72	90.82	79.23	65.22
−10°			79.71	79.71	77.78		

Figure 9.18. The directivity diagram of the light generated by a single cell of the quasi-periodic DOE.

Figure 9.19. Directivity diagram produced by the optical configuration of the headlamp (Fig. 9.7 without a diaphragm) with a binary quasi-periodic DOE.

complies with the EC standards, the total uniformity of the pattern meets the EC standards with a considerable margin.

In the course of testing, a binary quasi-periodic DOE focusing the light into a domain approximating the diaphragm in shape was used as the diffractive element in the headlamp optical scheme (Fig. 9.7). Figure 9.18 depicts the directivity diagram produced by a single cell of the quasi-periodic DOE. The cell was designed using the coordinated rectangles method [23], with the resulting phase function used for designing the quasi-periodic DOE [24,25].

Figure 9.19 depicts the results of testing of the headlamp (Fig. 9.7) with a binary quasi-periodic DOE but without the diaphragm. The use of the binary element in the tests accounts for the manufacturability of the binary microrelief. The resulting pattern is symmetric because of the binary character of the microrelief. Once a diaphragm is entered into the optical configuration, the diagram symmetry is eliminated, and the resulting pattern begins to show nearly complete compliance with the required pattern

(Fig. 9.6). In this case, the energy efficiency of the headlamp operation increases by 12 to 14 percent relative to the operation of an axially symmetric elliptical reflector that includes a diaphragm but lacks a binary DOE. A high-quality multilevel DOE used in place of the binary one may provide an additional 10 to 15 percent increase in the efficiency.

The efficiency of coplanar lighting devices was studied on prototypes realizing the optical schemes shown in Figures 9.10 and 9.12. Because the objective was to fabricate a full prototype of the car taillamp with minimal mass and weight, the original microrelief capable of generating the desired directivity diagram was computed for each taillamp function. The diffractive microrelief was fabricated using dry lithography techniques (plasma-chemical etching — see Chapter 4 or Ref. [27]) using photomasks generated by the Electronic(E)-beam lithography machine ZBA-20 by Carl Zeis (Jena, Germany) and a circular laser writing machine (see Section 4.2.1 or Ref. [28]) of the Institute of Automation and Electrometry, Siberian Branch of RAS (Novosibirsk, Russia). The external appearance of operative embodiments of various optical schemes is shown in Figure 9.20.

Table 9.5 gives the photometric pattern produced by a coplanar trafficator function for the taillamp embodiments utilizing the optical configuration in Figure 9.12. Comparison with the EC regulations (Table 9.1) testifies that the standards are met with great margin in terms of uniformity of the directivity diagram produced. Note that the performance of the embodiment utilizing the configuration in Figure 9.10 is somewhat better.

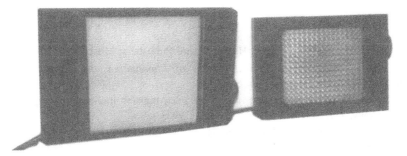

Figure 9.20. The external appearance of working coplanar illuminators fabricated using optical configurations of Figures 9.10 and 9.12.

TABLE 9.5. The Results of Testing a Coplanar Trafficator Function for the Taillamp Embodiment Utilizing the Optical Configuration in Figure 9.12

Vertical Angle	Horizontal Angle						
	−20°	−10°	−5°	0°	5°	10°	20°
10°			32.68	37.96	34.76		
5°	18.78	39.64	61.83	77.26	63.27	40.40	18.04
0°	20.53	46.16	78.67	100	77.06	45.17	18.83
−5°	18.06	34.85	52.84	60.93	50.27	34.29	16.50
−10°			28.63	30.79	27.50		

The studies of the developed prototypes of DOE-based lighting devices confirm their potential for such applications. A special gain in mass-weight characteristics is achieved when waveguide, diffractive, and other structures of modern optics are used in combination, as is the case with designing coplanar illuminators.

CONCLUSION

The use of DOEs to reduce mass and weight and enhance the efficiency of lighting devices was always considered to be mainly impeded by DOE chromatic aberrations and the complex design procedures of DOE-aided optical devices. Latest advances in techniques for fabricating "quasi-periodic" (or "harmonic") microreliefs of tens of wavelengths in height has made it possible to circumvent the former of the afore-mentioned impediments, although preserving the diffractive optics benefits. The theory set forth in the first sections of this chapter may form the basis for the development and optimization of DOE-based optical devices. The software developed following this theory has made it possible to design and produce prototypes of a number of original optical configurations for DOE-based lighting devices of high efficiency and unique functional characteristics.

The conducted tests of the developed prototypes have confirmed the potential for DOE use in lighting devices. The mass-weight characteristics and the efficiency are considerably improved when waveguide, diffractive, and other modern optics structures are used in combination, as is the case with designing coplanar illuminators.

REFERENCES

1. V.V. Trembach, *Lighting devices*, Higher School Publishers, Moscow (1990) (in Russian).

2. O. Kusch, *Computer-Aided Optical Design of Illuminating and Irradiating Devices*, "ASLAN" Publishing House, Moscow, 1993.

3. A.V. Volkov et al., Experimental studies of mass-transfer in liquid photopolymerizable compositions, *J. Tech. Phys.* **65**(9), 181–185 (1995).

4. D.W. Sweeney and G.E. Sommargren, Harmonic diffractive lenses, *Appl. Opt.* **34**(14), 2469–2475 (1995).

5. M.A. Golub et al., Synthesis of optical antennae, *Comput. Opt.* **1**(1), 25–28 (1989).

6. N.L. Kazanskiy, S.I. Kharitonov, and V.A. Soifer, Mathematical modeling of DOE-based lighting devices, *J. Comput. Opt.* **2**(14–15), 107–116 (1995) (in Russian).

7. N.L. Kazanskiy, S.I. Kharitonov, and V.A. Soifer, Simulation of DOE-aided focusing devices, *Opt. Memory Neural Networks* **9**(3), 191–200 (2000).

8. L.L. Doskolovich, N.L. Kazanskiy, and S.I. Kharitonov, Computer-aided design of DOE-based lighting devices, *J. Comput. Opt.* **18**, 91–96 (1998) (in Russian).

9. A.V. Volkov, N.L. Kazanskiy, and G.V. Uspleniev, Experimental investigation of DOE-based lighting devices, *J. Comput. Opt.* **19**, 137–142 (1999) (in Russian).

10. N.L. Kazanskiy, S.I. Kharitonov, V.A. Soifer, and A.V. Volkov, Investigation of lighting devices based on diffractive optical elements, *Opt. Memory Neural Networks* **9**(4), 301–312 (2000).

11. M. Born and E. Wolf, *Principles of Optics*, Pergamon Press, Oxford, 1968.

12. S.V. Karpeyev and V.S. Solovyov, Recording technologies for relief imagery with continuous profile, *Comput. Opt.* **2**(2), 155–156 (1990).

13. Yu.B. Boiko et al., Relief holograms recording on liquid photopolymerizable layers, *Proc. SPIE* **1238**, 252–257 (1990).

14. Yu.B. Boiko, V.S. Solovjev, S. Calixto, and D.-J. Lougnot, Dry photopolymer films for computer-generated infrared radiation focusing elements, *Appl. Opt.* **33**(5), 787–793 (1994).

15. M.T. Gale et al., Continuous-relief diffractive optical elements for two-dimensional array generation, *Appl. Opt.* **32**(14), 2526–2533 (1993).

16. M.T. Gale, M. Rossi, J. Pedersen, and H. Schutz, Fabrication of continuous-relief micro-optical elements by direct laser writing in photoresist, *Opt. Eng.* **33**(11), 3556–3566 (1994).

17. V.V. Popov, Materials and methods for flat optical elements, *Comput. Opt.* **1**(1), 125–128 (1990).

18. G.I. Greisukh, S.T. Bobrov, and S.A. Stepanov, *Optics of Diffractive and Gradient-Index Elements and Systems*, SPIE Optical Engineering Press, Bellingham, 1997.

19. M.W. Farn, Modeling of diffractive optics, *OSA Proc. Int. Opt. Design Conf.* **22**, 246–250 (1994).

20. M.A. Golub et al., Computer generated diffractive multi-focal lens, *J. Modern Opt.* **39**(6), 1245–1251 (1992).

21. V.A. Soifer, L.L. Doskolovich, and N.L. Kazanskiy Multifocal Diffractive Elements, *Opt. Eng.* **33**(11), 3610–3615 (1994).

22. M.V. Fedoryuk, *Asymptotics: Integrals and Series*, Nauka Publishers, Moscow, 1987 (in Russian).

23. L.L. Doskolovich, N.L. Kazanskiy, S.I. Kharitonov, and V.A. Soifer, A method of designing diffractive optical elements focusing into plane areas, *J. Modern Opt.* **43**(7), 1423–1433 (1996).

24. L.L. Doskolovich, N.L. Kazanskiy, V.A. Soifer, and A.Ye. Tzaregorodtzev, Analysis of quasi-periodic and geometric optical solutions of the problem of focusing into an axial segment, *Optik* **101**(2), 37–41 (1995).

25. L.L. Doskolovich, N.L. Kazanskiy, and V.A. Soifer, Comparative analysis of different focusators focusing into a segment, *Opt. Laser Tech.* **27**(4), 207–213 (1995).

26. L.L. Doskolovich, Designing binary dielectric gratings and 1-D DOEs using the electromagnetic theory, *Opt. Memory Neural Networks* **9**(1), 1–12 (2000).

27. M.A. Golub et al., The technology of fabricating focusators of infrared laser radiation, *Opt. Laser Tech.* **27**(4), 215–218 (1995).

28. V.P. Koronkevich et al., Fabrication of diffractive optical elements by direct laser writing with circular scanning, *Proc. SPIE* **2363**, 290–297 (1995).

CHAPTER 10

Optical Data Processing Using DOEs

10.1 OPTICAL GENERATION OF IMAGE FEATURES

In digital information processing, the operation most extensively employed is that known as the spatial filtration given by

$$f(\mathbf{u}) = \int_G h(\mathbf{x}, \mathbf{u}) w(\mathbf{x}) \, d\mathbf{x}. \tag{10.1}$$

where $w(\mathbf{x})$ and $f(\mathbf{u})$ are the input and output fields, $h(\mathbf{x}, \mathbf{u})$ is the system impulse response, or the dissipation function, and G is the domain of integration.

Coherent optics offers wide possibilities for conducting real-time spatial filtration of light fields. The most simply realizable space-invariant filters are as follows:

$$f(\mathbf{u}) = \int_G h(\mathbf{x} - \mathbf{u}) w(\mathbf{x}) \, d\mathbf{x}. \tag{10.2}$$

An example of the coherent optical system intended for the space-invariant filtration is depicted in Figure 10.1.

A transparency in the plane Π_1 illuminated by a plane monochromatic wave of wavelength λ generates the input field $w(\mathbf{x})$. The lens O_1 of focus f_0 generates in the frequency plane Φ a 2D Fourier image of the field $w(\mathbf{x})$:

$$W(\mathbf{v}) = \int_G w(\mathbf{x}) \exp[-i2\pi(\mathbf{xv})] \, d\mathbf{x}. \tag{10.3}$$

where $\mathbf{v} = (v_x, v_y)$ are the spatial frequencies related to the coordinates $\mathbf{u}$ in the plane Φ:

$$\mathbf{u} = (u, v) = (\lambda f_0 v_x, \lambda f_0 v_y).$$

The Fourier image $W(\mathbf{v})$ is multiplied by the transmission function

$$H(\mathbf{v}) = \int_G h(\mathbf{x}) \exp[-i2\pi(\mathbf{xv})] \, d\mathbf{x} \tag{10.4}$$

of a transparency placed in the frequency plane. The field emerging directly behind the plane Φ is as follows:

$$F(\mathbf{v}) = W(\mathbf{v}) H(\mathbf{v}). \tag{10.5}$$

673

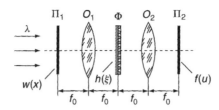

Figure 10.1. A coherent optical setup to realize the space-invariant filtration.

It can be seen from Eq. (10.5) that the transparency maps the frequency characteristics of the filter in Eq. (10.4). The lens $H(\mathbf{v})$ then performs the inverse Fourier transform, for which purpose the direction of the axes u and v must be the opposite of that of the axes x and y in plane Π_1 at the Fourier correlator output in plane Π_2. According to the convolution theorem, a field $f(\mathbf{u})$ will be produced in the plane Π_2.

The previously described filtration scheme by no means exhausts the entire diversity of schemes that are capable of implementing the operation in Eq. (10.2) by coherent optical methods. Note, however, that the general and the major component of those schemes is a spatial filter with the transmission function dependent on the plane coordinates.

The filtration operations may be faced when solving problems of matched filtration [1,2], image-quality enhancement [3], signal extraction from noised backgrounds [4], and image recognition [5–7].

The approach to image recognition, expanded upon in this section, is oriented to the coherent optical computation of coefficients of the orthogonal decomposition using computer-synthesized optical spatial filters [1,7–9], with the coefficients used as an array of image features in the subsequent digital classification procedure [11–13].

Assume that $\{\psi_{\mathbf{p}}(\mathbf{x})\}$ are the basis functions of the decomposition in an orthogonal series. The expansion coefficients $w_{\mathbf{p}}$ of the field with complex amplitude

$$w(\mathbf{x}) = \sum_{\mathbf{p}} w_{\mathbf{p}} \psi_{\mathbf{p}}(\mathbf{x}), \quad \mathbf{x} \in G \tag{10.6}$$

can be measured in two stages [14]. The first one involves an optical expansion of the field in terms of the basis functions using their property of orthogonality. In this situation, the energy distribution between the basis functions is transformed into the light intensity distribution at the output focal plane. In the second stage, photo-receivers with point apertures measure the light intensity that is proportional to the squared modulus of every coefficient $\sim |w_{\mathbf{p}}|^2$.

Let us demonstrate that if we place a spatial filter with the mathematical complex transmission function (CTF) $\psi_{\mathbf{p}}^*(\mathbf{x})$ at the Fourier stage input and generate a field $w(\mathbf{x})$ at the input, the coefficient $w_{\mathbf{p}}$ of one of the basis functions will be produced at the output plane center (see Fig. 10.2). Actually, directly behind the plane (x, y), we get the field

$$w(\mathbf{x})\psi_{\mathbf{p}}^*(\mathbf{x}) = \sum_{\mathbf{p}'} w_{\mathbf{p}'} \psi_{\mathbf{p}'}(\mathbf{x}) \psi_{\mathbf{p}}^*(\mathbf{x}). \tag{10.7}$$

The Fourier transform of Eq. (10.3) taken at the center $\mathbf{v} = 0$ of the output plane of spatial frequencies yields the operation of complex amplitude integration.

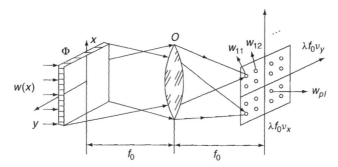

Figure 10.2. An optical setup for the parallel calculation of a set of coefficients of the light field expanded in terms of the orthogonal basis.

Owing to orthogonality, the basis functions interact in such a manner that while integrating the complex amplitude in Eq. (10.7) at point $\mathbf{v} = 0$ of the Fourier plane, the background from the basis functions numbered $\mathbf{p}' \neq \mathbf{p}$ becomes mutually destroyed, thus giving field values equal to the expansion coefficients:

$$w_{\mathbf{p}} = \int_G w(\mathbf{x})\psi_{\mathbf{p}}^*(\mathbf{x})d^2\mathbf{x}. \tag{10.8}$$

The power $|w_{\mathbf{p}}|^2$ of the basis function $\psi_{\mathbf{p}}$ may be measured by a usual photo-receiver with pinhole aperture, with the entire composition of the basis functions consecutively measured through the changed filters $\psi_{\mathbf{p}}^*$. For the parallel computation of the array of coefficients and their separation on the output plane (Fig. 10.2), a spatial carrier frequency method is used [14]. In subsections 10.2.2 to 10.2.4, this method will be applied to the particular bases.

10.2 EXPANSION OF THE LIGHT FIELD IN TERMS OF AN ORTHOGONAL BASIS

10.2.1 Optimal Karhunen-Loeve Basis

In image recognition, the representation of the image under analysis is most informative if the coefficients are statistically independent (or, at least, noncorrelated) [15]. It has been known [16,17] that for a random field with the pregiven correlation function, there is a unique orthogonal basis that can provide noncorrelated expansion coefficients. This is the Karhunen-Loeve basis [15,18] composed of the eigenfunctions of an integral equation with correlation function of the field under study serving as a kernel. The noncorrelated coefficients in the expansion of images in terms of the Karhunen-Loeve basis may effectively be used as image features.

With computer-aided synthesis of optical spatial filters matched to the basis functions of the orthogonal expansion, it is important to know how they are represented analytically. This becomes especially important with the Karhunen-Loeve expansion (KLE) because the numerical solution of the Karhunen-Loeve integral equation is very cumbersome and unstable for the practically employed filter sizes (greater than

1,000 × 1,000 pixels). A general approach to the analytical derivation of the Karhunen-Loeve basis functions for the linear fractional spectrum is taken in Ref. [19]. However, it calls for a great number of cumbersome operations, such as computation of complex determinants, and is inconvenient to algorithmize. Simple formulae for the exponential correlation functions are available [20], but in view of its importance for constructing the Karhunen-Loeve basis, it is desirable to have a more accurate, exponential-cosine [21,22] approximation of the correlation function. It is analytical expressions for the Karhunen-Loeve basis functions with the exponential-cosine correlation function that we deal with in this section.

With an optical implementation of orthogonal expansions, there is an unavoidable distortion of basis functions caused by sampling upon the computer-aided synthesis of an optical element, and quantizing upon fabrication. Therefore, one should take into account the effect of perturbations of basis functions on the recognition quality. It is most important to elucidate how the optical realization of the KLE [23,24] affects the preservation of its optimal properties. The theoretical estimates of the aforementioned perturbations described in Ref. [25] call for cumbersome computation of infinite matrix norms and other complicated operations. Therefore, in the present section we conduct experimental studies and determine numerically how such perturbations affect the KLE stability.

The basis KLE functions are derived from the correlation function of the images under recognition by solving the following integral equation in eigenvalues:

$$\int_G \overline{R}(\mathbf{x}, \mathbf{u}) \psi_{\mathbf{p}}(\mathbf{x}) d^2\mathbf{u} = \lambda_{\mathbf{p}} \psi_{\mathbf{p}}(\mathbf{x}), \tag{10.9}$$

where
$$\overline{R}(\mathbf{x}, \mathbf{u}) = \sum_{i=1}^{N_{cl}} R_i(\mathbf{x}, \mathbf{u}) P_i, \quad \sum_{i=1}^{N_{cl}} P_i = 1 \tag{10.10}$$

is the correlation function averaged in N_{cl} classes, $R_i(\mathbf{x}, \mathbf{u})$ is the correlation function of the ith class of the images under recognition, and P_i is the probability of emergence of the class.

Besides, quite a number of remarkable properties the KLE possesses place it in a special position among all kinds of random field expansions.

1. The expansion coefficients are not correlated

$$\langle w_{\mathbf{p}}, w_{\mathbf{p}'}^* \rangle = [\hat{R}(\psi_{\mathbf{p}}), \psi_{\mathbf{p}'}] = (\lambda_{\mathbf{p}} \psi_{\mathbf{p}}, \psi_{\mathbf{p}'}) = \lambda_{\mathbf{p}} \delta_{\mathbf{p}\mathbf{p}'}, \tag{10.11}$$

where
$$\hat{R}[\psi](\mathbf{x}) = \int_G R(\mathbf{x}, \mathbf{u}) \psi(\mathbf{u}) d^2\mathbf{u} \tag{10.12}$$

is the correlation operator. In Ref. [13], it has been demonstrated that the property of noncorrelation of linear features taking place when the Karhunen-Loeve basis functions are used affects the recognition quality and the clustering effect favorably [11].

2. The rms error of truncating an infinite series is minimal as compared with all orthogonal bases [13]. Let us approximate the field $w(\mathbf{x})$ by a finite number L of series terms

$$w(\mathbf{x}) \cong \hat{w}_L(\mathbf{x}) \equiv \sum_{\mathbf{p} \in K} w_{\mathbf{p}} \psi_{\mathbf{p}}(\mathbf{x}) + \overline{w}(\mathbf{x}), \quad |K| = L \tag{10.13}$$

The error of this approximation has the power

$$e_0^2(L) = \left\langle \int_G |w(\mathbf{x}) - \hat{w}_L(\mathbf{x})| \, d^2\mathbf{x} \right\rangle. \tag{10.14}$$

Note that the eigennumbers in the sequence $\{\lambda_\mathbf{p}\}$ are arranged in decreasing order so that the corresponding sequence produces the least error when approximated by a finite number of series terms.

Comparison between some orthogonal bases discussed in Ref. [25] is depicted in Figure 10.3 and corroborates the property of minimal error.

3. The entropy defined on the set of normalized variances of the KLE coefficients is minimal. The rigorous statement of this property and the proof may be found in Ref. [15].

4. The greatest eigen-number satisfies the inequality

$$\lambda \equiv \max_\mathbf{p} \lambda_\mathbf{p} \le \sup_{\mathbf{p} \in G} S(\boldsymbol{\omega}), \tag{10.15}$$

where $S(\boldsymbol{\omega}) = \int_G R(\mathbf{x}) \exp(-i\omega x) \, d^2\mathbf{x}$ is the spectral density and $\boldsymbol{\omega} = (\omega_1, \omega_2)$.

5. The eigen-numbers are monotone. The eigen-number $\lambda_\mathbf{p}(G)$ is a monotonically increasing function of the domain size, that is,

$$\lambda_\mathbf{p}(G) \le \lambda_\mathbf{p}(G'), \quad G \subset G' \tag{10.16}$$

6. The KLE is asymptotic if the domain G is expanded. In an infinite domain $G = R^n$, the eigenfunctions and eigen-numbers take the form

$$\psi(\mathbf{x}) = \exp(i\omega x), \quad \lambda = S(\boldsymbol{\omega}). \tag{10.17}$$

7. Assuming that the correlation function is factorable, that is $R(\mathbf{x}, \mathbf{u}) = R^{\mathrm{I}}(\mathbf{x}^{\mathrm{I}}, \mathbf{u}^{\mathrm{I}}) \cdot R^{\mathrm{II}}(\mathbf{x}^{\mathrm{II}}, \mathbf{u}^{\mathrm{II}})$, one can easily see that the eigenfunctions and eigennumbers are also

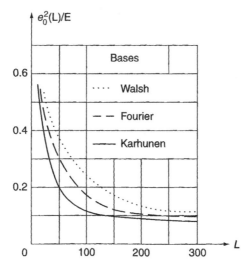

Figure 10.3. Comparing some orthogonal bases using the error of approximating by a finite number of series terms.

factorable

$$\lambda_{\mathbf{p}_m} = \lambda^{I}_{\mathbf{k}_m} \cdot \lambda^{II}_{l_m}$$

$$\psi_{\mathbf{p}_m}(\mathbf{x}) = \psi^{I}_{\mathbf{k}_m}(\mathbf{x}^{I}) \cdot \psi^{II}_{l_m}(\mathbf{x}^{II}), \quad m = 0, 1, 2, \ldots \tag{10.18}$$

and may be ordered so that $\lambda_{\mathbf{k}_m l_m} \geq \lambda_{\mathbf{k}_{m+1} l_{m+1}}$, $m = 0, 1, 2, \ldots$

For computing the KLE noncorrelated coefficients by digital holography methods [1,7,8], optical elements matched to the Karhunen-Loeve basis functions are synthesized. The use of an optical KLE [23,26] poses the problem of studying the stability of the KLE to the perturbations caused by the basis functions sampling (at the stage of computer-aided synthesis of an optical filter) and by the quantization (at the stage of lithographic fabrication) [27].

With the computer-aided synthesis of optical spatial filters matched to the KLE, it is important to have the analytical basis functions representations because the numerical solution of the Karhunen-Loeve integral equation is cumbersome and impractical for designing optical spatial filters with the number of pixels of the order $2 \cdot 10^3 \times 2 \cdot 10^3$.

It has been known [21,22] that the correlation function of stationary stochastic processes with linear fractional spectrum takes the general form

$$R(\tau) = \sigma^2 \sum_k \exp(-\alpha_k |\tau|) \cdot [A_k(\tau) \cos \beta_k \tau + B_k(\tau) \sin \beta_k |\tau|], \tag{10.19}$$

where $A_k(\tau)$ and $B_k(\tau)$ are the polynomials in τ; σ^2, α_k, and β_k are parameters.

In Ref. [19], one may find a general approach to the analytical derivation of the Karhunen-Loeve basis functions for the linear fractional spectrum. However, it calls for a great number of cumbersome operations and is inconvenient to algorithmize. There are simple formulae [20] for the exponential correlation function, but from Eq. (10.19) the exponential representation is seen to be only the first approximation of the general form of correlation function. Considering that the correlation function is very important in constructing the KLE, it is desirable to approximate it more accurately. Taking into account Eq. (10.19), it is proposed that the correlation function be described by a more accurate exponential-cosine formula that admits of a simple analytical representation for the KLE, as is the case with the exponential representation [20].

For image analysis, 2D KLEs are employed. Assuming that the correlation function is factorable [14], we can consider a 1D integral equation in eigenvalues on a symmetric interval $x \in [-A, A]$

$$\int_{-A}^{A} R(x - u)\psi(u)\, du = \lambda \psi(x). \tag{10.20}$$

The exponential-cosine correlation function

$$R(\tau) = \sigma^2 \exp(-\alpha |\tau|) \cos \beta \tau \tag{10.21}$$

has the spectrum

$$G(\omega) = \frac{2\alpha \sigma^2 (\alpha^2 + \beta^2 + \omega^2)}{\omega^4 + 2\omega^2 (\alpha^2 - \beta^2) + (\alpha^2 + \beta^2)^2}, \tag{10.22}$$

where ω is the spatial frequency.

In accordance with the algorithm for solving an integral equation of the 2nd kind for the kernel with linear fractional spectrum [19], the integral equation in Eq. (10.20) is reduced to the linear differential equation with constant coefficients

$$\psi^{(4)}(x) - 2\left(\alpha^2 - \beta^2 - \frac{\alpha\sigma^2}{\lambda}\right)\psi^{(2)}(x) + (\alpha^2 + \beta^2)\left(\alpha^2 + \beta^2 - \frac{2\alpha\sigma^2}{\lambda}\right)\psi(x) = 0.$$

(10.23)

The solution to this equation (for more details see Appendix) is given by the eigenfunctions $\psi_k(x)$ of the form

$$\psi_k(x) = \begin{cases} d_{1k}\cos\left(\varepsilon_k\frac{x}{A}\right) + d_{2k}\mathrm{ch}\left(\gamma_k\frac{x}{A}\right), & k = 0, 2, 4, \ldots \\ c_{1k}\sin\left(\varepsilon_k\frac{x}{A}\right) + c_{2k}\mathrm{sh}\left(\gamma_k\frac{x}{A}\right), & k = 1, 3, 5, \ldots \end{cases}$$

(10.24)

Here, ε_k and γ_k are the solutions to the system of transcendental equations [28]

$$\begin{cases} G_1(\gamma)G_2(i\varepsilon)\left\{\left(\frac{\alpha}{\varepsilon}F_1(i\varepsilon)\right)^P \pm \mathrm{tg}\,\varepsilon\right\}\{[F_2(\gamma)]^P + \mathrm{th}\gamma\} \\ -G_1(i\varepsilon)G_2(\gamma)\left\{\left(\frac{\alpha}{\gamma}F_1(\gamma)\right)^P - \mathrm{th}\gamma\right\}\{[F_2(i\varepsilon)]^P \mp \mathrm{tg}\varepsilon\} = 0, \\ \gamma^2 = (\alpha^2 + \beta^2)\dfrac{\alpha^2 - 3\beta^2 + \varepsilon^2}{\alpha^2 + \beta^2 + \varepsilon^2}, \end{cases}$$

(10.25)

where $\quad F_1(x) = \dfrac{\beta^2 + (\alpha^2 - x^2)}{\beta^2 - (\alpha^2 - x^2)} \quad$ and $\quad F_2(x) = \dfrac{\alpha^2 + \beta^2 + x^2}{2\alpha x}$,

for $k = 0, 2, 4, \ldots$: $G_1(x) = 1$, $G_2(x) = \beta^2 - (\alpha^2 - x^2)$, $P = 1$ and the upper sign is used; for $k = 1, 3, 5, \ldots$: $G_1(x) = \alpha^2 + \beta^2 + x^2$, $G_2(x) = \alpha^2 + \beta^2 - x^2$, $P = -1$ and the lower sign is used.

The solutions to the system (10.25) may be separated on nonintersecting intervals

$$\left(0, \frac{\pi}{2}\right), \quad k = 0; \left(\frac{\pi}{2}, \frac{3\pi}{2}\right), \ldots, \left(\frac{\pi(k-1)}{2}, \frac{\pi(k+1)}{2}\right), \quad k = 2, 4, 6, \ldots,$$

$$\left(\frac{\pi}{2}, \frac{3\pi}{2}\right), \left(\frac{3\pi}{2}, \frac{5\pi}{2}\right), \ldots, \left(\frac{\pi k}{2}, \frac{\pi(k+2)}{2}\right), \quad k = 1, 3, 5, \ldots.$$

The coefficients d_{1k}, d_{2k}, and c_{1k}, c_{2k} are determined from the normalization condition using the relations

$$\left.\begin{array}{l} d_{1k}, k = 0, 2, 4, \ldots \\ c_{1k}, k = 1, 3, 5, \ldots \end{array}\right\} = \left\{A\left[\left(1 \pm \frac{\sin 2\varepsilon_k}{2\varepsilon_k}\right)\right.\right.$$

$$\left.\left. + 4D_k^2\left(1 \pm \frac{\mathrm{sh}2\gamma_k}{2\gamma_k}\right) - \frac{4D_kB_k}{\varepsilon_k^2 + \gamma_k^2}\right]\right\}^{-1/2},$$

(10.26)

$$\left.\begin{array}{l} d_{2k}, k = 0, 2, 4, \ldots \\ c_{2k}, k = 1, 3, 5, \ldots \end{array}\right\} = -D_k\left\{\begin{array}{l} d_{1k}, k = 0, 2, 4, \ldots \\ c_{1k}, k = 1, 3, 5, \ldots \end{array}\right\},$$

where $\quad D_k = 2\dfrac{E_{1k}(\alpha^2 + \beta^2 - \gamma_k^2)}{E_{2k}(\alpha^2 + \beta^2 + \varepsilon_k^2)},$

$$B_k = \begin{cases} e^{\gamma_k}(\gamma_k \cos \varepsilon_k + \varepsilon_k \sin \varepsilon_k) - e^{-\gamma_k}(\gamma_k \cos \varepsilon_k - \varepsilon_k \sin \varepsilon_k), & k = 0, 2, 4, \dots \\ e^{\gamma_k}(\gamma_k \sin \varepsilon_k + \varepsilon_k \cos \varepsilon_k) - e^{-\gamma_k}(\gamma_k \sin \varepsilon_k - \varepsilon_k \cos \varepsilon_k), & k = 1, 3, 5, \dots \end{cases}$$

$$E_{1k} \begin{Bmatrix} k = 0, 2, 4, \dots \\ k = 1, 3, 5, \dots \end{Bmatrix} = (\alpha^2 + \beta^2 - \varepsilon_k^2) \begin{Bmatrix} \cos \varepsilon_k \\ \sin \varepsilon_k \end{Bmatrix} + 2\alpha \varepsilon_k \cos \varepsilon_k,$$

$$E_{2k} \begin{Bmatrix} k = 0, 2, 4, \dots \\ k = 1, 3, 5, \dots \end{Bmatrix} = (\alpha^2 + \beta^2 + \gamma_k^2) \begin{Bmatrix} (e^{\gamma_k} + e^{-\gamma_k}) \\ (e^{\gamma_k} - e^{-\gamma_k}) \end{Bmatrix} + 2\alpha \gamma_k (e^{\gamma_k} + e^{-\gamma_k}).$$

Note that the eigen-numbers are given by

$$\lambda_k = \frac{2A\alpha\sigma^2(\alpha^2 + \beta^2 + \varepsilon_k^2)}{\varepsilon_k^4 + 2\varepsilon_k^2(\alpha^2 - \beta^2) + (\alpha^2 + \beta^2)^2}. \tag{10.27}$$

Analysis of the results obtained suggests that the monotonically increasing sequences $\{\varepsilon_k\}$ and $\{\gamma_k\}$ specify a strictly decreasing sequence of the eigenvalues in Eq. (10.27) that allows, in accordance with the KLE theory, the fulfillment of one of the most important optimal properties of the KLE: the minimal rms error of truncating an infinite series.

For $\beta = 0$, the correlation function becomes exponential and Eqs. (10.24) to (10.27) are reduced to the solutions obtained earlier in Ref. [20]. Thus, for $\beta \neq 0$, we have obtained the generalization on the case of the exponential-cosine correlation function.

Example 1.1   Consider a 2D halftone image. For the centered image $w(x, y)$ shown in Figure 10.4, the 2D correlation function $R(\Delta x, \Delta y)$ (see Fig. 10.5) was calculated by [29]

$$R(\Delta x, \Delta y) = \frac{1}{4AB} \int_{-A}^{A} \int_{-B}^{B} w(x, y)w^*(x + \Delta x, y + \Delta y)\, dx\, dy, \tag{10.28}$$

Note that once the arguments $x + \Delta x$ and $y + \Delta y$ fell outside the image boundaries, we put $w(x + \Delta x, y + \Delta y) = 0$.

The 2D correlation function was then factored onto two 1D correlation functions, $R_1(\Delta x)$ and $R_2(\Delta x)$, for which the exponential and exponential-cosine approximations were constructed using a least-squares method. For comparison, Figure 10.6a depicts the estimated correlation function and Figures 10.6b and 10.6c show its exponential and exponential-cosine approximations, respectively.

From Figure 10.6, the exponential-cosine function is seen to better describe the central fragment, as compared with the exponential-only function. And from Figure 10.7 it can also be seen that the exponential-cosine function reflects the correlation-function oscillations.

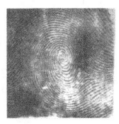

Figure 10.4. Halftone test image.

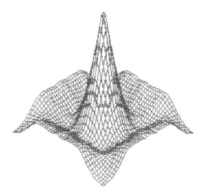

Figure 10.5. A 3D pattern of the correlation function for the image shown in Figure 10.4.

(a)   (b)   (c)

Figure 10.6. (**a**) The estimated correlation function, (**b**) its exponential and (**c**) exponential-cosine approximations.

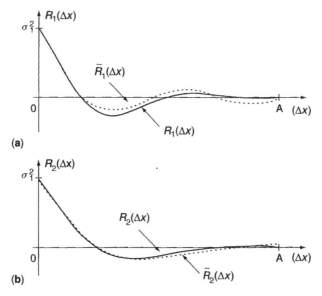

Figure 10.7. 1D cross sections of the estimated correlation functions (solid lines) and their exponential-cosine approximations (dotted lines).

For the approximating correlation functions of the image shown in Figure 10.4, we produced the following estimates of the exponential-cosine approximation parameters: $\sigma = 14.82$, $\alpha = 2.87$, $\beta = 0.41$, $\tilde{R}_2(\Delta x)$: $\sigma = 7.85$, $\alpha = 2.52$, $\beta = 0.86$.

The results of solving the integral equation for the kernel $\tilde{R}_1(\Delta x)$ and $\tilde{R}_2(\Delta x)$ are given in Table 10.1 and Table 10.2, respectively.

The form of the Karhunen-Loeve basis functions $\psi_k(x)$ on the interval $x \in [-A, A]$ is depicted in Figure 10.8, whereas the eigenfunctions can adequately be approximated by periodic sine and cosine curves, thus demonstrating the asymptotic behavior. However, taking into account the importance of the information aspect of the first KLE coefficients, the use of the asymptotic approximation seems to be justified only for the fairly high indices.

With the optical KLE implementation, it is digital holography that provides the most common methods for synthesizing spatial filters. Accordingly, for the synthesis of complex spatial filters, methods of computer-synthesized holograms are suited. Photocopies of spatial filters implementing Karhunen-Loeve basis functions for the exponential-cosine correlation function ($\alpha_x = \alpha_y = 3$, $\beta_x = \beta_y = 1$) are shown in Figure 10.9.

The use of the optical KLE necessitates taking into account of how the optical implementation errors affect the KLE stability.

There are many situations that can result in the KLE perturbations. With optical KLE realization, the perturbations are, most frequently, due to basis functions sampling in the course of computer-aided synthesis of an optical filter and also due to subsequent amplitude quantization at the lithographic fabrication stage.

TABLE 10.1. Basis-Function Parameters for the Correlation Function $\tilde{R}_1(\Delta x)$

Basis-Function Number, k	ε_k	γ_k	Eigennumber, λ_k
0	1.495	17.368	64.726
1	2.987	17.383	64.088
2	4.483	17.406	63.069
3	5.981	17.437	61.730
4	7.480	17.473	60.147

TABLE 10.2. Basis-Function Parameters for the Correlation Function $\tilde{R}_2(\Delta x)$

Basis-Function Number, k	ε_k	γ_k	Eigennumber, λ_k
0	1.513	13.349	38.387
1	3.024	13.440	37.341
2	4.529	13.582	35.620
3	6.030	13.759	33.268
4	7.529	13.960	30.363

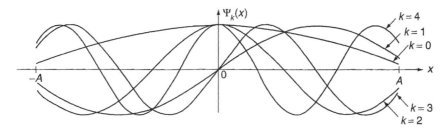

Figure 10.8. The form of the 1D Karhunen-Loeve basis functions.

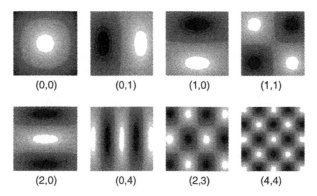

Figure 10.9. 2D Karhunen-Loeve basis functions.

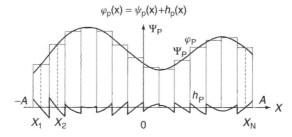

Figure 10.10. The effect of sampling and quantizing on basis function perturbations.

With sampling and quantizing, the eigenfunctions $\psi_{\mathbf{p}}$ are subject to the action of perturbations $h_{\mathbf{p}}$ and transformed into "perturbed" basis functions $\varphi_{\mathbf{p}}$ (see Fig. 10.10)

$$\varphi_{\mathbf{p}}(\mathbf{x}) = \psi_{\mathbf{p}}(\mathbf{x}) + h_{\mathbf{p}}(\mathbf{x}). \tag{10.29}$$

With the "perturbed" basis functions, instead of the coefficients $w_{\mathbf{p}}$ of the KLE, we get "perturbed' coefficients

$$\widehat{w}_{\mathbf{p}} = \int_G w(\mathbf{x})\varphi_{\mathbf{p}}^*(\mathbf{x})\mathbf{d}^2\mathbf{x}, \quad \mathbf{p} \in L, \tag{10.30}$$

which are weakly correlated.

Theoretical upper bounds for the Karhunen-Loeve basis function perturbations have been derived in Ref. [14], but they require the labor-consuming calculation of infinite matrix norms and other operations. Therefore, in the present section, the stability range for the KLE was determined in particularly posed tasks by constructing experimental curves for the aforementioned basis function perturbation effects.

Because the choice of the KLE is justified by its optimal properties, it seems natural to observe how perturbations induced by its optical implementation affect just these properties. The preservation of the optimal properties will count in favor of the KLE stability to the given perturbations. Among all properties of the KLE, we shall single out the two major ones: orthonormalization of basis functions and noncorrelation of expansion coefficients.

The orthonormalization condition for continuous basis functions is given by

$$\int_{-A}^{A} \psi_i(t)\psi_j^*(t)dt = \delta_{ij} = \begin{cases} 1, & i = j \\ 0, & i \neq j \end{cases}, \quad t \in [-A, A]. \tag{10.31}$$

When sampling the basis functions by replacing the integral by a sum, we get the numerical estimate of the condition in Eq. (10.31) in the form

$$\sum_{n=-N/2}^{N/2} \psi_i(n\Delta t)\psi_j^*(n\Delta t) = \mathrm{E}_{ij}^{\mathrm{KL}}, \quad N = \frac{2A}{\Delta t}, \tag{10.32}$$

where Δt is the sampling step.

Ideally, the matrix E^{KL} should be unit

$$\mathrm{E}_{ij}^{\mathrm{KL}} = \delta_{ij} = \begin{cases} 1, & i = j \\ 0, & i \neq j \end{cases}. \tag{10.33}$$

Consider the Karhunen-Loeve basis functions that are constructed using the exponential-cosine correlation function

$$R(\tau) = \sigma^2 \cdot \exp(-\alpha|\tau|) \cos \beta\tau, \quad |\tau| \leq 2A \tag{10.34}$$

with the following specific values of the parameters: $\sigma^2 = 1, \alpha = 3, \beta = 1, A = 1.28$.

For the first $M = 10$ basis functions with the sampling step of $\Delta t = 0.01$ (the number of pixels is $N = 2A \cdot \Delta t = 256$), the following results were obtained (a fragment of the matrix is presented):

$$\mathrm{E}^{\mathrm{KL}} = \begin{bmatrix} 1.0014 & 0.0000 & -0.0011 & 0.0000 & 0.0018 \\ 0.0000 & 1.0015 & 0.0000 & -0.0023 & -0.0000 \\ -0.0011 & 0.0000 & 1.0017 & -0.0000 & -0.0036 \\ 0.0000 & -0.0023 & -0.0000 & 1.0020 & 0.0000 \\ 0.0018 & -0.0000 & -0.0036 & 0.0000 & 1.0026 \end{bmatrix}.$$

The relative deviation from the ideal orthonormalization matrix in Eq. (10.32),

$$\varepsilon[\mathrm{E}^{\mathrm{KL}}] = \sqrt{\frac{\sum\limits_{i,j=1}^{M} (\mathrm{E}_{ij}^{\mathrm{KL}} - \delta_{ij})^2}{\sum\limits_{i,j=1}^{M} \delta_{ij}^2}} = \sqrt{\frac{1}{M} \sum\limits_{i,j=1}^{M} (\mathrm{E}_{ij}^{\mathrm{KL}} - \delta_{ij})^2} \tag{10.35}$$

amounts to the value of $\varepsilon[\mathrm{E}^{\mathrm{KL}}] = 0.016$, that is 1.6 percent.

The deviation depends on the relative parameters α/A and β/A because one can always reduce the interval under analysis to the unit line-segment. As α/A increases and β/A decreases, the value of $\varepsilon[E^{KL}]$ is decreased. Without changing the parameters α/A and β/A, let us observe the sampling effects, $\Delta t = 2A/N$, in more detail.

A twofold decrease in the sampling step $\Delta t = 0.005(N = 512)$ leads to an approximately twofold decrease in the relative deviation, $\varepsilon[E^{KL}] = 0.0083$, whereas a twofold increase in the sampling step, $\Delta t = 0.02(N = 128)$, results in a twofold increase in the relative deviation, $\varepsilon[E^{KL}] = 0.0321$. The same linear dependence holds for other values of Δt (see Fig. 10.11) up to a critical increase of $\Delta t_0 = 0.32(N = 8)$ when an abrupt jump of $\varepsilon[E^{KL}]$ takes place and the linear dependence is violated. This is because such a value of the sampling step allows inadequate "registration" of all basis functions variations. Thus, at $\Delta t \leq 0.16(N \geq 16)$, one can consider the dependence $\varepsilon[E^{KL}](\Delta t) \approx c \cdot \Delta t$, $c \approx 1.6$ as being linear.

Note that the dependence of $\varepsilon[E^{KL}]$ on the number of pixels N will be inverse (see Fig. 10.12). From Figure 10.12 it is clearly seen that at $N \geq 64(\Delta t \leq 0.04)$ the relative deviation $\varepsilon[E^{KL}](\Delta t)$ is no greater than 10 percent, thus suggesting that in the course of basis functions sampling the orthonormalization property is preserved.

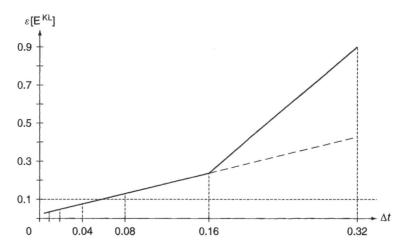

Figure 10.11. The deviation $\varepsilon[E^{KL}]$ as a function of the sampling Δt.

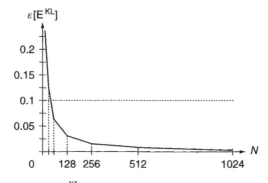

Figure 10.12. The deviation $\varepsilon[E^{KL}]$ versus the number of pixels N on the segment $[-A, A]$.

The preservation of orthonormalization property may also be observed at other basis function perturbations. It has been known [30] that quantizing resulting from the lithographic fabrication of optical elements may be described by the addition of a uniformly distributed white noise. In numerical simulation, the Karhunen-Loeve basis functions were distorted by the addition of white noise $\xi(n\Delta t)$

$$\tilde{\psi}(n\Delta t) = \psi(n\Delta t) + \xi(n\Delta t), \quad n = -\overline{N/2, N/2}, \tag{10.36}$$

and a variable $\varepsilon[\tilde{E}^{KL}]$ similar to that in Eq. (10.32) was calculated, where

$$\tilde{E}_{ij}^{KL} = \sum_{n=-N/2}^{N/2} \tilde{\psi}_i(n\Delta t)\tilde{\psi}_j^*(n\Delta t). \tag{10.37}$$

Because the noise $\xi(n\Delta t)$ is random, the variable $\varepsilon[\tilde{E}^{KL}]$ will also be random. Hence, its value can only be derived with some fiducial probability at a certain interval as a result of N experimental observations. In this case, the estimate $\hat{\varepsilon}[\tilde{E}^{KL}]$ is determined as an average over the observation results

$$\hat{\varepsilon}[\tilde{E}^{KL}] = \frac{1}{N_{\ni}} \sum_{i=1}^{N_{\ni}} \varepsilon_{\ni}^i[\tilde{E}^{KL}]. \tag{10.38}$$

From the central limit theorem [31] it follows that with increasing size of sampling, $N_{\ni}$, the sampling average distribution $\hat{\varepsilon}[\tilde{E}^{KL}]$ tends to a normal distribution irrespective of the form of the initial random variable $\varepsilon[\tilde{E}^{KL}]$. For practical purposes, the distribution $\hat{\varepsilon}[\tilde{E}^{KL}]$ may be considered as normal at $N_{\ni} > 10$ [31]. Hence, the fiducial intervals may be constructed using the following relation [31]:

$$P\left\{|\hat{\varepsilon}[\tilde{E}^{KL}] - \varepsilon[\tilde{E}^{KL}]| \leq \frac{\hat{\varepsilon}_{\varepsilon} \cdot t_{N_{\ni}-1;\alpha/2}}{\sqrt{N_{\ni}}}\right\} = 1 - \alpha, \tag{10.39}$$

where $\hat{\varepsilon}_{\varepsilon}^2$ is the sample value of variance $\hat{\varepsilon}[\tilde{E}^{KL}]$, $t_{N_{\ni}-1;\alpha/2}$ is the value of the tth student distribution, and $1 - \alpha$ is the fiducial probability.

For various values of the signal-to-noise ratio (SNR),

$$S/N = \sum_{n=-N/2}^{n=N/2} [\psi(n\Delta t)]^2 \bigg/ \sum_{n=-N/2}^{n=N/2} [\xi(n\Delta t)]^2, \tag{10.40}$$

and various number of pixels N, from $N_{\ni} = 1,000$ observations, we get the plots of $\varepsilon[\tilde{E}^{KL}]$ shown in Figure 10.13.

Having been given the fiducial probability of 95 percent ($\alpha = 0.05$) for $N = 1,000$ observations, we get that $t_{999;0.025} = 1.98$ and

$$P\left\{\hat{\varepsilon}[\tilde{E}^{KL}] - \varepsilon[\tilde{E}^{KL}] \leq \hat{\varepsilon}_{\varepsilon} \cdot 0.06\right\} = 0.95.$$

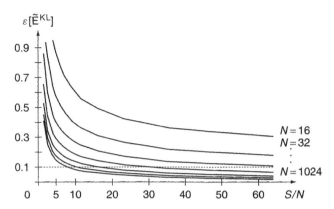

Figure 10.13. The deviation $\varepsilon[\tilde{\text{E}}^{\text{KL}}]$ versus SNR at different number of pixels N.

For convenience, we may consider the relative error

$$\mu_{0.95} = \frac{|\hat{\varepsilon}[\tilde{\text{E}}^{\text{KL}}] - \varepsilon[\tilde{\text{E}}^{\text{KL}}]|}{\varepsilon[\tilde{\text{E}}^{\text{KL}}]} \approx \frac{|\hat{\varepsilon}[\tilde{\text{E}}^{\text{KL}}] - \varepsilon[\tilde{\text{E}}^{\text{KL}}]|}{\hat{\varepsilon}[\tilde{\text{E}}^{\text{KL}}]} = \frac{\hat{\varepsilon}_{\varepsilon} \cdot 0.06}{\hat{\varepsilon}[\tilde{\text{E}}^{\text{KL}}]},$$

which turned out to be no greater than 2 percent: $\mu_{0.95}^{\max} \leq 0.02$, for the derived values of $\hat{\varepsilon}[\tilde{\text{E}}^{\text{KL}}]$ and $\hat{\varepsilon}_{\varepsilon}^2$. From Figure 10.13, the curves for $N = 256$–$1,024$ are seen to be very close to each other even at large noise levels SNR ≥ 2.5; hence, once $N = 256$ has been attained, a further increase in the number of pixels becomes ineffective.

On the basis of the results obtained, we can determine the range of the KLE stability as a function of the value of SNR: the relative deviation $\varepsilon[\tilde{\text{E}}^{\text{KL}}]$ does not exceed 10 percent for SNR ≥ 16 at $N \geq 256$ and for SNR ≥ 30 at $N \geq 128$.

For the Karhunen-Loeve expansion, another important criterion for the influence of basis functions perturbations on its stability is noncorrelated coefficients in the decomposition of the function x(t)

$$< x_i x_j > = \lambda_i \delta_{ij} = \begin{cases} \lambda_i, & i = j \\ 0, & i \neq j \end{cases}, \tag{10.41}$$

here $< \cdot >$ denotes averaging over a realization ensemble and x_i are the expansion coefficients

$$x_i = \int_{-A}^{A} x(t)\psi_i(t)\,dt, \quad |t| \leq A \tag{10.42}$$

in terms of eigenfunctions of the correlation operator

$$\lambda_i \psi_i(t) = \int_{-A}^{A} R(t-u)\psi_j(u)\,du, \quad |t| \leq A, \tag{10.43}$$

where λ_j are eigen-numbers and $R(t-u)$ is the correlation function of the process $x(t)$.

For conducting the numerical simulation, one must generate stationary stochastic processes corresponding to the pregiven correlation function. The stationary stochastic process for the exponential-cosine correlation function $R(\tau)$ in Eq. (10.36) with the same parameters as was the case in the previous section ($\sigma^2 = 1, \alpha = 3, \beta = 1, A = 1.28$) was simulated using a method of recurrent difference equations [21].

For K = 500 discrete realizations of such a stochastic process, we calculated the correlation matrix for expansion coefficients

$$\rho_{ij} = \frac{1}{K} \sum_{k=1}^{K} x_i^k x_j^k, \tag{10.44}$$

where $x_i^k = \sum_{n=-N/2}^{N/2} x^k(n\Delta t)\psi_i(n\Delta t)$, $k = \overline{1, K}$, $i = \overline{1, M}$ is the expansion coefficient of the ith discrete realization of the stochastic process $x(t)$ in terms of the ith basis function.

For $\Delta t = 0.01 (N = 256)$, the following correlation matrix for the Karhunen-Loeve expansion coefficients was obtained ($M = 10$, a fragment is only given):

$$\rho^{KL} = \begin{bmatrix} 0.5723 & -0.0011 & -0.0052 & -0.0009 & 0.0069 \\ -0.0011 & 0.3956 & -0.0031 & -0.0091 & 0.0040 \\ -0.0052 & -0.0031 & 0.2522 & 0.0020 & -0.0070 \\ -0.0009 & -0.0091 & 0.0020 & 0.1705 & 0.0038 \\ 0.0069 & 0.0040 & -0.0070 & 0.0038 & 0.1235 \end{bmatrix}.$$

The eigennumbers λ_i, $i = \overline{1, M}$, derived from Eq. (10.31) take the following values:

$$\lambda_1 = 0.5757, \quad \lambda_2 = 0.3992, \quad \lambda_3 = 0.2552, \quad \lambda_4 = 0.1649, \quad \lambda_5 = 0.1112.$$

From the preceding results, the correlation function perturbation is seen to introduce a correlation between the expansion coefficients $\rho_{ij}^{KL} \neq 0$ and $i \neq j$ and disturb the equality of diagonal elements to the eigen-numbers. However, the ordered arrangement for eigenvalues has been preserved [13]: $\lambda_1 \geq \lambda_2 \geq \lambda_3 \geq \cdots$.

In order to evaluate the perturbation introduced, the same experiment was conducted for the Fourier basis

$$f_m = \begin{cases} \dfrac{1}{\sqrt{A}} \cos\left(\dfrac{m}{2} \cdot \dfrac{\pi n \Delta t}{A}\right), & m = 0, 2, 4, \ldots \\ \dfrac{1}{\sqrt{A}} \sin\left(\dfrac{m+1}{2} \cdot \dfrac{\pi n \Delta t}{A}\right), & m = 1, 3, 5, \ldots \end{cases} \tag{10.45}$$

and the corresponding correlation matrix for the Fourier expansion coefficients was obtained:

$$\rho^F = \begin{bmatrix} 0.5866 & 0.0039 & -0.0074 & -0.0025 & 0.0154 \\ 0.0039 & 0.4118 & -0.0022 & -0.0061 & 0.0043 \\ -0.0074 & -0.0022 & 0.2715 & 0.0019 & 0.0149 \\ -0.0025 & -0.0061 & 0.0024 & 0.1793 & -0.0057 \\ 0.0154 & 0.0043 & 0.0149 & -0.0057 & 0.1312 \end{bmatrix}.$$

The correlation degree of the expansion coefficients was estimated through the following variable:

$$\varepsilon[\rho] = \sqrt{\frac{\sum\limits_{i,j=1}^{M} (\rho_{ij} - \lambda_i \delta_{ij})^2}{\sum\limits_{i,j=1}^{M} (\lambda_i \delta_{ij})^2}} \simeq \sqrt{\frac{\sum\limits_{i,j=1}^{M} (\rho_{ij} - \lambda_i \delta_{ij})^2}{\sum\limits_{i=1}^{M} \lambda_i^2}}, \tag{10.46}$$

which is analogous to Eq. (10.35) and denotes the relative deviation of the obtained correlation matrix from the ideal one.

For the Karhunen-Loeve expansion, this value was $\varepsilon[\rho^{KL}] = 0.0092$, whereas for the Fourier expansion, $\varepsilon[\rho^F] = 0.0186$, which is twice as large. The relative deviation $\varepsilon[\rho]$ as a function of the sampling step for the KLE and the Fourier expansion is shown in Figure 10.14 and suggests that the KLE curve lies below the Fourier curve for the entire range considered.

All results considered, one may infer that on basis function sampling, the KLE preserves its optimal properties and provides a lesser correlation degree of expansion coefficients compared with the Fourier basis.

The influence that the noise added to the Karhunen-Loeve basis functions for modeling the amplitude quantization, Eq. (10.36), exercises on the correlation matrix of expansion coefficients is given by

$$\tilde{\rho}_{ij}^{KL} = \frac{1}{K} \sum_{k=1}^{K} \tilde{x}_i^k \tilde{x}_j^k, \tag{10.47}$$

where $\tilde{x}_i^k = \sum\limits_{n=-N/2}^{N/2} x^k(n\Delta t) \tilde{\psi}_i(n\Delta t), \quad k = \overline{1, K}, \; i = \overline{1, M}.$

The relative deviation of the correlation matrix, $\varepsilon[\tilde{\rho}^{KL}]$ and $\varepsilon[\tilde{\rho}^F]$, for the KLE and the Fourier expansion as a function of the value of additive noise specified by the SNR

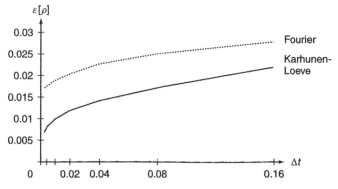

Figure 10.14. The deviation $\varepsilon[\rho]$ versus the sampling step Δt of basis functions for the KLE and the Fourier expansion.

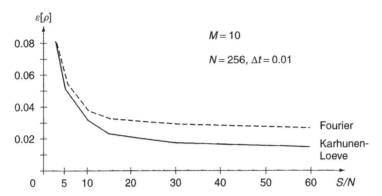

Figure 10.15. The deviation $\varepsilon[\tilde{\rho}]$ for the KLE and the Fourier expansion versus the level of noise added to the basis functions, SNR, at $\Delta t = 0.01(N = 256)$.

of Eq. (10.39) at $\Delta t = 0.01(\text{N} = 256)$, is shown in Figure 10.15. It can be seen that for SNR $\geq$ 15, the relation between the coefficient correlation degrees for the KLE and the Fourier expansion is almost the same as in the absence of noise, but with further increase in the noise background, the curves rapidly approach each other and at SNR $= 2.5$ the KLE is no longer optimal.

Thus, with a sampling step of $\Delta t \leq 0.01$ ($N \geq 256$) and a level of noise of SNR $\geq$ 15 of the basis functions, the major properties of the KLE are preserved, thus providing its stability to the perturbations resulting from optical implementation.

Example 10.2   To study the stability of the KLE-based system for image processing, we conducted a series of computer-aided numerical simulations, which involved the test image recognition using the coefficients of expansion of Eq. (10.10) in terms of eigenfunctions. Each image was interpreted as a random field realization. The correlation function of statistically homogeneous reference images was derived from one realization w_{ij} [29], with the averaged correlation function $\overline{R}$ determined as the arithmetic mean of all R_{ij}.

In the numerical simulation, $N_{\text{cl}} = 16$ classes of images were employed. The reference images were shaped as triangles, each of which had an inserted triangle, with the outer and inner triangles found in one of the four positions (see Fig. 10.16).

The 2D correlation function $\overline{R}(\Delta x, \Delta y)$ calculated for the reference images shown in Figure 10.16 was decomposed into two 1D factors: $R^{\text{I}}(\Delta x)$ and $R^{\text{II}}(\Delta y)$, with the exponential-cosine approximation constructed for each of them. With the use of the approximating correlation functions $\widehat{R}^{\text{I}}(\Delta x)$ and $\widehat{R}^{\text{II}}(\Delta y)$, we analytically solved the 1D integral equations (10.10) with the exponential cosine kernel, and derived 1D basis functions. The 2D basis functions calculated as a product of 1D functions according to Eq. (10.18) are shown in Figure 10.17.

In the computer experiment, we calculated $L = 25$ features, Eq. (10.9), using the ordered 2D basis functions (0,0), (0,1), (1,0), ..., (4,4) for the reference images and the objects, on the basis of class-average feature vector.

As the objects under recognition, we used slightly distorted reference images after they had been scaled (Fig. 10.18), turned (Fig. 10.19), and noised by the additive white noise (Fig. 10.20).

Figure 10.16. Reference images for 16 classes.

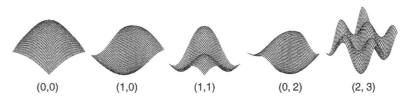

(0,0)   (1,0)   (1,1)   (0, 2)   (2, 3)

Figure 10.17. 3D Karhunen-Loeve basis functions.

(a) $0.85 < S < 1$ (b) $0.8 < S < 1$

Figure 10.18. Scaled objects under recognition.

(a) $-45°.. < P < 45°..$ **(b)** $P < -45°, P > 45°$

Figure 10.19. Turned objects under recognition.

(a) $S/N \geq 4$ **(b)** $S/N < 4$

Figure 10.20. Noised objects under recognition.

When conducting the experiment, the image-distortion parameters, the angle of turning, R, the scaling coefficient, S, and the signal-to-noise ratio, SNR, were gradually increased up to some values determining the limits of stable operation of the recognition system. Shown in Figures 10.18a, 10.19a, and 10.20a are the objects with the distortion degree allowing the stable recognition of the objects, whereas in Figures 10.18b, 10.19b, and 10.20b are the objects with the distortion degree beyond the range of KLE-based stable recognition.

Because with turning and scaling the distortion parameters are not random, the accuracy of the results obtained does not depend on the number N of the experiments conducted. With the addition of noise, the distortion is introduced by a stochastic variable and, hence, it is necessary to estimate the accuracy of the experimental results by making use of some formulae of mathematical statistics given in the Appendix. Given the 95 percent fiducial interval, we get the estimate of frequency of the successful outcome $W \in [\widehat{W} - \mu_{0.95}, \widehat{W} + \mu_{0.95}]$, with the accuracy

$$\mu_{0.95} = 2\sqrt{\frac{1-W}{W \cdot N_{\ni}}} \approx 2\sqrt{\frac{1-\widehat{W}}{\widehat{W} \cdot N_{\ni}}}, \qquad (10.48)$$

where $\widehat{W} = N_0/N_{\ni}$ is the estimate of frequency of the successful outcome N_0 in $N_{\ni}$ experiments conducted.

The results of the computer experiment on the recognition of distorted images are given in Table 10.3.

The experiment with model images has shown that the recognition system under study has good stability to the addition of noise and the turning of images (of the objects under recognition) and a considerable sensitivity to scaling.

Example 10.3 Consider the problem of recognition of real images — lachrymal-fluid crystallograms.

At present, ophthalmologists have studied the possibility of diagnosing a variety of eye diseases using a lachrymal-fluid crystallogram [32,33]. Different crystallization

TABLE 10.3. The Results of the Computer Experiment on the Recognition of Distorted Images

Character of Distortion	Parameters of Distortion	$N_{\ni}$	$\hat{W} = N_0/N_{\ni}$	Accuracy $\mu_{0.95}$
Scaling	$S = 1 \div 0.85$		1	—
	$S = 0.85 \div 0.8$	25	0.95	
	$R = -45° \div 45°$		1	—
Turning	$R < 45°, R > 45°^{(*)}$	100	1	
	$S/N = 30 \div 4$		1	
Noising	$S/N = 2.5 \div 1.5$	200	0.65	0.1

(*) In this case the object passed to another class and was adequately recognized as a representative of that class.

patterns of the lachrymal fluid in the patient with normal state of health and that showing different pathological signs form the basis of this method. However, the analysis conducted has demonstrated that it is very difficult, if not impossible, to visually separate some major pathological signs. Therefore, it is advantageous to formalize the disease signs and make the process of diagnosing automatic.

Aiming at preliminary studies of prospects for applying the aforementioned recognition procedure to this problem, we selected the lachrymal crystallogram photos that were previously classified as being normal and pathological on the basis of other diagnostic techniques. Figure 10.21a shows the normal crystallogram photos and Figure 10.21b shows those of pathological crystallograms.

Several formal features according to which normal crystallograms may be distinguished from the pathological ones were picked up in Ref. [34]. These are the crystal "transparency" (normal lines should be thin and fringeless), the number of crystallization centers (normally, there should be one), the existence of a global direction (normal lines should not have branches), and the line density on the crystal image (the normal distance between the lines is to be maximal).

In the posed problem of recognizing distortions in the microcrystal structure, the reference images are used to form two classes of images, the normal and pathologic, for each of which the class centers are constructed using the reference features represented by a set of orthogonal expansion coefficients. A newly entered image is classified according to the minimal distance from its vector to the class centers.

For conducting the numerical simulation, 17 reference samples of lachrymal-fluid crystallograms (3 normal and 14 pathological) were selected. The experiment was

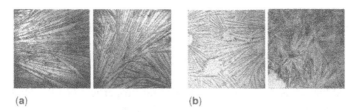

(a)   (b)

Figure 10.21. Images of real lachrymal crystallograms: (a) normal, (b) pathological.

TABLE 10.4. The results of recognition of lachrymal crystallograms

Fourier basis	Karhunen-Loeve basis
$W = 0.94$ at $L \geq 30$	$W = 0.94$ at $L \geq 19$

conducted in different variants. We put to recognition the initial crystallogram images using the coefficients of two orthogonal expansions, the Fourier and Karhunen-Loeve bases. The results of recognition for 15 newly entered images are given in Table 10.4 (W is the successful outcome frequency and L is the number of the expansion coefficients).

It can be seen from Table 10.4 that for attaining the same result the KLE requires 1.5 times less coefficients than the Fourier expansion, thus obviously corroborating the optimal character of the KLE and the efficiency of its application.

10.2.2   Use of the DOE for Decomposing the Field into the Hadamard Basis

Because Karhunen-Loeve basis functions are multilevel and alternating, their optical implementation calls for the fabrication of halftone amplitude-phase filters.

In this section we treat the Hadamard basis, which has been shown [35] to be well suited for the analysis of fingerprints. The advantages of the Hadamard basis are its universality and simple optical realization using binary-phase filters.

The Hadamard functions are defined as follows [36,37]:

$$\text{had}_m(t) = \frac{1}{\sqrt{T}} \prod_{k=0}^{\infty} [\text{rad}_{k+1}(t)]^{m_k^\Gamma}, \quad t \in [0, T], \tag{10.49}$$

where m_k^Γ is the kth digit of the Gray code with number m and $\text{rad}_m(t)$ are the Rademaher functions. The Gray code is formed from the binary number m by the rule

$$m_k^\Gamma = m_k \oplus m_{k+1}, \tag{10.50}$$

where k is the number of the binary digit (from right to left), m_k is the binary digit in the binary notation of the number m: $m = \sum_{k=0}^{\infty} m_k 2^k$, and $\oplus$ denotes the modulo 2 summation. The Rademaher functions are defined as follows:

$$\text{rad}_m(t) = \text{sign}[\sin(2^m \pi t / T)]. \tag{10.51}$$

The 2D Hadamard functions are defined as a product of 1D functions

$$\text{had}_{mn}(x, y) = \text{had}_m(x) \, \text{had}_n(y). \tag{10.52}$$

The Hadamard basis has the following interesting properties: (*1*) the Hadamard functions satisfy the zero condition, which means that their Fourier images are equal to zero at the central point; (*2*) they take only two values: $+1$ or -1; and (*3*) they are

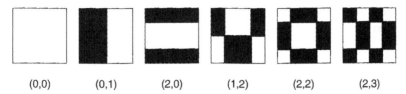

(0,0)   (0,1)   (2,0)   (1,2)   (2,2)   (2,3)

Figure 10.22. Examples of some Hadamard functions (white color corresponds to the value of +1 and black to the value of −1).

defined on a limited interval. Examples of some Hadamard functions are given in Figure 10.22.

In this section, we discuss an iterative algorithm for designing phase DOEs with the transmission function represented as an arbitrary linear combination of a finite number of Hadamard functions with different spatial carrier frequencies. An optical setup for calculating the image features vector, $w(x, y)$, is shown in Figure 10.2.

If a DOE with the transmission function represented by a linear combination of a finite number of basis functions $\{\Psi_{mn}(x, y)\}$ with different spatial carrier frequencies

$$\sum_{m=0}^{M} \sum_{n=0}^{N} C_{mn} \Psi_{mn}^{*}(x, y) \cdot \exp[i(\alpha_m x + \beta_n y)], \quad (10.53)$$

is complemented by a spherical lens and illuminated by a wave $w(x, y)$, the light intensity at pregiven points of the lens's focal plane ($u_m = (t/k)\alpha_m, \quad v_n = (t/k)\beta_n$) will be proportional to the squared modulus of the coefficients C_{mn} of the light field expansion into the basis $\{\Psi_{mn}(x, y)\}$

$$C_{mn} = \iint_{-\infty}^{\infty} w(x, y) \Psi_{mn}^{*}(x, y) \, dx \, dy. \quad (10.54)$$

Let it be required to compute the phase of an optical element $\varphi(x, y)$ that generates (when illuminated by the light beam of amplitude $[A_0(x, y)]$ the Hadamard expansion coefficients at desired points (α_m, β_n) of the frequency plane. The CTF of such an element should satisfy the following relation:

$$\tau(x, y) = A_0(x, y) \exp[i\varphi(x, y)] = \sum_{m=0}^{M} \sum_{n=0}^{N} C_{mn} \, \text{had}_{mn}(x, y) \cdot \exp[i(\alpha_m x + \beta_n y)].$$
$$(10.55)$$

If the difference $|\alpha_{m+1} - \alpha_m|$ between the neighboring frequencies is chosen to be sufficiently large, that is, such that the spatial spectra of the neighboring Hadamard functions be separated according to some criterion, the coefficients C_{mn} in Eq. (10.55) are

$$C_{mn} \cong \iint_{-\infty}^{\infty} A_0(x, y) \exp[i\varphi(x, y)] \, \text{had}_{mn}(x, y) \exp[-i(\alpha_m x + \beta_n y)] \, dx \, dy. \quad (10.56)$$

Note that the coefficients C_{mn} may be derived using a single Fourier transform through the equation

$$F(\xi, \eta) = \iint\limits_{-\infty}^{\infty} A_0(x, y) \exp[i\varphi(x, y)]\tau(x, y)\, dx\, dy. \tag{10.57}$$

In this case, the $F(\xi, \eta)$ function at points (ξ, η) of the plane (α_m, β_n) is equal to the corresponding coefficients

$$F(\xi = \alpha_m, \ \eta = \beta_n) \cong C_{mn}. \tag{10.58}$$

The previous calculations make it possible to propose an iterative algorithm [38] for deriving the phase $\varphi(x, y)$ of an optical element. As the initial phase estimate, we take the value of $\varphi_0(x, y)$. Suppose that in the kth iteration we get the kth phase estimate, $\varphi_k(x, y)$. The function $\varphi_k(x, y)$ is used for calculating the coefficients $C_{mn}^{(k)}$ of Eq. (10.56) or Eqs. (10.57) and (10.58), which are then replaced by the coefficients

$$\hat{C}_{mn}^{(k)} = B_{mn} C_{mn}^{(k)} |C_{mn}^{(k)}|^{-1} \tag{10.59}$$

with pregiven modules B_{mn}. The coefficients $\hat{C}_{mn}^{(k)}$ are then substituted in Eq. (10.55). The summation in Eq. (10.55) gives the $E_{k+1}(x, y)$ function whose argument serves as the subsequent phase estimate;

$$\varphi_{k+1}(x, y) = \arg E_{k+1}(x, y), \tag{10.60}$$

and so forth.

Example 10.4   The proposed algorithm was applied to calculating a phase optical element matched to the Hadamard basis. From Figure 10.23a, it is seen that the transmission function phase of such a DOE may have only four to five levels, thus making its microlithographic fabrication simpler. After 10 iterations, the deviation of squared modules of the coefficients generated by the designed DOE in the frequency plane (see Fig. 10.23b) from the ideal ones was less than 9 percent.

The algorithm proposed was also applied to designing a DOE intended to calculate the first 25 coefficients of the 2D Hadamard expansion, C_{mn}, $m, n = \overline{0, 4}$. The calculation parameters were as follows: the total number of pixels is 512×512, the number of terms of the sum in Eq. (10.55) is $N = M = 10$, and the illuminating beam amplitude $A_0(x, y)$ was constant.

Figure 10.24a depicts the phase of a DOE that generates the first 25 coefficients of the 2D Hadamard expansion in the spatial spectrum plane. The intensity distributions in the focal plane produced by the phase DOE illuminated by the light beam of amplitude $A_0(x, y) = \mathrm{had}_{00}(x, y)$ [peak at point (α_0, β_0) of the plane (ξ, η)] and $A_0(x, y) = \mathrm{had}_{32}(x, y)$ [peak at point (α_3, β_2)].

About 80 percent of the incident light energy contributes to the generation of desired coefficients. The rms error of the coefficients produced by such a DOE does not exceed 20 percent and is comparable to the fabrication process errors.

The designed DOE may find use in image analysis. In Ref. [35], it has been shown that the Hadamard expansion coefficients for the direction fields (see section 10.3) of fingerprints are well suited for recognizing such images.

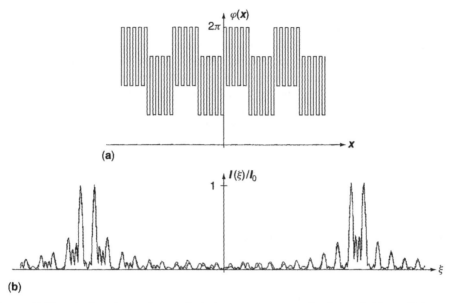

(a)

(b)

Figure 10.23. (a) The phase of an optical element generating the 3rd and 4th coefficients of the 1D Hadamard expansion and (b) the normalized intensity in the spatial spectrum plane (the plane of formation of squared modules of coefficients).

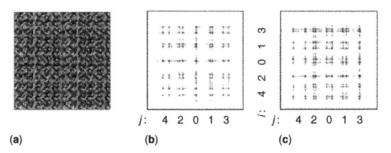

(a)   **(b)**   **(c)**

Figure 10.24. (a) The phase of a DOE that produces the first 25 coefficients of the 2D Hadamard expansion and the intensity distribution in the spatial spectrum plane that the DOE produces when illuminated by the light beam of amplitude (b) $A_0(x, y) = \text{had}_{00}(x, y)$ and (c) $A_0(x, y) = \text{had}_{32}(x, y)$.

Note that without essential modifications, the algorithm proposed may be applied to designing DOEs intended to perform optical computation of the Walsh and Haar expansion coefficients.

10.2.3   DOEs to Decompose the Field into Angular Harmonics

When dealing with the problem of turn-invariant image recognition, it is expedient to employ spatial filters that are capable of separating the coherent light field onto individual diffraction components of special orthogonal bases comprising angular harmonics. By the angular harmonics are meant complex functions with unit modulus and linear dependence on polar angle. Such harmonics appear, for example, in Bessel optics [39] as a result of optical implementation of the higher-order Hankel transform or generation of diffraction-free beams [40], diffraction-free images [41], axially periodic Bessel beams [42], and multimode rotating Gauss-Laguerre beams [43].

In this section we consider an iterative algorithm for designing phase DOEs, which may be referred to as *angular spectrum analyzers*, aimed at decomposing the coherent light field into an orthogonal basis with angular harmonics. The spherical lens, in fact, plays the part of a Fourier analyzer because it decomposes the light field into plane waves or spatial Fourier harmonics. Similarly, a "lens + DOE" combination may be called the *Bessel, Gauss-Laguerre,* or *Zernike analyzer* if the given optical element expands the laser light into the corresponding basis. The expansion in terms of Gauss-Laguerre modes is used to select transverse modes at the output of a multimode fiber with parabolic refractive index profile [44].

The complex amplitude $F(x, y)$ of the monochromatic light wave cast in polar coordinates can always be expanded into the functional Fourier series in terms of angular harmonics. Such a functional series is written as follows:

$$F(r, \varphi) = \sum_{n=-\infty}^{\infty} F_n(r) e^{in\varphi}, \tag{10.61}$$

where

$$F_n(r) = \frac{1}{2\pi} \int_0^{2\pi} F(r, \varphi) e^{-in\varphi} \, d\varphi. \tag{10.62}$$

The series in Eq. (10.61) gives an analogous expansion of the spatial spectrum of the given light field in terms of harmonics $e^{in\varphi}$. Actually, if we take a Fourier transform of the $F(r, \varphi)$ function, we get

$$G(\rho, \theta) = \Im[F(r, \varphi)] = \sum_{n=-\infty}^{\infty} G_n(\rho) e^{in\theta}, \tag{10.63}$$

where

$$G_n(\rho) = \frac{2\pi k i^n}{f} \int_0^{2\pi} F_n(r) J_n\left(\frac{k}{f} r\rho\right) r \, dr, \tag{10.64}$$

$$\Im[F(r, \varphi)] = \frac{k}{f} \int_0^{\infty} \int_0^{2\pi} F(r, \varphi) \exp\left[-i\frac{k}{f} r\rho \cos(\varphi - \theta)\right] r \, dr \, d\varphi, \tag{10.65}$$

k is the wave number, f is the lens's focal length, and $J_n(x)$ is the Bessel function of the first kind and of nth order. In Eqs. (10.61) to (10.65), the Fourier transform is assumed to be performed optically using a spherical lens of focal length f (see Fig. 10.2).

The expressions in Eqs. (10.61) and (10.63) are seen to be structurally similar, whereas the functions $G_n(\rho)$ and $F_n(r)$ are related through the Hankel transform of the nth order in Eq. (10.64).

The expansion in Eq. (10.61) is convenient to apply to the turn-invariant image recognition, because the turn of the image under analysis $F(r, \varphi)$ through an angle $\Delta\varphi$ will not result in a change of experimentally measured coefficient modules, $|F_n(r)|$. In this connection, the problem of turn-invariant image recognition may be reduced to measuring the coefficients of image expansion in terms of the bases proposed subsequently. Consider functions describing separate diffraction-free Bessel modes propagating in free space [41,46]

$$Q_{nm}(r, \varphi) = A_{nm} J_m \left(\gamma_{nm} \frac{r}{r_0} \right) e^{im\varphi},$$

(10.66)

$$A_{nm} = \left[r_0 \sqrt{\pi} J_m'(\gamma_{nm}) \right]^{-1},$$

(10.67)

where r_0 is the aperture radius limiting the Bessel beam, γ_{nm} are the Bessel function roots: $J_m(\gamma_{nm}) = 0$, $n, m = 0, 1, 2, \ldots$; and $J_m'(\gamma_{nm})$ is the derivative of the Bessel function at point $r = r_0$.

The set of functions in Eq. (10.66) is a complete orthogonal basis within a circle of radius r_0. Substituting them in Eqs. (10.61) and (10.63) gives

$$F(r, \varphi) = \sum_{n=0}^{\infty} \sum_{m=-\infty}^{\infty} C_{nm} Q_{nm}(r, \varphi),$$

(10.68)

$$G(\rho, \theta) = \frac{2\pi k}{f} \sum_{n=0}^{\infty} \sum_{m=-\infty}^{\infty} i^m C_{nm} A_{nm} e^{im\theta} \int_0^{r_0} J_m \left(\gamma_{nm} \frac{r}{r_0} \right) J_m \left(\frac{k}{f} r\rho \right) r \, dr.$$

(10.69)

At $\rho = \gamma_{mn} \left(\dfrac{f}{kr_0} \right)$, some terms in Eq. (10.62) are equal to zero according to the property of orthogonality of Bessel functions

$$\int_0^{r_0} J_m \left(\gamma_{nm} \frac{r}{r_0} \right) J_m \left(\gamma_{pm} \frac{r}{r_0} \right) r \, dr = \frac{r_0^2}{2} \left[J_m'(\gamma_{nm}) \right]^2 \delta_{np}.$$

(10.70)

The basis functions in Eq. (10.62) are convenient to use for selecting separate Bessel modes in a multimode beam. Such a multimode Bessel beam may occur at the output of a step-index light waveguide.

There exists another complete set of orthogonal functions with angular harmonics in a circle of radius r_0. These are circular Zernike polynomials [45], which are treated in detail in subsection 10.2.4.

The basis Zernike functions may be conveniently used when analyzing small wave front aberrations. An analyzer based on a superposition of these functions makes it possible to spatially separate the contribution made in the light beam by separate aberrations described by single Zernike polynomial. The output signal of such an analyzer may be used in adaptive mirror controlling that is aimed at compensating aberrations.

Generalized Gauss-Laguerre modes [43,44] form a complete set of orthogonal functions on the entire plane

$$S_{nm}(r, \varphi) = D_{nm} \left(\frac{r}{a} \right)^{|m|} \exp \left[-\frac{1}{2} \left(\frac{r}{a} \right)^2 \right] L_n^{|m|} \left(\frac{r^2}{a^2} \right) e^{im\varphi},$$

(10.71)

where $$D_{nm} = \frac{1}{a} \sqrt{\frac{n!}{\pi (n + |m|)!}},$$

(10.72)

$$L_n^m(x) = (-1)^m \frac{d^m}{dx^m} \left[L_{n+m}(x) \right], \tag{10.73}$$

a is the Gaussian-beam waist radius, and $L_n^m(x)$ and $L_n(x)$ are the generalized and common Laguerre polynomials.

In this case, the expansions in Eq. (10.61) and (10.63) in angular harmonics will be as follows:

$$F(r, \varphi) = \sum_{n=0}^{\infty} \sum_{m=-n}^{n} C_{nm} S_{nm}(r, \varphi), \tag{10.74}$$

$$G(\rho, \theta) = \frac{2\pi k}{f} \sum_{n=0}^{\infty} \sum_{m=-n}^{n} (-1)^n (-i)^m C_{nm} S_{nm}(r, \varphi). \tag{10.75}$$

Equation (10.75) follows from the fact that the functions in Eq. (10.71) are the eigenfunctions of the Fourier transform

$$\int_0^{\infty} \int_0^{2\pi} S_{nm}(r, \varphi) \exp\left[-i\frac{k}{f} r\rho \cos(\varphi - \theta) \right] r \, dr \, d\varphi = 2\pi(-1)^n (-i)^m S_{nm}(\rho, \theta). \tag{10.76}$$

The basis functions in Eq. (10.71) are used when designing an analyzer matched to the multimode beam at the output of a parabolic-index light fiber or a laser cavity with spherical mirrors. Such an analyzer makes possible the spatial separation of cylindrical modes in the beam.

Doe to Analyze the Angular Spectrum

The notion of modans — optical elements used as spatial filters — for analyzing the transverse-mode composition of coherent light beams has been introduced in Ref. [44]. In a similar way, one may consider optical elements intended for decomposing the light field into an arbitrary orthogonal basis as spectrum analyzers. An optical configuration for spectrum analysis of light beam is shown in Figure 10.2. Assume that the DOE transmission function of such an analyzer is represented by a linear combination of a finite number of basis functions $\psi_{nm}(x, y)$ chosen with pregiven inclinations, Eq. (10.53).

If such a filter is placed near a spherical lens and is illuminated by a light wave of wavelength $F(x, y)$, the intensity at the focal plane points given by

$$u_{nm} = \frac{f}{k}\alpha_{nm}, \quad v_{nm} = \frac{f}{k}\beta_{nm}, \tag{10.77}$$

where $(\alpha_{nm}, \beta_{nm})$ are the spatial carrier frequencies, will be approximately proportional to the squared modules of the coefficients C_{nm} of the complex amplitude expansion

$$F(x, y) = \sum_{n=0}^{N} \sum_{m=0}^{M} C_{nm} \psi_{nm}(x, y). \tag{10.78}$$

Actually,

$$\int_{-\infty}^{\infty} \int_{-\infty}^{\infty} F(x, y) \tau(x, y) \exp\left[-i\frac{k}{f}(ux + vy)\right] dx\, dy$$

$$= \frac{k}{f} \sum_{n=0}^{N} \sum_{m=0}^{M} \sum_{p=0}^{N} \sum_{q=0}^{M} C_{nm} \int_{-\infty}^{\infty} \int_{-\infty}^{\infty} \psi_{nm}(x, y) \psi_{pq}^{*}(x, y)$$

$$\times \exp\left[i(\alpha_{pq} x + \beta_{pq} y)\right] \exp\left[-i\frac{k}{f}(ux + vy)\right] dx\, dy$$

$$\approx \sum_{n=0}^{N} \sum_{m=0}^{M} \sum_{p=0}^{N} \sum_{q=0}^{M} C_{nm} \delta_{np} \delta_{mq} \delta\left(\frac{k}{f}u - \alpha_{pq}, \frac{k}{f}v - \beta_{pq}\right)$$

$$= \sum_{n=0}^{N} \sum_{m=0}^{M} C_{nm} \delta\left(\frac{k}{f}u - \alpha_{nm}, \frac{k}{f}v - \beta_{nm}\right) \tag{10.79}$$

In Eq. (10.79), the approximate equality takes place if the values of fast oscillating integrals at $p \neq n$ and $q \neq m$ are neglected:

$$\int_{-\infty}^{\infty} \int_{-\infty}^{\infty} \psi_{nm}(x, y) \psi_{pq}^{*}(x, y) \exp\left[i\left(\alpha_{pq} - \alpha_{nm}\right)x + i\left(\beta_{pq} - \beta_{nm}\right)y\right] dx\, dy. \tag{10.80}$$

The more effective the separation of the beams propagating at different angles, the more accurate is the approximate equality in Eq. (10.79).

For enhancement of the energy efficiency of the spatial filter in Eq. (10.77), it should be purely phase. The problem of designing phase DOEs intended for expanding the light field in different diffraction orders as applied to Gauss-Hermite and Gauss-Laguerre modes, without angular harmonics, has been treated in Refs. [47,48]. For the transmission function of a generalized phase analyzer, Eq. (10.53) may be written as follows:

$$\exp[i\Omega(r, \varphi)] = \sum_{n=0}^{N} \sum_{m=0}^{M} E_{nm} \psi_{nm}^{*}(r, \varphi) \exp[ir\rho_{nm} \cos(\varphi - \theta_{nm})], \tag{10.81}$$

where (ρ_{nm}, θ_{nm}) are the vectors of carrier spatial frequencies in polar coordinates and E_{nm} are the complex coefficients whose modules are given arbitrarily and the arguments are free parameters of the task, fitted in such a manner that Eq. (10.81) will be an exact equality.

For the effective spatial separation of individual diffraction orders in the Fourier plane, it is proposed that the functions

$$\psi_{nm}^{*}(r, \varphi) \exp[ir\rho_{nm} \cos(\varphi - \theta_{nm})] \tag{10.82}$$

should be considered as being approximately orthogonal and the coefficients in Eq. (10.81) be derived from the following relation:

$$E_{nm} = \int_{0}^{\infty} \int_{0}^{2\pi} \exp[i\Omega(r, \varphi)] \psi_{nm}(r, \varphi) \exp[-ir\rho_{nm} \cos(\varphi - \theta_{nm})] r\, dr\, d\varphi. \tag{10.83}$$

The proposed algorithm for computing the phase function of the filter $\Omega(r, \varphi)$ is based on a successive computation of the sums in Eq. (10.81) and integrals in Eq. (10.83) using the fast Fourier transform algorithm and considering definite limitations. For example, in the pth iteration, the coefficients $E_{nm}^{(p)}$ are derived from Eq. (10.83) and replaced by $\overline{E}_{nm}^{(p)}$ as follows:

$$\overline{E}_{nm}^{(p)} = \begin{cases} [(1+\alpha)T_{nm} - \alpha|E_{nm}^{(p)}|]E_{nm}^{(p)}|E_{nm}^{(p)}|^{-1}, & (n,m) \in W \\ E_{nm}^{(p)}|E_{nm}^{(p)}|^{-1}, & (n,m) \notin W \end{cases}, \tag{10.84}$$

where $T_{nm} > 0$ are the pregiven numbers characterizing the response of every channel of expansion, W is a set of index pairs with nonzero values of T_{nm}, and $0 < \alpha \le 2$ is adaptive or relaxation coefficient that makes it possible to control the algorithm convergence.

The next, $(p+1)$th, estimate of the filter phase function is derived from the equation

$$\Omega_{p+1}(r, \varphi) = \arg\left\{ \sum_{n=0}^{N} \sum_{m=0}^{M} \overline{E}_{nm}^{(p)} \psi_{nm}^*(r, \varphi) \exp[ir\rho_{nm}\cos(\varphi - \theta_{nm})] \right\}. \tag{10.85}$$

Then, the function $\Omega_{p+1}(r, \varphi)$ is substituted in Eq. (10.83) to give the coefficients $E_{nm}^{(p+1)}$ in the next iteration, and so forth. Similar to Ref. [48], one can prove the relaxation property of error of such an iterative process

$$\varepsilon_L^{(p+1)} \le \varepsilon_L^{(p)}, \tag{10.86}$$

where

$$\varepsilon_L^{(p)} = \left\{ \sum_{n=0}^{\infty} \sum_{m=0}^{\infty} [T_{nm} - |E_{nm}^{(p)}|]^2 \right\}^{1/2} \left\{ \sum_{n=0}^{\infty} \sum_{m=0}^{\infty} T_{nm}^2 \right\}^{-1/2}. \tag{10.87}$$

Example 10.5   In numerical simulation, the following parameters were used for Gauss-Laguerre modes: 128 pixels along the radius r and 128 pixels along the angular component φ; the range of values of the arguments is $r \in [0, 7 \text{ mm}]$ and $\varphi \in [0, 2\pi]$, the wavelength is $\lambda = 0.63 \text{ μm}$, the focal length is $f = 100 \text{ mm}$, and the Gaussian beam waist radius is $a = 1 \text{ mm}$. In Eq. (10.81), the series terms with the numbers $n, m \le N = 7$ were considered. The operation of the DOEs designed was simulated using the numerical Fourier transform.

Shown in Figure 10.25 is the generation of nine Gauss-Laguerre modes, $(0, 0)$, $(1, 0)$, $(1, 1)$, $(2, 0)$, $(2, 1)$, $(2, 2)$, $(3, 0)$, $(3, 1)$, and $(3, 2)$ in different diffraction orders: (a) the DOE phase, the orders generated: (b) the intensity, (c) the reference intensity distribution, (d) the arrangement of the mode numbers in the diffraction orders, (e) the phase, and (f) the reference phase.

The DOEs designed may find use not only as formers of Gauss-Laguerre beams with desired mode composition but also as spatial filters capable of determining the transverse-mode composition of the beam under study.

Figure 10.26 depicts a DOE matched to the Gauss-Laguerre mode $(5, 3)$ and operating as a filter (see Fig. 10.26b). From Figure 10.26 it is seen that as the mode $(5, 3)$ (Fig. 10.26a) passes through a Fourier stage, with the corresponding filter placed at its input, an abrupt intensity "peak" is formed at the focal plane center. If, however, the filter matched to the Gauss-Laguerre mode $(5, 3)$ is illuminated by another beam, for

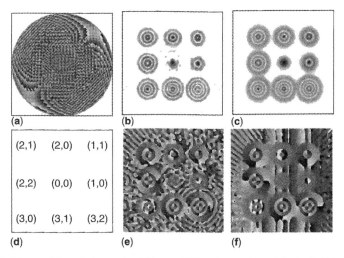

Figure 10.25. The multimode beam in different diffraction orders: (**a**) the DOE phase, (**d**) the generated mode numbers; the intensity distributions in the focal plane: (**b**) that produced with the use of the DOE, (**c**) the reference distribution; the phase distribution in the focal plane: (**e**) with the use of the DOE and (**f**) the reference phase distribution.

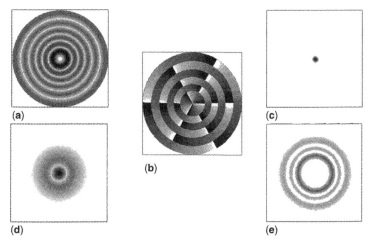

Figure 10.26. Operation of a unimode filter: intensities at the Fourier stage input corresponding to the Gauss-Laguerre modes (**a**) (5, 3); (**d**) (1, 0); (**b**) the phase of the filter matched to the (5.3) mode; the intensity at the Fourier correlator output for the mode (**c**) (5, 3); and (**e**) (1, 0).

example, the (1, 0) mode (Fig. 10.26d), a spot with the well-defined dip of intensity will be found at the center (Fig. 10.26e).

Similar patterns for the nine-mode filter are depicted in Figure 10.27. The beams composed of one mode, (2, 1), (Fig. 10.27a) and two modes, (2, 2) + (3, 1), (Fig. 10.27b,c) pass through a filter shown in Figure 10.25a (for correspondence of orders to modes, see Fig. 10.25d) and produce intensity "peaks" at the corresponding points on the focal plane (Figs. 10.27d and 10.27e,f) and spots with intensity dips at the centers of other orders. The beams shown in Figures 10.27b and 10.27c are mutually

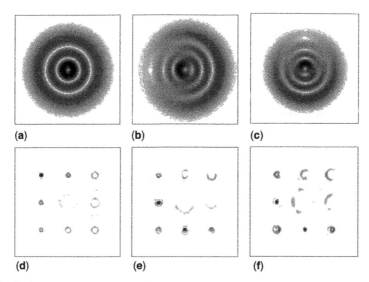

Figure 10.27. Operation of a multimode filter: the intensity at the input of a Fourier stage, corresponding to the Gauss-Laguerre beams with the numbers (**a**) (2, 1) and (**b, c**) (2, 2) + (3, 1); the intensity at the output of the Fourier stage for the beam with the modes (**d**) (2, 2) and (**e, f**) (2, 2) + (3, 1).

TABLE 10.5. Normalized Values of Intensity in Diffraction Orders

The number of the basis function	(0, 0)	(1, 0)	(1, 1)	(2, 0)	(2, 1)	(2, 2)	(3, 0)	(3, 1)	(3, 2)
The (2, 1) beam	0.002	0.001	0.039	0.046	1.000	0.066	0.042	0.025	0.003
The (2, 2) + (3, 1) beam	0.008	0.001	0.001	0.009	0.053	0.826	0.041	1.000	0.106

turned through 90 degrees. The results shown in Figures 10.27e and 10.27f corroborate that the generalized analyzers with angular harmonics are turn-invariant.

Table 10.5 gives normalized values of the intensity in each diffraction order, averaged over 5×5 central pixels of each order, which corresponds to the area of a minimal diffraction spot.

10.2.4 DOEs to Expand the Field into the Zernike Basis

Reconstructing the light field phase is one of the major problems of image processing. Being unable to directly measure the light field phase, one has to determine it indirectly by measuring the light intensity. By way of illustration, the light field wave front may be reconstructed by an interferogram [50] or by measuring the intensity distribution of spatial spectrum [51]. The Hartman-Shacke wave front sensor composed of an array of identical narrow slits or a microlens array [52] also serves to reconstruct the phase. The phase may also be reconstructed with the use of amplitude-phase filters that can expand the light field into an orthogonal basis [44,48,53,54].

In this section, wave front aberrations are analyzed using a phase spatial filter, with orthogonal circular Zernike polynomials used as a basis of the light field expansion [45]. Note that in this case, not the phase field but the complex amplitude is expanded into the Zernike basis, with the intensity generated in the spatial plane of Fourier spectrum and proportional to the field expansion coefficients. The coefficient modules measured are then used for computing the argument of the light field complex amplitude. In this section, we are also concerned with iterative algorithms for computing the Zernike filter phase and the phase of light field complex amplitude.

There is a complete set of orthogonal functions with angular harmonics in a circle of radius r_0. These are the circular Zernike polynomials [45]

$$\Psi_{nm}(r, \varphi) = A_n R_n^m(r) \exp(im\varphi), \tag{10.88}$$

where $$A_n = \sqrt{\frac{n+1}{\pi r_0^2}}, \tag{10.89}$$

$$R_n^m(r) = \sum_{p=0}^{(n-m)/2} (-1)^p (n-p)! \left[p! \left(\frac{n+m}{2} - p \right)! \left(\frac{n-m}{2} - p \right)! \right]^{-1}$$

$$\times \left(\frac{r}{r_0} \right)^{n-2p}, \tag{10.90}$$

$R_n^m(r)$ are the radial Zernike polynomials:

$$R_n^{-m}(r) = R_n^m(r), \quad |m| \le n, \quad R_n^{\pm 1}(r_0) = 1, \quad R_{2k+1}^{2l}(r) = 0, R_{2k}^{2l+1}(r) = 0,$$

$$R_0^0(r) = 1,$$

and (r, φ) are polar coordinates.

The expansion of the light field with complex amplitude $E(r, \varphi)$ into a series in terms of the functions in Eq. (10.88) is given by

$$E(r, \varphi) = \sum_{n=0}^{\infty} \sum_{m=-n}^{n} C_{nm} \Psi_{nm}(r, \varphi), \tag{10.91}$$

$$\int_0^{r_0} R_n^m(r) R_p^m(r) r \, dr = \frac{r_0^2}{2(n+1)} \delta_{np}, \tag{10.92}$$

$$C_{nm} = \int_0^{r_0} \int_0^{2\pi} E(r, \varphi) \Psi_{nm}^*(r, \varphi) r \, dr \, d\varphi. \tag{10.93}$$

In the plane of a spatial Fourier spectrum that may be generated by a spherical lens of focal length f, the light field complex amplitude $F(\rho, \theta)$ takes the form

$$F(\rho, \theta) = \frac{k}{2\pi f} \int_0^{r_0} \int_0^{2\pi} E(r, \varphi) \exp\left[-i \frac{k}{f} r\rho \cos(\varphi - \theta) \right] r \, dr \, d\varphi, \tag{10.94}$$

where $k = 2\pi/\lambda$ is the wave number of light, λ is the wavelength, and (ρ, θ) are the polar coordinates. On the basis of Eq. (10.91), the light field expansion, Eq. (10.94), in terms of the Zernike polynomials of Eq. (10.88) is given by

$$F(\rho, \theta) = \frac{k}{f} \sum_{n=0}^{\infty} \sum_{m=-n}^{n} (-i)^m C_{nm} A_{nm} e^{im\theta} \int_o^{2\pi} R_n^m(r) J_m\left(\frac{k}{f} r\rho\right) r \, dr. \qquad (10.95)$$

In deriving Eq. (10.95), we made use of the integral representation of the Bessel functions of the first kind and mth order

$$J_m(x) = \frac{i^m}{2\pi} \int_0^{2\pi} \exp[-ix\cos t + imt] \, dt.$$

The integral in Eq. (10.96) may be taken explicitly [45]

$$W_{nm}(\rho) = \int_o^{r_0} R_n^m(r) J_m\left(\frac{k}{f} r\rho\right) r \, dr = (-1)^{(n-m)/2} r_0^2 \frac{J_{n+1}(kf^{-1}r_0\rho)}{(kf^{-1}r_0\rho)}. \qquad (10.96)$$

From Eq. (10.96), one can see that at $n > 0$ the complex amplitude at central points $\rho = 0$ is equal to zero

$$W_{nm}(\rho = 0) = \begin{cases} 0, & n > 0 \\ \frac{1}{2}r_0^2, & n = 0 \end{cases}. \qquad (10.97)$$

Hence, at $n > 0$ the intensity distribution in diffraction orders of the Fourier plane will be circular in structure.

An optical configuration of the spectral Zernike analyzer to illustrate the use of a phase Zernike filter in analysis of the wave front of amplitude $E(r, \varphi)$ is shown in Figure 10.28. Similar to the Hartman-Shacke wave front sensor [52], the Zernike filter is mounted directly on the plane of the wave front to be studied, with a spherical lens L of focal length f placed immediately behind it. A photo-receiver array matched to the computer PC is placed in the rear focal plane of the lens L.

For the transmission function of the ZF to be phase-only

$$\tau(r, \varphi) = \exp[iS(r, \varphi)] \qquad (10.98)$$

it should be sought for in the form

$$\tau(r, \varphi) = \sum_{n=0}^{N} \sum_{m=-n}^{n} \Psi_{nm}^*(r, \varphi) \exp\left[ikf^{-1}r\rho_{nm}\cos(\varphi - \theta_{nm}) + v_{nm}\right], \qquad (10.99)$$

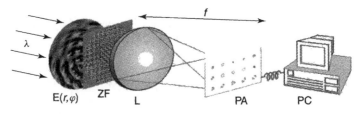

Figure 10.28. Optical configuration of the Zernike analyzer: ZF is the Zernike filter, L is a spherical lens, PA is a photo-receiver array, and PC is a computer.

where $(\rho_{nm}, \varphi_{nm})$ are the vectors of the carrier spatial frequencies in polar coordinates and v_{nm} are the free parameters of the task to be fitted in such a manner as to make Eq. (10.99) an exact equality. Once the light intensity proportional to the squared modulus of the expansion coefficients in Eq. (10.91)

$$I_{nm} = |C_{nm}|^2 \tag{10.100}$$

has been measured at discrete points of the Fourier plane (see Fig. 10.28), one must perform additional computation to find the light field phase from Eq. (10.91)

$$Q(r, \varphi) = \arg E(r, \varphi). \tag{10.101}$$

To do this, one may use an algorithm similar to the algorithm of Eqs. (10.93) and (10.94) and find the phase estimate of light field in the $(k+1)$th iteration in the form

$$Q_{k+1}(r, \varphi) = \arg \left\{ \sum_{n=0}^{N} \sum_{m=-n}^{n} \sqrt{I_{nm}} \Psi_{nm}(r, \varphi) \exp[i v_{nm}^{(k)}] \right\}, \tag{10.102}$$

where $v_{nm}^{(k)}$ are the free parameters in the kth iteration derived from the equation

$$v_{nm}^{(k)} = \arg \left\{ \int_0^{r_0} \int_0^{2\pi} \exp[i Q_k(r, \varphi)] \Psi_{nm}^*(r, \varphi) r \, dr \, d\varphi \right\}, \tag{10.103}$$

where $Q_k(r, \varphi)$ is the sought-for phase estimate in the kth iteration.

Because the wave front aberrations met within optical systems are described by even functions relative to the azimuth angle φ [45], the wave field $E(r, \varphi)$ may be written as

$$E(r, \varphi) = \exp \left\{ i \sum_{n=0}^{N} \sum_{m=-n}^{n} B_{nm} R_n^m(r) \cos(m\varphi) \right\}. \tag{10.104}$$

In this connection, instead of the general expansion in Eq. (10.100), one should use the expansion in terms of the even functions

$$E(r, \varphi) = \sum_{n=0}^{\infty} \sum_{m=-n}^{n} C_{nm} \overline{\Psi}_{nm}(r, \varphi), \tag{10.105}$$

$$\overline{\Psi}_{nm}(r, \varphi) = \varepsilon_m \sqrt{\frac{n+1}{\pi r_0^2}} R_n^m(r) \cos(m\varphi), \tag{10.106}$$

where $\varepsilon_m = \{2, \quad m \neq 0; \quad 1, \quad m = 0\}$.

For small aberrations, the relation between the expansion coefficients B_{nm} and C_{nm} is linear

$$1 + i B_{00} = \frac{C_{00}}{\sqrt{\pi r_0^2}}, \quad i B_{nm} = \varepsilon_m \frac{C_{nm}}{\sqrt{\pi r_0^2}}. \tag{10.107}$$

For arbitrary aberrations, the relation between B_{nm} and C_{nm} is nonlinear, and on measuring the modules $|C_{nm}|^2$, one has to use the algorithm of Eqs. (10.102) and (10.103) to derive the phase $Q(r, \varphi)$ of Eq. (10.101). Then, using Eq. (10.104), one derives the wave aberration coefficients, B_{mn}.

Note that because $R_0^0(r) = 1$, the Zernike polynomial basis contains the unit as an expansion term; this means that when illuminated by a plane wave of amplitude $E(r, \varphi) = $ const, the Zernike filter yields only one nonzero coefficient of the expansion in Eq. (10.91):

$$|C_{00}|^2 \neq 0.$$

From Eq. (10.96) it also follows that the diffraction orders corresponding to the basis functions with different numbers m, but with the same numbers n, will have similar diffraction patterns (circular structures at $n > 0$) in the Fourier plane

$$|W_{nm}(\rho)| = r_0^2 \frac{|J_{n+1}(kf^{-1}r_0\rho)|}{(kf^{-1}r_0\rho)}. \tag{10.108}$$

Example 10.6   The simulation parameters were as follows: 256 pixels on the radius r and 256 pixels on the angle φ, $r_0 = 1$ mm, $k = 10^4$ mm^{-1}, $f = 100$ mm. We designed a 25-channel filter [55] that generates diffraction orders for the basis functions with the numbers (n, m): $m \leq 8$ and $n \leq 8$, propagated at some angles to the optical axis.

Figure 10.29 depicts: (a) the halftone Zernike filter phase (black color corresponds to the phase value of 0 and white to 2π), (b) 25 diffraction orders generated in the lens's frequency plane (negative), and (c) the correspondence between the numbers (n, m) and diffraction orders.

The filter is assumed to be illuminated by a plane wave. In this case, the analyzer "splits" the incident beam into 25 beams of approximately the same energy. Eighty percent of the total illuminating beam energy is accounted for by these diffraction orders. From Figure 10.29b, the intensity is seen to be zero at all central points of the Fourier plane except for the zero order, (0, 0), implying that the illuminating wave front is aberration-free.

Figure 10.30 depicts the result of operation of the same 25-channel Zernike filter illuminated by the beam composed of three basis Zernike functions with the same

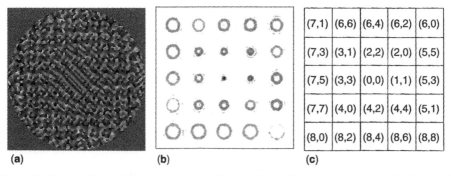

(7,1)	(6,6)	(6,4)	(6,2)	(6,0)
(7,3)	(3,1)	(2,2)	(2,0)	(5,5)
(7,5)	(3,3)	(0,0)	(1,1)	(5,3)
(7,7)	(4,0)	(4,2)	(4,4)	(5,1)
(8,0)	(8,2)	(8,4)	(8,6)	(8,8)

(a)   (b)   (c)

Figure 10.29. (a) The halftone phase of the Zernike filter, (b) the intensity distribution in the len's focal plane, and (c) the correspondence between the numbers (n, m) and diffraction orders.

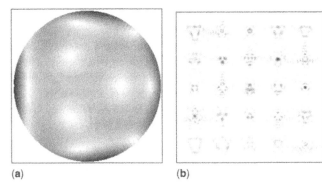

(a)   (b)

Figure 10.30. Operation of the Zernike filter (see Fig. 10.29a): (a) the illuminating beam intensity and (b) the diffraction pattern in the Fourier plane.

weights and numbers, (n, m): $(2, 0) + (5, 3) + (7, 7)$. Shown in Figure 10.30 are: (a) the illuminating beam intensity and (b) the diffraction pattern in the Fourier plane.

When compared with the distribution of mode numbers between the orders (Fig. 10.29c), Figure 10.30b suggests that the intensity is nonzero (black spots in Fig. 10.30b) at the central points of the diffraction orders with the numbers (2, 0), (5, 3), and (7, 7). Table 10.5 gives the corresponding averaged values in the vicinity of the central points for all orders (the vicinity size is 3×3 pixels).

One can see from Table 10.6 that the coefficients with the same weights in the input beam of the Zernike analyzer possess different weights at the output

$$|C_{20}|^2 = 0{,}977, \quad |C_{53}|^2 = 1{,}000, \quad |C_{77}|^2 = 0{,}683.$$

In addition, the intensity in the other orders is not zero. This is due to the fact that in an effort to obtain a pure-phase filter in Eqs. (10.98) and (10.99), the amplitude is replaced by a constant value. Thus, the squared modules of coefficients at the Zernike analyzer output are seen to have been measured with a relative error of 20 percent. There are two ways for reducing the error: a more accurate computation of the Zernike

TABLE 10.6. Averaged Intensity Values in the Vicinity of Central Points for the Fourier Plane Orders. The Zernike Filter (Fig. 10.29a) Is Illuminated by a Beam Composed of Three Modes: (2, 0) + (5, 3) + (7, 7)

(7, 1)		(6, 6)		(6, 4)		(6, 2)		(6, 0)	
	0.011		0.028		0.005		0.006		0.035
(7, 3)		(3, 1)		(2, 2)		(2, 0)		(5, 5)	
	0.103		0.013		0.018		0.977		0.008
(7, 5)		(3, 3)		(0, 0)		(1, 1)		(5, 3)	
	0.004		0.007		0.059		0.003		1.000
(7, 7)		(4, 0)		(4, 2)		(4, 4)		(5, 1)	
	0.683		0.056		0.000		0.001		0.001
(8, 0)		(8, 2)		(8, 4)		(8, 6)		(8, 8)	
	0.004		0.014		0.018		0.006		0.026

filter phase and the reduction of the vicinity (3×3 pixels) of the diffraction order centers in which the coefficient modules are measured.

If, in image recognition, it suffices to compute the modules of the coefficients expanded in some orthogonal basis, this procedure is insufficient when reconstructing the light field complex amplitude. The unique reconstruction of the light field also requires the knowledge of the phase of the expansion coefficients.

We can reconstruct the coefficient phases, if, to the filter in Eq. (10.99), some linear combination of neighboring basis functions is added [54]:

$$s_{nm}(r, \varphi) = \{\Psi^*_{nm}(r, \varphi) + \Psi^*_{n'm'}(r, \varphi)\} \exp[ikf^{-1}r\rho'_{nm}\cos(\varphi - \theta'_{nm}) + v'_{nm}],$$

$$p_{nm}(r, \varphi) = \{\Psi^*_{nm}(r, \varphi) + i\Psi^*_{n'm'}(r, \varphi)\} \exp[ikf^{-1}r\rho''_{nm}\cos(\varphi - \theta''_{nm}) + v''_{nm}].$$

$$(10.109)$$

In this case, the light intensity in the additional channels corresponding to the Fourier spectrum points with spatial frequencies $(\rho'_{nm}, \theta'_{nm})$ and $(\rho''_{nm}, \theta''_{nm})$ are as follows:

$$S_{nm} = |C_{nm}|^2 + |C_{n'm'}|^2 + 2|C_{nm}||C_{n'm'}|\cos(\phi_{n'm'} - \phi_{nm}),$$

$$P_{nm} = |C_{nm}|^2 + |C_{n'm'}|^2 + 2|C_{nm}||C_{n'm'}|\sin(\phi_{n'm'} - \phi_{nm}), \qquad (10.110)$$

thus allowing the derivation of the phases ϕ_{nm}, for example, assuming $\phi_{00} = 0$. The recursive relationship for the sought-for phases may be written in the form

$$\phi_{n'm'} - \phi_{nm} = \tan^{-1}\left(\frac{P_{nm} - I_{nm} - I_{n'm'}}{S_{nm} - I_{nm} - I_{n'm'}}\right). \qquad (10.111)$$

Thus, the optical method under consideration makes it possible to find the complex coefficients of the light field expansion in terms of an orthogonal basis and to reconstruct this field.

Example 10.7 We designed a 25-channel Zernike filter that can generate modes in different diffraction orders with the numbers (n, m): $n \leq 4$ and $m \leq 4$ (nine modes altogether) and their linear combination ($8 + 8$ altogether).

Figure 10.31 depicts (a) the halftone amplitude and (b) the phase of the Zernike filter, and (c) the distribution of modes with the numbers (n, m) and their linear combinations between the orders.

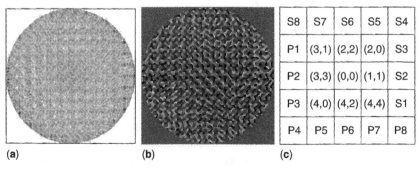

S8	S7	S6	S5	S4
P1	(3,1)	(2,2)	(2,0)	S3
P2	(3,3)	(0,0)	(1,1)	S2
P3	(4,0)	(4,2)	(4,4)	S1
P4	P5	P6	P7	P8

(a)   (b)   (c)

Figure 10.31. (a) The halftone amplitude and (b) phase of the Zernike filter, and (c) the distribution of modes numbered (n, m) and their linear combinations between the orders.

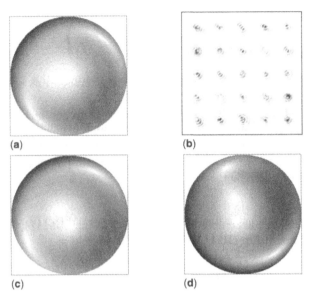

Figure 10.32. (a) The intensity of the beam under analysis, (b) the diffraction pattern in the Fourier plane produced by a pure-phase Zernike filter shown in Figure 10.31a,b, (c) the light field reconstructed by an amplitude-phase filter, and (d) the light field reconstructed by the pure-phase filter.

Figure 10.32 depicts how such a 25-channel Zernike filter operates when illuminated by a beam composed of three modes with the coefficients C_{nm}: $C_{11} = \exp(i0)$, $C_{33} = \exp(i\pi/2)$, and $C_{42} = \exp(i\pi)$. Shown in Figure 10.32 are (a) the intensity of the beam under analysis, (b) the diffraction pattern in the Fourier plane for a phase-only filter, (c) the light field reconstructed by a phase-amplitude filter, and (d) the light field reconstructed by the phase-only filter.

The example suggests that in image recognition, when it will suffice to measure the modules of expansion coefficients, a phase-only filter may be used to advantage (the error in measuring the modules of the expansion coefficients is less than nine percent). At the same time, reconstructing the full information about the light field also requires the knowledge of the phase of the expansion coefficients. In this case, an amplitude-phase filter should be used.

10.3 OPTICAL CONSTRUCTION OF THE DIRECTION FIELD AND SPATIAL FREQUENCY FIELD

The direction field is defined [56] as a geometric interpretation of a set of linear elements corresponding to an ordinary differential equation, which takes the following form for two variables [57]:

$$\frac{dy}{dx} = f(x, y). \tag{10.112}$$

The linear element is a set of numbers x, y, and $f(x, y)$ that may be represented as a set of coordinates of the point $(x, y) \in G \subset \mathbf{R}^2$ and a corresponding direction with direction cosines

$$\left(\frac{1}{\sqrt{1 + f^2(x, y)}}, \frac{f(x, y)}{\sqrt{1 + f^2(x, y)}} \right),$$

which is specified by a small-length segment passing through this point in parallel to the vector $[1, f(x, y)]$.

The direction field can be computed for well-defined contour images. Let us consider in the image plane an arbitrary light intensity distribution function $I(x, y)$, which is considered as being smooth, that is having continuous partial derivatives of the first order. Consider a set of curves on the plane (x, y), corresponding to constant values of the image intensity function

$$I(x, y) = I_0. \tag{10.113}$$

It can easily be seen that according to the definition in Eq. (10.112), the set of tangent direction to the lines in Eq. (10.113) form a direction field at

$$f(x, y) = -\frac{\partial I(x, y)/\partial x}{\partial I(x, y)/\partial y}.$$

Thus, the classical definition of the direction field leads to the function $\hat{\varphi}(x, y)$, which has the physical meaning of the angle of inclination of the tangent to the line of constant values of the image intensity function and is given by

$$\operatorname{tg} \hat{\varphi}(x, y) = -\frac{\partial I(x, y)/\partial x}{\partial I(x, y)/\partial y}, \quad 0 \le \hat{\varphi}(x, y) < \pi. \tag{10.114}$$

The formula for computing the direction field in Eq. (10.114) may be directly applied to the class of structurally abundant images [57], with the intensity function sufficiently smooth and, thus, allowing differentiation. Such an image class is represented, in particular, by interferograms for which the intuitive notion of the direction field is related to the direction of interference fringes and coincides with the definition in Eq. (10.114).

In an arbitrary, fairly small local domain (see the window in Fig. 10.33), the intensity function for such images may be described by the harmonic function

$$I(x, y) = A \cos[\omega_x x + \omega_y y] + B, \tag{10.115}$$

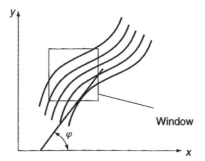

Figure 10.33. The angle of line inclination on a contour image.

where $\omega_x = 2\pi/T_x$, and $\omega_y = 2\pi/T_y$ are the local spatial frequencies, and T_x and T_y are the fringe periods of the contour image.

For the first time, the idea of optical computation of the direction field was suggested in Ref. [34]. If in some local domain Ω, the intensity function specified by

$$q(x, y) = \begin{cases} 1, & (x, y) \in \Omega, \\ 0, & (x, y) \notin \Omega, \end{cases}$$

can be approximated by a cosine grating of Eq. (10.115), it can be written in the form of two exponents

$$\cos(\omega_x x + \omega_y y) = \tfrac{1}{2}\{\exp[i(\omega_x x + \omega_y y)] + \exp[-i(\omega_x x + \omega_y y)]\}.$$

Then, the Fourier transform of the intensity function takes the form

$$A\cos(\omega_x x + \omega_y y) + B \xrightarrow{\ \Im\ } \frac{A}{2}[\delta(\xi - \omega_x, \eta - \omega_y) + \delta(\xi + \omega_x, \eta + \omega_y)] + B\delta(\xi, \eta),$$

$$(10.116)$$

where (x, y) and (ξ, η) are the Cartesian coordinates in the input and frequency planes, $\Im$ is a 2D Fourier transform, and $\delta(x, y)$ is the Dirac function.

Thus, the grating produces a δ-impulse at the center of the Fourier plane and two δ-impulses located symmetrically on the line that passes through the Fourier plane center at an angle of θ to the x-axis

$$\mathrm{tg}\,\theta = -\frac{\omega_y}{\omega_x}.$$

Then, the angle θ and the angle φ of the carrier direction (see Fig. 10.33) are related as follows:

$$\theta = \widehat{\varphi} + \frac{\pi}{2},$$

that is, the angle θ is orthogonal to the angle of inclination φ of the grating grooves.

If the grating is limited by a certain domain $q(x, y)$ in the frequency plane, we obtain the convolution of the Fourier image of a function $Q(\xi, \eta)$ describing this domain with the δ-impulses.

The convolution of the δ-function with any function is known to produce the same function with a corresponding shift

$$\delta(\xi - \omega_x, \eta - \omega_y) \otimes Q(\xi, \eta) \xrightarrow{\ \Im\ } q(-x, -y), \qquad (10.117)$$

which means that in the output plane the intensity will be nonzero only in a domain corresponding to the grating with groove inclination angle φ.

Note that this effect will take place irrespective of the frequency of the grooves, for the δ-functions found on the same ray (nearer to, or farther from the center) will correspond to them. Hence, while "cutting out" a segment along the $\theta = \mathrm{mod}_\pi(\widehat{\varphi} + \pi/2)$ direction, the spectra of all the gratings having the groove direction of φ are "caught," irrespective of the groove frequency and the limiting domains.

By rotating the slot (see Fig. 10.34a) and "cutting out" the segments in the upper part of the Fourier plane, one may scan all line direction found in the image in the range $[0, \pi)$. The existence of a mechanically moving part (the rotating slot) makes the realization of the method more difficult and increases the time it takes to generate

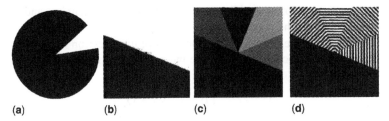

Figure 10.34. Spatial filters used in optically computing the direction field.

the direction field. It is expedient to exclude the moving element, as it has been proposed in Ref. [58]. For this purpose, two spatial filters are alternatively introduced into the setup and simple computation is performed:

1. An amplitude filter is placed in the Fourier plane, as shown in Figure 10.34c, with the transmission function $t(\varphi)$ given by

$$
t(\varphi) = \begin{cases} \sum\limits_{l=0}^{N-1} \psi_k \left(\widehat{\varphi} + \dfrac{\pi}{2N} - \dfrac{\pi}{N} l \right) \sqrt{\left[\dfrac{1}{2} + \text{sign}\left(l - \dfrac{N-1}{2} \right) \dfrac{l}{N} \right]}, \\ \qquad -\dfrac{\pi}{2N} < \widehat{\varphi} < \pi - \dfrac{\pi}{2N}, \\ 0, \quad \pi - \dfrac{\pi}{2N} < \widehat{\varphi} < 2\pi - \dfrac{\pi}{2N} \end{cases} \tag{10.118}
$$

where

$$
\psi_k(x) = \begin{cases} 1, & x \in [0, 1) \\ 0, & x \notin [0, 1) \end{cases},
$$

where φ is the polar angle in the polar coordinate system (ρ, φ) in the frequency plane

$$
\begin{cases} \xi = \rho \cos \widehat{\varphi} \\ \eta = \rho \sin \widehat{\varphi} \end{cases}, \tag{10.119}
$$

and N is the number of the direction extracted. Then, the lens is used to take another Fourier transform, with the output intensity distribution fed into the computer as a number array by a TV camera.

2. An amplitude filter is placed in the Fourier plane, as shown in Figure 10.34b, with the transmission function given by

$$
t(\widehat{\varphi}) = \begin{cases} 1, & -\dfrac{\pi}{2N} < \widehat{\varphi} < \pi - \dfrac{\pi}{2N} \\ 0, & \pi - \dfrac{\pi}{2N} < \widehat{\varphi} < 2\pi - \dfrac{\pi}{2N} \end{cases}, \tag{10.120}
$$

The Fourier transform is again taken and the output intensity to be stored in the computer as a number array.

3. The output intensity produced by the former filter is point by point divided by the intensity produced by the latter filter, the result of the division being the direction field approximation.

The presence of the division procedure in the method imposes strict requirements on the alignment of the optical system when conducting the real experiment, thus making the method poorly suitable for practical applications.

A method for constructing the direction field with the use of a spatial filter composed of binary diffraction gratings has been proposed in Ref. [59] and consists of the following.

In the frequency plane of the unit, there is an optical filter represented by a set of amplitude or phase sector diffraction gratings (Fig. 10.34d). If this is the set of amplitude diffraction gratings, its transmission function is given by

$$t(\rho, \widehat{\varphi}) = \sum_{i=0}^{N-1} \psi_k \left(\widehat{\varphi} + \frac{\pi}{2N} - \frac{\pi}{N}i \right) \sum_{n=0}^{M} \psi_k \left[2\frac{\rho \cos \left(\widehat{\varphi} - \frac{\pi}{N}i \right)}{T} - nT \right]. \quad (10.121)$$

If this is the set of phase gratings, the transmission function is

$$t(\rho, \widehat{\varphi}) = \exp \left[j \sum_{i=0}^{N-1} \psi_k \left(\widehat{\varphi} + \frac{\pi}{2N} - \frac{\pi}{N}i \right) \sum_{n=0}^{M} \psi_k \left(2\frac{\rho \cos \left(\widehat{\varphi} - \frac{\pi}{N}i \right)}{T} - nT \right) \right].$$
$$(10.122)$$

In the output plane of the Fourier correlator with such a filter, one gets in the -1st and $+1$st diffraction orders a set of images (Fig. 10.57) equal in number to the doubled number of direction. In the subsequent text, these will be referred to as *partial images*. In each of these partial images, the nonzero intensity should have been found only in those areas of the partial images where the lines of contour image had a proper direction. But because alongside the major fringes the image contains noise, the nonzero intensity is found on the entire area of the partial image. The partial images are entered into the computer by a TV camera as a number array of size 512×512 and taking values from 0 to 255. In order to select the partial images in the array, one should first detect their position. For this purpose, a point diaphragm is placed in the input plane of the Fourier correlator and a set of light spots is registered in the output plane, with their coordinates corresponding to the coordinates of the centers of the partial images. The size of the partial images is known and determined by

$$S_c = \frac{f_2}{f_1} S, \quad (10.123)$$

where S_c is the partial image size, S is the size of the initial input contour image, f_1 is the focal length of the first arm of the Fourier correlator, and f_2 is the focal length of the second arm of the Fourier correlator. The coordinates of the point in the general array are (i, j), and the coordinates of the point in the kth partial array are (i'_k, j'_k). They are connected by the relations

$$i'_k = i - I_k + \frac{S_c}{2\Delta l}, \quad (10.124)$$

$$j'_k = j - J_k + \frac{S_c}{2\Delta l}, \quad (10.125)$$

where (I_k, J_k) are the coordinates of the center of the kth partial image and Δl is the size of a minimal sensor of the TV camera.

The partial image is then computer-processed. In order to select unidirectional zones in the partial images, a binarization procedure is conducted. Every partial image is point by point compared with the others, and if the intensity at a given point of the partial image is maximal as compared with the intensities of the corresponding points of the other partial images, the intensity is taken to be equal to 1 at the given point of this partial image; otherwise the intensity value is assumed to be equal to 0. The direction field is formed from the set of partial images through an ordinary summation followed by the multiplication by a coefficient equal to the corresponding value of the angle of inclination of the grating sector. It is the method that we study further in this section. Optical methods for generating the direction fields give some error, which may vary widely with varying parameters of an optical setup. In particular, the direction field quality is affected by the number of direction selected, the grating period to the initial image width ratio, and the quality of the diffraction grating grooves. A number of computer simulations were aimed at elucidating the effects the aforesaid factors have on the accuracy of the direction field construction and also at determining optimal parameters of the optical setup. A set of 10 test images were used in the experiments, with two of them allowing the analytical computation of the direction fields (Fig. 10.35b,d) depicted in Figure 10.35a,c. The groove period on the test images was varied from 1/50th to 1/10th of the image size. Such a selection of the images was due to practical considerations of the direction field application to fingerprint identification. It is this range in which the periods of fingerprints are found. The images were recorded as number arrays of size 512×512 with 256 quantization levels. Then, the direction fields were determined by numerical simulation of the optical setup operation and compared with the fields derived analytically. The Fourier image of the initial image was taken using an algorithm of fast Fourier transform (FFT) and then multiplied by the transmission function of the spatial phase filter in Eq. (10.113) that was recorded as a numerical binary array of size 512×512. Then, using the FFT, a second Fourier transform was taken, with the result recorded as a number array of size 512×512 with 256 quantization levels. Further, following the devised technique, the partial images were selected and the direction field was generated. As the estimate

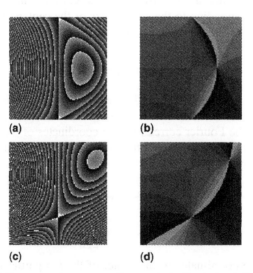

(a)   (b)

(c)   (d)

Figure 10.35. Images and corresponding analytically derived direction fields.

criterion, we used the value of the rms deviation of numerically simulated direction fields from those derived analytically. Let this value be denoted by the letter ε.

According to Ref. [60], ε is given by

$$\varepsilon = \sqrt{\frac{2}{n^2} \sum_{i,j=1}^{n} \sin^2 \frac{\hat{\varphi}_{ij} - \hat{\varphi}_{ij}^a}{2}} \tag{10.126}$$

where n is the dimension of the data array in which the direction field is recorded, φ_{ij} is the direction at point (i, j) derived optically, and φ_{ij}^a is the direction at point (i, j) derived analytically.

In the experiment, the number of sectors in the filter shown in Figure 10.34c was varied from 2 to 16, with the direction field computed with every filter for 10 test images. The direction fields constructed with selection of 2, 4, 8, and 16 direction for the image shown in Figure 10.35a are depicted in Figure 10.36a–d.

The plot for the error ε of direction field computation versus the number n of the direction selected is shown in Figure 10.37.

From Figure 10.37, it is seen that there is a minimum of the computation error at $n = 7-8$. With increasing n, the rms deviation at first decreases as a result of increasing number of the direction selected, but then, because of the fact that still narrower sectors are cut in the spectrum, the shape of local unidirectional domains becomes more and more distorted, and ε increases owing to the influence of diffraction grating's junctions.

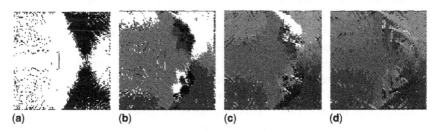

(a)   (b)   (c)   (d)

Figure 10.36. The direction fields constructed the image in Figure 10.35a in the course of computer simulation with the selection of (**a**) 2, (**b**) 4, (**c**) 8, and (**d**) 16 direction.

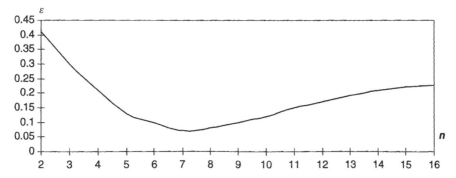

Figure 10.37. The error ε versus the number n of the direction selected.

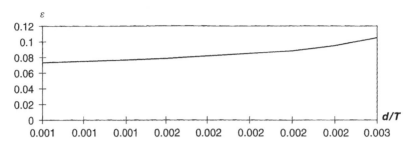

Figure 10.38. The error ε of direction field versus the ratio of the diffraction grating period d to the contour image spatial spectrum width T.

In the experiment, the diffraction grating period of the filter in Figure 10.34c was varied and the direction field from 10 test images was computed for every filter version. The error ε of the direction field computation versus the ratio of the spatial filter grating period d to the image spatial spectrum width T is shown in Figure 10.38. In this case, by the spatial spectrum is meant the minimal diameter of a circle centered at the system optical axis that fully covers the domains in the frequency plane with nonzero intensity. Because we used the image quantized in 256 levels in the experiment, the condition of nonzero intensity was replaced by the condition that the intensity should be in excess of 1/256th of the maximal spectrum intensity.

It can be seen that the smaller is the ratio d/T the smaller will be the error of determination of the direction field for the discussed computational technique. Certainly, there is a limitation on the decrease of the diffraction grating period caused by quantization and sampling effects appearing in the course of spatial filter synthesis, which have not yet undergone experimental studies. Another limitation on a further decrease in the diffraction grating period arises from restricted technological opportunities, whereas the expansion of the spectrum is limited by the geometric dimension of the optical setup. As a result, in a real optical setup one should choose the d/T ratio on the basis of the feasibilities of technical realization within the range from 0.0015 to 0.003.

The accuracy of the direction field computation by optical means may vary widely not only with varying parameters of the optical setup but also with varying parameters of the image itself. In particular, the quality of the direction field is affected by the signal-to-noise ratio, and also the ratio of the groove period in the image to the zone-size for a single direction. In a number of experiments, we revealed a set of images for which the direction field may be determined optically and, thus, derived the range of varying the parameters of the images to be processed.

In describing the initial image, the approximation in Eq. (10.124) was used. But most real contour images have considerable deviations from this approximation as a result of noise effects. Ten test images were chosen as initial. Each of the 10 test images was noised, with the signal-to-noise (SNR) ratio varying in the range from 11 to 1. Then, we determined the error of optical generation of the direction field in noised images. The images with SNR of 10, 2, and 1, respectively, are shown in Figure 10.39a,c,e, and their direction fields are depicted in Figure 10.39b,d,f.

From Figure 10.39, the noise is seen to weakly affect the direction field structure. The noise was generated using a pseudo-random number generator.

Because the error is likely to change not only with changing SNR but also with varying, that is, number of the direction selected in the image, we studied the stability

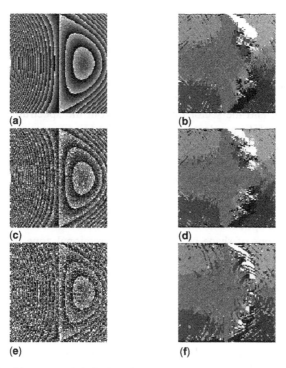

Figure 10.39. Noised images and their direction fields constructed with the selection of 8 direction: (**a**) the image with SNR = 10, (**b**) its direction field, (**c**) the image with SNR = 2, (**d**) its direction field, (**e**) the image with SNR = 1, and (**f**) its direction field.

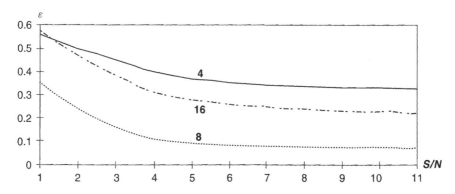

Figure 10.40. The plots of the error of direction field determination versus SNR for $n = 4, 8, 16$.

of the method to noise for a varying number of the direction selected from 2 to 16. The plots of the error of direction field computation versus SNR for $n = 4, 8, 16$ are shown in Figure 10.40.

From Figure 10.40, one can see that for SNR > 4, the rms deviation of the direction field is practically constant at fixed n and is almost not increased as compared with the rms deviation of the direction field in the noise-free image. At SNR < 4, the rms deviation begins to sharply increase and, on the average, for the given set of test images, achieves the value of 0.35 at SNR = 1 (at $n = 8$).

Obviously, the error of the direction field computation should increase with increasing period of fringes and decreasing size of unidirectional zones. The reason is the "spreading" of the Fourier spectrum of the unidirectional image zone, so that the spectrum falls simultaneously in several angular sectors. To illustrate this property, let us conduct a simple experiment. An image represented by a set of horizontal stripes bounded by a square is shown in Figure 10.41a. The result of the Fourier transform taken of this image and the sector that is "cut" from the spectrum in the method for selecting 4 direction [59] are depicted in Figure 10.41b.

It can be seen that not the entire spectrum falls to the sector, the result being the emergence in the direction field (Fig. 10.41c) of differently directed lines. Obviously, the lesser the size of the unidirectional zone, the wider is the spectrum, and the greater is its portion that does not fall into the sector, and the greater are the distortions in the direction field. Also, if the image line period is increased, the spectrum will be located nearer to the optical axis and its smaller portion will fall in the same sector. As a result, the distortions of shape of the local unidirectional zone in the direction field will be increased. By the unidirectional zone, we imply here an image domain in which the direction of lines lies in the interval $\hat{\varphi} \in (\hat{\varphi}_i - \pi/2n, \hat{\varphi}_i + \pi/2n)$, where $\hat{\varphi}_i$ is the selected direction and n is the number of the direction selected. As the characteristic parameter that determines the accuracy of the direction field computation we take the ratio of the line period to the size of the local unidirectional zone and denote it by the letter Q in the subsequent text.

One of 10 test images for which we determined how the error ε depends on the ratio Q, is shown in Figure 10.42. Both in numerical simulation and in the real experiment

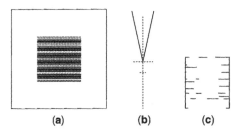

(a)   (b)   (c)

Figure 10.41. (**a**) Contour image, (**b**) the result of sector segmentation of its spatial spectrum, and (**c**) the direction field.

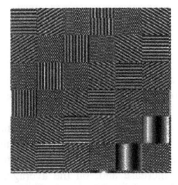

Figure 10.42. An example of the test image.

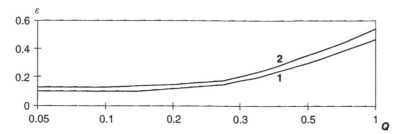

Figure 10.43. The rms deviation of the direction field resulted from the computer simulation (curve 1) and from the real experiment (curve 2) versus the ratio of the line period to the unimodal zone-size.

we selected 4 direction. For each unidirectional zone, the error ε was determined separately.

Figure 10.43 depicts the plot of the error ε as a function of Q. Curve 1 corresponds to the numerical simulation and curve 2 corresponds to the real experiment. In the real experiment, the test images were printed out on a transparent film using a laser printer. Using an optical setup that is comprehensively described in Section 10.3.1, the direction field was constructed for each image.

From the plot it can be seen that for the error of the direction field determination to be less than 10 percent, the value of Q should not exceed 0.2. Minor distinctions between the simulated and the real plot of the ε are due to technical errors of the real experiment: inaccurate alignment and small defocusing of the partial images and inaccurate fabrication of the diffraction gratings.

10.3.1 Optical Fingerprint Identification

Digital methods for fingerprint identification [61] take considerable time for computation. While shortening the time, the use of optical preprocessing allows one to attain a high degree of compression of the information-to-be and then process it digitally.

The familiar optical-digital systems [62–68] for fingerprint identification are based on either the correlation analysis or the spatial spectrum analysis. By way of illustrations, Ref. [62] is concerned with two variants (coherent and noncoherent) of an optical-digital system for fingerprint identification based on the optical construction of the fingerprint Fourier spectrum and its registration using a circular segment photoreceiver. As a result, instead of the fingerprint image pixels matrix, the computer memorizes a 64-component features vector (the photo-receiver is divided into 64 angular and 32 semicircular segments).

There are hybrid optical-digital devices in which contour image recognition is built upon the optical implementation of the Hough-Radon [69,70] transform or upon a cooperative correlation of two images with the use of photo-refractive crystals [71]. In some available systems, fingerprints are entered into computer in the real time using a prism operated in the mode of total internal reflection [71–73]. Fast optical input of fingerprints into the computer memory and optical image preprocessing essentially speed up the recognition process, thus providing the advantage of hybrid systems over the digital ones.

However, the available hybrid fingerprint identification systems are not free from disadvantages. Hence, the method that analyzes fingerprints using the Fourier spectrum will interpret images differing in the permutation of fragments as being identical. Note, in addition, that fingerprints belong to the class of structurally redundant images, because they are composed of a set of lines with a characteristic period of 0.5 to 0.7 mm. The spatial spectrum of such images is, for the most part, found in a narrow range of frequencies in the vicinity of the carrier spatial frequency. It is the carrier frequency that is perceived by the eye as a set of contour lines and constitutes the main factor of the structural redundancy of a fingerprint. In this connection, 32 semicircular photo-receivers placed in the Fourier spectrum to measure the light radial intensity distribution [62] are excessive in terms of information.

Analysis and classification of fingerprint fringes' structure using a neuron network that can extract straight-line segments in the image using the Radon transform [70] or through the determination of the Halton number (the number of fingerprint bifurcations and fringe centers) [69] are too time-consuming. This is due to the presence of high spatial frequency in the fingerprint, which hampers element-by-element image processing. A method for constructing the direction field of structurally redundant images using optical techniques has been proposed in Ref. [74] and allows one to effectively compress information contained in the images with carrier spatial frequency. With this method, the image fragment is practically replaced by a number defined as an average angle of line inclination in this fragment. A numerical simulation of fingerprint identification (for 10 different fingers) using the direction field algorithm (with 8 direction selected) has been discussed in Ref. [76] and showed highly reliable identification compared with the Fourier spectrum method [62].

Consider several variants of the optical-digital fingerprint identification technique using the direction field, which were computer-simulated in [76] and aimed at revealing the most effective technique, which was then implemented on a phototype model of the experimental setup.

In the first method, the direction field is constructed using the simulated optical setup shown in Figure 10.44a, where L is a laser, K is a collimator, LA and LB are spherical lenses, and TV is a TV camera.

A fingerprint on the glass is placed at the input of a Fourier correlator (Fig. 10.44a) in whose frequency plane is a spatial filter DF, performed as an amplitude transparency

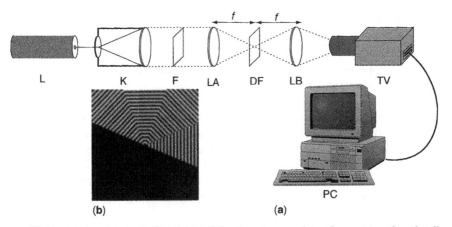

Figure 10.44. (a) An optical configuration of the Fourier correlator for constructing the direction field using (b) a spatial filter composed of sectored amplitude diffraction gratings.

composed of binary diffraction gratings dividing 180 degrees into 8 sectors, whereas the other part of the filter is opaque (Fig. 10.44b). At the correlator's output one registers a set of images, each of which is different from the initial (input image) by having only a portion of spectrum passed through the corresponding sector. Because each segment of the filter DF is a binary-amplitude diffraction grating, each sector produces a pair of symmetric images, which means that among 16 images generated, there are only 8 that are nonrecurring. These 8 images are then superimposed by computer to produce a single image, while the weight of each subimage corresponds to the sector and is equal to the angle of inclination of lines in the fingerprint image.

In this case, the direction field is approximated by the relation

$$\widehat{\varphi}(x, y) = \frac{\displaystyle\sum_{k=1}^{N} \widehat{\varphi}_k I_k(x, y)}{\displaystyle\sum_{k=1}^{N} I_k(x, y)}, \tag{10.127}$$

where $I_k(x, y)$ is the intensity function of the kth nonrecurring image generated at the output of the correlator in the optical setup shown in Figure 10.44, after the light had passed the kth sector of the filter grating with the central angle

$$\theta_k = \begin{cases} \dfrac{\pi}{2} - \widehat{\varphi}_k, \, 0 < \widehat{\varphi}_k < \dfrac{\pi}{2} \\[2mm] \dfrac{3\pi}{2} - \widehat{\varphi}_k, \, \dfrac{\pi}{2} < \widehat{\varphi}_k < \pi \end{cases}, \quad k = \overline{1, N}, \tag{10.128}$$

where $\widehat{\varphi}_k$ are the inclination angle pixels and $N = 8$ is the number of the grating sectors.

The direction field constructed by the aforementioned method is later referred to as *multichannel*. Note that the superposition of several partial images in the course of a real experiment is made digitally in computer, which requires high-precision positioning, thus leading to increased processing time. As a result, one has to use a simpler method for deriving the direction field, which allows a simpler implementation but gives a greater error ε relative to the method in Eq. (10.127). An optical setup for generating the alternative direction field is shown in Figure 10.45a.

A fingerprint on glass is placed at the Fourier correlator input (Fig. 10.45a), with spatial filters SF realized as amplitude transparencies alternatively placed in its frequency plane. One of the filters is composed of 8 sectors, with the absorption factor T proportional to the square root of the angle. These sectors occupy 180 degrees, whereas the other part of the filter is opaque to light (Fig. 10.45b). The other filter just serves to cover half the frequency plane (Fig. 10.45c). After the successive application of the two filters, two images are registered at the correlator's output, and then the computer uses them for derivation of their ratio approximating the direction field of the initial image

$$\widehat{\varphi}(x, y) \cong \frac{|f(x, y) \otimes g_1(\xi, \eta)|^2}{|f(x, y) \otimes g_2(\xi, \eta)|^2 + \alpha^2} \tag{10.129}$$

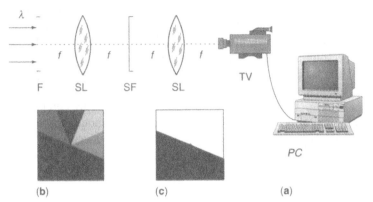

Figure 10.45. (a) An optical setup of the Fourier correlator for constructing the direction field using (b) sector amplitude spatial filter and (c) an amplitude spatial filter.

where $f(x, y)$ is the initial image function, $g_1(\xi, \eta)$ and $g_2(\xi, \eta)$ are the Fourier images of the transmission function for the filters shown in Figure 10.45b and 10.45c, $\otimes$ denotes the convolution operation, and α is a regularization constant. The direction field derived in this way will be referred to as *single channel*.

In both the methods considered, Eq. (10.127) and Eq. (10.129), one performs the operation of division by the function, which may result in considerable error ε of the direction field determination. In the direction field technique considered later, we managed to get rid of the division operation.

Owing to a number of technical limitations, the real experimental optical setup (Fig. 10.46) for the determination of the direction field is more complicated relative

Figure 10.46. Real optical setup for determining the direction field.

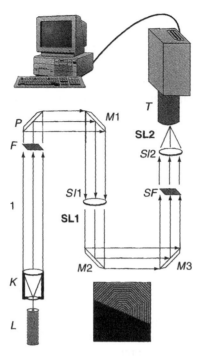

Figure 10.47. An optical setup for determining the direction field and the phase spatial filter.

to that used for the numerical simulation [79]. The real optical setup is shown in Figure 10.46.

An optical configuration for determining the direction field is shown in Figure 10.47. An amplitude transparency with fingerprint is illuminated by a coherent light beam from the He-Ne laser L. The beam is produced by the collimator K. The prism P allows one to enter the fingerprints in the real time. If the fingerprint is entered from the amplitude transparency, the prism serves as a turning mirror. The array of turning mirrors, M1, M2, and M3, made it possible to mount the optical setup in a small case. SL1 and SL2 are the Fourier correlator lenses. SF is the spatial phase filter shown in Figure 10.47b. Because the fingerprint field is 20 mm in size and the TV camera field is 20 mm in size, the Fourier correlator lenses have different focal lengths that should be fitted considering two conditions:

1. The partial images should be spatially separated.
2. All partial images should be found within the TV camera's field of view.

The partial image size is determined from Eq. (10.132) and the value r of the partial image deviation from the optical axis is given by

$$r = f_2 tg \left[\arcsin \left(\frac{\lambda}{d} \right) \right],$$

where λ is the light wavelength, d is the grating period, and f_2 is the focal length of the second arm of the Fourier correlator. The spatial filter SF is represented by a set of phase diffraction gratings of period 20 μm.

When selecting 4 direction, condition 1 (partial image separation) can be written in the form

$$r > \sqrt{2} S_c,$$

where S_c is the size of the partial image C.

Condition 2 (all images fit in the TV camera inlet window) is given by

$$L > 4 S_c,$$

where L is the TV camera's field of view.

From condition 2 and Eq. (10.132) follows the relation between the focal lengths of the Fourier correlator arms

$$\frac{f_2}{f_1} < \frac{L}{4S},$$

where S is the fingerprint size. Substituting the real value, we get that the focal lengths' ratio should be less than 0.125.

Condition 1 gives the minimal value $f_2 \approx 110$ mm, then the minimal value $f_1 \approx 880$ mm.

The TV camera allows one to read images quantized in 256 levels and arrange them as a graphic file of 512×512 pixels. The focal length of lens SL1 is 1,000 mm and the focal length of lens SL2 is 138 mm.

Figure 10.48 depicts two variants of sectors in the correlator's frequency plane: (*1*) an infinitely narrow sector defined by angle θ_0 (a) and (*2*) a finite-width sector limited by angles θ_1 and θ_2 (b).

The light field amplitude $A(x', y')$ at the output of a correlator with the filters shown in Figure 10.48 may be expressed through the input image amplitude $A_0(x, y)$ in the familiar manner [80]:

$$A(x', y') = \int_{-\infty}^{\infty} \int A_0(x, y) h(x + x', y + y') \, dx \, dy, \tag{10.130}$$

where $h(x, y)$ is the spatial filter frequency characteristic that is the Fourier image of the filter transmission function. For the narrow sector with pregiven angle θ_0 (Fig. 10.48a), the transmission function $H(r, \theta)$ and the frequency characteristic are given by

$$H_1(r, \theta) = \delta(\theta - \theta_0), \tag{10.131}$$

$$h_1(x, y) = [x \cos \theta_0 + y \sin \theta_0]^{-2}, \tag{10.132}$$

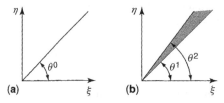

(a)   **(b)**

Figure 10.48. Variants of angular sectors placed in the frequency plane: (**a**) an infinitely narrow sector and (**b**) a finite-width sector.

where $\delta(x)$ is the delta function, whereas for the finite sector shown in Figure 10.48b, these functions take the form

$$H_2(r, \theta) = \begin{cases} 1, & \theta_1 \leq \theta \leq \theta_2 \\ 0, & 0 \leq \theta \leq \theta_1, \quad \theta_2 < \theta < 2\pi \end{cases}, \tag{10.133}$$

$$h_2(x, y) = \sin(\theta_1 - \theta_2)[x^2 \cos \theta_1 \cos \theta_2 + y^2 \sin \theta_1 \sin \theta_2 \\ + xy \sin(\theta_1 + \theta_2)]^{-1}. \tag{10.134}$$

If there are N such sectors in the filtration plane and there is a diffraction grating in each of them, a sequence of partial images will be generated at the correlator's output:

$$I_n(x', y') = \left| \int_{-\infty}^{\infty} \int A_0(x, y) h_n(x + x', y + y') \, dx \, dy \right|^2, \quad n = \overline{1, N}, \tag{10.135}$$

where the function $h_n(x, y)$ is derived from Eq. (10.131) or Eq. (10.133) with the following choice of angles: $\theta_k + \Delta n$, $k = 0, 1, 2$, $n = 1, 2 \ldots N$, where Δ is the pixel step of the angle.

Using a linear combination of the partial images taken with their weights proportional to the slit central angles, one may determine the function of direction field by Eq. (10.127).

Note that as the initial image $A_0(x, y)$ is described by a real function, the modulus of the Fourier image of such a function will be centrally symmetric, which means that the range of values of the angle φ_n is in the interval $[0, \pi)$.

Although the grating sectors generating the partial images do not intersect (Fig. 10.44b), every point of the initial image theoretically contributes to every point of the partial image. Structurally redundant images (contour images of fingerprint type) are composed of a great number of lines with characteristic period or of diffraction grating fragments, with the spatial spectrums each contributing only to a single filter's angular sector. Therefore, one should expect that the partial images will be nearly orthogonal, that is, the "integral of overlapping" for two partial images will be much less than the total energy of each of them

$$\int_{-\infty}^{\infty} \int I_n(x, y) I_m(x, y) \, dx \, dy \ll \int_{-\infty}^{\infty} \int I_n^2(x, y) \, dx \, dy. \tag{10.136}$$

If the inequality in (10.136) is not satisfied, one may perform the operation of orthogonalization of partial images by the rule

$$\tilde{I}_k(x, y) = \begin{cases} 1, & I_k(x, y) = \max_n\{I_n(x, y)\} \\ 0, & I_k(x, y) \neq \max_n\{I_n(x, y)\} \end{cases}, \tag{10.137}$$

where $\max_n\{\ldots\}$ is the maximal value of the function at a point among the functions with the numbers $n = \overline{1, N}$.

From Eq. (10.137), the partial images $\tilde{I}_k(x, y)$ are seen to form a nearly orthogonal set of binary functions. The orthogonality is violated only at pixels where the partial image intensities are coincident. Numerical simulation shows that these pixels do not outnumber 0.001 of the total number of image pixels. Having this in view, instead of

Eq. (10.127) one may do without the division operation and determine the direction field using a simpler formula

$$\hat{\varphi}(x, y) = \sum_{n=1}^{N} \hat{\varphi}_n \tilde{I}_n(x, y), \quad \hat{\varphi}_n = \frac{\pi n}{N}. \qquad (10.138)$$

From Figure 10.49c one can see that owing to orthogonalization and binarization of partial images, Eq. (10.138) involves procedures of partial regularization and filtration of the direction field that has been derived. For the same reason, Eq. (10.138) cannot be reduced, through the passage to the limit, to Eq. (10.114).

Figure 10.49a depicts the direction field (128 × 128 pixels) derived by numerical simulation of the correlator shown in Figure 10.45a and computed by Eq. (10.129) for the fingerprint shown in Figure 10.50a. The same direction field processed by a median filter is shown in Figure 10.49b, and the direction field for the same fingerprint computed by Eq. (10.127) is shown in Figure 10.49c. From Figure 10.50 the fields are seen to coincide in large-sized details.

Shown in Figure 10.50b,e,h,k are the direction fields (128 × 128 pixels) that are computer-generated by Eq. (10.127).

Consider now as to how the process of fingerprint identification is affected by the method for constructing the feature vector of the direction field. We shall form the feature vector using the coefficients of expansion of the direction field in terms of an orthogonal basis. For this purpose, we shall employ the Hadamard basis, Eq. (10.58), and the Fourier basis, Eq. (10.54) [57,58].

Table 10.7 gives the Euclidean distance d_{mn} between the feature vectors composed of components for 10 base and 10 analyzed fingerprints of 10 different fingers. The distance d_{mn} was derived from

$$d_{mn} = \sqrt{\sum_{k=1}^{K} [b_m^{(k)} - a_n^{(k)}]^2}, \qquad (10.139)$$

where $b_m^{(k)}$ and $a_n^{(k)} - "k"$ are the kth coefficients of the mth and nth vectors to be analyzed. In essence, $d_{mn}(a_n)m = \overline{1, N}$ represent a system of separating functions that describe a classifier that is schematically shown in Figure 10.52. The classifier is said to

(a)   (b)   (c)

Figure 10.49. (a) The direction field generated by numerical simulation of operation of the correlator shown in Fig. 10.45a, (b) the direction field generated by numerical simulation of operation of the correlator shown in Fig. 10.45a and then processed by a median filter, and (c) the direction field that is computer-generated by Eq. (10.138).

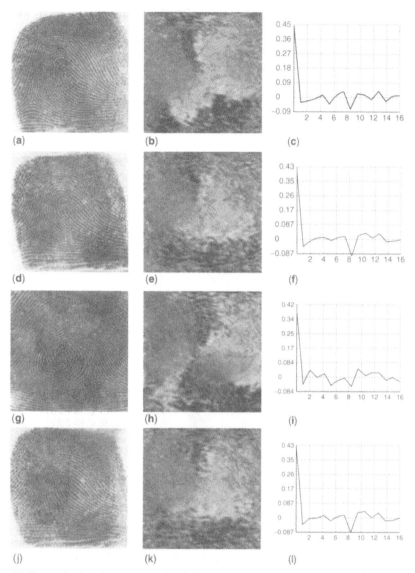

Figure 10.50. (**a,d,g,j**) Fingerprints, (**b,e,h,k**) their direction fields, and (**c,f,i,l**) the feature vectors composed of the first 16 coefficients of the Hadamard expansion.

put the feature vector a_n in correspondence with the class b_m if the following inequality is valid [93,94]:

$$d_{mn}(a_n) > d_{ln}(a_n), \quad m \neq l. \tag{10.140}$$

The distance values in each row of Table 10.8 present the result of identification of the vector a_n among the base vectors $\{b_m\}, m = \overline{1, M}$, whereas the column values present the result of identification of the vector b_m among the set of the vectors under analysis, $\{a_n\}, n = \overline{1, N}$. Because the number of the fingerprints under analysis is not large, it turns out to be impossible to directly estimate the method's reliability as the

TABLE 10.7. The Results of Reconstructing the Complex Coefficients by Purely Phase and Phase-Only Filters

Coefficients	$|C_{11}|^2$	$|C_{33}|^2$	$|C_{42}|^2$	Error	$\phi_{33} - \phi_{11}$	$\phi_{42} - \phi_{33}$
Initial	1	1	1		1,57	1,57
Reconstructed by the amplitude–phase filter	0,272	0,274	0,279	3,1%	1,46	1,54
Reconstructed by the phase-only filter	12,12	14,83	1,459	8,6%	0,95	1,53

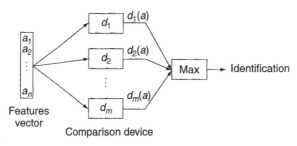

Figure 10.51. Schematic of the image classifier.

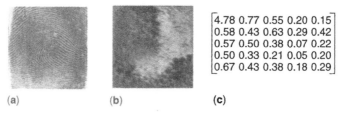

Figure 10.52. (a) Fingerprint, (b) its direction field, and (c) the coefficient matrix derived using the DOE designed (Fig. 10.24a).

TABLE 10.8. Distances Between the Feature Vectors Composed of 16 Expansion Coefficients in Terms of the Orthogonal Hadamard Basis for the Direction Fields Constructed Using 10 Base $\{b_n\}$ and 10 Analyzed Fingerprints of 10 Different Fingers

	b_1	b_2	b_3	b_4	b_5	b_6	b_7	b_8	b_9	b_{10}	R
A_1	5.13	13.00	9.73	8.83	11.07	12.56	7.99	10.12	11.42	13.39	0.22
A_2	13.37	3.97	9.52	10.20	10.03	7.96	12.14	10.13	7.39	8.17	0.30
A_3	8.70	7.09	4.56	8.21	6.05	10.65	8.24	7.64	7.66	9.29	0.13
A_4	8.31	8.84	5.90	4.58	6.79	9.78	6.61	8.16	8.75	11.41	0.12
A_5	9.42	9.53	6.18	6.36	2.07	9.15	7.58	5.94	8.21	9.71	0.48
A_6	11.74	7.76	9.86	9.22	9.03	3.47	10.01	7.23	7.84	9.32	0.35
A_7	8.92	10.54	5.99	5.64	4.71	10.52	4.22	7.34	10.61	12.52	0.06
A_8	10.94	9.25	9.04	9.42	7.09	8.53	9.78	3.52	5.31	6.10	0.20
A_9	11.11	7.82	9.56	9.69	9.80	9.63	10.85	7.75	3.60	5.25	0.18
A_{10}	12.74	8.52	11.63	11.90	11.17	10.15	12.74	8.94	4.36	3.58	0.10
R	0.24	0.28	0.12	0.10	0.38	0.39	0.22	0.15	0.10	0.18	0.21

ratio of correctly identified fingerprints to their total number. However, one may introduce a parameter characterizing the relative remoteness of classes from each other [76], thus making it possible to evaluate the reliability of the method indirectly:

$$R_i = \frac{d_{\min} - d_{mm}}{d_{\min} + d_{mm}}, i = \begin{cases} m, & d_{\min} \text{ determined in the row} \\ M + m, & d_{\min} \text{ determined in the column} \end{cases} \quad (10.141)$$

where d_{mm} is the diagonal matrix element and $d_{\min}$ is the minimal nondiagonal element.

The average parameter value, $< R >$, characterizes the average remoteness of classes for the identification method as a whole and is determined by the relation

$$\langle R \rangle = (2M)^{-1} \sum_{i=1}^{2M} R_i, \quad (10.142)$$

where $2M$ is the number of analyzed and base fingerprints.

Thus, the fingerprint identification method we consider involves the following sequence of steps.

1. For each analyzed or base fingerprint described by the transmission function $I(x, y)$, using a correlator, one optically generates N partial images $I_n(x, y)$, with their spatial spectrum confined in a narrow angular sector. The set of the partial images is then registered and entered into the computer as a number array.

2. Digital processing of the partial images involves the following stages:
   (a) a set of binary-orthogonal partial images $\tilde{I}_n(x, y)$ is generated;
   (b) the direction field $\hat{\varphi}(x, y)$ is computed using Eq. (10.127) or Eq. (10.138);
   (c) K coefficients ($\{a_k^{(n)}\}$, $\{b_k^{(n)}\}$) of the expansion of the direction field $\hat{\varphi}(x, y)$ in terms of the Hadamard basis are derived;
   (d) Euclidean distances d_{mn} are determined and their minimal is derived.

Because the vectors b_n and a_n with identical numbers correspond to different fingerprints of the same finger, the identification will be successful if the minimal distance values in every row and every column are found on the diagonal, the value d_{mn} being positive.

The result of identification using the feature vectors composed of the first 16 coefficients of the direction field expansion in terms of the Fourier basis showed the failure of complete fingerprint identification and the value of $\langle R \rangle (\langle R \rangle = 0.19)$ turned out to be less than the analogous value on using the Hadamard basis ($\langle R \rangle = 0.21$). Thus, the Hadamard basis is more effective in this case.

Note, also, that if the same fingerprints are identified using the simplified "single-channel" optical scheme (for the direction field, see Fig. 10.49a) and the feature vector composed of the first 16 Hadamard coefficients, the identification results are worsened too. Although in this case an identification takes place, the identification reliability is adversely affected by the presence of a small-scale structure in the direction fields (Fig. 10.49a): $\langle R \rangle = 0.17$.

The direction-field-based identification may be made more reliable if the initial fields are subject to processing by median filters. In this case, the complete identification takes place and the average relative distance between the classes is increased: $\langle R \rangle = 0.19$.

Table 10.9 provides the general comparison for the average distances between the classes for all the methods considered [95,96]. From Table 10.9, the method with the feature vector composed of the first Hadamard coefficients with the use of a "multi-channel" direction field is seen to have the best performance.

A DOE that may find use in image analysis is described in subsection 10.2.2. Figure 10.52 depicts: (a) a fingerprint, (b) its direction field, and (c) the matrix of the coefficients derived using the DOE shown in Figure 10.24a. The coefficients are proportional to the modules of the expansion of the fingerprint in terms of 25 basis Hadamard functions.

The general scheme of identification by means of the optical Karhunen-Loeve expansion is shown in Figure 10.53.

The advantage of the foregoing scheme lies in the fact that the most labor-consuming part ("initial training") is implemented only once at the initial stage. At the same time, the major part, analyzing the input image, possesses all the desirable characteristics: the high performance resulting from optical implementation and the high efficiency resulting from the use of the optimal expansion. Although the initial stage is thus complicated, one has to resort to it only once, making such an approach expedient.

TABLE 10.9. Reliability Values for Various Identification Methods

Image-processing method	Feature vector–generation method	$\langle R \rangle$
"Multichannel" direction field	16 coefficients of the Hadamard expansion	0.21
	16 coefficients of the Fourier expansion	0.19
"Single-channel" direction field	16 coefficients of the Hadamard expansion	0.17
"Single-channel," filtered direction field	16 coefficients of the Hadamard expansion	0.19

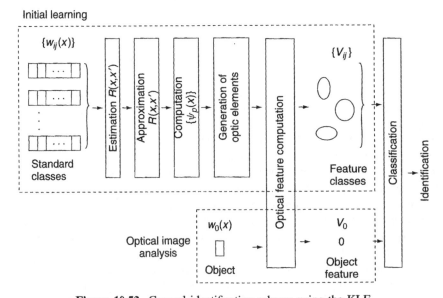

Figure 10.53. General identification scheme using the KLE.

When making classification in the feature space, one needs to choose the decision function, which is to classify the object depending on the "distance" r_i from the object to the ith class. Some classification methods are given in Ref. [11].

By way of illustration, the class-average vector method is as follows.

For each class, one finds the average feature vector among the vectors V_{ij}; the center of the class

$$V_i = \frac{1}{N_s} \sum_{j=1}^{N_s} V_{ij}, \tag{10.143}$$

then computes the Euclidean distance r_i^c from the object to the class center

$$r_i^c = |V_o - V_i| \tag{10.144}$$

and chooses the minimal value.

The minimal distance number is taken as the number of the class to which the object belongs (Fig. 10.54).

Table 10.10 gives the results of recognition of 10 classes of similar-pattern fingerprint images for an excerpt of 15 representatives on the KLE basis (subsection 10.2.1) with different types of the correlation function approximation (W is the frequency of successful identification and K is the number of the KLE coefficients). The direction field was constructed using both the optical and the variance method [74]. The direction field constructed using the variance method underwent the filtration operation.

The fact that the initial fingerprints practically defied identification [78] not only justifies but also makes necessary the use of the direction field in analysis of such

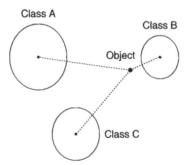

Figure 10.54. Scheme of determining the distance from the object to different classes.

TABLE 10.10. The Result of Fingerprint Identification

		KLE with Exponential Correlation Function	KLE with Exponential-Cosine Correlation Function
Initial Images		$W = 0.3$ for $K \geq 18*$	$W = 0.3$ for $K \geq 9*$
Direction fields	Variance	$W = 1$ for $K \geq 34$	$W = 1$ for $K \geqslant 31$
	Filtered variance	$W = 0.8$ for $K \geq 22*$	$W = 0.8$ for $K \geq 15*$
	optical	$W = 1$ for $K \geq 12$	$W = 1$ for $K \geq 11$

*An increase in K up to 100 does not result in enhanced identification

complicated images. The worsened identification quality of the filtered direction fields may be ascribed to the suppression of some minor, but essential, details in the course of filtration, and also by the KLE filtration property, allowing one to omit this fairly complicated stage. The optical method proved to be highly efficient in this experiment.

With the use of Eq. (10.127), the direction field reflects not only the structure of major fingerprint lines but also bye effect structural elements appearing as a result of image lines' contrast variations. Although the contribution from these to the partial images is not large on the whole, this may result in the misrepresented structure of the direction field. The plot of the normalized intensity for a single characteristic point in four different "partial" images is shown in Figure 10.55.

From Figure 10.55, one can see that the greatest intensity at the arbitrary point (x, y) is found in the partial image number 1. For this point, the intensity in the other partial images is essentially less, but the sum of the intensities at the point in the other three partial images is already comparable to the intensity at this point for the initial partial image. The analogous intensity ratio is found at the majority of the points. As a result the direction field was obtained using Eqs. (10.127) and (10.138) in the experiment. The experiment was conducted using the optical setup in Figure 10.47a and yielded the partial images shown in Figure 10.56a.

Four of the aforementioned images were employed in constructing the direction field computed by Eqs. (10.127) and (10.138), the fields being depicted in Figure 10.56b,c. The partial image size was 100×100 pixels, while the size of the entire image field was 512×512 pixels. The images are quantized in 256 levels. The geometric size of the TV camera field of view was 10×10 mm, whereas the geometric size of the partial image was 2 mm. As in numerical simulation, 10 fingerprints were chosen as base. The base-feature vectors were composed of the Hadamard expansion coefficients of the base fingerprints' direction fields. Ten analyzed fingerprints were chosen and the Euclidean distance d_{mn} from the vector of every fingerprint under analysis to the vector of every base fingerprint was determined using Eq. (10.148): in all experiments the first 16 Hadamard expansion coefficients were used.

Figure 10.57a depicts the plot of the Euclidean distance d_{mn} between the feature vector a_5 and 10 base vectors of different fingers. The plot of the Euclidean distance d_{mn} between the feature vector b_5 and 10 analyzed vectors of 10 different fingers is shown in Figure 10.57b.

From Figure 10.57, one can see that the distance is minimal between the vectors a_5 and b_5, that is, the recognition takes place. The same is true of any other pair of the vectors. When recognizing fingerprints by expanding the optically derived direction fields, Eq. (10.138), into the Hadamard-basis, the value of $\langle R \rangle$ is equal to 0.24,

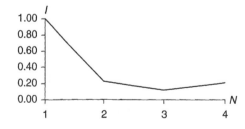

Figure 10.55. The normalized intensity for one point in different partial images.

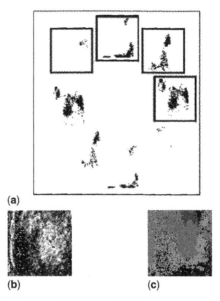

(a)

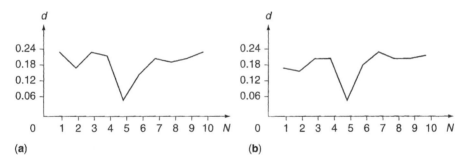

(b)   **(c)**

Figure 10.56. (a) Experimental partial images, (b) the corresponding direction fields derived from Eq. (10.127) and (c) Eq. (10.138) (framed images were used in constructing the direction field).

(a)   **(b)**

Figure 10.57. (a) The distances between the vector of the fingerprint under analysis, $\{a_5\}$, and the vectors of 10 base fingerprints, $\{b_n\}(a)$, and (b) the distances between the of base fingerprint vector, $\{b_5\}(b)$, and the vectors of 10 analyzed fingerprints.

which is somewhat greater than the analogous parameter resulting from the numerical simulation [74] of the Hadamard-based recognition of the same fingerprints using Eq. (10.127): $\langle R \rangle = 0.21$.

We also conducted a real experiment on fingerprint identification using direction fields optically derived from Eq. (10.127). In this case, we were unable to identify all fingerprints, and the relative average distance between classes turned out to be much less: $\langle R \rangle = 0.14$. The deteriorated reliability relative to the numerical simulation [59] is due to the fact that in the real experiment we extracted 4 direction, as opposed to 8 direction in the numerical simulation.

To enhance the identification reliability, one needs to construct the base vector as an average of the direction-field vectors for several variants of the same fingerprint.

Figure 10.58a depicts the distances between the vector $\{a_1\}$ and 10 base vectors, whereas Figure 10.58b depicts the distances between the same vector $\{a_1\}$ and 10 base vector, each of which has been derived by averaging over two vectors of different fingerprints of the same finger.

From Figure 10.58, the difference between the distances d_{11} and d_{21} is seen to be greater in Figure 10.58b. Hence, the parameter $\langle R \rangle$ is increased.

Table 10.11 gives the averaged base vectors, which means that not the coordinates of the base vector but the averaged coordinates of two base vectors are considered to be the center of the class.

From Table 10.11, the minimal distances are seen to be found on the diagonal, which means the complete fingerprint identification. Also, the averaging operation is seen to enhance the identification reliability from $\langle R \rangle = 0.24$ to $\langle R \rangle = 0.27$.

A number of experiments aimed at studying the field's stability to shifting and turning have been conducted in Ref. [82]. The feature vectors were composed of the

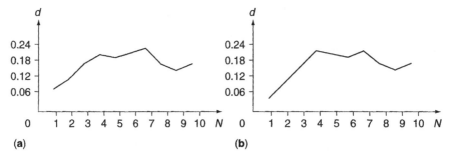

(a)   (b)

Figure 10.58. (a) The distances between the vector of the analyzed fingerprint $\{a_1\}$ and the vectors $\{b_n\}$ of 10 base fingerprints and (b) the distances between the vector $\{c_n\}$ and the vectors of 10 base fingerprints, derived by averaging over the vectors of two different fingerprints of the same finger.

TABLE 10.11. The Distances Between the 16-Component Feature Vectors of 10 Base Vectors $\{b_n\}$ Composed of Two Different Fingerprints of the Same Finger and 10 Analyzed Feature Vectors $\{a_n\}$ of Fingerprints for 10 Different Fingers; the Last Column and the Last Row Present the Values of R

	B_1	b_2	B_3	b_4	b_5	b_6	b_7	b_8	b_9	b_{10}	R
a_1	4.8	10.0	15.0	20.0	18.0	18.0	21.0	16.0	13.0	15.0	0.35
a_2	12.0	5.6	14.0	18.0	17.0	16.0	19.0	17.0	12.0	16.0	0.36
a_3	13.0	15.0	4.9	11.0	21.0	19.0	14.0	14.0	11.0	12.0	0.38
a_4	16.0	18.0	10.0	5.3	21.0	14.0	8.8	13.0	10.0	12.0	0.25
a_5	22.0	14.0	22.0	21.0	4.0	13.0	21.0	19.0	20.0	22.0	0.53
a_6	16.0	17.0	17.0	12.0	17.0	6.1	12.0	11.0	13.0	16.0	0.29
a_7	17.0	21.0	15.0	8.7	24.0	16.0	6.0	8.5	9.8	9.1	0.17
a_8	15.0	18.0	13.0	7.9	21.0	14.0	7.2	5.1	7.8	7.0	0.16
a_9	13.0	17.0	11.0	8.9	21.0	15.0	7.7	6.4	4.8	6.6	0.14
a_{10}	14.0	19.0	15.0	12.0	22.0	17.0	11.0	6.7	10.0	6.1	0.05
R	0.43	0.28	0.34	0.20	0.62	0.36	0.09	0.11	0.24	0.04	0.27

Hadamard expansion coefficients of the direction fields, and the Euclidean distance r_{mn} from every shifted fingerprint's vector to every nonshifted fingerprint's vector was derived: in all experiments, using Eq. (10.139), the first 16 Hadamard expansion coefficients were used. The shift was produced at 0.5-mm intervals at the distance of up to 4 mm.

The plot of the Euclidean distance r between the feature vectors a_3 and 8 feature vectors of the fingerprints shifted by the distance l for the same finger is shown in Figure 10.59.

In order to determine the stability to shift, it is necessary to know the average minimal distance between the feature vectors and the variance. The average minimal distance between 100 nonshifted vectors in the 16-dimensional feature space is equal to $\langle r \rangle = 0.085$ and the variance is $D = 0.00044$. For 50 vectors we found that $\langle r \rangle = 0.089$ and $D = 0.00045$. According to Ref. [83], the probability that $r < \langle r \rangle/2$ is given by

$$P\left\{ r < \frac{\langle r \rangle}{2} \right\} = 0.5 - \Phi\left(\frac{r - \frac{\langle r \rangle}{2}}{\sqrt{D}} \right), \tag{10.145}$$

where r is the distance from the vector to the center of the class.

Figure 10.60 depicts an averaged distance between the shifted and nonshifted fingerprint. Knowing this dependence and on the basis of Eq. (10.145), one may derive how the probability P of correct identification depends on the shift value. The corresponding plot is shown in Figure 10.61.

Figure 10.62 depicts how the $\langle R \rangle$ parameter depends on the shift value.

From comparison of Figures 10.61 and 10.62 it can be seen that at $\langle R \rangle = 0$ we have $P = 0.5$, that is, the positive value of $\langle R \rangle$ allows the conclusion that the correct identification is predominant over the false one.

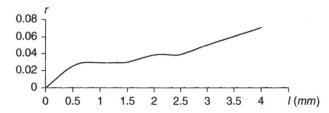

Figure 10.59. The plot of the distance between the feature vectors as a function of the distance l between the shifted and nonshifted fingerprints.

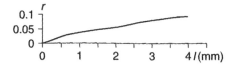

Figure 10.60. The distance between the shifted and nonshifted fingerprints, averaged over 100 feature vectors.

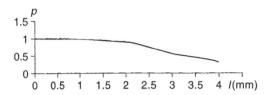

Figure 10.61. The probability P of correct identification versus the value of the initial image shift derived from Eq. (10.145).

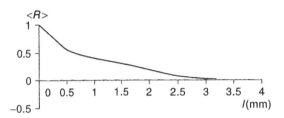

Figure 10.62. The $\langle R \rangle$ parameter as a function of the initial image shift.

In the experiment, the nonshifted fingerprints were used as base, whereas the shifted fingerprints served as those to be analyzed. Shown in Figure 10.63 is the plot of the identification reliability K versus the shift value, derived from experimental data, with K defined as

$$K = \frac{N_r}{N}, \tag{10.146}$$

where N is the total number of the analyzed fingerprints and N_r is the number of those correctly identified.

In the experiment with a great number of fingerprints, the values of K and P should coincide. From Figures 10.61 and 10.63, it is seen that in the experiment with 100 fingerprints, the values of K and P are coincident with the error of 5 percent. Because a decrease in the number of vectors in the experiment did not result in an essential change of values $\langle r \rangle$ and D, one can approximately evaluate the identification method reliability for a great number of fingerprints (>100) using Eq. (10.145) and on the basis of the parameters ($\langle r \rangle$ and D) derived in an experiment with a moderate number of base fingerprints.

A similar experiment was conducted in pursuit of studying the identification method stability to fingerprint turning. The same set of 100 fingerprints was employed. The

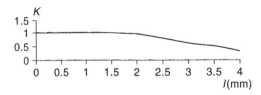

Figure 10.63. The experimental plot of the identification reliability as a function of the initial image shift.

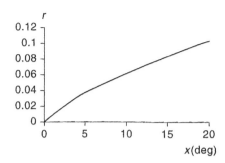

Figure 10.64. The distance between the shifted and nonshifted fingerprints, averaged over 100 feature vectors.

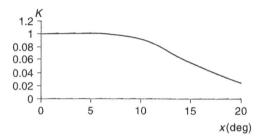

Figure 10.65. The experimental plot of the identification reliability K as a function of the angle of turning.

fingerprint was consecutively turned at 5 degree intervals from 0 degrees to 20 degrees. The plot of the average distance between the shifted and nonshifted fingerprints is shown in Figure 10.64. The experimentally determined identification reliability as a function of the angle of turning is shown in Figure 10.65. From Figure 10.65 it is seen that the identification reliability is high (>0.9) if the angle of turning is no greater than 10 degrees.

In summary, we can claim that optically constructed direction fields may be effectively used in systems for fingerprint identification intended to be operated with a fairly small number of base fingerprints (10^3 to 10^4).

10.3.2   Optical Interferogram Decoding

It is a common practice to process interferograms by computer using the method of Fourier transform [84] or the method of fringe-center extraction [50]. The main disadvantage of these methods lies in the fact that with increasing noise background in the image under processing and at a large number of speckle-effect-induced fringe disruptions, they cease to be reliable and may lead to large distortions of the phase reconstructed.

There are iterative methods [102,103] based on the regularization procedure that allow one to achieve a stable phase retrieval from a noised interferogram with the SNR no less than one. Note, however, that such methods require too much computational effort.

Optical methods for reconstructing the light field phase are based on the use of wave front sensors; they do not require the generation of interferogram and provide for the location of the sensor directly in the domain of the light field under analysis. The most popular wave front analyzer is Hartmann-Shacke sensor [52].

A hybrid optical-digital technique for interferogram processing based on the optical construction of the direction and frequency field has been discussed in Ref. [87]. Similar to the Hartmann-Shacke sensor, the values of two relevant readings in the frequency field (FF) and direction field (DF) specify the coordinates of a vector of inclination of the tangent plane at this point to the sought-for phase function.

Assume that the interferogram is described by the following function

$$I(x, y) = |\exp[i\,\Phi(x, y)] + \exp[i(\alpha_0 x + \beta_0 y)]|^2, \qquad (10.147)$$

where $\Phi(x, y)$ is the sought-for light field phase and (α_0, β_0) is the vector of the reference carrier frequency of a plane reference wave. Consider two scalar fields, $\widehat{\varphi}(x, y)$ and $\omega(x, y)$, specified by

$$tg\widehat{\varphi}(x, y) = -\frac{\partial I/\partial x}{\partial I/\partial y}, \quad 0 \le \widehat{\varphi}(x, y) < \pi, \qquad (10.148)$$

$$\omega(x, y) = \left[\left(\frac{\partial I}{\partial x}\right)^2 + \left(\frac{\partial I}{\partial y}\right)^2\right]^{1/2}. \qquad (10.149)$$

The functions $\varphi(x, y)$ and $\omega(x, y)$ are referred to as the *direction field* and the *frequency field*, respectively.

From Eq. (10.148) it follows that the DF is defined up to π. From comparison of Eqs. (10.147), (10.148), and (10.149) the relation between the DF, the FF, and the phase function $\Phi(x, y)$ is given by

$$tg\widehat{\varphi}(x, y) = -\frac{\dfrac{\partial \Phi}{\partial x} - \alpha_0}{\dfrac{\partial \Phi}{\partial y} - \beta_0} \qquad (10.150)$$

$$\omega(x, y) = A_0(x, y)\left[\left(\frac{\partial \Phi}{\partial x} - \alpha_0\right)^2 + \left(\frac{\partial \Phi}{\partial y} - \beta_0\right)^2\right]^{1/2}, \qquad (10.151)$$

where

$$A_0(x, y) = 2|\sin[\Phi(x, y) - \alpha_0 x - \beta_0 y]|. \qquad (10.152)$$

We may state that the light field phase $\omega'(x, y)$ can be retrieved from the functions IFF

$$\omega'(x, y) = \frac{\omega(x, y)}{A_0(x, y)}. \qquad (10.153)$$

$\Phi(x, y)$ can be retrieved from the functions $\widehat{\varphi}(x, y)$ and $\omega'(x, y)$. However, this retrieval will not be unique because we do not know the sign of $\partial\Phi/\partial x$ (or $\partial\Phi/\partial y$).

Imposing an additional requirement that the spatial frequencies of the reference wave should be chosen high enough so that the following condition will be valid:

$$\left|\frac{\partial\Phi}{\partial x}\right|_{\text{max}} < \alpha_0, \quad \left|\frac{\partial\Phi}{\partial y}\right|_{\text{max}} < \beta_0, \tag{10.154}$$

the phase can be retrieved uniquely from the DF and IFF. In order for the phase $\Phi(x, y)$ to be retrieved uniquely at any values of α_0 and β_0, including $\alpha_0 = \beta_0 = 0$, an additional a priori information about phase should be involved.

Assume that the interferogram F is implemented as a transparency and placed at the input of the Fourier correlator (Fig. 10.66) in whose frequency plane a binary-phase spatial filter DF is found. The filter transmission function is

$$H_{mn}^{(S)(C)}(\xi, \eta) = \begin{cases} S_n\widehat{\varphi}R_n(\xi, \eta), & \widehat{\varphi}_{n-1} < \widehat{\varphi} < \widehat{\varphi}_n, & n = \overline{1, N} \\ C_m(r)R_m(\xi, \eta), & r_{m-1} < r < r_m, & m = \overline{1, M} \end{cases}, \tag{10.155}$$

where
$$S_n(\widehat{\varphi}) = \tfrac{1}{2}[\text{sgn}(\widehat{\varphi} - \widehat{\varphi}_{n-1}) - \text{sgn}(\widehat{\varphi} - \widehat{\varphi}_n)], \tag{10.156}$$

$$C_m(r) = \text{circ}\left(\frac{r}{r_{m+1}}\right) - \text{circ}\left(\frac{r}{r_m}\right), \tag{10.157}$$

$$R_n(\xi, \eta) = \text{sgn}[\cos(\alpha_n\xi + \beta_n\eta)], \tag{10.158}$$

$S_n(\widehat{\varphi})$ and $C_m(r)$ are the sector and circular parts of the filter in which the binary-phase diffraction grating $R_n(\xi, \eta)$ remains unchangeable, (α_n, β_n) is the vector of the grating spatial carrier frequency that specifies the central coordinate of the partial image at the correlator's output

At the correlator's output, $2(M + N)$ images will be effectively generated. This is due to the fact that the binary-phase grating with a phase jump of π is able to generate with an 80 percent efficiency only two diffraction orders. The binary grating has been chosen in place of diffraction wedges as they allow simpler fabrication. If the spatial frequencies are properly fitted, N sectors and M rings will form just $2N + 2M$ partial

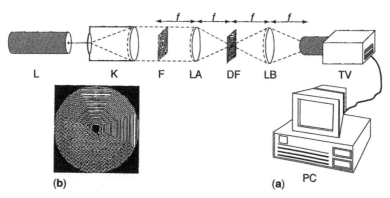

Figure 10.66. (a) The configuration of an optical setup for constructing the direction fields and frequency fields from interferograms and (b) the amplitude spatial filter.

images, with their intensities given by

$$I_m^{(c)}(u, v) = |\Im\{C_m\} * I|^2, \tag{10.159}$$

$$I_n^{(s)}(u, v) = |\Im\{S_n\} * I|^2, \tag{10.160}$$

where $\Im$ is the Fourier transform implemented by the correlator's lens. Of all partial images, only half is then processed. The partial image $I_n^{(s)}(u, v)$ has a narrow circular spectrum because it has been generated by filtering the initial image with the aid of the sector filter of Eq. (10.156). Contributing to this image are those portions of the initial image $I(x, y)$ whose interferogram fringes are inclined at an angle of $\hat{\varphi} + \pi/2$ from the range of angles $\hat{\varphi}_{n-1} < \hat{\varphi} < \hat{\varphi}_n$. Similarly, the partial image $I_m^{(c)}(u, v)$ has a narrow circular spectrum as having been generated by the circular filter of Eq. (10.157) and is made up of contributions from the points of the interferogram $I(x, y)$ characterized by a spatial frequency of $2\pi r/\lambda f$, (where $r_{m-1} < r < r_m$) in their vicinity.

The partial images spatially separated by diffraction gratings and so not intersecting at the correlator's output are then registered by the TV camera and entered into the computer as a number array. The centers of all partial images are again brought to the point.

Choosing N identical sectors of Eq. (10.156) of the filter (10.155), the angles are equal to $\overline{\hat{\varphi}_n} = \hat{\varphi}_{n-1} + \hat{\varphi}_n/2 = \pi n/N$, whereas with M identical rings of Eq. (10.157) of the filter (10.155) the central radii are given by $\overline{r_m} = r_{m-1} + r_m/2 = Rm/M$, where R is the radius of the filter's aperture.

The approximation algorithm is analogous to the Hough-radon transform [87] used in tomography and as follows. To a point (x, y) of the initial image one confers the value of an angle $\overline{\hat{\varphi}_n}$, for which the partial image intensity is greater than $I_n^{(s)}(u, v)$. It is the function relating the angles $\overline{\hat{\varphi}_n}$ to the coordinates (u, v), which will be the approximation of the DF

$$\hat{\varphi}(u, v) = \sum_{n=1}^{N} \overline{\hat{\varphi}_n}\theta\left[I_n^{(c)}(u, v) - \overline{I^{(s)}}\right], \tag{10.161}$$

where $\overline{I^{(s)}}(u, v) = \max_{n \in [1,N]}\{I_n^{(s)}(u, v)\}, \tag{10.162}$

and $\theta(x)$ is the Heavyside function: $\theta(x) = \begin{cases} 1, x \geq 0 \\ 0, x < 0 \end{cases}$.

The approximation of IFF is defined similarly

$$\omega'(u, v) = \sum_{m=1}^{M} \overline{r_m}\theta[I_m^{(c)}(u, v) - \overline{I^{(c)}}(u, v)], \tag{10.163}$$

where $\overline{I^{(c)}}(u, v) = \max_{m \in [1,M]}\{I_m^{(c)}(u, v)\}. \tag{10.164}$

Continuing the analogy with tomography, we may compare the partial images with interferogram's cross sections in the space of direction and frequencies.

Once the DF and IFF have been determined for every interferogram point (u, v), there are two numbers (φ and ω) defining, up to a constant, the vector of inclination (direction and magnitude) of the tangent plane at this point to the desired phase function

$$\Phi_0(x, y) = \omega'(u, v) \sin[\widehat{\varphi}(u, v)](x - u) + \omega'(u, v) \cos[\widehat{\varphi}(u, v)](y - v) + C.$$
(10.165)

In practice, the interferogram is broken down into k square areas, with the average DF, $\overline{\widehat{\varphi}_{ij}}$; $i, j = \overline{1, k}$, and average IFF, $\overline{\omega'_{ij}}$ determined in each area.

Then, the desired phase function is approximated in each square by the set of planes of Eq. (10.165) with average $\overline{\widehat{\varphi}_{ij}}$ and $\overline{\omega'_{ij}}$:

$$\Phi_{ij}(x, y) = \overline{\omega'_{ij}} \sin[\overline{\widehat{\varphi}_{ij}}]x + \overline{\omega'_{ij}} \cos[\overline{\widehat{\varphi}_{ij}}]y + C_{ij}, i, j = \overline{1, k}.$$
(10.166)

The constants C_{ij} are chosen to meet the condition that the function of Eq. (10.166) should be continuous on the boundary of neighboring squares. In the next step, the phase is reconstructed from the intensity data measured by the Shacke–Hartmann sensor (Fig. 10.69). Figure 10.67a depicts the initial phase

$$\Phi(x, y) = x^2 + y^2.$$
(10.167)

and Figure 10.67b shows the interferogram resulting from the interference of the light wave of phase in Eq. (10.167), with the plane light wave perpendicularly striking the registration plane. The size of the registration domain is 2 mm. Then, using the aforedescribed technique, we obtained from the interferogram the DF shown in Figure 10.67c and FF shown in Figure 10.67d.

Figure 10.68b depicts the interferogram resulting from interference of the light wave with phase in Eq. (10.167) with an oblique plane light wave.

Then, the interferogram was used to derive the DF shown in Figure 10.68c and the FF shown in Figure 10.68d. The reconstructed phase is depicted in Figure 10.68e.

Figure 10.69 gives 3D patterns of (a) the initial phase, (b) the phase reconstructed from the interferogram using the DF technique, and, for comparison, (c) the phase reconstructed from the Hartmangram.

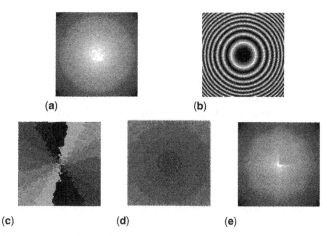

(a) (b)

(c) (d) (e)

Figure 10.67. (a) The initial phase, (b) interferogram, (c) the DF, (d) the FF, and (e) the reconstructed phase.

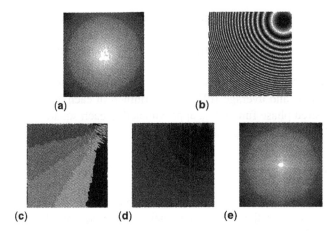

(a)   (b)

(c)   (d)   (e)

Figure 10.68. (a) The initial phase, (b) interferogram, (c) the DF, (d) the FF, and (e) the reconstructed phase.

(a)   (b)   (c)

Figure 10.69. (a) The initial phase, (b) the phase reconstructed using the DF and FF from the interferogram, and (c) the phase reconstructed using the Hartmann-Shacke technique.

The phase reconstruction error was determined by

$$\Delta^2 = \frac{\int_0^a \int_0^a |\Phi(x, y) - \Phi_r(x, y)|^2 \, dx \, dy}{\int_0^a \int_0^a |\Phi(x, y)|^2 \, dx \, dy}, \tag{10.168}$$

where $\Phi(x, y) \in [0, 2\pi]$ is the initial phase, $\Phi_r(x, y) \in [0, 2\pi]$ is the reconstructed phase, and a is the image size.

When reconstructing the phase in Eq. (10.167) using the DF technique, we have $\Delta = 0.045$, whereas the Hartmangram for the same phase provides the error of $\Delta = 0.039$. When the phase of Eq. (10.167) is reconstructed using the DF technique from the interferogram derived with an oblique reference wave, the error is $\Delta = 0.041$; when the phase is reconstructed using the DF technique from the light field, the error is $\Delta = 0.041$, that is, the error is the same. Thus, the examples suggest that the accuracy of the DF technique is close to that of the Hartmann technique, but the technique under consideration provides a fairly good accuracy when reconstructing the phase from heavily noised interferograms.

Figure 10.70 shows noised interferograms with different SNRs (SNRs), DFs, FFs, and the reconstructed phase.

From Figure 10.70, one can see that the greatest changes having appeared in the DF and the FF as the result of adding noise are found in the places of greater interferogram

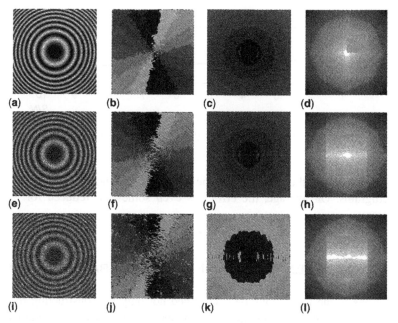

Figure 10.70. Noised interferograms: (**a**) $SNR = 10$, (**e**) $SNR = 2$, (**i**) $SNR = 1$, and (**b,f,j**) the corresponding DFs, (**c,g,k**) FFs, and (**d,h,l**) the reconstructed phases; $S = 2$, $\Delta = 0.061$ (middle row) and $S = 1$, $\Delta = 0.147$ (bottom row).

period. It is these fragments that make the greatest contribution to the increase in error. Thus, making the interferogram not have the fragments of great fringe period (oblique incident reference wave) would reduce the error of the method.

Figure 10.71 depicts the plot of the error Δ of phase reconstruction versus SNR for the interferogram produced as the result of interference of light wave with the phase in Eq. (10.167) and a plane light wave perpendicular to the registration plane. From Figure 10.71, at S > 2 the error of phase reconstruction is seen to be practically unvaried. As S approaches one, the error sharply increases. We pursued an experiment with a set of 10 interferograms that were each obtained as the result of interference of light wave with the phase in Eq. (10.167) and a plane light wave perpendicular to the registration plane, with the registration plane geometric size varied from 2 mm to 3 mm.

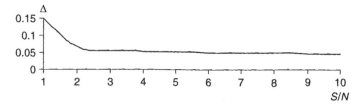

Figure 10.71. The error Δ as a function of SNR when reconstructing the phase from the interferogram produced as the result of interference of the light wave with the phase in Eq. (10.167) and a plane light wave perpendicular to the registration plane.

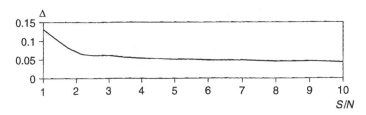

Figure 10.72. The error Δ versus SNR for the set of interferograms.

From Figure 10.72, the character of the curve is seen not to change for the set of interferograms. On average, the error has even somewhat reduced for the set of interferograms.

10.4   OPTICAL IMPLEMENTATION OF THE HOUGH-RADON TRANSFORM

Line directions in the image may be determined not only by constructing the DF but also by taking the Hough-Radon transform of the image. There is an optical-digital system for implementing the Hough-Radon transform (HRT) [89]. The system realizes the HRT property of translating an off axis point onto a shifted sine curve and comprises a matrix of $N \times N$ microholograms, each of which when illuminated by a plane beam forms a curve fragment defining a sinusoidal period shifted from the coordinate origin proportionally to the microhologram shift from the matrix center. When illuminated by a light segment, such a matrix will produce the output bright spot resulting from the intersection of many sinusoids.

The disadvantage of such kind of the HRT implementation lies in the tedious computation and fabrication of the matrix of $N \times N$ holograms, each having $M \times M$ elements and computed for L iterations. The entire matrix is computed for $L \times N \times N$ iterations, each involving the implementation of two Fourier transforms of dimensionality $M \times M$.

A modified optical realization of the HRT is discussed in the paper [90] and involves the use of N pairs of crossed cylindrical lenses. One lens of the pair produces an image of line in the transverse direction, whereas the other lens generates the spatial spectrum in the longitudinal direction (focuses the line at a point). The set of N pairs is necessary to focus differently oriented straight-line segments on the input plane. The disadvantage of this technique is that the other $(n - 1)$ pairs of lenses will also translate the line into the point with some efficiency, thus reducing the SNR.

A simpler technique for optically implementing the HRT has been proposed in [91] and employs the ability of the transform to translate the straight line into a point (Fig. 10.73). Such an optical setup comprises a correlator with one input and N outputs, with a phase spatial filter found in the spherical lens's rear focal plane. The filter consists of N angular sectors, with their apex angles equal to $\Delta \hat{\varphi} = 2\pi / N$.

Each such sector has the transmission function of a cylindrical lens

$$\tau(x, y) = \exp\left[-\frac{ik}{2f}(x \cos \hat{\varphi}_n - y \sin \hat{\varphi}_n - p_n)^2 \right], \qquad (10.169)$$

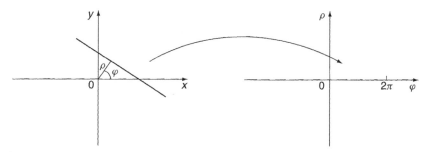

Figure 10.73. The Hough-Radon transform.

where

$$(x, y) \in \left\{ \hat{\varphi}_n - \frac{\Delta\hat{\varphi}}{2} < \text{arctg}\left(\frac{y}{x}\right) \le \hat{\varphi}_n + \frac{\Delta\hat{\varphi}}{2} \right\}, \quad \hat{\varphi}_n = n\Delta\hat{\varphi}, n = 0, 1, \ldots, N-1.$$

At the focal length 1 from the filter, one finds a photo-receiver that registers only the light leaving the center at definite angles. The corresponding optical setup shown in Figure 10.74 depicts the collimated illuminating beam, a spherical lens, a sector spatial filter with cylindrical lenses, a photo-receiver, and a computer.

In operation, the setup implements an integral form relating the HRT to the Fourier transform. The HRT of the function $f(x, y)$ takes the form

$$R(\rho, \varphi) = \int_{-\infty}^{\infty} \int f(x, y)\delta(\rho - x\cos\hat{\varphi} - y\sin\hat{\varphi})\, dx\, dy, \tag{10.170}$$

where δ is the Dirac function, ρ is the length of a perpendicular drawn from the coordinate center to a current point on the straight line, and φ is the angle between the previous perpendicular and the OX-axis (Fig. 10.73). It is easily shown that there exists a connection equation between the two integral transforms

$$R(\rho, \hat{\varphi}) = \int_0^{\infty} F(t, \hat{\varphi})e^{2\pi i \rho t}\, dt, \tag{10.171}$$

where $\quad F(t, \hat{\varphi}) = \int_{-\infty}^{\infty} \int f(x, y)\exp[-2\pi i(xt\cos\hat{\varphi} + yt\sin\hat{\varphi})]\, dx\, dy.$ $\quad$ (10.172)

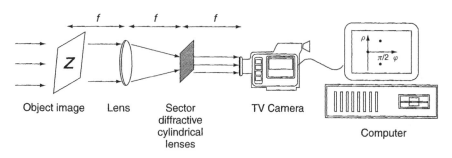

Figure 10.74. An optical configuration to implement the Hough-Radon transform.

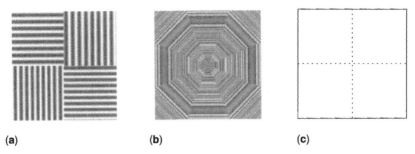

(a)   **(b)**   **(c)**

Figure 10.75. (a) the test image, (b) the phase spatial filter, and (c) the Hough-radon image of the object.

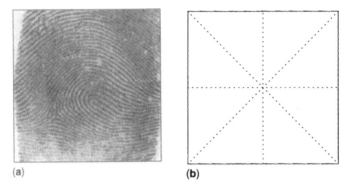

(a)   **(b)**

Figure 10.76. (a) The fingerprint and (b) its Hough-radon image.

From Eqs. (10.171) and (10.172), the HRT is seen to be the result of taking an 1D Fourier transform with respect to the radial coordinate of the 2D Fourier image of the original function.

The device shown in Figure 10.74 realizes Eqs. (10.171) and (10.172) approximately with a discreteness $\Delta\hat{\varphi} = 2\pi/N$ along the $\hat{\varphi}$-coordinate and with a discreteness $\Delta\rho$ equal to the photo-receiver's resolution along the $\Delta\rho$-coordinate.

A numerically simulated operation of the optical setup shown in Figure 10.74 is depicted in Figure 10.75. The test object (Fig. 10.75a) is made up of a set of straight-line segments directed at angles 0 and $\pi/2$ to the coordinate axes. An amplitude mask of 512×512 pixels of the spatial filter composed of eight cylindrical lenses found in angular sectors is shown in Figure 10.75b. Figure 10.75c depicts the output result as an array of light spots found on the OX- and OY-axes, with their number coinciding with the number of straight-line segments in the original image.

Figure 10.76 depicts (a) the fingerprint and (b) its Hough-radon image derived as a result of numerical simulation of the same device. To every line of the original image there corresponds a point of the Hough-radon image. Data compression similar to that occurring when constructing the DF is accomplished here.

CONCLUSION

In image processing, a number of topical problems, such as feature extraction in pattern recognition may be most adequately solved using hybrid optical-digital techniques.

In Chapter 10 we have developed an optical-digital method for constructing the DF and discussed its potential capabilities in fingerprint identification and reconstructing the light field phase from the interferogram. In numerous computer-aided and real experiments, we have studied the properties of the aforestated technique and justified its efficiency for the aforementioned problems.

With this method, the computational efforts needed for constructing the DF may be essentially reduced because of optical realization of the most cumbersome stage of calculation. The time it takes for the DF to be optically realized is the time the TV camera takes to input the image into the computer (about 0.1 sec). With digital processing, the modern computer takes about 100 sec to perform the same operation, so essentially impeding the computation. With the optical computation of the DF, the information is compressed because a high spatial frequency that plays the part of the carrier and is peculiar to fingerprints and interferograms disappears.

Because fingerprint banks in personal access systems and worldwide databases perpetually increase in volume, digital methods for fingerprint identification are likely to become insufficiently fast for practical use. In this situation, hybrid optical-digital techniques with use of the DF may adequately respond to the challenge.

REFERENCES

1. V.A. Soifer, *Digital holography and its applications*, Kuibyshev Aviation Institute, Kuibyshev, Russia, 1978.

2. W.H. Lee and M.O. Greer, Matched filter optical processor, *Appl. Opt.* **13**(4), 925–930 (1974).

3. G.W. Stroke, M. Haliowa, and V. Srinivasar, Holographic image restoration using fourier spectrum analysis of blurred photographs in computer aided synthesis of wiener filters, *Phys. Lett.* **A51**(7), 383–385 (1975).

4. V.A. Soifer, Simulation of holographic process in a stochastic medium, *Simulation of Multibeam Radio-Channels for Analysis and Synthesis of Data Transmission Systems*, Nauka Publishers, Moscow, Russia, 1978.

5. F.F. Veryaskin et al., An optical-electronic processor for image recognition, *J. Avtometriya* **3**, 73–77 (1975).

6. M.A. Golub and V.A. Soifer, Constructive approach to the use of the karhunen-loeve expansion in optimal signal processing devices, *Proc. 4th Int. Symp. Inf. Theory* **1**, 31–33 (1976).

7. V.A. Soifer, Digital holographic filters for scientific research automation systems, *Proceedings 9th All-Union Sch. on sci. res. automation*, Leningrad Nuclear Physics Institute Publishers, Leningrad, Russia, 1977, 350–354.

8. V.A. Soifer, Digital holography: achievements and challenges, *Proceedings 9th All-Union School on Holography and Coherent Optics*, Leningrad Nuclear Physics Institute Publishers, Leningrad, Russia, 1977, 199–228.

9. V.A. Soifer, Reconstruction of field parameters in systems for scientific research automation: algorithm synthesis and design of spatial filters, PhD Thesis, Leningrad Radioengineering Institute Publishers, Leningrad, Russia, 1984, 1–32.

10. M.A. Golub and V.A. Soifer, *Synthesis of Spatial Filters for Pattern Recognition Systems*, Moscow Physical & Technical Institute Transactions, Series: Radioengineering and Electronics, Dolgoprudny, (1977), pp. 120–125.

11. J. Too and R. Gonsales, *Principles of Pattern Recognition*, Nauka publishers, Moscow, Russia, 1971.

12. A. For, *Pattern Perception and Recognition*, Mashinostroyeniye Publishers, Moscow, Russia, 1989.

13. K.S. Fu, *Successive Methods in Pattern Recognition and Computerized System Learning*, Nauka Publishers, Moscow, Russia, 1971.

14. M.A. Golub, *Laser beam mode selection using computer optics methods*, PhD Thesis degree, Kuibyshev, Russia 1990.

15. S. Vatanabe, Karhunen-Loeve expansion and factor analysis, *Automatic Synthesis of Complex Images*, Mir Publishers, Moscow, Russia, 1969, 254–275.

16. B.V. Davenport and V.L. Root, *Introduction into the Theory of Random Signals and Noises*, Foreign Literature Publishers, Moscow, Russia 1960.

17. K. Karhunen, Uber Linear Methoden in der Wahrscheinlichkeitsrechnung, *Ann. Acad. Sci.* **A137**, Fennicae, Helsinki (1947).

18. D.D. Klovsky and V.A. Soifer, *Space-Time Signal Processing*, Svyaz Publishers, Moscow, Russia 1976.

19. D.C. Youla, The solution of a homogeneous Wiener-Hopf integral equation occurring in the expansion of second-order stationary random functions, *IRE Trans. Inf. Theory* **IT-3**(3), 187–193 (1957).

20. H.L. Van Trees, *Detection, Estimation, and Modulation Theory. Part 2. Nonlinear Modulation Theory*, New York, 1971.

21. V.V. Bykov, *Digital Simulation in Statistical Radioengineering*, Sovetskoye Radio Publishers, Moscow, Russia 1971.

22. S.M. Ermakov and G.A. Mikhailov, *Statistical Modeling*, Nauka Publishers, Moscow, Russia 1982.

23. M.A. Golub and V.A. Soifer, Optical-Digital Image Recognition Based on Non-Correlated Features. *Proceedings 3-rd All-Union Conference: Mathematical Methods of Pattern Recognition*, Institute of Physics and Mathematics of the Ukrainian Academy of Sciences, Lvov, Ukraine, 1987, pp. 141–142.

24. V.A. Soifer and S.N. Khonina, Stability of the Karhunen-Loeve expansion in the problem of pattern recognition, *Pattern Recog. Image Anal.* **4**(2), 137–148 (1994).

25. M.A. Golub and V.A. Soifer, Stability of the Karhunen-Loeve expansion and computer-aided synthesis of optimal spatial filters, *Spectral Methods of Data Processing in Scientific Research*, All-Union Workshop Transactions, Puschino, 1980, pp. 108–134.

26. V.A. Soifer, M.A. Golub, and S.N. Khonina, Decorrelated features of image extracted with the aid of optical Karhunen-Loeve expansion, *Pattern Recog. Image Anal.* **3**(3), 289–295 (1993).

27. V.A. Soifer, *Introduction into Computer Optics*, Samara State Aerospace University, Samara, Russia 1996

28. M.A. Golub and S.N. Khonina, Karhunen-Loeve expansion with the exponential-cosine correlation function, *J. Comput. Opt.* (13), 49–53 (1993).

29. A.A. Sveshnikov, *Applied Methods of the Theory of Random Functions*, Nauka Publishers, Moscow, Russia, 1968.

30. V.A. Soifer, *Theory of Information*, Kuibyshev Aviation Institute Publishers, Kuibyshev, Russia, 1975.

31. J. Bendat and A. Pirsel, *Applied Analysis of Stochastic Data*, Mir Publishers, Moscow, Russia, 1989.

32. O.B. Chentzova et al., A Crystallographic Examination Method as Applied to some Particular Diseases, Practical Methodics, Moscow, Russia, 1988.

33. T.P. Chuchman-Dvoryanova, A Modified Technique for Studying Lachrymal Fluid Crystallogram, Proceedings 6-th Congress of Russian Ophthalmologists, Moscow, Russia, 1994, p. 395.

34. S.N. Khonina et al., Optical-digital method for detecting distortions of microcrystal structure on a tear crystallogram, *Image Process. Comput. Opt., SPIE* **2363**, 249–255 (1994).

35. V.A. Soifer et al., Identification of fingerprints using the direction fields. *Proceedings 4-th Russian-German Workshop Pattern Recog. Image Anal."*, Valday, 1996, pp. 139–143.

36. L.P. Yaroslavsky, *Introduction into Digital Image Processing*, Sovetskoye Radio Publishers, Moscow, Russia, 1979.

37. W.K. Pratt, *Digital Image Processing*, Wiley-Interscience publication, New York, 1978.

38. R.W. Gerchberg and W.O. Saxton, A practical algorithm for the determination of phase from image and diffraction plane pictures, *Optik* **35**, 237–246 (1972).

39. A. Ye Beryezny et al., Bessel optics, *J. Rep. USSR Acad. Sci.* **234**(4), 802–805 (1984).

40. V.V. Kotlyar, S.N. Khonina, and V.A. Soifer, Algorithm for the generation of nondiffracting Bessel modes, *J. Mod. Opt.* **42**(6), 1231–1239 (1995).

41. V.V. Kotlyar, S.N. Khonina, and V.A. Soifer, Calculation of phase formers of nondiffracting images and a set of concentric rings, *Optik* **102**(2), 45–50 (1996).

42. V.V. Kotlyar, V.A. Soifer, and S.N. Khonina, An algorithm for the generation of laser beams with longitudinal periodicity: rotating images, *J. Mod. Opt.* **44**(7), 1403–1416 (1997).

43. Y.Y. Schechner, R. Piestun, and J. Shamir, Wave propagation with rotating intensity distribution, *Phys. Rev. E* **54**(1), 51–53 (1996).

44. V.A. Soifer and M.A. Golub, *Laser Beam Mode Selection by Computer-generated Holograms*, CRC Press, Boca Raton, Fla., 1994.

45. A. Vasara, J. Turunen, and A.T. Friberg. Regularization of general nondiffracting beams with computer-generated holograms *J. Opt. Soc. Am. A* **6**(11), 1748–1754 (1989).

46. M. Born and E. Wolf, *Principles of Optics*, Pergamon Press, Oxford, 1968.

47. V.V. Kotlyar, I.V. Nikolsky, and V.A. Soifer. Algorithm for calculating multichannel formers of Gaussian modes *Optik* **98**(1), 26–30 (1994).

48. V.A. Soifer, V.V. Kotlyar, and L.L. Doskolovich, *Iterative Methods for Diffractive Optical Elements Computation*, Taylor and Francis, London, U.K., 1997.

49. V.V. Kotlyar, S.N. Khonina, and V.A. Soifer, Light field decomposition in angular harmonics by means of diffractive optics, *J. Mod. Opt.* **45**(7), 1495–1506 (1998).

50. T. Yatagai et al., Automatic fringe analysis using digital image processing techniques, *Opt. Eng.* **21**(2), 432–435 (1982).

51. J.R. Fienup, Phase retrieval algorithms. a comparison, *Appl. Opt.* **21**(15), 2758–2769 (1982).

52. G. Artzner, Microlens arrays for shack-hartmann wavefront sensors, *Opt. Eng.* **31**(6), 1311–1322 (1992).

53. M.A. Golub et al., Synthesis of a spatial filter for investigation of the transverse mode composition of coherent radiation, *Sov. J. Quant. Electron* **12**(9), 1208–1209 (1982).

54. V.V. Kotlyar, Decomposition of the coherent field into an orthogonal basis, *J. Comput. Opt.*, (Moscow), **5**, 31–33 (1989).

55. V.V. Kotlyar et al., Coherent field phase retrieval using a phase zernike filter. *Comput. Opt.*, (Samara), (17), 43–48 (1997).

56. I.M. Vinogradov, *Mathematical Encyclopedia*, Vol 3., Sovetskaya Enziklopediya Publishers, Moscow, Russia, 1982.

57. V.A. Soifer et al., Image recognition using a directions field technique, *Proc. SPIE, Digital Image Process. Comput. Graphics* **3346**, 238–258 (1997).

58. V.A. Soifer et al., Fingerprint identification using the directions field. 13th Inter. Conf. on Pattern Recognition, Technical University of Vienna, August 25–29, 1996, pp. 586–590.

59. V.A. Soifer et al., Optical techniques for finger-print identification, *Comput. Opt.* Vol. 16, 78–89 (1996).

60. K. Mardia, *Statistical Analysis of Angular Observations*, Nauka Publishers, Moscow, Russia, 1978.

61. S.O. Novicov and V.S. Kot, Singular features detection and classification of fingerprints using hough transform, *Proc. SPIE, Digital Image Process. Comput. Graphics* **3346**, 258–269 (1997).

62. Z. Chen et al., Optical-digital access control using fingerprint identification, *Opt. Eng.* **34**(3), 834–839 (1995).

63. F.T. Gamble, L.M. Frye, and D.R. Grieser, Real time fingerprint verification system, *Appl. Opt.* **31**(5), 652–655 (1992).

64. D.H. McMahon et al., A hybrid optical computer processing technique for fingerprint identification, *IEEE Trans. Comput.* **C-24**(5), 358–368 (1975).

65. E.G. Johnson et al., Optical recognition of phase-encrypted biometrics, *Opt. Eng.* **37**(1), 18–25 (1998).

66. J.D. Javidi and A. Sergent, Fully phase encoded key and biometrics for security verification, *Opt. Eng.* **36**(3), 935–942 (1997).

67. J.D. Brasher and E.G. Johnson, Incoherent optical correlators and phase encoding of identification codes for access control or authentication, *Opt. Eng.* **36**(9), 2409–2415 (1997).

68. T.J. Grycewicz and B. Javidi, Experimental comparison of binary joint transform correlators used for fingerprint identification, *Opt. Eng.* **35**(9), 2519–2525 (1996).

69. H. Huh and J.K. Pan, Optical digital invariant recognition of two dimensional patterns with straight links, *Opt. Eng.* **35**(4), 997–1002 (1996).

70. M. Seth and A.K. Datta, Optical implementation of a connectionist model of Hough transform, *Opt. Eng.* **35**(6), 1779–1794 (1996).

71. J. Rodolfo, H. Rajbenbach, and J.P. Haignard, Performance of a photorefractive joint transform correlator for fingerprint identification, *Opt. Eng.* **34**(4), 1166–1171 (1995).

72. M. Dawagoe and A. Tojo, Fingerprint pattern classification, *Pattern Recog.* **17**, 295–303 (1984).

73. M.D. Drake, M.L. Lidd, and M.A. Fiddy, Waveguide hologram fingerprint entry device, *Opt. Eng.* **35**(9), 2499–2505 (1996).

74. V.A. Soifer, V.V. Kotlyar, and S.N. Khonina, Constructing the directions field using an optical technique, *J. Avtometriya* Vol. 1, 31–36 (1996).

75. R.O. Dooda and P.E. Hart, *Pattern Recognition and Scene Analysis*, Mir Publishers, Moscow, Russia, 1976.

76. N.G. Zagoruiko, *Recognition Methods and Their Application*, Sovetskoye Radio Publishers, Moscow, Russia, 1972.

77. V.A. Soifer et al., Fingerprint identification using the directions field. 13th Inter. Conf. on Pattern Recognition, Technical University of Vienna, August 25–29, **2**, 1996, pp. 586–590.

78. V.A. Soifer et al., Fingerprint Recognition Using Hardamard-expanded Partial Images. *Proc. SPIE, Optoelectr. and Hybrid Opt./Dig. Syst. for Im. Proc*, **3238**, 66–73 (1997).

79. V.A. Soifer, S.N. Khonina, Optical Structuring for Analysis of Contour Images, *Patt. Recog. Image Anal.*, **6**(1), 71–72, (1996).

80. S.N. Khonina et al., Optical-digital method for detecting distortions in microcrystal structure of tear crystallogramm. *Proc. SPIE, Int. Workshop Image Process. Comput. Opt.* **2363**, 249–255 (1994).

81. G. Stark, ed., *Application of Fourier-Optics Methods*, Radio i Svyaz Publishers, Moscow, Russia, 1988.

82. R.V. Skidanov, Shift-stability of the Method for Finger-print Identification Using Direction Field, *Comput. Opt.* Vol. 77, 130–134 (1997).

83. Ye. S. Ventzel and L.A. Ovcharov, *Probability theory and its technological applications*, Nauka Publishers, Moscow, Russia, 1988.

84. M. Takeda, H. Ina, and S. Kabayashi, Fourier transform method of fringe pattern analysis for computer-based topography and interferometry, *J. Opt. Soc. Am.* **72**(1), 157–160 (1982).

85. V.V. Kotlyar, P.G. Seraphimovich, and O.K. Zalyalov, Noise — insensitive method for interferogram processing, *Opt. Las. Technol.* **27**(4), 251–254 (1995).

86. V.V. Kotlyar and O.K. Zalyalov, An iterative algorithm for reconstructing a 3D object shape, *Comput. Opt.*, Samara State Aerospace University Publishers, Samara, (16), 71–74 (1996).

87. R.V. Skidanov, V.A. Soifer, and V.V. Kotlyar, A coherent optical-digital system for interferogram decoding using direction fields and frequency fields, Trans XXV School-Symposium on Coherent Optics and Holography, Yaroslavl State Pedagogical University, Yaroslavl, 1180–1182 (1992).

88. V.P. Aksenov and Y.P. Isaev, Analytical representation of the phase and its mode components reconstructed according to the wave-front slopes, *Opt. Lett.* **17**, 1180–1182 (1992).

89. P. Ambs et al., Optical implementation of the hough transform by a matrix of holograms, *Appl. Opt.* **25**(22), 4039–4045 (1986).

90. P. Woodford and D. Casasent, High accuracy and fast new format optical Hough-transform, *Opt. Mem. Neur. Net.*, (1), 1–16, 1997.

91. V.A. Soifer, V.V. Kotlyar, and R.V. Skidanov, Optical implementation of the Hough-Radon transform, *Comput. Opt.* (17), Samara, 143–144, 1997.

Printed and bound in the UK by
CPI Antony Rowe, Eastbourne

Printed and bound by CPI Group (UK) Ltd, Croydon, CR0 4YY

27/10/2024

14580343-0005